THE ORGAN,

ITS HISTORY AND CONSTRUCTION:

A COMPREHENSIVE TREATISE

ON THE

STRUCTURE & CAPABILITIES OF THE ORGAN,

WITH

SPECIFICATIONS AND SUGGESTIVE DETAILS FOR INSTRUMENTS OF ALL SIZES.

INTENDED AS A

HANDBOOK FOR THE ORGANIST AND THE AMATEUR.

BY

EDWARD J. HOPKINS,

Organist to the Honourable Societies of the Inner and Middle Temple.

PRECEDED BY AN ENTIRELY

NEW HISTORY OF THE ORGAN,

MEMOIRS OF THE MOST EMINENT BUILDERS OF THE SEVENTEENTH AND EIGHTEENTH CENTURIES, AND
OTHER MATTERS OF RESEARCH IN CONNECTION WITH THE SUBJECT,

BY

EDWARD F. RIMBAULT, LL.D.,

*Member of the Royal Academy of Music in Stockholm; Musical Examiner in the Royal College of
Preceptors, London, &c., &c.*

THIRD EDITION.

LONDON :

ROBERT COCKS & CO., NEW BURLINGTON STREET,

*Music Publishers to Her most Gracious Majesty Queen Victoria, H.R.H. the Prince of Wales, and
His late Imperial Majesty Napoleon III., Emperor of the French.*

SIMPKIN, MARSHALL, AND CO.   WHITTAKER AND CO.

MDCCCLXXVII.

Edward J. Hopkins and Edward F. Rimbault

Hopkins: The Organ, its History and Construction
… preceded by …
Rimbault: New History of the Organ.

Facsimile of the Third edition 1877.

First published by Robert Cocks in London, 1877.

Republished Travis & Emery 2009 and 2011.

Published by
Travis & Emery Music Bookshop
17 Cecil Court, London, WC2N 4EZ, United Kingdom.
(+44) 20 7240 2129
neworders@travis-and-emery.com

Hardback: ISBN10: 1-906857-47-4   ISBN13: 978-1-906857-47-9
Paperback: ISBN10: 1-906857-48-2   ISBN13: 978-1-906857-48-6

Edward John Hopkins (1818-1901). Organist and Composer.
He was a chorister at the Chapel Royal and trained under T.F.
Walmisley. In 1843 he became organist at the Temple church.

Edward Francis Rimboult. (1816-1876). Organist and Musicologist.
He studied under his father and then Samuel Wesley. His career was
centred on London, where he started as Organist of the Swiss church,
Soho.

More details are available from
 - C.W. Pearce: The Life and Works of Edward John Hopkins. 1910.
 - D. Baptie: The Late Dr. Rimbault. 1876.
 - Stanley Sadie: The New Grove Dictionary of Music and Musicians.

PREFACE TO THE FIRST EDITION.

———◆———

THE following work has been undertaken with the view of supplying what has hitherto been felt to be a great desideratum in this country; namely, a hand-book describing the construction of the English organ with the necessary minuteness to enable those not previously conversant with the subject to understand the formation, nature, and operation of every part of that most ingenious, complex, and noble of all musical instruments. In proceeding to carry out this design several plans presented themselves, but the one that appeared best calculated to place the subject in the most simple shape before the reader was that of arranging the various systems of mechanism and the several clever devices for giving speech and vitality to the organ into separate divisions, and then of describing the numerous parts which together form those main portions in the continuous order they are usually met with in modern English instruments. This course has therefore been adopted in the arrangement of the materials forming the following chapters; and each separate subject—as, for instance, some particular system of mechanism—is traced from its source to its termination, with a slight notice only (at the time) being taken of other portions of the intricate machine towards which it may occasionally approach closely, yet without having therewith any actual connection.

The endeavour has been made in the progress of the work to record the names of the originators of the numerous ameliorations and improvements that have been made from time to time in the details of organ-building. This part of the design, however, has not been found by any means so easy of accomplishment as at first it might appear to be, for but few records were ever kept either of the date or the builder by whom such advantageous modifications were effected. An internal examination of numerous organs, and a comparison of their dates of construction have been made, with the view of arriving at a correct conclusion on all these points, and the result has been given; at the same time a date or fact may here or there have escaped the research of the writer, who will therefore be glad to receive any such testimony as may come under the notice of others, and which will be gratefully accepted and carefully preserved for future use. To account for the frequent appearance of names and dates in the descriptions of some of the more recent improvements, it may be mentioned that these have in all cases been given, where positively known, in the hope of obviating future uncertainty.

Among the most vexed questions of the present time regarding the English organ are those relating to the compass and the temperament of the instrument. To each of these subjects, therefore, a full chapter has been devoted, which, it is hoped, may have some influence in conducting them nearer towards a settlement. In these discussions, and indeed throughout the work, great pains have been taken to preserve as much simplicity of language and freedom from technicality as seemed practicable. Other matters of importance are those relating to the musical pitch, the composition of the compound stops, and the position of the organ, all of which have also been considered at some length.

The Appendix will be found to present a collection of specifications of British and foreign organs more varied in size and details, and more extensive in number, than has ever before been brought together in any similar work in any country. A few of the English specimens are either accounts of instruments of past celebrity, or of such as were made according to a system now being fast superseded ; but most of the Continental descriptions, it is confidently hoped, will prove of the highest value to organists in exemplifying what are the general principles observed by the foreign artists, to the investigation of which the organ-builders and organists of this country, fortunately, are now almost universally turning their attention. The accounts of foreign organs have partly been prepared from notes made by the writer and other tourists at the instruments themselves, and partly from previously printed accounts, the stops, however, being in all cases re-arranged and classified according to one uniform and simple plan, so that they may be more convenient for purposes of reference and comparison. The descriptions of British organs have been drawn up, in some cases, from accounts kindly furnished by their respective organists ; in others, from well-known printed authorities ; while the particulars of the more recently constructed instruments have been extracted chiefly from the descriptions issued by their respective builders.

It remains for the writer to tender his thanks to those gentlemen who have kindly favoured him with their suggestions and opinions ; and he feels his acknowledgments to be particularly due to Mr. Hill and Mr. Walker, Mr. Robson and Mr. Jardine, for their exposition of certain technical matters ; and to the Rev. Sir Frederick Gore-Ouseley, Bart., and to C. Harwood Clark, Esq., for placing their MS. note-books, containing accounts of numerous foreign organs, so entirely at his disposal.

EDWARD J. HOPKINS.

69, TACHBROOK STREET, PIMLICO,
    June, 1855.

PREFACE TO THE SECOND EDITION.

THE arts of organ-building and organ-playing have made such rapid strides in England during the last few years that it was felt a new edition of " THE ORGAN : ITS HISTORY AND CONSTRUCTION," was urgently needed.

The practical portion of the work contains a full and minute description of the organ in every part of its manufacture. Not only has the material of the first edition undergone a complete and most careful revision, but two new chapters have been added ; *i.e.*, those on Joy's *Hydraulic Blower* and the *Electric Organ*. *The Pneumatic Draw-stop Action* has been carefully described, and the chapter on the important question of *Temperament* has been entirely re-written.

In the preparation of the additional material, my friend, Mr. Hopkins, has been assisted in his labours by some of the most eminent organ-builders, both English and foreign ; and through their co-operation correct and minute diagrams have been given, which will, it is confidently hoped, render the volume of the utmost possible practical use both to the organist and to the amateur. Special reference must here be made to the chapter and diagrams upon the most recent introduction, the *Electric Action*.

With regard to the " History of the Organ," I have bestowed some pains upon its revision and correction. Much curious and minute information has been added, the result of considerable labour and research. The Treatise of *Hero of Alexandria*, with its interesting notice of the ancient Greek organ, has received attention ; whilst the mediæval organ-builders and their works form an important and an entirely new chapter. The notices of the builders after the Restoration have received considerable and valuable additions, and the lists of their works have been carefully revised and extended.

For much curious and valuable information I am indebted to my friend, Mr. W. B. Gilbert, Mus. Bac., Oxon., late organist of Boston, Lincolnshire.

In the preparation of the "Specifications" (forming the APPENDIX), Mr. Hopkins has spared no time and labour. The descriptions and details given are the result, not only of much careful collating of the best authorities, but, in addition, a personal inspection of many of the most celebrated Continental instruments.

EDWARD F. RIMBAULT.

St. Mark's Crescent, Regent's Park, N.W.,
Christmas, 1870.

PREFACE TO THE THIRD EDITION.

IN the present (third) Edition of "THE ORGAN: ITS HISTORY AND CONSTRUCTION," the entire work has been subjected to a thorough revision, and the contents of the Appendix have received many important additions and substitutions. Improvements in the mechanism of the Organ have continued to be made since the publication of the second edition of this work, which have been duly detailed as far as space would admit ; and the same may be said with reference to the improvement in the general features of the specifications which have been issued and executed by some of the leading organ-building firms both in England and America.

All who enjoyed the personal acquaintance of the author of the Historical portion of this volume, the late Dr. Rimbault, will have felt the loss of so genial, accomplished, and unassuming a friend ; but they will be glad to know that the revision of his portion of the present edition was completed some weeks before his active and useful life was brought to a close.

EDWARD J. HOPKINS

23, ST. AUGUSTINE'S ROAD, N.W.,
June 1, 1877.

CONTENTS.

———◆———

THE HISTORY OF THE ORGAN.

———◆———

CONTENTS.

THE ORGAN : ITS STRUCTURE, &c.

CONTENTS.

CONTENTS.

CONTENTS.

CONTENTS.

CONTENTS.

CONTENTS.

CONTENTS.

APPENDIX.

COMPRISING AN ACCOUNT OF FOREIGN AND BRITISH ORGANS.

———◆‡◆———

CONTENTS.

CONTENTS.

CONTENTS.

LIST OF WOODCUTS, DIAGRAMS, &c.

CONTENTS.

THE CONSTRUCTION OF THE ORGAN.

PREFACE TO THE FIRST EDITION.

WHEN I undertook to prefix to my friend Mr. Hopkins's valuable treatise on the construction of the organ an historical account of that noble instrument, my intention was to give a *résumé* of what had already been written, with the addition of such new particulars as the course of years had accumulated in my note-books ; but, upon collating the various writers, their statements often appeared so vague and unsatisfactory that it became necessary to consider the subject more attentively, and in all cases, where it could be done, to consult *original* authorities. The result of this examination has been the clearing up of many doubtful points, and the discovery of some important particulars hitherto unknown.

All modern writers have been perplexed with the notices of the organ handed down to us by the ancient Greeks, and have endeavoured to reconcile them with our present ideas of the instrument. The *key-board* has been a constant source of difficulty, and the epigram, or rather enigma, of the Emperor Julian has been often cited to prove that it was known to the ancients. The discovery of a treatise on organ-building by a monk of the eleventh century (printed in the following pages) settles for ever this important question.

Another source of difficulty is the common expression, in mediæval times, of " a pair of organs." Some of our ablest antiquaries have exercised their erudition in endeavouring to explain this term, but with what degree of success the reader who peruses the following pages will have an opportunity of judging.

At a later period in the History of the Organ the biographies of Smith and Harris have been involved in much obscurity. Father Smith has *fathered* all our *old* organs, of whatever kind or description; and so little attention has been paid to dates that we are told "Harris's most celebrated organs are those of St. Sepulchre's, London, 1667; and Doncaster, Yorkshire, 1738!" I have been enabled to arrange the various members of these two celebrated families under their respective periods, and by so doing have cleared away many anachronisms, and reconciled a few seeming impossibilities.

The Jordans and the Byfields, and their foreign cotemporaries, the Silbermanns, have also received the same attention; and, if the information regarding them is somewhat scant, it is all my research has been able to bring together.

The section on the "Ancient Position of the Organ" is interesting at the present time, when architects are anxiously looking for precedents. I have carefully noted all the authorities upon the point, especially in this country, which, added to Mr. Hopkins's able chapter on the "Situation of the Organ," will, it is hoped, be found of some practical utility. The rescue of this noble instrument from the "holes and corners" to which modern ecclesiologists have ofttimes assigned it is part of the musician's creed.

It will be observed that my historical account deals more with facts than with opinions. For the latter I am content to refer to the body of the book, trusting with full confidence to Mr. Hopkins's superior judgment and intimate acquaintance with his subject.

The History of the Organ, from the period at which I leave it, chiefly consists in a series of inventions, all of which receive their full share of attention from Mr. Hopkins in the course of the volume.

PREFACE.

I ought not to pass unnoticed the aid I have received from several authors who have written upon the same subject. Amongst them I may especially name the Rev. Sir William Cope's paper on *Early Organ-builders in England*, inserted in the *Parish Choir;* Mr. Sutton's *Short Account of Organs built in England from the reign of King Charles the Second to the present time;* Herr Seidel's *Treatise on the Organ*, printed at Breslau; and M. Hamel's valuable reprint of "Dom Bedos," forming one of the publications of the *Encyclopédie-Roret.* If I have not named other modern works purporting to treat of the organ historically, it is because I have found them unworthy of credit.

It only remains to tender my obligations to those gentlemen who have kindly assisted me in the course of the following essay. I must especially thank my friend, F. W. Fairholt, Esq., F.S.A., for the valuable extracts from Mr. Rolfe's MSS., and for other information; William Chappell, Esq., F.S.A., for two or three curious notices; Mr. Hill, the eminent organ-builder, for the loan of G. P. England's Account Book; Alfred Price, Esq., of Gloucester, for his MS. translation of Herr Seidel's *Treatise on the Organ*, before mentioned · and lastly, Robert Hendrie, Esq., for his kindness in giving me permission to use his excellent translation of Theophilus's *Chapters on the Organ.*

EDWARD F. RIMBAULT.

29, St. Mark's Crescent, Regent's Park,
June, 1855.

THE

HISTORY OF THE ORGAN.

First Epoch.

THE ANCIENT ORGAN, ANTERIOR TO THE INVENTION OF THE
KEY-BOARD.

I. *Its Invention.*

THE early history of ancient musical instruments is surrounded
by mystery and fable; their invention being usually attributed to the heathen deities. Patient investigation is
required to sift the historical from the fabulous matter, and it then
remains a matter of doubt whether the result does not excite, rather
than satisfy, our curiosity.

The word *organ*, used in the Psalms and other parts of the Old
Testament, must not be confounded with the noble instrument now
bearing that name. The term was taken from the Greek translation;
but the ancient Greeks had no particular musical instrument called an
organ; for ὄργανον, with them, was a general name for an *instrument*,
a *work*, or an *implement* of any kind; hence, ὀργανικός, *instrumental*;
ὀργανοποιός, an *instrument maker*; and ὀργανοποιία, the *fabrication*
of *an instrument*. And, in all the Greek musical theorists, *organic*
is a general term applied to instrumental music.*

It is of much importance to the history of an art that the origin,
etymology, and primitive acceptance of its terms should be minutely
traced. In the present instance, the extended application of the word
organum, throughout the middle ages, has given rise to much confusion and misunderstanding. It is however perfectly clear, to those

---

* See note in Burney's *History of Music*, vol. i., p. 252; also Liddell and Scott's *Greek and
English Lexicon.*

B

who have investigated the subject, that the Greeks understood by the word ὄργανον, and the Romans by their *organum*, not an *organ*, in our sense of the term, but an instrument of any kind ; applying the expression, however, more particularly to musical instruments.*

The organ (*ougab*) mentioned in Genesis (chap. iv., *v.* 21) certainly little resembled the modern instrument of that name, although it may be regarded as furnishing the first hint.† It was probably a series of reeds, of unequal length and thickness, joined together ; being nearly identical with the pipe of Pan among the Greeks, or that simple instrument called a *mouth-organ*, which is still in common use.‡ The classical ancients ascribe its invention to Pan, the great sylvan god ; and, accordingly, he was usually figured with the instrument in his hands. The fable states that he formed it of reeds that grew by the river, and caused it to produce all kinds of agreeable sounds, while

---

* ORGANUM. A general name given to any instrument, machine, or contrivance, by which human labour is assisted, in agriculture, architecture, warfare, &c. ; differing, however, from *machina* in this particular, that it required a certain amount of skill from the person using it, whereas that only wanted brute force or numbers to work it. (Vitruvius, x., 1, 3. Columel, iii., 13, 12. Plin. *H. N.* xix., 20.) Hence the word is especially given to musical instruments (Quint. ix., 4, 10 ; xi., 3, 20), and, amongst these, more particularly to the one from which our *organ* is descended (Suet. *Nero*, 41. Lamprid. *Alex. Ser.* 27. Id. *Heliog.* 32) ; but which also had a special name of its own, in allusion to the water originally employed, instead of weights, for working it.—Rich's *Companion to the Latin Dictionary and Greek Lexicon*, p. 458.

† " And here we must not think that the organs in the Old Testament were any such things as those which we call so now. We read it in Job, chap. 30, verse 31, *and my organ into the voice of them that weep.* The Syriack rendreth it, *my psaltery*, clean another instrument of a triangular form, as you may see by the description of Mersennus (*De Instrum. Harm.* lib. 10, prop. 44). The Hebrew word in Job is *ougab*, which the Chaldee still turneth *abuba :* now *abub* signifieth properly an ear of corn with the stalk or straw : by translation it signifieth a pipe made of such a reed or stalk, *fistula ex novarum frugum calamo confecta * * *.* David's organ was but a kind of pipe, what kind soever it was."—Gregorie's *Discourse declaring what time the Nicene Creed began to be sung in the Church.* 4to. 1683.

‡ It is indeed remarkable that the lyre (*kinnor*) and syrinx (*ougab*) were the two first instruments of music the invention of which is recorded in Scripture, and the only ones that are mentioned before the Deluge ; and that subsequently the *ougab* is almost always mentioned in connection with the *kinnor*. The principle of the instrument is so simple, that it has been one of the most diffused of musical instruments. A syrinx, or *fistula Panis*, made of reeds tied together, exactly resembling that of the ancients, has been found to be in common use in the island of New Amsterdam, in the South Seas, as flutes and drums have been in Otaheite and New Zealand ; which indisputably proves them to be instruments natural to every people in a state of barbarism. They were first used by the Egyptians and Greeks, during the infancy of the musical art among them ; and they seem to have been invented and practised at all times by nations remote from each other, and between whom it is hardly possible that there ever could have been the least intercourse or communication. The combination of pipes in question is still used in different parts of Asia. The number of tubes which these instruments exhibit on ancient monuments varies from seven to eleven. See Burney's *History of Music*, vol. i., p. 267 ; and the *Pictorial Bible*, vol. ii., p. 665, *note.*

his goats were skipping around him, and feeding on the banks. This shows that it was regarded as properly a sylvan and pastoral instrument; and so it seems to be mentioned by Job (ch. xxi., *v.* 11, 12). Pan himself thought it superior to the lyre of Apollo, whom he challenged to a trial of skill; and, the challenge being accepted, the umpire, being no other than Midas, decided in favour of Pan's pipes.

The Greek and Latin shepherds made this primitive instrument of strong reeds, or some other suitable material. It originally consisted of seven or eight reeds of progressive lengths, fastened together with wax. The number was afterwards extended to ten or twelve.* The syrinx, or pipe of Pan, by its form and arrangement, may be regarded as the first kind of organ building; for it consisted of a number of pipes placed together in ranks, according to their succession of tones, and sounded by wind.

To obviate the fatiguing motion of the head or hands, by inflating the pipes in some other manner, seems to have been the object of desired attainment for centuries. At length this was accomplished. Among the Cilician antiquities discovered in Syria, and recently brought to this country by Mr. W. B. Barker, is the portion of a figure playing upon a musical instrument of singular curiosity and interest.† This instrument, of which we give a drawing, forms a connecting link between the pipes of Pan and the organ.

---

* This instrument is described by Virgil, and the use of it by Lucretius, lib. v. It is frequently depicted upon ancient medals.

† *Lares and Penates: or, Cilicia and its Governors.* By William Burckhardt Barker, M.R.A.S., 8vo, 1853. This interesting volume contains, in addition to the monument mentioned in the text, the representation of a youth playing the syrinx or Pandean organ. The pipes are more numerous, and those in the bass part of the instrument much larger than is usually represented.

Let us examine it. It consists of a vertical row of pipes, the length unknown, as the lower portion is wanting; they are inserted into a small air-chest, which appears inflated in the middle part. The right hand is operating upon it with a kind of cushion or compress, by which the performer forces the air into the pipes, and which he seems to apply to different parts of the instrument at will. There appears to have been a prolongation of the central part of the instrument across the left arm : the loss of this is much to be lamented, as that would have shown us more of its construction, and also how the left hand was employed in playing it. This curious relic may be looked upon as the earliest attempt to combine the pneumatic chest with the Pandean organ, which still retains its place on the breast of the player, though he no longer operates upon it with his mouth.

We need hardly say that this monument is of the highest importance in the history of the organ. It has never been pointed out by any musical writer, and the author may fairly take to himself the credit of giving it a place in our musical history.

Another step was the invention of a wooden box, the top of which was bored with just so many holes as there were pipes to stand on it. In these they now placed the pipes in the same order as they occupied in the Pan-pipes. From the chest (the modern *wind-chest*) proceeded a small reed (now the *wind-trunk*), into which they blew with the mouth. But as, by this means, all the pipes spoke simultaneously, they were obliged to stop with the fingers the tops of those pipes intended to be silent—a process which was soon found to be very troublesome, and, as the number of pipes increased, impossible. Now, in order to prevent the simultaneous intonation of all the pipes, a slider (now called the *valve*) was placed under the aperture of each pipe, which either opened or stopped the entrance of the wind into the pipes. Father Kircher, in his *Musurgia*, fol. 1650 (lib. ii., p. 53), has given us a drawing of this instrument, which is here copied.

The slides stood in an inclined position, and, in order to open them, levers were added, which were connected with the slides by cords or strings (the origin of the *pull-downs*). A furth·r increase of the number of pipes at length caused an enlargement of the pipe-chest (the modern *wind-chest*) ; consequently human breath was no longer sufficient to supply the instrument, and then a more suitable contrivance for the production of wind was devised. Thus we have a new class of instrument, called by the Greeks ὄργανον πνευματικόν, and by the Romans *tibia utricularis*. Virgil has an elegant passage, in which he describes the shepherd Tonius playing upon the *tibia utricularis* :—

> " Et cum multifori Tonius cui tibia buxo
> Tandem post epulas, et pocula, multicolorem
> Ventriculum sumpsit, buccasque inflare rubentes
> Incipiens, oculos aperit, ciliisque levatis,
> Multotiesque alto flatum e pulmonibus haustum
> Utrem implet ; cubito vocem dat tibia presso,
> Nunc huc nunc illuc digito saliente . . ."

When soberly considered, this instrument appears to be nothing more than the origin of the bagpipe. It consists of pipes pierced with lateral holes, and an inflating pipe, which the performer applied to his mouth to fill the leathern bag with wind. The application of the inflated tube, it is evident, related only to the smaller instruments, such as that described by Virgil ; the larger ones were supplied with wind by the compression of the leathern bag or bellows.* This contrivance proved of so much advantage to the improving instrument, that, in order to obtain a more powerful tone, a second row of pipes of the same pitch was added to the former. The pipes having been thus increased and enlarged, and the box widened, the next improvement was the enlargement of the wind-tube (*trunk*). It now became evident that the leathern bag was insufficient to supply the proper quantity of wind required. The want of wind thus occasioned by the enlargement of the instrument was remedied by the invention of *bellows*, yielding a continuous supply

---

* M. Fétis has written a long paper to prove that the *pneumatic-organ* of the ancients was nothing more than a *bagpipe!* This learned writer has, however, been led into an error by considering only a portion of the ancient authorities, *i.e.*, those relating to the *tibia utricularis*. See a translation of M. Fétis' paper in the *Harmonicon* for 1829, p. 4. M. Fétis is, no doubt, correct in saying, "The figure given by Bianchini, of a bagpipe joined to the pipes of an organ (fig. 13, tab. 2) in his Dissertation *De tribus generibus instrumentorum veterum*, is purely imaginary." The passage from Virgil is cited by M. Fétis, but it cannot be traced in the works of that author.

to the leathern bag, which, from this time, served the office of our modern *wind-chest*. Father Kircher's representation of the Hebrew instrument, called *Macraphe d'Aruchin*, affords an illustration of an *organ* of this kind.

From the progressive inventions here recorded, it will be observed that many portions of the modern organ were already to be met with in the instruments of the ancients, in a more or less complete state. We may, therefore, justly assign the invention of the organ to this period, though no precise date can be given ; thus much only can be stated with certainty, that all these inventions date from a period before the birth of Christ.

2. *The Hydraulic-Organ.*

Vitruvius, in his celebrated work on Architecture (but treating of other matters very little allied to that art), has left us a curious chapter on the *hydraulic* or *water organ*, which, from its complicated character, has much puzzled the learned. The *bellows* of the first organs, as we have seen, were very small, and so imperfectly constructed, that they could not supply a steady wind ; the organ in consequence did not produce a uniform tone. Thus, the improvement of the wind apparatus was now seriously thought of, and the result was the invention of the *water-organ*, the water being used in such a manner as to counterbalance the hitherto variable pressure.

Vitruvius' description, extracted from his work *De Architectura* (lib. x., cap. xi.), translated by Newton, is as follows :—

"OF THE HYDRAULIC-ORGANS.*

" I must not omit to discourse briefly, and as explicitly as I am able, on the

---

* The original Latin text is as follows :—

" De hydraulicis autem quas habeant ratiocinationes, quam brevissime proximeque attingere

construction of the hydraulic-organs. Upon a compact base of timber an arca (cistern), made of brass, is disposed; and to the right and left, upon the base, timbers united in the manner of ladders are erected; between these are included brass buckets, with moveable pistons, very carefully turned, and h ving bent and jointed irons fixed to their middle, with levers adjoined, and being covered with unshorn sheep skins: in the upper surface (of the buckets) are holes of about three digits; near to which holes are brass dolphins fixed on turning joints, and having cymbals hanging by chains from their mouths below the holes of the buckets.

"Within the arca which contains the water is a kind of inverted funnel, under which wedges, of about three digits high, are laid, to level the space between the under lip of the pnigeus and the bottom of the arca. Upon the neck of this (pnigeus) is fixed the little cistern which supports the head of the machine, called by the Greeks *canon musicus*. In the length of this (canon) are channels, in number four if tetrachordic, six if hexachordic, and eight if octachordic. In the several channels are epistomia (stoppers), having iron handles; which handles, when turned, open orifices from the arca (arcula) into the channels. The canon has also holes ranged transversely, communicating with the channels, and corresponding to orifices in the upper table, which in Greek is called *pinax*. Between the table and canon are disposed rulers, which, being perforated in the same

potero et scriptura consequi, non prætermittam. De materia compacta basi, arca in ea ex ære fabricata collocatur. Supra basim eriguntur regulæ dextra ac sinistra scalari forma compactæ, quibus includuntur ærei modioli fundulis ambulatilibus ex torno subtiliter subactis, habentibus fixos in medio ferreos ancones, et verticulis cum vectibus conjunctos pellibusque lanatis involutos. Item in summa planitie foramina circiter digitorum ternum, quibus foraminibus proxime in verticulis collocati ærei Delphini, pendentia habentes catenis cymbala ex ore infra foramina modiolorum chalata. Intra arcam, quo loci aqua sustinetur, inest in id genus uti infundibulum inversum, quod super taxilli alti circiter digitorum ternum suppositi librant spatium imum, ima inter labra pnigeos et arcæ fundum. Supra autem cerviculum ejus coagmentata arcula sustinet caput machinæ, quæ Græce κανὼν μουσικός appellatur: in cujus longitudine canales si tetrachordos est fiunt quatuor, si hexachordos sex, si octachordos octo. Singulis autem canalibus singula epistomia sunt inclusa, manubriis ferreis collocata: quæ manubria cum torquentur, ex arca patefaciunt nares in canales. Ex canalibus autem canon habet ordinata in transverso foramina respondentia in naribus, quæ sunt in tabula summa, quæ tabula Græce πίναξ dicitur. Inter tabulam et canona regulæ sunt interpositæ ad eundem modum foratæ et oleo subactæ, ut faciliter impellantur et rursus introrsus reducantur, quæ obturant ea foramina, pleuritidesque* appellantur, quarum itus et reditus, alias obturat, alias aperit terebrationes. Hæ regulæ habent ferrea choragia fixa et juncta cum pinnis, quarum pinnarum tactus motiones efficit regularum. Continentur supra tabulam foramina, quæ ex canalibus habent egressum spiritus. Regulis sunt annuli agglutinati, quibus lingulæ omnium includuntur organorum. E modiolis autem fistulæ sunt continenter conjunctæ ligneis cervicibus, pertingentesque ad nares, quæ sunt in arcula, in quibus axes sunt ex torno subacti et ibi collocati, qui, cum recipit arcula animam, spiritum non patientur obturantes foramina rursus redire. Ita cum vectes extolluntur, ancones deducunt fundos modiolorum ad imum, Delphinique, qui sunt in verticulis inclusi chalantes in os, cymbala replent spatia modiolorum, atque ancones extollentes fundos intra modiolos vehementi pulsus crebritate, et obturantes foramina cymbalis superiora, aera, qui est ibi clausus, pressionibus coactum, in fistulas cogunt, per quas in lignea concurrit, et per ejus cervices in arcam: motione vero vectium vehementiore, spiritus frequens compressus epistomiorum aperturis influit, et replet anima canales. Itaque cum pinnæ manibus tactæ propellunt et reducunt continenter regulas, alternis obturando foramina, alternis aperiundo, ex musicis artibus multiplicibus modulorum varietatibus sonantes excitant voces. Quantum potui," &c.—*M. Vitruvii Pollionis Architectura.* Utini, 1825-1830, tom. iv., pp. 169 et seq.

* Melius forsan *plinthides* a Græc. πλίνθις.

manner, and anointed with oil that they may be easily moved to and fro, stop these holes, and are called *pleuritides;* the passing and re-passing of which alternately stops and opens the holes.

"These rulers have iron choragia affixed to them, and are united to pinnæ, the touching of which pinnæ causes the motion of the rulers. Upon the table are the holes, through which the air from the channel passes. To the rulers are fixed rings, in which the tongues of all the organic pipes are inclosed. From the buckets proceed tubes, united to the neck of the pnigeus, and communicating with the orifices that are in the arcula ; in these tubes are fixed well-turned valves, which, when the arcula has received the air, stop their apertures, and prevent its return.

"Thus, when the handles of the levers are raised, the pistons of the buckets are drawn to the bottom ; and the dolphins that are fixed on axes lowering the cymbals that hang from their mouths, the cavities of the buckets become filled (with air). Then the pistons being raised into the buckets again, with frequent and strong pulsations, and thereby causing the cymbals to stop the upper holes, the air, which is there confined, is by the pressure forced into the tubes, from whence it passes into the pnigeus, and through its neck into the arca (arcula) ; and the frequent motion of the levers still violently compressing the air, it rushes through the apertures of the epistomia, and fills the channel with wind ; when, therefore, the pinnæ are touched by the hand, they thrust forward and draw back the rulers, alternately stopping and opening the holes ; and thus, by the art of music, sounds in an infinite variety of modulations may be produced.

"I have thus endeavoured to explain, as well as I could by writing, this complex machine ; but the construction thereof cannot be easily understood, except by those who are practised in things of this sort : those, however, who understand a little from the description, will, when they see the machine itself, more easily comprehend it, and will find the whole curiously and ingeniously contrived."

From this description, it seems that the water which forced the air into the pipes was pumped by men. Indeed, it has been much disputed whether the instrument was played with *fingers*, by means of levers, or *keys*. The latter was impossible, as they were not invented until perhaps a *thousand* years afterwards ! Yet, it has been remarked, the description of the *hydraulicon* by Claudian seems such a one as would suit a modern organ, only blown by the aid of water :—

> "Vel qui magna levi detrudens murmura tactu,
> Innumeras voces segetis moderatus aënæ ;
> Intonat erranti digito, penitusque trabali
> Vecte laborantes in carmina concitat undas."

Thus Englished by Dr. Busby :—

> "With flying fingers, as they lightsome bound,
> From brazen tubes he draws the pealing sound.
> Unnumber'd notes the captive ear surprise,
> And swell and thunder as his art he plies :
> The beamy bar he heaves ! the waters wake !
> And liquid lapses liquid music make."*

---

* *General Hist. of Mus.* 1819, vol. i., p. 220.

Kircher, in his *Musurgia* (lib. ix., p. 332), has given a lengthy description of the *Vitruvian hydraulicon*, and has accompanied his account by an engraving of the instrument, such as he conceived it to have been from the description handed down to us. Isaac Vossius, in his treatise *De Poematum Cantu et Viribus Rhythmi*, p. 100, gives another fancied representation of the instrument ; and a third may be seen in Perrault's* notes upon Vitruvius ; but, as all three differ considerably from each other, they cannot be received as authorities.

Dr. Burney says, " Neither the description of the hydraulic-organ in Vitruvius, nor the conjectures of his innumerable commentators, have put it in the power of the moderns either to imitate, or perfectly to conceive, the manner of its construction ; and it still remains a doubt whether it was ever worthy of the praises which poets have bestowed upon it, or superior to the wretched remains of the invention still to be seen in the grottos of the vineyards, near the city of Rome."†

Athenæus, who flourished in the third century, has left us an account of the *hydraulic-organ*, which is probably the most ancient and authentic extant.‡ He tells us that it was invented, in the time of the second Ptolemy Euergetes, by Ctesibius, a native of Alexandria (B.C. 200), and by profession a barber ; or rather that it was improved by him, for Plato furnished the first idea of the *hydraulic-organ*, by inventing a night-clock, which was a *clepsydra*, or water-clock, that played upon flutes the hours of the night at a time when they could not be seen on the index.

A very interesting treatise on pneumatics by one Hero of Alexandria, supposed to have been a pupil of Ctesibius, has lately been translated from the original Greek, and published by Mr. Bennet Woodcroft.§ Hitherto we have been content to rely on Vitruvius for our knowledge of the ancient organ, but now we have an independent authority ; for the work of Hero was unknown to Vitruvius, and both

---

* This author mentions, in his commentary on Vitruvius, a method of swelling an diminishing the force of each note in an organ : it is to communicate wind to one pipe, or to two, three, or more pipes, in proportion to the pressure of the key. This method has lately been introduced into the Harmonium.

† Reflections on the construction of Musical Instruments, *Hist. of Mus.* i., 491.

‡ Lib. iv., p. 174.

§ *The Pneumatics of Hero of Alexandria*, from the original Greek. 4to, 1851. It contains two separate descriptions of the organ : " An Altar Organ blown by the agency of a Wind-mill " (noticed in the text), and " An Altar Organ blown by Manual Labour."

describe, with considerable differences, the construction of the hydraulic and of the pneumatic organ.

The following is Hero's description of

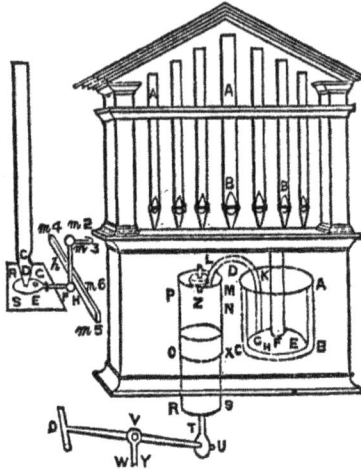

AN ALTAR ORGAN BLOWN BY MANUAL LABOUR.

The construction of an hydraulic-organ. Let A B C D be a small altar of bronze containing water. In the water invert a hollow hemisphere, called a *pnigeus*, E F G H, which will allow of the passage of the water at the bottom. From the top of this let the tubes ascend above the altar ; one of them, G K L M, bent without the altar, and communicating with a box, N X O P, inverted, and having its inner surface made perfectly level to fit a piston. Into this box let the piston, R S, be accurately fitted, that no air may enter by its side ; and to the piston attach a rod, T U, of great strength. Again, attach to the piston-rod another rod, U Q, moving about a pin at U, and also working like the beam of a lever on the upright rod, W Y, which must be well secured. On the inverted bottom of the box, N X O P, let another smaller box, Z, rest, communicating with N X O P, and closed by a lid above ; in the lid is a hole through which the air will enter the box. Place a thin plate under the hole in the lid to close it, upheld by means of four pins passing through holes in the plate, and furnished with heads, so that the plate cannot fall off ; such a plate is called a valve. Again, let another tube, F I, ascend from F G, communicating with a transverse tube, A' B', on which rest the pipes, A A A, communicating with the tube, and having at the lower extremities small boxes, like those used for money ; these boxes communicate with the pipes, and their orifices, B B B, must be open. Across these orifices let perforated lids slide, so that, when the lids are pushed home, the holes in them coincide with the holes in the pipes, but, when the lids are drawn outwards, the connection is broken, and the pipes are closed. Now, if the transverse beam, U Q, be depressed at Q, the piston, R S, will rise and force out the air in the box, N X O P ; the air will close the aperture in the small box, Z, by means of the valve described above, and pass along the tube, M L K G, into the hemisphere : again, it will pass out of the hemisphere along the tube, F I. into the transverse tube, A' B', and out of the transverse tube into the pipes, if the apertures in the pipes and in the lid coincide ; that is, if the lids, either all, or some of them, have been pushed home.

In order that, when we wish any of the pipes to sound, the corresponding holes may be opened and closed again when we wish the sound to cease, we may employ the following contrivance :—Imagine one of the boxes at the extremities of the pipes, C D, to be isolated, D being its orifice, E the communicating pipe, R S the lid fitted to it, and G the hole in the lid not coinciding with the pipe, E. Take three jointed bars, F H, H M, MM², of which the bar, F H, is attached to the lid, S F, while the whole moves about a pin at M³. Now, if we depress with the hand the extremity, M², towards D, the orifice of the box, we shall push the lid inwards, and, when it is in, the aperture in it will coincide with that in the tube. That, when we withdraw the hand, the lid may be spontaneously drawn out and close the communication, the following means may be employed. Underneath the boxes let a rod, M⁴ M⁵, run, equal and parallel to the tube, A B, and fix to this slips of horn, elastic and curved, of which M⁶, lying opposite C D, is one. A string, fastened to the extremity of the slip of horn, is carried round the extremity, H, so that when the lid is pushed out the string is tightened ; if, therefore, we depress the extremity, M², and drive the lid inwards, the string will forcibly pull the piece of horn and straighten it ; but, when the hand is withdrawn, the horn will return again to its original position and draw away the lid from the orifice, so as to destroy the correspondence between the holes. This contrivance having been applied to the box of each pipe, when we require any of the pipes to sound we must depress the corresponding key with the fingers ; and, when we require any of the sounds to cease, remove the fingers, whereupon the lids will be drawn out, and the pipes will cease to sound.

The water is poured into the altar that the superabundant air (I mean, of course, that which is thrust out of the box and forces the water upwards) may be confined in the hemisphere, so that the pipes which are free to sound may always have a supply. The piston, R S, when raised, drives the air out of the box into the hemisphere, as has been explained ; and, when depressed, opens the valve in the small box, Z. By this means the box is filled with air from without, which the piston, when forced up again, will again drive into the hemisphere. It would be better that the rod, T U, should move about a pivot at T also, by means of a single [loop] R, which may be fitted into the bottom of the piston, and through which the pivot must pass, that the piston may not be drawn aside, but rise and fall vertically.

I shall briefly call attention to this ancient author's drawing of " an altar organ blown by the agency of a wind-mill." The cylindrical vessel forcing the air into the pipes by means of a piston is here shown.

In our own days, in a journal of only twenty-five years back, we read that "a novel organ has lately been erected by the Prince Brancaforte, upon a hill in his park, near Messina ; it is supplied with wind *by a wind-mill,* and can be distinctly heard two or three miles distant." Probably the Italian prince thought that he had hit upon a novelty when he erected his wind-mill organ ; but we now find that his device had been anticipated more than eighteen hundred years before.

The mechanical operation of the *water-organ,* as we have said, is scarcely intelligible ; this much, however, is certain, that the *hydrauli-con* was provided with pipes and a wind-chest, and registered like the wind-organ. We must not suppose that the water directly produced the wind, but that it served merely to give the wind, by means of counter-pressure, equality, and power. Ctesibius' object was "to employ a row of pipes of great size, and capable of emitting the most fanciful, as well as the softest sounds." He is also said to have invented, or perfected, the perforated slide, by which means he was enabled to open and shut the mouths of the pipes with greater facility.*

Instruments of the *hydraulic* kind were made of different sizes, and in different forms. Athenæus, in his chapter on musical instruments, before mentioned, refers to a water-organ small enough to be trans-ported from place to place like the portable hand-organs of the Savoyards. A representation of this instrument is rudely indicated on a contorniate coin of the Emperor Nero, in the collection of anti-quities bequeathed to the Vatican by Christiana, Queen of Sweden. It is a medal of Valentinian, showing an organ of eight pipes placed upon a round pedestal. No performer or mode of performing appears ; but two figures, one on each side, are engaged in pumping the water by which it is worked.†

Kepler, the celebrated mathematician, had a mean opinion of this instrument. He says, "The water-organ, though it might have registers like the wind-organ, was not an admirable invention of the ancients, but mere *bagpiping !"‡*

Tertullian, the patriarch, who declares Ctesibius, of Alexandria, to

---

* Dr. Smith's *Dictionary of Greek and Roman Antiquities,* who cites, as authorities, Athenæus, Vitruvius, Drieberg, Brunck's *Anal.,* ii., 403, Claud. *De Mall. Theod. Cons.,* 316, Tertullian's *De Anima,* 14, &c.

† This coin is engraved in Rich's *Companion to the Latin Dictionary and Greek Lexicon,* p. 342 ; and in Dr. Smith's *Dictionary of Greek and Roman Antiquities,* p. 503.

‡ *Harmonices Mundi,* bk. iii.

be the *inventor*, and Archimedes the *improver* of the water-organ, expresses himself in the following extravagant terms of eulogy:—"Observe the extraordinary genius of Archimedes: I mean the water-organ; so many members, so many parts, so many joinings, so many roads or passages for the voices, such a compendium of sounds, such an intercourse of modes, such troops of tibiæ, and all composing one great whole! The spirit or air which is breathed out from this engine of water is administered through the parts, solid in substance, but divided in operation."*

A curious representation of an *hydraulic-organ* is exhibited in a poem by Publilius Optatianus, describing the instrument: it is composed of verses so constructed as to show both the lower part which contained the bellows, the wind-chest which lay upon it, and over this the row of twenty-six pipes. The latter are represented by twenty-six lines, which increase in length each by one letter, until the last line is twice as long as the first.†

The *hydraulic-organ* was occasionally used down to a comparatively late period. Vossius tells us that, in the French annals of an anonymous writer, he is informed that, in the year 826, a certain Venetian called Georgius, or rather Gregorius, constructed an hydraulic-organ for Louis the Pious, at Aix-la-Chapelle, and that after the manner of the ancients.‡

Dom Bedos, an industrious Benedictine monk, who wrote, about the middle of the eighteenth century, a voluminous work, entitled *L'Art du Facteur des Orgues*,§ cites a very curious passage from the Chronicle of William of Malmesbury, which is thus translated. Speaking of Pope Silvester II. (who died in 1003), he says:—"In the church

---

* The original passage, cited by Vossius, *De Poematum*, p. 106, is as follows:—"Specta portentosam Archimedis (Ctesibii rectius dixisset) munificentiam: organum hydraulicum dico, tot membra, tot partes, tot campagines, tot itinera vocum, tot compendia sonorum, tot commercia modorum, tot acies tibiarum, et una moles erunt omnia. Spiritus ille, qui de tormento aquæ anhelat, per partes administratur, substantia solidus, opera divisus."

† Wernsdorf's *Poetae Lat. Min.*, vol. ii., p. 394.

‡ *De Poematum*, 106.

§ This splendid work, containing 137 plates, was published at Paris in 1766-1778. The author styles himself "Dom François Bedos de Celles, Benedicton de la Congrégation de Saint Maur, dans l'Abbaye de Saint Denys en France; de l'Academie Royale des Sciences de Bordeaux, et Correspondant de celle de Paris." He is generally called *Don Bedos de Celles*. (Monks in the early ages were styled *Dominus*, afterwards *Domnus*, and finally abbreviated by the French into *Dom*. *Celles* is the name of the place where Bedos was born.) A copy of the original work is preserved in the King's Library, British Museum. It has lately been reprinted at Paris, and forms one of the numbers of the *Encyclopédie-Roret*. Par M. Hamel, 1849; 3 vols., 12mo and folio.

of Rheims are still extant (A.D. 1125), as proofs of his science, a clock constructed on mechanical principles; and an *hydraulic-organ*, in which the air, escaping in a surprising manner, by the force of *heated water*, fills the cavity of the instrument, and the brazen pipes emit modulated tones through the multifarious apertures."*

Mason, commenting on this passage, says, "I here suspect that by the word *ventus* the monk meant steam; because the sound was produced by hot water, *aquæ calefactæ violentia;* and if so, we have a new purpose, to which the ingenious steam engineers of the present time may, if they please, employ it."†

Dr. Powell, in his curious volume, *Humane Industry, or a History of most Manual Arts*, 12mo, 1661 (p. 109), mentions this instrument, but adds that it was self acting:—"Pope Silvester II. made, in his younger years, a pair of organs that should play without an organist; he used only warm water to give them motion and sound. Such hydraulics are frequent in Italy, that are moved with cold water as well as hot."

In another chapter of his book (*De Aquaticis Machinis‡*) Dr. Powell gives some curious notices of the water-organs of the seventeenth century. He says, "There are in sundry places of Italy and elsewhere certain *Organa Hydraulica*, that is, Organs that make good Musick of themselves, only by forcing the water up the pipes, and by the collision of the Ayr and Water therein: The lower part of the pipes are placed in the water (as Petrus Victorius describes them), which water being forced up with a scrue, or such device, doth inspire the pipes, as well as the wind that is made with a bellows. Among the water-works in the Duke of Florence his garden, there was an Hydraulic-Organ that with the turning of a cock would make sweet harmony, as Mr. Morison relates; the invention is ancient, for Ammianus Marcellinus makes mention of one, and Claudian describes one thus in his Poem *De Consulatu Mallii Theodori :—*

> ' Et qui magna levi detrudit murmura tactu
> Innumeras voces segetis moderatus Aënæ
> Intonat erranti digito penitusq. trabali
> Vecte, laborantes in carmina concitat undas.'

---

* Bohn's edition of *William of Malmesbury*, by Dr. Giles, p. 175.
† *Essays Historical and Critical, on English Church Music;* York, 1795, p. 35. The original Latin is as follows :—"Aquæ calefactæ violentia ventus emergens implet concavitatem barbiti, et per multiforatiles transitus æneæ fistulæ modulatos clamores emittunt."
‡ *Humane Industry*, p. 38.

Which invention is by some ascribed to Ctesibius, an ingenious artist of Alexandria; by others to Archimedes of Syracuse, as Tertullian writes, of which he speaks thus, *Specta potentissimam Archimedis*, &c."

As to the *hydraulic-organs* of modern Italy of which Grassineau* says there were several in the grottos of vineyards, "particularly one belonging to the family d'Este, near the Tiber, described by Baptista Porta, they were very different, and no way resembled the ancient *hydraulia.*" These, perhaps, as Sir J. Hawkins remarks,† will be found to be nothing more than the common organ played on by the barrel, which, by a very easy contrivance, is set in motion by a small stream of water.

3. *The Pneumatic-Organ.*

The various contrivances to introduce the wind into the pipes by means of water were not found to be successful, in spite of their seeming superiorities. A return was therefore made to the ancient bellows filled by manual labour. The Emperor Julian, called the Apostate (who died A.D. 363), is the reputed author of the following Greek enigmatical epigram, the solution of which is evidently the *pneumatic-organ.*

'Αλλοίην ὁράω δονάκων φύσιν· ἦπου ἀπ' ἄλλης
Χαλκείης τάχα μᾶλλον ἀνεβλάστησαν ἀρούρης,
Ἄγριοι, οὐδ' ἀνέμοισιν ὑφ' ἡμετέροις δονέονται,
Ἀλλ' ὑπο ταυρείης προθορὼν σπήλυγγος ἀήτης,
Νέρθεν εὐτρήτων καλάμων ὑπὸ ῥίζαν ὁδεύει.
Καί τις ἀνὴρ ἀγέρωχος ἔχων θοὰ δάκτυλα χειρὸς,
Ἵσταται ἀμφαφόων κανόνας συμφράδμονας αὐλῶν·
Οἱ δ' ἀπαλὸν σκιρτῶντες, ἀποθλίβουσιν ἀοιδήν.‡

Thus *literally* translated :—

"I see a species of reeds : surely from another and a brazen soil have they quickly sprung—rude. Nor are they agitated by our winds, but a blast rushing forth from a cavern of bull's hide makes its way from below the root of reeds with many openings ; and a highly-gifted man, with nimble fingers, handles the yielding rods of the pipes, while they, softly bounding, press out a sound."

---

* *Musical Dictionary*, 1743, p. 171.

† *Hist. of Mus.* bk. ii., chap. 14.

‡ *Anthologia Græca*, Edit. Lips. 1794, tom. iii., p. 111 ; also Du Cange, *Glossarium et infimæ latinitatis*, v. organum,

This passage is highly interesting, as showing the state of the instrument at this early period. From it we learn that the organ was still unprovided with a *clavier* or key-board, and that the bellows were made of a bull's hide. These facts have escaped the researches of former writers, who have alluded to the enigma, from their *mistranslation* of the original Greek.*

We have here a curious representation of an organ of this period, which shows a singular mode of giving weight to the bellows. It is copied from the sculptures on the obelisk at Constantinople, erected by Theodosius, who died A.D. 395.†

---

* Burney translates the passage thus : "I see reeds of a new species, the growth of another and a brazen soil, such as are not agitated by our winds, but by a blast that rushes from a leathern cavern beneath their roots ; while a robust mortal, running with swift fingers over the concordant *keys*, makes them, as they smoothly dance, emit melodious sounds."— *Hist. of Mus.*, ii., 65. Busby gives a metrical translation :—

> "Reeds I behold, of earth the rigid spoil,
> Reeds of a novel growth, and brazen soil !
> That not heaven's wind, but blasts mechanic breathe,
> From lungs that labour at their roots beneath ;
> While a skill'd artist's nimble finger bounds
> O'er dancing *keys*, and wakes celestial sounds."

—*Hist. of Mus.*, i., 263. Both these learned writers use the word *keys*, which cannot, by any forced application, be found in the original. The word κανόνας (*canonas*) means "any straight rod or pole, especially to keep a thing upright or straight—to regulate and order it." See Liddell and Scott's *Greek and English Lexicon*. Burney translates ἀγέρωχος "a tall, sturdy fellow ;" and then adds, "alluding to the force necessary to beat that kind of clumsy *carillon* keys of this rude instrument of new invention." This Greek enigma on the organ is given by Mr. Wackerbarth, in his *Music and the Anglo-Saxons*, p. 9, who adds—"It is obvious, from the sixth line, that it was played with finger-keys, and not by large carillon-keys." He then blames Dr. Burney for missing "the sense of the passage," but does not attempt a new translation. It is necessary to add that Mr. Wackerbarth's copy of the eight Greek lines contains no fewer than twenty errors.

† Didron's *Annales Archéologiques*, Paris, 1845, contains an article on Organs by M. Coussemaker. Our engraving is derived from this valuable work.

Another curious description of the pneumatic organ is given by Cassiodorus, who flourished under King Vitigas, the Goth, A.D. 514, in his Commentary on the 150th Psalm.* "The organ," he says, "is an instrument composed of divers pipes, formed into a kind of tower, which, by means of bellows, is made to produce a loud sound; and, in order to express agreeable melodies, there are, in the inside, movements made of wood, that are pressed down by the fingers of the player, which produce the most pleasing and brilliant tones."†

At the latter end of the seventh and beginning of the eighth century the organs of the Anglo-Saxons appear to have resembled, even in their external decorations, those now in use. The following passage from Aldhelm,‡ who died A.D. 709, will show that our ancestors at that time were accustomed to gild the external pipes :—

> " Maxima millenis auscultans organa flabris,
> Mulceat auditum ventosis follibus iste,
> Quamlibet auratis fulgescant cætera capsis."

4. *Its Introduction into the Church.*

The *organ* was early used in the public service of the church. Platina tells us§ that it was first employed for religious worship by Pope Vitalian I., A.D. 666; but, according to Julianus, a Spanish bishop who flourished A.D. 450, it was in common use in the churches of Spain at least 200 years before Vitalian's time.‖ The use of instruments in churches was much earlier; for we are told that St. Ambrose joined instruments of music with the public service in the cathedral church of Milan; which example of his was so well approved of, that, by degrees, it became the general practice of other churches. Nay, the antiquity of instrumental church music is still higher, if we may credit the testimony of Justin Martyr and Eusebius, the latter of whom lived fifty, and the former two hundred, years before the time of St. Ambrose.¶

---

* The passage is also quoted by Bede, tom. viii., 899, 900.

† Organum itaque est quasi turris quædam diversis fistulis fabricata quibus flatu follium vox copiosissima destinatur ; et ut eam modulatio decora componat, linguis quibusdam ligneis ab interiori parte construitur, quas disciplinabiliter magistrorum digiti reprimentis, grandisonam efficiunt et suavissimam cantilenam. In Psalm cl.

‡ *De laude Virginum. Bibliotheca Maxima Patrum,* tom. xiii., p. 3. This passage was first pointed out by Mr. Sharon Turner, *Anglo-Saxons,* iv., 447.

§ *Lives of the Popes ;* Rycaud's translation, p. 114.

‖ See Lorinus, Psal. 33.

¶ Hawkins, bk. iv., chap. 32.

We have seen, from the Epigram of the Emperor Julian, before quoted, that an organ capable of being used in religious ceremonies existed long before the erection of Christian churches ; we cannot then refuse to credit the testimony of Julianus, as to its admission into the service of public worship at an earlier period than that commonly assigned.*

It was some time before organs became common in the churches of Europe. Pepin, the father of Charlemagne, king of the Franks, an ardent worshipper of God, first introduced singing and the ceremonies of the Romish Church into France. He soon perceived the urgent need of an organ, both as an aid to devotion, and as a proper accompaniment and support to the choir. Accordingly, as the instrument was unknown at that time both in France and Germany, this pious king applied to the Byzantine Emperor Constantine, surnamed Copronymus, soliciting him to forward one to France. The emperor complied with the request, and in the year 757, or thereabouts,† sent him as a present, in charge of a special embassy,‡ a great organ with leaden pipes,§ which was placed in the church of St. Corneille, at Compiegne. It also appears that an organ, constructed by an Arabian named Giafar, was sent to Charlemagne by the renowned "Commander of the Faithful," the caliph Haroun Alraschid—an incident introduced with considerable effect by Madame de Genlis, in her romance, *Les Chevaliers du Cygne*. This was the instrument, in all probability, which Walafrid Strabo described as existing in the ninth century in a church at Aix-la-Chapelle. Its softness (query ?) of tone, he adds, caused the death of a female.‖ It is certain that this organ was very imperfect, and we must suppose

---

* Bingham (*Christian Antiq.*, bk. viii., c. 7—16) and his followers assert that the organ was first introduced into churches by Marinus Sanutus, in 1290 ! The authorities cited in the course of the present section completely refute this notion. Cardinal Bona supposes organs to have been used in churches in the fourth century.—*De Divin. Psal.*, 1653.

† Siegebert says 766 ; but Walter Odington, of Evesham (who wrote in the 13th century), is a preferable authority. His words are, "*Anno Domini* 757, venit Organum primo in Francium missum a potissima Rege Græcorum Pipino imperatori."—*De Speculatione Musicæ.*

‡ The deputation to King Pepin was headed by Stephanus, a Roman bishop.—Aventini, *Annales Bavariæ.*

§ Alex. Sardus, *De rerum Inventoribus*, lib. i.

‖ Eginhard, in his *Annals of Louis le Débonnaire*, and Nigellus, in his poem on the life and actions of Louis the Pious, printed in the *Scriptores Italici de Muratori*, both speak of the organ at Aix-la-Chapelle; but they allude to the *hydraulicon*, not to the *pneumatic-organ*. The former was in the palace of the king, the latter in the church. Historians have strangely confounded the two.

that poetical enthusiasm led Strabo a little beyond the truth. His words are these :—

> " Dulce melos tantum vanas deludere mentes
> Cœpit, ut una suis decedens sensibus ipsam
> Fœmina perdiderit vocum dulcedine vitam."[*]

Be this as it may, the French artists were eager to equal these speci·mens of foreign ingenuity ; and so successful were their efforts, that, in the ninth century, it is said, the best organs were made in France and Germany. Their superiority was acknowledged by John VIII., in a letter to Anno, Bishop of Friesingen, from whom he requested an organ, and a master for the instruction of the Roman artists. The passage runs thus :—" Precamur ut optimum organum cum artifice, qui hoc moderari, et facere ad omnem modulationis efficaciam possit, ad instructionem musicæ disciplinæ nobis aut deferas, aut mittas."[†]

Soon afterwards we find them in common use in England, constructed by English artists, with pipes of copper fixed in gilt frames.[‡] St. Dunstan, in the reign of Edgar, erected or fabricated an organ, the pipes of which were made of brass.[§] The following notice of this instrument is preserved by William of Malmesbury :—" Ideo in multis locis munificus, quæ tunc in Anglia magni miraculi essent, decusque et ingenium conferentis ostenderent, offerre credo. Itaque signa sono et mole præstantia, et organo ubi per æreas fistulas musicis mensuris elaboratas, ' dudum conceptas follis vomit anxius auras.' Ibi hoc distichon laminis æreis impressit—

> Organo de Sancto Præsul Dunstanus Aldhelmo ;
> Perdat hic æternum qui vult hinc tollere regnum."[‖]

This worthy prelate also caused an organ to be erected in the abbey church of Glastonbury.

In the same century Count Elwin presented an organ to the convent of Ramsey, on which it is said, " The earl devoted thirty pounds to make copper pipes of organs, which, resting with their openings in thick order on the spiral winding in the inside, and being

---

[*] Walaf. Strabo *apud Abb. S. Blasii*, p. 140.

[†] Sandini, in *Vit. Pont.* i., p. 294. See also Dr. Lingard's *Antiquities of the Anglo-Saxon Church*, ii., p. 376.

[‡] Aldhelm in *Gale*, pp. 266, 420, cited by Lingard, *Anglo-Saxon Church*, ii., p. 376. See also the curious passage from Aldhelm, quoted in a previous section, *ante*, 17.

[§] St. Dunstan died A.D. 988.

[‖] Gale, tom. iii., p. 366 ; Wackerbarth's *Music and the Anglo-Saxons*, p. 19.

struck on feast days with a strong blast of bellows, emit a sweet melody and a far resounding peal."*

In the old monastic church of Winchester was a monster organ, according to its description by the monk Wulston,† whose fidelity, as Lingard remarks, cannot be questioned, since he dedicated his poem to Bishop Elphege,‡ by whose order the organ was built about the close of the tenth century. The portion of Wulston's poem relating to the organ is as follows :—

> " Talia et auxistis hic organa qualia nunquam
>   Cernuntur, gemino constabilita solo.
> Bisseni supra sociantur ordine folles,
>   Inferiusque jacent quatuor atque decem.
> Flatibus alternis spiracula maxima reddunt
>   Quos agitant validi septuaginta viri ;
> Brachia versantes, multo et sudore madentes,
>   Certatimque suos quisque movet socios,
> Viribus ut totis impellant flamina sursum
>   Rugiat et pleno capsa referta sinu
> Sola quadringentas quæ sustinet ordine musas
>   Quas manus organici temperat ingenii.
> Has aperit clausas, iterumque has claudit apertas
>   Exigit ut varii certa camæna soni.
> Considuntque duo concordi pectore fratres,
>   Et regit alphabetum rector uterque suum.
> Suntque quaterdenis occulta foramina linguis,
>   Inque suo retinet ordine quæque decem :
> Huc aliæ currunt, illuc aliæque recurrunt
>   Servantes modulis singula puncta suis ;
> Et feriunt jubilum septem discrimina vocum
>   Permixto lyrici carmine semitoni :
> Inque modum tonitrus vox ferrea verberat aures,
>   Præter ut hunc solum nil capiat sonitum.
> Concrepat in tantum sonus hinc illincque resultans,
>   Quisque manu patulas claudat ut auriculas,
> Haudquaquam sufferre valens propiando rugitum,
>   Quem reddunt varii concrepitando soni :
> Musarumque melos auditur ubique per urbem,
>   Et peragrat totam fama volans patriam.
> Hoc decus Ecclesiæ vovit tua cura Tonanti,
>   Clavigeri inque sacri struxit honore Petri."§

---

* The original Latin of this passage is thus given in the *Acta Sanctorum :*—" Triginta præterea libras ad fabricandum cupreos organorum calamos erogavit, qui in alveo suo, super unam cochlearum denso ordine foraminibus insidentes, et diebus festis follium spiramento fortiore pulsati, prædulcem melodiam et clangorem longius resonantem ediderunt."—*Acta Sanctorum Ordinis Benedict. Sæc.*, v., p. 756. See also Gale, tom. iii., p. 420.

† Called Wulston or *Wolston* the Deacon. He died A. D. 963.

‡ Elphegus Calvus received the Bishopric of Winchester in A.D. 935, and held it till 951.

§ *Acta Sanctorum Ordinis Benedict. Sæc.*, v., p. 631-2.

Thus translated by Mr. Wackerbarth*:—

"Such organs as you have built are seen nowhere, fabricated on a double ground. Twice six bellows above are ranged in a row, and fourteen lie below. These, by alternate blasts, supply an immense quantity of wind, and are worked by seventy strong men, labouring with their arms, covered with perspiration, each inciting his companions to drive the wind up with all his strength, that the full-bosomed box may speak with its four hundred pipes which the hand of the organist governs. Some when closed he opens, others when open he closes, as the individual nature of the varied sound requires. Two brethren (religious) of concordant spirit sit at the instrument, and each manages his own alphabet. There are, moreover, hidden holes in the forty tongues, and each has ten (pipes) in their due order. Some are conducted hither, others thither, each preserving the proper point (or situation) for its own note. They strike the seven differences of joyous sounds, adding the music of the lyric semitone. Like thunder the iron tones batter the ear, so that it may receive no sound but that alone. To such an amount does it reverberate, echoing in every direction, that every one stops with his hand his gaping ears, being in no wise able to draw near and bear the sound, which so many combinations produce. The music is heard throughout the town, and the flying fame thereof is gone out over the whole country. This honourable church has your care dedicated to the Ruler of the thunder, and built up in honour of the key-bearing St. Peter."†

Although this curious description gives the idea of an instrument of large size and complicated mechanism, its construction must have been of a very primitive kind. Mr. Wackerbarth imagines that it possessed registers or stops ; a key-board furnished with semitones ; and a compass of three and a half octaves. Of the first position we have no proof whatever in the poem itself. Of the second all the writer says is, that it was provided with the seven sounds and the "lyric semitone," which latter clearly means the B flat. The alphabet alluded to was the handles of the rods or levers by which the instrument was played ; the key-board was not yet invented. Of the third

---

* *Music and the Anglo-Saxons*, p. 12—15.

† Mason (*Essays on English Church Music*, p. 37) gives the following metrical translation of eight lines of Wulston's poem. He was not aware of the original, but quoted from Dom Bedos, who in his turn took the passage from Du Cange's *Glossary* :—

> " Twelve pair of bellows, ranged in stated row,
> Are join'd above, and fourteen more below ;
> These the full force of seventy men require,
> Who ceaseless toil, and plenteously perspire ;
> Each aiding each, till all the wind be prest
> In the close confines of th' incumbent chest,
> On which four hundred pipes in order rise
> To bellow forth the blast that chest supplies."

Bedos, and after him Mason, erroneously say that this organ was erected at Westminster.

position it is clear that the compass did not exceed ten notes, "and for each note forty pipes," which makes up the number of *four hundred*. The *seventy* stout bellows-blowers must still remain a perplexing question. The brethren of Winchester were a rich and a large body, and the writer probably meant that it was the office of seventy inferior monks, at different periods, to succeed each other in this labour. Or probably *seventy* may be a corruption of the text for seven.

An interesting representation of the pneumatic-organ of about this period is preserved in a MS. Psalter of Eadwine, in the library of Trinity College, Cambridge.* It is here copied.

At the close of the tenth century many organs existed in the churches of Germany. Michael Prætorius, in his *Syntagma Musicum*, mentions (under the date 944) those in the Paulina Church at Erfurt, in St. James's Church at Magdeburg, and in the cathedral at Halberstadt. Notwithstanding the imperfection of these instruments, they everywhere produced the greatest astonishment, and the churches were desirous of possessing so efficacious a means of attracting a congregation. We therefore find in this century that organs multiplied not only in the cathedral churches of the episcopal seats, but also in many churches and monastic establishments.

---

* Under the press mark Insig. R, 17, 1. It is engraved in Strutt's *Horda*, i., pl. 33.

5. *Organ-Building in the Eleventh Century.*

The following very curious treatise upon the *Construction of Organs* is part of a larger work upon *Divers Arts*, by a monk named Theophilus.

There is a considerable diversity of opinion as to the exact period at which the writer flourished. Lessing, Leist, Raspe, and Emeric David, have placed him in the *tenth* century, a period too early. Guichard, Didron, and Texiér, consider that he belongs to the *twelfth* or *thirteenth* century. Mr. Hendrie, in his learned preface to the English translation of Theophilus,[*] shows pretty clearly that the work in question may be assigned to the early half of the *eleventh* century.

The most ancient manuscripts that have descended to us are of the latter part of the twelfth, or the early part of the following century. One is preserved at Wolfenbüttel; another in the Imperial Library, Vienna; a third is in the University Library, Cambridge; and a fourth among the Harleian MSS. in the British Museum. The three first-named manuscripts end abruptly, closing with the first chapter on the Construction of the Organ. The Harleian MS. enriches the musical inquirer with *three* new chapters upon the mode of building the "King of Instruments" in the eleventh century.[†]

Theophilus's treatise has escaped the notice of all writers, both foreign and English, who have devoted their time and talents to the consideration of musical antiquities. Such being the case, I have considerable pleasure in being the first to introduce it into that department of musical history to which it more particularly belongs :—

---

[*] *Theophili, qui et Rugerus, Presbyteri et Monachi Libri III., de Diversis Artibus.* Opera et Studio Roberti Hendrie. Londini, Johannes Murray, MDCCCXLVII. 8vo. I owe my knowledge of this curious treatise on the organ entirely to Mr. Hendrie's valuable book. The following translation is taken (with permission) from that gentleman's publication.

[†] This manuscript is upon vellum, in octavo, and is written in a clear German character of the very commencement of the thirteenth century. Sir F. Madden, the keeper of the manuscripts at the British Museum, and whose authority is conclusive, states that it is of that period, and that it was certainly written in Germany. It contains 115 folios of the books of Theophilus, and five folios of recipes relating to the arts, written by another hand of the period. A treatise, "De Unguentis," follows : it is a collection of medical recipes. The title and preface to the first book are unfortunately wanting : in so voluminous and superior a copy something might have been otherwise adduced from these which would have unravelled the mystery which shrouds the age and country of our author. The credit of discovering this important manuscript is entirely due to Mr. Hendrie. See his preface to *Theophilus*, p. xxvi.

𝔗𝔥𝔢𝔬𝔭𝔥𝔦𝔩𝔦 𝔏𝔦𝔟𝔯𝔦 𝔗𝔢𝔯𝔱𝔦𝔦 𝔡𝔢
𝔇𝔦𝔟𝔢𝔯𝔰𝔦𝔰 𝔄𝔯𝔱𝔦𝔟𝔲𝔰.*
(Original.)

CAPUT LXXXI.

DE ORGANIS.

FACTURUS organa primum habeat lec-
tionem mensuræ, qualiter metiri debeant
fistulæ graves et acutæ et superacutæ ;
deinde faciat sibi ferrum longum et
grossum ad mensuram, quam vult habere
fistulas, quod sit in circuitu, rotundum
summâ diligentiâ limatum et politum, in
unâ summitate grossius et modicè at-
tenuatum, ita ut possit imponi in alterum
ferrum curvum per quod circumdatur,
juxta modum ligni in quo volvitur run-
cina, et in alterâ summitate gracile,
secundum mensuram inferioris capitis
fistulæ, quæ conflatorio debet imponi.
Deinde attenueter cuprum purum et
sanissimum, ita ut unguis impressus
alterâ parte appareat. Quod cum fuerit
secundum mensuram ferri lineatum et
incisum ad longiores fistulas, quæ dicun-
tur graves, fiat secundum præceptum
lectionis foramen, in quo plectrum imponi debet, et circumradatur modicè ad
mensuram festucæ (fistulæ), ac super-
liniatur stagnum ferro solidatorio, rada-
turque in orâ longitudinis interiùs, in
alterâ orâ exteriùs eâdem mensurâ, et
superstagnetur tenuè. Quæ stagnatura,
priusquam rasi tractus noviter facti,
modicè calefacto cupro liniantur cum
resina abietis, ut stagnum facilius adhæreat. Quo facto, complicetur ipsum
cuprum circa ferrum et circumlige-
tur filo ferreo mediocriter grosso fortiter, ita ut stagnati tractus conveniant
sibi. Quod filum primo induci debet
parvulo foramini, quod est in gracili

𝔗𝔥𝔢𝔬𝔭𝔥𝔦𝔩𝔲𝔰'𝔰 𝔗𝔯𝔢𝔞𝔱𝔦𝔰𝔢 𝔬𝔫
𝔒𝔯𝔤𝔞𝔫 𝔅𝔲𝔦𝔩𝔡𝔦𝔫𝔤.
(Translation.)

CHAPTER LXXXI.

OF ORGANS.

THE manufacturer of organs should
first possess the knowledge of the measure, how the grave and sharp and treble
pipes should be meted out; he may then
make for himself a long and thick iron
to the size which he wishes the pipes to
possess ; this must be round, filed and
polished with great care, thicker at one
extremity and slightly diminished, so
that it can be placed in another curved
iron, by which it is encompassed, after
the fashion of the wood in which the
augur is revolved, and at the other extremity let it be slender, according to
the size of the lower end of the pipe
which should be placed on the bellows.
Then pure and very sound copper is
thinned, so that the impression of the
nail may appear on the other side.
When this has been marked out and cut
according to the size of the iron for the
longer pipes, which are called grave, an
opening is made according to the precept
of the lesson, into which the valve should
be placed, and it is rasped round a little
to the size of the rod,† and tin is anointed
over it with the soldering iron, and it is
rasped upon one edge of the length inside, and outside, upon the other edge,
and it is tinned over thinly. Which
tinnings, before the newly made lines
are scraped, are slightly anointed, the
copper being warmed with resin of the
fir, that the tin may the more easily adhere. Which being done, this copper
is folded around the iron and is strongly
bound round with an iron wire moderately thick, so that the tinned lines may
agree with each other. This wire should
be first carried through a very small hole
which is at the thin extremity of the iron,

---

* A few corrections have been made in the text, such as the grammatical construction
obviously suggested.

† " Pipe," in the Wolfenbüttel MS.

summitate ferri, et in eo bis contorqueri, sicque deduci in volvendo usque ad alteram summitatem, ibique similiter obfirmari. Deinde juncturis sibi convenientibus et diligenter conjunctis, ponatur ipsâ ligaturâ pariter cum ferro ante fornacem super prunas ardentes, et sedente puero et mediocriter flante, teneatur dexterâ manu lignum gracile, in cujus summitate fissâ, adhæreat panniculus cum resina, et sinistrâ teneatur stagnum longum gracile percussum, ut mox cum fistula incaluerit, liniat juncturam cum panniculo resina infecto, appositumque stagnum liquefiat, ipsamque juncturam (addidimus) diligenter consolidet. Quo facto, refrigeratâ fistulâ, ponatur ferrum in instrumento tornatoris more parato, impositoque curvo ferro et filo soluto circumvolvat unus ferrum curvum, alter vero, utrisque manibus chirothecis indutis, fistulam fortiter teneat, ita ut ferrum circumducatur et fistula quieta maneat, donec omnino oculis gratiosa sit, quasi tornata sit. Deinde educto ferro percutiatur ipsa fistula cum malleo mediocriter juxta foramen inferius et superius, ita ut pene usque ad medium descendat ipsa rotunditas spatio duorum digitorum ; fiatque plectrum ex cupro aliquantulum spissiori, quasi dimidia rotula, et superstagnetur circa rotunditatem sicut fistula superius, sicque ponatur in inferiori parte foraminis, ut sub ipsius ora æqualitèr stet, nec procedat inferius aut superius. Habeat quoque ferrum solidatorium ejusdem latitudinis et rotunditatis, quâ plectrum est. Quo calefacto ponat modicas particulas stagni super plectrum, parumque resinæ, et diligenter circumducat calidum ferrum ne plectrum moveatur, sed liquefacto stagno sic adhæreat ut in circuitu ejus nihil spiraminis exeat, nisi tantum in superiori foramine. Quo facto, apponat ori et sufflet primum modicè, deinde amplius, sicque fortiter, et secundum quod auditu discernit, disponat vocem, ut si eam vult esse grossam, foramen

and be twisted twice round in it, and so be carried down revolving to the other extremity, and be there similarly fastened. Then with its joinings agreeing together and carefully fastened, it is placed with its ligature, as with the iron, before the furnace upon the glowing embers, and the boy sitting and slightly blowing, in the left hand is held a thin wood, at the split top of which a small cloth with resin is fixed, and in the right can be held a long piece of tin beaten thin, so that directly the pipe has become hot he can anoint the joint with the rag filled with resin, and the tin applied may liquify, and he must carefully solder the join together. Which being done, the pipe cold, the iron is placed in the instrument prepared like that of a turner, and the curved iron being placed on, and wire loosened, one can revolve the curved iron, the other, both hands being provided with gloves, can hold the pipe firmly, so that the iron may be carried round and the pipe remain still, until it appear elegant to the eyes, as if turned. The iron being then taken out, the pipe is struck slightly with the hammer near the opening, above and below, so that this round shape may depress almost to the centre for a space of two fingers ; the valve may be made from copper somewhat thicker, like a half wheel, and be soldered over about the round part, as the pipe above, and be so placed in the lower part of the opening that it may stand equally under its edge, nor protrude below or above. He can have also a soldering iron of the same breadth and roundness as the valve. With this heated he can place small particles of tin upon the valve, and a little resin, and can carefully pass over the hot iron, that he may not move the valve, but that the tin being melted it may so adhere that no wind can come out in its circumference, unless only into the upper opening. Which being done, he can bring it to his mouth and blow at first slightly, then more, and then strongly ; and, according to what he discerns by hearing, he can arrange the sound, so that if he wish it strong

fiat latius ; si vero graciliorem, fiat stric-
tius. Hoc ordine omnes fistulæ fiant ;
mensuram vero singularum, a plectro
superius, secundum magisterium lectionis faciat, a plectro autem inferius, omnes
unius mensuræ et ejusdem grossitudinis
erunt.

the opening is made wider ; if slighter,
however, it is made narrower. In this
order all the pipes are made. He can
make the measure of each, from the
valve upwards, according to the rule in-
culcated, but from the valve below, all
will be of one measure and of the same
thickness.

CAPUT LXXXII.

DE DOMO ORGANARIA.

DOMUM vero facturus super quam stat-
uendæ sint fistulæ, vide utrum volueris
eam ligneam habere aut cupream. Si
ligneam, acquire tibi duo ligna de platano,
valde sicca, longitudine duorum pedum
et dimidii, et latitudine modicè amplius
quam unius, unum quatuor, alterum
duobus digitis spissum, quæ non sint
nodosa sed pura. Quibus diligentissimè
sibi conjunctis, in inferiori parte spis-
sioris ligni fiat in medio foramen
quadrangulum, amplitudine quatuor digitorum et circa quod relinquatur de eodem
ligno limbus, unius digiti latitudinis et
altitudinis, in quo conflatorium imponatur.
In superiori parte verò lateris fiant cava-
uræ, per quas flatus ad fistulas possit
pervenire. Altera vero pars ligni, quæ
et superior esse debet, metiatur interius
æqualiter, ubi disponantur septem vel
octo cavaturæ, in quibus diligenter jungantur linguæ, ita ut habeant facilem
cursum educendi et reducendi, sic tamen
ut nihil spiraminis inter juncturas exeat.

In superiori autem parte tonde cava-
turas, contra inferiores, quæ sint aliquantulum latiores, in quibus jungantur
totidem ligna, ita ut inter hæc et majus,
ligni cavatura remaneat vacua, per quam
ventus ascendat ad fistulas, nam in eis-
dem lignis foramina fieri debent, in
quibus fistulæ stabiliendæ sunt. Cavaturæ in quibus linguæ junctæ sunt in
anteriori parte procedere debent quasi

CHAPTER LXXXII.

OF THE ORGAN ERECTION.

IN the manufacture of the construction,
upon which the pipes are to stand, see
whether you intend to have it of wood
or copper. If of wood, procure for
yourself two pieces of wood of the plane
tree, very dry, two feet and a half in
length, and in breadth rather more than
one : one four, the other two fingers
thick, which must not be knotty, but
without blemish. Which being carefully
joined together, in the lower part of the
thicker wood a square hole must be
made in the centre, four fingers in
breadth, and about which a border must
be left of the same wood of one finger
in breadth and height, in which the
bellows can be placed. In the upper
part of the side, however, small hollows
are made, through which the wind can
arrive at the pipes. But the other part
of the wood, which should also be
uppermost, is measured out inside
equally, where seven or eight small
openings are disposed, in which the
stops are carefully joined, so that they
may have an easy means of being drawn
out and restored, so, however, that no
air can come out between the joins.
    In the upper part, however, cut small
openings opposite the lower ones, which
are to be rather wider, in which may be
joined so many pieces of wood, so that
between these and the larger the openings of the wood may remain empty,
through which the wind can mount to
the pipes ; for in these same pieces of
wood openings should be made in which
the pipes are to be made fast. The
openings in which the stops are fitted in

obliquæ fenestræ, per quas ipsæ linguæ introducantur et extrahantur.

In posteriori vero parte, sub fine ipsarum linguarum, fiant foramina æqualiter lata et longa, mensura duorum digitorum, per quæ ventus possit ascendere ab inferioribus ad superiora, ita ut cum linguæ impinguntur illa foramina ab eis obstinantur ; cum vero retrahuntur denuò pateant. In his vero lignis quæ super linguas junguntur fiant foramina diligenter et ordinatè, secundum numerum fistularum, uniuscujusque toni, in quibus ipsæ fistulæ imponantur, ita ut firmiter stent, et ab inferioribus ventum suscipiant. In caudis autem linguarum scribantur litteræ secundum ascensum et descensum cantus, quibus possit cognosci quis ille, vel ille tonus sit. In singulis autem linguis fiant foramina singula gracilia, longitudine dimidii digiti minoris, in anteriore parte, juxta caudas in longitudine, in quibus ponantur singuli clavi cuprei capitati, qui pertranseant in medio fenestellas, quibus inducuntur ipsæ linguæ a superiori latere domûs usque ad inferius, et appareant clavorum capita superius ita, ut cum linguæ cantantibus organis educuntur, non penitus extrahuntur. His ita dispositis conglutinentur hæc duo ligna, quæ domum organorum conficiunt, glutine casei ; deinde partes illæ quæ super linguas sunt junctæ, in quibus foramina stant, sicque circumcidantur diligentèr et radantur.

the front part should proceed, like slanting windows, through which these stops are introduced and removed.

In the hinder part, under the end of these stops, holes are made equally wide and long, of the size of two fingers, through which the wind can ascend from the lower to the upper parts, so that when the stops are placed upon them these holes may be stopped by them ; when, however, they are withdrawn, they may again lie open. In those pieces of wood which are joined upon the stops openings are made, carefully and in order, according to the number of the pipes of every tone, in which these pipes are placed, so that they may stand firmly and receive the wind from the lower parts. But in the handles of the stops letters are marked, according to the rise and fall of the sound, by which it can be known which tone it may be. In each one of these stops single slender holes are made, half of the little finger in length, in the front part, near the handles, lengthwise, in which single copper-headed nails may be placed, which may pass through the small windows in the middle, by means of which these stops are drawn from the upper side of the construction down to the lower, and the heads of the nails appear above, so that when the stops are withdrawn from the sounding instruments, they cannot be quite extracted. These things being thus arranged, these two pieces of wood, which perfect the organ-house, are joined together with cheese-glue ; then those parts which are joined over the stops, in which the holes exist, are also pared round carefully, and scraped.

CAPUT LXXXIII.

DE CONFLATORIO.

CONFLATORIUM facturus, conjunge tibi duo ligna de platano modo quo supra, longitudine pedis unius, quorum sit unum palma spissum, alterum tribus digitis, sintque in unâ fronte rotunda in

CHAPTER LXXXIII.

OF THE BELLOWS.

IN making the wind-chamber, join together two pieces of wood of the plane tree, in the above mode, of one foot in length, one of which may be a palm thick, the other three fingers, and let them be round at one end, like a shield,

modum scuti, et ibi pede et dimidio lata ; in alterâ fronte obtusa, latitudine unius palmi. Quæ cum diligenter conjuncta fuerint incide in spissiori ligno in rotunda fronte foramina quod volueris, secundum numerum follium, et in obtusa fronte unum, quod sit majus. Deinde incide ab unoquoque foramine fossam unam deductam usque ad majus, per quas viam possit habere ventus flantibus follibus. Sicque conglutinabis ipsa ligna glutine casei, et circumdabis panno lineo novo et forti, quem linies eodem glutine ut adhæreat, facies quoque ligaturas ferreas fortes, interius et exterius circumstagnatas, ne possint ex tigneâ (tignariâ ?) dissolvi, quas configes clavis longis capitatis atque stagnatis, ita ut inter duo foramina ligatura sit, quæ comprehendat utrumque lignum a superiore latere usque ad inferius. Deinde acquire tibi lignum curvum de quercu, sanum et forte, quod habeat in una fronte, a curvatura longitudinem pedis unius, in altera duorum, quod perforabis in utrâque fronte terebro magno, quo forantur modioli in rotis aratri. Sed quia foramina non possunt sibi obviare propter curvaturam, fac tibi ferrum quod habeat caput rotundum in modum ovi, et caudam longam gracilem, quæ imponatur manubrio, sitque juxta, caput modicè curvum, cum quo calefacto, combures foramina interius in curvaturâ, donec sibi æqualiter conveniant. Quo facto, incide ipsum lignum quadrico (quadratò ?) statum, ita ut in unoquoque latere uno palmo latum sit, ad mensuram conflatorii in obtusa parte. Post hæc conjunge ipsum lignum in longiori parte, ad inferius foramen domûs organariæ, ita ut eidem ligno cauda incidatur, unius pollicis longa, quæ ipsi foramini imponatur, vel inferatur, et junctura tam subtilis sit, ut nihil flatus inter eam exire queat. Alteram vero frontem conjunges eodem modo ad conflatorium, et ipsum lignum

and there a foot and a half wide, at the other end blunt, a palm in breadth. When these have been carefully fitted together, cut, in the round front in the thicker wood, the openings which you wish, according to the number of the bellows, and in the blunt end one, which must be larger. Then cut, from each opening, a hollow leading to the larger opening, through which the wind may have way to the working bellows ; and you will thus glue these woods together with the cheese-glue, and you will bind them round with a linen cloth, new and strong, which you anoint with the same casein glue that it may adhere : you also make strong iron bindings tinned over within and without, that they may not become disunited from the woodwork, these you will fix on with long nails, headed and tinned, so that between the two openings a binding may exist, which may include each wood from the upper to the lower side. Then procure for yourself a curved piece of oak wood, sound and strong, which must have at one end, from the curve, the length of one foot, in the other of two, which you will pierce in each end with a large auger, with which the middle portions are pierced in the wheels of ploughs. But because the openings cannot meet together, on account of the curve, make for yourself an iron which may have a round head, like an egg, and a long thin stem, which is fitted with a handle, and let it be slightly curved, near the head, with which, made hot, you burn the holes curved inside, until they meet together in an even manner. Which being done, cut this wood in a square manner, set so that it be one palm wide in each side, to the size of the windchamber in the blunt part. After these things join this wood on the longer part, to the lower opening of the organ construction, so that a projection may be cut to the same wood a thumb in length, which can be placed, or forced into this opening, and that the joint be so subtle that no wind can escape from it. You join on in the same manner the other end to the bellows, and will fasten this

glutine casei firmabis, atque circum-
volves panno totum lignum cum junctura, cui etiam circumfiges cuprum latum
quod utriusque ligni oram capiat. His
ita completis, si volueris organa ultra
maceriam muri stabilire, ita ut infra*
monasterium nihil appareat, nisi sola
domus cum fistulis, et ex altera parte
muri folles jaceant, ita oportebit te
ipsam domum convertere ut linguæ
versus folles extrahuntur, et in ipso muro
arcus fiat in quo cantor sedeat, cujus
sedes ita aptetur, ut pedes supra conflatorium teneat. Est autem foramen
quadrum in medio arcûs trans maceriam, per quod domus cum fistulis
exponitur ; et super collum conflatorii,
quod in muro infra foramen lapidibus
obfirmatum est, in sua junctura sistitur,
atque super duos clavos ferreos æqualiter in muro confixos nititur, cui foramini fenestra lignea appendet, quæ dum
clausa, sera et clave munitur, nemo ig-
notus superveniens cognoscere valet quid
in ea contineatur. Exterius quoque, super
organa, pannus spissus lignis interius ex-
tensus, in modum domunculæ, a laqueari
in funiculo ad arcendum pulverem dependeat, qui funiculus super ipsum
laquear circa rotulam arte compositus,
dum cantandum est organis trahitur, et
domunculam elevat, finitoque cantu,
denuò super organa deponitur. Habet
quoque ipsa domuncula pinnam ex
eodem panno, lignis quatuor in speciem
trianguli extensam, in cujus summo
sperula (sphærula ?) lignea stet, cui funiculus inhæret. Folles et instrumentum
super quod jaceant, secundum situm
loci ad libitos tuos dispone.

wood with cheese-glue, and will wrap
round the whole wood, with the join,
with cloth, to which you also fix a wide
piece of copper which may also compass
the edge of each wood. These things
being thus completed, should you wish to
establish the organ beyond the masonry
of the wall, so that nothing may appear
within the cloister, unless the erection
alone with the pipes, and that the
bellows may lie on the other side, you
must so turn the construction that the
stops may be drawn out towards the
bellows, and an arch may be made in
the wall itself in which the chanter can
sit, whose seat is so adapted that he can
keep his feet above the bellows. There
is also a square opening in the middle
of the arch through the masonry, through
which the construction with the pipes is
exposed to view ; and upon the neck of
the bellows, which is in the wall beneath,
the opening is made firm with stones, it
is supported at its junction, and is rested
upon two long iron nails evenly fixed in
the wall ; to this opening a wooden window hangs, which, when shut, is defended
by a lock and key, that no stranger
coming unaware be able to learn what
may be contained in it. Outside, also,
above the organ, a thick drapery, extended inside with wood like a dome,
for warding off the dust, can hang by a
rope from the ceiling, which rope, arranged with art around a wheel above
the ceiling itself, is drawn whilst the
organ is sounding, and thus raises the
roof, and the chant being finished, it is
lowered upon the organ. This dome
also has a spire, made from the same
cloth, extended by four pieces of wood
in shape of a triangle, at the top of
which a small wooden ball can stand,
to which the rope cleaves. The bellows,
and the instrument upon which they
may lie, arrange at your pleasure according to the situation of the spot.

---

* " Infra " seems to be a clerical error for "intra," " within the monastery."

CAPUT LXXXIV.

DE DOMO CUPREA ET CONFLATORIO EJUS.

SECUNDUM abundantiam fistularum dispone longitudinem et latitudinem domûs, et fac formam in argillâ maceratâ, siccatamque diligenter incide, quacunque mensurâ volueris, et cooperi cerâ, diligenter inter duas æqualiter spissas hastulas cum rotundo ligno attenuatâ. Deinde incide foramina linguarum in ipsâ cerâ, et foramen inferius, per quod ventus introeat ; additis spiraculis cum infusorio, cooperi eâdem argillâ semel, et iterum ac tertio. Cumque siccata fuerit forma, eodem modo funde quo supra formam turibuli. Conflatorium quoque formabis in argillâ procedentibus undique inferius venti aditibus, ad similitudinem radicis unius arboris, et in summo in unum foramen convenientibus. Quod cum mensurate dispositum cultello incideris, cooperi cerâ, et fac sicut supra. Cumque domum fuderis conjunges interius altitudine unius digiti a fundo, tabulam cupream ductilem sub foraminibus linguarum æqualiter, ut supra eam ipsæ linguæ jaceant, ita ut possint æqualiter produci et induci, illitisque ipsis linguis tenui argillâ, reliquum domûs perfundes liquefacto plumbo, per omnia, super ipsas linguas usque ad summum. Quo facto, ejicies ipsum plumbum diligenter designabisque foramina fistularum in linguis ; deinde in ipso plumbo et cum gracili ferro, vel terebro, perforabis diligentissime. Deinde sub linguis ventorum aditus facies, induces ipsas linguas singulas in suis locis, atque repones plumbum et cum malleo in percutiendo conjunges domui, ut nihil spiraminis exeat, nisi per foramina quibus fistulæ imponendæ sunt. Cum vero conflatorium fuerit fusum et limatum, atque uniuscujusque follis fistula suo inductorio coaptata, conjungi et firmiter consolidari debet ad domum

CHAPTER LXXXIV.

OF THE COPPER CONSTRUCTION AND ITS BELLOWS.

DISPOSE the length and width of the case according to the number of the pipes, and make a mould in beaten clay, and, being dry, cut it to whatever size you may wish, and cover with wax carefully thinned, between two rods equally thick, with the round wood. Then cut the openings of the stops in this wax, and the hole below through which the wind can enter ; the air-holes with the funnel being added, cover altogether with the same clay, and again, and a third time. And when the mould has become dry, cast in the same manner as the form of the censer above mentioned. You will also fashion the bellows in clay, the wind-issues proceeding everywhere below in the similitude of the roots of a tree, and meeting at the top in one opening. Which, when disposed in rule you have cut with a knife, cover with wax and act as above. And when you have cast the case, you join, inside, at the height of one finger from the bottom, a beaten copper plate, in an even manner under the openings of the stops, that these stops may rest upon it, so that they can be smoothly drawn forth and returned ; and lining these stops with thin clay, you pour over the rest of the case some melted lead everywhere, over these stops up to the top. This being done, you cast out this lead and will carefully mark the openings of the pipes in the stops ; then you will most carefully perforate in this lead with a thin iron or with a bore. Then you make the issues for the wind under the stops ; you introduce these stops singly in their places, and you replace the lead, and you fit them to the construction by beating with the hammer, so that no wind can issue, unless through the openings in which the pipes are placed. When the wind-case has been cast and filed, and the pipe of each air-issue fitted to its conductor, it should be joined together and firmly soldered below to the

organariam inferius, ita ut ventus suos aditus liberè inveniat, et per alias juncturas nullatenus exeat. Hoc quoque sollertius* procurandum est, ut in capite uniuscujusque follis, ante foram enfistulæ suæ, cuprum tenue dependeat ; quod spiraminis claudat aditum, ita ut cum follis flando deponitur illud cuprum se elevet, et ventus pleniter exeat ; cumque follis elevatur ut per ventilabrum suum flatum resumat, illud cuprum os ejus penitus claudat, et ventum quem emisit redire non permittat.

organ construction, so that the wind may find its access freely, and can in nowise issue through the other joints. This also is to be carefully provided, that a thin piece of copper may hang down before the opening of its pipe, which can close the access of the airhole, so that when by the breathing of the bellows this copper is displaced, it may rise, and the wind may freely issue ; and when the bellows is raised, so that it may recover air through its own ventilator, this copper can quite close its mouth and not permit the wind which it emitted to return.

* In MS. sollerterius.

Such is the highly interesting and valuable paper left us by this ancient monk—valuable in many points, but particularly so as to clearing up the debated point of the invention of the clavier or keyboard. THE ORGAN OF THEOPHILUS WAS UNPROVIDED WITH ONE.

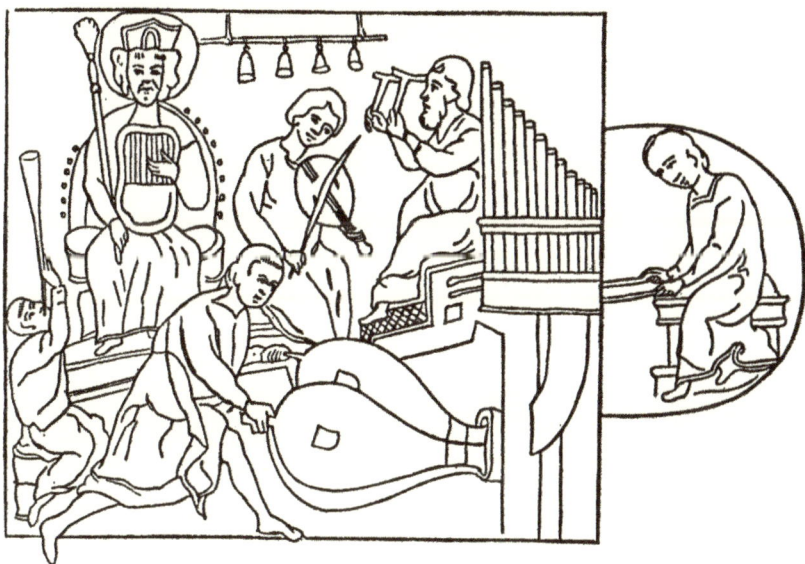

In a Saxon MS. of the eleventh century, preserved in the British Museum (*Cott. Tiberius*, B. 6) is a drawing of the "bumbulum cum fistulâ aereâ," with brass pipes. This *bumbulum* appears to be an organ, played upon in the same manner as that described by the monk.   But a better representation is preserved in Gori's *Thesaurus Diptychorum*, said to be from an ancient MS. of the time of Charlemagne, which is copied in the preceding page.

King David is depicted sitting on a throne, striking a lyre with his left hand, and holding a sceptre in his right.   His head is accompanied by two different kinds of ornaments.   One is the glory, the emblem of sanctity and eternity, and the other a turreted crown, representing a city with a gate.   This is, perhaps, the holy Jerusalem, or that happy Sion, "whose gates the Lord loveth," as David himself sings.   He is probably engaged in singing psalms, assisted by four musical instruments—the *pneumatic* organ, a sort of violin, a trumpet, and a set of bells.

Second Epoch.

THE MEDIÆVAL ORGAN, AFTER THE INVENTION OF THE KEY-BOARD.

6. *The First Key-board.*

THE close of the eleventh century forms an era in the history of organ-building, when an organ is said to have been erected in the cathedral at Magdeburg, with a *key-board* consisting of *sixteen* keys. In the earlier organs the number of notes was very limited. From nine to eleven was nearly their greatest extent, and the execution of the plain-chant did not require more. Harmony, it will be remembered, was still unknown.

The keys of the Magdeburg organ were an ell long and three inches broad. The following diagram, showing their form, is copied from Prætorius' *Theatrum Instrumentorum seu Sciagraphia.* 4to. Wolfenbüttel, 1620.

Dom Bedos speaks of some early organs whose keys were five inches and a half wide. The manner of performing upon these instruments was of course conformable to the size of the keys. They were struck down by the *fist* of the player, even to a considerable depth, whence, according to Seidel, arose the expression organ-*beater.* This method resembles that of *carillon*-playing,* still in use in some parts of France, Germany, and Holland.

---

* Burney gives an interesting account of his ascent of one of the belfries at Ghent, to witness a performance on the chimes. "The *carilloneur*," he says, "was literally at *work*, and *hard* work indeed it must be ; he was in his shirt, with the collar unbuttoned, and in a

The annexed very curious engraving, showing an organist performing upon an instrument with broad keys, is copied from Franchinus
Gaffurius's *Theorica Musica*, printed at Milan in 1492.*

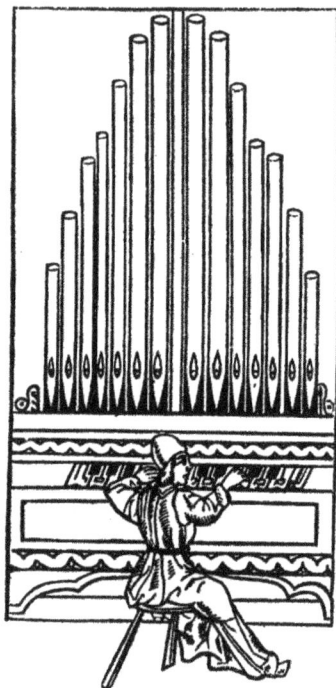

violent sweat. There are pedals communicating with the great bells, upon which, with his
feet, he played the base to several sprightly and rather difficult airs, performed with the two
hands upon the upper species of keys. These keys are projecting sticks, wide enough
asunder to be struck with violence and velocity by either of the two hands edgeways, without
the danger of hitting the neighbouring keys. The player had a thick leather covering for the
little finger of each hand, otherwise it would be impossible for him to support the pain which
the violence of the stroke necessary to be given to each key, in order to its being distinctly
heard throughout a very large town, requires."—*Present State of Music in Germany, the Netherlands, &c.*, 1775, vol. i., p. 14. An engraving of a *carilloneur*, performing in the exact
manner described by Burney, may be seen in the fourth book of Mersennus's *Harmonie
Universelle*: Paris, 1636.

* This engraving also occurs in the same author's *De Harmonia Musicorum*: Milan, 1518.
Mr. Wackerbarth, in his *Music and the Anglo-Saxons* (p. 8), says :—"Now it has been so
generally asserted by modern writers, though I know not on what authority, that the keys of
the organ were originally some inches wide, and played on, like carillons, with a blow of the
fist, that I dare not altogether reject, as untrue, so much concurring testimony." It is presumed that the writer of this passage will accept the names of Dom Bedos, Prætorius, and
Gaffurius, as *authorities*.

7. *The Bellows.*

We cannot but wonder at the perseverance of our ancestors, when we consider the various ineffectual efforts that were made from time to time to improve the bellows. For centuries they remained in the most imperfect state; sometimes twenty or more being necessary to supply the wind to a moderately sized organ. According to Wulstan, in the passage before quoted, the organ at Winchester was provided with twenty-six bellows. The great organ of the cathedral at Halberstadt had twenty, and that of Magdeburg twenty-four small bellows. They were fashioned in folds like the forge or smith's bellows, and were not provided with weights as in our modern organs. Our ancestors had no idea of proportioning the wind; but its force depended solely on the strength of the bellows-blowers. It is easy to conceive that by this means the organ could never have been in tune; because the wind was admitted unequally. Prætorius has left us a singular representation of the ancient mode of blowing, which is here copied from the *Theatrum Instrumentorum*, Wolfenbüttel, 1620.

Upon each bellows is fixed a wooden shoe; the men who work them hang by their hands on a transverse bar, and each man, placing his feet in the shoes of two bellows, alternately lowers one and raises the other.

We copy another curious representation of an early bellows, which is given by Mersennus, in his *Harmonie Universelle:* folio ; Paris, 1636. It shows that the *horizontal* bellows, though only brought into general use in the last century, was by no means a modern invention.*

The bellows is here placed at the top of the organ, and worked by a chain in the place of a feeder. Mersennus calls it bellows "à la lanterne."

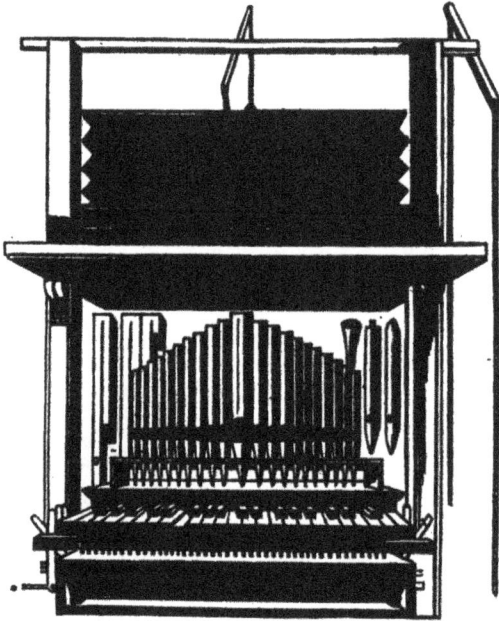

8. *Supposed Origin of the Mixture Stops.*

Seidel, in the introduction to his work on the organ,† has the following passage :—" In the twelfth century the number of keys was increased, and afterwards each note (or tone) multiplied by two, three,

---

* The horizontal bellows is an improvement upon the old one ; as a column of air by this machine is both supplied, and drawn at the same moment, by the action of a crank and other appendages, instead of levers, &c.

† *The Organ and its Construction: a Systematic Hand-book for Choristers, Organists, Schoolmasters, and Musical Students.* 2nd edit. Breslau, 1844. An English translation of this book was published by Ewer & Co., in 1852.

or more pipes, tuned to the fifth or octave, or to the third and tenth. By this alteration the organ became a mixture, and so remained until the idea occurred of classifying the pipes, by which means this mixture register received a separate slide." Forkel, also, in his *Geschichte der Musik* (part ii., p. 368), says that, even in the oldest organs, the mixture, as associated with $\frac{12}{8}$, was introduced, not as a stop or register, for there was nothing of the kind at that period, but as being invariably united to each tone.[*]

Burney[†] is inclined to ascribe the origin of harmony to this invention. His words are :—" With respect to the term *organum*, as used by musical writers of the middle ages for a voice part : if we could imagine, when the first organ was erected in churches and convents, that each of them was furnished with such a stop as is now called the *sesquialter*, or any other compound stop, consisting of 4ths, 5ths, and 8ths ; thus : &c., it might not only help to account for the introduction of such strange harmony into the church as that of Hucbald, Odo, and Guido, but even give a probable reason for the name by which it is called ; for, whether we supposed singers to have imitated such sounds as every *single key* produced or such as were produced by the fingers from *different keys* of the organ, it was natural to call the part which was added to a plain-song *organum*, and the art of producing it *organizare*."[‡]

Dr. Crotch[§] is of an exactly opposite opinion. He says :—" The method of accompanying the chants of the Christian Church by a succession of fifths, octaves, or fourths, used in and before the eleventh century, called organum, has been supposed to be the origin of harmony. The organ took its name from it ; and the stops called cornet, sesquialtera, twelfth, tierce, principal, fifteenth, &c., are thought to have been invented to facilitate the performance of this accompaniment.[||] But if the effect of this accompaniment was similar to that of the above stops of an organ,—if, by being performed comparatively

---

[*] Forkel cites Sethus Calvisius and Michael Prætorius as his authorities.

[†] *Hist. of Music*, vol. ii., p. 133.

[‡] *Organizare*, according to Du Cange, is *canere in modum organi ;* and among his authorities he gives the following definition from the *Catholicon* or *Lexicon* of John de Janua, written in 1286: Organizare, *Organo cantare ; Joer ou chanter en orgres, organiser ;* "to play or sing *like* the organ."

[§] Note in the second edition of *Elements of Musical Composition*, 1833, p. 33.

[||] This could not have been the case, as these stops were not invented till the *fifteenth* century, when the old *organum* had been discarded for something better.

soft, it only enriches the tone, without disturbing the melody,—then it should not be considered as the origin of harmony, having no more to do with it than the harmonies which constantly accompany the melody of a single voice or instrument. The invention of harmony may be said rather to have commenced when these fifths, fourths, and octaves, began to be *avoided."*

Kiesewetter, in his charming *History of the Modern Music of Western Europe,** has the following conclusions on the subject :—

" But in what manner, then, the organum may nevertheless have been, and really was, an imitation of the organ, and received its name from that instrument, may thus be explained. The oldest organs, of exceedingly coarse manufacture—the broad six-inch keys of which, separated from each other by a large space, must have been pressed down with the fists or elbows—were in truth as little adapted to harmonic performances as to harmonic experiments ; these instruments may, notwithstanding, have afforded the first opportunity of representing to our senses in a permanently continuous manner the physical effects of the then admissible consonances, at least in single unisons, by the pressing down and holding out at the same time a second key ; moreover, the organ-'thumper' might, whether intentionally or through awkwardness, have hit upon the idea of causing one key to remain sounding, whilst the singers, to whom he had given the note, proceeded with their melody above it, as in the bagpipes ; or it might also have happened that, at one time or another, he would accidentally, perhaps, press down the fifth to the fundamental note, and thus have caused an agreeable surprise by its pleasing effect. With this, indeed, there might not as yet have been a proper harmony discovered ; but effects would have been perceived calculated to produce, in speculative musicians, matter for reflection, and for hazarding other systems ; the union of different human voices, which now occurred to their thoughts, was an imitation, not altogether happy perhaps, of that which in various instances they had discovered with the organ ; and thus their diaphony, or polyphony, received the somewhat appropriate name of organum."

9. *The First Monastic Organs.*

In the thirteenth century the priests of the Greek and Roman churches thought the use of organs in divine service scandalous and profane. They preferred rendering divine worship as simple as possible, in order to distinguish it from that of the Jews and Pagans. Even to this day the Greek Church does not tolerate the use of organs in their public services. Notwithstanding these opinions, the use of organs and even other instruments became almost universal, not only in great churches, but in those of monasteries, convents, and small

---

* Translated by Robert Muller. 8vo. 1848.

towns. The historians of this era celebrate several monks, distinguished for the art of playing on the organ, and for their general musical abilities. For some time, however, organs were only used on great feasts and solemn occasions; they were not used in the ordinary celebration of the offices.*

The first monastic and conventual organs were very small, being merely used to play the melody of the plain-song with the voices. These organs were called *regals*.

10. *The Regal, or Portative.*

The term *regal* or *rigol* appears to have come from the Italian *rigabello*. Sir Henry Spelman tells us "that in the church of St. Raphael, at Venice, the figure of a certain musical instrument, called a *rigabello*, was to be seen; it was wont to be used in churches before organs came into vogue. Another instrument, called *turcello*, succeeded the *rigabello*, the use of which was introduced at Venice by a German."† This passage clearly shows the word *regal* to be a corruption or contraction of *rigabello*.‡

Musical writers have not explained the nature of the *regal*, which was evidently to give out and sustain the melody of the plain-song. Carter, the well-known antiquary, calls it "a portable organ, having

---

* On particular occasions, the performance of a band of minstrels was added to the organ. *Minstrels' galleries* are often seen in the continental churches, but are rarely met with in this country. There is a gallery of this sort over the altar-screen at Chichester Cathedral, and another, much more remarkable, near the middle of the north side of Exeter Cathedral. It is supported on thirteen pillars, between every two of which, in a niched recess, there is a sculptured representation of an angel playing upon some musical instrument. Among these are the cittern, bagpipe, harp, violin, pipe, tambourine, &c. The roof of Outwell Church, Norfolk, and the minstrels' column at Beverley, also exhibit a great variety of musical instruments anciently used in churches.

† "In Æde Sancti Raphaelis Venetiis, instrumenti musici cujusdam forma extat, ei nomen rigabello : cujus in ecclesiis usus fuerit ante organa illa pneumatica quæ hodie usurpantur. Rigabello successit aliud quod Turcello dictum est, cujus Venetias usum induxit homo Germanus."—Sansovinus, *Descript. Venetiarum*, lib. vi.

‡ Skinner, the etymologist, upon the authority of an old English dictionary, conjectures the word rigals or regals to signify a stringed instrument—namely, a clavichord. In this mistake he has been followed by numerous writers. Walther is more particular in his description of the regal: he makes it to be a reedwork in an organ, with metal and also wooden pipes and bellows adapted to it, so contrived that it may be taken out and set upon a chest or a table. He says that the name regal is frequently given to that stop in an organ called the Vox Humana; and in this sense Mersennus uses it, in his *Harmonie Universelle*, liv. vi. ; *Des Orgues*, Prop. viii. See Walther's *Musicalisches Lexicon*, Leipsic, 1732. Cotgrave and Florio write the word *rigols* and *rigoles*.

one row of pipes, giving the treble notes."* A writer in Rees's _Encyclopedia_ says that "the _regal_, in all Roman Catholic countries, is a portable organ used in processions, carried by one person, and played upon by another." This explanation is not quite accurate, as the representations in early manuscripts invariably exhibit the instrument carried and performed upon by the same person.

Snetzler, the celebrated organ-builder, remembered the regals in use in Germany ;† and, until nearly the end of the last century, an officer of the Royal Chapel at St. James's was styled "a tuner of the regalls."‡

In the accounts of the _Weavers' Pageant_, performed at Coventry in the sixteenth century, we have the following entries :—

" 1554. Payd to James Hewet for hys reyggals, viijd.
" 1556. Payd to James Hewet for playing of his _regols_ in the payggeant, viijd."

The _regals_ are mentioned in Edwards's play of _Damon and Pythias_, 1571 ; and in Jacobo Peri's opera of _Euridice_, composed for the royal nuptials of Mary de Medici with Henry IV. of France, in the year 1600.

In the Household Book of the Princess Mary, afterwards Queen Mary,§ under the year 1538, we have the following entry :—

" Item, payd for a payr of regalls, iiij. li. x s."

And in an inventory of Henry the Eighth's Musical Instruments, taken after his death,‖ we read of "thirteen pair of single regalls," and "five pair of double regalls." _Double_ regalls were furnished with two rows of keys.

Representations of regals of various kinds may be seen in the _Chronicon Nurembergense_, printed in 1493 ; and in Willemin's admirable work entitled _Monuments Français inédits_.

This instrument is also exhibited among the sculptures in the cornice of St. John's Church, Cirencester ; and on the crosier of William of Wykeham, preserved in New College, Oxford.

---

* _Gents. Mag._ 1804, Part i., p. 328.
† See the _Archæologia_, published by the Society of Antiquaries, vol. iii., p. 32.
‡ In 1767 Bernard Gates received a salary of £56, as "tuner of the _regalls_" in the Royal Chapel. The same gentleman, in 1770, is styled "tuner of the _organs_."
§ Edited by Sir Frederick Madden. 8vo. 1831.
‖ See Sir Henry Ellis's _Original Letters illustrative of English History_, Second Series, vol. i., p. 272.

The following early form of the regals is taken from Lucinius's *Musurgia, seu Praxis Musicæ*: Strasburg, 1536.

The regals were also called *portatives*, from the Latin word *portare*, " to carry." The old poets frequently allude to them under this name. Thus Gawin Douglas :—

> " On crowd, lute, harpe, with monie gudlie spring,
> Schalmes, clariouns, *portatives*, heard I ring."

Again, in the ancient romance of *Clariodus and Meliades :—*

> " The dulcet playit also with *portative*,
> Sad hevie myndis to make exultative."

Also in the poem of the *Houlate*, written in 1450 :—

> " Clarions loud knellis,
> *Portativis* and bellis."

In the codicil to the will of Richard Fitz-James, Bishop of London, proved 22nd May, 1522,* is the following bequest :—

" Item, I will that my payre of *portatives*, being in my chapels in the palace of London, mine organs, also being and standing in my chapels within my three manors of Fulham, Hadham, and Wykeham, shall there stand still and remain to my successor, next Bishop of London, that they may be used there to the honour and service of God."

In a curious account of the moveables of certain abbeys, at the dissolution of these establishments (dated 1538),† we read :—

" Item, sold an old payre of *portatyffes* organs to Mr. Besum, ij s."

II. *The Positive.*

In contradistinction to the portative we have the *positive* organ ; from the Latin word *ponere*, " to set down." This instrument was

---

* *Testamenta Vetusta*, by Sir Harry Nicolas, vol. ii., p. 598.
† *Letters relating to the Suppression of the Monasteries*, printed for the Camden Society, p. 269.

provided with a key-board of full compass, and was, of course, played upon with both hands.*

In the series of wood-cuts known as the *Triumphe de l'Empereur Maximilian*, drawn by Hans Burgmair, in 1516, and first printed at Vienna in 1796, is an engraving of Paul Hofhaimer, organist to the Emperor Maximilian,† playing upon a *positive* organ. The instrument is placed upon a table, an attendant blowing the bellows behind ; the whole being drawn upon a car, which forms part of the procession. In the descriptive letter-press which accompanies these plates it is said :—" In the car is a *regal* and a *positif ;* Paul Hofhaimer, master organist, touches the *last* instrument." The regal may be seen in the same engraving, behind the organist.

The following figure of the *positive* organ is copied from Ambrosius Wilphlingseder's *Erotemata Musices Practicæ*, Nuremberg, 1563.

The *positif* was afterwards added to the larger organ. In our musical dictionaries we find it thus explained—" *Positif*, the small organ which is placed before the great one in all churches where there

---

* Sir John Hawkins says:—" It is true when we speak of the organ we are to understand that there are two kinds of instrument distinguishable by that name; the one, for the smallness of its size and simplicity of construction, called the *portative ;* the other, the *positive*, or immoveable organ ; both of these are very accurately described by Ottomarus Luscinius, in his *Musurgia*, printed in Strasburg, in 1536. As to the first, its use was principally to assist the voice in ascertaining the several sounds contained in the system, and occasionally to facilitate the learning of any cantus. The other is that noble instrument, to the harmony whereof the solemn choral service has, ever since its invention, been sung, and which is now degraded to the accompaniment of discordant voices in the promiscuous performance of metrical psalmody in parochial worship."—*Hist. of Music*, vol. ii., p. 163.

Sir John has entirely mistaken the nature of the *positive* organ, as will be seen by the passages cited in the text.

† Luscinius speaks highly of Paul Hofhaimer. He says:—" He has received great honours from the Emperor Maximilian, whom he delights as often as he plays upon the organ. Nor is he more remarkable for skill in his profession than for the extensiveness of his genius and the greatness of his mind. Rome owes not more to Romulus or Camillus, than the musical world does to Paulus."—*Musurgia*, 1536. Burgmair's engraving is evidently a good por-trait of this eminent musician.

is an organ sufficiently large to be divided into two parts. The organist is placed between the *positif* and great organ, if the claviers or sets of keys are all attached to the great one, and of which the lowest belongs to the *positif*."*

We here see the origin of the *choir* organ, which was the *smaller* organ, called the positive, used in monastic· times to accompany the voices of the choir. Afterwards, when the organs were joined together, and the organist took his seat between them (or rather in a half-circle taken from the small organ), the *choir* organ became corrupted into the *chair* organ.† It has now re-assumed its ancient and original signification.

12. *The Meaning of " a Pair of Organs."*

This seems the proper place to explain a term which has frequently puzzled the enquirers after mediæval remains; *i.e.*, the common expression of "a pair of organs."

" It appears," says Mr. Albert Way,‡ " that the usual term 'a pair of organs' has reference to the double bellows, whereby continuous sound was produced." This, however, cannot be the case, as we often meet with "a pair of *virginals*," in which instrument wind was not required.

Douce,§ a high authority in these matters, tells us that a pair of organs means an instrument "formed with a double row of pipes." This explanation is obviously erroneous, as the *single* regals, always termed "a pair," had but *one* row of pipes. The *double* regals, mentioned in the curious inventory of Henry the Eighth's Musical Instruments (before alluded to), had two rows of keys.

Nichols, the learned historian of Leicestershire,‖ says:—"A pair of organs was the term at that time, when there were two kinds of organs, the one fixed and the other portable, adapted perhaps to the size of the church and its revenues." A recent writer,¶ improving upon this

---

* Danneley's *Musical Encyclopedia*, 1825—a work, notwithstanding some grave errors, of much more merit than is generally assigned to it.

† In one of Matthew Locke's organ pieces, printed in his *Melothesia*, 1673, the "great organ" and the "*chair organ*" are mentioned.

‡ *Promptorium Parvulorum*, published by the Camden Society, tom. ii. in v., *Organo*.

§ Cited by Mr. Way in the before-mentioned work.

‖ *Illustrations of the Manners and Expenses of Ancient Times in England.* 4to. 1797.

¶ A paper "On Organs in Churches," by Arthur Ashpitel, in the *Transactions of the British Archæological Association*, 1846, p. 289.

statement, adds :—"*A payre of organs*, consisting of two organs con-
joined, with two sets of keys, one above the other : one small and
called *the choir*, or more probably *the chayre* organ ; and the other *the
great organ*, built, as its name imports, on a large scale, and used in
forte passages." This is by far the most erroneous explanation of the
term yet given. An organ with two rows of keys was anciently called
" *a double organ*." Evelyn (July, 1654) speaks of his visit to Magdalen
College, Oxford, in the chapel of which " was still the *double* organ."
Matthew Locke, in his *Melothesia*, 1673, has some pieces for the organ,
one of which (p. 82), written for " chaire organ " and " great organ,"
is described as " For a *double* organ." When the organ with the rows
of keys became general, the term " pair of organs " went out of use.

Some authorities tell us that " a pair of organs " meant an organ
with two stops. But this could not have been the case ; as, in
Henry the Eighth's Household Book, we read of " a payer of
virginalls with *four* stoppes."

The truth is that " a pair of organs " meant simply an organ *with
more pipes than one*. Pepys, describing his visit to Hackney Church,
April 21, 1667, speaks of " a fair pair of organs," and then refers in
the singular number to " it," fully bearing out this explanation of the
term. Jonson, Heywood, and other of the older poets, always use
the term *pair* in the sense of an aggregate, and as synonymous with
set : thus we have " a *pair* of chessmen," " a *pair* of beads," " a *pair* of
cards," " a *pair* of organs,"* &c. When speaking of a *flight* of stairs,
we often say a *pair* of stairs. Therefore this ancient form of expression, although obsolete in most cases, is still in *use* at the present day.

13. *The Improved Key-board, and the Invention of the Pedal.*

The monks and friars, those zealous guardians and preservers of
learning and the fine arts in the dark times of the Middle Ages, not
only took great interest in the building and adornments of their

---

* " A *pair* of cards, Nicholas, and a carpet to cover the table."—*A Woman killed with
Kindness.* Heywood.   Printed before 1604.

" Have you ne'er a son at the groom porters to beg or borrow a *pair* of cards ?"—Jonson's
Masque at Christmas.   1616.

" Go, get a *pair* of beads, and learn to pray, sir."—*A Wife for a Month.* Fletcher.
1624.

" Was there no talk of a fair *pair* of organs, a great gilt candlestick, and a pair of silver
snuffers ?"—*A Mad World, my Masters.* Middleton.   1608.

churches and convents, but employed themselves in making improvements in the art of organ-building.

In the course of the fourteenth century they set about improving the clumsy clavier or key-board. In particular, they made neater keys, increased their number both upwards and downwards, to the extent of nearly three octaves, and so reduced their fall and breadth that they no longer required to be struck down by the fist, but were capable of being pressed down by the fingers, as in the organ of modern times.

In 1359 or 1361 Nicholas Faber, a priest, built the great organ in the cathedral at Halberstadt. It had fourteen diatonic and eight chromatic keys, the compass extending, on the key-board, from

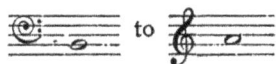

to ____ The great B stood in front, was thirty-two feet long, and three and a quarter inches (?) in diameter. According to Prætorius,[*] who gives us this account, this organ had four claviers, one being *pedals* for the feet, and twenty bellows, requiring ten men to supply the wind.

This is the earliest *authentic* account of an organ provided with the semitones of the scale. Dom Bedos,[†] indeed, tells us that "half-notes were invented at Venice in the twelfth century;" but, as his statement is unsupported by proof, we prefer following the *earlier* authority of Prætorius, who assigns their introduction to the middle of the fourteenth century—a period more in accordance with what we know respecting the progress of harmony in the Middle Ages.

Prætorius is, perhaps, wrong in fixing so early a date for the invention of the pedal. The Halberstadt organ was probably provided with this important addition by Gregorius Kleng, who restored the instrument in 1494.

The invention of the pedal is commonly attributed to a German, named Bernhard, organist to the Doge of Venice, between the years 1470-80;[‡] but it was certainly anterior to this date. A writer in the *Leipsic Musical Gazette*, 1836, states that, in the year 1818, a new organ was erected in the church of Beeskow, four miles from Frank-

---

* *Syntagma Musicum*, vol. ii., p. 98.
† *L'Art du Facture des Orgues.*
‡ It is sometimes claimed for Albert Van Os, who is said to have built an organ for St. Nicholas' Church, in Utrecht, in 1120. Traxdorf, in 1468, also (with more reason) has his advocates for the invention.

fort-on-the-Oder; on which occasion the organ-builder, Marx (senior), took some pains to ascertain the age of the old organ he had to remove. On a careful investigation it appeared that the organ had been built just four hundred years, the date of 1418 being engraved on the upper side of the partition *(kern)* of the two principal *pedal pipes ;* for that these two pipes did belong to the pedal was clear from their admeasurement. From this fact it may reasonably be concluded that the pedal may have been in use towards the end of the fourteenth century. Bernhard probably made some *improvements* in the pedal board which tradition has associated with the invention.

Marinus Sanutus, a celebrated Venetian patrician, and a zealous promoter of Christianity, caused, in 1312, an organ to be built for the church of St. Raphael, in Venice.* This was the first *organ* erected in that city. It was probably a large one, and the builder was a German. Hence we see that the Germans, at this early time, had acquired a considerable reputation for organ-building, which had even passed the limits of their fatherland ; and it will be observed, in the further progress of these pages, that the great improvements in this instrument almost exclusively proceeded from these thoughtful people.

14. *Monastic Organs in England.*

In England, as we have seen, a large organ existed at Winchester in the tenth century ; and probably, even at this early period, other cathedrals were supplied in a similar manner. Gervase, the monk, of Canterbury, describing the burning of that cathedral in 1174, mentions the destruction of the organ ; but does not allude to it as if it were an unusual thing in a church.† The organs of the abbeys of Malmesbury and Glastonbury we have already mentioned ; and, long before the close of the *fourteenth* century, all our abbeys and churches were plentifully supplied with instruments of this class.‡

---

* This organ had so many admirers in Venice, that Marinus Sanutus received the honourable fitle of *Torcellus*, organs being at that time called *Torcelli*, in Italy.—Seidel.

If this organ was the *first* erected at Venice—and we have reason to believe the statement —it is a sufficient refutation of Dom Bedos' story, that "half-notes were invented at Venice in the *twelfth* century."

† Gervas. Dorobern. *apud decem Scriptores de incendio*, &c. "Organa quæ supra fornicem in australi cruce."

‡ In Cotton MS. Nero, D. VII., in the British Museum, numerous curious particulars are recorded respecting the use of organs in England ; as at St. Albans, and Croyland, where there were "organa solemnia in introitu ecclesiæ superius situata," as well as smaller organs in the choir.

Chaucer in his tale of the *Cock and the Fox*, speaking of Chaun-
ticlere, the hero of the poem, says :—

> " His vois was merrier than the merry *orgon*,
>   On masse days that in the churches gon."

Again, speaking of St. Cecilia, the same poet says :—

> " And while that *organs* maden melodie,
>   To God alone thus in her heart sung she."

In the fourteenth century it became the practice to place two
organs in large churches ; one large, the other small. The *great*
organs was provided with two manuals, from ⟨music⟩ to ⟨music⟩
the upper manual forming the *treble*, the lower one the *bass*. This
arrangement, according to Seidel, suggested the invention of the
copula. The pipes of these instruments were always exposed ; and
such an organ (according to Fosbroke *) was, and perhaps is now, at
Uley Church, in Gloucestershire. The organist was usually one of
the monks, when little more was required than to accompany the
plain-song or chant. Afterwards, as musical composition improved,
and more skill was required for its performance, lay organists were
hired.†

---

* *British Monachism : or, Manners and Customs of the Monks and Nuns of England*,
edit. 1843, p. 204.

† In ancient times no distinct officer by the name of organist was appointed in churches
or colleges. This duty was subordinate, and appears to have been commonly preformed by
one of the clerks. In the statutes of Corpus Christi College, at Oxford, given in 1517, two
chapel clerks are established ; one of whom is also to be the *organorum pulsator*. The first
instance of the mention of an organ in any collegiate statutes occurs in those of Eton College,
made about the year 1440 ; where one of the four clerks who is appointed to instruct the
choristers is moreover ordered *jubilare organis*. Here also, for the first time, *cantus
organicus* is mentioned. In the new cathedral-foundations of Henry the Eighth, a master or
teacher of the singing boys is appointed ; and, besides, he is to be " cantandi, et organa
pulsandi, peritus." At New College, Oxford, King's at Cambridge, and Winchester
College, in each of which are ample choirs, there is no provision by statute, not even for an
Informator Choristarum ; although such an officer occurs in the early rolls of New College.
At Magdalen College, Oxford, founded about the year 1459, there is also no mention of an
organist ; but it is enjoined that one of the chaplains, or clerks, or some other skilful person,
shall educate the choristers in the plain-chant and pricked song. In the year 1446 the abbot
and convent of Muchelney, in Somersetshire, granted a corrody of five marks, with seven
gallons of ale, and seven loaves, every week, and a gown and four loads of wood annually, to
Ralph Drake, cantor, or chanter, *pro servicio nobis in illa scientia musica ;* and, on condition
that he attend the choir every day, and teach four boys, and one of the monks, or as
many as chose, to play on the organ.—See Warton's *Life of Sir T. Pope*, Appendix, p. 425,
for further information.

The precentor's accounts of Ely Cathedral, for the year 1407, give the earliest details of the " Expenses of making an Organ " with which I am acquainted.   Translated from the Latin they read as follows :—

			s.	d.
" 20	Stones of lead	. . . .	16	9
4	White horses' hides for 4 pair of bellows .	. . .	7	8
	Ashen hoops for the bellows	. . . . .		4
10	Pairs of hinges .	. . . .	1	10
	The Carpenter, 8 days making the bellows	. . .	2	8
12	Springs	. . . .		3
1	Pound of glue .	. . . .		1
1	Pound of tin	. . . .		3
6	Calf skins .	. . . .	2	6
12	Sheep skins	. . . .	2	4
2	Pounds of quicksilver	. . . .	2	
	Wire, nails, cloth, hoops, and staples	. . . .	1	
	Fetching the organ-builder, and his board 13 weeks	.	40	

Total   .   .   .   .   £3 17 8 "

The small proportion of tin, and the large quantity of lead made use of for the pipes, is remarkable.   The quicksilver was probably used to silver the latter ; or, perhaps, to soften the other metals.   It is to be regretted that the maker's name is not given, but we may be sure that he was a monk.

The Fabrick Rolls of York Minster are among the earliest and most interesting documents of their class.   Particulars of the "organs" commence as early as 1399, and in 1419 we have the following entries :—

" For constructing two pair of bellows for the organ, 46s. 8d.
" For constructing the ribs of the bellows of the same organ, by John Couper, 12d."

A representation of the instrument, of this date, is still existing in York Cathedral, beneath the great niche over the west window. The organ is carved in the pediment, the pipes appear without a case, and it has a single row of keys, on which an angel is playing from a music-book held by two small boys or choristers below, while another is behind blowing the organ with a pair of common bellows.   A similar device is carved over a door on the north wall of the cathedral of Utrecht.

It is doubtful whether John Couper was the builder of the organ, or merely the carpenter.   The ambiguity of the scribe has perhaps deprived this worthy of the honour of being the earliest English organ-builder on record.

The next entry, in 1457, is more clear :—

"To John Roose, brother of the order of Preaching Friars, who repaired and restored the organ at the altar of the B. V. M. in the Cathedral Church of the City of York, and one pair of bellows for the same, 36s. 8d."

Again, under date 1469, we have :—

"To brother John for constructing two pair of bellows for the great organ, and repairing of the same, 15s. 2d."

Both these entries undoubtedly relate to the same person ; and to Father John Roose must be awarded the distinction of being the first English organ-builder of whom we have any authentic account.

Other entries occur in the York records, where "organ menders" are mentioned. In 1470 we have the name of George Gaunte ; and, in 1473, of Richard Sowerby. But in 1485 we have the following specific and curious entry :—

"To John Hewe for repairing the organ at the altar of B. V. M. in the Cathedral Church, and for carrying the same to the House of the Minorite Brethren, and for bringing back the same to the Cathedral Church, 13s. 9d."

This is the earliest instance I have found of a practice afterwards common—that of one church *lending* another its organ.* Surely no further proof need be required of the *smallness* of our cathedral organs at the end of the fifteenth century.

But it was not uncommon before the Reformation for a cathedral to possess several organs. The York records particularly mention the organ at the altar, and the *large* organ in the choir. It was the *smaller* organ that was lent to the Minorite Brethren. There were doubtless several other organs in the various chapels.

Davies, in his *Ancient Rites and Monuments of the Monastical and Cathedral Church of Durham :* 12mo, 1672,† has left us a curious passage concerning the organs of that monastery :—

"There were," says he, "three pair of organs belonging to the said quire, for maintenance of God's service, and the better celebrating thereof. One of the fairest pair of the three stood over the quire door, only opened and play'd upon on principal feasts, the pipes being all of most fine wood, and workmanship very fair, partly gilt upon the inside, and the outside of the leaves and covers up to the top, with branches, and flowers finely gilt, with the name of Jesus gilt with gold. There

---

* 1508. "For bringing the organs of the Abbey (Westminster) into the church, and beryng them home agayne, ijᵈ."—*Accounts of St. Margaret's, Westminster.*

† Compiled from ancient MSS. before the dissolution of the monasteries. J. Davies, of Kidwelly, was the editor. Another edition of this curious volume was printed, in 1733, with some additions,

E

were but two pair more of them in all England of the same making ; one in *York*, and another in *Paul's*.

"Also there was a lantern of wood like unto a pulpit, standing and adjoining to the wood-organs over the quire door, where they had wont to sing the nine lessons, in the old time, on principal dayes, standing with their faces towards the high altar.

"The second pair stood on the north side of the quire, being never play'd upon but when the four doctors of the church were read—viz., Augustine, Ambrose, Gregory, and Jerome, being a pair of fair large organs, called the *Cryers*. The third pair were daily used at ordinary service."

In an inventory of the plate, jewels, ornaments, &c., belonging to the late Priory of Ely, Cambridgeshire, we read of "two paer of organs in the quyer," and "a paer of organs in the Ladye Chaple."*

In the ancient Cathedral of Worcester, the chapel of St. Edmund had a pair of organs ; that of St. George, another pair ; and in the choir was the *great* organ.†

Some of the entries in ancient documents respecting the organ are interesting, not only as showing its very general use in churches and monastic establishments in the fifteenth and sixteenth centuries, but also as exhibiting the progress—slow as it evidently was—of the art of organ-building, whilst it remained in the hands of the monks.

In the churchwardens' accounts of St. Mary's, Sandwich, are the following entries :—

"1444.	Ress^d [Rec^d] the bequeth of Thomas Boryner unto a payre of orgonys	iiij *li.*
——	To Sir John‡ for the amendyng of the organs . . .	xii *d.*
1462.	To a Preyst for the amending of the organys . . .	iiij *d.*
——	To a Preist that playth at organs	iiij *d.*
1463.	To Sir John for hys playying at organys . . .	vi *s.* viij *d.*
1496.	Payd for mendyng of the lytell organys . . .	iij *s.* iv *d.*
——	Item, for shepeskyn to mend the grete organyse . .	iij *d.*
1502.	Paid for mending of the gret organ bellowis, and the small organ bellowis	v *d.*
——	Item, for a shepis skyn for both organys, and for trying of the wax for the Paschall	ij *d.*
1521.	Payd Winsborough the Monke of Crists Churche [Canterbury] for mendyng the grete organys . . .	iij *s.* iv *d.*"§

---

* Bentham's *History of Ely Cathedral*, p. 225.

† Storer's *English Cathedrals*, vol. iv.

‡ This person was a priest. *Sir* was formerly a designation of an inferior member of the clergy. Bishop Percy says :—"Within the limits of my own memory all *Readers* in Chapels were called *Sirs*, and of old have been writ so ; whence, I suppose, such of the laity as received the noble order of knighthood, being called *Sirs* too, for distinction sake, had *knight* writ after them ; which had been superfluous, if the title *Sir* had been peculiar to them."—See Boswell's *Shakespeare*, vol. viii. p. 8.

§ Some of these entries are printed in Boys' *History of Sandwich*, but without the dates. They are here copied from the original transcripts now in the possession of his grandson,

In the accounts of Shipdam, Norfolk, is this entry :—

> " 1513. Payde to ye Clarke for mendynge ye orgaunys, and
> he shall take charge of ye pypes and ye bellows ye
> space of ij yeres at hys owne charge . . . . v *s.*"

Mr. Goddard Jonson, who quotes this extract in his *Illustrations of
Ancient Manners, &c., during the 16th and 17th centuries*, says, in a
note :—" The organs appear to have been a very considerable annual
charge upon the parish, as is shown by the various entries in the
books."

The Household Book of the Duke of Norfolk, an interesting
document of the fifteenth century, printed by the Roxburghe Club in
1844, has a valuable entry for our purpose. Under the date of 1482
we read :—

> " Item, the xxi day of March, my Lord payd Robert Borton of Stowmarket,
> the organ-maker, for mendyng of organys, vij^s."

This person, from his being called " organ-maker of Stowmarket,"
was, in all probability, a professional builder, not a priest. This
conjecture receives some confirmation from an entry that immediately
follows the one just given, where the person spoken of is styled
priest :—

> " Item, the same tyme my Lord toke Sir William Davyes, the pryst, to pay for
> a lok [lock ?] to the orgyns, iiij^d."

Some very curious illustrations of the history of the organ in
the fifteenth century may be gleaned from old wills. It is not
curiosity merely that is gratified by these inquiries, but we receive
ample scope for philosophical reflection in contemplating the customs,
habits, and superstitious bigotry, which prevailed at this distant era.

In the will of John Baret, of Bury, dated 1463, we have this
clause :—

> " Item, I wille y eche man y^t syngyit prykked songe on ye day of my enter-
> ment at our ladyes messe had ij^d and ye players at ye orgenys ij^d, and eche
> child i^d, and y^t yei preyid [be begged] to dyner the same day."

Lord John Beauchamp, who made his will in 1475, says :—

> " My body to be buried in the church of the Dominican Friars at Worcester,

---

W. H. Rolfe, Esq., of Sandwich. [Mr. Rolfe died soon after the publication of the firs
edition of this book.]

E 2

in a new chapel there now to be made on the north side of the quire, to which
house of friars, for my burial there I bequeath xx marks to be bestowed in vestments and stuff, besides an organ of my own."

I shall quote another piece of mortuary evidence, from the will of
John Baude, of Woolpett, dated 1501 :—

"I wyll that the tenement named the Cok w^t all the ptynaunce thereto belonging, be solde by the hande of my executors, and the mony thereof comying, the
fyrst p^t I will it be gwovyn to synge for me and all my benefactors by the term of
a holl yer, and the ij^de p^t of the mony, as fast as y^t may be receyuyd, I will ther be
bought one peyre of orgynys to the church of Wulpett."*

In the churchwardens' accounts of Lambeth are the following
items :—

"1517.   Paid to Sir William Argall for the organs .   .   .   .   x s.
1568.   Paid to Father Howe† for his fee for keeping the organes
one yere   .   .   .   .   i s."

The old accounts of St. Mary at Hill, London, contain, among
numerous interesting entries, several notices of the organ, i. e. :—

"1519.   For bringing the organs from St. Andrew's Church, against
St. Barnabas' eve, and carrying them back again .   .   v d.
1521.   To the organ maker for a pair of new organs, and for
bringing them home   .   .   .   .   .   .   x s. viij d."

Again, in the old books of St. Andrew Hubbard, Eastcheap :—

"1504.   Item, payd for mendyng of the organs   .   .   .   .   viij d.
1506.   Item, paid to John Smyth, organ plaier, for a quarter ending at our Lady Day in Lent   .   .   .   .   .   v s.
1568.   Paid to Hewe [probably Howe, before mentioned], the
organ-maker, for the kepinge of our orgaynes, his fee,
for ij yeres   .   .   .   .   v s."

As regards the prices paid for organs in ancient times we have
no very satisfactory information.

---

* These extracts from ancient wills are derived from Sir H. Nicolas' *Testamenta Vetusta*,
and the *Bury Wills ;* the latter printed for the Camden Society.

† The churchwardens' accounts of Blechingley, Surrey, show that, in 1542, they bought a
pair of organs at Lingfield, for £1 5s. In 1545 Mr. Howe, organ-maker, was paid, with his
man, for mending them—five days, 6s. 8d. Meat and drink for him and his servant, during
the time, and for "sawder," "lether," "glewe," "wyer," and other things, 4s. This
person was also employed in attending to the organ of St. Helen's Church, Bishopsgate. Mr.
Burgon, in his *Life and Times of Sir Thomas Gresham* (vol. ii., p. 466) says :—"Father
Howe's fee for the organes for a whole yere was 2s." Mr. W. B. Gilbert has discovered a
very curious document purporting to be "The Examination before Sir William Chester, Lord
Mayor of London, of Thomas Howe, of London, organ-maker." He appears to have been
suspected of Popery, and to have undergone, in consequence, a most rigid examination. I
regret that space will not allow me to print this most interesting record in the present work.

Whethamstede, abbot of St. Albans, about the year 1450, gave to his church a pair of organs; for which, and their erection, he expended the enormous sum, in those days, of *fifty pounds*. No organ in any monastery in England was comparable to this instrument, for its size, tone, and workmanship.[*] About the year 1476 Thomas Wyrcester, abbot of Hyde, near Winchester, gave eight marks and a horse to purchase an organ for his church. "*Octo Marcus et unum equum bonum pro nobis organis musicalibus*."[†] Organs were sometimes imported from the Continent, as appears from the Louth accounts, about 1500. The price of a pair of *Flemish* organs, suitable to be set up in the rood-loft of that noble church, was £13 6s. 8d.[‡] Grey, Archdeacon of Berkshire, bequeathed £4, in 1521, to St. Mary's Church at Oxford, "for a new payr of organs."[§] A new organ was bought, in 1529, for the large and beautiful Church of Holbeach, in Lincolnshire, for £3 6s. 8d.[||] In 1536 the churchwardens of St. Helen's, Abingdon, paid £8 for "a paire of organs."[¶]

According to Dugdale an organ was erected in the church of Sutton-Colfield, Warwickshire, by Vesey, Bishop of Exeter, in the reign of Henry the Eighth, at the cost of £14 2s. 8d.[**]

"A fair payr of organs" was placed in the chapel of Trinity College, Oxford, 1557, which, "with the carryage from London to Oxford, cost £10."[††]

These instances could readily be multiplied; but the present are sufficient for my purpose.

---

[*] *Chron. Whethamst.* per Hearne, vol. ii., p. 539.
[†] MSS. *Archiv. Wolves. apud* Winton.
[‡] *Archæologia*, vol. x., p. 91. [¶] Nichols' *Illustration of Expenses, &c.*, 1797.
[§] *Registr. Univ. Oxon.*, Archiv. A, 166. [**] Dugdale's *Warwickshire*, p. 667.
[||] Stukely's *Itin. Curios.*, p. 20. [††] Warton's *Life of Sir T. Pope*, p. 344.

Third Epoch.

THE FIRST ORGAN-BUILDERS BY PROFESSION.

---

15. *Early German Builders.*

THERE can be no doubt that many of the early organ-builders were ecclesiastics. Even down to a comparatively late period, as we have seen by the foregoing extracts, the latter continued to exercise a considerable influence over the art.

It is very difficult to distinguish the first organ-builders *by profession* from the priesthood ; but that such existed as early at least as the fifteenth century there cannot be a question.

Albert Van Os, emphatically called "Albert the Great," the earliest known organ-builder, was certainly a priest ; so were his followers, Ulric Engelbrecht and Nicholas Faber. Van Os built the organ of St. Nicholas' Church, Utrecht, in 1120 ; Engelbrecht, that of Strasburg Cathedral, in 1260 ; and Faber, that of Halbertstadt, in 1359 or 1361, before mentioned.

Heinrich Traxdorf, who built an organ at Nuremberg in 1455, and another at St. Mary Magdalen, at Breslau, in 1466, was probably a *layman ;* but this is by no means certain. Erhart Smid, of Peyssenberg, in Bavaria (whom Duke Ernest, in 1433, exempted from every species of impost and contribution, on account of his skill in constructing organs), and Andrè, who built, in 1456, the organ of St. Ægidea, at Brunswick, were cetainly lay-builders.

In 1475 Conrad Rosenburger, or Rothenburger, built an organ in the church of the Barefooted Friars, at Nuremberg ; and, in 1493, a still larger one in the Cathedral of Bamberg. The organ in the Cathedral at Erfurt was built, in 1483, by an artist of Breslau, named Stephen Castendorfer, who also built, in 1490, an organ for St. Ulrich's Church, at Augsburg, for 107 florins (£8 18s. 4d.). The great organ in the collegiate church of St. Blasius, at Brunswick, was built, in 1499, by Henry Kranx. Prætorius celebrates Frederick

Krebs and Nicholas Muller as skilful organ-builders. Probably all these eminent men were organ-builders by profession.

16. *Early English Builders.*

The Rev. Sir William Cope, in a brief but highly interesting paper on "Early Organ-builders in England," printed in the *Parish Choir*, was the first to bring forward the name of one William Wotton, of Oxford, as "the earliest organ-builder in this country" of whom any trace could be found. The writer, however, is constrained to deprive Wotton of this honour, having produced several claimants of an earlier date. With regard to William Wotton .an indenture exists, which was made, in 1487, between R. Fitzjames, warden of Merton College, and William Wotton, of the town of Oxford, by which the latter undertakes to make a pair of organs like the organs of the chapel of St. Mary Magdalen College, against the vigil of Whitsunday, 1489, for the price of £28. The organ in Magdalen Chapel had been set up by him not long before, as appears by an entry in the Libri Computi of that college, for the years 1486-7, of a payment to him of £13 in part for one pair of organs :—

"Sol. Willielmo Wotton, Orkyn-maker, pro uno pari organorum in parte, £13."

And, two or three years after, a further payment occurs to him for repairs to this organ :—

"1488-9, Sol. Willo. Wotton, pro reparacione organorum, 40s."

A very singular story in connection with this builder is told by Anthony Wood, in his *Annals*, A.D. 1486. It is to the following effect :—

"A certain poor priest of Oxford, named William Symonds, of the age of 28 years, having a youth of a crafty wit and comely presence to his pupil, contrived (in hope to raise himself to some great bishoprick), and brought it so to pass, that the said youth should be vulgarly reported by certain noble persons, that bore good will to the House of York, to be Edward, Earl of Warwick, son of the Duke of Clarence (who before, as 'tis said, had secretly conveyed himself out of prison), to the end that he might be king, and that the House of York might again flourish. But the said Symonds, being discovered, was apprehended, and the 10th Feb. confessed in St. Paul's Church, before divers bishops and nobles, as also the Lord Mayor, aldermen, and sheriffs of London, that he, by flattery, had seduced the son of *a certain organ-maker* of the University of Oxford, and had caused him to be sent into Ireland, where he was by many reputed to be the Earl of Warwick, and that he was with the Lord Lovell at Furnsell. Upon which confession he was sent to the Tower, and afterwards (as some say) suffered as a traitor ; though others not, but that he was only kept in close prison as long as he lived. Some report that the said youth was named Lambert Symnell, and that he was a baker's son in Oxford ; but the priest's confession was the truest, viz., that he was the son of *an organ-maker* of the University of Oxford. And who that should be but one William Wotton I cannot tell, knowing very well, from various obscure writs, that such an one, and nobody else, professed that art at that time in Oxford."

Wotton's organ in Magdalen College was probably soon replaced by another, or enlarged ; for, in 1509, a part-payment is entered for "organs" to John Chamberlayne.

John Chamberlyn, or Chamberlayne, and Thomas Smyth, were organ-builders, residing in London in the early part of the sixteenth century. A payment to the latter, in 1514, is thus recorded in the accounts of the churchwardens of St. Margaret's, Westminster :—

"1514. Item, paid to Thomas Smith, orgone-maker, for mendying of the grete orgones xl⁵, and for the small orgones v⁵."

An interesting document was discovered, in 1862, among the old papers in the church chest of Allhallows', Barking, London, of which a copy was kindly forwarded to me by the late Mr. George Corner, F.S.A. It purports to be "An Indenture or Contract between the Churchwardens of Allhallows', Barking, and Anthony Duddyngton for the Organs, A.D. 1519," and is as follows :—

"This endenture made the yere of oure lorde god mᴶ vᵉ xix. and in the moneth of July xxix day. Witnesseth that Antony Duddyngton, Citezen of London, Organ-Maker, hath made a full bargayn, condycionally, with Maister Willᵐ· Petenson, Doctour in Divinite, Vicar of Alhalowe, Barkyng, Robᵗ Whytehed and John Churche, Wardeyns of the same Churche, and Maisters of the P'isshe of Alhalowe, Barkyng, next yᵉ Tower of London, to make an instrument, that yᵃ to say a payer of organs for the foresed churche, of dowble *Ce-fa-ut* that yᵃ to say, xxvij. playne keyes, and the pryncipale to conteyn the length of v foote, so folowing wᵗ Bassys called Diapason to the same, conteyning length of x foot or more : And to be dowble pryncipalls thoroweout the seid instrument, so that the pyppes wᵗ inforth shall be as fyne metall and stuff as the utter [outer] parts, that is to say of pure Tyn, wᵗ as fewe stops as may be convenient. And the seid Antony to have ernest viᵘ xiii˙ iiijᵈ· Also the foresaid Antony askyth v quarters of respytt, that yᵃ to say, from the fest of Seynt Mighell the Archaungell, next following to the feast of Seynt Mighell the day twelvemonth following. And also undernethe this condicion, that the foresaid Antony shall convey the belowes in the loft abowf in the said Quere of Alhalowes, wᵗ a pype to the sond boarde. Also this p'mysed by the said Antony, that yf the foresaid Maister, Doctour, Vicare, Churche Wardeyns, Maisters of the p'isshe, be not content nor lyke not the seid instrument, that then they shall allowe him for convaying of the bellows xl˙ for his cost of them, and to restore the rest of the Truest [trust] agayn to the seid Maisters. And yf the said Antony decesse and depart his naturall lyf wᵗin the forseid v quarters, that then hys wyff or hys executours or his assignees shall fully content the foresaid some of iiijᵘ xijˢ iiijᵈ to the seid Vicare, and Churche Wardeyns, and Maisters of the said p'isshe w^tout any delay. And yf they be content w^t the seid instrument, to pay to the seid Antony fyfty poundes sterlinge. In Wittnesse whereof the said p'ties to these endentures chaungeably have set their sealls. Geven the day and yere abovesaid."

This contract was fulfilled, as the following receipt appended to the document proves :—

" M^{d.} Y^t Anthony Duddyngtoune have Rec^d of Harry Goderyk, Churche Wardeyn of Barkyng the som of xxx^{li} st., in p^t of paym^t of ı^{li} st., the which I shold have for a payr of orgens. In Wytnesse heyrof, I the foresaid Antony have sub-scrybed my name the xxij day of Mche, Aö xv^c xx

" Be me, ANTONY DUDDYNGTON."

The following remarks upon this early contract are from Mr. Hopkins' most interesting and valuable lecture " On the Progress of Organ-building in England," delivered before the Members of the College of Organists :—

" Duddyngton's contract furnishes us with several interesting particulars : from it we learn the important fact that the compass of the sixteenth century English organ was ' double C Fa-ut ;' that is to say, it was of CC or 8 feet downward range, and therefore corresponded in that respect precisely with the manual compass of the English and Continental instruments of the present day. The expression ' xxvij playne keyes' I take to mean that number of keys on a ' plane' or level :—in common language, that number of so-called naturals, the requisite number of short keys probably being understood. This would give the compass, if the scale were *unbroken*, as from CC to A3 in alt ; and, if broken, that is to say, having the CC pipes planted on the *apparently* EE key, a range corresponding exactly with the short octave CC four octave compass, still occasionally to be met with in some of the old German organs. The Allhallows' organ evidently had but one manual, and the English organs of the period appear never to have had more ; the expression ' payer of organs' in Duddyngton's contract having no reference whatever to the number of the manuals, but being used in a totally different sense.* No complete specification is presented by the various old documents under consideration, but the names of two stops are mentioned, and in a manner that clearly shows that they were applied precisely as in the present day. Thus we find the word ' pryncipale' used to indicate the octave sounding stop, and ' diapason' to distinguish the unison. The length of the stops—' v foote ' for the former, and ' x foote or more ' for the latter—would allow for a foot to the pipes of one quarter of the length of their speaking parts or bodies. The ' dowble pryncipalls thoroweout the seid Instrument' form a curious feature, and it becomes evident, on comparing several early contracts, but of successive dates, that the duplication of the four feet stop was as common and as favourite an arrangement in the sixteenth and seventeenth centuries as was the repetition of the eight feet, or open diapason, in the latter part of the eighteenth and first half of the nineteenth. With respect to the materials to be employed, it is specified that the inside pipes shall be of ' as fyne metall and stuff as the outer parts, that is to say, of pure Tyn ;' and from the manner in which this

---

* Duddyngton's contract is alone sufficient to refute Mr. Ashpitel's hypothesis, before noticed, about the meaning of this term.

condition is worded, it would seem that pure tin for the front pipes of an organ was at that time sufficiently understood, without its being distinctly mentioned in the agreement ; and, while it is interesting to note that the English organ-makers of that period used such an excellent material, it must not be forgotten that the value of that metal was then scarcely a tithe of what it now is."*

Nothing more is known of Anthony Duddyngton, "citizen of London ;" but it is more than probable that many of the old City organs, destroyed in the Great Fire, were of his construction.

William Lewes, organ-maker, was appointed in the year 1514 "keeper and tuner of the King's instruments," for which he received annually the sum of 100 shillings.

In the list of Henry the Eight's Musical Establishment we find, under the year 1526, the name of "John de John, *organ-maker.*" Again, in the King's Household Book, we have this entry :—

"May, 1531. Item, the 2d daye, paid to *Sir* John, the organ-maker, in rewarde, by the king's commandement . . . . . . xl\ˢ."

This person, who was a *priest*, was succeeded in the royal establishment by William Beton, or Betun, an organ-builder of some pretensions—if we may judge from the fact of his having built the organ for the old Cathedral of St. Paul, destroyed in the Great Fire of 1666.

In Rymer's (*Fœdera Pro Capitoli Organista Regis*) is a grant of £20 sterling per annum to William Betun, bearing date 1537 ; which annual stipend he appears to have received until the year 1544. He was retained in the royal service by Edward the Sixth and Mary. In the list of the musical establishment of the former we find :—

"Makers of Instruments, { William Beton, *Organ* Maker. { William Tresorer, *Regal* Maker."†

An eminent English builder of this period was named Wyght, or White. Entries of payments to him for work done to the organ of

---

* It is not known what was the ultimate fate of this organ, but it seems likely that it was sold for the value of the old metal—"the pure tyn" mentioned in the contract—during the reign of fanaticism in the century following. This seems the more likely, as the church was without an organ in 1675, when it was resolved at a vestry meeting to erect "an organ of convenient size and loudness for the due celebration of the psalmody of the church." According to this resolution money was collected, and arrangements entered into with Renatus Harris, who erected the present organ.

† There is an exceedingly curious licence preserved in the Cottonian MS. Galba C. 11., fol. 253, from which it appears that "WILLIAM TREASORER, a maker of musical instru-ments, his heirs and assigns," had letters patent for eight years, from King Philip and Queen

Magdalen College Chapel, Oxford, occur in the old account books, from 1531 to 1545. One of them runs thus :—

> "1531, Magistro White, organorum factore, pro reparat. duorum par organorum in choro."

From the title, *Magister*, here given him, it has been conjectured, with every appearance of probability, that he was the same person as Robert White, a well-known church composer, who may have united the art of constructing organs with his higher musical pursuits.[*]

Possibly, an entry in the old parish accounts of St. Andrew's, Holborn, may have some reference to this builder :—

> "1553. The parishe gave young Whyte £5 for ye great orgaynes which his father made for ye churche."

John Vaucks, "orgayn-master," as he is termed, is another new name in the annals of organ-building. He was employed, in 1533, to set up a new "pair of organs" in the rood loft of Wimborne Minster, for which he was paid by the contributions of the parish ; and his work appears to have lasted till the Great Rebellion, which brought it to an untimely end. In the year 1643, among entries for glazing the windows and new covering the roofs with lead (measures often found necessary after a visit of the Parliamentary forces), we find the following :—"Paid for some of the organ-pipes, 6d." Here, then, is the fate of John Vaucks' handiwork, after a century of use : its pipes scattered about the streets, or stolen for the sake of the metal, and the trouble of those who brought some of them back valued at sixpence. A considerable quantity of materials must, however, have been left, since, in the year following, the church-wardens sold off more than 140 lbs. of old tin—no doubt supplied by the organ pipes.[†]

Mary, dated July the 11th, in the first year of their reign, to provide and buy within the realm of England, in any place or places, one hundred thousand lasts of ashes, and four hundred thousand dozens of old worn shoes, and export the same to foreign parts." Queen Elizabeth, on the 13th March, in the second year of her reign, confirmed the same for an additional term of twelve years. Treasurer, as a consideration for the renewed patent, "having devised and given to the Queen a new Instrument Musicall, sending forth the sound of Flutes and Recorders ; and likewise promised and took upon him, at his labour, cost, and charges, to repair and amend before the feast of St. Michael next ensuing the great organs in the Queen's chapel at Greenwich."—Ellis's *Original Letters*, second series, vol. iii., p. 202.

[*] Sir William Cope's paper, before mentioned. I am also indebted to the same authority for the curious notices concerning Broughe and Chappington.

[†] I am indebted for these curious notices of John Vaucks, &c., to a *History of Wimborne Minster*, published by Bell & Daldy, 1860. 8vo.

To return again to Oxford. In 1520 one Barbye was employed in repairing the "little orgayns" in the chapel of Magdalen College ; but nothing seems to be known of him. We have also the names of John Hanson and John Schowt, shortly afterwards. They were probably all three local builders of no great note. The latter, from the spelling of his name, was probably a German.

The name of Richard Beynton, and the thoroughly English one of Thomas Browne, occur in old accounts as "mendyng," and otherwise restoring organs, about the middle of the sixteenth century.*

A little later we have a builder of the name of Broughe, who appears to have set up a new organ at St. Margaret's, Westminster, thus noticed in the churchwardens' accounts there :—

"1590, payde to Mr. Broughe, for changeing of our organs for a payre of his, viijᵘ."

An organ-builder flourished at the close of the sixteenth century, who, though his name is now forgotten, seems to have been extensively employed in his day—John Chappington. He appears to have built an organ for Westminster Abbey about 1596 ; at least we find him in this year (according to the following memorandum) selling the old organ of that collegiate church to the churchwardens of St. Margaret's :—

"Paid to Mr. Chappington for the organs of the Colledge, xiijᵘ· xiijˢ· iiijᵈ·, and the old organs do remayne in the parish church to be sold by the churchwardens."

The latter part of the entry possibly relates to the organ built by Broughe six years previously. In the following year a further payment was made "to Chappington for the organs, lxvjˢ· viijᵈ·"

One organ, at least, of Chappington's remains to this day—viz., that which he built, in 1597, for Magdalen College, Oxford ; and of the payment of which the following memorandum exists in the Libri Computi of that society :—

"Impensæ pro organis Mro. Chapington .   .   .   xxxv *l.* xiij *s.* viii *d.*
Pro color. et deaurat. eadem   .   .   .   .   .   .   ij *l.* ij *s.*
Pro wainscot circa eadem   .   .   .   .   .   .   iij *l.* xiv *s.*"

At the beginning of the following century there was an organ-builder living in London, named Gibbs. Alleyn, the founder of

---

* In the old accounts of King's College, Cambridge, as early as 1508, we find Thomas Browne receiving xxxiijs. ivᵈ ; "in partem solutionis viii librarum pro factura magnorum organorum." This may be the builder mentioned in the text.

Dulwich College, records in his diary, under the date April 27.
1618 :—"Bought a pair of organes of Mr. Gibbs, of Powles, £8 2s.;"
which organs were put up in the college chapel.*

We may mention two other builders of the seventeenth century
whose names have recently come to light :—Thomas Hamlyn, who
enlarged "the new organ at St. James's," in 1613 ; and Adam Fortess,
who built an organ for St. George's Chapel, Windsor, in 1635. For
the latter he received £140.

17. *Local English Builders.*

Organs were not mute in our country parish churches during the
sixteenth century, and constant mention of them is to be found in
old accounts.

Among the builders whose fame appears to have been purely
of a local character, and who have entirely escaped notice, was one
Robartt, who lived at Crewkerne about the time of the Reformation.
He was an "orgyn-maker," who let out organs to churches by the
year. Probably this might have been a prevailing practice, but this
is the only instance I have met with of it at an early date.

According to a notice preserved in Mr. G. Roberts' *Social History
of the People of the Southern Counties of England,*† this maker was
paid by John Hassard, Mayor of Lyme Regis, 1551, "his year's
rent, 10s."

Robartt's instrument seems to have been in the hands of an adept
whose services were appreciated, as we learn from the following
entry :—

"1552. The Mayor and his brethren grant to John Coke £5 yearly in
consideration of the good service that he hath performed in the church of King's
Lyme, from time to time, in singing and playing at organs, and which the said
John Coke was to continue during his life, in the best manner he could, as God
had endued him to do."

There was an organ in the parish church of Doncaster prior to
the magnificent instrument destroyed in the fire ; for, according to
the churchwardens' accounts of 1569, Mr. Fenton was paid " 13ˢ. 4ᵈ.

---

* See the *European Magazine* for June, 1792, p. 192 ; and Collier's *Memoirs of Alleyn*,
p. 157. From the latter it appears that, a year afterwards, Alleyn had "a diapason stop"
put to the organ by a person of the name of Barett, and "other alterations."

† 1856, 8vo, p. 233.

for an organe case." The parish registers of this church, under
the date of July 26th, 1567, record the burial of James Dempsey,
"organe-maker." It was in the establishment of this worthy, in all
probability, that the first Doncaster organ was made.

18. *English Builders in the Seventeenth Century.*

Among the eminent English organ-builders who belong to the
seventeenth century are the names of Preston, of York ; Thamar, of
Peterborough ; Robert Hayward, of Bath ; Loosemore, of Exeter ;
and the Dallans, or Dallams, of London.

Of the two first, no particulars, further than their mere names,
appear to have come down to us. Of the third our information is
not much more.

In the year 1663 a rate was made and levied at Wimborne,
Dorsetshire, amounting to £253 13s. 8d., towards the repairs of the
fine Minster Church in that town, and for buying a new organ ; and
an agreement was entered into with a provincial builder, Robert
Haywood, of Bath, "whose work," remarks Mr. Hopkins "(if it was
really his), which remains to the present day, proves that in skill he
was not a whit behind others of his countrymen, whose productions
are more numerous and better known."

The instrument was set up in the following year (1664), the price
being £180. When it was finished, two distinguished musicians, Mr.
Tomkins and Mr. Silver, from Salisbury, were sent for to "prove the
organ, whether it was sufficient according to our covenants," and
received £5 for their trouble.*

John Loosemore constructed the organ in the cathedral of his
native city, Exeter, shortly after the restoration of Charles II.†
This instrument is pointed out as worthy of especial notice on
account of its double diapason. The Hon. Roger North, in the
Life of the Lord Keeper Guilford (mentioning his brother's visit to
Exeter), adds :—

" His lordship, agreeably to his great mastership of musick, took great notice
of the organ in the Cathedral church of Exeter, where the two side columns that
carry the tower are lined with organ pipes, and are as columns themselves. His

---

* *History of Wimborne Minster.*

† On the outside of the instrument is this inscription :—"John Loosemore made this
organ, 1665." Henry Loosemore, M.B., organist of King's College, Cambridge (afterwards
of Exeter Cathedral), and George Loosemore, M.B., organist of Trinity College, Cambridge,
were brothers to our organ-builder.

lordship desired the dimensions of the great double diapason ; and the account, as returned, is thus :—

' Speaking part, long . . . . . 20 feet 6 inc.
Nose 4 0
Circumference 3 11
Diameter 1 3
Contents of the speaking part . . . 3 hogs. 8 gall.
Weight . . . . 360 lbs.'

" This is heard plainer at a distance than when near, as also louder ; and behind that, and the other large doubles, are placed large wooden pipes to help them into their sound, which otherwise would come on very slow, or perhaps not at all. One, being near enough, may, by the touch of the hand, discern when it speaks, and when not. How it is tuned, whether by measure or the beats, we were not informed ; and, bating their account of it, which was curious and diverting enough, I could not be so happy to perceive that, in the musick, they signified any thing at all, but thought them made more for ostentation than for use ; for there are terms in sound which will not be exceeded ; for, when the vibratory pulses are so slow as scarcely to be distinguished, sound vanisheth ; which is nearly the case with this great pipe." *

In the Choristers' Singing School, attached to the cathedral, is a small instrument of the same maker. Its stops, which are all of wood, are as follows :—

Stopped Diapason.	Twelfth.
Open Diapason.	Fifteenth.
Principal.	Flute.

The compass is CC (short octaves) to C in alt.

The following agreement between Loosemore and a customer is not devoid of interest :—

" February the 1st, 1665. Then made a bargain wth S^r G^o. Trevilyan, for an organ wth these stops in it, as follows :—

One Diapason . . . . . ⎫
One Flute . . . . . . ⎬ these in wood.
One Recorde . . . . . ⎪
One Fifteenth . . . . . ⎭
One Principall . . . . . ⎫
One Flagilett . . . . . ⎬ these in mettle.
One Trumpett . . . . . ⎪
One Shaking Stopp . . . ⎭

And for this organ I am to have one hundred pound, 20l. whereof at the 25th day of March next, and fourescore residue thereof when the work is finished.

" JOHN LOOSEMORE."†

---

* *Lives of the Norths*, vol. i., p. 246.

† See the preface to *A Short Account of Organs built in England from the Reign of King Charles the Second to the Present Time*. Lond., J. Masters, 1847. 8vo. The work is published anonymously, but the author is understood to be Mr. Sutton, of Jesus College, Cambridge.

This builder died on the 8th of April, 1681, aged 68.*

The accounts of King's College, Cambridge, at the beginning of the seventeenth century, introduce to our notice an organ-builder named Dallam, whose existence escaped my researches when collecting the materials for the first edition of the *History of the Organ.*

I was then enabled to show, for the first time, that there were *three* contemporary builders of the same name :—Dallam, or Dalham— namely, Robert, who built organs for York Minster, the Music School, and New College, Oxford ; Ralph, who was employed at St. George's Chapel, Windsor, at Rugby, Lynn Regis, and Greenwich ; and George Dalham, who is mentioned in 1672 as "that excellent organ-maker dwelling in Purple Lane, next door to the Crooked Billet." But the builder employed at King's College, Cambridge, in 1606, was clearly older than the three just mentioned, who may in all likelihood have been his sons, following their father's profession.

The accounts just mentioned purport to be " The charges about the organs, &c., from the 22nd of June, 1605, to the 7th of August, 1606." They are so highly interesting that I shall quote them *in extenso* :—

"Imprimis payd to Mr. Dallam for his journey from London to Cambridge before he took the woork in hand	xv *s.*
Item for his and his menes charges of their journey coming downe to work	x *s.*
Item for a thowsand six hundred of tynn at 3ll. 12s. le C . . .	lvij *li.* xij *s.*
Item for ebony for the kayes [*sic*]. , ...	iij *s.* iiij *d.*
Item for boxe	xij *d.*
Item for vij dozen of leather, unde iij dozen ad 6s. le doz. and 4 dozen ad vijs. le dozen	xlvj *s.*
Item for sodering coller and cyse	xxx *s.*
Item for vll. of white wyer ad 10d. lell.	iiij *s.* ij *d.*
Item for viill. of yeollowe wyer ad 18d. lell.	x *s.* vj *d.*
Item for Ashe woodd	xij *d.*
Item for xxijll. of tyn glasse ad 3s. lell.	iij *li.* vj *s.*
Item for viij dozen of glewe at 4s. 6d. le doz	xxxvj *s.*
Item for canves to put the glewe in	xviij *d.*
Item for a hamper to carry things in and corde to bynd yt . .	ij *s.*
Item for more corde to bynd up other things	x *d.*
Item for packthred to bynd the pypes	ij *s.*
Item for nayles of divers kyndes	x *s.*

---

* The following inscription is on his gravestone in the transept of Exeter Cathedral, near the south aisle of the choir :—" Hic jacet spe Resurrectionis JOHANNES LOOSMORE [*sic*], quondam Decano et Capitulo hujus Ecclesiæ Curator fidelissimus ; et inter Artifices sui Generis facile Princeps. Sit Organum hoc angustum prope situm perpetuum ipsius Artis et Ingenii Monumentum. Obiit 8° Aprilis An. 1681. Æta. suæ 68."

Item for carriage of the premisses being bought in divers places of
the Citie togeather with Mr. Dallam his Tooles . . . . iiij *s.*
Item to Walston Cruis for his paynes in seeing the things bought and
packed to be sent to Camb. . . . . iiij *s.*
Item for flannell clothe to laye under the kayes . . . . xij *d.*
Item for fustian to cast the mettell uppon . . . . . x *s.*
Item for preston clothe for the same use . . . . . vj *s.*
Item for chalke to lay upon the fustian . . . . . iiij *d.*
Item for brasse for the shaking stoppe . . . . . iiij *s.*
Item for a pan to make fyer in to remove . . . . . vj *d.*
Item for flaxe to glewe in the Conditts . . . . . vj *d.*
Item for carriage of the tyn from London at 2ˢ· 6ᵈ· le C . . . xl *s.*
Item for carriage of the hamper, Mr. Dallam's tooles, and other things
from London at dyvers tymes . . . . xv *s.*
Item for xx leaves of waynskott reddy sawne . . . . xx *s.*
Item to a Joyner for helping Mr. Dallam in his work . . . iiij *s.*
Item for planks for benches, &c. . . . . xiiij *s.*
Item for viii double quarters for frames for the said benches . . iiij *s.*
Item for bords for boxes, &c. . . . . ij *s.*
Item for popler to make the Maldrells, &ce . . . . . xiij *s.*
m for turning of the Maldrells . . . . . . viij *s.*
Item for planke about the sound borde . . . . . ij *s.* vj *d.*
Item for a C of planks for the bellowes . . . . . xxj *s.*
Item for Quarters to lyfte up the bellowes and other uses . . xxxj *s.*
Item for studds to make Claves [keys] . . . . . vj *s.*
Item for Joysts to lay over the bellowes and other uses . . viij *s.*
Item for ccxl foote of Inche board . . . . . . xxiij *s.* iv *d.*
Item for xiiij sparres of 12 foot long . . . . . . xiiij *s.*
Item for viij peeces tymber of 8 foote and ij of 10 foote . . x *s.* vj *d.*
Item for 4 planks of 16 foote long and 2 inches di. thicke . . v *s.* iiij *d.*
Item for three peeces of 11 foote long and 2 of 9 foote di. . . iiij *s.* v *d.*
Item for 83 foote of halfe ynche board to cover the organ . . iij *s.* iiij *d.*
Item for studes . . . . viij *d.*
Item for 44 foote of ynche board and a piller of 7 foote . . iiij *s.* iiij *d.*
Item for the carriage of this tymber at dyvers tymes . . . ij *s.*
Item for the mattes to sett the greate pypes on in the Vestrie . viij *d.*
Item payd to the Carpenter for the frame of tymber whereon the
organs . . . . xvj *li.*
Item to Chapman the Joyner for 82 yards of waynscott about the
sayd frame at vˢ· the yard . . . . xx *li.* x *s.*
Item for clxiii waynscotts bought unsawen for the case & wooddon
pypes of the organs, unde 60 ad 3ˢ· 8ᵈ·, 38 ad 4ˢ· 6ᵈ·, 23 ad
5ˢ·, 40 ad 5ˢ· 3ᵈ·, and 2 ad 6ˢ· in toto . . . . xxxvj *li.* viiij *s.*
Item payd for sawing the sayd waynscotts . . . . . vi *li.* ix *s.*
Item for carriage of them . . . . vij *s.*
Item for vi C of Lead at 10ˢ· le C . . . . iij *li.*
Item for casting of yt . . . . x *s.*
Item for sande & wood used about it . . . . . . iiij *s.*
Item payd to the Smithe for Iron worke ut patet . . . . vij *li.* vij *s.* iij *d.*
Item geven to one that went for the Joyner and bringing of his
Tooles . . . . viij *s.*
Item for the Joyner and his menes supper at their coming . . xij *d.*

F

Item paid for a grindlestone and hanging yt . . . . iij *s.*

Item paper and oyle for the Joyners windowes . . . . ix *d.*

Item for nayles &ce taken by Mr. Dallam & yᵉ Joyner at the Chandlers, ut patet . . . . xl *s.* iiij *d.*

Item payd to Hartop the Joyner for wages for him & his men for 10 monethes ad 18ˢ le weeke . . . . . . xxxvi *li.*

Item geven to him at his departure in regards above his sayd wages xxij *s.*

Item in regard to his men . . . . iij *s.* iiij *d.*

Item payd for a horse to carrye back his tooles . . . . vj *s.*

Item payd to Mr. Dallam the Organmaker, for his wages and his menes for lviij weekes di. viz. from the 22ⁿᵈ of June, 1605, untill the 7th of August, 1606, ad 30ˢ le weeke . . . lxxxvij *li.* xv *s.*

Item payd for the hyer of bedding for him and his men the first quarter . . . . xij *s.*

Item for the hyer of bedding for his men 3 qts. di. more ad 6ˢ le quarter . . . . xxj *s.*

Item payd for Mr. Dallams owne lodging the said 3 qᵗers di. at Brownings, Sampsons, and Knockells . . . . . xx *s.*

Item payd for his washing and his menes all the 58 weeks of his aboade . . . . xxv *s.*

Item payd for his owne and his menes frydays and fasting night suppers at 12ᵈ a supper being in all 87 nights . . . iiij *li.* vij *s.*

Item payd for his hoshier and charges of him and his men at their departure up to London . . . . x *s.*

Item for recarriage of his tooles &c. being iiijᶜ wayght . . x *s.*

Item payd to the Carver for the King's Armes standing upon the chayre organ . . . . iij *li.*

Item to him for the Scutchins of this College and Eton Armes . . . . xxx *s.*

Item to him for 2 figures or pictures that stand in the greate Organ . . . . xxx *s.*

Item payd for ixᵉ of leaf gould at 7ˢ 6ᵈ le C . . . . iij *li.* vij *s.* vi *d.*

Item payd to Knockle the Limber for laying the sayd gould &ce. upon the pypes, Armes and scutchins of the Chayre Organ . iiij *li.*

Item payd to him for imbossing and strawing with bice the 2 greater pypes of the chayre organ . . . . . . xxvj *s.* viij *d.*

Item to him for embossing and strawing with byce the 2 lesser pypes of the sayd organ . . . . x *s.*

Item to him for gould and gilding the crownes of the sayd organ xxvj *s.* viij *d.*

Item to him for the pastboard and byce strawed under the cutwoorke about the sayd organ & frame . . . . xx *s.*

Item payd to him for the 2 lesser pypes in the great organ imbossed & strawed with byce & for 12 wrought pypes gilded . vj *li.* x *s.*

Item for iiij pypes paynting with venice lake, &ce . . . xlviij *s.*

Item to him for gould & gilding 24 small pypes in the sayd Organ xl *s.*

Item to him for strawing with byce &ce & for gilding the embosses on the greate pype in the middle tower . . . xxvj *s.* viij *d.*

Item to him for strawing with byce and gilding the imbosses on the 2 greate pypes of the owtter towers . . . . iiij *li.*

Item payd for dyvers of the imbosses used upon the pypes in the litle and greate Organs . . . . xiiij *s.*

Item for mowlds to cast the rest of the imbosses . . . . x *s.*

Item payd more to Knockle for paynting &ce of the sixe fayre
    great pypes ad 50^s a pype . . . .   xv *li.*
Item to him for gilding the round towars of the sd Organ . .   iij *li.*
Item to him for gilding the finishing or square towars of the same
    Organ . . . .   iiij *li.*
Item to him for gilding the 2 starres . . . . . .   ij *s.*
Item for gilding and colloring the bracketts . . . . .   x *s.*
Item for colloring the 2 picktures or figures in the sayd organ .   xiij *s.* iv *d.*
Item to him for pastbord & byce strawed under the cut-woorke
    on the sayd organ . . . .   xxxij *s.* iij *d.*
                   Sm^a total . ccclxxi *li.* xvij *s.* j *d.*
Item more Mr. Dallams mens dyett in the hall . . .   xiij *li.* vj *s.* viij *d.*
Item bread and beer by Mr. Dallam the Joyner and their men
    for the whole tyme esteemyd at . . . . . .   v *li.*
Item fyering in charcoale about 5 load with candells . . .   vi *li.*"

There is something very primitive in this picture of the old organ-builder closing his workshop in London, and removing his whole "establistment," to Cambridge, to execute an order.

Dallam and his men were lodged in the town, but boarded in the College hall. From the item for suppers on Fridays and fasting nights, it appears they were not satisfied with the meagre fare there provided, but required extra dishes for their maintenance.

The whole of the materials used appear to have been bought in the rough, and made up on the spot; the metal purchased for the pipes, presuming that all the lead was used for that purpose, would be in the proportion of 16 to 6, or rather less than three-fourths tin. This was the composition of the original pipes of the Temple organ built by Father Smith.

No specification is extant from which any information may be obtained as to the compass and power of the instrument; the only stop mentioned in the account is the shaking stop, for which a special material was required; it was the original of the modern tremulant, and occurs in the specification for an organ given by John Loosemore, of Exeter, in 1665, already quoted. It is not found in later specifications, and went out of use owing to the noise it made in action, occasioned by its faulty construction.

The total cost of the organ and case was about £370; the outlay upon the organ, so far as the items may now be divided, amounting to £214, and that upon the case to £156.*

---

* I derive my information about the old King's College Organ from a paper in the *Ecclesiologist*, by the Rev. J. Brooklebank,

The name of Dallam still occurs in the College accounts after the completion of the organ. In 1607 he was paid xxxv⁵· for tuning the organ, besides xxxv⁵· received by the sale of the surplus tin, which had been purchased for the pipes; in 1617, £10, and, in 1638, £22, were paid to him for repairs. His name occurs for the last time in 1641. In no case is a Christian name given.*

The fate of Dallam's organ is soon told. The commissioners sent down to Cambridge by the Long Parliament ordered the organ in the chapel to be removed; and, in compliance with their edict, the pipes were taken out and sold. The case, with some alterations, remains to this day.

In 1613 Thomas Dalham, undoubtedly the builder just noticed, was employed to build an organ for Worcester Cathedral. The following extract is from the archives of the Dean and Chapter of that ecclesiastical establishment :—

"A.D. 1613. All the materials and workmanship of the new double organ in the Cathedral church of Worcester to Thomas Dallam, organ-maker, came to £211."

This entry is valuable as giving us the Christian name of this hitherto unknown builder.

Robert Dallam was born at Lancaster in 1602, and died in 1665 : he was buried in the cloisters of New College, Oxford.†

In the recently printed calendars of the State Papers is noticed "A Bill of Robert Dallam for work done for my Lordes Grace of Canterburie, his orgayne, A.D. 1635;" and an interesting notice of

---

* In the books of Magdalen College, Oxford, between the dates 1615 and 1637, several entries occur of payments to one Dalham for repairs to the organ. Dr. Bloxam, in his interesting account of the College Chapel, believes him to have been the *Robert* Dalham before mentioned; but this could hardly be the case, as he was not born till 1602, and consequently was only thirteen years of age in 1615. It was certainly the builder now brought to light whose name occurs in the Magdalen books.

† Wood, in his *Hist. and Antiq. Univ. Oxoniensis,* 1674, vol. ii., p. 155, gives the following inscription on this person :—" Hic jacet Dⁿᵘˢ Robertus Dallum, Instrumenti Pneumatici quod vulgo Organum nuncupant peritissimus Artifex ; filius Thomæ Dallum de Dallum in comitat. Lancastriæ. Mortuus est die Maii ultimo

Anno {Domini 1665.
      {Ætatis suæ 63.

Qui postquam diversas Europæ plagas hâc arte (quâ præcipue claruit) exornasset, solum hoc tandem, in quo requiescit, cinere suo insignivit." The records of the Blacksmiths' Company are said to contain many entries relative to Robert Dallam. A search amongst them would probably repay the trouble,

him is preserved among the memoranda of Dr. Woodward, Warden of New College, Oxford, at the time of the Restoration :—

"May 10, 1661.—Some discourse was then had with one Mr. Dalham, an organ-maker, concerning a new fair organ to be made for our College Chapel. The stops of the intended organ were shown unto myself and the thirteen seniors, set down in a paper and named there by the organist of Christ Church, who would have had them half a note lower than Christ Church organ, but Mr. Dalham supposed that a quarter of a note would be sufficient."

Robert Dallam built the organ in New College Chapel, and the small one in the Music School, Oxford; but his principal work appears to have been the organ in York Minster, destroyed when that noble building was partially burnt. The circumstances connected with the erection of the latter were these :—

In July, 1632, a fine of £1000 having been laid on Edward Paylor, Esq., for the crime of incest, the Dean and Chapter petitioned the King, who, in November, granted that sum to them, for repairing the church, *setting up a new organ*, furnishing the altar, and maintaining a librarian; whereupon, in March, 1632, articles of agreement were entered into by Dean Scott and the Residentiaries, with Robert Dallam, of London, blacksmith, who engaged to build a great organ for £297, with £5 more for his journey to York; and in which the price of each stop is distinctly specified. The following is a copy of this interesting agreement :—

"Articles of agreement, indented, made, concluded, and agreed upon, the one and twentieth day of March, anno dmi 1632, and in the eighth yeare of the reigne of our soveraigne Lord Charles, by the grace of God, Kinge of England, Scotland, France, and Ireland, defender of the Faith, &c. Betweene the right worshippfull John Scott, doctor of divinitie, deane of the cathedrall and metropoliticall church of St. Peter of Yorke; Phinees Hodson, doctor of divinitie, chancellor and canon residentiary of the said church; George Stanhope, doctor of divinity, precentor and canon residentiary of the same church; and Henry Wickham, doctor of divinitie, archdeacon of Yorke, and canon residentiary of the said church, of the one party; and *Robert Dallam*, citizen and blacksmith, of London, of the other party; touchinge the makeinge of a great organ for the said church (as followeth) :

"The names and number of the stoppes or setts of pipes for the said great organ, to be new made; every stopp containeinge fiftie one pipes; the said great organ containing eight stoppes.

"Imprimis two open diapasons of tynn, to stand in sight, many of
them to be chased . . . . lxxx *li.*
Item one diapason stopp of wood . . . . x *li.*
Item two principals of tynn . . . . xxiiij *li.*
Itm one twelft to the diapason . . . . viij *li.*
Itm one small principall of tynn . . . . vi *li.*
Itm one recorder unison to the said principall . . . . . vi *li.*

Itm one two and twentieth . . . . v *li*.
Itm the great sound-board with conveyances, windchestes, carry-
    ages and conduits of lead . . . . xl *li*.
Itm the rowler board, carriages, and keyes . . . . . xx *li*.

" The names and number of stoppes of pipes for the chaire organ,
every stopp containeinge fifty one pipes, the said chaire organ containeinge
five stoppes.

" Imprimis one diapason of wood . . . . x *li*.
Itm one principal of tynn, to stand in sight, many of them to be
    chased . . . . xii *li*.
Itm one flute of wood . . . . viij *li*.
Itm one small principall of tynn . . . . v *li*.
Itm one recorder of tynn, unison to the voice . . . . . viij *li*.
Itm the sound bord, windchest, drawinge stoppes, conveyances, and
    conduits . . . . xxx *li*.
Itm the rowler board, carriages, and keys . . . . . x *li*.
Itm the three bellowes with winde truncks, and iron workes and
    other thinges thereto . . . . x *li*.
                                    Sume total . cclxxxxvii *li*.

" It is agreed by and between the parties above said, and the said *Robert
Dallam* doth covenant, promise, and grant, for him, his executors and administrators, to and with the said Deane and Canons residentiary above named by these
presents, that he the said *Robert Dallam*, his executors or administrators, shall and
will well and sufficiently and workemanlike new make and finishe the said organ in
every the particulars before mentioned, accordinge to the true intent and mean-
inge hereof, before the feast of the nativitie of Saint John Baptist, which shall be
in the yeare of our Lord God one thousand six hundredth thirtie foure. In con-
sideracion of which worke undertaken to be done as aforesaid, the said Dean and
Canons residentiary above named have paid unto the said *Robert Dallam* in
hand one hundred pounds, and doe promise to pay unto him the residue of the
said sume of cclxxxxvii *li*. as soone as the said worke shall be finished ; and for the
more speedy finisheing of the said worke, the said Deane and residentiaries
are pleased to appointe the said *Robert Dallam* some convenient roome near unto
the said Cathedrall church to worke in. And further the said Deane and residentiaries doe promise to pay to the said *Robert Dallam*, towarde the charge of
himselfe and servants in comeinge from London hither about the said worke, the
sume of five pounds. In witnes whereof the parties above said to these present
articles indented have interchangeably sett their hands and seals the day and
yeare first above written."

It will be observed that this agreement does not provide for any
thing more than the pipes, sound-boards, and three pair of bellows.
The account of the chamberlain, relative to the appropriation of the
£1000, is dated 1634; from which it appears that a workman from
Durham was engaged for fifty-two weeks, at 20s. per week, to construct
the case. King Charles visited York in May, 1633, and on the 26th
he went to the top of the great tower, at which time it is presumable
that he directed the placing of the organ, then recently contracted for,

on the north side of the choir, which conjecture is strengthened by the entry of charges for work done at the *pillars* to support the organ loft.*

According to Sanderson's MS. collections for a history of Durham, Robert Dallam built organs for the Cathedrals of St. Paul and Durham. These instruments were similar to that of York. The Durham organ was removed by Father Smith and erected in the church of St. Michael-le-Belfry, York, in 1687. The diapasons and principal, as well as the case, form portions of the present instrument.

Ralph Dallans built the organ for St. George's Chapel, Windsor, at the Restoration ; an organ for the parish church, Rugby ; an organ for the old parish church, Hackney, in 1665 ; and the organ of Lynn Regis, which was removed by Snetzler in 1754.† This is all we know of him, except what is contained in the following inscription, formerly existing in the old church of Greenwich :—

" Ralph Dallans, organ-maker, deceased while he was making this organ ; begun by him Feb., 1672. James White, his partner, finished it, and erected this stone, 1673."

George Dalham has the following advertisement at the end of John Playford's *Introduction to the Skill of Musick*, 1672 (6th edit.) :—

" Mr. George Dalham, that excellent organ-maker, dwelleth now in Purple Lane, next door to the Crooked Billet, where such as desire to have new organs, or old mended, may be well accommodated."

This builder was living in 1686, when he added a "chaire organ " to Harris's instrument in Hereford Cathedral.

19. *Notices of English Organs.*

During the period that these various organ-builders flourished, our

---

* Crosse's *Account of the York Musical Festival*, 4to, 1825, pp. 134-5, and Appendix.

† Dr. Burney says :—" Part of the old organ a Lynn had been made by Dallans, the rest by some more ancient workman ; as the wooden pipes were so worm-eaten as to fall to pieces when taken out to be cleaned. Upon the churchwardens asking Snetzler what this old instrument would be worth if repaired, he said—' If they would lay out a hundred pounds upon it, perhaps it would then be worth fifty.' "—*History of Music*, vol. iii., p. 438.

The organ which Dallans built for the Royal Chapel at Windsor is still preserved in the church of St. Peter in the East, St. Albans'. A representation of it may be seen in Ashmole's *Order of the Garter.*

cathedrals were being supplied with organs on a much larger scale than those which had been used in the ancient monasteries.

In the British Museum, among the Lansdowne MSS. (No. 213), is preserved *An Account of a Tour made through a great part of England*, A.D. 1634.* This curious MS. contains some interesting notices of organs, which are worth extracting.

"YORK. There we saw and heard a faire, large, high organ, newly built, richly gilt, carv'd and painted ; and deep and sweet snowy row of quiristers."

"DURHAM. Away then wee were call'd to prayers, where wee were wrapt with the sweet sound and richnesse of a fayre organ, which cost £1000 ; and the orderly, devout, and melodious harmony of the quiristers."

"CARLISLE. The organs and voices did well agree, the one being like a shrill bagpipe, the other like the Scottish tone."

"LICHFIELD. And no sooner were we lighted, but the Cathedral knell call'd us away to prayers : there we entred a stately, neat fabricke ; the organs and voyces were deep and sweet, their anthems we were much delighted with, and of the voyces, 2 trebles, 2 counter-tennors, and 2 bases, that equally on each side of the quire most melodiously acted and performed their parts."

"HEREFORD. There we heard a most sweet organ, and voyces of all parts, tenor, counter-tenor, treble, and base ; and amongst that orderly, snowy crew of quiristers, our landlord guide did act his part in a deep and sweet diapason."

"EXETER. The organ here is rich, delicate, and lofty, and has more additions than any other ; and large pipes of an extraordinary length."

"GLOUCESTER. Here were wee admiring and whispering till the Cathedrall voyces whisper'd us away to prayers, and so soon as wee heard those voyces and organs, and had view'd their fayrely glass'd and carv'd work cloyster, wee hasted away."

"BRISTOL. In her wee found (besides that fayre and strong fabricke of the Cathedrall, which was newly finish'd) 18 churches, which all are fayrely beautify'd, richly adorn'd, and sweetly kept ; and in the major part of them are neat, rich, and melodious organs, that are constantly play'd on. In her [the Cathedrall] are rich organs, lately beautify'd, and indifferent good quiristers."

"WELLS. The Cathedral was beautify'd with ancient monuments and rich organs."

20. *Organs in Scotland, Ireland, and Wales.*

So far as I have ascertained, the earliest mention of the organ by any of the Scottish historians is by Fordun, who, upon the occasion of the removal of the body of Queen Margaret from the outer church, Dunfermline, for re-interment beside the high altar, in

---

* The full title is—"A Relation of a Short Survey of Twenty-six Counties, briefly describing the Cities and their Scytuations, and the Corporate Townes and Castles therein : observ'd in a Seaven Weekes' Journey begun at the City of Norwich, and from thence into the North,—on Monday, August 11th, 1634, and ending at the same Place. By a Captaine, a Lieutenant, and an Ancient [Ensign] ; all three of the Military Company in Norwich."

1250, describes the procession of priests and abbots, by whom the ceremony was conducted, as accompanied by the sounds of the organ, as well as the chanting of the choir. Mr. Tytler, the author of a *Dissertation on Scottish Music*, fell into a strange error, representing James I. of Scotland as the first introducer of the organ into that country; when all that he actually did, as Mr. Dauney has pointed out,* was to introduce organs of an improved construction. The principal churches and abbeys of Scotland had most probably been furnished with them more or less from the era to which we have referred. The Chapel Royal at Stirling, founded by James III., to all appearance upon the model of that of Edward IV., was a very complete and richly-endowed ecclesiastical establishment for the cultivation of church music; and several entries of sums laid out by the Scottish sovereigns in the upholding of the organs at Stirling and Edinburgh are to be found in the Treasurers' Books, of which the following are specimens:—

" 1507, Jan. 12. Item to the chanoun of Holyrudhous that mendit the organis in Strivelin and Edinburgh, vij^li."

" 1511. Item to Gilleam, organist, maker of the Kingis organis, for expenses maid be him at the sayd organis, in gait skynnis, and parchment for the belles, in naillis and sprentis of irne, in glew, papir, candill, coill, &c., viij^li. iiij^s."

The re-introduction of organs, episcopal vestments, decorations, &c., by James VI., into the chapel at Holyrood Palace, during his visit to Scotland in 1617, was regarded with great horror by his Scottish lieges.

" The Scots," says one of their own historians, " are, in all acts of religious devotion, simple, rude, and naked of ceremonial. The King, accustomed to the use of the organ and church ritual, commanded them to be used in his chapel of Holy-Rood, and in the moment of joy occasioned by the general expectation of his arrival did that, by exertion of authority, which he could not have done otherwise consistently with the actions and religious establishment of his native country. This was ill endured by the common people of Edinburgh, who considered it as staining and polluting the house of religion by the dregs of popery. The more prudent, indeed, judged it but reasonable that the King should enjoy his own form of worship in his own chapel; but then followed a rumour, that the religious vestments and altars were to be forcibly introduced into the churches, and the purity of religion so long established in all Scotland for ever defiled. And it required the utmost efforts of the magistrates to restrain the inflamed passions of the common people." †

---

* *Ancient Melodies of Scotland*, 4to, 1838.

† Johnston's *Historia Rerum Britannicarum, ad annum* 1617.

The organ introduced into the Chapel Royal of Edinburgh by James VI. must have been a magnificent instrument. I have been fortunate enough to meet with a very curious notice of it. John Chamberlain, writing to Sir Dudley Carleton, Dec. 7, 1616, speaking of the King's intended progress to Scotland, adds :—"We hear they made great preparations there to be in their best equipage ; and from hence (London) many things are sent, but specially a *pair of organs* that cost above £400, besides all manner of furniture for a chapel, which Inigo Jones tells me he hath the charge of."

Some years after this we are introduced, for the first time, to a *Scotch* organ-builder. The author of *Rouen : its History and Monuments,*[*] speaking of the church of St. Godard, says :—"In 1556 its organ was a very small one. It was afterwards enlarged ; but in 1562 it was destroyed by the Calvinists. The present organ, which was built in 1640, is the work of a Scotchman named George Leslie."

Of organs in Ireland I have not been able to meet with any particulars, and they would seem to have been almost unknown in that country in early times. In the Parochial Records of Cork, in the reign of Charles I., there is an order to pay £16 towards erecting a musical instrument called in English *organs*, as the custom is to have in cathedral churches."[†]

An organ-builder, a native of this country, seems to have acquired considerable fame on the Continent in the last century. He built an organ for the Cathedral of Lisbon about the year 1740, which is thus described in Joseph Baretti's amusing *Journey from London to Genoa*"[‡] :—

"The name of this man is Eugene Nicholas Egan, a native of Ireland. He is scarce four feet high ; but what body he has is all alive. He has obtained his place of *Masra* neither by chance nor protection, but by dint of skill. The King had caused eight famous organ-makers to come to Portugal from Italy, Germany, and other parts ; and he whose organ should prove best was to have that place. You may well imagine that each strove to conquer his rivals. But the immortal Castrato Caffarello, together with the celebrated composer, David Perez, having been deputed to judge of their several performances, unanimously decided in favour of little Egan's, and of course he had the place. His salary proved afterwards not so ample as he expected : but what is a salary to a genius ? He has defeated his enemies ; he has seen them quit Portugal with shame."

---

* *Rouen*, 12mo, p. 93.
† *Clerical and Parochial Records of Cork, Cloyne, and Ross*, by W. M. Brady, D.D. 1864.
‡ London, 1760, vol. i., p. 253. I am indebted to my friend, Mr. W. B. Gilbert, for the above curious notice.

With regard to Wales, Dafydd ab Gwilym, who wrote in the fourteenth century, makes particular mention of an organ and choir at Bangor in his time.* The Red Book of St. Asaph takes notice of a "loud organ" that existed at a very remote period in that church; and the organ at Wrexham enjoyed more than a local celebrity.

Fuller, in his *Worthies*, says:—"These organs were formerly most famous (the more because placed in a parochial, not cathedral, church) for beauty, bigness, and tuneableness, though far short of those in worth which Michael, Emperor of Constantinople, caused to be made of pure gold, and beneath those in bigness which George the Salmatian Abbot made to be set up in the church of his convent, whose biggest pipe was *eight-and-twenty* foot long, and four spans in compass." According to a *Gazetteer of England and Wales*, *temp.* Charles II., "At Wrexham is yᵉ rarest steeple in yᵉ 3 nations; and hath had yᵉ fayrest organes in Europe, till yᵉ late wars in Charles yᵉ 1st his raigne, whose Parliament forces pulled him and them downe with other ceremoniall ornaments."

21. *Improvements by German Builders.*

In Germany, and other parts of the Continent, the Reformer, Ulric Zuingle, had succeeded in banishing, for a time, the use of organs in public worship. But, early in the sixteenth century, this noble instrument was reinstated in the Church, and many improvements were made in its construction. It was in this century, according to Prætorius,† that *registers*, by which alone a variety of stops could be formed, were invented by the Germans. Improvements at this period were also made in the pipes, particularly the invention of the *stopped* pipe, whereby expense was saved, and that soft, pleasing tone obtained, which open pipes are unable to yield.

By employing the *small scale*, a number of registers with a penetrating, yet pleasing, tone were obtained, in imitation of the *violin, viol de gamba*, &c. By the *large scale*, on the contrary, was preserved that full, round tone which we always hear in good

---

* See *A Commendatory Ode, addressed to Hywel, Dean of Bangor* (Howel was made Dean in 1359), printed by Browne Willis.

† *Syntagma Musicum.*

organs. Besides these, certain kinds of pipes were made to *taper upwards*, whereby some other registers were added to the former, such as the *spitz-flute*, the *gemshorn*, &c.

In the course of the sixteenth century *reed* registers were invented, with which it was sought to imitate the tone of other instruments, and even the voices of men and animals—for instance, the *posaune, trumpet, shalm, vox-humana, bears-pipe*, &c.

In the same century the key-board was extended to four octaves; but the lowest octave was seldom or never complete. An instrument of this kind was called an organ with a *short octave*.

In 1570 Hans Lobsinger, of Nuremberg, invented the bellows with one fold, which is still found in old organs. In 1576 an organ with sixty practicable registers and a "back choir" was erected at Bernan, in the Prussian province of Brandenburg. This organ, which is still in existence, has forty-eight keys on the manual, and sixteen on the pedal. It has four bellows, each of which is twelve feet long, and six feet wide. The workmanship is said to be masterly, the whole mechanism bearing evidence of the great progress in organ-building at this period.

"Great organs and great organists," says Dr. Burney,[*] "seem, for more than two centuries, to have been the natural growth of Germany. The organ which is still subsisting in St. Martin's Church, at Groningen, in North Holland, and of which some of the stops are composed of the sweetest toned pipes I ever heard, was partly made by the celebrated Rodolph Agricola, the elder.[†] And, from that time to the present, the number of organ-builders whose names are well known to the lovers of that noble instrument, in Germany, is hardly credible in any other country. But, to show my English readers what a serious concern the erection of an organ is in this part of the world, I shall close my account of the progress of music in Germany, during the sixteenth century, by relating the manner in which the magistrates of Groningen contracted with David Beck, of Halberstadt, to construct an organ for the castle church of that city.

---

[*] *History of Music*, vol. iii., p. 255.

[†] A learned priest, born in the year 1442, at Bafflen, a village in Friesland. He is said to have been a prodigy in literature and science. Vossius says he was a great philosopher; that he understood Latin, Greek, and Hebrew, and was a *great musician*. He died in 1485, at Heidelberg, and was buried in the Minorite church of that city, where is the following inscription to his memory :—

> " Invida clauserunt hoc marmore fata Rudulphum
>   Agricolam, Frisii spemque decusque soli.
>   Scilicet hoc uno meruit Germania, laudis
>   Quicquid habet Latium, Græcia quicquid habet."

A fine portrait of Rodolph Agricola is preserved at Knole House, in Kent, the seat of Lord Amherst.

" In the year 1592 articles were drawn up between the magistrates and organ-builder, in which it was agreed by the former, that for an instrument, the contents of which were minutely described, a certain sum stipulated should be paid to the latter upon its completion, provided it was approved, after trial and examination by such organists as they should nominate for that purpose. The instrument in its construction employed the builder four years ; and in 1596 the most eminent organists in Germany being invited, the names of all those who signed the certificate of approbation, to the amount of fifty-three in number, are recorded in a book called *Organum Gruningense redivivum*, published by Andrew Werckmeister, 1705."[*]

22. *Italian Organ-Builders.*

The mechanism of the organ appears to have been well understood by the Italians in early times. The family of the Antegnati, of Brescia, were amongst the earliest famous organ-builders in Italy, in the fifteenth and sixteenth centuries. Zarlino, in his *Institutioni Harmoniche*, fol., Venice, 1558, mentions "Vincenzo Columbi and Vincenzo Colonna, two Italian organ-makers of the sixteenth century, inferior to none in the world." Columbi built the magnificent organ in the church of St. John Lateran at Rome, in 1549, which was afterwards enlarged by Luca Blasi Perugino, in 1600. Perugino built the organ for the church of Constantine at Rome, by order of Pope Clement VIII. ; also the organs in the Cathedrals of Orvieto and Trent.[†]

In later times Hermann, a Jesuit, acquired considerable fame in this department of art. He built the organ in the church of St. Ambrogio, at Genoa, in 1648 ; that in the Carignana Church, in the same city, in 1649 ; and one of the organs in the Cathedral of Como, in 1650.[‡]

23. *Notices of Foreign Organs.*

In the journals of some of our travellers in the seventeenth

---

[*] This voluminous writer on Music was born in 1645. He held the posts of inspector-general of organs in the Prussian dominions, and organist of the church of St. Martin, at Halberstadt. He died in 1706. His two books, called *Orgel Probe*, contain some interesting notices of the history and construction of organs in Germany.

[†] Padre Bonanni's *Gabinetto Armonico*, 4to, Rome, 1772.

[‡] In the eighteenth century there were in Italy many celebrated organ-builders, amongst whom Serassi, of Bergamo, and Callido, of Venice, each constructed upwards of *three hundred* organs.

century are scattered many curious notices of foreign organs, a few of which are here extracted.

First,—of Tom Coriat, the "Odcombian traveller," whose *Crudities* were published in 1611. Speaking of the Cathedral of Bergamo, he says:—"There are here two very rich paire of Organs on both sides without the Quire, most sumptuously gilt and imbossed, with many very excellent works."

In the church of the Augustine Friars, in the same city, "they have a wonderful rich paire of Organs (lately made) and decked with exceeding faire pillars ; made indeed but of wainscot, but so curiously handled, that it yieldeth a very faire shew : it is said it shall be all gilt."

At Verona, Coriat says :—"The fairest organs that I saw in Italy, or in any other country, are in this domo."

In the Cathedral of St. Mark, Venice, "at both sides of the choir are two exceeding faire payre of Organes, whose pipes are silver, especially those on the left hand as you come in from the body of the church, having the brasen winged lyon of St. Mark on the top, and the images of two angels at the sides : under them this is written in faire golden letters, *Hoc rarissimum opus Urbanus Venetus F.*"

The philosophical John Evelyn, writing in 1641, says :—"Generally all the churches in Holland are furnished with organs." He speaks of the "organs at Haerlem ;" and of that at Vienna (which place he visited in 1644), as being "exceedingly sweet and well-tuned." In 1645 he tells us that the organ at the Columna at Rome is "accounted one of the sweetest" in that city. Mentioning the Cathedral at Milan, in 1646, he adds :—"Here are two very fair and excellent organs."

Sir John Reresby, in his *Travels* (in the middle of the seventeenth century), says :—"At Venice are reckoned seventeen hospitals, sixty-seven parish churches, fifty-four convents of friars, twenty-six nunneries, eighteen oratories, and six schools. In these churches are the bodies of fifty saints, *one hundred and forty-three pair of organs*," &c. Speaking of the church of Santa-Croce, at Florence, he observes :—"The making of an organ in this church, besides the materials, cost *four thousand crowns.*"

William Carr, "gentleman, late consul for the English nation in Amsterdam," in his *Remarks of the Government of severall parts of Germanie*, &c., 12mo, 1688, makes mention of several interesting

particulars concerning organs.   In allusion to the city of Amsterdam
he says :—

" I will not say much of her churches, but only that they are in general large
and well built.   In one of them the States have spared no cost to exceed the whole
world in three things (viz.), an organ with sets of pipes that counterfeit a chorus of
voyces ; it hath 52 whole stops, besides halfe stops, and hath two rowes of keyes
for the feet, and three rowes of keyes for the hands.   I have had people of quality
to heare it play, who could not believe but that there were men or women above
singing in the organ, until they were convinced by going up into the organ roome,"
&c.

At Hamburg, the same writer tells us :—

" The churches are rich in revenues and ornaments, as images and stately
organs, wherein they much delight.   They are great lovers of musick ; in so
much that I have told 75 masters of severall sorts of musick in one church,
besides those who were in the organ-gallery.   Their organs are extraordinarely
large.   I measured the great pipes in the organs of St. Catherine and St. James's
Churches, and found them to be 3 foot and 3 quarters in circumference, and 32
foot long ; in each of which organs there are two pipes, 5 foot and 8 inches
round."

At Haerlem, we are told :—

" Here is one of the fairest and largest churches of the 17 provinces ; in the
walls whereof there remain to this day sticking, canon bullets, shot by the
Spaniards during the siege thereof.   In this church are three organs."

24.   *The Ancient Position of the Organ.*

Though it is not in the province of this work to enter upon the
subject of the ecclesiastical fitting-up of the chancel or choir, it will
not be out of place to say a word or two as regards the *ancient*
position of the organ.*

In the mediæval ages this instrument was placed on one side of
the choir ; a position which seems to have been almost universal
throughout Europe.   Gervase, the monk of Canterbury, whose curious
account of the burning of that Cathedral, in 1174, has descended to
our times,† informs us that the organ stood upon the vault of the
south transept.   After the re-building of the Cathedral, the instrument

---

* It will be right to mention that a pamphlet appeared, some few years back, entitled
Choirs and Organs : their proper Fosition in Churches ; by William Spark, Organist and
Choir Master, Leeds.   The *brochure* is merely an expression of the writer's *opinion* on the
subject.   He concludes "that, as historical data *do not* furnish any uniform rule for our
guidance in the locating organs and choirs," we are justified in placing them just where we
please.

† Dart's *Canterbury Cathedral,* p. 7 ; and the *Gentleman's Magazine* for 1772.

was placed upon a large corbel of stone, over the arch of St. Michael's Chapel, in the same transept.* In Dart's view the organ is shown on the north side of the choir, between the pillars three and four ; where it still remained in the time of Dr. Burney.

The organ in the old Cathedral of St. Paul was placed under one of the north pier arches of the choir, just above the stalls ; having a choir organ in the front, and shutters to close in the great organ. The case was Gothic, with a crocketted gable.† It occupied the same place during the Protectorate, and was destroyed in the Great Fire of 1666.

The organ of Westminster Abbey, upon which Purcell played, stood on the "north side of the choir," over the stalls; and seems, from the view of it in Sandford's *Coronation of James II.*, to have been a small instrument with diapered pipes.‡

At York, the Cathedral organ, built by Robert Dallam, in 1632 (before mentioned), was, by the express command of Charles the First, placed on the "north side of the choir," nearly opposite the bishop's throne. The reason given by the king was, that (placed on the screen which divides the choir from the nave) the organ was an impediment in viewing the interior of the church. King Charles's judicious decision was put aside in the year 1690, when Archbishop Lamplugh ordered the instrument to be removed to the stone screen.§

The organ of Winchester Cathedral, erected at the Reformation, was placed upon the screen between the nave and choir. It was removed, by the order of Charles the First, to the "north side of the choir."‖

"At Chester Cathedral," says Burney, "the small primitive organ is still standing on the left side of the choir, though that which is now used is at the *west* end."¶

---

* A representation of this corbel, with the organ as it then stood, over the screen, may be seen in Britton's *Canterbury Cathedral*, pl. iv. The corbel has since been removed.

† See an engraving of the choir, showing the organ, in Dugdale's *St. Paul's*.

‡ It would be interesting to know what became of this organ, hallowed by the fingers of Purcell. One account is that, when it was removed from the Abbey, in 1730 (the date of the present instrument), it was given or sold to the parish of St. Margaret's, Westminster ; and the remains of it, after lying for many years in the tower, were disposed of by the churchwardens, some thirty or forty years ago. Another account is that it was removed to Vauxhall Gardens, and was, in fact, the instrument in the orchestra of the Royal gardens at the time of their destruction.

§ Crosse's *Account of the York Musical Festival in* 1825.

‖ Milner's *History of Winchester Cathedral*.

¶ *History of Music*, vol. iii., p. 440.

The old organ of Rochester Cathedral is said to have originally stood in the north transept.* Fisher, in his *History of Rochester*, 1772, p. 67, says :—"Over the entrance to the choir is an ancient organ, which Browne Willis, when he surveyed the Cathedral, termed 'a sightly organ ;' but it now gives both the visible and audible indications of its great age. By the best information I can procure, it was erected very early in the last [the 17th] century, and so long since as 1668 it was styled 'an *old instrument*,' and one hundred and sixty pounds were then paid for its repair and a new '*chair*' organ." It was removed in 1791 to give place to the instrument by Green.

In the interior view of Lincoln Cathedral, in Dugdale's *Monasticon*, the organ is shown on the north side of the choir, above the stalls ; a copy of which is here given.

In Durham Cathedral the "large organ," erected at the Reformation, occupied a place on the north side of the choir ; and it is so depicted in Hollar's rare engraving of the interior of this Cathedral.

Previously to the year 1550 the "great organ" of the Cathedral of Worcester stood at the side of the choir ;† and such undoubtedly was the situation of other Cathedral organs, of which I have not succeeded in finding a record.

---

* MS. Archives of Rochester.   † MS. Archives of Worcester.

G

The practice of placing the organ on one side of the choir existed also in our College chapels.

At New College, Oxford, the organ given by William Port, in 1458, stood at the stall end of the "north side of the choir," near the vestry, supported by pillars.* This instrument was destroyed by the rebels in 1646. The present organ (improved by Green) was erected by Robert Dallam, in 1663 ; but the beautiful screen upon which it is placed (without any design of supporting the organ) was constructed in 1636.†

Previously to the year 1740 the organ of Magdalen College, Oxford, stood on the "south side of the choir."‡

The organ of St. John's College, in the same university, built in 1660, was placed in a little ante-chapel "on the north side of the choir."§ It was in that situation in 1768, when Byfield erected an organ on the present screen.

Quaint old Thomas Fuller, speaking of the Cambridge Colleges, under the date 1633, adds :—" Now began the University to be much beautified in buildings ; every college either casting its skin with the snake, or renewing it with the eagle. . . . But the greatest alteration was in their chapels, most of them being graced with the accession of organs."‖

The organ of Christ's College still remains on the south side of the choir ; and tradition assigns similar situations for the instruments of King's College, St. John's College, &c.

The same position, "at the side of the choir," is still retained in Winchester College ; the Royal Chapels at St. James's and Hampton Court ; and within memory it was so in Christ Church, Dublin.¶

Mr. W. B. Gilbert, in his paper *On the Musical Associations of Boston Church, Lincolnshire* (printed in the *Choir*, viii. 68), speaking of the organ presented to Croyland Abbey by Abbot Lyllyngton, who died in 1476, says :—

" This instrument, which was described as the ' Great Organ,' was placed at the *west* entrance of the Abbey Church ; a smaller one was situated in the choir, which latter organ was carried on the shoulders of two porters, who conveyed

---

* MS. Archives of New College.
† Warton's *Life of Sir T. Pope*, p. 344.
‡ MS. Archives of Magdalen College.
§ Warton's *Life of Sir T. Pope*, p. 344.
‖ Fuller's *History of the University of Cambridge*, folio, 1655.
¶ The Rev. John Jebb *On the Choral Service of the Church*, p. 197.

it from London to Croyland. The only other instance in this country of an ancient organ being placed over the west entrance is that of Beauchamp Chapel, at Warwick ; and the contract—A.D. 1440—for that beautiful building expressly mentions 'an organ-loft ordained to stand over the west door of the chappel.'"

The writer adds :—"We commend these two instances to musical antiquarians, some of whom have declared that organs were not placed at the west end of our churches before the Reformation."

A correspondent in the same volume of the *Choir* (p. 100) very aptly comments upon this statement in the following words :—

"Instead of this, I think his [Mr. Gilbert's] remarks only more strongly confirm the position of those who hold such an opinion, inasmuch as he himself admits that these *two* churches *were the only exceptions in this country* to the ordinary rule ; and surely that rule may fairly be taken as virtually universal when it had so small a number of exceptions."

As regards parish churches, the common situation for the organ, both before and after the Reformation, was in the chancel.*

Adam de Shakelsthorpe, by will, dated 1376, gave his organ, "then standing in Cawston Chancel," to Hickling Priory, Norfolk.† And, at a later date, George Preston, Esq., repaired the chancel of 'Coutmel Church, Westmoreland, "at his own great cost," in the year 1590, "and placed therein a paire of organs of great valewe."

The author of the Oxford *Glossary of Architecture*, edit. 1840, thus speaks of the ancient position of the organ :—

"The large instruments now in use were not put up in their present conspicuous situation in the place of the ancient rood-loft, until after the Reformation. On the Continent they were also introduced in the course of the seventeenth and eighteenth centuries ; but were usually placed at the west end of the church. In this country, previously to the Reformation, the organ was frequently placed on the north side of the choir, or in the north transept."

From the instances I have quoted it will be seen that, in England, the present usual position of the organ over the choir screen does not appear to have been *general* till the Restoration.

---

* Of course other positions were occasionally adopted. In the old church books of Sandwich, Kent, we have the following entry :—" 1473. For an orgayn boke for the organys in the Roode loft." In Neale's *Views of the Churches of Great Britain* (vol. ii.), there is an extract from a MS. account of Melford Church, in Suffolk, written about the time of the Reformation, in which the following notice occurs :—" There was a fair Rood Loft with the Rood, Mary and John, of every side, and with a fair pair of Organs standing thereby." In Britton's *Arch. Antiq.* (vol. iv.) the agreement for building the Beauchamp Chapel at Warwick, in the fifteenth century, is quoted ; where the carpenter covenants to make a parclose of timber about an organ to stand over the west door of the chapel. See Jebb *On the Choral Service*, p. 197, *note*.

† Blomefield's *History of Norfolk*, edit. 1805, vol. vi., p. 263.

On the Continent the *large* organs are generally placed in "lofts;" some at the west end, some over the doors, and very often against one of the piers. I particularise *large* organs, because it is a rare thing to find a church on the Continent, of any pretensions, without its two, three, four, and sometimes *six* organs.

The Duomo at Milan has two large organs, one on each side of the choir; so has also the Duomo at Verona, the Duomo at Cremona, the Chiesa del Carmine at Padua, and the Duomo at Lodi. The church of St. John in Monte, at Bologna, has two "immense" organs in similar situations. The church of St. Dominico, at Bologna, has two organs in the choir, and two more in the north transept. At Florence the two organs are placed in the north-east and south-east parts of the octagon.

The church of San Antonio, at Padua, has *four* large organs. At the entrance into the choir the majestic appearance of these instruments is very striking. The front pipes are of tin, highly polished, and have the appearance of burnished silver. The framework is richly carved and gilt; there are no panels to the frames, but the pipes are seen on three sides of a square.* These four organs exactly correspond in internal as well as external arrangement.

The church of St. Mark, at Venice, possesses *six* organs: two very large ones, and four small portable instruments used in the various chapels.

The only organs in St. Peter's, at Rome, were (and perhaps still are) three moveable ones on wheels, in the side chapels, and one fixed, of a larger size. The distance between the west door and the great altar is wholly a free and unbroken space.

The church of St. Annunziata, at Florence, has an organ on each side of the nave. The Duomo at Genoa has an organ in each transept.

The church of St. Bernardino, at Verona, has an organ with painted leaves, triptych-wise, bracketed out at the north-east of the nave. The church of St. Salvatore, at Venice, has an organ bracketed on the north wall of the north aisle. It has painted leaves like a triptych.

The church of St. Francesco, at Perugia, has an organ at the

---

* Burney's *Present State of Music in France and Italy*, p. 129.

south-east of the nave, matched by a sham one on the opposite side.

The Chiesa del Carmine, at Florence, has a small organ at the east end, and a large one at the west end, the case of the latter being painted with the scene of St. Simon Stock receiving the scapulary from the Blessed Virgin.

The church of Borgo St. Lorenzo, Perugia, has two organs in projecting galleries from the clerestory.

The Duomo at Viterbo has an organ over the south transept arch.*

At Ratisbon the organ is placed behind the high altar — an arrangement totally unworthy of this magnificent structure. The organs at St. Pietro Patriarcale and St. Giorgio, Venice, are in similar situations. The organ of the *Frauen Kirche*, or great Lutheran Church of Our Lady, at Dresden (one of the finest of old Silbermann's), is also placed at the *east* end of the church, over the communion table.†

At Treves there is a small organ on the north side of the choir, and a larger one at the west end.

The organ of the collegiate church of Notre Dame, at Courtray, is placed in a gallery at the west end of the building ; but, in order to preserve the window, which is necessary to light the body of the church, the organ is divided in two parts, one of which is fixed on one side of the window, and one on the other. The bellows run under the window and communicate with both parts of the instrument. The keys are in the middle, under the window.‡ The organ at the Jesuit's Church in Ghent is disposed in a similar way : in fact, it is no uncommon thing in the German and Flemish churches to divide the organ, in order to preserve a window."§

The organ in the church of St. Bavon, Ghent, is placed under the arch of the left side aisle, at the entrance into the choir.

---

* The last six notices are extracted from the Rev. Benjamin Webb's *Sketches of Continental Ecclesiology*. London, 1848.

† The organ is in a similar situation in the chapels of Versailles and the Tuileries ; and in England, at Little Stanmore, near Edgware. The latter is very slightly raised above the communion table, and is viewed through an arch, supported by Corinthian columns.

‡ Burney's *Present State of Music in Germany, &c.*, p. 12.

§ The fine church of St. Nicholas, at Prague, has an organ at the west end, arranged in this manner. The framework, pillars, base, and ornaments of this instrument are of white marble.

At Nancy the organ is above the entrance to the nave, just over the porch.

In the two Protestant churches of St. Sebald and St. Lawrence, at Nuremberg, the organ is in the gallery over the aisle, at the angle of the nave and transept, to the left of the entrance and opposite the preacher.

The Cathedral of Antwerp contains three organs: one very large, on the right hand side, at the west end of the choir; and two small ones, in chapels on each side of the broad aisle.

The Cathedral of St. Stephen, at Vienna, has *five* organs: a large one at the west end of the church, and four smaller ones in various chapels.

The Cathedral of Prague has three organs: the large organ, at the west end of the church, is only used on the great festivals of the year; the two smaller organs are used alternately on common days.

At Strasburg the magnificent organ of Silbermann's is over the second arch of the nave, to the left as you enter, about fifty feet above the pavement. It is supported by an enormous bracket, and is gilt and ornamented with figures playing on musical instruments, and otherwise much enriched. It rises to the roof of the Cathedral, and completely blocks up the clerestory window above the arch.* At Freiburg in Bresgau (on the borders of the Black Forest) the organ is placed like that at Strasburg, but above the *third* arch of the nave. It is richly decorated and gilt with sculptured figures.

The organ at Amiens Cathedral (perhaps the oldest in France) was built, in 1492, at the expense of Alphonso de Myhre, one of the

---

* "A word now about the great *organ*. If Strasbourg has been famous for architects, masons, bell-founders, and clock-makers, it has not been less so for organ-builders. As early as the end of the thirteenth century there were several organs in the Cathedral, very curious in their structure, and very sonorous in their notes. The present great organ, on the *left side* of the nave, on entering at the western door, was built by Silbermann, about a century ago, and is placed about fifty feet above the pavement. It has six bellowses, each bellows being twelve feet long and six wide; but they are made to act by a very simple and sure process. The tone is tremendous—when all the stops are pulled out—as I once heard it, during the performance of a particularly grand chorus! Yet is this tone mellow and pleasing at the same time. Notwithstanding the organ could be hardly less than three hundred feet distant from the musicians in the choir, it sent forth sounds so powerful and grand, as almost to overwhelm the human voice with the accompaniments of trombones and serpents. Perhaps you will not be astonished at this, when I inform you that it contains not fewer than two thousand two hundred and forty-two pipes. This is not the first time you have heard me commend the organs upon the Continent."—Dr. Dibdin's *Tour in France and Germany*, 2nd edit., vol. ii., p. 392.

chamberlains to Charles the Sixth. It is placed over the entrance to the nave, at the western extremity, thus allowing the eye to embrace the whole structure at one view.

At Chartres Cathedral the organ is placed over the sixth arch of the nave on the southern side, and at the height of the triforium, or gallery, which is continued all round the church. This organ was built in 1513, and was originally placed over the great western doorway.

In the church of St. Roch, at Paris, there are four organs; but *the* organ of the church stands over the west door.

25. *The Curiosities of Organ-Building.*

Foremost among the instruments demanding a place in this category are the organs of the Byzantine Emperor, Theophilus, who reigned from 829 to 841.

This renowned patron of poetry and music is said to have had "two great gilded organs, embellished with precious stones and golden trees, on which a variety of little birds sat and sung, the wind being conveyed to them by concealed tubes."

Prætorius tell us that a certain Duke of Mantua received from a Neapolitan artist an organ of which the keys, pipes, key-board, nay, even the outside of the bellows, were of alabaster.

Dr. Powell, in his curious volume, *Humane Industry, or a History of the Manual Arts*, 12mo, 1661, alludes to this organ in the following passage, which also makes mention of some other "curiosities of organ-building":—

"A Neapolitan artisan made a pair of organs all of alabaster stone, pipes, keys, and jacks, with a loud lusty sound, which he afterwards bestowed upon the Duke of Mantua, and which Leander Alberti saw in the said duke's court, as he relates in his description of Tuscany. The same Leander saw a pair of organs at Venice made all of glass, that made a delectable sound. This is mentioned also by Mr. Morison, in his *Travels.* . . . . Gaudentino Merula, in his 5th book *De Mirabilibus Mundi*, makes mention of an organ in the church of St. Ambrose in Milan, whereof the pipes were some of wood, some of brass, and some of white lead; which, being played upon, did express the sound of cornets, flutes, drums, and trumpets, with admirable variety and concord."

Ertel, who, in his celebrated *Atlas*, describes the treasures of the Bavarian Electorate Court Chapel, relates that the organ was of ebony, and ornamented with many precious stones; the key-board "glittered with pearls," and the bellows were "covered over with silver." And we are told that in the convent of the Escurial, near Madrid, are eight organs, one of which is of *solid silver.*"[*]

The author of a rare volume, published at Bologna in 1590, under the title of *Il Desiderio*, mentions some curious musical instruments that he saw in the palace of the Duke of Ferrari. He says some were preserved there for the sake of their antiquity, and others in respect of the singularity of their construction. Among these, he takes notice of a curious organ formed to the resemblance of a screw, with pipes of box-wood all of one piece like a flute ; and a harpsichord, invented by Don Nicola Vincentino, surnamed Arcimusico, comprehending in the division of it the three harmonic genera. He adds that the multitude of chords in this astonishing instrument rendered it very difficult to tune, and more so to play ; and that, for this latter reason, the most skilful performers would seldom care to meddle with it : nevertheless, he adds that Luzzasco, the chief organist of his Highness, who, it is supposed, must have understood and been familiar with the instrument, was able to play on it with wonderful skill. He says that this instrument, by way of pre-eminence, was called the Archicembalo ; and that after the model of it two organs were built ; the one at Rome, by order of the Cardinal of Ferrara ; and the other at Milan, under the direction of the inventor.

Don Nicola is reported to have died of the plague, in or about the year 1575, soon after the latter instrument was finished.

Father Bonanni, in his singular collection of engravings of musical instruments, entitled *Gabinetto Armonico*, 4to, Rome, 1722, gives a representation of a curious organ, fabricated by Michele Todino, of Savoy, for Signor Verospi, of Rome. It seems to be an organ with three "Spinette" attached to it ; the description tells us that they may be used "separately," or "all together." The worthy priest calls it a "prodigious artifice ;" but we question its claim to be anything more than a mere curiosity.

Worthy Master Mace's "*Chamber* Organ," made by himself, at his house in Cambridge, of which he gives an engraving in his *Musicks*

---

[*] Amongst the odd materials used by the old builders for organ pipes, I may add to those mentioned in the text, paper, burnt clay, porcelain, &c. Those who are curious in such matters may consult Jacob Adlung's *Musica Mechanica Organoedi*, 4to, Berlin, 1768 ; Part I, sections 85, 86, and 87.

Monument, folio, 1676, certainly comes under our notice in this place. His own account of the instrument is too quaint to be omitted :—

" Now as to the description of This Table Organ, I cannot more conveniently do it, than first, in giving you a view of it, by this figure here drawn, and then by telling you all the dimensions, and the whole order of it (I mean my Second, which is the Largest and the best), and take as here followeth. Two of such organs only (I believe) are but as yet in Being in the World ; They being of my own contrivance ; and which I caus'd to be made in my own House, and for my own Use, as to the maintaining of Publick Consorts, &c.

" It is in its Bulk and Height of a very Convenient, Handsom, and Compleat Table Seize ; (which may Become and Adorn a Noble-Mans Dining Room) all of the Best sort of Wainscot. The Length of the leaf 7 foot and 5 Inches ; the breadth 4 foot and 3 inches ; the Height 3 Foot, Inch, and Better.

" Beneath, the Leaf, quite Round, is Handsom Carv'd, and Cut-Work, about 10 inches Deep, to let out the Sound : And beneath the Cut-Work Broad Pannels, so contriv'd, that they may be taken down at any time, for the amending such faults as may happen : with 2 shelv'd cubbords at the end behind, to lock up your Musick Books, &c. The Leaf is to be taken in 2 pieces at any time for conveniency of Tuning, or the like, Neatly Joyn'd in the Midst.

" The Keys, at the upper End, being of Ebony, and Ivory, all cover'd with a Slipping Clampe, (answerable at the other End of the Table) which is to take off at any time, when the Organ is to be us'd, and again put on, and Lock'd up ; so that none can know it is an Organ by sight, but a Compleat New-Fashion'd Table.

" The Leaf has in it 8 Desks, cut quite through very neatly (answerable to that Up-standing One, in the Figure) with Springs under the Edge of the Leaf, so contriv'd that they may Open and Shut at pleasure ; which (when shut down) Joyn closely with the Table-Leaf ; But (upon occasion) may be Opened and so set up (with a spring) in the manner of a Desk, as your Books may be set against Them.

" Now the Intent of Those Desks, is of far more Excellent use, than for mere Desks ; For without those Openings, your Organ would be but of very slender use, as to Consort, by Reason of the Closeness of the Leaf ; but by the help of them, each Desk opened, is as the putting in of another quickning, or enliv'ning stop ; so that, when all the 8 Desks stand open, the Table is like a Little Church Organ, so sprightfully lusty, and strong, that it is too loud for any ordinary private use ; but you may moderate that, by opening only so many of those Desks as you see fit for your present use.

" There are in this Table Six Stops, the first is an Open Diapason ; the second a Principal, the third, a Fifteenth ; the fourth, a Twelfth ; the fifth, a Two-and-Twentieth ; and the sixth, a Regal. There is likewise (for pleasure and light content) a Hooboy Stop, which comes in at any time with the foot ; which stop (together with the Regal) makes the Voice Humane.

" The bellows is laid next the ground, and is made very large, and driven either by the foot of the player, or by a cord at the far end."

A passing notice of the grotesque decorations and machinery of old organ-cases is worthy of a corner in our cabinet of "curiosities." Seidel has a capital passage on this point. He says :—

" In the course of the seventeenth and early part of the eighteenth centuries great industry and expense were bestowed upon the external decoration of the organ.

The entire case was ornamented with statues, heads of angels, vases, foliage, and even figures of animals. Sometimes the front pipes were painted with grotesque figures, and the lips of the pipes made to resemble lion's jaws. This, perhaps, might have been tolerated, as in the course of time such artifices would naturally be rejected as useless and inappropriate. But people went further, and threw away the money which might have been expended in a worthier manner on the display of the most tasteless and absurd tricks of art, degrading thereby—doubtless unintentionally—a noble instrument, intended for sacred purposes, into a *raree-show*. Among these ornaments the figures of angels played a very conspicuous part ; trumpets were placed in their hands, which by means of mechanism could be moved to and from the mouth.* Carillons, too, and kettle-drums, were performed upon by the moveable arms of angels. In the midst of this heavenly host sometimes a gigantic angel would be exhibited hovering in a glory over the organ, beating time with his *bâton* as the conductor of this super-earthly orchestra !

" Under such circumstances the firmament, of course, could not be dispensed with. So we had wandering suns and moons, and jingling stars in motion. Even the animal kingdom was summoned to activity. Cuckoos, nightingales, and every species of bird, singing, or rather chirping, glorified the festival of holy Christmas, and announced to the assembled congregation the birth of the Redeemer. Eagles flapped their wings, or flew towards an artificial sun.† The climax, however, of all these rarities was the *fox-tail !* It was intended to frighten away from the organ all such inquisitive persons who had no business near it. Thus, when they pulled out this draw-stop, suddenly a large fox-tail flew into their faces ! It is clear that by such absurd practices curiosity was much rather excited than stopped, and that all this host of moving figures, and their ridiculous jingling, disturbed meditation, excited the curiosity of the congregation, and thus disparaged the sublimity of Divine service."

These absurd doings were not peculiar to the Continent ; records of such practices (although not to the full extent) formerly existed in England.

A correspondent of the *Gentleman's Magazine*, 1772, p. 562, who signs himself W. L. [William Ludlam], says :—" The old organ at Lynn, in Norfolk, had on it a figure of King David playing on the

---

* I must confess that I do not admire the " loud, uplifted angel-trumpets " on the case of the Antwerp Cathedral organ one whit more than the Gorgons and Hydras on that of the Dominican Church in the same city.

† Seidel seems to have had in view the ludicrous *outside* of the organ in the Garrison Church, Berlin. Burney, in his entertaining *Tour in Germany* (p. 104), describing his visit, says :—" I found a large organ in this church, built by Joachim Wagner ; it is remarkable for compass, having 50 keys in the manuals, and for its number of pipes, amounting to 3220 ; but still more so for the ornaments and machinery of the case, which are in the old Teutonic taste, and extremely curious. At each wing is a kettle drum, which is beat by an angel placed behind it, whose motion the organist regulates by a pedal ; at the top of the pyramid, or middle column of pipes, there are two figures representing Fame, spreading their wings when the drums are beat, and raising them as high as the top of the pyramid ; each of these figures sounds a trumpet and then takes its flight. There are likewise two suns, which move to the sound of cymbals, and the wind obliges them to cross the clouds ; during which time two eagles take their flight as naturally as if they were alive."

harp, cut in solid wood, larger than the life : likewise several moving figures which beat time, &c."

Dr. Donne, the eminent English satirist, alludes to these moving figures, evidently as no uncommon thing in his days. His words are :—" As in some organs, puppets dance above, and bellows pant below which them do move."*

When these figures were abolished, the organ-builders (perhaps in compliance with an absurd canon) set up the royal arms on the front of the organ ; and in place of the angel beating time, or King David playing on the harp, we had the British lion, with goggle eyes and shaggy mane, grinning horribly. Let us rejoice that these abominations no longer exist in our own country.† If they are still occasionally to be met with on the Continent, the increased feeling of true devotion will soon number them among the things that were.

26. *The Destruction of Organs in England during the Great Rebellion.*

An ordinance being passed in the House of Lords, dated January 4th, 1644, establishing a new form of divine worship, in which no music was allowed but plain psalm-singing, it was thought necessary, for the promotion of true religion, that no organs should be suffered to remain in the churches ;‡ that choral books should be torn ; painted glass windows broken ; sepulchral brass inscriptions defaced ; and, in short, that the cathedral service should be totally abolished. In consequence of this ordinance collegiate and parochial churches

---

* *John Donne, his Satires*, Anno Domini, 1593. This curious work is preserved among the Harleian MSS. (No. 5110) in the British Museum.

† There is great room for improvement in organ cases in England. We may walk many a weary mile without seeing a truly Catholic design. Mr. Faulkner published, in 1838, a volume of *Designs for Organs ;* but they are little more than an echo of what we see every day. Of a far different character are the designs of the late Mr. Pugin, appended to Mr. Sutton's *Short Account of Organs built in England, &c.,* 1847.

‡ A copy of the ordinances preserved in the library of the London Institution has the following title :—" Two ordinances of the Lords and Commons assembled in Parliament, for the speedy demolishing of all organs, images, and all matters of superstitious monuments in all Cathedralls, and Collegiate or Parish-churches and Chapels, throughout the Kingdom of England and the Dominion of Wales ; the better to accomplish the blessed reformation so happily begun, and to remove all offences and things illegal in the worship of God. Dated May 9th, 1644."

were stripped of their organs and ornaments: some of the instruments were sold to private persons, who preserved them ; some were totally, and others but partially, destroyed ; some were taken away by the clergy in order to prevent their being destroyed, and some few were suffered to remain.*

The puritanical spirit which doomed *organs* to destruction had long been gaining ground. Even as early as the reign of Elizabeth (Aug. 18, 1589), it was agreed at a parish meeting of St. Chad's, Shrewsbury, "that for the better providing and accomplishing the reparation of the bells, fencing the church-yard, and purchasing one decent and semely cuppe of silver for the use of the Communion, the *organs should be sould* to any of the parishe for the sum of £4, if any desyred the same : otherwise the said organs should presentlye bee sould to hym whosoever would give £4 or more for the same !" †

Some idea of the devastation committed by the Puritans upon organs may be gathered by a few extracts from *Mercurius Rusticus ; the Country's Complaint recounting the sad Events of this Unparraleld Warr*, 12mo, 1647.‡ At Westminster, we are told, "the soldiers of Westborne and Cæwoods' Companies were quartered in the Abbey Church, where they brake down the rayl about the Altar, and burnt it in the place where it stood : they brake downe the Organs, and pawned the pipes at severall ale-houses for pots of ale. They put on some of the Singing-men's surplices, and, in contempt of that canonicall habite, ran up and down the Church ; he that wore the surplice was the hare, the rest were the hounds." At Exeter Cathedral "they brake downe the organs, and taking two or three hundred pipes with them in a most scorneful and contemptuous manner, went up and downe the streets piping with them ; and meeting with some of the Choristers of the Church, whose surplices they had stolne before, and imployed them to base servile offices, scoffingly told them, '*Boyes, we have spoyled your trade, you must goe and sing hot*

---

* See an article on the Organ of St. Paul's Cathedral, in the *Musical Gazette*, No. 1, Jan. 1819.

† Two years before the passing of the ordinance just mentioned, a tract appeared, entitled *The Organ's Funerall, or the Quirister's Lamentation for the Abolishment of Superstition and Superstitious Ceremonies.* In a Dialogicall Discourse between a Quirister and an Organist, An. Dom., 1642. London, printed for George Kirby. 4to.

‡ Edited by Dr. Bruno Ryves, an unflinching opponent of cant and hypocrisy. At the Restoration he was rewarded with the Deanery of Windsor. The *Mercurius Rusticus* was originally published in numbers. In its collected form it went through several editions.

pudding pyes.'" At Peterborough Cathedral, after committing all kinds of destruction "when their unhallowed toylings had made them out of wind, they took breath afresh on two pair of organs."* At Canterbury "they violated the monuments of the dead, and spoyled the organs ;"† and, at Chichester Cathedral, "they leave the destructive and spoyling part to be finished by the common soldiers ; brake down the organs, and, dashing the pipes with their pole-axes, scoffingly said, '*Harke how the organs goe.*'" At Winchester "they entered the Church with colours flying, and drums beating : they rode up through the body of the ˙Church and Quire, until they came to the altar, there they rudely pluck downe the table and brake the rayle, and afterwards carrying it to an ale-house, they set it on fire, and in that fire burnt the Books of Common Prayer, and all the Singing Books belonging to the Quire : they threw downe the organs, and break the Stories of the Old and New Testament, curiously cut out in carved work."

Mr. W. B. Gilbert, in his recently published *Memorials of the Collegiate Church of Maidstone,* has the following interesting passage. which I quote at length :—

"The church still bears witness of the treatment received at this time. It seems pretty certain that up to 1642 the interior arrangement of the fabric had remained nearly the same as left during the reign of Edward IV., but now the

---

* Gunton is more particular in his account of the devastations here :—"The first that came was a foot regiment, under one Colonel Hubbard's command ; upon whose arrival come persons of the town, fearing what happened afterwards, desire the chief commander to take care the soldiers did no injury to the church ; this he promises to do, and gave order to have the church doors all locked up. Some two days afterwards comes a regiment of horse, under Colonel Cromwell, a name as fatal to minsters as it had been to monasteries before. The next day after their arrival, early in the morning, these break open the church doors, pull down the organs, of which there were two pair. The greater pair, that stood upon a high loft over the entrance into the choir, was thence thrown down upon the ground, and there stamped and trampled on, and broke in pieces, with such a strange, furious, and frantick zeal, as cannot be well conceived, but by those that saw it."—*History of the Church of Peterborough,* p. 333. Will modern writers tell us any more, after this, that "Cromwell himself was *partial* to the organ ?"

† In Culmer's *Cathedral News from Canterbury,* p. 19, we read :—"The news was that the troopers fought with God Himself in the Cathedral Quire at Canterbury. But the truth is that on the 26th of August, 1642, some zealous troopers, after they had (by command) taken the powder and ammunition out of the malignant Cathedral, they fought, it seems, with the Cathedral goods ; namely, altars, images, service-books, prick-song-books, surplice, and organs: for they hewed the altar rails all to pieces, and threw their altar over and over and over down the three altar steps, and left it lying with the heels upward : they slashed some images, crucifixes, and prick-song-books, and one greasy service-book, and a ragged smoke of the whore of Rome, called a surplice, and began to play the tune of 'Zealous Soldier' on the organs or case of whistles, which never were in tune since."

monumental brasses were torn up and destroyed, the sedilia damaged, and the painting over the first warden's tomb much mutilated. There is no doubt as to the period of this mischief, the date, with some wretched initials, are miserably scratched on the walls. About this time also the organ disappeared ; and from a rare tract, entitled *A perfect Diurnal of the several passages in our late journey into Kent, from August 19th to September 3rd, 1642*, we have a description of what was achieved in Maidstone and its neighbourhood at this period. During the Divine service at Rochester Cathedral on St. Bartholomew's Day, between the hours of nine and ten in the morning, a party of soldiers entered the church, and marched up to the Lord's Table ; but, finding that even this irreverence did not prevent the service from proceeding, they came down to the congregation, who were then kneeling, and demanded why they knelt ; not receiving any answer they returned to the altar, and seizing the Lord's Table, conveyed it to the middle of the choir ; they then tore down the communion rails, mutilated the altar steps, and gave the rabble, who had followed them, the pieces of the rails to burn, and ' So left the organs to be plucked down till we come back again ;' but it appears the Rochester people were a match for them, as the writer says, ' before we came back they took them down themselves.' "

" Leaving Rochester they marched on to Maidstone, where they were quartered that Thursday night, to the great terror of the inhabitants, who, notwithstanding that it was market day, closed all their shops. The town was completely at their mercy, and this seems by corroborative evidence to have been the identical day on which the church suffered so much by mutilation.

" On the Friday they proceeded to Canterbury, where, as Dr. Pask, the sub-dean, tells us, the soldiers entered the Cathedral at eight o'clock on the Saturday morning, overthrew the Lord's Table, tore the velvet covering, defaced the screen, violated the monuments of the dead, spoiled the organs, broke down the rails and seats, tore up the surplices, gowns, and bestrewing the pavements with the torn leaves of the Bibles and Prayer-books. A figure of our Lord placed over the south gate was destroyed by forty shots being fired at it.

" This amiable party then visited Faversham and other places, and returned to Maidstone on the evening of Thursday, and again quartered there, to the great indignation of some of the inhabitants, whose rage at their doings knew no bounds, and they made the place so hot, that the fellows were glad to depart the next day ; or, as the writer of the *Diurnal* says, ' the town being troubled with malignant spirits, who burned so inwardly with malice and hatred, that they could no longer forbear ;' and one Maidstonian, whose ire was raised, so disturbed the serenity of these fellows, that they carried him off as a prisoner, to be dealt with by the Parliament.

" This curious tract is embellished with a clumsily-executed sketch of soldiers destroying the east end of a church. Two men are removing the Lord's Table, one is pulling down a cross, another with a hatchet is chopping away at the communion rails, whilst a fifth is hastening, armed with a chopper, to assist his sacrilegious companions."

Sir William Dugdale, in his *Short View of the Late Troubles in England*, folio 1681, says :—" And when their whole (the Parliamentary) army, under the command of the Earl of Essex, came to Worcester, the first thing they there did was the profanation of the Cathedral ; destroying the organ ; breaking in pieces divers beautiful windows," &c.

The sacrilegious profanation of Norwich Cathedral is graphically described in Bishop Hall's *Hard Measure*, 1647* :—

"Lord, what work was here, what clattering of glasses, what beating down of walls, what tearing up of monuments, what pulling down of seats, what wresting out of irons and brass from the windows and graves, what defacing of arms, what demolishing of curious stone work, that had not any representation in the world, but only the cost of the founder, and skill of the mason ; what toting and piping upon the destroyed organ pipes, and what a hideous triumph on the market day before all the country, when, in a kind of sacrilegious and profane procession, all the organ pipes, vestments, both copes and surplices, together with the leaden cross which had been newly sawn down from over the green yard pulpit, and the service books and singing books that could be had, were carried to the fire in the public market place ; a lewd wretch walking before the train, in his cope, trailing in the dirt, with a service-book in his hand, imitating, in an impious scorn, the tune, and usurping the words of the Litany, used formerly in the church ; near the public cross all these monuments of idolatry must be sacrificed to the fire, not without much ostentation of a zealous joy in discharging ordnance to the cost of some who professed how much they had longed to see that day. Neither was it any news, upon the Guild day, to have the Cathedral, now open on all sides, to be filled with musketeers, waiting for the major's return, drinking and tobacconing as freely as if it had turned ale-house."

At the Nunnery, at Little Gidding, in Huntingdonshire, the same feats were carried on. We are told that

"Soon after Mr. Ferrar's death certain soldiers of the Parliament resolved to plunder the house at Gidding. The family, being informed of their hasty approach, thought it prudent to fly ; while these military zealots, in the rage of what they called *reformation*, ransacked both the church and the house ; in doing which they expressed a particular spite against the organ. This they broke in pieces, of which they made a large fire, and at it roasted several of Mr. Ferrar's sheep, which they had killed in his grounds. This done, they seized all the plate, furniture, and provision, which they could conveniently carry away. And in this general devastation perished the works which Mr. Ferrar had compiled for the use of his household, consisting chiefly of harmonies of the Old and New Testament."†

Similar examples of ignorant fanaticism might readily be adduced, but the passages cited are sufficient for my purpose.

After the Parliamentary ordinance of 1644, and the zeal of the Sectarians in putting their orders into force, it is somewhat remarkable that any church organs should have escaped demolition. But that some instruments were suffered to remain we have accredited evidence. Among the number were those of St. Paul's, York, Durham, and Lincoln Cathedrals ; St. John's and Magdalen Colleges, Oxford ; Christ's College, Cambridge ; and probably many

---

* Dr. Joseph Hall was successively Bishop of Exeter and of Norwich.
† See Izaak Walton's *Lives of Donne, Wotton, Hooker, &c.*, edit. 1845, *note*, p. 336.

others.* That the organ of St. John's escaped destruction is the more extraordinary, as it had been erected under the patronage of Archbishop Laud, and as Cromwell's visitors had ordered Sir William Paddy's donation for founding the choral service in that chapel to be entirely applied to the augmentation of the president's salary.

The popular account of the organ of Magdalen College is, that during the Rebellion it was conveyed by order of Cromwell to Hampton Court, where it remained in the Great Gallery till the Restoration, when it was restored to the College.†

The organ was still remaining in the College Chapel in 1654, when Evelyn, who was at Oxford in the July of that year, has this entry in his *Diary* :—

" Next we walked to Magdalen College, where we saw the library and chapel, which was likewise in pontifical order, the altar only, I think, turned tablewise ; *and there was still the double organ*, which abominations (as now esteemed) were almost universally demolished ; Mr. Gibbon [Christopher Gibbons], that famous musician, giving us a taste of his skill and talents on that instrument."

This notice seemed to refute the tradition that " in the Grand Rebellion, when the organ of Magdalen College, among others, was taken down, it was conveyed by order of Cromwell to Hampton Court, where it was placed in the great gallery." I accordingly treated the story as apocryphal in the first edition of the present work. Recently, however, the matter has been set at rest by the discovery of a memorandum in the College books, to the effect that, in 1660, £16 10s. was paid for the transportation of ·the organ from Hampton Court *back* to the College. It must, therefore, have been taken down and removed to Hampton Court between the years 1654 and 1660.

There was, in all probability, some amicable arrangement on the subject between Cromwell and the president and fellows. Nichols, in his *History of Leicestershire*, tells us that Stamford Church is decorated with a handsome organ, that formerly belonged to the banqueting room, Whitehall, which by order of Cromwell was taken

---

* The author of *A Short Account of Organs built in England, &c.*, makes a startling assertion at the commencement of his first chapter:—" During the rebellion *all* the Organs in England were destroyed by order of the Parliament, with all other church furniture, which was considered as appertaining to the Romish ritual."

† This anecdote may be traced to Warton (*Observations on the Fairy Queen of Spenser*, Lond. 1762, vol. ii., p. 236), who probably received his information from his father, a fellow of Magdalen College. Gutch, Chalmers, Hawkins, Burney, and Ingram copy Warton.

down and sold. It was intended, he says, to be placed in the chapel of Magdalen College, Oxford, but, being too small, was purchased by the Cave family. Dr. Bloxam suggests that it was offered in exchange for the Magdalen organ, which seems more than probable.*

The devastation committed upon organs by those misguided ruffians, the soldiers and commanders of the Parliamentary army, was not easily remedied. It was not until some time after the restoration of monarchy that these instruments could be reinstated. Pepys, that entertaining old gossip, has two or three interesting entries in his *Diary* bearing upon this point :—

"July 8, 1660. (Lord's day). To White-Hall Chapel, where I got in with ease, by going before the Lord Chancellor with Mr. Kipps. Here I heard very good musique, the first time that ever I remember to have heard the *organs*, and singing-men in surplices, in my life."

"April 5, 1667. To Hackney, where good neat's tongue, and things to eat and drink, and very merry, the weather being mighty pleasant ; and here I was told, that at their church they have a fair *pair of Organs*, which play while the people sing, which I am mighty glad of, wishing the like at our church at London, and would give £50 towards it."

"April 21, 1667. To Hackney Church, where very full, and found much difficulty to get pews, I offering the sexton money, and he could not help me. . . . . . That which I went chiefly to see was the young ladies of the schools, whereof there is great store, very pretty ; and also the *organ*, which is handsome and tunes the psalms, and plays with the people ; which is mighty pretty, and makes me mighty earnest to have a pair at our church ; I having almost a mind to give them a pair, if they would settle a maintenance on them for it."

The difficulty of procuring organs at this time seems to have been greater than that of finding either performers or music to perform. Dr. Burney says :—

"After the suppression of Cathedral Service and prohibition of the Liturgy, some of the ecclesiastical instruments had been sold to private persons, and others but partially destroyed ; these, being produced, were hastily repaired, and erected for present use.†

"A sufficient number of workmen for the immediate supply of cathedrals and parish churches with organs not being found in our own country, it was thought expedient to invite foreign builders of known abilities to settle among us ; and

---

* See Dr. Bloxam's *Registers of Magdalen College, Oxford*, a work to which I have been frequently indebted in the composition of these pages.

† It was not until the lapse of more than half a century after the Restoration that our parish churches began commonly to be supplied with organs. In 1708, when Hatton published his *New View of London*, a very large number of our places of public worship were without them. To what an extent other English cities were deficient in this particular may be gathered from Drake, who, at p. 338 of his *Eboracum*, published in 1733, says :—"There is now only *one* parish church in the whole city of York that possesses an organ ; and that came from the Popish chapel, the curators of which purchased it from Durham Cathedral."

the premiums offered on this occasion brought over the two celebrated workmen, Smith and Harris."

The establishment of these two eminent men in this country forms a new epoch in the history of organ-building.

27. Existing Old English Organs.

With regard to English organs prior to the Rebellion, very few are in existence at the present time. An instrument, said to be "the *first* organ made in England," may be seen at Ightam Moat-House, in Kent. Another instrument, called in Mr. Brady's catalogue "the *second* organ made in England," is preserved at Knole House, in the same county. Similar organs may be found at Hatfield House, and at an old mansion—the reputed residence of Cardinal Wolsey—at Cheshunt.

The three last-named organs are small chamber instruments, with wooden pipes, probably a little anterior to the Restoration, but of no greater antiquity. The Ightam organ has been much spoken about of late, and the author of a lecture delivered before the Society of Arts quotes it as an instrument of extraordinary interest, and of a date perhaps *earlier than the fourteenth century!* This strange illusion, however, I am compelled to dispel ; and I shall do so by the help of a note made some few years back by Mr. W. B. Gilbert, upon his inspection of the instrument in question. He says :—

" April 15, 1855.—Examined the remains of an old organ at the Moat-House, Ightam, Kent, which the guide told me was the *first* made in England. The wind-chest or sound-board had forty-eight small grooves ; a portion of the bellows and one feeder left ; one solitary pipe made of oak, open, and about tenor C pitch, but without a mouthpiece. The height of the instrument could not have been more than three feet, and the depth about eighteen inches. Attached to the grooves were a row of paper tubes (square), possibly used as conveyances. There were no slides or upper boards, nor anything like an 'action ;' neither were there any portions of case or manuals. Knowing several old organs well, especially those of Loosemore, at Exeter, it struck me, on a very close examination of the instrument, that it was either the remains of an old barrel organ, or something of village manu-facture, certainly not dating *beyond a century back!* Had it been a curiosity in the last century, the historians of the county, especially Hasted, would have mentioned it."

After this let us hear no more of the *great antiquity and curiosity* of the Ightam organ.

Other existing old organs are described in the course of the preceding pages ; it only remains to notice the curious remains of an old organ still preserved at Old Radnor, in South Wales. My knowledge of this relic is due to the Rev. Mr. Sutton, who has published a very interesting volume on the subject.[*]

The remains of the mediæval organ at Old Radnor, South Wales, are interesting upon two grounds—1st, architecturally, as regards the case, of which so few specimens exist ; 2nd, musically, with reference to the construction of organs of an early period. The very existence of these remains seems to have been unknown to the most diligent antiquaries in such matters, and they appear to have been brought under the notice of Mr. Sutton by Sir Henry Dryden, a well-known lover of antiquities and architecture, and a gentleman particularly versed in organs and church music.

Very few organ cases anterior to the Restoration have been preserved. The case of the organ at King's College, Cambridge, is the original one erected by Chapman and Hartop, the joiners, in 1606, to contain Dallam's organ, before mentioned ; for, though the action and pipes. of the organ appear to have been many times removed and renewed, there is every reason to believe that the existing case dates from 1606, and the choir organ from 1661.

Mr. Sutton does not assign any precise period to the organ case of Old Radnor, nor does he give us any tradition, or any extract from old records concerning its erection ; he simply describes it as "mediæval." It seems to me more than probable that the case is not older than the end of the sixteenth century, or it may present details of different periods. The heavy horizontal beam that supports the upper ornamental work can hardly belong to any good period of architectural ornamentation ; and the "napkin-pattern" panels are surely not older than the Jacobean period.

"The dimensions of the organ case," which is of oak, and elaborately carved and panelled, Mr. Sutton describes as follows :—

" Total height	18 feet	0 inches.
Width above wind-chest	9	4
Width below wind-chest	5	9
Height up to hang over	5	10
Height of cresting and pinnacles	1	8
Depth of the organ	2	6

[*] *Some Account of the Mediæval Organ-case still existing at Old Radnor;* with an Appendix, containing fifteen etchings illustrative of the construction of Gothic organs. By Frederick Heathcote Sutton, M.A., Vicar of Theddingworth. London : Hatchard & Co. ; Stamford : Langley. 1866,

"The front is divided into five compartments, three of which are occupied by the larger pipes standing in projecting towers, while the intervening spaces are flat, and contain two tiers of small pipes, each compartment being divided midway by a square panel of rich carved work. The rest of the case is almost entirely covered by napkin-pattern panels of the best description, and of very intricate design ; the whole composition being finished at the top of the organ with a deep bratishing of pinnacles and semicircles, upon which are seated grotesque animals. This cresting, though debased in style, compared with much of the detail in other parts of the case, has a very rich effect, and when painted and gilded, as no doubt it once was, must have looked extremely well."

To revert to the peculiarities of the mechanism—at least what remains of this old organ—Mr. Sutton sáys :—

"In this instrument (as probably would be found the case in all mediæval organs) there are several arrangements which it would be most undesirable to copy. The stops, for instance, appear at the east end of the organ, and seem to have been worked entirely by the blower, by means of iron levers about eighteen inches long. It is certainly difficult to conceive a stop sticking with such a tremendous power to act upon it. Still it is hardly to be expected that an organist, even for that great advantage, would resign all control over the instrument upon which he was expected to play, and be content only with the power of putting on an echo, or cornet, which seems, from a small aperture at the right hand of the player, to have been all that he could do in this instance. The Radnor organ is a small instrument, and contained five stops. It seems, however, to have had, in addition, an echo, or, perhaps, only a cornet, placed beneath the key-board. How this was used it is impossible now to tell, as all signs of the manual, or manuals, have disappeared. Part of the wind-chest remains, and also remnants of the bellows are in existence."

With regard to the draw-stops, many of the old organs built after the Restoration, with choir organs in front, had the stops of that department in the choir organ itself, consequently *behind the performer.* Numerous instances could be pointed out if required. It would then appear that the stops were not changed during the performance of a piece : they were arranged before commencing, and so remained until the end. The echo organ and cornet stop, which the author speaks of, were introductions into this country *after the Restoration,* and, consequently, if persisted in, would give a much later date for the erection of the Radnor organ than that contended for.

"Below the key-board," says Mr. Sutton, "the panels are plain, with the exception of the three central ones in the front ; these are perforated with a number of openings of different forms. The centre panel, and that on the right hand, have very elegant openings of Gothic tracery, the larger ones being formed of double triangles interlaced. These were no doubt intended to let out the sound of the echo organ." Surely it could not have been the intention of our old builders to *let out* the sounds of the echo organ, but rather to stifle them, or *keep them in*. But, as we have already said, the echo organ was unknown before the Restoration. Probably the "perforations" spoken of referred to a choir organ; at any rate it is a much more likely solution of the difficulty.

The public is much indebted to Mr. Sutton for his handsome volume and its accompanying etchings. Great interest attaches to the subject of organs at the present time, and anything that throws light upon the practice of our old builders is sure to be received with a hearty welcome. The appendix, illustrative of the construction of Gothic organ cases, is an important feature of Mr. Sutton's volume, and one calculated to do good, by calling attention to this most important branch of architectural art.

fourth Epoch.

THE FOUNDERS OF MODERN ORGAN-BUILDING.

---

28. *Bernard Schmidt, known as Father Smith.*

"ERNARD SCHMIDT, as the Germans write the name, brought over with him from Germany, of which country he was a native, two nephews, Gerard and Bernard, his assistants ; and to distinguish him from these, as well as to express the reverence due to his abilities, which placed him at the head of his profession, he was called Father Smith. The first organ he engaged to build for this country was for the Royal Chapel at Whitehall, which, being hastily put together, did not quite fulfil the expectations of those who were able to judge of its excellence. An organ is so operose, complicated, and comprehensive a piece of mechanism, that to render it complete in tone, touch, variety, and power, exclusive of the external beauty and majesty of its form and appearance, is perhaps one of the greatest efforts of human ingenuity and contrivance. It was probably from some such early failure that this admirable workman determined never to engage to build an organ upon short notice, nor for such a price as would oblige him to deliver it in a state of less perfection than he wished. And I have been assured by Snetzler, and by the immediate descendants of those who have conversed with Father Smith, and seen him work, that he was so particularly careful in the choice of his wood, as never to use any that had the least knot or flaw in it ; and so tender of his reputation, as never to waste his time in trying to mend a bad pipe, either of wood or metal, so that when he came to voice a pipe, if it had any radical defect, he instantly threw it away, and made another. This, in a great measure, accounts for the equality and sweetness of his stops, as well as the soundness of his pipes to this day." *

Such is the brief and unsatisfactory account of this eminent artist handed down to us by Dr. Burney. We are not told the period of his birth or decease ; the particular part of Germany from whence he came ; the builder or builders under whom he acquired the knowledge of his art, nor indeed any of those *minute facts* which it is the business of a faithful biographer duly to chronicle. This is the more to be regretted, because both Burney and Hawkins lived with many who could easily have supplied information which at this period of time we look for in vain.

---

* Burney's *History of Music*, vol. iii., p. 436.

In the middle of the seventeenth century Germany and Holland possessed many organ-builders whose fame had gone forth beyond their own countries: Christian Former, of Wettin (near Halle), Schnitker, of Hamburg, and Eugène Casperini, were foremost in the ranks; and under the able tuition of one of these builders Smith most likely learnt his art. Tradition, indeed, points out Christian Former as his master, and this seems to us more than probable.*

Father Smith was certainly in this country in the year of the restoration of King Charles the Second; and his first organ, that of the Royal Chapel at Whitehall, was built before the 8th of July, 1660. Pepys alludes to it in the extract from his *Diary*, quoted on a previous page.

Before the close of the same year Smith had erected an organ in Westminster Abbey. The old gossip Pepys, whose *Diary* is so full of valuable information, thus alludes to it under the date of December 30th, 1666:—"Lord's Day. I to the Abbey, and walked there, seeing the great confusion of people that came there to hear the organs."

In 1671 Smith built a new organ for the parish church of St. Giles's-in-the-Fields; and in 1675 he erected an instrument in the church of St. Margaret's, Westminster. On the 5th of April, in the following year, he was elected "organist" of the same church.†

Smith was now rapidly acquiring fame, and high in the favour of the King, who appointed him his "organ maker in ordinary," and allotted him apartments in Whitehall, called, in the old plan, "The Organ-builder's Workhouse."‡ He had, however, to contend with

---

* There is a curious note in Warburton's *History of Dublin*, 1818, vol. 1, p. 483; but the dates will not reconcile it with the subject of our memoir. Speaking of St. Patrick's Cathedral, Dublin, the writer adds:—"The organ is said to have been the gift of the Duke of Ormond: it was the work of *Smith the Father, of Rotterdam*, and intended for a church in Vigo, in Spain, where, however, it never was erected: when the Duke assisted in the attack made by the combined fleets of England and Holland on the ships in the harbour of that town in 1702, it had not been landed from the vessel which conveyed it from Rotterdam, and, of course, fell into the hands of the assailants."

The Cathedral Church of St. Canice, Kilkenny, is said to contain an ancient organ from St. Vigo, in Spain, from whence it was removed by Sir Francis Drake, when he plundered that town in 1587! Both stories partake of the marvellous, and seem to point to the same blundering origin.

† By an order of August 7, 1676, his salary was fixed at £20 a year. His predecessors in the same office were John Egglestone, John Parsons, and John Hilton. See the Rev. M. Walcott's *Memorials of Westminster*, p. 128.　　　‡ *Ibid.*

a formidable rival in Renatus Harris, who arrived in this country from France shortly after Smith came from Germany.

We now turn again to the pages of Burney's *History* for his account of the famous contention between these two rival builders concerning the Temple organ :—

"About the latter end of King Charles the Second's reign, the Master of the Temple and the Benchers, being determined to have as complete an organ erected in their church as possible, received proposals from both these eminent artists (*i.e.*, Smith and Harris), backed by the recommendation of such an equal number of powerful friends and celebrated organists that they were unable to determine among themselves which to employ. They therefore told the candidates, if each of them would erect an organ, in different parts of the church, they would retain that which, in the greatest number of excellences, should be allowed to deserve the preference. Smith and Harris agreeing to this proposal, in about eight or nine months each had, with the utmost exertion of his abilities, an instrument ready for trial. Dr. Tudway, living at that time, the intimate acquaintance of both, says that Dr. Blow and Purcell, then in their prime, performed on Father Smith's organ, on appointed days, and displayed its excellence ; and, till the other was heard, every one believed that this must be chosen.

"Harris employed M. Lully,* organist to Queen Catherine, a very eminent master, to touch his organ, which brought it into favour ; and thus they continued vieing with each other for near a twelvemonth.

"At length Harris challenged Father Smith to make additional reed-stops in a given time ; these were the vox-humana, Cremorne, the double Courtel, or doubl bassoon, and some others.

"The stops which were newly invented, or at least new to English ears, gave great delight to the crowds who attended the trials ; and the imitations were so exact and pleasing on both sides that it was difficult to determine who had best succeeded. At length the decision was left to Lord Chief Justice Jefferies, afterwards King Charles the Second's pliant chancellor, who was of that Society, and he terminated the controversy in favour of Father Smith ; so that Harris's organ was taken away without loss of reputation, having so long pleased and puzzled better judges than Jefferies.†

---

* This should be Baptist Draghi, organist to Queen Catherine, at Somerset House. See the curious anecdotes of him and M. Locke in the Hon. Roger North's *Memoirs of Music*, first printed from the original MS. by the present writer. Dr. Tudway (from whom Burney derived this account) wrote *Baptist*, which Burney interpreted to mean *Baptist* Lulli ; hence the mistake, which has been repeated *ad infinitum* by writers who ought to have known better.

† "The efforts of Smith and Harris were brought into, and heard by, an open court, supported by counsel, who exerted their best abilities in their defence, had a respectable variety of jurors, and Judge Jefferies gave sentence, which was in Smith's favour. In other words the organ made by Harris was placed on one side of the church, and that of Smith on the other ; the former played by Draghi, the latter by Dr. Blow and Mr. Purcell. Near a year elapsed before the contention ceased, and Jefferies made his fiat."—Malcolm's *Londinum Redivivum*, vol. iii., p. 106.

Jefferies' conduct seems to have been somewhat misrepresented in this affair. It has been suggested by a learned Templar that this famous contest was decided by *vote*. Jefferies happened to be "of the house," and it fell to his lot to give the *casting* one. Surely he is entitled to no obloquy on this account ! Jefferies had much to answer for ; but there is no evidence of 'bribery and corruption" in the present case,

" The Hon. Roger North, who was in London at the time of the contention at the Temple Church, says, in his *Memoirs of Music,* that the competition between Father Smith and Harris, the two best artists in Europe, was carried on with such violence by the friends of both sides, that they 'were just not ruined.' Indeed, old Roseingrave assured me that the partizans for each candidate, in the fury of their zeal, proceeded to the most mischievous and unwarrantable acts of hostilities ; and that, in the night preceding the last trial of the reed-stops, the friends of Harris cut the bellows of Smith's organ in such a manner that when the time came for playing upon it no wind could be conveyed into the wind-chest." *

The origin of the quarrel between this old worthy and Renatus Harris arose, probably, through the famous contest, or ." battle of the organs," as it was termed, at the Temple Church, in which, as is well-known, the former gained the day. That a bitter enmity afterwards existed between these two builders we may infer from the documents about to be produced. But first, of the circumstances connected with the dispute concerning the Temple organ.

When engaged in collecting materials for my notice of Father Smith in the first edition of this work, I was very desirous of obtaining some authentic particulars concerning this memorable dispute from the Books of the Societies of the Temple ; but, after several interviews with the Treasurer and other authorities, I was told that nothing could be discovered among the records : the matter was evidently of too trivial a nature to induce the slightest interest or research. This is now the less to be regretted, since a gentleman connected with the Temple, Edmond Macrory, Esq., M.A., has succeeded in bringing to light the documents that I was in search of, and has given them to the world in a charming little *brochure,* entitled *A Few Notes on the Temple Organ.†* From the new information furnished by these discoveries I avail myself of the following particulars.

In the latter part of the year 1682, the Treasurers of the Societies of the Temple had some conversation with Smith respecting the erection of an organ in their church. Subsequently Harris, who had some warm supporters among the Benchers of the Inner Temple, was introduced to their notice, and both these eminent artists were

---

* Burney's *History of Music,* vol. iii., p. 437. The substance of this account is derived from a letter written by Dr. Tudway to his son, and preserved in the Harleian Collection of MSS.

† First printed (anonymously) "at the private press of Duncairn," 1859 ; and afterwards, with fresh documentary matter, by Bell & Daldy, 1861. Both editions are charming little quartos of true Roxburghe-like appearance.

backed by the recommendations of such an equal number of powerful friends and celebrated organists, that the benchers were unable to determine among themselves whom to employ. They therefore, as appears by an order in the Books of the Temple, dated February, 1682, proposed that,

> " If each of these excellent artists would set up an organ in one of the Halls belonging to either of the Societies, they would have erected in their Church that which, in the greatest number of excellences, deserved the preference."

Smith believing that he had received the order for the organ felt, of course, much annoyed at the introduction of Harris on the scene. He accordingly obtained from five of the tradesmen in the employment of the Temple a memorial or memorandum, which was presented to the Benchers of the Middle Temple, and is as follows :—

> "MEMORANDUM. That I, Wm. Cleare, of the Parish of the Savoy in ye Strand, Surveyor, togeather with divers other workmenn whose names are herevnder also subscribed, was present and did heare Sr Francis Whitens, Knt., and then Treasurer of the Middel Tempell, London, and Sr Thomas Robinson, then also Treasurer of the Inner Tempell, both of them being in the Tempell Church together, in the month of September last, give full ordre and directions vnto Mr. Bernard Smith, the King's Organ Maker, to make an organ for the Tempell Church, and then also gave ordres to the said Smith to take care of and give directions for the setting up of the Organ Loft in the Tempell Church as the said Smith should judg most convenient, and accordingly the said Smith did give directions how and in what manner the said Organ Loft should be made, and the same was made and sett vpp accordingly, and that then neither Reny Harris, nor any other person whatsoever, was ever mentioned to have any Ordres or Directions to make any Organ for the Tempell Church, or in the least mentioned to stand in competition with the said Smith for or about making of the same, and this wee, whose Names are herevnto subscribed, shall be at all times ready to attest vpon oath, when that there shall be occasion, as witness our hands this eighth day of May, In the year of our Lord one thousand Six hundred Eighty and three."

> " The above memorandum," says Mr. Macrory, " had not the effect which Smith desired, for a committee composed of Masters of the Bench of both Societies was appointed in May, 1683, to decide upon the instrument to be retained for the use of the Temple Church ; and in about a year or fourteen months after each competitor, with the utmost exertion of his abilities, had an instrument ready for the trial. When Harris had completed his instrument, he presented a petition to the benchers of the Inner Temple, stating that his organ was ready for trial, and praying that he might be permitted to set it up in the church on the south side of the communion table. An order was accordingly made by the Benchers, granting the permission he sought. This petition of Harris is dated the 26th May, 1684 ; and thereby the date of the completion of his instrument is established. It is almost certain that Smith's organ was ready previous to the above date, and that for some reason (possibly to avoid the necessity of *re-voicing*, if he should be the successful competitor), he had obtained leave to depart from the order of February,

1682, so far as to place his organ in the church, and this suggested to Harris the propriety of adopting the same expedient."

The reader is already aware how Dr. Blow, and the celebrated Henry Purcell, were engaged to exhibit the powers of Smith's organ upon appointed days; and how Harris employed Baptist Draghi, one of the Royal organists, for the same purpose. The circumstance of Harris's challenge to Smith to make certain additional stops is also well known and need not be dwelt upon here.

The contention now became tedious and disagreeable, at least to the Benchers of the Middle Temple, who first made choice of Smith's organ, as appears by the following extract from the Books of that Society :—

"June 2, 1685. The Masters of the Bench at this Parliament taking into their Consideration the tedious Competicion betweene the two Organ-makers about their fitting an Organ to the Temple Church, and having in severall Termes and at severall Times compared both the Organs now standing in the said Church, as they have played severall Sundays one after the other, and as they have lately played the same Sunday together alternately at the same service. Now at the Suite of several Masters of the Barr and Students of this Society pressing to have a speedy Determination of the said Controversie ; and in Justice to the said Workmen as well as for the freeing themselves from any Complaints concerning the same, doe unanimously in full Parliam^t resolve and declare the Organ in the said Church made by Bernard Smith to bee in their Judgments, both for sweetnes and fulnes of Sound (besides ye extraordinary Stopps, quarter Notes, and other Rarityes therein) beyond comparison preferrable before the other of the said Organs made by — Harris, and that the same is more ornamentall and substantiall, and bothe for Depthe of Sound and Strengthe fitter for the use of the said Church ; And therefore upon account of the Excellency and Perfection of the said Organ made by Smith, and for that hee was the Workeman first treated with and employed by the Tre^{ors} of both Societyes for the providing his Organ ; and for that the Organ made by the said Harris is discernably too low and too weak for the said Church, their Ma^{r}pp^{es} see not any Cause of further Delay or need of any reference to Musicians or others to determine the difference ; But doe for their parts unanimously make Choise of the said Organ made by Smith for the Use of these Societyes—and Mr. Tre^{or} is desired to acquainte the Tre^{or} and Masters of the Bench of the Inner Temple with this Declaration of their Judgments wth all respect desiring their Concurrence herein."

So far so well, but the Benchers of the Inner Temple were not disposed to rest satisfied with the dictum of their brethren of the Middle Temple. Accordingly on the 22nd June, 1685, they made an order in which, after expressing their dissatisfaction that such a resolution and determination should be made by the Benchers of the Middle Temple, in a matter which equally concerned both houses, without a conference being first had with them, they declared

"That it is high time, and appears to be absolutely necessary, that impartiall Judges (and such as are the best Judges of Musick) be forthwith nominated by both Houses; to determine the Controversie betweene the two Organ-makers, whose Instrument is the best, which this Society are ready to doe, and desire their Mastershippes of the Middle Temple to join with them therein, in order to the speedy putting an end to so troublesome a Difference"—

and appointed a committee, of five members of their body, with instructions that they,

"or any three of them, doe at a Conference deliver the answer above mentioned, and they are hereby empowered to enter into a Treaty with a like number of the Masters of the Bench of the Middle Temple, in order to the speedy settling this Affair."

"The committee thus appointed," says Mr. Macrory, "appear to have entered upon their duties immediately, and to have fully considered the subject of the organs, not only with respect to the appointment of 'impartiall Judges,' but also the respective prices and number of pipes in each instrument ; for, two days afterwards, an answer was sent from the Middle Temple, from which the following extracts are taken":—

"*June 24th, 1685.*—The Masters of the Bench of the Middle Temple now say:—

"1. That they cannot imagine how the Masters of the Inner Temple can pretend any ill Usage or Disrespect offered towards them, either tending to a Breach of Correspondence or Common Civility by the Act of Parliament of the Middle Temple, of the second of this Instant June, for that the Masters of the Middle Temple thereby only on their own parts, with the Concurrence of the Barristers and Students, declare their Judgments and Choise of Smith's organ (not imposing but requesting) the Concurrence of the Inner Temple therein with all respect.

"2. As to the Matter of having the two Organs referred to the Judgment of impartiall Musicians, There yet appears not any Difference betweene the two Societyes concerning the same, the Masters of the Bench of the Inner Temple having not as yet in Parliament declared their Judgments and Choise of the other Organ, which if in their Judgments they shall think fit to doe, whereby a Difference shall appear betweene the two Societyes, then their said Mastershippes believe the Society of the Middle Temple will find some other expedient for the determination of the said difference.

"3. As to the Price of the Organs, Smith the Organ-Maker absolutely refuseth to set any price upon his Organ, but offers to submit the same to the Judgment of the Treasurers of both Societyes, or to such Artists as they shall choose, which their Mastershippes cannot but think reasonable.

"4. As to the Numbering the Organ Pipes and Stops, their Mastershippes think it below them to trouble themselves therein, because the Proposal can have no other ground than a Supposition of such Fraud in the Artist as is inconsistent with the Credit of his Profession."

These strange proceedings on the part of the Benchers of the two Temples do not reflect much credit upon the body. It were needless to carry on further this account of their petty disputes to determine which was the best organ.

"I have not," says Mr. Macrory, "been able to find anything in the Books of either Society to corroborate this statement, derived by Burney from a letter written by Dr. Tudway to his son, and it is not probable, if the decision had been left to Jefferies, that there would not have been some record either of his appointment, or of the decision. It is, however, certain that Jefferies was not 'Lord Chief Justice' at the time of the decision, as he became Lord Chancellor in 1685, and continued until 1690 in that office. It may be that the Middle Temple succeeded in their desire to have him decide 'the matter in difference,' or as suggested in a note to the above account in Dr. Rimbault's *History of the Organ,* p. 104, 'that the contest was decided by *vote*. Jefferies happened to be "of the house," and it fell to his lot to give the *casting vote*.' Many other writers have ascribed the decision to Jefferies, but I presume they all derived their information from the same source as did Burney."

The exact date of the termination of this celebrated "battle of the organs" does not appear, but it may fairly be stated as being about the end of 1687, or beginning of 1688. The original deed of sale bears date the 21st June, 1688, and is still preserved in the Middle Temple. It reads as follows :—

21st June, 1688.

"*Mr. Bernard Smythe's Bargaine and Sale of ye Organ in ye Temple Church to both ye Societys of ye Temple.*

"Know all men by these presents, That I, Bernard Smyth, of London, Gent., for and in consideration of one thousand pounds of lawfull money of England to me paid (to wit) Five hundred pounds, parte thereof, by the Treasurer of the Society of the Middle Temple, London, and the other moiety by the Treasurer of the Society of the Inner Temple, London, for wch I have given severall former acquittances, and in consideration of twenty shillings now paid to mee by the Hono^{ble} Roger North and Oliver Montague, Esq^{rs}, Benchers, and William Powlett, Esqr, now Treasurer of the s^d society of the Middle Temple, and by Sr Robert Sawyer, Knt., now Treasurer, and Charles Holloway, and Richard Edwards, Esq^{rs}, Benchers of s^d Society of the Inner Temple, Have granted bargained and sold and doe hereby fully and absolutely grant bargaine and sell vnto the s^d Roger North, Oliver Montague, and William Powlett, and the said Sr Robert Sawyer, Charles Holloway, and Richard Edwards, Esq^{rs}, all that organ which is now sett up and standing in the organ-loft in the Temple Church belonging to the said two Societyes; and all stops and pipes and other partes and appurtenances of the said organ, and particularly the stops and pipes in the Schedule hereunder written mentioned, and alsoe the curtaine rods and curtaines—and all other goods and chattles being in or belonging to the said organ and organ-loft. To hold to the said Roger North, Oliver Montague, and William Powlett, and the said Sr Robert Sawyer, Charles Holloway, and Richard Edwards, Esq^{rs}, their Exec^{rs} and Adm^{rs} In trust for and to the use of both the said Societyes of the Middle and Inner Temples. In witness whereof I the said Bernard Smyth have in these P^{r}sents (a duplicate whereof I am to seale to the said Treasurer and

Benchers of the Society of the Inner Temple) have sett my hand and seale this one and twentieth day of June one thousand six hundred eighty eight."

"THE SCHEDULE.

"GREAT ORGAN.

	PIPES.	FOOTE TONE.
" 1. Prestand of Mettle	61	12
2. Holflute of Wood and Mettle	61	12
3. Principall of Mettle	61	o6
4. Quinta of Mettle	61	o4
5. Super Octavo	61	o3
6. Cornette of Mettle	112	o2
7. Sesquialtera of Mettle	183	o3
8. Gedackt of Wainescott	61	o6
9. Mixture of Mettle	226	o3
10. Trumpett of Mettle	61	12
	948	

"CHOIR ORGAN.

	PIPES.	FOOTE TONE.
11. Gedackt Wainescott	61	12
12. Holflute of Mettle	61	o6
13. A Sadt of Mettle	61	o6
14. Spitts Flute of Mettle	61	o3
15. A Violl and Violin of Mettle	61	12
16. Voice humane of Mettle	61	12
	366	

"ECCHOS.

	PIPES.	FOOTE TONE.
17. Gedackt of Wood	61	o6
18. Super Octavo of Mettle	61	o3
19. Gedackt of Wood	29	
20. Flute of Mettle	29	
21. Cornett of Mettle	87	
22. Sesquialtera	105	
23. Trumpett	29	
	401	

" With 3 full setts of keys and quarter notes.

" BER. SMITH (L. S.).

" Sealed and delivered in the p'sence of Geo. Miniett, Tho. Griffin, Richard Cooke."

Smith's next large organ was the noble instrument for Durham Cathedral, a copy of the agreement for which possesses many points of interest to the curious in such matters :—

" A.D. 1683.

" Articles of agreement covenanted, concluded, and agreed upon the eighteenth day of August in the five and thirtieth year of the reign of our Sovereign Lord Charles the Second by the grace of God, King of England, Scotland, France, and Ireland, Defender of the Faith. Between the Rt. Hon. John Sudbury, Doctor of Divinity, Dean, and the Chapter of Durham of the Cathedral Church of Christ and blessed Mary the Virgin, of the one part, and *Bernard Smith* of the city of London, Organ-maker, of the other part as followeth.

"Imprimis. It is agreed by and between the said parties and the said *Bernard Smith* for himself, his Executors, and administrators, doth hereby covenant, promise, and agree to and with the said Dean and Chapter and their successors by these presents that he the said *Bernard Smith* for and in consideration of the severall sums of money hereinafter mentioned shall and will before the first day of May which will be in the year of our Lord one thousand six hundred and eighty five, at his own proper cost and charges make and fitt up in the Organ-loft of the said Cathedral Church of Durham, a good, perfect, laudable, and harmonious Great Organ and Choir Organ with a case of good sound and substantiall Oak wood, according to a draught or modell of an organ in parchment whereon or whereunto all the said partys have subscribed their names at or before the time of sealing and delivering of these presents.

"Item it is agreed by and between the said partys that the said *Bernard Smith* shall make in the said organ these seventeen stops, viz.':—

"Two open diapasons of Metall containing one hundred and eight pipes.
"A stop diapason of wood containing fifty four pipes.
"A principal of Metall containing fifty four pipes.
"A cornet of Metall containing nynety six pipes.
"A quinta of Mittall containing fifty four pipes.
"A super octave of Mitall containing fifty four pipes.
"A Holfluit of wood containing fifty four pipes.
"A Block flute of Mittall containing fifty four pipes.
"A small quint of Mittall containing fifty four pipes.
"A Mixture of three ranks of pipes of Mittall containing one hundred and sixty two pipes.
"A trumpett of Mittall containing fifty four pipes.
"And in the Choir organ five stops, viz. :—
    "A principal of Mittall in the front containing fifty four pipes.
    "A stop diapason of wood containing fifty four pipes.
    "A voice Humand of Mittall containing fifty four pipes.
    "A holfluit of wood containing fifty four pipes.
    "And a super octave of Mittall containing fifty four pipes.

"Item it is agreed by and between these parties that the said great Organ shall have a back front towards the body or west end of the Church which shall be in all things and respects like to the fore front both in pipes and carving. And all the pipes belonging to the two diapason stops shall speak at will in the said back front as in the fore.

"Item in consideration of which work by the said *Bernard Smith* to be done and formed in the manner and form aforesaid the said Dean and Chapter for themselves and their successors do covenant and grant to and with the said *Bernard Smith* his Executors and administrators by these presents in manner and form following, that is to say that the said Dean and Chapter shall and will well and truly pay or cause to be payd unto the said *Bernard Smith*, his executors, administrators, or assigns the sum of seven hundred pounds of good and lawful money of England at three several payments, that is to say two hundred thirty three pounds six shillings and eightpence thereof in hand at or before the sealing and delivering hereof the receipt whereof the said *Bernard Smith* doth hereby acknowledge and confess thereof and of every part and parcel thereof doth clearly acquit, exonerate, and discharge the said Dean and Chapter [blank in deed] by these presents other two hundred thirty three pounds six shillings and eightpence thereof when the said whole organ or organs is or are brought into the said Cathedral Church and ready for fitting up, and other two hundred thirty three pounds six shillings and eightpence being the residue thereof and in full amount of the said sum of seven hundred pounds when the whole organ is sitt up and in every respect finished according to the true intent and meaning of these articles. And further that the said *Bernard Smith* shall have and take to his own use, benefit, and charge, the old organ now belonging to the said Cathedral Church and all the Materialls thereunto belonging. Provided the said *Bernard Smith* shall not or do not remove, take nor carry away the said old organ till the new organ be ready for fitting up as aforesaid.

"And lastly, whereas the pipes of the two fronts of the said great Organ and the front pipes of the said Choir Organ are to be painted and guilt according to the best way and mode of painting and guilding of Organs, at the proper cost and charges of the said *Bernard Smith*. It is hereby agreed, by and between the said parties, that if the said *Bernard Smith* do well and sufficiently perform all the aforesaid works, in making, finishing, and sitting up the said new organ, to the ample satisfaction and content of the said Dean and Chapter ; that the said Dean and Chapter shall pay, or cause to be payd unto the said *Bernard Smith*, his executors, administrators or assigns, the sum of fifty pounds, of good and lawfull money of England, and in full satisfaction for the painting and guilding the said organ.

"In witness whereof to the one part of these articles remaining with the said *Bernard Smith*, the said Dean and Chapter have put this Chapter seal, and to the other part remaining with the said Dean and Chapter, the said *Bernard Smith* hath put his hand and seal the day and year above written.

Ber: Smith

" Signed, sealed, and delivered in the presence of

" WILLIAM WILSON.
" JO. SIMPSON."*

In consequence of the reputation which Father Smith had acquired by these instruments, he was made choice of to build an organ for St. Paul's Cathedral, then in the course of erection. A place was accordingly fitted up for him, in the Cathedral, to do

---

* In the year 1691 Smith made some additions to the organ, and the following is a copy of his receipt, preserved by the Dean and Chapter :—

" Received of John Rowell Twenty four pounds being the last payment and in full of Fifty pounds given to me by the Worsh[l] The Dean and Chapter of Durham for work done at y[e] organ.

" I say rec[d]
" By me
" BER : SMITH."

the work in, but it was a long time before he could proceed with it, owing to a contention between Sir Christopher Wren and the Dean and Chapter. Sir Christopher Wren wished the organ to be placed on one side of the choir as it was in the old Cathedral, in order that the whole extent and beauty of the building might be seen at one view ; the Dean, on the contrary, wished to have it at the west end of the choir ; and Sir Christopher, after using every effort and argument to gain his point, was at last obliged to yield.

Smith, according to his instructions, began the organ ; and, when the pipes were finished, found that the case was not spacious enough to contain them all ; and Sir Christopher, tender of his architectural proportions, would not consent to let the case be enlarged to receive them, declaring the beauty of the building to be already spoilt by the d——d box of whistles. Three of the stops were in consequence obliged to be kept out—viz., a bassoon, a clarion, and another stop of minor consequence, which were kept in the Cathedral for several years after ; Smith hoping he might get them in at some future period ; but he died a few years before Sir Christopher Wren.

After all this contention the architect, sorely against his will, was obliged to make an addition to the case. He not only had been niggardly in regard to the depth of it, where another foot would have been of no consequence whatever, but also in the height ; for, when Smith came to put in the large open diapason pipes in the two side flats, they appeared through the top nearly a foot in length, and spoiled the appearance entirely. Smith now entertained hopes of having a new case, but Sir Christopher, who before would not suffer any ornaments on the top, was now obliged to add several feet, or else alter the case, which vexed him exceedingly. These ornaments consist of angels with trumpets, standing at the side of a small altar. The colour of the wood, of which these are made, being lighter than the rest of the organ case, the addition is soon discoverable. The organ case (to the top of the ornaments) stands nearly thirty feet high ; the distance from the floor of the building being about forty-six feet. It is eighteen feet wide, and eight feet deep. The carving about the case is very good ; it was executed by Grinlin Gibbons, whose decorations embellish every part of the choir. The organ was opened with Divine Service, at the thanksgiving for the Peace of

I

Ryswick, December 2, 1697;* but the Cathedral was not entirely finished till 1715.†

The following highly interesting broadside, concerning Smith's organ, is reprinted from the original in the British Museum. It was unknown to me when the first edition of this work was printed. There can be little doubt that it emanated from Harris, or some of his partizans :—

"QUERIES ABOUT ST. PAUL'S ORGAN.

" I. Whether Sir Christopher Wren would not have been well pleas'd to have received such a Proposal from the Organ-builder of St. Paul's, as shou'd have erected an Organ, so as to have seperated [sic] 20 Foot in the Middle, as low as Gallery, and thereby given a full and airy Prospect of the whole length of the Church, and Six Fronts with Towers as high as requisite ?

" II. Whether the difficulty this Organ-builder finds in making Pipes to speak, whose bodies are but 16 Foot long, does not prove how much harder it would have been for him, to have made Pipes of 22 Foot speak, as those at Exeter ; or 32 Foot as several Organs beyond Sea ? And whether he has reason to complain of want of height, or room in the case for higher and larger Pipes, since those of a common size have put him to a Non-plus ? And whether he has not the greater reason because he gave the Dimensions of the Case himself ?

" III. Whether the double Bases of the Diapasons in St. Paul's Organ speak quick, bold, and strong, with a firm, plump, and spreading Tone, or on the contrary, slow, soft, and only buzzing, when touch'd singly ? And whether they may not more properly be called Mutes than speaking Pipes ?

" IV. Whether the Organ be not too soft for the Quire now 'tis inclosed ? And if so, what will it be when laid open to the Cupola, and Body of the Church ? And what further Addition of Strength and Lowdness will it require to display its Harmony quite through the large Concave of the Building, and answer the service of the Quire, which is the noblest for Eccho and Sound, and consequently of the greatest advantage to an Instrument, of any in Europe ?

" V. Whether the Sound-boards, and Foundation of the Instrument, as well as Contrivance and Disposition of the whole Work, will admit of more Stops to render the Organ in Proportion, five times as Lowd as now it is ?

" VI. Whether if 12 Stops (supposing there were so many in the great Organ) were plaid in full Chorus, 'twould not make St. Paul's Organ vibrate and faint ? And if so, how can it be render'd lowder by the Addition of Stops, since the Wind that does not well supply 12, must of necessity worse supply 13, and so onward ?

" VII. Whether 'tis possible to make an Organ lowder, that has all the Strength it can contain already ?

---

* The writer has in his library an original MS. anthem, subscribed at the end—" This was made by Dr. Blow Oct. yᵉ 15, 1697, at Hamton town, for the opening of St. Paul's Cathedral."

† The above account of the organ of St. Paul's Cathedral is copied from the first number of the *Musical Gazette*, January, 1819—a work which appears to have existed only a few months. The editor was Dr. Busby.

" VIII. Whether there been't Organs in the City lowder, sweeter, and of more variety than St. Paul's (which cost not one third of the Price) and particularly, whether Smith at the Temple has not out-done Smith of St. Paul's? And whether St. Andrew's Undershaft* has not outdone them both?

" IX. Whether the open Diapason of metal that speaks on the lower set of keys at St. Andrew Undershaft, be not a stop of extraordinary Use and Variety, and such as neither St. Paul's has, or can have?

" X. Whether Depth in the Case gives not Liberty for containing the greater Quantity and Variety of Work? And if so, why should not St. Paul's have as great Variety as other Organs, and the order of the Work be as well contriv'd, and disposed for Tuning and other Conveniences, since its case is near double the Depth to any in England?

" XI. Whether the great Organ-builder will condescend to submit his organ to the same Scrutiny, which all Artists of the same Profession do in all Countries? And if it be deny'd whether it will not give the World, and particular the Dean and Chapter of St. Paul's reason to fear, that this *Noli-me-tangere* proceeds from some secret Cause? And to Question—

" XII. Whether the Cupola, or the Organ at St. Paul's, will be first finished?"

Another famous instrument of Smith's is the organ in the chapel of Trinity College, Cambridge. It was built in 1708, during the Mastership of the celebrated Dr. Bentley, of whose club in London Father Smith was a member. The erection of this organ, together with the repairs of the chapel which were carried on under the auspices of the Master in direct opposition to the wishes of the Fellows, gave rise, amongst other things, to the serious quarrels which took place between Bentley and his College, and which nearly cost him his Mastership. Smith died before the instrument was finished, as will be seen from the following extract from a College document, quoted in Bishop Monk's *Life of Dr. Bentley*, p. 161 :—

" He (Smith) did not live to complete the organ of Trinity ; it was finished by tuning and voicing by his son-in-law, Xtopher Schrider, according to a resolution of the Master and Seniors, May 3, 1708."

Sir John Hawkins seems doubtful as to the exact time of Smith's death, but tells us "that the name of Smith occurs in the lists of the Chapel establishment, from 1703 to 1709 inclusive, as organ-maker to the Chapel, and also to Queen Anne." An entry, however, in the parish books of St. Margaret's, Westminster, sets the matter in question at rest :—

" On the sixth day of April, 1708, Henry Turner was elected Organist of St. Margaret's, Westminster, in the room of Bernard Smith, *deceased.*†

---

* Built by Harris at a cost of £1400, and opened May 31st, 1696.

† A memoir of Smith, chiefly extracted from Hawkins, may be seen in Noble's *Continuation of Granger's Biographical History of England*, vol. ii., p. 362 ; and a more elaborate

It would be interesting to give an account of all the organs built by Father Smith, but this is impracticable. The following list has been drawn up with some care, and is probably as complete as it can now be made. It has received considerable additions and corrections since the first edition :—

List of Father Smith's Organs.

1. The Royal Chapel, Whitehall. 1660.

Part of an organ by Smith still remains in the present Whitehall Chapel. Little of the original work, however, exists, as it was partly melted down in 1814, and a new inside put into the old case by Elliot. This organ is said to have been the instrument built by Smith immediately after his arrival in this country ; but this can hardly be the fact, as that organ must have been burnt in the great fire which consumed so many of the ancient buildings of Whitehall, including the old chapel, in 1697.

Paterson, in his *Pietas Londinensis*, 1714, p. 282, says :—" Whitehall was unfortunately laid in ashes by that dismal fire on Jan. 4, 1697 ; at which time the Royal Chapel was also consumed ; wherefore his late majesty erected a new one in that most spacious and beautiful room called the Banqueting House, built by King James I. ; and so it continues the Royal Chapel, for the use of the nobility, gentry, and other inhabitants thereabout."

Again, on the other hand, if Smith built this organ for the banqueting room, and not for the old chapel, in all probability it is the instrument alluded to as one of Smith's earliest works.

2. Westminster Abbey. 1660.

This was the organ on which Blow, Purcell, and Croft played. It appears, by the treasurers' books of the Abbey, to have cost £120.

3. Wells Cathedral. 1664.

4. St. Martin's-in-the-Fields. 1667.

5. St. Giles's-in-the-Fields. 1671.

The original cost of this organ is not given in the parish books. In Parton's *History of the Parish of St. Giles's*, p. 287, is this entry :—" 1698. The sum of £166 14s. 1d. was collected towards repairing the organ ; and the celebrated Smith, who had built it, offering completely to set it to rights for £200, was employed, and finished the same this year."

Again, in the following year, is this notice :—" 1699. Paid £200 to Mr. Christian Smith [the builder's nephew], for making and setting up the organ in the church."

This instrument is the one still in use.

---

notice in Mr. Sutton's *Short Account of Organs in England, &c.*, p. 17. An excellent painting of Father Smith still adorns the walls of the disused Music School, Oxford, which has been wretchedly copied in Hawkins' *History*,

6.   St. Margaret's, Westminster.   1675.

Malcolm, in his *Londinum Redivivum*, vol. iv., p. 165, has preserved the following entry respecting this organ :—" 1675. Item, to Mr. Bernhard Smith, for the charge of the organ newly erected in the parish church, £200."

Sir John Hawkins, in his *History of Music*, vol. iv., p. 510, speaking of the children of the celebrated Henry Purcell, says :—" Of these children we have been only able to trace one, viz., a son, named Edward, who was bred up to music, and, in July, 1726, was elected organist of St. Margaret's, Westminster. Upon inspection of the parish books, for the purpose of ascertaining this fact, it appears the organ of this church was built by Father Smith in 1676, and that he himself was first organist there, and played for a salary." The learned historian is in error *one* year as to the date of the erection of this organ. Smith was appointed organist, April 5, 1676 ; but the instrument, as we see from Malcolm, was built in 1675. Smith's organ was removed in 1804, and a new one supplied by Avery.

7.   Christ Church Cathedral, Oxford.   1680.

8.   St. Peter's, Cornhill.   1681.

This organ originally cost £210, inclusive of " painting and gilding."

Paterson (*Pietas Londinensis*, p. 231), speaking of this church, adds :—" Within it's beautified with a stately new organ, maintain'd by the gift of Mr. Benjamin Thorowgood, in 1682."

9.   St. Mary Woolnoth.   1681.

Hatton, in his *New View of London*, 1708, vol. ii., p. 411, says :—" The organ case is enriched with three large figures of Fame ; and on the front are, in gold letters, some texts of Scripture, relating to praising God with Church Musick." The date above given is also on the exterior of the case.

10.   The Temple Church.   1683-4.

The date usually assigned to this noble instrument is 1687 ; but it is manifestly incorrect, as contemporary authorities tell us that it was erected in the reign of Charles II., who ceased his career in 1685. The true date is that above assigned. Hatton tells us :—" The Temple Church having narrowly escaped the flames in 1666, it was in 1682 beautified, and the curious wainscot screen set up."

The swell-organ was added by Byfield at a subsequent period.

11.   Durham Cathedral.   1683.

Smith received £700, and the materials of the old organ, for this noble instrument. (See *ante*, p. 110.) It was repaired in 1748 by Abraham Jordan, who probably added the swell.

12.   St. Mary-at-Hill, Billingsgate.   1693.

Hatton, in his *New View of London*, 1708, vol. ii., p. 376, says :—" And here is a pretty organ, composed of these stops, and set up *anno* 1692-3." Then follows the following curious list of stops :—" A stop-diapason of wood. A recorder of wood. A fifteenth of metal. A mixture of 3 ranks of metal. A vox-humane. A trimeloe. A principal of metal. A cornet of 5 ranks, all of metal advanced exactly. A tierce of metal. A trumpet of metal throughout. An echo to the whole. To draw all in whole stops, except the great 12th, the 15th, the tierce, the mixture, the vox-humane, and the trumpet ; all which are broken, and made to draw in half stops, for the benefit of increasing the variety in the organ." This organ was removed late in the last century. Smith's original contract is preserved in the vestry.

13. St. Paul's Cathedral. 1694-7.

" Bernhard Smith entered into a contract with the commissioners, Dec. 19, 1694, to erect the great organ and a chair organ, for £2000."—Malcolm's *Londinum Redivivum*, vol. iii., p. 105.

The organ was opened Dec. 2, 1697, by Jeremiah Clark ; but the Cathedral was not entirely finished till 1715.

14. St. Mary's (University Church), Cambridge. 1697.

15. Trinity College Chapel, Cambridge. 1708.

16. Ripon Cathedral.

17. St. David's Cathedral.

The case and the diapason-pipes alone remain.

18. St. Mary's (University Church), Oxford.

19. The Theatre, Oxford.

This organ was taken down by Byfield about a century ago, and placed in the Church of St. Peter-in-the-East, Oxford.

20. St. George's Chapel, Windsor.

This organ remained in the Royal Chapel until 1788 ; when the king, upon the completion of the new organ by Green, presented it to Old Windsor Church. It was afterwards removed to the New Church at Haggerstone, Middlesex, where it now is.

21. The Chapel of Eton College.

22. Southwell Collegiate Church.

Repaired and completed by Snetzler in 1766.

23. The Chapel Royal, Hampton Court.

This organ is in a recess on the south side of the choir ; the case is richly carved by Gibbons.

24. Manchester Cathedral.

The choir organ only ; it still remains in its original state.

25. St. James's, Garlickhithe.

26. St. Clement Danes.

27. St. Dunstan's, Tower Street.

This organ was afterwards removed to St. Albans' Abbey.

28. High Church, Hull, Yorkshire.

Traditionally said to have been intended for St. Paul's Cathedral, in addition to the present instrument.

29. All Saints, Derby.

30. St. Margaret's, Leicester.

This organ has been rebuilt.

31. West Walton Church, Norfolk.

The case only remains.

32. All Saints, Isleworth, Middlesex.

Much improved by Green in 1776.

33. Pembroke College Chapel, Cambridge.

34. Emanuel College, ditto.

35. Christ's College, ditto.

The three last-named organs remain in nearly their original state; they have been disused for more than half a century. I have assigned them to Father Smith, upon the authority of Sir W. Cope, Bart.

36. St. Catherine Cree, Leadenhall Street.

The carved oak case of this organ is a fine specimen in its style. It is rich in well-cut mouldings, bold projections, and figures of angels.

37. Chester Cathedral.

This organ was removed in 1844. A small organ, probably by the same maker (formerly used to accompany the choir), is still preserved in an apartment in the cloisters.

38. St. Olave's, Southwark.

39. St. Martin's, Ludgate Hill.

40. Danish Church, Wellclose Square.

41. Sedgefield Parish Church, county Durham.

42. Whalley Lancashire.

43. Hadleigh, Suffolk.

44. Chelsea Old Church.

45. St. Nicholas', Deptford.

29. *John and Renatus Harris.*

According to Dr. Burney,

"Smith had not been many months here, before Harris arrived from France, with his son René or Renatus, an ingenious and active young man, to whom he had confided all the secrets of his art. However, they met with but little encouragement at first, as Dallams and Smith had the chief business of the kingdom; but upon the decease of Dallams, who died while he was building an organ for the old church at Greenwich, 1672, and of the elder Harris, who did not long survive him, the younger became a formidable rival to Smith."[*]

A slight digression is here necessary, which the reader will pardon, in order to introduce some new and curious particulars of Thomas Harris.

Organs, as we have seen, were generally demolished by the ordinance of 1644, but it was not carried into effect in Worcester Cathedral

---

* *History of Music*, vol. iii., p. 437.

till July, 1646 (the instruments having probably meanwhile been restored after their first damage by the troopers); and on the 23rd of that month many gentlemen went to six o'clock prayers at the College, to take their last farewell of the Church of England service, the organs having been taken down on the 20th. The account of that proceeding is thus narrated in *Townsend's Annals* :—

"July 20. The organs were this day taken down out of the Cathedral Church. Some parlaymenters hearing the music of the church at service, walkinge in the aisle, fell a skipping aboute and dancing as it were in derision. Others seeing the workmen taking them down said, 'you might have spared that labour; we would have done it for you.' 'Noe,' said a merry ladd about tenn yeres old, 'for when the Earl of Essex was here the first man of yours that pluckt downe and spoyled the organs broke his neck here, and they will prevent the like misfortune.'

"No sooner had monarchy been restored in 1660, than the Worcester quire petitioned the King for their salaries left unpaid when they were plundered and undone for their faithful service to the late King, of blessed memory, in regard of the said warrs and the King's enemies prevailing."

How the choristers fared does not appear; but in the same year an organ-loft was fitted up, the "gallery organ" painted, Turner, the joiner, received £1 "for mending pulpit organs," 1s. 6d. was paid "for postage of anthems from Cambridge," John Jones 6s. 6d. for an organ book, and "Thos. Harrison" had £5 for "coming from London to treat about making a new organ." Whether this negotiation failed, or the name was misspelt for Thos. Harris, of New Sarum, with whom a bond was entered into in 1666 for the making of new organs, is not shown on the books, but about this time there are several entries as to the repair and removal of the old organ, making a little organ gallery in the north aisle, etc. In the Bodleian MS., Tanner 45, fol. 19, is a letter from the Bishop of Worcester to Sheldon, Archbishop of Canterbury, interesting, though somewhat unintelligible, as pertaining to the musical affairs of Worcester Cathedral :—

"May it please your grace,—Tandem aliquando, I present your grace with all the papers that make (and as with humble submission I conceive) are requisite in Mr. Deane of Worcester's against Mr. Hathaway's pretences and allegations about the choire organ made and fixt, and the great organ to be made, but now bargained for, and the reason I sent these papers up no sooner was my longing hope and endeavour to have made Mr. George Dallow's (Dallam?) testimonie more pregnant and evident touching the promise of Hathaway and Dr. Gibbons to help him to this organ-worke at Worcester, but, to my satisfaction, there is more than probabilitie there had been money enough to have satisfied Gibbons and Hathaway and Talbot, had it been in the dean's power to have made a bargain, they well knew Mr. Deane's [Dr. Warmstrey] utter ignorance in re-musica. They knew he was, as it is in the Greek proverb, ονος προς λυραν, but no more skill in an organ than a beast that hath no understanding, and 'tis very considerable that Hathaway should dare to addresse a complaint at 'Council Board, when for above a whole yeare, Mr. Deane having forbidden him to procede to the worke of the great organ, he never applied himselfe neither to Mr. Deane nor to the chapter, nor to the visitor, continuing his visitacion for nine months at least, no complaint all this while ever heard of, and for ye materials provided it signifies nothing, unless it did appeare they were provided for this organ, when soon after he had made the choire organ he was forbidden to proceed any further. With Mr. Harrison (who was old Dallow's servant and married his daughter) I twice conferred about his testimonie, and he told me he would make good all he said upon oath, and make it good to all the organists in England, and if your grace shall secretly object, old Hesiod's testimonie in ye case, και κηραευs κηραμει φθονευει, an artist maligns his brother artist. I rely very much on Mr. Tomkins' skill, bred in his cradle, and all his life among organs, who is an excellent organist, and has ever maintained an organ in his house, his letter will show what his judgment was before this difference was started. Little reason have I had to interpose in the least in Mr. Deane's case, but I cannot forbear to stand up for innocence, though joined with much follie. I have returned a certificate to his Majestie's instructions about hospitalls, and by the grace of God shall returne a full answer to your grace's instructions about church affairs in ye due time. The Lorde in the meane time preserve your grace in health and safetie and ye comforts of his blessed Spirit. May it please your grace, I am your grace's most obliged and most obedient humble servant. "RO. WIGORN.

"Worcester, Aug. 5, 1665."

The following were the articles of agreement between Thos. Harris, of New Sarum, and the Dean and Chapter of Worcester, July 5, 1666 :—

"Within eighteen months he shall set up in the choyre a double organ, consisting of great organ and chaire organ. In the former, east and west side, both diapasons to be in sight and some of the principals ; two open diapasons of metal, a 10 ft. pipe as at Sarum and Gloucester, following the proportion of 8 in. diameter in the 10 ft. pipe, and 4 in. diameter in a pipe of 5 ft. The great organ case to be designed after the manner of Windsor church before the wars, a double prospective, the great pipes on the north and south ranging with the middle columns of the stone arch, and so the next great declining toward the east continually till the smallest in the middle meet within 2 or 3 ft., resembling the diminution of pillars in a prospect, and rising by degrees to that end ; the wainscot work on the top resembling architrave, freeze, and cornice, and lessening in proportion at the bottom bases ; two principals of metal, two 15ths of metal, one 12th metal, one recorder metal, one place for another stop ; in the chaire organ, one principal of metal in front, according to the design of Windsor before the wars, a cherub expanding its wings so as to returne downe perpendicular, and that the great pipes shall be in the place of the first and second quills [sic], on the north and south sides, and the rest proportionably less and less towards the cheeks of the cherub ; one stopped diapason of wood, one open diapason of wood, having nine pipes towards the bases beginning in A re, one 15th of metal, one two-and-20th (as they call it) ; the bellows, sound-boards, and all the timber and iron, as at Sarum and Gloucester, or wh. soever is the fairest ; the case of such wainscot as shall be judged by expert ones to equal those of either Sarum or Gloucester. Item, it is agreed upon and concluded, to pay £400 to the said T. Harris, of which £40 earnest money, £80 after setting up the chaire organ case and the lower part of the great organ case, £100 when the chaire organ is finished, £100 when the front of the great 'organ is set up, £80 when both perfected ; but if the organ shall be found not worth the amount it shall be lawful to stop £40 out of the last payment."

Here is Mr. Harris's acknowledgment of the settling, which seems to have been satisfactory to all parties :—

" Whereas the reverend dean and chapter of the cathedral church of Worcester, upon view by certain members of the said church taken of an organ built by Mr. Thos. Harrise in the said church, have been pleased to receive such satisfaction concerning ye whole work as to deliver up my bond given unto them for performance of certain articles concerning the said organ on my part undertaken, now I the said T. Harrise do hereby acknowledge that the said dean and chapter have not only paid unto me the full some belonging unto me by the said articles, viz., £400, and also the sum of £4 for a soft stop in ye choir organ, and ye sum of £5 for mending and removing ye old organ, but further the said dean and chapter have hereby given me the sum of £24 above my due, in which I do acknowledge their great kindness and bounty ; and I do hereby promise and oblige myself, in confirmation of what I have expressed, in my petition unto them, that I will constantly attend upon the said organ during my life and do all things touching the keeping of it in good order at my own cost, without any charge to ye said dean and chapter." *

Since the first edition of this book was printed Dr. Bloxam has done good service to the world by the publication of his *Registers of Magdalen College, Oxford.* From these Registers we learn that the Harrises were an English family, and that Renatus's grandfather was an organ-builder residing among us and practising his art with success.

The relationship between the two Harrises is established by an entry in the Magdalen College Registers, under the date 1672, where Renatus Harris, being at Oxford, offers his services to repair the organ, " the rather because his *grandfather* made it at first, and he was sufficiently known to be as skilful an artist as any in England."

The following documents connected with the Magdalen College organ will be read with interest :—

" THE PROPOSALS OF RENATUS HARRIS TO THE REVEREND THE PRESIDENT AND FELLOWS OF MAGDALEN COLLEGE IN OXFORD, FOR REPAIRING AND MAKING SEVERAL ALTERATIONS IN THEIR ORGAN, 17 JULY, 1686.†

" To make the three bellows new, to repair and perfect the inner trunks and wind-chests, to new hang both sets of keys, to rectify all defects in the roller-

---

* *The Monastery and Cathedral of Worcester.* By John Noake, 1866. A work of great interest.
† Harl. MS., No. 4240, fol. 116b.

boards, to repair the sound-boards and conveyances, and to make them as good as at the first.

" 2. To mend all the pipes and conduits in both organs, and perfectly to voice and tune them, which voicing shall be done after the modern, best, and sweetest manner that either the work or proposer is capable of.

" 3. Whereas the great organ consists of eight stops, namely two diapasons, two principals, two fifteenths, and two two-and-twentieths, one of which stops, and several pipes in the other, have been spoiled by Preston; finding by experience that when two unisons are together in an organ as two principals, two fifteenths, &c., that they never agree well together in tune, and one stop of each sort is in a manner as loud as two of the same name; for which reason neither in my organ at the Temple, nor in those which I make for the King, after the open and stopped diapasons, none of the rest are of the same denomination; so that I propose to make your eight stops to consist of these following, one open diapason, one stopped diapason, one principal, one great twelfth, one fifteenth, one tiers, one furniture of two or three ranks, according as there is room for it, in place of the two two-and-twentieths. In the choir organ there are one stopped diapason, two principals, one recorder, and one fifteenth, so that in these five stops there are no less than three unisons; which five stops ought to be reduced to these four, namely, one stopped diapason, one principal, one stopped twelfth, and one fifteenth; the recorder being left out will give more air to the rest of the work. With these amendments, alterations, additions, and varieties of stops, it will be an extraordinary good instrument, and the best old organ in England, and exceed the best organ in your University, with only the cost of one hundred and fifty pounds."

" HARRIS'S AGREEMENT WITH THE PRESIDENT AND FELLOWS OF MAGDALEN COLLEGE, OXFORD, TO IMPROVE AND ENLARGE HIS GRANDFATHER'S ORGAN.*

" Articles of Agreement had, made, concluded, and agreed upon the 6th day of June, in the Second year of the Reign of our Sovereign Lord and Lady, William and Mary, by the grace of God King and Queen of England, Scotland, France, and Ireland, Defender of the Faith, &c., Anno Domini 1690, between the Right Rev. Father in God, John [Hough] Lord Bishop of Oxford, President of the College of St. Mary Magdalen in the University of Oxford, and the scholars of the said College on their part, and Renatus Harris, of the City of London, Organ-maker on the other part, in manner following, that is to say :—

" *Imprimis*, It is covenanted, concluded, and agreed upon by and between the said parties to these presents, and me the said Renatus Harris, in consideration of the money to be paid unto him as hereinafter mentioned, doth for himself, his executors, and administrators, covenant and grant to and with the said President and Scholars, and their successors, by these presents, that he the said Renatus Harris, his servants, workmen, and assigns, shall and will in good and workmanlike manner put the great and choir organs in Magdalen College aforesaid into sound, good, and perfect repair in all ill parts and defects whatsoever, and shall new work and repair the three bellows and make them strong, staunch, and good; and all the wood-trunks and conveyances of wind shall repair, make good, and staunch, and shall new work and amend all

---

* Appendix to Dr. Bloxam's *Registers of Magdalen College.*

the defects in the sound-boards, and make them staunch and sound, and shall and will make new palletts, springs, and wind-chest to the sound-boards of the said organs, and shall and will make good and serviceable all the movements and roller-boards of the said organs, and shall make two sets of keys of good ebony and ivory, their fall to be as little as can be to give the pipes their due tone, and the touch to be ready, soft, and even under the finger.

" *Item*, That the said Renatus Harris, his servants, workmen, or assigns, shall and will make to the great organ a new great twelfth of metal, a cedrine of metal, and a furniture of three ranks, and a cymbal of two ranks, and shall and will repair, well voice, and tune, in the great organ, the open diapason, principal of metal, stop-diapason of wood, fifteenth of metal; which great organ shall consist of five hundred sixty and one pipes ; and make to the choir organ a new flute of metal and nason of metal, and repair, well voice, and tune in the choir organ the principal, stop-diapason, and fifteenth, which said choir organ shall consist of two hundred and fifty pipes ; and if the said new pipes or stops to be made in the said organs shall not be liked, or approved of, by such organist as the said President and Scholars shall appoint to inspect the same, that then the said Renatus Harris, his executors and assigns, shall take down such stops and pipes as shall be disliked of as aforesaid, and put in their places such new ones as shall be approved of under the same conditions as are hereby agreed to. And if any pipe or pipes belonging to the above-named stops cannot be made to speak well, and bear a good tone, strong, clear, and sweet, either through want of substance or any other defect ; that then in such case the said Renatus Harris, his executors, or assigns, shall and will put in new serviceable pipes in the places of such as shall be found so deficient and not useful ; and that the said Renatus Harris, his executors or assigns, shall and will alter the pitch of the said organs half a note lower than they now are ; and the said organs, being now Gamut in Do, Sol, Re, the said Renatus Harris, his executors or assigns, shall and will in good workmanlike manner completely finish on or before the Feast of All Saints next ensuing the date hereof.

" *Item*, In consideration of the said work and workmanship to be done and performed as aforesaid, the said President and Scholars, for them and their successors, do covenant and grant to and with the said Renatus Harris, his executors, administrators, and assigns, by these presents, that the said President and Scholars, or their successors or assigns, shall or will pay or cause to be paid to the said Renatus Harris, his executors or assigns, the sum of One Hundred and Fifty Pounds of lawful money of England, as followeth, viz., ten pounds at or before the sealing hereof, forty pounds on the Feast of the Nativity of Christ next ensuing, and one hundred pounds, being the remainder thereof, on the Feast of St. John Baptist, which shall be on the year of our Lord God 1691. For witness thereof, to the one part of these presents the said President and Scholars have put their common seal, and to the other part thereof the said Renatus Harris hath set his hand and seal, the day and year above written."

Renatus Harris seems to have been much employed, and to have been Smith's rival upon all occasions. The memorable " battle of the organs," at the Temple Church, has already been detailed ; and not long afterwards, upon the accession of James II., we find Harris rivalling his opponent in Court patronage. The evidence of this is contained in the following curious entries, extracted from *Moneys*

received and paid for Secret Services of Charles II. and James II.,
printed for the Camden Society.* The dates range between 1686
and 1688 :—

"To René Harris, by advances for an organ to be provided for the chappell in
Whitehall—£300."
"To René Harris, by advance, the same being intended to be employed in the
making and buying a new organ for the chappell in Whitehall—£200."
"To René Harris, for fitting and repairing an organ for the chappell in Whitehall, and for altering and preparing an organ for the chappell at Windsor, and
removing that organ from Winchester thither—£137 : 13."
"To René Harris, in full payment for making and finishing the organ in
yᵉ chappell at Whitehall—£600."

Without doubt, considerable jealousy existed on the part of Harris
towards his rival Smith. The "quarter tones" in the Temple organ,
which gained the latter such reputation, appear to have been a sore
subject with Harris. The following interesting advertisements, which
are quite a new feature in the lives of these distinguished artists, are
here reprinted from my *Lecture on the Early English Organ-
Builders and their Works.†* The first is from the *Post Boy*, April 12,
1698 :—

"Whereas the Division of half a Note (upon an organ) into 50 Gradual and
distinguishable parts has been declar'd by Mr. Smith, as also by the generality of
Masters to be impracticable : All Organists, Masters, and Artists of the Faculty,
are together with the said Mr. Smith, invited to Mr. Harris's house in Wine Office
Court, Fleet Street, on Easter Monday next at Two of the clock in the Afternoon,
to hear and see the same demonstrated."

Again, in the same paper, April 30, the following appeared :—

"Whereas the Division of half a note (upon an organ) into 50 Gradual and
distinguishable parts, was performed by Mr. Harris on Easter Monday to the
full satisfaction of the Persons of Quality and Masters that were present : And
Whereas the said Mr. Harris intends a further Division of half a Note, viz., into
One Hundred parts (and this, as before, not mathematically, but purely by the
Ear), all Masters and others of curious and Nice Ears are invited to the said Mr.
Harris's House, in Wyne Office Court, Fleet Street, on the 10th day May, at Three
of the clock in the afternoon, to hear and see the Performance, and to be informed
(if any doubt) of its usefulness."

It would be interesting to know more of these trials, but nothing
appears on record, as far as I have discovered.

---

* Edited by J. Y. Akerman, from a MS. in the possession of W. L. Lowndes, Esq. The
entries occur, pp. 144, 169, 180, 196.
† Delivered before the College of Organists, Nov. 15, 1864. London : Alf. Whitting-
ham. 12mo.

Harris built a noble instrument for the Cathedral of Salisbury; the only record of which seems to be an engraving fortunately extant. This curious print measures thirty-three inches by sixteen, and purports to be " The East Front of the New Organ in Salisbury Cathedral, made, in the year 1710, by Mr. Renatus Harris, Organ-Builder." At the bottom, " John Lyons, delin ;" " Francis Dewing, sculp." Running along the top of the engraving is this passage :—" Vitalianus, the 74th Bishop of Rome, about the year 662, ordained organs first to be used in the Church. He was born in Segni, a city of great antiquity, on ye top of a Mountain in Italy ; in this city organs were first invented, or first brought to perfection." And on each side of the engraving (at the top of the print), is the following very curious description :—

" This Instrument, consisting of four sets of keys, and fifty stops, stands over the choir door, and is above 40 foot high and 20 foot broad ; the arch under which it stands, being lofty and but narrow, would admit no larger extention in breadth ; and yet it was judged necessary to carry the finishing very high, to render this figure more lively and proportionable to the structure of the church (which is, from the pavement to the vaulting thereof, 80 foot high). The organ blower, as well as the bellows which are very large, have room in the body of ye case, in which are all ye movements, keys, roller-boards, and eleven stops of Echos, and yet the sight of the work is conceal'd from him, as he is from the people in the Church or Gallery. This organ is a new contrivance, and on it may be more varietys express'd, than by all ye organs in England, were their several excellencies united. The figures designed for the finishings of the choir organ are not as yet set up, neither are ye finishings of ye great organ fore shortned in this print according to perspective, because all parts of the Instruments should answer the Scale." *

It seems as if Harris had been a candidate for building the organ of St. Paul's Cathedral, as well as that of the Temple ; for, in the *Spectator* (No. 552, for Dec. 3, 1712), a proposal of Mr. Renatus Harris is recommended in the following words :—

" The ambition of this artificer is to erect an organ in St. Paul's Cathedral, over the west door, at the entrance into the body of the church, which in art and magnificence shall transcend any work of that kind ever before invented. The proposal in perspicuous language sets forth the honour and advantage such a performance would be to the British name, as well as that it would apply the power of sounds in a manner more amazingly forcible, than perhaps has yet been known, and I am sure to an end much more worthy. Had the vast sums which have been laid out upon operas without skill or conduct, and to no other purpose but to suspend or vitiate our understandings, been disposed this way, we should now perhaps have an engine so formed, as to strike the minds of half a people at once,

---

* A copy of this rare engraving, which seems to have been unknown to Gough and Upcott, is in the possession of the writer.

in a place of worship, with a forgetfulness of present care and calamity, and a hope of endless rapture, joy, and Hallelujah hereafter."

In the latter part of his life, according to Sir John Hawkins,

"Renatus Harris retired to Bristol, and, following his business there, made sundry organs for the churches in that city, and in the adjacent parishes, as also for churches in the neighbouring counties. He had a son named John, bred up under him, who followed the business of organ-making, and made a great number of very fine instruments." *

Renatus Harris died in or about the year 1715 ; and his latest organ seems to have been that in St. Mary's Church, Whitechapel.

In regard to the following list of organs, it may be remarked that the first four were built by Renatus in conjunction with his father Thomas.

List of Renatus Harris's Organs.

1. Salisbury Cathedral (before 1665).
2. Gloucester Cathedral (before 1665).
3. Worcester Cathedral. 1665.

In Valentine Green's *Survey of the City of Worcester*, 8vo, 1764, p. 54, the following notice occurs :—" The organ of this church, which, with its gallery, terminates the west-end of the choir, is esteemed a fine instrument, consisting of nine stops : The trumpet stop is justly allowed to be the finest of that sort in the kingdom. The last reparation of it cost three hundred pounds, which sum was raised by a voluntary contribution of several noblemen and gentlemen, whose arms are emblazoned on the west-front of its gallery. * * * The east-front of this gallery, towards the choir, has a pretty deception of marble, well imitated ; and presents a view of the lesser or *choir* organ, which has communication with the great one, and consists of five stops."

4. St. Sepulchre's, Snow Hill. 1670.

Two dates are assigned to this organ, 1667 and 1677 ; but a document in the author's possession gives it (probably correctly) as above. The date 1667 is evidently wrong, as the following extract from Hatton's *New View of London*, 1708, vol. ii., p. 546, will testify :—"St. Sepulchre's being almost demolished (except part of the wall and steeple) by the fury of the devouring flames in 1666, it was again re-erected and finished *anno* 1670."

5. St. Botolph's, Aldgate. 1676.

Upon the front of the organ is this inscription :—" This organ is yᵉ gift of Thomas Whiting to the hole [*sic*] parish, 1676."

---

* *History of Music*, vol. iv., p. 356. Sir John adds :—" In the *Mercurius Musicus* for September and October, 1700, is a song inscribed : ' Set by René Harris.' " Father Smith and Renatus Harris, following the example of their predecessors, united a knowledge of the science of music with the more mechanical art of organ-building.

6. St. Dunstan's, Stepney. 1676.

The case of this organ is beautifully carved in oak ; and the instrument is said to be a very fine one.

7. St. Nicholas', Newcastle-upon-Tyne. 1676.

A trumpet stop was added in 1699, and in 1710 the instrument was thoroughly repaired. Snetzler added the swell in 1749.

8. Allhallows Barking, Great Tower Street. 1675-7.

This church escaped the flames of 1666. Hatton (*New View of London*, 1708, vol. i., p. 98), speaking of the organ, says :—" There is likewise a handsome organ case enrich'd with Fames, and the figures (about 6 foot high) of Time and Death, carved in *basso relievo* and painted." " A new chaire organ " was added in 1720 at a cost of £100 ; and the " old organ" was at the same time repaired at a further cost of £80.

9. Chichester Cathedral. 1678.

A trumpet stop was added by Byfield in 1725 ; a choir organ some twenty years later ; and a swell in 1778.

10. Lambeth Old Church. 1680.

11. Winchester Cathedral. 1681.

Subsequently rebuilt by Avery in 1794.

12. Winchester College Chapel. 1681.

Rebuilt by Green in 1780.

13. St. Michael's, Cornhill. 1684.

14. Bristol Cathedral. 1685.

" In the years 1681 and 1685, in the Deaneries of Towgood and Levett, £300 or more was laid out in mending the floor and beautifying the church, painting the east-end of the choir and other works, and in making a fine timber case for the new organ, erected by the contribution of the Dean and Chapter, and many other well-disposed persons, at the expense of £550 in the whole, to Mr. Renatus Harris, organ-builder."—Barrett's *History of Bristol*, p. 290.

15. Hereford Cathedral. 1686.

The cost of the instrument was £515, exclusive of the case, which cost (carving included) £185. In the same year " George Dallam " was paid £5 for a " chaire organ." In the first edition this organ was erroneously assigned to Smith.

16. King's College Chapel, Cambridge. 1686.

The builder received £350 for the instrument when erected ; £70, in 1688, for three additional stops ; £30, in 1695, for a trumpet stop ; and £60, in 1710, for a diapason. David Loggan published an accurate engraving of the interior of the chapel, between 1675 and 1691, which gives the west front of the organ as it then appeared. The present case is the original one, erected by Chapman and Hartop, in 1606, to contain Dallam's organ ; for, though the action and pipes of the organ appear to have been many times removed and renewed, there is every reason to believe that the existing case dates from 1606, and the choir organ from 1661. When Avery was employed, in 1804, to reconstruct and enlarge the instrument, he probably incorporated much of the old work with his own.

17. St. Lawrence, Jewry. 1687.

Paterson, in his *Pietas Londinensis*, 1714, p. 131, calls it "a fine organ ;" an opinion in which the writer concurs. The case, with its choir organ in front, is one of the finest specimens of its kind in London.

18. St. James's, Piccadilly. 1687.

This organ was made for James II., and designed for his Popish chapel at Whitehall. His daughter, Queen Mary, presented it to the church. On the front was this inscription :—" The gift of the Queen, in the year 1691." Some valuable entries respecting it have already been given (see *ante*, p. 125).

Ambrose Warren, in his curious tract, entitled *The Tonometer*, 1727, p. 8, tells us :—"About the year 1707, when Father Smith, the organ-builder, died, I was by the honourable vestry of St. James's parish chosen to keep their organ in tune and order in his stead, which I found to be in a very mean condition in many respects. And, in 1708, I was by the same authorities ordered to reform divers stops, and put in several new ones, which I with help performed to the full satisfaction of all concerned, as well as myself."

19. St. Mary's, Ipswich. 1690.

20. Christ Church, Newgate Street. 1690.

21. St. Ann's, Westminster. 1691.

Hatton says :—" Here is a fine organ made by Mr. Harris" (p. 132). Paterson adds :—" Given by King William III." (p. 27). It was formerly in one of the royal apartments at Whitehall, and was presented to the church by the King in 1691. It is now in the church of St. Michael's, Paternoster Royal.

22. Allhallows, Lombard Street. 1695.

This church was opened in 1695, which is the probable date of the organ. Paterson (*Pietas Londinensis*, p. 11) speaks of its "fine altar-piece and pulpit, and stately organ, made by Mr. Harris, by the contributions of forty-two benefactors." Hatton says "the names of the benefactors to the organ are inscribed in gold letters on the gallery."—*New View of London*, vol. i., p. 109.

23. St. Andrew's, Undershaft. 1696.

Paterson (*Pietas Londinensis*, p 22) calls it "a most excellent and costly organ, made by Mr. Harris." Hatton (*New View of London*, p. 174) calls it "a fine *large* organ," and adds, "several gentlemen (whose names I am not allowed to mention) contributed for the organ, &c., the sum of £1400."

This organ was opened on the 31st of May, 1696, when Dr. Towerson preached a sermon on Vocal and Instrumental Music in the church.

24. St. Patrick's Cathedral, Dublin. 1697.

The following extracts are from the old Chapter Book :—" 12th August, 1695. The Dean and Chapter agrees with Renatus Harris, of London, organ-builder, to make and set up a Double Organ for the sum of £505. In the great organ—Open Diapason of metal, Stop Diapason of wood, Principal of metal, Nason of wood, a great 12th of metal, 15th of metal, a Cornet of metal. In the little organ—a Principal of metal, Stop Diapason of wood, 15th of metal, and a Nason of wood, being in all 13 stops, consisting of 800 pipes, sound-board, &c., &c. The pipes of the old organ to be removed, and to allow £65 for the same."

" 11th March, 1697. Organ erected and examined by the several Vicars."

" 10th May, 1697. Further contract for additional stops for £350, to be paid at Strongbow's Tomb, in Christ Church, on stated times named—viz., Trumpet stop, Echo stop, *Time* stop [*sic*] entire, Open Diapason, Flute of metal, Great Furniture of 3 ranks."

K

25.   St. Andrew's, Holborn.   1699.

Harris's organ, after its rejection at the Temple, was part of it erected a: St. Andrew's, Holborn, and part in the Cathedral of Christ Church, Dublin Sir John Hawkins records the following anecdote in his *History of Music*, vol iv., p. 539 :—" Dr. Sacheverell, having been presented to the living of St. Andrew's Holborn, found an organ in the church, of Harris's building, which, having nevei been paid for, had, from its erection in 1699, been shut up.   The Doctor, upon his coming to the living, by a collection from his parishioners, raised money enough to pay for it."

Some curious notices respecting the earlier organs of this church occur in the old churchwardens' books :—" 9 *Henry VIII*.   The little organs were made and bought at the charges of the parish, and devotion of good people, and cost, as I can gather, £6."   " 2 *Edward VI*.   My Lord of Lincolne gave a pair of organs."   " 1 *Mary*.   The parish gave young White £5 for the great organs which his father gave to the church."—See Malcolm's *Londinum Redivivum*, vol. ii., p. 197.

26.   St. John's Chapel, Bedford Row.   1703.
27.   St. Giles's, Cripplegate.   1704.

In Malcolm's *Londinum Redivivum*, vol. iii., p. 274, is the following curious extract from the parish books :—" 1672.   Mrs. Charnock shall have thanks given her, for her affection in bestowing a faire organ upon the parish church of St. Giles ; and that some convenient place shall be found for setting it up."   The double duty of organist and sexton was performed by James Brookes, who was " chosen by the King's Majesties letter."   It was provided that, if the sexton did not, or could not play, he should find an organist.

In 1726 a proposal was made, and accepted, by Abraham Jordan, organist, to take the organ to pieces, the builder having left it in a very imperfect state, and repair it *gratis*, on condition of his having his salary secured to him for 21 years.— See Malcolm, *Ibid*, p. 279.

28.   St. Clement's, Eastcheap.   1709.

"A pretty organ, made by Mr. Harris."—Hatton, vol. i., p. 208.   This instrument was probably built in 1709, when the church "was repaired and beautified."

29.   Salisbury Cathedral.   1710.

See the account of a curious engraving of this organ, *ante*, p. 126.   This noble instrument was probably removed in 1792, when Green erected the present organ.   *The Modern British Traveller*, 1779, thus describes it :— " The organ, which is fixed over the entrance to the choir, is very large, being 20 feet broad, and 40 feet high to the top of its ornaments.   It has 50 stops, which are 18 more than there are in the organ of St. Paul's Cathedral, in London, but the latter is much superior in the sweetness of its tone."

30.   St. Mary's, Whitechapel.   1715.

This organ was opened on the 29th of May, 1715.   See the Parish Clerk's *Remarks on London*, 1732, p. 246.

31.   St. Bridget's (now St. Bride's), Fleet Street.

Hatton, in his *New View of London*, vol. i., p. 175, says :—" Here is a very fine organ, and a curious carved case adorned with two large Fames, &c.   This organ was made by Mr. Harris."

32. Ely Cathedral, Cambridgeshire.

33. Jesus College Chapel, Cambridge.

This instrument is now in All Saints' Church, Cambridge.

34. Wolverhampton Collegiate Church.

This organ, with that of St. Andrew's, Holborn, was constructed out of the rejected Temple organ. Burney says "that part of the organ for the Temple church by Harris, and sent to Dublin, was sold, after the death of the elder Byfield, to Wolverhampton for £500. It still stands in the church of that town, and is thought a very good instrument."

35. Norwich Cathedral.

This organ is attributed to Harris. Sir Thomas Browne, in his *Repertorium of the Antiquities of Norwich Cathedral*, thus alludes to the earlier organs :— "There was formerly a fair and large, but plain, organ in the church, and in the same place with this at present. It was agreed in a Chapter by the Dean and Prebends that a new organ be made, and timber fitted to make a loft for it, June 6, *Anno* 1607, repaired 1626, and £10 which Abel Colls gave to the church was bestowed upon it. That, in the late tumultuous time, was pulled down, broken, sold, and made away. But since his Majesty's restoration another, a fair, well-tuned, plain organ was set up by Dean Crofts and the Chapter, and afterwards painted and beautifully adorned by the care and cost of my honoured friend, Dr. Herbert Astley, the present worthy Dean."—*Posthumous Works of the Learned Sir Thomas Browne*, 8vo, 1712, p. 31.

36. St. John's, Clerkenwell.

37. Bideford Church, Devon.

38. Cork Cathedral.

The specification is signed "Renatus Harris," but the organ was probably finished by John Harris.

39. St. Mary's, Dublin.

30. *Father Smith's Nephews.*

Upon Father Smith's arrival in this country, he was accompanied (according to Hawkins and, after him, Burney) by his two nephews, Bernard and Gerard. There is reason to believe that the historian was in error as to the first name. Horace Walpole, in his corrected copy of Hawkins's *History*, altered the name of Bernard to *Christian*, and evidently upon some good authority, as we find, in the case of the repair of the organ of St. Giles's-in-the-Fields (before quoted), *Christian* Smith received payment, and signed the receipt for the same.[*]

---

[*] These two young men, in all probability, were the sons of *Christian* Smith, one of whose organs, with the date 1643, is in the possession of a gentleman at Norwich. All the pipes

The names of Christian and Gerard Smith are so little known, that they have not hitherto been registered in our roll of organ-builders. Nevertheless, they built several fine instruments.

In Chamberlayne's *Magnæ Britanniæ Notitia* for 1755 we find, among the officers of Chelsea Hospital, "Organ Repairer, Mr. Gerard Smith." This person was probably Father Smith's grand-nephew. The date almost precludes the possibility of his being a nephew.

Organs built by Christian Smith.

1. Tiverton Church, Devon. 1696.

Among the conditions, dated March 6, 1695, the rector, burgesses, &c., "do undertake to procure an excellent and well-contrived organ, of a sufficient bigness, and with decent and proper ornaments of carved work, answerable for the Parish Church," &c. Articles accordingly were entered into with "the excellent artist, Mr. Christian Smith, a very honest and ingenious man, who lives in Hart Street, nigh Bloomsbury Market, London," who built the instrument.

2. Boston Church, Lincolnshire. 1717.

Organs built by Gerard Smith.

1. Parish Church, Bedford. 1715.

This instrument was sold by the parish, when the church was restored in 1832, for £50—about the price of its case. It is now in the Moravian Chapel at Bedford.

2. Allhallows, Bread Street. 1717.

An echo was added to this organ, by the original builder, in 1722 ; the whole cost being £422. It is probable that Schrider assisted in this instrument.

3. Finedon Church, Northamptonshire. 1717.

This organ was built at the cost of Dr. Dolben, of Finedon, a great patron of music and musicians. In *A Collection of Anthems, as the same are now Perform'd in the Cathedral Church, Durham*, Durham, 8vo, 1749, p. 159, is one beginning " Praise God in His sanctuary," " Compos'd for and Perform'd at the Opening a new Organ at Finedon, in Northamptonshire, May 17, 1717," by Dr. Croft.

The instrument is in its original state : the pipes are diapered.

4. Little Stanmore Church (Whitchurch), Edgware.

This organ is sometimes attributed, by mistake, to Jordan.

---

are of wood, and the date and name of the builder, *Christianus Schmidt*, are inscribed in three places, in different parts of the instrument. Query—Did Christian accompany his brother to England ?

5. St. George's, Hanover Square. 1725.

"This organ was erected, in 1725, by Smith, nephew to the great artist of that name ; and the choice of an organist is thus mentioned in the *St. James's Evening Post* of Nov. 16 :—'On Friday last came on the election of an organist of St. George's, Hanover Square ; and, the salary being settled at £45 *per annum*, there were seven candidates : Mr. Rosengrave ; Mr. Cole, organist of the Chapel of the Royal Hospital of Chelsea, and of St. Mary Hill, London ; Mr. Monro, organist of St. Peter's, Cornhill ; Mr. Stanley, the ingenious blind youth, aged 13 years and a half, organist of Allhallows, Bread Street ; Mr. Centlivre, organist of Oxford Chapel, near Oxford Square ; Mrs. Sweet, organist of the Chapel in Duke Street, Westminster ; and Mr. Obbel, organist of St. Bartholomew the Great, in West Smithfield. The vestry, which consists of above 30 lords and 70 gentlemen, having appointed Dr. Crofts, Dr. Pepusch, Mr. Bononcini, and Mr. Geminiani, to be judges which of the candidates performed best, each of them composed a subject, to be carried on by the said candidates in the way of fuguing ; and one hour was allowed for every one to play upon the four subjects so appointed, one not to hear another unless himself had done before ; only the four first performed, and all of them very masterly. In the conclusion the judges gave it for the famous Mr. Rosengrave, who made that way of performance his study great part of his life ; and he was accordingly chosen.'"—Malcolm's *Londinum Redivivum*, vol. iv., p. 234.

This organ was removed in 1790.

31. *Renatus Harris, Jun.*

In the first edition of this work I only knew of this builder from a notice on the fly-leaf of an old MS. collection of voluntaries for the organ—*i.e.*, "John Harris, given me by my *brother* Renatus, A.D., 1712." I am now enabled to cite an organ built by the younger Renatus. He doubtless built several others, although they are not recorded, and it is certain he died young.

Organ built by Renatus Harris, Jun.

St. Dionis Backchurch. 1724.

It would seem, from the parish books, that the first steps for erecting an organ in this church were taken in the year 1722, when a subscription was set on foot, and a committee appointed by the vestry for that purpose, the Rev. Dr. Smith (President of Queen's College, Oxford) being the rector of the parish. In the same year the committee were empowered by the vestry to enter into a contract with Mr. Renatus Harris,* an organ-builder, and to obtain a faculty from the ecclesiastical authorities.

The sum raised by voluntary subscription for the erection of the organ and for every expense connected with it amounted to £741 9s. ; Mr. Deputy Hankey (afterwards Sir Henry Hankey, Knt., and Alderman), taking charge

---

* In the first edition of my *History of the Organ* (pp. 100-101), I followed the common error in ascribing the building of this organ to the firm of Messrs. Byfield, Jordan, & Bridge.

of the several contributions, a detailed list of which is preserved in the parish ledger.

During the year 1723 the only entries relative to the organ are three payments in advance to Mr. Renatus Harris, who, when in the following year he was paid the balance due to him, appears to have received from beginning to end the sum of £525 for the instrument.*

In 1724, at a meeting of the vestry, the organ was ordered to be opened on the second Sunday in June, and Mr. Philip Hart was chosen the first organist. It is supposed that the organ was accordingly opened on the day appointed, as there is an entry in the parish ledger, June 15th, that £10 10s. was paid for singing two anthems.

As regards the structural arrangements, the organ continued nearly in its original state until 1867, when, being much out of repair, and of course deficient in many points deemed necessary in the present day, its condition was brought under the attention of the vestry, who elected a committee to consider the question. The committee presented a report to the vestry, recommending Messrs. Gray and Davison to be instructed to rebuild the organ according to specifications, and obtained leave to lay out thereon a sum not exceeding £200.

The organ having been rebuilt was opened February 7th, 1868.

32. *John Harris and John Byfield.*

John Harris, another son of Renatus, seems to have been overlooked by all who have written upon the subject of our early organ-builders since the time of Sir John Hawkins. Indeed so little attention has been paid to dates that, we are told, "Harris's most celebrated organs are those of St. Sepulchre's, London, which, however, is now much changed since its first erection in 1667 ; and Doncaster, Yorkshire, 1738." (!) †

In 1738, March 19, articles of agreement were entered into "Between John Harris, of Red Lion Street, in the Parish of St. Andrew, Holborn, in the County of Middlesex, organ-maker of the one part, and the Reverend Hollis Piggot, Vicar of the Parish of Doncaster, in the County of York, William Seaton, John Hancock, James Buckley Wilford, and John Gibbons, Churchwardens of the said Parish of Doncaster, of the other part."

Harris undertakes, for the sum of Five Hundred and Twenty-five pounds,

"To make, compleat, finish and erect, on or before the 24th day of June, 1740, a Good, Tuneful, and compleat Organ with One Handsome Front and a Case according to the Modell or Draught. The said Organ to contain the

---

* The parish ledger mentions that on September 18th, 1724, the sum of £52 10s. was paid to "Jno. Harris for some additions and to take care of it for five years."

† *A short Account of Organs built in England, &c.*, p. 60.

severall stops and other particulars hereinafter mentioned, without any communication or any Sett of Pipes made to serve in a double capacity in or upon both organs (that is to say) The Great Organ to contain Twelve Stops (to wit) One open Diapason of Mettal in the front, with fifty-two speaking pipes. One open Diapason in the inside, with fifty-two Pipes. One Stop'd Diapason with fifty-two Pipes. One Principall of Metall with fifty-two Pipes. One Twelfth of the like. One Fifteenth of the like. One Tierce of the like. One Sesqualtra of five rows of Pipes. One Cornet of five rows of Pipes. Two Trumpets with One Hundred and four Pipes. And One Clarion with fifty-two Pipes. The Choir or Quoir Organ, to contain One Stop'd Diapason with Fifty-two Pipes. One Flute with Fifty-two Pipes. One Fifteenth with Fifty-two Pipes. And one Bassoon with Fifty-two speaking Pipes. The Eccho Organ to contain the following Stops, which shall Eccho and Swell to express passion in degrees of Loudness and Softness, as if inspired by human breath (viz.) One open Diapason with twenty-seven Speaking pipes. One stop'd Diapason with twenty-seven pipes. One Principall with twenty-seven pipes. One Cornet of three Rows with Eighty-one pipes. One Trumpet and one Hautboy with twenty-seven pipes to each. For the Great and Choir Organ, fifty-two pipes in each Sett, being from G G to D la sol. The Keys of the Ecchos and Swelling from C sol fa ut Cliff, to D la sol, in all being twenty-seven keys, and the Speaking Pipes in the whole Organ to be in number one thousand three hundred and thirty-nine, and the front to be gilt with Leaf Gold."*

John Harris was probably in partnership with John Byfield; at any rate he built most of his organs in conjunction with the latter. The connection between the two builders was still closer, by Byfield's marriage with Harris's daughter. They resided at Red Lion Street, Holborn, and were living there when they built the Doncaster organ.

According to a power of attorney, dated September 16, 1740, signed John Harris, and sent from London, "John Byfield, organ-builder, of the Parish of St. George the Martyr, but now at Doncaster," is empowered to receive the money due to Harris; and on the 2nd of October in the same year Byfield signs a receipt for Five Hundred and twenty-five pounds, "by order and for ye use of Mr. John Harris."

Organs built by Harris and Byfield.

1. St. Mary's, Shrewsbury. 1729.

There was an organ in this church in the sixteenth century; and on the 31st of August, 1589, it was agreed at a parish meeting that "the organs should be sould to any of the parishe for the sum of £4, if any desired the same; otherwise the said organs should presentlye be sould to him whosoever would give £4 or more for the same." In 1590 it appears that the Dean of Worcester, "at the motion of Mr. John Tomkins, gave that sum for them, and an additional present to the churchwardens of a communion booke worthe 7s. 4d."

---

* Communicated, some few years back, by Mr. W. Sheardown, the well-known bookseller of Doncaster, to the *Doncaster Chronicle.*

2. Grantham Church, Lincolnshire. 1736.

3. St. Mary's, Haverfordwest. 1737.

4. St. Albans', Wood Street. 1738.

5. St. Bartholomew's, Change. 1740.

6. Parish Church, Doncaster. 1740.

The agreement for this organ (before cited at length) is dated March 19, 1738. The money for the organ was raised by subscription, and the Corporation agreed to pay £20 per annum for an organist's salary, "when and so soon as a good and complete organ shall be set up."

The celebrated Snetzler was employed upon the instrument in 1758, as appears by the following receipt :—"April 26, 1756. Received of Mr. Francis Caley, church-warden, the sum of Twenty pounds for Repairing and Tuneing the Organ, by me, John Snetzler."

7. St. Mary Redcliffe, Bristol.

"The entrance into the church is at the great west door, to which you ascend by steps. The door is 8 feet in breadth and 12 high, within which is built a great stone gallery, on which is a grand magnificent organ, being in all 53 feet high fro m the ground to the top of the crown panel ; the great case, about 20 feet square, contains one great and lesser organ ; the musical part executed by Messrs. Harris and Byfield, and the whole cost £846 7s."—Barrett's *History of Bristol*, 1789, p. 574.

8. St. Thomas's, Bristol.

9. St. James's, Bristol.

This and the previous organ are assigned to Harris and Byfield, upon the authority of Robert Broderip of Bristol.—See the Preface to his *Organists' Journal*, 1802.

10. St. Thomas Southover, Lewes, Sussex.

Traditionally said to have been made for the Duke of Chandos, and removed here from Cannons in 1747.

33. *Christopher Schrider.*

Schrider, or Schreider, a German, was a workman in the employ-ment of Father Smith, and, previous to the year 1708, had attained a closer connection, by becoming his son-in-law.* After the death of Smith he succeeded to his business ; and, in the year 1710, to the appointment of organ-builder to the Royal Chapels. His organs, as far as we know, are not very numerous, that of Westminster being his *chef-d'œuvre.*

* He probably married again, as we find the following entry in an old register of burials in the library of St. Peter's, Westminster :—"Mrs. Hellen Shrider died March 21, 1752, aged 65 years, and was buried y" 27, in the South Cloyster, on her father, Mr Thos. Jennings." Jennings was a Gentleman of the Chapel Royal, and of the Choir at West-minster. Many notices of Schrider's family occur in the same volume. The present entry may refer to the wife of Christopher Schrider, jun.

The date of his death is not recorded, but it probably took place in 1754 ; as, in the following year, among the " Servants in Ordinary to the King," in Chamberlayne's *Magnæ Britanniæ Notitia*, we find, "Organ Maker, Mr. Christopher Shrider, son of the *late* Mr. Schrider."

The following *quibbling* epitaph, upon the subject of our notice, appeared in Webb's *Collection of Epitaphs*, 1775 (vol. ii., p. 76) :—

> " ON THE CELEBRATED MR. CHRISTOPHER SHRIDER.
>
> " Here rests the musical *Kit Shrider*,
> Who organs built when he did bide here :
> With nicest ear he tun'd 'em up ;
> But Death has put the cruel Stop :
> Tho' Breath to others he convey'd,
> Breathless, alas ! himself is lay'd.
> May he, who us such Keys has giv'n,
> Meet with St. Peter's Keys of Heav'n !
> His Cornet, Twelfth, and Diapason,
> Could not with Air supply his Weasand :
> Bass, Tenor, Treble, Unison,
> The loss of tuneful Kit bemoan."

Organs built by Christopher Schrider.

1. **The Royal Chapel, St. James's. 1710.**

This organ was removed in 1819, and, after undergoing the necessary repairs, was purchased, for the Episcopal Chapel in Long Acre, for £200. In 1866 it was taken down and re-erected in the chapel of Mercers' Hall. Mr. Thomas Hill, in a communication to the *Church Choirmaster* (Jan. 1867), says, speaking of this instrument :—" It is clearly a work of *Father Smith's*, and presents the unusual feature of having escaped any attempt at modernising." The old accounts of the Chapel Royal say :—" 1710, organ erected by *Mr. Schrider.*" It is difficult to reconcile these two statements, but the high authority of Mr. Hill deserves attention.

2. **St. Mary Abbot's, Kensington. 1716.**

Faulkner, in his *History of Kensington*, says :—" This instrument was built by subscription at a cost of £500, in the above-named year."

John Harris appears to have added the swell in 1730.

3. **St. Martin's-in-the-Fields. 1726.**

This organ was the present of George the First, as the following note from Dr. Burney shows :—" Schreider, who built the organ of St. Martin's-in-the-Fields, which King George the First presented to the Church upon being chosen church-warden of the parish, soon after his Majesty's arrival in England."

In a list of Exchequer Payments, 1725, occurs this entry :—" To Zachary Pearce, Vicar of St. Martin's, as of Royal bounty, to erect an organ there, £1500."

Malcolm, writing in 1807, says :—" The instrument has however been worn out and replaced."—*Londinum Redivivum*, vol. iv., p. 195.

Schrider's organ is now in a church at Wotton-under-Edge, and is said not to be *worn out.*

4. Westminster Abbey. 1730.

The following memorandum occurs in a MS. book in the custody of the Precentor of Westminster :—"The new organ, built by Mr. Schrider and Mr. Jordan, was opened on the 1st August, 1730, by Mr. Robinson ; the Anthem, Purcell's 'O give thanks.'"

From the treasurer's accounts we learn that the cost of the instrument was £1000. Jordan's share in building this noble organ is not defined ; but it was, in all probability, the *swell*, of which, as we shall presently show, he was the inventor.

5. St. Mary Magdalen, Bermondsey.
6. Whitchurch Shropshire.

34. *Thomas Schwarbrook.*

This eminent artist, who was also a German, was in the employment of Renatus Harris. Early in the eighteenth century he left the metropolis, and took up his abode at Warwick, at which place he probably lived until his death. He built many noble instruments ; but his masterpiece is said to be the organ of St. Michael's, Coventry. *Henry* Schwarbrook was organist of Hereford Cathedral in 1730 ; but it is not known if he was any relation.

Thomas Schwarbrook, in 1720, received an annual salary of £8 for keeping the organ of Worcester Cathedral in repair. In 1748 he supplied the instrument with a new set of keys ; and in 1752 an order was made—

"That whereas it appears upon experience that £200 formerly agreed on will not be sufficient to add the stops that are wanting in the great organ, and to make it full, perfect, and complete in all its parts, ordered that £100 more be allowed—in all £300, effectually to repair and finish the same."

This is the latest notice I find of him.

Organs built by Thomas Schwarbrook.

1. St. Saviour's, Southwark. 1703.

This organ is commonly ascribed to Schwarbrook. If so, it must be one of his *earliest* instruments.

Hatton, in his *New View of London*, 1708, vol. ii., p. 538, says :—"The organ-case is also of oak, very lofty, elevated on 10 square pillars, the upper part whereof is adorned with 3 Fames, carved, standing in full proportion about 42 feet from the area of the isle."

2. St. Chad's, Shrewsbury. 1716.

" At the west end of the church of St. Chad, Shrewsbury, in a gallery, supported on Corinthian pilasters, was a large and remarkably handsome organ, in a case profusely adorned with carving. On the summit stood a figure of St. Chad, in his episcopal vestments. This noble instrument is said to have cost £1500, raised by subscription, towards which £100 was contributed by the Drapers' Company. It was made by Thomas Schwarbrook, a German artist of considerable eminence in his day, and erected in 1716. There is a tradition that the small organ in the Collegiate Church of Wolverhampton once belonged to St. Chad's, and preceded this."—MS. *History of Shrewsbury.*

This organ was removed in 1794.

3. St. Mary's, Warwick. 1717.

Samuel Ireland, in his *Picturesque Views of the Upper, or Warwickshire Avon,* 1795, p. 145, says :—" Within this church a very judicious alteration, that of removing the organ from the centre of the building to the west end, is now carrying into execution. The custom of placing the organ in the former situation, so universally prevalent, is matter of astonishment to those who are capable of feeling the full effect of beautiful symmetry in the works of architecture ; by this barbarism in taste, the sublime interest we take in the ' Long drawn aisle and fretted vault ' of our Gothic cathedrals is in a great degree destroyed, and the most striking and impressive works of human invention obscured by a range of gilded pipes, that can only be entitled to a secondary consideration." Schwarbrook's organ was erected by subscription.

4. Trinity Church, Coventry. 1732.

This instrument cost £600, and the old organ.

5. St. Michael's, Coventry. 1733.

This noble instrument (Schwarbrook's masterpiece) cost £1400.

It originally contained three remarkable stops—the *harp, lute,* and *dulcimer ;* but, in consequence of the " difficulty of keeping the *strings* in tune," they were removed in 1763.

6. Magdalen College, Oxford. 1740.

7. Lichfield Cathedral.

Removed in 1789.

8. Stratford-upon-Avon Church.

Now removed.

9. All Saints', Northampton.

35. *The Jordans, Father and Son.*

Sir John Hawkins, in his *History of Music,* tells us :—

" About the year 1700 one Jordan, a distiller, who had never been instructed in the business, but had a mechanical turn, and was an ingenious man, betook himself to the making of organs, and succeeded beyond expectation. He had a son, named Abraham, whom he instructed in the same business ; he made the organ for the chapel of the Duke of Chandos, at Cannons, near Edgware, and many organs for parish churches."*

Mr. W. B. Gilbert, in his *Antiquities of Maidstone*, shows that the Jordans were an ancient family located in that town as early as the fifteenth century. He says :—

"Thomas Jordan resided [in 1477] at the ancient family seat in Stone Street, called for some centuries 'Jordan's Hall.' Many members of this family have at various times been concerned in the affairs of Maidstone, and one of the Jordans in the last century was a distiller in the town. Having a genius for organ building, he removed to London, where he made many fine instruments. When the parish of Maidstone, in 1746, decided to have an organ in the church, Jordan was unanimously selected to build it, which he did to the entire satisfaction of the committee. Jordan's organ still remains in the parish church. Others of this family have also in their day been celebrated, and many descendants are yet to be found in the neighbourhood of Maidstone."

The Jordans are especially deserving of our notice, as to them we are indebted for the invention of the *swell*. Among the advertisements in the original edition of the *Spectator* (Feb. 8, 1712), is the following announcement :—

"Whereas Messrs. Abraham Jordan, senior and junior, have, with their own hands, joynery excepted, made and erected a very large organ in St. Magnus' Church, at the foot of London Bridge, consisting of four sets of keys, one of which is adapted to the art of emitting sounds by swelling the notes, *which never was in any organ before;* this instrument will be publicly opened on Sunday next, the performance by Mr. John Robinson. The above-said Abraham Jordan gives notice to all masters and performers, that he will attend, every day next week at the said church, to accommodate all those gentlemen who shall have a curiosity to hear it."†

Many of the old English organs, as we have seen by the specifications quoted, contained a department called the *Echo*. This consisted in a duplicate of the treble portion of some of the stops enclosed in a wooden box, which rendered the sound softer and more distant. Jordan's improvement was that of a sliding shutter, which was made to open and shut at the performer's pleasure, thus producing a "swelling" effect. The invention of the *swell* was well received, and Jordan soon found sufficient employment in carrying out his contrivance in many of the London organs.

---

* Although this is the *only* biographical notice of the Jordans handed down to us, yet, strange to say, their names are omitted in the index to the new edition of Hawkins's elaborate work.

† This curious advertisement was first noticed by Malcolm (see his *Londinum Redivivum*, vol. iv., p. 234) ; it was afterwards copied into Hone's *Every Day Book*, and the *Chronicles of London Bridge*.

With regard to the introduction of this important improvement upon the Continent, Burney has some interesting passages in his *Continental Tours*, which I extract.

Writing in 1771, he says :—

"It is very extraordinary that the *swell* which has been introduced into the English organ more than fifty years, and which is so capable of expression and of pleasing effects that it may well be said to be the greatest and most important improvement that ever was made on any keyed instrument, should be utterly *unknown* in Italy ; and, now I am on the subject, I must observe that most of the organs I have met with on the Continent seem to be inferior to ours by Father Smith, Byfield, or Snetzler, in everything but size ! As the churches there are very often immense, so are the organs ; the tone is indeed somewhat softened and refined by space and distance ; but, when heard near, it is intolerably coarse and noisy ; and, though the number of stops in these large instruments is very great, they afford but little variety, being for the most part duplicates in unisons and octaves to each other, such as the great and small 12ths, flutes, and 15ths ; hence in our organs not only the touch and tone, but the imitative stops, are greatly superior to those of any other organs I have met with."[*]

Again, in another of his works, a few years later, he says :—

"Before I left England M. Snetzler had told me that I should doubtless find *swells* in Berlin organs, though he was not certain that this improvement, which was English, had been adopted in other places on the Continent ; for Mr. Handel, several years ago, had desired him to describe in writing the manner in which the swell was produced, that he might send it to a particular friend in Berlin, who very much wished to introduce it there. But I enquired in vain of musical people in that city, whether they knew of any such machine as a swell, worked by pedals, in any of their organs : no such contrivance had ever been heard of, and it was difficult to explain it."

The first *swell* introduced into Germany appears to have been in Hildebrand's organ for the church of St. Michael, at Hamburg, built in 1764.[†] Burney says :—

"A swell has been *attempted* in this instrument, but with little effect ; only three stops have been put into it, and the power of *crescendo* and *diminuendo* is so small with them that, if I had not been told there was a swell, I should not have discovered it."[‡]

The Jordans also lay claim to other important inventions. The following advertisement is from the *London Journal* of Feb. 7th, 1729-30 :—

"An organ made by Jordan, being the first of its kind, the contrivance of which

---

[*] *Present State of Music in France and Italy*, 8vo, 1771, p. 375.

[†] *Present State of Music in Germany, the Netherlands, and United Provinces*, 8vo, second edit., 1775, vol. ii., p. 103.

[‡] *Present State of Music in Germany, the Netherlands, and United Provinces*, 8vo, second edit., 1775, vol. ii., p. 275.

is such that the master when he plays sits with his face to the audience, and, the keys being but three foot high, sees the whole company, and would be very useful in churches. This organ has but one set of keys, but is so contrived that the trumpet base, and trumpet treble, the sesquialtera and cornet stops, are put off and on by the feet, singly or altogether, at the master's discretion, and as quick as thought without taking the hands off the keys. The said Mr. Jordan invites all masters, gentlemen, and ladies, to come and hear this performance at the workhouse against St. George's Church, Southwark, and will give his attendance from 2 till 4 o'clock all next week, Ash Wednesday only excepted.

" N.B.—This organ was play'd on and approv'd by several masters, in publick, the latter end of November, and is fit for any small church or chappel."

Very little more remains to be said of the Jordans. In the parish books of St. Giles's, Cripplegate, under the date 1726, "a proposal was made, and accepted, by Abraham Jordan, organist, to take the organ to pieces, the builder having left it in a very imperfect state, and repair it *gratis*, on condition of having his salary secured to him for 21 years."[*] This entry, we presume, relates to the younger Jordan, whose latest work appears to have been the repair of the Durham Cathedral organ, in 1748.

List of Organs built by the Jordans.

1. St. Michael's, Paternoster Royal. 1700.

In the Parish Clerks' *Remarks on London*, 1732, it is said that this church has " no organ." Tradition, however, says that an instrument was given to this church by Abraham Jordan, in the year 1700. This organ was removed, in 1798, to make room for the old instrument from St. Ann's, Westminster, which was erected here with additions by the elder Gray.

2. Fulham Church, Middlesex. 1701.

An excellent instrument ; it still remains in almost its original state.

3. St. Antholin's, Watling Street. 1703.

4. St. Saviour's, Southwark. 1703.

5. The Chapel of the Duke of Chandos, at Cannons. 1720.

Handel used to perform upon this organ. When the Duke of Chandos died, the magnificent mansion, being thought to require an establishment too expensive for the income of his successor, was pulled down, and the materials sold by auction, in the year 1747. The organ, by the Jordans, forms an item in the sale catalogue. It is now in Trinity Church, Gosport, having been purchased at the dispersion of Cannons. A curious document, printed in 1748, is in the possession of Mr.

---

[*] Malcolm's *Londinum Redivivum*, vol. iii., p. 279.

Howlett, the organist of the church, being a sort of a debtor and creditor account connected with the purchase of the organ. It contains the following items :—

	£	s.	d.
" To cash paid Mr. Ch. Cock [the auctioneer] for the organ as it stood at Cannons	117	12	0
To do. paid Mr. Jordan for taking it down, and carriage to London	16	0	0
To ditto ditto for repairs	105	0	0
To ditto for a new swell	30	0	0
To ditto for repairs and carriage to Gosport	8	0	0 "

Several other curious items make the total outlay £344 15s. 6d. One is, "To cash paid Mr. Richard Mullings for painting the organ, as per bill, £1 14s." There is no name or date on the organ, but the Chandos arms are carved in gold on the top of the instrument. In the first edition it was said the organ is "now in Spa Fields Chapel." The name of the farm and glebe attached to Trinity Church is *Speed Field.* May not this have originated the mistake?

6. St. Magnus the Martyr, London Bridge. 1712.

This organ was the gift of Sir Charles Duncomb. It is exceedingly interesting, as being the first instrument in which the swell was used. (See the curious advertisement, *ante*, page 136.) It has been much altered and modernised by Parsons ; three only of the original four sets of keys remain.

7. Chelsea College. 1715.

8. Parish Church, Southampton. 1731.

In the St. James's *Evening Post*, for Feb. 13th and 24th, 1731, the following satirical notice occurs :—" Whereas it has been advertised that an organ had been lately set up by the ingenious Mr. Jordan, in the parish church of Holy-rood, in the town and county of Southampton ; this is to give notice that the churchwardens of the same parish are willing to show all manner of encouragement to any one who shall offer himself as organist, provided he understands nothing of his business ; the candidates to be approved of by the clerk of the said parish, who, according to his profound judgment and skill in music, promises, on his part, to determine the controversy fairly and impartially in favour of him that shall perform the worst."

" N.B. If any one who is an ingenious man in his profession (though never so strongly and with justice recommended by the ablest masters in the kingdom), should, notwithstanding this advertisement, presume to offer himself, he must expect to be rejected : it being fully resolved that none but bunglers, or those who know the least of their business, shall be entitled to the place. The latter are desired to meet in the said town of Southampton, on Lady-day next, being the 25th March, 1731, where they may be assured to find a very kind reception and a suitable encouragement."

9. St. Luke's, Old Street. 1733.

A MS. note by Pennant, the London historian, ascribes this organ to Jordan. This church was consecrated by Dr. Hare, Dean of St. Paul's and Bishop of Chichester, Oct. 18, 1733. The organ was presented to the parish by Mr. Buckley, an eminent brewer of Old Street.

10. Parish Church, Maidstone. 1746.

11. St. Bennet Fink, Threadneedle Street

" Madam Sarah Gregory, of this parish, gave four hundred pounds for building an organ, and a gallery for it ; which is now perfectly finished, and built by Mr. Jordan, besides ten pounds per *annum* to keep it up."—Paterson's *Pietas Londinensis*, 1714.

12. St. Dunstan's, Fleet Street.

Ascribed to Jordan, upon the authority of William Russell's MS. account of English organs. It is not mentioned by Hatton in 1708, or Paterson in 1714; but it is noticed in the Parish Clerks' *Remarks on London*, 1732. It must therefore have been erected some time between the two last-named dates.

13. St. Paul's, Shadwell.

14. The Portuguese Chapel, London.

15. The Abbey Church, Bath.

16. Covent Garden Theatre.

17. St. George's, Botolph Lane.

36. *Richard Bridge.*

This artist enjoyed considerable celebrity, and it is to be regretted that nothing is known of his biography. He is supposed to have been trained in the factory of the younger Harris. According to an advertisement in the *General Advertiser*, for Feb. 20, 1748, "Bridges, organ-builder," probably the same person, then resided in Hand Court, Holborn. We learn incidentally, from a note in Burney's *History*, that he died before 1776.

Organs built by Richard Bridge.

1. St. Paul's, Deptford. 1730.

2. Christ Church, Spitalfields. 1730.

This is esteemed the maker's best instrument. Its original cost was £600, not half its value. In point of number of pipes and stops, it is one of the largest parish organs in London.

3. St. Bartholomew the Great. 1731.

"We hear that the curious new organ made by Mr. Bridge, for the church of St. Bartholomew the Great, is to be opened on Sunday next with an anthem."— *Daily Advertiser*, Oct. 27, 1731.

4. St. George's-in-the-East, 1733.

5. Cuper's Gardens, Lambeth. 1740.

6. St. Anne's, Limehouse. 1741.

This instrument was burnt in 1851.

7. Enfield Church, Middlesex. 1753.

8. Faversham Church, Kent. 1754.

9. St. Leonard's, Shoreditch. 1757.

10. Eltham Church, Kent.

11. Spa Fields Chapel, Clerkenwell.

12. St. James's, Clerkenwell.
Removed in 1796 to Beccles, Suffolk.

13. Parish Church, Paddington.

Organs built by Byfield, Jordan, and Bridge, conjointly.

In consequence of the many new churches that were erected at the commencement of the last century, an equal number of organs was required, which induced many persons who were totally unskilled in the art and mystery of voicing organ-pipes to become builders. To prevent, therefore, the sad consequences which must have naturally followed, a coalition was formed between the three eminent artists of the day, Byfield, Jordan, and Bridge, who undertook to build organs at a very moderate charge, and to apply their united talents to each; the result of which was a fair, though moderate, compensation to themselves, and superior instruments to our churches.

I regret that I can name only two instruments in which the joint efforts of these eminent men were united :—

1. Great Yarmouth Church, Norfolk. 1733.
An instrument celebrated for its many beauties.

2. St. George's Chapel, Great Yarmouth. 1740.

37. John Byfield, Jun.

This is the next builder that comes under my notice. Nothing whatever is known of his biography; in fact, he is not named, as far as I can learn, by any writer upon the subject of organs, or organ-building. The works of the two Byfields pass current under one head.

According to a MS. note in the handwriting of Dr. Benjamin Cooke, he died in 1774.

Organs built by John Byfield, Jun.

1. St. Botolph's, Bishopsgate. 1750.
2. Christ Church Cathedral, Dublin. 1751.
3. St. Mary's, Rotherhithe. 1764.
4. St. John's College, Oxford. 1768.
5. Charlotte Chapel, Pimlico. 1770.
6. Drury Lane Theatre. 1769.

L

7. Magdalen College Hall, Oxford.
8. Woolwich Church, Kent.

Also ascribed to Bridge.

9. Cardiff, Glamorganshire.
10. Highgate Chapel.
11. St. Bartholomew the Less.
12. The Chapel of Greenwich Hospital.

Destroyed in the fire which consumed the chapel in 1779.

13. Berwick Street Chapel, Soho.   1768.
14. The Theatre, Oxford.   1768.
15. Barking Church, Essex.   1770.
16. Newbury Church, Berks.   1770.
17. St. Mary's, Islington.   1771.
18. St. Lawrence, Reading, Berks.   1771.

The six last-named organs were built conjointly with Green.

38. *Messrs. Glyn and Parker.*

The above names are new in the annals of organ-building. Although eminent builders, their celebrity was of a local character. They resided at Salford, near Manchester, and built a number of instruments for Lancashire and the neighbouring counties. One organ, that of Poynton Church, attracted the notice of Handel, who is reported to have been so pleased with it, that he employed Parker to erect the famous instrument for the Foundling Hospital.*

The following is a list of organs by these builders :—

Organs built by Glyn and Parker.

1. Collegiate Church, Manchester.   1730.
2. St. Ann's Church, Manchester.
3. St. John's Church, Manchester.
4. Bury Church, Lancashire.

---

* Dr. Burney, in his " Sketch of the Life of Handel," prefixed to his *Account of the Commemoration*, 4to, 1785, says :—" The organ in the chapel of this hospital was a *present* from Handel." But how are we to reconcile this statement with the following notice in the *European Magazine*, for February, 1799?—" Handel *did not give* the organ to the Foundling Hospital. It was built at the *expense* of the Charity, under the direction of Dr. Smith, the learned Master of Trinity College, Cambridge, who added demitones, &c., and some of the niceties not occurring in other organs." Handel conducted the performance at the opening of this organ in 1749.

5. Poynton Church, Lancashire. 1748.
6. Chapel-en-le-Frith, Derbyshire.
7. Prestbury Church, Gloucestershire.
8. Leek Parish Church, Staffordshire.
9. Foundling Hospital, London. 1749.
10. Allhallows the Great, Thames Street. 1749.

39. Thomas Griffin.

This person, a barber, and Gresham Professor of Music ! is said to have built several City organs, but I can only name one, upon the authority of Malcolm's *Londinum Redivivum*, iii., 553.

Organ built by Thomas Griffin.

St. Helen's, Bishopsgate, 1741.

" 1741. Thomas Gryffin agreed to build an organ, value £500, on condition he should receive £250, and £25 *per annum* during his life. To play himself or provide an organist."—*Parish Books.*

40. John Snetzler.

This truly eminent builder was born at Passau, in Germany, about the year 1710, where several of his organs are still to be seen. He acquired some fame by his restoration of the Cathedral organ in that city, and was afterwards induced to settle in England. After building several excellent organs, he erected the noble instrument at Lynn Regis, in Norfolk, being recommended to the Corporation of that town by Dr. Burney. The double diapason and dulciana stops in this organ were novelties which attracted attention, and fully established his fame in this country.

Snetzler had but an imperfect pronunciation of the English language, which gave him, like many foreigners, a very quaint way of expressing himself. Two stories are current of his peculiarities in this respect. One was on the occasion of the erection of his new organ at Halifax, in Yorkshire. Wainwright (afterwards Dr. Wainwright, and organist of the Collegiate Church, Manchester) and Herschel (subsequently known as the great Astronomer) were amongst the candidates for the situation of organist. The former so annoyed Snetzler by his rapid playing, that he paced the church

L 2

exclaiming :—" He do run over de keys like one cat, and do not give my pipes time to speak." He also told the churchwardens of Lynn, upon their asking him what their old organ would be worth if repaired, " If they would lay out a hundred pounds upon it, perhaps it would be worth fifty."

Snetzler lived to a very advanced age, and died either at the end of the last, or the commencement of the present century. He is said to have saved sufficient money to return and settle in his native country, which he accordingly did ; but, having been so long accustomed to London porter and English fare, he found in his old age that he could not do without them, so he came back to London, where he died.

Organs built by Snetzler.

1. Chesterfield Church, Derbyshire.   1741.
2. Finchley Church, Middlesex.   1749.
3. St. Mary's, Hull, Yorkshire.   1750.
4. St. Margaret's, Lynn Regis, Norfolk.   1754.

Built, under the superintendence of Dr. Burney, at a cost of £700.

5. St. Paul's, Sheffield.   1755.
6. Christ Church, Broadway, Westminster.   1760.

This organ is said to have been originally built for the Duke of Bedford.

7. Leatherhead Church, Surrey.   1760.
8. St. George's, Hanover Square.   1761.
9. Cambridge, U.S.   1761.
10. Ludlow, Shropshire.   1764.
11. Halifax Church, Yorkshire.   1766.
12. Louth Church, Lincolnshire.   1769.
13. Beverley Minster, Yorkshire.   1769.

This organ was opened with the performance of two Oratorios, Sept. 20 and 21, 1769.

14. Richmond Church, Surrey.   1770.

The gift of S. Sprags, Esq.

15. Edmonton Church, Middlesex.   1772.
16. St. Martin's, Leicester.   1774.

A remarkably fine instrument.

17. Scarborough Church, Yorkshire.   1780.
18. Pontefract Church, Yorkshire.
19. Sculthorpe, near Fakenham, Norfolk.

20. Rotherham Church, Yorkshire.

It appears from a short account printed by Dr. Sewell, the present organist, that this organ was completed and opened on St. Thomas's Day, Dec. 21, 1777. It was built by subscription, the total amount of which was £678 0s. 11d. Dr. Sewell adds :—" The stopped diapason in the choir organ, and also the flute stop, are allowed by some of the most eminent judges now living to be equal, if not superior, to anything they have ever heard. The pedal pipes, which were added with the dulciana stop about twenty-six years ago, by Gray and Davison, of London, are very fine."

21. Whitehaven Church, Cumberland.

22. St. John's (formerly St. Augustine's), Hackney.

23. St. Clement's, Lombard Street, City.

24. St. Margaret's Chapel, Bath.

25. St. Peter's College, Cambridge.

This instrument is remarkable for having the *Echo* (the predecessor of the swell) still remaining.

According to Mr. Hopkins it is really a *swell* of three stops, acting on choir organ keys.

26. The German Lutheran Chapel in the Savoy.

The late Charles Wesley, in a letter in my possession, says, this was the first instrument in this country provided with a pedal clavier.

27. The German Calvinistic Church, Savoy.

Presented by the builder.

28. St. Ann's Church, Belfast.

29. Hillsborough Church.

30. The Chapel at Donegal.

Removed from Armagh Cathedral, and burnt on the same evening that it was removed.

31. Parish Church, Leeds.

32. Buckingham Palace.

Now in the German Chapel, St. James's.

33. St. Mary's, Nottingham.

34. St. Mary's, Huntingdon.

35. All Saints', Huntingdon.

41. *Messrs. Crang and Hancock.*

Crang was a Devonshire man, and, after settling in London, became a partner with Hancock, a good voicer of reeds. Hancock added new reeds to many of Father Smith's organs. Crang appears to have been chiefly employed in altering the old echoes into swells.

He made this improvement in the organs of St. Paul's Cathedral ; St. Peter's, Cornhill ; St. Clement Danes ; &c.

It appears that there were two Hancocks, probably ·brothers, John and James ; and they are specially mentioned in the contract for an organ at Chelmsford in 1772. The following payments relating to these makers are extracted from the accounts of the church-wardens of Maidstone, printed in Mr. W. B. Gilbert's *Memorials of the Collegiate Church of Maidstone* :—

		£	s.	d.
" 1755.	Mr. Crang for cleaning and repairing the organ . .	8	8	0
1760.	Mr. John Crang's bill for cleaning the organ . . .	8	8	0
1765.	Mr. Crang's bill for repairing and making additions to the organ	52	7	0
1770.	Mr. Crang for cleaning the organ	8	8	0
1790—Oct 13.	Mr. James Hancock, as per bill for organ . .	10	10	0."

Mr. Gilbert tells me that John Hancock, "organ-builder of Wych Street, London," who had been employed for some time in super-intending the repairs and additions to the Maidstone organ, died very suddenly near that town, in January, 1792. James Hancock was living in 1820, and probably some years later.

Organs built by Crang and the Hancocks.

1. St. John's, Horsleydown. 1770.
2. Barnstaple Church. 1772.
3. Chelmsford, Essex. 1772.
4. St. George the Martyr, Queen's Square. 1773.
5. St. Vedast, Foster Lane. 1780.
6. Brompton Chapel.
7. St. Margaret's, Leicester.
8. St. Mary's, Scarborough.
9. St. Mary's Cray, Kent.

This organ was built by James Hancock.

42. *Samuel Green.*

Although generally considered a contemporary of Snetzler, this eminent artist was not born till 1740 ; thirty years after the birth of the former. In all probability he was brought up in the establishment of Byfield, Bridge, and Jordan, as in the earlier part of his career he was in partnership with the younger Byfield. He seems to have been greatly patronized by King George the Third, and, in consequence, to have been employed in all parts of the kingdom.

The organs built by Green are characterised by a peculiar sweetness and delicacy of tone, entirely original ; and, probably, in this respect he has never been excelled.

"We possess more cathedral and collegiate organs of this builder's construction than of any other ; and although patronized as he was by his Majesty George the Third, and long at the head of his profession, this admirable artist scarcely obtained a moderate competency. His zeal for the mechanical improvement of the organ consumed much of his valuable time in experimental labours, which to him produced little or no emolument ; and it is painful to know that a man so eminent in his profession should not, at his decease, be able to leave even a slender provision for his family." *

The newspapers of the day record that "Mr. Samuel Green, organ-builder to the King, died at Isleworth, Sept. 14, 1796, at the age of 56."

The following list of Green's organs is taken *verbatim* from the *Gentleman's Magazine*, for June, 1814, as extracted from the builder's own account book. I have added a few dates, &c., in brackets :—

Organs built by Samuel Green.

CATHEDRAL AND COLLEGIATE ORGANS.

1. Canterbury Cathedral. 1784.
2. Wells Cathedral. 1786.
3. St. George's Chapel, Windsor. 1790.
4. Lichfield Cathedral. 1789.
5. Salisbury Cathedral. 1721.
6. Rochester Cathedral. 1791.
7. Bangor Cathedral. 1779.
8. York Cathedral (restoration only). 1803.
9. Cashel Cathedral. 1786.
10. New College Chapel, Oxon (restoration only). 1776.
11. Trinity College Chapel, Dublin.
12. Winchester College Chapel. 1780.

---

* *Christian Remembrancer*, Jan., 1834. One of a series of excellent papers on old organs and organ-builders.

LONDON ORGANS.

13. St. Katherine's Hospital. 1778.
14. St. Botolph, Aldersgate Street.
15. St. Peter-le-Poer. 1792.
16. St. Mary at Hill. 1788.
17. St. Michael's, Cornhill (restoration only). 1790.
18. St. Olave's, Hart Street. 1781.
19. Broad Street Chapel, Islington.
20. Magdalen Chapel.
21. Freemasons' Hall.
22. Concert Room, Opera House. 1794.
23. Broad Court Chapel. 1796.

LOCAL ORGANS, &c.

24. St. Petersburg.
25. Greenwich Hospital. 1789.
26. Sleaford, Lincolnshire.
27. Manchester (St. Thomas Ardwick). 1787.
28. Helston, Cornwall. 1799.
29. Walsal, Staffordshire.
30. Wrexham.
31. Wycombe.
32. Nayland, Essex.
33. Wisbeach, Cambridgeshire. 1789.
34. Cirencester.
35. Macclesfield.
36. Stockport (St. Peter's). 1788.
37. Bath.
38. St. Michael's, Cornwall.
39. Tunbridge, Kent. 1788.
40. Loughborough.
41. Tamworth.
42. Walton.
43. Leigh.
44. Chatham.
45. Bolton, Lancashire. 1795.
46. Cranbourne, Cornwall.
47. Aberdeen Episcopal Chapel.
48. Kingston Church, Jamaica.

49. Pomfret Parish Church.
[50. Oudwick, St. Thomas's, 1787.]

43. *John Avery.*

Very little is known of this builder. He is said to have been a dissipated character : he was certainly an excellent workman. The dates of his organs range between 1775 and 1808. He died in the latter year, during the time he was engaged in finishing the organ of Carlisle Cathedral, his last work.

Organs built by Avery.

1. St. Stephen's, Coleman Street, City. 1775.
2. Croydon Church, Surrey. 1794.

Avery considered this instrument his best work. This fine organ, together with the church, was destroyed by fire in 1866.

3. Winchester Cathedral. 1799.
4. Christ Church, Bath. 1800.
5. St. Margaret's Church, Westminster. 1804.
6. King's College Chapel, Cambridge. 1804.

Some of the earlier work of Dallam's organ was, no doubt, incorporated in this instrument by Avery. The case is the original one, erected by Chapman and Hartop in 1606. Cole, the antiquary, gives a description of its appearance in his time :—

"Over each side of the choir door towards the choir are the coats of arms of this and Eaton College, in shields neatly carved and blazoned, and directly over it stand the organs. The small choir organ hangs somewhat over the door into the choir, and is elegant and carved about the mouldings and wainscot part with beautiful gilt and painted pipes, adorned with the two aforesaid college arms, and other devices, as portcullises, fleurs-de-lis, roses, all crowned. Over the middle part of this organ, which is the lowest, are the college arms again carved, and over the two side parts, where the pipes are much larger, are two large royal crowns. This choir organ was put up about the year 1661, and cost about £200, and is a mighty neat one : this stands just before the great organ, the pipes of which on this side are neither gilt nor painted, but quite plain. Over the lower middle part of it are the royal arms, supported by a lion and unicorn, garter round them, and crowned. Over the middle part, fronting the antechapel, is an image of King David playing on his harp, and on each side of him, over the large pipes, are two Gothic carved pyramids. The pipes on this side are painted, gilt, and adorned as those of the choir organ. These organs were put up again, after they had been demolished by the Puritans of 1643, in 1661, and, though they are not the best of the sort, yet they are not by any means the worst."

7. Sevenoaks Church, Kent.   1798.

The following is a copy of a curious handbill in the possession of Mr. W. B. Gilbert, Mus. Bac. :—

" Sevenoaks, Oct. 17, 1788.   This is to give notice that the magnificent organ left to the parish of Sevenoaks by James Wright, Esq., late of Greenwich, will be opened in a *grave* and *patriotic* manner by the celebrated Mr. Wesley, on Sunday, the 28th of October.   At the same time a collection will be made for the relief of the widows and children of those brave seamen that fell, and also those wounded, in the late glorious victory of Admiral Nelson over the French fleet on the 1st of August.   Service at 11."

8.   Carlisle Cathedral.   1808.

44.   *The Englands, Father and Son.*

These two organ-builders are generally confounded.   George England flourished between the years 1740 and 1788, and George Pike England, his son, between 1788 and 1814.   The former married the daughter of Richard Bridge.

The elder England built many noble organs, a few of which may be enumerated.

Organs built by George England.

1.   St. Stephen's, Wallbrook.   1760.
2.   Gravesend Church, Kent.   1764.
3.   Ashton-under-line, Lancashire.   1770.
4.   St. Michael's, Queenhithe.   1779.
5.   St. Mary's, Aldermary.   1781.

The last two organs were built in conjunction with Hugh Russell.

6.   St. Matthew's, Friday Street.
7.   St. Mildred's, Poultry.
8.   German Lutheran Church, Goodman's Fields.
9.   The Chapel of Dulwich College.
10.   St. Margaret Moses.
11.   St. Alphege, Greenwich.

With regard to the son, our information is more satisfactory ; the following list of organs built by him being copied from his own account book, kindly lent me by Mr. Hill, the eminent organ-·ilder :—

Organs built by G. P. England.

1. St. George's Chapel, Portsmouth Common.   1788.
2. St. James's Church, Clerkenwell.   1790.

This organ cost £500 and the old organ, which was valued at £105.   It was afterwards sold by England to the parish church of Beccles, Suffolk, for £220.

3. Fetter Lane Chapel.   1790.
4. Warminster Church, Wiltshire.   1791.
5. The Adelphi Chapel.   1791.
6. Gainsborough Church, Lincolnshire.   1793.
7. Newington Church, Surrey.   1794.
8. Blandford Church.   1794.
9. Carmarthen Church, South Wales.   1796.
10. St. Margaret's, Lothbury.   1801.
11. The Sardinian Chapel.   1802.
12. Newark Church, Notts.   1803.
13. Parish Church, Sheffield.   1805.
    This organ cost £770.
14. St. Philip's, Birmingham.   1805.
15. St. Martin's, Outwich.   1805.
16. Hinckley Parish Church.   1808.
17. Stourbridge Church.   1809.
18. Richmond Church, Yorkshire.   1809.
19. High Church, Lancaster.   1809.
    This organ cost £672.
20. Shiffnall Parish Church, Salop.   1811.
21. Ulverstone Parish Church.   1811.
22. St. Mary's Chapel, Islington.   1812.

45. *Paul Micheau.*

This builder was a native of Germany. He came to England about 1780, and settled in the city of Exeter. He built several organs for churches in Devon, and was largely employed in restorations and repairs. He had the care of Loosemore's noble organ in Exeter Cathedral, and made several improvements in that instrument. He was also employed to keep the organ of the Parish Church of Tiverton in order, for which he received the sum of £10 per annum. For the information concerning this builder I am indebted to Mr. W. B. Gilbert.

Organs built by Paul Micheau.

1. St. Mary Arches, Exeter.
2. St. Mary Major, Exeter.
3. Etwall Church, Derbyshire.

46.   *Organ-builders of the end of the Eighteenth Century.*

The *Musical Directory for the year* 1794, a curious and perhaps unique little book, in the library of the Sacred Harmonic Society, gives the following names, and places of residence, of the organ-builders living in London in that year :—

" Avery, St. Margaret's Church-yard, Westminster ; Cummins, Pentonville ; Elliot (Thomas), 10, Sutton Street, Soho ; England, Stephen Street, Rathbone Place ; Flight & Kelly, Exeter Change ; Green (Samuel), Isleworth ; Holland (Henry), Little Chelsea ; Maher, Lower Lambeth Marsh ; Pister (E. & J.), 116, Leadenhall Street ; Russell, Theobald's Road."

The most important of these builders have been carefully chronicled in these pages, and, if I have not mentioned all, it is because the records of their labours are not easily attainable. Other well-known names might be added to this list, such as Gray, Lincoln, and the two Allens ; but they more properly belong to a somewhat later period, to which my historical sketch does not extend.

47.   *Progress of Organ-building in Germany.*

During the eighteenth century Germany was especially prolific in large organs, and most of these instruments still remain as honourable memorials of the talents of their builders.

48.   *Andreas Silbermann.*

Amongst the most renowned organ-builders that the world has produced are the celebrated Silbermann family.   The founder of this race of talented men was Andreas Silbermann, born at Frauenstein, Saxony, in 1678.   The particulars of his life are not recorded ; but, during the space of twenty-seven years in which he flourished, he built at least twenty-nine organs.   He died in 1733.

Organs built by Andreas Silbermann.

1. St. Nicholas, Strasburg. 1707.
2. Convent of St. Margaret, Strasburg. 1709.
3. Protestant Church of St. Pierre, Strasburg. 1709.
4. Mauerstein, Lower Rhine. 1710.
5. Basle Cathedral. 1711.
6. Convent of Guillelmines, Strasburg. 1712.
7. Oberenheim. 1713.
8. Giedertheim. 1715.
9. Strasburg Cathedral. 1714-16.
10. St. Etienne, Strasburg. 1717.
11. Andlau. 1717.
12. The Madeleine Convent, Strasburg. 1718.
13. Ebersheimmünster, Lower Rhine. 1718.
14. St. Leonard's, Basle. 1718.
15. Hanau. 1719.
16. Grendelbach. 1719.
17. Lautenbach, Upper Rhine. 1719.
18. St. Jean, Weissemburg. 1720.
19. St. Leonard's, near Oberenheim. 1721.
20. Altenheim, near Offenburg. 1722.
21. Kolbsheim. 1722.
22. Church of the Dominicans, Colmar. 1726.
23. St. Guillaume, Strasburg. 1728.
24. Bischweiter. 1729.
25. Altorf, Lower Rhine. 1730.
26. Kœnigsbrük Abbey, Lower Rhine. 1732.
27. Hospital Church, Colmar. 1732.
28. Protestant Church, Colmar. 1733.
29. Rosheim. 1733.

49. *Gottfried Silbermann.*

Gottfried Silbermann, brother of the preceding, was born at Frauenstein, in 1684. After remaining some years in the workshop of his brother, he went into France, where, we are informed, "he worked and resided many years."[*] He was the inventor of the

---

[*] Burney tells us that "the French organ-builders are much esteemed by the Germans themselves, for the simplicity of their movements and the mechanism of the whole."—*Tour*

" Clavecin d'amour," and one of the earliest makers of the pianoforte. He died in 1754, during the period in which he was engaged on the Royal Catholic Church organ at Dresden, which noble instrument was completed by his nephew, Jean Daniel Silbermann.

Organs built by Gottfried Silbermann.

1. Freiberg Cathedral. 1714.
2. St. Pierre, Freiberg. 1720.
3. The Royal Church of the Evangelists, Dresden. 1720.
4. St. Sophia, Dresden. 1740.
5. Church of Notre Dame, Dresden. 1736.
6. Poenitz, near Altenburg. 1737.
7. The Royal Catholic Church, Dresden. 1754.

50. Johann Andreas Silbermann.

This branch of the Silbermann family was the eldest son of Andreas, and consequently the nephew of the last-named. He was born at Strasburg, where his father resided, in 1712. He enjoyed considerable reputation as an organ-builder, and was beloved by his fellow-citizens for his social qualities. He died at Strasburg in 1783, with the title of Member of the Council of that city, leaving two sons, one of whom, Johann Josias, afterwards distinguished himself as a maker of musical instruments.

Johann Andreas Silbermann built fifty-four organs, the most important of which are :—

1. St. Thomas, Strasburg. 1740.
2. St. Etienne, Basle.
3. St. Theodore, Basle.
4. The Abbey of St. Blaise in the Black Forest.

---

in Germany, vol. I., p. 21. During the period that Gottfried Silbermann studied in France, the best builders were Charles Dallery and François Clicquot. These builders chiefly worked together, and among their organs we may name those in the churches of St. Gervais, St. Nicolas des Champs, St. Méry, St. Sulpice, the chapel at Versailles, and the Abbey of Clairmarais. Pierre Dallery built the organ of Notre Dame, and those in the churches of St. Lazare and St. Suzanne at Paris. A descendant, Pierre François Dallery, was living as late as 1833. M. Danjou, the late organist of Notre Dame, Paris, discovered, in 1843, in the church of Soliez Ville, in the department of the Var, an organ built as far back as the year 1450. It is in many respects an interesting discovery. Up to that time the oldest organ known in France was that of Gomesse, near Paris.

51. *Johann Daniel Silbermann.*

This builder, the last of the family whom I shall particularise, was the second son of Andreas. He was born, in 1717, at Strasburg, and studied organ-building, under his uncle Gottfried, at Dresden. Upon the death of the latter, in 1754, whilst constructing the noble organ of the Royal Catholic Church at Dresden (before mentioned), he succeeded to his uncle's business. He died at Leipsic, in 1766.

52. *Contemporaries and Successors of the Silbermanns.*

The family just mentioned had many contemporaries and successors, some few of which, if not equally eminent, are deserving of a notice in these pages. Zacharias Thessner built, in 1702, the great organ in the Cathedral of Merseberg ; it had 68 registers, 5 manuals, and pedal. Adam Sterzing built, in 1707, a noble organ for the Court Church at Eisenach ; it had 58 registers, 4 manuals, and pedal. Eugenius Casparini (then an aged man), in conjunction with his son, Adam Horatius, built, in 1703, an organ for the Church of St. Peter and St. Paul at Görlitz, in Upper Lusatia ; it had 82 registers, 57 of which were whole stops. Henrich Herbst and his son built, in 1718, an organ at Halberstadt, with 74 registers, 3 manuals in front, 2 manuals at the sides, and pedal.

Michael Engler, of Silesia, who flourished between 1688 and 1760, built many noble instruments ; amongst which we may instance those in the churches of St. Salvator and St. Elizabeth at Breslau. He was succeeded by his son and grandson, Theophilus Benjamin and Jean Theophilus. The latter flourished between 1775 and 1822.

Johann Michael Roder, of Berlin, built the great organ in the church of St. Mary Magdalen, at Breslau. It was erected in 1726. Then we have Joachim Wagner, who, in 1725, built the instrument in the Garrison Church at Berlin, of which Dr. Burney has left us a curious description, in his *German Tour.*

The Hildebrands—Zacharie, who flourished between 1680 and 1743, and Johann Gottfried, his son—were eminent artists. The latter built the noble organ in St. Michael's Church, Hamburg, in 1762, at an expense of £4000.

But the two best-known organ-builders of the latter half of the eighteenth century are Johann Gabler, of Ulm, and Christian Müller, of Amsterdam ; the former, by his glorious organ in the Benedictine Abbey of Weingarten ; the latter, by the "world-famed" Haarlem organ.

In this slight sketch of the history of the organ, from the earliest time to the close of the eighteenth century, I have doubtless omitted some names deserving of "honourable mention," and left untold many things of importance to the inquiring student during this long period of progress. But all I professed to do was to treat the subject in an historical point of view, avoiding all details of a technical nature, keeping my attention strictly to facts. The labours of the principal builders towards the perfection of the "king of instruments" will receive their proper amount of attention, and their merits be duly chronicled, in the able Treatise which follows this Introduction.

THE ORGAN:

A COMPREHENSIVE TREATISE, ETC.

BY

EDWARD J. HOPKINS.

M

THE ORGAN.

———o———

PRELIMINARY OBSERVATIONS.

THE Organ, as it is usually met with in cathedrals and large churches, town-halls and concert-rooms, is divided interiorly into four principal parts. The chief of these divisions, or *departments*, is that styled the Great Organ; the others are the Pedal Organ, the Choir Organ, and the Swell Organ. Some instruments of the first magnitude have, in addition to the foregoing, a fourth Manual Organ, which is usually a Solo Organ, as at St. Paul's Cathedral, Westminster Abbey, St. George's Hall, Liverpool, the Parish Church, Leeds, &c.; while in a few instances there is even a fifth Manual Organ, or Echo, in addition to a Solo Organ, as at the Parish Church, Doncaster, and the Town Hall, Leeds. In the former example the Echo has a separate manual, in the latter it is attached to one of the other rows of keys.

The several departments just enumerated are, in one sense, so many separate and distinct organs. This is the case so far, that each has usually its own *sound-board, stops, clavier,* &c.; but the whole of them being generally enclosed in one case (the choir organ sometimes excepted), with the different claviers so arranged as to be under the control of one performer, they are thus made to assume the appearance of one vast and comprehensive instrument. The choir organ is occasionally enclosed in a separate case, placed in front of and below the chief one,[*] as at St. Sepulchre's, Snow Hill; St. Lawrence, Jewry; St. James's, Piccadilly; St. Martin's-in-the-Fields, &c.; though not so arranged as to give it the appearance of being a detached portion, but harmonising with the main body of the

---

[*] In England it is customary to speak of the separate choir organ *as seen from the body of the church;* while in Germany it is better known in reference to its position to that of the organist when seated at the keys. Thus in England it is described as "the choir organ in front," and in Germany as the "back-choir organ." In the estimates and accounts of the early seventeenth century organs, the two departments, which formed the entire musical portions of the largest instruments of the period, were frequently described as the "greate and litel organs;" while in other instances they were spoken of collectively as "the double organ."

instrument; so that, when viewed from the church, the two present one handsome and noble façade.

In a few instances the main body of the organ is *divided*, leaving between a clear prospect of the building from end to end, as at Westminster Abbey, Rochester Cathedral, &c.; in which case a general unity in the design and grouping of the several parts of the case is more or less observed.

The several departments already named have, generally speaking, certain fixed situations allotted to them in the instrument. For instance:

The *Great Organ* is generally placed immediately behind the front pipes of the instrument (see *fig.* 1); many of which "show pipes" form a portion of those belonging to that department.

The *Choir Organ*, when not located "in front," is stationed behind, and at a convenient distance from the great organ (*fig.* 2), a foot-way (marked 3, in the general section) sixteen or eighteen inches wide being left between the two as a pathway for the convenience of tuning, &c., called the *passage-board*.

The *Swell Organ* is placed above the choir organ, when the latter is not situated in front (*fig.* 4). In small instruments, where the choir organ is altogether omitted, the swell is often, though not advisedly, stationed over the great organ.

The *Pedal Organ* is either placed, in an entire state, behind, and parallel with the others (as shown in *fig.* 5), or it is divided, and a part arranged on each side of them. When there is no choir organ, or when that department appears in front, the pedal organ is frequently stationed to the rear of the great organ (occupying the usual position of the choir organ), with the swell above.

The structural portions of an organ are classed into three great divisions, namely (1) the machine by which the wind is collected for the production of sound, the channels through which it is conducted to the various departments of the instrument, and then re-distributed among the numerous pipes of each; (2) the mechanism by which the several departments are individually or conjointly brought into use, and their stops brought under perfect control; and (3) the sound-producing parts, namely, the pipe-work.

These several divisions, together with the case, constitute what is known, *par excellence*, as "THE Organ;" the construction and operation of which form the subject-matter of the following chapters.

Division I.

THE EXTERIOR OF THE ORGAN.

CHAPTER I.

THE ORGAN CASE.

Its nature and use, and the materials of which it is formed.
1. MOST organs are enclosed, at the back, sides, and front, in a case of wood—a covering that is of service to the instrument in protecting its mechanism and pipe-work from external injury, and rendering the working of its movements, when in operation, less audible. The case is of great utility, also, in rendering the instrument an ornament to the church, by bringing its appearance into perfect keeping with the other carved wood-work of the edifice. The organ-case is usually constructed either of oak, mahogany, walnut-tree wood, or of deal. When made of the last-mentioned material, it is either grained to imitate one of the fore-mentioned woods, or, what is much better, more real and light-looking, it is simply varnished. The case to the choir organ, in the chapel of Magdalen College, Oxford, is of stone.

The general structure of the organ-case, and the means of ingress.
2. The organ-case is usually divided, horizontally, into two stages, either by an impost or by a bold moulding ; and vertically, into numerous *compartments*, by pilasters, or by buttresses. The compartments below the impost are usually filled in with panelling work all round, except in front, towards the centre, where the claviers are, generally speaking, located. The upper divisions are also frequently filled in similarly with panelling work, except where intended to receive pipes, as is the case in most small organs, where the chief wooden pipes are ranged immediately above the impost along the two sides, and, being lightly varnished and otherwise decorated, present a pleasant appearance. Some of the panelled parts are hung on hinges, or are otherwise made moveable, so as to form entrance doors, for the purpose of tuning, or for facilitating admittance to the mechanism and other work.

3. The front of the organ-case above the impost is generally formed into a series of open-work compartments—an arrangement that is so far advantageous to the tone of the instrument, that it admits of many of the pipes of some of the chief stops being placed in these openings, whereby the predominance of their tone is more effectually secured ; the interstices between the bodies and feet of the pipes being calculated to assist the egress of the sound produced by those inside. Cathedral organs that occupy a central position have generally two fronts, facing east and west respectively—an arrangement that materially assists the progress of the tone of the instrument through the building laterally ; while many church organs of recent construction have no case above the impost, but pipes sustained by light wooden framework, or by elegantly designed iron-work.

The general arrangement of the front pipes.
4. The front pipes are very rarely arranged to succeed each other according to the sound they produce in the musical scale. like the keys—semitonally—as, in that case, all the large ones would be

on one side and the small on the other, giving to the whole the appearance of a huge set of Pan-pipes ; but they are placed so as to present a symmetrical appearance.

5. The first and most obvious arrangement is into groups of large and small pipes, forming separate compartments. The admixture of these large and small compartments constitutes one of the principal features of the design.

The various figures in which the front pipes are arranged.   6. Next, the pipes occupying the large and small compartments are arranged according to one or more of many different plans, and in varied forms, with the view to gaining greater contrast and elegance in the appearance of the organ.

7. The chief of these diversified plans, and the names by which they are known, are as follow :—

8. Pipes that are placed in a projecting semicircle are said to form *Towers.* (See *a a, fig.* 6.) Examples of this kind of pipe arrangement occur in the graceful cases of the organs at Whitehall Chapel ; St. Clement's, Strand ; and indeed in most organs.

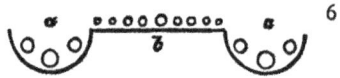

9. Pipes standing in an angle are termed *Pointed Towers* (*a a, fig.* 7) ; specimens of which may be seen at St. Sepulchre's, Snow Hill ; and at St. Nicholas's, Newcastle-on-Tyne.

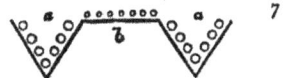

10. Groups of pipes inclining inwards, semicircularly, are said to form *Niches* (*b, fig.* 8) ; of which an example occurs in the centre of the case of the organ at St. Philip's, Stepney.

11. A *Breasted* compartment is that of which the middle part is a little rounded forwards, as shown at *a,* in *fig.* 9. Examples occupy the centre of the handsome organ-cases at St. Mary's, Islington, and St. John's, Horselydown.

12. If the pipes are placed curvilinearly, the compartment is said to be of the *Ogee* form. (See *fig.* 10.) Of this kind of pipe arrangement examples exist at St. Olave's, Southwark, and at St. Helen's, Bishopsgate.

13. When the pipes are continued in a straight line, they are called *Flats* (see *figs.* 11, 12, 13, 14 ; also *b b, figs.* 6 and 7) ; of which examples occur in all organs.

14. Some organ-cases have what are denominated *Flat Towers,* of which very fine examples occur at St. Paul's Cathedral. Such are formed by arranging the pipes that in some organ-cases stand in a semicircle, or in an angle, parallelwise. Others, again, have what are called "circular ends" ; *i.e.,* the case, instead of being flanked at each side by a tower, has a curved compartment, resembling half a circular tower, furnished with a greater number of narrow pipes. The organ at Exeter Hall has circular ends.

15. The front pipes are generally planted in tonal succession in *each half* of the case; that is to say, those which occur in the compartments to the left of the centre give one or other of the following six sounds, namely, C, D, E, F sharp, G sharp, or A sharp: the pipes occupying those to the right sounding either C sharp, D sharp, F, G, A, or B. This alternate distribution may readily be discovered by first drawing the open diapason, or whatever other stop may have most of its pipes appearing "im prospect" (as the Germans have it), and then slowly playing the chromatic scale in its ascending form; when the sounds will be noticed to proceed first from the left, and then from the right hand side of the front. Occasionally, however, the order is reversed.

16. As to the precise *situation* in the front where these alternate speaking pipes will be found, this depends on the design of the case. If it comprises three towers, a large centre one and two smaller flanking ones, as in most of Harris and Snetzler's organs, the largest pipe will generally be found in the middle of the centre tower, those which follow standing right and left alternately, the arrangement being continued in the lateral towers; if there are two large lateral towers, and a smaller one in the centre, the alternate plantation will commence from the sides. In Smith's four-tower fronts the distribution is usually among the entire number of towers. In the majority of instances, therefore, a pipe which on the second side *replies* to a particular one on the first will occupy the corresponding position *on* the second side. Thus supposing the CC pipe of the open diapason to stand in the middle of the tower on the left side of the case, the CC sharp pipe will probably be in the centre of the similarly situated tower on the right; the D D and E E pipes will stand one on each side of the C C; while those giving D D sharp and F F will appear immediately on the right and left respectively of the C C sharp pipe.

17. The alternate assortment of the front pipes materially facilitates the power of giving to the organ a symmetrical appearance. The C C sharp pipe differs so slightly from the C C in its diameter (in a decreasing ratio), that the eye fails, at a distance, to discover the deviation; hence the two pipes—as indeed any other two, of which the sounds are only separated by a semitone—are placed in corresponding positions, without the slightest ill, but, on the contrary, good effect resulting.

18. The necessary deviation in *length*, however, would be sooner detected; hence both pipes are made to agree in this respect: but the one that is to give the higher sound has an opening cut in the back, at the top, which produces the same influence on the tone as slightly shortening the pipe.

19. The next pipe on the "C C side," F F sharp (supposing the towers already spoken of to contain three pipes each only), will probably appear in another compartment; perhaps in a smaller tower, or in a flat, or in one of the ogee or the breasted form; and so on. When the pipes become too small to appear externally, the few remaining ones are disposed inside, and members of other stops brought into prominence, if more pipes are required in sight to complete the design.

20. The pipes in the flats are arranged in a far greater number of different ways than are those in the towers. In compartments of the fore-mentioned kind the largest pipes are sometimes placed outside, and the small ones in the middle, as represented in *fig.* 11,

11 ⃝◯◯◯ooooo◯◯◯

at others, the small ones occupy the extreme positions right and left, and the large ones the centre (*fig.* 12),

12   oooOOOOOOOOooo

while occasionally they are disposed in a graduated series; the largest being at one end and the smallest at the other; as in *figs.* 13 and 14.

13   OOOOOoOooooooo   ●●●●oooooOOOOOO   14

Of the decoration of the   21. The surface of the front pipes of most English organs is
front pipes   adorned either with gilding or diapering. In former times the front pipes were more commonly *diapered; i.e.*, figured in various colours; and many of Smith and Harris's organs were so ornamented. That, by the former builder, at Finedon, in Northamptonshire, still retains its original embellishments of this nature; so also does the old organ in the chapel of Christ College, Cambridge. The front pipes of the organ built by Harris for King James' Chapel, at Whitehall, and now in St. James's Church, Piccadilly, were diapered; and, on being transferred to their present locality, were cut open and turned inside out. Frequent instances have of late occurred of the revival of this kind of pipe-decoration. The instruments in Westminster Abbey and the Temple Church have their front pipes both gilded and diapered.

22. The front pipes of the organs in Holland, some parts of France, and most of the German States, being frequently made of pure tin, are simply polished or burnished, giving them the handsome appearance of bright silver. The front pipes of the organ, in the Roman Catholic Church in Leicester Square, by Mr. Gern, are of burnished tin, so also are the 32-feet pipes by Mr. Willis in the front of the organ in the Albert Hall.

Division II.

THE WIND-COLLECTING PORTION OF THE ORGAN.

CHAPTER II.

THE BELLOWS.

Their use. 23. THE use of the bellows is to collect and enclose a quantity of atmospheric air, and, after compressing it, to propel it through the various wind-channels up to the pipes. These are, in fact, the lungs of the organ : without their aid it would be but a voiceless machine.

The different kinds of organ bellows ordinarily met with ; which the oldest ; their names ; and why so called. 24. There are two kinds of bellows to be met with in church organs, namely, *diagonal* and *horizontal* bellows. Previously to the introduction of the kinds now understood by these names, organ bellows were made like the ordinary household bellows. As an improvement upon these, bellows were next constructed on a plan identical with those still used in smiths' forges, namely, with a feeder below, and a *diagonal* reservoir above to produce a continued blast of air, the folds or sides being made of thick hide leather. Some bellows of this latter species were in existence, lying in a lumber-room in the (once collegiate) Church of Tong, in Shropshire, as late as the year 1789. But such primitive machines, from the nature of the material of which they were made, were liable to frequent injury from the friction to which their folds were unavoidably subject whenever they were worked ;[*] and their constantly recurring unsoundness from this cause gradually led to the adoption of a more durable material in their construction. Thus wood came to be used in lieu of leather for the folds, with pieces of horse-sinew and strips of leather for the hinges, which substitution rendered the bellows far less liable to destruction from attrition. Of this more substantial kind of bellows specimens are still occasionally to be seen in the small cabinet organs of Father Smith. In the church organs, however, of that celebrated artist, and also in those of his worthy competitor, Harris, only diagonal bellows—the kind represented in *fig.* 15, except that they were worked by a handle and not a treadle—were used. These bellows are said by some to have been first introduced by Lobinger, of Nuremberg, in 1570. According to other accounts they were invented by Hennings, of Hildesheim, in the seventeenth century. But Dr. Rimbault, in his valuable *History of the Organ*, p. 48, quoting from the Fabrick Rolls of York Minster, under the date 1419, states that John Couper, *a carpenter*, received, "for constructing *the ribs* of the bellows of the organ, 12d." If these were made *of wood*, of which there can scarcely be a doubt, the improvement in question is not only much older than is generally supposed, but was made by an Englishman.

25. Diagonal bellows continued to be almost exclusively[†] employed in church

---

[*] Hence the repeated appearance in so many old parish accounts of entries such as "for mendyng of ye organ bellowis," or "for the amendyng of the organys."

[†] It will have been seen, from the illustration on page 35 of the Historical Introduction, that

organs till towards the latter part of the last century, when a new kind was brought forward in this country, which was considered by the English organ-builders of the time to present so many advantages over that previously used for church-work, that, soon after the commencement of the present century, the construction of bellows of the diagonal species was entirely abandoned. The fine organ in St. Margaret's Church, Westminster (built by Avery, in 1804), appears to have been one of the latest instruments made with bellows of the single or diagonal kind.

26. At the present time the horizontal is the only description of bellows made by English and French organ-builders ; though, in Germany, the diagonal still remains in favour. In the magnificent organ erected by Schulze, of Paulinzelle, in the Parish Church, Doncaster, in 1862, diagonal bellows are used.

27. The names given to the two kinds of organ bellows sufficiently indicate the distinctive principle upon which each operates. The diagonal, or, as it has some-times been denominated, the wedge-shaped bellows, is so called because, when blown, the top rises diagonally ; that is to say, one end ascends while the other remains stationary ; thus giving to the bellows a wedge-shaped appearance, as shown in the following engraving, when charged with air.

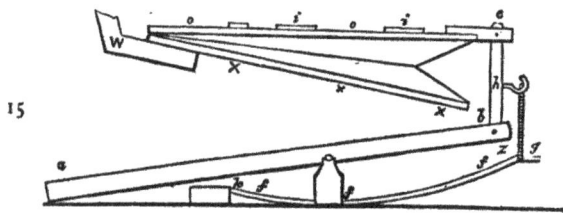

15

28. A horizontal bellows (*fig.* 16), on the contrary, preserves its level surface in all stages of its operation, whether it be wholly distended, quite empty, or at any intermediate point between the two extremes. Hence *its* distinctive appellation.

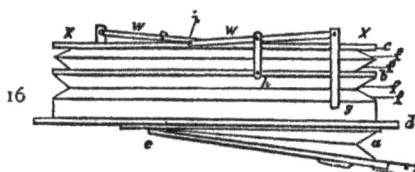

16

Particulars concerning the diagonal bellows.   29. Diagonal bellows are, as already mentioned, seldom, if ever, now made in England. Numerous specimens, however, still exist in our old town and village church organs. Of such kind of bellows two, at the least, are found in even the smallest church organs ; one for supplying the instrument while the other is being replenished. As, during the process of inflation, the top of the bellows is gradually raised, and, therefore, the weights on its surface

a reservoir similar to the upper member of a horizontal bellows was known in the time of Prætorius, 1620 ; but, being made without a feeder, it was the same in principle as the old diagonal bellows, so far that it was inflated by raising the top. Although somewhat similar to the modern bellows in appearance, it was as different in the method of its working, as it was inferior in actual utility.

exercise no compressing influence on the contained air, it follows that, for the time being, the wind within that bellows can be of no greater density than the air without, and therefore is of no service in supplying the organ. A practical proof of this fact may be obtained, where there are two diagonal bellows, by pressing the handles of *both* down at once, when the organ will become for the time quite silent. Hence arises the necessity for a second bellows, to supply wind while the first is being charged, and *vice versâ*.

Their number. 30. And while small and moderate-sized organs have from 2 to 6 diagonal bellows, many large instruments have 8, 10, 12, or even as many as 14. Thus the Meresburg organ has 6 bellows ; that at Wismar, 8 ; that at Haarlem, 12 ; while that at St. Sulpice, in Paris, had, until lately, 14 bellows. Smith's organ in St. Paul's Cathedral had originally 4 large diagonal bellows, measuring 8 feet by 4. The new organ at Doncaster has 12.

Arrangement. 31. The several diagonal bellows are usually placed in a row, side by side, outside the case ; or, when too numerous to be so disposed, they are often ranged in *two* rows, one over the other. In the latter case the upper row of bellows is generally furnished with ropes, by means of which the same blowers are enabled to work both rows. Such was the arrangement at the church of St. Owen, at Rouen, previous to the recent improvement of the organ by Cavaillé-Coll. The blower depressed the handles of the lower row of bellows as he leisurely walked across the platform behind the organ from one side to the other, and drew down the ropes of the upper row as he returned. In Smith and Harris's organs they were placed outside, and generally to the rear of the case. They were placed, for the first time, inside the case by Harris, in 1703, in his Salisbury Cathedral organ. In many of the Continental organs the bellows are inflated by means of treadles instead of handles. The illustration numbered 15 represents a bellows worked in this manner. The treadles lie in a row near the ground, and the blower, stepping from one treadle to another, by his weight lowers each of them, and thus the bellows are distended. The bellows of the Doncaster organ are blown in this way.

32. The wind supplied by the several diagonal bellows is received into a chief or head canal, consisting of a long square and (generally) horizontally disposed wooden tube ; from which canal it is distributed among the several sound-boards, through smaller tubes shooting forth from it and traversing the organ in all necessary directions. Such are the general arrangements for collecting and compressing, for receiving and distributing the organ-wind. To an enumeration of these may be added the following details :—

Method of operation. 33. Diagonal bellows are blown by pressure upon the near end of the governing handle or treadle (*a, fig.* 15). On this descending, the other end (*b*) ascends, raising with it the moveable end of the top of the bellows (*c*). As this is taking place, some of the external air rushes in through the bottom of the bellows, at openings or gratings made for the purpose, and fills the cavity of the bellows. Valves placed over the apertures then fall over them and close in the wind. The surface weights (*i i*) now exercise their influence, by pressing heavily on the top of the bellows (*o o*) ; and the top of the bellows, by descending, in its turn, forcibly on the enclosed wind, compresses it and so prepares it for use ; in which state it rushes towards the chief wind-receiver, through the wind-trunk (*w*). As the air in the bellows is by degrees exhausted, the top descends, the handle as gradually rising ; when the latter reaches its full height and becomes stationary, it indicates that the contents of the bellows are exhausted. The wind from the several bellows does not enter the receiver at the same time; but that from one bellows is first consumed, and then the supply is continued by the next. So that the bellows do not all sink down together, but one after the other, as is indicated by the consecutive rising of the handles.

34. This successive transmission of the wind from the several bellows is brought under regulation by means of valves or traps, one between each bellows and the chief wind-receiver, which act in the following manner. The wind from the first bellows not only supplies the organ, but by its force alone keeps the traps of the other bellows closed so long as the wind lasts. When this supply is just exhausted, then the trap of the second bellows suddenly opens, the condensed air from which not only keeps the traps of the remaining bellows still closed, but also shuts that of the one just emptied, and so prevents the entrance of any of the wind which the bellows now in operation is supplying. On the stock of wind from the second bellows being exhausted, the trap of the third opens and continues the supply, that of the second closing; and so on with all the remaining bellows. Sometimes a certain number of the bellows supply one department only of the organ. Thus, of the 14 originally at St. Sulpice, 6 were devoted to the great organ, 4 to the pedal, the remaining 4 supplying the smaller departments of the organ. The description just given must therefore be understood as referring to the working of one set or series of bellows only, of which an organ may contain 1, 2, or 3, according to circumstances.

Their original defects.   35. Although the bellows of every large organ were more or less numerous, yet for a long period there lacked the means for ascertaining whether they all produced a supply of wind of equal strength or intensity. Improvements had been made by which the evils of this defect had been lessened by increasing the size, and, therefore, by decreasing the number of the bellows, but the uncertainty remained in respect to the fewer bellows that had still to be employed. It was not until the seventeenth century that the wind-gauge or *anemometer* was invented by a German organ-builder of the name of Förner. This little machine enabled builders to "weight" the bellows of an organ so that they all produced a wind of the same general force. But a source of inequality was discovered to exist in the bellows itself. It was found that a diagonal bellows produced a comparatively light wind when fully distended, and a gradually increasing one as it collapsed; the consequences being that the organ did not always produce precisely the same strength of tone, neither did it always sound strictly in tune. The causes of this inequality in the strength of the wind were as follow. A diagonal bellows, on being charged with air, would have the top-board (*o o, fig.* 15, and *b, fig.* 17) raised to its greatest height; the *side* and *end ribs* (*c c, c c, fig.* 17) taking as nearly a perpendicular position as a regard   17

to the stability of the bellows would allow, and having their *middle joints*, or points of conjunction (*d d*), inclined inwards. The sides and end would then present an obtuse angle to the wind, as shown in *fig.* 17, which is a *cross* section of a diagonal bellows. But as the top-board descended, the angle they described would become more and more acute, as illustrated at *e e,* in *fig.* 18. As the contents there-   18 fore of the bellows were gradually exhausted, not only was the *height* of the space within the bellows lessened, *but also the length and breadth.* The wind within, consequently, was not simply influenced by the calculated pressure of the surface-weights, but also by the com-pressing power of the inward folding ribs, which, pressing forward, wedge-fashion, into the confined air, gave it more force. An accurately made anemometer showed

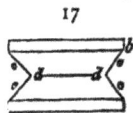

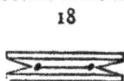

that the wind was $\frac{1}{14}$ stronger when the bellows was at its *least* elevation, and nearly empty, than when at its *greatest* elevation.

36. Another circumstance that tended to bring about the inequality complained of was the irregular influence of the surface-weights, which did not press with the same effect on the bellows in all stages of its sinking. A weight will, according to one of the simplest laws of mechanics, operate with its fullest effect only upon a *level* surface. Now, when a diagonal bellows was distended, at which time the top-board presented an *inclined** plane, the weights could only press *obliquely* on the wind, and therefore with something less than their greatest effect. This imperfect pressure gradually disappeared as the bellows closed; that is to say, as the top gradually approached the *horizontal* line; the result being that the bellows completed its work by the production of a stronger wind than was the case at the commencement of its sinking.

37. These were the defects which existed in the diagonal bellows, as originally made, and which the German organ-builders succeeded in rectifying, by means as simple in their nature as they were successful in their effect.

How remedied. 38. Instead of the bellows being fixed with the under-board (*x x x, fig.* 15) perfectly level, as heretofore, they were now placed with the spreading end somewhat *below* the other end (as illustrated in *fig.* 15); so that, when expanded, the *top* (*o o*), instead of the *bottom*, formed the horizontal line. This slight alteration of position secured to the wind the full influence of the surface-weights (*i i*) at the *commencement* of the bellows' sinking, instead of at the end; and therefore at the time when the ribs would be producing the *least* effect. As the top descended below the level, the weights would lose some of their influence; the closing ribs, however, pressing in on all sides, at the same time increased theirs. This is the arrangement of the bellows at Doncaster. To counteract any greater influence which the inward folding ribs might still exercise, a long wooden spring was applied, which operated during the earlier stages of the bellows' sinking, in addition to the surface-weights; but by degrees ceased to do so as the influence of the ribs was more and more felt.

39. This spring, consisting of a long rule of box-wood (*fig.* 15, *f f f*), was laid under the bellows, and fastened down at one end (*k*), the other having a rope attached (*g*), communicating with the wooden rod (*h*) that lifts the top of the bellows. On raising the top-board, the rope and free-end of the box-wood spring were drawn up; the latter, from its own elasticity of course, operating with the greatest force when most curved upwards. Additional compressing power was thus brought to bear upon the wind when the ribs pressed inwards but slightly; but as they gradually did so more acutely, giving to the wind more strength, the elastic power of the spring as gradually became less, and finally became powerless. Thus was a uniform strength of wind secured throughout the sinking of the diagonal bellows.

40. In England, also, various ingenious devices were had recourse to for equalising the wind-pressure. Renatus Harris, in his organ at St. Dionis, Backchurch (1724), applied accumulative springs to the four bellows for this purpose. Green, in the organ erected by him in St. George's Chapel, Windsor (1790), inserted an apparatus consisting of a system of gradually increasing counterpoise, acting, by

---

* Diagonal bellows were originally fixed with the *under-board* (*x x x, fig.* 15) in a perfectly horizontal position.

means of a rope coiled round a small pulley, in opposition to the descent of the bellows.

41. An ingenious mechanician, of the name of Cumming, a clock-maker by trade, appears to have been the first to whom the idea occurred of making a bellows on the *horizontal* principle. According to his own pamphlet, the principle was sketched out by him in 1762, and first carried into practice in the organ completed under his direction for the Earl of Bute in 1787. It was also tried by Samuel Green in the beautiful little organs erected by him in St. Thomas's Church, Ardwick, in 1787, and in St. Peter's Church, Stockport, in the following year. On the other hand the organs by the same admirable maker in Lichfield Cathedral (1789, now removed), and St. George's Chapel, Windsor (1790), had *diagonal* bellows, from which circumstance it would seem that Green was not at first entirely satisfied with the then new kind of bellows. The one main fact, at any rate, is certain, as well as satisfactory, namely, that the horizontal bellows is an invention of English origin.

The horizontal bellows.   42. A horizontal bellows (see *fig.* 16) comprises two separate and distinct chambers, one immediately over the other. The lower one (*a*), closely resembling a diagonal bellows, is called the *feeder*, from its supplying or " feeding " the upper division with wind. The upper chamber (*x x*) is called the *reservoir*, because it *receives* the great body of wind collected by the feeder for compression, and holds it in " reserve " for after-distribution among the various departments of the organ.

43. One circumstance connected with the horizontal bellows—and a very important one it is—is, that one of this kind will with ease supply an organ that would require perhaps half-a-dozen of the diagonal species. How this should be the case is soon explained. A feeder, as already stated, closely resembles a diagonal bellows. Now supposing a horizontal bellows to be supplied by a feeder of a given size, and that six full charges therefrom are necessary to fill the reservoir, it follows that the supply from that one reservoir will be as plentiful and efficient as that from six bellows of the diagonal species of the dimensions of the feeder (*a*). This fact is the more apparent, when it is born in mind that diagonal bellows do not all afford their supply at the same time.

Its structural features.   44. On examining a horizontal bellows, it will be seen to consist of three stout horizontal layers or plates of wood, called respectively the *top-board* (*c, figs.* 16 and 23, also *figs.* 19 and 20) ; the *middle-board* (*d, figs.* 16 and 23, also *fig.* 21) ; and the *bottom-board* (*e, figs.* 16 and 23, also *fig.* 22) : which " boards " are joined together all round by side and cross-fold boards called *ribs*. (See *f f f f*, in *figs.* 16 and 23 ; also *figs.* 24, 25, and 26).

45. The *top-board* is usually made of pine, from one to three inches in thickness ; and, in small bellows, consists simply of a plain, substantial board, *ledgered* near to each end, as shown in *fig.* 19. The top-board for larger bellows is frequently composed of a stout frame, divided crossways and lengthways by rails, resembling the *stiles*, &c., of a common door (*fig.* 20) ; with the interstices filled in, or in some instances covered in, with thick wooden panels. Very large bellows frequently have the top-board framed all round, and also across, with a lining two or three inches in height ; which increases its stability and its freedom from tremor. Moveable panels offer an easy means of getting at the valves of the middle-board below, if they become deranged from damp, excessive heat, or any other cause.

19

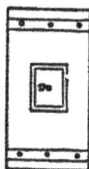

46. The *middle-board* (*fig.* 21) is made of rather larger dimensions than the top-board ; a slight additional portion being required all round to form a substantial ridge for the support of the bellows on their sustaining frame-work. This is clearly shown at *d*, in *fig.* 16 ; also in *figs.* 23 and 35. To the middle-board are attached, at the sides and ends, and marking as nearly as may be the outline of the top-board, four thick boards (*e e e e*, *fig.* 21), some four or five inches broad, and set up edgeways (*g*, *fig.* 16), called the *trunk-band*, or *lining*, which "band" permits the various wind-trunks to be joined to the bellows at *any part* most convenient to fix them. (See *o* and *v*, *fig.* 23.) In some bellows pieces of wood, the same *height* as the band, and of the same *width* as the ribs, are placed inside the band, and at right angles to it, which, with the band itself, form a firm resting place for the ribs. Besides this three or four posts are inserted down the centre of the middle-board, of the same height as the trunk-band, with the thickness of the ribs, &c., *added*, which bear up the top-board and weights. Or, in very *long* bellows, instead of a few posts, a rib of inch pine (of the same height as the posts) is carried through the whole length of the middle-board (inside the band, glued to the middle-board and screwed through from the under side), which not only supports the top-board *from end to end*, down the middle, but also serves as a *brace* to the middle-board, These several insertions add materially to the stability of the bellows. The middle-board and trunk-band together form a kind of large, shallow trough, in the bottom of which lie the several "valves" or "suckers," marked *f f f* in the adjoining figure. Sometimes the middle-board, like the top, has moveable panels, to facilitate the repairing or cleaning of the valves in the bottom-board, when required.

47. The *bottom-board* (*fig.* 22) is made of good substance, like the other "boards" of the bellows. It is provided with suckers, like the middle-board, and forms the bottom of the feeder, as already exemplified in *fig.* 16. It is therefore ledgered on the under side, to prevent its "springing," when in forcible operation. The bottom-board sometimes approaches the top-board in dimensions ; at other times, not nearly so ; this often depending on the kind of feeder by which the reservoir is fed.

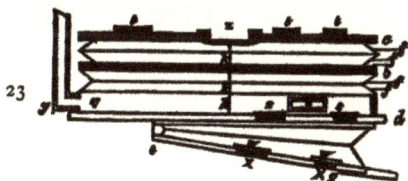

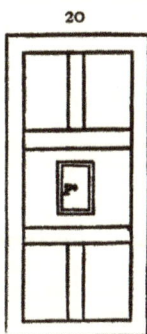

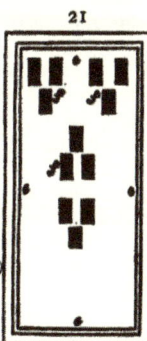

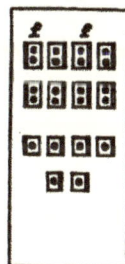

48. The *ribs* are the variously shaped pieces of wood that form, chiefly, the folds of the bellows. They measure from 3-8ths to an inch in thickness, according to the size and general strength of the bellows.

49. Two general forms of rib are made use of—the *parallel* and the *triangular*. The former kind, represented in figures 24 and 25, is employed in the formation of the reservoir

25

of the bellows, and the spreading end of the feeder (*fig.* 17) ; the latter (*fig.* 26), for the sides of the feeder. Those constituting the sides and ends of the reservoir are narrow and long, measuring usually three or four inches in breadth, and from three or four to ten or twelve feet in length, or even more, according to circumstances.

50. The *parallel ribs* are classified into *direct* and *inverted*, in regard to a certain peculiarity in their shape. The former kind are those which have their *shorter* sides hinged together ; the latter, those which have their *longer* sides so united. The direct ribs (25) are used in the formation of the *lower* half of the reservoir ; the inverted (24), for the *upper* half—at least, in modern bellows. In addition to this classification the parallel ribs are further divided into *side-ribs* and *end-ribs*, in reference to the position which they occupy.

51. The *triangular-shaped ribs*, which are identical in shape with the side-ribs of a diagonal bellows, are made broadest at the end where the feeder opens widest (*o, fig.* 26 ;

26

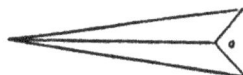

also *e, fig.* 16, and *fig.* 23); from whence they gradually diminish in width towards the other end, finishing off in a point. In the formation of the reservoir of a horizontal bellows sixteen ribs are used ; four on each side, and as many at each end. These ribs are divided all round into two series of two each, by a frame called the *middle-frame ;* of which, however, only the edges are to be traced in a completed bellows. (*b, figs.* 16 and 23.)

52. The *valves* in the middle and bottom boards are formed of one, two, or three thicknesses of leather, glued together. They are made rather larger than the openings which they are designed to cover, that the closing may be effectual. (See

figs. 27 and 28 for the plan and section of the valves.) The valves are usually hinged on at one end (*b*) to the "board," the other end and both sides being left quite free to rise and fall.   The end forming the hinge consists of one thickness only of leather, (*figs.* 27 and 28), that it may be perfectly flexible. Occasionally the valves are attached with pieces of tape ; one piece at each of the four corners, with the other ends nailed to the board. The entire valve then rises ; the pieces of tape preventing its shifting from over the orifices or gratings.

27

28

53. These several openings or gratings are technically called *suckers*. They are sometimes made of an oblong form ; as shown at *f f f*, in *fig.* 21, and at *w w*, in *fig.* 23, and filled in with a metal or wooden grating ; or they consist of clusters of circular holes ; as shown at *f f*, in *fig.* 22, and on an enlarged scale, in *figs.* 27 and 28.   The gratings in the square suckers, and the wooden substance that separates the holes of each circular cluster from one another, prevent the compressed air from forcing the valves downwards through the suckers.

54. As their names imply, the bottom-board forms the bottom to the feeder ; the middle-board occupies the intermediate position, and so serves the double

purpose of roof to the feeder and bottom to the reservoir ; while the top-board forms the top to the reservoir.

55. Of these three great layers of wood-work the middle-board is the fixture, and supports the entire bellows. Below hangs the feeder, and above rests the reservoir. The bottom and middle-boards are furnished with perforations or gratings, with leather valves lying over the upper sides ; the use of which will be clearly understood from an explanation of the manner in which a horizontal bellows is worked.

The working of the horizontal bellows ; and the room which the compressed air makes for itself between the plates and folds of the reservoir.

56. As the free end (g, *fig.* 23) of the feeder descends, the external air throws back the valves (w w) in the bottom-board, and rushes through the gratings (x x), filling the cavity of the feeder ; after which the valves descend again over the gratings and close in the wind. The hanging end of the feeder is then drawn upwards, by which movement the enclosed air is strongly pressed against the surface above ; that is, against the under side of the middle-board (d). The exercise of this force throws back the valves (s s) that lie over the apertures in the middle-board—the valves not being intended to resist the pressure of the wind in this direction, but only *downwards*—and the wind, having thus cleared a way for itself, passes from the feeder into the reservoir. The valves on the upper side of the middle-board (s s) then in their turn fall over the openings and prevent the return of the wind into the feeder.

57. At the moment wind is being thus transmitted, the folds ($f f f f$) open and the top-board (c) rises so as to form a sufficiently capacious receptacle for it.

58. While the several processes just detailed are going on, some of the wind is, under the pressure of the surface weights (t t t), constantly flowing through the various exits or *wind-trunk holes* (o and v) into wooden tubes (y) or *wind-trunks*, and thence to the several departments of the organ supplied by that bellows ; the top-board of the bellows descending and the folds collapsing as the quantity of the wind in the reservoir is reduced, and rising again and the sides expanding as more wind is supplied. In *figs.* 16, 23, 35, and also in the general section, the reservoir is represented as being fully distended or charged with wind ; and in *fig.* 32 it is shown in a collapsed or resting state.

59. The folds of the bellows are subject to a constant strain in consequence of the antagonistic powers exercised by the feeder on the one hand, and the compressing weights on the other ; the former forcing air upwards, while the latter press the top-board downwards.

60. To give them the power of resisting the outward pressure of the contained air, arising from these circumstances, a piece of frame-work an inch or more in thickness, some three or four inches in breadth, and of nearly the same outer measurement as the top-board (see *fig.* 29), is inserted between the two series of ribs.

61. This *middle-frame* holds the ribs so firmly in their proper positions, that there is no liability, under ordinary circumstances, of the folds bulging from the force above alluded to.

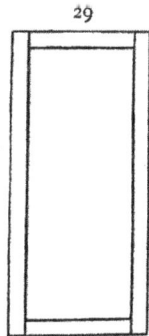
29

The construction of the reservoir.

62. The several parts of the reservoir already described are worked together in the following manner. The ribs are first assorted into pairs ; the proper sides of each couple being brought close together. A long strip of white-dressed leather is then glued over the contiguous edges ;

N

a second piece being attached in a similar manner to the same edges on the other side. These pieces together form a strong hinge, which is called the *middle-joint.*

63. All the other couples of the ribs are then firmly united together in like manner.

64. The lower edge of the under series of ribs is then fastened to the lining ; secondly, the upper edge of the upper ribs is united to the edges of the top-board ; thirdly, the lower edge of the upper series is bound to the inner edge of the middle-frame ; and, fourthly, the upper edge of the lower series is joined to the outer edge of the middle-frame. The openings at the four angles or corners, where the ends of the ribs nearly meet, marked *a a a a*, in *fig.* 30, are then closed with leather, which form what are technically called the *gussets.* The adjoining figure (No. 30) is a plan of the folds of the reservoir.

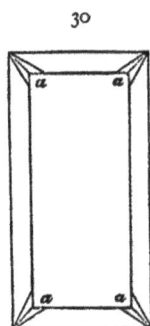

The construction of the feeder.   65. The folds and boards of the feeder are joined together in much the same manner, only that the end of the bottom-board is strongly fastened to the middle-board with several pieces of shoe-leather, rope, girth-webbing, or something of the sort, to form the working part of the great hinge. Over these is glued a stout coating of white leather, to render this joint equally air-tight with the others. A piece of wood running across the end of the feeder (*c c, fig.* 31), and about equal in thickness to the folds when they are closed against the middle-board, admits of the feeder being drawn up without straining the hinge. Both corners, where the end of this cross-piece and the points of the side-ribs nearly meet, are covered in with leather *corner-pieces.* The adjoining figure (No. 31) is a plan of the folds of a single feeder, which are formed of six ribs, two to form each side, and two for the hanging end.

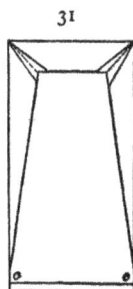

The blowing action.   66. The apparatus by which the feeder of the bellows is put in motion is called the *blowing-action,* one of the simplest kinds of which, namely, that for a single feeder, consists of a vertical pump-rod, a horizontal bellows-handle, and an upright standard, to which must be added the fork-shaped piece of wood that projects from the hanging end of the feeder, called the *lug.* The lower end of the pump-rod (*a, fig.* 35) is placed between the two prongs of the lug (*w*) and secured by an iron bolt (*v*) ; the upper is placed in a *mortice* cut in the near end of the bellows-handle, and similarly secured, while the bellows-handle itself rests in a deep cutting made in the upper part of the standard to receive it, where also it is secured by a bolt. Where there are double feeders, there are of course also *two* pump-rods (*a a*), which then communicate with a large lever (*o o*), from which latter a rod (*c*) communicates with the bellows-handle (*d*). (See *fig.* 35.)

67. The disengaged end of the bellows-handle usually passes through a high and narrow cutting in the organ-case, and is worked outside. As, however, it is necessary that the bellows-blower should at all times know at what rate the wind in the reservoir is being exhausted, which will at times be rapid, and at others slow, and as the bellows themselves are generally hidden from view, a kind of index, or, as it is commonly called, a *tell-tale,* is introduced to convey this necessary intelligence. This usually consists simply of a plummet fastened to a piece of whip-cord, which whip-cord is carried over a little wheel in the organ-

case near to the bellows-handle, and then fastened to the top-board. As the reservoir fills and the top rises, the weight *descends ;* as it is emptied, the top descends and the weight *rises.* When the weight is down, the bellows are understood to be "full ; " and, when up, "empty." The most proper place to keep the weight is about midway between the two extremes.

The action of the inverted folds. 68. By making the upper "fold" to open *outwards,* while the lower does so *inwards,* the former affords *more* space for the wind, just in proportion as the latter provides *less.* Thus the disadvantageous influence that would certainly be exercised by the one fold is neutralised by the opposite action of the other.

The counter-balances. 69. The "*inverted folds*" formed a part of Cumming's original improvement. One condition, however, necessary towards securing their corrective influence was, that both should always be at the same *relative* degree of openness and closeness ; for otherwise an unequal wind would still result. To obtain this proportionate action, some light, moving, directing frame-work (*fig.* 16, *w w*) was applied to the two sides (or sometimes to the two ends) of the reservoir, and attached to the trunk-band (*g*), middle-frame (*h*), and top-board (*c*) of the reservoir, which "guide-work" always kept those three portions at equal distances apart, and so effectually secured the required and exact contrary action of the two series of ribs which occurred in the spaces between them. The *counterbalances,* as the adjuncts in question were called, serve the additional purpose of preventing the top-board, with its heavy weights, swerving to the right or to the left, instead of rising and falling. In large bellows the influence of the folds is far less than in small ones, as the width of the ribs is by no means increased in proportion to the superficial measurement of the bellows. The folds, therefore, of large bellows are narrower in proportion than in small ones, and their influence consequently less perceptible.

The waste-pallet. 70. Another cause of inequality in the strength of the wind had to be guarded against. The consumption of wind would, under certain circumstances, be very slow and gradual ; the rate of the fresh supply from the feeder being then, most probably, much greater than that of the outflowing. This additional wind, accumulating in the reservoir, would soon fully distend it. If, while in this inflated state, more wind were attempted to be introduced, as the reservoir could expand no farther, the extra wind could only make room for itself by compressing that which was already within into a still smaller space. By doing this, the density of the organ-wind would be increased beyond the required degree. Besides causing the pipes to produce a shrill scream rather than a musical sound, the soundness of the reservoir itself would be endangered by the consequent overtension, and the leather hinges liable to be strained or even rent by the violence. To obviate such evils, a clever contrivance, called the *waste-pallet,* was devised. This, in its earliest form, much resembled the key of a wind instrument on an enlarged scale, and consisted of a plate covering a vent, with a lever (or tail) working on a centre, by which the plate could be raised. This pallet occupied the centre of the top-board, and was so disposed that when the top-board had risen to a certain and its proper height, the tail of the waste-pallet came in contact with some wood-work. If more wind were then passed into the reservoir, the retention of which would involve a further distension of the reservoir, and consequently a farther rising of the top-board, the tail of the pallet struck against this wood-work ; the other end was lifted up, the vent uncovered, and the extra wind thus allowed to escape. A spring, placed either above the waste-pallet or under the tail, kept the pallet closed, except when purposely opened.

71. With a view to the saving of room, and other circumstances, the waste-pallet was, after a time, transferred from the upper to the under-side of the opening, as shown in *fig.* 23, *z*, also at *a* and *d* in *figs.* 19 and 20, and there hinged on at one end to the top-board. It was, therefore, changed in plan from the key to the valve kind. The waste-pallet was now worked by a piece of rope (*fig.* 23, *k k k*) or a leathern thong, one end of which was fastened to the pallet, and the other to the middle-board. This rope or throng was just long enough to allow the top-board (*c*) to rise to the desired height, without checking the pallet, and no farther. If any more wind were now attempted to be introduced, the top-board would, indeed, rise somewhat higher, but the pallet would be held stationary by the rope now stretched at full length ; and, the vent being uncovered, the superfluous air would escape.

72. In modern bellows the waste-pallet is often situated in the middle-board, to which part it was removed, because dust or *cuttings* sometimes worked their way on to the edges of the pallet and prevented its closing properly. When so placed, it consists simply of a reversion of the one just described. The vent is cut in the middle-board ; the pallet is laid over it, and raised by a rope fastened to the top-board, which latter, after rising to a certain extent, draws it up, allowing the wind to escape underneath, outside and to the rear of the feeder. Some organ-bellows have two waste-pallets, one opening into each feeder. In this case, as superfluous wind is introduced by one feeder, an equal amount is discharged into the other.

73. But whatever may be its situation, the waste-pallet is always introduced to serve the same end, in regard to the reservoir of a bellows, that a safety-valve does to the boiler of a steam engine ; namely, to guard it from more than the intended strain, by letting off all that might otherwise peril its soundness.

74. The above are the most important improvements for equalising the wind made in the horizontal bellows up to within the last thirty years.

The unsteadiness of the organ-wind arising from unskilful blowing, or from irregular consumption.   75. There were other ways, however, in which the strength of the organ-wind might be disturbed, besides those arising from the irregular compression of the weights and ribs of the reservoir, and ways which were beyond the power of the devices just enumerated to correct. For instance, if, instead of the bellows-handle being pressed down gradually—as it always should be—it were thrust down with a jerk, the wind in the feeder would be forced into the reservoir so suddenly that there would not be time for the top and sides to rise and unfold to receive it ; the result for the moment being an over-compression of the wind.

The several kinds of feeder.   76. In the earliest kind of horizontal bellows the reservoir was too small and the feeder too large ; the consequence being that every stroke of the feeder elevated the upper-board too suddenly ; and, as the resistance arising from the inertia of the weight upon a bellows is increased in proportion to the velocity with which it is elevated, it followed that a blast of very varying strength was produced. The reservoir was therefore increased in size, and a plan devised for transmitting the wind more gradually and continuously by means of a feeder made on the principle of the little bellows of the common cuckoo toy, and hence called the *cuckoo feeder*. In this feeder the bottom-board instead of being fastened to the middle-board at one end, as in the instance of the *single feeder* (see *figs.* 16 and 23), was hung about midway between the two ends to a cross-board running transversely beneath the middle-board (see *e e* fig. 32, which presents a side view of a bellows with a cuckoo feeder). Each

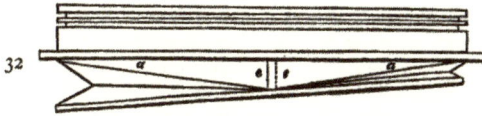

32

half was provided with two end-ribs and four side-ribs, the latter with their points (*o o o o, fig.* 33) towards the cross-board. These several parts were fastened together in the usual way, and, with the addition of an *under-lining*, of the same depth in the centre as the cross-board, but inclining upwards towards each end (*a a, fig.* 32), formed two separate though smaller feeders. On referring to *fig.* 32, the two feeders will be distinctly traced.

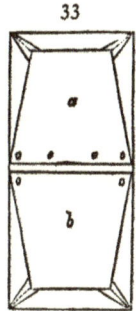

33

77. A cuckoo feeder gives a supply of wind with the up-stroke of the bellows-handle as well as with the down, which was not the case with the single feeder; and the quantity of wind pumped in by the two strokes is about equivalent to that supplied by the one stroke from the older kind of feeder.

78. In some cuckoo feeders the under-lining (*a a, fig.* 32) is transferred from the under-side of the middle-board to the upper-side of the bottom-board, and *reversed*, as shown at *a a*, in *fig.* 34. This has the effect of greatly strengthening the feeder, the bottom-board of which is subjected to a considerable strain across the middle, where there is consequently a possibility of its " springing," but which tendency is entirely removed by placing the lining as shown in the figure below. This transfer of the under-lining does not weaken the middle-board, which is amply strengthened by the trunk-band and the inside bracings.

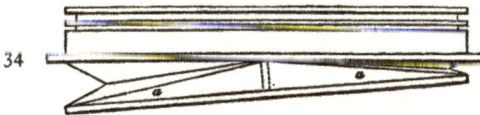

34

79. A third kind, called the *double* feeder, differs from the cuckoo feeder, in having a separate bottom-board to each feeder, instead of one long board to

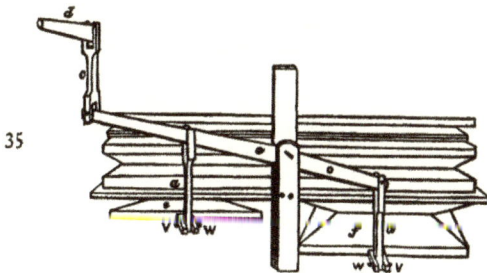

35

serve for the two. Feeders of this class are not simply " separate " feeders, as in the cuckoo, but are also " independent " feeders (*e f, fig.* 35), like those of the single species. They usually extend the cross-way of the reservoir, as shown in *fig.* 35 ; though occasionally they run lengthways. Double feeders present this advantage : if one becomes unsound, the other still can be used while the repair of the first is being proceeded with, which could not be the case with the cuckoo feeder.

80. In some large organs of recent construction, or renovation, the feeder and the reservoirs of the bellows have been made quite separate and distinct from each other. This has been done so that the feeder might still be placed in some convenient and remote part of the instrument, or even in a dry chamber below or behind it, and yet the reservoir be located close to the sound-board it has to supply. In some cases the number of separate reservoirs has been increased, and they have been distributed in various parts of the organ. For the purpose of yielding a more ample supply of wind to large organs, the *vertical feeder* has been devised. This differs from the ordinary feeder not only in position, but in having the same amount of motion at both ends, and through its length. (See *fig.* 36.) It is formed of three vertical parallel boards (*i i i*), the outer two of which

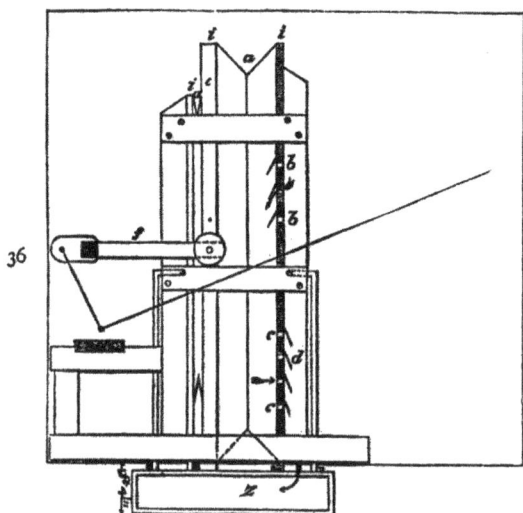

are fixtures, and the inner one (*e*), corresponding to the " bottom-board " of the ordinary feeder, moveable.   The feeders are shown at *a a ; f* is the blowing-rod ; *o*, a wheel travelling on a plane to steady the motion ; *b b* the suckers through which the feeder receives the wind ; *c c*, the valves through which it is passed into the wind-trunk (*d*), whence it is conducted into the receiver (*z*) for after-distribution.

81. Other causes of unsteadiness in the wind were perceived to exist, besides those attributable to defective bellows or unskilful blowing. The wind became agitated—as indicated by the altered speech of the pipes—when many bass keys (the pipes of which consumed a great quantity of wind) were pressed down simultaneously ; and a similar effect was also noticed on their being suddenly allowed to rise. The disturbing cause in the former case originated with the large pipes, which consumed so much of the wind in the wind-chest, that what remained expanded by its own elasticity.   Having thus lost some of its intensity or strength, the smaller pipes of the keys higher up in the scale supplied by it would in consequence speak with a kind of hesitation, which would continue till

the flow of wind from the bellows had been accelerated in proportion to the increased demand, and the general mass had thus regained its accustomed power.

82. The agitation in the second case arose from the wind continuing to flow in the same rapid and copious manner into the wind-chest for an instant after the great demand for it had ceased. The wind there, meeting with a check, accumulated, causing an over-compression ; and, by its thus acquiring greater force for the moment, brought about the defect the other way.

83. Some apparatus, therefore, was required, possessing the power of adding a small quantity of wind to the usual supply, when that supply, from extraordinary circumstances, would be scarcely sufficient, and of deducting some, when, from opposite causes, it would be too great and too strong. Such a wind-regulating apparatus the late Mr. Bishop devised, whose invention is now so generally known as the *concussion-bellows*. He adapted it, for the first time, to the organ he built for old Covent Garden Theatre many years ago.

The concussion-bellows. 84. This apparatus for steadying the wind is usually formed of a board and six ribs (see *fig.* 37), like a single feeder ; though occasionally it is composed of a board and eight ribs, resembling the top and lower ribs of a reservoir. These form a small wedge-shaped reservoir (see *fig.* 37), which is fixed around and over a hole cut through one side of the wind-trunk (*a*), or sometimes through the bottom of the wind-chest, with a metal spring behind (*b*), the strength of which is so adjusted as precisely to balance the ordinary pressure of the compressed wind. When the bellows are blown, the concussion-bellows immediately becomes partly charged from the wind-trunk, or wind-chest, to which it is attached ; and, partly expanding, is then ready to operate either way. If any jerking now occurs at the bellows, or if the consumption of wind be suddenly reduced—either of which circumstances would cause a momentary over-compression of the wind—the concussion-spring gives way, and the concussion-bellows opens farther. More room being thus afforded to the wind, its density is reduced to the proper strength, and its extra force is expended on the concussion-bellows, instead of on the pipes that are speaking.

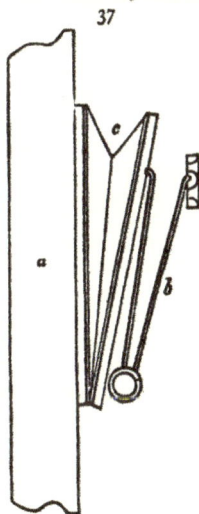

37

85. On the other hand, when a large and sudden demand is made on the wind, and the supply is likely to run short, the concussion-bellows, now acting in the opposite manner, collapses, as it always has a tendency to do under the influence of the spring, when the wind-resistance from within decreases ; and, adding so much of the wind previously contained as the exigency of the occasion requires, preserves the strength of the organ-wind at its proper force.

86. When the organ is not being played upon, but the "wind is in," the concussion-bellows remains about half-way open.

The Anemometer. 87. The organ-wind is required to enter the pipes with not less than a certain prefixed and uniform force. This required strength the bellows do not give to the wind unassistedly ; hence slabs of iron or large lumps of stone are placed on the top of the bellows to compress the wind. Stones are, however, very unfitted for the purpose ; for, in *damp* weather, they absorb a great deal of *moisture* and *gain* weight ; and, in *hot* weather, the moisture again *dries out* and they *lose* weight ; the organ, in consequence, continually changing both in tone and tune. Slabs of iron are best, although they are of course more costly. The exact amount of weight to be used depends partly on the size of the bellows, and partly on the " strength of wind " they are desired to produce.

88. The precise power of the blast from the bellows is ascertained by the aid of a little machine, called the *anemometer*, or wind-gauge ; and the process is termed " weighing the wind."

. 89. The anemometer consists of a glass tube, bent in the manner represented in *fig.* 38, having the lower end (*d*) fixed into a socket, with the other (*a*) open to the atmosphere. When the wind-gauge is about to be used, a small quantity of water is poured in at the upper end, some of which passes through the lower bent part and finds its level on the other side (*b b*). The socket is then placed over one of the holes in the upper-board of the sound-board, through which one of the pipes is to receive its supply of wind ; and the bellows are inflated. Under the influence of the surface-weights, the wind, on the opening of the pallet, rushes up to the sound-board, and, entering the socket, traverses the glass tube till it reaches the surface of the water, which it depresses, raising that on the other side to a corresponding extent. At first, the water oscillates ; but when it has ceased to do so, the deviation between the two surfaces is ascertained with a rule ; and if found to be, say two and a half inches, the bellows are said to give a " two and a half inch wind."

38

90. If a " stronger " wind than this is required, more weights are gradually added to those on the surface of the bellows, till the index shows the desired difference by a still further rising and falling of the water in the anemometer.

91. The " weight of wind," to which the manual portions of a church organ are usually " voiced," ranges from two and a half to three inches. The pedal stops, when supplied by a separate bellows, are usually voiced to a wind a quarter or half an inch stronger than the above, which is supposed to accelerate the speech and improve the tone of the large pipes. The *amount* of surface-weight necessary to produce the compressed organ-wind is about *three pounds and a quarter* per superficial foot of the top-board, to give an *inch* wind. This is the *average*, for the thickness of the top-board makes a little difference. In large bellows, with inch-and-a-half timber in the top-board, the weight would only be about *three pounds and two ounces ;* while in small bellows, with only inch timber in the top-board, the weight required will be about *three pounds and six ounces ;* the variation in the weight of the timber accounting for the difference. On a bellows, therefore, that produces a *three-inch* wind, the average amount of surface-weight will be *nine pounds and three quarters* per superficial foot.

92. Some of the French builders use different weights of wind for even their manual stops, and without increasing the number of bellows. This they manage by placing one or two reservoirs over that of the bellows, with expanding wind-trunks (like the sides of an accordion), reaching from the latter to the former. The upper reservoirs are then loaded with different proportionate amounts of surface-weights, thus producing the varied pressure of wind. The organ in the Carmelite Church, Kensington, built by MM. Cavaillé-Coll, of Paris, is alimented after this manner ; so also is the organ recently erected by Mr. A. Gern in the French Church in Leicester Square. The custom of applying different weights of wind, where necessary, is now common among the English and American organ-builders.

Division III.

THE WIND-DISTRIBUTING PORTIONS OF THE ORGAN.

CHAPTER III.

THE WIND-TRUNKS.

The wind-trunks. 93. THE wind, having been collected and compressed in the manner detailed in the preceding chapter, is next distributed among and conveyed to the several main divisions or departments, *i.e.*, great, swell, pedal, &c., of the organ, through the medium of wooden tubes, called *wind-trunks*.

94. In the early mediæval organ the apparatus for conducting the wind was little more than a large nozzle reaching from the bellows to the wind-chest. In the seventeenth century organ it was a wooden tube, projecting from the under-side of the hinge end of the bellows ; and the tubes of the several bellows were connected with a chief canal communicating with the great organ wind-chest, from which those for the choir and "echo" branched out. Conjointly, however, with the introduction of the horizontal bellows, a more independent method of winding the several divisions of the organ was introduced ; each wind-chest then having a separate wind-trunk devoted to it, proceeding directly from the bellows.

95. The original wind-trunks of many old organs were not large enough to allow the quantity of wind to pass that was necessary to supply modern demands. The old system of English organ-playing was very "light" and "thin" as compared with the modern ; that is to say, but few keys were held down at a time, seldom more than three or four. Moreover, old English organs seldom possessed the advantage of "double stops" (which would exhaust much wind), neither were there even pedals to draw down the lower keys of the manual, the *occasional* use of which, therefore, had to be made with the fingers. The old wind-trunks, therefore, were, no doubt, sufficient for all cotemporary purposes. But, as a more dignified style of playing, in broad and well distributed harmony, has since come into vogue, and the bass of, not simply one, but both or even all the manuals (if there be three), are brought under the proper use of the feet, the demand on the wind has been considerably augmented. Hence the insufficiency of most of the old trunks for modern purposes, and also of the necessity, in most "restorations," for new and larger wind-trunks—increased means for *distributing* the wind being of as much importance as increased means for *supplying* it by new horizontal bellows.

96. The size of a wind-trunk varies according to circumstances ; *i.e.*, according to the number and size of the stops to be supplied through it, the distance at which the sound-board on which they stand is placed from the bellows, and so forth ; and, thus governed, it ranges from four or five to sixteen or eighteen inches in width ; from three to about six inches in depth ; and from two or three to twelve or fifteen feet in length.

97. The course that a wind-trunk follows, in traversing an organ, is direct or circuitous, according to circumstances ; but the organ-builder makes the route as short as possible, for the important reason, that the nearer the bellows and sound-boards are to each other, the more prompt and decided will be the speech of the pipes. The wind is apt to become weakened by a long passage—to compensate for which, the wind-trunk has to be made larger, as well as longer, whereby a needless expense is incurred—besides which, the wind becomes more susceptible of disturbance, from the greater elasticity of the then lengthened column. To guard against this latter objection, organ-builders not unfrequently place, at the end of the long wind-trunk, a special reservoir immediately underneath the sound-board, so that the wind-store and source of consumption may be close together.

98. As the bellows and the wind-chests are seldom, if ever, on the same level, the direction of the wind-trunks is changed after their advance from the bellows, and turned towards the particular wind-chest which each has to supply. They are, for this purpose, jointed in one or more places, and the contiguous parts glued and nailed together in such relative positions as will direct the wind to its destination by the least circuitous route (*y, fig.* 23). The parts are seldom jointed at right angles to each other, as that forms checks, and disturbs and renders irregular the current of wind. To render the joints thoroughly air-tight and strong, they are covered with pieces of parchment, leather, or paper. Parchment or leather is best for the purpose, though the most costly ; paper is very perishable, and therefore almost useless. Some organ-builders cover the whole wind-trunk, internally, with a thin coat of glue, to fill up the pores of the wood ; and externally, as well as a great portion of the wood-work, including much of the wooden pipe-work, with a coat of colouring mixture, compounded of glue and red ochre, called red size. A more agreeable looking compound for the last-mentioned purpose is of a dark slate colour, on which ground the lettering of the pipes, in white capitals, stand out very distinctly. The most cheerful and light-looking covering for the wind-trunks, &c., is the light blue paper used by the French and German organ-builders, and also by some of the English.

CHAPTER IV.

THE WIND-CHEST.

The wind-chest ; its use. — 99. THE wind thus conveyed from the bellows is received into what are called *wind-chests.* And now that the more minute distribution of the wind is about to be traced, it will be well, for the sake of perspicuity, to confine the remaining observations on this subject to a single division of the organ ; more especially as the arrangements for the further distribution of the wind are the same in principle in every part of the organ ; and, consequently, one description will serve for all its departments.

100. *A wind-chest* is a long and broad, but rather shallow, wooden case or box, a *cross* section of which is shown in *fig.* 40 ; and a front view at *c c,* in *fig.* 39. It is made of the same length as the *sound-board* above, to which it belongs ; from half to two-thirds the breadth of the same ; and about equal to it in depth, or perhaps a little deeper.

101. These general dimensions refer to modern work. The wind-chests of old organs, in some instances, measure little more than *one-fourth* the breadth of the sound-board, and are therefore, of course, far less efficient than the later examples, and for the reason before explained, when speaking of the smaller wind-trunks of old organs.

102. In the wind-chest the compressed air accumulates ; and there it remains in a state of readiness for further and more minute distribution. A wind-chest, therefore, is in reality a local wind-reservoir, or cistern, so to speak, disposed, and designed to receive a due portion of the great body of organ-wind collected in the great reservoir, and to retain it for the supply of that special department or division of the organ to which the particular chest belongs.

39

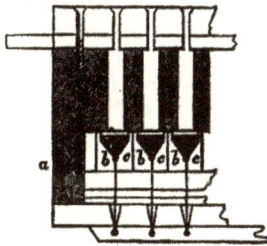

Front view of a portion of a wind-chest.

Its attendant parts.   103. Through one of the *ends* (*a*, *fig.* 39), or sometimes through the *bottom* (*c c c*, *fig* 40) of the wind-chest, the aperture is generally cut, at which the wind is to enter from the wind-trunk. The *back*, called the wind-bar (*d*), passes under all the sound-board bars crossways, and is made of very substantial material, because it serves a second purpose, namely, that of affording additional support to the sound-board above it, and so prevents the sound-board yielding under the weight of the superincumbent pipe-work.

40

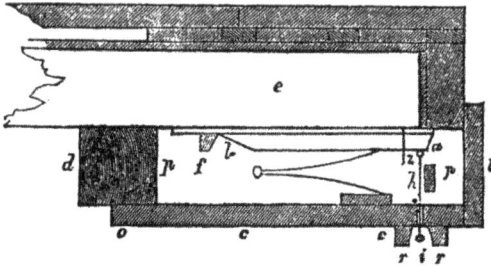

Side view of a wind-chest.

104. The ends, bottom, and back of the wind-chest are all firmly wrought together, and to the sound-board, which forms the *top* thereto. The *front-board* (*l*, *fig.* 40), as the front is called, is made moveable, because the *sound-board pallets* (*a*, *fig.* 40, and *c c c*, *fig.* 39) are immediately inside, and are liable to temporary derangement from a variety of causes; they are therefore required to be easy of access. The front-board, then, is simply fastened on with screws (see *fig.* 70, *e e e*), so that it may be soon removed, if the pallets require cleaning or repairing. In old sound-boards the front-boards were secured with hooks, and the plan is still followed by some of the French organ-builders.

105. Immediately under each pallet a hole is drilled in the bottom of the wind-chest, through which the necessary communication is established between the sound-board pallets inside the wind-chest and the *key-movement* without. These holes, which are ranged in a line, are made much larger than the thickness of the pieces of wire that pass through would require (see *figs.* 39 and 40), for, in wet seasons, wood-work is very apt to swell; and the holes, if in the first instance made so as nearly to fit, might, from their becoming, through this cause, smaller, prevent the pull-downs from passing freely, and so produce a "sticking." To prevent, however, an escape of wind through these enlarged holes, a long, narrow plate of brass is fixed over, or rather under them—for it is outside the wind-chest;—and through this plate holes are drilled, just sufficiently large to allow of the *pull-downs* working through them freely. The plate of brass is securely fastened on, by its edges being covered over with a small wooden beading (*r r*, *fig.* 40), which, at the same time, guards the loops (*i*) of the pull-downs from injury.

CHAPTER V.

THE SOUND-BOARD.

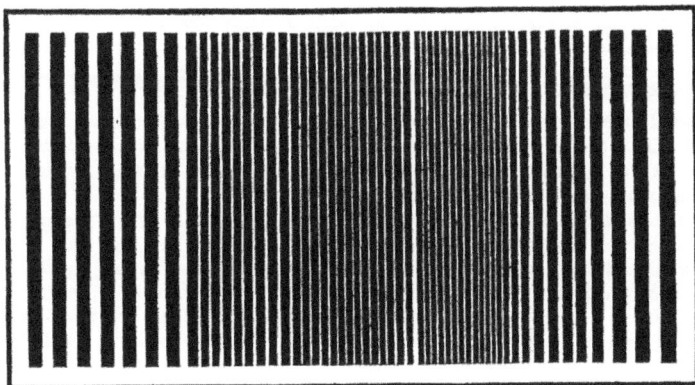

41

106. THE air that enters the wind-chest, in the manner already described, forms a sort of reserve, from which the several pipes of each key on the corresponding clavier receive their supply of wind. The ingenious arrangements and contrivances by which some of the wind is conducted from the chest to the pipes of any one of such keys, independently and exclusively of those belonging to the rest, next demand attention.

107. For every key on the clavier a small special channel is usually provided; so that if there be, say 56 keys on a manual, there will be the same number of *grooves* (as they are called) prepared to conduct wind to the respective pipes of those 56 notes. This is the general rule, to which, however, there are a few exceptions, which it is necessary to point out.

108. Some manuals, of which the *keys* indeed extend throughout, are nevertheless entirely without sound-board and pipes of their own, to the 8-feet octave (as is the case with a "tenor c swells"), and which, therefore, would produce no sound at all below that key, were it not that the bass octave usually communicates with the corresponding twelve semitones on the choir or great organ, or even with the "pedal pipes." And some pedal organs, and more particularly "pedal pipes," after extending the about an octave of their scale, suddenly turn back or repeat on the remaining pedals. In all such examples the number of grooves in their sound-boards will be *less* than the number of the keys.

109. On the other hand, where the pipes to a key are numerous and large, as is frequently the case in the bass of great manual organs, one groove is not

always considered sufficient to ensure a satisfactory supply to the whole ; and *two* grooves are accordingly devoted to each key in the "great octave." Here, therefore, the number of grooves would *exceed* that of the keys. John England is said to have been the first English organ-builder who introduced "double grooves" for the bass keys of the great organ sound-board.

The formation of a sound-board.   110. The manner in which the grooves are formed is as follows :—A large and strong layer of wood, that is ultimately to form the *roof* of the grooves, is turned upside down, so as to bring the under surface uppermost. Several pieces of wood, called *sound-board bars*, having been previously cut and planed to the requisite degrees of thickness, one of them is well glued on to the so-called *table*. To this are attached two pieces of wood, called the *fillings in*—one piece at each end—of the exact width that the space or groove is to be ; to which again is fastened a second bar ; and so on, a bar and fillings-in alternately, until the required number of channels or grooves are formed. Next, a shallow piece of wood, a few inches in length, is let a little way into each groove, to form a hold, to which the tail pieces of the pallets, presently to be noticed, can be attached ; and similar pieces are also let in, in other places, to increase the amount of surface, to which the sheet of leather, forming the bottom, can be glued.

111. After the sound-board has been "glued up," as the process just detailed is sometimes designated, its two long sides, presenting the rough ends of the sound-board bars and the intermediate fillings-in, are planed down ; and a stout piece of mahogany, from an inch to an inch and a half thick, is firmly glued and pinned on over them, to secure the bars, to strengthen the sound-board, and to give it a neat and finished appearance. These front and back surfaces are called the *cheeks* of the sound-board.

112. A large sheet of leather is then glued over the whole under surface of the sound-board, except in that part of the grooves which is to be enclosed within the wind-chest, where openings are left as entrances for the wind. The sheet of leather (in old sound-boards, parchment) usually forms the only closing the greater portion of the grooves have underneath.

113. The *sound-boards* of old organs are generally of the *frame* kind ; that is to say, the bars are at each end let into a frame, about an inch and a half thick, instead of being separated by fillings-in ; and the grooves are closed in above with wood, there then being no separate table ; after which a sheet of leather is glued over the whole, on which latter the sliders work. In Germany and France the sound-boards are still generally made in this way ; and Mr. Bishop retains the custom of making the sliders run on leather.

114. The grooves run parallel to one another, as represented in *fig.* 41. When the sound-board is turned right side upwards, about half of the under-side of every groove lies immediately over the wind-chest, as shown in *fig.* 40 ; the long openings already referred to being enclosed therein.

115. If all these wind entrances were to be left open, air would of course pass through all alike into the pipes, and thus cause every note in the scale to sound at once. To prevent this, the wind-entrances are first of all closed beneath by moveable pieces of wood, which, however, are so adjusted that any one or more of them can be drawn open at pleasure, and wind admitted into the corresponding groove. By these means the power is admirably secured of admitting wind to, or of excluding it from, the pipes of any of the keys. These pieces of wood are called *sound-board pallets ;* and from them the openings which they cover are named *pallet-holes.*

116. To ensure the pallets closing firmly against and over the pallet-holes, a spring of brass or steel wire is inserted underneath each, which presses them upwards. (See *fig.* 40.) The springs in question are, in old sound-boards, generally made of brass wire, with two or three curls; in modern examples they are frequently of steel-wire.

How the sound-board pallets are brought under control.   117. The orderly arrangement of the sound-board pallets, side by side, in a row, will be found illustrated in *figs.* 39, *c c c*, and 51, *c ç c*. As an organ cannot be played without some of the sound-board pallets being drawn open, and as the pallets themselves are completely shut up in the wind-chest, means are taken for bringing them under *outward* control.

118. A small loop of wire (*fig.* 40, *z*) is inserted into the moving end of the pallet (*a*), called the *pallet-eye;* to this is attached a piece of steel wire (*h*), of sufficient length to pass through one of the holes (*o*) bored through the bottom of the wind-chest; outside which it is finished off in a loop (*i*). Every pallet is similarly provided with a *pull-down*, as this piece of wire is called (see *fig.* 51); and thus the first step is taken towards making the pallets answer to the touch on the keys. To ensure their keeping their proper course, each pallet is furnished with two other pieces of wire, one placed on each side, called *direction-pins* (*fig.* 39, *b b b;* see also *fig.* 51); which prevent the pallet turning during its opening and closing, and thus secure its closing truly and entirely over the pallet-hole. Some of the above features may now be noticed somewhat more in detail.

The sound-board bars.   119. The *bars* of a sound-board are all made of the same pre-arranged *length* and *depth;* but there is a considerable variation in their *thickness.* This is because they have a *second* office to perform; for, besides separating the groves, they have to sustain and resist the pressure of the pipe-work above. As, however, the pipes belonging to the treble portion of a manual sound-board are all comparatively small and light, narrow bars afford sufficient support for them, and are therefore employed; whereas in the bass, where the pipes are both larger and heavier, bars of greater substance are necessary to ensure stability, and are consequently introduced. For the intermediate bars two or three graduated thicknesses are adopted, according to their situation.

120. In addition to the variation in the substance of the bars in the *same* sound-board, the thickness and indeed all the proportions of sound-board bars vary much, according to the number and size of the stops that have to be supported. Thus, the thickness of the bars ranges from one-third of an inch to an inch and a half; their length, from about two to five or six feet; and their depth, from two and a half to five inches.

121. Among the narrow bars of a sound-board a stout bar is interspersed here and there, in order to give additional strength to the work, and to offer a good hold to the screws that fasten down the upper-boards. Two pieces of wood of extra stoutness, resembling sound-board bars in all other respects except their greater substance, form the extreme ends—also introduced to ensure stability—called the *end-bars.* The entire sound-board rests on a stout and substantial frame.

122. The sound-board bars are represented in *fig.* 39 by the *white* lines.

The sound - board grooves.   123. The *grooves* in a sound-board, like the bars, are frequently made of three or four different widths. The narrow ones are of course for the treble keys, and the broad ones for the bass, where the pipes are large and a plentiful supply of wind is demanded. In all other respects the dimensions of the gooves are the same throughout a sound-board ; an increase in their width alone, or if not, then double pallets in the bass, being ordinarily sufficient to secure an adequate supply of wind to *the same* stops in the lower part of the scale or gamut. When even this addition is not likely to prove so, the groove is not further enlarged, but a second one is allotted to the same bass key, as already explained. For *more* stops, the grooves are made *longer*, to allow the additional pipes standing and speaking room above ; and also *broader* and *deeper*, that the cubic space in each groove may be adequate to the reception of the increased quantity of wind now necessary to feed the augmented number of stops. When these conditions, or any one of them, are not sufficiently attended to, the pipes do not all get enough wind to make them speak properly, and they are then said to " rob " each other. If the reed-stops are to be on a heavier wind than the flue, a piece of wood is glued in across every sound-board groove, to divide it into two : the wind-chest, which is then made as large as the sound-board, is divided longitudinally, and of course there are double pallets to the grooves. If the treble pipes are to be in a heavier wind, the wind-chest is divided transversely. Sometimes separate smaller sound-boards are made for the several purposes last mentioned ; particularly when there is a pneumatic action, or ventils.

124. It will be seen, then, that there are no fixed dimensions for sound-board grooves, but that they vary according to the number and size of the stops. The extent of this variation is ordinarily from one third of an inch to about an inch and a half in breadth ; from two to about five or six feet in length ; and from two and a half to five inches in depth. In large pedal sound-boards the grooves are sometimes made as much as four inches in width.

125. The grooves are represented in *fig.* 39 by the *light* lines.

The sound-board pallets.   126. The *sound-board pallets* are so many long and narrow pieces of wood, of a triangular shape. (See *fig.* 39, *c c c*.) One of the three flat surfaces is laid against the *pallet-hole*, to cover it and exclude the air from the groove. And, that the closing may be the more effectual, the surface so placed is coated with two or three thicknesses of white dressed leather (sheepskin), which allow the pallet to " bed " more closely against the pallet-hole than the bare wood could possibly do. Besides assisting in completely excluding the wind, the leather silences the return of the pallet against the sound-board ; which takes place with rather a smart blow, under the combined influence of the metal spring and the compressed air in the wind-chest.

127. The second and third surfaces of the pallet, constituting the sides, slope off gradually downwards, and ultimately meet and terminate in a long edge. This edge, pointing downwards and presented to the wind, enables the pallet, by its sharpness, to cut its way through the compressed air with comparatively little difficulty.

128. The ends of the pallet (*a b, fig.* 40), as well as the sides (*c c c, fig.* 39), are bevelled off, upwards ; that forming the front, nearest the front-board, somewhat acutely (*a, fig.* 40), and the other much more gradually (*b, fig.* 40). By the latter, the pallet is attached to the sound-board, by glueing a long and narrow piece of leather to the tail of the pallet and to the under-side of the sound-board ; and, so that the pallet may not accidentally become detached, from damp, &c., a piece of wood, called the tail-piece, is nailed over the end of the leather that is glued to the sound-board, which secures it (*f, fig.* 40). By the front end the pallet is drawn down or " open."

The pallet-holes.   129. Now, as the grooves are made gradually broader as the scale descends, that they may hold the required quantity of wind, so are the pallet-holes made gradually longer, that they may admit the increased quantity of wind, and, consequently, the pallets themselves are also made larger. The pallet-holes range from about five to twelve inches in length, according to circumstances. The pallets are always made rather larger than the holes they govern, that they may ledge firmly against the bars and wood-work all round, and so thoroughly exclude the wind. Thus a pallet to cover a hole an inch wide is made an inch and a quarter in width. A twofold object has here to be attained, namely, of allowing *sufficient* margin to the pallet for the purpose just mentioned, without unnecessarily increasing its *size*, and, therefore, its resistance and tendency to ciphering. The *less* the pallet projects beyond the pallet-hole all round, of course the *less space* will there be for the *lodgment* of "cuttings," or any other substance that might fall through the sound-board on to the pallet ; and an eighth of an inch on *each side* is amply sufficient to render a pallet perfectly "sound," if it is quite "true" in all other respects.

130. Some pedal pallets are made as much as sixteen or eighteen inches in length, and from four to five inches broad. The resistance, however, which the wind offers to so large a surface moving through it being very great, several organ-builders have devised means for overcoming this difficulty.

131. Mr. Hill, some years since, invented a new pallet, which allows of the passage of a large quantity of compressed air, without making so great a demand on the muscular powers of the performer to set into motion as did the old *clack-pallet*. This new kind, called the *box-pallet*, is formed like a small box (*a a, fig.* 42), the bottom of which is open, but furnished with a moveable covering. On pressing down a key, this covering is drawn sideways, and up by the side of the box, as shown in *fig.* 43 ; returning again under the influence of a spring at each end, when the pressure ceases. The circular motion enables it to escape the pressure of the wind during the opening ; an edge only, instead of a broad surface, being all that is presented to it ; and the calculation is, that it thus reduces the resistance to *one-fourth* of that presented by one on the old plan ; and admits, at the same time, *double* the quantity of wind. The leathered faces of the valve-seat are so arranged (the centre of motion of the valve being slightly eccentric to the curvature of the valve-seat) that all parts are thrown out of contact at the first moment of motion, consequently there is no friction of surfaces. A silver medal was, in 1841, awarded by the Society of Arts to Mr. Hill for his ingenious invention.

132. The *jointed-pallet* of Mr. Holt, of Bradford, consists of a pallet of the usual kind, with the front end (*a, fig.* 44) divided from the remainder, though jointed by means of the leathering above, so that the front may descend about the

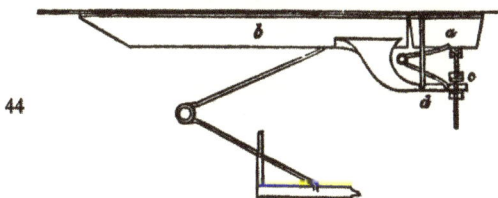

sixteenth of an inch before the hinder portion is set in motion. In a pallet fifteen inches long, about two inches and a quarter is thus separately hinged. The front

O

part descends first, admitting air into the groove; after which the button *c* takes hold of the fork (*d*), and by it draws down the remainder of the pallet without the finger having to overcome more than the resistance offered by the spring. The great organ pallets of the instrument in Leeds Parish Church were some years ago altered agreeably to this plan, and the average resistance reduced from nineteen ounces to seven.

133. The *valve-pallet*, invented by Mr. Jardine, of New York, and introduced by his nephew (of Manchester) into this country, is formed, as its name would imply, by attaching a second pallet, of diminutive size, to the back of the first one, covering a small circular orifice through the free end of the latter. See *b*, *fig.* 45, in which *c* represents a brass wire, tapped at both ends, screwed firmly

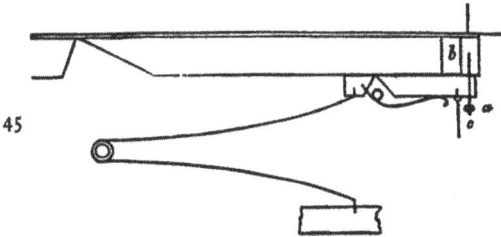

45

into the large pallet above, and furnished with a strong button (*a*) below; the middle part—passing through a hole in the small valve of sufficient size to allow the pallet to work freely—being left smooth, to prevent friction. On pressing down the controlling key, the small valve is lowered about the sixteenth of an inch, uncovering the orifice, and allowing some of the compressed air to pass through into the groove above. The atmospheric pressure now becoming the same over as well as under the pallet, there is only the resistance of the spring—necessary to ensure the *return* of the key-movement—to be overcome. The small valve, in descending, touches the button (*a*); resting on which, it now draws down the large pallet with it. The jointed-pallet and the valve-pallet are obviously the same in principle, although the manner in which the ultimate object is attained in the two is totally dissimilar. There is no disagreeable "second" touch discernible in the action of either of the last-mentioned pallets.

134. The *relief*-pallet (*fig.* 46), invented by Messrs. Hill & Son, is simple in construction, and conduces to lightness and elasticity in touch. It is completely surrounded with wind, except at the shaded parts (*a b c*); so that the pressure has the least possible amount of influence upon it. A small piece of "filling-in" (*e*), in the groove prevents the passage of wind through the division in the pallet immediately below.

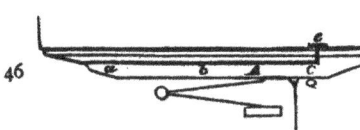

46

The pull-down lowers the under part of the pallet (A) until it touches the bottom (*c*), resting on which the remainder of the motion draws down the second member of the pallet, reaching from between *c* and *e* to the back end of the pallet.

CHAPTER VI.

THE TABLE.

The Table.　　　　　135. THE grooves, as already described, are entirely closed or roofed in by a layer of stout and tough wood-work, called the *table*. Through this table the wind has to make its exit. For this purpose, there are bored over each groove as many holes, or nearly so, as there are pipes to be supplied from each groove.

136. The accompanying engraving (*fig.* 47) represents the table of a sound-board thus perforated. On referring to it, and comparing it with *fig.* 41,

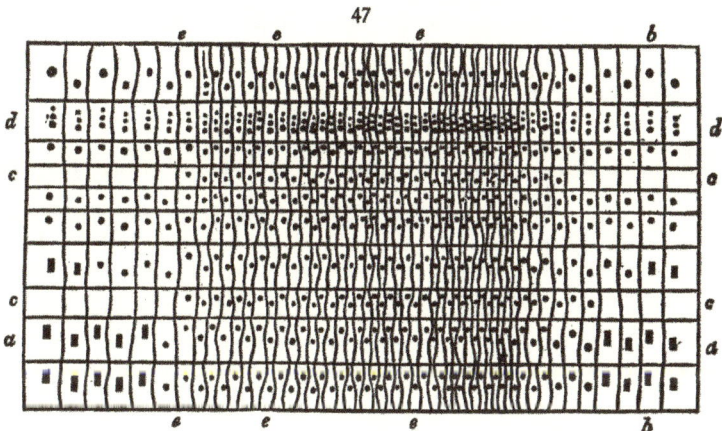

47

p. 29, showing the grooves of a sound-board, it will be at once seen that the rows of dots, circles, and squares, that may be traced by casting the eye in a line directly *across* the table, as from *b* to *b*, represent the several holes which occur in the roof of a *single* groove. And, on turning to the general section that forms the frontispiece to this volume, the reader will there see represented the several pipes belonging to a single groove in each of the four sound-boards drawn to a comparative scale.

137. But other series may be detected in the above diagram. For instance, if the eye be now directed *along* the table instead of *across* it, as from *a* to *a*, it will select from each of the transverse series a single aperture, with certain deviations presently to be noticed. Each *longitudinal* series thus compounded constitutes the outlets for the wind from the grooves to the several pipes of some single and independent *stop*. A portion of a longitudinal series, with pipes above, will be found represented in *figs.* 51, 52, and 53, pp. 44 and 45.

138. Some of the longitudinal series in the foregoing illustrations are so drawn as to illustrate certain peculiarities in either the arrangement of the perforations, their boring or grouping, which require to be explained.

Q 2

139. In England the room allowed for a church organ is seldom of sufficient width to permit the pipes of the stops being arranged in a parallel and unbroken series. What is wanting, therefore, in width, has to be secured in the depth of the organ. Only every *alternate* pipe of a stop is therefore usually ranged in a straight line, the other pipes being planted at a short distance behind.

140. Now, as the holes in the table are bored in the first instance to suit the arrangement of the pipes, each longitudinal series has the zig-zag appearance shown in the drawing. Sometimes, when the pipes of a stop are very large, as is the case with those of the manual 8-feet posaune at the upper end, only every *third* pipe is placed in a straight line, thus necessitating a *three-fold* distribution of the corresponding series of holes.

141. In some instances, again, the longitudinal series of holes is not continued over the entire length of the table, as indicated at *c c c c*. This is generally the case when the stop to be placed above is not to be of the full compass, but *minus* the pipes to those grooves over which a blank is left, and, consequently, to those keys which govern them ; and which, moreover, are not to be "grooved" into the bass of any other stop. Thus the blanks at *c c*, over the six wide grooves at each end of the table, indicate that the stop above will have no pipes to the bass or 8-feet octave.

142. In other cases, instead of there being simply *one* hole over each groove in a longitudinal series, there will be a cluster of from *two* to *five* smaller ones (*d d*) over every *treble* groove, and either the same number or an *oblong* one over each *bass* groove. These groups of little holes indicate the part of the table over which a *compound* or *mixture* stop is to be planted, and which always has from two to five pipes to a key.

143. The holes forming a longitudinal series are not made of a uniform size, but of graduated dimensions ; the smaller holes being over the treble and the larger above the bass grooves. The latter are also sometimes made square instead of round, as shown at *a a*, in *fig.* 47. Neither are the several longitudinal series of holes bored of the same size, as all stops do not require the same amount of wind. For instance, a 4-feet stop consumes little more than half as much wind as one of 8 feet ; while one of 16 feet requires nearly three times as much. The size of the holes in the table, therefore, obviously depends on that of the pipes and stop to be *fed* through those holes. At the same time, in order to secure the plump and ready speech of a pipe, the sound-board hole is made much larger than what would be necessary to feed the pipe, that the "flush of wind" may be ample. Thus the hole for the lower C in the Great Open Diapason is made an inch, that for the Principal, four-feet, three-quarters of an inch in diameter. To ensure an energetic and unhesitating tone from an organ, all the wind-courses, from the bellows to the pipes, should supply twice as much wind as is required for actual consumption.

144. Sometimes a small quantity of air will escape through a groove-hole, and make its way up to some pipe, and cause it to produce a low, disagreeable, and continuous humming. This is called a "running ;" to prevent which, little cuttings are made in the surface of the table, or in the upper-boards, in a zig-zag or waving course, passing between some of the holes, as shown at *e e e*, in *fig.* 47. If now any wind escapes before it can reach the next pipe, it is caught in some one of these channels, and by it conducted to the edge of the sound-board, where it escapes through a small triangular hole, without doing any mischief.

145. A running is sometimes caused by a sound-board bar "springing" (*i.e.*, becoming partially separated) from the table ; thus allowing a "leakage" of wind from one groove to the next. An accident of this kind can only be *thoroughly*

cured by taking the wind-chest to pieces ; but an expedient is in such cases often resorted to, technically called "bleeding," which consists in making a small hole in the groove through the "cheek," which allows the air to escape ; or the sound-board is disconnected, turned upside down, and hot glue poured into the grooves between which the leakage has occurred, which closes the fissures.

CHAPTER VII.

THE UPPER-BOARDS.

146. THE detection of the several transverse series of holes just now will assist in illustrating the next particular to be noticed.

147. If the pipes belonging to the grooves were to rest on the table immediately over the series of holes just described, the wind, on entering any one of them, would pervade all the pipes of that groove, and the organ would in consequence be incessantly pealing forth its tones at their greatest power ; none of the numerous modifications so necessary to accommodate the strength and character of the organ-tone to required purposes would be attainable ; but all would be powerful, monotonous, and meaningless alike. Such, nevertheless, was the case up to the sixteenth century, at which period the organ had, as to number of pipes to a single key, been to some extent developed, but not so the mechanism whereby to separately control those pipes. Up to the twelfth century the organ appears to have consisted of unison pipes only. In that century two or three pipes were added to each key ; sounding the fifth and octave, or the third and tenth. The organ thus became, as it were, a great mixture-stop, which it continued to be until the idea occurred of devising some mechanical means by which these added pipes could be allowed to sound or be silenced. This first step in the construction of *registers* or *stops* had been taken in the fourteenth century,—when so many other improvements in the organ are recorded to have been effected, if, indeed, it were not made before. It consisted in placing under every tier of pipes required to be under individual control a separate row of pallets, like the usual sound-board pallets. These complicated "spring sound-boards" remained in use up to the beginning of the sixteenth century, when the slider sound-board, still in use, and about to be described, was invented by a German. The power of subduing the organ-sound, even to a mere whisper, if required, is now secured by the introduction of two additional layers of wood-work over the table, by means of which the wind from the grooves can be excluded from or admitted to any or every longitudinal series of pipes at pleasure.

148. The upper layer of wood-work is, as nearly as possible, a counterpart of the table, and is placed at a distance of about one-third or half-an-inch from it. (See *fig.* 48.) Indeed, it may be said to be a repetition of that part of a sound-board, rendered necessary by the introduction of the mechanical work that is to control the speech of the pipes, and which must be over the air-tight grooves, yet under the pipes. The area of its surface is similar in all respects to that of the table ; the holes also correspond, for the most part, both in number, situation, and arrangement. It is not, however, made in one connected piece, like the table, but in several pieces, much *narrower* than the sound-board, though of the same *length* (at least frequently so in England), and which, when laid collectively side by side, present a plain surface, as shown in the above figure.

149. A sound-board is, in consequence, said to have, not one, but several upper-boards ; and it is an advantage to have as many of these as possible ; a separate upper-board for every stop, if practicable. The reason of this is, that if a slider below warps or "binds," it can only be effectually set right by being first

removed, and then planed ; and as, by way of preliminary thereto, the upper-board must be taken off, and, of course, the pipes above it disturbed, this can be done, if there be a separate upper-board to each slider, without displacing more pipes than those the disarranged slider governs ; but, if there are one or two other stops on the same upper-board, those stops must also be removed before the upper-board can be taken off.

150. A narrow upper-board is also less liable to "cast."

151. One exception to the general rule, that "the perforations in the upper-boards agree with those in the table," occurs in the case of "conveyanced-off pipes." When the sound-board, from whatever cause, is made so short that all the pipes cannot have proper standing and speaking room thereon, a situation has to be found for some of the larger pipes elsewhere, and the wind has to be con-ducted from over the holes in the sound-board to their new locality. If this situa-tion be on nearly the same level with the sound-board, a groove is cut in the substance of a kind of second upper-board, called the *groove-board*, from over the former to the latter, and then the surface outlet is made ; and when the pipe is below or above the level of the sound-board, a metal tube, called a *conveyance*, is introduced to conduct the wind from the groove or the groove-board to the pipe. The conveyances that conduct wind to the front pipes can generally be traced with ease.

152. It sometimes happens, particularly in modern churches, that the site for the organ is so circumscribed that there is neither adequate width for the sound-boards nor height for the pipes. It is this latter circumstance that renders it necessary for the organ-builder to place some of the large pipes one or two feet below the sound-board.

153. Another exception to the general rule sometimes occurs in the case of mixture or compound stops. In the bass part of the table, the preparation for a stop of this kind sometimes consists simply of one long hole. But as each key is provided with from two to five pipes, the upper-board on which they rest is required to have an equivalent number of punctures, instead of a single hole, and so causes the deviation in question.

48

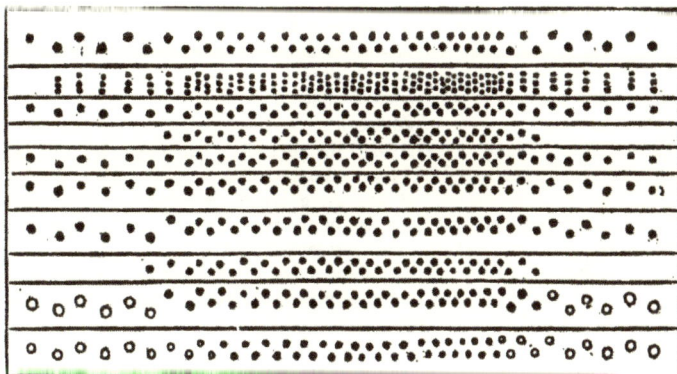

CHAPTER VIII.

THE SLIDERS, BEARERS, AND PIPE-RACKS.

154. BETWEEN the table and upper-boards (the first and third layers) is the second layer of wood-work. Certain portions or longitudinal strips of this layer, like those above and below it, are *fixtures;* while the intermediate parts are *moveable.* The fixed parts are called *bearers* (*f f f f, fig.* 49) ; and the moveable, from their being so, *sliders* (*a b c d e*). The latter are the wind-regulating features.

49

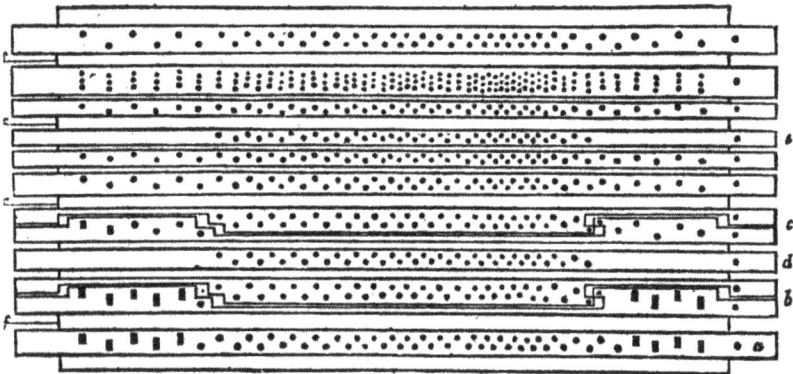

155. The *sliders* are so many long and flat pieces of oak or mahogany, lying over the longitudinal series of holes in the table. Each of these sliders is pierced with holes corresponding precisely with those in that part of the table on which it rests, and with those in the upper-board above.

156. This may be seen by comparing the above woodcut (representing the slides and intermediate bearers) with the preceding two cuts, *figs.* 47 and 48, pp. 35 and 39, illustrative of the table and upper-boards.

157. The relative position of the three layers of wood-work, between the grooves of the sound-board and the feet of the pipes, could not of course be shown in the preceding plans ; but they are represented in the "front section of a portion of a sound-board," *fig.* 51, p. 44, where they are marked *a d e,* and to which section the reader might here refer, as it will illustrate the following explanation of the manner in which a slider operates.

The action of a slider. 158. On drawing a slider (*a*) a little way out, its perforations are brought exactly *over* those in the table (*e*), and therefore immediately *under* those in the upper-board (*d*). The three series of apertures now agreeing, the air can pass up uninterruptedly from any groove into which it may be admitted, through all of them, into the pipe of the stop that stands immediately above ; the pipe being thus made to sound. The grooves are, in *fig.* 51, represented by the *unshaded* vertical divisions.

159. On moving the slider back into its former position, the holes in it are brought over the sound-board bars, the *shaded* parts, and the blank substance of the slider substituted for the holes over the grooves. The wind now, instead of finding a free outlet as before, is checked by the intervening material of the slider. The wind-passage between the first and third layers of wood-work being thus intercepted, and the communication for the wind from the grooves to the pipes of this particular stop consequently cut off, it becomes silent, and the stop is said to be "in."

160. Every separate slider, as a rule, controls a separate stop ; so that any stop may be allowed to sound or not, according as the slider is "in" or "out."

161. In some sound-boards certain of the sliders are "cut," so that the portion which controls the bass part of the stop above can be drawn independently of the remaining part. The stop is then said to "draw in halves." In *fig.* 49 the sliders marked *b* and *c* are represented as being constructed in this manner.

162. Other sliders, again, which do extend through the whole length of the sound-board, are not perforated, in some cases, in that part which lies over the bass grooves. (See *fig.* 49, *d e.*) Sliders that are thus only partially bored are intended to control stops that are of inferior range to the manual.

163. When all the sliders are drawn, the organ peals forth its amplest tones ; when all are in, no sound is heard, because the wind cannot reach any of the pipes.

164. The sliders measure from one and a half to three or four inches in breadth ; from one-third to half-an-inch in thickness ; and a few inches more in length than the sound-board itself. Two additional holes are cut through each slider ; one in that portion which, in consequence of its greater length, projects beyond the sound-board (*a, fig.* 49); the other, in some part that is convenient for the purpose. The former receives the end of the lever by which the slider is moved to and fro, on the drawing out or the pushing in of the controlling knob at the side of the manuals. The second hole receives a stout iron pin, which is fixed into the table, and allows the slider just sufficient motion to cover or uncover the holes in the table. If this motion were to exceed or to fall short of what is necessary, the holes in the table would, in either case, be partly shaded, thus cutting off a portion of the supply of wind from the pipes, and preventing their speaking with proper strength or in tune.

165. Other holes are sometimes cut through the opposite end of the slider. This is often the case when the "composition pedals" act directly on the sliders.

The bearers. 166. The *bearers* receive and support the edges of the upper-boards, which are screwed down to them, and sustain the weight of the upper-boards and pipes above—hence their name. The sliders are thus relieved from all pressure, and left entirely free to work.

167. In modern sound-boards there is commonly a bearer between every slider and its neighbour ; but in old sound-boards there is more frequently only one bearer between every two or three sliders. The modern plan is obviously the best, as one slider cannot, in moving, rub against another and disturb its position.

The pipe-racks. 168. The greater number of the pipes stand on the upper-boards, but cannot of course support themselves on their apex without more assistance : a frame-work, therefore, is used to keep them in an erect position.

169. The frame-work consists of some thin planks of oak, mahogany, or pine

wood, called *rack-boards* (*d, fig.* 50), laid parallel with, but four or five inches above, the upper-boards (*a*), and is there sustained at all corners, and in other convenient situations, either by wooden pins, called *rack-pillars* (*fig.* 50, *h h*), or by some other connecting wood-work. These rack-boards are furnished with holes cut immediately over those in the upper-boards. Through these rack-board holes the lower and narrow ends of the pipe-feet pass (*s s*), while the upper and broad ends of the pipe-feet (*b b*) are made to fit tightly into them; and to prevent the feet from shifting about, and the pipes getting out of the perpendicular, the "noses" (*s s*) of the pipes are sunk a little way into the upper-boards, which are "counter-sunk" to admit of this.

170. Most of the metal flue pipes, all the small and moderate-sized wood-pipes, and also the boots of the reed pipes, are racked in this manner.

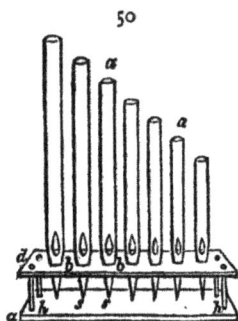

50

CHAPTER IX.

THE ARRANGEMENT OF THE GROOVES AND STOPS.

The situation of the large and small grooves in the sound-board. 171. IT has been explained, on pp. 31 and 32, how the grooves lie, side by side ; and how some are broad, others narrow. Nothing, however, has yet been said concerning the *order* in which these broad and narrow grooves are arranged with regard to one another. The primitive and most natural arrangement would be *semitonal*, and this is shown to have been a not unfrequent one in old times by the position of the pipes, as illustrated by some of the wood-cuts in the Historical Introduction. This plan is followed by some organ-builders even in the present day.

172. Several other ways or " plans," however, are in use, the selection of the particular one from among which is influenced by many considerations ; as, for instance, the size of the sound-board ; the department of the organ for which it is destined ; the terms on which the organ is to be constructed, &c. ; some description of groove arrangement calling for a more complicated and costly kind of *key-movement* than others.

173. The organ-builders of the seventeenth and earlier part of the eighteenth centuries, when fixing on the situation of their sound-board grooves, were often influenced much by the design of the case in which the instrument was to be enclosed. For instance, if the case was to have three towers, with the largest one in the centre, say of five pipes each, some of the largest grooves,—namely, those for some of the lowest keys,—were placed on each side of the centre passage-board, *i.e.*, at the *inner* end of the two halves of the sound-board ; the grooves next in size, at each *outer* end of the two halves ; and the smaller grooves in between the larger. In distributing the grooves after this fashion, the builders had two objects in view : (1) to keep the front pipes, which, of course, were " conveyanced off," and the grooves from which they were to receive their supply of wind, as near to each other as possible ; and (2) to distribute the large and the medium-sized grooves throughout each half of the sound-board ; doubtless from an impression that if all the large grooves were placed at one end of the " half," and the small grooves at the other end, the consumption of wind at one end of the wind-chest might at times be so great as to risk the partial withdrawal of that required for the smaller grooves at the other end.

174. The peculiar and complicated " plantation " of pipes, however, which such a distribution of the grooves rendered necessary, was most inconvenient. It caused a cluster of large pipes to accumulate at each end of the halves of the sound-board ; while there were the " prospect pipes " in front, and the large reeds in the rear. The small pipes were thus walled in on all sides ; and although little pipes are much sooner affected by change of temperature, dirt, &c., and therefore require looking to more frequently than any other pipes in an organ, except the reeds, yet they were thus rendered the most difficult of access. Several of the large pipes had, in the majority of cases, to be removed before the tuning or cleaning could be commenced ; which handling and shifting about, in addition to involving considerable trouble and loss of time, was not unattended with danger to the instrument.

175. These manifest disadvantages soon led to an amelioration of the then prevalent method of laying out and winding an organ. The sound-board grooves were made deeper, the pallet-holes lengthened, the wind-chests made broader and deeper, and the dimensions of the wind-trunks much increased. The grooves appear generally to have been made of a satisfactory *width* originally ; and the borings in the table, sliders, and upper-boards, were of ample size. These several improvements, and more particularly the subsequent introduction of *double grooves* in the bass, admitting of the introduction of conveyances of larger bore, the close proximity of the large pipes to their grooves, although at all times an arrangement most desirable, no longer remained a matter of such vital importance as before ; and, as the old plan of groove arrangement was so very objectionable in all other respects, it was allowed to fall into disuse, and was entirely and finally abandoned before the middle of the last century.

176. At the present time the English organ-builders usually adopt one of four different plans of groove arrangement, according to circumstances. Some of these plans require the adoption of a special kind of key-movement ; and, as it will be convenient to refer to these plans separately, the terms " first plan," " second plan," "third plan," and " fourth plan," are here adopted ; and, in the description of the key-movement, they will be briefly referred to under these heads.

First plan of groove arrangement.   177. In the first plan the grooves are placed alternately on each side of the organ, *i.e.*, the groove belonging to the C C key is planted at the extreme or outer end of one half of the sound-board, the groove belonging to the C C sharp key being similarly situated at the extreme end of the other half. The grooves throughout the sound-board are then arranged in the like alternate manner ; ultimately bringing those belonging to the upper two keys (*e³* and *f³*, say), one on each side of the passage-board. (See *fig.* 51.) In this first plan, therefore, the grooves occur in *tonal* succession on each half of the sound-board. (See *fig.* 51.) The " half " to the left, as the performer sits at the keys, contains the grooves for C C, D D, E E, F F sharp, gamut G sharp, A sharp, and their octaves. To the right are the grooves for C C sharp, D D sharp, F F, gamut G, A, and B, with their replicates. As a consequence of this distribution, the largest pipes stand at the *outer* extremities of each half of the sound-board, and the smallest in the *centre*.

51

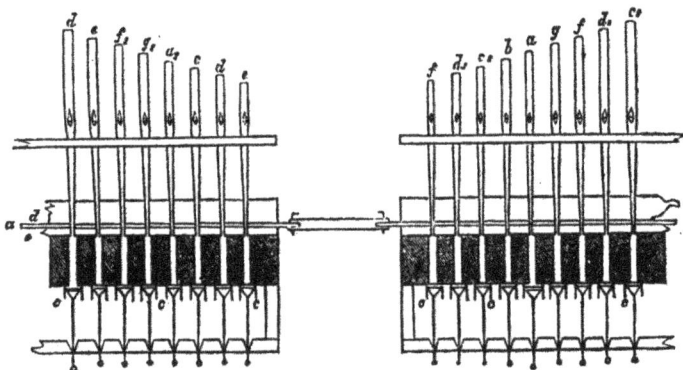

178. This groove arrangement is much used for large great organ (chief manual) sound-boards, both on account of the symmetrical arrangement of the pipe-work to which it leads, and the facility it offers for the purpose of tuning, &c. The shortest pipes standing, as they then do, immediately on each side of the passage-board, with the largest farthest off, and those of intermediate length between ; the tuner can, without difficulty, adjust either of the small pipes at his feet, or, reaching over them, arrive at larger pipes, if they require his attention.

179. The half of the sound-board on which the C C groove occurs is called the C side ; and the other half, the C sharp side. The " sides " are named after the lowest note on that half of the sound-board. Thus, in a G G organ, the side on which the G G groove is placed is called the " G " side ; and so on.

Second plan.   180. The second plan (*fig.* 52) may be described as a *reversion* of the first plan. The groove for the *lowest* key in the scale, instead of the *highest*, is placed in the centre of the sound-board ; while the other grooves, instead of *increasing*, decrease as they diverge from the middle. The *largest* pipe of each stop, therefore, is planted in the centre of the sound-board ; the *smallest* two standing one at each end. The pipes on a sound-board, having the grooves arranged in this manner, present a pyramidal outline, as shown in the accompanying woodcut.

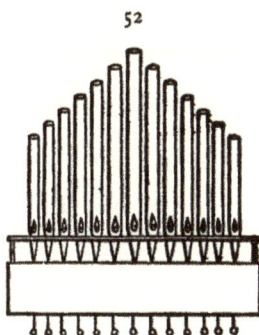

181. This second plan of groove arrangement is very generally adopted for swell sound-boards. It is very seldom that room can be spared inside the swell-box either for a passage-board down the centre or for one round the pipes. The pipes are therefore arranged according to the second plan ; and each side of the swell-box is furnished with a moveable panel. On removing this panel, the pipes of one half of the sound-board present themselves arranged in a graduated series from small to large ; and the remaining half the pipes are reached by the same simple means from the other side of the swell-box.

Third plan.   182. In the third plan the smallest groove is placed somewhat to the right of the centre of the sound-board—as it is viewed from the front of the case—and those for every semitone, as far as tenor *c*, are arranged in regular *chromatic* succession to the left of the first groove. Those for the lowest or "great octave" are then disposed alternately to the right and left, as in the first plan, occupying, as before, the extremities of the sound-board. (See *fig.* 53.)

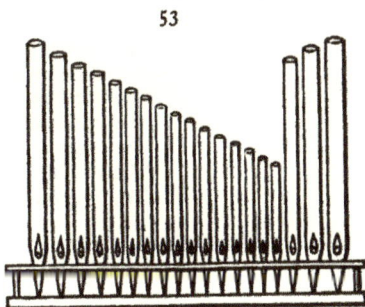

183. This third plan is most frequently adopted for the chief manual sound-board of small-sized church and chamber organs ; and admits of a much more simple kind of key-movement than the first and second plans.

Fourth plan.   184. In this plan the grooves and pipes follow the semitonal arrangement throughout the entire scale. It is much used by Schulze, of Paulinzelle ; Walcker, of Ludwigsberg ; Kirtland and Jardine, of Manchester ; Brindley, of Sheffield, &c., and admits of the most simple kind of key-movements possible.

The arrangement of the stops on the sound-board.   185. The stops—or, to use the technical phrase, " contents " —of the great organ are usually so arranged that the flue stops stand in front and the reeds behind ; and the largest flue stops, such as the unison and double diapasons, are generally placed first, the remaining stops being planted in rotation according to their size, the mixtures thus being brought next to the reeds. This arrangement of the stops is illustrated by *fig.* 1 in general section. When there were duplications of any stop, as two open diapasons or two trumpets, the old builders usually placed other stops between the first stop and its replicate. Thus, in Harris's organ, at Doncaster, the second open was placed between the two trumpets ; and in the organ at Ripon Cathedral, by Father Smith, the second open diapason stood between the trumpet and the sesquialtera.

186. The inside choir organ has its stops planted the reverse way to the above, *i.e.*, with the flue stops behind and the reeds in front, that the latter may be under the immediate inspection of the tuner. Thus, in *fig.* 2 in general section, the clarinet and bassoon are placed nearest the passage-board.

187. In the swell, the reeds are usually placed in front—as in the choir—because the tubes offer less impediment to the egress of the sound than would the more bulky flue pipes. (See *fig.* 4.)

188. The pedal stops are also planted in the same manner, and for the same reason.

The mechanism of the organ.   189. Having described the apparatus by which wind is collected for the use of the organ, traced its course from that source through the various channels, great and small, till it reaches the pipes, and noticed the sound-board pallets and the sliders by which the organ-wind is made subservient to musical purposes, we will now proceed to investigate, in detail, the several systems of mechanism, through the intervention of which the pallets and sliders of the several sound-boards, and, by consequence, the several pipes and stops of the organ, are brought so admirably under the control of one performer.

190. Of those numerous distinct systems of mechanism there remain the following to be considered, viz. :—

> The key and pedal movements,
> The draw-stop action,
> The composition pedals,
> The coupling movements,
> The sforzando coupler,
> The pneumatic action,
> The swell action, and
> The tremulant.

The sound-board pallets, sliders, and the blowing-action, have already been described.

CHAPTER X.

THE CLAVIERS AND KEY MOVEMENTS.

191. BEFORE, however, describing the appliances, through the agency of which the impulse given by the fingers or the feet of the performer is conveyed to the sound-board pallets, a few words may be said concerning the several ranges of keys assigned to *receive* such impulse, namely, the claviers.

The manuals.　　192. The organ, as is well known, is played partly by the pressure of the fingers, and partly also by the pressure of the feet, upon suitable claviers or keys. A *clavis* (a word derived from the Latin, and signifying a key, in French called *touche*) is a small lever (from *levare*, to lift up); and a clavier is an assemblage of such *levers* or "keys," rightly assorted. The various sets of keys (of which every perfect organ contains several, and among these at least one for the use of the feet*) are classed under one general term, *clavier;* and those intended to be used with the hands are called "manual claviers," or simply "manuals" (from the Latin word *manus*, a hand); and that for the feet, "pedal clavier," "pedal-board," or simply "pedals" (from the Latin word *pedes*, the feet). The keys, as well of the pedals as the manuals, are divided into long and short keys like those of a pianoforte; and the former are readily distinguishable from the latter by their magnified scale.

193. It is necessary to bear in mind the great distinction that exists between the terms clavier, manual, and pedal-board; as, otherwise, frequent uncertainty is likely to arise. The word clavier is of *general* application, and means simply *a set of keys;* which, however, may be for the use of the hands, or for the use of the feet; while the two other words, manual and pedal, are of *special* application, and define for what purpose, and by which members of the body, the clavier so named is to be employed.

194. In Germany the terms manual and pedal are used in a more extended sense than is usual in England. In that country they refer to the department of the organ on which the *claviers operate*, as well as to the *claviers themselves:* hence we frequently find it stated that there are so many stops on the "pedal," or so many "on the chief manual." Moreover, when a *manual* is said to be of 8-feet compass —*i.e.*, descends to C C—the manual *organ* is understood to be of corresponding range.

195. In the present work the word clavier will be used whenever the passing observation refers equally to the keys for the hands or for the feet. In all other cases the more explicit terms will be employed.

196. It has been already stated in the Historical Introduction that, so late as the thirteenth century, the keys of the organ were so heavy and clumsy in their touch, that they had to be played with blows of the fist, the keys being made many inches in width for this purpose. When it is borne in mind that there were as many sets of pallets and springs, of rude and primitive construction, as there were separate stops,

---

* Some Continental organs have, in addition to three or four manuals, *two* sets of pedals as at St. Paul's, Frankfort, &c.

it is easy to understand why the touch should have been so ponderous and resisting. A very few stops must have been sufficient to have made it so. In the fourteenth century the keys were made smaller and neater, so that they could be pushed down with the fingers ; and in the fifteenth century we read, for the first time, of different materials being used for the keys; as, in the year 1475, Conradus Rosenburger built an organ for the Barefooted Friars' Church in Nuremberg with ebony naturals, and ivory "sharps and flats." The keys of the English organs of the seventeenth century, made usually of oak, were *capped* in a similar manner; though this arrange-ment of the black and white keys remains only in such specimens in which the subsequent alterations have not kept pace with the progress of modern improve-ment. The original keys of many of the instruments of this time, as those of Smith and Harris, were very short and disagreeable to play upon, the short keys of those by the last-mentioned builder being 2½ inches only in length, and the longer keys 4⅜ inches. Those of Snetzler's organs were generally longer, and therefore more pleasant to the fingers. Previous to the year 1720 the thumbs had been but little used in organ-playing, and usually hung down in front of the manual ; consequently the portion of the naturals that projected forward in front of the short keys was made to do so as little as possible, that the fingers might reach the so-called sharps and flats with the more ease. It was the custom, moreover, instead of raising the fingers from the knuckles, to draw them under towards the palm of the hand, which accounts for the short naturals of old organs being scooped out into hollows in the centre by the friction of the nails.

197. When the thumbs came to be more freely used on the naturals—a method of fingering that was introduced by Francis Couperin, organist and court musician to Louis XIV. and XV., who printed the first fundamental instructions in 1713, and who died in 1733—the front part of the naturals was made a little longer ; and when they were also employed on the short keys—a system dating as far back as the time of John Sebastian Bach—those in their turn had to be slightly elongated. Thus, from the naturals being, in old organs, little more than four inches in length in front of the cross-beading, they are in modern instruments sometimes made from five to six, and with the short keys in proportion.

Side view of manual keys.

198. The manual keys of modern organs are usually made of lime tree wood, with the surface of the long keys covered or capped with ivory ; and that part of the short keys which rises above the level of the naturals is either made of ebony or some other wood stained black. Each manual key is punctured towards its centre with a small hole, passing downwards, to admit a metal pin (*a, fig.* 54), that rises from a piece of wood or pin-rail beneath (*b*), and which pin serves as a pivot for the key to work upon. The hole through the key is not cut exactly midway between the two ends, but rather nearer to the back end, leaving about five-ninths of the entire length in front of the pin. A second hole is bored in the under-side of the front end of each key, to admit a pin that rises from a rail (*c*), running across under the front of the keys, and upon which pin the key descends as it falls. This pin renders the fall of the key true and steady under the finger. Two or three *thicknesses* of green baize, or some such woollen stuff, laid at the root of the pins, prevent the keys from coming into noisy contact with the front-rail. These two rails are strongly united to two pieces of wood, called *key-checks*, the front ends of which appear on each side of the set of keys, finished off in some ornamental

form in keeping with the style of the case. As the manual keys would, on the removal of the finger, spring up beyond their proper level under the influence of the returning "key-movement," unless something were done to check them, a piece of wood is laid transversely across the keys, immediately to the rear of the veneered part, so as to be just out of sight, which is loaded with lead on the upper side to make it so heavy as to stop the rise of the key, and lined underneath with green baize to silence the blow of the key against the board.   This piece of wood is called the *thumping-board*.

The pedals.   199. The pedals are made either of oak, mahogany, beech, or some other hard wood, and are, as before said, chiefly distinguishable from the manual keys by their magnified scale ; the order of the keys, long and short, being the same in both cases.   The pedals work on a centre at the back (*a, fig.* 55), and fall under the pressure of the foot, in front (*b*), that is, at the end under the manuals. A spring under each pedal (*c*) causes them to resume their original position on the removal of the foot.   The pedals are placed at a proper distance below, and under the manuals, that they may be conveniently played upon by the feet of the performer.

Side view of pedal keys.

The situation of the   200. The claviers of an organ are usually placed in the front
claviers.   of the organ-case, in the centre, just beneath the impost ; though want of room and other circumstances sometimes render other arrangements necessary.   Thus they are occasionally found at the side, as at Hanover Chapel, Regent Street ; or even at the back, as at Ely Cathedral, Christ's Chapel, Maida Vale, &c. In some instances the claviers are not in the instrument itself, but separate, and, to all appearance at least, unconnected with it.   This is the arrangement observed in the organ at Windsor Castle, constructed on a plan suggested by His Royal Highness the late Prince Consort, where the keys appear in a kind of manual table, situate twenty-two feet from the body of the instrument.   At Westminster Abbey, again, the claviers are similarly detached ; the great organ being in front, the swell behind, the choir to the right, and the pedal organ, with its large pipes lying horizontally, to the left of the organist.   The Apollonicon had its numerous claviers so arranged that the several performers sat looking towards the audience.

201. Concert-room organs were formerly furnished with what is called a "long movement," a modification of the usual mechanism that admits of the keys being placed in the front of the orchestra, while the instrument itself stands at the back. The first long movement made in England is said to have been that attached to the organ in Vauxhall Gardens, by Byfield, and which served Green as a model for the long movement applied by him to the organ he erected for the Handel Commemoration in Westminster Abbey in 1784.   At All Saints' Church, Manchester, the communication between the keys and sound-board pallets is established by means of a movement 87 feet in length.

202. But the most remarkable long movement is that attached to the organ in the church of St. Alessandro in Colonna, at Bergamo, built by Serassi in 1782.   The organ has three manuals, the first and second of which serve for the great and choir organs, in the same part of the church ; while the third, by means of a long movement passing underground, acts upon another great organ situated at a distance of nearly 115 feet from the keys.

203. Some organs have two, three, or even four manuals.   These are arranged

P

one above another, and in such a manner that the lowest stands out farthest and each succeeding one recedes.

204. In an organ having two manuals the keys of the great organ form the lower row, and those of the swell the upper. Where there are three manuals, the great manual is usually in the middle, with the swell above and the choir below. In Avery's organ, at St. Margaret's, Westminster, however, the great manual was originally below, and the choir organ keys in the centre.

The key-movement.   205. The key-movement is that system of the mechanism of an organ which establishes the communication between the keys just noticed and the sound-board pallets that control the entrance or otherwise of the wind from the wind-chest into the grooves.

206. In the ancient organ, with its spring sound-board and large keys, this consisted of strings and ropes. In a modern organ there is usually a separate "move. ment" for each clavier. And as the clavier and its corresponding sound-board are variously located in regard to each other, according to circumstances—sometimes being placed in close proximity, at other times at a long distance apart ; sometimes in a direct line with each other, at others at right angles ; sometimes so that the performer faces the organ, and at others so that he sits with his back to the organ— it is obvious that the "movement" introduced for the purpose above mentioned must not only vary very much in detail in various examples, but in some cases must be far more complex than in others. This would be the case even if the grooves were always arranged in the same order ; but as they are sometimes disposed agreeably to the regular semitonal "fourth plan," and sometimes according to the crossing "first or second plans," the key-movement, from this cause, becomes in some respects still more diversified.

207. Yet, although so multifarious as to detail, there are in reality only two distinct kinds of key-movement in common use in England, namely, the *lever* or *fan-frame* movement, and the *roller-board* movement. Two other kinds are noticed in a subsequent chapter.

208. The *fan-frame movement* is the simpler kind of the two. It consists of three parts only, namely, a small upright rod, called the *sticker* (*c, fig.* 56) ; a horizontal lever, called the *backfall* (*h*); and a second vertical rod, called the *tracker* (*f*). The lower end of the sticker (*c*) rests on the tail (*b*) of the key (*a*), and the near end (*d*) of the backfall (*h*) on the top of the sticker. The far end (*e*) of the backfall is attached to the tracker (*f*), which latter passes up perpendicularly, and communicates with the pull-down that draws open the pallet (*g*).

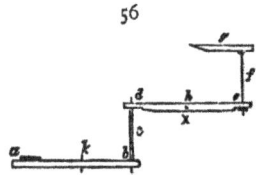

209. The *stickers*, which are made of pine or cedar, and of a round or square shape, reach from the key-tails to the backfalls—a height varying from a few inches to a foot or two, as may be requisite. From the top of each sticker a wire pin rises about an inch (*a, fig.* 57), and passes through a puncture in the backfall, to prevent its slipping off instead of rising with the sticker. A small piece of woollen stuff, placed over the top of the sticker, prevents that and the backfall rattling together ; a similar noise at the lower end being obviated by the leather on the tail already noticed.

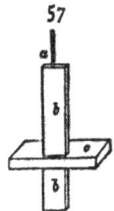

210. Sometimes the stickers are made to pass through a *register* —a rule of wood laid transversely and flatways above the tails of the keys, and perforated (*c*) ; in which case they have each a small piece of wood

or leather attached. This, by resting on the register, prevents the sticker falling through, and so allows of the temporary removal of any key, or even the entire set, without disturbing the arrangements of the stickers.

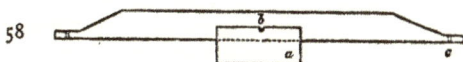

58

211. The *backfalls* are made of some hard wood, such as oak or cedar, and of the shape indicated in the adjoining cut (*fig.* 58). They range from one to about three feet in length, according to the distance, in a direct line between the pallets and the keys; from one to two inches in depth; and from three-sixteenths to one-quarter of an inch in thickness. A small wooden beam, called the *backfall-frame,* sustains them in their proper situation; the frame itself being scored crossways with numerous narrow cuttings, made to receive that portion of the backfalls which is below the centre. The centre consists of a piece of stout iron wire passed through the middle of each backfall, and fastened down with small staples.

212. The *trackers* (*fig.* 59) are so many strips of some light wood, as pine, measuring about five-sixteenths of an inch in width, one-eighth in thickness, and, in the situation under consideration, not more than about two feet in length. Each tracker is furnished at the lower end with a *tapped-wire* (*b*)—a piece of brass wire about three inches long, incised or *tapped* at one end like a screw, and slightly hooked at the other, by which it is bound to the tracker with thread, afterwards covered with size. The upper end is provided with a hook (*a*) of copper wire, that communicates with the pull-down.

213. The tapped-wire at the lower end is passed through a small hole in the free end of the backfall, indicated by dotted lines at *c*, in *fig.* 58; and the latter is then firmly secured to the former with a small circular piece of leather, about one-third of an inch in diameter, turned out of thick leather, like that used for the soles of shoes, and called a button (*c, fig.* 59).

The action of the key-movement.   214. The several parts just described operate one on the next in the following manner :—On pressing the key (*a, fig.* 56) down, which moves on a centre (*k*), the tail (*b*) rises, lifting with it the sticker (*c*) This in its turn raises the near end (*d*) of the backfall, which, by moving on the centre (*h*), causes the far end (*e*) to descend. In doing so, it draws down the tracker (*f*), which pulls the pallet (*g*) open.

215. Some of the wind from the wind-chest now rushes through the pallet-hole into the groove, and from thence makes its escape through such apertures in the roof as have been uncovered by the drawing of the sliders above, as explained in detail in previous sections; but, in doing so, it is compelled to pass into pipes placed over those holes, which are thus made to sound; and, having thus performed its destined duty, it regains its freedom.

216. The key-movement just described is found chiefly in conjunction with a sound-board, made according to the "third plan," and, therefore, most frequently in small organs. Where the grooves follow in semitonal succession, rollers are not usually required; and, as simplicity in the mechanism is always desirable, the above movement, as the least complex, is preferred, where and so long as the consecutive groove arrangement is observed. This accounts for the omission of rollers, as also for the presence of the backfalls as doors; though not for their taking the *fan* form, which latter circumstance arises from another and independent cause.

217. A sound-board is always wider than the manual, sometimes extending to twice its width, or even more. It follows, therefore, that the grooves, instead of running *parallel* with their respective keys, and differing only in being located at a

higher level, are, with few exceptions, more or less *out of the line* with them. This being the case, and yet it being necessary that the far end of every backfall shall be under its own groove, at the same time that its near end shall still rest on its proper sticker, all the backfalls, with the exception of the middle two or three which swerve but slightly, are made to diverge, until at last the extreme ones are at one end considerably out of a line with their near end.

218. The spreading out of the backfalls causes the set to bear a sufficient resemblance to the ribs of an open fan, to account for the adoption of the name by which this portion of the movement is generally known.

219. In the notice of the "third plan" of groove arrangement, it was mentioned that the grooves for the lowest or bass octave were placed alternately at each end of the sound-board. While, therefore, all the bass keys are to the extreme left of the manual, six of the corresponding grooves, at the least, are at the extreme right of the sound-board. To bring these, through the governing pallet, under the control of their respective keys, a horizontal rod or roller is provided for each key, extending along behind the backfalls, to transmit the motion the requisite distance to the right.

220. These rollers—of which the accompanying engraving (*fig.* 60) is a plan—

(*a a*) are each provided with two arms (*b c*), one (*b*) projecting immediately *over* the descending end of the backfall, the other (*c*) directly *under* the pallet. Instead of the tracker now drawing down the pallet as before, it lowers the first roller-arm (*b*); and the roller itself (*a a*), being thus made partly to revolve, conveys the downward motion to the second roller-arm (*c*), which, descending, draws with it a second tracker in communication with the pallet-wire, which latter opens the pallet. The rollers just referred to are made from an inch to an inch and a half in width, from five-eighths to one inch in depth, and from an inch or two to about five feet in length. They are each provided with two metal *centre-pins*, projecting about an inch from each end, which pass into holders or *studs* standing out from the *roller-board*. These pins form the centre at each end on which the roller partly revolves, while the studs hold them suspendedly over the keys.

221. The rollers are mostly ranged one over the other ; though in some cases, if more convenient, two are placed in a line. Wooden rollers are omitted from all the best modern work, and iron ones substituted. They are, however, more costly. The eyes in the arms of iron rollers are sometimes advantageously bushed with leather ; and the holes in the studs which support the rollers are lined with cloth to render the action noiseless.

The roller-board movement.

222. The second variety of key-movement is that known as the *roller-board movement.* This description of movement is a usual accompaniment to all sound-boards in which the grooves are disposed according to the alternate or any other *irregular* arrangement, and is, therefore, a common adjunct to such as are made agreeably to the "first and second plans," among others.

223. In a sound-board so constructed the CC and CC sharp grooves and pallets occur, in separate halves of the sound-board, at a distance sometimes of seven or eight feet from one another, while the keys lie side by side on the manual. And all the other grooves, as already explained, are arranged alternately right and left, while the keys of course continue their scale gradually and uninterruptedly upwards. In consequence of the order of the keys and grooves never agreeing, every key is

generally furnished with a roller. After the motion of the key, therefore, has been conveyed *inwards* to the necessary distance, which is effected, in this case, either by *parallel* backfalls, or by squares and trackers, it is transferred to the *right* or *left* by a long or short roller, until it is brought under the right pallet. The groove arrangement therefore leads to the introduction of a great number of rollers, and the movement is in consequence named after them. The roller-board, which sustains the rollers, is the large irregularly shaped board, or sometimes a frame, that may be placed edgeways, and occupying the necessary space under the wind-chest, and extending to nearly the entire width of the sound-board.

Square and tracker-work. 224. But in most organs some of the sound-boards are necessarily situated at a greater distance from their manuals than that to which the key-movements, in the condition already described, can reach ; more particularly those for the choir and swell departments, as will be obvious on referring to the general section. A modification and extension of one of the movements just noticed—usually of the roller-board movement—therefore becomes necessary, and is effected by first dividing it. The roller-board still occupies its usual position underneath the sound-board, and the stickers theirs on the tails of the keys. The backfall frame is altogether dispensed with, and the communication between the stickers and now distant rollers is established by "square and tracker-work."

225. The "work" last mentioned has a familiar illustration in the crank and wire-work of bell-hangers (see general section). The trackers traverse distances either horizontally, perpendicularly, or diagonally, like the wires, while the squares transmit the motion round corners, from one tracker to the next, like the cranks.

226. The trackers in the modified movement now under consideration are often made very long, extending to ten or twelve feet, or even more ; or, what comes to the same end, several shorter trackers are hooked together, so as collectively to make up the necessary length. These great "lengths" of tracker are generally carried through registers or bridges, which afford them support, if they run horizontally, and also prevent their flapping together. The pedal movement, which in most examples closely resembles the last-mentioned, is noticed in conjunction with the pedal coupling movement.

227. The *squares* mentioned just now are so many centres (see *fig.* 61), formed of some tough wood, furnished with two arms each (*a b*), about three inches in length, also of the same material as the square, or sometimes of iron, or even of brass. The angle (*c*) of each square is placed in a corresponding cutting made in the *square-frame* (*d d d*) to receive it, and the squares are sustained in their proper positions by a small metal rod (*e*), on which they move freely to and fro.

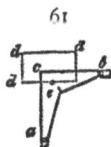

228. Occasionally, squares are cut out of a single piece of wood ; but that is not a good way of making them ; for, in that case, one arm must necessarily be the cross way of the grain, and will not long bear the "tug," but will snap off short. A much better kind of square is that wherein two pieces of wood are dovetailed together, at a right angle, the strong way of the wood ; these are more expensive, but at the same time they are much more durable. Mr. Forster, of Hull, has a plan of fixing his squares so that any one can be taken out separately, without disturbing the set of fifty or sixty to which it may belong. The French builders also frequently set their squares in independent holders. The organs in the Carmelite Church, Kensington, and in the French Church, Leicester Square, have their squares adjusted in this manner.

CHAPTER XI.

THE COUPLERS AND SFORZANDO PEDAL.

229. BESIDES the several *primary* systems of mechanism already described, which are indispensably necessary for working the organ at all, most instruments are provided with a greater or less number of members belonging to an important *subsidiary* class, called *coupling movements*, or, more briefly, *couplers*.

230. A coupler is an appliance by which either a second clavier and its stops can be brought into play while the performer's hands or feet are engaged upon the first, or the same clavier can be united to itself in the octave above or below ; in any case, the result being an increase of the resources of the department receiving such accession. For the time being, the stops or pipes, according to whether the coupler be another clavier altogether, or the pipes of the same clavier, but united in the octave above or below, appear to belong to the key *actually struck*, and new combinations and effects become thus producible, which are not otherwise attainable on the same instrument. Seidel* supposes the idea of the manual copula to be as old as the fourteenth century. It is certain that, so long ago as the year 1651, some movement of the kind existed in Geissler's celebrated organ in the Cathedral at Lucerne, in Switzerland ; and the circumstantial manner in which the operation of the registers in question was described in the account over the keys of the old organ, now removed, leaves little doubt that couplers were at the above date great rarities, if not absolute novelties, at any rate in Switzerland. The account states that originally the organ contained " several registers, whereby one may make use of the three manuals together, or one or two of them separately."

Manual couplers.   231. Couplers are classed under two heads, viz., manual couplers and pedal couplers. Of the former kind there are three varieties, viz., the unison, octave, and double or sub-octave couplers.

232. The *unison* manual coupler unites any key of one manual to the corresponding key of another. One of the most usual couplers of this nature is that for uniting an upper manual to a lower ; in other words, for attaching the " swell to great." This is commonly formed of a set of short stickers (*d, fig.* 62), one to each key, reaching from the upper surface of the great organ key to the under side of the swell key. These stickers pass through a rod (*e*) extending over the great organ key-board from side to side, between the centre and tail of the keys, and between the two manuals. This rod is capable of being turned partially round by drawing out a handle at the side of the keys, communicating with appropriate medium work, which places the stickers in a perpendicular position, as shown in the accompanying cut. If any key of the low manual (*a*) be pressed

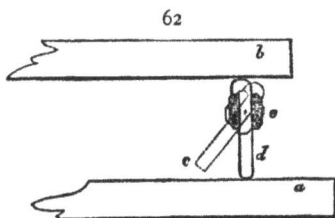

---

* See Historical Introduction, p. 47.

down while the " coupler is out," the sticker above will be raised, lifting the tail of the corresponding key on the upper manual (*b*,) so that whatever is played on the lower manual is also executed on the upper. When this union of manuals is not required, the governing handle is thrust in, causing the rod, and, consequently, the sticker, to resume their original positions, as shown by the dotted lines. That of the latter at such times is at an angle of about 45 degrees with the great manual keys ; their lower ends (*c*) being then raised sufficiently far to admit of the keys of the under manual being set in motion without coming in contact with them. The *tumbler* coupler has a tendency to throw the fingers off the keys, when drawn on while the great organ is being used, or, if not this, to disarrange itself, or even become broken. This defect does not appear in the *sliding* coupler represented in *fig.* 63, which is formed in the following manner :—The great organ key has a portion of its upper side cut away, leaving an inclined plane (*a*) covered with leather and black-leaded. The under side of the swell key is similarly hollowed (*b*), the shape of the cutting being reversed. The coupler, when not *in action*, is stationed as indicated by the dotted lines, the sticker (*l l*) dropping into the register (*n n*). The hollow in the great organ key then allows the key to rise without touching the sticker. When required to be used, the register, which is held and moves freely in a *slot* in each key frame, is carried

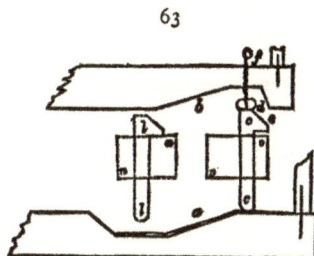

a little backwards (*o o*), the sticker (*c c*) glides up the inclined plane (*a*), is raised a little way out of the register, and brought directly under the regulating button (*d*), by which it raises the swell key. The back part of the knob of the sticker is bevelled (*e*), so that, in the event of a great organ key being down when the coupler is drawn on, the sticker may raise the swell key gradually without causing any jerk to the finger, and the button (*d*) is rounded to assist its coming into operation smoothly and quietly. Through the swell key a tapped wire passes (*f*), by which the action of the coupler is so nicely regulated that the swell key will begin to descend at the same moment that the finger commences the depression of the key of the great organ. This improvement on the tumbler coupler is due to Messrs. Kirtland and Jardine, organ-builders, of Manchester.

233. Another kind of mechanism for the coupler "swell to great," called from its shape the "*ram* coupler," also possesses the merit of being capable of being drawn while the keys are down, without causing any disagreeable resistance, and without being liable to derangement from being brought into operation under such circumstances. This kind of movement was invented by the Messrs. Robson, and has been applied by them to the pedal couplers, as well as to those for the manuals.

234. An organ with three manuals occasionally has, in addition to the coupler above described, another for uniting the lower manual to the middle one, *i.e.*, " *choir* " to " *great*." A third kind of unison coupler unites the upper manual to the lower ("*swell*" to "*choir*"), of which examples occur in the organ at the Temple Church, &c. Other couplers take down the octave above or the octave below the key pressed down by the finger. These occur in numerous organs.

235. An "*octave* manual coupler," *i.e.*, one acting in the fore-mentioned way, was introduced into the organ at St. James's Church, Bristol, by Smith, of that city, in the year 1824 ; another, and, like that just noticed, forming part of the original work, occurred in the York Minster organ, built in 1829 by Mr. Hill. Both these unite the *swell* to the *great organ* in the octave above. Octave couplers are

frequently found in the organs of Italy, where they are called *Terzo Mano*, third hand.   In England this kind of coupler is called by the organ-builder who *re*-invented it—for Mr. Holdich does not appear to have been conscious of its pre-existence elsewhere—the Diaocton.   A "*double* manual coupler" either unites one manual to the other in the octave below, or a manual to itself in the same manner ; generally the former.   The organ in St. Dunstan's Church, Fleet Street, erected in 1834 by Robson, has one that attaches the choir organ to the great in this way. This acts on separate pallets in the sound-board, and therefore does not move the keys.   Octave and double couplers sometimes take down the keys, and sometimes not.   Composed usually of a series of diagonal backfalls, they either communicate with separate pallets, when the keys, of course, do not fall, or they operate upon the same set of pallets ; the working of the movement being then made obvious by the motion of the keys, as in the case of the ordinary couplers, unless indeed the key-tails are weighted (as they sometimes are) to balance them.   The swell manual of the organ at St. Luke's Church, Old Street, made by Gray and Davison, has both an octave and a double coupler.   By the aid of such couplers "an 8-feet stop may be converted into a 16-feet, or a 4-feet (or all three), at pleasure ; and a great variety of effects and combinations may be produced, which otherwise would be unattainable without increasing almost indefinitely the size of the organ."[*]

The sforzando coupler.   236. The *sforzando coupler* is a movement for reinforcing the strength of the swell instantaneously, and to a far greater extent than is attainable by the aid of the swell pedal alone.   It is worked by a pedal, on pressing down which the great organ becomes coupled to the swell.   On removing the pressure from the pedal, it returns (by means of a spring), and the action is disconnected.   The action simply is a backfall in connection with the swell key, and operating on the great organ key movement, as shown in *fig.* 64, in which *a* represents the swell tracker, *b* the great organ tracker, *c* the connecting backfall in question, which rises and falls on the sticker (*e*), the pin being free, while *d* marks out the regulating button.   In a few instances, where the swell has been provided with octave and double couplers, the sforzando pedal has been made to bring on those couplers simultaneously, and *not* act on the great organ ; and where the swell is to C C, and is powerful, this latter kind of movement is in some respects more effective than the other, as the *reinforcement* is also under the influence of the swell.

64

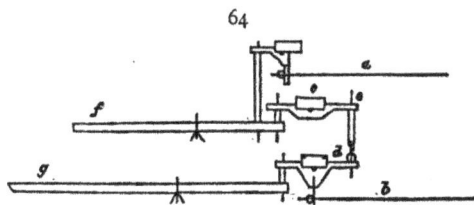

237. A sforzando pedal, uniting the great to swell, was introduced by Lincoln into his organ at St. Olave's, Southwark, built in 1844, and it has subsequently found admission into several other instruments.

Pedal couplers.   238. The second class—*i.e.*, the *pedal couplers*—are such as either unite the manuals to the pedals, or cause the pedal organ to play in the

---

[*] Pole, *On the Musical Instruments in the Great Exhibition of 1851*, r. 75.

octave, one way or the other, as well as in unison. Of pedal couplers there are as many varieties as there are of manual couplers. The most common form of the pedal coupling movement is the following :—First, in consequence of the pedals occupying much more room in regard to width than the corresponding number of manual keys, rollers similar to those in the key-movement are introduced (see *b b, fig.* 65), having one arm (*a*) *over* the controlling pedal (*e*), and a second (*f*) directly *under* the key to be communicated with (*c*). The action of the pedal having thus been brought into a line under the key, a backfall (*d, fig.* 66) occurs running underneath and parallel thereto. From each of these a sticker (*a*) reaches thence to the under side of the manual key (*c c*) to be acted upon ; a pin in the lower end (*e*) of each sticker, descending through the end of the backfall, to render the former in one sense a

65

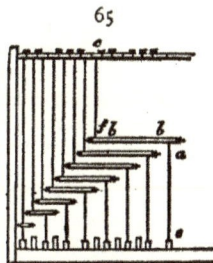

fixture, the upper end being left free to be moved forward or backward as occasion may require. The stickers pass through a register (*b*), which, among other purposes, serves as a support thereto. When the manual is to be coupled to the pedals, the

66

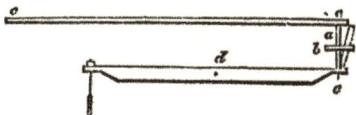

register is drawn forward a little, the upper end of the stickers being thus brought immediately under the tails of the manual keys. They are represented as being thus situated in the last illustration. When the pedal coupling action is in operation, the two trackers, the roller arms, and the near end of the backfall (*e*) rising, lifting with it the sticker (*a*), which in its turn raises the tail of the manual key (*c*), and this, setting the key-movement in motion, produces the same effect as pressing the key down with the finger would do. When the union of the "manual to pedal" is no longer required, the handle is pushed in, which moves the register back again, the upper end of the stickers being by this guided in the same direction till they get just beyond the key-tails. The stickers now appear in a slanting position, as shown by the dotted lines in *fig.* 66, and *miss* the keys. Sometimes there are two or even three couplers for uniting the different manuals to the pedals in the same pitch ; as " great to pedal," " choir to pedal," and " swell to pedal ;" in which case there are as many sets of these stickers rising from the backfalls, each communicating with a particular manual.

239. Thus much concerning the *mechanism* by which the manuals are coupled to the pedal. With regard to the *pitch* in which this union is effected, great dis-similarity used unfortunately to prevail in England. In some organs the key acted upon by any given pedal would be identical with the one that the finger would have touched, *i.e.*, corresponding with the bass note written and sounding in unison with the bass voice. This is the case when the manual organs are of the CC compass. In such cases the manual unison stops are said to give the 8-feet or legitimate pitch. In GG, FFF, and CCC organs, however, the pedal couplers more often attached the manuals to the pedal in the octave below, that is, in the 16-feet pitch. This want of systematic arrangement arose from there being no recognised *compass* as the invariable one for the manuals of English organs. Some organs of long manual compass have pedal couplers acting in the 8 *and* 16-feet pitch on the great manual, as in those in St. George's Hall, Liverpool, Westminster Abbey, &c.

240. In the organ in Trinity College Chapel, Cambridge, is, or was, a coupler, called the *Canto Fermo* coupler, that unites the treble of the choir organ from middle c[1]

upwards to the pedal to the extent of two octaves and a third.   This causes the 8-feet stops of that manual organ to produce the effect of so many 2-feet pedal stops.   Other organs have a coupler for uniting the tenor C of the swell to the CCC of the pedal, as in the instrument at the Irvingite Church in Gordon Square, built by Gray and Davison, which obtains, from the unison stops of the fore-mentioned department, a sound resembling that of so many 4-feet pedal stops.

241. Besides couplers for uniting the manuals to the pedals in various ways, others are occasionally met with which attach one octave of the pedal *organ* to the other.   The octave coupler brings the CC pipe on to the CCC pedal, the effect being similar to that of the addition of an 8-feet principal to the 16-feet open diapason.   The double coupler brings the CCC pipe on to the CC pedal, thus giving the effect of a 32-feet stop on the pedals from thence upwards.   Both kinds were added by Walker to the organ in Tonbridge Church, though they do not exist in the instrument as rebuilt by Gray and Davison in 1855.

CHAPTER XII.

THE PNEUMATIC ACTION.

242. It has already been shown that every sound-board pallet is provided with a spring beneath, to ensure the return of the key-movement on the withdrawal of the pressure from the key; and it has also been mentioned that the compressed air in the wind-chest becomes a second source of resistance to the touch of the performer. This latter fact is perceptible, even in small organs, of which the sound-boards are palleted in the ordinary way, by striking a chord in the bass part of the manual, first without the bellows being blown, then with the "wind in," when the additional resistance which the organ-wind causes will at once be felt. In larger organs which have pallets of increased size throughout the sound-boards, with two pallets in the bass, the amount of spring and wind resistance is of course much increased, which again is augmented when there are also octave and double couplers, causing perhaps six or seven pallets to operate upon a single key. In instruments, again, containing some stops on a heavy pressure of wind, the resistance becomes too great for even the most muscular finger to control without experiencing much fatigue. In such cases, it being probably beyond the power of any of the relief pallets to *remove* the stiffness from the touch, some contrivance is required that shall boldly *overpower* the resistance. The pneumatic lever performs this duty most efficiently; and, in doing so, ingeniously converts that which would otherwise be the organist's antagonist into his assistant.

243. The first idea of establishing such pneumatic assistance occurred to the late Mr. Joseph Booth, organ-builder, of Wakefield, who applied his invention to the organ he built for the church at Attercliffe, near Sheffield, in the year 1827. He placed the lower pipes (wood) of the open diapason of the GG manual on a small separate sound-board, and to the pull-down of every separate pallet he attached a small circular bellows below. A conveyance from the great organ sound-board groove conducted wind into this bellows, which, opening downwards, drew with it the pallet. These small bellows Mr. Booth used to call *puffs*. The second step in establishing pneumatic agency was made by Mr. David Hamilton, of Edinburgh, who, in 1835, added a movement of the kind to the organ in St. John's Episcopal Church in that city. In the year 1839 a paper was read at a meeting of the British Association at Birmingham, explanatory of a pneumatic lever which he then exhibited. It was left, however, for Mr. Barker, a native of Bath, but for many years a resident in Paris, to fully appreciate the importance of, and to develop, and make generally known, this new agency in organ manipulation. Mr. Barker's first attempts were made with a cylinder and piston, which were afterwards abandoned in favour of a small bellows. "In the first instance he endeavoured to introduce his apparatus in England, about 1832. Experience, however, in large organs was then wanting in this country, and his endeavours were unsuccessful; he therefore went to France, where the subject was better known, and where the value of the new principle was at once appreciated. It was introduced immediately in the great organ, being built at St. Denis (1841), and has since been

applied to a considerable number of large instruments in the principal churches of France ;"* as, for instance, at the Madeleine, St. Vincent de Paul, &c.

244. The pneumatic lever, as made by different organ-builders, varies slightly in detail ; but the following is the general plan and principle of all. The upper member of the lever is formed very like a small concussion valve (see *a, figs.* 67 and 68) ; the former of which shows the lever *closed*, the other *open*. Beneath the lever are two little chambers (marked *c c* and *d d*), between which passes a third (*e e e*). Below, again, is a kind of backfall (*o o*) which controls two circular pallets (*b b*) in such a manner that when one is open the other must be closed. Lastly, to the rising end of the lever a small lug (*w*) is attached, which draws up a tracker (*f*) that sets the several key-movements in motion.

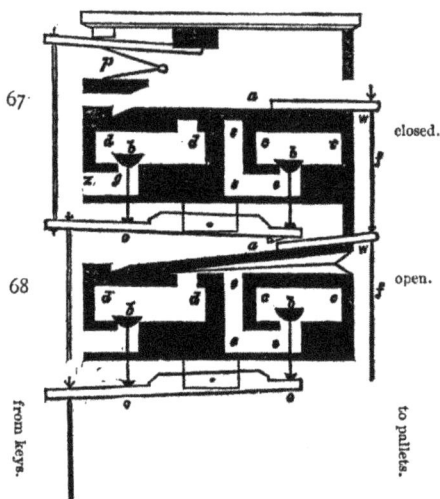

The pneumatic action shown at large.

245. On pressing down a key on any one of the manuals, the movement draws down the near end of the backfall (*o o*), causing the far end to rise, which motion places the circular pallets (*b b*) in the positions shown in *fig.* 68. Some of the wind from the chamber (*c c*) now passes downwards through the uncovered pallet-hole, traverses the passage (*e e e*), raising and filling the pneumatic lever (*a*), which draws up the tracker (*f*), communicating the impulse to all the sound-board pallets that may be attached to the controlling key. The circular pallet in the second chamber (*d d*) at the same time closes and prevents the escape of any wind.

246. When the finger is withdrawn from the key, the position of the backfall, and consequently the circular pallet, is reversed, as shown in *fig.* 67. The supply of air from the wind-chamber is now cut off by the descent of the pallet. At the same time the second pallet in the chamber (*d d*) is raised, allowing the wind to descend through the pallet-hole (*g*), escaping through the opening (*z*) into the atmosphere. The contents of the lever being thus exhausted, it returns to its state of rest, as shown at *fig.* 67 ; the rapidity of the change being accelerated by the

---

* Pole, *On the Musical Instruments*, &c., p. 77.

spring (p). In consequence of the width of the pneumatic levers, about three inches, only every *fifth* lever is placed in the same row ; hence the pneumatic action always appears in five tiers, as shown in the general section.

247. A very simple kind of pneumatic action has been devised by Messrs. Hill and Son. This is shown in the accompanying cut. The circular pallet (a) in the wind-chamber (b) being drawn open by the square (c), wind passes through the orifice (d) into the receiver ($e\,e$), and hence into the pneumatic bellows ($f\,f\,f$), the square pallet (g) being at the same moment closed by the motion of the wire (i). On the key being released, the *lug* (k), under the influence of the spring (l), returns, drawing with it the wire (m), closing the pallet (a), and uncovering the aperture (o), through which the wind escapes, the bellows ($f\,f\,f$) then descending.

69

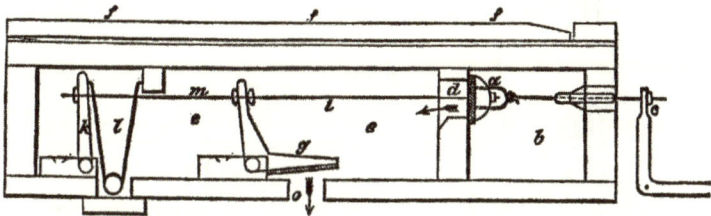

248. For Messrs. Bishop and Son's compact pneumatic action the merit is claimed of its requiring less space than the usual lever attachment, without sacrificing either efficiency or facility of touch. The two diagrams on page 62 exhibit the constructive peculiarities of these appliances, the working of which is elucidated by the letterpress that immediately follows :—

$A\,A$ are chambers or wind-chests containing compressed air ; $B\,B^1$ are valves commanding the entrances to the pneumatic bellows or motors ; $C\,C\,C^1\,C^1$ are the pneumatic motors themselves, the lower series of valves and motors being shown *closed*, and the upper series *open ;* $D\,D^1$ are exhaust valves ; $E\,E$ are tubes conveying the compressed air to series of motors above the two wind-chests ($A\,A^1$) ; $F\,F^1$ are backfalls, to one end of which is attached the mechanism set in motion by the organ-keys, and to the other a flexible tape ; $G\,G^1$ connected with the exhaust valves (D). When the backfall (F) is pulled down by the rod (H) into the position shown at F^1, it carries with it the valve (D^1), which has hitherto been retained in its position by the spring ($\mathcal{J}\,\mathcal{J}\,\mathcal{J}^1\,\mathcal{J}^1$) ; this allows the compressed air to enter the opening ($I\,I$) and inflate the motor ($C\,C$) into the position shown at $C^1\,C^1$, which conveys the motion of the key to the rod (K), or any other rods that may be connected to the arms ($L\,L\,L\,L$). The position of the backfall (F^1) also relaxes the tape (G^1) and permits the exhaust valve (D^1) to close by its spring. On releasing the key the backfall returns to the position shown at F; the spring ($\mathcal{J}$) returns the valve (B) to its seat and opens the exhaust (D), by which, and by the pressure of the spring of the organ-pallet with which the rod (K) is in connection, the motor ($C\,C^1$) is exhausted and falls to the position indicated at C. In the series of motors above the wind-chests (A and A^1) the wind, instead of passing direct through the passage ($I\,I^1$), passes through the openings ($I\,I^1\,e\,e^1$, $E\,E^1\,e\,e^1\,e\,e^1$). This, it will be seen from the front section, is necessary by reason of each motor occupying the width of two of the valves (B).

249. The tubes marked $M\,M$ are for pneumatic tubular actions intended to take the place of the troublesome long tracker-actions, or the present unreliability of the magneto-electric actions now generally employed where the key-boards

or " console " of the organ are separated from the instrument itself. In this case
only the supply and exhaust valves of the pneumatics are placed within the console,
the pneumatic bellows being immediately beneath their separate pallets of the
wind-chest at the other extremity of the tubes. The motors (C C C^1 C^1) are then
only auxiliary ones to act on the manual couplers ; the same supply and exhaust
valves serve for the two sets of bellows attached to the apparatus.

Front view.   Side view.

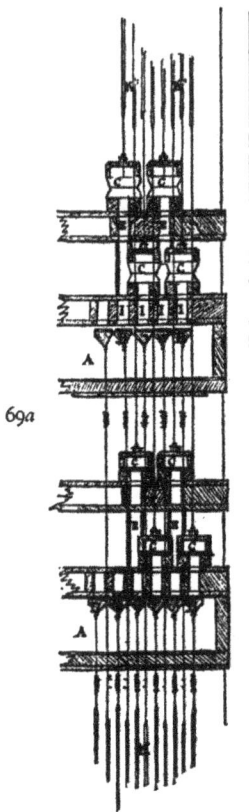
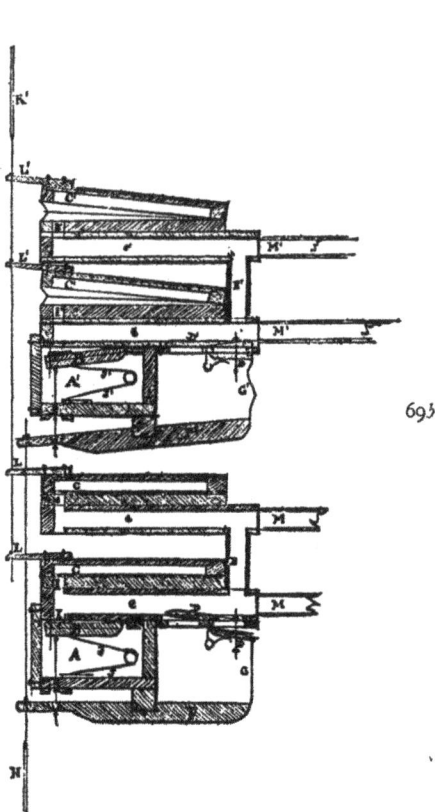

69a   69b

CHAPTER XIII.

THE DRAW-STOP ACTION.

250. THE several longitudinal series of pipes on the various sound-boards have already been explained to be governed by sliders, which either permit the wind to enter the pipes or not, as circumstances may require. The sliders, as already mentioned, are an invention of the sixteenth century. The earliest mechanism for moving them consisted simply of so many levers, the sliders, doubtless, being too "stiff" to be drawn or closed by the fingers unaided. This "first kind" of draw-stop action appears to be shown in the engraving on p. 36 of the Historical Introduction, where the free ends of the levers are directed *upwards*. In the interesting remains of an old organ at Radnor, similar levers, of iron, about eighteen inches in length, were the only means by which the five stops of that instrument were originally controlled. Before the end of the century a complete draw-stop action had been invented, although it was not always brought into the most convenient position for the use of the organist. Even in some of the English organs erected soon after the Restoration, a troublesome arrangement still existed. For instance, in the organ by Father Smith in Manchester Cathedral, and in Pembroke and Emanuel Colleges, Cambridge, the choir organs of which were "in front," the draw-stops of those departments were in the choir organs themselves, and therefore *at the back* of the player. In the organ at St. Paul's Cathedral, by the same builder, and in Harris's instrument in Worcester Cathedral, the choir stops were indeed made to draw through the great organ case, but through the jambs below the manuals, and quite out of convenient reach ; and not many years ago the choir stops of Silbermann's celebrated organ in the Cathedral at Strasburg could only be drawn from the choir organ itself, which stood at least six feet to the rear of the player. The reason why in English organs arrangements such as the foregoing proved to be sufficient for their time was that, in the church music then existing, "musical colouring" formed by no means a general feature, and, therefore, "instrumental colouring" had not become, as it has since, a necessary and looked-for contingent. In organs built to meet modern necessities the draw-stops of *all* the departments are brought within easy reach of the performer. Of the mechanism introduced to effect this end, called the *draw-stop action*, there are many varieties, designed to meet the exigencies of particular cases.

251. The first kind proposed to be noticed is that which may be described as the *wooden-trundle draw-stop action*.

The wooden-trundle draw-stop action.

252. To understand the necessity for the presence of the several parts of the action just named, it is requisite to point out the relative position of the performer and the end of the sliders to be operated upon. We will suppose the sound-board to be ranged longitudinally immediately behind the front pipes—the usual position occupied by the great organ sound-board. The situation of the slider-ends, then, as compared with that of the organist, would ordinarily be inwards ; to the right we will suppose, though it may be the left; and upwards to a higher level. This route is, in the above action, followed by the draw-stop rod (*a, fig.* 70), which traverses the organ inwards ; the trundle (*b b*),

w̦hich conveys the motion round an angle, the trace (*c*), which continues the motion at right angles with the draw-stop rod, and the lever (*d*), which conveys it upwards.

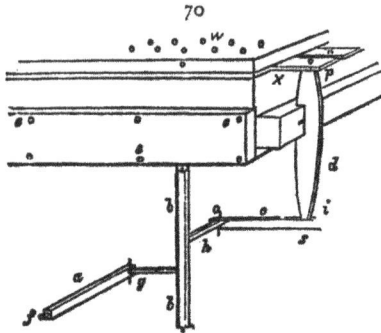

70

A description of the several parts.   253. *The draw-stop rods* usually measure about an inch across, for they are made round or square according to fancy, and from about one and a half to ten feet or more in length, according to the distance of the trundle from the manuals. The front end is made of oak or other hard wood, and the remainder of pine, the two parts being neatly spliced together. The near end of each draw-stop rod is furnished with a handle, formed of some dark-coloured and handsome-looking wood, into which is inserted a circular plate of ivory, bearing an inscription, announcing the kind of stop that is controlled by that particular handle and attendant parts.* The farther end of the rod has a horizõntal mortise made in it to receive the trundle-arm, a small iron bolt fastening the two together, so that the one cannot be drawn forward without the other accompanying it. The draw-stop rods run horizontally from the front of the case inwards, in the direction of the back of the organ, bordering the manuals (with which they run parallel) usually on each side, where they are arranged one over another, forming one, two, or three tiers, as the case may be.

254. *The wooden trundles* are made of good thickness, to prevent their springing, which casualty, were it to occur, would prevent the perfect drawing or closing of the slider. Each trundle is furnished with a stout pin at both ends, which passes into frame-work above and below, and which form pivots for it to revolve upon. The *arms* (*g h*) are made of wood or iron. They have no fixed positions ; but the first arm (*g*) is placed as nearly as possible in a line with the draw-stop rod (*a*) that is to act upon it, and which may be high or low in the row wherein it appears ; while the second (*h*) is placed in a line with the lower end of the lever (*d*).

255. The trundles usually stand under the sound-board to which they belong, bordering the draw-stop rods perpendicularly, as the rods do the manuals horizontally.

256. *The traces* are rods of deal, reaching from the second arm of the trundle to the lower end of the lever ; hence their name. They are mortised at each end ; at the one (*o*), horizontally to receive the second trundle-arm ; at the other (*i*),

---

* The custom of distinguishing stops one from the other by a particular name was introduced in the sixteenth century.

vertically, to admit the lower extremity of the lever. The traces may usually be seen under the sound-board, running in the direction of its length.

257. *The levers* are generally constructed of some hard wood, as oak, beech, etc., though in some old organs they are met with of iron. They are hung on a centre about two-thirds from the lower end, and the lower extremity is narrowed to allow of its admission into the mortise in the trace; while the upper is made altogether smaller, that it may pass into a hole prepared for its reception in the projecting end of the slider.

How the draw-stop action operates.   258. When the organ is about to be used, the inscriptions that are on the stop-handles, or sometimes over or at the side of them, are referred to, and the handle bearing the desired name is drawn *forward*. The rod brings with it, in the *same direction*, the first arm of the trundle (*g, fig.* 70), and the trundle itself (*b*), partly revolving, causes the second arm (*b*) to swerve round and draw the trace (*c*) in the direction from the *side* towards the *middle* of the organ. This latter having the lower end of the lever (*i*) fastened to it draws that with it *inwards;* the upper end (*p*) in consequence taking an *outward* motion, and moving the slider the *same* way. The passage way is thus made clear for the wind from the grooves through the holes (*w*) in the upper-board into the pipes.

259. In the draw-stop action for small organs wooden trundles are not usually employed, but iron squares are more frequently used.

The iron trundle draw-stop action.   260. In the second or iron trundle draw-stop action (*fig.* 71), the trundle and the arms are formed of wrought iron. The trundle itself (*a a*) stands at the edge of the sound-board (*b b b*), instead of underneath it, as in the former case, with its upper end (*c*) rather above the level of the bottom of the sound-board. There is no trace used, the bottom arm (*d*) being made much longer, that it may extend from the trundle to the draw-stop rod (*e*), and the top arm (*f*) is placed quite at the upper end of the trundle, from whence it gradually inclines upwards, until it reaches the slider (*h*), where it is finished off with a small bolt (*g*), that passes through the slider (*h*), and acts upon it.

71

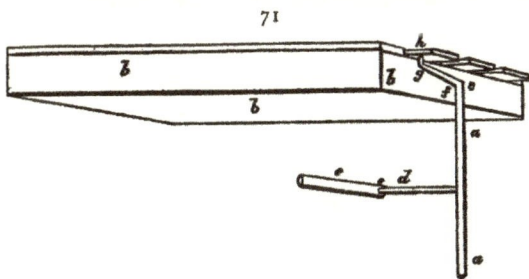

261. When a sound-board is remotely situated, its draw-stop action is modified, and the trundles are sometimes placed horizontally, instead of perpendicularly; all such matters of detail being of course regulated by the nature of the situation to which the organ is being adapted.

262. In the organ originally built by Messrs. Hill and Son for the Panopticon, and now at Clifton, the draw-stop action was made upon a principle then entirely new to this country, the sliders being put in motion by small bellows, and the weight of the long vertical trace rods was ingeniously balanced by counter weights attached to the end of short horizontal levers.

The pneumatic draw-stop action. 263. The bellows now mostly used for the pneumatic draw-stop action consists, like the vertical feeder already explained, of three vertical boards, the two outer of which (*a a*) are fixtures, the middle one (*b*) being moveable. The two sets of ribs in between are marked *c* and *d*; *e e e* is the wind-chest ; *o o* the D valve, the hollow of which is long enough to reach from the wind entrance to one member of the bellows to the exhaust, marked *m*. The draw-stop movement is attached to *k*, and *l* communicates with the slider. The wind passes from the wind-chest (*e*) through *f f* into *g g*, distending it. On drawing out *k*, the condition of the two members of the bellows becomes reversed. The hollow of the D valve is drawn sufficiently to the right to uncover the wind entrance (*r*), and consequently to reach to the second one (*i*). Wind from *e* now passes through *r*, following the course (*s s*), entering *t t*, carrying *b* close up to *a*. The wind from *g g* at the same time *descends* through *f f i* into the D valve, and is conducted through the exit (*m*) into the vacant space (*n n*).

72

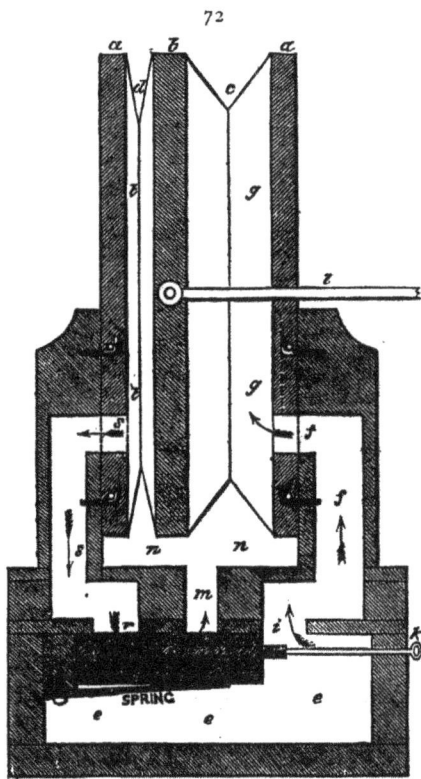

CHAPTER XIV.

BLOWING MACHINES.

264. Among the most agreeable additions to the mechanical appliances of an organ must be classed the blowing machines for pumping the bellows of the instrument, and keeping them duly supplied with wind under all possible and varying circumstances. One of the greatest drawbacks to the pleasure of playing upon a large organ used to be the consciousness that one's own performance frequently could only be carried on at the toil and exhaustion of fellow-beings. Hence, the discovery of some mechanical means for inflating the bellows, and of blowing quickly or slowly, according as much or little wind might be required, became a great desideratum. The first hydraulic engine patented was that invented by Mr. David Joy, of Middlesbrough, and originally arranged by him for the large chamber organ of his brother, Mr. Walker Joy, of Leeds. The engraving (*fig.* 73) is taken from a photograph of one of the engines now at work in the Leeds Town Hall.

73

265. The engine consists of a cylinder similar to that of an ordinary steam engine, the piston having a reciprocatory motion given to it by the pressure of a column of water, admitted alternately to the top and bottom of the piston by suitable passages. The admission of the water to the cylinder is regulated by a slide valve, the back of which is attached to a small double piston working in cylinders formed at the top and bottom of the valve-box. The pistons are actuated by the water-pressure, the ingress and egress of which are regulated by a four-way cock. The plug of this cock is attached to, and moved by, means of a small lever, which is connected to a vertical rod, the upper end of which is secured to an arm fitted to the piston-rod. The vertical rod is fitted with set nuts, by means of which the action of the four-way cock may be adjusted. In the outlet port of the four-way cock is a set screw, by which the area of the port can be diminished so as to retard the escape of the water, and thereby regulate the speed of the valve. The water-main is fitted with an ordinary stop-cock, to which is attached a lever connected with the reservoir of wind. This lever is so arranged that when the reservoir is full the cock is closed, and when the reservoir is about one-quarter exhausted the cock is full on. By means of this self-regulating action the wind-reservoir is kept constantly filled. Under this arrangement of the engine the motion of the valve can be adjusted to suit any pressure of water that may be at command.

266. The Liverpool Water Meter, as made under the patent of the late Mr. Thomas• Duncan, by Messrs. Forrester and Co., of Liverpool, consists of two cylinders, with pistons and slotted piston rods working a short crank-shaft. The water under pressure is admitted alternately to each side of the pistons, and thus a rotary motion is given to the shaft, to which a counter is attached, and a correct register is kept of the quantity of water passing through the cylinders. Many of these meters have been adapted as power engines for working the bellows of organs, and have proved most successful. They are silent, and under the immediate control of the organist. They can be placed either horizontally or vertically, and are attached to the levers which work the bellows by means of the crossheads on the connecting rods. The sizes usually made are for ½ in., 1 in., 1 ½ in., 2 in., and, occasionally, 3 in. pipes.

Other blowing machines are noticed in the Appendix.

CHAPTER XV.

THE ELECTRIC ACTION.

267. HAVING explained the several kinds of organ mechanism in ordinary use, notice may now be taken of the recent application of *electricity* to the purposes and uses of organ construction and manipulation. It has been shown in what manner the communication between the claviers and the sound-board pallets, and between the draw-stops and the sound-board sliders, is established in compactly built instruments. An explanation has also been given of the way in which these systems of mechanism are developed in large organs, or in organs of which the claviers are placed at some distance from the main body of the instrument; and the means by which the organist is at the same time relieved from unnecessary toil, through relief pallets or pneumatic agency, have likewise been illustrated. For such situations—of claviers in relation to sound-boards—the electric action is applicable in common with, and possesses advantages and conveniences over, the mechanism in general use, to compensate for its greater cost, though it will probably be employed mostly for large organs, unless there be unusual peculiarities to be met and overcome. There are some positions or circumstances in which the intermediate space, as to width and depth between the two parts, takes such a direction, or is so small, that such situations have hitherto been considered extremely difficult of treatment, or altogether impossible. The usual mechanism, besides travelling horizontally and vertically, can turn an angle—equal, obtuse, or acute—or can follow a diagonal, splayed, or spreading course. But it cannot climb an incline, as from the front to the back of an orchestra. The downward drag of the action was always considered too much for the pallet strings, and the alternative action, running horizontally inwards to the organ, then upwards to the Instrument, rendered so much valuable space under the orchestra useless for all other purposes, that the plan, which originally existed at the Hanover Square Rooms, and the concert room of the old Opera-house in the Haymarket, has been abandoned in nearly all modern orchestras. At the Gloucester Festival, September, 1868, the electric action allowed the organist again to be placed near the conductor, while the organ itself stood at the top of the orchestra, and not in a line, but on the right-hand side.

268. The electric wire, having no motion, attaches no weight to the pallet; and it can be laid down in any required or conceivable direction. Any circumscribed positions are sufficient for its accommodation, and it can describe any *curves* as well as follow any regular course. It can traverse round pillars, or ascend in any form or direction where there may be an inch of space for it to pass through. In fact, it is as free and unfettered in its power of adaptation as the gutta percha tube of a garden engine. It has been mentioned that the speciality of the electric action recommends itself for very large organs, in which instruments the "pneumatic lever" is almost a necessity. The following particulars, therefore, referring to Mr. Barker's invention of the latter, and to his development of the same, taken almost *verbatim* from his own "notes," will, without doubt, prove interesting. Before giving them, however, a few more words may be said respecting relief pallets.

269. *Fig.* 74 is a pallet patented by Mr. Willis in 1861. The outside resembles an ordinary pallet, but is hollowed out on the top side, leaving only the portion of its surface that laps its seat ; the top is covered all over with the usual soft leathern packing. Holes communicate through the outside into its interior ; several bars, forming a grating, are placed inside the groove between the sound-board bars to prevent the leathern packing being blown in by the pressure of air on the underside ; on opening this pallet the edges leave their seat first and offer little resistance ; the air having passed in, in sufficient quantity, relieves the pressure on the underside.

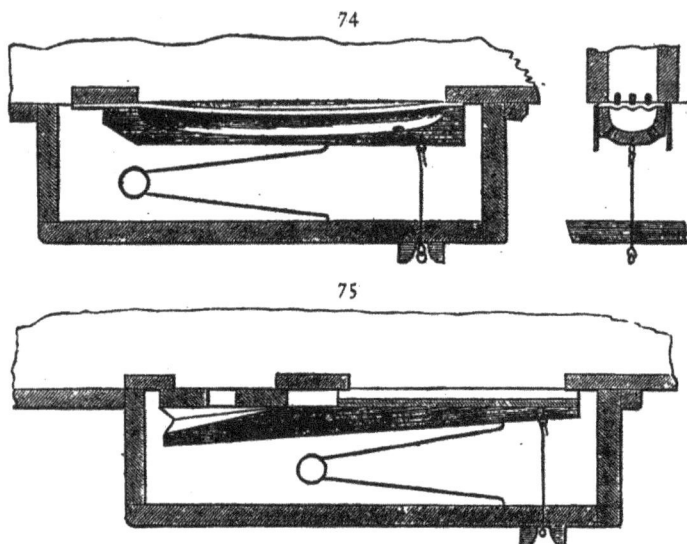

74

75

270. *Fig.* 75 is a compensating pallet. The small bellows attached to the tail have a communication from their interior with the atmosphere; the compressed air in the sound-board has therefore an inclination to collapse them, and the force expended in this direction counterbalances the pressure against the pallet.

271. *Fig.* 76 represents the section of a single pneumatic lever showing the action of the throttle-valve (*a*) (patented by Mr. Willis in 1853) and the double exhaust-valves (*b*), an auxiliary spring which closes them with the first motion of the key, instead of being pressed home only by the last, thus ensuring rapidity of action as well as certainty. Many modifications of the original form have been used, but the following explanation will suffice :—

272. The lowest chamber on the right (*d*) contains highly-compressed air, derived from a reservoir ; the lever (*e*), carrying the valve (*f*) which cuts off the communication between this chamber and the one immediately above it (*g*), works through the air-tight leathern purse (*h*) in the centre, and the left-hand end of the lever moves the double exhaust-valves (*b*), and is attached at the extremity by a tracker (*i*) or connecting-rod to the tail of the key. On raising this end of the lever the double exhaust-valves are immediately closed, cutting off or preventing the atmosphere from entering the interior of the power-bellows (*j*) ; at the same time the valve at the other end is opened, so as to allow the compressed air to pass through the chamber above into the power-bellows, and so inflate them. As

they rise they draw up the throttle-valve, which is attached to the top-board, so that, on its reaching the seat provided for it, it cuts off further supply of compressed air, and checks the motion of the power-bellows almost noiselessly (*fig.* 77). This movement of the top-board is communicated to the sound-board pallets by the usual train of mechanism. Immediately the key is released by the finger it is returned to its former position by the spring underneath, the compressed air escapes by the exhaust-valves, and the power-bellows collapses and allows the sound-board pallet to close. These pneumatic power-bellows are usually arranged in a frame of seven or eight tiers, the width of the manuals, and placed as near to them as possible.

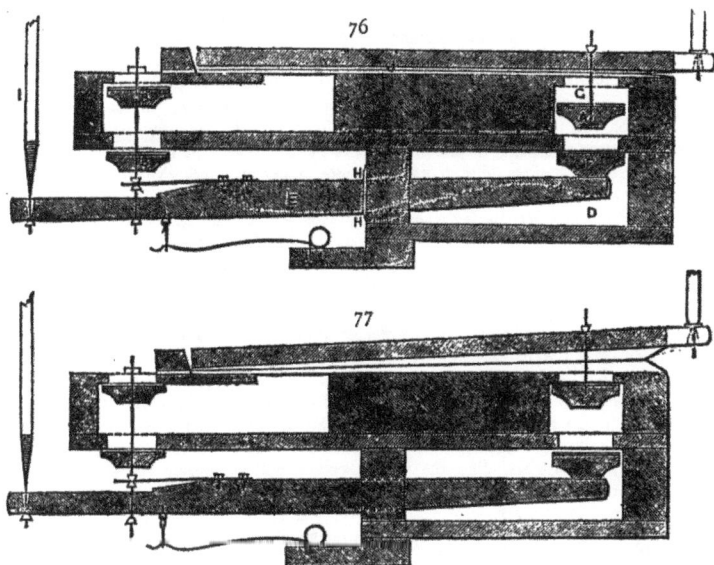

273. The following are the observations of Mr. Barker already referred to :—

"It was in 1832 that Mr. Barker, then established as an organ-builder in Bath, his native city, was led to reflect on the serious inconvenience arising from the extreme heaviness of touch in all large organs, and as more particularly exemplified in the one then but recently constructed for York Minster Cathedral. His persevering studies having revealed to him an efficacious remedy of this defect, by the invention of what has since been called the pneumatic lever, he wrote, in 1833, to Dr. Camidge, then organist of the Cathedral, announcing his discovery, and begging to be allowed to give a proof of its efficacy, by applying it in a temporary way to one of the heaviest keys of the organ. Dr. Camidge in his reply wrote : 'To such an instrument as ours it (*i.e.*, the discovery) would most certainly be very important, where four organs have to be played occasionally by ONE set of keys, and I should be most happy to recommend its adoption. Mr. Hill, of the late firm of Elliot and Hill, has erected our organ, and, I assure you, the playing it is no sinecure ; on the other hand, it is most laborious work to go through a grand chorus or last voluntary with the whole power of the instrument Such a difficult touch as that of York Cathedral organ is doubtless sufficient to paralyse the efforts of most men, I assure you. I, with all the energy I rally about me, am sometimes inclined to make a full stop from actual fatigue in a very short time after the commencement of a full piece.' Notwithstanding Dr. Camidge's wish and recommendation, financial difficulties stood in the way of Mr. Barker's invention being adopted in York ; nor was he more successful in his proposition for applying it to the Birmingham organ opened in

1834 or 1835. It was about this period that the eminent French builder, M. Cavaillé, was occupied in building a colossal organ for the royal church of St. Denis, near Paris, and it was already sufficiently advanced to convince Mr. Barker that, for heaviness of touch, it would rival or even surpass the York Minster and Birmingham organs in their then conditions; indeed, it might have been fairly questioned whether any organist of acknowledged talent would risk his reputation by attempting to play it. Mr. Barker heard from a friend who visited the Continent occasionally that such an instrument was building, and Mr. Barker wrote immediately to M. Cavaillé to propose the introduction of his pneumatic lever, accompanying his letter with a certificate from his since lamented friend, Mr. Merrick, who had played on a small instrument Mr. Barker had fitted up for demonstration, each key of which presented a resistance of several pounds. This was in 1837. M. Cavaillé replied, engaging Mr. Barker to go over to France, and examine the possibility of applying his invention to the magnificent organ in question. Mr. Barker visited Paris, and the application was decided on, under his immediate superintendence. However, in order to establish his priority as inventor, and protect at the same time his interests, previous to doing anything more in the matter, he took out, in 1839, a French patent, and soon after the pneumatic lever was applied with the greatest success, and, for the first time, to the St. Denis organ. After having passed an agreement with M. Cavaillé to grant him licence, under Mr. Barker's patent, as he might require, and which led to its application to the organs in St. Roche, La Madeleine, St. Vincent de Paul, &c., Mr. Barker's connection with M. Cavaillé ceased, and he was then led to undertake the direction of a large organ-building establishment recently formed in Paris, under the name of Daublaine and Callinet, where he had frequent opportunities of introducing his invention. This company having been dissolved about 1845, Mr. Barker undertook to carry on the concern for a M. Ducroquet, a capitalist who had purchased it, and built for him, among other important instruments, that of St. Eustache, as also the small but very complete organ which appeared in the French department of the London Universal Exhibition of 1851, and for which M. Ducroquet received, in addition to the English prize medal, his nomination of Chevalier of the Legion d'Honneur from the French Government."

Reverting to the English Exhibition of 1851, Mr. Barker's French organ presented, for the first time, a *complete* specimen of the application of the pneumatic lever to the fingerboards; that is to say, including the unison, octave, and sub-octave couplers. Mr. Hill exhibited an organ in which the pneumatic lever was applied to the draw-stop action only; and Mr. Willis, a large organ in which the lever was applied both to the key and draw-stop action, but to the former without acting on the couplers.

From this time the advantages of the pneumatic application were more appreciated; and the adoption of the system became more frequent in England, France, and Germany.

In fact, workmen who had been familiarised with the construction of the lever in the workshops of M. Cavaillé, lent aid and assistance in England, so that when Mr. Barker proposed to take out—alas! too late—a patent in this country, he found he would be only bringing coals to Newcastle.

At length came the great Paris Exhibition of 1855, to which Mr. Barker was admitted as an exhibitor on his own account, independently of M. Ducroquet, who was on the point of retiring from business, but for whom Mr. Barker had built for the last time, and for the Exhibition, an organ of twenty stops, three manuals, and separate pedal organ, in which the pneumatic lever was turned to good account, and enabled him to place all the powerful reeds of the great organ in the swell-box, and to obtain by that means unusual powers of *crescendo*. At the close of the Exhibition he was honoured with a first-class medal and his nomination as Chevalier in the Imperial Order of the Legion d'Honneur.

Mr. Barker cannot, in this rapid and imperfect biographo-historical sketch respecting the pneumatic lever, pass over in silence the claims of priority which have been put forth by other parties to the invention. In the first place, that of Mr. Joseph Booth, organ-builder in Wakefield, and who, it is alleged, introduced a contrivance of this nature into the Brunswick Chapel organ in Leeds, in 1827.

"A small bellows, called a puff-valve, is said to have been placed in connection with one of the double grooves of the sound-board, and by its inflation, on one of the pallets being drawn, to have acted automatically on the second. In suffering this description to be correct, there would be evidently here the germ of the pneumatic lever, as in the early trials of Papin was contained implicitly that of the steam engine, perfected later by Watt, Stephenson, and others, but in the one as in the other case, how great the distance which separates the elementary fact from its ultimate results—how great the difficulties to be overcome. Free to admit that Mr. Booth was in possession of a fruitful idea, he kept his light so completely under a bushel, that, sterile in its consequences, no one heard of it till twenty-four years after, when it had long ceased to exist. It is superfluous to say that Mr. Barker had no previous knowledge of this attempt or any other in the direction of his pneumatic lever, which, it is well known, constitutes in the organ as constructed by him a motive power directed by the finger of the performer *to all* the mechanical parts of the instrument. The foregoing remarks are, in part, equally applicable to the pneumatic apparatus of Mr. Hamilton, but with this difference, that this gentleman does not substantiate any claim to an application anterior to 1835, two years later than Mr. Barker's correspondence with Dr. Camidge. It might seem, in the presence of the comparatively satisfactory results obtained by the pneumatic lever, that, as a means of facilitating execution on large instruments, nothing better could be wished for. This, however, is not so absolutely the case as might be inferred at first view, as will fully appear from the following considerations. The great defect of the organ, and especially large instruments with several key-boards, lies in the number and excessive complication of its mechanical parts, all of which, however accurately adjusted, are, from their nature, particularly subject to the effects of atmospheric, or, to speak more exactly, hygrometric influence. Thus, under the effect of damp, the long trackers lengthen, the levers swell and move with difficulty on the bearings. The solid framing which supports the sound-boards and the mechanism adds by its swelling or shrinking to the general disorder ; and every organist is aware that in summer the touch of his instrument is often reduced to zero, whilst in winter it is deepened, and he is exposed to continual cypherings. To remedy as far as possible these serious inconveniences, the parts of attachment of the various mechanical parts of the instrument are provided with regulating screws and nuts, by which means the virtual length of these organs of transmission may be *integralement* established when changed. But how many difficulties have to be got through before accomplishing this labour of Sisyphus, which is *considerably increased* by the introduction of the pneumatic lever and its couplers. It occurred to Mr. Barker, as it already had to many others, that seeing what has been accomplished in telegraphy, by which the most delicate movements are transmitted to indefinite distances, with rapidity and precision, it might be possible to apply the same principle to the organ, in which the key-board represents the manipulator and the pallets of the organ the receptors of the telegraphy *bureaux*. Now this has been actually and successfully accomplished by Mr. Barker, in presence of repeated and uniform failure on the part of his predecessors. The reasons for this will appear in the course of the explanations of his system, as applied by Mr. Barker, in France, to the large St. Augustine organ, in which the key-boards have not offered the slightest derangement although the instrument has been erected more than a twelvemonth, and, consequently, has been during that time subject to great vicissitudes of temperature. The applications of Mr. Barker's patent in England by Messrs. Bryceson Brothers and Co. have been equally successful.

"An essential condition in the electric transmission in the organ, and which had been generally overlooked by Mr. Barker's predecessors in this direction, is to diminish the resistance of the pallets to a minimum by means of a peculiar construction, or to attack them by the intervention of a pneumatic lever reduced to a simple inflating bellows and debarrassed of all its usual accessories in the shape of couplers, &c., which can now be all affected electrically.

"This new system offers three inestimable advantages in its application :—

"1. A great simplification, by the suppression of a multitude of moving parts, replaced by simple insulated wires.

"2. The possibility of transmitting the movements to any required distance, irrespective of the relative positions of the organ and its key-board.

"3. The invariability of the key-boards under the greatest changes of temperature.

"It is now about five years since Mr. Barker made his first experiment for the application of electricity to the organ, and proposed applying it to the large organ which he had just received the order to construct for the church of St. Augustine, upon the favourable report of the commission charged to examine the new mode of construction. This organ was opened about three months since, and the commission having made another and final report in most favourable terms, Mr. Barker is now charged with the construction of another large organ for the new church of St. François de Xavier, which, with those of St. Augustine, Salons, and Montrouge, is the fourth application of the electric principle in France."

274. During the Paris Exhibition of 1867 the attention of Mr. Bryceson was directed to the electric organ in St. Augustine's Church, in Paris, then nearly completed, and he at once determined to introduce the electric system into England, and made arrangements with Mr. Barker for that purpose.

275. Dr. Gauntlett, who had done much towards the introduction of the Continental or CC compass of organs in this country, now universally adopted, may claim to be the first who conceived the idea of applying electricity to organ mechanism. The following notice occurs in the *Orchestra* of March 28th, 1868 :— " The using of electricity as a motive power in organ building was first mooted about twenty years ago by Dr. Gauntlett, who, at the time of the Great Exhibition of 1851, proposed a scheme for playing all the organs in the place at one and the same time. The plan met with great opposition, and nothing was done ; but, on the announcement of the Crystal Palace Company, Dr. Gauntlett met the Provisional Committee, and proposed the erection of *fac-similes* of the eight most celebrated organs in Europe, and playing them altogether or separately in the centre of the building. The original prospectus of the company put forth the Exhibition as one of still life, and one which might be grasped in one view. All such exhibitions fail unless accompanied with music, and Dr. Gauntlett's proposition was to supply the place with a continual stream of music at an outlay much less than that for the maintenance of an orchestra. Messrs. Anderson and Fuller, two gentlemen of the committee, met the proposition with a decided negative. ' Dr. Gauntlett,' said Mr. Fuller, ' you will never hear a note of music in the Crystal Palace ; the Exhibition is intended for far higher purposes. We do not want music and we shall never have it !' And thereupon Dr. Gauntlett departed, but not without telling the committee that without music the whole affair would become bankrupt. Dr. Gauntlett patented his speciality in 1852, and in 1863 another plan was patented by Mr. Goundry."

276. Dr. Gauntlett's patent of 1852 comprehends playing organs, both finger and barrel, as well as seraphines and pianofortes, through the electrical agency. For organs he proposed placing a powerful electro-magnet immediately beneath each pallet, and fastening the armature on the end of the pallet itself, an arrangement that would require much space and an expenditure of electric force requiring a very large battery to supply a sufficient current. He mentions that an apparatus known as the " pneumatic lever" may be worked with the electro-magnets and armatures, though he does not describe any form of arrangement. The draw-stop and swell action are also alluded to, but there is no explanation as to how they are to be accomplished. Dr. Gauntlett's contact at the key did not act till the key was quite down, and, being simply a touching contact, would soon become oxidised.

277. In 1863 Mr. Goundry patented a very elaborate electric system, chiefly in connection with the introduction of the enharmonic scale, which requires, at the least, forty sounds to the octave. He describes several known forms of light pallets, and proposes to open them direct by the electro-magnet in a similar manner to Dr. Gauntlett. The pneumatic lever is also mentioned, and a form given for its application. Mr. Goundry shows a very elaborate arrangement for coupling purposes, and also for throwing up the melody. In his draw-stop action he proposes that a

spring should pull the slider in, and that it should be drawn by a pneumatic power-bellows, actuated by an electro-magnet, around which the current of electricity would be passing all the time the slider remained drawn, thus involving a great consumption of battery power.

278. No organ-builder embarked in either of these patents ; and no organs, to illustrate their practicability, appear to have been attempted.

279. Mr Barker's English patent, taken out in January, 1868, protects his special arrangements of the following applications, which, with the exception of the draw-stop action, were then based on his actual experience, gained in the construction of three electric organs, which he had already erected in France :—

1st. His arrangement of the electro-pneumatic action to the keys and pedals, including a method of making the contacts by means of immersing copper points in mercury cells.

2nd. A contrivance for coupling the various manuals as well as the pedals, either in unison or in octaves.

3rd. An arrangement for drawing the stops.

4th. The manner of commanding the large valves in wind trunks, known in England as ventils.

5th. An automatic system for suspending all waste of electrical agents in the battery when not actually in use.

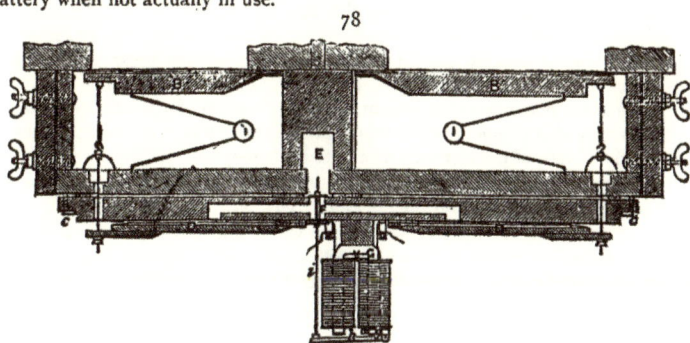

78

280. *Fig.* 78 is a copy of the drawing attached to Mr. Barker's English patent, dated January 28, 1868. It represents the end section of a divided sound-board, such as would be used when two different pressures of wind are required, or where the number of stops is so great as to require two pallets to supply a sufficient quantity of wind. The chamber (*e*) in the wind-bar is supplied with compressed air, and is continued the whole length of the sound-board. This is to supply the pneumatic power-bellows (*d*), which are all fixed externally on the bottom side of the sound-board, one of these power-bellows being provided beneath each pallet (*b*). Immediately below the air-chamber and upon the fixed table of the power-bellows is a small double-action disc-valve (*f*) attached to a vertical rod. In a state of rest, as shown in the drawing, the top disc-valve is closed, cutting off the compressed air ; and the lower one is open, so as to establish a communication from the interior of the power-bellows with the atmosphere, and allowing the sound-board spring (*i*) to hold the power-bellows shut. The disc-valve is actuated by the armature (*h*) of an electro-magnet (*g*) placed below, and attached to the vertical rod (*f*), so that when the electro-magnet becomes excited by the current of electricity, and, therefore, attracts the armature, the position of the disc-valve is

reversed : the lower one being shut and the top one opened, it allows the compressed air from the chamber above to rush in and inflate the power-bellows, which, being attached to the sound-board pallet, immediately pulls open the same. Directly the electric current ceases the armature is of course released ; the disc-valve returns to its former position ; the compressed air is cut off ; the sound-board spring collapses the pneumatic power-bellows, and the air escapes by the bottom disc or exhaust-valve, which is now open again.

281. The draw-stop action for each slider in the sound-board consists of two large pneumatic bellows, acting alternately in opposite directions, the inflation of which is governed by two double-action disc-valves, worked again by small accessory power-bellows and two electro-magnets, acting positively and negatively.

282. A sound-board, therefore, with its electro-pneumatic power-bellows applied to both pallets and sliders, requires no train of moving mechanism to connect it to the key-board and draw-stop knobs, however distant, but simply the necessary number of insulated copper wires to conduct the electric currents from the console, or stand, which holds the manuals, pedals, &c. The console, thus detached from the main body of the instrument, contains a vast amount of accurate and beautifully-arranged work. Its dimensions may be compared to those of a large harmonium ; and, besides holding the various key-boards, it contains, first, the rocking-lever beneath each key, which, being furnished with copper points, plunges them in mercury cells directly it is depressed, and so establishes the electric current ; secondly, the various couplers, which are bars of wood, on which are screwed copper springs for each note (when drawn by the knob these metallic springs press against corresponding copper-plates, and so cause the electric current to divide and actuate the additional electro-magnets and pallets at the same time); thirdly, the draw-stop knobs and traces, to which contacts of a similar nature are attached, and which, likewise, complete the circuit of the electric current to their respective positive and negative magnets ; fourthly, all combinations which act mechanically upon the draw-stop traces, and other accessory movements and pedals, &c.

283. To prevent the waste or destruction which would take place in a powerful and active battery if the electrodes were left immersed in the exciting liquid, it is necessary to lift them out of their cells when the organ is not in use ; and, as this operation would probably often be forgotten, the last provision of Mr. Barker's patent refers to a self-acting arrangement. For effecting this object, he places the jars containing the liquid on the top of a wind-reservoir supplied from the main bellows, and suspends the electrodes in a frame above them. When the bellows are blown the reservoir becomes inflated, raising the cells so as to immerse the electrodes ; when the wind ceases the reservoir gradually collapses, and the jars sink down, leaving the electrodes suspended dry above. Mr. Barker also protects the reverse action, the cells remaining stationary, and the electrodes being made to descend into the liquid ; this is effected by the same agency, and amounts to the same thing. Mr. Barker does not patent a battery of his own, having found his requirements satisfied by modifications of more than one already known and in common use. The battery is not placed within the console, and close to the keys, as some have supposed, but in any convenient position within or near the organ itself.

284. From what has already been explained with regard to electric key-action, it will have been perceived that two intermediate agents are employed to make the depression of the key open the pallet in the sound-board, viz., electricity and pneumatics, and it might seem that such an arrangement would tend to cause a certain amount of delay or slowness in its operation. This, however, is not the case in actual practice ; the velocity of electric currents requires no comment, and,

in the short circuit employed in the organ electric action, electricity performs its work simultaneously with contact being made at the key. The pneumatic power-bellows, unlike those employed in a mechanical organ, where they have to be large enough to pull open several pallets at once, besides moving long trains of action, are now only required powerful enough to open one pallet, and are therefore so small that very little compressed air is sufficient to inflate them ; moreover, their small and sensitive valves are not impeded by mechanical attachments. The practical result is, that no perceptible difference of time can be discovered between the depression of the key and the speech of the pipe. This is best proved by the excellent repetition touch obtained ; in this it far surpasses any mechanical action.

285. It was, however, obvious that a great advantage and saving of work would be gained if, as Mr. Barker suggested, a perfectly new form of pallet could be contrived which would offer no resistance in opening, and admit of being acted on direct by the electro-magnet instead of being attacked by the intermediate pneumatic lever as heretofore. To effect this, Mr. Bryceson turned his utmost attention, and at length succeeded in constructing a pallet fulfilling all the requirements.

79

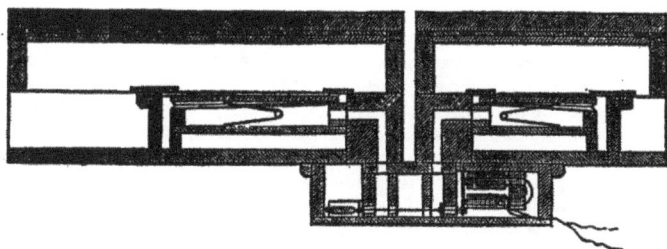

80

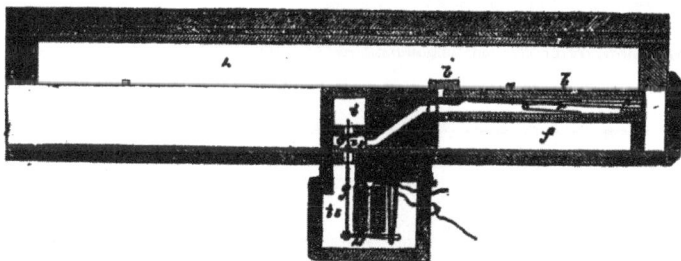

286. *Figs.* 79 and 80 are copies of drawings attached to Mr. Bryceson's patent, dated April 6th, 1868, and show the complete arrangement of his new pallet as applied in a double and single palletted sound-board ; *fig.* 81 (p. 78) being enlarged to show a section of the pallet of the latter. The pallet consists of a small diagonal bellows, formed with top and bottom-boards attached to each other by flexible leathern ribs (*k*). The upper-side of the top-board (*a*) is covered with soft leather, and forms the valve which beds close against the under-side of the sound-board bar (*b*); it is kept in this position when at rest by a common spring (*c*) pushing upward from the fixed bottom-board. The back or tail-end of the bottom-board is hollow, and is fitted into a square mortise in the wind-bar, through which a channel (*d*) is continued to a chamber (*i³*) on the other side. The front end of

the bottom-board is fixed sufficiently below the top-board, so as to distend the leathern ribs (*k*) nearly to their full extent. On the other side of the wind-bar are two chambers (*i i²*). The upper one (*i*) runs the whole length of the sound-board, and contains compressed air of the same pressure as is supplied to the sound-board. The lower chamber (*i²*) is the one in communication with the interior of the pallet ; it is partitioned off separately for each note, and contains a double-action disc-valve (*g*) fixed on a vertical rod. The position of this valve determines the communication with the chamber above containing compressed air or the atmosphere below outside. In a state of rest the top disc-valve is open so that the compressed air from the chamber above is inside as well as around the pallet, and of course by its pressure holds the top-board firmly against the sound-board bar—indeed, if the wind could always be kept in there would be no necessity for a spring at all, which is only to keep up the top-board till the pallet is inflated. The lower disc-valve is now closed, and prevents the escape of the compressed air. If the position of the disc-valve is altered and reversed by raising the vertical rod (*g*) by means of the armature of an electro-magnet (*m*) the compressed air is at once stopped from entering the interior of the pallet, and the pressure on the outside of the leathern ribs collapses them, and they draw down the upper-board and allow the wind to enter the groove of the sound-board, and thence, if the sliders are drawn, supply the pipes above. The air in the interior of the pallet is allowed to escape into the atmosphere through the lower disc-valve, which is now open. When the vertical rod is released by the armature of the electro-magnet, the disc-valve returns to its original position, the escape-valve is closed, the compressed air again enters the interior of the pallet and shuts it firmly against the sound-board groove. In cases where it may be considered necessary to open the pallet very wide, as in pedal sound-boards, &c., a third chamber (*i³*), running the whole length of the sound-board, from which the air is exhausted, could be placed beneath the lower disc-valves instead of allowing them to open direct into the atmosphere ; the top-board would then be drawn hard down on the bottom-board, which can be fixed at a greater distance, and thus secure either a horizontal or diagonal opening to provide a great supply of wind to the sound-board groove for distribution to the pipes.

81

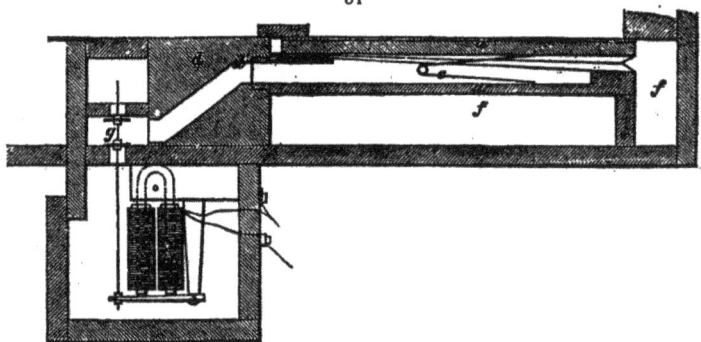

287. This new pallet might appear to resemble a form known for many years, and used in several instances by both Messrs. Gray and Davison and Mr. Willis for pedal sound-boards, but in reality it differs widely in its condition and mode of action, inasmuch as it is held closed by the pressure of wind in its interior, and

opened by the disc-valves allowing this wind to escape or exhaust, so that the pressure around it is enabled to force in the ribs of leather, which, in yielding, actually pull the top-board away from its seat against the sound-board bar ; whereas the old form of pallet just alluded to had ribs sufficiently distended only to counterbalance the resistance of the wind, and was pulled open by a connecting link in the same way as an ordinary or common pallet. Neither disc-valves nor attenuated air were used in conjunction with it, and the interior was in communication with the atmosphere instead of being filled with compressed air when in a state of rest. In Mr. Bryceson's pallet he gains the advantage, that, when closed, it has the full force of the wind to press it soundly against its seat, and thereby prevent any tendency to leakage, a fault common to all other compensating or balanced pallets, which must be closed by strength of the spring. Again, the ribs of his pallet, being distended to their full extent when at rest, present the most favourable position for being acted upon by the compressed air in the sound-board directly the escape-valve is opened, at which time the first movement of the pallet from its seat requires most force to be expended. Any single pallet can be easily taken out for repair by raising it from the fixed rail in front, and pulling it out of the mortise in the wind-bar. As no pull-down, link, or connecting rod is attached to it, and guide-pins are unnecessary, these very frequent causes of derangement are thus entirely avoided. The dimensions of the pallet can be varied from that required for the smallest treble note to the largest necessary for any pedal sound-board. It is equally available for mechanical and non-electric action, in which case a spring would have to be introduced just sufficiently strong to return the key and action ; this would constitute all the resistance presented to the finger of the performer. The cost, as well as the space required, is less than when the ordinary pallet is employed with a separate pneumatic power-bellows placed externally.

288. In most cases where organs already built are to be re-constructed on the electric system, the old arrangement of the sound-boards will prevent this new pallet being conveniently used ; Mr. Bryceson has therefore found it best to apply externally a pneumatic power-bellows beneath each original pallet, similar to Mr. Barker's arrangement, but placed in two tiers, to get them in the length of the sound-board. These he works with exhaust or attenuated air instead of pressure, for the following reasons :—The ribs or sides of pneumatic power-bellows, if not made very rigid, and lined with cardboard, are subject to be overstrained and inverted when inflated, and thus either locked open or destroyed. If made stiff enough to be secure from this defect, they will not work as freely as desirable in the treble or smaller sizes. By the use of exhaust instead of pressure, no stiffening for the ribs is necessary, the cost of manufacture is reduced, and greater durability and freedom from noise are attained. Mr. Bryceson is not aware that exhaust or attenuated air has been proposed or applied for pneumatic power-bellows by any other firm besides his own. Mr. Willis, however, took out a patent almost simultaneously with himself, in which exhaust and pressure are proposed to be employed alternately for actuating what Mr. Willis terms a " floating valve " in connection with a novel arrangement of draw-stop action. From the way in which provisional patent specifications are lodged it is impossible either could be aware of the conclusion arrived at by the other ; and it is a singular coincidence that a new principle in organ-building, which is likely to be of great service for intermediate purposes, should have been thus introduced for the first time. Mr. Bryceson was led to adopt exhaust for reasons already stated, and because the saving effected in a single power-bellows, however small, was a great consideration in the aggregate or large number employed in electric organs.

289. *Figs.* 82 and 83 show the section of two electro-pneumatic arrangements,

as patented by Mr. Bryceson, for moving the sliders. In large organs, where highly-compressed air is used for supplying certain stops of pipes, as well as exhaust-bellows for working the pneumatic key-action, he has used the arrangement shown in the left-hand figure, and the method of its action is as follows :—A large pneumatic power-bellows (*n*), connected by a lever and trace to the slider, is fixed on a table (*l*), and at the back of this table are three chambers (*k k k*). The top one is supplied with compressed air, and the bottom one has the air exhausted from it. The middle chamber communicates with the interior of the power-bellows, and also with either the top or the bottom chamber, according to the position of a large double-action disc-valve (*m m*). The drawing shows the top chamber cut off by the valve being closed, and the bottom or exhaust-chamber in communication. The power-bellows is therefore collapsed, and the end of the lever

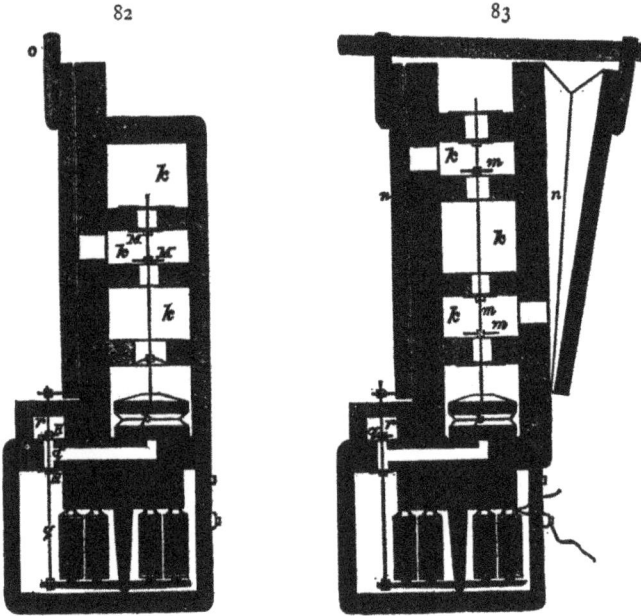

82   83

drawn to the right hand. When the double-action disc-valve is reversed the exhaust-chamber is cut off, and the communication opened with the top or pressure-chamber, the compressed air rushes in and inflates the power-bellows, causing the end of the lever to be moved to the left hand. To gain rapidity of action it is necessary that the ports covered by the double-action disc-valves should be of considerable size, and also that the valve itself should have a movement of at least one-quarter of an inch. As this would require a very powerful electro-magnet and great expenditure of battery power, it is found advantageous to introduce a small accessory pneumatic power-bellows (*p*). This is placed immediately under and attached to the rod carrying the large disc-valve, and its position will be determined by its inflation or collapse. This accessory power-bellows is commanded by a very small double-action disc-valve (*h*) attached to a vertical rod (*g*) connected to the double armature of two electro-magnets (*s s*) ; the chamber (*r*) above this small double-action disc-valve is supplied with compressed air. The drawing shows that the left-hand electro-magnet was last used. It attracted its end of the double armature and the little double-action disc-valve, admitting the compressed air to inflate the small accessory power-bellows. When the right-hand magnet is actuated the small double-action disc-valve will be drawn down, the compressed air will be cut off from, and allowed to escape by, the bottom valve

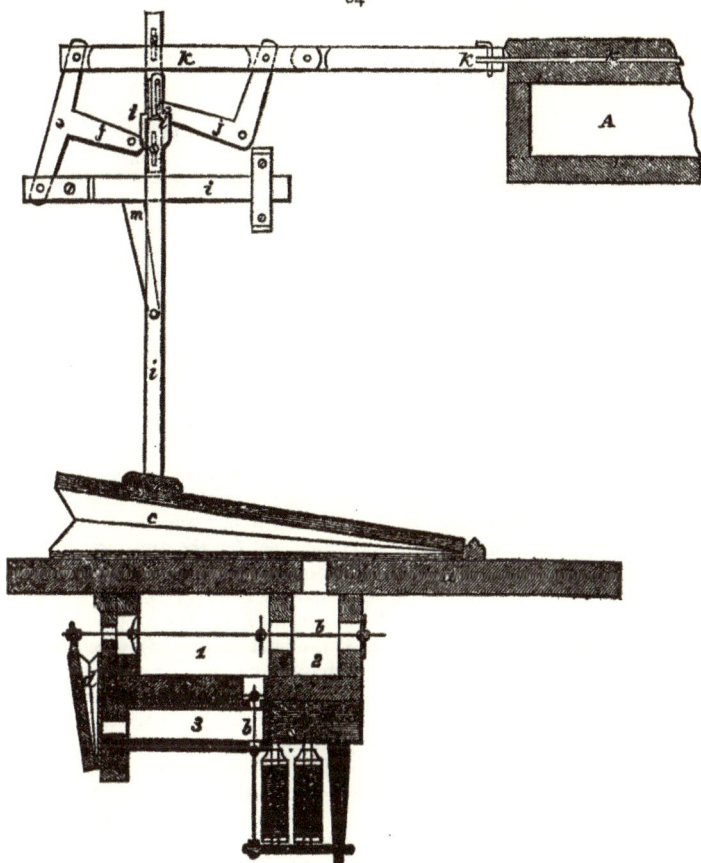

84

from the accessory pneumatic power-bellows, which will immediately collapse. The two electro-magnets are connected to the positive and negative contacts of the draw-stop trace in the console by insulated copper wires. In organs, when highly-compressed air is not required for other purposes, the expense is avoided of constructing such bellows expressly for working the draw-stop pneumatic power-bellows, and both the on and off movements are obtained from the exhaust alone. For this purpose Mr. Bryceson has employed the arrangement shown in *fig.* 83, and finds it acts most satisfactorily. Two large

R

pneumatic power-bellows (*n n*) are coupled together with a connecting-rod (*o*) in such a way as to ensure the expansion of one on the collapse of the other.   Three chambers (*k k k*) are placed between their fixed tables (*l l*); the centre chamber has the air exhausted from it, the top chamber is in communication with the left-hand power-bellows, and the bottom chamber with the right-hand one.   The communication of these chambers with the middle one is alternate, and governed by two double-action disc-valves (*m m*), arranged similarly to the one in the first figure already explained.   These are also commanded by small accessory power-bellows (*p*) and two electro-magnets (*s s*) in the same way as before described ; therefore, as the contact is made at the conso. , ' e corresponding power-bellows is collapsed, drawing the slider in the desired direction.   As combination pedals are not used in France, but only ventils, which cut off and introduce the wind to certain groups of stops by means of pedals, provision had to be made for an elaborate system of combination movements when required, as in England these most useful accessories for changing the stops are held in high estimation by our organists.   It will be sufficient for the present to remark that electricity is most favourable for the extension of combination movements in novel ways.

290. *Fig.* 84 (p. 81) represents Mr. Bryceson's patent double-action draw-stop movement, with one electro-magnet and one pneumatic power-bellows to be used in conjunction with an electric signal at the key-boards.   The pneumatic power-bellows (*c*) is fixed on the table (*a*).   On the under-side of this table are three chambers, 1, 2, and 3.   These chambers communicate with each other, and also with the atmosphere by four holes in their partitions.   This communication is regulated by the position of the double-action valve (*b*), composed of a rod and two discs.   The end chamber (2) communicates through the table (*a*) with the interior of the power-bellows (*c*).   The chamber (1) contains compressed air.   The double-action valve is operated by an accessory bellows (*d*), which, when required, is inflated by air from the chamber (1), which passes therefrom through the valve (*b*) into the chamber (3); and from thence to the bellows (*d*). The valve (*b*) is controlled by the electro-magnet (*e*), the armature of which is connected to its rod, as shown in the drawing.

291. The electric circuit is completed, and the magnet (*e*) caused to act on its armature by the depression of the button-knob (*f*, *fig.* 85), at the console.   To the stem of the button-knob are attached two light springs (*f*), which rub against the blocks (*g*) made of some non-conducting substance.   Strips of metal (*g*) are secured to the lower part of these blocks, and are connected to the electro-magnets and battery by insulated wires.   The button-knob is also provided with a spring underneath that always returns it to its original position when the pressure of the performer's finger is removed therefrom.   It will be obvious that every time the button (*f*) is depressed it will complete the electric circuit and will electrise the magnet (*e*), which, by attracting its armature, will lift the valve-rod (*b*) and open its valve so as to allow wind from the pressure-chamber (1) to pass through the chamber (3) into the accessory bellows (*d*) and inflate them, and by so doing will draw back the valve-rod (*b*) and open the communication between the chambers (1 and 2) so as to allow the wind to pass into and inflate the large pneumatic power-bellows.

292. This motion will raise a rocking-rod (*i*) which is provided at its upper end with two shoulders (*i i*).   Two bell-crank levers (*j j*) are connected by a link motion (*k*) to the draw-stop slider of the sound-board (*a*).   The upper arms of the levers (*j j*) are jointed to the link (*k*), and therefore both of them move simultaneously.   The lower arm of the lever (*j*) is jointed to a slide (*i*) which

is provided with a flat spring (m), the lower end of which bears against pins fixed in the rocking-rod (i). The horizontal arms of the levers (jj) are provided with projecting pins, against which the shoulders (ii) of the rocking-rod are caused to act alternately. When the bellows (c) are inflated, as shown in the drawing, one of the shoulders (i) of the rocking-rod will come against the pin of one of the levers (j), and by lifting the same will push forward the link (k), and at the same time will draw back the slide (i), and thus put tension on the spring (m). On the performer taking his finger off the button (f, $fig.$ 85), and allowing it to rise, the electric circuit will be broken and the position of the valves (b) will consequently be reversed ; and the bellows '(c and d) will then collapse and be ready for a second operation. Upon the button (f) again being depressed, the same operation will be repeated, but the rocking-rod will, by the tension of the spring (m), be thrown over in the opposite direction to the last time, and will bring the other shoulder under the pin of the other lever so that when the rocking-rod rises by the inflation of the bellows the link and draw-stop slider will be drawn in the opposite direction to that before described.

85

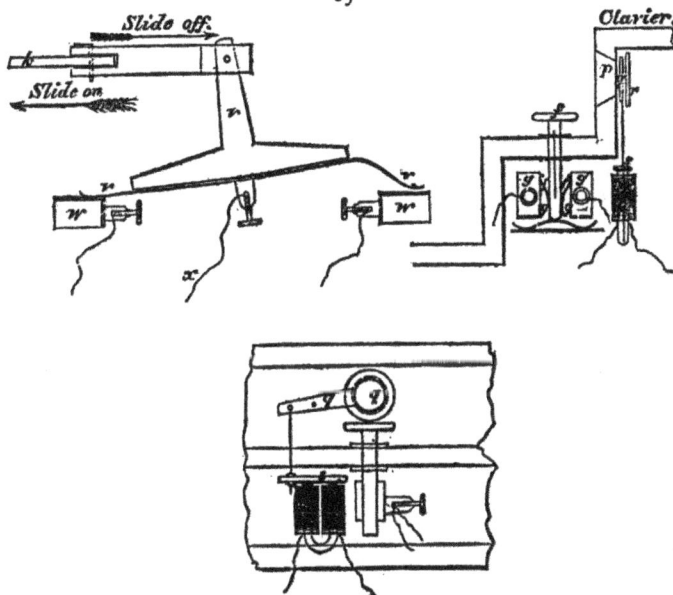

293. As the depression of the button or knob (f) at the keys or manuals either brings the draw-stop slider on or takes it off (and in both cases the button returns to the same position), it is necessary for the convenience of the player that an index should show the actual position in which the slider had been moved and left. The index is arranged as follows. Immediately behind the knob or button a hole (p) is made in the draw-stop jamb ; behind this hole works a lever (q) carrying at one end a coloured disc or label. This lever is so balanced on its centre of motion that when at rest a fixed disc (indicating that the stop is closed) appears behind the hole.

294. The opposite end of the lever is attached by a rod or wire to the armature

R 2

of a small electro-magnet which is connected with a special battery and the draw-stop slider. Near the end of the slider is a fixed block of some non-conducting material provided with two metal plates to form terminals.

295. On the end of the slider itself is fixed a forked spring. When the slider is moved back this spring will be brought into contact with the terminals on the block ; and, by completing the circuit, the electric current will pass through the electro-magnet (*s*), which, by acting on its armature, will draw down one end of the lever and raise the coloured disc behind the hole, and thus indicate that the slide is on. Upon depressing the button the next time to close the draw-top slider, as already explained, the slider will be drawn back away from the terminal block, and, the electric circuit being thereby broken, the lever, with its disc, will fall into its original position, indicating to the player that the stop is off.

296. For combination movements in connection with this draw-stop action, a bell-crank lever (*v*) is connected to each slide by its upper arm, as shown in *fig.* 85. Two metal springs (*v*) are fixed at the ends of the other two arms, so that by the movement of the draw-stop slider they are alternately brought into contact with the metal surface of the blocks (*w w*). These metal springs are, by means of the conducting wire (*x*), in connection with one of the poles of the electro-magnet, which works the slide of that particular draw-stop. On the depression of the combination knob or pedal, an electric communication will be established from one pole of the battery to the terminals of each of the bell-crank levers. The current can, however, only pass through those levers which are in a suitable position. For instance, *fig.* 85 represents the slider on—that is, with the spring of the lever in contact with the block (*w*), thereby completing the circuit so as to allow that slider to be withdrawn. Should any of the stops of that combination be already withdrawn or closed, the lever would be in the opposite position, the circuit would be broken, and therefore no effect would be produced, as the slider would be in the required position without alteration. Should these stops be required to be brought on, another combination knob or pedal must be depressed, when the electric current would pass to the blocks (*w*), and from thence through such of the springs as were in contact therewith to the lever, and thence to their magnets. If, however, any of the stops should happen to be open, the lever would be in the position shown in *fig.* 85, and, consequently, their springs would not be in contact with their blocks ; and, the circuit not being complete, no effect would be produced on those particular sliders, as in the opposite case. No insurmountable difficulty stands in the way of opening the swell louvres by means of an arrangement of electro-pneumatics, but as it is necessary, for the purpose of gaining a gradual *crescendo* effect, to employ more than one electro-magnet, and, as the electric current would have to be in circulation around them during the long intervals that the swell is locked open, it becomes an expensive arrangement as far as battery power is concerned. Mr. Bryceson has, therefore, adopted a hydraulic means of communicating the motion of the swell pedal at the console to the swell louvres at the organ. To effect this he uses two small brass cylinders —one placed immediately under the pedal, and the other beneath the connecting-rod of the swell louvres. These two cylinders are connected together by a small lead pipe filled with water. When the plunger at the pedal is depressed, the one under the swell is raised to a corresponding degree,—the motion being as much under the control of the player as if a connecting-rod was carried through, and of course with far less friction in long distances. The principal has been used with success in connection with the steering of vessels : Mr. Bryceson does not therefore claim it in his second patent as an invention, but only as a new adaptation to the organ.

297. In the first organs Mr. Bryceson built on the electric system he was unable

to overcome a certain difficulty connected with the draw-stop action, which did its work perfectly, except under the following circumstances :—If the knobs at the console were moved at a time either before the blowers had commenced or after they had ceased, no corresponding movement of the sound-board slider could of course take place, therefore the organist would be misled as to the real position of the sliders. It was also possible to move the knob so rapidly that the large pneumatic power-bellows had not time for inflation, before the momentary contact had again broken. These shortcomings no longer exist, as he has invented an arrangement which provides that, however quickly the knobs are moved, either singly or collectively, the contact will be prolonged to any length of time found necessary to insure the inflation of the large pneumatic power-bellows, and also on the bellows being filled, every slider will be moved so as to correspond with the position of the knob to which it belongs, although these may have been moved during the time there was no wind in the organ. This arrangement Mr. Bryceson patented Feb. 3, 1869, and describes as follows :—Each draw-stop trace is provided with a metallic forked spring. Three metal plates are fixed near it in such positions that one arm of the spring is always in contact with either the second or the third plate, according to the position of the draw-stop trace. These two plates are respectively connected by two insulated wires with the positive and negative electro-magnets of the draw-stop apparatus, by means of which the slider in the organ is moved, and thence with one and the same pole of the battery. The first plate is connected by an insulated wire to one of a pair of mercury cells placed near each other, and the other mercury cell communicates by another insulated wire with the other pole of the battery. Hence when the two mercury cells are connected together an electric circuit is completed round either the positive or negative electro-magnet of the draw-stop apparatus. The position of the draw-stop trace will show whether the forked spring is connecting the second or third plate with the first, and will therefore determine round which electro-magnet the electric circle is completed.

298. The mode of establishing a connection between the two mercury cells is as follows :—A small pneumatic bellows, called the *contact*-bellows, is fixed on a table, and kept distended by a suitable spring. The end of the top-board of this contact-bellows carries two metallic points connected together and fixed in such a position as to dip into the two mercury cells on the depression of the top-board. Each draw-stop trace is also provided with a double incline, and one arm of a roller or lever is raised by this each time the trace is moved out or in. The other arm of the roller or lever thus pushes down the top-board of the contact-bellows (the air being allowed to escape from the interior by a valve placed externally for that purpose), and, by immersing the two metallic points in the mercury cells, establishes a connection between them.

299. When the draw-stop trace is either quite out or in, the arm of the roller or lever will exert no pressure on the top-board of the contact-bellows, which will be slowly raised by the spring, and thus the electric current will be broken. The duration of the contact, and, therefore, of the current of electricity, can be regulated by the dimension of the bellows, the depth of the immersion of the metallic points in the mercury, the strength of the spring that returns the top-board, and the size of the inlet to the bellows.

300. One contact-bellows may be made to serve for a group of draw-stop traces, by connecting all the first plates together and arranging each trace so as to move the roller or lever that depresses the top-board of the contact-bellows.

301. In order to insure a correspondence between the position of each slider and the position of the knob at the key-board to which it belongs in case such

knob has been moved while the wind was not in the bellows of the organ, a small tube is connected with the interior of the contact-bellows and carried into one chamber of a double box near the battery. In this box there is another chamber which communicates by another tube with the interior of the main exhaust-bellows. The partition between these two chambers is fitted with a valve, which is connected by means of a lever and trace or other suitable mechanical contrivance to the frame holding the electrodes in such a manner that, when the electrodes are only partially immersed, the communication between the two is open.

302. When the bellows begin to rise, the electrodes are gradually immersed, and, consequently, the communication between the main exhaust-bellows and the contact bellows is at first open and then closed. The result of the communication being open is that the top-board of the contact-bellows is depressed ; hence, if, at the time the blowers begin to blow, the position of the slider does not correspond with the position of the knob at the key-board to which it belongs, it is at once moved into its corresponding position by the action of the electric current on one of the electro-magnets ; and then, the communication being closed between the main exhaust-bellows and the contact-bellows, the top-board of the contact-bellows rises, and the electric circuit is again broken. If a battery be used in which the electrodes are always immersed, a separate pneumatic bellows can be used to open and shut the valve between the two chambers of the box, which can then be placed in any convenient part of the organ. Valves are placed in the contact-bellows to prevent the air in the tube from passing into them when they are depressed by the draw-stop traces. The same patent protects Mr. Bryceson's arrangement of opening and closing the swell louvres by a column of water and two cylinders with plungers, as before described ; also, the application of hydraulic cylinders and a pressure of water for working the combination movements, so that they can be commanded by the performer without offering the usual great resistance.

303. The construction of an electric organ, as regards the sound-board, key, and draw-stop action, combination movements, method of opening the swell-box, automatic battery attachment and console, has now been explained in detail. The grouping of these parts so entirely depends on the nature and extent of the organ which is to be built, that it is impossible to present any diagram which will show properly the relative positions they will occupy in an entire instrument.

304. Before dismissing the matter of construction, it may be well to observe that the battery employed is simple, inexpensive, and easily replenished by any careful person. It will not require attention more than four or five times a year. ... are no grounds for supposing electricity to be a treacherous or uncertain agent. It is well known that chemicals of the same quality will, under similar circumstances, give the same result in their action. Ample notice of any decline in the power of the battery is given by the galvanometer placed in the console for that purpose, which serves as well to show whether or not the wind is in the organ, as indicated by the immersion of the electrodes. Thunder storms, or the electric condition of the earth, have no effect on an electric organ, as earth currents are not employed as in telegraphy. The adoption of electricity and insulated wire to replace or supersede the mechanical action in large organs is not merely a new process to attain the same end, but, independently of the suppression of a multitude of moving parts, many new advantages are presented otherwise unattainable. The touch is more delicate, rapid, uniform, and invariable. The durability is increased owing to the absence of wear and tear. The key-boards can now be placed at any required distance from, and quite irrespective of, the relative position of the organ ; therefore the organist may choose a position where he can hear the effects he produces, and the voices he leads or accompanies, without in any way

increasing the complication or proportionate liability to derangement. Many positions that formerly were utterly impracticable can now be utilised with the grandest effect. Powerful west-gallery organs may be played from the east end of the church, entirely through a cable of insulated wire an inch in diameter, or attached to additional manuals provided for that purpose at a mechanical organ placed close to the choir. Again, in Roman Catholic churches, an altar organ, to accompany the priests, can be similiarly played from the west-gallery organ, and thus one organist will be able to accomplish the duty performed by two, as in foreign churches. Many other novel dispositions and architectural arrangements suggest themselves now as perfectly practicable.

305. The electric principal is applicable to the re-construction of organs already built, though in such cases all existing mechanical action must be thrown away ; consequently it is more expensive than when applied in new organs. The cost must necessarily exceed that of ordinary construction, unless similiar conditions are imposed, in which case comparison will be favourable, although in addition much more valuable and imperishable materials are employed in the electric organ, and the larger it is, the less the proportionate cost of the application, besides the greater the advantages gained. Should the manuals not require removal, but occupy the ordinary position, close to the organ, an electric key-action, to ensure a light touch, may be employed with a mechanical or common draw-stop action, and so save expense.

306. Mr. Bryceson's first electric organ was built for Her Majesty's Opera, Theatre-Royal, Drury Lane, carried on there on account of the destruction of the old house in 1867. This organ, erected within three months of the time he obtained the concession from Mr. Barker, was placed behind the scenery on the O.P. side, fifty feet away from the key-board, which was in the orchestra, where the organist could see the conductor and instantaneously realise his suggestions and directions. It was first publicly used on the 25th of May, 1868, and continued in operation till the end of the season without the slightest derangement or requiring attention. He then erected it in the Polytechnic Institution, Regent Street, where it has been performed on twice daily ever since. This was the first organ which had an electric draw-stop action and a cable of insulated wire through which it was played. No such example yet exists in France.

307. The next was built for Christ Church, Camberwell. It contains two manuals and independent pedal organ, twenty sounding-stops and five couplers. It stands above the vestry, in a chamber on the south side of the chancel, and the console is on the opposite side amongst the stalls for the choir ; fifty-five feet of cable intervenes, and runs beneath the encaustic tiles, passing through a drain-pipe provided for it. Exhaust is used for the key pneumatics, and exhaust and pressure for the draw-stop action. This organ was previously erected for the Festival, Gloucester Cathedral, September 7th, 1868. Mr. Bryceson has also re-constructed the large organ in St. Michael's, Cornhill, upon the electric principle. This fine instrument contains three manuals and independent pedal organ, thirty-seven sounding-stops, and seven couplers. The console is opposite, and facing the organ at a distance of thirty feet, thus placing the choir between the organist and organ. The cable contains 336 insulated wires, and measures $1\frac{1}{4}$ inch in diameter ; it is carried through a small drain-pipe under the chancel floor, and this constitutes, with the exception of the lead pipe for the swell cylinders, the only connection between the organ and the console. Exhaust is used for the key pneumatics, and exhaust only for the draw-stop action. He has also finished a large electric organ for St. George's Church, Tufnel Park, placed over the west door, and others for St. Augustine's Church, Highbury, Minley Manor, near Farnborough, &c., all on the electric system. The tubular pneumatic action is noticed in the Appendix.

CHAPTER XVI.

THE SHIFTING MOVEMENT AND THE COMPOSITION PEDALS.

The shifting movement.   308. BESIDES the means just described for bringing the sliders under the control of the *hands* of the organist, others were in the course of time devised for bringing some of the stops of the great organ under the control of the *feet* of the performer, called *shifting movements.* Many of Father Smith's smaller church organs consisted simply of one manual organ of full compass, with perhaps also an " echo " to middle c^1. This was the case in respect to his instruments in the churches of St. Mary-at-Hill ; St. Mary's Oxford ; the Theatre, Oxford ; &c. There being no choir organ for softer playing, Smith attached to most of such instruments—perhaps to all of them—a movement worked by a pedal, the depression of which silenced particular stops—usually all the flue-stops of smaller size than the principal, and also the reed-stop—and so they remained as long as the pedal was held or *hitched* down ; and, on raising or releasing it, they again came into play. Snetzler also made use of a similar appliance for his small organs. The shifting movement had to be supplied with springs to draw back the sliders on the removal of the foot, the resistance of which had to be overcome before the pedal would act ; and this must have rendered its frequent use a matter of some toil and difficulty.

The composition pedals.   309. These drawbacks led, soon after the commencement of the present century, to the invention of the *composition pedals ;* a system of mechanism in which springs acting in the way just described are entirely done away with, and wherein the sliders are left to remain as the pedal arranges them, until the hand, or another pedal, effects a readjustment. The merit of this invention is due to the late Mr. Bishop, although a counter claim to something of the same kind was made by the late Mr. Flight. The circumstances, as related by the late Mr. Bishop to the present writer many years ago, were briefly these. Mr. Bishop, then a very young man, and former apprentice of Mr. Flight's, laid before the Society of Arts the plans of his invention, which invention Mr. Flight then claimed as having been made by himself, and at a date prior to that named by Mr. Bishop ; and he put in drawings in support of his assertion. On close examination, however, the paper on which the drawings were made, was discovered from the paper-mark not to have been manufactured until after the date at which the drawings were declared to have been completed, that date also being subsequent to the one affixed to Mr. Bishop's diagrams. This irresistible discovery, of course, brought the investigation to a close, and Mr. Bishop's claim to the invention was never afterwards contested.

310. Of composition pedals there are two kinds—the " single-action " and the " double-action."

The single-action composition pedal.   311. A single-action composition pedal operates in *one* way only ; that is, it either *draws out* or *thrusts in* a given number of sliders, but does not do *both.*

312. For example, one composition pedal of this kind will simply *draw out*

stops, say Nos. 1, 2, and 3 ;* a second, stops Nos. 4, 5, and 6, and so on.   But the first pedal will not *draw in* all the stops, *except* Nos. 1, 2, and 3 ; this, if done at all, must be accomplished by a third pedal.   Some single-action composition pedals, therefore, only draw out stops ; others merely draw some in.   They are now seldom if ever made.

The double-action composition pedal.   313. A double-action composition pedal performs *both* offices. It will either draw out all the stops *up* to a certain one, or it will draw in all *to* the same certain one.   Or, supposing a combination to have been previously prepared, composed partly of stops below and partly above the number acted upon by a certain pedal—as, for instance, Nos. 1, 2, 5, and 6—on pressing down the composition pedal that throws out stops Nos. 1 to 3, the stop No. 3 will be *added* to Nos. 1 and 2, and Nos. 5 and 6 will be *drawn in.*

314. The full operation of the "double-action" can be interestingly brought under observation in the following manner :—If the mixtures and reeds *only* be drawn, and the pedal that acts on the great organ stops "to fifteenth" be pressed down, the stop handles that were previously in will all be thrown out, and those that were out will be drawn in.

315. To modern organs of moderate size there are usually 3, 4, or 5 double-action composition pedals, controlling the great organ stops ; and sometimes there are also others which affect the swell and pedal stops.

316. The second composition pedal is usually designed to prepare a *louder* combination than the first ; and the third, if there are only three, generally brings into operation the remaining and most powerful stops.

317. The second one will therefore draw the sliders up to, say No. 6, if *fewer* are out ; or it will draw *in* to that number, if *more* are out.   The third will generally draw out all the remaining sliders, or such of them as may previously have been left undrawn ; and so increase the tone of the great organ to its fullest power. Occasionally, indeed, the trumpet is not thus drawn, but is left to be added by the hand.

The composition pedal action.   318. Of the composition pedal action there are many varieties, almost every organ-builder having some plan which differs, either in principle altogether, or in some matter of detail, from that adopted by all the others. The kind of action represented in the following engraving, however, has been very generally used.   It consists of two iron rods, or "composition irons," disposed horizontally (*a a b, fig.* 86), furnished with vertical iron arms (*c c e e*); the whole of which are brought under control in the region of the manuals, through the aid of some simple mechanism, such as that indicated at *d f.*

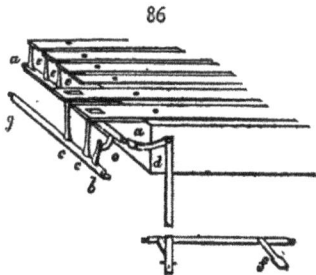

86

The way in which the action operates.   319. On pressing down the composition pedal (*f*), the horizontal arm (*d*), projecting from the first composition iron (*a a*), is drawn downwards, partly turning the composition iron on its axis.   The upright arms at the end (*e e*) are by this motion turned *inwards*, towards the

---

* Instead of making use of the names of stops in this explanation, figures are employed, as it is thought the description will be rendered more clear by being divested of all technicality.

sound-board, thrusting back the sliders with which they are brought into contact. The composition irons are supposed to be placed at the *opposite* end of the sound-board to the draw-stop action ; consequently their motion produces an effect the *reverse* of what they would do were they placed at the *same* end of the sound-board. Thus, *thrusting in* the sliders at the one end is of course equivalent to *drawing them out* at the other. The first three sliders being thrust back, the draw-stops acting thereupon start forward, and the three stops governed by those draw-stops and sliders respectively are now ready for use.

320. As the *first* composition iron revolves, the *contact* (*o*) strikes against the contact (*h*) belonging to the second composition iron (*b*), and causes the second composition iron to revolve the *contrary* way to the first. The arms (*c c*), being made to move only with the body, take also the contrary course, moving the other sliders with them ; and thus it is that the "double-action" is established, and the power secured of restoring any combination of stops to one particular form, by simply the pressure of the foot upon a pedal.

321. Every "double-action composition pedal" made upon this principle is provided with two of these composition irons, one for drawing off such sliders as the other does not draw on.

322. The composition pedals are usually placed immediately over the German pedals in a row, and nearly parallel with the swell pedal ; but occasionally they project through the jambs, as that of the swell often does, some on each side of the pedal-board.

323. Mr. Willis constructs his composition appliances so that they may be worked with the thumbs by the aid of pneumatic levers ; and for which method of putting them into operation he has secured a patent. No pedals are used, but simply studs or pistons, which project through the beading under the manual keys. Messrs. Bryceson sometimes use both the pneumatic buttons and the composition pedals in the same instrument.

324. Mr. Hill introduced into the Panopticon organ a piece of mechanism, worked by a pedal, which drew out all the great organ stops, singly and in succession, producing thereby a gradual and complete *crescendo ;* after doing which, it drew them in again, one by one, producing as complete a *diminuendo.* Herr Walcker, of Ludwigsburg, produces a *crescendo* of the entire organ, which he has done at Ulm Cathedral, and also in his famous Boston Music Hall organ in America.

325. In the modern French organs by Cavaillé-Coll, and others, the combination pedals do not act upon the draw-stops, but upon the *wind.* For instance, if you put down the pedal to take off the reeds, it does not shift the sliders, but cuts off the communication of the wind from the reed sound-board, which, of course, effectually silences the stops. The Festival organ at the Crystal Palace has pedals of this kind ; so have Cavaillé-Coll's at the Carmelite Church, Kensington, and Mr. Gern's at the French Church in Leicester Square. Schulze's combination pedals in the new organ at Doncaster Church act in the same manner.

326. In Germany composition pedals are scarcely known ; consequently the organs of that country are mostly without one of the greatest modern advantages. Batz, of Utrecht, is beginning to introduce composition pedals.

327. In arranging the composition pedals, some of the English organ-builders place the "loud pedal" to the left and the softest to the right, while others reverse this order. The adoption of a uniform plan is most desirable. Some of them, however, have a movement for disconnecting the powerful pedal stops—as will be seen on reference to some of the Foreign Specifications—which practically answers the same end.

CHAPTER XVII.

THE ECHO AND SWELL.

328. Most of the old English organs originally possessed, and a few of them still retain, a department called the "echo."

329. The Echo organ consists of a duplication of the treble portion of some of the stops found on the other manual organs closed in a wooden box, to render their tone soft and more distant sounding than that of the stops of the same name in other parts of the instrument, planted on a small sound-board of their own, and provided with a separate half row of keys. The name of this now nearly obsolete department in English organs plainly indicates the purpose for which it was originally designed. In the year 1712 a most important improvement on the old echo was effected by Abraham Jordan, whereby the sound produced from its stops could be made to rise or fall on the ear with increasing or decreasing strength. This power was gained by making the front of the box that enclosed the pipes *open* instead of solid, as before, and furnishing it with a moveable shutter, fitting closely to, and entirely covering, the opening, and running up and down in a sash, like a window. A rope or lever attached to the shutter raised it, on the performer pressing down a pedal placed to his right and near to the ground, which action, gradually raising the sliding shutter, uncovered the opening in the box, and allowed the sound produced by the pipes within to emerge. The echo, in this greatly ameliorated form, was called the "swelling organ" or "swell," and rose so rapidly into repute, that the echo in its former primitive state fell into entire disuse in a very short space of time.

330. The "*nag's-head swell*," as the above early kind of swell was called, was not well designed, nor happily adapted to its purpose in a mechanical point of view. The weight or resistance to be overcome by the pressure of the foot was so great that the shutter could be set in motion only with difficulty; and, when it was in motion, there was equal difficulty in regulating the rate or extent of its ascent; for it would then not unfrequently run up almost of itself. Its descent was similarly beyond control, and it would often fall with an audible noise. The nag's-head swell continued in use for upwards of half a century, till it was superseded by what has since been denominated the "Venetian swell." This kind of swell was adapted to the organ by Samuel Green; it having previously been applied successfully to some of the better class of harpsichord.

331. The peculiarity of the *Venetian swell* consists in the front being composed of a series of "shades" or "shutters," measuring from six to ten inches in breadth, and from one and a half to two and a half inches in thickness. Each shutter is hung on an axis placed one-third from the top of its breadth. The edges of each shutter are bevelled away at an angle of about 45 degrees, so that the bevelled surfaces are parallel to each other, and each two contiguous boards are made to overlap each other, the bevelled surfaces meeting, so that the whole front may be quite flush or even when the shutters are closed. An arm projects a few ... es from each shutter, in a line one above another, and these are all connected with a perpendicular rod, so that when the rod is raised, which is done by means of a pedal, all the shutters are opened. The bevelled surfaces of the shutters are covered with felt, or some such substance, to make them fit closely and shut in the sound. Cloth and matting were for some time used as a lining to the box to deaden the sound when the swell was

closed ; but they exercised a similar influence also when it was open ; besides which the former material harboured moths, and the latter crumbled into dust, some of which found its way into the pipes. Brown paper, well coated with glue, covers the pores of the wood of the box, and so keeps in the sound when the shutters are closed, at the same time that it presents a hard surface to reflect the sound when they are open.

332. The resemblance which the shutters of a modern swell bear to Venetian window-blinds readily suggested the designation by which they are now so generally known.

333. When the shutters of a swell are narrow, they are of course more numerous ; and in such cases, when open, they present a greater number of thicknesses of wood to check the egress of the sound. On the other hand, when they are broader, and, consequently, fewer in number, they are more liable to " cast."

334. The swell-box and shutters are shown in profile in the general section. (See *fig.* 4.)

335. On a well-constructed Venetian swell a practised performer can imitate, not only a gradual *crescendo* and *diminuendo,* but also a *sforzando ;* a very small opening being sufficient to make an immediate burst on the ear, while, when the shutters are closed, a close imitation of an echo is produced. When the shutters are closed, they take that position either from their own weight, or from the influence of springs or weights.

336. In the lower part of the swell-box, in front, or at the back, or sometimes in both places, according to the plantation of the reed-stops, there is usually either a long moveable panel or a wooden flap, corresponding in length with the swell-shutters, behind which are ranged the pipes forming the reed-stops, to which access for tuning purposes is thus easily gained.

337. Other facilities for tuning are usually provided, having special reference to the adjustment of the flue-stops. These consist of large openings in each side of the swell-box, ordinarily closed by doors or panels. By removing these, the tuner can reach the top of any flue-pipe that may require his attention.

338. Large swell sound-boards have frequently a centre passage-board, in which case there is an entrance door provided through the centre of the front of the swell, and the shutters are divided into two smaller sets.

339. A good Venetian swell, constructed on the ordinary principle, is capable of producing great effects of light and shade ; yet attempts have been made from time to time to increase its contrasting powers.

340. One plan consisted in enclosing the original box in a second case, with a space of a few inches left between the two at the sides, back, and top, and filling the interstices with shaving, sawdust, or any other material that would prevent the escape of sound. In the front were placed two or even three sets of shutters, which did not all open simultaneously, although acted upon by one pedal ; but, by a suitable arrangement of cranks and levers, on the gradual depression of the pedal, one set commenced its motion, then a second, and finally the third, each of the latter two with an accelerated pace, as compared with that of the one that preceded it ; so that all three sets arrived at their extreme opening at the same moment, the shades falling into parallel lines, presenting scarcely any obstacle to the free escape of all the sound which the enclosed pipes were capable of producing. The box of the swell in the organ at St. James's Church, Bristol, built by Smith of that city in 1824, under the direction of Dr. Hodges, was constructed in the manner just detailed.

341. Another plan provided the *back* as well as the front of the swell-box with Venetian shutters, as was the case at the parish church, Doncaster ; while the chief peculiarity in the third plan, devised for the same purpose, consisted in furnishing *both the sides* as well as the front of the box with shutters, as at York Cathedral.

In this latter example the side shutters were made to work *vertically*. The shutters of the swell in the fine organ in the church of St. Vincent de Paul, in Paris, made by Cavaillé-Coll, work in this manner, and the plan has been followed with excellent effect by Mr. Lewis in some of his recent organs. The swell-box at St. Vincent de Paul presents the peculiarity of having its sides and back provided with plate-glass panels, by which means not only is a perfect view of what is within obtained from without, but the inside of the swell is nearly as free from darkness as the other interior parts of the organ.

342. A swell imparts to the sound of an organ an agreeable undulating effect, similar to that produced by the wind on the sound of a peal of bells when it bears their tones first *towards*, then *from* the listener. An organ with a swell is, in fact, as much in advance of an organ without one, so far as the power of giving expression to music is concerned, as a modern pianoforte is superior to the old harpsichord; on which account it is rapidly finding admission into the organs of France and Germany.

343. The compass of the early swells was very limited, usually extending only to middle c^1, fiddle g, or at most to tenor f. The swell of the fine organ in St. Mary Redcliff Church, Bristol, built by Harris and Byfield, in 1715, descended to gamut G; while that of the equally fine instrument at Great Yarmouth, erected by Jordan, Bridge, and Byfield, in 1733, went to tenor c. The shorter ranges, nevertheless, were generally adhered to until the time of Samuel Green, who held this department of the organ in special estimation, and improved it in a variety of ways. In two of his instruments he again extended the swell compass by nearly a whole octave. The admirable organs in which these evidences of Green's sound judgment are to be found are those in St. Katherine's Church, Regent's Park, brought from the demolished structure of that name, near the Tower, and in the chapel of Greenwich Hospital; in the former the swell descends to gamut G, and, in the latter, a tone lower—namely, to FF. Green originally enclosed even the great manual organ of his instrument in St. George's Chapel, Windsor, in a great swell. Cavaillé-Coll's organ at Kensington is so enclosed.

344. Some of the old swell-boxes were furnished with a wooden tube, not unlike a wind-trunk, projecting from the back of the box, and passing out into the tower of the church. This was the case with the organ at St. Martin's-in-the-Fields, built by the elder Gray. The end of the tube attached to the swell-box was furnished with a trap, which opened when the swell was closed, and closed as the swell was opened; by which means the subdued effect of the swell, when shut, was increased, on account of an outlet being thus afforded for the sound. This contrivance suggests a method of overcoming a difficulty with regard to the larger swells of modern organs. If the swell is much used without being opened, and the shutters fit accurately, the atmosphere within the swell-box becomes increased in density by the great quantity of wind that rapidly passes through the large pipes into the circumscribed area of the box, which has the effect of flattening the pitch of some of the pipes. If, on the other hand, a little leakage be allowed, the escaping air, by carrying some of the tone with it, renders the softened effect of the swell less perfect. By adapting a tube, as above, there would be free ventilation within the swell-box, when closed as well as when open, whereby the freedom of speech of the large as well as small pipes would be better secured; the pipes would not be thrown out of tune by being smothered; and the fullest contrasting powers of the swell would be preserved. If the swell were likely to be exposed to *two* temperatures—a second and lower one from the tower when the shutters were closed—this might be rectified by a small gas jet placed at a safe distance from the mouth of the tube. In his Exhibition organ Mr. Willis secured a free circulation of air by putting the swell bellows inside the swell-box.

CHAPTER XVIII.

THE TREMULANT.

345. THE tremulant is a small apparatus that gives to the tone of any department of an organ to which it may be applied a waving or undulating effect,
resembling the *vibrato* in singing, and the *tremolando* in violin playing. It has
long been known in England by tradition. A "shaking stoppe" formed part of
the organ made by Dallam, in 1606, for King's College, Cambridge ; another
was included in Loosemore's organ for Sir George Trevelyan, built in 1665 ; a
"Trimeloe" occurred in Smith's organ at St. Mary-at-Hill, 1693 ; and another formed
a portion of the original work of Snetzler's organ in the Lutheran Church, at the
Savoy, Strand. The old tremulants, however, were very noisy contrivances ; hence
they were not favourably received in this country, and they were latterly also
omitted from most of the new organs in Germany. In Paris a better kind of
tremulant action was devised, not many years ago, on which, nevertheless, the
English builders have succeeded in making considerable improvements ; the first
church organ in this country to which a tremulant of the new kind was applied
being that at St. Luke's, Old Street, the addition being made by Mr. Davison.

346. The accompanying engraving (*fig.* 87) represents one of the most successful

87

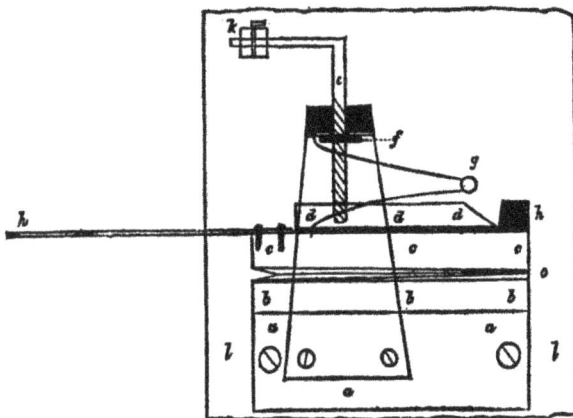

tremulant actions. It is supposed to be fixed to one of the broad sides of the
wind-trunk. The wind passes through a hole in the wind-trunk (*l l*), into the
wind-box (*a a a*), and hence, through an internal aperture in the slab (*b b b*), into the
tremulant (*c c c*), which also has an aperture through it, covered by the pallet (*d d d*)
held firmly down by the screw (*e*). The tremulant is thus set in motion. The rod
(*k*) turns the screw half-round in the socket (*f*), the pallet (*d d d*) being thereby
raised slightly ; the tremulant (*c c c*) immediately follows the pallet (*a*), by reason

of the internal pressure of air on its under surface ; but it is immediately thrown back by the spring (*g*), which, in power, just counterpoises the upward pressure of the tremulant (*c c c*). These two opposing forces, viz., the wind inside and the spring outside, impart a trembling motion to the tremulant, which motion is communicated to the elastic bar (*h*). The rapidity and regularity of the vibrations depend upon the length and thickness of the vibrating bar, influenced, in some examples, by a small sliding weight at the end, on shifting which nearer to or farther from the tremulant, the vibrations are accelerated or retarded.

347. The tremulant is here described in connection with the swell, because that is the department to which it is the most usually attached in England ; besides which, its effect is considerably enhanced when brought into conjunction with the numerous other resources of the division of the organ just named. The effects of *forte, piano, crescendo, diminuendo, sforzando,* and *tremolando,* are then all attainable from that one department alone.

348. The tremulant effect in an organ is of *older* date than the *tremolando* and *vibrato* effects in instrumental and vocal performance. This fact may be gathered from the following passage taken from *Grassineau's Musical Dictionary,* ed. 1740, p. 289 :—

349. " TREMOLO, *Tremolante,* or *Tremente,* 'tis not often used, except thus abbreviated—*Trem.* or *tr.;* to intimate to the *instrumental* performers of a piece that they make several notes on the same degree or pitch of tune, with one draw of the bow, *to imitate the shaking on the organ,* though this is often placed in the *vocal* parts of a song." We have examples of both in Mr. Tully's opera of *Isis.*

Division O.

THE SOUND-PRODUCING PORTIONS OF THE ORGAN.

CHAPTER XIX.

THE MATERIALS USED FOR ORGAN PIPES.

350. HAVING now described the wind collecting and distributing portions, as also the mechanism of the organ, the next subject to be considered is the nature and construction of those parts from which the *tone* of the organ is more immediately produced.

351. The sound of an organ emanates from an assemblage of pipes, which are made either of tin, metal, or wood; are round, square, or triangular shaped; long or short, broad or narrow, according to circumstances. But first of the materials.

352. The various *substances* of which organ pipes are made are tin, metal, lead, antimony metal, zinc, and wood of various kinds.

Tin.　　　　353. Of all the materials just specified as being used for organ pipes tin ranks first in point of excellence; and, of the many existing varieties of this substance, that found in England is held in the highest esteem, not only by some of the organ-builders of this country, past and present, but also by the Continental artists, by the latter of whom it still continues to be used in liberal quantities. Thus we find English tin mentioned as being used for a greater or less number of stops in some of the specifications of foreign organs contained in the Appendix to this book; while in other cases other kinds of tin are named, as Prussian tin, probe tin, or simply " tin."

354. Tin has occasionally been used by English organ-builders for organ stops for many years past. Greenwood, of Leeds, introduced a dulciana of this material into the organ in Brereton Hall upwards of twenty-five years since; Mr. Hamilton, of Edinburgh, has employed it exclusively for many years past; and more recently it has been used by Mr. Davison, for the Great Open Diapason, and an interior stop in the Eton College Chapel organ (built 1852); also for the Choir Open Diapason in the Glasgow Town Hall organ (erected in 1853); by Mr. Walker, for the Open Diapason and Dulciana, forming the Bass continuation to the Viol di Gamba, in the organ at Holy Trinity Church, Vauxhall Bridge, finished in the year 1852; and by Mr. Willis, for the 32-feet front pipes of his organ in the Royal Albert Hall.

355. Tin recommends itself as a material for organ pipes by its great durability, its superior silver colour, and its lightness. It is very ductile, on which account pipe-work made of such material does not nearly so soon become cracked or broken round the top by the force necessarily exercised with the tuning-horn during the process of tuning. Neither are pipes of this metal so soon attacked by the strong acid in the wood-work that sustains them (the upper-boards), but which will eat away the lower part of pipes made of many other materials that are more frequently used. It undergoes but little change, either from exposure to the

atmosphere, or to the impure exhalation produced by the breathing of a closely packed audience ; and it resists the influence of sulphurous vapours, such as the fumes from gas. Nor is it oxidised even by the combined action of air and moisture ; on which account it has always been liberally used for the pipes of organs in those countries where there is a humid atmosphere, as in Holland, and the use of wood pipes at the same time avoided, as far as possible, on account of their tendency to swell from the damp. Of the sixty stops in the Haarlem organ only one is of wood, namely, the pedal Sub-bass, and that is a subsequent insertion. The front pipes of that celebrated instrument, the largest of which is nearly forty feet in length, are of pure tin ; while the inside pipes are made of metal compounded of half tin and half lead.

356. Tin, again, is less susceptible of change of temperature than are many of the compounds in common use, on account of its greater hardness ; consequently pipes of this material stand much better in tune.

357. Tin does not soon become tarnished ; hence its peculiar appropriateness for ungilded front pipes, for which purpose it has indeed been used for centuries in even the humblest village church organs in Germany ; and, when it does at length become dulled, its splendour is easily recovered. When it dulls, it never changes below a dark grey tint.

358. The lighter specific gravity of tin, again—fully one-third less than that of lead—is in its favour, a given quantity of the former going much farther than an equal weight of the latter. This is supposing the pipes to be made from sheets of the *same thickness;* but as this is but seldom the case—the 16-feet front pipes of the organ at St. Roque's Church, in Paris, however, forming an exception, they being of tin, and of remarkable *substance*—the tin would probably go as far again as the lead. The great cost of tin—five or six times that of lead—and more particularly the baneful " low-contract " spirit which unfortunately pervades most *modern* transactions in organ-building matters, preclude its use to any great extent in this country, although it would, on account of the greater durability of the material, prove to be the cheapest in the end. The easy fusibility of tin renders the joining together of the edges of sheets of that metal a work demanding great care, as it is possible otherwise for the melted solder to fuse them instead of uniting them into a seam ; hence a small portion of alloy (lead) is frequently added, which renders the substance less susceptible of heat. According to a late experiment, tin fuses at 442°, whereas lead requires 612° of Fahrenheit's thermometer. Cavaillé-Coll, the eminent organ-builder of Paris, generally proportions 1-10th of lead to 9-10ths of tin ; and Schulze, one of the most excellent builders in Germany, uses 1-4th of lead to 3-4ths of tin ; and, for his ordinary metal, half tin and half lead. The two ingredients just named are said to form the hardest compound, when the proportions are 1-4th of lead to 3-4ths of tin.

359. Some German organ-builders draw a distinction—and a very good one—between "pure tin " and "tin." The term " pure tin " of course explains itself ; but the material is still called "tin " so long as the proportion of alloy is so small as to *improve* the mass ; and this is considered to be the case so long as the alloy forms no more than 1-4th of the total weight of the metal. Pipes composed of this material are said to produce the greatest amount of tone, combining brightness with fulness. When the pipes are of "pure tin," if they are also made of good substance and well blown, the tone has a tendency to become rather piercing ; if, on the other hand, they are made thin and less copiously winded, the sound will be very musical, though not so weighty as that from more solid pipes of the same scale made of the alloyed tin. Hence the latter material is preferred for the strongest-toned stops ; and the former for others of a clear, cutting, crisp, or light

S

intonation. Thus the Gambas, Salicets, &c., in Germany, and the Choir Open Diapason and Dulciana of English organs, are not unfrequently made of " pure tin."

360. The original front pipes of the Temple organ, made by Father Smith, are rather more than 3-4ths tin. The specific gravity of the metal of the last-mentioned organ is 7·911 (that of water = 1) ; and its composition is as follows :—

$$
\begin{array}{lr}
\text{Tin} & 76\text{·}9504 \text{ per cent.} \\
\text{Lead} & 21\text{·}9017 \quad \text{„} \\
\text{Copper} & \text{·}5183 \quad \text{„} \\
\hline
& 99\text{·}3704
\end{array}
$$

361. The presence of copper, which is only about a half per cent., is no doubt accidental, and was in combination with the tin ; a small quantity of copper being commonly found in ordinary commercial tin. The above composition very nearly accords with what would be called by the German organ-builders " 12¼ löthig metal," that is, one pound (= 16 löth) of the metal contains 12¼ löth of tin, or 12¼ oz. of tin to 3½ oz. of lead. The proportions of tin and lead, therefore, lie between 4 of tin and 1 of lead, and 3 of tin and 1 of lead, as above intimated.

362. In *Die Orgel*, by Töpfer (Erfurt, 1843), page 175, a table is given of the specific gravity of metal with different proportions of tin and lead, from which it appears that the specific gravity of that consisting of 4 of tin and 1 of lead is 7·8830, and that containing 3 of tin and 1 of lead is 8·0380 ; the specific gravity of the Temple metal being *between* the two, namely, 7·9111. The front pipes of the organs at St. Paul's Cathedral and Trinity College Chapel, Cambridge, are also of very fine metal, and of considerable thickness ; hence the rich and resonant character of the Diapasons of all the instruments above named.

Metal.   363. Metal is a word used technically by organ-builders, and is understood to signify a mixture of tin and lead, which compound is valued according to the quantity of the former ingredient contained in its composition. The metal ordinarily used abroad consists of half tin and half lead. The distinction between tin and metal stops, as well as the proportion of tin and lead used in the composition of the metal, will be found interestingly illustrated in some of the Specifications of Foreign Organs included in the Appendix.

Spotted Metal.   364. There is a compound now much used in England, and held in high repute, called " spotted metal," from its surface being mottled or covered with spots. The spots gradually appear on the surface as the metal cools after being cast into sheets, and " rise " when the ingredients contain about 1-3rd of tin. They are, therefore, generally viewed as an evidence of the goodness of the material. Spotted metal was frequently made use of by the younger Harris and Green, also by Lincoln. In the present day it is constantly used by most of the English organ-builders.

Lead.   365. Lead, either alone or with but a slight admixture of tin, from its inability to sustain itself for any lengthened period, is, as a material for metal organ pipes, comparatively worthless. The greater thickness to which a sheet of this metal must necessarily be made, to compensate for its natural softness, added to its greater specific gravity, are circumstances that render the bodies of leaden flue pipes so heavy that their feet are very liable to become depressed at the apex from the weight, and the languid to sink, whereby the intonation of the pipe is endangered, if not lost. The tubes of reed pipes, especially, are very apt to bend at the narrow end or stork, from this weakness. Bad metal is discernible in a variety of ways; to the eye, by its dark blue tint;* to the touch, by its producing a dull hollow sound on being rapped, whereas pipes of good thick metal produce a clear ringing sound; and to the nail, by its being easily scratched, whereas tin can scarcely be marked in that manner. Metal composed chiefly of lead also easily soils paper rubbed upon it. The organ in the Minoreten Church at Bonn—the instrument on which Beethoven used to play—has its metal pipe-work composed entirely of lead, including the 16-feet front. It is not a very good instrument.

Antimony Metal.   366. Antimony metal is compounded chiefly of lead and antimony, or lead and type. The antimony imparts considerable hardness to the mass; so that the possibility need scarcely exist of a pipe-foot or languid of antimony metal sinking. The drawback is its brittleness; pipe-work of this compound being very liable to crack round the top after being subjected to the action of the tuning-horn for a few years. A proof of this lack of tenacity in the metal in question is obtained by bending a piece of it to and fro, when it will be found to break asunder on reversing the bend. In some instances the antimony has been known to separate itself from the lead, leaving the pipes covered with little indentations; and reed-pipes of antimony metal have been known to snap off suddenly at the stork, and fall from their situations.

Zinc.   367. Zinc has frequently been used of late years in England by Hill and Son, Willis, Lewis, and others, for the structure of large metal pipes; and it is a material that undergoes but little alteration at common temperatures, under even the combined influences of air and moisture. The tone produced from pipes of this substance, when voiced by the hands of a master, is very fine and weighty. Its cost, again—far less than that of good metal—much favours its introduction. The tubes of the 32 and 16 feet reed-stops in many of the Continental organs are made of this material. The 32-feet Posaune on the pedal at St. Roque's, Paris, is of zinc; so also is the 16-feet Bombarde in the organ at St. Martin's, Liege. The front Double Open Diapason (32 feet) in the Birmingham Town Hall organ is likewise of the same material; and there is a Double Open Diapason of the same size and metal also in the Cathedral organ at York, and a very fine 16-feet Pedal Diapason of the same substance in the transept front of the organ in Doncaster Church. The 32-feet front pipes in the Alexandra Palace organ, by Willis, are of zinc.

The casting of the Metal.   368. In order to prepare the metal for use, of which organ pipes are to be formed, the ingredients are melted together in a copper, and then cast into *sheets;* a process effected by pouring it, in a molten state, into a wooden trough, and running the trough rapidly along a bench faced with *tick*. The metal escapes from the trough through a narrow horizontal opening at the back, leaving a layer of metal behind it as it proceeds; and the wider the cutting is, of course the thicker will be the sheet of metal

---

* "In the Continental organs, the pipes visible in front of the case are carefully finished and burnished, and show the bright natural lustre of the white metal; but, in England, where the ignoble alloy is incapable of retaining its polish, the pipes are obliged to be gilt or painted, to make them appear respectable."—*Musical Instruments in the Great Exhibition.* By Wm. Pole, p. 49.

produced. After being cast to an *approximate* thickness, the metal is planed down to the precise thickness required. It is then cut into portions of the shape necessary to give to the pipes the required size and form, and is thus finally worked up.

Wood.   369. A great number of the large pipes, as well as some of the smaller, are made of wood; and experience proves that pipes made of good wood do better service, and are of longer duration, than inferior metal ones.

370. Dr. Burney was assured by Snetzler, who had seen Father Smith work, that he was so particularly careful in the choice of his wood, as never to use any that had the least flaw or knot in it; and so tender was he of his reputation, that he would never waste time in trying to mend a bad pipe, but would immediately throw it away and make another, which accounts for the soundness of his wood pipes to this day. The woods chiefly made use of for modern pipes are cedar, deal, and pine. Oak was employed by Father Smith, but not frequently, in consequence of its cost and the expense of working it. The bass of the Stopped Diapason in the great organ at the Temple is however of this material. So also is the Flute in the great organ. Mahogany is occasionally adopted for the pipes of organs destined for hot climates, as in the organ at Calcutta Cathedral, built by the late Mr. Gray. Other woods are sometimes made use of in Continental organs, as maple-wood, pear-tree-wood, cypress-wood, box-wood, &c. (See Foreign Specifications.)

The seasoning of the   371. The wood of which organ pipes are to be made is
wood.   first well seasoned; that is to say, it is thoroughly exposed to the air for a few years, and, to a certain extent, also to rain water, to destroy all its vital properties; after which it is kept in a dry place, where the air can get to it freely, to prevent its decaying. If any sap were to remain in the timber—*i.e.*, if the wood were not to be thoroughly seasoned—it would be very apt, after being worked up into pipes, to split on becoming dry, and so render the intonation faulty.

372. With the view to rendering the wood pipe-work thoroughly sound, such knots in the timber as cannot be avoided are covered well with glue and leather, or paper, to prevent their falling out; or they are extracted, and their places filled in with other wood. After this, the wooden pipes are often covered on the outside with a coat of red size (which by no means improves the appearance of the interior of the organ), and inside with a layer of thin glue, to fill up the pores of the wood, which, by rendering the surface smooth, improves the tone of the pipes.

CHAPTER XIX.

THE PLAN, OUTLINE, AND STRUCTURE OF ORGAN PIPES.

The plan and outline of the pipes.

373. THE next particulars to be noticed are the *plan, outline,* and *proportions* of the pipes that are formed out of the several materials just enumerated.

374. In regard to *plan* organ pipes are divided into three classes : *round, four-sided,* and *triangular ;* the respective kinds of plan almost necessarily arising from the employment of the flexible and the stiff substances.

375. In regard to *shape* and *outline* organ pipes are very diversified ; and every variation in these respects causes more or less alteration in the *strength* or *character of the tone* of the pipe.

376. The chief varieties of metal round-bodied pipes are the

> Cylindrical,
> Conical,
> Conical, surrounded by a bell,
> Inverted cone, and
> Inverted cone, surmounted by a bell.

377. Wood pipes are divided into

> Four-sided,
> Three-sided,
> Cylindrical,
> Pyramidal, and
> Inverted pyramidal pipes.

Cylindrical pipes.

378. Pipes classed under this head are such round ones as preserve the same diameter in body all the way up. There are three varieties of cylindrical pipes—the open, the stopped, and the half-stopped.

Open cylindrical pipes (*fig.* 88, p. 102).

379. Open cylindrical pipes are the most numerous in all organs ; the stops called Open Diapason, Principal, Fifteenth, and Mixture, among others, being ordinarily composed of pipes of this shape. Open cylindrical pipes are therefore used for the strong-toned flue-stops.

Stopped cylindrical pipes (*fig.* 89, p. 102).

380. Stopped cylindrical pipes are such as have their top closed or covered in by a metal covering or cap (*a, fig.* 89). Stops composed of pipes so formed are rarely to be met with in England, except in old organs ; and there they are only occasionally to be seen. There was an excellent one in Father Smith's organ in Chester Cathedral ; and the pretty (so-labelled) Stopped Diapason in the swell of the small organ in All-Hallows, Bread Street (now removed), was formed of pipes of this description. Stops of covered pipes, however, are of common occurrence in the German organs, under the names of " Gedact " and " Quintaton."

381. The " Gedact 8 fusston," which is sometimes made also of wood, is a full,

yet mellow-toned Stopped Diapason. The "Quintaton 8 fusston" is a Stopped Diapason of smaller scale, which sounds the Twelfth or Octave-fifth as well as the fundamental or ground-tone.

Half-stopped cylindrical pipes (*fig.* 90).   382. Half-stopped cylindrical pipes are far more common in English organs than are the last mentioned. They are formed much after the manner of the covered pipes just noticed, the chief difference consisting in the cap being perforated in the centre with a small tube or chimney rising therefrom, and hence called *flute à cheminée* by the French. (See *e, fig.* 90.) Stops of this kind are frequently to be seen in old organs, and occasionally also in modern ones, under the names Stopped Diapason (metal), Flute (metal), &c. ; although the stop-labels seldom indicate their presence, so far as the *material* is concerned.

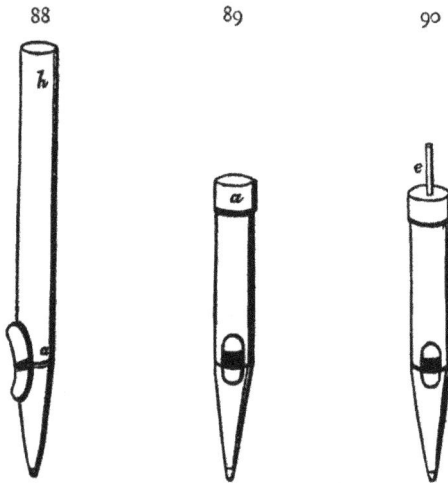

383. The great and swell Stopped Diapasons and the swell Flute in the organ at the Temple Church are of metal ; so were those in Harris's fine organ at Doncaster, destroyed in 1853. There is a fine metal Stopped Diapason in Bridge's great organ at Christ Church, Spitalfields.

Perforated cylindrical pipes.   384. Perforated cylindrical pipes are used in the formation of certain stops. Thus the small pipes of the Keraulophon are pierced through the body, near to the top ; those of the English Hohl-flute have two holes near to the top, and opposite to each other ; while those of the Flute Harmonique have each a small perforation half way up the body.

385. Besides the foregoing varieties, cylindrical pipes are made of *wood* in Germany, and produce a most exquisite tone. They are used for the "Flauto Traverso," among other stops, which stop, like the French Flute Harmonique, blows its octave in the upper portion of the scale.

386. Besides the flue-stops already enumerated, some soft-toned reed stops are composed of cylindrical pipes. These are the Clarionet (*fig.* 91) and Vox Humana (*fig.* 92) stops. The former is constructed of moderately long and narrow pipes which are quite open at the top ; the last mentioned are of shorter and broader pipes, and half-stopped at the top.

Conical pipes.

387. Conical pipes are such that the bodies lessen from the mouth upwards more or less rapidly. Pipes of this conical shape are rather rare in old English organs ; nor can they be traced very readily when they do occur, as their presence is seldom notified in any way on the stop handles. Two varieties of conical pipes are here engraved. *Fig.* 94 represents the German " Spitz-flöte," which is little more than half the width at the top ; and *fig.* 95 the German " Gemshorn," which is scarcely more than ⅓ at the top than it is at the mouth. Father Smith occasionally made use of conical pipes. A Spitz-flöte and a Gemshorn of his make still exist on the choir manual of the organ in the Temple Church. There was a " Gemshorn Twelfth " in the choir of Smith's organ at St. Paul's Cathedral. Within the last few years the use of conical stops has become rather general with the English organ-builders.

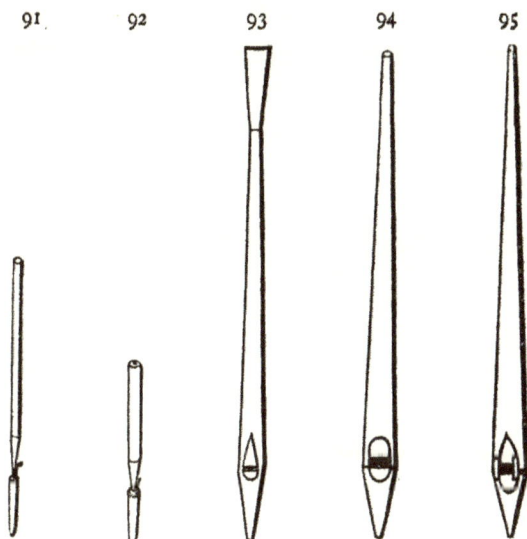

91 92 93 94 95

388. Messrs. Hill and Son frequently insert into their organs a stop of conical outline, and rather crisp tone, which they call " Cone Gamba, 8 feet."

Conical pipes, surmounted by a bell or outspreading top (*fig.* 93).

389. Conical pipes, surmounted by a bell, are used in the formation of the English Viol di Gamba ; the pipes of which stop, however, differ from those of the German one of the same name, in having the bell at the top, besides being conical. This kind of pipe is peculiar to the English organ, and was first introduced by Mr. Hill.

Inverted cone (*fig.* 96).

390. Pipes of the inverted conical form—*i.e.*, narrow at the lower extremity, and spreading out thence upwards (see *fig.* 96)—are employed to a great extent in most organs ; the greater portion of the reed stops, as Trumpet, Posaune, Clarion, Horn, Basscon, &c., being composed of pipes partaking of this outline, the chief difference perceivable to the eye being in the proportion. Flue

pipes are made of this shape on the Continent, and form the stop called the "Dolcan" (*fig.* 97). A stop of this shape and name occurs in the organ at St. Stephen's Church, Westminster, built by Mr. Hill, producing a light, agreeable, and rather fluty tone.

Inverted cone, sur-mounted by a bell (*fig.* 98).

391. Pipes of the shape of an inverted cone, surmounted by a bell, increase in diameter more gradually and to a less extent than the preceding, the bell expanding more suddenly. Pipes of this construction (*fig.* 98) are only used in the formation of the Hautboy and its octave, the pipes of which stops more nearly resemble the shape of their orchestral prototype than those of any other in the organ, excepting some of the Continental Flutes.

Wooden pipes.

392. *Four-sided pipes* (*fig.* 99) are those of which the bodies are of the same width and depth throughout their length. They are freely employed in most organs, and are of two kinds ; the first open, the second stopped, entirely or partially.

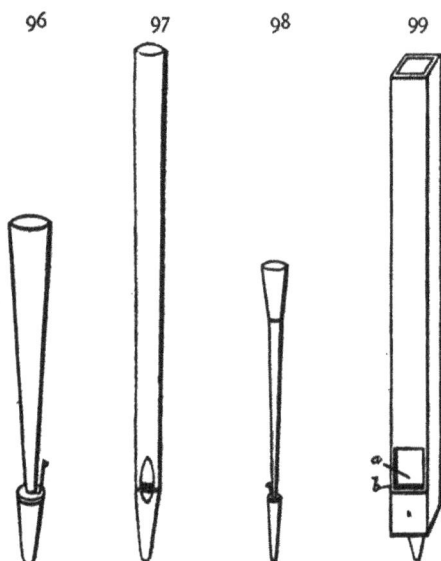

96   97   98   99

Open four-sided pipes.

393. Open four-sided pipes are often introduced in lieu of the large metal bass ones of the Dulciana and Open Diapason. Some stops are formed exclusively of pipes of this class, as the Clarabella, the English Wald-flöte, &c. The Pedal Open Diapason is very commonly composed of pipes of the above kind.

Stopped four-sided pipes (*fig.* 100, p. 105).

394. Stopped four-sided pipes are closed or covered at the upper end with a *stopper*. Like the preceding, they are used to a great extent in most organs ; the Double and Unison Stopped Diapasons, and the Stopped Flute, being in modern instruments usually composed of pipes of this description.

Half-stopped four-sided pipes. 395. The difference between a stopped and a half-stopped pipe consists in the latter having a hole bored down through the handle and stopper. The treble portion of the stops mentioned under the last head is frequently perforated in this manner ; so also is the Clarionet-flute. Large stopped pipes are seldom bored.

Three-sided pipes. 396. Three-sided pipes are of rare occurrence. They are the invention of Mr. Edmund Schulze, who has recently used them for his Hohl-flötes. Specimens by him are to be found in the Doncaster organ, and in the organ recently erected by Messrs. Foster and Andrews at Halifax.

Cylindrical wood pipes. 397. Cylindrical pipes of *wood* are frequently made in Germany, and produce an exquisite tone. They are used for the " Flauto Traverso " of 8 and 4 feet, among other stops. Examples, by Schulze, occur in the Doncaster, the Temple, and the Leeds Parish Church organs.

Pyramidal pipes (*fig.* 101). 398. Pyramidal pipes, broadest at the mouth and lessening upwards, are sometimes introduced (*fig.* 101) to form the bass of the metal conical stops, in the same way that the open four-sided pipes are employed for the completion of some of the cylindrical stops. Occasionally entire stops are formed of pipes of this shape.

399. In the choir department of the large organ in the Wesleyan chapel at Boston, built by Messrs. Gray and Davison, are two stops made of this shape, and called " Gamba " and " Gemshorn."

Pyramidal and inverted (*fig.* 102). 400. Pipes of the inverted pyramidal shape—*i. e.*, narrow at the bottom and broad at the top (*fig.* 102)—are frequently used for large reed stops, as the 16 and 32 feet Posaunes. Smaller reed stops are sometimes formed of pipes of this description ; as, for instance, the Bassoon. The pipes constituting the lower portion of the " Dolcan " (*fig.* 103) are also sometimes made of the pyramidal and inverted shape.

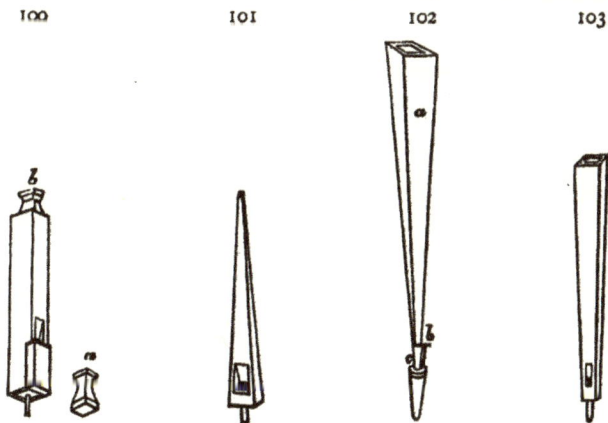

100   101   102   103

401. The varied *proportion* in the dimensions of a pipe, and its influence on the sound, are noticed in a subsequent page.

The classification of the pipes into *flue* and *reed* pipes.   402. The numerous kinds of pipes just noticed are divided, in regard to the distinct manner in which that part is made which in reality produces the tone, into two great classes, namely, *flue pipes* and *reed pipes*.

Flue pipes.   403. Lip, mouth, or flue pipes—for they are called by all these names—are such as have an oblong opening, called the *mouth*, at the junction of the body with the foot of the pipe ; bounded above and below by two edges called the *lips*, which are made to sound by the wind first passing through a narrow fissure, *flue*, or *wind-way*, and which depend chiefly on the length or shortness of their *bodies* for the gravity or acuteness of the sound they produce.

Reed pipes.   404. Reed or tongue pipes are, on the contrary, those which are made to sound through the medium of a mouthpiece (not unlike that of a Clarionet), furnished with an elastic plate of metal, and which do *not* depend on the length of tube* of the pipe, but on the size of the mouthpiece and the vibrations of the *tongue*, for the gravity or acuteness of the sound.

405. For the purpose of illustrating the difference between these two classes of pipes, it may be observed that, while an open flue pipe must have a body of eight-feet standard length to produce the CC sound, a reed pipe may only require a tube of about eighteen inches, as in the case of a Vox Humana. Indeed, a tube of any sort is not indispensable, as is evidenced in accordions, seraphines, harmoniums concertinas, and such like instruments, all of which produce their sounds from metal tongues of various sizes, closely resembling those belonging to the reed pipes of an organ, but the dimensions of which instruments must be sufficient to indicate that tubes cannot therein be contained. The tubes, however, acting like speaking-trumpets, exercise a great influence on the strength and fulness of the tone produced, both being much increased by their presence.

The separate parts of a metal flue pipe.   406. An open metal flue pipe is composed of three distinct parts, called the *body*, *foot*, and *language*, or *languid*.

407. *The body* is that part of the pipe that, commencing at the mouth, extends thence *upwards*. (See *fig*. 88, *a h*, page 102.) It is formed by rolling a sheet of metal of the requisite dimensions round a wooden cylinder or cone, called a "mandrill," and uniting the edges together with solder. The joint thus formed is called a "seam," and occurs in the back of the pipe. On the opposite side, forming the front of the body, and near to the lower end, an indentation is made, as shown in *fig* 104, at *a*, called the "leaf," which is continued to nearly the bottom, where a small portion of the flattened part is cut away, leaving a broad opening *b*. The edge that is left immediately over this opening (*c*) is called the "upper lip."

104

408. *The foot* is that part of the pipe, of an inverted conical shape, that extends from the mouth downwards (*fig*. 105). It is made in a similar manner to the body ; *i.e.*, it has a seam running vertically up the centre of the back, and an indentation in the front ; though, in this instance, in the upper part (*a*), corresponding with that in the body of the pipe, forming an "under lip." The foot serves as a conductor of wind from the upper board up to the mouth of the pipe ; hence, in the apex (*e*), a hole is made for the entrance of the wind. It further answers as a support to the pipe, to which end it is made very thick and strong, that it may resist the weight and pressure of the body.

105

---

* Flue pipes are said to have *bodies*, and reed pipes *tubes*.

409. *The language*, or *languid* (*fig.* 106), is the flat plate of metal that lies horizontally over the top of the foot, just inside the mouth. It is made of much thicker material than any other part of the pipe, because it is entirely unsupported, except at the sides and back. In front, it presents a straight edge, corresponding with the lips of the body and foot, but slightly behind that of the latter, leaving a narrow fissure or "wind-way" between. The front is also bevelled inwards and upwards. The *languid* is made very strong and thick, that it may not sink in front or in the middle—casualties that would cause the "sheet of wind" to miss the upper lip, and so render the speech of the pipe defective.

106

410. *The mouth*, as already intimated, is the horizontal cutting or opening that occurs at the junction of the body and foot of the pipe. Its use and influence will be noticed hereafter.

411. *Open metal pipes.*—The separate parts of an open flue pipe are joined together in the following manner :—The straight edges of the language and foot are first arranged parallel, and then the back and sides of the two are soldered together, the narrow slit in front being left open so as to form a passage or "wind-way" for the current of air that enters at the foot of the pipe. In the next place, the lips of the body and foot are placed precisely opposite to each other, and the body and foot are then strongly united together at the back and sides. The languid is thus entirely enclosed within a finished pipe.

The way in which the several parts of metal pipes are united together.

412. *Stopped metal pipes* are sometimes furnished with a moveable cap, that fits tightly over the top of the pipe, completely enclosing it ; or a metal cap is soldered on to the top of the body ; while in some examples a wooden stopper covered with leather is fitted into the end of the pipe, the pipe in that case being made somewhat longer to receive it.

413. *Half-stopped metal pipes* have, in addition to the cap, the fixed covering, or the stopper, a small cylindrical tube, or "chimney," soldered into a hole in its centre ; or in the case of a wooden stopper, a hole is burnt through it.

414. It may be as well to explain here the precise meaning of the German name given to a stop composed of pipes of the kind just noticed. The literal translation of the German name Rohr-flöte is reed flute, which has sometimes been supposed to imply a reedy-*toned* flute stop; such interpretation, however, being accompanied by a difficulty arising from the fact that half-stopped metal pipes, with chimneys, produce a peculiarly smooth and liquid tone. The name really refers to the formation of the pipe, not to the character of its tone ; and signifies that the distinguishing feature of the pipe is a small tube resembling the hollow-stalk that grows in wet grounds, and which all English dictionaries describe as a *reed* (rohr). Rohr-flöte, therefore, simply means a stop belonging to the *flute*-work, the pipes of which are furnished with a tube or *reed*. Furthermore, *reed* pipes are always so called in England, from the circumstance of their being provided with a small metal tube by way of mouthpiece ; while, in Germany, they are called *tongue* stops.

415. The three kinds of metal flue pipes are frequently furnished with *ears* ; *i.e.*, pieces of metal projecting from each side of the mouth. In stopped and half-stopped pipes the ears are large ; but in open ones they are smaller and more neat, giving to the front pipes, which are mostly furnished with them, a finished appearance. Metal pipes have sometimes a strip of metal running horizontally across, under the mouth of the pipe, and reaching from ear to ear. This is the case with the large pipes of the Transept Pedal Diapason at Doncaster.

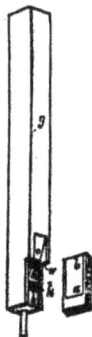

Wood flue pipes; open, stopped, and half-stopped.   416. An open *wood* pipe is formed of four separate parts, namely, the body, block, cap, and foot.

417. *The body* (*g*, *fig.* 107) consists of a right-angled tube, formed of four planed boards; the cross section of which is not usually a square, but an oblong. At the lower end the body is closed by the block (*h h*), which is nearly divided in two by a deep cutting, called the *throat* (*k*). The block and throat are closed in front by the *cap* (*b a*)—a piece of hard wood, hollowed out (*n*)—leaving the two sides and the bottom edges to be glued or screwed to the sides and block of the pipe. The upper edge (*b*) of the cap recedes a little, to form the wind-way. *The pipe-foot* (*m*) is a cylindrical or four-sided tube, introduced at the bottom of the pipe, to serve as a conductor of the wind into the pipe, and also as a support thereto.

418. In wooden stopped and half-stopped pipes the stopper is well covered with leather at the bottom and sides, to make the stopping quite sound. Were it not so, the tone would be false.

419. The proportion of the breadth, as compared with the depth, of wood stopped pipes is varied very much, according to the quality of tone that is desired to be produced. Father Smith and Bridge frequently made their stopped pipes nearly square; the former sometimes making the proportions of the block of his CC Stopped Diapason 5 inches by 4¾. The German builders make some of their wood pipes narrow and deep, as in the Lieblich Gedact, the CCC pipe of which measures 5 inches by 3⅞; while those for other stops are made wider than they are deep, as in the Hohl-flöte, shown in *fig.* 108, the tenor C pipe of which is made 1¹¹⁄₁₆ deep and 2⁷⁄₁₆ wide. A pipe that is nearly square gives a full and weighty tone; one that is narrow and deep, a soft and sweet (*Lieblich*) tone; and one that is shallow and wide, a powerful and hollow (*Hohl*) tone. Father Smith made his Hohl-flöte perfectly square, the block of the 2-feet pipe measuring exactly 1 inch in depth and width; and, when placed on the same manual with a Stopped Diapason, he then made the latter narrow and deep, *i.e.*, of the Lieblich Gadact shape, by which means he secured great individuality in the tone of the two stops. An interesting illustration of this arrangement of scales will be found in his charming choir organ that is or was in the Cathedral at Manchester.

How the several parts are worked together.   420. In working together the separate parts of an open wood flue pipe, the sides are first glued and nailed, or pinned, to the block; and, when the glue has thoroughly "set," the back and front are attached to the edges of the sides by similar means. The pipe-foot is then glued in; and, when the pipe is voiced, the cap is fastened on.

421. *The mouth of a wood flue pipe* is formed by discontinuing the front of the body of the pipe just above the (block as shown at *w*, in *fig.* 107), and bevelling off the front of the surface just above, downwards and inwards (*o*), till an edge is produced, called the upper lip. Just below this, leaving, however, an opening of sufficient depth to form the mouth, is the upper edge of the cap, which constitutes the under lip of the mouth.

422. There are certain modifications sometimes effected in the manner of making the mouth of wooden pipes that may here be noticed.

423. *Block pipes* occasionally have their mouths *inverted*. (See *fig.* 109.) In such cases, the front of the block (*a*) is made to project as far as the *outer* surface of the front of the pipe (*b*), instead of being only in a line with the inner

one, as in the case of block pipes of the usual kind : and the bevelled part that forms the upper lip (*c*) is cut on the *inner* surface of the front of the pipe, instead of outside, the exterior then presenting an unbroken appearance, as though there were no lip at all. The arrangement of the mouth, in fact, as compared with that of simply block pipes, is precisely reversed. The English Wald-flute of 4 feet, and sometimes the Clarabella, and even larger stops, are sometimes composed of block pipes with inverted mouths.

109

424. *Languid Wood Pipes* (*fig.* 110) are sometimes made, the peculiarity in which is sufficiently indicated by the term employed for distinguishing such from the other varieties of pipe, namely, that, instead of a wooden block, they are simply furnished with a plate or languid of wood, as shown in the accompanying section. Large wood pipes are often made on this principle.

425. *The double-mouthed pipe* is but seldom seen in England. Its name is a key to the peculiarity observable in the nature of its formation, namely, that of having *two* mouths instead of one ; and the mouths are placed opposite to each other. Greater strength of tone is said to be produced from pipes with two mouths. The German Doppel-flöte is composed of pipes so formed.

426. The G G G Open Pedal pipe introduced into the Westminster Abbey organ by Elliott and Hill, in Dr. Cooke's time, had two mouths, and was also of the pyramidal form. Its situation in the organ-case, however, was a confined one, consequently it was never heard to advantage ; and when the large pedal pipes were afterwards laid horizontally in a pile on the screen, as its outline was inconvenient for its new position, it was removed and another pipe substituted.

110

427. The only difference between an open and stopped wood pipe consists in the latter being closed at the top (*b*, *fig.* 100) by a plug or stopper, illustrated at *a* in the same figure. A half-stopped wood pipe has a hole drilled down the stopper.

428. Wood flue pipes are sometimes furnished with ears on each side the mouth, and occasionally also with a cross-piece fastened on immediately beneath the under lip, called a *beard*. Ears and beards are chiefly attached to pipes of very narrow scale, or have small mouths. These additions, by keeping the wind together, accelerate the speech of the pipe.

Origin and continuance of the tone in flue pipes. 429. Something may now be said concerning the speech of flue pipes. A *metal* flue pipe is made to sound by the admission of a jet of wind at the apex of the foot, which, rushing upwards, passes through the wind-way and strikes against the upper lip, producing a concussion which prevents the air from issuing in a continuous manner from the mouth, and causes to proceed intermittingly. The vibrations thus caused are communicated to the column of air within the body of the pipe ; and, the air being set in motion, a sound is produced ; which sound, however, cannot strictly be said to be produced by the pipe itself, nor by the elastic motion of its body, but by the vibrations at its mouth, and the motion of the column of air contained within its body. The former circumstance is sufficiently evidenced by the fact that the pitch is nearly the same, whatever may be the thickness or the character of the material employed in the construction of the pipe. The stoutness, toughness, and elasticity of the material, have, nevertheless, something to do with the *quality* and *strength* of the tone, as will presently be explained. A slight motion of the body of the pipe may indeed be detected: which, however, is a consequence, and not a cause; and arises from the friction of the column of air within, having nothing to do with the *production* of the sound, which is to be attributed solely to the circumstances already mentioned.

430. A *wood* flue pipe is made to sound in much the same manner as a metal pipe of the same kind. The wind, on being admitted, passes up the pipe-foot into the throat, and from thence into the hollowed part of the cap, up which it forces itself; then, after passing through the wind-way between the upper edge of the cap and block, it strikes against the upper lip, and is thus made to vibrate, the vibrations, as already described, being communicated to the air in the body of the pipe.

431. It is worthy of remark that, whereas the sides of a wooden pipe beat violently while the pipe is speaking, the front and back remain perfectly quiescent.

432. The sound from a pipe continues so long as the organ wind is allowed to enter that pipe, and at the same unabated strength.

433. In a stopped pipe the current of air in the body of the pipe takes a somewhat altered course, and produces a remarkably different result from what it does in an open one.

434. The consideration of this subject affords an opportunity for explaining what might otherwise appear to be an inaccuracy in regard to flue pipes depending on the dimensions of their bodies for the gravity or acuteness of their sound. A stopped flue pipe of a given length will produce a sound as low as that of an open pipe of *twice the length*. This fact, however, is soon accounted for. Instead of the air escaping out at the top of the shorter pipe, as it does out of the longer, it is checked by the stopper that closes the upper end. In consequence of this interruption, the wind is reflected back again down the pipe before it can make its exit, which it does through the mouth. The wind in a stopped pipe, therefore, traverses the distance of the length of the body twice over—first up, then down—and, consequently, produces a sound of increased gravity in proportion. Thus, a stopped pipe of 2 feet gives the same sound as an open one of 4 feet; a stopped pipe of 8 feet the same sound as an open one of 16 feet; and so on.

The mouth of a flue pipe; and the influence of its proportions on the tone of the pipe.
435. The size and proportions of the mouth of a *metal* flue pipe exercise great influence on the strength, character, and quality of the tone of the pipe. The usual proportions, which, however, are subject to considerable modification, are, for the width, $\frac{1}{4}$ the circumference of the body, and $\frac{1}{16}$ of the same measure for the height. According to this rule, therefore, the mouth of a pipe that is 16 inches in circumference inside—or, what is the same thing, $5\frac{1}{3}$ inches in diameter, the diameter being about $\frac{1}{3}$ of the circumference—would be 4 inches in width and 1 inch in height. Some organ pipes have a wider mouth than this, others a narrower one; some have a higher mouth, and some a lower one. A wide and high mouth produces a round, powerful tone; a narrow one, a sharp tone; a narrow and low mouth, a delicate tone; and a wide and high mouth, a full, thick, and hollow tone. But even these deviations have their assigned limits; for, if the upper lip be cut up too high, the pipe will be slow to speak, or will not speak at all; and, if the mouth be too narrow, the pipe will speak the octave above its real sound. The greatest deviations are found in wooden stopped pipes, the mouths of those of small scale being in height equal to one-half or even two-

thirds of their width.   Large scale stopped pipes, on the contrary, have sometimes very low mouths.

The voicing of metal and wooden flue pipes.   436. The careful conformation of the mouth of the pipe ; setting the lips ; regulating the quantity of wind to be admitted ; conducting it through the wind-way in a sheet of the precise thickness ; and carrying out other such details necessary to secure the true tone, character, and speech of the pipe, are matters of great delicacy ; demanding the nicest skill as well as a just perception of tone on the part of the operator. These and other duties are included under the one general term *voicing ;* and some idea will be formed of the importance and influence of this branch of organ-building from the following observations in reference to the speech of an organ pipe.

437. The wind on entering a pipe is carried through the wind-way in a thin sheet, and is directed against the upper lip ; the mouth or intermediate space being covered by this stream of air.   This " sheet of wind," as it is called, is exposed externally to the outward air, while on the inside it is defended from it by the back and sides of the pipe.   The wind that comes out at the mouth of the pipe passes fairly upwards against and above the leaf ; causing an inward draught underneath, towards and indeed through the mouth.   The former fact may be ascertained by blowing *smoke* into a pipe and watching its progress ; the latter, by holding a lighted candle just below or in a line with the mouth of a pipe while speaking, when the flame will be drawn towards or even through the mouth.   The inward-bearing draught outside the mouth being stronger than the quiescent air within, the sheet of wind gives way for an instant, and the draught bears into the pipe, but is immediately overcome by the sheet of wind, which in its turn prevails, until the draught overcomes it again.   Hence the periodical concussions of the sheet of wind against the upper lip of the pipe.

438. This alternate crossing of streams will, under ordinary circumstances, of course take place with greater or less rapidity, according to the dimensions of the mouth, and the strength of the wind exciting the column of air within the body of the pipe ; and the elastic motion of the lower end of the column of air in the region of the mouth, by compression and expansion, assists in the alternate restitution of the sheet of wind and the inward-bearing draught by turns.   The pitch of the sound of a flue pipe, therefore, is regulated as much by the number of pulsations which take place at the *mouth* of the pipe in a second of time as by the number of vibrations that occur in the *body* of the pipe in the same time, with the latter of which the former doubtless correspond.   This hypothesis is borne out by the fact that, if a pipe be shortened, as in transposing a GG metal Open Diapason into a CC, it does not then require *less* wind, but *more ;* the additional quantity no doubt being required to *accelerate* the vibrations at the mouth, so that they may be in proportion to the quicker vibrations of the shorter column of air inside the body of the pipe.

439. It has already been explained that some proportion is preserved between the dimensions of the mouth and the *diameter* of the pipe ; but the *length* of the vibrating column of air may be *somewhat* increased or decreased without much affecting the speech, as may be ascertained by temporarily covering one or more of the lower holes in the back of a front pipe which has openings in it.   If, however, the length of a pipe be very great in proportion to its diameter and the dimensions of its mouth, the pulses at the mouth will not be *slow* enough to correspond with the waves of the lengthened column of air ; and the pipe will then either not speak at all, or it will break into its octave. This circumstance accounts for Dulciana pipes, usually the smallest in scale

of any open pipes in an English organ, and with even narrower mouths in proportion, having so decided a tendency to "speak their octave" when in the slightest degree out of order. For some stops, it is required that the pipes *shall* speak their octave and *not* give their unison sound, as in the German "Flauto Traverso;" in which case the voicer regulates the 'dimensions and proportions of the mouth accordingly. At the same time, a pipe in which the proper proportions are preserved, in regard to length, diameter, and mouth, will break off into a higher sound, if it has more than a certain amount of wind, or a stronger wind; as in the "Flute Harmonique" of the French and English organ-builders.

440. In cutting the wind-way, if the opening be made too deep, the "sheet of wind" will be too thick, and the inward-bearing draught will be unable to break through; in which case the pipe will not speak with the proper strength, but will simply produce a humming or whizzing sound. Or if the mouth of a pipe be "cut up too high," the sheet of wind will not entirely cover the space forming the mouth; in organ-builders' phraseology "the wind will not reach;" and the speech of the pipe will be dull and unsteady.

441. In *wood*, pipes of the four-sided shape, the width of mouth, of course, corresponds with the inside measure of the same side of the pipe in which it is cut. Its height is commonly one-fourth of its width, or a little more; but, inasmuch as wood pipes are, as already explained, sometimes made narrow and deep, the mouth being on the narrow side, while at others the mouth is placed on the wide side, it is evident that its measure in the direction just mentioned must be subject to much greater variation than in metal pipes.

442. In some German *wood* pipes, the blocks and other parts connected with the speech of the pipes are made on a plan so different from any of the English methods already noticed, and yet produce so firm and full a tone, even when the scale is small, that a few particulars concerning them are here introduced. Instead of the block being formed with its face at a right ⟨111⟩
angle to the top, it is bevelled back and downwards, as shown at
a, in *fig*. 111. The cap is made straight and smooth inside, instead
of being hollowed as in *figs*. 107, 109, and 110; and, in lieu of the
wind-way being made by filling a portion from off the cap, it is
formed by filling from off the *block;* and the upper edge of the cap
is set on a *level* with the top of the block, instead of *a little
below it.*

443. A glance at the accompanying diagram (*fig*. 111) will be
sufficient to show that in a pipe thus formed the wind must gradually
undergo increased compression as it ascends through the wedge-
shaped hollow between the block and cap, and that it must, in consequence, be thrown with much greater force against the lip; a
stronger and clearer tone being thus secured. The mouth is cut
up much higher than ordinary, it frequently being equivalent to
half of its width, and even more; and the lip is left thick, that
the wind may take good hold. There are no nicks either in the
block or the cap; the latter of which is made about half as thick again at the mouth end as at the foot end, to prevent the inward-bearing draught being too strong. The hole in the pipe-foot is made very large, and is perfectly round; there is no *plugging*, and the speech is plumper than when the wind is carried through four three-quarter apertures, as in most plugged pipes. The lower end of the foot is leathered, so as to prevent any escape of wind between it and the upper-board.

444. The modern German *metal* pipes are made and voiced more nearly as in England, except that in some cases the *bevel* on the languid is made *more acute* than in English pipes. *Fig.* 112 shows the English languid and bevel in profile; *fig.* 113 exhibits the German in a similar manner. The acute bevel has the effect of throwing the wind more *into the pipe*, which permits the mouth to be cut up higher, the tone produced being remarkably full and bright. The mouth is then cut up $\frac{4}{7}$ths.

445. The *mechanical* part of voicing, as far as the *eye* can detect, consists, in the instance of a metal pipe, chiefly in cutting with great nicety a series of notches or *nicks* in the front part of the languid. The "nicking" is made on the lower edge of the bevelled surface of the languid, and the notches run parallel to each other, and sometimes, though not always, at an angle to the axis of the pipe. There are different methods of voicing, which produce different results. A pipe that is not voiced at all will frequently not sound at all, or will give a wrong note, or will not speak with adequate strength.

446. Large pipes, and sometimes comparatively small ones, will however occasionally present exceptions to the rule, if the mouth and parts adjacent are proportioned with mathematical accuracy. The front-pipes of the organ at St. Giles's-in-the-Fields, made by Smith, had no nicking, neither have several of the metal and wood Stopped Diapasons in the Temple organ. Pipes that have but few nicks will frequently produce a round sonorous tone, as is evidenced in many of Smith's Open Diapasons; while others, that are much and regularly nicked, will produce a softer and very musical tone, as in Green's Diapasons.

447. The voicing of a wood flue pipe consists of several small parallel lines filed on the front or face of the upper part of the block. These little cuts do not quite run at right angles to the upper lip, neither are they made of the same width right down; but they are deepest and widest at the mouth, and gradually decrease as they recede from it, until at last they are lost in the plain surface of the block. In voicing the pipe, which of course is done before the cap is put on, the upper edge of the block is slightly pared away opposite the under lip, so as to direct the wind against the upper lip. If the angle be pared off too much or too little, the pipe will be slow to speak, or will speak ill, or perhaps not at all; or, if the sheet of wind be suffered to strike against the upper lip with rather too much force, the tone produced will be imperfect, and perhaps accompanied with a chirping at the commencement of the pipe's speaking.

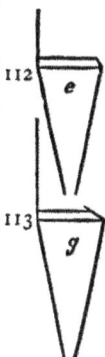

The influence of the material, form, and scale on the tone of a pipe. 448. Besides the many modifications or *characters* of tone (so to speak) which are produced by the particular method of voicing adopted, the tone of a pipe is influenced by many other circumstances.

449. And first, of the *material*. Supposing all other circumstances to be the same, it may be said in regard to metal flue pipes that the thicker and more elastic the body of the pipe, the more decided, clear, and distinct will be the sound. According to some of the first German works on the subject, the tone of a pipe is improved by the material being well hammered before being worked up.

450. In regard to wood pipes, the same phenomenon may be observed as to the influence of the material on the tone; a pipe made of some hard wood, as

T

oak, giving the clearest and strongest tone, while one of the softer kind produces the most mellow tone. When the old builders used a soft wood, they sometimes cut the planks the *cross-way* of the grain, probably from the circumstance of the wood of the bellies of violins being cut in that manner. The deal pipes in the Finedon organ, Northamptonshire, built by Gerard Smith, are formed out of boards cut in the direction just mentioned. If a comparison be drawn between the quality and strength of the tone of metal and wood pipes generally, a large open metal pipe will be found to give the clearer and more sonorous sound, and an open wood pipe a thicker and heavier sound. This is of course supposing their measurement and all other circumstances to be about the same. The voicer's art, however, has quite the power of not only disguising the quality of tone that might be expected from the two kinds of material, but even of reversing them. In an old MS. book in the library of the Hon. Society of the Inner Temple is a memorandum to the effect that "Father Smith sayes he can make metall pipes speak like those made of wood ; and them of wood to speak like those of metall." Herr Schulze excels in thus matching the tone of wood and metal pipes, of which several admirable specimens occur in the Doncaster organ.

451. Then of the *form*. Pipes having the open cylindrical outline, when made to the full proportionate diameter, give the strongest, clearest, and fullest tone of any metal flue pipes. Those of the conical shape produce a rather more subdued sound than the cylindrical ; accompanied either by a tender, reedy, or a *crying* character of tone, according to the extent of their conicality and the manner in which they are voiced. Pipes of the covered species emit the weakest sound.

452. By an alteration of *scale*, that is to say, an increase or decrease of diameter, while the same length is preserved, a further modification in the strength and character of the tone is produced.

453. The width or narrowness of a pipe alters the strength of the sound produced, and to such an extent, that an open cylindrical pipe (already described as giving the more powerful sound) may, by the reduction of its scale, be made to sound as lightly as a covered one, as will be perceived on comparing the strength of the tone of a Dulciana pipe with that of a stopped Diapason pipe. Moreover, by enlarging the scale sufficiently, a pipe of soft wood—Christiana deal, for instance —may be made to produce a stronger and heavier sound than a pipe of hard wood, as oak.

Influence of the strength and quantity of the wind on the character and strength of the tone.   454. In addition to the influence which the material, form, and scale of a pipe exercise on the tone produced, the strength of the wind by which it is made to speak, or the quantity allowed to enter the pipe, or both, effect a further alteration in the strength of the sound. A stronger and a greater "flush of wind," within certain bounds, causes a pipe to give a fuller and brighter tone. If the jet of wind, however, be too great or too strong, the pipe will "overblow," and give the octave of its true sound. A strong wind causes the sound produced to be also rather higher in pitch, as well as stronger and brighter. An illustration of the influence of a *lessened* strength of the wind on the quality, power, and pitch of the sound of a pipe occurs when the wind is being "let out." The sound then gradually becomes duller, weaker, and *lower*, until it altogether ceases ; or it will *rise* in pitch, and speak louder and clearer again, as more wind is supplied just before the sound dies away.

455. Experiments have proved that reed stops acquire a considerable accession of power and splendour by being placed upon a heavier wind than the flue stops.

The first organ in England that had a reed stop voiced to a heavy pressure of wind is that in the Town Hall, at Birmingham; into which instrument the stop alluded to, called the "*Tuba Mirabilis*," was introduced in the year 1840. Stops of this kind are now made by nearly all the English organ-builders.

456. In France the influence of different strengths of wind has been turned to still greater account by the ingenious artists, Messrs. Cavaillé-Coll, organ-builders to the late French Government, in the fine instruments built by them for the Abbey Church of St. Denis, near Paris, and the Church of St. Sulpice and the Madeleine, in Paris, as well as in many other of their organs. In these admirable specimens of their skill, they have not only placed the reed stops on a heavier wind than the flue, but have increased the weight in the treble by an inch. This latter application was suggested by the fact of performers on wind instruments, in order to render the acute tones of equal strength with the grave, exercising a greater effort of the muscles of the lungs when sounding high notes than when producing low ones. By supplying the pipes of the upper keys with a stronger wind, the weakness at times observable in the treble of organs is entirely rectified. These systems have, of late years, been frequently introduced by Messrs. Hill and Son, Willis, Gray and Davison, Lewis, Bryceson, and other builders, into their larger organs.

457. The French builders have further succeeded in making reed and flue stops produce an harmonic instead of a ground tone, and hence called "Trompet Harmonique" and "Flute Harmonique." (See Foreign Specifications.) The pipes are made of double length, and, by a strong and copious wind, made to "overblow," and so sound their octave.

458. In the new organ erected in St. Paul's Cathedral, by Mr. Henry Willis, the builder has incorporated not only the several modern Continental improvements above referred to, but also several new mechanical inventions of his own. The organ in the Glasgow Town Hall, by Gray and Davison, has also the great reeds and two harmonic flutes on a heavy wind, and the treble of the organ on a stronger wind than the bass.

Formation of a reed pipe. 459. A reed pipe of an organ is formed of a *mouthpiece*, composed of a *block*, *reed*, *tongue*, and wooden *wedge*, with a *tuning-wire* and *boot*; and a *tube* or *body*.

460. The *block* of a reed pipe (*fig.* 114) is, in modern specimens, usually a circular and rather solid mass of metal, cast in a mould, though in old reed

115 pipes the blocks are frequently of box-wood, turned in a lathe. From the block the reed and tongue hang suspended *below*, and the tube rises *above*. Through the block two round holes (*b c*) are left in the casting, the largest of which (*b*) forms the passage-way for the wind from the reed into the tube; and the smallest, which occurs a little in advance of the first, admits a wire that is required for regulating the precise length of the vibrating portion of the tongue, presently to be noticed. The upper part (*a*) of the block is made rather wider than the lower, forming a rim that rests on the upper edge of the boot.

461. The *reed* is a small cylindrical tube of brass (*fig.* 115), slightly conical in shape, being usually widest at the lower end, and having the lower end closed by a piece of brass, which slants a little upwards and backwards. In the front of the reed an opening is left (*d*), running lengthways, presenting an appearance as though a portion of the reed had been cut away, at which the wind enters. The upper end of the reed is fitted tightly into

T 2

the larger hole of the block already mentioned, with the opening towards the smallest hole.

462. *The tongue* (*fig.* 116) lies immediately over the opening just noticed in the reed, covering also the edges which border it. It consists usually of a thin, tough, and elastic plate or spring of brass, and is fixed in its position by the upper end being passed a little way up into the block, and then a small wooden wedge being driven into the part of the circular hole of the block left vacant on the flattened side of the reed. The lower end of the tongue, therefore, is left entirely free, and is slightly curved.

463. *The tuning-wire* (*fig.* 117) is a moveable piece of bent steel wire, that passes through the small hole in the block, in front of the reed and tongue. The lower part of it is bent up (as shown at *f* in the accompanying illustration), so as to press against and across the tongue. So much of the tongue as may be *above* the point where the tuning-wire crosses it is pressed firmly against the reed and prevented from vibrating : the wind, therefore, only agitates that part that is *below* the wire. As, however, the wire is moveable, the vibrating portion of the tongue can be lengthened or shortened as required ; and the upper end of the tuning-wire is hooked, so that the " tuning-knife " may move it upwards or downwards the better.

464. *The boot* of a reed-pipe is the short upright and strong tube of metal into which the greater portion of the block sinks. (See *fig.* 96, page 104, and *fig.* 114, page 115.) It therefore has to support the weight of the entire pipe ; in addition to which it receives the wind, through a hole in the lower end, from one of the borings in the upper board, over which it rests, and indeed sinks into a short distance, and directs the wind up to the reed.

465. *The tube* of a reed-pipe, as already explained, presents the outline of a cylinder, an inverted cone with a bell, or an inverted pyramid, according to circumstances ; and rises from the surface of the block, to which it is soldered, in the instance of small metal pipes. In larger pipes this is not so, but a short tube called a *socket* is introduced, which receives the narrow end or " neck " of the longer tube, and sustains it firmly and steadily. Sockets are of course necessary for reed pipes of all sizes that have *wooden* tubes, as illustrated in *fig.* 102, page 105 ; and the lower end of each tube has then to be rounded off to make it correspond in form with the circular shape of the socket that is to receive it.

466. It might prove interesting to the reader now to refer to the various kinds of reed pipes represented on pages 102, 103, 104, 105, and 109 ; and trace out for himself their several peculiarities and points of difference, as well as their separate parts, so far as they are in sight.

The formation of the tubes.   467. Metal tubes, like the bodies of flue pipes of the same material, are formed of sheets of metal, cut to such a shape as will, when rolled and soldered up, give to the tube the required form and proportion. The bell, if the addition of one be required, is of course applied afterwards. That part of the metal plate which is to form the neck of the tube is left much thicker than the other end, in order that it shall neither sink nor snap off under the pressure of the upper and broader part. Wooden tubes are formed of four boards each, comparatively wide at the upper end and narrow at the lower, glued and nailed together.

The different kinds of mouthpieces or reeds. The open, closed, and free reeds. 468. The opening, already noticed as occurring in the front of the reed, either extends all the way up, as shown in *fig.* 105, or only partially so, and gradually contracting to a point. The former is called the "open reed," and is the same in kind that has been in use for centuries; the latter is termed the "closed reed," and is of modern invention.

469. *The open reed* admits by far the greater quantity of wind into a pipe, the influence of which increased volume excites the tongue to vibrate against the reed with more force, and so to produce a stronger and clearer tone. Hence it is generally considered to be the description of reed the best adapted for all powerful and prompt-speaking reed pipes. It requires a rather longer tube than the closed reed.

470. *The closed reed* allows only of a lessened draught through it, and is on this account considered by some organ-builders to be well adapted for reed-pipes, the tone of which is required to be of a quieter character; though it is not indispensable to employ them to obtain a subdued tone, inasmuch as some organ-builders eschew the use of closed reeds altogether. Moreover, they present a much larger surface between the reed and tongue, whereon dirt may lodge.

471. *The free reed.* A third kind of reed is used on the Continent, called the free reed. In this variety the size of the tongue and the opening in the reed are so adjusted in regard to each other, that the former almost exactly fits the latter; the tongue, therefore, instead of striking on the edges of the reed, is impelled into the opening by the wind; when, from its own elasticity, it resumes its former position; and the sound is produced by its rapid vibratory motion to and fro through the air. The tone of a *free* reed is not usually so strong as that of a *striking* reed, but it is particularly smooth and free from rattling. Some fine 16 and 32 feet Posaunes have been made in Germany of free reeds, and there are admirable specimens of stops of both sizes in Schulze's organ at Doncaster.

The influence of the tube, its shape, scale, and material, on the strength and character of the tone of a reed-pipe. 472. It will be remembered to have been stated that a reed pipe does not depend upon its tube for the gravity or acuteness of the sound produced, but chiefly on the dimensions and other circumstances connected with its tongue. The tube, however, makes a considerable difference in the *strength* and *character* of the tone. Were it otherwise, there would exist no sufficient reason for its introduction. The dimensions of the tube are so adjusted to the size of the tongue, that the vibrations of the column of air contained in the former shall correspond with the vibrations of the latter. Where this accordance does not exist, the sound produced is inferior in quality. It is not absolutely necessary that the tongue and the column of air in the tube should be in unison to produce a musical sound; but the tone of small scale reeds is always more pleasing, and that of larger reeds more full and rich, when the unison is perfect. Short-bodied pipes of the cylindrical shape give a comparatively light sound; as may be ascertained by trying any Clarionet or English Vox Humana stop. Pipes with tubes of the inverted conical form give a more sonorous tone than the last mentioned—the strength and character of the sound being governed to some extent by the scale and length of the tube. When it is of narrow measure, the tone is rather thin and somewhat nasal, as in most Bassoon stops. When the pipe is similarly shaped, but with a bell added, the tone becomes somewhat clearer, more wailing and attenuated, as in a Hautboy stop. The weight and power of the sound increases with the further increase in the scale, the Trumpet being louder and more smart than the Bassoon, and the Posaune more ponderous than the Trumpet.

The influence of the reed and tongue on the tone of the pipe. 473. The strength of tone, again, depends much on the shape of the opening in the reed ; whether the tongue be made of common brass, or a composition containing a larger proportion of copper ; the equal thickness and evenness of the tongue ; its curvature ; and the smoothness and flatness of the edges of the aperture against which the tongue vibrates. Reed-stops of delicate intonation, as the Hautboy, Clarionet, and Bassoon, have long, narrow, and thin tongues ; others of strong and full tone, as the Trumpet, Horn, and Posaune, have shorter, broader, and thicker tongues. Many of the old Trumpet stops have reeds that are either larger or broader than those now used, and shorter tubes, which accounts for their tone being thin, and devoid of the power and impressiveness which characterise all good stops of the kind.

How a sound is produced from a reed pipe. 474. When the tongue of a reed-pipe is in a state of rest, it is curved, leaving the opening in the reed free to the passage of the air. The peculiar *tone* of a reed-pipe is, in the instance of a *striking* reed, produced by the tongue beating against the reed, and rebounding again by the force of its own elasticity. The tongue is excited by a current of air being thrown on to it from below, which, as it rushes through the opening in the reed, draws or sucks the tongue with it towards the reed, against the edges of which it strikes, and then returns.

475. In a *free* reed, the sound is produced by the motion of the tongue to and fro ; and, as that motion is never checked or interrupted by the tongue striking, the tone is as smooth and continuous as that of a flue pipe.

How the pitch of the sound of an organ pipe is determined. 476. The *pitch* of the sound produced by a reed pipe is determined by the number of beats or regular vibrations made by the tongue in a second of time ; and the reeds are accordingly made small or large, depending on the acuteness or gravity of the sound each is required to emit. The higher the pitch of the sound, the smaller must be the reed, and the quicker the vibrations of its tongue ; the deeper it is, the larger must be its reed, and the slower the beats of its tongue upon the reed, and perhaps even audible. In a flue pipe the pitch is governed by the length of the body of the pipe, or, more strictly speaking, by the length of the column of air within that body ; which follows the simple geometrical law, that by doubling the length, it sounds an octave lower ; and by halving the length, it sounds an octave higher.

477. The following table exhibits at one view the number of vibrations which take place in a flue pipe, and the number of blows made by striking a reed in a second of time, in producing the several C sounds used for organ stop measurement ; while, to the right, the shortened length of the pipe is given.

Name of C.	Vibrations in flue pipe.		Blows of tongue in reed pipe.		Length of open flue pipe.
C C C C	32	...	16	...	32 feet.
C C C	64	...	32	...	16 ,,
C C	128	...	64	...	8 ,,
Tenor c	256	...	128	...	4 ,,
Middle c¹	512	...	256	...	2 ,,
Treble c²	1024	...	512	...	1 ,,

478. It is necessary to mention that the above table of vibrations refers to *single* and not to *complete* or *double* ones. As the latter are used by some writers on harmonics, the difference might create confusion, if not explained. The tongue of a reed pipe strikes when vibrating *towards* the reed, but of course *not* when

vibrating *from* it ; hence the beats made by the tongue in a reed pipe only amount to *half* the number of vibrations taking place in a flue pipe in the same time, as shown in the above table, which accounts for those beats often being perceptible to the ear in the speech of even 16-feet reed stops. When, therefore, the rustling of the tongue of large reed pipes cannot otherwise be silenced, the front of the reed is lined with a thin coat of leather—simply the dressed part, the *fleshy* part being cut or scraped away—so as to form a soft surface for the tongue to strike against. Schulze preferred all powerful striking reeds below Tenor C to be leathered, as being then more musical.

479. The wind having passed through the mouthpiece of a reed pipe, the *size* of which has defined the *pitch* of the sound, it passes into the tube ; the shape, material, or scale, or all combined, imparting to such sound the *character* and *strength* required.

CHAPTER XX.

THE STANDARD LENGTH OF ORGAN PIPES.

480. ORGAN PIPES are made to a great variety of sizes, and those of the flue species to a greater extent than reed pipes. The greatest standard length of a speaking pipe is 32 feet; the shortest, $\frac{1}{4}$ of an inch. The foot is not of course taken into calculation, as that is nothing more than a supporter and wind-channel to the pipe. The sound of the two pipes of the extreme measurement just mentioned would be nine octaves apart; consequently, a complete range of organ pipes, including all the semitones, would present a series of 109 different sizes.

481. Organ pipes do not measure the *exact* length quoted, but fall a little short of, or, in some cases, rather exceed, that measurement, as the case may be. Hence a distinction is drawn between the *literal* length and the *standard* or *quoted* length of a pipe, the latter presenting an *approximation* only to the former. Many circumstances tend to render an adherence to the literal length almost impossible; as, for instance, a stronger or lighter wind, which would demand a somewhat longer or shorter pipe to produce a sound of the same pitch; or more copious winding of a pipe, which again would cause it to "blow sharp," and require a longer body to produce a sound of the original pitch; the difference in the foot measurement in various countries; the variation of pitch; or an alteration in the scale, or in the outline of the pipe.

The names of the sounds produced from organ pipes.   482. From the circumstance of every septave of pipes and sounds included in the extensive range just mentioned being called by *the same* seven letters, it becomes a matter of necessity that, in order to obtain a clear view of the whole, some means should be adopted for distinguishing each septave from the others. This advantageous classification is established either by the aid and use of some special kind of letter—capital or small; by some particular kind of letter, with a sign added thereto; or by two, three, or four capital letters grouped closely together. In some few cases a particular *name* is also given to a particular pipe or sound, though it considerably simplifies the nomenclature by confining the application of such names solely to the *keys*.

483. For most musical purposes, the *notation* indicates with sufficient precision the gravity or acuteness of the sound that may be expected to be heard, because many instruments, and all voices, produce but a sound of one unvarying pitch for each note, and that one agreeing with the music written. With the organ, however, the case is different; for, in some instances, eight or ten different sounds are concentrated on one key, produced from as many separate pipes, of nearly as many varying lengths; therefore, a definite *pitch* cannot invariably be associated with the *note* written, nor with the *key* struck, in the case of an organ, or of organ music, since the sound produced may be in accordance therewith, or it may be one or two octaves lower, or one or two octaves higher, or a combination of all, according to the nature of the stop or stops drawn.

484. Nevertheless, the several octaves and keys on a manual, and also some of the intermediate keys in those octaves, have distinctive names, by which they are

conveniently referred to in the course of writing, or in conversation. These names have originated from various sources.

The classification of those sounds into octaves, and the different methods by which the several octaves are distinguished from one another.

485. In olden times the twenty-one degrees, comprehended in the great stave of eleven lines, and indicated in modern notation as commencing on the first line in the bass, and ascending to, and ending on, the fifth line in the treble, were termed the *gamut*, or musical scale, which gamut comprised a range of two octaves and a minor seventh. The several sounds therein contained were represented by letters, which at the same time corresponded with the names of those sounds ; but to distinguish such sounds as were represented by the same *letter*, but which differed in *pitch*, a different *kind* of letter was used, sometimes accompanied by another attendant characteristic. Thus, the first septave was represented by *capital* letters ; the second, or next above, by *small* letters ; and the third and upper one by *two small* letters ; thus,

EXAMPLE.

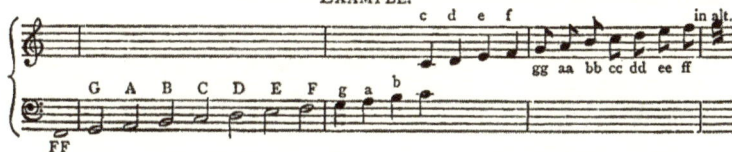

486. On this gamut* being in the course of time extended, the next seven keys and diatonic sounds represented by notes immediately *below* the bass stave were in England termed *double*, and were marked with *two* capital letters, as CC, DD, etc. ; while those forming the first septave *above* the treble stave were said to be *in alt*. The *second* series of seven diatonic sounds below the original "gamut," commencing with F, the fourth line below the bass stave, were distinguished by *three* capital letters, as CCC, DDD, and so on ; and the remaining four diatonic sounds, from GGG to the C below, were marked with *four* capital letters, as CCCC, DDDD. Then *upwards*, the sounds in and higher than the second octave above the treble stave, *i.e.*, from *g*, the fourth line above the treble stave, were said to be *in altissimo*. This completed the English tablature.

487. But it will be perceived that it presents neither the names nor signs by which the highest two and a half octaves of pipes and sounds can be distinguished from each other ; and is therefore so far incomplete. Moreover, the terms *in alt* and *in altissimo* are inconveniently long for the practical purpose for which the distinguishing terms are so useful in organ-building, namely, for marking the composition of the mixture stops in various parts of the scale.

488. From the above nomenclature, however, two of the most useful *names*, as well as one of the *terms* used at the present day by organ-builders as part of the tablature applied to the *keys* of the manual, have been borrowed ; while as many of the remaining terms are preserved to distinguish the deeper sounds that are below the unison range of the modern manual. The former are (1) gamut G, or the lowest G of Guido's gamut ; (2) middle c¹—the "mean" or middle cleff c¹ of the

---

* Guido Aretinus, a Benedictine monk of Arezzo, in Tuscany, in the tenth century, was the inventor of the gamut above referred to ; though it is not perhaps so strictly an invention as an improvement on the *diagrammo*, or scale of the Grecians. Previous to the time of Guido, the septaves were reckoned from A ; but that ancient theorist added or adopted the G below, and denoted it by the Greek *gamma*, Γ. Hence arises the word gamut, or gamma ut, it being the Ut, or first sound of the G hexachord.

same gamut, represented by the note on the ledger line between the bass and treble staves ; and (3) the term *in alt* for the keys above the treble stave.

EXAMPLE.

489. Some of the other keys are named after certain string instruments, from the circumstance of their unison sound corresponding with the lowest sound produceable on such instruments ; as tenor (or viola) c, and fiddle (or violin) g. These several names and terms, with the additional three, viz., "double C," "g¹ above middle c¹," and "treble c²"—the latter applied to the c represented by the note of that name in the treble stave—form a complete tablature for the several C and G keys of the organ manual, as shown in the following table.

EXAMPLE.

490. The several septaves—or octaves, as they are more frequently, though less strictly, called—which occur on a manual comprising the above gamut, are sometimes distinguished by the name given to the C with which each commences ; as the bass octave, tenor octave, middle octave, treble octave, and top octave, or half octave, as the case may be. In addition to this, they are sometimes referred to by the standard length of the C that commences each octave ; as the 8-feet octave, the 4-feet octave, &c.

491. But, as before observed, the number of different *sounds* in an organ far exceeds that of the *keys* on the clavier ; hence arises the necessity for some method of grouping the *additional* sounds, and indeed all sounds, into octaves, and of calculating and measuring them. And first, of the classification of the sounds *within* the usual manual compass. According to the old English system, G was made the starting sound for this purpose, as being the first note in the "gamut ;" while, in Germany, C has for a long period been recognised as the standard sound, as being the first note in the "natural scale." In the latter country the lowest octave on the manual, corresponding with the "bass octave" of the table above given, is called the "great octave," and is represented by single capital letters, as C, D, E, &c. The next octave, identical with the English "tenor octave," is termed the "small octave," and is distinguished by small letters, as c, d, e. The third octave, or "middle octave" of the English, is called the "once-marked octave," represented by small letters with a small figure ¹ to the right and a little above the letter, thus—c¹, d¹, e¹ ; while the "treble octave" is called the "twice-marked octave," c², d², e² ; the remaining half octave, from "c³ in *alt* to f³ in *alt*" forming a portion of the "thrice-marked octave," c³, d³, e³. Sometimes so many little horizontal lines are used instead of figures, thus c̄ ; which system, however, has an air of complication about it.

492. Then, of the sounds *above* the compass of the ordinary organ manual, the

octave commencing with c in *altissimo* is termed the "four-times marked octave," as c⁴, d⁴, e⁴; and the octave higher again, the "five-times marked octave," as c⁵, d⁵, e⁵. Of the sounds *below*, the 16-feet octave is called the "first sub-octave," distinguished by capital letters with a line underneath, C, D, E, and the 32-feet octave, counting downwards from the "contra C," as the Germans call the 16-feet C, is termed the "second sub-octave," distinguished by capital letters twice underlined, thus—C, D, E.

493. The English tablature for distinguishing the several octaves of manual keys, including some of the intermediate keys, is so complete, distinct, and satisfactory, that nothing advantageous would be gained by relinquishing it in favour of the German; but as the English tablature presents no means for classifying the higher sounds, the German nomenclature above given might, under such circumstances, be beneficially received. It will therefore be adopted in the chapter which treats of the composition of mixtures; and, in order to give an easy clue thereto, the English names which refer to the several C and G sounds comprehended in the compass of the manual will also be introduced, that the *names* in the one case may explain the *tablature* in the other.

494. For the 16 and 32 feet octaves of pipes and sounds, we have in England a tablature of our own, and one that is so thoroughly understood and generally received that their exists no necessity for adopting any other.

The size of the pipes mostly used for stop measurement.   495. Many of the pipes, especially those sounding C, E, or G, form the lowest of a separate series, or organ stop, and therefore fix the standard length of that stop. It is necessary, therefore, to refer to these.

496. *The C of 32 feet length.* The sound of this pipe is below that of any other musical instrument. It is called either the "32-feet C pipe," from its standard length, or the "C C̄C̄ C" (pronounced *four* C) "pipe," from its English designation; or the "twice under-marked C," according to the German tablature. Its sound is an octave below the lowest C of the grand pianoforte.

497. *The C of 16 feet length.* The sound of this C is in unison with the lowest C of the grand Pianoforte; and is represented by a note in the sixth space below the bass staff. It is the "CCC" (pronounced *three* C) of the English tablature; the "contra C," or "once under-marked C," of the German, and the "16-feet C" pipe.

498. *The C of 8 feet length.* The pitch of this pipe is in unison with the lowest sound (produced from the open fourth string) of the violoncello; and is represented by a note on the second ledger line below the bass staff. It is the English "CC" (double C); the German "great C"; or the "8-feet C pipe."

499. *The C of 4 feet length.* The sound of this pipe is in unison with the lowest note of the tenor violin, or viola, and also of the old tenor hautboy, or tenoroon;* on which account it is frequently called "tenor C." It is represented in the English tablature by a capital C: but in the German by a small c. Its sound is indicated by a note in the second space of the bass staff.

500. *The C of 2 feet.* This pipe sounds in unison with the lowest C of the hautboy and flute. Its pitch is represented by a note placed on the ledger line between the two staffs. According to the English tablature, this sound would be denoted by a small c; according to the German, by the once-marked c¹. This is called most frequently "middle c," from its being the C on the middle line of

---

* The name tenoroon has sometimes been given to an organ stop, which, however, does not resemble the instrument named in the text, either in regard to pitch or quality.

the ancient great stave of eleven lines ; and also from its being the cleff C of the middle, *mean,* or intermediate parts—the counter-tenor and tenor—in vocal compositions.

501. *The C of* 1 *foot.* The sound of this pipe (in unison with the lowest note of the Flauto Piccolo) is represented by a note placed in the third space in the treble staff. It is distinguished in the English tablature by two small letters, c c ; in the German by the twice-marked c². It is also known as treble c².

502. *The C of* 6 *inches.* This is the English " c in *alt,*" and the German " thrice-marked c," c³. Its sound is represented by a note on the second line above the treble staff.

503. *The C of* 3 *inches.* The English " c in *altissimo,*" and highest c on the pianoforte, and the German "four-times marked c," c⁴. A note in the sixth space above the treble staff denotes its sound.

504. *The C of* 1½ *inch.* The five-times marked c of the German tablature, c⁵.

505. *The C of* ¾ *inch.* The six-times marked c, c⁶. This is the smallest pipe made. Its sound is 2 octaves above c in *altissimo.*

506. The Cs are the most important class of organ-pipes, not only because they are the most convenient and proper ones that can be adopted as a foundation for the purpose of stop measurement, of which more in another chapter ; but also because pipes of that sound commence and conclude the great series. The class next in importance are the G pipes, which denote the foundation measurement of G G organ stops, and also the size of the fifth-sounding stops of C organs.

507. The following are the lengths of the chief G pipes.

508. *The G of* 21⅓ *feet* (24 feet) standard length. The sound of this pipe is a fifth above that of the 32-feet C. It is the " G G G " (three G) of the English tablature, and the "twice-undermarked G̿" of the German.

509. The different lengths are here given for the G pipes. The first is in every case the correct one, and therefore the best one to be written down or engraved ; the other, in brackets, is necessarily made use of in conversation for convenience, and for brevity sake. The latter is not so well adapted for the stop labelling, because it would lead to some confusion in regard to the lengths. For instance, the standard length of a Twelfth is one-third the length of the Diapason ; therefore, if the former were to be marked 3 feet, the latter would appear to be wrong at 8 feet, and might be supposed to be a misprint of 9 feet, which would be a second error.

510. *The G of* 10⅔ *feet* (12 feet). The sound of this open pipe is represented by a note placed in the fourth space below the bass staff. It is the " G G " (double G) of the English tablature, and the "once under-marked G̱" of the German.

511. *The G of* 5⅓ *feet* (six feet). The sound of this pipe is represented by a note placed on the first line of the bass staff. It is the "great octave G" of the Germans, and the English " gamut G."

512. *The G of* 2⅔ *feet* (3 feet.) The sound of a pipe this length is represented by a note in the third space below the treble staff. In both the English and German tablature it is denoted by a small g. It is the English " fiddle g."

513. *The G of* 1⅓ *foot* (1½ foot). A note placed on the second line of the treble staff represents the sound of this pipe. It is marked in the English tablature by two gs (g g) ; and in the German by a g once-marked (g¹). It is known as "g¹ above middle c."

514. A third class of pipes may be noticed, as being used for the purpose of stop measurement ; viz., some of the E, or third-sounding pipes.

515. *The E of* 6⅖ *feet.* The sound of this pipe is a major third above that of the C C or 8-feet pipe. The gravity of its sound is represented by a note on

the first ledger line below the bass staff. It is the English E E (double E) ; the German "great E."

516. *The E of* 3⅕ *feet.* The sound of this pipe is a third above that of the tenor C, or the 4-feet pipe. Its sound is represented by a note in the third space of the bass staff ; and is denoted by a small e in the German tablature, and by the term " tenor e," mostly in England.

517. *The E of* 1⅗ *foot.* The sound of this pipe is a third above that of the middle c^1, or 2-feet pipe. A note placed on the first line of the treble staff represents its sound. It is the small e of the English tablature ; the "once-marked e^1" of the German ; and is the " middle e^1" of ordinary phraseology.

CHAPTER XXI.

THE SIZE OF TONE OF ORGAN PIPES.

518. BESIDES the description of pipe, *i.e.*, the open, noticed in the preceding section, wherein the standard length of the body accords with the pitch of its sound, there are other kinds, the sound produced from which is much lower or "larger" than what the length of the body would indicate. The chief of these are the stopped pipes, which produce a sound as deep as that of an open pipe of twice the length, or nearly so, for the reason explained when speaking of the form of pipes.

519. As the *length* of such pipes would be no criterion of their sound, and yet it is most necessary to know what pipes of different conformation will speak *in unison* with each other, the standard *length* of the several kinds of *short-bodied* but *low-sounding* pipes is dispensed with, and, in lieu of this, they are measured according to the gravity of the sound they produce, or, in other words, according to their *size of tone*.

520. In speaking, therefore, of pipes, the bodies of which measure much less than the "standard length," they are said to give the 8, 16, or 32 feet *tone*, according to whether the sound they produce be in unison with an open pipe of 8, 16, or 32 feet *measurement*. To prevent, however, their being confounded with the open pipes of superior length, the word "tone," "sound," or "pitch," is added, which, of itself, implies that the bodies are not of that approximate or *standard* size.

521. The difference between "standard length" and "size of tone" may be familiarly illustrated in the following manner. If an open pipe, say a Clarabella, be blown with the mouth, and the top be covered with the flat palm of the hand, its pitch will be lowered to the extent of a major seventh. And a similar lowering of the sound would take place in a larger pipe, say the 8-feet C. The latter would not, however, on that account be transformed from an 8 into a 16 feet *pipe;* its sound or "size of tone" only would be altered, its *length* would remain the same. A shorter pipe would simply be made to produce the sound of a longer.

522. Besides the class of pipes that gives a sound *larger* than what the length of their bodies would indicate, there is another that produces a *smaller* sound than that which would be expected, as the 2-feet tone from a 4-feet pipe. These are the harmonic speaking stops, as the Flauto Traverso, &c., of the German builders, and the Harmonic Flutes of the French and English builders.

523. The full range to which stopped pipes have been made is 7 octaves, namely, from the 32-feet C tone to c⁴ in *altissimo*, or perhaps a note higher. Reed pipes have been made to the same range:—*downwards* in numerous German, French, Belgian, and Dutch organs, also in the York Minster organ, by Elliott and Hill (1829) ; the Liverpool Town Hall organ, by J. Willis ; Gray and Davison's organ in the Town Hall, Leeds ; and in Hill and Son's pedal organ, in the Parish Church, Leeds ; *upwards* occasionally in some of Harris's organs, who, at times, carried his clarions right through in octave reeds, as in the late parish church organ at Doncaster, the manuals of which were up to d³ in *alt.*

524. The question here presents itself why the pipe in the
above experiment did not speak the *full* octave below, instead
of a major seventh only, if the column of air travelled the
double distance. It was because the *bulk* or scale of the
body remained *of the same size*. A stopped pipe is required to be of a somewhat
larger diameter than an open one of the same length to produce the true octave
below, as will be at once ascertained by comparing a middle c^1 Clarabella with
a tenor c Stopped Diapason pipe. A middle c^2 Clarabella will measure $2\frac{1}{16}$ inches
in depth, by $1\frac{4}{8}$ inches in width; whereas the latter will be about $2\frac{7}{10}$ inches,
by $1\frac{1}{8}$ inch in depth.

525. The width or narrowness of any pipe, in proportion to its length, is
termed its "scale;" and a pipe is spoken of as being of a "large scale" or a
"small scale," according to the ratio which its diameter bears to its length.
A pipe in which this width is carried to the full legitimate extent, is said to be
of "full scale;" and when the diameter is narrow as compared with the length,
it is said to be of "small scale."

526. An alteration of scale causes a slight difference in the length of a pipe
producing a given sound; the length being reduced by an increase in the scale,
and *vice versâ*. Thus, a large scale Open Diapason pipe sounding, say middle c^1,
is rather shorter than the corresponding pipe of a similar stop of smaller scale;
while that of a Dulciana producing the same sound will be longer than either,
on account of its measure being narrower than either. These variations are,
however, subject to modification, from the influences mentioned in sec. 481, p. 120.

527. If the three pipes of different scales were to be made to the same length,
all their sounds would differ in pitch from each other.

528. The length of a pipe producing a given sound is also slightly affected
by an alteration in the outline of its body. Thus, a conical pipe will be rather
longer than a cylindrical pipe of full scale, and its length will increase with the
extent of its conicality. The following short table will suffice to illustrate the
above several particulars.

2-FEET (MIDDLE C^1) FLUE-PIPES.

Name.	Circum. at mouth		Circum. at top		Length.
Open Diapason	$6\frac{7}{8}$ in.	...	$6\frac{7}{8}$ in.	...	1 ft. $10\frac{3}{4}$ in.
Dulciana	$4\frac{5}{8}$ in.	...	$4\frac{1}{8}$ in.	...	1 ft. $11\frac{5}{8}$ in.
Gamba	$4\frac{1}{2}$ in.	...	$4\frac{1}{2}$ in.	...	2 ft. $0\frac{5}{8}$ in.
Spitzflöte	$6\frac{1}{4}$ in.	...	$4\frac{5}{8}$ in.	...	1 ft. 11 in.
Gemshorn	$6\frac{3}{8}$ in.	...	$2\frac{5}{8}$ in.	...	1 ft. $11\frac{1}{2}$ in.

529. The foregoing observations refer to flue pipes; but the length of reed
pipes is also modified by the outline and scale of the tube; the length increasing
as the scale is enlarged or made to deviate from the cylindrical outline. A
cylindrical reed, or clarionet pipe, is very short, being little more than half the
speaking length; a bassoon pipe, slightly outspreading, rather longer; a hautboy pipe, with a wider bell, longer again; a trumpet longer still; and a
trombone, or posaune pipe, the largest in scale of any, also the longest of any.

2-FEET (MIDDLE C^1) REED PIPES.

Name.	Circum. at top.		Length.
Clarionet	$3\frac{1}{8}$ in.	....	1 ft. $1\frac{1}{2}$ in.
Bassoon	$3\frac{3}{4}$ in.	....	1 ft. 8 in.
Hautboy	$6\frac{1}{2}$ in.	....	1 ft. $8\frac{1}{2}$ in.
Trumpet	$8\frac{1}{2}$ in.	....	1 ft. $8\frac{3}{4}$ in.
Horn	10 in.	....	1 ft. 9 in.

CHAPTER XXII.

ORGAN STOPS.

Definition of a stop; and an explanation of the various kinds.

530. THE gross number of pipes contained in an organ consists of so many distinct longitudinal series or sets ; some of which are for the separate use of the manuals, and others for the pedal. A series of pipes, the range of which extends from the lowest to the highest key of a clavier ; gradually diminishing in length and size ; having the same quality and strength of tone throughout ; and the mechanism of which will allow of their being sounded independently of those of the other series, is called a stop. Or, viewed in another way, a stop may be described as consisting of a certain number of octaves of pipes, extracted from the greater series—such as that of 9 octaves mentioned in the preceding chapter—commencing with some pre-arranged pipe. Thus, four octaves and a half of pipes from the open series, commencing with 8-feet C, would form a Manual Open Diapason ; two octaves and a half, beginning with gamut G, would form a pedal Twelfth ; four octaves and a half, commencing with 2-feet c¹, would be a Manual Fifteenth ; four octaves and a half from the stopped series, commencing with the C C C pipe, 16-feet tone, would form a Manual Bourdon ; the same compass from the reed series, commencing with the 8-feet C pipe, would form a Manual Trumpet ; or two octaves and a half, from C C C, 16-feet pipe, a Pedal Posaune. Allowing a little for variation of scale, this will convey a very good idea of what an organ stop is.

531. Organ stops may, in regard to their compass, the way in which they are made to " draw," and other circumstances, be divided into five classes, namely,

> Whole stops ;
> Half stops ;
> Incomplete stops ;
> Short stops ; and
> Repetition stops.

532. *Whole stops* are such as have their compass extending through the entire range of the manual or pedal. To this class rightly belong the Open and Stopped Diapasons, the Dulciana, Double Diapason, Principal, Fifteenth, Mixture, Trumpet, &c.

533. *Half stops* are those which are so far complete that they comprise an unbroken series of pipes inside the organ, throughout the manual range—like the whole stops—but with the difference, that the draw-stop action and sliders are so contrived that the bass portion of such stops can be drawn independently of the treble, by means of a second handle. Half stops occur the most frequently on those manuals which have some incomplete stops, and where the bass of one stop is therefore used as a substitute for the omitted part of other stops. The Stopped Diapason is very frequently "cut" for this purpose ; the 8-feet octave being employed to complete the range of the Dulciana, when the latter stops at tenor c. Many of Father Smith's smaller instruments, consisting of great manual and echo, were furnished with several half stops, "for the benefit of increasing the variety in

the organ." These stops were divided between middle b and middle c¹, and the object obviously was to allow of a melody being played in a stronger tone, or a different quality of tone, or both, on that part of the compass *above* middle C, to the accompaniment played *below* that note.

534. *Incomplete stops* are those which ought, from their nature, to extend through the entire compass of the Manual—which should, in fact, be whole stops—but which, from some reason, are made in an incomplete form. A Dulciana without pipes to the bass, or 8-feet octave of the Manual, or a Bourdon (Double Stopped Diapason), not having its full complement of pipes upwards, are incomplete stops. The difference between an incomplete and a half-stop is that the former is altogether *without* pipes in some portion of its compass, either in the treble or in the bass, as the case may be; whereas a half-stop has its remaining pipes really in the organ, commencing where the first half or portion of the stop leaves off, but which can only be drawn on by means of a *second* draw stop.

535. *Short stops* are such as do not extend completely through the compass of the manual, and are not, therefore, whole stops; and which yet cannot strictly be classed either as half or as incomplete stops, since they are of limited range by nature. To this class belong many of the imitative stops. These, in many instances, take the extent of their compass from that of the instrument which they each individually represent, without reference to the compass of the manual on which they may happen to be placed. Thus, a Clarionet stop that descends to tenor c sharp has the full range downwards of the instrument the name of which it bears, and, therefore, cannot fairly be ranked as an incomplete stop; nor can a Bassoon stop that ascends to b¹ flat above middle c¹ be correctly so classed, since it then has the full upward range of the ordinary orchestral Bassoon. When their compass is *less* than that just given, then they, of course, become incomplete stops. The old builders made the " Cremona " and Bassoon stops of equal compass with the Manual, and this was a very advantageous plan.

536. Some imitative stops are classed as incomplete stops even when their compass equals that of their prototypes, unless their range corresponds with that of the Manual on which they are placed. This is the case with the Trumpet, Hautboy, Cornopean, and Flute, among others. The reason of this is that such stops are used as frequently, if not more so, as combination than as solo stops, for the purposes of accompaniment; and are hence required to be of the same compass as the other stops of the organ employed for the same end.

537. *Repetition stops* are only met with in pedal organs, and only in such specimens of those as are of too short a range. A repetition stop is that whereof one octave of pipes is made to sound on a second octave of pedals, or on a portion of them, when there is not quite a complete second octave of pedals for them to act upon. They are found most frequently in G G organs. They are incomplete stops with a return to hide the deficiency.

538. *Accessory stops.* Organ stops are further divided into sounding stops and accessory stops; the former being all such as produce tones like those already described, while under the latter head are classed the numerous mechanical devices, operated upon by handles, or pedals, which aid in bringing the organ and its several resources more completely under control. The several manual and pedal couplers, therefore, are accessory stops; so also are the wind-trunk valves, or ventils, found more frequently in Continental than in English organs. The distinction is a necessary one, for otherwise it would be possible in many organs to draw out six or eight so-called " stops " without any sound whatever being producible from the instrument; whereas, by their being recognised as " accessory stops," no sound would be *expected* from them.

U

The size of the stops;
how ascertained.
539. The numerous effects of which all well-planned organs are susceptible result partly from the presence and use of stops of diverse form, nature, and character of tone; and partly from stops varying in pitch as well as in quality of tone, and other distinctive conditions. The most important and useful stops for the Manuals are those of 8-feet, because they are in unison with the human voice, and are, therefore, particularly required for the accompaniment of singing. For the Pedal the 16-feet is the most useful, which, being twice the size of the most important Manual stops, will of course sound an octave below them, as they form the true bass to the Manual 8-feet stops. The size of a stop is ascertained and fixed by the standard length of the pipe that speaks on the lowest key of the clavier on which it appears. If it be a C C Manual, and the 8-feet or C C pipe be placed on the lowest key, as in the Open Diapason, the series of pipes are said to form an "8-feet stop." If it be a tenor c or 4-feet pipe that is so placed, as in the Principal, the series of pipes compose a "4-feet stop." If it be a 16-feet pipe that is so situated, as in the Double Open Diapason, then the pipes are said to form a "16-feet stop," and so on. These quoted measurements refer more particularly to stops composed of open pipes, the low C pipe of each of which is of the standard dimension given. Covered and other stops composed of short-bodied pipes are, as already explained, measured according to their "size of tone," irrespective of their length of pipe. A stop so composed and having attached to the C C key a pipe that gives the C C or 8-feet sound, as in the Stopped Diapason, is a stop of 8-feet *tone;* one giving the 16-feet sound, as in the Bourdon, is a stop of 16-feet *tone.*

540. Some incomplete and short stops are, as already explained, without pipes to the 8-feet octave of keys; the size of which, therefore, is calculated in another way, viz., by their pitch, so far as their compass *does* extend. An Open Diapason or Dulciana, for instance, that stops at tenor or 4-feet c, is, nevertheless, an 8-feet stop, *as far as it goes.* The circumstance of its longest pipe measuring but 4 feet arises from the omission of the entire 8-feet octave; the introduction of which would make the true standard length of the stop quite apparent. Even a Clarabella to middle c^1 (2-feet *length*) is an 8-feet stop so far as it extends; but is without both the 8 and 4 feet octaves of pipes.

541. To be a 4 or 2 feet *stop*, the 4 or 2 feet pipe must be on the C C or 8-feet *key*. The 4-feet pipe on the 4-feet key, as in the case of a tenor c Dulciana, or the 2-feet pipe on the 2-feet key, as in a middle c Clarabella, still leaves the sound in unison with the Diapasons, so far as any sound at all can be obtained, and is therefore of unison or 8-feet pitch.

The classification of
the stops, in regard to
their tone - producing
part, into Reed stops
and Flue stops.
542. The peculiarity by which the two great classes of organ-pipes are distinguished has been already so fully explained, that it is only necessary to add, in this place, that the same classification is observed with the stops, and that a Reed stop is a series of pipes which speak through the medium of a reed and tongue; and a Flue stop, a similar series of lip pipes.

543. Among those of the former class are included the Trumpet, Clarion, Double Trumpet, Horn, Cornopean, Trombone, Hautboy, Bassoon, Clarionet, and Vox Humana stops; among the latter, the Diapason, Principal, Fifteenth, the Mixtures; and, in short, all the stops not included in the fore-mentioned class.

Classification of the
Flue stops, in regard to
their structure, into Diapason-work, Covered-
work, and Flute-work.
544. The several kinds of Flue stops are so numerous, and some kinds are so much more important than others, and require to be introduced in so much greater abundance, that, for the sake of recognition, they are conveniently distributed

and arranged under three separate heads. Flue stops are, therefore, grouped into

Diapason-work,
Covered-work,
Flute-work.

545. *Diapason-work.* Under the head of Diapason or Principal work are placed all the open cylindrical stops of Open Diapason measure, or which have their scale deduced from that of the Open Diapason; such stops are the chief, most important, or "*principal*," as they are also the most numerous, in an organ; and hence the origin and appropriateness of the term under which stops of this shape and proportion are classed. The Unison and Double Open Diapasons, the Principal, Fifteenth, and Octave Fifteenth, the Fifth, Twelfth, and Larigot, the Tenth and Tierce, and the Mixture stops, when of full or proportionate scale, belong to the Diapason-work.

546. *Covered-work.* This class comprises all stops composed of pipes that have their bodies stopped, closed, or covered at the upper end. The Unison and Double Stopped Diapasons (Bourdon), the Stopped Flute, and the Stopped Piccolo, therefore, are members of the Covered-work.

547. *Flute-work.* This division includes all Flue stops, of whatsoever kind or shape, that do not come under either of the preceding divisions.

548. All four-sided pipes, therefore, that are open at the top, and so distinguished from the Covered-work, belong to the "Flute-work"—a term adopted for convenience of classification, and not intended to imply that all the stops arranged under that head produce a *flute quality of tone.* The "Diapason" and "Covered" stops have occasionally been included with the above, under one general term "Flute-work;" but "Flute" stops are never placed under the head of "Diapason," or "Covered-work."

549. The Clarabella, Wald-Flute, Hohl-Flute, Oboe-Flute, Suabe-Flute, the English and German Gambas, the Flageolet, Keraulophon and Piccolo stops, therefore, belong to the "Flute-work." Also the conical stops, as Spitz-Flöte and Gemshorn; and all stops of cylindrical shape, the scale of which is either *below* or *beyond* that of the Diapason-work, as the Dulciana of 16, 8, and 4 feet, the Block-flute, &c.

Classification of Organ stops, in regard to the sound they produce, into Foundation, Mutation, and Compound stops.   550. A third classification of Organ stops is made, in regard to the *sound* they produce, *i.e.*, whether that accords with the key struck or not. The three divisions into which the stops are thrown for this purpose are

Foundation stops,
Mutation stops, and
Compound stops.

551. *Foundation stops* are such as produce a sound corresponding with the key pressed down; that is to say, that give the C sound when the C key is touched. They are so designated, because their sound is the very "foundation" of the organ tone; so much so, that such stops cannot be dispensed with, and therefore receive priority of selection; without them, and that in good proportion, the tone of an organ would be confused and undefined; although they again are, to a certain extent, dependent on members of the other classes of stops for a complete and satisfactory result. The Foundation stops are of various lengths, consequently their sound may be high or low; but this does not affect their *classification*, so long

as the key and the name of the sound agree.   They are of 32, 16, 8, 4, 2 feet, and 1 foot in length or sound, and include members of all classes of stops ; Reed and Flue ; Open and Stopped ; Diapason, Covered, and Flute-work ; the chief conditions being that they are of the standard lengths, or the size of the tone indicated above.

552. The 8-feet stops on the Manual and the 16 on the Pedal are called the Chief Foundation stops, as being the unisons of their respective departments, and giving the "ground-tone." All the 4-feet on the Manual and 8-feet on the Pedal are classed as Octave stops, and those of 16-feet on the Manual and 32 on the Pedal as Double stops.

553. *Mutation*, or *Filling-up, stops* do *not* give a sound corresponding with the key pressed down ; but some sound g on the C key, others e. Those giving the fore-mentioned sound are called "fifth-sounding," or Quint stops ; those giving the latter, "third-sounding," or Tierce stops. They are of various lengths, like the Foundation stops ; the size, or size of tone, of the fifth-sounding stops being as follows :—$10\frac{2}{3}$ (12), $5\frac{1}{3}$ (6), $2\frac{2}{3}$ (3) feet, and $1\frac{1}{3}$ ($1\frac{1}{2}$) foot.

554. An Open stop of $5\frac{1}{3}$ feet on the Manual, or $10\frac{2}{3}$ on the Pedal, sounds the *fifth* above the Unison stops of those departments respectively, and is called the *Fifth* or *Quint*. One of the $2\frac{2}{3}$ feet on the Manual, or $5\frac{1}{3}$ on the Pedal, gives the octave of the Fifth, or the *Twelfth*, by which name it is hence called. A stop, sounding the second octave above the Fifth, that is a *nineteenth* above the unison, measuring $1\frac{1}{3}$ on the Manual and $2\frac{2}{3}$ feet on the Pedal, is called the *Larigot* or *Octave Twelfth*. A still smaller rank of fifth-sounding pipes, speaking a *twenty-sixth* above the unison tone, is often included among the ranks in the bass part of the Manual Compound stops, where, indeed, the last-mentioned series is more frequently met with than as a separate stop.

555. In German organs the fifth-sounding stops are called "Quints," in reference to the *sound* they produce. The *pitch* of that sound is not usually indicated by any peculiarity in the name on the draw-stop, but by the length being marked in figures. (See Foreign Specifications.)

556. The lengths of the third-sounding stops or Tierces are $6\frac{2}{5}$, $3\frac{1}{5}$ feet, and $1\frac{3}{5}$ foot. Except on the Pedal, they are rarely found in modern organs, unless of great magnitude.

557. An Open stop, measuring $3\frac{1}{5}$ on the Manual, or $6\frac{2}{5}$ on the Pedal, gives the major third above the Octave stops, or the *tenth* above the unison, and is called the Tenth. One measuring $1\frac{3}{5}$ foot on the Manual, or $3\frac{1}{5}$ on the Pedal, sounds a major third above the Super-octave stops, or a *seventeenth* above the Unison stops, and is called the Tierce.

558. The Mutation stops impart a certain roundness and fulness to the general organ-tone, by "filling up" some of the bare octave sounds of the Foundation stops, by the mixture therewith of certain intermediate, harmonical sounds, of fixed and determinate pitches. They also have the further effect of binding together the extreme sounds of the Compound stops, and the Unison and Double stops ; and of blending the whole into one great mass of musical sound. The laws which regulate the admission of Mutation stops, and decide which are required and which are not, are fully explained in a subsequent chapter.

559. *Compound* or *Mixture stops*. The stops which have 1 pipe to each key have been termed "Simple" stops. The kind now under consideration are called "Compound" stops, because they have more than 1 pipe to each key, often 5 of various sizes ; and "Mixture" stops, because those several pipes consist of certain members of the two preceding description of stops, "mixed" or "compounded" together. These pipes are so uniformly required to be used in conjunction, that

they are rarely made to draw separately. The Compound stops give to the Foundation stops a distinctness and clearness of effect in the bass, especially necessary to the quick recognition by the ear of the pitch of the larger pipes ; and great vivacity, as well as a kind of ringing character, to the general organ tone. The German organ-builders recognise a class of stops which they call " Simple Mixed stops." These are stops which, consisting of a set of single pipes, produce *two* sounds. To this class belong the *Quintatons* of 32, 16, 8, and 4 feet size of tone. These stops not only produce their fundamental tone, but, from a certain peculiarity in their voicing, also the *twelfth or octave fifth above* that tone. Hence their name. It is in this particular that they are distinguished from the similar class of stops which, producing only their pure, deep, humming tone, are called *Bourdons.*

CHAPTER XXIII.

THE NAMES OF ORGAN STOPS.

The name and description of stops found in English organs; together with their length or size of tone on the Manual and Pedal.

560. THE custom of distinguishing the different stops from one another, as Principal, Octave, &c., dates from the sixteenth century. A list of stops usually found in English organs will now be given. Among the names inserted therein will occasionally be found one of Continental origin, and for which no English equivalent is known to exist. Where this is the case, of course, the original name has been allowed to stand ; but where a translation of the foreign name could be given this has been added within brackets. It has happened that, in a few instances, Continental names have been applied by English organ-builders to stops of somewhat different construction or character of tone, which will be duly pointed out.

561. With regard to the *arrangement* of the stops mentioned in the list, the flue and reed species have been treated separately, priority being given to the former ; and the members of each have been taken in the order of their length or their size of tone, commencing with the largest, and ending with the smallest.

562. *Sub-Bourdon, Manual-Untersatz.* This Manual stop is composed of stopped pipes, and is, in pitch, two octaves below the unison or 8-feet stops : it is, therefore, of 32-feet tone. The Sub-Bourdon is best suited for organs of the first magnitude, in which it has a grand effect. Its compass is usually to the middle c^1, fiddle g, or, at most, to the tenor c key. At Stuttgardt the 32-feet tone is produced in the bass octave acoustically by the union of a Bourdon 16 feet and a Great Quint of $10\frac{2}{3}$ tone. Examples will be found in the Doncaster Parish Church organ, built by Schulze ; also in the organ at St. Olave's, Southwark, built by Lincoln, which, however, has open pipes in the treble. Various Foreign Specifications in the Appendix contain notices of other specimens.

563. *Double Open Diapason.* This stop belongs to the " Diapason-work," and is of 16 feet length on the Manual, and 32 on the Pedal. It is made either of tin, metal, zinc, or wood. The Manual Double Open Diapason is most frequently made of metal in this country, and is sometimes continued right down in metal, as is the case in the organ at Brunswick Chapel, Leeds, built by Booth of Wakefield ; one of GG compass, where the largest metal pipe is consequently $21\frac{1}{2}$ feet in length. In some instances the lower half-octave or octave of pipes are of wood—as in that of the late St. George's Church, Doncaster—from FFF to CCC. In other specimens the pipes, to the lowest octave or so, are omitted and stopped pipes, substituted to save room or expense ; or the stop is altogether discontinued below the tenor c key. In the latter case the stop is on that account called *Tenoroon.* The oldest authentic specimen of the Double Open Diapason known to exist in England is the one in the very interesting organ in Exeter Cathedral, made by Loosemore, 1664-5. The instrument just named, together with that in St. Saviour's, Southwark, also said to be made by the same builder, were the only two organs in this country that possessed a Double *Open* Diapason until of late years.

564. The Pedal Double Open Diapason is made of either of the four materials mentioned above. Specimens of wood stops of this kind occur at Westminster

Abbey; St. Paul's Cathedral; at the Parish Church and at Brunswick Chapel, Leeds; at York Minster; at the Birmingham Town Hall; and at the Parish Church, Doncaster. The instruments at York and Birmingham have also each a 32-feet stop of this description made of zinc; the Town Hall organ at Leeds has also a stop of this kind; while 32-feet stops of tin occur 'at Haarlem, Hamburg, Weingarten, Albert Hall, &c. The pitch of the Double Open Diapason, whether of the Manual or Pedal, is an octave below the Unison stop.

565. *Double Dulciana.* An open metal cylindrical stop, belonging to the Flute-work, of small scale and delicate tone, and somewhat slow of speech. It is a Manual stop of 16 feet, of which but a few specimens have been made in a complete form. There is one, however, in metal throughout, to the 16-feet pipe, in the Choir organ of the large instrument at Brunswick Chapel, Leeds. Occasionally the pipes to the lowest octave, or octave and a half of keys, are of stopped wood, as in the swell at Christ Church, Newgate Street; though more frequently there are no pipes at all provided for the 8-feet octave of keys; in which case the stop is usually called Tenoroon Dulciana.

566. *Contra-Gamba.* An effective 16-feet open metal Flue stop, frequently introduced into the Swell by Mr. Henry Willis.

567. *Double Stopped Diapason,* or Bourdon; on the Pedal, Sub-Bourdon, or Untersatz. This is a covered stop, of 16-feet tone on the Manual and 32 on the Pedal. It is, rightly, a whole stop, like the two preceding; complete specimens occurring on the Great Manual organs at the Temple Church; St. Luke's, Old Street; the Exchange, Northampton; All Saints', Northampton; St. Michael's, Chester Square, &c. In many organs which have a Tenoroon Open Diapason or Dulciana the Double Stopped Diapason consists of one octave only of pipes, producing the 16-feet octave of sounds, acting on the 8-feet octave of the Manual, commencing where the Tenoroon leaves off. The English Double Stopped Diapason is generally made of wood throughout. This is the case also with many Continental specimens; while others, again, are either wholly or in part metal, as in the Choir organ at the Temple Church. Of the Manual Double Stopped Diapason numerous specimens were in existence in this country about the middle of the last century. The organ built by Jordan, Bridge, and Byfield, in the year 1740, for the church at Great Yarmouth, had a stop of this kind. So also had the organ in the Foundling Hospital, constructed by Parker, and erected in 1759. The instrument at St. Margaret's, Lynn, made by Snetzler, in 1754, originally contained one throughout the Great Organ; and another, by Schwarbrook, formed part of his masterpiece at St. Michael's, Coventry. Sir John Hawkins, in his *History of Music*, mentions another specimen as occurring in an organ at Manchester (at the Cathedral) in his time.

568. The *Pedal Double Stopped Diapason* (32-feet tone) appears to have been introduced, for the first time in this country, by Smith, of Bristol, in the organ he built for the church of St. James in that city, in 1824. Other examples of the stop occur in organs at St. Pancras Church, and St. Olave's, Southwark, where it is called Sub-Bourdon, 32-feet tone; and at Trinity College, Cambridge.

569. *Pyramidon.* This is a Pedal stop of 16 or 32 feet tone, invented by the Rev. Sir Frederic Gore-Ouseley, and made by Mr. Flight; the peculiarities in which consist, first, in the shape of the pipes, which are more than four times the size at the top that they are at the mouth; and, secondly, in their producing sounds of remarkable gravity for their size. From a pipe, measuring only 2 feet 9 inches in length, 2 feet 3 inches square at the top, and 8 inches at the block, the CCC, or 16-feet sound, is obtained. The quality of the tone bears some resemblance to that of a stopped pipe.

570. Open Diapason. The Open Diapason is the chief member of the "Principal-work." It is a whole stop of 8 feet on the Manual, and 16 feet on the Pedal; and is called Open in contradistinction to the Stopped Diapason, the pipes of which are closed or covered in at the top. From its being the chief Foundation stop on the Manual and Pedal, its goodness or badness exercises an important influence over the effect of the organ generally. The Manual Open Diapason is generally formed of tin or metal pipes, many of which are those usually seen in front of the case. Sometimes the lowest half-octave or octave of pipes are made of wood.

571. Large organs frequently have two Open Diapasons on the Great Manual; of tin or metal throughout, usually, in old instruments, but with the bass of the second one of wood in many later organs. When the organ is placed on the choir screen, as is often the case in cathedrals and other cruciform structures, the majority of the pipes of one *Open* appear in the east, and those of the other in the west front of the case. The second Open Diapason is made to a different scale from the first, usually one pipe smaller, to destroy the sympathy. Zinc is sometimes successfully used for the 8-feet octave of this stop.

572. The *Pedal Open Diapason* is almost invariably made of wood. Metal ones, however, are sometimes met with; as in the Pedal organs at St. Sepulchre's, Snow Hill; Christ Church, Newgate Street; Exeter Hall; St. John's, Chester, &c. A magnificent specimen, of which the pipes in the 8 and 16 feet octaves are of zinc, occurs in the new organ at Doncaster, where it faces the transept.

573. It may be worth while to mention here that the use of the word "Diapason" has, in some instances, been objected to, as having no definite signification; and its retention as a name for an organ stop proposed to be discontinued in consequence. There seems, however, to be no sufficient reason for discarding it.

574. That it is no longer applicable to its *original* signification is indeed true. The word, which is of Greek origin, means an "octave;" and, applied to the first pneumatic organ, which is recorded to have had but *one octave* of pipes, and those only of the diatonic scale, offered the most fit name that could have been given. But in proportion as the subsequent increase in the compass of the organ and the number of its stops took place, the appropriateness of the term in its *original* sense decreased.

575. These developments, however, prepared the way for the application of the word in a more extended sense. The term "Diapason," coming as it does from two Greek words, signifying "through all," is applied by makers of musical instruments to the rule, standard, or scale, by which they make their flutes, hautboys, &c. In a similar manner the set of Unison Open pipes under consideration forms the rule, standard, or scale, by which the organ builder regulates the size of the harmonic corroborating series of stops; not only in the first instance, in regard to their length and breadth of body, but afterwards, in regard to their strength and quality of tone. Its influence extends "through all" the stops in question; hence, the name "Diapason" appears to be just the most appropriate one that could be given to a set of pipes exercising so much power.

576. *Dulciana.* This is an 8-feet Manual stop, belonging to the Flute-work. It is sometimes of metal throughout, as at the Temple Church, and St. Giles's, Camberwell; or the lowest octave is made of wood, and the remainder of metal, as at St. Dunstan's, Fleet Street. The Dulciana, in most organs, stops at tenor c; the stop then frequently being grooved into the Stopped Diapason in the 8-feet octave; or the bass of the Stopped Diapason is made to draw separately to meet it. The pipes of the Dulciana are much smaller in scale than those of the Open Diapason, the fiddle g, or tenor f sharp pipe of the former, being of the same diameter as the middle c^1 pipe of the latter, and its tone is peculiarly soft and gentle.

577. The Dulciana Stop was either invented or introduced into this country by

Snetzler, who acquired great reputation from the entire success that attended his first public specimen, which forms a portion of the organ erected by him, in the year 1754, in St. Margaret's Church, at Lynn, in Norfolk.

578. *Harmonic Flute.* This is a Manual open metal Flute stop, extending to fiddle g, at the farthest, in its Harmonic form ; is of cylindrical form, of 8-feet pitch, and either blown by a heavy wind or simply copiously winded. The pipes are of double length, *i.e.*, 16 feet ; and the bodies have a hole bored in them midway between the foot and the top. ·The tone of ·the Harmonic Flute is exceedingly full, fluty, and powerful, and imparts great breadth and thickness to the general organ tone. It was invented by Cavaillé-Coll, of Paris, an'd has of recent years been adopted generally by the English builders.

579. *Voix Céleste.* The Voix Céleste is another stop of French invention, formed of a delicate Gamba and a Dulciana, which are first tuned in unison, and then the pipes of the second one are lightly touched again with the tuning-horn, and their pitch slightly raised. This gives to the tone of the stop a waving, undulating character, which in this respect resembles the German stop called *Unda Maris* (wave of the sea), which will be found mentioned in some of the Foreign Specifications, which see.

580. The Voix Céleste was first employed in this country in the Panopticon and Glasgow organs.

581. *Stopped Diapason. Gedact.* The Stopped Diapason is an 8-feet sounding stop on the Manual, and 16 on the Pedal. It is the most important member of the Covered-work—its sound being in unison with that of the Open Diapason. The Manual Stopped Diapason is sometimes composed of metal pipes as far as tenor c, and of oak thence downwards, as on the Great Manual at the Temple Church ; or of metal to middle c^1, and of deal below, as at Christ Church, Spitalfields. More frequently, however, it is of wood throughout. The different materials slightly modify the tone, which may, in general terms, be described as being fluty and mellow.

582. On the Pedal the Stopped Diapason is generally made of wood. Its tone adds a quiet solidity to that of the Pedal Open Diapason, and, if purely and fully voiced, is one of the most useful stops a Pedal Organ can contain.

583. *Clarionet Flute.* This stop is formed much after the manner of a Stopped Diapason, except that the perforations in the stoppers are much larger, and its tone is of a reedy quality. It is of 8-feet tone on the Manual. The tone is very rarely even or equal throughout the stop.

584. *Clarabella.* The modern stop thus called, which was invented by the late Mr. Bishop, is of 8 feet on the Manual. It is formed of open wood pipes of a large scale, producing a thick and powerful fluty tone, and is sometimes introduced instead of the treble portion of the Stopped Diapason. The Clarabella is seldom disposed otherwise than an incomplete stop ; its compass generally only extending to middle c^1, or, at most, to tenor c. A complete one, however, occurs in the Swell of the Brunswick Chapel organ, Leeds, by Booth of Wakefield. The English Clarabella much resembles the German "Hohl-flöte" in character of tone, except that its sound is scarcely so strong or so full.

585. *Dolcan.* This is an Open Manual Stop, of 8 feet, the pipes of which are of larger diameter at the top than at the bottom, producing a very agreeable tone. It is not much known in England ; a specimen, however, exists in the organ at St. Stephen's Church, Westminster, made by Hill.

586. *Viol di Gamba,* or *Gamba.* This is one of the most highly-esteemed 'and most frequently-disposed stops in Continental organs ; as may be gathered from reference to the Foreign Specifications in the Appendix. The German Gamba is usually composed of cylindrical pipes of small scale, though occasionally it is formed of conical pipes. In England the Viol di Gamba was, until very recently,

made exclusively of the conical shape, surmounted by a bell, as represented in *fig.* 81, page 103, and which kind of pipe was first introduced by Mr. Hill.

587. In compass the Viol di Gamba usually descends no lower than tenor c ; that at Christ Church, Spitalfields, however—which is a Bell Gamba—descends to CC. Examples of the German Gamba occur in the organ at Doncaster Parish Church, in the Exchange organ at Northampton, and in the organ at the Temple Church, the latter specimen descending to CC. The proper Pedal bass to the Gamba and other unison string-toned stops is the *Violone*, 16 *feet*, a stop composed of wooden pipes of small scale, the CCC measuring about 5 inches by 7. An admirable specimen of this stop occurs on the Pedal of the Temple organ, and another at Doncaster.

588. The tone of the Bell Gamba is very agreeable and reedy, and quick in its articulation ; while that of the (German) Gamba is much stronger, pungent, and cutting, and sometimes of slower intonation (imitating the bite of the bow on the string), in which case the Stopped Diapason, or, still better, the " Hohl-flöte," is drawn with it, which performs the same office, in regard to this and all other slow-speaking stops, that the " percussion " does to the tongues of harmoniums.

589. *Keraulophon.* This also is a Manual stop of 8 feet, of metal, and, like the one last noticed, of a reedy and pleasant quality of tone. It seldom extends lower than tenor c. It is formed of cylindrical pipes, like the Open Diapason and Dulciana, the peculiarity in the character of the tone being produced by the boring of a small round hole in the body of the pipe near to the top, or through a sliding cap. The Keraulophon was invented by Messrs. Gray and Davison, and used by them for the first time in the organ of St. Paul's Church, Knightsbridge, built in 1843.

590. *Hohl-flöte* (Hollow-toned Flute). A German name, applied of late years to an English open metal stop of 8 feet, that is nearly identical with the stop last described.

591. The Hohl-flöte was occasionally introduced by Father Smith into his organs. There were originally *two* in his instrument at Durham Cathedral, one on the Great and the other on the Choir Manual, each of wood, and two in the Temple organ, similarly disposed ; all of which, however, have long since disappeared. That introduced by the same builder into the Choir organ at the Cathedral, Manchester, still remains under the name " Dulciana." The German Hohl-flöte, when of metal, is made to a very large scale, *i.e.*, larger than the Open Diapason, producing a powerful and thick or, as the name distinctly intimates, a *hollow* tone. In the organ erected by Schulze, in 1851, in the Exchange at Northampton, there is a Hohl-flöte of wood, and having the mouth on the broad side of the pipe. That in the Doncaster organ is formed of *three*-sided pipes, and is the first Mr. Schulze made of that shape.

592. *Geigen Principal* (Violin Diapason) is a Manual stop of 8 feet, producing a pungent tone, very like that of the Gamba, except that the pipes, of larger scale, always speak quick, and produce a fuller tone. Examples of the stop exist at Doncaster, the Temple Church, and in the Exchange organ at Northampton.

593. *Salicional*, or *Salicet*. Another reedy-toned 8-feet Manual Stop, of small scale, of which an example occurs in the Swell of the old Panopticon organ. It may not be uninteresting to many to have the peculiarities of the several string-toned stops briefly pointed out :—

> The fiddle g————————Geigen Principal,
> tenor d sharp ———————— Gamba, and
> tenor c sharp ———— of the Salicional, are all of the same
> diameter as the middle c¹————of the Open Diapason—*i.e.*, 1¼ in.

594. All the above-named stops differ in respect to the "height of mouth;" the *smallest* in scale (the Salicional) being cut up *most*, and the Open (the *largest*) the *least*. Moreover, they differ very much in their speech; the Salicet being the slowest, but the most penetrating; the Open the quickest and fullest.

595. *Fifth, Quint. Double Twelfth, Diapente.* The fifth is the largest Mutation stop commonly introduced into an organ. On the Manual it is sometimes composed of open pipes of proportionate scale to the Double Open Diapason, in which case it of course forms a portion of the "Diapason-work;" at others it consists of stopped pipes, as in the Chester Cathedral organ (built by Gray and Davison), in the Doncaster organ, and in St. Margaret's Church, Gotha (built by Schulze)—when it belongs to the Covered-work (Gedact-Quint—see Foreign Specifications). In a few English examples the Manual Quint has been formed of Dulciana pipes, which, however, are of weak intonation, and less prompt in speech. The Quint on the Pedal is almost invariably composed of stopped pipes, and are most effective. (See Foreign Specifications.) The greatest size of the Quint is usually 5⅓-feet on the Manual, and 10⅔-feet tone on the Pedal. In the great organs at Stuttgardt and St. Paul's, Frankfort, are Quints of 10⅔ on the Manual; and in the Cathedral organ, at Bremen, built by Schulze, is a "Quintet-Bass" of 21⅓-feet tone, of stopped wooden pipes.

596. A Manual Open Quint was made in England, so long back as the year 1730, by Bridge the organ-builder, who introduced it into the instrument erected by him in Christ Church, Spitalfields, in that year. The Pedal Stopped Quint, 10⅔-feet tone, was first introduced into this country by Robson, in the organ at Huddersfield, built in 1850. A second specimen was introduced, by Kirkland and Jardine, with excellent effect into their organ in Holy Trinity Church, Manchester, made in 1852.

597. *Principal, Octave.* A 4-feet stop on the Manual, and 8 feet on the Pedal. Its usual material is either tin or metal, though, in some organs, where there are two Principals on the Great Manual, the second one is sometimes of wood, as at Christ's Hospital, &c.; the second one is then more correctly an open wood Flute of 4 feet. At the Temple Church, St. Giles's, Camberwell; Christ Church, Spitalfields, &c., both Principals are of metal. The English Principal is the octave stop to the Open Diapason; and, where there are two metal Principals, the scale of the second one is generally regulated by the measure of the second Open Diapason, to which stop it is usually designed to form an appropriate octave.

598. *Dulciana Principal, Dulcet.* A delicate and sweet-toned Manual stop of 4 feet, formed of metal pipes, of small scale. It was first introduced by Green, who, in several of his later instruments, placed this, as well as a Unison Dulciana, in the Swell. Examples occur, thus disposed, in the organs erected by him at Rochester and Salisbury Cathedrals, Greenwich Hospital, &c.

599. *Flute Octaviente harmonique.* The *Harmonic Flute* of 4 feet, that has recently become so great a favourite with most English organ-builders.

600. *Flute.* A stop of either 4-feet standard length or 4-feet tone on the Manual (for both species of stop are met with indifferently and indiscriminately under the same name), and 8-feet tone on the Pedal. The old Flute stops are sometimes composed of metal pipes throughout, as in the Swell organ at the Temple Church; St. Andrew's, Undershaft; and, until lately, at St. Paul's; sometimes partly so, as at St. Michael's Cornhill; while in many instances they are of wood throughout, as at Finedon. The old organs often have a Flute stop of octave pitch on both the Great and Choir Manuals. Where this is the case, one is often of metal, either wholly or partially, and the other of wood, the different materials being used as an auxiliary to secure an individuality in the character of the tone of each. The

majority of the modern Flute stops, when not "Harmonic," which they frequently are, are of wood, and open; and hence are 4-feet stops, as those already noticed are of 4-feet tone. The quality of the tone of a Flute stop usually bears a close resemblance to that of the wind instrument after which it is named.

601. As a Pedal stop, the Flute is now much used in this country, and is of the greatest utility. A Bass Flute stop occurs in the organ at St. Mark's, Hamilton Terrace, Regent's Park, built by Gray, in 1847; and in instruments by Brindley, of Sheffield, at Papworth Everard, and Little Drayton.

602. *Spitz-flöte* (literally, pointed or spire-flute). This stop is found of 8, 4, and 2 feet length in German organs. An example of 8 feet occurs in the Choir Organ at the Temple Church. The pipes of the Spitz-flöte are slightly conical, being about ¼ narrower at the top than at the mouth, and the tone is therefore rather softer than that of the cylindrical stop, but of very pleasing quality.

603. *Gemshorn.* The Gemshorn is a member of the Flute-work, and is met with of 8, 4, or 2 feet length in Continental organs. A stop of this kind, of 4 feet, occurs on the Choir Manuals of the organs at the Wesleyan Chapel, Poplar, built by Mr. Hill; and at the Temple Church. The pipes of this stop are only ⅓ the diameter at the top that they are at the mouth; and the tone is consequently light but very clear and travelling.

604. *Nason.* This name is sometimes found applied in old organs to a wood-stopped Flute of 4-feet pitch on the Great Manual, as at the Temple Church; and, until a few years since, at St. Paul's Cathedral. It is generally a quiet sweet-toned stop, producing a most lovely effect when combined with the Diapason.

605. *Wald-flöte* (Wood or Forest-flute). The name given in England to a Manual stop of 4 feet, formed of open wood pipes of a large scale, with inverted mouths. It is a full-toned and powerful-speaking stop, and, in all essential particulars, may be considered as an octave Clarabella. It seldom ranges lower than tenor c. Mr. Hill first used it in the Cheetham Hill organ, Manchester, built by him in 1841. The English Wood-flute is a distinct stop from the German one of the same name. The German stop is made either of tin, metal, or wood; the English one always of the last-mentioned material. The former is also made to a scale larger than that of the Open Diapason, and produces a thick and full tone.

606. *Clear-flute.* An open wood flute of 4 feet, invented by the firm of Kirtland and Jardine, of Manchester. It resembles the Wald-flöte so far, that the pipes have the inward-bevelled mouth; but, in addition to this, they have also the bevelled block, shown in *fig.* 111, page 112; are copiously winded; have no nicking, and are more nearly square in shape. The tone is exceedingly firm, clear, and full.

607. *Oboe-flute.* Another 4-feet Manual stop, composed of wood pipes of small scale. Its usual range is tenor c. The tone of the Oboe-flute is very delicate and reedy, and not so strong as that of the Viol di Gamba.

608. *Saube-flöte* Also a tenor c Manual stop of 4 feet, formed of wood pipes, with inverted mouths. Its tone is liquid and clear, and not so loud as the Wald-flöte. The Saube-flöte was invented by Mr. Hill.

609. *Celestina.* A 4-feet Manual stop, formed of open wood pipes, of small scale, producing a delicate and subdued tone. It is not often met with. Its usual place is in the Swell organ, as at Christ's Hospital, &c.

610. *Tenth, Double Tierce, Decima.* This is an open metal cylindrical stop, of 3⅕ feet length on the Manual, and 6⅖ feet on the Pedal. It is the second Double Mutation stop, taking them in the order of their size or gravity of tone; and the largest of the third-sounding species. The first English organ in which the Tenth was legitimately introduced is the one in the Mechanics' Institution, Liverpool. The pitch of the Tenth is a major third above the Principal, or a tenth above the Diapa-

sons ; all *numerical* names giving the altitude of the sound above that of the unison stops. The great Tierce of 6⅖ tone, on the Pedal, at Doncaster, is the first stop of the kind made in England.

611. *Twelfth, Octave-quint, Duoaecima.* An open metal stop of 2⅔ feet on the Manual, and 5⅓ feet on the Pedal, belonging to the Diapason-work. Its pitch is a perfect fifth above the Principal, or a twelfth above the Diapasons.

612. *Fifteenth, Super-octave.* Also an open metal stop belonging to the Diapason-work of 2-feet length on the Manual, and 4-feet on the Pedal. The Fifteenth sounds the octave above the Principal, and consequently a fifteenth, or super-octave, above the Unison stops. In some organs, where there are two Fifteenths on one Manual, the second is made of wood, forming, in fact, a Piccolo ; at Christ Church, Spitalfields, both the Fifteenths on the Great Manual are of metal.

613. *Block-flute* (Common or Ordinary Flute). This is an open metal stop, tuned in unison with the Fifteenth. It is composed of pipes of a very large scale, the 4-feet c pipe measuring very nearly 4½ inches in diameter, the measure of the 4-feet pipe of the Open Diapason being about 3½ inches. The tone of the Block-flute is very full and broad. The Block-flute was a favourite stop with Father Smith, who introduced it into his organs at Durham and St. Paul's Cathedrals. Both specimens have now disappeared.

614. *Octavina Harmonique.* The *Harmonique Piccolo* of the French and English organ-builders.

615. *Piccolo.* A 2-feet Manual stop, formed of wood pipes, producing a bright, clear, and travelling tone. Its pitch, as its accordance of length thereto would imply, is in unison with the Fifteenth, *i.e.*, two octaves above the Diapasons. The Piccolo is sometimes a Whole stop, as at St. Michael's, Chester Square ; but more often it only extends to tenor c.

616. *Flageolet.* Another small member of the Flute-work, usually of 2 feet on the Manual. It is formed of open wood pipes, and the tone is smaller and sharper than that of the Piccolo.

617. *Tierce, Seventeenth.* A stop formed of open metal cylindrical pipes, the pitch of which is a major third above the Fifteenth, or a seventeenth above the Diapasons. The Tierce frequently constitutes one of the ranks of the Sesquialtera, though, in old organs, it is occasionally made to draw separately, as at St. Sepulchre's. It is, however, found in both ways, in ancient as well as modern instruments.

618. *Larigot, Nineteenth, Octave-Twelfth.* This also is a small metal Mutation stop, of 1⅓ foot on the Manual, and 2⅔ on the Pedal. It is occasionally met with as a separate stop, as at Christ Church, Spitalfields, and St. Sepulchre's ; but generally it is embodied in the Sesquialtera, of which it forms, strictly speaking, an integral part. The Larigot sounds a perfect fifth above the Fifteenth, and therefore a nineteenth above the Unison stops.

619. *Octave-fifteenth, Twenty-second.* A small open metal stop, of 1 foot on the Manual and 2 feet on the Pedal, of bright and sharp tone. It sounds the octave above the Fifteenth, and the third octave above the Diapasons. This rank of pipes, like the Tierce and Larigot, is but seldom disposed as a separate stop. It occurs in this manner in the organs at St. Phillips, Sheffield, and Stratford-on-Avon. A "Two-and-twentieth" also appears as one of the stops in the original specification of the old organ at York Minster, built by Dallam, in 1633.

620. *Doublette.* The French name for the Fifteenth ; but in England applied, of late years, to a two-ranked Foundation stop, sounding a fifteenth and twenty-second above the unison, the two sounds being an octave apart.

Compound Stops.   621. *Sesquialtera.* This Compound stop is composed of either 5, 4, 3, or 2 ranks of open metal pipes, tuned in thirds, fifths, and octave to the Diapasons. The altitude of the several sounds of a 5-ranked Sesquialtera above the unison pitch, used, under ordinary circumstances, to be, in the bass, a Seventeenth (3), Nineteenth (5), Twenty-second (8), Twenty-sixth (5), and Twenty-ninth (8), from the ground tone. Where, however, there was a separate Tierce, it was not usual to include a duplicate of that rank in the Sesquialtera, unless, indeed, the ranks of mixture were sufficiently numerous to demand this arrangement. At Doncaster, where there was a Tierce and a 5-rank Sesquialtera, in Harris's organ, now destroyed, the latter was compounded of a Nineteenth (5), Twenty-second (8), Twenty-fourth (3), Twenty-sixth (5), and Twenty-ninth (8) : that is, with an octave Tierce in lieu of the unison (separate) one. Another composition for a 5-rank Sesquialtera with separate Tierce, was—Fifteenth (8), Nineteenth (5), Twenty-second (8), Twenty-sixth (5), and Twenty-ninth (8). A 4-rank Sesquialtera was generally, though not always, composed of a Fifteenth (8), Seventeenth (3), Nineteenth (5), and Twenty-second (8), as at St. Mary's, Nottingham (Snetzler), and at St. Botolph's, Aldgate. Sometimes it consisted of a Seventeenth (3), Nineteenth (5), Twenty-second (8), and Twenty-fourth (3) (Tierce and octave Tierce), as was the case at St. Magnus, London Bridge. This again, and indeed all Sesquialteras, however numerous or few may be the number of ranks of its pipes, are, in regard to their composition, influenced very much by the presence, or otherwise, of the Tierce, the Larigot, the temperament to which the organ is tuned, and even also by the occurrence, or not, of other Compound stops on the same Manual.

622. As the pipes of the Sesquialtera would become exceedingly small, keen, and prominent in the treble, and, moreover, their presence is not demanded by the acoustical phenomenon on which the introduction of the Compound stops is founded, as is fully explained in a succeeding chapter, the smaller ranks are usually discontinued from middle c^1, or c^1 sharp, at their original altitude of pitch above the Diapason, and larger pipes, sounding an octave lower, are substituted. In this manner the Twenty-second, or Octave-fifteenth, the smallest rank in a Sesquialtera of three ranks, is turned into a Fifteenth, and the Nineteenth, or Larigot, into a Twelfth. The Tierce, if present, is usually allowed to remain unbroken throughout the Manual. In the real Sesquialtera the Third-sounding rank is smaller than the Fifth-sounding ; and the pitch of the two is a major sixth apart. The old English Sesquialtera was therefore correct in the treble, but was a *Mixture* in the bass.

623. In consequence of these " breaks," as they are termed, there are then of course two Twelfths and two Fifteenths in the treble. All such duplicate ranks are, in England, usually made to a different scale.

624. The German Sesquialtera, when of 2 ranks, which is seldom met with except in old organs, is composed of a Twelfth and Tierce, sounding a major sixth.

625. *Mixture.* This stop consists of from 5 to 2 ranks of open metal pipes, which are, in England, generally of smaller dimensions than those of the Sesquialtera, particularly where the last-mentioned stop is not very numerously ranked, and has nothing higher than a Twenty-second.

626. The Mixture, then, if of two ranks only, usually consists of a Twenty-sixth (5) and Twenty-ninth (8) in the bass and tenor octaves ; changing to a Nineteenth (5) and Twenty-second (8) at middle c^1, or middle c^1 sharp, *i.e.*, on the same key where the Sesquialtera breaks into a Twelfth, Fifteenth, and Seventeenth. In some Mixtures the breaks occur sooner. In some modern examples, on the contrary, both the Sesquialtera and Mixture are carried up to the smallest pipe commonly

made, namely, f⁵, occurring on the treble f² key in the Sesquialtera, and on the f¹ above middle c¹ key in the Mixture, before any break is made.

627. The Mixture of 5 ranks occurs the most frequently on such Manuals as have no other Compound stop, as in the Swell at Christ Church, Newgate Street. In such cases its composition is nearly identical with that of a numerously ranked Sesquialtera, and closely resembles the Continental Mixture.

628. In Germany the Mixture is usually the first Compound stop, as the Sesquialtera is in England, and not the second, as we generally make it. Their second Compound stop is generally either a Scharf (sharp) or Cymbel.

629. On the Great Manual of the organ in the Town Hall at Birmingham is a 5-rank Mixture, besides a Sesquialtera and Furniture of the same number of ranks.

630. *Furniture.* This Compound stop consists of from 5 to 2 sets of small open metal pipes, the number of ranks, as well as the intervals they sound above the Unison stops, varying with circumstances. Where there is a Sesquialtera and Mixture on the same Manual, the Furniture is sometimes above both, as at St. Giles's, Camberwell. For instance, if it be of two ranks, they will probably be a Thirty-third (5) and a Thirty-sixth (8) above the unison, *i.e.*, a fifth and eighth above the (usual) upper rank of the Mixture ; but the ranks will break in every octave, on account of even its longest pipes being but very small. In other examples the Furniture is nearly identical in composition with the usual 3-rank Sesquialtera, as at St. Sepulchre's. In many organs the Furniture appears as the second Compound stop, as at St. Leonard's, Shoreditch, &c. ; in which case it is nearly, if not quite, identical with the usual Mixture.

631. The Furniture appeared on the Choir Manual of Avery's organs, at St. Margaret's, Westminster, and Croydon Church.

632. *Cornet.* This name is applied to several distinct kinds of stops.

633. *The Mounted Cornet* is a Compound stop, consisting usually of 5 ranks of pipes, three, four, or five pipes larger in scale than the Open Diapason, and voiced to produce a full and broad tone. It is only a treble stop in English organs, ranging from middle c¹, or c¹ sharp, upwards ; but, in German examples, its usual compass is to tenor c. The Mounted Cornet is composed of a Stopped (or sometimes an Open) Diapason, a Principal, Twelfth, Fifteenth, and a Tierce. The pipes are planted on a small sound-board of their own, raised some three or four feet above that of the Great Organ (hence its name), and the wind is conducted from the Great Organ sound-board up to that of the Mounted Cornet through metal tubes. The Mounted Cornet is mostly found in old organs ; but examples occur on the Great and Swell Manuals of the new organ at Doncaster. It was chiefly used for playing out the melody of the Chorales upon, and for the performance of a now obsolete kind of voluntary ; but it is of great use in large organs in hiding the breaks in the several Compound stops, as it proceeds itself without any "repetitions." In Father Smith's organs the Cornet was never "mounted," but stood on the sound-board. It was afterwards raised, probably to economise room.

634. *Echo Cornet.* This variety is also a Compound stop, and is sometimes mounted. It is composed of the same number of ranks of pipes as the Mounted Cornet, and usually, though not always, of pipes of the same pitch, but of Dulciana scale. This stop frequently extends to tenor c. Its usual situation is in the Swell as at St. Peter's, Cornhill ; its tone, besides being in itself light and delicate, was further subdued by being enclosed within a box.

635. The name of Cornet is often found applied to the Compound stop so frequently met with in the short Swells of the last century. It is generally of

3 ranks, Twelfth, Fifteenth, and Seventeenth ; though, where there is no separate Principal, as at St. George's, St. George's Street, E., that stop is usually incorporated with it, which then, of course, contains 4 ranks.

636. In small organs the Sesquialtera is not uncommonly made to "draw in halves ;" the treble of which is then often labelled " Cornet."

637. The name is, in German organs, further applied to a small Pedal Reed stop, of 4 feet and 2 feet. (See Foreign Specifications.)

Reed stops.   638. *Double Trumpet.* This is a Manual stop of 16 feet, with pipes either of metal throughout, as at St. George's, Doncaster ; or having the tubes to the lowest octave of wood, as at Ashton-under-Lyne. Sometimes the pipes of the lowest octave are omitted ; in which case the stop is frequently called " Tenoroon Trumpet." Its tone is weaker—though only slightly so—than the Unison Trumpet, to which it of course sounds the octave below.

639. *Double Bassoon. Contra Fagotto.* Also a Manual 16-feet Reed stop, but of smaller scale and softer tone than the Double Trumpet. Specimens occur in the Swells at the Temple Church, and at All Saints', Northampton.

640. *Double Hautboy.* Another 16-feet Manual Reed stop, of small scale. An example occurs in the Swell of the organ in Cranbrook Church, Kent.

641. *Trumpet.* An 8-feet Reed stop, both on the Manual and the Pedal. Its tone is clear and penetrating, somewhat resembling that of the well-known wind instrument after which it is named. The Tubes of the Trumpet-pipes are usually made either of tin or metal, though occasionally they are of zinc or wood.

642. *Horn.* An 8-feet Manual Reed stop, formed of tin or metal pipes of much larger scale than those of the Trumpet. The tone of the Horn stop is fuller and smoother than that of the Trumpet, and without the clang peculiar and necessary to that stop. A Horn stop forms part of the original work of the organ in Christ Church, Spitalfields, made by Bridge, who appears to have been its inventor.

643. *Cornopean.* Also a Manual Reed stop of 8-feet, consisting of a set of tin or metal pipes of nearly the same scale as the Horn, but of a different style of voicing. Its tone is more sonorous than the Trumpet ; and smoother, though scarcely so powerful, as that of the Horn.

644. *Trombone. Posaune.* A very powerful and full-toned Reed stop, of 8 feet on the Manual, and 16 or 32 feet on the Pedal. Its pipes are made to a very large scale, and of tin, metal, or wood—of tin or metal for the Manual ; and of metal, zinc, or wood mostly, for the Pedal.

645. There are 32-feet *Contra* Posaunes in churches at Hamburg and Copen-hagen, and of tin. Those at Birmingham and York are of wood. Specimens of metal are to be found in the parish churches at Leeds and Doncaster. A 16-feet Pedal Posaune of metal occurs in the organ at Exeter Hall, built by Mr. Walker ; and one of zinc at the New Church, Cheetham Hill, near Manchester, built by Mr. Hill. Wooden ones are of common occurrence throughout the country.

646. *Ophicleide. Tuba Mirabilis.* The most powerful 8-feet Manual Reed stop known. The majestic effect produced by this stop arises partly from its scale, but more particularly from the great strength of the wind that gives it utterance—three or four times that of the ordinary organ-wind. The stop is usually placed on a sound-board of its own with a separate bellows, &c., &c.

647. The Ophicleide was first introduced by Mr. Hill into the large organ in the Birmingham Town Hall.

648. *Hautboy*. An 8-feet Manual stop, formed of metal pipes. The tone of the stop is thin, penetrating, and of a wailing character, like that of the instrument of the same name, the sound of which it, of course, is intended to imitate.

649. *Bassoon, Fagotto*. This is a soft and slightly nasal-toned Reed stop, of 8 feet on the Manual, and 16 on the Pedal. Its tubes are made either of metal or of wood. In old organs the Bassoon is generally a whole stop, as at Christ Church, Spitalfields; St. Michael's, Cornhill; &c. In modern instruments it is more frequently an incomplete one, sometimes consisting of a single octave of pipes only, acting on the Great octave of Manual keys, and therefore, as an imitative stop, comparatively useless.

650. *Clarionet, Cormorne, Cromorne*, or *Krumm-horn, Cremona, Corno di Bassetto*. This is another agreeable Reed stop, of soft intonation, of 8-feet size of tone. It possesses great sweetness and beauty of tone ; and, when finished by the hand of a master, is a close imitation of the orchestral Clarionet, invented at the commencement of the last century, by Denner, of Nuremberg. This stop is met with under a great variety of names. The word Cormorne, from which Cromorne is derived, signifies a soft-toned Horn. The name Krumm-horn is compounded of the adjective krumm—*i.e.*, crooked—and horn ; and signifies a Cornet or small Shawm of irregular form. These names have, in England, been corrupted into "Cremona ;" and as the stop has, in the majority of modern examples, also been reduced from its former full manual compass to one of *fiddle* g range, the idea is thus in two ways conveyed that it is a *Violin* stop ; whereas the last-mentioned (*Geigen-Principal*) is a flue and not a reed stop, as already explained.* As the stop in question is estimated in proportion as its tone approximates that of a Clarionet, and as all organ-builders alike strive to make it imitate that instrument, "Clarionet" is obviously a better name to apply to it than "Cremona," that is, when it is of Clarionet compass, namely, to tenor c sharp, or to c natural.

651. A Clarionet of deeper pitch, *i.e.*, descending to FF, composed of a longer tube, bent towards the middle, and forming an obtuse angle—is known in England as the *Corno di Bassetto*, and in Germany as the *Krumm-horn* (crooked-horn). The appropriateness of this name for a Clarionet stop of similarly extended compass is therefore obvious. Fine examples of this stop occur in the organs of the Temple Church and at St. Mary-at-Hill. A *Bass Clarionet*, having a compass down to CC, or even BB flat, has recently been introduced.

652. *Corno-flute*. The name given to a Manual Reed stop of 8 feet, having wooden tubes, and producing a soft and agreeable quality of tone. As it is a reed stop, it is not easy to say why it is named as belonging to the flute work.

653. *Vox Humana*. This stop is intended to represent the human voice which it often does, but very faintly. It is of 8-feet tone, and generally extends throughout the entire compass of the Choir or Swell organ. Its tubes are very short, like those of the Clarionet, but broader.

654. *Clarion*. A 4-feet Reed stop, both on the Manual and Pedal, formed of pipes of tin or metal. The tone of this stop is sharp and clear, giving great brilliance to the Full organ. The upper octave of this stop is, on the Manual,

---

* The "names and descriptions of several instruments instruct us as to the nature and design of many stops in the organ, and what they are intended to imitate. To instance, in the Krumm-horn ; the tone of it originally resembled that of a small Cornet, though many organ-makers have corrupted the word into Cremona, supposing it to be an imitation of the Cremona Violin."—Hawkins's *History of Music*, vol. ii., page 245, note.

generally composed of open flue pipes, because reed pipes above F³ in alt seldom remain long in tune. The Clarion at Doncaster, however, by Byfield, was carried up to the top in reed pipes. In many French organs the Clarion has trumpet pipes in the upper octave; and this is the case with the two Clarions in the Temple organ.

655. *Octave Hautboy* (*Hautboy Clarion*). This is a 4-feet Reed stop, composed of pipes of the Hautboy species. It is not a common stop; but one of the kind occurred in the old Swell of the organ at St. George's Church, Hanover Square.

656. *Octave Clarion.* This is the smallest Reed stop used in an organ. It is a 2-feet stop, both on the Manual and Pedal. When it occurs as a Manual stop, it usually extends through 2¼ octaves in reed pipes, CC to f¹ above middle c¹ (sounding from middle c¹ to f³ in *alt*), and then carried hence to the top in flue pipes. Sometimes, however, it consists of reed pipes throughout; breaking first into a Clarion, then into a Trumpet.

Table of the Sounds produced by the several leading Manual and Pedal Stops from the low C key.

MANUAL.

PEDAL.

The sound of the 32-feet C is an octave below the first note above written.

CHAPTER XXIV.

THE ORIGIN AND NECESSITY OF FOUNDATION, MUTATION, AND COMPOUND STOPS.

The introduction of stops of various sizes, founded on a pheno-menon in nature. 657. THE preceding chapter presents a list of all the different organ stops ordinarily found in English organs, with their sizes and other particulars annexed. The lengths of these are not only very diversified, as will already have been perceived ; but the sound of some might, at first, be imagined to be so opposed to that of others, as to be quite irreconcilable with them for any *musical* pur-

pose. For example, if the 3-part chord of c be struck with the

Open Diapason drawn, the true sounds will be heard ; but if the Twelfth be

substituted, the chord of g¹ major will be sounded ; or, if the

Tierce be drawn, then the chord of e² major So that, in fact,

we find the following apparently opposed sounds, namely, c, e, g—g¹, b¹, d²—e², g² sharp, b²—concentrated on the same three keys.

658. Some organs have no separate Tierce wherewith the last example can be illustrated ; in which case some Compound stop, containing a Tierce, may be drawn for the purpose, if the organ contain one, by which substitution the disso-nance will appear to be still more egregious.

659. Now, it would seem that no agreeable effect could possibly be obtained from the union of sounds so hostile ; but, so far from this being the case, not only are most of these sounds capable of the most satisfactory reconciliation, but their presence is positively indispensable to the production of true organ tone. The fact of their sounding so disagreeably, when tried as above suggested, arises from the peculiar manner of using them, which is *not* in accordance with the generally received method. The object, however, was simply to show that such combinations of sounds *exist* in organs : it has now to be explained *how* it is they are found there, and *why* it is they sound so well there, when well balanced and properly tuned.

660. If, when all is perfectly still, one of the bass strings of a pianoforte, or the fourth string of a violoncello, be set in vibration, other and higher sounds will be heard to accompany the fundamental sound or *ground tone*.

661. A deep-toned string is best to select, in order to obtain a favourable illus-tration of this experiment ; because the higher the fundamental sound is, the quicker will the harmonics follow each other, and consequently the less audible will they be—particularly the higher ones.

662. These concomitant sounds are what are called the harmonic sounds ;

and they stand, in relation to the principal or ground tone, in the following ratios :—

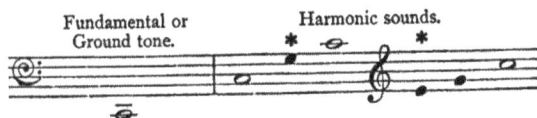

Some of the smaller harmonics, as being of no importance here, are not noted down.

663. On examining the above notation, representing the series of harmonic sounds, it will be discovered that the sounds which at first appeared to be so much out of place (distinguished above by asterisks) correspond exactly with two of those suggested by Nature. In fact, they, and indeed the sounds of all the smaller Foundation, Mutation, and Compound stops, are introduced to *corroborate* Nature's dictates, and to reduce into the form of actual sounds what she indicates in the shape of *harmonic* sounds.

664. Nor are these harmonic corroborating stops voiced so as to sound as weakly as the harmonic sounds themselves ; yet they blend so well with the other stops in all good organs, that together they produce the effect but of one full, brilliant, and magnificent whole.

665. This unity of effect and due subordination of the Mutation stops are secured partly by the greater number and power of the Foundation stops ; partly by the weaker intonation of the Mutation ranks ; partly by the restricted and correct method of using them ; and partly by their being of the proper relative sizes.

How the sizes of the harmonic - corroborating are deduced and fixed.   666. We have now to ascertain what those rightly decreasing sizes are, and to what stops those sizes direct us, as being necessary to represent the harmonic series of sounds.

The former point may be the most easily illustrated by a reference to the measurement of a string, and the extent to which its vibrating portion must be successively lessened, to reduce those harmonic sounds into a series of natural sounds.

667. A string of a certain length, thickness, and tension will produce a given sound. To make that string produce the *octave* of its full-length sound (corroborating the first acoustic sound), the vibrating portion must be shortened to *one-half*. To produce the fifth of that octave, or the *twelfth* of the original sound (the second acoustic sound), it must be reduced to one-third ; to one-fourth, to obtain the second octave of the full-length sound ; to one-fifth, to produce the seventeenth ; to one-sixth, for the nineteenth ; and to one-eighth of the original length to produce the twenty-second, or third octave of the original sound.

668. According to this scale the fixed length of the harmonic series of stops should be $\frac{1}{2}$, $\frac{1}{3}$, $\frac{1}{4}$, $\frac{1}{5}$, $\frac{1}{6}$, and $\frac{1}{8}$ the length of the chief Foundation or Ground stop, whatever that may be. That is to say, if an 8-feet Manual Open Diapason be taken as the basis of the organ tone, the smaller stops should measure in length 4 feet ($\frac{1}{2}$), $2\frac{2}{3}$ feet ($\frac{1}{3}$), 2 feet ($\frac{1}{4}$), $1\frac{3}{5}$ foot ($\frac{1}{5}$), $1\frac{1}{3}$ foot ($\frac{1}{6}$), and 1 foot ($\frac{1}{8}$).

669. Or if a 16-feet stop be taken for the Foundation, as would be the case for the Pedal, the length of the harmonic series would be 8 feet ($\frac{1}{2}$) $5\frac{2}{3}$ feet ($\frac{1}{3}$), 4 feet ($\frac{1}{4}$), $3\frac{1}{5}$ feet ($\frac{1}{5}$), $2\frac{2}{3}$ feet ($\frac{1}{6}$), and 2 feet ($\frac{1}{8}$).

670. And such we find to be the case ; for, on comparing the first of the above codes of " lengths " with those given in the list of stops in the last chapter, they

are found to single out the identical stops from the great number which are so constantly found in all organs. This fact is still more clearly illustrated in the following example :—

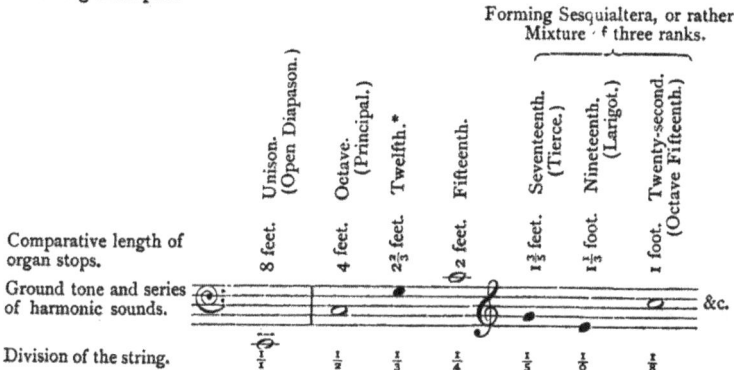

Forming Sesquialtera, or rather Mixture · f three ranks.

	Unison. (Open Diapason.)	Octave. (Principal.)	Twelfth. *	Fifteenth.	Seventeenth. (Tierce.)	Nineteenth. (Larigot.)	Twenty-second. (Octave Fifteenth.)
Comparative length of organ stops.	8 feet.	4 feet.	$2\frac{2}{3}$ feet.	2 feet.	$1\frac{3}{5}$ feet.	$1\frac{1}{3}$ foot.	1 foot.
Ground tone and series of harmonic sounds.								&c.
Division of the string.	$\frac{1}{1}$	$\frac{1}{2}$	$\frac{1}{3}$	$\frac{1}{4}$	$\frac{1}{5}$	$\frac{1}{6}$	$\frac{1}{8}$

671. In the above table the notes represent the harmonic series of sounds, the figures beneath show the extent to which a string must be shortened to produce those sounds, the figures above show the precisely corresponding reduction that is made to transfer the series from a string to columns of air within pipes ; and the names over all are those of the organ stops to which the lengths have directed us.

Reasons for marking the length of the stops on the knobs.   672. We are thus made sensible of the advantage and importance of having the *length* of the stops placed on all the draw-stop knobs, *in addition* to the *names* of the stops. Their names are *variable*, and may be *familiar*, or *not;* but their lengths, or size of tone, are *fixed*, and therefore give an unerring clue to their *pitch*, when the names may, perhaps, be wholly unintelligible. It is now also obvious why the Fifth-sounding stops should not be marked as being of "6 feet" and "3 feet," those figures placing the length of those stops beyond their deducible admeasurement. These lengths would imply that the ground-tones were 9 feet and 18 feet respectively, which any organ-builder's apprentice boy ought to know must be wrong.

Theoretical exceptions sometimes taken to certain organ stops.   673. It should not be omitted to be noticed that some theorists take exception to some of the harmonic corroborating stops ; some objecting to the Tierce because of its sounding the *major* third to the key struck, which it is thought must be offensive in a *minor* key ; others to the Twelfth, on the ground that it causes all musical progressional passages to be played in *consecutive fifths;* and others, again, to the Double Diapason downwards, and the Principal and smaller Foundation ranks upwards, as they play in *consecutive octaves* to the Diapasons. According to the laws of musical composition, all such progressions, in strict writing, are forbidden, and all the above objections are equally strong and entitled to attention.

674. The rules of musical composition, however, are not the tests by which the admissibility of organ stops can be truly judged. An organ never sounds so well as when it contains most of these "theoretically" objectionable stops. This fact may be soon evidenced on an organ that contains them ; though it will be necessary

to proceed inversely.   It may be ascertained thus : first draw all the open flute work ; if the Twelfth—the " consecutive fifth " stop—be shut in, there is then nothing to break the bare octave work from the Diapason, till you come to the Mutation ranks of the Compound stops, and the tone consequently loses some of its roundness—becomes top and bottom.   Close the Mutation ranks of the Compound stops, and the tone becomes more thin and cutting, because the sounds designed to fill up some of the intervals between the Foundation ranks, to bind the whole together, are silenced.   Next shut in all the " consecutive octave " stops upwards, and the tone will be deprived of all brightness ; and lastly, put in the Double Diapason—the stop which sounds in unison with the adult male voices in the melody of a chorale—and the manual will lose its greatest gravity.   Nothing but the Open Diapason will be left ; the organ will be theorised down from a magnificent instrument to certainly a solemn, but, at the same time, dull and monotonous single set of pipes.

675. The laws of musical *progression* and the phenomenon of harmonic *attendant* sounds are, in reality, two very distinct subjects.   As an illustration of this, it is only necessary to play on a full organ, with the Mutation and Compound stops drawn, first a series of single notes, and then the same succession in fifths, when the difference between harmonic *attendant* sounds and harmonic *progressional* sounds must at once become apparent.

CHAPTER XXV.

PARTICULARS CONCERNING THE SCALE AND THE BALANCING OF ORGAN STOPS.

The comparative scale of the Foundation and Mutation stops, and ranks of pipes. 676. IT was stated in the preceding chapter that the sounds of all the Mutation stops and ranks of pipes are kept in a certain degree of subordination; and various means were mentioned by which this end is attained. In German organs, where the 8 and 4 feet flue stops are generally more numerous than in English instruments, to their great improvement, and where double stops are such common as well as excellent features, the Mutation stops are made to as large a scale as the Foundation; the predominance of the latter being secured by their great number. Great breadth, as well as fulness of tone, is obtained by these means.

677. The old English builders made very little ·· :ation in the scale of the different stops, but kept to nearly the same measure through them all. This accounts for the remarkably full as well as brilliant tone of the *Chorus-work* of the best of their organs. This ringing, cheerful quality, however, is by no means a general, or even common, characteristic of old organs. In some cases the scale of the small pipes was either too large, according to modern views, or the pipes were not sufficiently blown; consequently, the tone of the small stops and Mixtures became dull and thick, or, as it is technically called, "horny." On the other hand, when the scales run too small, the tone indeed becomes bright, but without sufficient fulness; "keen and sharp," as the Germans have it.

678. Father Smith made his Principal, Twelfth, and Fifteenth *one* pipe smaller than his Open Diapason; and the several ranks of his Mixtures *two* pipes smaller; so that the Twelfth was of the same scale as th·· Fifteen ..., and the Tierce as large as the octave Fifteenth. By the requisite voicing, the ..one of the Mutation stops and ranks was rendered smooth and mellow, and th:.t of the Foundation ranks full and bold; the effect of the whole being exceedingly firm and clear, although occasionally lacking sufficient body, firmness, and depth of tone, consequent on the smallness of the number of unison and octave stops, and the entire absence of double Manual stops. As this circumstance involves a matter of some moment, where the renovation and enlargement of an old organ is concerned, it may be briefly discussed here.

679. Much pains was taken by the writer, while abroad, to test several Continental organs, with precisely the same stops drawn that are usually found in old English organs, and the experiments were invariably attended with the same effect as that witnessed from some of the best old instruments of this country, namely, the production of a clear and ringing character of sound, but accompanied by rather an over-amount of Mixture tone. It was also observed that, on adding the *remaining* stops, the accurate balance of tone was immediately restored. An indisputable proof was in this manner obtained of the *cause* of the misproportion originally existing in so many English organs, as well as a clear illustration of the most correct way of *remedying* that defect. The "fathers of modern organ-building in England," Harris and Smith, studied their art *abroad*, where it was the custom to produce a fine and well-balanced organ by disposing a certain proportion of

Mixture work to secure clearness, boldness, and vivacity; one or more double stops to impart gravity and dignity; and a good number of 8 and 4 feet stops to give *firmness* and definitiveness to the whole, by blending the various elements in harmonious amalgamation. On arriving in this country they encountered a serious difficulty in being compelled to keep their organs within restricted dimensions Perhaps they were also sometimes straitened in the matter of terms; and they might even have had to contend with a want of appreciation and co-operation on the part of contemporary organists.

680. Being denied the necessary room wherein to complete their Manual organs —even independently of a separate Pedal organ, which was invariably omitted— they had to relinquish some of those stops which would require the *most space* for their accommodation; hence the double stops were generally expunged, and, in some cases, even some of the unison and octave stops also.

681. The due proportion of the three great elements being thus disturbed by the entire omission of one and the weakening of a second, the third then naturally stood out with undue prominence. To give an instance: Dr. Burney, in his *History of Music*, vol. iii., page 440, note, speaking of the St. Paul's Cathedral organ, says: "Notwithstanding the power of the chorus of this admirable instrument, several more excellent stops were made for it, which lay many years useless in the vestry, but for which Sir Christopher Wren, tender of his architectural proportions, would never consent to let the case be sufficiently capacious to receive." In the *English Musical Gazette* for January, 1819, page 6, it is stated what some of those stops were. After mentioning that Sir Christopher Wren "would not consent to let the case be enlarged to receive them," the narrator proceeds to say: "Three of the stops were in consequence obliged to be kept out, viz., a Bassoon, a Clarion, and another stop of minor consequence, which were kept in the Cathedral for several years after, Schmidt hoping he might get them in at some future period; but he died a few years before Sir Christopher Wren." The stop of "minor consequence," as it seems then to have been considered, the late Mr. Bishop imagined to have been a *Double Diapason;* and Mr. Sutton, in his *Short Account of Organs*, page 34, adds: "This conjecture seems highly probable, as there is no doubt that, to contain a Double Diapason in addition, the organ-case would necessarily have to be much enlarged."

682. Again, in the building of the Temple organ, Smith had to confine his work within certain limited dimensions, in order that, if his instrument should be accepted, it might remain within the western arch of the choir; hence it was not only made without doubles, but with one Open Diapason only to support six ranks of Mixture in the bass, and nine in the treble; and the Great and Choir organs had to be crowded on to one sound-board.

683. At St. Paul's, in consequence of the omission of all double stops, one unison, and one octave stop, what then remained as "the organ" was of course thrown out of proportion; and "the power of the chorus," noticed by Dr. Burney, becoming thus excessive, the trebles of the Mixtures were ultimately taken out, and new ones of softer tone introduced. The influence of "large" and "small" stops on the general effect of an organ is a subject concerning which nearly as much misapprehension prevails in England now as in the days of Smith and Harris. Many imagine that, because the introduction of a few double 8 and 4 feet stops will increase the "bulk" of an organ by perhaps one-half, therefore their striking and arresting effect must be in proportion; and that, as the addition of more Mixture would not call for the addition of six inches to the depth of the organ, its introduction would exercise as little appreciable difference to the ear as it would to the eye. These are the *popular* ideas on the subject, whereas the

facts are exactly the contrary. The large stops increase the fulness, roundness, depth, and sonority of the organ, imparting great richness to the general effect; whereas more Mixture may increase the "din" of the organ to such an extent as to be almost intolerable. Dr. Burney appears to have been, to some extent, under the influence of the general misapprehension; for, in the extract already given— "*Notwithstanding* the power of the chorus, *more* excellent stops were made," &c.— he writes as though the effect of the omitted stops would have been to *increase* that "power;" whereas they would certainly have tended to *subdue* it. Sir Henry Dryden, in his pamphlet on *Church Music*, when writing concerning *modern* church organs (pages 28 and 29), says: "Generally the Pedal organs are too weak, the Great organs too noisy, the Choir organs too small, and the Swell organs too short in compass. We have a great deal too many Mixtures and such like cheap stops, and too few of large and expensive open metal pipes. It is difficult to have too much bass to an organ. No sound below a voice will drown it. The Pedal pipes at Westminster Abbey will not drown the weakest boy's voice. Mixtures and Sesquialteras drown voices." It is manifest from this how permanently injurious it must be to limit the space for an organ to such an extent that the organ-builder cannot introduce all the stops necessary to produce a well-balanced instrument.

684. The stops that have a tendency, from their brightness, to interfere with the just predominance of the voices, always find ready admission; while those that are necessary for sustaining and supporting the voices are almost as invariably limited in number and efficiency.

685. The Mixtures in Father Smith's organs were, from the causes already explained, so uniformly made to appear "too shrill," or "too screaming," that, in the great majority of instances, they have since been melted down and replaced by others of weaker intonation. Many of Harris's organs also have been brought into proportion by a like process. Another way of obtaining this end would have been to *add* stops similar in pitch to those which the original builders had, from the good influence of early education, learnt to consider as necessary, and which the experience of more recent times has proved to be indispensable, but which they were, from the first, compelled to relinquish, and to the omission of which the original misproportion was to be ascribed. This would not only have *restored* the balance of tone, but would have *raised* those instruments towards the state of completeness and efficiency contemplated by their respective makers, and upon an acoustic principle with which they were perfectly familiar; for it is important to bear in mind that most of the large organs constructed in England during the last ten years, with double Manual stops and an independent Pedal organ, are, in reality, only on an equality in these respects with many of the instruments which Smith and Harris left behind them in their native countries upwards of a century and a half ago, and with some of which they could not fail to have been well acquainted.

686. Organs having double stops on the Manual and a 16-feet Pedal were of most common occurrence in France, Holland, and German, not only in the seventeenth century, but even in the *sixteenth*. For instance, those at Freiburg, in Bresgau, built in 1520, contained 24 stops; at Amsterdam, *enlarged* in 1673, 44 stops; at Rouen, 1630, 49 stops; at Amiens Cathedral, built as long ago as 1429, and yet with a 16-feet front; and at Antwerp, 1645 and 1670 (see Foreign Specifications);—all those just mentioned, among a number of others, included the above-mentioned features among their original constituent parts; the Pedal organs comprising from 4 to 10 stops—a proportion that is considered liberal, even in the nineteenth century, in England.

687. There were even some 32-feet organs also existing in Germany as far

back as the sixteenth century. At St. Mary's Church, Lübeck, an organ was erected in the year 1517, with a 32-feet front of polished tin; and at St. Peter's Church, Hamburg (since destroyed), was a 32-feet organ, erected before the year 1548. The several foregoing facts and dates are important, and necessary to be introduced here, as being calculated to allay the groundless fear occasionally expressed that the present race of English organ-builders are getting their instruments "too large;" whereas, in reality, they are only introducing certain stops requiring much space, that are necessary to produce a full and well-balanced tone. The organs of Harris and Smith were originally little more than "8-feet organs," destitute of Pedal; the "Great organ" departments being, in most cases, scarcely so complete as the "Echo" or "Choir" of many old Continental organs, as may be ascertained by comparing the original specifications of their instruments with those of the last-named parts of foreign organs, described at the end of this work. Modern builders, in striving to raise the standard of English organs above that to which the excellent makers just named were permitted by circumstances to work, are really doing no more than placing their instruments, in regard to number and distribution of stops, *on a par* with those made nearly *two centuries since* abroad— of course, introducing such beneficial alterations into the list of stops as modern science has placed at command, and also incorporating numerous improvements in the mechanism that were not even so much as dreamt of at the former period; —and it seems needless to treat this attempt to place the nineteenth century English organ at least on an equality with the seventeenth century foreign organ as an alarming advance or as a hazardous enlargement.

688. As bearing upon the subject of the great improvement to be effected by the judicious development of a really good old organ, an extract may be made from the late Mr. Edward Holmes's entertaining volume, entitled *A Ramble among the Musicians of Germany*, of which the author, after mentioning Silbermann, "one of the most renowned builders of Germany, and whose name (Silvermann) very well describes the quality of his tone," proceeds to say, in a foot note, page 193: "As a matter of science, it is worthy consideration how far the structure of our organs might be improved by uniting the sweet *cathedral* quality of tone, for which those of the Temple, Westminster Abbey, &c., are noted, with the magnificence of Silbermann." Had Harris and Smith worked unfettered, there is little doubt but the two attributes above specified would always have been found combined in as eminent a degree in their organs as in those of the great Strasburg builder. In the absence, however, of this, and in proceeding to renovate organs of their make, the choice lies between "wedging up," "papering up," or "melting down" the original Mixtures, supplying their place by others of softer tone, and of *reducing* their comparative strength of tone by *increasing* that of the 8 and 4 feet tone, by adding to the number of stops producing those pitches, and by also engrafting one or more double stops. The former course has the charm of economy to recommend it, although it involves a greater departure than ever from the calculation of the original builder, while the latter and more expensive process effects a nearer approach to it.

689. In some of the organs built soon after Smith and Harris's time a better balance of Manual tone was attempted, by giving the small stops less wind at the foot; but, the former large scale being at the same time also retained, the result was the production of an indistinct, dull, horny quality of tone, as already mentioned.

690. The organs of John Schreider, Smith's son-in-law, are distinguished from those of Smith by having the Diapasons voiced stronger in the treble. The extent to which his organs were susceptible of improvement by the introduction

of double stops, &c., has been satisfactorily evidenced in the enlargement of his fine instrument in Westminster Abbey, the additions to which were made by Hill.

691. Renatus Harris's organ at St. Sepulchre's, Snow Hill, has also been considerably improved, by additions made by Gray and Davison, and would, by the introduction of Double Manual stops to the Great organ, be rendered quite magnificent.

692. The younger Harris (John) made the Tierce in his organs of the same scale as the Principal, Twelfth, and Fifteenth, *i.e.*, one pipe smaller than the Diapason, and the Mixtures two pipes smaller.

693. In conjunction with his partner, Byfield, he increased the strength of the 8 and 4 feet sound by the more frequent introduction of a second Open Diapason and of a Trumpet and Clarion of great power and beauty of tone. In the organ at St. George's, Doncaster, erected in 1738, those builders introduced *two* Trumpets. The Mixtures of Harris and Byfield were usually carried up higher in the musical scale without a break than were those of Smith; hence a greater amount of brilliancy, though with scarcely so much boldness, from the omission of the duplicate ranks for which the higher ones were substituted. It may be mentioned that the firmness is imparted by the number or strength of tone of the 8 and 4 feet stops; while the boldness, brilliancy, or keenness, depends a great deal on the composition, scale, and winding of the Mixtures. The younger Harris's Compound stops were wonderfully animated and ringing, which properties seemed to indicate that their maker included Double Manual stops in his conception of what a complete organ should be; and this opinion was afterwards confirmed at Doncaster, when such stops were added, by the increased beauty which they imparted to the tone of that originally fine organ. The organ built in 1740, by the same Byfield, in conjunction with his *other* partners, Jordan and Bridge, for the church at Great Yarmouth, actually had, according to Dr. Burney's account, printed in Ree's *Cyclopædia*, under the article " Organ," a *Double Diapason;* also two Open Diapasons, two Trumpets and Clarion, and nine ranks of Mixture.

694. Both Schwarbrook and Snetzler (Germans) succeeded in also incorporating a Bordun as a part of their organs at St. Michael's, Coventry, 1733, and Lynn Regis, 1754. In reference to that in the last-named organ, Dr. Burney *(History,* vol. iii., page 438, note) says : " One of the metal stops of this instrument, called the *Bordun*, is an octave below the Open Diapason, and has the effect of a double bass in the chorus." The double stops have since disappeared from the Yarmouth and Lynn organs ; and, as stops of that nature were but very rarely introduced into other instruments, these circumstances clearly indicate that even at so recent a period as a century since the prevailing taste, or prejudice, or both, of English organists, continued to run counter to the attempted advances of the most eminent builders towards the production of a complete and well-balanced organ. It would be interesting to ascertain, if it were possible to do so, whether the trifling and irreverent notions concerning organ-playing in church, so much in vogue throughout the last century, were so at the time of Smith and Harris's arrival in this country ; and, consequently, whether the incapacity to appreciate, and therefore to advocate, the broad and dignified instruments which those builders were prepared to construct, was to be attributed to the then prevailing musical taste ; or whether the frivolous and tasteless manner in question of using the organ was the *consequence* of their usually being composed chiefly of "little" stops, as some of the Germans have expressed themselves, somewhat contemptuously, when speaking of our old organs. One thing is at any rate certain : that the organs were not calculated to *encourage* the conception of elevated musical ideas ; nor, if they arose, independ-

ently of external assistance, were they capable of *realising* them ;* hence the production of so much music, specially written for such instruments, that now reflects nought but discredit upon the contemporary musical taste of this country. Dr. Crotch, in his *Elements*, page 89, felt it necessary, in addition to directing the taste of students, also to state what they should avoid. " Organ voluntaries," he says, "should consist of fugues, with introductions for the full organ, upon the model of Sebastian Bach and Handel. Soft movements for the Diapason and Swell should be slow and sweet, or mournful and pathetic, and may be in the Italian style of the seventeenth century. *English voluntaries* for the Trumpet, Echo, Vox Humana, Cornet, Oboe, and other solo stops, are too often vulgar, trifling, and ridiculous ; being equally void of science, taste, and that decorous gravity of style which should ever characterise church music." It is an important fact that in Germany, where Double Manual stops have been common for centuries, the vicious style of organ music above referred to *never existed*, so far as we are aware ; whereas, in England, it never *ceased to exist*, until an appreciation for that class of stops, and for firmer "medium work," began to spread itself, that is, within the present century.

695. George England made his Principal one pipe smaller than his Open Diapason, his Fifteenth two pipes narrower, and every rank of his Mixtures to a varied scale.

696. In a Compound stop of 4 ranks, comprising seventeenth, nineteenth, twenty-second, and twenty-sixth, he would make the seventeenth a small scale, the nineteenth rather larger, the twenty-second large scale and powerfi ..y voiced, and the twenty-sixth small again, and voiced almost as a Dulciana. This last rank, nevertheless, made itself heard, and gave to the Mixture a sound as ot bells. England's Mixtures were of a very silvery and sparkling quality, though not so bold as Smith's, nor so full as Harris's, on account of their different composition and smaller scale. His larger organs commonly had the advantage of four 8-feet stops and three 4-feet stops, which, in conjunction with the lighter Mixtures, presented a twofold modification greatly in favour of a well-balanced tone ; though, from the greater comparative firmness thus imparted to the medium work, they are generally quite capable of "carrying" a 16-feet stop of light intonation.

697. Green's scales were, in some respects, larger than those of any of the preceding ; that is to say, he made his seventeenth and nineteenth *one* scale smaller only than the Diapason, and the twenty-second alone *two* scales less. The Open Diapason itself was made one pipe smaller in the treble than Father Smith's scale, but several pipes larger in the bass ; and was generally of remarkable excellence, the treble part being very pure in quality, though not very loud, and the bass full and ponderous. His Mixtures varied but slightly in their composition from those of Smith ; while, in the voicing, Green's pipes were closely and finely nicked, and not cut up much, and with comparatively but little wind passing in at the foot ; hence his soft, rich, and pleasant tone, which, however, generally lacked the boldness and energy of the organs of Harris and Smith.

698. The system of scaling frequently followed in modern times is as follows. To speak first of the Foundation stops : the Open Diapason is made to the largest scale, because, being the *chief* Foundation stop, it is essential that its sound should predominate. The Principal is made one scale smaller than the Open Diapason ;

---

* Those who, like the writer, heard Mendelssohn extemporise, in 4 or 5 pure parts, on an essentially *English* organ, will remember how destitute of breadth and dignity was the effect which emanated from what present organ-builders call the "thin-toned old organ."

the Fifteenth one scale less than the Principal—and so on, each successive Foundation rank rather smaller than its predecessor. Thus, the 2-feet pipe of the Principal, speaking on the Tenor c key, is made of the same diameter as Middle c¹ *sharp* pipe of the Open Diapason ; and the 2-feet pipe of the Fifteenth, speaking on the CC key, the same width as the Middle d¹ pipe of the Open Diapason.

699. Each Foundation stop, however, commencing from the Open Diapason upwards, is voiced rather brighter, as may be ascertained by first drawing the Open Diapason and striking the Middle c¹ key, when a full and sonorous sound will be heard. Change the Open Diapason for the Principal, and press down the Tenor c key ; the sound, identical with the first one in pitch, will be rather louder, but less full. Substitute the Fifteenth for the Principal, and strike the CC key, which will reiterate the same pitch, and the sound will be yet brighter, though there will be less again of it.

700. The Twelfth is much varied in scale, according to circumstances. If there be but few ranks of Mixture, the Twelfth is made only of the same diameter as the Fifteenth, although its pitch is a fourth lower, and its pipes consequently more than one-fourth longer. At other times it is made of the same scale as the Fifteenth.

701. The Third-sounding stops are made to a still smaller scale, as their sound has to be more subdued even than that of the Fifth-sounding stops.

702. The Foundation stops, then, are the largest scaled and the loudest ; the Fifth-sounding stops the next ; and the Third-sounding the smallest and the softest in tone of all in much modern work.

703. Towards the commencement of the present century the usual method of balancing the stops was much disturbed by the influence of certain theoretical organists of the time, who would have the Compound stops voiced so as to sound nearly as weakly as the acoustic sounds they were introduced to corroborate. At the present time those organ-builders enjoy the highest reputation in England whose instruments are voiced the most directly *at variance* with these theoretical notions.

704. Organ-builders are frequently heard to speak of an Open Diapason being made to a 12, 13, 14, or 15 inch scale, as the case may be. These figures refer to the width of the sheet of metal out of which the gamut G pipe is made, and which pipe, therefore, when finished, ordinarily measures from nearly 4 to about 5 inches in diameter.

705. According to the scale of the Open Diapason, those of the harmonic series of stops are of course regulated.

The increase of scale in a stop as the pipes become shorter ; and why necessary.

706. It was shown in Chap. XX., *ante* pp. 123, 124, and 125, that a pipe which sounds the octave above another of the same kind is only half the length of the first one. Thus, in a Manual Open Diapason, the CC pipe of which is 8 feet in length, the Tenor c is but 4 feet ; the Middle c¹, 2 feet ; the Treble c², 1 foot ; and the c³ in alt, 6 inches. The *diameter* of these several pipes might, at first thought, be imagined to decrease in proportion to the reduction in their *length*. This, however, is not really the case. As the pipes gradually become shorter, they are made *rather wider* in proportion. As an illustration of this, suppose the 8-feet pipe of an Open Diapason to be 6 inches in diameter ; the 4-feet pipe will not be simply 3 inches, but about 3½ inches in width ; the 2-feet, not 1½, but 1⅝ inch in diameter ; the 1-foot, not ¾ of an inch, but 1½ ; and the 6-inch pipe, not ⅜, but ⅞ of an inch in diameter. Thus we find that the diameter of a metal open pipe, as compared with its length, is, in the course of four octaves, sometimes just doubled.

707. A still greater increase is made upwards in the scale of a reed stop. Take, for instance, an 8-feet Posaune. In some examples, the CC pipe, 8 feet, measures 5 inches in diameter; the Tenor c, 4 feet, $4\frac{1}{2}$ inches; the Middle c¹, 2 feet, $3\frac{1}{2}$ inches; Treble c², 1 foot, $2\frac{1}{4}$ inches; and the c³ in alt pipe, 6 inches in length, 2 inches in diameter at the bell.

708. The object for which an increase is made in the scale of organ pipes, whether of the flue or reed species, is to secure, as far as possible, an equality and uniformity in the strength and tone-character of the stop throughout its range, and which could not be otherwise obtained; for the pipes of an Open Diapason would ultimately become smaller than those of a Dulciana, the c³ in alt pipe of which stop measures $\frac{7}{16}$ of an inch, good, in diameter, and those of a Posaune less than those of a Bassoon.

709. It has already been explained that a performer on a wind instrument has to exercise a *greater* effort of the muscles of the lungs, in order to secure the high sounds being of *the same* strength as the low ones. In like manner an organ-builder first *increases* the scale of his stop gradually from the longest pipe up to the shortest, as a preliminary to his obtaining even *the same* amount and kind of tone. He then admits an increased quantity of wind in at the foot, for the purpose of blowing from each successive pipe of the series an undiminished strength of tone; an *additional* amount of wind of the same density producing nearly an equal effect to that which the same amount of wind of greater density would do. In some of the modern French organs, and also in the organ at St. Paul's, built by Mr. Willis, and that in the Town Hall, Glasgow, built by Mr. Davison, the treble portion of the stops is supplied with a wind much heavier than the bass part, which brings the method of producing high sounds from organ stops and from wind instruments into closer analogy.

710. Many of the German builders have for a long series of years obtained a similar result, either by introducing two pipes to each key in the treble, as in Müller's celebrated organ at Haarlem, finished in 1738 (see Foreign Specifications, No. 1); and in Batz's organ, at Utrecht, erected in 1826; or by putting larger pipes in the treble of their Compound stops than is usual in England. The latter plan, which is one of great utility, will be more fully explained in a following chapter.

A variation is made in the scale of the stops of the same name on the different claviers, and also in the duplicates on the same clavier. The reason and necessity thereof. 711. The stops belonging to each separate division of an organ are made to a different scale to what the corresponding stops are on the other departments; that is to say, the Open Diapason in the Swell is made to a somewhat less diameter than the like stop in the Great organ, and that of the Choir organ smaller again, which variation of scale in the fundamental stop or "Diapason" of each clavier leads, as a matter of course, to a corresponding variation in that of the harmonic series of stops of each department.

712. One of the main objects in this variation of scale is to secure to each department the requisite distinctness of character and proportionate strength of tone. Thus a large scale is adopted for the Great organ, the tone of which is required to be full, broad, and strong; a somewhat smaller scale for the Swell, which combines in its sound much of the dignified character of the Great organ tone, united with the sprightly tone of the Choir; the smallest for the Choir organ, the sound of which is lighter than that of the other Manual organs, yet full of life and vivacity; and the largest for the Pedal, which should possess weight, depth, and fulness.

713. The way in which a variation of scale is effected is by taking the diameter of, say, the CC sharp pipe of the first stop as the scale for the CC pipe of the second stop, and by following out the same relative and reduced measure throughout the series of pipes.

714. For another scale, the width of the original DD pipe would be taken for the CC pipe.

715. Where two stops of one kind are placed on the same Manual, as, for instance, two Open Diapasons, or two Principals, the second is usually made to a different scale from the first ; and not only so, but to a scale varying, however slightly, from that of the similar stop on all the other Manuals. One reason for this is, if two stops are made to the same scale, and voiced alike, they are very likely to "sympathise."

716. When two pipes sympathise, a beating or waving is heard when they are sounded together, although they are perfectly in tune when tried separately, and do not "rob." Sometimes the two pipes together will even sound weaker than either when used separately.

717. Varying the scale is one of the means taken for preventing sympathy ; not indeed that this step is *indispensable* to that end, since some organs exist having two Open Diapasons in the treble, of *the same* scale, which *do not* sympathise ; while in other examples, having two Open Diapasons of *different* scale, a tremulousness *does* appear. It is, nevertheless, one of the most advisable as well as most usual methods adopted to prevent it. A "beating" between two pipes made to *different* scales will arise from their being placed too near to each other on the sound board.

718. In that case the defect does not arise from "sympathy," but *proximity*. To prevent any waving occurring from this second cause, it is essential that the two stops should be placed at some distance apart, and, if possible, be separated by other stops.

719. An additional reason to that given above for making the corresponding stops of the several claviers to different scales is to avoid, as far as possible, any beating occurring when any of, or all, the departments of the organ are coupled together.

720. Again, the repetition ranks in the Compound stops of a department, *i.e.*, the duplicate ranks which are introduced where the "breaks" occur, and which appear in greater or less abundance in all Mixture stops, as already explained, are sometimes made to diversified scales in England, with the view to preventing any tremulousness appearing among them.

721. For this reason, also, the duplicates in the Compound stops—that is, the repetition of certain ranks of pipes which always occur in greater or less abundance where there are many ranks of mixture, particularly in the treble part of the stops—are generally made to diversified scales, otherwise a beating or waving is likely to arise from the phenomenon just noticed.

722. Father Smith not only used to vary the scale slightly, but also to make the feet of the duplicate ranks to a different length, so that the pipes might speak on a different level to the others. Green and England also varied the length of their pipe-feet for a similar purpose.

CHAPTER XXVI.

THE TUNING AND TEMPERAMENT OF THE ORGAN.*

723. FROM very early times the interval of the perfect octave has, by philosophers and musicians, been divided into 53 equal parts, called *commas;* and the successive sounds of the diatonic scale have, by the aid of these commas, been shown to be separated by intervals of the following "sizes" or comparative dimensions:—

	Major tone.		Minor tone.		Semitone.		Major tone.		Minor tone.		Major tone.		Semitone.	
I.		II.		III.		IV.		V.		VI.		VII.		VIII.
C	9	D	8	E	5	F	9	G	8	A	9	B	5	C
o		9		17		22		31		39		48		53

724. The foregoing are the sizes of the several intervals as deduced from Nature's suggestions; and it is quite probable that the organ was, at a very early period, tuned in recognition of this system of "perfect attunement." The extremely simple nature of the early church music; the non-existence of harmony; and the peculiar construction of the ancient *octo-chords* or *modes*—produced by taking, in succession, each different sound of the old diatonic gamut as the initial note, and proceeding thence to its octave, thus—

```
G  f  e  d  c  b  a  g
   F  e  d  c  b  a  g  f
      E  d  c  b  a  g  f  e
         D  c  b  a  g  f  e  d
            C  ♮  a  g  f  e  d  c
               B  a  g  f  e  d  c  b
                  A  g  f  e  d  c  b  a
```

did not call for or suggest any departure from it; and an organ having scarcely two octaves of perfectly attuned diatonic sounds must have been equal to all the musical requirements of the time.

725. But when the idea occurred of *transposing* some of the ancient chants, to bring them within the compass of a less extended range of voice—the higher into a lower pitch to suit bass voices, and the lower into a higher to suit tenor voices—and the gradual introduction of the five chromatic semitones to facilitate this among other ends;—then the preservation of the primitive method of attunement could no longer have been possible. Take, for an example, the natural major diatonic scale of C. That could not be transposed into G, because the tones between G and A and A and B were each of the wrong "dimension"

---

* Only an outline of what might be said on this subject is given in the present chapter. Its fuller treatment is reserved for separate publication.

for the purpose; nor could D be taken as a key-note, inasmuch as the interval between that sound and E was a *minor* tone only.

I.		II.		III.		IV.		I.		II.
G	8	A	9	B	5	C		D	8	E.

726. Such misuse of the distinctive tones would have produced a "wolf" in all the scales except the primary one, as unequal temperament afterwards did in all the keys beyond A major and B flat major.

The union of perfect attunement with the power of transposition impossible. 727. For a long time the question as to the attuning of the scale, so as satisfactorily to adapt it to the gradually increasing requirements, was, to quote the words of an old writer, "found to be an unmanageable thing." Nor was the division of the octave into a given number of intervals of the *exact dimension* suggested by nature at all practicable. The number *twelve*—that of the semitones in the octave—is divisible into 6 twos, 4 threes, or 3 fours, representing the whole tone, the minor third, and the major third respectively. But 6 major tones, of 9 commas each, would amount to 54 commas; 4 minor thirds, of 14 commas each, to 56 commas; while 3 major thirds, of 17 commas each, would only amount to 52 commas; 53 commas being the number that represented the perfect octave. There would therefore have been an excess, or shortcoming, as the case might be, had the octave been divided according to any of the smaller "exact" intervals.

The susceptibility of certain intervals being tempered discovered. 728. At length it was observed that certain intervals would bear being tuned a little in excess of, or short of, perfect, without offending the ear. This discovery led to the introduction of a system of *tempering*,* in which the thirds and fourths were tuned rather sharp, and the fifths rather flat. The result of this tuning was the *distribution* of the "three commas" by which the major tones exceeded the minor, and a slight augmentation of the minor tones, so that the five tones in the diatonic series were rendered equal in dimension.

Unequal temperament, and the practicable scales it introduced. 729. The first modern who urged the necessity of a temperament was Bartholomew Ramis, a Spaniard, who wrote before the year 1482. By the date just named all the five short keys had been added to the seven different diatonic sounds of the key-board. Of these five three were tuned as the first three sharps, namely, F, C, and G; and two as the first two flats, namely, B and E. The short keys were, further, tuned as pure thirds, or nearly so, to the long keys represented by the black notes in the following example:—

---

* In all instruments having the usual number of keys to the octave the natural inequalities between the tones and semitones are softened down and hidden, as far as possible, by *distribution*; and any sound that is slightly raised or lowered in receiving its small allotted share of the dissonance is said to be "tempered;" while the *principle* on which the dissonance is distributed—whether equally among all the scales, as on the pianoforte and harmonium; or unequally, so as to appear rather less obviously in a few of them, at the sacrifice of all the rest, as on old organs—constitutes the *system* of temperament adopted.

Y

Ex. 6. *Double Chant.* LORD MORNINGTON.

Ex. 7.   *Behold! now praise the Lord.*   ROGERS.

Ex. 8.   *O where shall wisdom.*   BOYCE.

Ex. 9.   *I will love Thee.*   CLARK.

Music written in either of the foregoing ten scales, on being played on an unequally tempered organ, could not fail to produce an effect very offensive to sensitive ears ; and a little investigation would reveal that the main cause of the untunefulness arose from the fact that each of the five short keys was tuned *either* as the *sharp* to the long key to the *left*, or as the *flat* to the long key to the *right;* but in no case so as to serve in the two capacities, thus :—

The unequal tuning left the scale of E flat without a proper fourth (A flat); and the scale of A flat not only had no suitable tonic, by reason of the omission of that same A flat, but it was also without any proper fourth (D flat). The scale of E major had no leading note (D sharp) ; and B had neither a proper third (D sharp) nor a seventh (A sharp—see preceding examples).   And so on with the other scales. The consequence of such tuning may be best shown to English readers by extracts from works well known in England, which are accordingly subjoined ; or it may be *heard* if they be played on an unequally tempered organ.

Ex. 1.   *Single Chant.*   Dupuis.

As written.

As sounded on an unequally tempered Organ.

Ex. 2.   *Single Chant.*   Hayes.

Ex. 3.   *Single Chant.*   BATTISHILL.

Ex. 4.   *Single Chant.*   DR. BLOW.

Ex. 5.   *Double Chant.*   DAVY.

This step was a great one in advance in the cause of *practical* music. It brought into existence, on keyed instruments having thirteen sounds and twelve intervals in the octave, *six* practicable major scales—C, G, D, A, F, and B flat—in place of the one perfect one ; and *three* minor scales, instead of one, viz., A, D, and G.

Bontempi, writing in the seventeenth century, and reviewing the progress that music had made during the two centuries that had elapsed between the era of the establishment of the unequal temperament and his own time, could not refrain from describing that method of tuning as "that sublime and memorable operation which so improved the noble science of counterpoint."

The introduction of unequal temperament strongly opposed, but nevertheless established. 730. The greatest opposition was, nevertheless, offered to the system by the purists of the time ; and an animated controversy ensued, which continued to rage with great violence for more than a century, between the adherents to ancient proportions, on the one hand, and the friends of tempered scales, on the other. The contest, however, ended in favour of practical progress.

731. At first, little more than half the number of the available scales were made use of. Those almost exclusively employed were C, G, D, and F major, A and D minor, and a few of the ancient modes more or less modified. Nor did the music of the fifteenth century present much modulation ; for, in whatever key a piece of music commenced, in that key it remained almost rigorously throughout. For such want of constructive variety and contrast—as it would now be considered—some compensation was, however, afforded by the more nearly accurate intonation of the few progressions of melody and harmony that *were* used ; for us the agreeable relief arising from a change of scale was a resource almost unknown,

the earlier tuning had not been required to be much modified to provide for it. The altered tuning, on the other hand, admitted of greater freedom in writing, of which composers gradually learnt to avail themselves.

732. In this way the remaining practicable scales, namely, A and B flat major,

were, by degrees, taken into requisition ; and, as those two scales employed all the five short keys of the clavier, they necessarily marked the farthest limits as to range of scales established or allowed by the unequal temperament.

The musical art progressing required other scales beyond those provided by unequal temperament.

733. The art of musical composition continued to progress ; and as "form" began to take the place of the rather fragmentary style of writing that had previously and of necessity prevailed, and as the "attendant keys" of the *boundary* scales were first touched, then dwelt upon, the use of other scales was required that had not been provided by the framers of the prevailing temperament, and which had not, in fact, any practicable existence on keyed instruments as then tuned. Some of those were E flat major, A flat major, E major, E minor, B minor, F sharp minor, and F minor.

After a time other scales, again, came to be required, among which were the following :—

Ex. 10.   *By the waters of Babylon.*   BOYCE.

Ex. 11.   *The Father everlasting.*   ROGERS, in D.

Ex. 12.   *Turn Thee unto me.*   BOYCE.

Ex. 13.   *Surely He hath borne our griefs.*   HANDEL.

Ex. 14.   *Surely He hath borne our griefs.*   HANDEL.

740. The great question that had to be solved was not
whether it were possible to make an instrument that, whatever
its merits, could not pass into general use—for that had already been demonstrated
conclusively more than once—but whether it were practicable, *without* increasing
the number of twelve sounds in the octave, so to tune or "temper" those that
they would *practically* meet the then increased and all future possible musical
requirements. It was in Germany, and in the early part of the last century, that
this important theme was first started and discussed ; and the glory of its elucida-
tion in the affirmative was chiefly due to the genius of the great John Sebastian
Bach, who produced and advocated the system of tuning now so generally known
as that of "equal temperament."

741. This wonderful yet simple system consists in dividing
the octave into twelve semitones by fixed sounds, as uniform in dimension to
the *ear* as are the inch marks of the foot-rule to the *eye*. The results of that
tuning are as follows :—Firstly, every one of the twelve different sounds can
be made the key-note from which a well constituted and equally useful *diatonic*
scale can follow ; and which diatonic scale, further, may be either in the
major or the minor form. Thus the *twenty-four* major and minor scales are
at once rendered available, and equally so for melodic or harmonic progressions. Secondly, any one of the twelve different sounds can be taken as the
commencing note of an even and uniform chromatic scale. Thirdly, the
numerous beautiful enharmonic transitions and modulations can be realised in
the manner intended by the great composers who originated them, without the
destructive distinctions which would result if the *altered notation* were accompanied by an *altered intonation* that, despite its theoretical propriety, in practice
is *not* wanted.

742. From what has been said it will be seen that every note is, according to
this system, designed to serve in "different capacities ;" some in several. For
example, the sound representing C may be either a key-note or a natural diatonic
second, third, fourth, &c., or another key-note, or it may be treated as B sharp or
D double flat, or it may be changed, *upon paper*, from C natural to B sharp, as by
an enharmonic change. Every one of the other eleven sounds is designed to serve
in a similar manner. In a word, this wonderfully constituted *compound* scale comprises the twelve major and twelve minor scales and the chromatic and the enharmonic scales *all in one*.

743. Nor did Bach simply "theorise" respecting his scale. His writing, teaching,
and playing were in consonance with his artistic conviction. In the year 1722 he
produced the first book of his well known 48 Preludes and Fugues, under the title
of "The Well-tempered Clavier, or Preludes and Fugues through all the tones and
semitones concerning the major third, or *C, D, E*, as well as touching the minor
third, or *D, E, F*. For the use and study of young eager musical students ; as also
for the leisure hours of those who are already advanced. Composed and revised
by John Sebastian Bach," &c.* In the year 1744 he issued a second set of the
same number of Preludes and Fugues, and again in the 24 different major and

---

* "Das wohl temperirte Clavier oder Pæludia und Fugen durch alle Tone und Semitonia
sowohl tertiam majorem oder *Ut, Re, Mi,* anlangend, als auch tertiam minorem oder *Re, Mi,
Fa,* betreffend. Zum Nutzen und Gebrauch der Lehrbegierigen Musicalischen Jugend, als
auch derer in diesem studio schon babil seyenden besondern Zeit Vertreib aufgesetzet und
verfertiget von Johann Sebastian Bach, *p. t.* Hochfürstl. Anhalt. Cöthenischen Capell-
Meistern und Directore dorer Cammer Musignen. Anno 1722."

minor keys. In these works Bach made use of the following members of his "compound" scale. (The diatonic and chromatic notes are distinguished by their initial letters D, C, and such of the enharmonic as are included are marked by *En* and a bind.)

In his "Chromatic Fantasia" Bach put upon paper many notes, which, differing in appearance, and being also unlike in theory, were yet intended to be the same in sound.

744. Nor did he leave his opinion as to the necessity for a compound diatonic, chromatic, enharmonic scale for the organ less indelibly stamped upon the works he wrote expressly for that instrument. In those works he allowed himself the utmost freedom in the choice of "initial" keys; also as to the other keys into which he passed, as well as the most unfettered use of chromatic progressions and enharmonic modulations whenever he required their introduction.

The part Bach took in the establishment of equal temperament.

745. In the biographies of Bach, by Forkel and Hilgenfeldt, occur several passages that describe the condition in which Bach found clavichord playing and tuning, what he did to develop the capabilities of that instrument, and how he effected that end. Hilgenfeldt says : "At the end of the seventeenth century it was *not* customary to play in *all* the keys. Those with *more* than *three* sharps or flats were seldom used. The reason of this was, undoubtedly, the 'unequal' mode of tuning the instrument, which was obstinately adhered to in preference to the system now known as 'equal temperament.'" Forkel writes to the same effect : "Before his (Bach's) time, and in his younger years, it was usual to play *not* in all the twenty-four modes. The clavichord could not be perfectly tuned; people played therefore only in those modes which *could* be tuned with the most purity. Bach *extended* the use of the modes, partly by deviating from the ancient modes of church music, and partly by mixing the *diatonic* and *chromatic* scales. He learnt (or discovered how) to tune his instrument, so that it *could* be played upon in all the twenty-four modes. Bach tuned both his harpsichord and his clavichord *himself;* and he was so practised in the operation that it never cost him above a quarter of an hour. But *then*, when he played from his fancy, *all the twenty-four modes were in his power;* he did with them whatever he pleased. He combined the *most remote* as easily and naturally together as the *nearest;* the hearer believed he had only modulated within the compass of a single mode. He knew nothing of harshness in modulations ; his transitions in the chromatic scale were as soft and flowing as if he had wholly confined himself to the diatonic scale. His 'Chromatic Fantasia,' which is now published, may prove what I here state. *All his extempore* VOLUNTARIES *are said to have been of the same description, but frequently* MUCH MORE FREE, *brilliant, and expressive.*"

chromatic scale, the distances of the fixed sounds being neither what nature nor art required for the last-mentioned purpose.

The defects of the un-
equal tuning known in
the sixteenth century. 735. Nor was the detection of these inherent defects in the then existing organ scale a discovery only of the eighteenth century. So far back as the *middle of the sixteenth century* several organs existed in Italy having two extra keys in each octave, inserted for the purpose of hiding some of the asperities of the unequal scales. Salinus, in his treatise, *De Musica*, published in 1577, relates that many organs in his time had what in England have since been denominated *quarter-tones*, one between A natural and G sharp (A flat), and a second between D natural and E flat (D sharp). On many such organs he had often played, particularly on a very famous one at Florence, in the monastery of the Dominicans, called Santa Maria Novella. Rather more than a century afterwards, that is, in 1685, the same two extra notes were introduced into the Temple organ by Father Smith,* namely, the third flat (A flat) and the fourth sharp (D sharp), which brought into a musical and available form two more major and two more minor scales, namely, E flat major, C minor, and E minor.

Further ameliorations of a similar kind were subsequently made in England. For instance, the organ of the chapel of the Foundling Hospital, erected in 1759, had two more quarter-tones, namely, the fourth flat (D flat) and the fifth sharp (A sharp). These, again, moulded two more major and two more minor scales into a musical form, A flat major, B major, F minor, and B minor.

* An old MS. book, preserved in the Library of the Honorary Society of the Inner Temple, thus notices these additions:—"The organ at the Temple hath quarter notes, which no organ in England hath, and can play any tune ; as, for instance, ye tune of ye 119 Psalm (which was set in E minor), and severall other services set by excellent musicians, *which no other organ will do.*"

736. About the year 1808 Hawkes took out a patent for an organ which, in addition to the foregoing, presented the fifth flat (G flat). This rendered one more major and one more minor scale practicable, D flat major and B flat minor.

The scales up to five sharps and up to five flats inclusive were thus made available. The remaining four sharps and flats, two of each, were not, however, represented.

Enharmonic organs.   737. Nearly a quarter of a century before the date just given the elder Russell had made an organ with twenty sounds in the octave, among which were doubtless included all the foregoing.   At subsequent periods other organs were built with a still greater number of sounds in the octave, until those erected for the late Rev. Mr. Liston and Colonel Thompson, which had forty-three and forty sounds in the octave respectively.   Nor were instruments of this nature so modern an invention as some might imagine.   Vincentino, in the middle of the sixteenth century, invented an instrument of the harpsichord kind, to illustrate the three ancient genera, which had such an accumulation of wires to represent the great variety of intervals, that the instrument had to be furnished with six rows of keys ; and a modern organ specimen has three elaborate key-boards for the manipulation of a single stop, and *then* only incompletely illustrates the theory it is intended to elucidate.

Perfect attunement.   738. Such instruments presented several varieties of every degree in the musical scale, as C, D, E, tuned a comma sharper or flatter than others ; so that the distinction between the major and the minor tones, &c., of every separate scale could be rigorously produced.   They not only answered their purpose well, but served theoretically to illustrate the exact difference between a multiplicity of sounds, which, from the force of habit, some might be apt to consider identical.   Their general adoption, however, could not follow, for many reasons, such as the enormous cost of the extra pipes ;* the great additional room necessary to accommodate them ; the complex machinery or key-boards that would be required to bring them into active use, &c.

739. Moreover, in proportion as *theoretical perfection* was approached, as to intonation, by the introduction of additional sounds, the *practical disadvantages* were *increased;* for it destroyed the ambiguity in certain harmonic combinations, which is one of the greatest and richest resources of the musician's art. The beauty of an enharmonic modulation consists, as all musicians know, in " the theoretical change *without* the practical difference."

* An enharmonic organ, with one stop and three manuals to play it with, costs about £300.

Ex. 15.   *And with His stripes.*   HANDEL.

Ex. 16.   *O Lord God of my salvation.*   DR. CROFT.

Ex. 17.   *And all flesh shall see it together.*   HANDEL.

734. The foregoing musical extracts, although but few in number, are sufficient to show that the system of unequal temperament, which had so admirably facilitated the progress of music up to a certain extent, had, in the course of time, become "insufficient" for the greatly increased and still increasing requirements. The musical art had been undergoing *continuous* and *rapid development* during the two centuries that had elapsed between the time of the introduction of that temperament and the beginning of the eighteenth century, while the system of tuning *had remained stationary*. Thus the resources presented by the latter, which were, at the time of its establishment, not only sufficient for, but far in advance of, the current musical necessities, had not only passed into common use, but many others had come to be much required. Indeed, if investigated by the clearer vision of increased musical intelligence, the result could only have been the discovery that an organ, tuned according to the then prevailing system, was, in one sense, *an extremely incomplete enharmonic organ.* It was an instrument that, on the one hand, presented C sharp as distinguished from D flat, E flat as distinguished from D sharp, and so on ; yet, on the other, presented but half the major diatonic scales in a practicable form, only one quarter of the number of the minor scales, and no

Equal temperament opposed, as unequal tuning had been before it. 746. The equal temperament system, nevertheless, met with the greatest opposition, as the unequal method had before it. While it was admitted that equal temperament moulded into practicable form fifteen scales that were non-existent on an unequally tempered organ, it was objected that it also left the first nine scales in not so good a condition as they were before. This was, in substance, a repetition of the argument that had held good for centuries against unequal temperament; which latter, while it rendered seven scales practicable that were not so before, left the first nine that previously were pure no longer in that condition. It was a line of reasoning that told against all temperament whatever, and could be applied until the perfect attunement of many centuries before were restored, and with it the comparatively primitive state of the art of musical composition; or—the improved state of the latter partially preserved—enharmonic organs became general, and with them their theoretical beauties, practical imperfections, complexity of manipulation, and impossible pedipulation. Such a position, in fact, was assumed not many years ago by a writer whose advocacy of just intonation forbade his admitting any merit in any temperament whatever. Bontempi, in his *History of Music*, page 188, 1695, spoke of temperament as a "divine thing," while the writer just alluded to described it in the same words without the adjective, namely, as "a *thing!*"

747. One of the strongest opponents to the adaptation of equal tuning to the organ is said to have been Silbermann, the celebrated organ-builder; and the tradition runs that whenever Sebastian Bach observed Silbermann among his select circle of auditors he used to say to him, in perfect good humour, "You *tune* the organ in the manner *you* please, and I *play* the organ in the key *I* please;" and thereupon used to strike off a fantasia in A flat major, the contest invariably ending in Silbermann's retiring to avoid the "howling of his own wolf."

748. Equal temperament was opposed also on the ground that it destroyed the "distinctive character of key" which unequal temperament imparted to the different scales. A slight acquaintance with unequal temperament would disclose, as shown on pages 162 and 163, that a few of the commonest scales were by it rendered nearly, if not quite *alike*, by reason of the removal of the difference between the major and minor tones; consequently, but little distinction of "character" existed among them, but rather was to be found among the remaining fifteen scales, some of which are shown on page 163. And it appeared among the latter in consequence of the dissonance produced, in greater or less quantity, by the unavoidable use of the wrong *dieses*, or quarter-tones, as indicated by the black notes. All those scales contained at least one instance, and some two, of the same degree of the scale occurring *twice over;* some other degree, or degrees, being omitted altogether. This is shown by the *figures*, as well as notes, in the foregoing examples. Those wrong fixed sounds brought into those scales intervals as whole tones that were, in dimension, *greater* than the *major* tones of perfect attunement—the REDUCTION of which was one of the grounds on which unequal temperament was originally devised—and other intervals as semitones that were considerably too small and dissonant for the purpose. Yet for those scales the exaggerated or contorted intervals of which were not in the least degree produced by design, but appeared, both as to number and situation, just where accident had chanced to throw them during the process of tempering the first nine scales—for those scales a merit and advantage was claimed on the plea that they established a variety of "character" that was useful and desirable to the musical art! Scheibler* spoke much to the purpose when he said: "Such a

* *An Essay on the Theory and Practice of Tuning*, by Scheibler, page 26. Cocks and Co.

modification, or rather *corruption* of the scales, was called *temperament;* and, strange to say, the old theorists advocated the adoption of such *unequally* tempered scales, on the plea that the different degrees of deviation from the mathematical purity tended to give them a greater characteristic difference of effect, and thereby give a greater power of colouring to the musical art ; a plea that represented a *necessary evil* in the colour of a *real advantage* and benefit."

749. No record seems ever to have been made of what were supposed to be the " characters" of the several keys as presented by unequal temperament ; nor does it appear that anything was advanced in support of the plea, beyond a few broad statements and generalities.

Equal temperament re-commended on the same grounds.

750. The case was very different with equal temperament. In the English translation of Bombet's *Life of Haydn*, published in the year 1818, the editor gave, on pages 98, 99, and 100, a list of keys, with observations, in reference to this very subject of " character," which are here quoted. Those to which a * is attached are keys which have no practical existence on an unequally tempered organ.

" F major . . . } This key is rich, mild, sober, and contemplative.
D minor . . . } Possesses the same qualities, but of a heavier and darker cast ; more doleful, solemn, and grand.

G major . . . ⎱ Gay and sprightly. Being the medium key, it is adapted to the greatest range of subjects.
*E minor . . . ⎰ Persuasive, soft, and tender.

*A flat major . ⎱ The most lovely of the tribe. Unassuming, gentle, soft, delicate, and tender, having none of the pertness of A in sharps. Every author has been sensible of the charm of this key, and has reserved it for the expression of his most refined sentiments.
*F minor . . . ⎰ Religious, penitential, and gloomy.

A major . . . } Golden, warm, and sunny.
*F sharp minor } Mournfully grand.

B flat major . ⎱ The least interesting of any. It has not sufficient fire to render it majestic or grand, and is too dull for song. (Handel's 'O Father, whose Almighty power,' Mozart's ' Benedictus,' in the *Requiem*, and Mendelssohn's ' O come, every one that thirsteth,' are in this key.)
G minor . . . ⎰ Meek and pensive. Replete with melancholy.

*B in sharps . Keen and piercing. Seldom used. (Mendelssohn's 'I am He that comforteth ' is written in this key.)

C major . . . ⎱ Bold, vigorous, and commanding ; suited to the expression of war and enterprise.
A minor . . . ⎰ Plaintive, but not feeble.

*D flat major . Awfully dark. In this remote key Haydn and Beethoven have written their sublimest thoughts. They never enter it but for tragic purposes.

D major . . . ⎱ Ample, grand, and noble. Having more fire than C, it is suited to the loftiest purposes. In choral music it is the highest key, the treble having its cadence note on 4th line.
*B minor . . . ⎰ Bewailing, but in too high a tone to excite commiseration. (Handel's 'Vouchsafe, O Lord,' and Mendelssohn's ' O God, have mercy,' are written in this key.)

z

*E flat major . ⎫ Full and mellow ; sombre, soft, and beautiful.   It is a key
in which all musicians delight.   Though less decided in
its character than some of the others, the regularity of its
beauty renders it a universal favourite. (Bach's St. Ann's
Fugue is written in this key ; also, Mendelssohn's chorus,
'Thanks be to God.')

*C minor. . . ⎭ Complaining ; having something of the whining cast of B
minor.   (Bach's *Passacaglia* and several of his most
beautiful fugues are written in this key.)

*E major. . .   Bright and pellucid ; adapted to brilliant subjects.   In this
key Haydn has written his most elegant thoughts.   Handel
mistook its properties when he used it in the chorus, 'The
many rend the skies with loud applause.'   Though higher
than D, it is less loud, as it stretches the voice beyond its
natural powers.

It is sufficient to have hinted at these effects.   To
account for them is difficult ; but every musician is sensible
of their existence."

751. Enough is set forth in the above quotation, after allowing something for
over-colouring, to show the immeasurable superiority of equal temperament over
the unequal on the question of "character of key" under consideration ; not the
least of its greater excellencies consisting in its transforming the otherwise "wolfish
key" of A flat major into "the most lovely of the tribe."

Temperament, as the   752. It is doubtful, however, whether the question of
only source of distinc-   "character of key" should ever have been *so much* mixed up
tion of key, questioned.   with that of "temperament" as it has been, since writers are by
no means unanimous as to the precise source from which springs that distinction.

Pitch supposed to ex-   753. In unequally tempered instruments a distinct cha-
ercise an influence in   racter of key undoubtedly exists ; but it is of so untuneful a
establishing the cha-
racter of key.   nature that, instead of proving an *advantage*, it is a source
of pain to sensitive ears.   To cite one further example: Dr.
Burney, in his *Musical History*, vol. iii., page 608, says of the work from which
Ex. 16, on page 170, is taken : "The anthem for three voices, from the eighty-
eighth Psalm, is truly pathetic and expressive, from beginning to the end ; but,
unluckily, the key in which it is composed (F minor) is so much out of tune on
the organ, as it is usually tempered, that the effect must be doubly offensive to
those who, though possessed of good ears, are unable to account for it." Equal
temperament removes the cause of this crude distinction.   But in doing so, it
must, in the opinion of some, destroy all difference between one key and
another.   Clear as this conclusion seems to be, experience shows that on an
equally tempered instrument a distinction of key nevertheless *does* exist.   The
equality of the tuning can be proved *mathematically;* yet a difference in the
keys is perceived *practically*, and reason has hitherto failed to fathom this
subtile phenomenon.   Some have attempted to account for it by supposing
that an *unintentional* temperament must find admittance ; that the tuner, un-
consciously, has perhaps a bias in favour of certain keys.   Others would
attribute the distinction to the influence of a second and independent agency,
namely, *pitch*, or the grave and acute qualities of sound.   As to the manner
in which that influence is exercised, they propose to account for it by supposing
that, when an author composes a piece of music, he first determines his

key, and then confines his ideas to the proper compass of the voices or instruments for which he is writing. Thus, in penning a vocal piece for a treble voice of average compass, if c^2 be taken as the key note, the available range would be half an octave upwards, and a whole octave downwards; if f^1, it would be a whole octave upwards, and half an octave downwards; if a^1 flat, it would be a sixth upwards, and a sixth downwards, and so on; and that each separate melodial range has perforce its own distinct series of attendant harmonies. That *students* and *auditors*, by performing and hearing music so written, are thus gradually led to ascribe to each of the keys a specific character. In this case, however, the primary influences would appear to be the limits of the voice, and other circumstances under which the music was written, rather than any inherent and peculiar property in the *pitch*. If any specific quality ever belonged to certain sounds—of which sounds the musical scales are formed —that quality would continue to exist; therefore, on *an alteration of pitch* taking place, such as has actually occurred, by ascent, to the extent of a semitone, since the time of Haydn, the scales that formerly had sharps for the signature, though now having flats, would still be brilliant; and those which had flats, though now having sharps, would be the reverse. Music written in the last century, in the "golden, warm, and sunny" scale of A major, would now be heard in the "least interesting key" of B flat major, and so on; whereas no such perversion of sentiment has ever been declared to have taken place.

The internal resources of the musical art capable of giving any character to any key. 754. The probability is that neither *temperament* nor *pitch* have so much to do with giving "greater power of colouring to the musical art," by means of the establishment of the so-called "character of scale," as the *internal resources of the art itself.* For since music has become a *language*, as well as a *science* and *art*, composers have been enabled to express *whatever they please* in any *scale* they please. They have drawn music of a given "character," *and its opposite*, from one and the same scale. Thus, if Handel selected the "bold, vigorous, and commanding" scale of C major for "The horse and his rider" chorus, he employed it with equal success also for his "Dead March" in *Saul*. If Mendelssohn adopted the same scale, "expressive of war and enterprise," for his "Military Duet," he used it no less felicitously for his sweet and peaceful aria, "O rest in the Lord." If he fixed upon the scale of G minor, "replete with melancholy," for his most pathetic second movement in the instrumental introduction to the *Lobgesang*, he adopted the same "meek and pensive scale" with equally perfect success also for two of his most vivacious *scherzos*, those in the *Otteto* and the *Midsummer Night's Dream* music. Weber selected the "awfully dark and tragic" scale of D flat major for his inspiriting "Invitation to the Dance." But to whatever circumstance, or combination of circumstances, the distinction of scale is observable, all musicians are sensible of its existence.

Characteristics of equal temperament. 755. We have *heard* how "out of tune" the unequal tuning makes some of the scales that are even in constant use; and we have *seen* the cause. We have also noticed in what way equal temperament removes that cause, namely, by, among other things, tempering the sound of all the short keys, so that they will serve either as the *flat* to the white key *to the right*, or as the *sharp* to the white key *to the left*. Its influence in the enharmonic scales, which is considerable, is not here dwelt upon. The equal temperament, by rendering each of the twelve fixed sounds susceptible of answering two or three distinct purposes, possesses advantages, as well as a degree of practical simplicity and efficiency, quite peculiar to itself.

756. In distributing the wolf equally among all the scales, the major thirds in a few of the more common keys are made rather sharper than in the unequal temperament.   This, the most grave objection taken to the equal system of tuning, never amounts to a striking defect, while, under certain circumstances, it becomes a positive beauty.   It is well known that the most perfect organ and instruments in existence, the human voice and the violin, can produce all the gradations of the enharmonic scale ; yet both singers and performers on string instruments *prefer* making the leading note *not* a perfect third to its root, but *sharp*.   And as every major triad, at the same time that it forms the *tonic* triad of one scale (c for instance), also forms the *dominant* of the *fifth below*, f ;

it follows that its third, e, as the leading note of that dominant harmony, accords more closely with the custom observed by the best practical musicians, from the very circumstance of its being sharper than perfect.   Besides this, the sharp thirds infuse a freshness and spirit into the common keys, which, according to the old temperament, they do not possess.   Besides this, the equal temperament much improves the effect of the whole series of minor scales ; in which, it will be recollected, a very considerable proportion of the English church music is written.   Again, as nearly all well-cultivated voices have been tutored at an equally tempered pianoforte, a similarly tempered organ must prove the best accompaniment to them. No singer would think of sounding for semitones such intervals as those which occur on an unequally tempered organ between G natural and G sharp, or between E flat and E natural ; or such as those between G sharp and B flat, or between C sharp and E flat for whole tones ; or such as those between G sharp and C, or between B and E flat for major thirds :—

In this respect, singers have frequently been censured for "singing out of tune," when the fault has rested solely with the barbarous temperament of the organ by which they have been accompanied.

757. Then, in practice, the equal temperament is the only system that affords unfettered facility for the transposition of a piece of music (when that may be required), without distorting the intervals of its melody, or rendering the progress of its harmony crude and exaggerated.   In this variable climate it frequently happens that, by transposing a psalm tune or a chant a semitone or a whole tone lower, the voices of a choir or congregation may be spared much exertion and unnecessary fatigue.   Besides this, organs vary more or less in pitch ; and, if an instrument be tuned very high, the music can then be transposed without harshness being imparted to it.   In the *Harmonicon* for 1824, a correspondent states that "till of late years the organ in St. Paul's Cathedral was half a note above the usual standard, and the organ part of the music performed at the Feast of the

Sons of the Clergy was therefore obliged to be transposed half a note lower than the other parts for the accommodation of the organist."

758. As to the manner in which tempered sounds are received by the musical sense, Mr. G. A. Macfarren has explained this matter very clearly in his *Lectures on Harmony*, published by Longman and Co., Paternoster Row. On pages 43 and 44 he says :—" The system, I believe, first practised by Sebastian Bach—which has now become general—of tuning keyed instruments by equal temperament, consists in prevaricating the enharmonic diesis—that is, the distinction between D sharp and E flat, &c.—by tuning notes too sharp for the one and too flat for the other of their names, and by making a like compromise between the still minuter discrepancies of the diatonic scale, so that, while no interval is perfectly true, the ear is in neither case shocked by false intonations. It is, however, a beautiful and a wonderful property of the musical sense, so to adjust these tempered notes, that in every key they produce the same effect upon us in relation to other notes that the perfectly attuned notes would produce which they represent." And on page 141 he further adds that, " in despite of equal temperament, the ear has the admirable facility of so adjusting the tempered sounds which enter it, that they seem to us not what we hear, but what we should hear, were all the notes perfectly attuned to the true natural scale." At the same time, another fact cannot be concealed, which is, that it is quite possible for the ear, under the influence of a firm imagination, to be encouraged to refuse to receive tempered sounds when presented in a particular shape—or even in any shape whatever—and yet tolerate the far more egregious effect of the use of the wrong diesis. The painful effect, however, of such unequal tuning on sensitive ears may be gathered from the following :—The late Adolph Hesse was in England in the year of the first Great Exhibition, together with his father-in-law, Louis Spohr. Both were at Westminster Abbey on the occasion of the Purcell Festival, and, after service, Hesse was asked to try the organ—then *unequal*—which he proceeded to do. He had not played many chords before he discovered the condition of the tuning ; when, directing Spohr's attention to it, he positively declined to touch another note, and, with Spohr, closing his ears, left the organ gallery. On his return to Germany, Hesse had occasion to write "something about English organs," in which he said, in reference to the unequal tuning: "It is inconceivable to me how, in the neighbourhood of the best orchestral music, and of the most splendid and perfectly well-tuned pianos, the ear can reconcile itself to such barbarisms."

759. One of the earliest and most earnest advocates, in England, for the application of equal temperament to the organ was the late Dr. Crotch—himself a very great authority—who directed attention to the subject, on the last page of the second edition of his *Elements of Musical Composition*, in the following words :— " The author cannot but regret that the preference of English organists for the old method of tuning has been (as he is informed) hitherto so strong and determined, as to have resisted and repelled the attempts made to introduce the equal temperament into our cathedrals and churches. He has for many years uniformly recommended that this system should have a fair trial, upon the principle that, as all tempered fifths and thirds offend the ear, those systems which contain such as are most tempered and most discordant cannot be preferable, especially in an age when the keys which have four sharps and three flats can no longer be excluded from general use. It has at length been fairly tried, and, having carefully examined it, he feels convinced that its practicability and superiority are as unequivocal on the organ as they are allowed to be on the pianoforte, and on all other instruments which contain only twelve different notes on each octave. He continues to press

these opinions, not merely because they are his own, but because, in so doing, he is contending for the far higher authority of the judgment and practice of one whom, he trusts, his opponents must venerate and admire—the greatest of all composers for his sacred instrument—

SEBASTIAN BACH."

Mr. George Hogarth, in an article on the organ, printed in the *Musical World* for 1836, page 21, observes :—" The organ in England is tuned according to a system of temperament different from that which prevails on the Continent, and the effect of which is that the harmony is intolerably impure in all keys which require more than three sharps or three flats." And the late Chevalier Neukomm, in the preface to his *Organ Voluntaries,* inquired—" Why do the English organists continue to follow a barbarous system no longer adequate to the improved state of modern instrumental music, and which renders the organ unfit for accompaniment when in concert with other instruments ?" Mr. Hullah, again, in his *History of Modern Music,*[*] page 9, observes :—" The modern European system, though the exigencies of practice prevent its being absolutely true, is nearer the truth than any other system ; and its inaccuracies are so slight as to cause little disturbance to the most refined ear. I mean by this that all our music is, of necessity, a little out of tune ; for our intervals vary, *however slightly,* from those deduced from the division of a musical string into aliquot parts. But the discrepancy, I repeat, is so slight, and distributed, by the system of *equal temperament,* over so many instances, that it is practically of no consequence." To these several observations it may be added that the preference of English organists is *not* now for the " barbarous system,". but has become almost as universally " strong and determined " *in favour* of J. Sebastian Bach's tuning. A few of the instruments thus tempered may here be enumerated. St. Paul's Cathedral (both organs) ; Westminster Abbey ; St. Sepulchre's, Snow Hill ; Temple Church ; All Saints', Margaret Street ; St. Andrew's, Wells Street ; Foundling Hospital ; Crystal Palace (both organs) ; all the Town Hall organs in the Kingdom, &c., &c. Equal temperament is *universally* adopted on the Continent.

---

[*] Longman and Co., Paternoster Row.

CHAPTER XXVII.

THE TUNING OF THE ORGAN.

Laying the bearings, and extending their influence to the stops generally. 760. IF the sounds of a set of pipes, or a stop, are to be adjusted according to "perfect attunement," the thirds, fifths, &c., will of course be tuned mathematically true; but if so as to present some kind of *tempered* scale, then the first step taken is to "lay the bearings." This process, after adjusting the starting sound to the pitch of the tuning-fork, consists in tuning the remaining eleven sounds of the octave, by intervals of a third, fourth, fifth, sixth, or octave, up or down, as the case may be, and at the same time of making those intervals, except the octave, which is always tuned absolutely perfect, "bear" nearer towards or farther from the sounds from which they are being calculated than if they were being tuned justly.

761. The following scheme exhibits one of the most approved methods of laying the bearings on the unequal temperament principle :—

The bound note is in each case supposed to be tuned; the other is the one to be adjusted. In laying the bearings, all the thirds, fourths, and sixths that are tuned upwards are made a little sharp, and those that are tuned downwards rather flat. The fifths, on the contrary, are tuned a slight degree flat upwards and sharp downwards. As the tuner proceeds with his work, he occasionally tries the temperament of a note just tuned with some other note previously adjusted, to ascertain whether the bearings are being laid correctly. These references are called *trials* or *proofs*, and are made by adding the major third, fourth, or sixth, above or below, to the note just tuned. If the intervals upwards prove to be rather greater than perfect in all cases, except between c sharp and f sharp, which should be rather flat, all is right; but if otherwise, then some of the previous bearings are not quite correct. The proofs are, in the above scheme, indicated by the initial letter p.

762. In laying the bearings according to the equal temperament system, the tuning is frequently proceeded with by fifths and octaves only, as shown in the following example :—

763. The bearings are laid in and about the middle octave and a half of the stop, as will be perceived on referring to the notation of the two last examples ; and the stop usually selected for the purpose is the Principal, the pitch of that stop being the medium one between the unison and small stops. The bearings having been laid, the remainder of the stop is tuned in octaves to the pipes already adjusted. After this, the unison flue stops are tuned, and then the smaller stops, the reeds being left till last. The fifth and third-sounding stops, as also the fifth and third-sounding ranks of the Compound stops, are tuned in absolutely perfect thirds and fifths to the Foundation stops.

How the pitch of the several kinds of organ pipe is altered.   764. *A large open metal flue pipe* has its pitch raised by cutting away a ring of the metal from off the top of the pipe, and is lowered by soldering a ring on. Or the pipe is furnished with a sliding cap or cylinder, which is slipped up or down, according to whether the pitch of the pipe is to be lowered or raised. Sometimes a large pipe is tuned by a slit made in its back at the upper end. This is particularly the case with front pipes. By bending the two edges apart, so as to leave an aperture, the pitch of the pipe is sharpened, and by closing them it is flattened. Sometimes all the pipes, except the small ones, are left rather long, and a " tongue " of metal cut near to the top, which is inclined inwards or outwards, according as the pitch of the pipe requires flattening or sharpening.

765. *A small open metal flue pipe* is tuned by an instrument constructed for the purpose, conical in shape, called a *tuning-horn*. Tuning-horns are of many different sizes, all of which come into requisition in the course of " tuning an organ through." The larger ones consist simply of a hollow cone (*fig.* 118), made of brass ; the smaller, of a handle (*fig.* 119) with a solid metal cone at one end (*a*) and a hollow cone at the other (*b*). Through the instrumentality of a tuning-horn, the top of a pipe may be slightly contracted or expanded, *i.e.*, its edge may be drawn in or turned out as occasion may require.

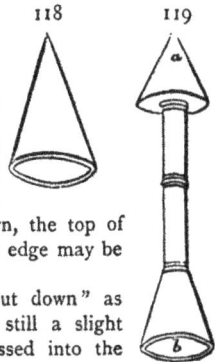

766. All the flue pipes in an organ are first " cut down " as nearly as possible to the exact pitch. If any pipe is still a slight degree too flat, the pointed end of the cone is pressed into the aperture at the top of that pipe, which turns the edge a little outwards, and so slightly raises its pitch. If, on the contrary, a pipe is a little too sharp, the hollow part of the cone is forced over the top of that pipe, which draws its edge inwards, and thus has the same effect that very slightly lengthening the pipe would have.

767. *A large open wood flue pipe* is sharpened by cutting the body of the pipe shorter, and flattened by nailing a piece of board as far over the open end of the pipe as may be necessary to make it give its true note.

768. *A small open wood flue pipe* has a metal shade fixed into the upper end of the back of the pipe. To flatten the pitch, this shade is bent down towards the orifice of the pipe ; to sharpen it the shade is raised.

769. As the Compound stops have several pipes to a note, and all these would of course sound at the same time, a small *mop* (*fig.* 120) is thrust into each pipe of the given key, excepting the one about to be tuned, to silence them. Sometimes the various ranks of pipes that form a Compound stop are governed by as many small sliders, capable of being drawn separately. Where this is the case, mops are not used, as

the small special slider to a single rank of pipes can then be drawn without disturbing any of the others.

770. *Stopped metal pipes*, whether entirely or partially closed, are furnished with a cap, and by this they are occasionally tuned. By pressing this cap down, the vibrating column of air within the pipe is shortened, and the sound of the pipe is therefore raised, and *vice versâ*. In England, stopped metal pipes, which have generally very large ears, are more frequently tuned by those ears. By bending them nearer towards the mouth of the pipe, they lower the pitch ; and by bending them outwards, they, on the contrary, raise it. In modern specimens, both in England and Germany, the pipes are made sufficiently long to receive cylindrical wooden stoppers covered with leather.

771. *Stopped wood pipes* are closed with a stopper, that is, forced *into* the upper end of the pipe ; and in this respect differs from the cap of the stopped metal pipe, which *encloses* the top of the body. Its influence, however, is the same, namely, that of sharpening the pitch of the pipe the further it is pressed down, and of flattening it the more it is drawn upwards.

772. *Reed pipes* are tuned by means of the tuning-wire, on raising which the vibrating portion of the tongue is lengthened, causing it to give a deeper tone ; and on depressing which the vibrating portion of the tongue is shortened, and the pitch consequently raised.

The pitch of the organ altered by the heat and cold in different seasons. The extent of this alteration. 773. The pitch of the organ is affected to a considerable extent by the altered temperature of the atmosphere at different seasons of the year. This fact was satisfactorily elucidated by the late Dr. Smith, Master of Trinity College, Cambridge, who has given the result of his experiments in his work on *Harmonics*, page 192, 2nd edition :—" I found," he says, " that the particles of air in the cylindrical pipe, called d^1, in the middle of the open diapason, made 262 complete vibrations, or returns to the places they went from, in one second of time. This experiment was made in the month of September, at the time when the thermometer stood at temperate, or thereabouts. But, upon a cold day in November, I found, by a like experiment, that the same pipe gave but 254 complete vibrations in one second ; so that the pitch of its sound was lower than in September by something more than $\frac{1}{4}$ of a mean tone."

774. "And, upon a pretty hot day in August, I collected, from another experiment, that the same pipe gave 268 complete vibrations in a second of time ; which shows that its pitch was higher than in November by almost half a mean tone."

775. "By some observations made upon the contraction and expansion of air, from its greatest degree of cold in our climate to its greatest degree of heat, compared with Sir Isaac Newton's theory of the velocity of sounds, I find also that the air in an organ pipe may vary the number of its vibrations made in a given time in the ratio of 15 to 16, which answers to the major hemitone, or about $\frac{7}{12}$ of the mean tone, and agrees very well with the foregoing experiments."

776. The influence of a change or rise in the temperature on the pitch of an organ is sometimes rather strikingly illustrated during the evening meeting of large congregations, and also in concert-rooms ; and it is not unfrequently also attended with some temporary inconvenience. On account of the church or room being filled with people, the temperature soon rises, the atmosphere in and around the pipes of those parts of the organ that are exposed to it undergoing a similar change. The metal pipes themselves also become warm from the heated air coming in contact with them, some metals and compounds, however

being sooner influenced than others. When the parts of the organ in question are played, supplied as they then are by a warm air, and with their pipes also warm, they are found to sound much sharper than before. The Swell pipes, however, supposing the shutters of the box to have been kept closed, are surrounded by an atmosphere of the original temperature, the heat not having been able to penetrate through the box, they, therefore, remain cool, and the warm air from the bellows as it passes into them becomes chilled, and is reduced to its original density; the consequence being that the Swell, at its unaltered pitch, sounds, perhaps, a quarter of a tone flatter than the Great organ. This non-accordance of pitch is often very detrimental in its effect; but it can generally be obviated by fixing the Swell open, whenever the organ is not being used during the evening, so as to allow the warm air to reach its pipes, and raise their pitch with the rest of the organ. Care should afterwards be taken to leave the Swell open all night, that its pipes may cool with the other parts of the organ, or it may be too sharp when next used. The writer has known a concert-room organ to rise as much as a semitone in pitch in the course of an evening's performance, when the temperature has very much increased.

777. When an organ has been thrown much out of tune by a great change of temperature, it will be found that the flue stops are not so much at variance among themselves, nor the reeds, as that one class of stops has bodily separated from the other. This change is commonly attributed to the reeds, which are said to have "gone flat"—reed pipes being rather proverbial for their instability of pitch;—but in this instance the alteration appears to rest rather with the flue stops.

778. A simple and ready illustration of the influence of heat in raising the pitch of a flue pipe may be obtained in the following way :—Take out the top pipe of the Dulciana, if it be in tune, and hold its body in the hands until it becomes perfectly warm, and then return it into its place, and sound it with the stopped Diapason. It will then be found to sound very sharp. This is because the warm pipe raises the temperature of the air as it passes through it. If the two pipes are allowed to continue to sound together, a rapid beat will at first be heard ; but, as the current of air gradually cools the pipes, the beats will become slower, until they at last entirely disappear, as the pipe, on attaining its first temperature, returns to its original pitch.

779. As to the cause of the change of pitch, from alteration of temperature, some have been inclined to attribute it partly to the expansion of the metal in warm weather and its contraction in cold, and partly to the lighter density of the atmosphere in summer than in winter. Dr. Brewer, in his little work on *Sound and its Phenomena*, page 255, says : "The reason is, an increase of temperature increases the *elasticity* of the pipes, in consequence of which they vibrate somewhat more quickly, and render a higher note." This refers to flue pipes. With regard to the tongues of reed pipes, which are of brass, as the heat expands them, it would be supposed that they would vibrate slower, and produce a lower sound ; but, if their elasticity also is increased, the one influence may to some extent balance the effect of the other.

780. As being connected in some degree with this subject, reference may be made to the cause of the draught that is so generally felt to issue from the region of the keys of the organ. The warmer atmosphere, as it comes in contact with the numerous metal pipes, becomes chilled ; and, its density being increased, it descends. In this manner a constant eddy is produced, resulting in the disagreeable effect referred to, and which has been attributed to almost every cause but the right one.

CHAPTER XXVIII.

THE PITCH TO WHICH AN ORGAN SHOULD BE TUNED.

The question a most interesting one. 781. THE question as to the pitch to which an organ should be tuned introduces to consideration several very interesting particulars. A concert-room organ would probably be tuned up to the prevailing concert pitch, in order that it may accord with the orchestral instruments. With regard to church organs, however, this same question cannot be so easily disposed of. Several circumstances first demand attention, particularly when the organ is for a church where choral service is celebrated.

The presumed lower pitch of two centuries since. 782. Much has been written at various times to show that the musical pitch has been gradually rising for the last two centuries; and the opinion has even been expressed that in Tallis's time it was some two tones lower than it is now.

The difficulties inseparable from that theory. 783. The difficulty, or rather impossibility, has been to reconcile this theory with the *notation* of the venerable pieces of church harmony of the sixteenth and early part of the seventeenth centuries. All who have been accustomed to assist in the choral performances of the services and anthems of the early English church composers must have observed that the parts, generally speaking, lie so low for the voices that they can be sung only with some difficulty, even at the present supposed elevation of a major third above the original pitch; and this circumstance has naturally led to much speculation as to whether they ever *could* have been sung at a pitch much, if at all, below that in present use.

784. Several different theories have been propounded, with the hope of settling this by no means unimportant question.

785. Some have supposed that the range of the human voice must have been lower at that period than it is now; others, that the composers could not have studied the compass and convenience of the voices for which they wrote; while others maintain that the compositions in question were not contemplated by their authors to be sung to any definite pitch, but were intended to be transposed, to suit the voices, as occasion might require. All these explanations, however, are accompanied by some circumstance that proves fatal to its unqualified reception. Let us examine them in the order they are given above.

The compass of the human voice supposed to have changed. 786. It must be needless to insist on the extreme improbability of the supposition that nature has found it necessary to *revise* that which has always been ranked among her most perfect works—namely, the vocal organ of the human species—particularly as there exists no real difficulty to render the retention of so unseemly an hypothesis necessary. But were it otherwise, the questionableness of such a theory is soon rendered evident by making an analysis of the music of the period already alluded to. In the Services of Tye, Tallis, Byrd, Gibbons, Bevin, Farrant, Hilton, and others, the *notation* of the treble part in no case ascends higher than d², the fourth line in the treble ; while in a few instances it descends as low as tenor a, the second line below. The bass constantly ranges down to FF, and sometimes even to EE ; and the inner parts lie proportionably low. The anthems of the same composers slightly exceed the above upward range in the treble part ; but that only rarely. Now, if the *pitch*, at the time alluded to, were some two tones lower than at present, the above writers must have considered the *sound* corresponding with the modern b¹ flat, or b¹ natural, the third line in the treble, as marking the full average upward range of treble voices, and an occasional tenor f, the fourth line in the bass, as not too low for them ; and further, they must have viewed DD flat, and even CC, the second line below the bass, as sounds quite within the range of ordinary bass voices ;—ideas certainly most opposed to our knowledge and experience of the compass and capabilities of the several voices in existence in the present day. But inasmuch as the theory of the former existence of a complete series of different, that is, deeper voices, rests solely on the presumed lower pitch of the seventeenth century—and this latter point is not yet proved—its further consideration may, for the present, be withheld.

The old composers supposed not to have consulted the convenience of the voices they wrote for.

787. With regard to the second suggestion—"that the composers could not have studied the compass and convenience of the voices for which they wrote "—the answer to this must depend entirely on the decision arrived at in reference to the former question, and, therefore, may also stand over for a time.

The early English composers supposed to have written without regard to any definite pitch.

788. The third supposition is "that the compositions in question were not contemplated by their authors to be sung to any definite pitch." This, however, does not meet the difficulty. Unless the old English treble voices were as deep as the modern counter-tenors, and all the other voices proportionably low, Tallis, Gibbons, and the other church composers of the period, must invariably and intentionally have written their music in a pitch in which it could *never* have been sung, and have thus rendered recourse to transposition not simply a matter of *occasional expediency*, but one of *constant necessity*. Nay, more, as the services, &c., were *from the first* intended to be accompanied by the organ (the composers themselves, in many cases, taking their seat at the instrument), and as the organs of that day were tuned according to the *unequal* temperament ;—as, moreover, the music was generally written in the scales *provided* by that temperament, but *out* of which, according to the above theory, they must uniformly have been transposed ;—it follows, if the above hypothesis be correct, that the learned composers referred to must have avoided the *good* keys in performance, and used the *bad*. Now, it is not possible that proceedings so needlessly complex and objectionable as those just detailed could have been recognised, still less have received *preference*, at the hands of those who were, in all other respects relating to their art, such methodical and deep-thinking men.

Everything questioned except the presumed lowness of the old pitch.

789. In the attempted solutions hitherto advanced, the judgment of the great English composers of the time referred to, and even the original perfectness of some of Nature's own work, the compass of the human voice, have been questioned, while one thing, the mutability of which is so well known, namely, the *pitch*, has been treated as though it was indisputably a very low one in the sixteenth century

Strong grounds for believing in the former existence of a high ecclesiastical pitch.

790. Now, although the opinion is directly at variance with all the hitherto received notions on the subject, there are the strongest reasons for believing that the ecclesiastical pitch of the sixteenth and early part of the seventeenth centuries, so far from being some two tones lower than now in use, was a *whole tone higher than the present concert pitch.*

The sixteenth and seventeenth century organs in Germany a whole tone sharp.

791. During several visits to the organs of Germany, the writer was frequently struck with the extreme *sharpness* of the pitch of the *old* organs. Of the three great instruments at Hamburg, two—namely, those in St. Catharine's Church, which is the oldest, and that in the Church of St. Jacobi, built in the seventeenth century (see Foreign Organs in Appendix)—proved to be a *whole tone* above the writer's tuning-fork, marked "Philharmonic" pitch. The transept organ in St. Mary's Church, at Lübeck, another *old* instrument, on being tested, was also found to be a whole tone above the same pitch; while that in one of the other churches in the same old town was a full semitone above the same pitch. On the inquiry being made of the organists of the three fore-mentioned churches how they accounted for this circumstance, they explained that their organs were tuned to the *church* pitch; and it subsequently transpired that in Germany three distinct standards of pitch had at different periods been used to which to tune organs; namely, orchestra pitch, which was the lowest; chamber pitch, a semitone above the former; and church pitch, which was the highest. On extending these inquiries to an organ-builder of that country, that person stated that he had almost invariably found the old organs, which he had been called upon to tune, repair, or replace by new ones, a semitone or a whole tone sharper than the present concert pitch. Not the least interesting proof of the former existence of a high church pitch is to be found in the fact that Sebastian Bach, in his church Cantatas, in most cases, wrote the *organ* part *a note lower than the other parts;*—which circumstance is alluded to by Mr. Macfarren, in his analysis of the contents of the first volume of Cantatas, published by the Leipzig Bach Society, printed in the *Musical World* for 1853.

A high ecclesiastical pitch believed to have existed formerly in England as well as in Germany.

792. The above facts, in conjunction with others, tended to confirm an opinion the writer had long previously entertained, namely, that in England, as in Germany, there must have existed at the period of the Reformation, and from that time to that of the Rebellion, a church pitch quite separate from the orchestral or instrumental pitch; and not only so, but even higher than the modern concert pitch. Every circumstance directly supports this hypothesis, which at the same time removes and reconciles all the difficulties and improbabilities which have encumbered every other view of the same subject.

The very low notation of ancient church music favourable to this view.

793. To begin with a reference to the English church music. If we read the notation of the old services *a tone higher*, the average compass of the treble parts will then be made to the extent from middle b or c¹ up to e² or f²; and the bass parts, as a rule, not lower than gamut G or F F; precisely the ranges which are known to be the best for the corresponding voices in church music. By this very simple means the necessity is obviated for supposing that the range of the human voice has undergone any modification; it removes all occasion for suggesting that the whole race of church composers of the sixteenth and early part of the seventeenth centuries understood

or studied the convenience of the voices so little as invariably to have written *too low* for them ; and it renders it quite superfluous to suppose that that industrious class of writers made a practice of setting their services and anthems in *wrong keys*, leaving singers and organists to transpose them into the correct ones.   William Turner, writing in 1724, says : " When Guido Aretinus reduced the Greek scale into the form now used, there was no sound practised above *E la*, which gave birth to the common proverb, viz., He strains a note above E̶ la." Without going back so far as this quotation would take us, if the pitch in Tallis's time had been some two tones lower than at present, it is difficult to comprehend a cause for treble voices having to strain at c^2 ; but, if it were a tone higher, it is easy to understand that then, as now, the *sound* of f^2 sharp could only be produced by some exertion.

794. Soon after the above observations were first written, two interesting facts came to the writer's knowledge, which strongly supported the opinion as to a former high church pitch.   In the library at Exeter Cathedral is preserved a MS. copy, written about the beginning of the last century, of Tallis's Service in D, transposed into E ; and in Dr. Rimbault's library is a copy of Gibbons' Service in F, transposed into G ; in both cases the *notation*, no doubt, being *raised* to compensate for the *lowering* of the *pitch*, in order that the originally intended sounds might be preserved.

795. In 1644 church organs were ordered to be demolished by Act of Parliament ; and so implicitly was the nonsensical decree obeyed that very few organs escaped the general destruction ; and even the two or three that were spared have subsequently undergone so much alteration in the course of improvement that they could afford little or no assistance in solving the question which has just been considered.

796. A few incidental references as to the pitch of old organs have, however, from time to time come to light, which clearly proves the existence of a high *church* pitch in the seventeenth century.   The elder Harris built an organ for Magdalen College, Oxford, in the early part of the seventeenth century, which was repaired by his *grandson* in the years 1690-91. Among other necessary improvements he undertook to " alter the pitch of the said organs *half a note lower* than they now are." Among the memoranda of Dr. Woodward, Warden of New College, Oxford, under the date " March 10th, 1661," occurs the following :—" Some discourse was then had with one Mr. Dalham, 'an organ-maker, concerning a new fair organ to be made for our college chapel. The stops of the intended organ were shown unto myself and the thirteen seniors, set down in a paper and named by the organist of Christ Church, who would have had them *half a note lower* than Christ Church organ, but Mr. Dalham supposed that a quarter of a note would be sufficient."

Father Smith's pitch flatter than the ecclesiastical pitch of preceding times.   797. The organs built by Smith and Harris after the Restoration were not tuned to so high a pitch as the choir pitch of the time of Tallis and Gibbons, and Smith's pitch was higher than Harris's.   Smith's pitch was, however, higher than some have supposed, as may be gathered from the following passage, extracted from *The English Musical Gazette* for January, 1819 :—" It is a remarkable circumstance that all Schmidt's organs were a quarter, and some even half, a tone above pitch ; this was so severely felt by the wind instruments, at the performances of the Sons of the Clergy, that they could not get near the pitch of the organ. In consequence of this, it was agreed upon that the organ should be altered to concert pitch, by transposing the pipes, so that the present DDD was formerly CCC, and so on through the organ."   To this it may be added, that the pipes to the CCC key are new ones, the two open Diapason pipes, of wood, standing in the angles of the case to the left of the manuals. The pitch of the Temple organ was also originally rather sharp. Harris's organs were lower in pitch than Smith's. The lower pitch of Harris's organ was one of the specified causes of its rejection at the Temple. The matter is thus referred to in an extract printed in Mr. Macrory's excellent little book, *A Few Notes on the Temple Organ* :—" The organ made by the said Harris is discoverably *too low* and too weak for the said church." The portion of this organ that was afterwards erected at Wolverhampton remained at the low pitch until about twenty years since, when it was raised by the late Mr. Bishop. Smith's pitch was almost the mathematically correct one, if not absolutely so. Harris's lower pitch he no doubt brought with him from France, where the organ in the King's Chapel and all the famous organs in Paris and in the country were tuned *a semitone lower* than the King's chamber pitch. As the pitch of the C in the time of the eminent violin maker, Stradivarius, was that of 512 variations in a second of time, and very probably agreed with the chamber pitch, the greater gravity of Harris's pitch can be traced to its source and cause, and its disagreement with Smith's accounted for.

The flattened pitch accompanied by a raised notation.

798. On referring to the sacred compositions by the contemporaries of Smith and Harris, we perceive this coincidence in support of the opinion that the pitch of that period was flatter than the earlier choir pitch ; namely, that certain notes, such as e² and f², which scarcely ever appeared in the treble part of the earlier church music, were now of quite common occurrence.

The pitch lower again, at the commencement of the eighteenth century, in England.

799. Soon after the commencement of the eighteenth century the pitch had again fallen. Possibly Harris's flatter pitch was preferred, and accepted as the standard. It is known that the organ in the chapel of Trinity College, Cambridge, commenced by Father Smith, and " cut down " and finished by his son-in-law, Schrider, in 1708, was originally adjusted to the pitch which has been shown mathematically to have been a minor tone below the present pitch. The writer of the *Reformation of Cathedral Music*, page 25, says : " Dr. Smith (*Harmonics*, 1749) gives 393 as the number of vibrations of A in a second. Fisher, in 1823, gives 430. Woolhouse ascertained the Philharmonic pitch, in 1835, to have 424. The same note referred to the scale of vibrations C = 512, and derived as a prime harmonic from the subdominant F, will have 426·6. Now the ratio of any of these to 393 is almost exactly as 10 : 9, which is the ratio of a minor tone, showing the rise of pitch within a single century."

A similar alteration of pitch, at the same period, in France and Germany.

800. What is very remarkable is, the pitch had, soon after the commencement of the last century, fallen as much in France and Germany as in England. Of the three fine organs at Strasburg, built by Silbermann, those in the cathedral, finished in 1716, and that in the Protestant church, proved, on trial in 1853, to be *a whole tone below the pitch of the same fork* by which the Hamburg organs were tested the preceding year, and found to be *a whole tone sharp*. The third organ, in St. Thomas's Church, is nearly as flat. The organ in the Church of St. Maria di Capitol, at Cologne, built in 1767 by Konig, was also originally flat, and, like the Trinity organ, has since been sharpened.

The lower pitch in the last century accompanied by a further ascent in the notation. 801. In this case, again, the greater *depression* of the *pitch* is manifested by the increased *upward* range of the *notation*, as is clearly demonstrated by the music of Handel and other composers of the last century, even without the authority of Handel's tuning-fork, the existence of which further authenticates the supposition. William Turner likewise speaks of the treble voices in his time going some three or four degrees higher than Guido's gamut, which, however, would then have consisted of the same range of *sounds* as in Tallis's time, or within a semitone of it.*

802. It is evident, then, (1) that the organ pitch has within three centuries varied to the extent of two whole tones ; (2) that there have at different times existed three distinct pitches, the highest being the oldest ; that in use soon after the commencement of the last century being the lowest ; and (3) that the present pitch is about midway between the extreme high and low pitches of former times, and is as nearly as possible identical with Father Smith's.

To which of the three church pitches formerly in use should a church organ be tuned ? 803. The question now is, to which of these three different pitches a *church* organ had better be tuned, seeing that music has been written to *all* of them, yet but *one* can be adopted? As the *medium* pitch is at the same time also the true mathematical one, there can be no doubt but that, theoretically speaking, it would be better that all organs be adjusted to a fork that gives that true mathematical pitch, such as that published by Mr. Hullah, and issued by Messrs. Longman and Co., Paternoster Row ; but complaints are so frequently made by members of congregations, on the one hand, and by singers who have to perform the solo and verse music of the last century, on the other, of the inconvenience of singing to the present high pitch, that it is worthy consideration whether it would not be as well to have organs tuned exactly a semitone flat, for the general convenience of the voices, and then for such music to be transposed as may be required, and into such keys as would best suit the particular congregations or choirs. At any rate, it is clear that, to be adequate to the purposes of transposition, all organs should be tuned on the equal temperament system. In that case, music could be transposed by easy semitonal gradations, either upwards or downwards, or by whole tones, without involving crude results, which could not be accomplished on an organ tuned in any other way. Recently the question as to the desirability of a recognised lower Diapason has been under the consideration of the Royal Society of Arts, and has also met with two able advocates in Mr. John Hullah and Mr. G. A. Macfarren.

---

* It is, perhaps, worth mentioning, that several pieces by Handel have lately been transposed into *lower* keys, and printed, with the view of *restoring* their original pitch.

Division CIII.

CHAPTER XXIX.

ON THE CORRECT USE OF THE STOPS.

804. HAVING, in a preceding chapter, given an account of the several organ stops commonly found in English organs, a few words may now be added as to their object and use, as well as their effect when sounded singly or in combination.

805. On a correct knowledge of the nature, quality, and pitch—whether indicated by name or by figures—of the different organ stops depends the good or bad effect of even the best organs. Without a clear perception of what is right in these matters, it is impossible that a performer can be *sure* how, under what circumstances, and for what ends, this or that combination of stops may be the most seasonably employed. However scientifically the organ-builder may have fixed and deduced his scales, voiced his pipes, and truly balanced their tone; however strictly every rule necessary to the production of a "good organ" may have been observed in constructing the instrument; all these important preliminaries, necessary towards a becoming and decent accompaniment to the music of the church, will be of little avail if the mind that is to direct their use is but imperfectly stored with the knowledge necessary to secure their proper application. Nor can this knowledge be obtained from books beyond a certain extent; for a combination of stops that will answer a particular purpose in one organ often will not do so, at any rate to the same extent, in another, on account of the different size or proportions of the building in which the organ stands; the varied strength of tone of the similar stops of different instruments; the situation of the organ in the church; or even the locality of the stops in the organ itself—for the exigencies arising from which circumstances, or a combination of them, no book could provide. It is, therefore, incumbent on every organist rather to endeavour to ascertain for himself the peculiar excellencies, and, perhaps, defects, of the individual instrument at which he is chosen to preside, and so discover the method of applying the former to special purposes with the best effect, and of hiding the latter as far as may be.

806. There are certain general and fundamental rules, however, concerning the appropriate method of combining the stops which may be pointed out. Besides the combinations about to be specified, others of a less common kind will be found to follow the suggestions for the introduction of certain stops in the specifications given in a subsequent chapter; beyond which, as has been already said, all must be left to the organist's good judgment and the capacity of his instrument.

General rules for the use of the stops.   807. The first step essential towards a correct knowledge of the right use of the stops is an acquaintance with the general method of combining the members of the three great classes of

" Foundation, Mutation, and Compound " stops, so as to secure, in all cases, the predominance of the foundation tone.

808. The Foundation stops, as explained in a preceding chapter, produce a sound agreeing in name with the key pressed down ; and are of 16, 8, 4, and 2 feet on the Manual, and of double size on the Pedal.

809. The larger Foundation stops will, for certain purposes, produce an appropriate effect alone ; as, for instance, the 8 and 4 feet flue stops, or the 16, 8, and 4 ; or, in some cases, the 16, 8, 4, and 2 feet.

810. The Mutation stops—*i.e.*, the Fifth, Tenth, Twelfth, Tierce, Larigot, &c.—are not intended to be used alone, the class to which they belong being designed expressly for the filling up of some of the intervals between the Foundation stops, and for so doing away with the leanness of bare octave-work. They depend on the first class of stops for their good effect, and must not, therefore, be employed without them. In using the Mutation stops care should be taken that the Foundation rank, the *next smallest* in size, is also drawn with it to *cover* it ; otherwise its sound will appear too remarkable, and perhaps even offensive. Thus the Twelfth should always have the Fifteenth drawn with it ; and the Tierce or Larigot, the octave Fifteenth, at any rate in the bass.

811. The Fifth and Tenth, being *Double* Mutation stops, forming the Twelfth and Tierce to the Double Open Diapason, constitute no part of the *Unison* harmonic series ; for which reason they should never be drawn without their fundamental stop of 16 feet. An exception to this rule is sometimes made abroad, with good effect, on the Pedal, concerning which more further on.

812. The Compound stops can only be successfully used when blended with some Foundation and Mutation stops.

813. The Foundation stops give distinctness, the Mutation stops fulness, and the Compound stops brightness and point to the general organ tone.

The character of tone of some of the leading stops ; and the purposes to which they may be applied.   814. The Unison stops are, of course, the most important in an organ, as they are also generally the most numerous. In drawing any of these separately, or blending them together, attention should be directed to their various qualities of tone. Some stops possess a character that renders them more applicable to one kind of music than to another ; and, again, some mix better than others together.

815. *Open Diapason.* The tone of this stop is full, sonorous, and solemn. It is the one best, adapted for the performance of slow music in dispersed harmony, particularly when there are many suspensions occurring in the progress of the piece. The Stopped Diapason is advantageously added to the Open Diapason, when used as above, to give body to the pure sounds of the open pipes ; and the Dulciana, if there be one on the same clavier, is also drawn, as adding slightly to the general effect. All reedy-toned flue stops, as the Gamba, &c., are foreign to the purpose, as interfering with the smooth and *velvety* tone of the best English Diapasons.

816. The *Stopped Diapason* is fluty in its character of tone, and free from all reediness or roughness. Generally speaking, it tells better, when used singly, for solo purposes than for full harmony, its tone not usually being sufficiently sonorous for the latter purpose. In short passages of tranquil character it can be used with charming effect. As a combination stop, it is one of the most useful in an organ. It is the best one to use with the Clarionet, with the tone of which it blends admirably, or with the Swell Hautboy, when the latter is to

be employed as a solo stop. In certain cases it forms an excellent accompaniment to a single voice, being very prompt in its speech, as well as light and travelling in its tone. The Lieblich Gedact, as a Choir organ stop, forms an excellent accompaniment to the Swell Hautboy.

817. *The Dulciana* is usually a stop of great delicacy, smoothness, and gentleness of tone. Its sound is lighter than that of the Stopped Diapason, but clearer and of a more singing character. It is the most used singly as an accompanimental stop to some of the solo stops on the other Manuals, as the Stopped Diapason in the Great organ or the Hautboy in the Swell, its own situation being usually on the Choir Manual. The Dulciana may, however, be effectively employed as a solo stop in the treble part in cantabile passages, with the Diapasons in the Swell (closed) by way of accompaniment, and also much in the same way as the Open Diapasons ; *i.e.*, in full harmony, to which stop it may be considered as a diminutive or echo.

818. *The Gamba*, from the resemblance of its tone to that of stringed instruments, is peculiarly well adapted for four-part playing, particularly for music that has many chromatic progressions in the harmony. When of weak intonation, it tells best by itself ; but, when of strong tone, it sounds better when blended with the Stopped Diapason, Clarabella, or German Hohl-flöte. For accompanimental purposes it requires to be used with some caution. A Gamba of strong intonation, used alternately with Stopped Diapason and Stopped Flute (one of them of metal) on another Manual produces a most charming effect. The pungent tones of the former, followed by the liquid tones of the latter combination, presents a most exquisite contrast. What has been said of the Gamba applies mostly also to the Keraulophon and other *reedy*-toned unison flue stops.

819. *The Clarabella*, from its powerful fluty quality, forms an excellent unison solo stop by itself at times when a strong and decided flute tone is required. As a combination stop, for use with the Clarionet or Hautboy, it sometimes imparts too much body to render the imitation close.

820. *The Trumpet* in the Great organ is seldom used as a solo stop. When it is so, it should always be accompanied by the Diapasons. When thus blended it sounds well, if played in harmony ; in major keys its effect being grand and dignified, and, in minor, solemn and impressive. Diatonic progressions of harmony are better suited to the tone-character of this stop than chromatic. The Swell Trumpet is much used for choral accompaniment, as well as for solo playing ; and the same may be said of all the other full scale unison reed stops of that department. When employed for the former purpose, it has the Diapasons drawn with it ; and often, also, the Principal and smaller stops, according to circumstances. As a rule, all reed stops should have some unison flue stop or stops combined with them, to add body to the penetrative and powerful character of that produced by the reeds.

821. *Clarionet.* The best flue stop to draw with the Clarionet is the Stopped Diapason ; as this not only mixes well with the former, but does not give more body and thickness to the tone of the stop than it should have in its imitative capacity, and it is not generally used in any other. This stop is often used, among other purposes, for playing out the whole or a portion of the melody of a psalm tune upon. For an accompaniment thereto the Swell Diapasons and Hautboy answers well, with a couple of soft stops (16 and 8 feet pitch) for a Pedal bass.

822. *The Hautboy*, as already intimated, when about to be used as a solo stop, will tell best with the Stopped Diapason only added. The instrument itself

(Hautboy) is by nature but of thin tone; hence, to preserve the resemblance between the tone of the original and the prototype, a flue stop of light but firm tone is the most appropriate to be employed. When used for the purpose of accompaniment to voices, the Hautboy stop tells best combined with both the Diapasons, and perhaps, also, though not always, with the Principal, which latter stop will sometimes blend and sometimes not, according to the exact character of the reed stop.

823. In blending together some of the smaller Foundation stops with the unison, for the purpose of accompaniment, they are generally taken in their regular octave progression. Thus, after the 8-feet stops are drawn, some of those of 4 feet are next brought on; and then, if necessary, those of 2 feet; but not those of 2 feet first, and then others of 4 feet. The Flute or Principal, or both, according to the strength of the unison tone, therefore follow the unison stops; and then the Piccolo or the Fifteenth, if necessary; and not *vice versâ*. For particular effects, unusual combinations are made; as for instance, 16 and 4 feet stops without any of 8; or 8 and 2 feet stops, omitting those of 4 feet. Such combinations produce the best effect when compounded of members of the covered or light-toned Flute-work. The tone of stops of the Open Diapason species is generally too strong and sonorous for such purposes.

On the combination of the stops for the production of any required strength of tone. 824. By means of an appropriate combination of the stops which all well-arranged or complete organs contain, any strength of organ tone may be obtained, from the softest to the loudest. The kinds of stop arrangement that will produce these several desirable and necessary gradations of sound may be distinguished by a particular letter or letters, thus: P P, P, M P, M F, F, and F F; under which heads may be conveniently given such combinations as will produce the strength of tone that the musical meaning of those letters are understood to indicate.

825. P P. For the production of a *pianissimo*, a single soft-toned 8-feet flue stop* on the Manual will be sufficient, as a Stopped Diapason, Dulciana, or Gamba, &c. On the Pedal, its own bass (16 feet) may be drawn, or, if that is not present, some other stop of an equally subdued tone. It is generally of advantage to add a "helper" (that is, a stop giving the octave above) to the Pedal; this can either be a soft Pedal stop of 8 feet, or the Manual stop coupled to the original Pedal stop.

826. P, for *piano*, all the smooth-toned Manual 8-feet flue stops. On the Pedal, the corresponding 16-feet stops should be drawn. The addition of an 8-feet open stop will in many cases improve the effect of the Pedal; but, if a stop of this kind should not exist in that department, one of a similar nature can be borrowed from the second Manual; or the first Manual may be coupled to the Pedal.

827. M P, a *mezzo piano*, is gained by adding the 4-feet flue stops of the Manual (Principal, Flute, &c.) to those already named, and those of 8 feet to the Pedal.

828. For the production of a medium strength of tone between the two last-given gradations, combine all the *soft* 8 and 4 feet Manual stops, as the stopped Diapason, Dulciana, and Flute. These together possess more brightness, but less fulness, than the former, and less roundness than the latter.

---

* The size of stop here spoken of may or may not be its standard size. When, in organ music, "8-feet flue stops" are directed to be used, the expression is understood to mean the combination of all stops, except the reeds, that give the 8-feet sound. This interpretation is always accepted when speaking of the *use* of the stops.

829. M F. A *mezzo forte* is produced by adding the 2⅔-feet and 2-feet stops (Twelfth, Fifteenth, &c.) on the Manual to those of 8 and 4 feet and those of 5⅓ and 4 feet to the Pedal.

830. F. For a *forte*, the collected Compound stops may be brought into play. When a medium between the two last-mentioned gradations is required, only one Compound stop need be drawn.

831. FF. A full climax is secured by adding the reed stops (Trumpet, Clarion, &c.) to the foregoing.

832. A medium may here again be obtained by adding the 8-feet reed stop only to the flue stops previously drawn out.

833. The Manual 16-feet flue stops (*doubles*) have not been specified in any of the above gradations, because it is not so much the nature of such stops to add power as weight, gravity, and solemnity to the tone of the other stops. Their use with or rejection from any particular combination, therefore, does not so properly come under consideration when the question of *strength* of tone is being discussed as when that of *character* of tone is being treated of. Almost any combination, whether loud or soft, may receive the accession of a 16-feet stop with advantage under particular circumstances. Thus, some soft or moderately strong combinations that would, perhaps, give a tone approaching towards joyfulness become imbued with a more serious character when a stop of 16-feet pitch is added thereto, and is therefore rendered a more fit accompaniment to music of a sad character. A strong combination which possesses the brilliance and point of the Mixture work, and perhaps also the impressiveness of the reed stops, acquires weight and magnificence from 16-feet Manual stops, particularly if they are accompanied by double Mutation stops and a 16-feet reed stop.

834. Moreover, the organ should be used in a somewhat different manner when any 16-feet Manual stops are drawn ; otherwise the excellent effects which that class of stops are especially calculated to produce will be to some extent obscured. The omission of all "doubles," as a rule, from the Manuals of English organs until of late years rendered it compulsory on organists to invent a sort of substitute for them *in effect;* for it was found that the organ tone lacked the requisite gravity and dignity, however numerous the *unison* stops might be. Performers on that instrument, therefore, had to lay aside the purer and more strict style of playing as being "ineffective," and to fall back upon the system of keeping some eight or nine notes down at a time to draw from their instruments anything approaching a broad and massive character of tone. Latterly, the serious omission above adverted to has been supplied by addition to old organs and by incorporation with new ones ; and the care already hinted at, as being required in playing on an instrument possessing so valuable an acquisition, consists in not adopting so full a style of playing when the 16-feet stops are drawn as when they are not. The former is viewed as rather a complicated *substitute* for the latter ; and if *both* are had recourse to simultaneously, the one is most likely to destroy the effect of the other. A very charming contrast may, however, frequently be produced by accompanying a chant or chorale, sometimes in four parts *with* the doubles drawn, sometimes in about six *without* them.

835. It may be mentioned here that many object to the doubles being used in accompanying vocal compositions in the fugal style, particularly at those points where the subject is led off by one of the higher parts. There is much reason in this objection, although it only applies to the precise times specified. The doubles may between whiles be introduced with even greater effect when the voices are

moving in harmonic masses. For the best illustrations of the occasions when the 16-feet stops may or may not be used in choral accompaniment, the organ part to *Israel in Egypt*, written by Mendelssohn for the Handel Society, may be consulted with the greatest advantage.

836. When the organ is being used as a *solo* instrument—*i.e.*, in voluntaries —the above objection does not hold good. The doubles cannot then interfere with or mislead any voices. Moreover, the tradition throughout Germany is that Sebastian Bach *generally* played his fugues with the doubles drawn ; therefore those who would aspire to perform his works after his own manner can only do so by frequently availing themselves of that dignified class of stops. As to the " octave below " being discernible at the starting of a fugue, there is no doubt that any moderately educated musical ear can detect *any* interval or stop in an organ that it cares to listen for, whether it be the Double Diapason, the Tierce, the Twelfth, or what not ; but that affords no sufficient ground for the exclusion of any of those stops. Besides, even supposing the doubles to have an undesirable effect for some half dozen bars in the course of a musical composition, if it has a most advantageous influence in the remaining hundred or so, which fact is beyond question, the far greater evil would arise from their *exclusion*. The fact is, no single rule would be a good guide in this matter. The " lead " in the first movement of the " St. Ann's Fugue " sounds bad with the doubles ; that of the last movement as ill without them.

837. Neither has the influence of the *Swell* been included in the foregoing scheme for producing various degrees of strong or weak tone. The Swell is of inestimable advantage for all classes of accompaniment, as it enables the performer to increase the tone when the voices may be getting flat, and to decrease it when all is going well. This power is independent of, and supplementary to, that of imparting expression to the music, which latter attribute is of such peculiar value, as well as being highly acceptable to those who have true appreciation and sound musical feeling.

On the adaptation of the organ tone to the true purposes of choral accompaniment.   838. In applying the various combinations and resources already specified to the purposes of choral or congregational accompaniment, there are many circumstances to be taken into consideration, and which ought always to influence the selection. The first and greatest of these is, of course, the prevailing character of the words about to be sung, whether they are jubilant or supplicatory, and with which the accompaniment should always accord, so that it may produce a suitable impression. A musical composer, when scoring a secular work for an orchestra, employs those instruments the quality and character of tone of which are the most applicable to the subject of the words and the spirit of the music. An organ being the more seemly substitute for an orchestra in a church, and containing, as it does, imitations of most of the orchestral instruments, an organist should, by a skilful combination of its different stops, adapt the tone of the instrument to the sense of the words and the character of the music that are being sung, in order that the result of his rightly directed efforts may be as appropriate and acceptable as possible. When it is recollected how much pains is taken with the accompaniment to heighten the effect of music, some of which is avowedly written chiefly for man's amusement and pastime, it is obvious that at least the same amount of care should be exercised to secure an equally appropriate accompaniment to those vocal strains which occur in the edifying services of the church. An organist cannot be too mindful of this, nor can he exercise too much forethought and discretion in making this most important condition of the utility of his office legitimately perceptible. It is in this particular, of all others, that he has the opportunity of showing his superiority over the mechanical work of a self-acting instrument. A barrel organ can be made to execute music with the utmost precision and finish; it may even be made to shift its own stops; but it cannot be endowed with the *reason* necessary wherewith to direct the *application* of these combinations to their special purposes. A *mind* must be in active operation to do this worthily; and herein lies the secret of an organist's great advantage in performance over an instrument from which the choral accompaniment is "ground" out. Nothing can be less acceptable than to hear bright stops used, and an animated style of playing adopted, when the words are prayerful or supplicatory; or, on the other hand, to hear only heavy stops brought into requisition when the subject is a jubilant one. Every large and well-designed organ necessarily contains many stops that are appropriate and inappropriate for *all* occasions; and it is, therefore, capable of considerably heightening or of injuring the effect, according to whether its powers be rightly directed or not; and an organist who misses their judicious application, whether from causes resting with himself or from the influence of others, is open to the supposition of being disregardful of the trust reposed in him, and may, therefore, hazard the respect due to his office —consequences against which every organist should guard himself by the exercise of his best powers of discrimination.

839. After ascertaining the prevailing character of the words, the next point to be considered is the exact *quantity*, as well as description, of loud or soft tone that the circumstances of time and place would seem to suggest as the most appropriate to the occasion. As the number of the congregation will vary on different occasions, so also will the strength of the united voices of its members. The amount of organ tone, therefore, necessary for directing and giving support to the voices of a full congregation will consequently be too much when there is but a "thin attendance." Particular care, therefore, should be taken to modify the tone in some way, so that it may not be too strong for a reduced number of voices, and yet strong enough to prevent the congregation singing out of tune or time. The simplest way of lessening the strength of the accompaniment, without destroying its spirit and character, is to draw, on the second or third Manual, stops of the same size, and perhaps name, that one would use on the first, if the concourse of persons were larger. Any modification in this combination that the peculiarities of the particular organ might render necessary would, of course, be taken into account. With the resources at his command which every parish church organ ought to possess, and which many do, an organist ought to find no difficulty in accommodating its tone to any exigency that may arise.

840. At the same time that every organist should view his calling as a high one, demanding the exercise of great intelligence as well as technical knowledge in the fulfilment of its duties, it should also be borne in mind that the introduction of organs into churches, and their judicious employment there, are but means to the attainment of certain ends. What those ends and objects may be will be best gathered from the following quotation from the introduction to Schneider's *School for the Organ*, which well describes what is looked for from the church organs and organists of Germany:—"An organ consecrated to the sanctuary and to sacred music is intended to be subservient to the edification of a congregation assembled together for divine worship; to support and to accompany, in a proper manner, the singing; and to be instrumental in promoting a devotional frame of mind and the edification of the soul, and its elevation above everything earthly, to the contemplation of things invisible and divine—a noble object, which can only be obtained by a style of performance suited to the holiness of the place and the

sacredness of the subjects. The proper management of this sublime instrument can induce a devotional spirit and an elevation of mind in the scientific hearer, as well as in any individual of feeling. The sound of the organ is able to insinuate itself by mild and tender tones, and then the mind is filled with the pious tranquillity of filial devotion ; but it can also elevate itself to majesty and pomp, and peal and roll like storm and thunder, and then it elevates our hearts with sublime emotions. Whilst most other instruments can only express individual feelings, this kingly instrument can produce a variety of emotions. The organ alone can best fill with its tones the lofty vaults of the vast cathedral, support the singing of large congregations, and, by its power, operate upon the religious feelings."

THE CAUSE OF MANY FAULTS IN AN ORGAN, WITH THEIR REMEDIES.

CHAPTER XXX.

841. IT is important that an organist should be in a position to ascertain the cause of the faults existing, or occasionally appearing, in his organ ; and also what are the steps necessary to be taken to remedy them. Some derangements arise from such simple causes, and can be so easily set right, that an organist might remove them himself, if quite certain of the seat of the disorder ; and, by so doing, save the organ-tuner perhaps a long journey to rectify what may not occupy him ten minutes when he is there. Schneider, in his *Organ School* (page 60, first English edition), expresses himself on the above subject in the following words :—— " It is, generally speaking, necessary for the organ-player that he should make himself as intimately acquainted as possible with the internal construction of the organ, with the nature of every single part, the combination of which constitutes its whole ; as well of the particular parts of the mechanism which cause the pipes to sound, as also of the nature, peculiarities, and properties of the pipes themselves, in the manifold variety of their make and the various kinds of sounds which are constantly produced ; by which means alone a right and appropriate style of managing the instrument, and one in all respects suitable to its nature, can be attained. But as regards a regularly appointed organist, the knowledge is absolutely indispensable ; for it is his first duty to take care of his instrument, to preserve it, and carefully to look after it—a duty which can only be fulfilled when he is able to discover immediately the cause of those derangements in the mechanism, &c., which are unavoidable in that instrument, composed of so many diversified parts ; and even to remedy the defects himself, in many cases, when an organ-builder may not be immediately at hand. If the organist, thus acquainted with the construction of the organ, fulfils that duty to the fullest extent, and, in those cases for which he does not find himself competent, procures promptly the assistance of some qualified person, an organ may continue for a long time in a sound condition, and a more extensive repair be rendered unnecessary for a considerable period. On the contrary, an ignorance of the construction of the organ, and negligence in the care of the instrument, and also with respect to getting small defects remedied, always leads to inevitable and more considerable damage ; and not only do expensive repairs become requisite, but also an instrument thus neglected can often only be restored in a very imperfect manner."

THE UNBIDDEN SOUNDING OF A PIPE FROM CAUSES IN THE REGION OF THE PALLETS.

Ciphering caused by dirt on the pallet.

842. Among the numerous faults and derangements to which all organs are at times liable, one of the most frequently

recurring is that known as a "ciphering;" in other words, the sounding of a pipe, on the drawing of a stop, without any key being pressed down. A ciphering may arise from various causes. Some grit or chips may have worked down from the pipes, through the table and the channels of the sound-board, to the surface of the pallet; and, by resting on its edge, and holding it a little way open, thereby admit sufficient wind into the groove to make the first stop sound that is afterwards drawn. A derangement from this cause is frequently indicated by the controlling key being a little below the level of the others. To remedy it, the front-board of the wind-chest must be taken off, the pallet drawn open, and its surface carefully wiped, as well as that part of the groove against which it "beds," with some dry, rough substance, to remove the impediment.

843. To facilitate the rectification of such casualties, some German organ-builders fasten on the front-board with large wooden screws, having sexagon heads, so large that they can be turned by the fingers alone; so that, in the event of a pallet becoming deranged during the service, the organist can get at it with little loss of time, without the aid of noisy tools, and perhaps put it to rights before the organ is again required.

Ciphering from a pallet-spring being too weak.

844. Or the ciphering may be caused by the pallet-spring being too weak to cause the key-movement to return quickly, and the pallet to thoroughly close over the pallet-hole. If this is the cause, the key will rise sluggishly, and only partially; and the ciphering will continue till the key has been raised to its proper level by the hand. In this case, a piece of coiled wire, similar to that on the fourth string of a violin, and called by organ-builders "check-spring," may be fastened to the tracker, outside the wind-chest, and to some neighbouring wood-work, which will assist the return of the movement, and accelerate the closing of the pallet. Or, still better, the weak spring can be removed, and replaced by a stronger one.

Ciphering caused by the pallet catching on a direction-pin.

845. Sometimes a ciphering will be caused by the pallet descending too low, and catching on one of the side direction-pins, an accident that is likely to occur if a key be struck too violently and suddenly. To cure this, the front-board must be taken off, and the pallet released. In some German organs the two side direction-pins are omitted, and one pin of extra stoutness introduced instead, and placed in the centre of the *front* of the pallet, where a small vertical groove is cut in the pallet, to allow the pallet to descend and ascend without leaving the pin.

Ciphering from damp loosening the leather; or heat warping the pallet.

846. A ciphering will frequently arise—particularly in instruments that are so situated as to be exposed to the changes of atmosphere in an aggravated form—from the damp in winter loosening the leather from the surface of the pallet, allowing it to swerve from its place over the pallet-hole, and admitting wind into the groove; or from the heat in summer warping the pallet as it dries it, and, by destroying its evenness of surface, preventing its bedding properly over the pallet-hole. To remedy either of these derangements, the pallet has to be taken out; and, in the one case, the leather has to be fresh glued on to the pallet; while, in the other, the pallet has to be planed down afresh, newly faced with leather, and then re-fastened to the sound-board.

847. The pallet in some French sound-boards is made without leather pallet-hinges, but with simply a pin passing through a puncture in the tail end of the pallet for the pallet to work upon. This arrangement presents the advantage of allowing an almost instantaneous substitution of a sound pallet for a defective

one ; and it also admits of the immediate resumption of the use of that pallet, instead of its remaining idle for many hours while the glue is drying. It also admits of the easy cleaning of the joint end of the pallet, which is always a tiresome operation with pallets fastened on in the usual way.

Ciphering caused by a pull-down being rusty. 848. A ciphering is sometimes caused by a pull-down having become rusty, which causes it to become fixed in the hole in the brass plate through which it ought to pass, and holding the pallet a little way open. This fault can generally be remedied by drawing the pallet open, and cleaning the pull-down with scouring paper ; care at the same time being taken not to bend the wire, which would establish another source of ciphering.

THE UNBIDDEN SOUNDING OF A PIPE FROM FAULTS IN THE KEY-MOVEMENTS.

Ciphering from some adhesive substance falling between the keys. 849. A ciphering will sometimes be caused by some derangement of the key-movement. Commencing at the keys, one of the commonest causes of ciphering is the falling of melted wax or tallow on and between the keys, which will attach two together. This is soon remedied by carefully scraping the sides as well as the surface of the keys with a penknife, to remove the cause of adhesion. Or it may be caused by dirt or a pin having fallen between two keys. The best way to proceed to remove the impediment, in that case, is to " work it out," which may be effected by taking hold of the two keys, in front, with the thumb and forefinger of each hand, and raising the one key at the same time that the other is lowered ; drawing them apart with a certain amount of firmness, without violence, to encourage the impediment to fall.

Ciphering caused by a key warping. 850. Another cause of a sticking at the key is its warping from excessive heat, which causes it to rub against its neighbour, and become fixed. The eye will easily discover whereabouts the key is out of the parallel, if it is in the fore part of the key, as well as the probable point of contact. To remedy this, the key has to be removed from its place, and either scraped, or a few very fine chips pared off from the part where it touches the next key ; which may be done sufficiently to ease the key, without disfiguring it. To remove the key, the book-desk has first to be taken out ; and, if the disarranged key is in one of the lower sets, the upper must be lifted out, to lay the right Manual bare. Modern organs are usually so constructed that the Manuals can be moved in or out with little more difficulty than the drawers of a chest of drawers, which is a most convenient arrangement.

Ciphering from a sticker binding. 851. Sometimes a sticker will " bind " in the hole in the register through which it should move, from damp swelling both portions of the wood-work, whereby the hole in the register becomes smaller, and the sticker larger. This can be cured by taking out the sticker, and either filing the hole in the register a little larger, or by scraping the sticker. Or the sticker may bind, from the black-lead having worn away from its surface ; in which case more might be added with a black-lead pencil, without, however, damping it.

Ciphering caused by a backfall getting off the sticker. 852. In a backfall movement, a ciphering will sometimes be caused by the backfall shooting off the sticker, under the influence of a violent blow on the key, and catching on the top of the sticker-pin. To set this right, it is simply necessary to press the sticker-pin carefully, but firmly—without, however, bending it—into its place under the drill-hole in the backfall, and lowering the backfall into its right place. On doing this, the key will resume its proper level.

Ciphering from grit in the centre-holes ; or by swelling of the movement.

853. A ciphering will sometimes be caused by grit, dirt, or small wood or metal chips working into the pin-holes of some part of the movement, or between a square or backfall and the frame ; which, by preventing the complete action of the movement, will hold the pallet a little way open, and also cause the key to remain a little way down. By tapping the key rapidly, the fault will frequently correct itself, and save further trouble : if not, it must be sought for through the movement, and removed. Or some part of the movement may have swollen, and be thus made to bind too tightly on the pin. This might be rectified by cutting the centre-hole the least degree larger ; but if the fault only appears in damp weather, and then only slightly, it is usually better to leave it to be corrected by a drier and warmer atmosphere : particularly as the wood, by contraction at such a time, might otherwise leave the pin-hole sufficiently large to cause a looseness of action and a rattling.

THE UNBIDDEN SOUNDING OF A PIPE FROM DEFECTS IN THE SOUND-BOARD.

854. A running. One of the most tiresome and vexatious defects which can occur in an organ is a *running*, because the region of the disarrangement is frequently one of the most hidden parts of the organ. Its seat is always the sound-board, or immediately adjacent parts, and it consists of an unbidden sounding of a second pipe on the sounding of a first, which may arise from a variety of causes. The pitch of the second sound, however, will sometimes assist one in discovering the seat of the disorder, if some allowance be made for its pitch being *flat*, and its sound not well defined, on account of the defect frequently being produced by a very small quantity of wind, which *breathes* rather than *blows* into the pipe. For this reason, the evil is not apparent when all the stops on the sound-board are drawn ; for then there are so many outlets for the fugitive wind, that it disperses and escapes without producing any audible effect ; but when one or two soft stops only are drawn, then it frequently becomes painfully so.

A running caused by an upper-board being too loose.

855. A running may arise from an upper-board not being screwed down sufficiently ; which is soon remedied by tightening the screws in the immediate vicinity of the pipe originally sounded. Or it may be caused by a leakage from one groove to the next. Whether it arises in this manner will be indicated by the pitch of the unbidden sound, when compared with the plantation of the pipes. If the pipes are planted semitonally, as in plan 2, and the secondary sound is the half-tone above or below the tone sounded ; or if the pipes are disposed tonally, as in plans 1 and 3, and the unbidden sound is a tone above or below that produced in the usual way, the defect will, in either case, be traceable to the above-mentioned cause.

A running caused by a sound-board bar separating from the table ; or by an unsound bar.

856. Or a sound-board bar has "sprung"—*i.e.*, has become partially separated from the table ; or a small crack has "started" in the sound-board bar itself, allowing a little wind to pass through from one groove to the next. To stop this, the crevice

is well covered with paper, coated, and saturated with glue. Sometimes, to cure this fault, recourse is had to "bleeding," which, however, is only an objectionable method of hiding the fault.

A humming caused by one slider touching and partly drawing a second. 857. A disagreeable humming, not unlike a running in effect, although it is not in reality one, will sometimes be caused by one slider rubbing against the next as it is being drawn, and partially drawing that also, causing a little wind to pass into the pipes of a second stop. In this case the effect will be like a running of an aggravated kind, inasmuch as the defect will appear to exist on nearly every key of the Manual. The unbidden sounds will be rather lower in pitch than the correct sounds, though scarcely amounting to a semitone. To remedy this evil, a peg might be driven in between the two sliders, or one of them might be planed at the edge to prevent its touching the other. As the objectionable custom of placing two, or even as many as three, sliders together, without intermediate bearers, is entirely discarded by all modern organ-builders, the liability of a humming from the disarrangement last named is confined to old organs. When it occurs, all the stops that are not actually in use should be pressed in.

A humming caused by pipes standing in too close proximity. 858. Sometimes the unbidden sounding of a second pipe will arise from the pipes being packed too closely together, so that the wind that passes out at the mouth of one pipe enters that of another, causing it to produce a moaning sound. This evil is frequently not an easy one to remove. The primary cause of this is the sound-board being too small, which leads to the pipes being placed in too close proximity. In some cases this defect can in a manner be cured by turning the mouth of one of the pipes in another direction; or by mounting the pipe on a longer foot; or by conveyancing it off to another situation. The most thorough cure for such an evil, however, is the introduction of a new and larger sound-board.

DEFECTS IN THE KEY-MOVEMENT.

A springing in the key-movement. 859. A Manual key will sometimes go down about half-way, under the pressure of the finger, without causing any sound; after which something will appear suddenly to snap, and the key will descend the remainder of the distance with a run, the organ at the same moment sounding. This disagreeable effect is caused by the roller being too weak. Instead of its setting the second arm in motion, the instant the first one is operated upon by the key, the roller "springs" or twists for a time, until it has in this manner derived a sufficient accession of power to give a tug at the pallet; the resistance at which being thus overcome, the pallet starts down, giving to the touch the tiresome breaking sensation already noticed. This can only be cured by introducing stronger, or thicker, or iron rollers.

A dead resistance opposed to the finger by the key movement. 860. In some cases, a key will at first altogether resist the touch of the finger, and will not move until the pressure has been much increased, when it will suddenly give way, and descend, accompanied by a sharp clacking noise. This defect, quite as annoying as the last, is found more frequently in old organs than in new, where the roller-arms are of iron, instead of wood, with metal tracker-hooks attached in both cases. The iron, after a few years, rusts, causing a grating and biting, instead of a free and immediate action, which leads to the dogged resistance experienced at the keys. New wooden roller-arms are the only cure for this fault.

A thumping at the keys.   861. A thumping will sometimes be heard as the keys go down. This will be the case if the layers of cloth or baize under the front of the keys have become hard, or are too thin. The fault is easily remedied by the substitution of soft and thick baize, or by the addition of an extra layer.

A rattling in the key-movement, from the noisy nature of the materials.   862. The original key-movements of old organs were frequently so noisy, rattling, and squeaking, and their every motion so audible, that whatever the organist played seemed to have the questionable addition of a "castanet" accompaniment. This offensive interruption arose from metal having been used where wood has subsequently been found to be so much superior. The cause of the rattling was this. On touching a key, the first tracker-hook produced a "click" as it struck against the first *iron* arm ; the second iron arm produced a similar noise on coming in contact with the second tracker-hook ; the "metal against metal" not only produced a squeaking or a grating as the parts moved, on the finger descending, but, when the finger left the key, and the movement returned, the tracker-hooks vibrated and chattered in the holes of the iron arms. Thus a rustling and sometimes also a chirping noise accompanied the action of the movement when it ascended, as well as when it descended. The removal of the cause of the defects noticed in the two preceding sections will lead to the disappearance of those just noticed.

863. In modern organs iron roller-arms are almost always avoided, even when the rollers themselves are of that metal, and wooden ones introduced, as being far more quiet in their action. Even in the few instances where the contact of metal with metal cannot be avoided, as at the junction of the tracker-hook with the pull-down, some organ-builders do not allow the two pieces of metal to touch, but "bush," *i.e.*, line the loop of the pull-down with cloth, to silence the action. For the like purpose of lessening the friction and quieting the motion, other organ-builders introduce into each of the studs which support the rollers a kind of leather button, in the centre of which the roller-pin noiselessly works.

A rattling sometimes caused by trackers flapping together.   864. Sometimes, in "extended" key-movements, a noise will be caused by the long trackers flapping together. This is soon remedied by introducing an additional register. As, however, every additional register, or comb, adds to the friction, to avoid this latter, some Continental builders carry the trackers over little box-wood or ivory reels, by which means they are supported and steadied, without the touch being made heavier or more sluggish.

A key down without producing any sound.   865. Occasionally a key will be found to have sunk—*i.e.*, it will be down—without, however, causing any ciphering. This will arise from some connecting portion of the key-movement having slipped or given way. For instance, it will occur if either of the tracker-hooks is broken ; and it can, in that case, soon be remedied with a fresh piece of wire. Or, if the rollers are provided with wooden roller-arms, and the union of the roller-arms with the trackers is effected by means of tapped wires and buttons, it will sometimes arise from the button slipping down the tapped wire. In this case, all that is necessary to correct the disarrangement is to screw the button up again, which is done by turning it to the *right*. The tracker, however, should be held firmly, immediately above the tapped wire, to prevent its twisting, or a cause of second derangement may arise while the first is being removed. A dumb key will sometimes be caused by the breaking of a square, a casualty to which squares are very liable if they are formed of one piece of wood only, so that the grain of the wood necessarily crosses one of the arms. To cure this fault thoroughly, and prevent its recurrence, a new and stronger square must be provided.

The touch of the Manuals too shallow at certain seasons and too deep at others.

866. In warm, dry weather the touch sometimes becomes "shallow," and the pallets do not open sufficiently; consequently the pipes sound out of tune, from the inadequate supply of wind, particularly in the bass. In cold, wet weather the touch on the contrary, becomes "too deep;" which change renders the playing more difficult, and also causes a tendency to ciphering, from the keys then pressing against the thumping-board, and producing the same effect as its being slightly held down by the finger. The variations in the depth of the touch are caused solely by atmospheric change; the heat, by drying and contracting the building frame and key-movements, slackening it; and the damp, by swelling and expanding them, tightening the touch. There are several ways of remedying these faults.

867. Most modern organs are provided either with small wedges, placed under each end of the square or backfall frame, immediately over each Manual, or with screws; the former of which are pressed in or drawn out, and the latter turned down or up, according as the touch requires deepening or being made shallow. The touch of the entire row of keys can thus be altered in a very few minutes. In older organs which have not these facilities, the depth of touch can only be regulated by screwing or unscrewing the button of every key separately, which process consumes a great deal of time. To make a key "higher," the button must be turned to the right; to make it "lower," it must be screwed to the left. While this is being done, some one should be at the keys, who, by passing the fingers lightly over the key being regulated and its neighbours, will ascertain whether the key is on an exact level with the others; and if it is not, he will call out whether it is required to be "higher" or "lower" to make it so.

An unevenness in the level of the keys of the manual.

868. A single key will sometimes be out of the level with the other keys. If it is below, without causing a ciphering, the irregularity is most probably caused by the button having slipped, which, in that case, must be screwed up again; and a second one might be added, and screwed up close to the first one, to assist it. If a key is above the proper level, without causing a ciphering, it has probably risen from the rapid return of the movement, on the quick or sudden removal of the finger from the key. A slight tapping on the key will generally be sufficient to cause it, or the movement, to adjust itself.

A key screwed up too high sometimes causes the speech of the pipes to tremble.

869. A key that is screwed up rather too high will frequently cause the pallet to open and close slightly and rapidly, admitting a small quantity of wind into the groove by fits and starts, and imparting to the speech of the pipes an effect not unlike that produced by a tremulant when in motion. To stop this it is simply necessary to unscrew the button a little. A key that has slightly deepened from change of weather will sometimes produce this effect.

A ciphering caused by the breaking of a pedal-spring.

870. A ciphering is sometimes caused by the spring that should raise a pedal having broken, whereby the weight of the pedal-key drags on the movement, and has the same effect as the weight of the hand on a Manual key. If a Manual remains coupled to the Pedal while this fault exists, it will cause an apparent ciphering there also, but which will be found to have no real existence on disconnecting the Manual, as the supposed derangement will then immediately disappear. If the Pedals are only furnished with bell-springs, they will be very noisy, as well as more liable to the above accident, and should be removed, and better springs provided.

DISARRANGEMENTS CONNECTED WITH THE DRAW-STOP ACTION AND SLIDERS.

A draw-stop rod will sometimes come out too far, or go too far in.

871. A draw-stop rod will occasionally come out far beyond its proper distance, and will also return too far, and that without affecting the stop, which will be either always in or always out. This fault arises from the connecting-pin at one of the centres having worked out ; and it may therefore occur either at the junction of the draw-stop rod with the trundle-arm, of the second trundle-arm with the trace, the trace with the lever, &c. All that is in general required is the restoration of the pin to its original position, or its place supplied by a new one.

A draw-stop is sometimes very stiff.

872. Sometimes, on the contrary, a draw-stop is very diffi-cult to draw ; in the language of organ-builders, it is " stiff." This derangement is generally caused by atmospheric change. In damp weather the upper-board and slider become swollen, and, by pressing against each other, increase the amount of friction. The consequent stiffness is usually removed by slightly loosening the screws, which fasten down the upper-board, which allows the slider more liberty. On the re-appearance of warm weather, and the subse-quent drying, shrinking, and return of the wood-work to its original and precise dimensions, the screws should of course be tightened again. In hot weather, however, as well as in cold and damp, a stiffness will sometimes appear in the action of the draw-stops ; but in this case the cause would be the warping of the upper-board or slider, which would lead to a "binding" of those parts. An abatement of the heat would be accompanied by an abatement of the fault. In the course of time, however, it may happen that if the screws of the upper-board are loosened sufficiently to remove all stiffness from the draw-stop, a running will be heard ; and, on tightening them, the stiffness will return. This is an evidence that the repeated changes of temperature and condition of the atmosphere have had the effect of permanently disturbing the accurate adjustment of the several parts to one another. When this is the case, the upper-board requires to be removed, the slider taken out, and the several parts "eased" at those points where the binding occurs.

DEFECTS IN THE BELLOWS AND THE WINDING OF THE ORGAN.

A creaking from fric-tion at the centres.

873. One of the most frequently recurring faults in a bellows, fortunately, is generally one of the most easy to cure ; namely, a squeaking or creaking. This commonly arises either from the friction of the bellows-handle on its centre, or from a similar rubbing at the junction of the

pump-rods with the lever or feeders ; and is removed by simply applying a little grease.

A clacking, caused by hard valves.
874. A clacking will sometimes be heard at the moment that the feeders are drawn up. This is only perceived in old bellows, and is caused by the valves being made of wood, covered with leather that has become hard, descending on the bottom-board with an audible blow. To remedy this, new leather valves must be substituted for the noisy old ones.

A gasping, from the valves being too few and small.
875. A rushing, gasping sound may occasionally be discerned, as a feeder descends and inhales a fresh supply of wind. This occurs when the valves are too few in number, or are too small, or do not open sufficiently. The wind then forces its way through the gratings or orifices under the valves with so much additional force as to cause a whistling as it goes. To cure this, additional valves must be made.

Bellows work quicker in hot weather.
876. In very dry seasons the contents of the bellows will sometimes be exhausted much sooner than at other times. This is partly owing to the contraction of the wood of the ribs, which opens the pores, and partly to the shrinking or curling of the leather valves, which together cause more or less wind to escape. Generally this is only a temporary derangement, which a change of weather will rectify ; but, should it prove otherwise, the assistance of the organ-builder should be at once secured, as the restoration of a firm and steady wind is of vital importance to the intonation of the organ.

Bellows produce a cracking sound after damp weather.
877. After damp weather the bellows will frequently produce a sharp, tearing sound when they are first blown, particularly if they have not been used for some days. This, however, does not announce any real accident, though its cause might lead to one. In damp weather the coat of glue with which the inside of the ribs is covered, to close the pores, becomes softened, which causes the ribs, as they lie together, to adhere slightly. When the bellows are subsequently blown, the sticky and adhering surfaces of the ribs are separated after some resistance, producing at the same time the sound above noticed.

Tremulousness, from the length and elasticity of the column of wind.
878. Sometimes the working of the bellows affects the speech of the pipes, i.e., a slight waving or forcing of the tone will be heard at the moment the feeders commence and complete their operation. This arises from the additional compression which takes place at the moment that the feeder and the surface-weights alternately exercise their influence. The feeder, before it can introduce fresh wind, has to overcome the pressure of the surface-weights by the exercise of *more* than an equivalent force ; and, when this under and upward pressure ceases, the surface-weights and top-board return and descend upon the wind with all their original pressure. In this manner a series of little jerks are given to the wind at the commencement and completion of each stroke, which are sometimes communicated to the speech of the pipes, particularly if the wind-trunks are small or long. To remove this defect, a concussion-bellows is usually applied ; but a more effectual remedy would be the introduction of wider, shorter, and more direct wind-trunks. When the wind-trunks are small or long, and the supply of wind to the sound-board barely adequate, the column of wind becomes more elastic ; in consequence of which, not only is every little and perhaps unavoid-

B B

able defect at the bellows conveyed to the pipes, but it is also exaggerated. When, on the contrary, the wind-trunks are broad and short, the column of air has greater firmness, from its greater bulk, and is less elastic from the same cause, aided by its lesser length, consequently, it is not nearly so liable to communicate every little disturbance at the bellows to the speech of the pipes. In many large organs built in recent years the admirable custom of inserting a second or local wind reservoir near to the sound-board has been resorted to, which is of course the most thorough way of guarding against the evil.

Tremulousness, from shortness of supply. 879. Sometimes if a chord be held down with the right hand in the treble, on adding a three-part chord with the left hand in the tenor, the treble pipes will be weakened in their speech for a moment, and then will recover themselves ; and, on withdrawing the left hand from the keys, the treble pipes will "raise their voices" for an instant, and then reduce their tone to the usual strength. These defects are sure indications of the wind-trunk, or the wind-chest, or both, being too small. In other cases an organ will stand the above test successfully ; but if chords be held down in the treble and tenor with the two hands, and a disjunct passage be played upon the pedals in the bass of the Manual, a tremulousness in the tone will appear in the upper parts. This will show that the wind-supply at the grooves is still inadequate, from one or other of the causes already mentioned.

Unequal intonation, caused by small grooves and pallet-holes. A robbing. 880. In some organs it is found that certain stops sound sharper : brighter, or stronger, when tried by themselves ; and flatter and duller, or weaker, when used with the others. This serious fault rests either with the grooves which do not hold sufficient wind to supply all the pipes effectually, or with the pallet-holes which do not admit the necessary quantity. The "robbing" usually manifests itself most strongly in the lowest octave or octave and a half of the sound-board. It almost invariably appears in old sound-boards, and is not always absent from new ones. There are many simple ways of ascertaining whether a Manual organ is properly supplied, or not, with wind in the bass. If, on drawing the Mixtures by themselves, and holding down one of the lowest keys, the pipes sound firmly in a certain pitch, and with a certain amount of strength, and if, on adding the other stops, the Mixtures fall in pitch and become more quiet in their tone, it is clear that the grooves either do not hold, or do not receive sufficient wind. Or, if the reeds be drawn alone, and they speak with a certain amount of crispness, promptness, and strength, but, on adding the other stops, the reeds sound tamely, sluggishly, and more quietly, it is evident that the demand on the wind in the grooves is greater than the supply. The only effectual remedies for this defect are either "double palleting," or the introduction of a new and larger sound-board with more capacious grooves in the bass (or, with double grooves), and with larger pallet-holes and pallets. In the absence of this the small stops have to be tuned in the bass, with all the stops on the sound-board drawn, that allowance may be made for the *flattening* effect caused by the robbing ; and this is why the small stops sound sharper and, perhaps, tremulously when tried by themselves, at which time they receive their full supply of wind. The excellent plan has sprung up within the last few years of introducing two or three sound-boards instead of one, and of making the treble part distinct from the bass. This effectually puts an end to all "robbing."

881. Sometimes a hissing or whizzing sound is heard to emanate from some part of the organ. The sound itself is, perhaps, scarcely perceptible, but it arrests the attention by its continuance. The exact place where it occurs is frequently difficult to discover. An engineer has an advantage over an organ-builder under parallel circumstances, for in a steam engine the locality of a slight leakage is immediately made evident by the escaping steam turning to vapour and attracting attention; whereas no such assistance appears in an organ to guide the builder to the seat of an analogous fault. This is frequently ascertained by means of a lighted candle, the flame of which will flicker as it draws near to the place where the escape is taking place, and as it gets into the unusual draught caused by it.

A hissing, arising from an escape of wind.

882. The hissing frequently arises from an escape of wind at the joint of one of the wind-trunks; which will be caused by the leather covering having become loosened, from damp, age, or decay. This is remedied either by glueing the eather down again; by applying a fresh strip of leather if the other is unsound; or even by fastening a piece of thick paper over the little hole, saturating the stopping with glue. An escape of wind will sometimes take place at the side of a pull down, through the hole in the brass plate; particularly if the action of the pull-down has worn the hole into an oval shape.

FAULTS CONNECTED WITH THE SPEECH OF THE PIPES.

Small pipes are frequently dumb, tremulous, or weak in their speech.

883. It frequently happens, particularly with regard to small open flue pipes, that a pipe will be "off its speech," *i.e.*, will not sound, or it will sound tremulously, or with less than its proper strength. A most frequent cause of this fault is *dust;* a very small portion of which—so small that it would not affect the speech of a large pipe at all—being sufficient to render a small one dumb. If the fault is a general one throughout the organ, it can only be remedied by a thorough cleaning. If there are only isolated instances here and there, they can be rectified by taking the few pipes out, one by one; wiping the surface of the languid, and carefully dusting the nicking, and clearing the wind-way with a fine brush, or by blowing into it with the mouth.

Flue pipes become unequal in their strength and quality of tone from various causes.

884. Sometimes an irregularity will be caused in large or small pipes by some disarrangement of the pipe itself. The upper lip may be pressed in too far, or not far enough; the under lip may have met with a similar temporary derangement; or the languid may be too high or too low. The foot-hole may have become slightly contracted from the pressure of the body of the pipe upon the foot; or it may have become too large from the partial decay of the apex of the foot. Any one of these accidents would affect the intonation of the pipe, causing it to sound too loud or too soft, tremulously, or in the octave above; and it is often more difficult to discover what may be the true cause of the fault in any individual instance, than to correct it when it is found out. A pipe that sounds too loud sometimes has its tone softened by pressing the under lip a little nearer to the languid, which reduces the width of the wind-way, and therefore allows less wind to enter the pipe; and by altering the position of the upper lip in the same direction. A pipe that sounds too weakly frequently has its power increased by the opposite process.

885. A pipe will sometimes "sound its octave;" and stops of small scale, as the Dulciana, are particularly liable to such derangement. This may be caused by a little dust having fallen into the wind-way, or by the pipe having rather too much wind, or even by simply a change of temperature. All stops of slow speech, "heavy intonation," as the Germans have it — as, for instance, the German Gamba—also are liable to casualties from similar causes; and, like the Dulciana, may be thrown off their speech, if the bellows do not give a perfectly equal blast. A pipe that has too broad a wind-way, or an insufficiently high mouth, will also speak its octave.

A pipe sometimes sounds its octave, from the effects of dirt or over-blowing.

886. Wood pipes are much influenced by change of temperature. In rainy weather the damp, by swelling the fibres of the wood, presses and closes the pores; and, by thus rendering the wood more compact, firm, and sound, improves and strengthens the tone. In very wet seasons, however, it is possible that the change may so far affect a pipe as to lessen the height of its mouth; and, by swelling the block, lessen the breadth of the wind-way, which would have the effect of slightly flattening its pitch, as well as perhaps affecting its speech. In an organ that is placed in a damp situation, these vexatious changes and derangements are both frequent and unavoidable. In dry weather the wood may shrink and become more porous, the tone then being weaker. The height of the mouth, from the excessive dryness and contraction of the wood, may be increased, as well as the breadth of the wind-way, which would raise the pitch of the pipe, and perhaps also alter its speech. The influence of these changes is the most discernible in the large open wood pedal pipes, which frequently will sound fuller in wet than in dry weather.

The tone of wood pipes influenced by change of temperature.

887. Stopped wood pipes are in summer occasionally put out of order by the stopper shrinking and falling into the pipe, raising the pitch, and destroying its quality. The stopper must, in that case, be taken out and restored to its proper place; some means being at the same time taken to make it fit tightly. This can frequently be done by putting a layer of paper between the stopper and the leather cover on all four sides. Or an additional covering of thin leather might be put over the stopper, if this will not make it fit too tightly. If a stopper that fits too tightly be driven into a pipe, it may cause the front or back to separate slightly from the sides at the joints; and, by so causing the pipe to become unsound, render the tone false and weak. A defective intonation will arise also if the stopper is not driven in perfectly level, but sideways. Mr. Lewis adopts the ingenious device of making the stoppers of all his small stopped pipes of cork, which material is, of course, self-adjusting.

Stopped wood pipes sometimes deranged by heat and drought.

Division IX.

SUGGESTIONS FOR THE CONSTRUCTION AND ERECTION OF AN ORGAN.

CHAPTER XXXI.

888. THE preceding chapters of this work having been devoted to a descriptive analysis of the structural details, &c., of an organ, it now remains to treat of other essentials which call for the attention more particularly of those to whom the duties of preparing the specification and superintending the construction of an organ are entrusted.

THE COMPASS OF THE CLAVIERS, AND OF THE SEPARATE DIVISIONS OF THE ORGAN.

889. The first subject to be considered is the compass necessary for the Manuals and Pedal, together with their respective departments of the organ.

890. It is most desirable that patient attention should be devoted to this question, since nearly every separate compass yet devised has its advocates ; yet whose opinions, when compared, are found to be conflicting. As, moreover, what is advanced in favour of one compass is not unfrequently accompanied by something else by way of objection against all or most others, it behoves all who would desire to arrive at a just conclusion on this very important subject to weigh all the arguments for and against each plan, before making a decision ; otherwise, with the best intention, their efforts may only end in a perpetuation of the existing confusion.

Precedents for nearly every variety of clavier range. — 891. There are precedents for almost every imaginable variety of range, both of Manual as well as Pedal ; and if the selection of any one from among the number were a question of no greater moment than the gratification of individual taste, or did not involve some violation of artistic arrangement that would not militate against the proportionate development of the separate departments of which an organ should consist, nor entail the sacrifice of funds and room in its consequences, there could be no difficulty in the way of any compass whatever being adopted that fancy might dictate. But the case is far otherwise. On a just view of this matter depends the successful issue of the work ; its influence pervading the arrangements of the entire instrument. It is very important, then, that the most careful consideration should be given to this subject, before proceeding any further in the work, particularly as a false step in this direction, once taken, cannot afterwards be retraced.

892. In the Historical Introduction to this book Dr. Rimbault[1] has mentioned that in the earlier organs the number of notes were very limited : from

nine to eleven (inclusive of the one chromatic note, B flat), being nearly their greatest extent, the execution of the plain-chant not requiring more, and harmony being then unknown. At the close of the eleventh century an organ was made for the Cathedral of Magdeburg, containing *sixteen* notes, and A KEY-BOARD. In the twelfth century the number of keys was increased, and every key was furnished with two or three additional pipes, sounding the fifth and octave, or the third and tenth. In the fourteenth century an organ was built, at Thorn, with *twenty-two* keys; and besides this increase in the compass, which extended upwards and downwards, the keys were made smaller and neater, and with a lesser fall, so that they could be played with the fingers collectively and the thumb alternately. The most notable improvement effected in this century, however, was the gradual introduction of the four remaining chromatic keys. F sharp, the first sharp, was inserted in the early part of the century; afterwards came the second sharp and second flat, C sharp and E flat; and lastly the third sharp, G sharp. In 1359, or 1361, Nicolas Faber built the great organ in Halberstadt, with fourteen diatonic and eight chromatic

keys, extending from to . From this time the

organs for large churches were frequently made with a compass of three octaves,

from to In the early part of the sixteenth century

we begin to glean something authentic respecting the compass of English organs. In 1520 Antony Duddington made an organ for Allhallow's Church, Barking, the lowest key of which is distinctly set forth in the contract as being *Double Ce-fa-ut;* the 8-feet note that marks the full downward range of the Manuals of all the English and Continental instruments of the present day. Consisting of " xxvij playne keyes " (or naturals), and, doubtless, the requisite number of short keys, the compass, if *unbroken*, must have extended to a³ in alt; and if *broken*, that is to say, having the CC pipes planted on the *apparently* EE key, it would then have been of the four octave CC short octave compass. The latter is the more probable range, as it is that of many of the old German organs of about the same date. In 1637 Thomas Harris built an organ for Magdalen College Chapel, Oxford, which was also " Gamut in Do, Sol, Re ; " and Dr. Burney mentions that, in Father Smith's time, the usual organ compass was four octaves, from CC ; which range, however, was frequently departed from.

The compass of the Manuals; the confused state in which the question was involved in England; and the importance of a correct view of the subject.

893. Indeed, those who a few years ago were much in the habit of visiting English church organs, and of observing their general arrangements, were much struck with the remarkable *variation* that existed in the compass of the Manuals and Pedal of different instruments. A dozen organs might have been visited promiscuously, without any two being found to agree precisely in the above respects. Some had short-octave GG Manuals; others, GG Manuals with long octaves. Some had Manuals descending a note lower to FFF ; others, Manuals to CCC ; while a fifth class would have Manual organs of the orthodox CC range. There were not wanting some having three Manuals all of different ranges. Then of the Pedal : some organs had an octave of pedals commencing at GG ; others, an octave and a half beginning on the same note, or perhaps on FFF. Some had two octaves of GG pedals, while others

had one octave, an octave and a half, two octaves, or two octaves and a half of CCC pedals. Such was the undecided state into which these divisions of organ arrangement had fallen in this country, previous to the commencement of the now widely-spread desire for their amelioration.

894. **How the true Manual compass is to be ascertained.** That *all* the compasses for Manual and Pedal just cited can be *equally* correct, is impossible; either some are too long, or others must be too short; or, supposing a medium range to be the true one, then some must be as much too short as others are too long. The question, then, is, of the number, which is the correct compass and which not?

895. The presence of a certain number of keys on the Manual and Pedal claviers, and an equal number of semitones in their respective organs, must be necessary to render an instrument adequate to all the purposes and uses of a church organ. Do those Manuals—the question of the compass of the Pedal is deferred for the present—then, that extend only to CC, *fall short* of this needful range; or do the various kinds of long octave ones *exceed* it by just so much as their Manuals descend below that key? Or, is the medium compass, the GG, the correct one, and consequently the CC range as much too short as the CCC is too long for the required purposes? The sources to which alone reference can be made, with the certainty of finding a correct solution to the above problems, are the choral and instrumental compositions that are most frequently heard in, and which are held in the highest esteem as accessories to, the church service; and for the accompaniment of the one, and the performance of the other, the organ itself is employed in our ecclesiastical edifices. If reference then be made to the works of the long list of English choral writers, and to the scores of Handel, Beethoven, Bach, Mendelssohn, &c., this examination will be attended with the following results.

896. In the selected movements from the works originally written with orchestral accompaniments, such as the solos and choruses in oratorios, masses, &c., it will be observed that the violoncello part, which comprehends within its downward range also that of all vocal basses, *never* descends below the CC note, which note (as all musicians know) is the lowest one on that instrument. The double bass, indeed, is a deeper-toned instrument; yet, as it does not give a sound in accordance with the notes written, but the *octave below*, as far as its compass permits, its representative is correctly to be found among the unison (16-feet) flue-work of the pedal organ. Again, if the compositions written expressly for the organ by Bach, Mendelssohn, Hesse, Wèly, Henry Smart, and others, be consulted, it will be seen that the greatest extent to which the Manual part of those works descends is also CC. The most elaborate sacred musical productions, then, whether they be essentially choral, originally written with instrumental accompaniments, or composed exclusively for the organ, neither require nor *recognise* a greater extent of compass downwards than that possessed by the *shortest* of the various kinds of Manual above mentioned. A few exceptions to this otherwise universally supported fact may indeed be found in the organ compositions of Samuel Wesley, Thomas Adams, and Dr. S. S. Wesley; yet these examples would scarcely be deemed sufficient to outweigh the united authority established by the various and voluminous works presented to us by the writers previously named. That the CC Manual *does* afford ample scope for the perfect execution of the *hand* parts of all descriptions of music used in the church, excepting the few excellent works already specified, has never been disputed. And that the CC Manual range is the best one for concert-room organs,

is equally beyond a doubt. So much, therefore, is greatly in favour of the CC Manual organ.

Arguments against the CC Manual compass, and in favour of a longer range.

897. Against it, and in favour of a longer compass, it has sometimes been urged (1) that in accompanying the choral service, and more particularly the quieter parts, a soft bass is frequently required (though not written) *below* CC ; (2) that if the Manual keys are made to *end* on that note, then the deeper sounds have to be obtained from the Pedal ; and (3) if that department be furnished with a fair proportion of stops, a shifting of these with every change from "Full" to "Verse," &c., becomes necessary ; or (4) if there be but one stop on the Pedal, as is too frequently the case, the choice then lies between a ponderous and heavy bass and none at all.

898. These objections are founded on the manner in which CC organs *are* sometimes made in England, rather than on the Continental system, according to which they *should be,* and occasionally are, built. It is not a correct conclusion that, if the Manual *keys* stop at CC, the Manual *sounds* must also cease there, any more than it would be that the *upward* range of an organ must cease at f³ in alt, if the keys do so. In all two-Manual instruments of average pretension, the Great organ should have a Double Stopped Diapason (Bourdon) throughout. This is one of the *fundamental* laws of the German system of organ-building, and is *constantly* adhered to in the construction of the average church organs of that country ; and it does not follow, because the Great Manual of an English CC organ is sometimes made without a stop of 16-feet size of tone, that the inconveniences which must arise from such omission are to be attributed to a principle of organ-building, from which it is a departure. Where a stop of the kind in question *is* disposed, instead of the downward range of the deep Manual sounds being *limited* by the termination of the keys at CC, it is *increased* to the extent of seven semitones *beyond* what an old-fashioned GG Manual could produce ; so that, even on the question of "depth of tone," a CC Manual organ on the Continental principle has the decided advantage over a GG Manual organ on the English principle. Furthermore, the concentration of so many deep sounds on the Manual obviates the " necessity " for employing the Pedals so constantly, if the performer cares to dispense with the use of the latter ; and thus the second objection to the CC Manual is, to a great extent, done away with. But, even supposing the continued use of the Pedals to be desired, so far from the shifting of the Pedal stops to obtain a soft bass being a matter of "necessity," some German Pedal organs are made with a wind-trunk valve (Sperventil) to cut off the wind from the Pedal Reeds and Chorus stops, and worked by a stop-handle that is shifted as quickly as a Pedal coupler ; by means of which a soft or loud Pedal may be obtained with the greatest facility.

899. One fact relating to the subject of the deep Manual tones should not here be omitted. While the extra keys below CC are said to be so necessary for soft accompaniments, the Second Manual (Swell), on which the quieter parts would frequently be played, is always made not only *without* those very keys, but, in the great majority of cases, also *without the next whole octave above.* This important circumstance much weakens the position, as to the "necessity" for the Manual keys descending below CC, to meet the requirements of *soft* playing.

900. Nay, more ; when the Second Manual organ (Swell) in GG instruments is made to the short tenor c compass, it is usual to arrange the keys beyond to act

either on the Great organ, or on the "Pedal pipes." Now, in the former case, a shifting of the Great organ stops must be made with every change from *forte* to *piano*, and back again ; in the latter, there will be the strong and unseasonable bass ; so that the second and third objections, if they are such, exist, to at least an equal extent, in organs of long compass, and are not by any means peculiar to those of shorter range.

901. The CC is the only Manual range now accepted on the Continent. In Germany, Holland, Belgium, the Netherlands, Switzerland, France, America, &c., no organ is ever made to any other compass. The celebrated organs at Haarlem, Frieburg, Frankfort, Hamburg, Rotterdam, Dresden, St. Denis, Boston, U.S., &c., are all CC Manual organs.*

902. Among the 300 or 400 English organs that have been either built or re-modelled conformably with this range may be mentioned the new organ in St. Paul's Cathedral ; the organs at Christ Church, Newgate Street ; St. Paul's, Knightsbridge ; St. Peter's and St. Michael's, Cornhill ; Temple Church ; St. James's, Piccadilly ; All Saints', Margaret Street ; St. Andrew's, Wells Street ; and St. Giles's Camberwell, &c. Also those in the Birmingham, Leeds, Newcastle, Brighton, Glasgow, Edinburgh, and Dundee Town Halls ; the Collegiate Institution, Liverpool ; the Parish Churches at Doncaster, Leeds, Newark, Ashton-under-Lyne, &c.

Much room and a great expenditure of funds required to extend the compass of a Manual organ below CC.

903. The CC compass for a Manual organ, at the same time that it is quite satisfactory as to completeness and convenience, is far *less costly* than one of longer range ; not that *cheapness* ought to be made a consideration in any case, where the object is to be devoted to the service of the church, and where the question should not be "what will do," but *what is best*. Still, it does so happen that a given number of stops to CC will cost very considerably less than when extended down to GG, or lower ; and the money and space saved by observing the distinction between what is essential and what is not, are of vital importance where funds and room are objects (and where are they not ?), since they can then be devoted to the proper proportionate development of other departments which are too often straitened, or altogether excluded, in order to allow of the lengthening out of a Manual organ.

904. Some idea may be formed of the extra cost of a long octave Manual organ, from the increase that is made in the price of *one stop alone* by this downward elongation. The charge for an Open Diapason to CC used to be about eighteen pounds. The cost of the same stop, extended to GG, was increased to nearly thirty pounds ; with the FFF and FFF sharp added, to about forty pounds ; and, when further extended down to CCC, the 16 feet pipe, and a good quality of metal preserved throughout, its cost was not far short of seventy pounds. From these few facts it will easily be seen that a hundred pounds may be soon expended in extending the stops of even a single Manual, and this, too, without extending its resources as a *Manual* organ, in any shape or way.

---

* It is worth mentioning that the Manuals of Spanish and Italian organs sometimes descend below CC. Those of the new organ at the Cathedral at Seville go down to AA ; those of the two organs at Milan Cathedral descend to FFF ; those of the chief organ at St. Peter's at Rome range to CCC, short octaves ; while those of the organ at St. Alessandro at Milan are of CCC range, and of complete compass. (See accounts of these organs in the Appendix.)

The true method of in-
creasing the resources
of a Manual organ.
905. For an illustration of this latter fact, try two Manual organs by the same builder, furnished with stops similar in every respect only that the compass of those of the one shall stop at CC, while those of the other shall extend to GG, or anywhere else. If this

or any other chord be struck in pure four-part harmony, first on one of those Manuals, and then on the other, the sound will be found to be precisely the same in each case, both as regards quantity as well as quality ; in other words the tone of the GG Manual organ will possess no advantage over that of the CC one. The reason of this is obvious. Increasing the *compass* of a Manual, and increasing its *resources* as to tone and variety, are two widely different things, and they are worked out by totally opposite processes. The former end is attained by keeping to the same stops, and augmenting their range ; which is like adding a fifth or sixth string to the stringed instruments in a band, with the view to increasing their efficiency. The latter is effected by preserving the original compass (that compass being a full and complete one), and engrafting thereon other stops that emit sounds differing in pitch, or quality, or both, from those produced by the original ones ; a course which is equivalent to increasing the number and variety of instruments as the means of augmenting the resources of an orchestra. As the capabilities of a band would be amplified—both in regard to its power of varied combination in the detail, and its grandeur of tone in the aggregate—by increasing the number of distinct instruments, so are the analogous powers of the organ correspondingly augmented by increasing the number of distinct stops ; and they are increased *only* by this principle of development. A Manual can but be complete, let its compass be extended below CC as far as it may ; even as a violin could be no more, were the number of its strings to be doubled, or even trebled. Supposing such an experiment to be tried with a violin, music for that instrument would have to be *altered*, before any use could be made of the additions as *violin* features. In like manner all church music has to be altered, before any use can be made of the keys below CC as *Manual* features.

How it may be ascer-
tained whether certain
keys are essential or
not as Manual ones.
906. The best proofs of there being no legitimate use for the long octaves with the *hand* are to be gathered from the deviations which it is necessary to make from the musical text, in order so to employ them. The keys, acting upon these additional tones and semitones, are placed, as a matter of course, *beyond* the CC key ; and, as the Manual part of all descriptions of church music alike only extends *to* that note (as has been already shown), they are not available as above, so long as a composer's notation is adhered to. To make use of the extra notes with the hand, the hand must be transferred an octave lower than the music directs ; and single notes, octaves, or even full chords, played down there ; the tenor part of the composition, meanwhile, being either entirely abandoned, or thrown an octave higher ; the consequence being in either case a material departure from the musical text, and a most undesirable transposition of the parts.

907. Speaking of the superior effect that divided harmony produces upon the

organ over close harmony, Forkel says : " By this means a chorus, as it were, of four or five vocal parts, *in their whole natural compass*, is transferred to the organ.

Let the following chords in divided harmony be tried :—

and then compare how the following,   a more common way

of rendering the same sounds in comparison, and it will be evident what injury must accrue to the effect from playing a whole piece in such a manner. *In the former manner* BACH *always played the organ.*" (*Life of Bach*, Boosey's edition, page 33.)

908. Taking all the foregoing circumstances into consideration, it seems clear that the "long octaves" do not possess any real advantages as *Manual* adjuncts to compensate for their enormous cost. And it is as indisputable that their application to certain departments—say the Chief Manual, or Great organ—is often the means of excluding many of those which are so from others, of reducing the number and amount of their contents, or even of necessitating their entire omission, by absorbing for their construction a sum from the gross amount which would be sufficient to secure the amelioration of one, if not more, of the above material blemishes. A few general illustrations may be given of these last-mentioned facts. To advance more specific ones would be inconsistent with the object of the present work.

The ameliorations that might be effected on a given specification, by regulating the outlay otherwise than in the construction of unessential Manual notes.

909. If the general arrangements of a modern £400 or £500 GG organ be examined, they will in the majority of cases be found to be as follows :—

Compass of Great organ, GG to f³ in alt, with
    GG sharp . . . . 59 notes.
Compass of Swell organ, tenor c to f³ in alt . 42 notes.

The Swell Manual continued down to GG, and made to act either on the Bass of the Great organ, or on the Pedal pipes at pleasure.

Compass of Pedal board, GG to tenor c . . . . 18 notes.
Compass of Pedal pipes, from CCC to CC . . . . 13 pipes.

910. From these particulars we perceive that, while the Chief Manual or Great organ is carried *half an octave lower* than CC at a considerable cost, the second Manual organ (Swell) is discontinued *a whole octave above* that note—the funds *then* not admitting of the latter department being made complete—and the Pedal organ consists of " half" a stop, and *that* sounding an octave out of pitch. Now

it need scarcely be urged that the only particular in which the two Manual organs ought to differ from each other are the number of stops, or their strength of tone, and not in the *compass*, which should be the same in either case; for what is required for "soft accompaniments" is a Manual with stops of a subdued tone, and not without any bass to it. In fact, the longer compass has sometimes been declared to be more specially needed for soft accompaniments.

911. The old organ-builders, although compelled to make instruments to all kinds of compass, and thus to give an air of vacillation to some of their arrangements, but for which they must not be held responsible, and, for reasons already shown, were yet fully sensible of the propriety of making both Manual organs to consist of the same number of keys; unless, indeed, as was sometimes the case, particularly in their very small instruments, one was only designed as a Solo or Echo organ, and not calculated for use in choral accompaniments. A few remarkable exceptions only to this rule are known to exist. In the generality of instruments built during the latter part of the seventeenth, throughout the eighteenth, and even at the commencement of the present century, we constantly find the Second Manual (Choir) of equal range with the First, or Great.

912. No doubt the Second Manual organ is in the present day sometimes made shorter than the requisite compass, through lack of funds; and, when such imperfectness is really the work of necessity, nothing can be said against it. That, however, is a separate question. When there are funds sufficient to pay for a GG Great organ and a tenor c Swell, there *must* be sufficient also to procure a Second Manual organ of nearly, if not quite, perfect compass, if the expenditure be so directed; so that the above plea is not admissible under such circumstances, since the lessened range of that department can then no longer be attributed to the smallness of the grant, but to the mode of its outlay.

913. The Swell being thus limited in its compass, some substitute is usually devised to supply the place of the omitted octave. The most usual expedients are to extend the Second *Manual* downwards to the same range as the First or Great organ, and make the continuation keys communicate either with the Pedal pipes or with the bass keys of the Great organ. It is only necessary, however, to advert to the derivation of the terms Manual and Pedal ("manus," a *hand*, and "pes," the *foot*), when the inaccuracy of bringing on to a *Manual* certain pipes designed exclusively for the use of the *feet*, and distinctly designated "Pedal" pipes, will become apparent. Besides, the Pedal pipes are the most ponderous-toned pipes in an organ, and, therefore, as a bass to the Manual, designed for *soft* accompaniments, are singularly inappropriate. Again, in many examples where there are "Double" Pedal pipes, instead of there being an interval of a semitone only between the unison sound of the last key acting on the Swell and the first one on the Pedal pipes, the two sounds are separated by an interval of a minor ninth; so that not only is the sound of the borrowed bass opposed to its newly applied purpose in the several respects of character, strength, and quality of tone, but in pitch it is of "16 feet;" whereas, for the Manual, the 8-feet pitch is most required.

914. Neither does the bass octave of the loud or Great organ form a satisfactory continuation to the soft or Swell organ, for the reason that, if the same combination be drawn on both Manuals, the strength of the bass (Great organ) will be too strong to match well with the remainder (Swell); or if, to obviate this, fewer stops be drawn on the Great organ, there will exist but slight affinity between the tone-character of the bass and the other parts. As before observed, if such arrangements as these arise from unavoidable causes, it is one matter; but if they are purely voluntary, as they must of

necessity be when they appear in conjunction with a GG Great organ, it is quite another.

915. The next point to be illustrated is the extent to which "long octaves" limit the specification of the different departments of an organ.

916. A good average specimen of a GG Great organ contains the following ten stops; viz. :—

1. Open Diapason.
2. Open Diapason.
3. Stopped Diapason.
4. Principal.
5. Twelfth.
6. Fifteenth,
7. Sesquialtera—III. ranks.
8. Mixture.   II. ranks.
9. Trumpet
10. Clarion.

917. By confining the above ten-stop Great organ to the CC compass, instead of extending it down to GG, the sum so saved would nearly, if not quite, defray the cost of the following stops; viz. :—

1. Double Stopped Diapason 16 feet tone.
2. Open Diapason . . . . 8 feet.
3. Open Diapason . . . . 8 feet.
4. Stopped Diapason . . . 8 feet tone.
5. Dulciana to Tenor c . . . 8 feet.
6. Stopped Fifth . . . . . 5⅓ feet tone.
7. Principal . . . . . . 4 feet.
8. Flute . . . . 4 feet.
9. Twelfth . . . . 2⅔ feet.
10. Fifteenth . . . . 2 feet.
11. Piccolo . . . . 2 feet.
12. Sesquialtera . . . IV. ranks.
13. Mixture . . . . III. ranks.
14. Trumpet . . . . 8 feet.
15. Clarion . . . . 4 feet.

That is to say, the number of pipes to most of the keys could be increased from thirteen to twenty; the range of deep sounds extended downwards to the extent of seven semitones; and the capabilities of the department for varied combination nearly doubled.

918. Or, supposing the sum saved were expended on the improvement of an originally contemplated tenor c Swell, containing the following six stops; viz. :—

1. Double Stopped Diapason.
2. Open Diapason.
3. Stopped Diapason.
4. Principal.
5. Trumpet.
6. Hautboy.

919. Not only could its specification be made to take the following improved form :—

1. Double Stopped Diapason 16 feet tone.
2. Open Diapason . . . . 8 feet.
3. Stopped Diapason . . . 8 feet tone.
4. Principal . . . . . . 4 feet.
5. Fifteenth . . . . 2 feet.
6. Mixture . . . . III. ranks.
7. Trumpet . . . . 8 feet.
8. Hautboy . . . . 8 feet.

but its compass could be extended downwards to at least Gamut G. That is to say, besides increasing the number of pipes to each key from six to ten, about half of the 8-feet octave could be added to the Swell Manual organ, which would be far more useful than half of the 16 feet octave to the Great Manual organ.

920. Or again, if the amount saved as above were to be laid out in getting rid of the ordinary "Pedal pipes" of a single octave only in compass—in which the unison and double pitches are so strangely mixed together—and

providing something more intelligible in their stead, the following stops could be secured :—

PEDAL ORGAN, COMPASS CCC TO TENOR D.

1. Open Diapaso . . wood . . . 16 feet.
2. Stopped Diapason. . . wood . . . 16 feet tone.
3. Trombone . . . . . wood . . . 16 feet.

921. The questions that here suggest themselves are, first, whether the principle of organ-construction that *necessitates* the confusing of the Manual organ with the Pedal organ, and the Pedal organ with the Manual—making the one too long and the other too short—each rendered dependent on the other, while neither of them are in themselves complete, nor even capable of forming a satisfactory whole when united,—whether such a system should be perpetuated, in preference to the other principle, which has for its foundation the requirements expected of each department, and which, from its well-tested merits, has become the standard principle of nearly all other countries.

922. Or, secondly, if either of the three modifications just suggested on the original specification were to be followed, whether there would not result a much more satisfactory instrument ?

923. It should be remarked that the *shortest* and *least expensive* of the various long octave Manual organs was selected wherewith to draw the foregoing parallel specifications. Had a longer compass been chosen, a still more surprising difference would have resulted ; which would also have been the case even with the same compass, had two Manual organs been taken into account instead of one ; or even one Manual organ, but having more stops.

Other views in favour of GG Manuals, and against CC, considered. 924. There are other grounds yet to be noticed, on which the desire for the perpetuation of elongated Manuals is founded.

925. It is urged—(1) that the introduction of the extra keys offers scope for the production of many fine effects ; (2) that their presence is absolutely essential to serve as Pedal tones ; and (3) that shortening the compass is going backwards instead of forwards.

926. That *sounds* below CC on the Manual are of the greatest use, and capable of most impressive results, has already been admitted, and is, indeed, self-evident. What is maintained is, that the desirability for their introduction does not call for a *lengthening of the key-board.*

927. When, for example, such sounds are required, it is very easy to draw the 16-feet stop alone, when they will be obtained not only to GG, but seven semitones lower. For this method of using the organ we have the authority of the greatest organist and organ composer that ever lived. Sebastian Bach not only played, but actually wrote some of his music to be executed with the left hand on a 16-feet stop only ; by which means he drew from his instrument the practical effect of a CCC Manual, without overturning the theory of organ-building to obtain it. (See translation of Forkel's *Life of Bach*, page 86.)

928. No rules, or specific directions, setting forth the manner of using the extra keys of a GG organ with the hand, with fine effect, have ever appeared in print ; and music for the organ, of what kind soever, offers little or no assistance on the subject ; but, on the contrary, generally discountenances them. So that all is left to chance ;—one has to *invent* a mode of using them, if they are to be *touched* at all ;—and it is but a natural consequence that the attempts should, in different cases, be attended with various degrees of success. That the

Manual keys below CC are seldom made use of with the *hands* when they are introduced is clearly evinced by the comparatively *perfect* state in which those keys are *invariably* found, when most of the others are so much worn as to require renewal.

929. But whatever may be the effects attendant on the lengthening of the Manuals, if they be placed in juxtaposition with the decrease sustained in the number of the stops; the loss of the numerous soft combinations that could have been made with the aid of those stops for accompanimental purposes; and the impossibility of playing the best music even *correctly*, still less with adequate effect; it will then be seen what sacrifices must be made to secure the presence of five semitones—the advantages of which, when they are obtained, is very generally questioned.

930. The next position, "that the presence of the extra notes on the Manual is essential, that they may serve as Pedal tones," offers anything rather than assistance to the principle of organ-construction it is intended to support. The anomaly of attaching to the *Manual* keys pipes that are expressly adapted for the *feet* has already been pointed out. The above plea is in favour of placing certain keys and tones on the *Manual*, which are conceded to be chiefly for the use of the *Pedals*. This creates a fresh discrepancy, and one that assumes a more prominent form, when it is considered for what purpose the extra tones are said to be introduced, and how far it is possible they can effect the end desired. If the Manual unison stops are required to serve as substitutes for the Pedal Diapason, they should descend as far as those Diapasons, namely, to CCC; if as Octave stops, only to CC. The GG range is 7 semitones too short for the one purpose, and 5 too long for the other; therefore the peculiar unfitness of the notes in question, from BB to GG, for rendering the assistance sought, in a correct and intelligible manner, becomes obvious.

931. In suggesting the adoption of the CC compass for the Manual, it must not be concluded that the notes below CC are not required *anywhere*, but simply that they are not required on that clavier as *Manual* notes. This leads to the third objection, that "shortening the compass is going backwards instead of forwards." This appears, at first, to be a well-grounded objection; yet, in reality, it admits of a ready reply. The great question is not which is the *longest*, but which is the *most correct*, complete, convenient, compact, and economical compass. These questions have already been once considered, but they may be further illustrated by a return to our former parallel. Supposing a fifth and sixth strings to have been added to a violin, and, no legitimate use being found for them, they were taken off again; the violin would not, on that account, become a less perfect instrument;— there would be no "going backwards." Or, to draw the parallel more closely, if, to supply the two extra strings for the violin, two had been abstracted from the violoncello; and it was afterwards desired that *both* should be rendered efficient; there could be no question as to the propriety of reducing the former and increasing the latter to the proper and precise dimensions. This latter comparison is the more exact one to draw; for the essential lowest octave of the swell, or the equally essential upper octave of the pedal organ have been but too often omitted, where the one or the other might have been introduced but for the unessential notes from BB to GG on the Great organ. It is believed there could be but one opinion as to the most correct course to pursue in regard to the stringed instruments; and it would seem surprising there should be a second one against an equally consistent proportioning of the different departments of an organ.

932. It may be mentioned, by the way, that although the "viols" of former times had *six* strings, and the modern violins had but *four*, yet the latter have

always ranked as the *more perfect* instruments; while the advancement in the composition of music for string instruments, as well as of the playing on them, dates from the time of the general adoption of the instrument having *fewer* strings. The parallel holds good in every respect in regard to organs and organ playing in England.

933. The advocates for the long and for the short Manuals appear to be agreed on one very important point, namely, that the 16-feet range is the most correct one for as many of the organ *stops* as possible; the point of difference between them being as to where the large pipes should be planted, whether on the Manuals or on the Pedal.

934. In Germany, also, the CCC or 16-feet range is viewed as the most correct one for the organ *stops*, even more generally so than in England, but not for the organ *Manuals*. The *Pedal* is justly considered as the only proper place for their *bass*. This is conclusively shown in German specifications, where may frequently be seen disposed to a " Principal 8 feet " on the Manual a " Principal *bass* 16 feet " on the Pedal; to the " Octave 4 feet " on the Manual, an " Octave *bass* 8 feet " on the Pedal; to the " Flöte 4 feet " on the Manual, a " Flöte *bass* 8 feet " on the Pedal ; to a " Quint 5⅓ feet " on the Manual, a " Quinten *bass* of 10⅔ feet " on the Pedal ; and so on. A reference to the German specifications in the Appendix— taken either from German organ books or copied from the stop labels themselves —will fully illustrate this fact.

How the CC Manual compass was first exceeded. 935. The question here suggests itself how the CC compass ever came to be exceeded. The Manual range of the organs built immediately after the Restoration generally consisted of four octaves, from CC to c³ in alt. (See Dr. Burney's article on the organ before referred to.) The Double Diapason at that time was scarcely known in this country, and was certainly not appreciated ; the Pedal organ was entirely unknown ; so that the English instruments of the date in question lacked those deep and sonorous tones which render an organ so peculiarly well adapted to its place in the church, and so superior to all other instruments for religious purposes. In proceeding to supply the existing deficiencies, without regarding either of the two systematic courses that were open for adoption, the third and only remaining mode of doing so was by extending the Manual downwards. Two notes were therefore added; one, sounding AA, placed on the CC sharp key ; and the other, giving GG, on an additional key placed next beyond the CC one. A Manual of this kind is now called a " short octave " Manual, to distinguish it from the still longer ones that are to be met with. The result of this experiment being favourable *as to the effect*, the intermediate semitones from CC to GG were applied (excepting, perhaps, the GG sharp); and thus the GG long octave Manual organ was formed. Further extensions were subsequently made ; first to FFF, then to CCC. It is now, however, admitted by the great majority of English organists that these added keys do not so properly belong to the Manual as to the Pedal ; and that no sufficient grounds exist for introducing them as adjuncts to the former-mentioned departments in new work. It is not considered a sufficient reason for so doing, that the Manuals were made to GG in our fathers' time. Besides, if the key at which the Manual ought to stop is still to be passed—if the rules which should keep its compass within proper bounds are to be disregarded—there then exists nothing to prevent the introduction of a GGG or even a CCCC Manual, if individual taste should desire it. Such an extension would be but carrying out, to the extent of a second octave, the elongating principle, which many would advocate to the extent of one octave, and which, moreover, would be equally justifiable on the same ground of individual fancy.

936. That the CC is the only true Manual compass would not then seem to be so much a matter of individual opinion (as must be the supposition on behalf of any other), as a self-manifesting fact—all church music clearly showing it to be so. That it is also the only one that facilitates the perfecting of the range and proportionate development of the other departments, by avoiding an undue outlay on the chief Manual organ, is also beyond a doubt. Under all these circumstances, independently of others about to be mentioned, the CC compass is the only one that can be suggested with confidence for adoption as the best for the Manuals of new organs.

The confusion in the size of the stops caused by their elongation. 937. But there is a disadvantage in lengthening out the Manual stops that has not as yet been hinted at, and one, moreover, that seems to be always overlooked by the promoters of long Manuals, namely, the confusion into which such elongation throws the question of the standard length and the literal pitch of the stops. It must have been observed that in much organ music, to save specifying any particular stop that the instrument might or might not contain, the direction given is often simply an open one; as, for instance, "one 8-feet stop," meaning, of course, thereby, a unison stop. Now, by extending the compass of the stops downwards, their size is altered; and so great is the confusion caused in consequence, that many of the lengthened stops on a GG, FFF, or CCC organ are made to assume a size identical with that of certain other stops, correctly ranged, to which they are quite opposed, either in nature and method of usage, or both, and which ambiguity is eminently calculated to throw those who are desirous of identifying the size and pitch with the use of the stops into the greatest doubt and perplexity. For example, an Open Diapason would be of 8-feet length on a CC Manual; on a FFF Manual the *Quint* would be the stop of that size; and, on one of the CCC compass, the *Principal.* If, therefore, an 8-feet stop were really to be drawn as directed, it would in the first case produce the right effect, but in the second would sound the music a fifth higher than written; and in the third the octave above. Again, in the instance of a GG organ, the Diapason and Principal ($10\frac{2}{3}$ and $5\frac{1}{3}$ feet), which should be freely available for the majority of combinations, and understood to be so, are, from their altered size, made to be identical in measurement with the *Quints* of better arranged organs; while the *Twelfth* and *Larigot* of a FFF organ (4 and 2 feet), which require to be used with much care, are by the same process made to correspond in size with the *Principal* and *Fifteenth* of a CC organ, which are scarcely at all restricted in their use. In fact, the sizes of the Unison, Octave, and Mutation stops are mixed, crossed, and inextricably confused together.

938. But, it might be suggested, if the confusion of lengths could somehow be got over (which of course it cannot), and the Manuals were to be extended down to CCC, whether then there would not result a satisfactory substitute for a proper Pedal organ, and one, moreover, that would offer great conveniences for the purpose of duet-playing. In one sense it would, but at the same time new difficulties would be created. What is required of an efficient Pedal organ is not simply a bass to the Great Manual stops, neither more nor less, but a Pedal bass to as *many* of the leading stops of *all* the Manuals as circumstances will permit, with the addition of such others as will stamp that department with a character of individuality. All these ends can never be attained by extending the compass of the Great organ, even to CCC.

939. And with respect to the conveniences for duet-playing, a principle of organ-building, that takes two performers to produce the effect that one could manage under proper circumstances, can hardly be said to be an advantageous one.

940. Again, if the Manual unison stops be increased to the 16-feet size, the Doubles will become 32 ; and, 32 being then the unison size for the Pedal, the Doubles will be 64 feet in length. The full development of a long Manual organ would demand the introduction of pipes nearly the height and bulk of factory chimneys, which would be destitute of definite tone when made.

941. In suggesting the adoption of the CC compass for the Manual, it will not of course be supposed that discontinuing the Manuals at that key will, alone and of itself, render an organ a better and more perfect instrument. It is nothing more than one necessary step towards a successful issue—a means to one end. Two of the most prominent faults of the long Manual systems are, they allot *too much* to certain Manuals, and *too little* to the Pedal, *both* of which faults require correcting. But if the 16-feet octave, or even a portion of it, be omitted from the Manual, and *nothing* be added to the Pedal by way of compensation, then the organ is left practically less efficient than it was before, in spite of the theoretical corrections. This is because the "bass" of the stops, instead of being simply transferred from the Manual to the Pedal, is omitted altogether, giving strong ground to justify the opinion of the promoters of the long Manual systems, that "shortening the Manual compass is going backwards." The *minimum* number of "Pedal basses" which a CC organ should have is *one third* as many as there are stops on the Great organ. The *maximum* number is one-third as many Pedal basses as there are stops in the entire Manual organs. Below the former proportion the Pedal stops are never reduced in Continental organs of pretension. (See Foreign Specifications, in the Appendix ; also the works of Töpfer, Kützing, Seidel, Schlimbach, &c.) These observations, however, are not intended to qualify in the slightest manner the ample proofs already adduced of the great superiority of the CC organ, when consistently carried out. As compared with it the inferior and patchy Pedal effect of the GG organ is only equalled by a second unsuccessful imitation, also peculiar to long Manual organs, namely, that of mimicking the effect of a 16-feet stop by coupling the Choir organ to the Great in the octave below. Such expedients in co-existing organs that have only been partially remodelled are innocent enough, but they offer no satisfactory precedents for their adoption in new work.

The upward range of the Manuals. 942. With regard to the upward range of the Manuals, organ music very seldom ascends beyond c^3 in alt ; while the psalm-tunes and chants, of course, do not reach anything like so high ; but as the pipes to the keys above that c^3 are small, do not occupy much room, and cost but little, and moreover are very useful in a variety of ways—particularly where there are octave couplers—the Manuals are generally continued up to g^3, a^3, or even to c^4 in altissimo. The latter range is in some respects desirable for concert-room organs. The late Dr. Gauntlett was one of the earliest and most strenuous advocates for the CC organ, and for the concentration of a grand body and variety of tone on the Manuals.

CHAPTER XXXII.

OF THE PEDALS AND PEDAL ORGAN ; THEIR INTRODUCTION INTO ENGLAND; AND CORRECT COMPASS.

943. AMONG the most important additions and improvements that have been made to the organ in modern times in England are to be classed the introduction of Pedals, and the establishment and subsequent development of the Pedal organ. These features, the importance and utility of which have for *centuries* been appreciated so justly on the Continent that a place has been assigned to them in every instrument of even moderate pretensions, are even now only just beginning to be adequately valued in this country. Yet, as Forkel observes, in his *Life of Bach*, page 99, " the Pedal is an essential part of the organ : by this alone it is exalted above all other instruments ; for its magnificence, grandeur, and majesty depend upon it. Without the Pedal, this great instrument is no longer great; it approaches those little organs called in Germany *Positivs*, which are of no value in the eyes of competent judges."

944. A few particulars concerning the date, compass, and number of stops found in some early Continental Pedal organs may be of use, as showing at how early a date an independent Pedal was appreciated abroad.

NAME OF PLACE.	DATE.	NUMBER OF STOPS.	COMPASS.	NO. IN FOREIGN SPECIFICATIONS.
Amiens Cathedral	1429	7		14
Constance Cathedral	1518	8	CCC to Gamut G	115
Freiburg in Bresgau	1520	4	CCC to CC	37
St. Peter's, Hamburg, earlier than	1548	13, including 2 of 32 feet		69
Rouen	1630	8	CCC to tenor c	17
Lucerne Cathedral	1651	13, including 1 of 32 feet, and 5 of 16 feet	CCC to tenor c, short	114
St. Nicholas, Hamburg	1686	16, including 2 of 32 feet		68

945. It is not a little remarkable that Smith and Harris—the former of whom studied his art in Germany, and the latter in France—should never have made a Pedal organ, nor even Pedals, in England. What the cause of this striking omission could have been cannot now be positively ascertained ; but we know that nearly every other real improvement in its turn met with the greatest opposition—as the introduction of Doubles, the establishment of equal temperament, the restoration of the CC compass, &c.—and probably the idea of introducing Pedals met with no better reception. Be this as it may, Pedals were not introduced into England till nearly the end of the last century. According to an autograph letter, written by the late Charles Wesley, and which was in the possession of the late Dr. Rimbault, the Savoy organ, by Snetzler, was the first that had a Pedal-board, without, however, any pipes, and which formed part of Snetzler's original work. Another account states that the organ in St. Matthew's Church, Friday Street, was the first to have Pedals ; and, further, that they were of the two-octave CCC in compass, with a complete set of Stopped Diapason pipes of 16 feet tone attached ; and were made, in 1790, under the direction of the late Rev. Mr. Latrobe. A third account is that the first Pedals made in England were those applied to the organ in Westminster Abbey by Avery ; that they were a *ninth* in compass, GG to Gamut A, with an octave of unison Open Pedal-pipes attached ; that they were such a novelty and

curiosity that people used to go from far and near to hear and see them ; and that Dr. Benjamin Cook, who died in 1793, composed his fine Service in G for the opening of the instrument after receiving those additions.

946. Whichever of the preceding accounts is right or wrong, one fact is certain, namely, that the range of the Pedal-board and Pedal-organ, like that of the Manual and *its* organ, have in England been subject to great diversification. In seeking to form a governing opinion on this subject—*i.e.*, of the correct Pedal compass—the only sure course is to consider for what end the Pedal is introduced into the organ, and to take as a guide the result to which that consideration may direct us. The primary object, then, is to enable the organist to play the bass part of any church composition with his feet,* so that the necessity of his deserting the tenor and perhaps other inner parts may be obviated ; to which, it is scarcely necessary to say, his left hand should be chiefly devoted.†

947. In Germany, Holland, &c., where the true principles of organ-construction and organ-playing are more generally understood and appreciated than was the case till lately in England, the question concerning the compass necessary for the Pedal-clavier and organ has long been set at rest ; whereas in this country no attention at all commensurate with the importance of the subject was bestowed upon it, either by organists or organ-builders, until within the last few years ; but the Pedals were generally made to accord with the incorrect GG Manuals.

948. But, as music had to be more or less altered and injured to suit such Pedals, a proper spirit of inquiry was awakened ; the contents of the English and German sacred musical storehouses were diligently consulted ; and from those unimpeachable sources a solution to the problem was obtained—"What is the proper compass for the Pedal?" The result of these examinations was the decision, that, to be competent for their purposes, a Pedal-clavier and organ should possess a range of from 27 to 30 keys and tones, commencing at CCC, and ascending to tenor e or f.

949. This CCC scale has accordingly been almost uniformly adopted in England during the last few years. Occasionally, however, the old GG, or some other long octave range, has been adhered to, consequently it will not be superfluous to set forth on what substantial grounds it is considered wholly unsuitable to the present advanced state of organ-playing in this country.

The insufficiency and incorrectness of GG Pedals for practical purposes. 950. The first disadvantage attendant upon a GG pedal-board is, that a very large proportion of the music written expressly for the church cannot be correctly played thereon. Even many of the little pieces in the instruction books of Rink, Hesse, &c., are beyond their capabilities. In fact, Pedals that have descended no lower than GG are precisely in the same imperfect state that a violoncello would be without its fourth string, that is, also descending only to G ; and the straits to which a violoncellist would be reduced by such a curtailment of the proper compass of his instrument, may well be adduced to faithfully illustrate the difficulties which

---

* Bach "produced with the Pedal, not only the lower notes, or those for which common organists use the little finger of the left hand, but he played a real bass melody with his feet."—Forkell's *Life of Bach*, page 33.

† The Tenor was formerly the Canto Fermo, Plain-Song, or principal part in a composition, and derived the name Tenor from the Latin word *tenuo, I hold ;* because it held or sustained the air, point, substance, or meaning of the whole *Cantus ;* and every part superadded to it was considered but as its auxiliary. In Tallis's Responses the Plain-Song is preserved in the tenor.

an organist who desires to play correctly has to contend with when performing on Pedals so incomplete in their downward range.

The wrong pitch in which GG Pedals execute on the Manual stops such passages as do come within their range. 951. In such case, even passages which ac.ally lie within their compass are not sounded in the right pitch on the Manual stops. It is the true nature of a Manual unison stop to produce sounds in *exact accordance* with the notes written; whether the keys be pressed down with the fingers, or drawn down by the Pedals; but this, usually, is what is *not* the case on GG organs. For instance, if some simple progression, such as the following,

be played first on the Manual unison stops, and

then repeated on the Pedals coupled thereto; instead of the same sounds

being produced we have the following, . In fact,

we find this singular confusion of "size" and "sound" presented by a GG Open Diapason; while the stop itself is of 10⅔ feet standard length, its pitch will be of 8 feet if played with the hands, and of 16 if played with the feet.

The impossibility of satisfactorily uniting CCC Pipes to GG Pedals; and the false pitch in which the pipes sound when they are so united. 952. The second disadvantage attendant on a GG Pedal-board consists in the impossibility of satisfactorily attaching thereunto an octave of pipes having CCC for their lowest sound. The Pedals do not extend low enough to admit of the pipes being applied to the right keys; hence they are made to act on the only perfect C octave which the Pedals *do* present, namely, the octave above. But, in applying them in this manner, the pipes undergo transposition, which materially alters their nature. Instead of forming the *lowest* octave of a 16-feet stop, they then constitute the *upper* octave of a 32-feet stop, and produce a sound *two* octaves lower than the notation, thus :—

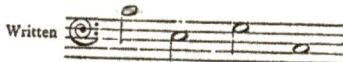

Written   Sounded

953. The incorrect Manuals suggest wrong Pedals; and the wrong Pedals necessitate a defective application of the "CCC Pedal pipes." The pipes being attached to the Pedals, in the manner just noticed, the remaining half-octave of Pedals (*i.e.*, the five treadles from BB down to GG) are either made to communi-cate with the same pipes as their octave above, or they are furnished with pipes in unison therewith; the result in either case being virtually the same. A "return" or "repeat" is caused in the series of Pedal sounds, which leads to this singular anomaly—that the pipe which produces the *lowest* sound is attached to one of the *middle* Pedals, while another that gives one of the *medium* sounds is made to act on the *lowest* Pedals.

The false readings which the CC Pedal pipes create. 954. The third disadvantage attendant on a GG Pedal-board arises from the compulsory attachment of the CCC pipes to the wrong octave of Pedal keys, and the consequent "return" that takes place on the half-octave of keys below. By this "return

Pedal pipe system" the GG, G sharp, A, A sharp, and B Pedals are made to produce precisely the same sounds; so that whether the upper half-octave

of Pedals be used or, the lower,

or both together, no contrast or relief of any kind can

be gained. The consequence of this identity in the sound produced from both ends of the GG Pedal-board is, that such musical progressions as can be played on the treadles are altered, transposed, and reversed in their sounds, in the most remarkable manner; often producing effects of the most startling and grotesque description. A few illustrations of this fact will now be given.

955. The first is taken from the well-known Chorus in Handel's *Messiah*. "And with His stripes." The subject, on its first entry in the bass, stands thus in the score:—

956. On " return Pedal pipes" it is given in the following form:—

the subject being, in a musical sense, destroyed by the "return," marked by an asterisk, and a grammatical error of the worst description introduced.

957. The next illustration is the subject of the concluding Chorus in Mozart's *Litany*:—

958. The above—one of the most dignified subjects ever written—is thus altered by the "return Pedal pipes":—

959. The reading conveyed of the first five bars of this subject then consists of a tame and meaningless reiteration of a single note.

960. The following few chords exhibit the progress of the harmony in the opening phrase of the introductory symphony to Handel's Coronation Anthem, *Zadok the Priest*:—

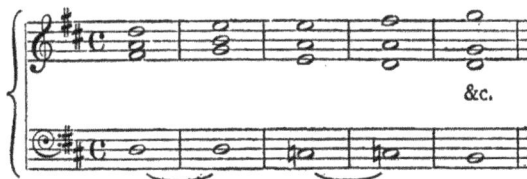

and the following notes show the very objectionable form the resolution of the seventh in the bass is made to take by the return Pedal pipes :—

961. The foregoing selections are from works written for voices and instruments. The two following are subjects from strict organ compositions.

962. No. 1 is taken from Bach's well-known Fugue on the German Chorale, "*Wir glauben all' au einen Gott,*" and which stands thus in the composition itself :—

963. This is given out in the following form on the "return Pedal pipes":—

964. The next is from Mendelssohn's Fugue in C minor :—

965. The Pedal pipes give the following version of the above :—

966. It would scarcely be possible to recognise either of the foregoing subjects when played on the Pedal pipes alone ; for the original order and nature of the intervals from note to note are so frequently altered, that but few vestiges of the original progression remain.

967. Here are two of the simplest subjects that are to be found in the whole range of our standard choral works for the Church :—

Opening subject of the Anthem, "I will exalt Thee," by Dr. Tye.

As given on a return Pedal organ :—

Opening subject of the Anthem, " Almighty and everlasting God," by
Orlando Gibbons :—

Subject as given by a return Pedal organ :—

968. The list of examples of false reading rendered unavoidable by the principle of organ-construction already adverted to might be increased *ad infinitum;* but this must be needless. The above specimens will be sufficient to show how defec-tive is the GG Pedal and " Double Pedal pipe " system. For concert-room organs it is absolutely worthless.

The introduction of " Double Pedal pipes " as the first Pedal stop not in accordance with the laws of organ-building.   969. But, independently of violating the rules of the Grammar of Music when they are being used, the " Double Pedal pipes," by their introduction as the first stop on the Pedal, involve a departure from the very rudiments of organ-building ; one of which is, that the unison stops of each Clavier, as being the most important, shall be *first* introduced. Others are (1) that the sound of the unison stops shall predominate ; and (2) that the first stops proposed for the Pedal shall be the bass to some of the Manual stops. That it must be impossible for the organ-builder to balance the tone of his instrument properly, if the most important Pedal stops—the 16-feet—are designed to be excluded, and another—the *Double*—which should be subservient, is to be introduced, is self-evident. Moreover, the specification itself presents great want of unity and clearness of design, when the " Double " is the only stop proposed for the Pedal, and yet is the stop that is omitted from perhaps all the Manuals, as is generally the case with GG organs.

970. It might be urged that the above important omission from the Pedal is very well supplied by coupling the Manuals thereto in such a manner as to obtain a 16-feet from the elongated stops of those departments, so far as their compass will permit. This, however, is not really the case ; for, instead of the scale of the single Pedal stop being so deduced from that of the borrowed unison as to secure the predominance of the tone of the latter, it is generally so much larger, and the power and density of its sound so much greater, that it cannot be reduced into proper proportion, even if the Diapasons of all three Manuals are coupled together and brought to bear against it.

971. In fact, after carefully considering what are the characteristics· of a GG organ, with Pedals of the same compass and return Pedal pipes, and ascertaining its theoretical and practical defects, it scarcely becomes a subject of wonder that such a system (or rather no system) should be considered unworthy of perpetuation in the present day.

972. For, in the first place, it is as necessary to have the bass part of a composition played in an intelligible and correct manner as any other—more particularly as part-singing, and consequently part-playing, is now more often encouraged and appreciated in the English Church than it used to be ; and in the next, on an instrument so defective in the main points we have described, the greater part of the music of the church can either not be played at all, or without due effect ; as is but too well known to many an organist

whose misfortune it is to have so inconsistently arranged an organ whereon to play. Even the very name "Pedal pipes," as applied to the single half-stop on the Pedal of a GG organ, is devoid of definiteness and intelligibility. From such a name it cannot be gathered whether a stop, so called, sounds in unison with the Manual Diapasons, or whether it gives the octave below; or if it does neither the one nor the other in particular, but partly both. Neither can it be discovered whether its pipes are made of wood, or of metal, or whether they are Open or Stopped. Then of the Scale : the CCC pipes will in some instances be scarcely 10 inches deep ; while in others it will be 20 inches —that is to say, there will be a greater difference than between the Dulciana and Open Diapason on the Manuals—yet there will be nothing whatever in the name or labelling to announce the difference. All these varieties of pitch, material, scale, and structure, are alike to be met with under the one indefinite term, "Pedal pipes."

The premature intro-
duction of Double
Pedal pipes often a
hindrance to the in-
troduction of more
important Pedal stops.

973. Besides the defects above ennumerated, which they bring with them, the premature introduction of Double Pedal pipes is an injudicious step on other grounds. They are often the means of preventing the subsequent introduction of the more important unison Pedal stops, on account of the false impression which they convey of the "size" of the instrument of which they form a part. Instances might be cited, where an organist has represented to the authorities the imperfect state of his instrument ; and has been told, in reply, that the organ is "too large" or "too loud" already ; and this, too, when there has been but half a Swell, no Choir organ, and no Open Diapason, Stopped Diapason, &c., on the Pedal. Nor is such an answer made without some justification, although founded on a serious misconception. Those who have had neither the requisite leisure, nor opportunity to make themselves acquainted with the technical details and practical working of an organ, can only speak of the instrument from the effect which it produces on them in the church ; and an octave of Pedal *pipes* (in a small organ), sounding *two* octaves below the corresponding octave of the bass voice, of a larger scale than those forming any other stop in the organ, and often supplied with a wind of extra strength, are just the very things to betray one who so forms his judgment into a wrong conclusion. Their tone, standing apart from the remainder of the instrument, as it must do under such circumstances, arrests the attention of the auditor ; who, erroneously taking that as a sample of the sound of all Pedal stops, feels opposed to the introduction of the latter. It may seem paradoxical to those who are not sufficiently masters of the subject to be aware of its perfect truth, that an organ will possess more adequate means for being played *soft*, if the *one* octave of Pedal *pipes* be omitted, and some *three or four complete* Pedal *stops* be introduced ; but such is nevertheless the fact. It is constantly the case in accompanying church music that a soft Pedal unison bass (that is, one of 16-feet pitch) is the only appropriate bass, while one of a heavier and deeper tone is quite opposed to the purpose ; yet when, instead of some of these most important Pedal stops, there are only the "Double Pedal pipes" at command, the organist has no alternative but either to use those, in spite of their manifest inappropriateness, or none at all ; and with the certain prospect of missing the true effect, do what he may, and perhaps of being held responsible afterwards for the result. What has been here advanced in relation to church organs applies with even greater force to concert-hall organs.

The arrangements of a C C organ contrast favourably with those of GG compass.

974. How strongly do the simple, systematic, and perfect arrangements of the Pedal of a genuine CC organ contrast with the complicated, faulty, and incomplete attributes of the GG plan, many of the particulars of which have just been detailed ! For instance, on a correctly planned CC organ, the bass part of any piece of church music can be executed on the Pedals in all its integrity, let the instrument be ever so small. In the next place, music that is played thereon, with the Manuals coupled thereto, is not only sounded in the *correct pitch*, but is also given in *octaves*, consisting of the actual sounds represented by the notation, with the addition of *the octave below*, as would be the case in duet-playing on a CCC Manual organ. The most skilful left-hand would fail to play passages in octaves on a long Manual key-board, which can be executed with ease on a properly arranged CC organ. The *Manual* unison stops (8 feet) give the various progressions as they stand (just as bass voices or violoncellos would), while the *Pedal* unison stops (16 feet) give it as faithfully in the octave below ; that is, in the pitch corresponding with that of the double basses ;—so happily does an artistically planned organ facilitate, and render comparatively easy, the perfect execution of music of the highest and most difficult class.

975. It should be the aim, then, of those to whom is entrusted the task of designing an organ (if it really be desired that the instrument shall be as applicable and adequate to all its purposes as circumstances will permit, and be worthy of recognition as a work of art when completed), to eschew all plans that involve the violation of those rules and principles of which every organ-builder and organist is naturally supposed to be an upholder. All attempts to produce an artistic instrument will prove futile, unless the stunted GG Pedal-board and the imperfect and defective 32-feet stop be given up ; and, in their lieu, a CCC set of Pedals, and at least one intelligible stop of 16-feet pitch, be substituted. In organs, even of the most diminutive kind, this is quite attainable. A Covered stop of that size of tone might, in extreme cases, be disposed on the Pedals ; in moderate-sized organs, two or three 16-feet stops should be introduced. In instruments of larger dimensions a 32-feet *sounding* stop may be added ; and in those of the first magnitude (*and in those* ONLY) should a 32-feet Open stop appear. The 32-feet stop, therefore, is one of the *last*, instead of the *very first*, to be proposed. The rules which regulate the admission of these and smaller Pedal stops, form a subject for separate consideration.

976. It need only be added here that the CC Manual key should be capable of being united to the CCC Pedal ; the tenor c to the CC Pedal ; and the middle c¹ key to the tenor c Pedal. The intermediate Manual notes would of course be attached to the respectively positioned Pedals.* Thus would be secured the presence and union of the 8 and 16 feet scales, even in an instrument of the most prescribed limits.

---

* In adding C Pedals to a long octave Manual organ, it would be necessary, in order to prevent the notes below CC from becoming useless, to have *two* Pedal-couplers ; one of the kind above recommended, and another to unite the GG Manual note to the GG Pedal, and so on. In many existing cases, where there are CCC Pedals and GG Manuals, the Pedals from CCC to FFF take down the Manual keys from CC to FF, and then the GG Pedal draws down GG on the Manual. This creates a *second* return.

CHAPTER XXXIII.

THE SITUATION FOR THE ORGAN.

977. The next subject for consideration—the situation for the organ—is of no less importance to those already discussed ; since on it depends, in a great degree, the best effect of the instrument when finished. So great an influence, indeed, does the position exercise on the power and quality of an organ, that an inferior instrument favourably situated will sound better than a superior one that is unfortunately placed ; and a weak-toned instrument in a good position will sound louder than a fuller-toned one in an unfavourable situation.

Acoustical facts to be consulted. 978. Before entering upon the inquiry as to which are good situations and which are not, it may not be unimportant to mention certain facts connected with the production and propagation, the absorption and weakening, the interception and reflection of sound ; as a recollection of these will materially assist in illustrating the relative excellence, or otherwise, of the several sites that will have to be brought under notice.

How sound is produced and propagated. 979. First, then, as to the production and propagation of sound. "When bodies are brought into sudden contact," says the author of the volume entitled *The Art of Improving the Voice and Ear*, "or a single body is made to vibrate or expand suddenly, it must displace a quantity of the surrounding air. The air which is thus displaced in its turn displaces that portion of air which is next to it or beyond it on every side, above and below, before and behind, on the right and on the left. This displaced portion of air displaces again what is beyond it, and so on, in a manner similar to the circles of water which arise from throwing a stone into a pond. In the case of sound, however, the waves are not in *superficial* circles, but in *spheres*, like the coats of an onion. Sound, then, travelling, as it does, in all directions, this circumstance clearly accounts for the excellent musical effect which an organ produces that occupies a *central* position in a building ; as, for instance, the choir screen of a cathedral, or other large cruciform church."

How brief sounds disperse. 980. A sound that is only an instant in duration and not continuous does not spread like a flood of water, pervading every part over which it passes ; but, like a ripple made in a lake, which leaves in repose the part that it has quitted. This may be ascertained by striking a full staccato chord on a cathedral organ that occupies a central position, when the sound will be distinctly perceived retiring from the instrument to the remotest parts of the building, gradually lessening in power, and ultimately dying away.

How sustained sounds more completely occupy space. 981. A continuous sound, on the contrary, pervades the entire space through which it has travelled ; because fresh sound-waves are constantly being engendered, which successively occupy the space the preceding ones have left. This is the reason that the first sound of a sustained chord on a cathedral organ is *not* heard receding. The greater strength of the sound-waves nearer the instrument, from being less spent by divergence, prevents the original sound being heard. On raising the hands, however, from the keys, the sound will again be heard fading away.

The distribution of a sound that cannot travel backwards.   982. A sound that is produced in such a situation that it cannot travel backwards, on account of there being a large reflecting surface to check its progress in that direction, as in the example of an organ placed at the west end of a church, spreads somewhat after the manner of the rays of light through the bull's-eye of a lantern. It travels forwards and sideways, upwards and downwards, and spreads as it proceeds. It is also reflected forwards by the surface behind; and derives some accession of strength from being so reflected. Sound, however, being greatly more reflexible than light, it spreads more rapidly, makes its way into recesses, round columns, and passes great walls or corners of buildings, where the solid interpositions would, in the example of light, only cast shadows.

983. An illustration of the fact of sound spreading as it proceeds may easily be found in a galleried church having the organ at the west end. The tone of the instrument is heard the most completely, *not* by stationing one's self immediately inside the door, at the side of the organ, leading into one of those appendages; but by traversing the gallery some little distance. In a similar manner, an illustration of the fact of sound descending as it progresses, is given in the circumstance of an auditor in the nave having to place himself at some *distance* from the instrument to hear it to the greatest advantage; and in his having to *increase* that distance in proportion to the *elevation* of the organ above the ground.

984. The extent to which the sound of a west-end organ is strengthened, by reflection from the surface behind, does not meet with a familiar illustration in a church that has the instrument so situated; but, in those cathedrals wherein the organ occupies a central position, a good example is presented by the effect of the "Choir organ in front;" the tone of which sounds strong in the choir, into which part it is directly reflected by the Great organ case behind; but which sounds weak outside the choir, on account of the Great organ case standing between the Choir organ and the auditor, and, therefore, presenting an interposition to the tone travelling in that direction. The extent to which the Great organ case assists the tone of the Choir organ in its forward progress into the choir, and checks its backward course into the nave, are points that received distinct illustration in St. Paul's Cathedral in the year 1854, on the occasions of the Sunday Morning Service being celebrated in the choir of the church, and the afternoon under the dome. In the fore-mentioned part of the building the tone of the Choir organ, as far as the Principal, reflected as above, sounded louder, and afforded more support to the vocal choir, than did the same stops, with the Twelfth and Fifteenth added, impeded as above, when the singers sat outside the choir screen. Another proof, though of a negative kind, of the extent to which a sound is strengthened by reflection, is afforded by the circumstance of its being so much weakened by the removal of the reflecting surface from behind. An illustration of this fact was given at Westminster Abbey, when the Great organ was removed from the centre of the screen; which alteration, allowing more of the tone of the Choir organ to travel backwards into the nave, caused it to appear more "faded" in the choir.

Sound weakened by divergence.
985. As the circular waves on the surface of a piece of water become more faint as they proceed and diverge, so sound becomes weaker the farther it travels and the more it disperses. "Whenever," says Dr. Brewer, in his work on the *Phenomena of Sound*, "sound can diffuse itself freely round its centre of propagation, it loses in *intensity* what it gains in *extent;*" consequently, a sound that has travelled *twice* a certain distance will only be heard with *one-fourth* its original strength, the loudness not diminishing inversely as the distance increases, but inversely to the *square* of that distance. This is the case in the open air; but in a building—as a church or a concert-room—the walls and roof limit the extent of the divergence of the sound, and so prevent its fading away so rapidly. Moreover, after the sound has struck against them, and is checked by them, it is by them reflected back; and, if the original sound has ceased, the reflected sound forms an echo; but, if it continues, the latter mingles with the former, and enriches and strengthens it.

Echo.
986. When the return of the sound is perceptible to the ear, it is termed an echo. A certain time, however, must elapse between the production of the sound and its being reflected, or no echo will be perceived; and that time at least must be the twelfth part of a second, within which interval the ear is incapable of receiving separate impressions. The distance of the reflecting surface, therefore, must be at least forty-seven feet from the place whence the sound emanates to cause an echo.

Resonance.
987. But the strength and quality of a musical sound are much increased and improved by the reciprocation of bodies in the more immediate neighbourhood whence the first sound emanates. Thus the vibrations of a tuning-fork will, on the tip of the handle of the fork being placed on a table, acquire a marked accession of strength. This augmentation of sound is due to *resonance*. The sonorous vibrations created by the tuning-fork set the wood upon which it is placed in a similar state of citation; the simultaneous vibrations of which, being communicated to the superincumbent air, greatly increase the strength of the original sound. The front, back, sound-post, and all the air contained in the body of a double-bass or violin, in like manner contribute to produce the volume of tone elicited from the instrument, by vibrating in unison with the strings and with each other. If only the *strings* vibrated, the sound would be comparatively insignificant; but, when the entire body of the instrument is set in motion, the impulse is sufficient to produce sounds of considerable power.

988. A sound thus increased and enriched is capable of further augmentation from resonance, if it is produced under circumstances favourable to the extension of that influence. The tone of a double bass, for instance, is much increased in power by the instrument resting on a hollow platform—as the reciprocating floor of a concert-room orchestra. "The platform receives from the musical instrument a vibratory motion, imparts the same to the air between it and the floor of the building, and the whole combined gives a powerful impulse to the air in the concert-room." (Dr. Brewer, page 277.)

989. These several examples illustrate precisely the effect of resonance on the tone of an organ. The tone of an organ is much improved by the instrument being placed on a wooden floor; and it is still more beneficially affected when that floor is a raised one. The reasons are these. The sound-board acting somewhat after the manner of the belly of a violin; the frame-work

as the sound-post ; and the *wooden* floor as the back ; all are thrown into a state of greater or less vibration by the sounds, which in this case are produced by pipes and not strings.

990. The vibratory motion of portions of the frame-work is sometimes perceptible to the touch, even when a single stop only is being sounded on the sound-board above, as, for instance, the Stopped Diapason ; while that of the floor is frequently felt by the feet, when all the stops are in full play.

991. The air between the sound-board and the ground is also set in motion, like that in the body of a violin ; and sometimes its tremulousness is sufficiently great to cause the trackers to vibrate in their registers. The tone of a large pipe, again, is much strengthened by standing on a wooden floor, even as that of a double-bass is by resting on the platform of an orchestra. This is one of the reasons why organ-builders place their great Pedal Diapason pipes as near to, if not actually on the floor, whenever this arrangement is practicable.

992. The wooden portions of the case of an organ, again, are frequently of essential service in increasing the resonance. It has sometimes happened that a pipe that has produced but a weak sound has, when tried in its situation, and been assisted by the vibrations of the case, produced one of the finest notes in the instrument.

993. When the wooden floor on which an organ stands is a raised one, the platform, together with its supports, and also the free air about the whole, are all thrown into a state of vibration, to the augmentation and improvement of the sound ; and when the heavy-toned bass pipes are being used, the vibrations of the flooring or platform are sometimes communicated to the wooden fittings of the church, or even to the very walls of the edifice.

994. Echo and resonance, therefore, each exercise great influence on the tone of an organ. Echo imparts to it that inexpressibly charming, etherial, lingering effect which is so perceptible in cathedrals and other large buildings that are comparatively free from absorbents, after the actual sound has ceased. Many buildings which do not produce a *perceptible* echo yet impart a certain buoyant, free effect to musical sounds produced within them, that is highly beneficial to the quality of their tone, as well as favourable to their distribution.

995. Resonance is the cause of the agreeable, pleasant, humming effect which is heard to come from within the organ itself. In low, broad, galleried buildings, where but little room has been allotted to the organ, and where the contents of the instrument have in consequence been so crowded together as to leave but little free space inside it, the resonance is much decreased : and an effect is frequently perceived as though the sound of the organ were struggling to develop and disperse itself, in spite of the impediments with which it is beset. The effect of an instrument so constructed and situated is frequently dead and *palpable*. Instead of the many different sounds which in an organ are concentrated on each key, mingling together, and producing the effect of one excellent whole, every "item" falls on the ear as a distinguishable separate and isolated sound.

Impediments to the equal distribution of sound.   996. The most common impediments to the equal dispersion of the tone of an organ occupying a west gallery are the lateral galleries. These catch the sound as it spreads, and prevent its descending into and pervading the aisles beneath so effectually as it would otherwise do.

Absorbents of sound.   997. The materials and fabrics common in churches that soften and deaden sound are wool, cloth, hair, tow, matting, &c. "They shut up a large quantity of air between their minute and detached parts, so that they cannot readily transmit an impulse." (Dr. Brewer.) Cushions, hassocks, curtains, people's dresses, and matting, therefore, are all absorbents of sound.

Church arrangements that are favourable to sound. 998. The exclusion of lateral galleries from modern churches, together with their baize linings ; the introduction of low open seats, in place of high closed pews ; the removal of hassocks in favour of kneeling-boards ; and the substitution of Minton's tiles for matting up the avenues ; these are all favourable steps towards the preservation of the acoustical properties of the building.

Absorbents sometimes introduced to subdue excessive echo. 999. While the influences of impediments and absorbents are, generally speaking, highly detrimental in their effect, there have been instances of the latter being made to serve a beneficial purpose ; as when the echo in a building has been so great as to render sounds, whether of the voice or of music, confused and indistinct. At the Chapel Royal, Whitehall, the echo was found to be so excessive, a few years ago, after the building was restored, that the clothing of an assembled congregation was insufficient to check the remarkable prolongation of sound ; and crimson cloth was therefore hung in festoons round the building, which, not presenting a sufficiently hard surface to throw off all the tone, but, on the contrary, a sufficiently soft one to absorb some of it, produced the desired effect.

Velocity of sound. 1000. The average rate at which sound travels in atmospheric air is 1,120 feet in a second of time ; and high and low sounds, soft and loud sounds, all proceed with the same velocity. Thus the tones of the lightest treble voice will reach the extremities of an extensive building as rapidly as those of the heaviest bass voice ; and the sounds of the most delicate Dulciana as quickly as the tone of the most ponderous Posaune. Were it otherwise, the acute and grave tones of voices, and the weak and strong-toned stops of an organ would be heard confusedly jarring after one another.

1001. But for the same reason that the ripple caused by dropping a small pebble gently into a smooth piece of water will not spread so far as those produced by casting a large stone into it, the sound-waves produced by a soft musical sound will not extend so far as those excited by a powerful one. Its precise strength depends, in the first instance, on the force of the shock that is imparted to the air ; and which produces sound-waves of correspondingly decided character. The distance to which it will travel depends on the extent to which the sound-waves can spread without meeting with an obstruction. When there are no impediments, and but few absorbents in their course, the sound not only reaches farther, but mellows as it progresses ; when they meet with many obstructions or absorbing circumstances, it not only does not reach so far, but its strength is lessened and its quality impoverished.

1002. The distance to which a sound will travel depends upon its intensity, density, and perhaps gravity. A dense sound will travel farther than an intense one, as is proved by the fact of the beat of the great drum of a military band playing in the open air being distinctly audible at a greater distance than the united sounds of the trombones and ophicleides. Grave sounds also appear to travel farther than acute ones. The Open Pedal Diapasons of an organ may be heard at a greater distance outside a church than the higher organ sounds ; and the tone of the double-basses in an orchestra may be distinguished sooner than the treble instruments, as you approach a concert-room. The "tenor" of a peal of bells is also frequently heard at a greater distance from a church, or at any rate more distinctly, than the other bells.

The apparent strength of a sound dependent on the position of the auditor, &c.   1003. The *apparent* strength or weakness of a sound will depend on the relative position of the sounding body and the auditor ; that is to say, whether they be near to each other or far apart ; and also, to a material extent, whether there be many absorbing substances between them. A sound of a given strength will sound louder at a greater distance, when the intermediate space is comparatively free, than it will at a less distance with impediments interposed ; hence the fact, mentioned at the commencement of this chapter, of the tone of an inferior organ being improved, and of a better one being injured, by its position, the acoustic capacity of the church, and the nature of its fittings. If the auditor is stationed below the level of the sounding body, he will hear the sound as it diverges downwards ; if he is on either side of it, he will hear it as it spreads ; but if he is on the same level with it, and near to it, he will experience its full and direct force, at the same time that his clothing will present an absorbing impediment to its free progress ; while, on the contrary, if he is stationed at a distance, and other persons intervene, the sound will reach him in a weakened and faded form.

1004. When the amount of absorbing substance in a church is needlessly increased, and the organ occupies a position unfavourable to the equal distribution of its tone, the instrument will sometimes sound "too loud" in some parts of the church, at the same time that it will appear "too soft" in others. This inequality of effect, however, is, under such circumstances, unavoidable.

Penetration of sound.   1005. Sound possesses the power of penetrating and passing through hard substances ; hence the circumstance of the tone of an organ being heard so plainly outside a church. When an organ is placed in a chamber built out from a church, and is accompanied by other arrangements disadvantageous to the free dispersion of its tone, it will even be heard almost as distinctly outside the building as in it. Another illustration of the penetration of sound is presented by the swell of an organ, the tone of which is heard perfectly well, though in a sweetly subdued form, through the thick wooden box, when the shutters are perfectly closed.

1006. Having noticed such phenomena connected with sound as appeared to be necessary to illustrate our present subject, we may now proceed to consider the various situations occupied by church organs, as well as the merits of each.

The west end of a church as the situation for the organ.   1007. The most usual position assigned to the organ in Continental churches, for at least the last three hundred years, has been the west end.

Old examples of west-end organs in Continental churches.   1008. A few examples and dates may be cited, illustrative of this fact. The organ in Amiens Cathedral, which has a 16-feet front, and was completed in 1429, originally stood and still stands at the west end. The organ in Chartres Cathedral, built in 1513, was first erected over the great western doorway. In the Cathedral at Constance, in Switzerland, the organ at the west end was originally erected in that situation, in the year 1518, which date appears on the case of the instrument. The organ at the west end of the nave of the cathedral at Freiburg, in Bresgau, was built in 1520. At Hamburg, the oldest organ in the town, previous to the conflagration of 1842, in St. Peter's Church, stood at the west end, and had a 32-feet front. It was not known when or by whom it was originally built; but the last two manuals—it had four—were made at Hartzogen-bach, in Brabant, by Mister Nargenhof, in 1548, and sent to Hamburg by sea. This, M. Pfiffer, the organist to the church towards the latter part of the last century, informed Dr. Burney was upon record. Again, at Lübeck, in St. Mary's Church, the Great organ, which has lately been rebuilt, but originally made in 1518, is similarly situated. This instrument is a "hanging" organ, with a 32-feet front of tin; and the beams which support it are built into and project from the wall behind.

1009. There were three old west end organs standing a few years ago in churches at Liege. That in the church of St. Denis, which had the Choir organ in front, bore the date of 1589 carved on the case; the second, in St. Jaques', also with Choir in front, was built in 1600; and the third, in St. Anthony's Church, had the date of 1624 carved and gilt on the case.

The merits of the west end, as the situation for the organ, considered. 1010. In selecting the west end of the church as the situation for the organ, the ecclesiastics, architects, organ-builders, organists, or whosoever fixed on that position, no doubt gave it the preference for the same reasons which in old times led to the end of a baronial hall being selected as the site for the "Minstrels' Gallery;" and in after times the extremity of a concert-room being generally recognised as the best place for an orchestra;—namely, because the tone could travel "forwards, sideways, upwards, and downwards;" in fact, could be dispersed throughout the building more equally from that available situation than from any other.

1011. An orchestra so placed has the area of the entire length of the room before it, into which the sound, from the great concourse of instruments, can travel, and, in a united state, fall on the ear of the auditor. In the same manner an organ, similarly situated in a church, has the area of the entire length of the nave and chancel before it, into which the sound from the several pipes can travel, and, in a united and mellowed form, reach the ear of the clergy and congregation.

1012. The west end afforded sufficient space to admit of the organ being erected on an elevated platform or gallery—as a modern orchestra is elevated above the level of an audience—whereby the resonance was increased, and additional free-dom also imparted to the tone.

1013. By elevating the instrument, the full force of its tone passed over, instead of overwhelming those nearest to it, into the open space before it, whence it was diffused throughout the edifice. A sound is distributed more equally from a raised position in *any* part of a church than from a low one; hence the necessity for a reading-desk, pulpit, and steps to the altar, to elevate the minister, so that his voice may travel to the remote parts of the building.

1014. The west end, at the same time that it admitted of the organ being sufficiently elevated, presented facilities for this being done, and yet plenty of space being left between the top of the instrument and the roof of the church, whereby the tone was still further and beneficially affected. Into this space the numerous pipes poured forth their separate sounds, which, there meeting and amalgamating, entered the church with united and mellowed effect.

1015. Had the organ, however, been placed too near the roof, its tone would have been partially "smothered" in effect, and the instrument itself exposed to

D D

considerable injury from the excessive heat of the sun in summer, which might then often have been conducted into it through the roof, and from the cold and damp in winter. A certain amount of derangement from atmospheric change would at times be unavoidable, as explained in a former chapter ; but such variations would have told with much greater severity, had the organ been placed close to the roof ; where, in addition to its pipe-work being more frequently thrown out of tune by the excessive alterations of temperature, the mechanism would, by its exceeding dryness at some seasons and dampness at others, have been rendered more subject to sticking, swelling, warping, ciphering, and many other evils of a like kind, with which casualties subsequent organ-builders were compelled to become familiar when they had to erect instruments in " second galleries."

1016. The west end, again, generally admitted of more space being devoted to the organ, which obviated the necessity for crowding the mechanism and the pipe-work.

1017. When an organ-builder is " cramped for room " the mechanism has often to be crammed so closely together that, on the occurrence of some trifling fault, much additional derangement must be caused before the seat of the original failing can be arrived at. And the same with the pipe-work ; but with the additional disadvantage that, when the pipes are "packed too closely together," there will sometimes arise a beating or a jarring, or a weakness or unsteadiness of speech, in some of the pipes that will defy correction.

1018. Another very important object attained by placing the organ at the west end of the church was this. An efficient organ was necessarily also a large one ; and the larger the organ, the greater probability of its becoming an eyesore. By erecting it, however, at the west end, it would not be within sight of, but at the *back* of the congregation, and would only be visible to its members on their turning to leave the church.

1019. The reasons, musical, acoustical, and structural, in favour of the west end, as an eligible situation for the organ, therefore, were very great.

An architectural ob-   1020. *Architecturally* considered, however, it was frequently
jection to the organ open to one great objection. Most churches had a west
occupying the west window ; generally one of the most handsome in the building ;
end.   to hide which would have been a serious sacrifice. Many organs were therefore made, so as still to occupy the west end for the sake of the musical effect, but so that the architectural feature should not be hidden, nor the light through it excluded from the church. Several instruments so constructed are mentioned by Dr. Burney in his tour through Germany and Italy, the particulars of which are here extracted :—

Examples of divided   1021. " In the town of Courtray, the organ, at the collegiate
west end organs in church of *Notre Dame*, is disposed of in a very singular manner ;
Continental churches. it is placed in a gallery at the west end of the building ; but in order to preserve the window, which was necessary to light the body of the church, the organ is divided in two parts, one of which is fixed on one side of the window, and one on the other ; the bellows run under the window, and communicate with both parts of the instrument, which is a large one of sixteen feet, with pedals, and seems to have been but lately erected (1772). The keys are in the middle, under the window, but not to be seen below."

1022. " The organ at the Dominicans' Church, at Frankfort, has an arch cut through it, to let the light into the church from the west window ; it is in a handsome case, the ornaments over the arch are in good taste, and the side columns are well disposed. The keys are on the right hand *side* of the instrument, over which there is a small front ; the compass is from C to C, the pedals have an octave below double C."

1023. "In the cathedral at Passau, which is a very beautiful modern building, of the Corinthian order, there is a very magnificent organ to look at. The case is finely carved and gilt, and the pipes are highly polished. It is divided into two columns of large pipes, one on each side, and has a complete little organ in the middle, which joins them together, and saves the west window. It is what builders call a 32-feet organ. The front pipes are of burnished tin."

1024. St. Michael's Church, Vienna. "This instrument has no front. The great pipes are placed, in an elegant manner, on each side of the gallery ; and there is a box only in the middle, of about four feet square, for the keys and stops ;—so that the west window is left quite open. The compass of the organ, in the Manuals, extends only from double E* in the bass to C in alt ; but the Pedals of most German organs have an octave lower than the lowest note of the keys that are played by the hands, which is the case with this instrument. It has forty stops and three sets of keys, which, by a spring of communication, can be played all together."

1025. Prague. The organ in the church of St. Nicholas "is divided into two parts, placed one on each side the gallery ; and the keys, with a *positif*, or small Choir organ, are in the middle, but placed so low as to leave the west window clear ; instead of wood, the framework, pillars, base, and ornaments of this instrument, in front, are of white marble."

1026. To these examples may be added the organ at Weingarten, in Suabia, which is so constructed as to admit light into the church through six semi-circular-headed windows, ranged in two rows of three each. The organ at the Minoreten Church, at Cologne, is also pierced with several window-like openings, to admit light from the west window into the body of the building.

Smith and Harris's parish church organs usually placed at the west end. 1027. When Smith settled and Harris returned to England, towards the latter part of the seventeenth century, to take part in supplying our churches with new organs, in place of those that had been so needlessly destroyed, they followed the custom, usual in their own countries, of placing their organs at the west end of churches not of cruciform shape ; but they at the same time erected them in that situation, whether there was a window there or not. No instances are known of a *divided* organ having been made by either of those artists, for the purpose of preserving an architectural beauty. The earliest English specimen of an organ constructed in this manner appears to have been that made by Green, for New College, Oxford. Many others have since been constructed in this way ; one of the most successful in its treatment being that by Hill, in the church of the Immaculate Conception, Farm Street Mews.

Their cathedral organs usually placed on the choir screen. 1028. The cathedral organs built by Harris and Smith were usually placed on the Choir screen. This situation appears to have been selected for two reasons. The instruments they were

---

* The organ is really of CC compass, but having short octaves ; which fact appears to have escaped the Doctor. (See Foreign Specifications.)

called upon to build for those spacious and venerable piles were scarcely a whit larger than those they made for ordinary parish churches; and it must, therefore, have been obvious that, if they were placed at the west end, the *firmness* of their tone would have been utterly spent before it could have reached the choir. They were accordingly erected some 150 or 200 feet nearer to the vocal choir, and generally in such a situation as a knowledge of acoustics prescribed as the best.

Harris's proposal for a grand west end organ in St. Paul's Cathedral.   1029. Renatus Harris, indeed, made a proposal in 1712, and, therefore, after the death of Smith, to erect an organ in St. Paul's Cathedral, "over the west door, at the entrance into the body of the church," which was to be such a one as· " in art and magnificence should transcend any work of that kind ever before invented;" and in its construction it was intended to "·apply the power of sounds in a manner more amazingly forcible than had, perhaps, before been known." (See Hawkins's *History of Music,* vol. iv., page 356; quoting the *Spectator,* No. 553, for December 3, 1712.) Is it possible, as this quotation would imply, that Harris had some partial acquaintance with the principle that Cavaillé-Coll has in our own times carried out with such fine effect in his Harmonic Flute-work, and Hill in his " Tuba" Reed-work? At any rate, to *equal* " any work before invented," Harris's must, in size, have been a 32-feet organ. But, whatever the details of his plan might have been, the plan itself was not accepted.

The erection of Father Smith's organ on the Choir screen of St. Paul's opposed.   1030. Father Smith had previously erected an organ on the Choir screen of St. Paul's; but whether it should occupy that position or not, had been a subject of warm contention between Sir Christopher Wren and the Dean and Chapter of the Cathedral.

1031. " Sir Christopher Wren," says the article in the *Musical Gazette,* from which we have before quoted, " wished the organ to be placed on one side of the Choir, as it was in the old Cathedral, that the whole extent and beauty of the building might be seen at one view; and the Dean, on the contrary, wished to have it at the west end of the Choir; and Sir Christopher, after using every effort and argument to gain his point, was at last obliged to yield. Schmidt, according to his instructions, began the organ, and, when the pipes were finished, found that the case was not spacious enough to contain them all; and Sir Christopher, tender of his architectural proportions, would not consent to let the case be enlarged to receive them, declaring the beauty of the building to be already spoiled by the '—— box of whistles.' After all this contention, the architect, sorely against his will, was obliged to make an addition to the case. He not only had been niggardly in regard to the depth of it, where another foot would have been of no consequence whatever, but also in the height; for, when Schmidt came to put in the large Open Diapason pipes in the two side flats, they appeared through the top nearly a foot in length, and spoiled the appearance entirely. .Schmidt now entertained hopes of having a new case; but Sir Christopher, who before would not suffer any ornaments on the top, was now obliged to add several feet, or else alter the case, which vexed him exceedingly. These ornaments consist of angels, with trumpets, standing at the side of a small altar. The colour of the wood that these are made of being lighter than the organ-case, the addition is soon discoverable."

1032. In this struggle Smith evidently viewed the question *musically,* while Sir Christopher Wren considered it *architecturally;* and both had reason on their side. Sir Christopher was, of course, correct in asserting that an organ in the centre would prevent the whole extent of the building being seen at one view ; but then the objection applied with equal force against the Choir screen, to defend which and condemn the organ involved a manifest inconsistency.

1033. The result of the contention was, as we have seen, that

"Music won the cause ; "

and the arrangements just detailed were uniformly followed in cathedral and other churches, from the time of Smith and Harris, down to within the last few years.

The comparative merits of the several side situations considered.
1034. In recent times the west end of a parish church, as the position for the organ, has been strongly objected to, particularly where there is a choir ; and there is no doubt that a much better musical effect results from the choir and organ being near to each other, as a more united effect is produced in a concert-room by the band and singers being together.

1035. Next to the west end, the best place for the organ, as indicated by the laws regarding the propagation of sound, will be some elevated position, having space above, and both sides free. These conditions point to the *side* of the church ; and in every instance, where all or most of them have been complied with, a very good effect has resulted.

1036. The organ in the church of St. Mary Magdalene, St. Pancras, built by Gray and Davison, may be cited as a successful example of an instrument so placed. It is supported on stone brackets, about eight feet above the ground ; has good head room ; is entirely free at one side, and has a reflector immediately behind, in the south wall of the aisle.

1037. In some instances, where sufficient room could not conveniently be found in the church itself for the organ, a recess or organ-chamber has been built out from one of the sides for its reception. An old example of such an organ-chamber exists in the chapel of Christ's College, Cambridge ; a second occurs in the chapel of Hampton Court Palace. The tone of an organ so placed is much weakened in consequence, as it cannot begin to spread and disperse till it has passed through and over the front of the case. The natural disadvantages of such a situation, however, can be considerably modified by making the chamber of ample dimensions, by lining it with wooden boards, and by furnishing it with a hollow wooden flooring. It is also of the highest consequence that there should be plenty of space between the top of the case and the turn of the arch ; otherwise there will be no possible means of egress for the tone, which will then be smothered. All these precautions were taken in the construction of the organ-chamber at the Temple Church, the flooring of which is eight feet above the level of that of the church, the great organ soundboard being nearly another eight feet above the chamber flooring. There is also plenty of space between the top of the organ and the roof of the chamber.

1038. An organ that stands in a recess certainly appears to possess less strength of tone than if it were placed at the west end ; but if there be plenty of head room over the pipes, and attention is paid to other circumstances favourable to resonance, what the instrument loses in power it frequently gains in sweetness of quality and cathedral-like character of tone ; and, as the loss of power can be easily compensated for by disposing additional stops, there appears to be no reason why an organ should not tell fully as well at the side as from the west end, if every means be taken to make it do so. This is specially the case with the organ in the Temple Church.

1039. By this it is not meant that an organ placed in a side recess will tell as well as the same kind of organ would at the west end with space around it ; but that if it be judiciously *enlarged*, in proportion to its *loss of power*, so as to counteract the otherwise ill effect exercised by the recess, it will then sound at least as well as the unenlarged west end organ. The distinction here intended to be drawn is well illustrated by the difference produced by a choral staff of a given number singing *forte*, as compared with a more numerous body singing *sotto voce*. Supposing the strength or abstract power of sound produced by each to be about the same, yet there will be a marked difference in the *quality* of the tone, which, under many circumstances, will be in favour of the larger, but softer, sounding body. The subduing influence of a recess, in a similar way, frequently imparts to the tone of an organ a certain chasteness and kindliness of character, as well as a slight haziness—as though a fine veil were drawn over it—that is exceedingly pleasing, and even beneficial, if the volume and fulness of tone at the same time remain unreduced. The organ in Leeds Parish Church is a very successful example of an instrument placed in a transept, and causes one to regret that the magnificent new organ at Doncaster does not enjoy the advantage of a similar position.

1040. At Lübeck, the "little" organ in St. Mary's Church—which, by the way, has upwards of thirty stops, including ten on the Pedal—partly projects from the east wall of the south transept, and partly stands in a recess in that wall. The Choir organ, containing ten ranks of Mixture, stands in front ; and the effect of the instrument is altogether most admirable. The treatment of the position, so as to give to a moderately deep organ only a shallow projection into the church, is both ingenious and successful. Neither the view of the building, on the one hand, nor the tone of the instrument, on the other, is destroyed. This organ is said to be about two hundred years old.

1041. A most unfavourable plan, usually, for the tone of an organ is that of putting the instrument in a recess, and placing the front pipes so as to form an ornamental *filling up* of the arch. With walls on three sides, and a tier of large pipes entirely occupying the fourth, the tone can only force its way through the interstices between the pipes, as water escapes through the fissures in a flood-gate. The contrivance is frequently more calculated to keep the tone back than to let it out. The organ at All Saints' Church, Manchester, built by Kirtland and Jardine, of that town, is most picturesquely treated, it being divided, and a portion placed in a recess on each side the chancel ; but the Pedal Open Diapason, which produces a very bold effect in the recess where it stands, sounds in the church as weak as an ordinary Pedal Stopped Diapason. At the church of St. Mark, Old Street Road, the organ was similarly placed in a chamber ; and the calculation of the organ-builder, Bevington, was that only *one-fourth* of the tone of the instrument found its way into the church. The melody of a chorale played out on the Great Diapasons, Principal, and Trumpet of this organ sounded no stronger than it would have done on the Stopped Diapason and Clarionet of most instruments that are favourably situated. The good taste of those in authority, however, had this mistake satisfactorily remedied long since.

1042. The worst possible arrangement is that of putting the *organist*, as well as the organ, into a chamber at the side ; filling up the arch, as before, with pipes, which form an ornamental wall between the player and the congregation. This arrangement *did* exist at St. Mark's, Old Street Road, where three-fourths of the organ-tone was boxed in, and which, returning and descending on the organist, produced a din around him like that heard from a peal of bells in a belfry. The wall of pipes was not only a serious impediment in the way of the organ tone travelling into the church and reaching the congregation ; but, telling both ways, it was as effectual a check to the voices of the congregation entering the recess and reaching the organist. Added to this double impediment, the deep humming sound which the ornamental pipes, forming the bass portion of one of the stops in most constant use—the Open Diapason—was producing between the congregation and organist presented another difficulty in the way of the one hearing the other. This arrangement was, therefore, soon abandoned.

The east end of an aisle, or a chancel chapel, as the situation of the organ considered. 1043. It has been a frequent custom during the last few years to place the organ either at the east end of one of the aisles, or in an organ chapel on one side of the chancel. These arrangements are preferable to the one last noticed. In such a situation it is necessary (1) that the ground should be of wood, and hollow ; (2) that the sound-boards should be kept as high as possible ; (3) that there should be a good amount of clear space over the organ ; and (4) that as much ground space as possible should be allowed for the organ.

1044. The wooden floor increases the resonance, concerning which all has been already said that is necessary. The elevation of the sound-boards to a satisfactory height causes the mouths of the pipes to range above the heads of the congregation, whereby their tone is more likely to travel before it becomes partially absorbed, instead of being partially absorbed before it travels. It may easily be surmised how comparatively dull and muffled a clergyman's voice would sound were he to stand only on the same level as the congregation ; and the tone of an organ that has its sound-boards kept low will have a decided tendency towards the same fault. If the mouths of the pipes generally can be kept as much above the level of the vocal choir as those of the choir are above the level of the congregation, it will be so much the better both for singers and organ.

1045. The space over the organ relieves the tone of the instrument from the force and hardness which its contracted situation, as compared with the west end, is otherwise very liable to impart to it ; while the greater space allowed for the organ admits of the pipes being planted in a less crowded and confused manner. Of the quantity of wind that enters at the foot of the pipes something like three-fourths of it passes out again at the mouth, a comparatively small portion only entering the body of the pipe. From this it must be obvious how necessary it is to allow the pipes the utmost available room to *speak* in. When this is not the case, some pipes have to be mounted on longer feet ; others turned this or that way ; and others grooved off here and there ; not from design, or preference, but from necessity ; and which "packing and contriving" give to the interior of an organ a very unsystematic and disorderly appearance.

1046. If the organ be placed in a chancel chapel, there should be an arch—the more lofty and wide the better—opening into the aisle, as well as one towards the chancel. The importance of this arrangement is explained by the first fact mentioned at the commencement of this chapter, regarding the propagation of sound ; and its object is to allow the tone of an organ to pass down the aisle as well as across the chancel. When there is no second arch, the whole strength of the organ tone is directed towards the vocal choir in the chancel, which is then more liable to be overpowered by it at the same time that the congregation will experience scarcely any support from it. If there be two arches, and they are simply separated by a column or a pier, this will be more favourable to the egress of the tone than an angle formed by the junction of two walls, and having a hollow angle inside ; which latter is apt to catch and throw some of the tone back, while the former would allow it to pass round and proceed onwards, diagonally, into and across the nave of the church.

1047. As much free space as possible should also be left near to the organ. This enables the tone to get fairly from the instrument before it begins to be absorbed by the dresses of the congregation. The organ in the "Catholic and Apostolic Church," Gordon Square, built by Gray and Davison, which stands at the end of the south transept, on the ground, has plenty of free space around and over it, and sounds very freely in consequence. Space being left and the congregation not being seated so near to an organ, together, allow of the instrument being voiced more boldly and church-like, with little ill effect and much good resulting. The conditions necessary to cause the tone to travel to the extremities of the church can then be better attended to, without causing inconvenience to anyone ; but if seats be placed too near to the organ, those who occupy them will hear more of its tone than they wish, while their clothing will prevent its getting away, and reaching those at a distance so effectually, by absorbing some of it before it can do so.

1048. If the several precautions just enumerated be taken to prevent deadening the sound of the organ, and to lessen the partial and unequal distribution of its tone, to which all side situations have an unavoidable tendency, an organ may be made to tell very fairly in either of the positions just considered.

The chancel an eligible position for a divided organ. 1049. Another and more rare arrangement is that of dividing the organ, and placing a portion of it on each side the chancel, where there is room, as at St. Margaret's, Leicester. This plan is in every respect a most excellent one. It is scarcely, if at all, inferior, even in a musical point of view, to that of a divided west-end organ ; while, under its working, the organ is accommodated, without being sacrificed, to other arrangements that are now considered essential in most churches. In the first place, as the chancel is generally more lofty than the side chapels, this circumstance admits of the sound-boards being kept up higher, the important advantage of which arrangement is already known to the reader. Next, as the chancel is sometimes not very much less in height than the nave, it affords nearly as much space over the instrument for the mellowing and sweetening of the tone. Thirdly, the chancel being only occupied by the clergy and choir, it is comparatively unencumbered by absorbents and impediments, which is highly beneficial to the tone. Again, the organ will still be at the "end" of the church—although the opposite one to that which it frequently occupies—with the whole length of the edifice before it, into which its harmonious tones can travel. Moreover, by being placed to the east, with the vocal choir nearer to the nave, it will occupy its proper subordinate position in regard to the voices. No one would ever think of placing the instrumental staff between the vocal choir and the audience in a concert-room ; and an analogous arrangement is equally ineligible in a church. (In a theatre, the arrangement is different ; but the *sunken* position of the band there tends to its subordination.) Such a distribution of the organ might lead to a new use of the instrument, of an antiphonal character ; of the advantage of which, however, we have at present had no practical experience in this country, although it would perhaps prove a source of many very fine and legitimate effects. The two parts could ordinarily respond to each other, after the manner of the separate sides of the choir ; and be united, by means of couplers, when the entire choir joined in bursts of joyful exultation. Many Continental churches are furnished with divided organs in the choir, or with two separate and distinct organs ; the effect of which, when used as above, is said to be singularly fine. Then, with regard to the construction of such an organ, as the two parts would stand *sideways*, and therefore would be seen only in *profile* from the church, their projection could be lessened, if room for greater breadth be allowed, whereby the view from west to east would be less interfered with. For the interior arrangements, the Abbé Vogler's system of pipe arrangement might be advantageously employed, as being admirably calculated to facilitate the progress of the tone through the side of the case towards the church. At All Saints' Church, Margaret Street, the organ is divided, and a part placed at the extreme of each transept. The result of this arrangement is quite satisfactory.

The relative position of the vocal choir and organ. 1050. Respecting the relative position of the choir and organ in a church, concerning which a few words may here be said, it may be accepted as a good general rule that, if the organ is to be in a line with the choir, it should not be on a level with it ; and, if it is to be on a level with the choir, it should not be in a line with it. That is to say, the choir should never be subjected to the direct force of the tone of the instrument. When it is so—as, for instance, when the organ is placed immediately behind one-half of the choir—that half hears the tone too strongly and palpably, while the clothing of its members deadens it before it reaches the other part of the choir. No given amount of organ tone, whether much or little, is then so equally and agreeably distributed to both. When the organ is out of a line, but on a level, with the choir, the choir hears its tone, as it is spreading, with less force, but with equal distinctness ; when it is in a line with the choir, but elevated above it, the choir catches its sound as it descends in the course of its propagation. But, inasmuch as the sound produced at an elevation is necessarily less under the absorbing influence of the clothing of the congregation below, the plan of putting the organ "in a line with the choir, but above its level," is the preferable one. The tone of the organ can then reach the congregation and support its voice, as well as that of the choir. Hence the excellence of the arrangement at the Temple Church. At the church of St. Mary Magdalene, St. Pancras, the organ is above the level of the choir, but out of a line with it, and also produces a good effect.

Recent arrangements in cathedrals. 1051. Much pains have been taken within the last few years to find a better place, architecturally speaking, for our cathedral and minster organs.

1052. At the time the alterations in the interior of Westminster Abbey were in contemplation a very excellent article appeared in the *Parish Choir*, No. 20, for August, 1847, from the pen of the Rev. Sir William Cope, in which it was proposed to erect the organ at the west end of that church, and at the same time to strengthen its tone as much as possible. The solid stone Choir screen was proposed to be placed at the west end, so as to extend across between the first pair of pillars of the nave, with its architectural face to the east. The entire expanse of the minster, from west to east, from the ground to the roof, would then have been seen at one view. "Let our readers," says the article alluded to, "now consider how splendid the whole expanse of the church thus laid open would be. Looking to the east end, the eye would rise from the altar to the screen, and be led up by the beautiful apse to the vaulting of the roof ; and, if the spectator turned toward the west, he would see the stone screen surmounted by the organ; above that would appear the whole extent of the perpendicular window, with its coloured glass running up into the vaulting of the roof. And if, besides these architectural beauties, the eye of the Christian spectator were to rest on the vast multitude who (we are sure) would throng the expanse, and to see a reverent and attentive congregation joining, as they would then be able to do, with one mind and one heart and, we trust, with one voice with the clergy and choir of that glorious church, in those majestic hymns which form the Choral Service of the English Church, would it not be a sight to which English Churchmen might point with an honest exultation?" This proposition possessed the unusual recommendation of treating the question musically as well as architecturally; and, besides this, of providing for the orderly arrangement of a vast congregation. As the arrangements were subsequently carried out, the choir screen was retained in its former position; the organ was divided into four portions, the Great organ being placed within an arch on the north side of the church, the Swell under the corresponding arch on the south side; the 32-feet Pedal pipes were laid horizontally along the west side of the screen, while the Choir organ hung over the east side in the usual way. The tone of the organ, on the whole, tells exceedingly well, although the instrument is so much broken up, which, no doubt, arises partly from the two main portions not being put too much under the side arches, but partly projecting out from under them; and, again, from the organ having been *considerably enlarged* at the same time.

1053. At Ely Cathedral the organ, as reconstructed by Mr. Hill, under the direction of the able architect, Sir Gilbert Scott, is a *hanging* one, the appearance of which is most gorgeous. It projects from the *side* of the choir, overhanging the stalls. The keys are placed behind—that is to say, on the aisle side—so that some portion of the organ is directly between the organist and the singers. The organ thus arranged is pleasant to sing to, and the organist can hear the *Choir* organ quite distinctly. The vocal choir, also, he can hear pretty well; but the tone of the Great organ does not reach him so readily.

1054. At Canterbury Cathedral the organ is placed in the triforium over the south side of the Choir, at a great altitude, and the keys are placed behind the stalls. The touch being both heavy and deep, it is a most laborious organ to play upon; and on account of the length of the action between the keys and the pallets, and the manner in which the tone has to find its way down into the Choir, a perceptible interval occurs between the keys being struck and the sound being heard.

1055. In making praiseworthy endeavours to find a less prominent locality for our cathedral organs, every facility should be provided for the organist hearing and seeing the choir, and *vice versâ*. For this purpose it would be an admirable plan to make the organ play *at the side*. This arrangement has so many recommendations, and not one drawback, that it is surprising it should not long since have been generally adopted. The organist, by a mere turn of the head, would then have at least half the choir under his view, and could, by a gesture imperceptible to the congregation, convey a suggestion down to its members. Moreover, the organist would in all cases hear the voices much better. In the instance of an organ on the Choir screen, if the keys were placed in the manner here suggested, the organist could probably see *both* sides of the Choir, instead of *neither*, as at present, and at the same time he could also see to both ends of the cathedral. Another important end would be gained by placing the keys of a cathedral organ in the manner under consideration. The space of the organ-loft could be taken into the Great organ case, by moving the east front forward to the back of the Choir organ, and inserting new panels to fill up the openings in the sides, which would admit of a material improvement in the organ, by admitting of the introduction of many large pipes, on the tone of which the true dignity of the organ so much depends. The arrangement above recommended may be met with in Snetzler's organ at Beverley Minster, which instrument, standing on the Choir screen, has the keys on the north side. It has also been recently adopted by Sir Gilbert Scott in the restoration of the organ in Rochester Cathedral.

CHAPTER XXXIV.

THE SIZE OF THE ORGAN.

The organ should be proportioned to the congregation and church.   1056. THE size or contents of the organ should, as a rule, be regulated by the number of the congregation whose united voices the instrument will have to sustain, and by the dimensions of the church in which it is to be placed. This is assuming that usefulness of instrumental support, as an aid to the voice in devotional exercises, is admitted; which point, however, is not conceded by some religious denominations. The question before us, however, is not whether an organ is admissible for the purpose above specified, but—that opinion being supposed to be acquiesced in—what should be the properties and attributes of the instrument to render it adequate to its purpose. The size of the organ would also be influenced by the kind of stops chosen, whether they are chiefly of loud or soft intonation; Dulcianas, Flutes, and Piccolos usually having little to do with the power of an organ, although they increase the number of its stops, and materially add to the number and variety of its soft and agreeable combinations.

Certain influencing circumstances to be taken into account.   1057. The acoustical capacity of the church, again, must be taken into account; some churches being as good for sound as others are bad, as is well known to most clergymen, who find little difficulty in filling some, while they have great trouble in making themselves heard in others. If there be much echo—a circumstance that may soon be ascertained by sounding the voice in various parts of the church—such a natural advantage will be much in favour of the organ; but if the sound do not get away, but immediately fall dead, then more stops should be disposed, to enable the organ-tone to make its way; or a greater proportion of loud stops might be introduced; or the whole should be more strongly voiced and blown. Some such steps would also have to be taken if the organ is to be placed where its tone is likely to be weakened; as, for instance, in a recess.

An approximate calculation of the number of stops necessary for an organ to have.   1058. From what has just been said, it is obvious that the number of stops necessary for an organ to have cannot be deduced with absolute certainty from the number of the congregation, although an approximation to it may be drawn from that source. According to Seidel, for a congregation of from 200 to 300 persons, an organ with from 8 to 10 stops may suffice; for one of from 400 to 500, an organ of from 12 to 16 stops; and for a congregation of from 1,000 to 2,000, an organ of from 24 to 30 stops. In this calculation allowance is not made for half-stops; still less are the couplers and other mechanical contrivances taken into account. Half-stops are of comparatively rare occurrence in German organs, although short stops are common enough, particularly among the flute-work. When a stop only extends to tenor c, it is usually grooved into the bass octave of some other stop below, instead of that other stop being cut to draw in halves, as is the more frequent custom in England. Neither are couplers included in the calculation, since they have no "voice"* at all. With these exceptions, and making some allowance for the addition to the number of a few soft stops that are in great favour in this country, the above calculation is a very good one.

Too small an organ in a church most undesirable. 1059. As it is quite as great an evil to design too small an organ for a large church as it is to plan too large a one for a small church, it may be well to explain why an instrument of fair proportions may with confidence be admitted into a place of worship. The primary purpose for which an organ is introduced into a church is to support and direct the voices of the congregation. It therefore becomes necessary to ascertain, if possible, what may be the strength of that congregational voice which the organ is expected to sustain.

The strength of the human voice as compared with that of the organ wind. 1060. To this a clue may be obtained by a very simple experiment. If an anemometer be provided with a flexible tube, furnished at the end with a large mouthpiece, and the breath be freely expired into it, the index prepared at the side will show that the human lungs produce, without any very great exertion, a current of air of 9 or 10 inches pressure, the Manual departments of a church organ being ordinarily voiced to a wind of from $2\frac{1}{2}$ to 3 inches pressure. This result, perhaps scarcely expected by many, makes it apparent that the human voice, when firmly delivered, is sounded by a wind 3 or 4 times the strength of that which ordinarily gives speech to a church organ. Then the sound-waves which surround every singer—as they encircle an organ pipe that is speaking—are proportioned in strength to the power of the voice that originates them ; and at the same time they to some extent prevent his hearing other external sounds distinctly.

The general requisites of a church organ. 1061. Now a church organ should possess sufficient fulness, depth, and *travelling* character of tone, to make its way through all other sounds to the ear of the congregation, and support, keep in tune, and lead the united voices of its members. Whether much or little organ will suffice for this is a question that much depends not only on the number of the congregation, and the dimensions of the church to which its size and power should in the first place be adapted, but also on whether the entire congregation takes part in the singing, or only a portion, and whether the many or few who tune their voices do so boldly or timidly. In those large churches abroad, wherein great numbers assemble, and among whom the singing is both general and zealous ; where, in fact, may be heard the finest congregational music—namely, in some of the Protestant churches of Germany and Holland—there will also be heard the largest organs in the world. The "music mill" has long been considered the necessary concomitant of the "vocal thunder ;" and the two have been exercised conjointly, from week to week, for centuries ;—the one in uttering, in unison, the melody ; the other, in playing, in fine progressive harmony, the simple and magnificent chorales of the former country, without the one injuring the effect of, or obscuring, the

---

* In German Specifications the stops are generally called *Klangbare Stimmen* (sounding voices), and the couplers and other mechanical contrivances, *Nebenregistern* (accessory or secondary registers).

other in the slightest degree.* And it is now tolerably clear why no ill effect should have resulted from this union of instrumental with vocal sound. It would not be easy for an organ voiced to a 2½ or 3 inch wind to interfere with an assemblage of 800 or 1,000 voices, singing with a strength equal to a 9 or 10 inch pressure of organ wind, if its tone be rich and full, and its stops well balanced.

An organ of sufficient dimensions in a church a great acquisition.

1062. A fine organ, then, may fairly be considered as a great acquisition for a church to possess ; provided, of course, that its powers only be fully exercised on rare and befitting opportunities. Dr. Spark, in his pamphlet on *Choirs and Organs*, page 11, gives a good instance when the full peal of an organ may be beneficially employed. "Who," he writes, "can have heard a crowded congregation in a large church sing with heart and voice that glorious, time-honoured tune, the Old Hundredth Psalm, accompanied with the full power of a great and beautiful organ, and not acknowledge the powerful aid and thrilling effect which a grand organ gives to some portions, at least, of our Church Service ? " At such times the propriety of a cheerful accompaniment is at once recognised by the members of the congregation ; they raise their voices, energetically and earnestly, under the combined influence of the service, the occasion, and the appropriate tone-character of the organ—the trebles, singing in unison with the melody, and the tenors and basses below, add immense strength, in the *Unison and Double Diapason pitch*, to the mass of musical sound, the result being that the choral song stands out distinctly in bold and grand relief through the dignified and impressive peal of the full organ.

1063. Thus much has been said to illustrate what an organ should be *capable* of when the upraised voice of the congregation may put its powers to the test. Of course, there are times and seasons when the hymn of praise and thanksgiving would be hushed, and the song of sadness raised in its stead, and on which occasions the organ tone would, of course, be reduced to accommodate it to the altered sentiments of the words. The strength of the congregational voice itself would also, at such times, be much subdued. With regard to the organ, however, this forms an entirely separate question ; and presents no subject for consideration, while the power requisite for the instrument to possess is being discussed, but rather bears on an important matter connected with its after-use. On this latter head much has been said in a former chapter ; it need, therefore, only be added in this place that when a subdued tone is desired—produced, of course, by using a portion only of the organ—those stops should be selected that will give the requisite "tone-colouring" to the words, *in addition to* affording the exact amount of support required. On this point a very correct idea will be obtained of the manner in which an organ should be used, by a reference to the vocal and instrumental scores of Mozart, Spohr, Mendelssohn, &c. ; from which it will be seen that, however extensive the orchestra at disposal, their authors have not yielded to the temptation of using a single additional instrument beyond what was necessary for the particular purpose ; but have first confined themselves within the proposed limits, then

---

* It should be mentioned that, while unison singing is at once the most simple in kind, the most easy of execution, and the most appropriate for a congregation to adopt, it is at the same time the most powerful in effect, from its concentrating all the vocal force into one part ; and is, therefore, the kind of congregational singing that requires the most organ for its support.

proceeded to select such instruments for use as would sympathise the most closely with the words to be sung, and yet at the same time produce so *transparent* an effect that the voice could be heard clearly and definedly through the whole. These are precisely the several processes that should be gone through to secure the best, because the most appropriate, kind of subdued organ tone for accompaniment ; that is, if the organ admit of a choice.

The power of an organ partly due to its extent of tone. 1064. It was stated just now that, while an organ is commonly voiced to a 2½ or 3 inch wind, the human voice is frequently produced by a current of air equal to a 9 or 10 inch wind. This fact would seem to imply that the tone of an organ must be much weaker than that of voices ; and, although the above figures may or may not represent the *exact* comparative strength of the two, yet there is no doubt of the fact that *Unison* stops alone in an organ would be quite unequal to the support of a large body of strong voices. Organs, therefore, are never made with this one class of stops alone, because they then could not possess the requisite nerve, ring, and power. The "power" of an organ is, in a great measure, due to its greater *extent* of tone, as compared with that of voices, *pitch* exercising a marked influence on its loudness. Everyone is aware that in a quartet sung by the four varieties of male voices the treble part always sounds the most prominent, *not* because the boy's voice is the most powerful, for it may be the weakest, but because it is the *highest*. So great is the influence which acuteness of pitch exercises that the general ear, and consequently voice, will follow the upper part of a four-part harmony, whether it should do so or not. Of this a remarkable instance is given on all occasions when Tallis's Responses are sung in cathedrals, *i.e.*, on church festival days. The chief melody, or "Plain-song," is set in the tenor, for which reason it remains unrecognised by the congregation generally, who never follow it, but, on the contrary, take the treble or acute part, which in reality is only a portion of the choral accompaniment.

1065. Now, for the same reason that the adult male members of a congregation hear the trebles so much more clearly than the choir voices that are in unison with their own, the trebles hear those of an organ stop that sounds the octave above their voices much more distinctly than those that are in unison therewith. This fact must be familiar to all who have had much experience in accompanying a choir, and who will have noticed this illustration of it, that, if the treble voices get flat, they will be set right much sooner by drawing the Principal, or by playing the melody in octaves, which will produce the same kind of effect, than by adding a number of other Unison stops. The addition of one Principal to the Great Diapasons will at such times be heard more distinctly by the trebles, and will exercise a far greater corrective influence than the addition of three or four Unison stops from the Swell, by means of coupling, even if there be one or two reeds included among the number. This, however, does not arise from any greater *power* possessed by the Principal (for in that respect it is rather inferior to the other accessory mentioned), but from its *acuteness*. The influence of high-toned stops extends still further. For the same reason that the Principal adds clearness to the Diapasons, the Fifteenth and Twelfth impart a cheerful ring to the tone, while the Mixtures add brilliance and vivacity, perhaps keenness, if they be voiced too loud, as is too frequently the case. So much for the stops sounding *above* the Unison. But the remaining stops also fulfil certain important conditions. The Unison and Double stops impart a fulness to the tone that is appreciably felt by a choir and congregation, and conduces, in conjunction with the

Pedal bass, to convey that sensation of *nearness* of accompaniment to the singer that is of such essential consequence in infusing confidence and affording encouragement to those who need support. The Pedal bass, in its turn, marks the progress of the music, and that much more effectually than any of the other stops could do. Summing up, then, in a few words, the influence which the three classes of stops exercise : the Octave and other acute stops tend to keep the voices in tune ; the Unison and Double Manual stops afford them support ; while the Pedal Diapasons, by marking the time in the course of the onward movement of the music, keep them together.

How the acoustic capacity of a Manual organ is increased to adapt its tone to a large building.

1066. What has hitherto been said has had more especial reference to the requirements of an organ as an accompanimental instrument. But it is necessary also to consider by what process of development an organ, as an independent instrument, is made to fill, with its musical tones, a building, however large its dimensions ; particularly as this point has not the less bearing on the question concerning its efficiency and excellence in the capacity already considered. The presence of a Double Diapason has already been mentioned as being necessary in an organ to support the tenor and bass voices in a congregation, as the Unison do the trebles. But a stop or stops of that size are required to fulfil another end, totally distinct, but of not inferior consequence. If a chord be played in the treble part of the Great organ of an instrument placed in a large building, and not having any stops lower in pitch than the Unison, there will be perceived a certain *smallness* of effect, which makes it evident that, although the treble may possess sufficient brightness and intensity, perhaps even amounting to shrillness, yet it lacks the amount of fulness and volume necessary to produce an ample and dignified tone. This arises from the fact of even the Unison pipes in the treble being comparatively acute in their sound, and, therefore, in the very nature of things, unpossessed of stately impressiveness. It thus becomes obvious that the harmonic corroborating series of stops alone do not present *all* the resources necessary to form a satisfactory organ. Something that is essential appears to be wanting, and a fresh element is felt to be necessary to supply that absent property.

The acoustical grounds on which Double stops are introduced into an organ.

1067. The property wanting is *gravity*, which possesses a character peculiar to itself, and for the absence of which no amount of *intensity* in the other sounds will compensate. Of the travelling and filling-up character of grave sounds we have already spoken, and of the fact itself a sufficient illustration is given in the circumstance of a chant sung by twenty tenor and bass voices in unison pervading a building more completely than if sung by thrice the number of trebles. Again, the deep tone of a Pedal Diapason will travel through a building more entirely than a double chord of six or seven notes played on the Manual Diapasons, from middle c^1 upwards. Its sound will certainly not be nearly so well defined, but it will be of a more pervading character. The want felt, and above specified, however, is not a *substitute* for the harmonic sounds, but a new element, which, *added* to them, shall render the general tone larger and more ample. It is worth mentioning that this want was so much felt abroad nearly three centuries and a half ago, that means were, even at that period, taken to supply the deficiency. It was about the year 1508 that a covered stop of 16-feet size of tone was invented in Holland ;

and which, to some extent, imparted the necessary, deep, resonant, *humming* effect to the other stops, and was hence expressly called *Bourdon;* a name that means a hum or drone ; and which stop has never ceased to be highly valued abroad to this day.

1068. The strength of this under-sound has to be regulated by the size of the organ and the dimensions of the building in which it is to stand. For a small church organ a *Lieblich* Bourdon is sufficient ; for one of ordinary size a full scaled Bourdon (Double Stopped Diapason) will be ample ; for a larger instrument a Double Open Diapason is also required, perhaps accompanied by Double Mutation stops ; for a still larger one a 16-feet Double Trumpet is necessary ; and for organs of first-class magnitude a small Sub-Bourdon, in addition, of 32-feet tone, as far as the fiddle g or tenor c key, sounding GG or CCC. In the bass octave the 32-feet sound can be produced *acoustically* by means of a Bourdon and Quint of 10⅔-feet tone. When a Manual organ is thus developed, the tone of its Treble is so ample, that it may be used by itself without any insignificance of effect in the largest buildings.

The effect of a large organ not constructed on acoustic principles as well as on harmonic.   1069. It has been thought necessary to enter thus fully into this subject, because there are many who hold that all double stops are inadmissible, from the circumstance of their not being included in the harmonic suggestions of nature. This opinion, however, does not imply a complete view of the question. The rearing of a large organ is not governed simply by the laws of *harmonics*, but also by the laws of *acoustics*. The former have already been sufficiently considered in the previous chapter ; and it only remains here to point out what an organ becomes, when the claims of the latter are overlooked. The greater the number of stops introduced into the Great organ, and the greater the quantity of chorus-work, the more is the tone of the Treble *drawn upwards*. The greater the number of ponderous stops put on the Pedal, the more the bass is *drawn downwards*. As the size of the instrument is increased, so is this effect of the *severance* of the two parts in proportion ; which accounts for the fact of the largest organs, built *not* on acoustic principles *as well* as on harmonic, being the greatest failures. The two parts contain no one property or characteristic that is common to both. Instead of the Manual tone being extended downwards to meet the Pedal, by means of Doubles, &c., and the Pedal being extended upwards to meet the Manuals, by means of small stops, &c., the 8-feet and smaller tones of the former, and the 32-feet tone of the latter, draw the two asunder. The sharpness and acuteness of the one, and the depth and fulness of the other, instead of producing the effect of harmonious amalgamation, convey an impression of the two parts being engaged in an altercation. It then becomes necessary for the left hand of the organist to be employed in holding down nearly every concordant note within reach, and as low down on the Manual as possible to disguise the deficiency.

1070. It is not consistent with the real dignity of the instrument that its good or bad effect should depend on the player's power of hiding a defect. All the properties and attributes for producing the best and a perfect effect should be embodied in *the organ itself;* but this will not be the case unless what is acoustically necessary is provided, as well as what is harmonically so. Besides, a certain combination of concordant sounds, as a note and its fifth, will generate *sub*-harmonics or undertones—in this case, the octave below ; and this phenomenon, without doubt, first suggested the introduction of "Doubles." Deep tones were felt to be a necessity ; and the laws of acoustics suggested what those sounds should be.

CHAPTER XXXV.

VARIOUS MATTERS CONNECTED WITH THE DIVISION OF STOPS, AND THEIR SELECTION ACCORDING TO SIZE.

The proportionate division of a given number of stops among the several departments. 1071. IN distributing a given number of stops among the several departments of an organ, care has to be taken not to devote too great a proportion of that number to one department, and so few to another that the latter will be insignificant beside its compeer; but the endeavour should be made to develop all the departments that are proposed to be introduced gradually and proportionably.

1072. The Great organ, as being the most important department, and the one required to have the fullest tone, should have the greatest number of stops. The second Manual (Swell) need not have quite so many, although the difference ought not by right to be great. The third Manual, if there be one (Choir), would have somewhat fewer again. For the Pedal the *minimum* proportion should be one third as many stops as there are on the Great Manual. When even this proportion cannot be secured, there should always be an Octave Pedal Coupler, which is a stop of great use. Below the ratio just given the German and French organ-builders never descend, except for instruments of the most unpretending description. The *maximum* number for the Pedal is as many stops as on the Great Manual. The German proportion often exceeds this.

1073. According to the size of the proposed organ, the stops would thus be assorted into from 2 to 4 or 5 separate divisions. In so appropriating them two extremes have to be avoided; namely, of reducing a moderate number of stops into too many divisions, and of confining a large number of stops to too few claviers. By the former course, in consequence of the stops of every clavier having to commence with the unison, several and minute varieties of the same stops must necessarily be introduced, which might, under the circumstances, be very well dispensed with; while the effect of the whole is small as compared with what it might be. On the other hand, if a great number of stops be assorted into too few divisions, the stops that produce the more delicate gradations or shades of tone, if introduced, cannot then be used with the same facility, advantage, or convenience. A greater number of Manuals will always possess advantages over a smaller, provided the organ tone be not dispossessed of its proper dignity to secure them.

1074. As a rule, possessing sufficient accuracy to answer all general purposes, it may be laid down that an organ with 6 to 12 stops might have 1 or 2 Manuals; one having from 12 to 30 stops, 2 or 3 Manuals; and one with from 24 to 60 stops, 3 or 4 Manuals. In each case there should be separate stops for the Pedal, as far as possible.

1075. It may in some cases happen that there are large funds at disposal. If, under such circumstances, it be thought desirable to add to the comparative completeness and efficiency of the organ, without increasing its strength of tone, or throwing it out of proportion with the church, this could be done either by adding a second Manual organ (Swell); or, if that be already designed, a third

Manual organ (Choir); or it might be effected by proposing extra stops of a delicate character of tone.

1076. The next point to be observed is the size of the stop *The size of stop that should form the basis of the Manual and Pedal tone.* that forms the unison or basis of the Manual and Pedal tone. For all the Manuals this would be the same—namely, 8 feet—but for the Pedal, 16 feet. The stops first to be selected for the former must therefore be of 8 feet, or 8 feet size of tone; and for the latter, 16 feet, or 16 feet size of tone.

1077. At the same time it would be incorrect, for reasons *Stops of one size only for Manual or Pedal incorrect.* already assigned, to place only 8-feet stops on the Manual, and only 16 feet on the Pedal. The effect of such a selection of stops, at first serious and solemn, would gradually become dull and monotonous, and then oppressive and dispiriting. Other and smaller stops are required to give life and energy to the organ tone, and to serve the numerous other purposes mentioned in former chapters.

1078. A table of the smaller stops just referred to was given *The proper size for the stops, and the order in which they should be selected.* on a previous page. All these, of course, cannot be placed in *every* Manual organ in the first instance. They are not indeed required; for the individuality of character in the tone of the several Manual departments depends as much on the size and proportion, as on the choice and scale of the stops with which they are each furnished.

1079. Where, however, fulness and power are required, as is always the case with regard to the Great organ, the series of smaller harmonic or corroborating stops should be introduced in a complete form as soon as possible, or the above-named essential requisites will not be secured to the full extent. The Principal, 4 feet, is the first stop of the series to be introduced, after the Unison stop itself. Next to that, the Fifteenth. It is a rule never to propose a Third or Fifth-sounding rank without the Octave-sounding rank the next smallest in size to itself being also introduced to cover its tone. This is why the Twelfth is never disposed before the Fifteenth; although its size is 2⅔ feet, and that of the latter only 2 feet. In like manner the Nineteenth, or Larigot, should always be accompanied by the Twenty-second or Octave Fifteenth, otherwise the Mutation tone may appear remarkable, or even offensive.

1080. As the tone, on the one hand, would tend towards *The stop from which the harmonic corroborating stops must be measured.* thinness if any of the requisite Mutation ranks were to be omitted, so, on the other, it would become thick and vague if Mutation ranks of too great size were to be introduced. It is necessary, therefore, to bear in mind from which stop the harmonic series should be measured, as this will prevent the occurrence of either error. The proper stop to be used for this purpose is the largest one of the Open Diapason species proposed to be placed on the same Manual. If that stop is to be of 8 feet, the harmonic corroborating series would, for the theoretical reasons before explained, be as follows:—

1	8	12	15	17	19	22	26	29
8 feet.	4 feet.	2⅔ feet.	2 feet.	1⅗ foot.	1⅓ foot.	1 foot.	8 inches.	6 inches.

1081. The order of the harmonic corroborating sounds will easily be committed to memory if the series be viewed in this way. All the octave sounds are required. The interval of the first octave from the fundamental tone must not be broken; the second should be broken by a Fifth only; while the third may be broken by a Third* and Fifth. In the above example the filling-up sounds in their correct situations are represented by minim notes.

1082. If a large organ is proposed, having a 16-feet stop, Double Open Diapason, the harmonic corroborating series of that fundamental sound will be of the following sizes and pitch :—

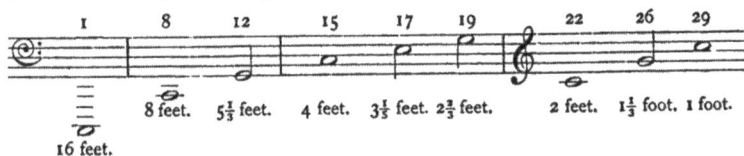

1	8	12	15	17	19	22	26	29
16 feet.	8 feet.	5⅓ feet.	4 feet.	3⅕ feet.	2⅔ feet.	2 feet.	1⅓ foot.	1 foot.

1083. For a small Choir organ, having no larger stop of the Open Diapason species than the Octave or Principal of 4 feet, the following would be the proper sizes for the harmonic series :—

1	8	12	15
4 feet.	2 feet.	1⅓ foot.	1 foot.

1084. As to the naming of the stops of the Manuals, this point is always decided in England by their pitch in relation to the unison tone of those departments, as shown in the following scheme :—

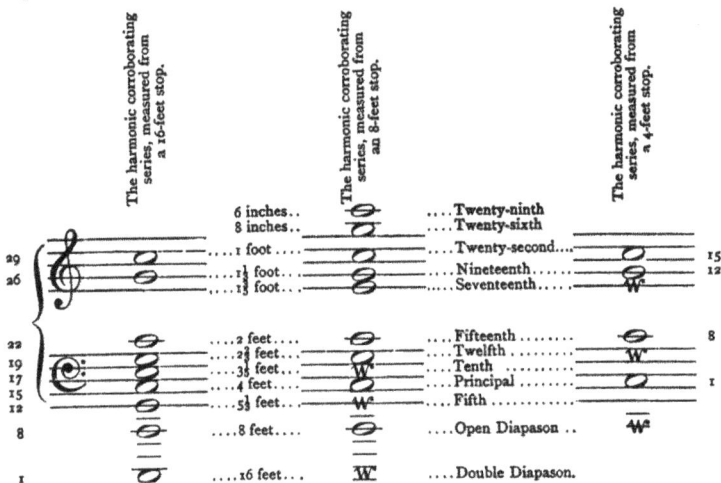

The harmonic corroborating series, measured from a 16-feet stop.		The harmonic corroborating series, measured from an 8-feet stop.		The harmonic corroborating series, measured from a 4-feet stop.	
	6 inches..		....Twenty-ninth		
	8 inches..		....Twenty-sixth		
29	....1 foot....		....Twenty-second....		15
26	....1⅓ foot...		....Nineteenth....		12
	....1⅗ foot...		.....Seventeenth.....		
22	....2 feet....		....Fifteenth........		8
19	....2⅔ feet...		...Twelfth.........		
17	....3⅕ feet..		...Tenth..........		
15	....4 feet...		....Principal.......		1
12	....5⅓ feet..		....Fifth...........		
8	....8 feet....		....Open Diapason ..		
1	....16 feet...		....Double Diapason.		

* In Germany the Tierce is not commonly introduced into new organs of moderate dimensions, on account of its not harmonising so well with the slightly sharpened thirds of the equal temperament. The flat Twenty-first is never included, even in the largest organs of that country.

1085. We perceive, from the middle column of the above scheme, that, when the largest open cylindrical stop of full scale is only of 8 feet, it would be wrong to introduce either a Fifth or Tenth (see directs); because they form no portion of the 8-feet harmonic series, but of the 16. Or, to put the fact in a *practical* instead of a *theoretical* form, the Fifth would break the first octave from the fundamental tone, and the Tenth would introduce a second filling-up sound into the second octave. In *effect*, these would, under such circumstances, obscure the Foundation tone, and render the whole thick and indistinct.

1086. The Twelfth, on the contrary, would be a necessary stop to dispose to an 8-feet ground tone. This, however, in its turn becomes inadmissible, when the largest stop of the Diapason species is only 4 feet in length; as shown in the third column of the above scheme.

The meaning of the German terms, 16-feet Manual, 8-feet Manual, and 4-feet Manual.   1087. As the meaning of the German terms, " 16-feet Manual," " 8-feet Manual," and " 4-feet Manual," are by no means generally understood, an explanation of them may not be uninteresting in this place. They have by some been supposed to signify a CCC Manual, a CC Manual, and a Tenor c Manual respectively; whereas, in reality, they refer to nothing of the kind. The German Manuals never descend below CC, and in modern specimens they seldom fall short of that compass. The terms refer to the size of the greatest stop of the Open Diapason kind on the Manual to which either of the three may be applied. If the stop in question be of Sub-octave pitch, corresponding with the English Double Open Diapason of 16 feet, the Manual on which it stands is said to be a 16-feet Manual. If it be of 8-feet length, the Manual is said to be an 8-feet one. If it be of Octave pitch, it is said to be a 4-feet Manual. The fact of there being a Bourdon of 16-feet tone, and perhaps even a " Gedact-Quint," or a " Rohr-Quint" (Stopped Fifth, 5⅓-feet tone), does not affect the classification. In the same manner, the presence of the Stopped Diapason, and perhaps other Unison stops not of the governing kind, are again not permitted to affect the classification.

Stops of one class alone not sufficient to produce the best organ effect.   1088. Two facts have already been mentioned, that the harmonic corroborating series of stops are usually formed of pipes of the Open Diapason species, and that the presence of that series is essential to the production of a full and satisfactory organ tone. At the same time, those stops do not present *all* that is necessary to produce the best attainable effect. No single class of stops can do this. For instance, Open stops of the Diapason kind, alone, would produce rather a cutting tone; an organ entirely of Covered stops would sound weak and muffled; while one composed entirely of Reeds would be too strong and penetrating. The four great classes of organ stops—Open, Covered, Flute, and Reed—are, in fact, to a great extent dependent on each other for the production of the most satisfactory result. The Covered stops impart a quiet solidity to the Open stops; the Open stops bestow roundness and firmness on the Covered stops; the Flute stops give variety and increased character to the soft combinations; while the Reed stops impart to the full organ stateliness and splendour, and in return receive fulness and brightness from the Open series of stops.

The proportion to be observed in the number of stops of different sizes.   1089. In selecting stops from the Covered, Flute, or Reed species, for addition to those of the Diapason kind, certain proportions should be observed in regard to the number of each size proposed to be introduced, or the proper balance of the general organ tone will not be preserved. The foundation tone should in all cases predominate over the mutation sounds ; and, in like manner, the unison sound should predominate over all the octave sounds. The former point is attained by *doubling* the number of 8, 4, and 2-feet ranks or stops ; and the latter by introducing more 8-feet stops than of 4-feet, and a greater number of 4-feet stops than of 2-feet. For the regulation of these matters, certain general rules are laid down in Germany, which are embodied in what follows.

1090. A Great Organ Manual should ordinarily have, besides the Open Diapason, from one to three or four other 8-feet stops, according to the size of the instrument. In addition to these there should be a good proportionate number of 4-feet stops. Those latter should be, at the least, half as numerous as the 8-feet ; and, if of those of 8-feet there should be an odd number, the balance should be given in favour of the 4-feet stops.

> Thus—(1) to two 8-feet stops, there should be
> > one 4-feet stop ;
> (2) to three or four 8-feet stops, there should be
> > two 4-feet stops, and
> > one 2-feet stop ;
> (3) to four or five 8-feet stops, there should be
> > three 4-feet stops, and
> > two 2-feet stops.

1091. The stops should, in fact, in regard to their proportion and size, be arranged after the manner of a pyramid ; lessening gradually as they rise.

> Thus, for a small Great organ they should stand thus :—
> > to three 8-feet stops,
> > two 4-feet stops,
> > one 2⅔-feet stop, and
> > one 2-feet stop.

The Twelfth would be required, to give that kind of " chorus " effect which is so desirable a characteristic for even the most limited Manuals of the kind to possess.

1092. A Great Manual that is to have 9 or 10 stops should include a Twelfth, a Compound stop, and a Bourdon. This would make the second of the three tables just given take the following form :—

> One 16-feet sounding stop,
> three or four 8-feet stops,
> two 4-feet stops,
> one 2⅔-feet stop,
> one 2-feet stop,
> one Mixture of III., IV., or V. ranks—9 or 10 stops.

1093. If the Great Manual is to have 16 stops, it should include two 16-feet stops and a Quint of 5⅓ feet. These would give to the third table the following form :—

> Two 16-feet stops,
> five 8-feet stops,
> one 5⅓-feet stop,
> three 4-feet stops,
> one 2⅔-feet stop,
> two 2-feet stops,
> two Mixtures, comprising VIII. ranks—16 stops.

1094. It will be understood, from a glance at the foregoing tables, that it must be improper to propose two Twelfths with but one Fifteenth to cover them. If they were to speak out properly, the fifth sound would certainly be stronger than the octave, and the predominance of the foundation tone would be to some extent obscured. There would then appear a certain thickness and nasal quality in the tone. It would be equally wrong to propose a greater number of 4-feet stops than of 8-feet, or a greater number of 2-feet than of 4-feet. Either of these latter mis-calculations would have the effect of drawing the tone up from the unison pitch, whereby the requisite fulness and gravity would be lost, and an undue brightness and thinness substituted. It is equally bad to dispose a full-toned and powerful 4-feet stop with only a delicate 8-feet stop to support it ; yet this is frequently done in modern Choir organs.

1095. The foregoing schemes and observations have more immediate reference to the properties requisite for the Great organ to possess. They, however, apply equally to all the Manuals, and indeed to the Pedal also ; but the Swell and Choir organs are seldom furnished with as many stops as the Great ; and, moreover, are not developed in the same manner. For instance, the harmonic series of stops are among the first to be proposed for the Great organ ; their importance is shared by the Reeds in the Swell ; while, in the Choir organ, they are the very last that find admission.

1096. The Swell may be considered as an Echo to the Great organ in one sense, and as a Solo organ in another ; and the stops that are selected for it in these two capacities render it a most valuable division of an organ for accompanimental purposes.

1097. To serve as an Echo to the Great organ, the Swell should have, besides two Unison Flue stops, the harmonic-corroborating series of ranks complete, as far as practicable ; and it should be the first, after the Great organ, to have a Bourdon. As a Solo organ, it requires at least one soft Unison Reed, even sooner than the Great organ. The proportion in the number of Unison and Octave stops, even in a small Swell, will, therefore, almost of necessity stand in the following ratio, namely :—

to three 8-feet stops,
one 4-feet stop.

For a larger Swell there should be two Unison Reeds and a second 4-feet stop, which might be a Clarion. The proportion could then be as follows :—

to four 8-feet stops,
two 4-feet stops.

It is quite wrong, as to effect, convenience, and completeness, to propose a Bourdon for the Swell before a Compound stop. One of the reasons why Reeds are so soon and so freely introduced into a Swell is that, on account of the stops being enclosed in a box, the tone must be of a more penetrating quality to make itself heard ; and a strong and a weak Unison Reed are therefore proposed. It is also for the above reason that the second 4-feet stop proposed for the Swell is almost always a Clarion in preference to a Flute.

1098. The Choir organ should be of a *lighter* tone than either the Swell or the Great organ. By this it is not meant that it should be so very much *softer*. Choir organs have sometimes been voiced with the delicacy of a chamber organ ; and have, therefore, for church purposes, been of little use. Excellent examples of what the comparative strength of the like stops in the Great and Choir organs should be will be found in some of the best old instruments which still remain :

not, indeed, that the Choirs of those organs present good models for literal reproduction ; for they are, or were, in their original form, very much out of proportion. It was a constant practice with the old builders to propose a Stopped Diapason only to stand against two 4-feet stops and one 2-feet stop. Instead of the unison tone being properly maintained by such a specification, it was completely overbalanced by the higher sounds, and a quality of tone was produced that was characterised by excessive thinness, in spite of its sprightliness. Probably this misproportion in the old Choir organs arose from the same cause which operated against the proper balancing of the old Great organs—namely, lack of room, want of funds, or both. In later examples of Choir organs a Dulciana was generally introduced ; but so weak a unison, even as an addition, was insufficient to reduce the strong-toned Principal and Fifteenth into proportion ; hence the custom was introduced of voicing the last-mentioned stops much more quietly than before ; and this twofold modification, while it certainly had the effect of producing a more equally balanced Choir organ, at the same time brought in the chamber quality, as already mentioned. The attributes for a Choir organ are lightness and variety, rather than fulness and power ; hence a given number of stops, that would in the case of the Great organ require a Twelfth and a Compound stop, neither call for the one nor the other when appropriated to the Choir organ. A good number of 8 and 4-feet stops, comprising delicate accompanimental and Solo stops, are among the first that should be selected for this department.

1099. The Pedal organ should contain a "Bass" to as many of the leading Manual stops as circumstances will allow. A good complement of 16 and 8 feet stops should first be disposed for this department, particularly as all smaller stops can be conveniently borrowed by coupling the Manual to the Pedal. The 16-feet Unison stops are the most indispensable, because their tone forms the true basis of the Pedal tone. Of scarcely less importance are the 8-feet, or Octave, stops. When there is a choice of stops of this latter size, the Pedal can then, in soft playing, be freely used without there existing any necessity for coupling either of the Manuals thereto to produce a good effect. The left hand, moreover, will not then be constantly deceived by descending on a key that is already down, or the melodic progression of a tenor part be broken from the same cause. If these stops cannot be introduced, or not in sufficient proportion, an "octave coupler" to the Pedal stops should be introduced.

1100. With regard to the proportion between the 16 and 8 feet stops on the Pedal, this should, if practicable, be the same as in the Great organ. When there are 5 or 6 Pedal stops, these should include a Quint of $10\frac{2}{3}$-feet tone ; and when there are 10 Pedal stops, a double open Bass of 32-feet might be included.

CHAPTER XXXVI.

THE COMPOSITION OF THE MIXTURES.

1101. WE have now arrived at the consideration of the composition of the Mixtures; that is, of the Compound stops generally, under whatever name they may appear—as Sesquialtera, Mixture, Furniture, Cornet, &c. The subject is one of great interest and importance. So great, indeed, is the influence which the class of stops in question exercises, that, after taking the greatest care to preserve the harmonic-corroborating series of stops entire, and to secure the proper proportionate number of stops of the different sizes, it is quite in the power of incorrectly compounded Mixtures to disturb those pre-arrangements, and to qualify the perfect effect of the work. For this reason, it becomes necessary to inquire what may be the several requisites of the class of stops above named.

Why should there be breaks in a Compound stop? 1102. The first question that presents itself is, *Why* should there be any "breaks" in a Compound stop? In the first place, because there is a practical difficulty in the way of continuing the smaller ranks throughout at the original altitude of pitch above the unison, although to do this is not impossible. It is far from easy to make pipes small enough for the purpose; and, when made, are difficult to tune, and are put out of tune again by the slightest change of temperature or by the smallest particle of dust.

A Compound stop without a break, not in accordance with the suggestions of nature. 1103. Moreover, there exists no *necessity* for continuing a Compound stop up without a break. The Mixtures are intended to *corroborate* certain of the higher harmonic sounds. But these sounds are not heard to rise to so great an altitude when the fundamental tone is higher up in the scale as when it is lower down. So long a series of harmonic sounds will not be traced rising above the middle c^1 as from the CC string of a pianoforte. To continue a Compound stop throughout would be to "corroborate" what cannot be heard.

The same Compound not productive of the same effect in different parts of the scale. 1104. Furthermore, there is a very important practical fact, connected with the sound of the small stops of an organ, that should be here mentioned. It is no other than this: that the same combination or compound does *not* produce the same effect in different parts of the scale, but possesses more prominence in the upper than in the lower part. For example, if the Great organ stops, as far as the Fifteenth, be drawn, and this, or any similar passage, be played in the Treble,

a certain completeness of effect will be produced that will be satisfactory to the ear. Repeat the progression in the Bass,

and an equally perfect effect will not be experienced. The Mutation sound (Twelfth) will appear to be stronger than before ; and, besides this, there will be a sensation of dulness as compared with the effect resulting from the previous experiment. If there be a III. rank Sesquialtera, and that stop now be drawn, on repeating the same low notes, the Bass will be found to be brightened up, and the Twelfth tone to be covered. If, however, the treble of the added stop be of *the same* composition as the lower part, and the foregoing passage be repeated in the higher part, the treble will again appear to be in *advance* of the Bass, in regard to comparative brightness. These facts clearly show that there is a close connection between the extent of the audible harmonic series of sounds in nature and the good effect of the harmonic corroborating stops, when of approximate range. It is evident, moreover, from their works, that the old English-builders were aware of this, and that they worked accordingly, so far as circumstances permitted.

Might not a rank " die out," instead of pre- senting a break?   1105. The second question is, Might not a rank, as its continuation becomes unadvisable or impracticable, be al- lowed to "die out?" No. For, in that case, the Treble, from having fewer pipes, would sound weaker than the Bass, and consequently would be overpowered by it. To prevent this, the same number of ranks should be maintained throughout ; and, when it becomes advisable to discontinue a rank at its original altitude of pitch above the fundamental sound, a duplication of some larger rank should be introduced in its stead ; which, by strengthening one of the most important *remaining* tones, will add fresh energy to that tone, and so compensate for the loss of *extent* in the harmonic series.

The valuable aid ren- dered to the Treble of an organ by the return ranks.   1106. These duplications, introduced where the breaks occur, and increasing as the harmonic series decreases, per- form a most important and valuable office when rightly managed. It has already been mentioned more than once in the course of this work that there is always a tendency in organ stops to become weaker and of lighter tone in the Treble than in the Bass. The duplications in question offer one means for almost entirely removing this defect from organs of average dimensions, which they do by presenting a great accession of tone to the ranks that are "repeated." These advantageous duplications, of course, alter the proportions as to the number of stops and ranks of different sizes *in the Treble*, which modification takes place without any detriment, but, on the contrary, improvement, to the general effect. The two chief rules to be observed in regard to the Treble are (1) that, of the Foundation ranks, those of a smaller size shall never *exceed* those of a larger, as more Fifteenths than Principals ; and (2) that those of a Mutation rank must not be greater than those of the Foundation rank next below, as more Twelfths than Principals, or more Nineteenths than Fifteenths, &c. The more nearly the return ranks present a general duplication of the entire Treble, the better. The reinforced Treble then more nearly matches in strength the brighter Bass.

On what keys the breaks had better take place. 1107. The breaks, then, being not only unavoidable, but even *advantageous* when judiciously managed, the next question is, On what keys had they better be made? For these changes no fixed positions were recognised by the old builders, nor have any been uniformly adopted by the modern. They are met with on c, c sharp, f, f sharp, and g, in different organs. In the following plans for Compound stops they occur chiefly on c sharp and g sharp.

Where the broken ranks should return to. 1108. The next point to be considered is, Where should the broken ranks return to? Seidel says, "In the repetition of a Mixture, Fifths and Octaves must be used alternately." This refers to the Compound stops of many modern Continental organs tuned on equal temperament, in which there are no Tierces, and is the best arrangement. Smith sometimes broke his Mixtures by Octaves in the bass, and used Fifths, Thirds, and Octaves successively in the Treble; England and Green more frequently used Fifths as well as Octaves for the breaks in the Bass, and Fifths, Thirds, and Octaves alternately in the Treble. But, in whatever way the breaks be made, the consequent duplication should be introduced with the view of preserving the predominance of the Foundation tone and the subordination of the Mutation.

1109. These precautions were not uniformly taken; hence certain misproportions will sometimes be met with in the old Mixtures of even some of the best builders. For example, in some old organs there will be found in the Tenor octave, to three Unison Flue stops, one Principal and *two* Twelfths, the Fifth-sounding ranks being in consequence more numerous than the Octave-sounding ranks the next below them in pitch; and from middle c¹ upwards to two Principals, three Twelfths and one Fifteenth—the misproportion being thus increased. When the sound of the Mutation ranks is strengthened beyond the necessary degree, it then no longer simply gives roundness to the tone, but imparts a slightly nasal quality to it that has nothing to do with the production of the peculiarly rich and musical effect that so frequently distinguishes the old Mixtures, but, on the contrary, to some extent it deteriorates it.

1110. In one organ the writer examined not very long since there were, in the treble of the Great organ, to

1 Open Diapason—2 Principals—3 Twelfths—4 Fifteenths.

The tone was extremely bright, on account of the Fifteenths being so much more numerous than the Principals and Diapasons; but the fundamental sound was far from being properly maintained. In another there were, to

3 Principals—2 Twelfths—2 Fifteenths—3 Tierces—4 Nineteenths.

In this case, the "Chorus" was anything but brilliant, although there was a great quantity of it, on account of the Tierces and Nineteenths being more numerous than the octave sounds immediately above and below them. On the Mixtures last referred to being subsequently revised, and the Foundation and Mutation ranks brought into better proportion, their power and clearness were considerably increased without a single rank being added to the original number.

Plans for Compound stops.   1111. Some compositions for Mixtures will now be given, in the preparation of which special care has been taken to guard against the appearance of any of the misproportions already alluded to. Advantage has been taken of a personal examination of all the finest English and Continental Mixtures, the best points in which have been freely incorporated, so far as the proposed number of ranks would in each case allow. As, however, two Mixtures of even the same number of ranks will produce a very different effect according to their composition, scale, and strength of voicing, the one giving a sharp and clear tone, the other a full and bold tone, the terms "Full Mixture" and "Sharp Mixture" have been used, after the German manner. The term "Mixture" has also been applied alike to all the Compounds ; for which, however, any other name would, of course, be substituted that might be preferred.

1112. The first kind of Compound stop that is required for a small organ is one that will brighten up the Bass and Tenor, and add fulness, body, and firmness, to the Treble, without, however, imparting sharpness or keenness thereto. The kind of stop that is usually proposed for this purpose is a 3-rank Sesquialtera, consisting of 17—19—22 in the Bass and Tenor octaves ; and 12—15—17 from Middle c¹ upwards. Almost the only fault to be found with this composition is that it places two Twelfths to one Principal in the Treble. This misproportion would be entirely removed by arranging the composition thus :—

I. COMPOSITION FOR A FULL MIXTURE OF III. RANKS.

Key on Manual.	Intervals in relation to the Unison.		The corresponding sounds in Tablature.
CC to middle c	15—19—22	————	c^1—g^1—c^2.
Middle c¹♯ to the top .	8—12—15	————	c^2—g^2—c^3.

1113. This alteration is effected entirely by substituting some other rank for the Tierce, which is not required where equal temperament is adopted. The advantages presented by the *substituted* rank are that the Fifteenth gives increased clearness to the Bass and the Principal fulness to the Treble.

1114. The goodness of a Mixture composition depends, as already explained, on the extent to which the predominance of the Foundation tone and the rules of proportion are preserved, when its ranks are added to the other Flue stops of the same Manual. Let the above composition, then, be tested in this manner. Suppose it to be added to a small organ, such as that proposed as the First Specification immediately preceding the Appendix. The proportion to the size of the stops as there given is as follows :—

3 Unisons—2 Octaves, 1 Twelfth, and 1 Super-octave throughout.

With the above addition, it would stand thus :—

From CC to Middle c¹ . . . . 3 Unisons—2 Octaves—1 Twelfth—2 Super-octaves—19 and 22 ; and

From Middle c¹♯ to the top . . . 3 Unisons—3 Octaves—2 Twelfths—2 Super-octaves.

1115. For a somewhat larger organ, such as Specification No. IV., a IV. rank Mixture would be required. This might be of the following compound :—

II. COMPOSITION FOR A CLEAR MIXTURE OF IV. RANKS.

Key on Manual.	Intervals in relation to the Unison.		The corresponding sounds in Tablature.
CC to Fiddle g . . .	19—22—26—29	———	g^1
Fiddle g♯ to Middle c¹ .	15—19—22—26	———	g♯—d♯—g♮—d♯.
Middle c¹♯ to Treble c² .	12—15—19—22	———	g^2♯—c^2♯—g^3♯—c^4♯.
Treble c²♯ to the top . .	1— 8—12—15	———	c^2♯—c^3♯—g^3♯—c^4♯.

1116. The duplication of the four principal ranks of the organ from Treble c²♯ upwards (an octave and a half) imparts great breadth and dignity to the upper part of the Manual.

1117. If a keener tone should be required, the compound might have the following form :—

III. COMPOSITION FOR A SHARP MIXTURE OF IV. RANKS.

Key on Manual.	Intervals in relation to the Unison.		The corresponding sounds in Tablature.
CC to Middle c¹ . . .	19—22—26—29	———	g^1 —c^2 —g^2 —c^3.
Middle c¹♯ to Treble f² .	12—15—19—22	———	g^2♯—c^3♯—g^3♯—c^4♯.
Treble f²♯ to b² above .	8—12—15—19	———	f^3♯—c^4♯—f^4♯—c^5♯.
c³ in alt to the top . . .	1— 8—12—15	———	c^3 —c^4 —g^4 —c^5.

1118. As compared with the preceding composition, the above presents a *twofold* contrast from Treble c² to b² in alt—nearly a complete octave. In the first half of that octave it has a 19 and 22 in place of the Open Diapason and Principal ranks before proposed ; and in the second half octave, nearly, it has a 19 in lieu of the Open Diapason.

1119. The 29 is continued unbroken through the Bass and Tenor octaves. The upper rank, however, might have been changed at Tenor c♯ ; and at Treble c²♯ the 22nd might have been discontinued, leaving the 19th at top. These modifications would have caused the composition to stand thus :—

IV. COMPOSITION FOR A QUINT MIXTURE OF IV. RANKS.

Key on Manual.	Intervals in relation to the Unison.		The corresponding sounds in Tablature.
CC to Tenor c	19—22—26—29	———	g^1 —c^2 —g^2 —c^3.
Tenor c♯ to Middle c . .	15—19—22—26	———	c^2♯—g^2♯—c^3♯—g^3♯.
Middle c¹♯ to Treble b¹ .	12—15—19—22	———	g^2♯—c^3♯—g^3♯—c^4♯.
Treble c²♯ to b² above .	8—12—15—19	———	c^3♯—g^3♯—c^4♯—g^4♯.
c³ in alt to the top . .	1— 8—12—15	———	c^3 —c^4 —g^4 —c^5.

1120. A break here occurs on every c♯ key throughout the scale ; and the octaves and fifths are discontinued alternately, after the manner proposed by Seidel. The changes are therefore very gradual. In some respects this composition resembles that frequently adopted by England, who was very partial to the 26th as the top rank in the Tenor octave, and sometimes in the Bass octave also. In connection with the discontinuance of the Octave Fifteenth at Treble c²♯, it may be mentioned as a circumstance worthy of observation that the tone of that particular rank has a decided tendency to fall on the ear with great prominence above that note, unless it be very carefully treated and well balanced.

1121. If a very full tone be desired from the Mixture, the following composition would produce that effect :—

V. COMPOSITION FOR A FULL MIXTURE OF IV. RANKS.

Key on Manual.	Intervals in relation to the Unison.		The corresponding sounds i Tablature.
CC to Tenor c	15—19—22—26	———	c^1 —g^1 —c^2 —g^2.
Tenor c♯ to Middle c¹ .	12—15—19—22	———	g^1♯—c^2♯—g^2♯—c^3♯.
Middle c¹♯ to the top . .	1— 8—12—15	———	c^1♯—c^2♯—g^2♯—c^3♯.

1122. At Tenor c♯ this composition is exactly like that adopted by Green in the organ at Rochester Cathedral, excepting the omission of the Tierce ; and the Treble is also the same as that planned by that builder for the same instrument, excepting the same omission and the substitution of the Unison rank in its stead.

1123. Let these several IV. rank Mixtures now be tried in the manner prescribed in an earlier part of this chapter. The Great organ, in Specification No. IV., would have, without the Mixture, Reed, and Double—

3 Unisons—2 Octaves—1 Twelfth—and 1 Super-octave throughout.

With the clear Mixture of IV. ranks, it would have—

From CC to Fiddle g . . . . .   3 Unisons—2 Octaves—1 Twelfth—1 Super-octave—19—22—26—and 29 ;

From Fiddle g♯ to Middle c¹ . .   3 Unisons—2 Octaves—1 Twelfth—2 Super-octaves—19—22—and 26 ;

From Middle c¹♯ to Treble c² . .   3 Unisons—2 Octaves—2 Twelfths—2 Super-octaves—19—and 22 ; and

From Treble c²♯ to the top . . .   4 Unisons—3 Octaves—2 Twelfths — and 2 Super-octaves.

With the Sharp Mixture of IV. ranks, it would have—

From CC to Middle c¹ . . . .   3 Unisons—2 Octaves—1 Twelfth — 1 Super-octave—19—22—26—and 29.

From Middle c¹♯ to Treble f² . .   3 Unisons—2 Octaves—2 Twelfths—2 Super-octaves—19—and 22.

From Treble f²♯ to b² in alt . .   3 Unisons—3 Octaves—2 Twelfths—2 Super-octaves—and 19.

From c³ in alt to the top . . . .   4 Unisons—3 Octaves—2 Twelfths — and 2 Super-octaves.

With the Quint Mixture of IV. ranks, it would have—

From CC to Tenor c . . . . .   3 Unisons—2 Octaves—1 Twelfth — 1 Super-octave—19—22—26—and 29.

From Tenor c♯ to Middle c♯ . .   3 Unisons—2 Octaves—1 Twelfth — 2 Super-octaves—19—22—and 26.

From Middle c¹♯ to Treble c² . .   3 Unisons—2 Octaves—2 Twelfths—2 Super-octaves—19—and 22.

From Treble c²♯ to b² in alt . .   3 Unisons—3 Octaves—2 Twelfths—2 Super-octaves—and 19.

From c³ in alt to the top . . . .   4 Unisons—3 Octaves—2 Twelfths — and 2 Super-octaves.

With the full Mixture of IV. ranks, it would have—

From CC to Tenor c	3 Unisons—2 Octaves—1 Twelfth—2 Super-octaves—19—22—and 26.
From Tenor c$\sharp$ to Middle c^1 . .	3 Unisons—2 Octaves—2 Twelfths—2 Super-octaves—19—and 22.
From Middle c$^1\sharp$ upwards . . .	4 Unisons—3 Octaves—2 Twelfths—and 2 Super-octaves.

1124. We here see that the composition of a Mixture, consisting of a specified number of ranks, may be varied in many different ways, to adapt it to special purposes, or to cause it to suit individual tastes or feelings, and yet without creating any misproportion in any one instance. For a V. rank Sharp Mixture, the following composition would answer well :—

VI. COMPOSITION FOR A SHARP MIXTURE OF V. RANKS.

Key on Manual.	Intervals in relation to the Unison.		The corresponding sounds in Tablature.
CC to Middle b . . .	15—19—22—26—29	——	c^1 —g^1 —c^2 —g^2 —c^3.
Middle c^1 to Treble f$^2\sharp$	8—12—15—19—22	——	c^2 —g^2 —c^3 —g^3 —c^4.
Treble f$^2\sharp$ to b^2 in alt.	1— 8—12—15—19	——	f$^2\sharp$—f $^3\sharp$—c$^4\sharp$—f $^4\sharp$—f $^5\sharp$.
c^3 in alt to the top . .	1— 5— 8—12—15	——	c^3 —g^3 —c^4 —g^4 —c^5.

1125. In the Bass and Tenor octaves the above composition is identical with that used by Harris in the fine organ at Doncaster, lately destroyed, excepting that a 15 is substituted for the octave Tierce. The composition from Middle c$^1\sharp$ to Treble f^2 is also the same, with the exception of the substitution of a 22nd for the Tierce. The Fifth at c^3 in alt, introduced after the manner common in German Mixtures, should be scaled and voiced as a Dulciana, when the Double is a Bourdon. It is a noteworthy fact that scarcely any of the old organs contain a 22nd in the Treble, even when there are as many as six ranks of Mixture. The writer has not met with it in the Treble of any of the organs by Smith, Harris, Snetzler, or England, that have come under his notice ; and he has only met with it in one of Green's—namely, that in St. Katherine's Church, Regent's Park—and there it stops at Treble c^2.

1126. The omission of the 22nd from the Mixture compound in the Treble of old organs, and the occasional appearance of the misproportion in that part of those instruments, seem to have arisen from three causes :—(1) the omission of Doubles, which deprived the Treble of all depth of tone, and so prevented its successfully resisting the upward-directing influence of the octave Fifteenth ; (2) the non-return of any Mixture rank to the Unison tone, which further militated against the effectual balancing of the acute rank in question ; and (3) the comparatively few intervals left to which the broken ranks could return, and which therefore were certain to be thrown out of proportion with the Unison the more they were doubled.

1127. In the organ at Newcastle-on-Tyne, built by Renatus Harris, and also in that at Halifax, by Snetzler, an Open Diapason rank, however, as well as a Principal, is comprised in the Mixture compound in the Treble.

1128. In compounding two separate Mixtures, the same attention should be paid to the preservation of the proportion in the Bass, and the regular duplication of the ranks in the Treble, that has already been bestowed on the single Mixtures.

VII. COMPOSITIONS FOR

	a Full Mixture, III. ranks,		and a Sharp Mixture, III. ranks.
CC to Middle c¹	15—19—22	———	22—26—29.
Middle c¹♯ to Treble c² . . .	8—12—15	———	15—19—22.
Treble c²♯ to f² above . . .	1— 8—15	———	12—19—22.
Treble f²♯ to b² in alt . . .	1— 8—15	———	12—15—19.
c³ in alt to the top	1— 8—15	———	8—12—15.

1129. Although the 19 and 22 cannot be traced among nature's suggestions in the *higher* parts of the musical scale, yet those tones have a good effect in the Treble of an organ, when they are well balanced. Moreover, there are several arrangements which will aid in bringing those acute sounds into due subordination, without the two ranks which produce them being voiced weakly ; as, for instance, the duplication of their octaves below, *i.e.*, of the Twelfth and Fifteenth, which will be found to occur in all the best modern Mixtures, as well as in the old ; the presence of a 4-feet or second Principal rank, which, however, is met with more frequently in old organs than in modern ; and more particularly the insertion of a Sub-octave sounding stop, which is always found in new organs of pretension, and never in old. These, in connection with the usual proportion of stops—as, for instance, those in Specification No. VIII.—would produce so great a body of tone that there would be little chance of the 19 and 22 predominating in the Treble octave. At Treble c²♯, where the 22 begins to produce an effect of remarkable acuteness—a fact, no doubt, observed by Green, as he discontinued that rank on that note—an Open Diapason rank might be introduced, as suggested in the Full Mixture of the preceding composition ; which, in conjunction with the Double, would certainly tame down that otherwise noisily-inclined rank.

VIII. COMPOSITIONS FOR

	a Full Mixture, III. ranks,		and a Sharp Mixture, IV. ranks.
CC to Middle c¹	15—19—22	———	19—22—26—29.
Middle c¹♯ to Treble c²	8—12—15	———	12—15—19—22.
Treble c²♯ to f² above	1— 8—15	———	12—15—19—22.
Treble f²♯ to b² in alt	1— 8—15	———	8—12—15—19.
c³ in alt to the top	1— 8—15	———	1— 8—12—15.

1130. On examining the above compounds, it will be seen that *either* of them could be used separately with the larger stops as far as the Fifteenth, according as a full or a ringing tone might be required, without any lapse appearing in the progression ; while *both* could be united for a third and fuller effect, without any misproportion occurring. This idea is taken from some of the Continental Mixtures. A separate Tierce might be drawn with either of them, and thus the possible usefulness of that rank be doubled without its being repeated, which would certainly have a very disagreeable effect.

IX. COMPOSITIONS FOR

	a Full Mixture, III. and IV. ranks.		and a Sharp Mixture, V. ranks.
CC to Tenor c	15—19—22	———	15—19—22—26—29.
Tenor c♯ to Middle c¹ . .	12—15—19—22	———	15—19—22—26—29.
Middle c¹♯ to Treble f² .	1— 8—12—15	———	8—12—15—19—22.
Treble f²♯ to b² in alt . .	1— 8—12—15	———	1— 8—12—15—19.
c³ in alt to the top . . .	1— 8—12—15	———	1— 5— 8—12—15.

1131. It may be as well, before proceeding further, to explain why one of the most generally received names for a Compound stop, that of Sesquialtera, has not, in the foregoing schemes, been retained.

1132. The Continental Sesquialtera, from which the English stop was originally derived, is a II-rank Mutation stop, composed of a Fifth and a Third-sounding rank, the Fifth being the lowest, and the Third the highest; the two thus sounding a major sixth, as g, e¹ on the CC key.   Hence the name Sesquialtera, from Sexta, a sixth.   The size of the two ranks was usually 2⅔ feet and 1⅗ foot, which therefore corresponded exactly with the English Twelfth and Tierce.   Sesquialteras of this kind will be found in the Great and Positif departments of the Rotterdam organ; also on the Choir manuals of the organs at Amsterdam, the Hague, Freiburg, &c.   When the Sesquialtera consisted of 3 ranks, a Fifteenth was frequently added to the Twelfth and Tierce, making it sound g, c¹, e¹; and it was in this form that the stop was introduced by Smith and others into the *Treble* of their English organs.   Sometimes the Sesquialtera consisted of IV ranks in the Treble, in which case a Principal was usually incorporated, as in Snetzler's excellent organ at St. Mary's, Nottingham.   In the Tenor and Bass octaves the Third was *lower* than the Fifth-sounding rank—thus on the CC key, e¹, g¹, c²—so that the stop was not a Sesquialtera at all, but essentially a Mixture.   Occasionally Harris made a sort of *octave* Sesquialtera, consisting of 19, 22, 24—g¹, c², e²—on the CC key.

1133. Another II-rank Mutation stop used frequently to be admitted into Continental organs, called a Tertian, from Tertia, a third.   This consisted of an *inversion* of the two Sesquialtera ranks; that is to say, the Fifth-sounding rank was the *smallest*, and therefore the *highest* in pitch.   The two ranks thus sounded a third, as e¹, g¹ on the CC key, and therefore agreed precisely with the Tierce and Larigot of English organs.   A Tertian of II ranks occurs on the Great Manual of the Haarlem organ.

1134. It will be seen, however, that the two stops in question were named after the interval which their own two distinctive ranks conjointly produced, without reference to the relation in which they might stand to the fundamental tone of the organ; and in this respect they differed from all the other stops in the organ-builder's vocabulary.   In fact, the Sesquialtera was, in a few cases, simply labelled "Sexta," as on the Great Manual of the organ at Mülhausen, and on the same department of that in the Church of St. Dominico, at Prague. A third stop, of II ranks originally, and mostly composed of a Twelfth and Fifteenth on one slider, used also to be frequently introduced by German organ-builders, under the name of Rausch-quint or Rausch-pfeif.   This combination is still in use.   To the Sesquialtera composition in the Treble many modern organ-builders and organists have taken great exception; some proposing to substitute in its stead a continuation of the 19 and 22 through the next octave and a half; thus forming a sort of III-rank Sharp Mixture, while others suggest the introduction of a Principal in place of the Tierce, after the manner of the III-rank Full Mixture already given.   Both the compositions recommended remove almost every vestige of the original Sesquialtera, even from the only half of the Manual range in which it usually appeared in English organs; and on this account it becomes a subject well worthy of consideration whether the name should continue to be applied to a stop to which it is no longer in the least degree appropriate.   Following the modern German custom, the name was relinquished with the composition in the plans for Mixtures just now proposed; and other names were adopted, which very simply, yet clearly, announce, even to the uninitiated, what are the distinctive properties of each, as "Full

F F

Mixture" and "Sharp Mixture." The only deviations from the Continenta nomenclature consist in the addition of the adjective "full" to the *largest* Mixture, which appeared to be necessary, inasmuch as fulness of tone is by ho means a common attribute of an English Mixture, although it is one of the leading characteristics of a German one in the Treble, and, in the addition of the word "Mixture" to that of "Sharp," to intimate that such a stop *is* a stop of that kind; a fact known sufficiently well abroad to be understood without the announcement being placed on the stop-label, but which probably would not be so at first in this country, supposing that name to be adopted.

1135. One of the chief objects for which the Sesqualtera was originally used abroad was to place a second Twelfth on the Manual of those large instruments, in which the Mixture ranks were sufficiently numerous to require it, to bind their tone more firmly to the large work of the same Manual. In the modern instruments of German builders, from which the stop in question is mostly omitted, the second Twelfth is usually incorporated with the "Full Mixture," as illustrated in the 9th Composition already given. That plan might be followed for new Mixtures; or, if the introduction of a separate and genuine Sesqualtera were desired, this would be well secured by arranging the composition after the following manner :—

X. COMPOSITIONS FOR

	a Sesqualtera, II ranks.	a Full Mixture, III and IV ranks,	and a Sharp Mixture, V ranks.
CC	12—17	15—19—22	15—19—22—26—29.
Middle c'♯ . .	12—17	1— 8—12—15	8—12—15—19—22.
Treble f²♯. . .	12—17	1— 8—12—15	1— 8—12—15—19.
c³ in alt . . .	12—17	1— 8—12—15	1— 5— 8—12—15.

1136. The Tierce, or second rank of the Sesqualtera, is, in modern German organs, usually incorporated with the Sharp Mixture, and not the Full Mixture, *i.e.*, with the *second* Compound stop, and not the *first*—and for this reason : When the unequal temperament was in vogue abroad, the slightly sharpened thirds in the common scales nearly accorded with the Third-sounding rank of the Mixtures, and the latter effected a direct improvement on the general tone of the organ. On the equal temperament being adopted, and the thirds sharpened a little more, the Tierce was found to harmonise less agreeably than before; hence arose the plan of not introducing a Third-sounding rank so soon as had previously been the custom. Five ranks of Mixture thus came to be generally proposed without a Tierce; and in its stead a duplication of the Fifteenth was usually introduced, which substituted rank added materially to the distinctness and the silvery character of the Mixture sound.

1137. With regard to the incorporation of the Tierce with the Sharp Mixture, this Continental custom was not followed in the preparation of the foregoing schemes, because in England the prevailing feeling is at present more frequently in favour of the *early* use of the Tierce than not; therefore, by leaving it to be disposed as a separate stop, it could be drawn either with the first Mixture or not, according as the inclination of the organist might dictate.

1138. There is another German Compound stop, sometimes met with in large organs, that might here be noticed, called the Cymbal. This frequently consists of a duplication of the two or three upper ranks of the Sharp Mixture, with sometimes an octave Tierce added. In connection with a stop of this kind it may be mentioned that, when the Mixtures ascend very high, and are particularly strong in the Tenor octave, there is always a danger of the Treble being overpowered and obscured by them ; and it is then that Cavaillé-Coll's increasing pressure system is useful. For the Treble Reeds of large organs the heavy pressure system is often very desirable. The tendency to weakness as the scale ascends was observed by the Dutch and German builders nearly two centuries since, who proceeded to rectify it by furnishing the leading Manual stops of their organs with two pipes to a key from Middle c, Fiddle g, or even Tenor c upwards ; and also by increasing the number of ranks in the upper part of the Mixtures, as at Haarlem, Rotterdam, Amsterdam, Hamburg, &c. The repetitions which occur in the Treble of the Mixture stops also exercise a material influence in that direction. The increasing pressure system attains the same end without such re-duplications. At the same time all the proportions which have already been detailed, and the duplication of all larger ranks before smaller ones, must be duly observed, otherwise it is not in the power even of a heavy wind to secure a well-balanced effect.

1139. The Cornet is a very useful stop for a large organ to contain, and it is frequently the only stop that contains a Tierce, as at Doncaster. The Cornet was originally used for giving out the melody of a chorale upon, and hence was usually only a Treble stop in English instruments ; but in Germany, where the Canto Fermo is frequently announced in the Tenor, à la Bach, it generally descends to Tenor c, or even to CC. For a large organ the Cornet is also useful in another way. Not having any "breaks" itself, it covers up those in the other Compound stops very effectively. It is sometimes made to increase or "progress" in the number of its ranks, from two to three, and three to four, in the following manner :—

CC . . 15—17   Tenor c . . 12—15—17   Middle c¹ . . 8—12—15—17,

or it is made to consist of 8—12—15—17 from Tenor c upwards.

1140. In regard to scale, the Mounted Cornet is larger than the Open Diapason ; the Principal and Twelfth ranks being three pipes larger, and the Fifteenth and Tierce two pipes larger, with narrow mouths, arched lips, and voice of a flute-like quality of tone.

1141. Herr Franz Weber, the late excellent organist of Cologne Cathedral, constantly used the Mounted Cornet as an accompaniment to the priests' voices.

1142. As the Mixtures of many of the old English builders have been so frequently referred to in the present chapter, the composition of some of them may prove interesting to many readers, and are therefore subjoined.

SMITH.
(*Temple Church.*)

	Sesquialtera, III ranks.	Mixture, III and II ranks.
CC	17—19—22	22—26—29.
Tenor c♯ . . .	17—19—22	19—22.
Middle c¹♯. . .	15—17—19	12—15.
Treble c²♯. . .	12—15—17	12—15.
Treble f²♯. . .	8—12—15	12—15.

HARRIS AND BYFIELD.
(*Doncaster Church.*)

	Tierce.	Sesquialtera, V ranks.
CC to middle b . . .	17	19—22—24—26—29.
Middle c¹♯ to the top	17	8—12—15—17—19.

F F 2

SNETZLER.

(*St. Mary's, Nottingham.*)

	Sesquialtera, IV ranks.
CC to Fiddle g	15—17—19—22.
Fiddle g♯	12—15—17—19.
Middle g¹♯	8—12—15—17.

GREEN.

(*Rochester Cathedral.*)

	Sesquialtera, III ranks.		Mixture, II ranks.
CC	17—19—22	. . . . . .	15—19.
Tenor c	17—19—22	. . . . . .	12—15.
Fiddle g	15—17—19	. . . . . .	12—15.
Middle c² . . .	12—15—17	. . . . . .	8—12.

GREEN.

(*St. Katherine's, Regent's Park.*)

	Sesquialtera, III ranks.		Mixture, II ranks.
CC	17—19—22	. . . . . .	22—24.
Fiddle g	17—19—22	. . . . . .	17—22.
Middle c¹ . . .	15—17—19	. . . . . .	17—22.
Treble c² . . .	12—15—17	. . . . . .	15—17.

ENGLAND.

(*Lancaster Church.*)

	Sesquialtera, IV ranks.		Mixture, II ranks.
CC	17—19—22—26	. . . . . .	24—29.
Gamut G . .	17—19—22—26	. . . . . .	22—24.
Tenor c . . .	17—19—22—26	. . . . . .	12—22.
Tenor . . .	15—17—19—22	. . . . . .	19—22.
Middle c¹ . .	8—15—17—19	. . . . . .	15—19.
Middle f¹ .	8—12—15—17	. . . . . .	15—19.
Treble c² . .	8—12—15—17	. . . . . .	12—15.

The Mixture-work in the Newcastle-on-Tyne organ, made as long back as the year 1676, includes an *Open Diapason* rank in the Treble, and is of the following composition :—

NEWCASTLE-ON-TYNE MIXTURES, BY HARRIS.

	Tierce.		Sesquialtera, II ranks.		Mixture, III ranks.
CC	17	. . . .	19—22	. . . .	24—26—29.
Middle c¹♯ . . .	17	. . . .	19—22	. . . .	17—24—26.
Middle d¹	17	. . . .	19—22	. . . .	15—17—24.
Middle a¹	17	. . . .	1— 8	. . . .	15—17—24.
Treble d²	17	. . . .	1— 8	. . . .	12—15—17.

The chorus stops of the organ at St. Peter Mancroft, Norwich, by the same builder, included *two* Open Diapasons, *two* Principals, and *a Quint*. The following is the scheme :—

ST. PETER MANCROFT MIXTURES, BY HARRIS.

	Tierce.	Larigot.	Sesquialtera, III ranks.	Mixture, II ranks.	Furniture, III ranks.
CC	17	19	19—22—26	29—33	22—26—29.
FF♯	17	19	19—22—26	29—33	15—19—22.
Tenor c♯ . .	17	19	12—15—19	22—26	15—19—22.
Tenor f♯ . .	17	19	12—15—19	22—26	8—12—15.
Middle c¹♯ .	17	19	8—12—15	19—22	8—12—15.
Middle f¹♯ .	17	19	8—12—15	19—22	1— 8—12.
Treble c²♯ . .	17	19	1— 5— 8	15—19	1— 8—12.

Snetzler also incorporated an Open Diapason rank in the Treble of his Mixtures at Halifax. The composition he adopted was as follows :—

HALIFAX MIXTURES, BY SNETZLER.

	Sesquialtera, IV ranks.		Furniture, III ranks.
CC	15—17—19—22	. . . .	22—26—29.
Tenor c	15—17—19—22	. . . .	15—19—22.
Middle c¹ . . .	8—12—15—17	. . . .	15—19—22.
Middle g¹ . . .	8—12—15—17	. . . .	8—12—15.
g³ in alt	1— 8—12—15	. . . .	8—12—15.

CHAPTER XXXVII.

THE EXTERIOR ARRANGEMENT OF THE ORGAN.

The organ case.   1143. THE two great desiderata in an organ case, the one referring to its appearance, the other to its influence on sound, are that it should correspond in style with the building in which it is erected, and that it should impede the egress of the tone as little as possible.

1144. The most appropriate style for a church organ case, generally speaking, is one of the periods of the Gothic; because in some one of those the great majority of our finest ecclesiastical edifices, both ancient and modern, are built. No authentic examples, however, of cases in this style of early date are known to exist in England. In Germany a few still remain. One of the most beautiful is in the "Marien-Kirche" at Lübeck, at the west end of the building. It consists of three main compartments, flat; the centre one being the largest, and containing the 32-feet tin pipe. The main compartments are separated by two subordinate ones, containing smaller pipes. All the front pipes are of pure tin, burnished, and slightly but exquisitely diapered about the mouth; and the case, of some dark wood, has a great quantity of carved and gilt work about it, which gives a gorgeous effect to the whole. Underneath it is groined, and handsomely illuminated and gilded.

1145. There was an old organ case existing in Tong Church, Shropshire, towards the end of the last century, ornamented with "tabernacle work." That at Radnor has already been described. The handsome old cases at Exeter, Shrewsbury, and Cambridge, are Italian in their detail. So also are those made by Smith and Harris immediately after the Restoration. Literal copies of these are therefore unsuitable for churches of pointed design, even though the originals may stand in buildings erected in that style. Nevertheless, many of the specimens just referred to possess an air of great dignity, as well as considerable beauty and elegance of outline. Their various compartments are often very finely proportioned, while their relative sizes have been adjusted to each other with consummate judgment and taste. In most of the old organs the largest pipes of the original work—*i.e.*, the lower pipes of the Open Diapason—are almost always found in the front of the case, in the towers. They were originally placed there for two reasons : (1) to impart dignity to the general appearance of the instrument, and (2) to secure for them plenty of speaking room. The larger the pipe, the greater is the gust of wind emitted from its mouth; and, consequently, the more space must there be in the vicinity of the mouth to admit of the pipe speaking clearly and firmly. By mounting the large pipes in the manner already noticed, they not only had plenty of this necessary room, but, from the direction in which their mouths were turned, they could produce their sounds freely, without encroaching on the speaking room inside the case necessary to ensure the correct enunciation of the interior pipe-work.

1146. In some modern organs the case has been made with carved woodwork in front, instead of pipes, giving the instrument a "shrine-like appearance,"

If a case of this kind is proposed—although it is not clear what may be the merit of making an organ look like what it is not—additional space should be allowed inside for the accommodation of the dismounted pipes; for if one pipe be placed too near to the back or side of a second, so that its mouth becomes shaded, the tone of the former will become muffled and flattened in pitch, or if the mouth of one pipe be placed so near to that of a second that when both are made to speak the current of air emitted from the one intersects that from the other, the tone will be false and tremulous. The organ-builder's greatest care is required to guard against the appearance of these casualties, even when circumstances are most favourable; but when standing and speaking room have to be found inside for several additional and large pipes, without the necessary extra space being allowed internally, the organ-builder's difficulties and the chances of the tone of the organ being unequal are needlessly and vexatiously increased.

1147. The principle of arranging large pipes with their mouths turned outwards has in several instances been carried farther by the modern organ-builders than by their predecessors, and with equally good results. The Pedal organ is usually planted either at the back of the instrument, or it is divided into two portions, and a part arranged at each side of the organ, just inside the case. When there is sufficient clear space outside the organ case in the vicinity of the Pedal organ, the larger pipes of that department are often turned round and made to speak through openings or gratings in the case made for the purpose, as at Christ Church, Newgate Street; St. Olave's, Southwark; St. Peter's, Cornhill, &c. This plan is a very good one, not only because it prevents the possibility of the tone from the large pipes being smothered and uncertain, but also because it admits of some of the other inside pipes being planted close to them, back to back, as at St. Olave's, Southwark, whereby a great saving of room is effected.

1148. In a few instances the organ case has been made with metal pipes at both sides, as well as in front, as in the instrument recently destroyed at Croydon Church, built by Avery, in 1794, and also in that at St. Katherine's Church, Regent's Park, by Green. Organs on a central screen mostly have an east and west front, not simply for ornament, but to allow the tone to travel up and down the building.

1149. It would greatly add to the beautiful appearance of the organ, as well as be beneficial to the quality of some of its tones, if the front pipes were to be made of pure tin, and the natural lustre of the material to be left unobscured, instead of their being formed of an inferior compound, and then gilded or painted. This improvement might be the more easily effected, since the sum necessary to defray the cost of gilding, &c., added to the value of the metal pipes of lower standard, would probably go some way towards securing substantial pipes of the more handsome and durable material. Moreover, the bright metal pipes, by catching and throwing back the rays of light, after the manner of a reflector, would relieve the appearance of the organ from some of the dulness it wears in the dismal holes and corners to which it is too frequently consigned.

The Manuals and Pedals; their width, and their proper situation in regard to each other.

1150. The width for a Manual that ranges from CC to f³ in alt (54 keys) is 2 feet 6 inches. For the Pedal board there is in England at present no fixed width, which is a circumstance much to be regretted. On this subject Dr. Burney wrote, eighty years ago :—" Scarcely two organs in the kingdom have their Pedals alike, either with respect to number or position; so that every performer who comes to an organ with which he is not previously acquainted (be he ever so skilful in the use of

Pedals) has the whole of his business to learn again." The want of uniformity complained of by Dr. Burney as existing in his time remains in full force in the present day.

1151. The natural Pedal keys should, if possible, be a good inch in thickness, about 20 inches in length, and from 2 to 2½ inches in depth. If they are either too narrow, too long, or too shallow, they will have a tendency to spring. Their upper surface should not be much rounded off towards the sides, as in that case the foot would only touch the crown of the Pedal. The angles, however, would of course be bevelled off, to remove splinters, &c. The upper surface is sometimes rounded to assist the foot in slipping from one Pedal to the next ; but this is reversing the order of things. The Pedal should be constructed to *retain* the foot steadily and firmly. It is the organist's province to be able to change from one Pedal to its neighbour with facility when necessary.

1152. The two great points to be observed in the construction of a good Pedal board are that space should be economised, as far as practicable, in order that as complete a compass as possible may be secured, and yet that the Pedals be not placed so closely that they can only be made of the thickness of mere sticks.

1153. A good medium scale is obtained by planting the Pedals so that the naturals measure 2⅜ inches from centre to centre. This is about the scale adopted by Mr. Hill, among other builders, and it admits of the introduction of a complete compass of Pedals without throwing the upper keys so much to the right as to be out of reach of the performer. In Germany the Pedals usually measure as much as from 3⅛ to 3¼ inches from centre to centre, while in England they are as frequently placed too closely together.

1154. The Pedals are more agreeable to play upon when the naturals are about half an inch higher at the back (under the stool) than at the other end ; then the heel of the foot sooner reaches the key. The upper part of the short Pedal keys, which need not be more than five inches in length, are also the better for not being quite level. They should slightly incline upwards as they recede, leaving the front or lowest part about an inch above the neighbouring part of the naturals. When so shaped they meet the point of the foot more accurately. A frame should run across beyond the short Pedal keys, to serve as a foot rest, but *not* at the sides, as it would be in the way of the extreme keys.

1155. Several experiments have at various times been made with the view of bringing the Pedals more conveniently under the control of the performer. In the organ at York Cathedral, erected in 1829, Mr. Hill made the Pedal board on the radiating principle. In Germany the Pedal board is frequently made concave in shape, i.e., the Pedals to the extreme right and left are made to rise gradually in a curve. This was the case with Schulze's organ in the Great Exhibition of 1851.

1156. Lately, Willis of London and Heinrich of Cologne have been making Pedal boards in which it has been the object to combine the peculiarities of the radiating with the concave principle. Indeed, most of the English organ-builders now occasionally make " concave and radiating " pedal-boards.

1157. The Manual keys should not be too short in front of the centre, otherwise the touch will be too shallow and too heavy. On the other hand, they should not be too long, otherwise the touch will be too deep, and most likely also destitute of firmness. About ⅜ of an inch is the proper depth for the Great organ keys to fall ; and all the Manuals should descend to the same depth. The performer, nevertheless, soon accommodates himself, for ordinary purposes, to a rather deeper or slightly more shallow touch than the average one, or even to one that is a degree heavier or lighter than usual.

The condition of the greatest importance to him is that, whatever be the general depth and resistance, all the keys on a Manual shall be *alike in both these respects*. If one key requires more power than its neighbours to press it down, or descends lower, or not so low, the playing is rendered more difficult by such vexatious inequalities. Check-springs, put on by a lazy attendant to save a little trouble, are a prolific source of unequal resistance.

1158. A springy resistance of greater or less amount, according to circumstances, is all that the finger or foot should have to overcome. Unequal, stiff, or sluggish touches are all defective. A little allowance, however, may fairly be made in favour of lately renovated or newly constructed organs. In new mechanism of all kinds there will be a little friction at first, in proportion to the accuracy with which it is made ; and the mechanism of an organ offers no exception to the rule. If the key movement works "too easy" at first, it may rattle after a few years' use.

1159. When the Manual couplers are drawn, the resistance offered by the chief Manual to the finger will, of course, be increased. The touch, however, should still preserve its *elasticity*. Sometimes a very disagreeable grating sensation is experienced by the finger, as though the coupler stickers were working through scouring paper.

1160. With regard to the arrangement of the Manuals, the best and most generally received plan is that of placing the one belonging to the Great organ in the middle, with that of the Swell three inches above, and that of the Choir as many inches below. Sometimes, to lessen the distance to which the upper Manuals recede behind the lower, the front of the Great organ keys is made to project over those of the Choir about an inch and a half, and those of the Swell to stand forward in the same manner and to the same distance over the Great organ keys. There are two ways of doing this : either by making the beading in the front of the keys take the form of an ogee projection, or by bevelling away the under side of the key, upwards, commencing about an inch from the front, as in the Birmingham and St. Paul's organs, &c. The latter plan is the best, as the hands can then be raised from one Manual to the next without danger of striking the knuckles.

1161. Thirty-one inches below the Great organ Manual is a convenient position for the Pedals. The centre C of the Pedals—that is, the middle one of the three bearing that name—should be planted immediately underneath the middle c^1 of the Manuals ; and the front of the short keys should come just under the front of the Great Manual short or black keys.

1162. In many organs the Pedals are placed too far from the Manuals, and often also too forward. The organist should be able to use either of the three Manuals or the Pedals freely, without experiencing the slightest tendency to fall from the seat. This firmness of location and command over the instrument will be secured if (1) the Pedals are placed at twenty-eight inches from the Choir Manual, with the front of the short keys placed as already described ; (2) if the stool be arranged at a distance of twenty-two inches above the Pedals ; and (3) if the stool be placed about six inches in front of the Choir Manual.

1163. When seated at the organ, the feet should be suspended immediately in front of the short Pedals. If, when seated at a distance of twenty-two inches above the Pedals, the Manuals appear too high; or if, on increasing the height of the stool, so as to bring the Manuals more under command, the feet are too far from the Pedals, it is a proof that the Pedals are at too great a distance from the Manuals. If, after placing the organ stool in such a position as will allow of the free use of the Pedals, the Manuals are too far off, and if, on adjusting it so that

the Manuals are within convenient reach, the feet hang over the short Pedals—
this shows that the Pedal board is too forward.

The organ stool.   1164. It adds much to the comfort of playing if the top of
the organ stool be made of a good width, as it enables the player to sit with more
firmness at the instrument.   For this purpose it should be made about fourteen
inches in width, and should *not* incline downwards towards the front, as this has a
tendency to make the player slip forward when actively employed.   For the same
reason it is better not to cover the seat with a smooth substance, as certain kinds
of leather or horse-hair cloth ; but simply with either a piece of carpet, or with
rough leather, with a *little* stuffing.   The plain wood is often left for the top.   In
such case it is much better for it not to be polished.

1165. In the top of the stool one or two drawers can be conveniently introduced,
which are always useful to hold music or books.   A rail across under the stool,
from end to end, about four inches above the Pedals, and five or six inches from
the front, will be found a great convenience for resting the feet upon, as the frame
under the composition Pedals is too far off for constant use.

The Swell Pedal.   1166. The Swell Pedal is not at all times conveniently
placed, it frequently being too high and too forward.   About seven inches
above the Pedal board will be found a very convenient position for it.   Sometimes it is so arranged that, when the Swell is fixed open, it *crosses* the upper
short keys of the Pedals.   This, of course, is not good.   It might conveniently
be made to project parallel with the composition Pedals, so as to meet the
foot, instead of through the jamb, and in such a position that, when fixed down,
it would lie over some place where two naturals come together ; as, for instance,
over the upper e and f of the Pedals.   On fixing open the Swell, it would then
be far less in the way of the Pedals than it frequently is when it projects from the
side.

1167. When the Swell Pedal projects from the side, and the leg has to be
turned out so much before the Pedal can be got at that the position of the body at
the keys becomes disturbed, it is a proof that the Pedal is too forward.   If the
thigh-joint as well as the foot have to be raised before reaching the Pedal, it is an
indication that the latter is too high.   Sometimes the organist has to throw his
body backwards in order to preserve his equilibrium, or to place his thumbs on the
beading in front of the keys to prevent his falling forward.   Either inconvenience
is the consequence of some misarrangement in the region of the keys.   Either the
Swell-Pedal will prove to be too high or too forward, or the stool or Pedals will be
too low or too forward.

The music desk.   1168. It is a matter of great convenience to have the music
desk properly adjusted.   When there are three Manuals, the desk should not be
farther back than the *front* of the Swell keys, and it may be placed nearly as forward as the front of the Great Manual.   It is a great fault if the desk is placed at
the back of the Swell keys, as, from this cause, the music is needlessly carried five
or six inches farther from the organist than there is any occasion for, and nearly as
much too low also, thus rendering it necessary that he should look *down upon* the
music, instead of *forward at* it.

The Composition Pedals.   1169. The Composition movement should be of the
" double-action " kind.   The Pedals which operate upon them are sometimes
made to project in a line with, and just above, the German Pedals ; at other

times from the sides, like so many long Swell pedals. The former is not only
the most neat, but the most convenient arrangement. It is a good plan to
place the Composition pedals immediately over where two naturals come together,
as there is then no chance of the heel touching a short key when either of them
is being pressed down, or they can be kept up a little higher to prevent this
accident. The Composition pedals should not remain down so as to be in the way
of the short pedal keys.

The arrangement of the
draw stops. 1170. The draw stops should be so placed that they will
not only be under the convenient control of the player, but
also present a handsome and symmetrical appearance.

1171. In many of the old English organs half the stops belonging to each
department are arranged on each side of the Manuals. A great number of the
German and other Continental organs also have their stops assorted in a similar
manner. The plan, however, is not by any means a good one, as it apportions the
stops into twice as many divisions as there is any occasion for, without serving
any beneficial result.

1172. A far better arrangement is the modern English one of placing all the
stops of each department together, as the contents of each division can then be
so much more easily distinguished from the rest.

1173. Besides keeping them separate, as above, the stops of each department
should further be placed where they can be combined or changed with the
least difficulty to the performer. With a view to the attainment of this end,
it is important to bear in mind the two following facts : (1) that, as a rule, the
left hand can be more easily spared for a moment than the right ; and (2) that
the Great organ stops are more frequently brought under the control of the
feet of the performer by means of Composition pedals than those of any other
department.

1174. The right-hand side is therefore the best side on which to place the
Great organ draw stops, as they can be drawn in or out, in all the ordinary
and most frequently required combinations, without any assistance whatever
from the hand.

1175. The Swell and Choir organ stops are not nearly so often acted upon
by Composition pedals. Moreover, as the numerous delicate shades and varieties
of tone are produced from those departments chiefly, leaving the Great organ for
the broad contrasts, the left side appears the most proper one whereon to place
their draw stops. As the bass part of the music can be continued by the pedals,
the left hand can, with a little contriving, be for a moment spared for effecting the
necessary changes in the combinations, without in the least degree disturbing the
progress or completeness of the music.

1176. The Pedal organ stops and the various *Manual* couplers might be
placed on the right-hand side, with a view to securing as nearly as possible
an equal number of stops on both sides of the keys, which is always desirable.
But the *Pedal* couplers should, whenever practicable, be ranged on the left-hand
side, to facilitate the making of those quick changes from one Manual to another
that are so constantly required in accompanying the musical service, as well as
in solo playing.

1177. If there is a large Pedal organ, it will be advisable to have some
contrivance for reducing the full Pedal organ to a few 16 and 8 feet Flue stops
of soft intonation, to form a Pedal bass to the Choir or Swell. This can
either be a Composition Pedal, or, by placing all the louder stops on a second
sound-board, and introducing a valve into the second wind-trunk—as is ordinarily

done in small English organs which have only "Pedal pipes" by way of Bass—they can then be silenced by shutting off the wind. A third plan would be to have a movement, worked by the hand or foot, to disconnect the action of the loud-stop sound-board from the Pedal. If a "Ventil" be introduced, and it be intended to work it by the hand, the handle should be placed near to the Great Pedal coupler, that both may be changed together.

1178. In arranging the places for the several stops of any one department, it is best, first, to keep the Reed and the Flue stops quite separate.. The Reed stops should be placed above, and the Flue stops below.

1179. Next, the members of the different classes of stops should be arranged according to their standard length or their size of tone, giving to the largest the lowest positions, and the smallest the highest. According to this rule, all the Flue stops of 16 feet on the Manual, as being usually the largest, should occur at the bottom, with those of 8 feet next, and so on through the series in regular gradation. And the same with the Reeds. The disposition of even a large organ may soon be learnt, as well as the places where the several draw stops are to be found, when the latter are arranged in a methodical and intelligible manner. As an example, the size and comparative completeness of any of the German organs described in the Appendix may at once be ascertained from a perusal of the list of its contents arranged in the simple manner there given.

1180. The several draw stops are generally arranged in single, double, or triple *vertical* rows on each side of the Manuals, according to their number and the size of the organ. The draw stops of the organ in Cologne Cathedral are arranged in four *horizontal* rows, and so are those of many other Continental organs. At Westminster Abbey the draw stops are also placed in this manner. Regarding the best method of distinguishing such draw stops as belong to one department from the remainder, this matter must necessarily depend in some measure on individual circumstances.

1181. In small organs of two Manuals the Great and Swell stops are generally arranged so as to form each a separate row—one on the right, the other on the left. An ivory or brass plate inserted above each row, bearing the name of the clavier to which that tier belongs, is, in that case, all that is required to mark the requisite distinction. This plan of identifying the draw stops with the clavier to which they belong is far preferable to that of crowding such announcement on every individual stop handle, in addition to the name. The less there is engraved on the knob, besides the name and length of the stop, the better. What *is* engraved not only then appears more distinct, but there is room to cut it in a bolder and more legible type.

1182. If the draw stops are intended to be placed in double rows, it will be found a convenient arrangement to let the Swell stops comprise one portion of the two tiers on the left-hand side, and those of the Choir the remainder. The list of contents of each department is then brought within much more convenient range of the eye than when extended over a long tier of draw stops. In that case the Swell stops should occupy the upper position, and the Choir the lower. This arrangement also presents an analogy with the situation of the respective Manuals.

1183. When the draw stops are numerous, they are frequently arranged in triple instead of double rows. This plan is a good one, as it prevents the tiers becoming inordinately long, and, therefore, keeps the upper draw stops more within reach. The best method of then classifying the stops is to make those belonging to one department occupy the upper portion of the three rows, and those of another, the lower. A little extra space, if possible, left where those of one clavier leave off, and those of another begin, in addition to the engraved plate, will be found most advantageous in making the point of separation more distinct.

1184. Other means are sometimes taken, in addition to those already mentioned, for distinguishing the draw stops of each department. Thus, in addition to their being arranged in tiers or in clusters, the ivory plates in the face of the stop handles of some of the departments are sometimes stained red, blue, green, or some other colour. If colours be used, for which there is no absolute occasion, they should be of the lightest possible tint, or they will render the inscriptions indistinct. Different substances are also occasionally used for the name plates, for increasing the distinction; as ivory for those of one department, mother-of-pearl for a second, porcelain for a third, tortoise-shell for a fourth, and so on. These, however, give to the general appearance of the draw stops a motley effect, as the colours, if deep, give them a heavy and patchy appearance. Another plan is to have the names of one department on each side printed in black, and the other in red. This has a light and handsome effect, particularly when the character chosen is the old church text. The red-lettered labels should be above, and the black below. Every stop should have its name engraved on the handle, in preference to being placed over or at the side of it; as this prevents the possibility of the inscription being by mistake read as referring to any other than the right draw stop. The names are sometimes engraved on plates of zinc or brass, and inlaid; but those metals soon become tarnished. Many organs have the names of the stops printed on pieces of paper, which are pasted on, near to the handles; but such labels are apt to become soiled or rubbed off, and at the best present but a mean appearance.

1185. The head of each stop-handle is usually turned out, and a plate of ivory or some other bright material inserted, bearing the requisite inscription.

1186. The inscriptions should be engraved boldly and legibly. For this reason, italics with long flourishing tails to the g's, &c., should be avoided, as not being so easily deciphered. Capital letters are the most appropriate; and those of the Egyptian, German, Old English, or modern English character are available according to taste. Old English text for the names has a handsome appearance, and is particularly appropriate for church organs. It is better to have the names engraved in horizontal lines rather than in a circle, following the outline of the plate. It is then deciphered more easily and more quickly.

1187. In connection with the question of distinctness of labelling, it may not be out of place to mention that the person who plans the organ will most probably have also to decide on the nomenclature for the stops. When settling this by no means unimportant matter, it will be well to bear in mind the purpose for which the labelling is introduced; namely, to *assist* and *guide* the player. To carry out this object, the labels should describe in as simple and clear a manner as possible the stops to which they apply. And to facilitate this end, names in English would appear to be clearly the best for English organs, whenever they are applicable. Sometimes, however, it is preferred to call the stops after some Continental fashion. When this is done, care should be taken to apply the names, so that an organist or organ-builder from the country whence the terms are derived shall understand them. This necessary precaution has not always been attended to.

1188. It is of importance that the draw stops should move with freedom and noiselessly. A stiff and stunted draw-stop action is most disagreeable. If, however, the table of the sound-board is covered with leather, *i.e.*, if the sliders work upon leather—they will move rather stiffly at first, until the leather has become tolerably smooth, for which stiffness some allowance should be made.

1189. From $2\frac{1}{2}$ to 3 inches is a good distance for the draw stops to move backwards and forwards.

1190. The draw stops, which are better for being of a good medium size, should not be placed too closely together. If the knobs are $1\frac{1}{2}$ inch in diameter, with ivory plates $1\frac{1}{8}$ inch wide, and have the inscriptions cut in letters $\frac{3}{16}$ of an inch high, they will have a bold and handsome appearance.

CHAPTER XXXVIII.

THE INTERIOR ARRANGEMENT OF THE ORGAN.

The building frame. 1191. The building frame that is to support the entire organ should be very strong and substantial, and should be so constructed as to resist the great weight and pressure of the sound-boards and pipes without sinking or giving in any manner.

The platform. 1192. It is not a less important and necessary precaution to see that the platform—when the organ is to stand on one—is not only fully capable of supporting the entire weight of the instrument, but also that of any assembly that may be gathered around it from time to time, as the members of an orchestra and chorus in a concert-room, or the choir and children in the gallery of the church. Instances are known where this preventive course has not been sufficiently taken in music-halls, the consequence being that, while the organ is entirely free from cipherings and stickings at all other times, during concerts it is subject to both.

1193. With regard to the general arrangement of the interior of an organ, the sound-boards and other main portions of the work would be distributed chiefly according to local circumstances.

The distribution of the sound-boards. 1194. The most usual positions assigned to the different sound-boards in English organs were mentioned on page 4, and need not, therefore, be again described here.

1195. In some German organs, occupying a very broad, high, and shallow site, the "8-feet Great organ" (*Haupt-manual*) is placed in the centre, with the "4-feet Choir" above (*Ober-manual*), and the "16-feet Pedal" half on each side; the largest pipes of the "Principal" of each department, 8, 4, and 16 feet, being placed in the front of the case.

1196. In the organ of St. Peter's Church, Cornhill, built by Hill, the large Swell is placed over the Great organ, resembling in this respect the arrangement just mentioned; and when a church is very lofty, or an organ is to stand at a great elevation above the ground, the Swell may be placed in this manner without producing any disadvantageous effect, but rather the reverse, provided it be kept well up at the same time. The under side of the Swell sound-board then acts as a sort of reflector to the Great organ, and directs its tone into the church before it is too much spent. The old English builders frequently put a top or covering to the case of their cathedral organs for the above-named purpose, as at St. Paul's Cathedral.

1197. In other German organs, where the site is about the same width as before, but lower and deeper, the Choir organ is placed in the centre, with the Great organ, divided, flanking it on each side, and the Pedal behind. The object in placing the Great organ partly on each side, rather than in the centre, no doubt, was to prevent its force being too sensibly felt at the keys. Other plans were sometimes adopted by the old English builders for shielding the organist from the full strength of the instrument; such as keeping the impost of the case high, or placing a passage board completely across the front, between the Great organ sound-board and the front pipes, as was originally the case at St. Michael's, Cornhill. When there are three Manuals, the third Manual organ is frequently placed "in front," as it is termed in England, but "at back," as they say in Germany, where that division is hence called *Ruckpositiv* (Back-choir). In very large instruments the Pedal organ frequently occupies three separate sites, forming what are called "side Pedal Basses" and "back Pedal Basses," an English example of which arrangement will be found in Mr. Hill's organ in St. Paul's Cathedral; or, where the largest metal "Principals" appear in front of the case, a fourfold division of the Pedal will sometimes be met with, forming "front Pedal Basses," "back Pedal Basses," and "side Pedal Basses." Of this latter distribution an English example occurs in the Town Hall organ at Birmingham, by Hill.

1198. These particulars are given here to show that an organ may be made to suit almost any site, provided only that the necessary room be allowed in some direction or other.

The cause of the bad proportions of many English organs. 1199. English organs have frequently been found fault with, on account of their square, solid, inelegant form, and their projecting so far into the buildings wherein they stand. But this has in almost every case arisen from the builder being, in regard to room, so much restricted in the direction of width and height. In churches which have west-end organs this has been more particularly the case, and for no better purpose than that of providing room for a mass of children up each side the instrument. In Continental churches, where the whole width of the west end is frequently devoted to the organ, much larger instruments project to a far less distance into the buildings than do the smaller instruments in English churches.

1200. It may be mentioned, as in some degree illustrating this point, that the performers in an orchestra are placed in a comparatively few long rows, from the correct supposition that such an arrangement has a more beneficial effect than if they were ranged in several shorter rows, behind one another, as though stationed on a wide staircase. For the same reason it will be conducive to the best musical result if the organ be made broad, high, and shallow, rather than narrow and deep.

1201. In one or two instances the analogy between the interior arrangement of an organ and the distribution of an orchestra has been carried to a still greater extent in German organs; for sound-boards have occasionally been made to slope upwards from front to back, like a concert-room platform, upon which the pipes have been ranged in terrace-form, and with the largest Flue stops at the back and the smallest in front. It was in the organ at the Church of St. Maurice, at Halle, built by Schulze, that this last arrangement was for the first time practically brought to bear.

Much room conducive to the orderly arrangement of the organ. 1202. But whatever general arrangements may be considered best to adapt an organ to a particular site, it will be of essential service in a variety of ways to allot as much room to the instrument as can conveniently be spared.

1203. One of the first things which arrests the attention of a visitor, on entering a modern German organ, whether of large or small dimensions, is the appearance of roominess which it presents; and this is speedily perceived to be accompanied by a very simple, yet orderly and systematic, distribution of the several parts of which the organ is composed.

The advantages of large sound-boards.

1204. The roominess is soon discovered to arise, in a great measure, from the ample size of the sound-boards, which, even in instruments of ordinary dimensions, frequently measure 9, 10, and 11 feet in length ; and in large instruments, 15, 16, and even 17 feet from end to end. The orderly appearance of the stops also is seen to result from the fact of the sound-boards being sufficiently large to admit of their pipes being placed "over their wind," whereby all *compulsory* recourse to the conveyancing off of pipes is avoided.

1205. This plan—of planting all the pipes on the sound-board—might at first sight appear to involve a great "loss of room," as the phrase goes; but, on account of the admirable manner in which the stops are sometimes planted, this is not the case to nearly the extent that might be imagined. The 8 and 4 feet members of the Flute-work are, in German organs, as in English, frequently of tenor c compass ; and the way in which a sound-board is sometimes laid out so as to receive them is as follows :—

1206. The two stops which form the basis of the Manual tone, corresponding to the English Open and Stopped Diapasons, of course extend to CC ; and the twelve pipes which form the 8-feet octave of each are ranged in a single row. The room which they require for their accommodation, therefore, is in the direction of width rather than of depth. At tenor c, where the pipes are little more than half-size, the two 8-feet members of the Flute-work commence, and occupy the standing and speaking room now at liberty. For the sake of illustration, these may be supposed to be a tenor c Gamba and a tenor c Hohl-flöte. To give to these two members of the Flute-work the effect of a complete range, when either may be used singly, the Hohl-flöte is grooved into the Stopped Diapason in the 8-feet octave ; and the Gamba ; which is usually of fuller tone than most English stops of the same name, is grooved into the Open Diapason in the Bass octave. At about middle $d^1\sharp$, where the pipes of the four stops will have become reduced to half dimensions, the single row plantation is discontinued in favour of the double row zig-zag plan, described in a former chapter ; and this arrangement is continued up to the top. In a similar way one or two additional 4-feet Flue stops are also frequently worked in from the tenor c groove upwards.

1207. From measurements taken of existing specimens, it was found that the average dimensions of a German sound-board furnished with nine stops, of which the following are the English equivalents—

1. Bourdon	16 feet tone	6. Principal	4 feet
2. Open Diapason . . .	8 feet	7. Twelfth	$2\frac{2}{3}$ feet
3. Gamba to Tenor c .	8 feet	8. Fifteenth	2 feet
4. Stopped Diapason . .	8 feet tone	9. Full Mixture, V ranks . .	2 feet
5. Dulciana to Tenor c .	8 feet		

were 3 feet in breadth, from back to front, and 11 feet in length.

1208. If we may judge from their works, the old English builders attached as much importance to placing the pipes of their organs over their respective grooves as the Germans do in the present day ; for we find this system carried out in even their smallest organs ; the front pipes and the largest pipes of the Stopped Diapason frequently offering the only exceptions to the rule. They also followed the same plan in their larger instruments, as far as practicable ; hence it is no very unusual circumstance to find the original sound-boards by Smith and Harris, Byfield and Bridge, measuring 8, 9, and 10 feet in length.

A Great organ sound-board by the first-mentioned builder, furnished with the
following ten stops, viz. :—

1. Open Diapason	6. Fifteenth
2. Stopped Diapason	7. Sesquialtera, III ranks
3. Principal	8. Mixture, II ranks
4. Flute	9. Cornet
5. Twelfth	10. Trumpet

measured 2 feet 10 inches in width, and 9 feet in length.

1209. In the Dome organ from St. Paul's Cathedral, recently removed to
Bristol, the late Mr. Hill introduced Great organ sound-boards about 10 feet in
entire length ; while, for the Pedal basses, occupying the side wings and back, he
provided others which were patterns for spaciousness and efficiency.

1210. In some German Manual sound-boards of the size indicated above,
the grooves measured in the bass octave 1 inch in width ; in the tenor and
Middle octaves, $\frac{3}{4}$ of an inch ; and in the treble octave and upper half octave,
$\frac{1}{2}$ an inch. The pallet-holes were of one length *throughout*, namely, 11 inches ;
and the grooves measured $3\frac{1}{2}$ inches in depth. The continuation of the pallet-
holes at an unreduced length, in the 4-feet octave, was for the purpose of feeding
the extra 8-feet stops that commenced there ; and their further continuation in
the treble was to supply the large Mixture ranks, which there returned to an
Open Diapason.

1211. It may be added that, although the Mixture included a duplication of
the Open Diapason, Principal, Twelfth, and Fifteenth in the treble, there was
not the slightest symptom of sympathy, robbing, or unsteadiness in the speech
of the pipes, when all the stops were drawn.

"Unoccupied space"   1212. The difference between the sound-board measurements
in an organ not "lost   just quoted is not so great as many might have anticipated it to
room."   have been. This, however, is partly due to the bass of the
German scales being in some cases somewhat smaller than the English, concerning
which more is said further on. But, had it been otherwise, it can never be
correctly said that "unoccupied space" in an organ, within reason, is "lost room ;"
since, next to the Pipes themselves, which are of course necessary to emit the
primary sounds, free air is the most important element in the production of a
resonant quality of tone. It is, indeed, true that English organ-builders have
frequently been called upon to "get in" a great number of stops into an unrea-
sonably small space ; and one cannot help admiring the manner in which they
have frequently grappled with the difficulties which have beset them ; at the same
time England is in consequence by no means destitute of organs that are
nearly as crowded, and almost as destitute of resonance, as a broker's shop.
It is a fact always worth the remembrance of those who would limit an organ-
builder too strictly in regard to space, that one of the secrets of the good effect
of many old instruments is their *comparative emptiness*. They have not only
pipes to produce tone, but breathing room to improve it.

The Abbé Vogler's   1213. Some notice should here be taken of Abbé Vogler's
simplification system.   "simplification system ;" of which Seidel has given a brief
account in his work on organ-building. (See Ewer's English edition, page 26.)
"At the end of the eighteenth and the beginning of the nineteenth centuries,"
says Seidel, "George Joseph Vogler, the famous musician, composer, and organ-
player (born 1749, in Wurzburg—died 1814), tried to reform thoroughly the whole
former mode of organ-building, an experiment in which he succeeded to a great

degree. His system, aiming at a *simplification of the whole mechanism* of the organ, created great sensation at the time, and found as many admirers as opponents. All that was superfluous, inappropriate, or too costly, he endeavoured to do away with. First of all, he rendered the action simpler by arranging the keys (grooves) in their natural succession ; in consequence of which, the construction of the roller-board (key movement) became easier and simpler, and the touch lighter. Vogler's system was adopted in several places, and even now some organ-builders make use of it." Among other Continental builders who construct their organs on Abbé Vogler's system may be mentioned Schulze, of Paulinzelle, near Erfurt, who placed an instrument so made in the Great Exhibition of 1851 ; which organ was afterwards purchased, and erected in the Exchange Room at Northampton : while, in England, the same plan has for some years past been adopted by Kirtland and Jardine, of Manchester. Some disadvantages, as well as advantages, attend the semitonal arrangement ; though, according to the account given to the writer by those builders in Germany and England who have had experience in making sound-boards on this principle, and of whose reports use is here freely made, the former are far outweighed by the latter.

1214. In Vogler's system the grooves are arranged in their natural or semitonal succession throughout the sound-board ; that is to say, the CC groove is placed to the extreme left, and the f³ in alt groove to the extreme right. The pipes of all the stops are arranged in the same order ; so that in the Open Diapason, for instance, the CC or 8-feet pipe is placed to the left of the Claviers, and the 4-inch f³ in alt pipe to the right ; the intermediate pipes forming a graduated series. The end of the sound-board to the right is therefore left clear of all but small pipes.

1215. Among the disadvantages attendant on this system of groove arrangement are mentioned the facts of the chief weight of the pipe-work being thrown to one end of the sound-board and building-frame ; an increased consumption of wind taking place at that same end of the sound-board ; longer conveyances being required to the front pipes to the right, or a special little sound-board for them, or "mute" pipes instead of speaking pipes. The additional weight, and greater consumption of wind at one end, however, have each their ascertained limits, like the greater tension of the bass strings of a pianoforte, and are provided against by a stronger building frame and larger wind-trunks, as the greater tension in a pianoforte is by stronger bracings ; while a diminutive sound-board rids the organ of long conveyances.

1216. The advantages attendant on the semitonal system of groove arrangement are stated to be as follows :—The pipes, being chiefly or entirely planted on their own wind, speak more promptly and plumply, and with a firmer tone, than if grooved or conveyanced. But few pipes, if any, being removed from over their grooves, few, if any, conveyances are required ; hence a fertile source of loss of wind, hissings of escaping air, impediments to the wind from lodgment of chips, accidental damage of conveyances, and occasional repairs, are removed. The pipes, when planted consecutively, have better speaking room.

1217. *Below* the sound-board, the action being in a direct line from the key to the pallet, no rollers are required ; and, there being no rollers, there are fewer centres, and consequently less friction. The abbreviation thus secures a lighter touch, and more instantaneous response to the finger. The omission of the roller-boards clears the interior of the organ of those walls of mechanism which not only impede the view of the instrument from front to back, but also prevent light penetrating to its remote parts. The tone, moreover, has then more room to *spread*, and is not thrown back, as must be the case to some extent when two or three roller-boards are in the organ. Roller-boards being dispensed with, the remaining mechanism can be constructed or "set it" more compactly. There is also less liability to stickings in a radiating tracker movement, and less chance of its getting out of order ; or, if out of order, it is easier and sooner repaired. The movement, by reason of its greater simplicity, is less effected by changes of temperature ; and on account of its whole extent, from the key to the pallet, being under the eye, an organist can at once detect and remedy any trifling disarrangement that might arise. An organ built on Vogler's principle is more convenient to tune than one built in any other manner ; and a large organ can be built on the simplification system without the *necessity* for the Pneumatic Lever Action, than on the ordinary system. The larger and more ample sound-board will not increase the cost of the entire work, on account of the omission of the roller-board and numerous conveyances effecting a saving in the expense.

1218. Without waiting to discuss the validity of all the claims that are made in favour of the semitonal arrangement, or whether they are such as are likely to lead to the system in question superseding others, a few words may yet be said concerning certain situations in churches, in the construction of organs for which the semitonal groove arrangement seems to be peculiarly suitable.

1219. The semitonal system of groove arrangement seems to be well adapted for an organ that is to occupy some side or corner position ; from either of which points the sound would have to travel in *two* directions. Suppose, for example, an organ so made to be placed on the south side of a church, or in an organ chapel on that same side, with its back towards the south wall ; the back of the case would reflect the tone forward, *i.e.*, through and over the front, in the usual way, and therefore *across* the church ; while the left side of the case would reflect it to the right, and therefore *down* the church. The small pipes to the right would present no impediment to the sound of the large ones passing over them into the church ; while the side of the case to the right, facing the church, by being filled with perforated panelling, or with pipes, would facilitate the egress of the tone in that direction at the same time that it would form an additional adornment to the instrument itself. Or, supposing an organ so constructed to be stationed at the east end of the north aisle, or in a north chapel, with its keys towards the west, the sound would travel through the front, down the aisle, in the usual way, and through the right side, across the chancel and church.

1220. For a divided west-end organ, also, the semitonal groove arrangement appears to be very suitable.

Passage-boards advantageous in more ways than one. 1221. It is very advisable that an organ should be well furnished with wide passage-boards. These will enable one to move about the instrument, either for purposes of tuning or for examination, without unintentionally disturbing any of the pipes, or of injuring the mechanism. Moreover, they are indirectly of beneficial service to the tone of the organ, by being instrumental in securing a free current of air round the various masses of pipes on the sound-boards.

The pipes should be so arranged that the small ones are accessible. 1222. The pipes should be so arranged on the sound-boards that they may all be easy of access for the purpose of cleaning, tuning, and regulating. If large and small pipes be planted together in such a manner that the former present a barrier in the way of the tuner reaching the latter, a frequent and "unnecessary touching or taking out of the pipes" will have to be resorted to, which, as Seidel truly observes, is injurious ; as pipes are soon bruised or bent. "Besides," he continues, "if a pipe, after having bee 1 taken out, is not replaced exactly in its former position, it will sound too flat or too high, too strong or too weak."

1223. With regard to the construction of the sound-boards, nearly all that was necessary has been said in a former chapter. The leathering of the table, which is so much dwelt upon in many foreign works on organ-bu'.ding, is almost universally considered by English organ-builders to be superfluous, if the table, sliders, and upper boards are accurately adjusted to one another.

Double grooves in the bass of large sound-boards advisable. 1224. If there are many stops on a Manual to be supplied, it is better to have two distinct grooves to each key in the bass octave, than one larger groove and one great pallet ; and for this reason the large pipes rapidly exhaust the wind from the groove, diminishing the pressure or the density of the air therein ; therefore, when drawn, they have the effect of flattening the pitch of the Mixtures, destroying their brightness, and of making the reeds speak slow. By introducing two grooves, the Unison and Double Diapasons and Principal can be placed on one groove, and the Twelfth, Fifteenth, Mixtures, and Reeds, on the other. The rollers would then, of course, be provided with two pallet-arms instead of one only ; or, if squares were used, their second arm should be furnished with a small cross-bar, to each end of which a pull-down would be attached. John England, who first introduced double grooves into English organs, used to perforate the sound-board bar that separated the two. Or two pallets, one at each end of the groove, might be employed. It is now a frequent custom to place the 16, 8, and 4 feet flue stops on one sound-board, the smaller flue stops on a second, and the reeds on a third, supplied by a heavy wind. The "trebles" are further placed on separate sound-boards, and blown by a stronger blast.

The roller-boards. 1225. The rollers should be so disposed that the tapped wires, buttons, hooks, &c., that communicate with them can be easily got at for purposes of regulation, renewal, &c., when occasion may require. Wooden rollers and arms are now generally cancelled in favour of those of iron, and some builders also bush the iron studs which support the rollers, i.e., line their perforations with cloth, or make the centre-pins work in leather buttons, to quiet the noise otherwise consequent on their motion.

The bellows. 1226. The bellows should be made of such dimensions that they will easily yield, and continue to give an abundant supply of wind, when all the Manuals are coupled together, with every stop drawn, and the fullest chords are played on the Manuals and Pedal. The first thing Sebastian Bach used to do, when requested to examine a new organ, was to draw out all the stops, and play on the full organ. He used to say, he must first know whether the instrument had good lungs. (Forkel's *Life of Bach*.) A copious supply of wind is more particularly necessary, in the first instance, if the organ is intended to receive subsequent additions. There should be no unsteadiness perceivable in the tone of the organ at the moment when the feeders commence and complete their work ; neither ought any clacking to be heard when the valves fall over the suckers in the feeders and the bottom-board ; nor should there be any sucking or gasping noise heard when the feeders are being replenished ; but which will be the case if the suckers are too few or too small. The feeders and blowing-action should also work with but little noise. Many organs have the Pedal as well as the Manual organs supplied from the same bellows. When this is the case, the tone of the Manual organs should remain perfectly firm and unaffected when any disjunct or staccato passage is being played on the Pedals.

1227. The reservoir of the bellows should of course have inverted ribs, counterbalances, and a waste pallet, which latter will cause the least noise if it be made to discharge the superfluous air into the feeders. The shape of the bellows is a matter of no importance; their proportions must necessarily be influenced in a great measure by local circumstances.

1228. As regards the situation for the bellows, the lower part of the organ near to the ground is the place usually assigned to them in modern English instruments. In German organs they are more frequently put outside the case; as they were indeed in many old English instruments. Where the necessary additional room can be spared, the latter arrangement is the most advantageous, as it allows so much more space for the convenient distribution of the mechanism, as well as admitting of more ready means of access to its several parts for purposes of regulation, repair, &c., besides which the free space then left is beneficial to the resonance of the organ. At Westminster Abbey the bellows are in two chambers under the organ, in the choir screen; at the Temple Church they are in a bellows room below; at St. Martin's-in-the-Fields, and at St. Philip's, Waterloo Place, they are placed in the belfry behind the organ. In many large modern organs the feeders and reservoirs are made quite distinct, and the former placed in some convenient situation outside the organ, where they are blown by one of Joy's hydraulic machines, while the latter are placed close to the sound-boards. This is the arrangement at King's College Chapel, Cambridge. In many large instruments, where there is plenty of room, a special reservoir is placed near to every sound-board, which is an admirable arrangement.

1229. If the bellows are to produce different pressures of wind—to do which they will require to be furnished with upper reservoirs—much additional height will be required for bellows room. Under these circumstances, and if they are to be placed under the sound-boards, the latter must be well elevated; or the bellows might even be kept out of the organ altogether.

The wind-trunks. 1230. The wind-trunks should be large enough to convey an ample supply to the wind-chests; otherwise it will be of little use, the bellows yielding a good quantity. Concussion bellows should also be applied, if found necessary; but if the wind-trunks are capacious, and are not very long, such appliances will probably be less required. If not absolutely necessary, they are almost better omitted than introduced. The writer is acquainted with an instance of a concussion bellows being attached to a new organ, in obedience to one of the conditions of the contract; and of its disturbing the wind, which, before its introduction, was perfectly steady. It is a question whether concussion bellows are not occasionally made too large. When it is seen how small a bellows, in the shape of a tremulant, will disturb the wind, it seems that one four or five times the size can scarcely be necessary to correct the far less accidental disturbance that would be likely to occur in a well-winded organ.

The Swell-box. 1231. The Swell-box should not be less than 2 inches in thickness; and it would be the better for being $2\frac{1}{2}$, particularly if it be a large one. The edges of the shutters should be faced with leather, cloth, or felt, to make them bed closely and shut in the tone. Walker lines the interior of his swell-boxes with very stout brown paper, about $\frac{1}{8}$ of an inch thick, to further subdue the tone when the shutters are closed.

The scale for the pipe-work. 1232. The general dimensions of an organ containing a given list of stops are influenced by no one thing more than by the scale adopted for the bass pipes. Or, to put the fact in another shape, no single circumstance affects the question as to the number of stops which may be satisfactorily placed in a given space, more than the wide or narrow measure selected for the large pipes. Continental organs of moderate dimensions ordinarily contain from 4 to 6 Pedal stops ; while those of the first class frequently have from 15 to 18. (See all the Foreign Specifications, in the Appendix.) To any one who might be led to calculate the standing-room of such instruments by the amount of space necessary to accommodate a single English stop of the scale to which many sets of "Pedal pipes" have been made, it would seem that such organs must occupy a site almost sufficient for a small church. Such, however, is not the case. It was stated in the first chapter of this division that in Germany most of the Pedal stops are properly viewed as simply "Basses" to some of the Manual stops. This being the case, their scales exhibit but a very slight advance on those of the Manuals ; one pipe only frequently being the extent of the difference. The 16-feet Open basses of Continental organs, moreover, are frequently made of wood, as in English. Of the three fine instruments by Silbermann at Strasbourg two contain "Principal Basses" of this material (see Foreign Specifications) ; and of these organs the latter has two open wood Pedal stops of 16 feet ; yet the largest of these only measures 9 inches by 11. In some very large German organs, having about 16 stops on the Pedal, and including two 16-feet open wood stops, independently of the Violone, the scale of one is sometimes advanced, and the stop hence called " Major-Bass," *i.e.*, *Great*-Bass ; but even the CCC pipe of this stop seldom exceeds 10 inches in width by 12 in depth. In two instances only could the writer trace the existence of stops of greater calibre in foreign organs. The "Contra Violone" at Cologne Cathedral (Foreign Specifications) measures 12 inches across the mouth, and a stop approaching the scale of English Pedal pipes occurs in the St. Eustace organ at Paris. (Foreign Specifications.)

1233. In English organs, even of ordinary size, the CCC Pedal pipe not unfrequently measures 18 inches in width and 20 inches in depth : some examples are as much as 2 feet in depth.

1234. Then, of the Continental scales of longer wooden pipes ; in the organ at St. Paul's, Frankfort (Foreign Specifications), built by the famous Walker, of Ludwigsburg, which has two Pedal stops of 32 feet, one measures 11 inches across the mouth, the other 15¾ inches. The CCCC wood pipe in the Cathedral organ at Bremen (Foreign Specifications), and in St. Mary's Church, Wismar (Foreign Specifications), both by Schulze, measure exactly 12 inches each across the mouth. Comparing these dimensions with the English scale given above, it is seen that the 16-feet Pedal pipe, as it exists in many of our ordinary-sized organs, exceeds in bulk the 32-feet pipe of cathedral and other first-class instruments of the Continent.

1235. The vast disparity of breadth in proportion to length between English and foreign organ pipes naturally suggests these three questions—(1) How have pipes of such huge bulk come into use ? (2) What may be their effect ? and (3) Is that effect such as will justify the allotment of so much space, not easily spared, to their accommodation ?

1236. The first open wood Pedal pipes made in England were those added by Avery to the organ in Westminster Abbey. They were "Unisons ;" and, from that circumstance, being designed simply to reinforce the Manual Diapasons in the bass, no doubt proved sufficient for that purpose. What may have been the scale of those pipes the writer has not been able to ascertain ; but, subsequently, the measure for the GG unison Pedal pipe became, and for several years continued to ' ordinarily, 12 inches for the depth ; that is to say, the 10⅔ feet pipe was equal in bulk to the 16-feet major bass pipe of Continental organs. When Pedal pipes came to be altered in pitch from Unisons to Doubles, a single set, of the scale and power before in use, was incapable of asserting its independence.

1237. As, in former days, the compass of the Manuals was extended downwards, as a primitive method of obtaining from it deeper tones, so the calibre of the "Pedal pipes" was now augmented, gradually, from little to more, in the hope of obtaining from them the effect of a proper Pedal bass, until they at length assumed the dimensions already quoted. The huge scale, therefore, originated from a correct feeling, namely, a consciousness of the necessity for a Pedal bass, proportioned in power to the Manual departments of the organ, but accompanied at the same time by a misconception as to the proper method of carrying that feeling into effect. A "Bass" to the entire organ was attempted to be forced from a single rank of pipes, and with astonishing success, had one only, and that of an unvarying kind, been required from the Pedal. The effect of such a Pedal stop was certainly most powerful and commanding, but not *amalgamating*. It formed no suitable bass to any one stop in the organ. As a Pedal continuation to the Manual Diapason, it was without the true, serious, calm, deliberate, and mixing characteristics of that stop. It was also too powerful and predominating for the numerous softer effects in constant requisition in all organs, and only appeared to be in proportion when used in conjunction with the loud organ ; but the employment of the full organ being the exception, rather than the rule, the heavy sound of the great stop constituted, in the great majority of cases, a very unsuitable bass. Then, with regard to standing room, the large scale Pedal pipes in some cases occupied as much room as would have accommodated *three* 16-feet Pedal stops made to a more strictly correct measure ; and it must be obvious that a Pedal organ possessing an Open Diapason, Stopped Diapason, and Trombone, would have formed a far more efficient and *tractable* bass to an instrument.

1238. Experiments subsequently made, together with a closer acquaintance with the Continental principles of the art, conduced to make evident the nature and extent of the original misconception to which reference has already been made ; and to bring into clear view the true means by which it was to be rectified and superseded. These included a reduction of the measure previously adopted for Pedal *pipes*, and an increase in the number of independent Pedal *stops*. Among the first to revise their Pedal bass scales were the late Mr. Hill and Mr. T. Robson. Mr. Hill, who had built a greater number of large organs than any other man in England, and had therefore given the large Pedal pipe scale the most extended trial, thought it not inconsistent with the high position and character as a true artist to scrutinise his former work, and to materially modify the previously received proportions for large wood pipes. Added to this, he insisted on the importance of securing several stops instead of one ; an honourable course, which he ceased not to follow stedfastly and consistently up to the time of his death.

1239. Reverting to the scales of Continental stops before given, some of them will be viewed as being extremely small. The quantity of tone, however, produced from the largest of them is really most astonishing. Being copiously winded, they speak with a promptness and fulness that is highly satisfactory. A very careful trial and comparison of the smaller-scaled open wood stops of Continental organs with the huge scale Pedal pipes of English instruments, however, leads to the firm impression that the most useful scale for musical purposes lies between the two. And that such a scale is equal to the production of the best effects is exemplified in the excellent 32-feet open pipes of the West-minster Abbey organ, made by Mr. Hill, the sound of which is sufficient to fill the Minster, yet does not overpower even a single voice, which is detected the moment it is added to that of the other stops by the richness which it imparts, yet does not obtrude itself, but on the contrary, blends in the happiest manner with the sound of the rest of the organ. The scale of the 16-feet pipe of this stop is 10 inches by 11½ inches, which is a slight advance on Silbermann's Strasbourg scale, already quoted, and of the 32-feet pipe, 19 inches by 22 inches, which is a little in advance of the Frankfort scale. For a unison Pedal Open, the German major bass scale already given, namely 10 inches by 12 inches for the 16-feet pipe, was adopted by Robson in his organ in Trinity Church, Sloane Street, where, for a moderate-sized organ, it answered as well as could possibly be desired. At West-minster Abbey, where the Great organ is extended down to CCC, to serve as a substitute for an independent Pedal, the 16-feet pipe of the Pedal Open Diapason measures 13½ inches by 16 inches. This, although far below the old Pedal pipe measure, yet forms an admirable and ample "Major Bass" scale to the rest of the organ.

1240. Then, with regard to large metal pipes, great variation has likewise, at different periods, been made in their scale, also, in English instruments. The organ in St. Paul's Cathedral had two Open Diapasons, part of the original work of Father Smith, on the Great Manual. The article in the *Musical Gazette*, so often quoted, says of them, "They have always been esteemed the finest Schmidt ever made, and are regular and uniform in the quality of tone throughout." The largest of the two 8-feet or CC pipes of those stops measures somewhat less than 6 inches in diameter. The original FFF pipe at the Temple was 7 inches in diameter, and the largest of the two original CCC or 16-feet pipes at St. Paul's is a little under 10 inches across. Towards the latter end of the last century Green effected a considerable increase on the measurement above given. This was before the introduction of Pedal pipes (which either originated with Avery or about his time), and no doubt was intended by Green to impart additional weight to the bass of his organs. The CC pipe he increased in diameter from 6 inches to 8 inches, his GG to 11 inches, and his FFF from 7 inches to 12 inches; that is, to 2 inches beyond Smith's scale for the 16-feet pipe. Avery and England, who succeeded Green, availing themselves of the advantage which a set of small Pedal pipes presented, reduced the scale again for the bass of the metal Diapasons.

1241. In specifications for modern organs, even those for small churches, it is sometimes stipulated that the CC metal pipe shall measure 8 inches in diameter, or, in other words, shall be wider than Smith's large cathedral scale for the FFF pipe. As a matter that materially affects the question of room, it is worthy of consideration whether the advantages of so greatly an enlarged scale are com-mensurate with the increased quantity of space required to accommodate pipes of such a measure. Metal pipes of so great a scale no doubt produce a somewhat heavier, thick, and more ponderous tone than others of less bulk, but not so close, firm, and *clean* a sound. There is always sufficient difficulty in obtaining an even tone from a stop that increases in scale gradually from the lowest pipe up to the top one. It was, in fact, this difficulty which led Muller of Amsterdam and Batz of Utrecht to apply duplicate pipes to the trebles of their organs, and Cavaillé-Coll to adopt a heavier wind in the upper part of the Manual compass to overcome it. But if the scale be enlarged from the tenor *downwards* also, and a more powerful tone *really* be produced in that direction, it seems clear that the tendency to an inequality in the general effect must be increased. It is well known that, for richness, fulness, and power, the bass of Smith's Diapasons have never been surpassed. If they ever failed, as they occasionally did, it was in the upper part. Moreover, it is by no means a matter of course that an enlargement of scale will result in the production of a tone of an improved quality, as the following extract will show. The *Christian Remembrancer* for October, 1833, page 624, speaking of the Temple organ, says, "It is somewhat remarkable that Schmidt should be able to produce so ponderous a tone in the lower notes of the Open Diapason out of so small a scale pipe, the FFF measuring only 7 inches in diameter, whereas the same pipes in Green's organ at Greenwich Hospital measures 12 inches, and does not give so fine a note. The fact is, when the scale is increased the pipes then no longer remain members of the "Principal-work," but, from that enlargement, merge into the "Flute-work," and at the same time also cease to retain that clear and pure character of tone which is so closely associated with the idea of a true Diapason, and which then is exchanged for a heavier and less silvery tone. This refers to the large pipes. As the "Diapason-measure" is exceeded higher up in the musical scale, the cornet-scale is approached. For instance, if a Pedal Principal were to be made to a much-increased measure, so that its middle c^1 pipe (2 feet) were to be advanced from about 2 inches to nearly $2\frac{1}{4}$ inches in diameter, it would produce a tone, powerful and broad indeed, but utterly unlike that of a member of the Diapason-work.

1242. It has already been mentioned that the largest of the two 16-feet pipes at St. Paul's Cathedral does not measure quite 10 inches in diameter, neither do those made by Cavaillé-Coll, in his magnificent new organs at the Madeleine and St. Vincent de Paul, at Paris. And of upwards of twenty examples in German organs which the writer measured, not one exceeded 10 inches across, while the smallest was $9\frac{1}{3}$ inches only. The corresponding pipe in modern English work has occasionally been made as much as 14 inches across, that is, within an inch of the 32-feet pipe at Haarlem, which measures but 15 inches over. There seems, however, to be no essential advantage arising from the use of such very large scales, while the waste of room which they involve is very great.

1243. The subject of the scale of large Open wood and metal pipes has been entered into thus fully, because those who have to decide on the comparative merits of different specifications are sometimes apt to attach undue value to those which promise "good bumping scales," and think lightly of others which do not— to consider the necessity for great scaled pipes as an unquestionable fact, and their advantages as being beyond doubt.

1244. Stopped wood pipes present a no less variation in regard to scale than do those of the Open kind. The ordinary English measure for the CCC Bourdon or Double Stopped Diapason pipe, 16-feet tone, is $7\frac{1}{4}$ inches in width, by 9 inches in depth. Occasionally this scale has been increased to 12 inches in depth, but it has seldom been much lessened in England. The Swiss scale for Stopped pipes is somewhat larger than the first of the above-mentioned English measures; *i.e.*, it is about $9\frac{1}{2}$ inches by 11 inches for the CCC pipe. In some modern German organs the scale of the large Stopped pipes has been much reduced, and that without involving any loss of tone, so that a great saving of room has been effected. The unreduced quantity of tone from the narrower pipe is secured by allowing a more copious supply of wind to enter the foot, instead of shutting part of it off by plugging, making a wider wind-way, and by cutting the mouth high. In this way a perfectly firm, plump, and pure tone is obtained from a CCC pipe, measuring $6\frac{1}{4}$ inches by $4\frac{3}{4}$. A Bourdon of the above scale occurs on the Great Manual of the German organ in the Exchange Room at Northampton, and produces a remarkably full tone. The smaller scaled pipes present the additional advantage of being more easily planted over their own wind on the sound-board. It should be mentioned that the pipes of a stop, made to the German scale just referred to, sometimes decrease in size or bulk more gradually than is common with English scales; that is to say, the scale is not reduced to half measure until it has reached the pipe that sounds the interval of an *eleventh* from the pipe whence the calculation commences. The following therefore presents an outline of the scale in question :—

GREAT MANUAL BOURDON SCALE.

Pipe.	Depth.	Width.	Diameter of foot-hole.
CCC.	$6\frac{1}{8}$ inches . .	$4\frac{5}{8}$ inches . .	$1\frac{5}{8}$ inch.
GG	$4\frac{3}{4}$ inches . .	$3\frac{1}{4}$ inches . .	$1\frac{1}{2}$ inch.
CC	$3\frac{5}{8}$ inches . .	$2\frac{13}{16}$ inches . .	$1\frac{3}{16}$ inch.
FF	$3\frac{1}{16}$ inches . .	$2\frac{7}{16}$ inches . .	$1\frac{1}{8}$ inch.
Tenor c. . . .	$2\frac{3}{16}$ inches . .	$2\frac{11}{16}$ inches . .	$\frac{15}{16}$ inch.
Middle b flat. .	$1\frac{1}{2}$ inch . .	$1\frac{3}{16}$ inch . .	$\frac{7}{8}$ inch.

1245. The height of mouth for a 3-inch wind is, on the average, about equal to half the width.

1246. Another class of covered stops, producing a delicate tone, and called, in Germany, Lieblich Gedackt (Lovely-toned Stopped Diapason), is made to a smaller scale again than the Bourdon. It occurs in many foreign instruments; and is also frequently introduced by Schulze to form the Unison and Double Stopped Diapasons of his Choir or Swell organs. Its scale decreases in the same ratio as that of the Bourdon already noticed.

LIEBLICH GEDACKT SCALE, FOR CHOIR OR SWELL COVERED STOPS.

Pipe.	Depth.	Width.	Diameter of foot-hole.
CCC . . .	5 inches . .	$3\frac{3}{8}$ inches . .	$1\frac{1}{8}$ of an inch.
GG	$3\frac{1}{2}$ inches . .	$2\frac{11}{16}$ inches . .	$\frac{11}{12}$ of an inch.
CC	3 inches . .	$2\frac{1}{16}$ inches . .	$\frac{3}{4}$ of an inch.
FF	$2\frac{1}{2}$ inches . .	$1\frac{11}{16}$ inch . .	$\frac{11}{16}$ of an inch.
Tenor c . .	$1\frac{3}{4}$ inch . .	$1\frac{3}{8}$ inch . .	$\frac{9}{16}$ of an inch.
Middle b flat	$1\frac{1}{4}$ inch . .	$1\frac{1}{16}$ of an inch . .	$\frac{3}{8}$ of an inch.

1247. The peculiar value of the Lieblich Gedackt scale for the Swell-covered stops consists more particularly in the comparatively small amount of standing and speaking room required for the accommodation of pipes made to that measure. The CCC pipe is scarcely any wider or deeper than the CC pipe of some English scales, that is to say, the lowest pipe of a Double Stopped Diapason made to the Lieblich Gedackt scale does not call for more standing room than the lowest pipe of some Unison Stopped Diapasons made to the English scale. It consequently admits of the entire stop being placed inside the Swell-box, whereby its whole range derives the advantage and benefit of the crescendo and diminuendo; whereas, on account of the size of the bass pipes of a Bourdon made to the usual English scale, the lowest octave of the stop has generally to be placed outside the box, even in the largest Swells. Examples of Lieblich Gedackts, as Choir organ stops, of 16 and 8 feet tone, occur on the upper Manual of the organ at the Exchange, Northampton; and of 16, 8, and 4 feet tone at the Temple.

1248. It will now be seen why a German organ should not cover the great space that might at first have been imagined. The lowest Open Stopped and Pedal pipes of an ordinary GG organ frequently equal in bulk the 16-feet pipes of a German organ.

1249. There is one thing in connection with the question of large and small scales that is well worth mentioning in this place. It does not answer to plant large scale Bourdons semitonally. This fact was proved by an organ-builder in the following manner. The CCC pipe was voiced, put in its place, and tuned; then the CCC♯ was completed in a similar manner, when it was found that the CCC pipe had become uncertain and windy in its speech. The DDD was next added, and, having in its turn been tuned and voiced, the CCC♯ was tried, and that was found to be spoiled by the DDD, as the CCC had been by the CCC♯. Four more pipes, up to FFF♯, were added, one by one, and every successive pipe destroyed the speech of the one below it. There was not a single exception; the only good sound was from the FFF♯ pipe which completed the series. It was shown by this experiment, (1) that the speech of a Stopped pipe is not affected by the note its *semitone below*, but by the *semitone above ;* and (2) that the vibration at the mouth of a large scale Stopped pipe has an influence upon the pipe its semitone below, that does not appear in *small* scale Stopped pipes; and it is argued from this that the semitonal arrangement *and* the large scale English Stopped-work could not be satisfactorily combined. If this be true, it is curious that, in the system of semitonal arrangement, the scale should be required to be small, and for two very opposite reasons (at least, having no intermediate relation); 1st, that they may be planted without loss of room; and 2nd, that an acoustical phenomenon or law requires them to be so, *if* planted semitonally; and, of course, it would be absurd to set out a sound-board semitonally to simplify the action, and then by conveyances, groove-boards, or such like means, to plant the pipes otherwise.

The materials for the pipe-work.   1250. The different metals, woods, and compounds used in the construction of organ pipes were enumerated in a previous chapter. In the specification for which the organ-builder's estimate is afterwards to be obtained, it ought to be distinctly specified what materials are desired to be used in the formation of the pipe-work; which stops, if any, are to be made of pure tin, which of metal, and which of wood; also, if some are designed to be made partly of tin or metal, and the remainder of wood, on what note the metal pipes are to be discontinued and the wood ones to commence; and lastly, the proportions of tin and lead to be employed in the composition of the metal. One of the particulars on which the ultimate cost of an organ rightly depends is the standard of the metal that is to be used, and the gross weight of it to be embodied in the instrument; and an organ-builder who proposes to employ tin or the best metal, in good quantity, must necessarily require a higher sum for his work than he would demand, were a less valuable metal and a smaller quantity of it understood to be all that was desired. An estimate, therefore, that would appear to be a high one, were not these circumstances to be taken into consideration, will often prove to be both just and reasonable when it is more closely examined. But English organ-builders are by no means agreed on certain questions relating to metal pipes; some considering that "substance" in material is of more importance than quality, while others view quality as of more consequence than substance. Preparatory to offering any observations on these points, it may be observed that the bodies of metal pipes should *vibrate*, but not *tremble;* that is to say, they should vibrate from the natural elasticity of the metal or compound of which they are made, but not tremble from thinness of material or weakness of texture.   Of the two materials which form the chief ingredients in organ pipe metal tin is light, firm, and elastic ; and lead, heavy, weak, and comparatively inelastic.

1251. Strictly speaking, it is the periodical motion of the column of air that is within a pipe, rather than the pipe which encloses it, that is the source of the tone.   The substance and quality of the walls of the pipes, however, have a great deal to do with the strength and character of the sound produced ; and in this way, if the material of which a pipe is made be thin in substance, it will be weaker, more pliant, and consequently less impatient to return to its state of repose.   The pipe therefore will not bear much blowing, as, in that case, its sides would not be strong enough to resist or counterbalance the power of the wind ; and would tremble, and produce a blurring sound.   Being thus unable to resist any *violent* excitation of the column of air within, a thin pipe can only be *slightly* blown, and hence will produce only a light tone. If thin material, however, be pure tin, or good spotted metal, it will on that account be firmer ; and the sharp and rapid vibration of a pipe made from such sheets will cause the tone to be of a more refined and silvery quality.   The pipes of a Gamba are the better for being thin and of fine metal.

1252. A pipe made of thick metal will bear much more blowing, without its vibratory motion being exaggerated into a trembling ; consequently it will be capable of producing a much fuller tone than a thin pipe of the same scale. For instance, the stronger the organ-wind, or the greater the quantity of it entering a pipe through a larger foot-hole, the more powerfully will the column of air within the pipe be excited, and consequently the greater will be its friction against the sides of the pipe.   If the strength and firmness of the pipe have been correspondingly increased, it will successfully resist the influence of the stronger current ; the whole resulting in the production of a clearer and better tone.   If, added to its substance, the metal of the pipe be compounded chiefly of tin, this will cause it to be firmer still, and therefore more *resisting* at first ; but if fully excited by the more copious blowing which it will bear, it will prove more elastic, and more impatient to return to its state of rest ; and, from the great strength and power of its vibrations, will produce a sound remarkable for clearness as well as for a ringing character.   A heavy pipe is therefore good for a Diapason.

1253. It has been customary to attribute the distinction in the tone of the organs of different builders to the voicing and winding of the pipes, which is of course true to a great extent ; but the substance and quality of the metal are by no means unimportant agents in the matter.   Father Smith used metal of fine quality and of great substance, usually, for his front pipes.   His inside pipes were of a metal of less high standard, but were very thick and heavy.   Green employed good spotted metal, but of less thickness ; and Smith could no more have obtained Green's light, playful, and musical tone from his thick pipes, than could Green have produced Smith's powerful and ringing tone from his thin pipes.   Green was aware of this, particularly in regard to bass pipes : hence his great enlargement of the scale ; though, from the thinness of their material, they would not bear so much blowing.

1254. But, whatever difference of opinion may exist as to whether and to what extent the tone is influenced by the metal or compound used, there can be no doubt of the greater *durability* of pipes formed of tin, or chiefly so, over every other composition that has been commonly employed for the purpose. The metal used by Harris and Smith, for the chief part of the pipe-work of their organs, contained a great proportion of tin among its ingredients ; and the present condition of the original pipes of many of the instruments constructed by those makers fully confirms the correctness of the opinion as to the lasting character of organ pipes made, in the first instance, of metal of good quality and thick in substance. Harris's organ, at St. Sepulchre's, was built in 1667 ; Smith's, at the Temple, in 1685 ; and that at St. Paul's Cathedral, by the last-mentioned builder (the front pipes of which still remain), in 1695. The comparative durability of metal compounds, of various kinds, was well illustrated in an organ which passed not long since into the hands of an organ-builder. The organ had been made rather more than a century ; and while the original pipes, of spotted metal, were found to be quite sound, the feet of others of *subsequent* introduction, formed of inferior metal, had been so attacked by the strong acid in the wood of which the upper-boards were made, that the apex of the feet of several of them was completely eaten away.

1255. Other evidences of the great durability of substantial pipes of tin, or good metal, are afforded by the great age of several Continental organs, the dates of the erection of which are authenticated. The organ in the Cathedral at Constance, in Switzerland, was built in 1518 ; that in the Cathedral of Freiburg, in Bresgau, in 1520; that in the Cathedral at Antwerp, in 1645 ; and that in the Cathedral at Lucerne, in Switzerland, in the year 1651. The last has recently been replaced by a new organ. The particulars of numerous other old organs are contained in the Appendix ; but, from the *approximate* age only having been ascertained, they cannot be quoted here.

1256. Moreover, the writer put the question distinctly to a German organ-builder, how long he considered an organ ought to last ; and he gave it as his deliberate opinion that, if well constructed, out of the best and most substantial materials, and taken the best care of, it ought to continue good for 400 years. An organ lasting for so protracted a period will no doubt appear strange to many ; but the undoubted age of numerous Continental instruments, together with the good state of preservation the pipes of many of them are in, fully justify the above calculation ; while the fact of certain of the stops of old organs being in some cases retained in their successors, as at Cologne and Liège, further supports it.

1257. That pipe-work made of metal of good quality and substance retains its fulness, brilliance, and "ring," for a very lengthened period, is a fact fully borne out by the effect of numerous old English organs. Age also may have exercised some influence in imparting to the tone that peculiar richness, purity, and healthy clearness for which many old instruments are so remarkable ; although, as there are good, bad, and indifferent old instruments, and in some cases by the same maker, it cannot always have had so much to do with the production of the peculiar mellowness that some imagine.

1258. And if time really effects so much for an organ, how important must it be to secure the use of the most durable metal for its pipe-work ; otherwise, when the mellowing hand of time ought to be bringing the instrument to perfection, the pipe-work will have seen its best days, and be becoming useless when it ought to be enhancing in value. Zinc is now much used for large metal beyond 4 feet speaking length, and, when properly prepared, is very efficacious. It is particularly useful for organs that are to be exported, as the pipes do not flatten during the journey.

1259. While, in some instances, the scale has been increased for the large metal pipes, it has been decreased for the small ones forming the "chorus." When the scale of the harmonic series of stops is "kept up," and the pipes are well blown, a tone is produced that is remarkable for fulness, breadth, and power.   When, on the contrary, their measure is reduced more rapidly, the small stops are less full and more penetrating in tone, and require the frequent, or even constant, addition of a reed stop to modify their keenness and impart strength to the sound.   In some German organs, both codes of scales are adopted ; that is to say, a rather large scale is followed for the harmonic series of stops, including the *first* Mixture, and a smaller for the second Compound stop ; the 2-feet pipe (c¹) of the latter being usually of the same diameter as the e¹ or f¹ pipe of the Diapason, *i.e.*, of Geigen Principal scale.   The second stop is then sometimes called " Scharf," or " Cymbal," either of which names would suggest the idea of a ringing, sharp-toned stop.   The third Compound stop is usually a Cornet, so that on many German Great Manuals will be found, first, a Mixture of nearly full Principal scale, a second rather below, and a third one above that measure.

1260. Wood pipe-work is introduced to a greater proportionate extent in modern than it was in old organs, as it effects a judicious saving in the expense. Many of the largest pipes in the Pedal organ are almost invariably made of this material ; so also is some of the Flute-work of recent invention or introduction into this country.   The Stopped Diapason and Flute stops of modern organs, too, are frequently made of wood ; so are the bass pipes of the Open Diapason ; while, in old instruments, the treble of the former and the bass of the latter were more commonly made of metal.   When long wood pipes are made to a small scale, they are capable of producing a very close imitation of the " metal tone," and in that case form a most efficient substitute for good metal pipes, in the bass, when the latter are not attainable.   In some foreign organs a wood bass of this kind is united to a metal treble so successfully, that it is scarcely possible to trace on what note the one material is discontinued and the other commenced.

The price of the organ.   1261. We have now arrived at the last, but by no means the least important question for consideration, namely, the *price* of the organ, This matter necessarily rests, to some extent, with the builder chosen, but remains to a much greater degree in the hands of the purchasers.

1262. From what has been explained in the preceding sections it must be obvious that there is a durable, complete, but *costly* way of building an organ, and an unsubstantial, incomplete, and *cheap* way of making it.   It is also equally evident that organ-building may be viewed as a calling of high art, or treated merely as a matter of business ; and it will be exercised in either the former or the latter spirit, according to circumstances.

1263. Under the most extreme circumstances, the organ-builder must *exist* by the exercise of his calling ; but at the same time it is only consistent with the proper feeling of ambition that actuates every genuine artist, that he would prefer *also* rearing specimens of his art to which he might point with pride, as well as his successors for generations after him.   But this second condition must obviously depend on the means placed at his disposal.

1264. On being applied to to make proposals for the construction and erection of an organ, an organ-builder may draw up a specification for an instrument of given contents, and, intending to use certain materials, and to devote much attention to various matters of detail and finish which cannot be specified in an estimate without extending to the length of a pamphlet, place his charge at, say, £1000.   He may, however, have good reason to know that that figure will ensure him the *loss* of the "order;" accordingly, without altering one of the *written* conditions of his contract, or foregoing one penny of his own fair profit, but simply by reducing the standard or substance, or both, of his metal, and paying less regard to the minute excellencies of his work, he can, "to meet circumstances," at once lower his estimate from £1,000 to £850. It is in this sense that "the price of the organ" is said to remain so much in the hands of the *purchasers*. But when the organ is completed, will it rank as highly, *as a work of art*, as it was originally intended by its designer it should do? Will it reflect more than *temporary* credit on its builder? A few years pass, and *the organ itself* probably solves these problems. And, as though to reduce its existence to the shortest span, the crowded organ has perhaps been consigned to a site bounded by cold or damp walls, where the leather-work has quickly rotted, the brass-work corroded, the iron-work rusted, the glue soddened, and the accurate adjustment of the several parts of the wood-work, by swelling, been disturbed. Crooked or bruised metal pipes, cracked wooden pipes, running sound-boards, twisted rollers, double frictional resistance opposed to the fingers at the keys, and numerous other such fatalities, too frequently indicate what are and must ever be among the most probable distinctivenesses of the "cheap organ." Nor is the builder exactly to be held responsible for all this, if he gave timely advice and warning.

1265. So far it has been shown by how easy a course the price of an organ of a given size may be materially reduced, to accommodate the estimate to particular circumstances. But the process may be reversed; *i.e.*, the size of an organ may undergo great *apparent* increase, when "a grand organ" is desired for the price of one of ordinary dimensions.

1266. An organ with, say, fifty stops will cost either about £1,000 or nearly £2,000, according to circumstances. If its specification be drawn up in a spirit consistent with the magnitude of the work, as *implied* by the number of its stops—if the stops chosen are introduced mostly in a "complete" form, and if a just proportion be observed in the distribution of the stops between the Manuals and Pedal—the cost of such an instrument will certainly approach the higher of the two rough estimates above given. But then it will also be a genuine specimen of high art organ-building, carried out in its amplitude and integrity. Among the fundamental laws of that system are these: if a great Manual be furnished with sixteen stops, these should include at least two double stops, one of which must be a Double Open Diapason throughout. Or, to follow the German form of expression more closely, the Great organ should be a "16-feet Manual." Then all the Manuals—by which is meant the *organs* as well as the *keys*—should be of equal, that is CC range; and the Pedal moreover should, as a *minimum* proportion, have at least one-third as many stops as the Great Manual.

1267. These and other governing rules of the science, however, can only be recognised, or, at least, followed, when "the price" will admit of their being so. But it too frequently happens that the approximate price for the organ has already been fixed, and the hoped-for number of stops also considered; in which case, all that is left for an organ-builder to do, who desires to secure the order, is to prepare a design that will as little as possible run counter to these performed expectations. He sees clearly that a plan for an instrument on the most artistic principle will exclude itself by its appended estimate; that there is every probability of the prize falling into the hands of one who can prepare the most "promising" specification; therefore ideas about "art" must subserve to those relating to "business."

1268. Nor can organ-builders fairly be held accountable for adopting the obvious alternative thus imposed upon them, and which amounts to this in effect, if not in words : he who will prepare the specification that seems to promise the most extensive instrument for the stated terms—who, in fact, can the most successfully make what would form a smaller organ look like a larger upon paper—will stand the best chance of securing "the order." And the ingenuity sometimes displayed in estimates drawn up to meet such expectations almost calls for admiration. First, instead of the specification stating that the proposed instrument shall be built on the German *system*, which would be embodying a great deal, all it will promise, if it be prudently drawn up, is that it shall be made to the German *compass*, which is, at the same time, the old English compass of two centuries ago, and implies but little. Next, several of the stops are planned to draw in *halves*, every such divided stop thus appearing as *two ;* or they are introduced in an incomplete form to meet other incomplete stops.* In this manner a great step is made towards securing the necessary array of " stops," many persons judging of the excellence of an organ by the number of its *handles* rather than by the excellence and completeness of what those handles *govern.* The *couplers* even, to swell the number, are sometimes enumerated as " stops." Then the important distinction between " standard size " and " size of tone " is overlooked, and the two portions of the Stopped Diapason, which together form in reality but one stop of 8-feet *tone*, in consequence bear the aspect of two stops of 8 *feet.* The Bourdon, also, if divided, appears as two stops of 16 *feet.* In this manner the stops in question, and by consequence the department to which they belong, are left open to a flattering estimate of their real dimensions.† The *one* Sesquialtera of V ranks, again, which is to be found in all the most important organs of Germany, as well as those of Bridge, Byfield, Harris, and Snetzler, has to be made to draw as two or even three stops. Then the Swell *organ,* which is essentially of English invention and development, and is more highly and justly appreciated in this country than in any other in Europe, is a department in the construction of which an organ-builder takes peculiar pride and interest ; this must be cut short at tenor c, which denudation deprives the Swell of its finest octave, though at the same time it affects a saving of nearly £100 in the cost of that department alone, in the instance of a design for a large Swell, and must therefore be resorted to as one means of keeping down the price of the instrument. The Swell *Manual,* indeed, perhaps runs " throughout," though that is of little value without its proper pipes. Numerous small, inexpensive, and incomplete stops, again, find admission, particularly in the Choir organ, which assist in making up the required number at no great outlay ; while many large and costly ones are excluded, to bring the instrument within the narrow bounds prescribed by the

---

* As a matter of fact, it may be mentioned that two of the modern organs that are the most free from half and incomplete stops are those in the church of St. Mary at Hill, and St. Walburgh's Catholic Church, Preston, both by the late Mr. Hill. The former has but four such stops among a series of thirty ; the second, not one stop of broken range among thirty stops. Many other builders are now equally averse to the half-stop system.

† It has already been explained that it is not the *tone* of the deepest *sounding* covered stop, but the "standard length " of the largest stop of the Open Diapason species, that fixes the size of a Manual or Pedal organ. Among other instruments, of which the Great organ department is a 16-feet Manual in the strict sense of the term, must be classed those at St. Paul's, by Willis ; and at Buxton Road and Highfield Chapels, Huddersfield, by Robson and Walker.

H H

stipulated terms. In this manner the admirable rule which lies at the very foundation of the German and French *systems* of organ-building—that the Pedal shall have, at the least, one-third as many stops as the Great Manual—and which is specially intended to check all excess in small or incomplete stops, as well as the slighting of large and more important ones, is treated as though it had no existence. By the above and other such means, a specification for an organ of almost any number of stops—*i.e.*, handles—may be provided, to suit almost any sum that may be named. But it cannot be supposed that any organ-builder who has a real love for his art can *prefer* building an instrument according to so unhealthy a system, however readily he may *consent* to do so. Yet, despite the discouraging influences under which it has been sometimes carried on, organ-building has nevertheless progressed marvellously within the last fifteen years, particularly in respect to those mechanical details which ensure quietness in the action generally, and which relate to lightness and promptness in the touch of large instruments, as well as in the selection and variety of the stops ; and in regard to the completeness of the compass of the stops, and the excellence of the metal used in their conformation, great "progress" has also been made, particularly by some of the younger firms, by *going back* to the customs of a century or more since. These latter returns, it is but reasonable to hope, are accompanied by a corresponding return to something akin to the fair and liberal terms paid to the artists of former times. What these might have been may be gathered from the following extracts, taken quite at random, from a list of many which were ready to hand. It is recorded that Father Smith had 1,000 guineas for the organ (about 20 stops) at the Temple Church, and 500 more for the case ; for the St. Paul's Cathedral organ (about 28 stops), £2,000 ; and for that in Durham Cathedral (17 stops), £700 and the old organ. For the Westminster Abbey organ (21 stops), Schrider had £1,000 ; and Green, for the organ at Greenwich Hospital (26 stops), £1,000, exclusive of the case. Harris had for the St. Patrick's Cathedral organ, Dublin (13 stops), £505. Then, for a single stop, Byfield received £50 for the Trumpet in the cathedral organ at Chichester. It is, indeed, true that most of the stops in the organs above mentioned were "whole" stops, and not only so, but were even beyond the full necessary CC range. Still, after making an ample reduction for the costly extra notes below, a sum remains that is far beyond what an English organ-builder is sometimes supposed to be fairly entitled to in the present day for a similar amount of work. We need not wonder, then, at the completeness, so far as they went, goodness of material, excellence of finish, beauty of tone, and durability of old instruments made under such favourable auspices.

1269. For the organ in the church of St. Vincent de Paul (40 sounding-stops), at Paris, Cavaillé-Coll received £2,000 ; and for that at the Madelaine (48 sounding-stops), £2,500. The above matters relating to the price, excellence, and completeness of an organ, have been entered into thus fully and unreservedly in this place, first, because, emanating as they do from one who is wholly unconnected with the organ-building business, and who, therefore, can in no way be interested in the issue, beyond what is shared by all who admire excellence, irrespective of size, they may perhaps be permitted to exercise some influence with those who have to detect the actual merits of competing estimates ; and, secondly, because they really involve the permanent interest of the purchaser, the credit of the builder, and the progress of the art in equal degrees. It need only be added that a builder of high reputation will naturally expect, and will be entitled to receive, higher remuneration for his work than one of less eminence.

CHAPTER XXXIX.

PLANS FOR ORGANS OF VARIOUS SIZES.

1270. SOME plans or specifications for organs of various sizes will now be given, which will illustrate the several rules that have been explained in detail in preceding chapters of this book ; and will also serve to show by what easy and successive steps an instrument may be gradually developed from a small chancel or schoolroom organ into a large cathedral or town hall organ, without any of the primary laws of the science being overturned or modified in any way. In their preparation, the schemes of the best English and foreign organs, of old as well as of recent times, have been consulted, and their best features embodied, so far as has been found practicable, or seemed to be in accordance with the requirements of a modern English organ. As, however, nearly every organ-builder and organist has his predilection in favour of particular stops, some of the details of the following specifications would, of course, be modified to adapt them to particular tastes.

POSITIF ORGANS.

1271. Before entering upon these several matters, a few words may be said on a kindred subject. The question has frequently been raised as to the most economic mode of using the funds and space—both usually too limited—that may be available for organs for small village and mission churches, and where the use of the instrument will only be needed as an accompaniment to simple vocal harmony. For an organ built for the *sole* purpose indicated, and under the close restrictions mentioned, as great a proportion as possible of the small funds should be expended on *pipes*, and as little as possible on *mechanism;* as much on the most efficient attainable production of those notes specially required for the guidance and support of the voices, and as little as possible on anything and everything beyond. The first question, then, that presents itself is that as to the compass that would be sufficient for such an instrument. If we refer back some centuries to the time when the organ could have been used for no other purpose in the church than as an accompaniment to the voices, we find its range agreeing very nearly, if not exactly, with that of the human voice ; and that compass is fully represented by the ancient great stave of eleven lines with the notes immediately below and above :—

1272. For an organ for the purpose indicated a compass of three octaves and a tone—FF to g³ in alt, 39 notes—would be sufficient. With regard to the stops, it should be mentioned that a single stop, and that in unison with the voices, never can keep the voices in tune long together. Singers find a difficulty in hearing a stop that is in unison with their voices, but readily detect one that sounds in the octave above them. The smallest organ, therefore, should have two stops, a Unison and an Octave. For a small delicate toned instrument there might be—

I.

1. Lieblich Gedact.
2. Dulcet, or Octave Dulciana.

For a two-stop organ of fuller tone the following would be suitable :—

II.

1. Stopped Diapason.
2. Principal, Gemshorn, or Spitzflöte.

For an organ of three stops :—

III.

1. Stopped Diapason.
2. Open Diapason to Middle c¹.
3. Principal.

1273. Father Smith, in numerous small organs, made the Open Diapason to range simply from middle c¹ upwards ; and, as that note marked the full average range downwards of the treble voice, there was a certain completeness and distinctness of adaptibility about the little stop. It is, therefore, proposed above.

IV.

For a four-stop organ the following registers will be quite satisfactory :—

1. Lieblich Bourdon.
2. Open Diapason.
3. Stopped Diapason.
4. Principal.

1274. As the Bourdon appears in these plans for Positif organs for the first time in the foregoing, a few words may be said in reference to that stop. Deep-sounding bodies generate large and ample sound-waves ; and large sound-waves exercise an impressive effect on the feelings of auditors within their influence. In drawing up plans for small organs, advantage should be taken of this fact to introduce those deep-sounding bodies as soon as practicable, that they may exercise on those engaged in acts of devotion the wholesome influence just adverted to.

1275. If the Bourdon be made to the small scale, and voiced to the sweet tone implied by the adjunct " Lieblich," it will be found to enrich and deepen the general tone, without obscuring or disputing the predominance of the unison pitch. The compass of the above organ is supposed to be the same as before ; but as the pipes to the keys in the *upward* direction would be small and inexpensive, and yet would be most useful in a variety of ways, the range might be continued another octave, as being everything short of a *necessity*. The first and most obvious use of the upper octave of keys would consist in its being available for playing the melody "in octaves" when the voices might be showing a tendency to get flat, and of its thus offering an ever-ready means of checking such tendency without the player having to remove a hand from the Manual to draw the Octave stop.

1276. The extra octaves of keys would, in conjunction with the Bourdon, admit of a very pretty combination, resembling that produced by the Stopped Diapason and Flute on ordinary organs.

1277. A desire is sometimes evinced to have introduced, into organs even of the very small kind under consideration, the movement called by the Spanish organ-builders of the last century "Terzo Mano," and by Mr. Holditch, who introduced it into England, "Diocton." It is a question whether it be advisable to introduce any mechanical appliance whatever into so small an organ. If, however, its insertion be proposed, some care will be required as to the selection of the stops. The effect of an "octave coupler," it may be as well to explain, is to repeat all the sounding stops at *half size*, and add them in that new form to the stops in their actual size. There is a great risk, therefore, of the 4-feet tone being made to exceed the 8-feet tone by a movement of the above kind, and of the general tone becoming top-heavy. If an octave coupler be desired, the stops in their half size, as well as their full, should be written down, and the size and proportion of the whole then tested. No scheme of four stops will bear this trial better than the following :—

V.

1. Bourdon . . 16.
2. Open Diapason 8.
3. Dulciana . . 8.
4. Flute . . . 4.

"Reproduced" as above, the scheme would stand thus :—

VI.

1. Bourdon . . . . 16.
2. Open Diapason . . . . 8.
*3. Stopped Diapason . . . . . 8.
4. Dulciana . . . . 8.
*5. Principal . . . . 4.
6. Flute . . . . 4.
*7. Dulcet . . . . 4.
*8. Piccolo. . . . . 2.

That is to say, like one stop 16 feet, three of 8 feet, three of 4 feet, and one of 2 feet.

For an organ capable of sustaining some hundreds of voices the following five stops would be good :—

VII.

1. Bourdon.
2. Open Diapason.
3. Stopped Diapason.
4. Principal.
5. Mixture, II ranks—12 and 15.

These organs might well be distinguished as *Positif Organs*, as that is not only the old English name for small instruments, but is one that has not hitherto been appropriated in modern days.

CHANCEL ORGANS.

1278. Another kind of small organ is appropriately called the Chancel organ. This consists of at least one Manual of full compass, and a good complement of pedals ; and two stops at the least, one of 8 feet and one of 4.

For a delicate toned organ of this kind the following stops would answer well :—

VIII.

Manual compass CC to g³, 56 notes.   Pedal CC to d¹, 27 notes.

    1. Lieblich Gedact . . . . 8 feet tone.
    2. Dulcet . . . . 4 feet.

For a somewhat fuller tone :—

IX.

Compass as before.

    1. Stopped Diapason . . . . 8 feet tone.
    2. Gemshorn. . . . . 4 feet.

For a stronger tone the following three stops :—

X.

    1. Stopped Diapason . . . . 8 feet tone.
    2. Open Diapason to Middle c¹ . . . . 8 feet.
    3. Principal . . . . 4 feet.

For an organ of six sounding stops the following would answer well :—

XI.

Manual Organ.

    1. Open Diapason . . . . 8 feet.
    2. Stopped Diapason . . . . 8 feet tone.
    3. Dulciana to tenor c, grooved into
        No. 2 below . . . . 8 feet.
    4. Principal . . . . 4 feet.
    5. Mixture, II ranks . . . . 12 and 15.

Pedal Organ.

    6. Bourdon, CCC to tenor d, 27 notes   16 feet tone.

1279. In drawing up plans for organs, however small, advantage ought to be taken of the experience and successful experiments of the early builders and their successors, and to propose, as soon as practicable, not only the tone *to* CC, but below them as far as FFF, to obtain a greater or less number of which the makers of past times did not hesitate to depart from what they knew to be the proper compass, rather than lose those tones altogether. Without those tones *somewhere,* all the simple church music, written in the scales of B flat, A, G, and F, forming a considerable portion of the whole, would be deprived of its deep-toned tonic, as well as many of its grave-sounding progressions. In the above plan for a Chancel organ the Manual presents the range not only indispensable for an accompaniment organ—like the Positifs, already proposed—but also the compass necessary for the unfettered study and practice of the *Manual* parts of the greatest works ever written for the instrument; while the Pedals present not only the deep tones necessary to afford a satisfactory interpretation of any of the bass progressions of vocal church music, but likewise the still freer parts of essentially church organ music. This subject cannot be followed any further in this place. Probably it may be treated of more fully in a separate form of publication.

CHURCH ORGANS.

1280. The next subject to be touched upon is the smallest kind of church organs, from which point the subject may be continued forward uninterruptedly.

XII.

For a small organ of two Manuals and Pedal and 10 sounding stops :—

Great Organ.

1. Open Diapason . . . 8 feet.	grooved into No. 2
2. Stopped Diapason . . 8 feet tone.	below . . . . . . 8 feet.
3. Dulciana to tenor c,	4. Principal.

Swell Organ.

5. Violin Diapason, or Spitzflöte, to tenor c, grooved into No. 6 below . . . . . . 8 feet.	7 Violino, or Gemshorn . 4 feet.
	8. Mixture, II ranks, 12
	and 15 . . . . . 2⅔ feet.
6. Rohr-gedact . . . . 8 feet tone.	9. Oboe . . . . . . 8 feet.

Pedal Organ.

10 Stopped Bass . . . . 16 feet tone.
Bass Flute, 8 feet tone by means of octave coupler.

Accessory Stops, Movements, &c.

1. Swell to Great.	3. Great to Pedal.
2. Swell to Pedal.	4. Octave Coupler, Pedal.

1281. An "octave coupler," to produce the effect of a "Bass Flute," is proposed for the Pedal. A stop of this kind is very useful, even when the extra octave of pipes, to complete its upward compass, is not attainable, as is supposed to be the case in the present instance. The 8-feet "helper" quickly defines the deep tones of the 16-feet octave, and has the advantage of doing this, according to the present plan, without either of the Manuals being coupled to the Pedal for the purpose. The Manuals are thus left free to be used with their own separate and special soft combinations whenever required. The higher tones of the 16-feet range are quite distinct, and not far removed in pitch from the Manual tones; hence the omission of the 8-feet sound is not felt to be material. In place of No. 8 a 2-feet stop of some kind might be substituted.

XIII.

SPECIFICATION FOR AN ORGAN OF TWELVE SOUNDING STOPS, TWO MANUALS,
AND PEDAL.

Great Organ.		*Swell Organ.*	
1. Open Diapason . . .	8 feet.	7. Violin Diapason, Open	
2. Stopped Diapason . .	8 feet tone.	Diapason, or Spitz-	
3. Dulciana to tenor c,		flöte, to tenor c . .	8 feet.
grooved into No. 2		8. Lieblich Gedact. . .	8 feet tone.
below	8 feet.	9. Violino, Principal, or	
4. Principal	4 feet.	Gemshorn. . . .	4 feet.
5. Flute, Stopped, Open, or		10. Mixture, II ranks . .	2⅔ feet.
Harmonic	4 feet.	11. Trumpet, Horn, or	
6. Mixture, II ranks, 12		Cornopean . . .	8 feet.
and 15.	2⅔ feet.		

Pedal Organ.

12. Stopped Bass . . . . 16 feet tone.

Bass Flute by means of octave coupler.

1282. A difficulty that frequently attends the planning of a small English organ of two Manuals, on the modern principle, is the satisfactory treatment of the bass or 8-feet octave of the second Manual, or Swell, owing to the size of the stops that are justly considered to be indispensable for even the most limited departments of that kind to possess. In the instance of the second Manual or Choir organ of the instruments of the last century no such difficulty existed, on account of the stop generally selected for that department being comparatively small ones—as Stopped Diapason, 8-feet *tone* (4 feet *literal* length) ; Principal, 4 feet, and so on ; but now that the Swell invariably takes the precedence of the Choir organ, and an Open Metal Flue stop of 8 feet and at least one Reed stop of the same size are required for even the smallest specimen of that division of an organ, the case is very different.

1283. By way of illustrating the extent of this alteration and increase in the size of the stops, the following experiment might be tried on a tenor c Swell, containing the following six stops :—

1. Bourdon	16 feet tone.	4. Principal	4 feet.
2. Open Diapason . .	8 feet.	5. Mixture II ranks .	2⅔ and 2 feet.
3. Stopped Diapason .	8 feet tone.	6. Hautboy.	8 feet.

First, press down the tenor c key, then draw the Bourdon, when a sound like that from a CC Stopped Diapason will be heard. The Open Diapason, when added, will sound like a Principal, the Stopped Diapason like a Flute, the Principal like a Fifteenth, the Twelfth and Fifteenth like a II-rank Mixture, and the Hautboy like a Clarion. Thus it will be exemplified that the tenor c pipes of those six Swell stops are as large as the CC pipes of the following six Choir stops :—

1. Stopped Diapason . .	8 feet tone.	4. Fifteenth	2 feet.
2. Principal	4 feet.	5. Mixture, II ranks.	
3. Flute	4 feet tone.	6. Clarionet . . .	8 feet tone.

That is to say, the Swell stops of a modern organ are ordinarily twice the size of the Choir stops of old organs. This will at once give an idea of the great amount of extra standing-room a Swell must require beyond what is necessary for a Choir organ of the same number of stops, even supposing the necessary additional funds to secure the more costly stops in a complete form to be forthcoming ; added to which there is the price of the expensive "large wooden room," or box, to hold them, to be taken into account. A Swell, therefore, with all its stops of complete compass, could scarcely be expected in an organ for so small a church as the above would be calculated ; yet, on the other hand, it is very disadvantageous to the effect of the music, as well as unsatisfactory to the player, when the range of the second Manual organ is far short of what it should be.

1284. To overcome this difficulty, the bass octave of the Stopped Diapason and Principal in the Great organ has sometimes been "borrowed ;" that is to say, they have been made to act on the corresponding octave of the Swell Manual without the remaining Great organ stops sounding. Something analogous to this in principle used to be effected by Harris, Bridge, and other builders, who, in some of their organs, borrowed the two lower octaves of their "Choir organ" from the Great, as at St. Andrew Undershaft, by means of double grooves, one set for each Manual, and two sliders to each borrowed stop, of which also one was for each Manual. Conveyances or grooves extended from the upper-boards over the one slider to the bass pipes over the other, and small leather valves were placed over each set of sound-board holes to prevent any of the wind that came up from one department of the organ passing down into the other division. The borrowing, however, has been effected in various ways, as, for instance, by partitioning off a small portion of the single sound-board grooves, and providing pallets and sliders as before. All such contrivances are designed to arrive at the same end, though a borrowed bass is far better than the plan of making the Swell keys below tenor c act on the entire Great organ, which is a very primitive device. Another plan has been to introduce a small "Choir bass" to act on the bass octave of the second Manual to meet the Swell. This is a better arrangement still, as the Stopped Diapason bass and Principal, of which it is usually composed, can be scaled and voiced with some reference to the strength of the Swell stops. Still this is not entirely satisfactory, as, of course, it cannot be made to match the Swell stops equally well, whether the Swell-box be open or closed. Of the several methods that have been devised none appear to be open to so little objection as the following.

1285. The Open Diapason might, to save room, be discontinued at the 4-feet c pipe, as in the ordinary tenor c Swell; but the Stopped Diapason could be carried down to CC, the longest pipe of which would even then only be of the same 4-feet *length*, although its sound would be of 8-feet *pitch*. The Principal might also be carried right down, the lowest pipe of which octave stop would even then be no longer than the Open Diapason pipe of the octave above, that is, 4 feet. About the Mixture, smaller again, yet so pretty in its effect, there would be no difficulty. Lastly, the Reed could be mitred down without any detriment to its tone, but rather the contrary, and so be reduced to the 4-feet height. In this way the 8-feet octave of Manual tones could be secured to the Swell without increasing the height of the Swell-box at all, by adding to its breadth to some extent, and to its depth to a less degree, while its sounds would be rendered susceptible of being increased or diminished with the rest of the Swell, which power, of course, cannot be secured by any of the other plans. Within the last few years this plan has been frequently and successfully followed by Foster and Andrews and other organ-builders. The lowest septave of the Principal might be made to draw on the Open Diapason slide, in conjunction with the bass of the Stopped Diapason, to which it would act as a helper. In that case the Principal, as a separate stop, would not sound below the tenor c key; but, as it is never used as a separate stop without the Diapason, this would practically be no disadvantage. The 8-feet septave of the Stopped Diapason as a bass to the Open always sounds somewhat dull and muffled without some such " helper."

1286. A mistake sometimes finds its way on to the labels of the Pedal couplers which it is worth while to point out. It is generally understood that, of the two claviers named on the label of a coupler, the *first* is that of the row of keys coupled, and the second that of the one to which it is united. Thus, " Swell to Great" is understood to mean that the former is coupled to the latter, which is the case ; but with the Pedal coupler the names frequently get reversed, and although the mechanism attaches the Great organ to the Pedal, yet the label announces that it unites the " Pedal to Great."

XIV.

SPECIFICATION FOR AN ORGAN WITH SEVENTEEN SOUNDING STOPS, TWO MANUALS, AND PEDAL.

Great Organ, 9 *Stops.*

1. Bourdon . . . . . 16 feet tone.	6. Flute . . . . . . 4 feet tone.
2. Open Diapason . . 8 feet.	7. Twelfth . . . . . $2\frac{2}{3}$ feet.
3. Dulciana to Tenor c. 8 feet.	8. Fifteenth . . . . . 2 feet.
4. Stopped Diapason . 8 feet tone.	9. Mixture, III, IV, or V
5. Principal . . . . 4 feet.	ranks.

Swell Organ, 6 *Stops.*

10. Open Diapason . . 8 feet tone.	13. Mixture, II ranks . $2\frac{2}{3}$ and 2 feet.
11. Stopped Diapason . 8 feet.	14. Hautboy . . . . 8 feet.
12. Principal. . . . . 4 feet.	15. Horn . . . . . 8 feet.

Pedal Organ, 2 *Stops.*

16. Open Bass . . . . 16 feet.	a. Octave Bass {borrowed by} 8 feet.
17. Stopped Bass . . . 16 feet tone.	b. Flute Bass . {means of a coupler} 8 feet tone.

Accessory Stops, Movements, &c.
1. Swell to Great.
2. Great to Pedal.
3. Pedal Octave.

Compass.
Great. CC to g³ in altissimo, 56 notes.
Swell. CC to g³ in altissimo, 56 notes.
Pedal. CCC to Tenor f, 30 notes.

4, 5, 6, 7, 8. Five double-action Composition pedals, to act on the stops of the Great organ in the following manner :—

4, to draw out the Dulciana, and reduce the full organ to the same.

5, to draw out the Diapasons, and reduce the full organ to the same.

6, to draw out to the Fifteenth, and reduce the full organ to the same.

7, to draw out the full organ.

8, to compound a Choir organ by drawing out the Stopped Diapason, Dulciana, Principal, and Flute, and reducing the full organ to the same.

1287. The last Composition pedal mentioned in the above scheme, although but seldom introduced, would prove of the greatest possible use in all small organs which have no separate Choir organ. It was tried for the first time (at the writer's suggestion) in the organ built by Walker, for Trinity Church, Vauxhall Bridge, in 1852. As a Pedal of the kind does not belong to the series for increasing the strength of the organ tone by gradations from *piano* to *forte*, and for reducing it back again, but is designed to answer a distinct and special purpose, it had better be placed quite apart from the rest, say, to the extreme left, opposite to where the Swell Pedal is usually situated. The Bourdon is proposed to be acted on only by the Composition Pedal that is to draw out the full organ, as its use is not governed by any laws analogous to those which regulate the employment of the other stops, but is sometimes required in soft combinations, while at others it is not desired for much louder ones. For these reasons it will be better for it to be controlled chiefly by the hand.

1288. In many small English organs a Bourdon of 16-feet tone is placed on the second Manual, while all stops of the same pitch are omitted from the first. This is not in accordance with the Continental custom, as will be perceived on referring to any of the specifications of small organs contained in the Appendix.

1289. Two independent Pedal stops are included in the specification last given. Both those stops are proposed to be of 16 feet; Flue stops of that size or size of tone being the most important ones for the Pedal to have first, they forming the "Open and Stopped basses" to the Diapasons of the Manual. Of scarcely less importance are the 8-feet Pedal stops, for which a Pedal octave coupler is proposed, as before.

1290. At the same time, a plan for compounding a second independent stop out of a first has been quite successfully tried by Schulze, Jardine, Wadsworth, Robson, and others. It is as follows :—CCC and CC grooves are placed side by side ; the CCC sharp and CC sharp grooves the same ; and so on throughout the sound-board ; an extra octave being added at the end to complete the 8-feet range. Each Pedal roller is then provided with two lowering arms, one communicating with the CCC pallet, the other operating on a second pallet in the CC groove. On the table are twice the usual number of sliders, say four instead of two ; that is to say, in addition to those for the two actual stops, the same number is introduced for the borrowed octaves, and those for the 16-feet stop and the borrowed octave are in each case placed side by side. The CCC and CC pipes also stand side by side on the sound-board, to save conveyancing or grooving ; and all the other pipes are arranged in the same manner. By these means the independence of the 8-feet range is so completely established that it is scarcely possible to discover that there are less than twice as many actual stops as really exist.

XV.

SPECIFICATION FOR AN ORGAN WITH TWENTY SOUNDING STOPS, TWO MANUALS AND PEDAL.

Great Organ, 10 Stops.

1. Bourdon	16 feet tone.		5. Principal	4 feet.
2. Open Diapason	8 feet.		6. Stopped Flute or Harmonic Flute	4 feet tone.
3. Dulciana, or Gamba, to tenor c	8 feet.		7. Twelfth	2⅔ feet.
4. Stopped Diapason, Clarabella, Hohlflöte, or Harmonic Flute	8 feet tone.		8. Fifteenth	2 feet.
			9. Mixture, III, IV, or V ranks	2 feet.
			10. Trumpet	8 feet.

Swell Organ, 9 Stops.

11. Lieblich Bourdon .	16 feet tone.	15. Principal	4 feet.
12. Open Diapason . .	8 feet.	16. Mixture, III ranks.	2 feet.
13. Stopped Diapason .	8 feet tone.	17. Hautboy	8 feet.
14. Keraulophon or Viola	8 feet.	18. Horn	8 feet.

Pedal Organ, 2 Stops.

19. Open Bass . . .	16 feet.	a. Octave Bass {borrowed}	8 feet.
20. Stopped Bass . .	16 feet tone.	b. Bass Flute {as before}	8 feet tone.

Accessory Stops, Movements, &c.	*Compass.*
1. Coupler Swell to Great.	Great. CC to g³ in altissimo, 56 notes.
2. Swell Octave.	Swell. CC to g³ in altissimo, 56 notes.
3. Coupler Great to Pedal.	Pedal. CCC to tenor f, 30 notes, with
4. Pedal Octave.	extra octave of organ, to complete
5, 6, 7, 8, 9. Composition Pedals as	the octave range.
before.	

1291. In Germany a satisfactory specification for a 10-stop Great organ always includes one Flue stop of 16-feet tone, three or four of 8 feet, two of 4 feet, and a Compound stop of from III to VI ranks. This skeleton scheme cannot be improved upon ; and there is the less occasion for even making the attempt, since there is so much room for indulging individual taste in making the selection of stops wherewith to fill it up.

1292. It will be seen that the "Double" in the Great organ is proposed to be stopped throughout (Bourdon), and not open in the tenor and treble, as it is sometimes made in England. The Continental rule is that when there is but one stop of 16-feet pitch on a Manual that should be a covered stop (see Specifications in Appendix) ; and to this rule very few exceptions indeed exist. A Bourdon or kindred stop is first introduced, because it is more prompt in its speech than a Double Open Diapason ; because it deepens the organ tone so admirably, without rendering the sub-octave sound so weighty and sonorous as to confuse it with the unison pitch in soft combinations ; and because it is the less expensive stop, and also requires less standing and speaking room. For these several reasons its adoption has been recommended above. Sometimes a Quintaton, 16 feet (Fifth-sounding covered stop, 16-feet size of tone) is found proposed in foreign specifications. A stop of the kind is not designed to give its actual tone purely, but to produce its twelfth, of 5⅔-feet, as strongly as its ground tone. The original design of such a stop is to obtain the effect of two from one rank of pipes, on which account the stop in question is in Germany termed a "simple mixed stop." It, of course, is never intended to be used by itself.

1293. The Flute on the Great Manual of the organ at Hampton Court, by Father Smith, is really a Quintaton of 4-feet ground tone. It is formed of metal pipes, with metal caps *without* chimneys.

1294. A Swell octave coupler is proposed above, that is, one to unite the Swell to itself in that interval. A movement of this kind is very useful for solo playing in the middle and tenor octaves, as *either* reed can then have its 4-feet effect brought into conjunction with its 8-feet. Moreover, where the Swell is coupled to the Pedal, a very excellent effect, by additional distinctness, is imparted to the latter by it. Lewis has introduced this very successfully into some of his recent instruments.

XVI.

SPECIFICATION FOR AN ORGAN OF TWENTY-EIGHT SOUNDING STOPS, THREE MANUALS, AND PEDAL.

Great Organ, 10 Stops.

1. Bourdon	16 feet tone.	6. Stopped Flute, or Flute Harmonic .	4 feet tone.
2. Open Diapason . .	8 feet.	7. Twelfth	$2\frac{2}{3}$ feet.
3. Spitzflöte, or Gamba.	8 feet.	8. Fifteenth.	2 feet.
4. Stopped Diapason, Metal Treble, Clarabella, or Hohlflöte	8 feet.	9. Mixture, III, IV, or V ranks	2 feet.
5. Principal.	4 feet.	10. Trumpet	8 feet.

Swell Organ, 9 Stops.

11. Lieblich Bourdon. .	16 feet tone.	16. Mixture, III and IV ranks	2 feet.
12. Open Diapason . .	8 feet.	17. Hautboy.	8 feet.
13. Rohr Gedact . . .	8 feet tone.	18. Horn	8 feet.
14. Principal	4 feet.	19. Clarion	4 feet.
15. Fifteenth	2 feet.		

Choir Organ, 5 Stops.

20. Dulciana. . . .	8 feet.	23. Flute	4 feet tone.
21. Lieblich Gedact . .	8 feet tone.	24. Clarionet, to tenor c	8 feet.
22. Principal, or a Taper stop	4 feet.		

Pedal Organ, 4 Stops.

25. Open Bass	16 feet.	27. Principal Bass. . .	8 feet.
26. Stopped Bass . . .	16 feet tone.	28. Posaune, wooden tubes	16 feet.

Accessory Stops, Movements, &c.

1. Swell to Great.
2. Great to Pedal.
3. Choir to Pedal.

Compass.

Great. CC to g³ in altissimo, 56 notes.
Swell. CC to g³ in altissimo, 56 notes.
Choir. CC to g³ in altissimo, 56 notes.
Pedal. CCC to tenor f, 30 notes.

4, 5, 6, 7. Four double-action Composition Pedals to act as follows :—

4, to draw out Diapasons (2, 3, and 4), and reduce full organ to the same.
5, to draw out to Fifteenth, and reduce full organ to the same.
6, to draw out full organ without Reed, and draw in Trumpet.
7, to draw out full organ.

1295. The effect of a second Open Diapason has generally been to increase the quantity of smooth unison tone. Most English organs of the size represented in the preceding specification used to contain the repetition in question ; whereas very few of the Continental instruments include any such duplication of the equivalent stop, *i.e.*, of the " Principal, Prestant, or octave of 8 feet." The organs at Rotterdam, Freiburg, and Tours, offer exceptions to the rule, which, however, are all much larger instruments. (See Foreign Specifications.) It might, therefore, be supposed that the foreign organs do not contain any stop corresponding with the English "second Open;" which inference, however, would only be correct so far as the *name* is concerned, for they very generally do possess a second Unison Open Metal Flue stop of rather strong tone. It is true, indeed, that they usually present but one "Principal, or *most* important stop of 8 feet," which, forming the basis from which the length and scale of the whole series of harmonic corroborating stops are calculated, thus constitutes the *Diapason* thereto; but then they have, in lieu of a second stop of that same name and size, some member of the Flute-work, which is selected according to the character of tone it is desired the "second Open" shall produce.

1296. The point of difference, therefore, in this particular, between the English and the Continental system is this: that whereas in this country the second open stop is almost always labelled "Open Diapason," although its tone may differ much, and advantageously so, from the full and sonorous character of that of the first stop of the same name; in Germany, the several varieties of tone are, on the contrary, produced from as many different kinds of stops, each of which has something peculiar in its *form* to distinguish it to the organ-builder, something special in its *tone* to distinguish it to the auditor, and something distinct in its *name* to distinguish it to the organist. Thus, in some German organs, we find a "second Open," slightly conical in form, producing a rather lighter tone than the first, of a slightly flutey quality, and bearing the inscription "*Spitzflöte 8 feet*." In others, we find the second 8-feet open stop more conical than the last-mentioned, producing a clear, piping, and chirping quality of tone, and labelled "*Gemshorn 8 feet*." Other organs contain a second open stop that is more or less reedy in tone, and smaller in scale, bearing the name *Gamba, Salicional, Geigen Principal*, &c., as the case may be. Any Specification in the Appendix may be referred to for an illustration of these particulars.

1297. The origin of the introduction of a second Open Diapason into the English organ is possibly connected in some way with the custom, prevalent in the seventeenth century, of erecting the organ on the choir screen, which rendered a "double front" necessary, demanding two sets of *cylindrical* pipes wherewith to adorn them. And it is worthy of observation that, although Father Smith frequently introduced "two Opens," he generally voiced the smallest one so that it produced a tone partaking in some degree of the peculiar flutey quality of the German *Spitzflöte*. The custom of introducing two Open Diapasons has prevailed very generally in England, from the time of Smith and Harris down to our own. The fault generally was that they did not possess sufficient individuality of tone, nor, consequently, the amount they might have done when combined.

1298. The particular in which the English system is felt to be insufficient is in its not possessing any nomenclature whereby the stops producing the several characters of tone can be distinguished and specially referred to. That the adoption of something of the kind would prove advantageous, there can scarcely be a second opinion. All must have experienced the convenience of being able, for instance, to distinguish a Dulciana from an Open Diapason by a *name* instead of a *description*, and a Keraulophon from both by the same simple means. Perhaps "smooth Open" and "clear Open" would be sufficiently definite for the purpose.

1299. The second Open Diapason is sometimes, indeed, labelled "*small* Open;*" but this addition only refers to the *scale* of the stop, and not to the *quality* of its sound, which may vary considerably in different examples. Moreover, one builder's "small" Open will not unfrequently nearly equal in size the "large" Open of another. What the performer requires most especially is a key to the tone-character of the stop; and, if some special term could be applied to every stop, the sound of which differed from that of the actual "Diapason," such a series of names would doubtless prove most acceptable. Under this impression, the second Unison Open stop on the Great Manual of the last specification is marked "Spitzflöte 8 feet;" for which, however, some other 8-feet stop could be substituted, or even the hitherto usual English stop and terminology, if preferred.

1300. In selecting the particular kind of Stopped Diapason and Flute for the Great and Choir Manuals, a better opportunity is afforded for the exercise of individual choice than is the case with almost any other class of stops in an organ. It was a frequent custom with the younger Harris to make the Treble of his Choir Stopped Diapason and Flute of metal, as in the late Doncaster organ; while the younger Smith as often made his both of wood throughout, as at Finedon. The elder Smith, on the contrary, frequently made the two stops of a different kind of material; so that if the Stopped Diapason was of wood, the Flute would be of metal; and when the Stopped Diapason was of metal, the Flute was of wood. In a few cases he made the one Stopped and the other Open, as in the Durham Cathedral organ, where to a Stopped Diapason of wood on the Great and Choir organs a Hohlflöte of octave pitch was placed in each instance.

1301. The "crossing" of the Stopped Diapason and Flute, in regard to their material, after the manner adopted by the elder Smith, has long been a prevalent practice, though by no means an invariable one, with the German organ-builders. It was followed by Silbermann in his fine instruments at Dresden, in the Choir organs of each of which it will be seen, on referring to their Specifications in the Appendix, that to a "Gedact of 8-feet tone" he introduced a "Rohrflöte of 4-feet tone." It will be noticed, also, that to the "Gedact of 8-feet tone" in the Choir he in each case disposed a "Rohrflöte of 4-feet tone" in the Great organ.

1302. By making one of the covered stops on the same Manual of wood, and the other of metal, greater individuality of character in the tone is obtained from each than is usually secured by the voicing alone; and by making two stops of similar nature on two different Manuals—as, for instance, the Stopped Diapasons on the Great and Choir organs—of different materials, a nice, mild contrast is caused to exist even between stops which (in England, at any rate) usually bear the same name. Much variety is also to be obtained by crossing the Clarabella of 8 feet and the Flute Harmonic of 4 feet; also by the use of the Rohrflötes, Gedacts, and the numerous Flutes that have been invented or introduced within the last few years.

1303. The plan of making the covered stops of 8 and 4 feet tone "cross" was adopted by the late Mr. Hill for the Choir organ of his instrument at the Panopticon, and also by the late Mr. Walker.

1304. It is the nature of all good stops of Flute quality of tone, whether they be stopped or open, metal or wood, to impart to the metal tone of those members of the Diapason-work with which they sound in unison a certain fulness and mellowness of effect not attainable without them; and this mollifying influence is exercised to the most beneficial extent when the Flute sound is fully proportioned to that of the metal, yet without being so strong as to prevent its mixing perfectly with, and merging, as it were, in the metal tone. For an organ that is to be lightly and sweetly voiced, somewhat after the Green model, for instance, a Stopped Diapason and Stopped Flute would answer best ; as a Clarabella and Flute Harmonic would in that case be likely to produce rather a "hooting" effect through the light foundation and chorus-work. Instead of simply imparting body and breadth to the Open Diapason and Principal, they would tend to obscure the predominance and "glisten" of the metal quality by their nearer equality of strength, and would thus serve only to thicken and deaden the tone. But, if the Diapason and Harmonic series of stops are to be boldly and fully voiced, a Clarabella and Flute Harmonic might be advantageously introduced ; for the reasons that, while they would be covered by the peal of the ringing Mixtures, they would in their turn assist in supporting them by the broader effect which they would impart to the unison and octave sounds.

1305. The Clarabella is generally of excellent quality in the upper octave and a half of its compass, being clear and smooth, yet powerful ; but in the middle octave its tone is sometimes thick and woody, probably on account of the largeness of its scale, and its not being blown sufficiently. In the German equivalent for the above-named English stop—the Hohlflöte—the pipes increase in bulk far more gradually downwards, yet the most perfect evenness of quality is preserved.

1306. A singular mistake is sometimes made in the labelling of the Swell octave coupler, which it is necessary to notice. The coupler in question is frequently marked *super*-octave, which means not "the octave above," but "above the octave," and therefore indicates that it operates in the 2-feet pitch, whereas it in reality acts in the *single* octave or 4-feet pitch. This error is the more confusing where the terms octave or super-octave are applied to any of the 4 or 2-feet organ stops.

XVII.

SPECIFICATION FOR AN ORGAN OF TWENTY-FOUR SOUNDING STOPS, TWO MANUALS, AND PEDAL.

Great Organ, 12 *Stops.*

1. Bourdon	16 feet tone.		7. Twelfth		$2\frac{2}{3}$ feet.
2. Open Diapason	8 feet.		8. Fifteenth		2 feet.
3. Dulciana	8 feet.		9. Harmonic Piccolo		2 feet.
4. Stopped Diapason or Clarabella	8 feet tone.		10. Mixture, V ranks		2 feet.
5. Principal	4 feet.		11. Trumpet		8 feet.
6. Harmonic Flute	4 feet tone.		12. Clarionet		8 feet tone.

For No. 9 a Gamba might be substituted.

Swell Organ, 10 *Stops.*

13. Bourdon	16 feet tone.		19. Mixture, III and IV ranks		2 feet.
14. Open Diapason	8 feet.		20. Hautboy		8 feet.
15. Rohr Gedact	8 feet tone.		21. Horn		8 feet.
16. Gamba to tenor c	8 feet.		22. Clarion		4 feet.
17. Principal	4 feet.				
18. Fifteenth	2 feet.				

For No. 18 a Flute or a Flageolet might be substituted.

Pedal Organ, 4 Stops.

. Open Bass, wood . . 16 feet.	25. Principal Bass, metal . . 8 feet.
. Stopped Bass, wood . 16 feet tone.	26. Posaune, wooden tubes . . 16 feet.

Accessory Stops, Movements, &c.   *Compass.*

1. Swell to Great.
2. Great to Pedal.
3. Swell to Pedal.
4. Swell Octave.
5. Swell Sub-octave.
6, 7, 8, 9. Four Composition Pedals, as before.

Great. CC to g³ in altissimo, 56 notes.
Swell. CC to g³ in altissimo, 56 notes.
Pedal. CCC to tenor f . . 30 notes.

1307. The Piccolo, which now appears in the Great Organ Specifications for the first time, completes the Flute or wood organ, consisting of the Bourdon, Stopped Diapason, Flute, and Piccolo—a series of stops of the greatest service for purposes of accompaniment and for solo playing. A Harmonic Piccolo or Flageolet of 2 feet might take the place of the wood stop, if preferred.

1308. The Octave and Sub-octave Couplers are sometimes made to attach the "Swell to Great;" at others they unite the Swell to itself in the octave above and below. In the latter case, the octave sound, each way, can be concentrated on a single Swell key, provided the octave be within the standard compass of the Manual. The Octave and Sub-octave Swell Couplers are then freely available, without the independence of the Great organ being *of necessity* lost for the time being. If either the Octave or the Sub-octave effects, or both, were required *in conjunction* with the Great, they are then obtainable by drawing the usual Coupler Swell to Great; when, of course, every key united *to the Swell unison* would also descend on that key, being drawn down by the corresponding key of the Great organ. The only effect lost is that of attaching the Swell to the Great in the Octave and Sub-octave *without* the Swell unison.

1309. Several excellent Pedal effects are placed at the organist's command, when the Swell unites to itself. For instance, the Swell—with the "Swell Octave" drawn—on being coupled to the Pedal, would, by means of the Clarion, produce the effect of a 2-feet Reed, and thus impart to the Pedal entry of a subject a great amount of point and brightness; or, with the Sub-octave drawn, which would attach the CC Swell key to the second c of the Pedals, and consequently bring the 16-feet CCC Bourdon *tone* on to the same CC Pedal, the effect of a light Pedal stop of 32-feet tone would be obtained through the octave and a half of the Pedal range from that key upwards.

1310. Octave and Sub-octave Couplers occur in most of the Italian organs, whether of ancient or recent date. It would be interesting to know positively the exact period of the introduction of such useful movements. The Unison Coupler would naturally be the first kind thought of; and, from the prominent way in which that description of accessory stop is mentioned in the old account of the Lucerne organ (Foreign Specifications), it is not improbable that a clavier coupler was, at the period of the construction of that instrument (1561), then either a new feature or a great novelty in the science.

I I

XVIII.

SPECIFICATION FOR AN ORGAN OF THIRTY-SIX SOUNDING STOPS, THREE MANUALS, AND PEDAL.

Great Organ, 13 Stops.

1. Bourdon . . . . . 16 feet tone.	7. Twelfth . . . . 2⅔ feet.
2. Smooth Open Diapason . . . . . . 8 feet.	8. Fifteenth . . . . . 2 feet.
3. Clear Open Diapason . 8 feet.	9. Piccolo . . . . . . 2 feet.
4. Stopped Diapason, Clarabella, or Hohlflöte . . . . . . 8 feet tone.	10. Full Mixture, III ranks . . . . . . 2 feet.
5. Principal . . . . . 4 feet.	11. Sharp Mixture, III, IV, or V ranks . or 2 feet.
6. Stopped Flute, or Flute Harmonic . . 4 feet tone.	12. Trumpet . . . . . 8 feet.
	13. Clarion . . . . . . 4 feet.

For No. 10 a Gamba might be substituted.

Swell Organ, 10 Stops.

14. Bourdon . . . . . 16 feet tone.	19. Fifteenth . . . . . 2 feet.
15. Open Diapason . . . 8 feet.	20. Mixture, IV ranks . . 1⅓ foot.
16. Stopped Diapason, metal treble. . . . 8 feet tone.	21. Hautboy . . . . . 8 feet.
17. Bell Gamba . . . . 8 feet.	22. Horn . . . . . . 8 feet.
18. Principal . . . . . 4 feet.	23. Clarion . . . . . . 4 feet.

Choir Organ, 7 Stops.

24. Open Diapason . . . 8 feet.	27. Spitzflöte . . . . . 4 feet.
25. Stopped Diapason, wood . . . . . . 8 feet tone.	28. Metal Flute . . . : 4 feet tone.
26. Dulciana . . . . . 8 feet.	29. Gemshorn . . . . . 2 feet.
	30. Clarionet to tenor c . 8 feet tone.

a—Pedal Organ, 6 Stops.

31. Open Bass, wood . . 16 feet.	34. Principal Bass, metal . 8 feet.
32. Stopped Bass, wood . 16 feet tone.	35. Flute Bass, wood . . 8 feet tone.
33. Great Quint Bass, wood, stopped . . . 10⅔ feet tone.	36. Posaune, wooden tubes 16 feet.

b—Pedal, 6 Stops.

1. Open Bass . . . . 16 feet.	5. Mixture, II ranks, 12 and 15 . . . . . 5⅓ feet.
2. Stopped Bass . . . 16 feet tone.	6. Posaune . . . . . 16 feet.
3. Quint Bass . . . . 10⅔ feet tone.	
4. Principal Bass . . . 8 feet.	

c—Pedal, 6 Stops.

1. Open Bass . . . . 16 feet.	4. Posaune . . . . . . 16 feet.
2. Principal Bass . . . 8 feet.	5. Trumpet . . . . . . 8 feet.
3. Fifteenth Bass . . . 4 feet.	6. Clarion . . . . 4 feet.

Accessory Stops, Movements, &c.

1. Coupler Swell to Great.	6. Swell to Pedal.
2. Swell Octave.	7. Choir to Pedal.
3. Swell Sub-octave.	8, 9, 10, 11. Four Composition Pedals to Great.
4. Choir to Great.	
5. Great to Pedal.	12, 13. Two Composition Pedals to Swell.

Compass.

Great, CC to g³ in altissimo, 56 notes.	Choir, the same.
Swell, the same.	Pedal, CCC to tenor f, 30 notes.

1311. Three distinct plans are given for a Pedal of 6 stops in the foregoing specification. The first contains a Great Quint Bass, of 10⅔-feet tone, which stop, though but little used in England, is capable of great effect. Many German and Flemish organs produce a mild, yet distinct, 32-feet tone from a Pedal organ, which, nevertheless, contains no stop of that pitch. The sounds which would be supposed to proceed from such a stop are in reality only an "acoustical illusion," resulting from the introduction of a stop of the above kind; every *third* vibration of which coinciding with every *second* vibration of the 16-feet stops and with every *fourth* vibration of the 8-feet stops together, so reinforce the periodical vibrations which occur thirty-two times in a second, that they produce the effect above mentioned. Where room and expense are objects, and no Sub-Bourdon is therefore obtainable, the above plan of obtaining the deepest musical tones, by making the phenomenon of sub-harmonic sounds subservient to practical use, might advantageously be adopted, particularly as the additional stop necessary to produce them is of no greater length than the Pedal Twelfth.

1312. The second plan for a 6-stop Pedal organ is a favourite English scheme; while the third is almost a literal reproduction of one held in high esteem by Silbermann and other German builders. (See Specifications in Appendix.) The first of the three schemes appears, on the whole, to be the best adapted for the accompaniment of the English Church Service, whether choral or congregational; while the second unquestionably would form the best chorus organ. In many Continental churches the Canto Fermo, or melody of the old church chant, thundered forth in unison by a large choir of priests, is made the *bass* in the accompaniment, the harmony appearing as a kind of superstructure, the effect of which arrangement of the parts is frequently most commanding. For this kind of use the third specification, with its three octaves of Reeds—16, 8, and 4 feet—would be the best, it being equal to the production of most impressive effects when employed in this manner.

1313. The consideration of the above three Pedal specifications offers a striking illustration of the immeasurable superiority of the system of organ-building which treats the Pedal as an independent department of an organ over that which recognises the extension of the Manuals down below CC as a substitute for it. In the former case several plans, consisting of the same number of stops, but very dissimilar in their selection, each possessing merits of its own, and each specially adapted to answer a distinct end, can be prepared, and from these a final selection be made, according to special requirements; whereas in the latter this is not possible, for the very existence of the Pedal as an independent and important division of an organ is then scarcely recognised.

XIX.

SPECIFICATION FOR AN ORGAN OF FIFTY SOUNDING STOPS, THREE MANUALS, AND PEDAL.

Great Organ, 17 *Stops.*

1. Double Open Diapason	16 feet.	9. Stopped Flute, wood	4 feet tone.
2. Bourdon	16 feet tone.	10. Twelfth	2⅔ feet.
3. Open Diapason	8 feet.	11. Fifteenth	2 feet.
4. Spitzflöte	8 feet.	12. Piccolo*	2 feet.
5. Stopped Diapason, metal Treble	8 feet tone.	13. Full Mixture, III ranks	2 feet.
		14. Sharp Mixture, V ranks	1⅓ foot.
6. Quint	5⅓ feet.	15. Double Trumpet	16 feet.
7. Principal	4 feet.	16. Posaune	8 feet.
8. Gemshorn	4 feet.	17. Clarion	4 feet.

* Or another 8 feet stop.

Swell Organ, 12 Stops.

18. Bourdon . . . . . 16 feet tone.	24. Twelfth* . . . . . 2⅔ feet.
19. Open Diapason . . 8 feet.	25. Fifteenth . . . . . 2 feet.
20. Stopped Diapason . 8 feet tone.	26. Mixture, IV ranks . . 1⅓ foot.
21. Gamba to tenor c . 8 feet.	27. Hautboy . . . . . 8 feet.
22. Principal . . . . . 4 feet.	28. Horn . . . . . . 8 feet.
23. Flute . . . . . . 4 feet.	29. Clarion . . . . . . 4 feet.

. * Or a Vox Angelica.

Choir Organ, 10 Stops.

30. Lieblich Bordun . . 16 feet tone.	35. Gemshorn . . . . . 4 feet.
31. Spitzflöte . . . . . 8 feet.	36. Lieblich Flöte . . . 4 feet tone.
32. Lieblich Gedact . . 8 feet tone.	37. Flute Harmonic . . 4 feet.
33. Dulciana to tenor c . 8 feet.	38. Mixture, II ranks* . . 2⅔ feet.
34. Keraulophon to tenor c . . . . 8 feet.	39. Corno di Bassetto, throughout . . . . 8 feet tone.

* Or a Flageolet or Piccolo.

Pedal Organ, 11 Stops.

40. Sub-Bass, Stopped or Open . . . . . 32 feet.	46. Flute Bass, wood . . 8 feet tone.
41. Open Bass, wood . . 16 feet.	47. Twelfth and Fifteenth Bass . . . . . . 5⅓ feet.
42. Violone . . . . . 16 feet.	48. Trombone . . . . . 16 feet.
43. Stopped Bass, wood . 16 feet tone.	49. Trumpet . . . . . 8 feet.
44. Quint Bass, Stopped 10⅔ feet tone.	50. Clarion . . . . . . 4 feet.
45. Principal Bass, metal 8 feet	

Accessory Stops, Movements, &c.

1. Coupler Swell to Great.	8. Pedal Ventil.
2. Coupler Choir to Great.	9. Tremulant to Swell.
3. Swell Octave.	10, 11, 12, 13. Four Composition Pedals to the Great organ.
4. Swell Sub-octave.	
5. Great to Pedal.	14, 15. Two Composition Pedals to the Swell organ.
6. Swell to Pedal.	
7. Choir to Pedal.	

Compass.

Great, CC to g³ in altissimo, 56 notes.	Swell, CC to g³ in altissimo, 56 notes.
Choir the same.	Pedal, CCC to tenor f, 30 notes.

As a solo organ to the above, the following four stops would form a good addition to be operated upon by a fourth Manual :—

1. Diapason Harmonic 8 feet.	3. Tuba . . . . . . 8 feet.
2. Flute Harmonic . . 4 feet.	4. Tuba Clarion . . . 4 feet.

There should in that case be two extra couplers, namely, one to unite "Solo to Great," and a second to attach "Solo to Pedal."

1314. A German Great Manual organ, containing 16 stops, is usually furnished with two or three stops of 16 feet, a Quint, and two metal Open Flue stops of 4 feet. All these excellent features are embodied in the plan for the Great organ department of the preceding specification. The Great organ has, in fact, now become strictly a "16-feet" organ. Two Principals, like two Open Diapasons, have frequently been introduced into large English organs, as in the fine instruments at St. Sepulchre's, Snow Hill; Temple Church; Christ Church, Spitalfields; Hereford Cathedral, &c.; and, when there is much Mixture work above, a second stop of the kind, or nearly allied to it, is a most advisable one for an organ to have, as it strengthens the medium tone of the instrument materially. As, however, German organ-builders seldom "repeat themselves," the second 4-feet open metal stop in their specifications is never a repetition of the Principal, but frequently a member of the taper Flute-work, as a Gemshorn or a Spitzflöte of 4 feet. Sometimes the stop in question is an octave to the 8-feet stop, occupying the position corresponding to our second Open Diapason; sometimes, however, the Spitzflöte and Gemshorn "cross" after the manner of the Stopped Diapason and Flute, as already detailed; i.e., if the 8-feet stop be a Gemshorn, the 4-feet will be a Spitzflöte. The latter plan is the most highly esteemed in Germany, and is therefore suggested above.

1315. But the above Great organ specification contains 17 stops. This number has been preferred, since it allows of the incorporation of the Piccolo of 2 feet, which stop is less highly esteemed in Germany than in England or France, and therefore does not usually appear on the 16-stop Great manuals of the former country.

1316. As the full-compass Swell presents a second complete Manual organ composed of cylindrical stops, a few stops of tapering outline might be proposed for the Choir organ, for the purpose of obtaining greater individuality of tone, if preferred. Thus a Spitzflöte of 8 feet and a Gemshorn of 4 feet have been suggested in lieu of the usual Open Diapason and Principal. In some German organs the taper Flute-work of the Choir is made to "cross" that of the Great organ, after the manner of the covered work. Thus, if the Great has a Spitzflöte of 8 feet and a Gemshorn of 4 feet, the Choir would have a Gemshorn of 8 feet and a Spitzflöte of 4 feet; so that there are many ways of varying a specification with good effect. A stop of 8 feet of string tone, as a Gamba, Salicional, Viol d'Amour, &c., might be proposed for the Choir organ, if preferred.

1317. It is a rule with German organ-builders that, when a Pedal organ contains 10 stops, it should include a stop of 32-feet size, or size of tone. Sometimes a stop of that pitch occurs even in a Pedal of 7 or 8 stops. A Mixture, however, is seldom included in a 10-stop German Pedal.

1318. Most German Pedals of 4 stops and upwards contain a "Violone of 16 feet." This is a particularly fine stop, and one of which several good specimens by the late Mr. Hill were made. It is an open stop, usually of wood, and of small scale, the block of the 16-feet CCC generally measuring only $5\frac{1}{2}$ inches by 7 inches. It forms the "Pedal bass" to the Gamba and other string-toned Manual stops. Its intonation is very crisp and pungent, and is in close imitation of the bowing on a large string instrument; hence its name Violone (Double Bass).

1319. In the organ at Cologne Cathedral the 16 feet Violone pipe measures as much as 12 inches across the mouth, and is, from its great scale, called "Contra Violone." When heard from the choir of the cathedral, its tone is very like a fine Pedal Diapason combined with a soft 16-feet Reed of equal quality and accurate intonation.

XX.

SPECIFICATION FOR AN ORGAN OF EIGHTY-SEVEN STOPS, FOUR MANUALS, AND
PEDAL.

Great Organ, 22 Stops.

1. Sub-Bourdon to the tenor c key . . . 32 feet tone.	11. Principal . . . . 4 feet.
2. Double Open Diapason . . . . . 16 feet.	12. Flute . . . . . . 4 feet.
3. Bourdon . . . . . 16 feet tone.	13. Twelfth . . . . . . 2⅔ feet.
4. Open Diapason . . 8 feet.	14. Fifteenth . . . . . 2 feet.
5. Open Diapason . . 8 feet.	15. Piccolo . . . . . 2 feet.
6. Gamba . . . . . 8 feet.	16. Full Mixture, III ranks 2 feet.
7. Stopped Diapason, metal . . . . . 8 feet tone.	17. Sharp Mixture, V ranks 2 feet.
8. Clarabella to tenor c . 8 feet.	18. Cornet, II, III, and IV ranks.
9. Quint . . . . . . 5⅓ feet.	19. Double Trumpet . . 16 feet.
10. Principal . . . . 4 feet.	20. Posaune . . . . . 8 feet.
	21. Trumpet . . . . . 8 feet.
	22. Clarion . . . . . 4 feet.

Swell Organ, 20 Stops.

23. Bourdon . . . . 16 feet tone.	34. Octave Flute . . . 2 feet.
24. Open Diapason . . 8 feet.	35. Mixture, V ranks . . 2 feet.
25. Gamba . . . . . 8 feet.	36. Echo Dulciana Cornet, V ranks . . 4 feet.
26. Echo Dulciana . . 8 feet.	37. Double Bassoon . . 16 feet.
27. Rohr Gedact . . . 8 feet tone.	38. Hautboy . . . . . 8 feet.
28. Voix Celeste . . . 8 feet.	39. Trumpet . . . . . 8 feet.
29. Principal . . . . 4 feet.	40. Horn . . . . . . 8 feet.
30. Gambette . . . . 4 feet.	41. Clarion . . . . . 4 feet.
31. Flute . . . . . . 4 feet.	42. Vox Humana . . . 8 feet tone.
32. Twelfth . . . . . 2⅔ feet.	
33. Fifteenth . . . . 2 feet.	

Choir Organ, 15 Stops.

43. Lieblich Bourdon . . 16 feet tone.	51. Flute . . . . . . 4 feet tone.
44. Open Diapason . . 8 feet.	52. Twelfth . . . . . 2⅔ feet.
45. Lieblich Gedact . . 8 feet tone.	53. Gemshorn . . . . 2 feet.
46. Flauto Traverso . . 8 feet tone.	54. Flageolet . . . . 2 feet.
47. Dulciana . . . . 8 feet.	55. Mixture, IV ranks . 1⅓ foot.
48. Keraulophon . . . 8 feet.	56. Corno di Bassetto . 8 feet tone.
49. Spitzflöte . . . . 4 feet.	57. Bassoon, throughout 8 feet.
50. Dulcet . . . . . 4 feet.	

Solo Organ, 12 Stops.

58. Bourdon . . . . . 16 feet tone.	64. Contra Fagotto . . 16 feet.
59. Violin Diapason . . 8 feet.	65. Clarinet . . . . . 8 feet tone.
60. Flute Harmonic . . 8 feet.	66. Hautboy . . . . . 8 feet.
61. Violino . . . . . 4 feet.	67. Hautboy Clarion . . 4 feet.
62. Flute Octaviant . . 4 feet.	68. Tuba . . . . . . 8 feet.
63. Piccolo Harmonic . 2 feet.	69. Tuba Clarion . . . 4 feet.

Pedal Organ, 18 *Stops.*

70.	Double Open Bass, wood	32 feet.	79. Flute Bass	8 feet tone.
71.	Double Open Bass .	32 feet tone.	80. Twelfth Bass. . . .	$5\frac{1}{3}$ feet.
72.	Open Bass, wood .	16 feet.	81. Fifteenth Bass . . .	4 feet.
73.	Great Bass, wood .	16 feet.	82. Mixture, VI ranks .	$3\frac{1}{5}$ feet.
74.	Violone	16 feet.	83. Contra Posaune . .	32 feet.
75.	Stopped Bass. . .	16 feet tone.	84. Posaune	16 feet.
76.	Great Quint Bass .	$10\frac{2}{3}$ feet tone.	85. Bassoon	16 feet.
77.	Principal Bass, metal	8 feet.	86. Trumpet	8 feet.
78.	Violoncello, wood .	8 feet.	87. Clarion.	4 feet.

Accessory Stops, Movements, &c.

1. Coupler Swell to Great.	9. Pneumatic Lever attachment.
2. Choir to Great.	10, 11. Pedal Ventils.
3. Solo to Great.	12, 13, 14, 15. Four Composition Pedals
4. Great to Pedal.	to Great Organ, acting on Pedal
5. Swell to Pedal.	Organ in proportion.
6. Choir to Pedal.	16, 17, 18. Three Ditto to Swell.
7. Solo to Pedal.	19. Piano Pedal.
8. Tremulant to Swell.	

Compass.

Manual, CC to C⁴ in altissimo, 61 notes. | Pedal, CCC to tenor f, 30 notes.

1320. The length of the slides in large Pedal organs is so great, and the weight of the superincumbent pipe-work so considerable, that the slides frequently can only be set in motion by the exercise of great force. This motive power is sometimes provided in the shape of a pneumatic action. But this is not always sure in its operation, and is, moreover, liable to extra resistance from atmospheric causes. Walcker, of Ludwigsburg, puts every stop of his large Pedal organs on a separate sound-board, furnished with mushroom valves; and the stops are controlled by ventils, which can then be worked by a simple tracker. This plan has so many conveniences to recommend it, that Messrs. Hill and Sons are adopting something of the same kind in principle for the Yarmouth organ they are now rebuilding, and for the Great organ for Melbourne Town Hall.

1321. It will be seen that the German custom of attaching the word "Bass" to the Pedal stops of double size to the Manual stops of like kind has been followed in all the preceding specifications. This has been done, not only because it is the most simple system of nomenclature that has yet been devised, but also because it is the only system that appears to be likely to clear away the confusion that has so long existed in England as to the only correct manner of naming and classifying the Pedal stops. It has frequently been the case that the 8-feet Pedal stops have been classed as Diapasons instead of as Octaves; whereas the Pedal stops are, in nearly every instance, twice the length of the similarly labelled Manual stops. Exceptions to this rule, however, are presented by the Trumpet and Clarion, which are 8 and 4 feet stops respectively, whether placed on the Manual or Pedal.

1322. There are several excellent stops in German organs that are not at present made in England, for which reason their names have not been included in the foregoing specifications. They will, however, be readily traced in the plans of foreign organs that will now be given in the form of an Appendix. An examination of these schemes and a comparison of different specifications, comprising the same number of stops, with the view of ascertaining their points of difference, will be found not only a very interesting, but also a very instructive employment.

APPENDIX.

APPENDIX,

CONTAINING

AN ACCOUNT OF FOREIGN AND BRITISH ORGANS.

———————◆———————

I. HAARLEM.

THE organ in the Cathedral Church of St. Bevan, in this city, has long been celebrated in the annals of organ-building as one of the largest, as well as one of the finest, instruments in the world. It was built by Christian Muller, of Amsterdam, and was nearly three years and a half in course of construction ; it having been commenced on the 23rd of April, 1735, and finished on the 13th of September, 1738. The Haarlem organ has 60 sounding stops, among which are two of 32 feet, and eight of 16 feet ; and all the stops are whole ones, excepting the Cornets and the Hautboy in the Great organ. Many of the stops, further, have two pipes to each key in the treble. This is the case with the Prestant of 16 feet (Double Open Diapason), which not only extends throughout the entire range of the Great Manual, but has duplication pipes from the middle b key (gamut B pipe) upwards. The octave, of 8 feet (Open Diapason), also has two pipes to a note, commencing on the same key. The Prestant of 8 feet (Open Diapason), on the Choir Manual, similarly has two pipes to every note, commencing as low down in the scale as gamut G ; and the corresponding stop (Prestant) in the Echo also has double pipes, beginning at middle b. The ranks of Mixture likewise increase in number as the scale ascends. All the stops are made of metal, excepting the Pedal Sub-Bass, which is of wood, and is a subsequent insertion. The front pipes, which include the Pedal "Sub-Principal" of 32 feet, are of pure English tin, burnished ; and all the interior metal pipes are formed of a composition consisting of half tin and half lead. The 32-feet pipe, which is 15 inches in diameter and nearly 40 feet long, stands in one of the chief towers. The instrument, with its magnificent case, altogether cost about £12,000. The following is a list of its stops :—

Great, 16 Stops, 1209 Pipes.

			Pipes.					Pipes.
1. Prestant	....	16 feet	....	78	9. Quint Prestant	2⅔ feet	....	51
2. Bourdon	....	16 feet tone	......	51	10. Woodfluit	.... 2 feet	....	51
3. Octaav	....	8 feet	....	78	11. Tertian, II ranks	1 foot	....	102
4. Roerfluit	....	8 feet tone	......	51	12. Mixture, VI, VIII, and X ranks	...	339
5. Viol di Gamba	...	8 feet	....	51	13. Trompet	.... 16 feet	....	51
6. Roerquint	....	5⅓ feet tone	......	51	14. Trompet	.... 8 feet	....	51
7. Octaav	....	4 feet	....	51	15. Hautbois	.... 8 feet	....	51
8. Gemshorn	....	4 feet	....	51	16. Trompet	.... 4 feet	....	51

Choir, in front, 14 Stops, 1268 Pipes.

			Pipes.
17.	Prestant	8 feet	95
18.	Quintadena	8 feet tone	51
19.	Hohlfluit	8 feet	51
20.	Octaav	4 feet	51
21.	Fluit-doux	4 feet	51
22.	Speelfluit	2⅔ feet	51
23.	Super-octaav	2 feet	51

		Pipes.
24. Sesqualtera, II, III, and IV ranks	144
25. Mixtur, VI, VII, and VIII ranks...	360
26. Cimbel, II ranks	102
27. Cornet, V ranks	108
28. Fagot .... 16 feet	51
29. Trompet .... 8 feet	51
30. Regal .... 8 feet	51

Echo, 15 Stops, 1098 Pipes.

31.	Quintadena	16 feet tone	51
32.	Prestant	8 feet	81
33.	Baarpyp	8 feet	51
34.	Quintadena	8 feet tone	51
35.	Octaav	4 feet	51
36.	Flagfluit	4 feet	51
37.	Nassat	2⅔ feet	51
38.	Nachthorn	2 feet	51

39. Flageolet .... 1½ foot	51
40. Sesqualtera, II ranks	102
41. Mixtur, IV, V, and VI ranks	246
42. Cimbel, IV ranks	108
43. Schalmey .... 8 feet	51
44. Dulcian .... 8 feet	51
45. Vox Humana ... 8 feet	51

Pedal, 15 Stops, 513 Pipes.

46.	Sub-principal	32 feet	27
47.	Prestant	16 feet	27
48.	Sub-bass	16 feet	27
49.	Roerquint	10⅔ feet tone	27
50.	Octaav	8 feet	27
51.	Hohlfluit	8 feet	27
52.	Quint	5⅓ feet tone	27
53.	Octaav	4 feet	27

54.	Hohlfluit	2 feet	27
55.	Ruisquint, V ranks	2⅔ feet	27
56.	Buzain	32 feet	27
57.	Buzain	16 feet	27
58.	Trompet	8 feet	27
59.	Trompet	4 feet	27
60.	Cinq	2 feet	27

Accessory Stops, Movements, &c.

1. Coupler, Choir to Great.
2. Coupler, Echo to Great.
3. 4. Two Tremulants.
5. Wind to Great organ.
6. Wind to Choir organ.
7. Wind to Echo organ.
8. Wind to Pedal organ.
   Twelve Bellows, 9 feet by 5.

Compass.

Manuals, CC to d³ in alt., 51 notes.
Pedals, CCC to tenor d, 27 notes.

Number of Pipes.

Great	1209
Choir	1268
Echo	1098
Pedal	513

Total............ 4088

2. ROTTERDAM.

The organ in the Cathedral Church of St. Lawrence, situated at the upper part of Rotterdam, is a very fine and powerful instrument, and will, when completed, be one of the largest in the world. It already contains 75 stops, and is designed to have 92. Its pipes at present amount in number to about 5,700, the largest of which, standing in front, measures 32 feet speaking length, and 16 inches in diameter. Among the stops are included 3 of 32 feet, and 12 of 16 feet. The distribution of its stops is as follows :—

Great, 18 Stops.

1.	Prestant	16 feet.
2.	Bourdon	16 feet tone.
3.	Octave	8 feet.
4.	Prestant	8 feet.
5.	Holpfeif	8 feet.
6.	Quint	5½ feet.
7.	Octave	4 feet.
8.	Speelfluit	4 feet.
9.	Quint	2⅔ feet.

10.	Octave	2 feet.
11.	Woudfluit	2 feet.
12.	Sesqualtera, II ranks	2⅔ feet.
13.	Mixtur, IV, V, and VI ranks.	
14.	Scharf, IV and V ranks.	
15.	Cornet, VI ranks.	
16.	Trompet	16 feet.
17.	Dulcian	16 feet.
18.	Trompet	8 feet.

Positif, 18 Stops.

19.	Bourdon	16 feet tone.	28.	Gemshorn	2 feet.
20.	Prestant	8 feet.	29.	Sesquialtera, II ranks	2⅔ feet.
21.	Roerfluit	8 feet tone.	30.	Mixtur, VI and VII ranks.	
22.	Fluit Traverse, discant	8 feet.	31.	Mixtur, IV and V ranks.	
23.	Dolce	8 feet.	32.	Cornet, VI ranks.	
24.	Octaav	4 feet.	33.	Fagot	16 feet.
25.	Roerfluit	4 feet tone.	34.	Trompet	8 feet.
26.	Gemshorn	4 feet.	35.	Oboe	8 feet.
27.	Octaav	2 feet.	36.	Fagot	8 feet.

Choir, 15 Stops.

37.	Quintadena	16 feet tone.	45.	Octaav	2 feet.
38.	Prestant	8 feet.	46.	Fluit	2 feet.
39.	Quintadena	8 feet tone.	47.	Flageolet	1 foot.
40.	Gamba	8 feet.	48.	Cornet, III ranks.	
41.	Holpfeif	8 feet.	49.	Vox Humana	8 feet tone.
42.	Octaav	4 feet.	50.	Schalmey	8 feet.
43.	Open fluit	4 feet.	51.	Carillon, III ranks.	
44.	Roerfluit	4 feet tone.			

Echo, 8 Stops.

52.	Bourdon	8 feet tone.	56.	Vox Angelica	8 feet.
53.	Salicional	8 feet.	57.	Salicional	4 feet.
54.	Barpfeif	8 feet.	58.	Fluit	4 feet.
55.	Gamba	8 feet.	59.	Gemshorn	2 feet.

Pedal, 16 Stops.

60.	Prestant	32 feet.	68.	Octaav	8 feet.
61.	Sub-bass	32 feet tone.	69.	Octaav	4 feet.
62.	Prestant	16 feet.	70.	Octaav	2 feet.
63.	Sub-bass	16 feet.	71.	Buzian	32 feet.
64.	Bourdon	16 feet tone.	72.	Buzian	16 feet.
65.	Prestant	16 feet.	73.	Trombone	8 feet.
66.	Quint	10⅔ feet.	74.	Trompet	4 feet.
67.	Prestant	8 feet.	75.	Cinq	2 feet.

Accessory Stops, Movements, &c.

1. Coupler, Echo to Choir.		4. Coupler, Great to Pedal.
2. Coupler, Choir to Great.		5, 6. Two Tremulants.
3. Coupler, Positif to Great.		7, 8, 9, 10, 11. Five Wind-trunk valves.

Compass.

Manuals, CC to f³ in alt., 54 notes. | Pedal, CCC to tenor f, 30 notes.

3. ROTTERDAM.

The organ in the Octagon Church at Rotterdam was built by Batz, of Utrecht, in 1850, and is a very fine instrument. It has three Manuals and a Pedal of 8 stops, and is one of the very few German organs which have a Swell and Composition Pedals. The following is an enumeration of its Stops, &c.:—

Great, 13 Stops.

1.	Prestant	16 feet.	8.	Octaaf	2 feet.
2.	Octaaf	8 feet.	9.	Mixtur, VIII ranks.	
3.	Gemshorn	8 feet.	10.	Cornet, V ranks.	
4.	Bourdon	8 feet tone.	11.	Fagot	16 feet.
5.	Octaaf	4 feet.	12.	Trompet	8 feet.
6.	Fluit	4 feet.	13.	Clarinet	4 feet.
7.	Quint	2⅔ feet.			

Choir, 11 Stops.

14.	Bourdon	16 feet tone.	20. Nazard	2⅔ feet.
15.	Prestant	8 feet.	21. Woudfluit	2 feet.
16.	Viol di Gamba	8 feet.	22. Cornet, V ranks.	
17.	Roerfluit	8 feet tone.	23. Trompet	8 feet.
18.	Octaaf	4 feet.	24. Dulcian	8 feet.
19.	Open-fluit	4 feet.		

Swell, 8 Stops.

25.	Gamba	8 feet.	29. Roerfluit	4 feet tone.
26.	Salicional	8 feet.	30. Gemshorn	2 feet.
27.	Holpyp	8 feet.	31. Schalmey	8 feet.
28.	Salicional	4 feet.	32. Vox Humana	8 feet.

Pedal, 8 Stops.

33.	Prestant	16 feet.	37. Octaaf	4 feet.
34.	Sub bass	16 feet tone.	38. Buzian	16 feet.
35.	Octaaf	8 feet.	39. Trombone	8 feet.
36.	Fluit Bass	8 feet.	40. Trompet	4 feet.

Accessory Stops, Movements, &c.

1. Swell to Choir.
2. Choir to Great.
3. Tremulant Swell.
4. Great to Pedal.

5. Octave Pedal.
6, 7, 8, 9. Four Wind-trunk valves.
10, 11, 12. Three Composition Pedals.

Compass.

Manuals, CC to f³ in alt., 54 notes. | Pedal, CCC to tenor f, 30 notes.

4. AMSTERDAM.

The organ in the old church at Amsterdam was begun by R. B. Druyschot in 1683, and finished by him in 1686. It is a most effective instrument; all the Foundation stops are *doubled*, which increases the fulness and solidity of the tone. The Reed stops and Mixtures are also very good, and the mechanism is very fair for so old an organ. This instrument contains 51 stops, distributed as follows :—

Great, 16 Stops.

1.	Prestant	16 feet.	9. Octaaf	2 feet.
2.	Bourdon	16 feet tone.	10. Fluit	2 feet.
3.	Octaaf	8 feet.	11. Flageolet	1 foot.
4.	Holpyp	8 feet.	12. Sesquialtera, IV ranks	2⅔ feet.
5.	Quint	5⅓ feet.	13. Mixtur, VI, VII, and VIII ranks.	
6.	Octaaf	4 feet.	14. Scherp, VI ranks.	
7.	Roerfluit	4 feet tone.	15. Trompet	16 feet.
8.	Roerquint	2⅔ feet tone.	16. Trompet	8 feet.

Choir, 12 Stops.

17.	Prestant	8 feet.	23. Quint	2⅔ feet.
18.	Gedact	8 feet tone.	24. Octaaf	2 feet.
19.	Quintaton	8 feet tone.	25. Sesquialtera, IV ranks	2⅔ feet.
20.	Dulciana	8 feet.	26. Mixtur, VII and VIII ranks.	
21.	Octaaf	4 feet.	27. Scherp, VI ranks.	
22.	Fluit	4 feet.	28. Trompet	8 feet.

Echo, 13 Stops.

29. Quintadeen	16 feet tone.		36. Super-octaaf	2 feet.
30. Prestant	8 feet.		37. Sesqualtera, III ranks...	2⅔ feet.
31. Baarpyp	8 feet.		38. Cimbel, III ranks.	
32. Gamba	8 feet.		39. Fagot	16 feet.
33. Octaaf	4 feet.		40. Trompet	8 feet.
34. Gemshorn	4 feet.		41. Vox Humana	8 feet.
35. Nasat	2⅔ feet.			

Pedal, 10 Stops.

42. Prestant	16 feet.		47. Nachthorn	2 feet.
43. Sub-bass	16 feet tone.		48. Buzian	16 feet.
44. Octaaf	8 feet.		49. Trompet	8 feet.
45. Roerquint	5⅓ feet tone.		50. Trompet	4 feet.
46. Octaaf	4 feet.		51. Cornetin	2 feet.

Accessory Stops, Movements, &c.

1. Coupler, Echo to Great.		3. Coupler, Great to Pedal.
2. Coupler, Choir to Great.		4. Tremulant Echo.

Compass.

Manuals, CC to d³ in alt.		Pedal, CCC to tenor d.

5. AMSTERDAM.

The organ in the new Church at Amsterdam is also a very old one, like the last. The original builder's name is unknown, but it was repaired and enlarged in 1673 by J. Duyschor van Goor, of Dordrecht. It is a most excellent instrument, though scarcely equal to that in the old church. The Mixtures, however, are very brilliant, and the Reeds are very well voiced. It has 44 stops, of which the following is a list :—

Great, 12 Stops.

1. Prestant	16 feet.		7. Quint	2⅔ feet.
2. Quintadena	16 feet tone.		8. Siflet	2 feet.
3. Octaaf	8 feet.		9. Mixtur, VI ranks.	
4. Holpyp	8 feet.		10. Scherp, VII ranks.	
5. Octaaf	4 feet.		11. Fagot	16 feet.
6. Gemshorn	4 feet.		12. Trompet	8 feet.

Choir, 14 Stops.

13. Prestant	8 feet.		20. Fluit	2 feet.
14. Holpyp	8 feet.		21. Siflet	1 foot.
15. Quintadena	8 feet tone.		22. Sesqualtera, II ranks ...	2⅔ feet.
16. Octaaf	8 feet.		23. Mixtur, III ranks.	
17. Fluit	4 feet.		24. Scherp, VI ranks.	
18. Quintfluit	2⅔ feet.		25. Quartane, IV ranks.	
19. Octaaf	2 feet.		26. Cornet, V ranks.	

Echo, 10 Stops.

27. Prestant	8 feet.		32. Fluit	4 feet.
28. Quintadena	8 feet tone.		33. Octaaf	2 feet.
29. Baarpyp	8 feet.		34. Sesqualtera	2⅔ feet.
30. Gamba	8 feet.		35. Trompet	8 feet.
31. Octaaf	4 feet.		36. Vox Humana	8 feet.

Pedal, 8 Stops.

37. Prestant	16 feet.	41. Octaaf	4 feet.
38. Bourdon	16 feet tone.	42. Buzian	16 feet.
39. Octaaf	8 feet.	43. Trompet	8 feet.
40. Roerquint	5½ feet tone.	44. Trompet	4 feet.

Accessory Stops, Movements, &c.

1. Coupler, Echo to Great.	4. Tremulant Echo.
2. Coupler, Choir to Great.	5. Tremulant, Choir.
3. Coupler, Great to Pedal.	6, 7, 8, 9. Four Wind-trunk valves.

Compass.

Manuals, CC to d³ in alt., 51 notes. | Pedal, CCC to tenor d, 27 notes.

6. NYMENGEN.

The organ in the Church of St. Stephen, at Nymengen, in Holland, was built, in 1766, by König, of Cologne. It is a much larger as well as more complete instrument than any which König built for his own city. It contains altogether 53 stops, 3 Manuals, and Pedal; the latter comprising 12 stops. The following is the specification of the above-named instrument, which is one of the best in Holland, particularly in regard to its solo stops :—

Great, 13 Stops.

1. Prestant	16 feet.	8. Tertian	3⅓ feet.
2. Octaaf	8 feet.	9. Super-octaaf	2 feet.
3. Gemshorn	8 feet.	10. Mixtur, VI ranks.	
4. Roer Gedact	8 feet tone.	11. Fourniture, III ranks.	
5. Quint Gedact	5⅓ feet tone.	12. { Trompet Discant } { Trompet Bass }	... 16 feet.
6. Octaaf	4 feet.		
7. Roerflote	4 feet tone.	13. Trompet	8 feet.

Choir, 14 Stops.

14. Bourdon	16 feet tone.	21. Klein octave	2 feet.
15. Prestant	8 feet.	22. Flageolet	1 foot.
16. Flauto Traverso	8 feet.	23. Mixtur, VI ranks.	
17. Klein Bourdon	8 feet tone.	24. Carillon, II ranks.	
18. Octaaf	4 feet.	25. Trompet	8 feet.
19. Flaut a becq	4 feet.	26. Bassoon	8 feet.
20. Quint	2⅔ feet.	27. Vox Humana	8 feet tone.

Echo, 14 Stops.

28. Quintadeen	16 feet tone.	35. Quint Fluit	1½ feet.
29. Koppel	8 feet.	36. Mixtur, V ranks.	
30. Viol di Gamba	8 feet.	37. Cornet, V ranks.	
31. Weide Gedact	8 feet tone.	38. Echo, II ranks	8 & 4 feet.
32. Octaaf	4 feet.	39. Hautbois	8 feet.
33. Nazard and Composita, II ranks	2⅔ feet.	40. Vox Humana	8 feet tone.
34. Super-octave	2 feet.	41. Vox Angelica Bass	4 feet.

Pedal, 12 Stops.

42. Principal	16 feet.	48. Quint	5⅓ feet.
43. Violin	16 feet. -	49. Octaaf	4 feet.
44. Sub-bass	16 feet tone.	50. Bombarde	16 feet.
45. Quint Bass	10⅔ feet tone.	51. Trompet	8 feet.
46. Octaaf	8 feet.	52. Clarion	4 feet.
47. Roer Bass	8 feet tone.	53. Cornet Bass	2 feet.

Accessory Stops, Movements, &c.

1. Great to Pedal.
2. Choir to Great.
3. Echo to Great.

4. Tremulant to Choir.
5, 6, 7, 8. Four Wind-trunk valves.

Compass.

Manuals, CC to f³ in alt, 54 notes. | Pedal CCC to tenor d, 27 notes.

7. GOUDA.

The organ in the Church of St. John the Baptist, at Gouda, was built by Moreau, of Rotterdam, in 1736. One of the chief features in this instrument is its Vox Humana stop, which is particularly fine ; but the tone of the whole organ is most excellent. It has 3 Manuals and Pedal, and 51 stops, the names and distribution of which are as follows :—

Great, 13 *Stops.*

1. Prestant .... 16 feet.
2. Prestant .... 8 feet.
3. Holpyp .... 8 feet.
4. Quint .... 5½ feet.
5. Octaaf........................ 4 feet.
6. Roerfluit........................ 4 feet tone.
7. Open-fluit .... 4 feet.

8. Octaaf .... 2 feet.
9. Mixture, IV and VI ranks.
10. Cornet, V ranks.
11. Trompet .... 16 feet.
12. Trompet .... 8 feet.
13. Schalmey .... 8 feet tone.

Choir, 15 *Stops.*

14. Bourdon........................ 16 feet tone.
15. Prestant .... 8 feet.
16. Holpyp .... 8 feet.
17. Fluit Traverso .... 8 feet.
18. Octaaf........................ 4 feet.
19. Fluit Douce .... 4 feet.
20. Quint .... 2⅔ feet.
21. Octaaf........................ 2 feet.

22. Woudfluit........................ 2 feet.
23. Mixture, VI ranks.
24. Scherp, VI ranks.
25. Cornet, VI ranks.
26. { Carillon Discant, III ranks. { Carillon Bass, II ranks.
27. Trompet........................ 8 feet.
28. Dulcian .... 8 feet.

Echo, 12 *Stops.*

29. Prestant........................ 8 feet.
30. Salicional .... 8 feet.
31. Echo Holpyp................... 8 feet.
32. Quintadon .... 8 feet tone.
33. Octaaf........................ 4 feet.
34. Echo Fluit .... 4 feet.

35. Octaaf .... 2 feet.
36. Nachthorn .... 2 feet.
37. Sesquialtera, II ranks ...... 2⅔ feet.
38. Flageolet .... 1 foot.
39. Echo Trompet .... 8 feet.
40. Vox Humana .... 8 feet tone.

Pedal, 11 *Stops.*

41. Prestant .... 16 feet.
42. Sub-bass........................ 16 feet tone.
43. Prestant .... 8 feet.
44. Wyd Gedact .... 8 feet tone.
45. Rohrquint .... 5⅓ feet tone.
46. Octaaf........................ 4 feet.

47. Hohlfluit .... 2 feet.
48. Bazuin .... 16 feet.
49. Trompet .... 8 feet.
50. Clarion .... 4 feet.
51. Cornetin .... 2 feet.

Accessory Stops, Movements, &c.

1. Great to Pedal.
2. Choir to Great.
3. Echo to Great.

4. Tremulant Echo.
5, 6, 7, 8. Four Wind-trunk valves.

Compass.

Manuals, CC to d³ in alt, 51 notes. | CCC to tenor c, 25 notes.

8. THE HAGUE.

The organ in the Lutheran Church at the Hague is a very good instrument, possessing 3 Manuals and Pedal, and 39 stops, the names and distribution of which latter are as follows :—

Great, 14 Stops.

1. Bourdon	16 feet tone.	8. Octaaf	2 feet.
2. Prestant	8 feet.	9. Woudfluit	2 feet.
3. Roerfluit	8 feet tone.	10. Mixture, VI ranks.	
4. Quintadon	8 feet tone.	11. Cornet, V ranks.	
5. Octaaf	4 feet.	12. Fagot	16 feet.
6. Nachthorn	4 feet.	13. Trompet	8 feet.
7. Quint	2⅔ feet.	14. Trompet	4 feet.

Choir, 9 Stops.

15. Prestant	8 feet.	20. Sesqualtera, II ranks	2⅔ feet.
16. Holpyp	8 feet.	21. Flageolet	1 foot.
17. Octaaf	4 feet.	22. Mixture, III ranks	2 feet.
18. Fluit	4 feet.	23. Dulcian	8 feet.
19. Octaaf	2 feet.		

Echo, 8 Stops.

24. Prestant	8 feet.	28. Roerfluit	4 feet tone.
25. Baarpyp	8 feet.	29. Fluit	2 feet.
26. Quintadon	8 feet tone.	30. Schalmey	8 feet tone.
27. Salicional	4 feet.	31. Vox Humana	8 feet tone.

Pedal.

32. Prestant	16 feet.	36. Octaaf	4 feet.
33. Bourdon	16 feet tone.	37. Trompet	16 feet.
34. Prestant	8 feet.	38. Trompet	8 feet.
35. Roerquint	5⅓ feet tone.	39. Trompet	4 feet.

Accessory Stops, Movements, &c.

1. Choir to Great.	4. Tremulant, Echo.
2. Echo to Great.	5. Tremulant, Choir.
3. Great to Pedal.	6, 7, 8, 9. Four Wind-trunk valves.

Compass.

CC to c³ in alt., 49 notes. | Pedal CCC to tenor c, 25 notes.

9. DELFT.

The organ in the New Church at Delft was built by Batz, of Utrecht, and is altogether a very fine organ, especially the reed stops. It has 3 Manuals and Pedal, and 43 stops, of which latter the following is a list :—

Great, 13 Stops.

1. Prestant	16 feet.	8. Octaaf	2 feet.
2. Bourdon	16 feet tone.	9. Mixture, IV, VI, and VIII	
3. Octaaf	8 feet.	ranks.	
4. Roerfluit	8 feet tone.	10. Cornet, V ranks.	
5. Octaaf	4 feet.	11. Fagot	16 feet.
6. Gemshorn	4 feet.	12. Trompet	8 feet.
7. Quint	2⅔ feet.	13. Trompet	4 feet.

Choir, 11 Stops.

14.	Prestant	8 feet.	20.	Octaaf	2 feet.
15.	Holpyp	8 feet.	21.	Mixture, III, IV, and VI ranks.	
16.	Quintadon	8 feet tone.	22.	Cornet, IV ranks.	
17.	Octaaf	4 feet.	23.	Trompet	8 feet.
18.	Roerfluit	4 feet tone.	24.	Dulcian	8 feet.
19.	Quint	2⅔ feet.			

Echo, 9 Stops.

25.	Prestant	8 feet.	30.	Salicional	4 feet.
26.	Holpyp	8 feet.	31.	Woudfluit	2 feet.
27.	Viol di Gamba	8 feet.	32.	Trompet	8 feet.
28.	Quintadena	8 feet tone.	33.	Vox Humana	8 feet tone.
29.	Open-fluit	4 feet.			

Pedal, 10 Stops.

34.	Prestant	16 feet.	39.	Octaaf	4 feet.
35.	Sub-bass	16 feet tone.	40.	Bazuin	16 feet.
36.	Octaaf	8 feet.	41.	Trompet	8 feet.
37.	Fluit Bass	8 feet.	42.	Trompet	4 feet.
38.	Roerquint	5⅓ feet tone.	43.	Cinq	2 feet.

Accessory Stops, Movements, &c.

1. Echo to Great.	4. Tremulant.
2. Choir to Great.	5, 6, 7, 8. Four Wind-trunk valves.
3. Great to Pedal.	

Compass.

Manuals, CC to f³ in alt., 54 notes. | Pedals, CCC to tenor e, 29 notes.

10. UTRECHT.

The organ in the principal Protestant Church at Utrecht is a very fine one, and is remarkable for having two pipes to each key, from Middle c upwards, throughout all the stops of the great organ. It was built by Batz, of Utrecht, in 1826, and contains 51 stops, 3 Manuals, and Pedal. The following is a list of its contents :—

Great, 13 Stops.

1.	Prestant	16 feet.	7.	Quint	2⅔ feet.
2.	Bourdon, metal Treble, wood Bass	16 feet tone.	8.	Octaaf	2 feet.
			9.	Gemshorn	2 feet.
3.	Octaaf	8 feet.	10.	Sesquialtera, IV ranks.	
4.	Roerfluit	8 feet tone.	11.	Mixture, VII ranks.	
5.	Octaaf	4 feet.	12.	Fagot	16 feet.
6.	Gemshorn	4 feet.	13.	Trompet	8 feet.

Choir, 13 Stops.

14.	Prestant, 2 pipes all through	8 feet.	21.	Fluit	2 feet.
15.	Holpyp	8 feet.	22.	Mixture, V ranks.	
16.	Quintadena	8 feet.	23.	Scherf, VIII ranks.	
17.	Octaaf	4 feet.	24.	Cornet, V ranks.	
18.	Roerfluit	4 feet tone.	25.	Trompet	8 feet.
19.	Quint	2⅔ feet.	26.	Dulcian	8 feet.
20.	Octaaf	2 feet.			

Echo, 13 Stops.

27. Prestant	8 feet.	34. Quintfluit	2⅔ feet.
28. Bourdon	8 feet tone.	35. Woudfluit	2 feet.
29. Gamba	8 feet.	36. Flageolet	1 foot.
30. Flute Traversie to tenor c...	8 feet.	37. Trompet	8 feet.
31. Barpyf	8 feet.	38. Voix Humaine	8 feet.
32. Octaaf	4 feet.	39. Carillon, II ranks.	
33. Fluit, open, large	4 feet.		

Pedal, 12 Stops.

40. Prestant, metal in front ...	16 feet.	46. Mixture, VI ranks	2⅔ feet.
41. Sub-bass, wood	16 feet tone.	47. Bazuin, CCC, 10 inch	16 feet.
42. Octaaf, metal	8 feet.	48. Trombone	8 feet.
43. Fluit Bass	8 feet tone.	49. Trompet	4 feet.
44. Roerquint	5⅓ feet.	50. Cinq	2 feet.
45. Octaaf, of metal	4 feet.	51. Clarion	1 foot.

Accessory Stops, Movements, &c.

1. Positif to Great.
2. Echo to Great.
3. Great to Pedals.

4. Tremulant Positif.
5, 6, 7, 8. Four Wind-trunk valves.

Compass.

Manuals, CC to f³ in alt., 54 notes. | Pedal, CCC to tenor d, 27 notes.

11. TRIEBEL.

The organ in the State Church at Triebel, in the Netherlands, has 22 sounding stops, 2 Manuals, and Pedal. The following is a list of the stops :—

Great, 10 Stops.

1. Bourdon, 10 loth metal in the treble ; the bass of wood	16 feet tone.	5. Octave, 12 loth English tin	4 feet.
2. Principal, 14 loth tin, polished, and in front	8 feet.	6. Fullfluit, 10 loth metal ...	4 feet.
3. Salicional, 14 loth English tin	8 feet.	7. Quint, 12 loth tin	2⅔ feet.
4. Hohlfluit, 10 loth metal to tenor c; the 8-feet octave of wood	8 feet.	8. Super-octave, 12 loth tin...	2 feet.
		9. Mixture, IV ranks	2 feet.
		10. Trompet	8 feet.

Choir, 8 Stops.

11. Viol di Gamba, 14 loth English tin	8 feet.	15. Wald-fluit, 10 loth English tin	2 feet.
12. Flaut d'amour	8 feet.	16. Flageolet, 12 loth English tin	2 feet.
13. Principal, 14 loth English tin, in front	4 feet.	17. Cornet, 12 loth English tin, III ranks	
14. Nazard, 12 loth English tin	2⅔ feet.	18. { Oboe, 12 loth English tin } { Fagot, 12 loth English tin }	8 feet.

Pedal, 4 Stops.

19. Principal, 14 loth Eng. tin, in front ; the five lowest Pipes of Pine, and Stopped	16 feet.	20. Sub-bass, wood	16 feet tone.
		21. Octave, wood	8 feet.
		22. Posaune	16 feet.

Accessory Stops, Movements, &c.

1. Choir to Great.
2. Great to Pedal.

3, 4, 5. Three Wind-trunk valves.
Three Bellows, 10 feet long.
Six Sound-boards.

Compass.

Manuals, CC to f³ in alt., 54 notes. | Pedal, CCC to tenor d, 27 notes.

12. ST. DENIS.

The organ in the Abbey Church of St. Denis, near Paris—the Westminster Abbey of France—is a particularly fine instrument. It was made by MM. Cavaillé-Coll, organ-builders of Paris, and was opened on the 21st of September, 1841. It contains sixty nine sounding stops, among which are twelve for the Pedal; and there are three Manuals. The "Clavier de Bombardes" is not furnished with a separate Manual, as at the Madelaine, but communicates with the Great organ keys. Among the most remarkable features in this organ is the adjustment of the wind. Not only are the Reed stops placed on a heavier wind than those of the Flue species, but the upper octaves of all the stops are in common supplied with a stronger blast than the lower ; upon the principle that wind instrument players exercise a greater pressure of the muscles upon the lungs when producing the acute sounds. There are also several stops of a novel kind, called by Cavaillé "Harmonique," which sound the octave above the note that the length of the pipe would indicate. This was the first organ that had Barker's Pneumatic Lever attachment for lightening the touch. The Combination Pedals, eight in number, are of novel and convenient construction. The following is a list of its stops :—

Clavier du Grand Orgue, 20 Stops.

		Pipes.			Pipes.
1.	Montre, throughout; of spotted metal to CCC; last octave of wood .... 32 feet	54	12.	Grosse Fourniture, IV ranks	216
2.	Montre .... 16 feet	54	13.	Grosse Cymbale, IV ranks	216
3.	Bourdon .... 16 feet tone...	54	14.	Petite Fourniture, IV ranks	216
4.	Montre .... 8 feet	54	15.	Petite Cymbale, IV ranks	216
5.	Bourdon............... 8 feet tone...	54	16.	Première Trompette Harmonique ...... 8 feet	54
6.	Viola .... 8 feet	54	17.	Deuxième Trompette Harmonique ...... 8 feet	54
7.	Flute Traversière Harmonique .... 8 feet	54	18.	Basson et Cor Anglais 8 feet	54
8.	Prestant............... 4 feet	54	19.	Cornet à pavillon 8 feet	54
9.	Flute Octaviante Harmonique...... 4 feet	54	20.	Clarion Octaviant... 4 feet	54
10.	Nazard .... 2⅔ feet	54			
11.	Doublette .... 2 feet	54			

Clavier de Bombardes, 12 Stops.

21.	Bourdon............... 16 feet tone...	54	28.	Bombarde... .... 16 feet	54
22.	Flute .... 8 feet	54	29.	Trompette de Bombarde .... 8 feet	54
23.	Bourdon............... 8 feet	54	30.	Trompette Harmonique............ 8 feet	54
24.	Prestant............... 4 feet	54	31.	Clarion Harmonique 4 feet	54
25.	Quint .... 2⅔ feet	54	32.	Clarion Octaviant... 4 feet	54
26.	Doublette .... 2 feet	54			
27.	Cornet, VII ranks 210				

Clavier de Récit.-Echo Expressif, 8 Stops.

33.	Bourdon............... 8 feet tone...	54	38.	Trompette Harmonique .... 8 feet	54
34.	Flute Harmonique 8 feet	54	39.	Voix Humaine Harmonique............ 8 feet	54
35.	Flute Octaviante Harmonique .... 4 feet	54	40.	Clarion Harmonique .... 4 feet	54
36.	Quint .... 2⅔ feet	54			
37.	Octavin Harmonique 2 feet	54			

Clavier du Positif, 17 Stops.

			Pipes.
41.	Bourdon	16 feet tone...	54
42.	Salicional	8 feet	54
43.	Flute Harmonique	8 feet	54
44.	Bourdon	8 feet tone..	54
45.	Prestant	4 feet	54
46.	Flute	4 feet	54
47.	Flute Octaviante ...	4 feet	54
48.	Quint	2⅔ feet	54
49.	Doublette	2 feet	54
50.	Flageolet Harmonique	2 feet	54

			Pipes.
51.	Tierce	1⅗ feet	54
52.	Cymbale, IV ranks		216
53.	Fourniture, IV ranks		216
54.	Trompette Harmonique	8 feet	54
55.	Clarion Octaviant...	4 feet	54
56.	Cor d'harmonie et Hautbois	8 feet	54
57.	Cromorne	8 feet	54

Clavier de Pedales, 12 Stops.

58.	Flute Ouverte		32 feet ...	25
59.	Flute Ouverte	(24 ft.)...	16 feet ...	25
60.	Contre Basse	...(24 ft.)...	16 feet ...	25
61.	Flute Ouverte	(12 ft.)...	8 feet ...	25
62.	Grosse Quint	...(8 ft.)...	5⅓ feet	25
63.	Flute Ouverte	(6 ft.)...	4 feet ...	25
64.	Bombarde	......(24 ft.)...	16 feet ...	25

65.	Première Trompette	.........(12 ft.)...	8 feet ...	25
66.	Deuxième Trompette	.........(12 ft.)...	8 feet ...	25
67.	Basson	.........(12 ft.)...	8 feet ...	25
68.	Première Clarion	(6 ft.)...	4 feet ...	25
69.	Deuxième Clarion	(6 ft.)...	4 feet ...	25

Combination Pedals, &c.

1. Recit. (Swell) to Great.
2. Bombardes to Great Manual.
3. Swell Stops.
4. Positif to Great.
5. The Treble of Positif Reed and Harmonic Stops to Foundation Stops.
6. The Bass of Positif Reed and Harmonic Stops to Foundation Stops.
7. Manuals, Basses to Pedal.
8. Sub-octave Manual.
9. Tremulant Swell.

Compass.

Manuals, CC to f³ in altissimo, 54 notes. | Pedal, FFF to tenor f, 25 notes.

13. St. Vincent de Paul, Paris.

The organ in the Church of St. Vincent de Paul, at Paris, was built by Cavaillé-Coll, and is quite on an equality with the same builder's admirable instrument at the Madelaine, both in regard to refinement of tone and perfectness of finish in the mechanism. It stands at the west end of the church, and is divided, so as not to obstruct the light through the west window. The stops are forty in number, of which the following is a list :—

Great Organ, 14 Stops.

1.	Montre	16 feet.
2.	Bourdon	16 feet tone.
3.	Montre	8 feet.
4.	Gamba	8 feet.
5.	Bourdon	8 feet tone.
6.	Prestant	4 feet.
7.	Flute	4 feet.

8.	Quint	2⅔ feet.
9.	Doublette	2 feet.
10.	Fourniture, V ranks.	
11.	Cymbale, III ranks.	
12.	Trompette	8 feet.
13.	Cornet à pavillon	8 feet.
14.	Clarion	4 feet.

Choir Organ, 10 Stops.

15.	Bourdon	16 feet tone.	20. Flute Octaviante	4 feet.
16.	Flute Harmonique	8 feet.	21. Doublette	2 feet.
17.	Salicional	8 feet tone.	22. Octavin Harmonique	2 feet.
18.	Bourdon	8 feet tone.	23. Trompette	8 feet.
19.	Prestant	4 feet.	24. Cromorne	8 feet tone.

Swell Organ, 8 Stops.

25.	Flute Harmonique	8 feet.	29. Voix Celeste	8 feet.
26.	Bourdon	8 feet tone.	30. Trompette Harmonique	8 feet.
27.	Prestant	4 feet.	31. Cor Anglais	8 feet.
28.	Flute Douce	4 feet.	32. Voix Humaine	8 feet tone.

Pedal Organ, 8 Stops.

33.	Grand Bourdon	32 feet tone.	37. Bombarde	16 feet.
34.	Montre	16 feet tone.	38. Contre Basse	16 feet.
35.	Contre Basse	16 feet.	39. Trompette	8 feet.
36.	Flute Ouverte	8 feet.	40. Clarion	4 feet.

Accessory Stops, Movements, &c.

1 to 8. Manual and Pedal Couplers.	23. Pneumatic Lever attachment.
9 to 22. Fourteen Composition Pedals.	

Compass.

Manuals, CC to f³ in alt., 54 notes.	Pedal, CCC to tenor c, 25 notes.

14. The Madelaine, Paris.

The fine instrument in the Church of the Madelaine, at Paris, was built by the eminent artists who constructed the St. Denis organ, MM. Cavaillé-Coll. It was completed in 1846, and was opened in the church on the 29th of October of that year, with a performance of vocal and instrumental sacred music. The organ has 4 Manuals and Pedal, and 48 stops, distributed in the following manner :—

Clavier du Grand Orgue, 12 Stops.

1.	Montre	16 pieds.	7. Prestant	4 pieds.
2.	Violon Basse	16 ,,	8. Quint	2⅔ ,,
3.	Montre	8 ,,	9. Doublette	2 ,,
4.	Bourdon	8 ,,	10. Plein Jeu, X ranks.	
5.	Salicional	8 ,,	11. Trompette	8 ,
6.	Flute Harmonique	8 ,,	12. Cor Anglais	8 ,,

Clavier de Bombardes, 10 Stops.

13.	Soubasse	16 pieds.	18. Octavin	2 pieds.
14.	Basse	8 ,,	19. Bombarde	16 ,,
15.	Flute Harmonique	8 ,,	20. Trompette Harmonique	8 ,,
16.	Flute Traversière	8 ,,	21. Deuxième Trompette	8 ,,
17.	Flute Octaviante	4 ,,	22. Clarion	4 ,,

Clavier du Positif, 10 Stops.

23.	Montre	8 pieds.	28. Dulciana	4 pieds.
24.	Viol di Gamba	8 ,,	29. Octavin	2 ,,
25.	Flute Douce	8 ,,	30. Trompette	8 ,,
26.	Voix Celeste	8 ,,	31. Basson et Hautbois	8 ,,
27.	Prestant	4 ,,	32. Clarion	4 ,,

Clavier de Récit. Expressif, 8 Stops.

33.	Flute Harmonique	8 pieds.	37. Octavin.........................	2 pieds.
34.	Bourdon...........................	8 ,,	38. Voix Humaine..............	8 ,,
35.	Musette	8 ,,	39. Trompette Harmonique...	8 ,,
36.	Flute Octaviante	4 ,,	40. Clarion Harmonique	4 ,,

Clavier de Pédales, 8 Stops.

41.	Quintaton	32 pieds.	45. Grosse Flute	8 pieds.
42.	Contre Basse	16 ,,	46. Bombarde.....................	16 ,,
43.	Basse Contre.................	16 ,,	47. Trompette	8 ,,
44.	Violoncelle	8 ,,	48. Clarion	4 ,,

Combination Pedals, &c.

1. Positif to Great.	8. Tremulant to Choir and Swell.
2. Great to Pedal.	9. Great Reeds.
3. Bombarde to Positif.	10. Bombarde Reeds.
4. Pedal to Great.	11. Choir Reeds.
5. Great Organ Sub-octave.	12. Swell Reeds.
6. Bombarde Sub-octave.	13. Pedal Reeds.
7. Pedal octave above.	

Compass.

Manuals, CC to f³ in alt, 54 notes. | Pedal, CCC to tenor d, 27 notes.

15. ST. EUSTACHE, PARIS.

The magnificent new organ in the Church of St. Eustache was built by Ducroquet, of Paris, and was opened in May, 1854. It contains 68 sounding stops, 4 Manuals, and a Pedal of 18 stops. The following is a list of its contents :—

Great Organ, 16 Stops.

1. Montre	16 feet.	9. Doublette	2 feet.
2. Grosse Flute	8 feet.	10. Fourniture, V ranks.	
3. Flute	8 feet.	11. Cymbale, IV ranks.	
4. Flute à pavillon..............	8 feet.	12. Cornett, V ranks.	
5. Bourdon.........................	8 feet tone.	13. Euphone	16 feet.
6. Prestant	4 feet.	14. Trompette.....................	8 feet.
7. Flute	4 feet.	15. Trompette.....................	8 feet.
8. Nazard	3 feet.	16. Clarion	4 feet.

Clavier des Bombardes, 10 Stops.

17. Gamba	16 feet.	22. Gamba	4 feet.
18. Bourdon.........................	16 feet tone.	23. Salicional	4 feet.
19. Gamba	8 feet.	24. Bombarde.....................	16 feet.
20. Salicional	8 feet.	25. Trompette.....................	8 feet.
21. Bourdon.........................	8 feet tone.	26. Clarion	4 feet.

Positif, 14 Stops.

27. Montre	8 feet.	35. Trompette.....................	8 feet.
28. Bourdon.........................	8 feet tone.	36. Hautbois to tenor f	8 feet.
29. Flute Harmonique to tenor c	8 feet.	37. Hautbois (free Reed) to	
30. Keraulophon	8 feet.	tenor f	8 feet tone.
31. Salicional	4 feet.	38. Cromorne	8 feet tone.
32. Flute Ouverte	4 feet.	39. Basson	8 feet.
33. Plein Jeu, V ranks.		40. Clarion	4 feet.
34. Cor Anglais	16 feet.		

Recit. Expressif, 10 Stops.

41.	Bourdon	16 feet tone.	46.	Trompette	8 feet.
42.	Flute Harmonique	8 feet.	47.	Hautbois	8 feet.
43.	Bourdon	8 feet tone.	48.	Euphone	8 feet.
44.	Flute Harmonique	4 feet.	49.	Voix Humaine	8 feet tone.
45.	Trompette	16 feet.	50.	Clarion	4 feet.

Pedale, 18 Stops.

51.	Flute, montre	32 feet.	60.	Salicional	4 feet.
52.	Flute, wood	16 feet.	61.	Bombarde	32 feet.
53.	Contre Basse	16 feet.	62.	Bombarde	16 feet.
54.	Bourdon	16 feet tone.	63.	Basson	16 feet.
55.	Flute	8 feet.	64.	Trompette	8 feet.
56.	Salicional	8 feet.	65.	Trompette	8 feet.
57.	Violoncello	8 feet.	66.	Basson	8 feet.
58.	Flute	8 feet.	67.	Clarion	4 feet.
59.	Flute Ouverte	4 feet.	68.	Basson	4 feet.

16. St. Sulpice, Paris.

The organ in this church was rebuilt by Aristide Cavaillé-Coll, and inaugurated 29th April, 1862.

Grand Chœur d'ut à Sol, 56 Notes.

1.	Salicional	8 feet.	8.	2 E Trompette	8 feet.
2.	Octave	4 feet.	9.	Clarion	4 feet.
3.	Grosse Fourniture, IV ranks.		10.	Clarion Doublette	2 feet.
4.	Grosse Cymbale, VI ranks.		11.	Basson	8 feet.
5.	Plein Jeu, IV ranks.		12.	Basson	16 feet.
6.	Cornet, V ranks.		13.	Bombarde	16 feet.
7.	Ier Trompette	8 feet.			

Grand Orgue, d'ut à Sol, 56 Notes.

1.	Principal-harm	32 16 feet.	8.	Bourdon	8 feet.
2.	Montre	16 feet.	9.	Diapason	8 feet.
3.	Bourdon	16 feet.	10.	Flute à pavillon	8 feet.
4.	Flute Conique	16 feet.	11.	Prestant	4 feet.
5.	Flute Harmonique	8 feet.	12.	Grosse Quint	5⅓ feet.
6.	Flute Traversière	8 feet.	13.	Doublette	2 feet.
7.	Montre	8 feet.			

Bombarde d'ut à Sol, 56 Notes.

1.	Soubasse	16 feet.	11.	Grosse Quint	5⅓ feet.
2.	Flute Conique	16 feet.	12.	Grosse Tierce	3⅕ feet.
3.	Principal	8 feet.	13.	Quint	2⅔ feet.
4.	Flute Harmonique	8 feet.	14.	Octave	4 feet.
5.	Bourdon	8 feet.	15.	Octavin	2 feet.
6.	Gamba	8 feet.	16.	Cornet, V ranks.	
7.	Violoncello	8 feet.	17.	Trompette	8 feet.
8.	Keraulophon	8 feet.	18.	Clarion	4 feet.
9.	Flute Octaviante	4 feet.	19.	Baryton	8 feet.
10.	Prestant	4 feet.	20.	Bombarde	16 feet.

Positif d'ut à Sol, 56 Notes.

1.	Violon Basse	16 feet.	11.	Quint	2⅔ feet.
2.	Quintaton	16 feet.	12.	Doublette	2 feet.
3.	Quintaton	8 feet.	13.	Plein Jeu-harm, III-VI ranks.	
4.	Flute Traversière	8 feet.	14.	Tierce	1⅗ foot.
5.	Salicional	8 feet.	15.	Larigot	1⅓ foot.
6.	Viol di Gamba	8 feet.	16.	Piccolo	1 foot.
7.	Unda Maris	8 feet.	17.	Trompette	8 feet.
8.	Flute Octaviante	4 feet.	18.	Clarinette	8 feet.
9.	Flute Douce	4 feet.	19.	Clarion	4 feet.
10.	Dulcian	4 feet.	20.	Euphone	16 feet.

Recit. Expressif d'ut à Sol, 56 Notes.

1.	Quintaton	16 feet.		
2.	Bourdon	8 feet.		
3.	Violoncello	8 feet.		
4.	Prestant	4 feet.		
5.	Doublette	2 feet.		
6.	Fourniture, IV ranks.			
7.	Cymbale, V ranks.			
8.	Basson et Hautbois	8 feet.		
9.	Voix Humaine	8 feet.		
10.	Cromorne	8 feet.		
11.	Cor Anglais	16 feet.		
12.	Voix Celeste	8 feet.		

Jeux de Combinaison.

13. Flute Harmonique	8 feet.
14. Flute Octaviante	4 feet.
15. Dulcian	4 feet.
16. Nazard	2⅔ feet.
17. Octavin	2 feet.
18. Cornet, V ranks.	
19. Trompette	8 feet.
20. Trompette-harm	8 feet.
21. Bombarde	16 feet.
22. Clarion	4 feet.

Clavier de Pedale (ou Pedalier d'ut à Fa, 30 Notes.)

1. Principal Basse	32 feet.
2. Contre Basse	16 feet.
3. Soubasse	16 feet.
4. Flute	8 feet.
5. Violoncello	8 feet.
6. Flute	4 feet.

7. Clarion	4 feet.
8. Ophicleide	8 feet.
9. Trompette	8 feet.
10. Basson	16 feet.
11. Bombarde	16 feet.
12. Contre Bombarde	32 feet.

Pedales de Combinaison.

1. Orgue.	11. Anches Bombardes.
2. Tirasse Grand Chœur.	12. Anches Positif.
3. Tirasse Grand Orgue.	13. Anches Recit.
4. Anches Pédalle.	14. Copula Grand Chœur.
5. Octaves Grand Chœur.	15. Copula Grand Orgue.
6. Octaves Grand Orgue.	16. Copula Bombardes.
7. Octaves Bombardes.	17. Copula Positif.
8. Octaves Positif.	18. Copula Recit.
9. Octaves Recit.	19. Tremblant.
10. Anches Grand Orgue.	20. Expression.

Registeres de Combinaison.

1. Combinaison Pedal G.	6. Combinaison Pedal G.
2. Combinaison Grand Orgue G.	7. Grand Orgue D.
3. Bombardes G.	8. Bombarde D.
4. Combinaison Positif G.	9. Positif D.
5. Combinaison Recit. G.	10. Recit. D.

Registeres Accessoires.

1. Sonnette du Haut G.	3. Sonnette du Haut D.
2. Sonnette du Bas G.	4. Sonnette du Bas D.

Total—100 Stops, 118 Registers, 20 Composition Pedals, 6706 Pipes.

17. AMIENS.

The organ in the Cathedral at Amiens, which has a 16-feet front, was completed in the year 1429, and was built at the expense of Alphonse de Myrhe, one of the chamberlains of King Charles the Sixth. It still retains its interesting antique appearance, and stands at the west-end of the nave, with the west entrance below, and a handsome circular window, filled with stained glass, above. The Amiens Cathedral organ has 3 Manuals and Pedal, and 40 stops, of which latter the following is a list :—

Great Organ, 16 Stops.

1. Montre	16 feet.	9. Tierce	1⅗ foot.
2. Bourdon	16 feet tone.	10. Fourniture.	
3. Montre	8 feet.	11. Cornet.	
4. Bourdon	8 feet tone.	12. Bombarde	16 feet.
5. Flute	8 feet.	13. Trompette	8 feet.
6. Prestant	4 feet.	14. Trompette	8 feet.
7. Nazard	2⅔ feet.	15. Clarion	4 feet.
8. Doublette	2 feet.	16. Vox Humaine	8 feet.

Choir Organ, 11 Stops.

17.	Montre	8 feet.	23. Tierce	1⅗ foot.
18.	Bourdon	8 feet tone.	24. Plein Jeu.	
19.	Flute..........................	8 feet.	25. Cornet.	
20.	Prestant......................	4 feet.	26. Trompette	8 feet.
21.	Nazard	2⅔ feet.	27. Cromorne	8 feet tone.
22.	Doublette	2 feet.		

Recit., 6 Stops.

28.	Bourdon	8 feet tone.	31. Cornet.	
29.	Flute	8 feet.	32. Trompette	8 feet.
30.	Prestant......................	4 feet.	33. Hautbois	8 feet.

Pedal Organ, 7 Stops.

34.	Flute	16 feet.	38. Bombarde	16 feet.
35.	Bourdon	16 feet tone.	39. Trompette	8 feet.
36.	Flute	8 feet.	40. Clarion......................	4 feet.
37.	Flute	8 feet.		

18. AMIENS.

The organ in the Church of St. Remy, at Amiens, was built by the monks of St. Basil, and finished by them in the year 1842, at a cost of £1,000. It has 34 sounding stops, 3 Manuals, and Pedal. The following is an enumeration of the stops :—

Great Organ, 14 Stops.

1.	Bourdon	16 feet tone.	8. Doublette	2 feet.
2.	Montre	8 feet.	9. Fourniture.	
3.	Bourdon	8 feet tone.	10. Cornet.	
4.	Prestant......................	4 feet.	11. Trompette	8 feet.
5.	Dulcian	4 feet.	12. Trompette	8 feet.
6.	Flute	4 feet.	13. Voix Humaine	8 feet tone.
7.	Nazard	2⅔ feet.	14. Clarion......................	4 feet.

Choir Organ, 10 Stops.

15.	Bourdon......................	8 feet tone.	20. Quarte de Nazard	2 feet.
16.	Prestant......................	4 feet.	21. Fourniture.	
17.	Flute	4 feet.	22. Cornet.	
18.	Nazard	2⅔ feet.	23. Cremona (throughout) ...	8 feet tone.
19.	Doublette	2 feet.	24. Clarion......................	4 feet.

Swell Organ, 6 Stops.

25.	Bourdon	8 feet tone.	28. Nazard......................	2⅔ feet.
26.	Prestant......................	4 feet.	29. Hautbois	8 feet.
27.	Flute	4 feet.	30. Trompette	8 feet.

Pedal Organ, 4 Stops.

31.	Flute	16 feet.	33. Bombarde	16 feet.
32.	Flute	8 feet.	34. Trompette	8 feet.

Compass.

Great CC to f³ in alt., 54 notes.	Swell, tenor c to f³ in alt, 42 notes.
Choir CC to f³ in alt., 54 notes.	Pedal, FFF to tenor f, 25 notes.

19. TOURS.

There were two cathedrals at Tours. That dedicated to St. Martin was destroyed. The large organ here described was destroyed in the Revolution ; but its specification is worth preservation. The instrument was built by J. B. U.

Le Fevre, of Rouen, was of immense power, and had 4 Manuals and 60 sounding stops, supplied by 13 bellows. The stops were distributed in the following manner :—

Great Organ, 23 Stops.

1.	Grosse Principal to FFFF	32 feet.	13. Quint	3 feet.
2.	Sub-bourdon.................	32 feet tone.	14. Doublette.....................	2 feet.
3.	Prestant......................	16 feet.	15. Tierce	1⅗ foot.
4.	Bourdon	16 feet tone.	16. Quint	1⅓ foot.
5.	Montre	8 feet.	17. Mixture, XV ranks.	
6.	Prestant......................	8 feet.	18. Cornet, V ranks.	
7.	Principal	8 feet.	19. First Trompette	8 feet.
8.	Bourdon	8 feet tone.	20. Second Trompette	8 feet.
9.	Quint..........................	6 feet.	21. Third Trompette............	8 feet.
10.	Octave	4 feet.	22. First Clarion	4 feet.
11.	Octave	4 feet.	23. Second Clarion	4 feet.
12.	Tierce	3⅕ feet.		

Choir Organ, 16 Stops.

24.	Bourdon	16 feet tone.	32. Tierce	1⅗ foot.
25.	Principal	8 feet.	33. Quint	1⅓ foot.
26.	Prestant......................	8 feet.	34. Mixture, IX ranks.	
27.	Bourdon	8 feet tone.	35. Cornett, V ranks.	
28.	Octave	4 feet.	36. Trompette	8 feet.
29.	Quint..........................	3 feet.	37. Clarion......................	4 feet.
30.	Octave	2 feet.	38. Cromorne	8 feet.
31.	Doublette	2 feet.	39. Voix Humaine	8 feet.

Bombarde, 6 Stops.

40.	Bourdon	8 feet tone.	43. Bombarde	16 feet.
41.	Octave	4 feet.	44. Trompette	8 feet.
42.	Cornet, V ranks.		45. Clarion......................	4 feet.

Fourth Manual.

A general Echo to the Great organ.

Pedal, 15 Stops.

46.	Grosse Principal	16 feet.	54. Octave	2 feet.
47.	Octave	8 feet.	55. Tierce	1⅗ feet.
48.	Prestant......................	8 feet.	56. Bombarde	32 feet.
49.	Quint..........................	6 feet.	57. Trompette	16 feet.
50.	Octave	4 feet.	58. Trompette	8 feet.
51.	Flute	4 feet.	59. Clarion......................	4 feet.
52.	Tierce	3⅕ feet.	60. Clarion......................	2 feet.
53.	Quint..........................	3 feet.		

20. ROUEN.

The organ in the magnificent Church of St. Ouen, at Rouen, was built in the year 1630. It has recently been renovated by MM. Cavaillé-Coll. It had 5 Manuals, a Pedal organ of 2 octaves in compass, 12 pairs of bellows, and 49 sounding stops, distributed as follows :—

Great, 13 Stops (Fourth Manual).

1.	Montre (throughout, in metal)	16 feet.	7. Quart	2 feet.
			8. Tierce	1⅗ foot.
2.	Bourdon (throughout)	16 feet.	9. Fourniture.	
3.	Montre	8 feet.	10. Cymbale.	
4.	Bourdon	8 feet.	11. Bassus de Trompette	8 feet.
5.	Prestant	4 feet.	12.' Voix Humaine	8 feet.
6.	Quint..........................	2⅓ feet.	13. Clarion......................	4 feet.

Choir, 14 Stops (*Lower Manual*).

14.	Prestant	8 feet.	21.	Cornet.	
15.	Bourdon	8 feet.	22.	Galonbel.	
16.	Prestant	4 feet.	23.	Plein Jeu.	
17.	Flute	4 feet.	24.	Cromorne	8 feet.
18.	Nazard	2⅔ feet.	25.	Basson et Hautbois	8 feet.
19.	Doublette	2 feet.	26.	Trompette	8 feet.
20.	Tierce	1⅗ foot.	27.	Clarion	4 feet.

Echo, 4 Stops (*Upper Manual*).

28.	Flute	8 feet.	30.	Trompette	8 feet.
29.	Cornet.		31.	Clarion	4 feet.

Recit., 6 Stops (*Second Manual*).

32.	Bourdon, Recit.	8 feet.	35.	Hautbois, Recit.	8 feet.
33.	Flute, Recit.	4 feet.	36.	Trompette, Recit.	8 feet.
34.	Cornet, Recit.		37.	Clarion, Recit.	4 feet.

Bombarde, 4 Stops (*Third Manual*).

38.	Bombarde	16 feet.	40.	Clarion	4 feet.
39.	Trompette	8 feet.	41.	Cornet.	

Pedal, 8 Stops.

42.	Prestant	16 feet.	46.	Prestant	4 feet.
43.	Gamba	16 feet.	47.	Bombarde	16 feet.
44.	Prestant	8 feet.	48.	Trompette	8 feet.
45.	Quint	5⅓ feet.	49.	Clarion	4 feet.

21. ABBEVILLE.

The organ in the Cathedral at Abbeville is placed over the west entrance, where it has a majestic appearance. The case of the Great organ has five towers, with the smallest one in the centre; the Choir organ has three towers, with the largest one in the centre. The 16-feet Montre stands in front, and is of polished tin. The organ is an old one, and originally belonged to the Church of St. George, which building was completely demolished in the Revolution of 1793. The organ escaped sharing the same fate through the care of Honoré Blondin, the nephew of whom was for many years, and, perhaps, still is, organist. The instrument was enlarged and thoroughly repaired by M. Charles Lefevre, of Abbeville, some years since, but both cathedral and instrument were in a dilapidated condition when we last saw them. The organ contains 42 stops, distributed as follows :—

Great, 18 Stops.

1.	Montre (throughout)	16 feet.	10.	Doublette	2 feet.
2.	Bourdon (throughout)	16 feet tone.	11.	Flute	2 feet.
3.	Montre	8 feet.	12.	Fourniture	
4.	Bourdon	8 feet tone.	13.	Grand Cornet	
5.	Flute	8 feet.	14.	Trompette	8 feet.
6.	Prestant	4 feet.	15.	Trompette	8 feet.
7.	Flute	4 feet.	16.	Clarion	4 feet.
8.	Flute Tacet	4 feet.	17.	Cromorne (throughout)	8 feet.
9.	Nazard	2⅔ feet.	18.	Voix Humaine	8 feet.

Choir, 12 Stops.

19.	Bourdon	8 feet tone.	25.	Petit Nazard	1⅓ feet.
20.	Montre	4 feet.	26.	Fifre	1 foot.
21.	Flute à Cheminée	4 feet.	27.	Fourniture.	
22.	Nazard	2⅔ feet.	28.	Hautbois Tacet	8 feet.
23.	Super Octave	2 feet.	29.	Clarion	4 feet.
24.	Doublette	2 feet.	30.	Cromorne (throughout)	8 feet.

Swell, 6 Stops.

31.	Dulcian	8 feet.	34. Flute	2 feet.
32.	Flute	4 feet.	35. Hautbois	8 feet.
33.	Nazard	2⅔ feet.	36. Trompette	8 feet.

Pedal, 6 Stops.

37.	Flute Allemande	16 feet.	40. Musette	
38.	Flute	8 feet.	41. Bombarde, wood	16 feet.
39.	Flute	4 feet.	42. Trompette, metal	8 feet.

There are four Manuals : the lower one for the Choir organ, the second for the Great ; the third for the Pedal organ, which is of the same compass as the other organs ; and the fourth for the Swell. The compass of the Great, Choir, and Pedal is from CC to f³ in alt. The Swell, to tenor f ; the Pedal-board is from CCC to tenor f, two octaves and a half. The Manuals are coupled together by being drawn out about half an inch.

22. BEAUVAIS.

The organ in the Cathedral at Beauvais has 5 Manuals and Pedal, and 64 sounding stops, of which the following is a list :—

Grand Orgue (Great), 19 Stops.

1.	Montre	16 feet.	11. Quarte de Nazard	2 feet.
2.	Bourdon	16 feet tone.	12. Tierce	1⅗ foot.
3.	Montre	8 feet.	13. Grosse Fourniture.	
4.	Flute	8 feet.	14. Fourniture.	
5.	Gamba	8 feet.	15. Cymbale..	
6.	Bourdon	8 feet tone.	16. Great Cornet.	
7.	Gros Nazard	5⅓ feet.	17. Première Trompette	8 feet.
8.	Prestant	4 feet.	18. Deuxième Trompette	8 feet.
9.	Grosse Tierce	3⅕ feet.	19. Clarion	4 feet.
10.	Nazard	2⅔ feet.		

Positif (Choir), 14 Stops.

20.	Montre	8 feet.	27. Fourniture, III ranks.	
21.	Bourdon	8 feet tone.	28. Cymbale, II ranks.	
22.	Flute	8 feet.	29. Cornet, V ranks.	
23.	Prestant	4 feet.	30. Trompette	8 feet.
24.	Nazard	2⅔ feet.	31. Clarion	4 feet.
25.	Doublette	2 feet.	32. Cromorne	8 feet tone.
26.	Tierce	1⅗ foot.	33. Basson	8 feet.

Bombarde, 4 Stops.

34.	Bombarde	16 feet.	36. Clarion	4 feet.
35.	Trompette	8 feet.	37. Grand Cornet.	

Recit., Echo, 14 Stops.

38.	Salicional	8 feet.	45. Doublette	2 feet.
39.	Bourdon	8 feet tone.	46. Quintadena	2 feet.
40.	Flute	8 feet.	47. Tierce	1⅗ foot.
41.	Flute Harmonique	8 feet.	48. Trompette	8 feet.
42.	Principal	4 feet.	49. Cor Anglais	8 feet.
43.	Flute Douce	4 feet.	50. Hautbois	8 feet.
44.	Quint	2⅔ feet.	51. Voix Humaine	8 feet tone.

Swell, 3 Stops.

| 52. Conoclite. | 53. Euphone. | 54. Terpomele. |

Pedal, 10 *Stops.*

55. Flute Ouverte	16 feet.	60. Flute	4 feet.
56. Contre Basse	16 feet.	61. Bombarde	24 feet.
57. Bourdon	16 feet tone.	62. Trompette	12 feet.
58. Flute	8 feet.	63. Clarion	6 feet.
59. Quint	5½ feet.	64. Dermogloste.	

Compass.

| Manuals, CC to f³ in alt., 54 notes. | Pedal, FFF to tenor f, 25 notes. |

23. ANTWERP.

The organ in the Cathedral at Antwerp was built by De la Haye, of Antwerp, in 1645, and repaired by Folder, of Brussels, in 1834. It has 44 stops, 3 Manuals, and Pedal. The following is a list of its contents :—

Great Organ, 18 *Stops.*

1. Montre	16 feet.	11. Tierce	1⅗ foot.
2. Bourdon	16 feet tone.	12. Fourniture.	
3. Montre	8 feet.	13. Cymbale.	
4. Bourdon	8 feet tone.	14. Cornet.	
5. Flute traversière	8 feet.	15. { Bombarde Discant / Bombarde Basse }	… 16 feet.
6. Gros Nazard	5⅓ feet.		
7. Prestant	4 feet.	16. { Trompette Discant / Trompette Basse }	… 8 feet.
8. Flute	4 feet.		
9. Nazard	2⅔ feet.	17. Clarion	4 feet.
10. Doublette	2 feet.	18. Voix Humaine	8 feet tone.

Choir Organ, 10 *Stops.*

19. Montre	8 feet.	25. Fourniture.	
20. Bourdon	8 feet tone.	26. Cornet.	
21. Prestant	4 feet.	27. { Trompette Biscant / Trompette Dasse }	… 8 feet.
22. Flute	4 feet tone.		
23. Nazard	2⅔ feet.	28. Hautbois	8 feet.
24. Doublette	2 feet.		

Swell Organ, 6 *Stops.*

29. Montre discant	8 feet.	32. Flute	4 feet.
30. Bourdon	8 feet tone.	33. Doublette	2 feet.
31. Prestant	4 feet.	34. Cromorne	8 feet.

Pedal Organ, 10 *Stops.*

35. Montre	16 feet.	40. Flute	4 feet.
36. Bourdon	16 feet tone.	41. Fourniture.	
37. Prestant	8 feet.	42. Bombarde	16 feet.
38. Bourdon	8 feet tone.	43. Trompette	8 feet.
39. Prestant	4 feet.	44. Clarion	4 feet.

Compass.

| Manuals, CC to f³ in alt. | Pedals, FFF to tenor f. |

24. ANTWERP.

The organ in the Church of St. Paul, at Antwerp, was built by Terbrugen, of Antwerp, in the year 1670, and was repaired and improved in 1825. It has 3 Manuals and Pedal, and 51 stops. The Pedal-board is very inconveniently arranged, and the touch is disagreeable ; otherwise it is a very satisfactory instrument, and rather superior to that in the Cathedral. The following is a list of its stops :—

Great Organ, 19 Stops.

1. Principal	16 feet.	11. Nazard	3 feet.
2. Bourdon	16 feet tone.	12. Doublette	2 feet.
3. Montre	8 feet.	13. Fourniture.	
4. Bourdon	8 feet tone.	14. Cymbale.	
5. Quintaton	8 feet tone.	15. Cornet.	
6. Grand Nazard	6 feet.	16. Bombarde.	16 feet.
7. Prestant	4 feet.	17. { Trompette Discant } { Trompette Basse }	8 feet.
8. Flute	4 feet.		
9. Flute Traversière	4 feet.	18. Clarion	4 feet.
10. Grosse Tierce	3⅓ feet.	19. Voix Humaine	8 feet.

Choir Organ, 15 Stops.

20. Bourdon	8 feet tone.	28. Tierce	1⅗ foot.
21. Viol di Gamba	8 feet.	29. Fourniture.	
22. Prestant	4 feet.	30. Cornet.	
23. Flute	4 feet.	31. Trompette	8 feet.
24. Flute Traversière	4 feet.	32. Hautbois	8 feet.
25. Nazard	3 feet.	33. Vox Angelica	8 feet.
26. Doublette	2 feet.	34. Basson	8 feet.
27. Flute Champ	2 feet.		

Echo Organ, 10 Stops.

35. Bourdon	8 feet.	40. Tierce	1⅗ foot.
36. Prestant	4 feet.	41. Fourniture.	
37. Flute	4 feet.	42. Cornet.	
38. Nazard	3 feet.	43. Trompette	8 feet.
39. Doublette	2 feet.	44. Voix Humaine	8 feet.

Pedal Organ, 7 Stops.

45. Prestant	16 feet.	49. Bombarde	16 feet.
46. Quintaton	16 feet tone.	50. Trompette	8 feet.
47. Flute	8 feet.	51. Clarion	4 feet.
48. Prestant	4 feet.		

Compass.

Manuals, CC to f³ in alt.	Pedals, CCC to tenor c.

25. BRUSSELS.

The organ in the Cathedral Church of St. Gudule, at Brussels, contains 47 stops, 3 Manuals, and Pedal containing a 32-feet reed. The following list shows the distribution and names of the stops :—

Great Organ, 18 Stops.

1. Bourdon Discant	32 feet tone.	11. Quint	1⅓ foot.
2. Montre	16 feet.	12. Fourniture.	
3. Bourdon	16 feet tone.	13. Cymbale.	
4. Prestant	8 feet.	14. Cornet.	
5. Bourdon	8 feet tone.	15. Cornet, lowest rank, Bourdon	16 feet.
6. Octave	4 feet.		
7. Flute	4 feet.	16. Bombarde	16 feet.
8. Nazard	2⅔ feet.	17. Trompette	8 feet.
9. Doublette	2 feet.	18. Clarion Bass	4 feet.
10. Tierce	1⅗ foot.		

Choir Organ, 12 Stops.

19. Bourdon	16 feet tone.	25. Octave	2 feet.
20. Bourdon	8 feet tone.	26. Tierce	1⅗ foot.
21. Flute	8 feet.	27. Larigot	1⅓ foot.
22. Prestant	4 feet.	28. Fourniture.	
23. Flute	4 feet.	29. Cornet.	
24. Nazard	2⅔ feet.	30. Hautbois	8 feet.

Echo Organ, 7 Stops.

31. Prestant	8 feet.	35. Doublette	2 feet.
32. Bourdon	8 feet tone.	36. Fourniture.	
33. Octave	4 feet.	37. Trompette	8 feet.
34. Flute	4 feet.		

Pedal Organ, 10 Stops.

38. Montre	16 feet.	43. Flute	4 feet.
39. Bourdon	16 feet tone.	44. Quart	2 feet.
40. Flute	8 feet.	45. Buzain	32 feet.
41. Bourdon	8 feet tone.	46. Bombarde	16 feet.
42. Quint	5⅓ feet.	47. Trompete	8 feet.

26. LIEGE.

The organ in the Church of St. Martin, at Liege, built by Clerinex, at a cost of £1,000, has 3 Manuals and Pedal, and 35 sounding stops, of which the following is a list :—

Great Organ, 14 Stops.

1. Bourdon	16 feet tone.	8. Super-octave	2 feet.
2. Principal	8 feet.	9. Sesquialtera, III ranks ...	3 feet.
3. Bourdon	8 feet tone.	10. Fourniture, IV ranks.	
4. Gamba	8 feet.	11. Cornet, IV ranks.	
5. Flute Traversière	8 feet.	12. Trompette	8 feet.
6. Prestant	4 feet.	13. Clarion	4 feet.
7. Flute pointue	4 feet.	14. Cromorne	8 feet.

Choir, 9 Stops.

15. Salicional	8 feet.	20. Sesquialtera.	
16. Bourdon	8 feet tone.	21. Cornet.	
17. Prestant	4 feet.	22. Trompette	8 feet.
18. Old Flute	4 feet.	23. Hautbois	8 feet.
19. Super-octave	2 feet.		

Echo, 6 Stops.

24. Bourdon	8 feet tone.	27. Super-octave	2 feet.
25. Prestant	4 feet.	28. Cornet.	
26. Flageolet.		29. Trompette	8 feet.

Pedal, 6 Stops.

30. Montre, metal	16 feet.	33. Montre	8 feet.
31. Flute, wood open	16 feet.	34. Bombarde*	16 feet.
32. Soubasse	16 feet tone.	35. Bombarde	8 feet.

---

* The CCC pipe, 12 inches in diameter.

27. COLOGNE.

The organ in the Cathedral of Cologne was built in the year 1572, and repaired in 1734 by J. J. Schmitt, of Mülbeim. It was re-constructed and considerably enlarged by Engelbert Maas, of Cologne, in the years 1817 and 1821 ; more than half the pipes, the mechanism, &c., being made by him. The organ, since the completion of the nave of the cathedral, has been re-erected in the north transept. It has now 40 stops, 3 Manuals, and Pedal, the names and distribution of the former being as follow :—

Great, 11 Stops.

1. Principal, tin, in front......	16 feet.	7. Rauschwerk, V ranks......	2⅔ feet.
2. Octave	8 feet.	8. Cymbale, IV ranks.	
3. Viol di Gamba...............	8 feet.	9. Sesquialtera, II ranks......	2⅔ feet.
4. Hohlflote	8 feet.	10. Posaune	16 feet.
5. Super-octave......	4 feet.	11. Trompette	8 feet.
6. Flautin	2 feet.		

Choir, 11 Stops.

12. Principal	8 feet.	18. Cornett, IV ranks.	
13. Rohrflote	8 feet tone.	19. { Bourdon, Discant } { Contrafagot, Bass }	... 16 feet.
14. { Viol di Gamba, Discant } { Violoncello Bass }	8 feet.	20. Clarion.......................	8 feet.
15. Queerflote, Discant	8 feet.	21. Krumhorn	8 feet tone.
16. Rohrflote	4 feet tone.	22. Glockenspiel.	
17. Super-octave..................	2 feet.		

Echo, 9 Stops.

23. { Hohlflote, Discant } { Hohlflote, Bass }	8 feet.	28. Super-flote	2 feet.
24. Queerflote, Discant.........	8 feet.	29. Quint-flote	1½ foot.
25. Prestant........................	4 feet.	30. Cymbale.	
26. Hohlflote	4 feet.	31. { Clarinett, Discant } { Clarinett, Bass }	... 8 feet tone.
27. Super-octave..................	2 feet.		

Pedal, 9 Stops.

32. Contra Violin	16 feet.	37. Posaune	16 feet.
33. Sub-bass	16 feet tone.	38. Trompette	8 feet.
34. Violin	8 feet.	39. Clarion.......................	4 feet.
35. Octave Sub-bass	8 feet tone.	40. Clarinett	2 feet.
36. Super-octave..................	4 feet.		

Compass.

Manuals, CC to f³ in alt., 54 notes. | Pedal, CCC to tenor c, 25 notes.

28. COLOGNE.

The organ in the Minorets Church is said to be no less than 400 years old. Its tone is exceedingly good, and it has 33 stops, of which the following is a list :—

Great, 15 Stops.

1. Bourdon	16 feet tone.	9. Salicena, oder Quint	2⅔ feet.
2. Prestant........................	8 feet.	10. Super-octave	2 feet.
3. { Gamba, Discant } { Gamba, Bass }	8 feet.	11. Quint	1½ foot.
4. Violoncello	8 feet.	12. Mixture, III and IV ranks.	
5. Hollpfeife.....................	8 feet.	13. { Trompette, Discant } { Trompette, Bass }	... 8 feet.
6. Octave	4 feet.	14. Clarion........................	4 feet.
7. Flote	4 feet.	15. Vox Humana	8 feet tone.
8. Wald-flote.....................	4 feet.		

Choir, 12 Stops.

16.	Hollpfeife	8 feet.	22. Octave	2 feet.
17.	Flaut Traversière	8 feet.	23. Cymbale, III ranks.	
18.	Prestant	4 feet.	24. Carillon, II ranks.	
19.	Flaut Douce	4 feet.	25. Hautbois	8 feet.
20.	Vox Angelica	4 feet.	26. Clarinett	8 feet tone.
21.	Quint-flaut	2⅔ feet tone.	27. Vox Humana	8 feet tone.

Pedal, 6 Stops.

28.	Principal, in front	16 feet.	31. Posaune	16 feet.
29.	Octave Bass	8 feet.	32. Trompette	8 feet.
30.	Super-octave	4 feet.	33. Clarion	4 feet.

Accessory Stops.

1. Choir to Great. | 2. Great to Pedal.

Compass.

Manuals, CC to d³ in alt., no top c³ sharp, 50 notes. | Pedal, CCC to EE, 17 notes.

---

29. COLOGNE.

The organ in the Jesuits' Church at Cologne is a particularly fine instrument. It was originally built about the year 1750, and was repaired and enlarged in 1822. It has now 34 Stops, 3 Manuals, and a Pedal of 5 Stops.

Great, 11 Stops.

1.	Principal	16 feet.	7. Super-octave	2 feet.
2.	Prestant	8 feet.	8. Mixture, IV ranks.	
3.	Gamba	8 feet.	9. Cornett, V ranks.	
4.	Bourdon	8 feet tone.	10. { Trompette, Discant } { Trompette, Bass }	8 feet.
5.	Octave	4 feet.		
6.	Quint	2⅔ feet.	11. Clarion	4 feet.

Choir, 11 Stops.

12.	Prestant	8 feet.	18. Flautino	4 feet.
13.	Gamba	8 feet.	19. Super-octave	2 feet.
14.	Hollpfeife	8 feet.	20. Carillon, II ranks.	
15.	Travers-flote	8 feet.	21. Cornett, V ranks.	
16.	Octave	4 feet.	22. Clarinett	8 feet tone.
17.	Flote	4 feet.		

Echo, 6 Stops.

23.	Gemshorn	8 feet.	26. Flote	4 feet.
24.	Hollpfeife	8 feet.	27. Hautbois	8 feet.
25.	Prestant	4 feet.	28. Vox Humana	8 feet tone.

Pedal, 6 Stops.

29.	Sub-bass	16 feet.	32. Posaune	16 feet.
30.	Octave	8 feet.	33. Trompette	8 feet.
31.	Violone	8 feet.	34. Clarion	4 feet.

Accessory Stops, Movements, &c.

1. Choir to Great. | 3. Great to Pedal.
2. Echo to Choir. | 4. Tremulant to Choir.

Compass.

Manuals, CC to f³ in alt., 54 notes. | Pedal, CCC to FF, 1½ octave, 18 notes.

30. COLOGNE.

The Church of Maria de Capitol, at Cologne, contains an imposing-toned organ, erected by Ludwig König, of Cologne, in 1767.   In the year 1839 a Cornett and Flautino were added, and the organ raised to its present pitch by Engelbert Maas, of Cologne.   It has now 40 stops, 3 Manuals, and Pedal of 10 stops.   The following is the disposition :—

Great, 12 Stops.

1. Principal	16 feet.	7. Quint	2⅔ feet.
2. Octave	8 feet.	8. Mixture, IV ranks	2 feet.
3. Viola di Gamba	8 feet.	9. Cymbale, III ranks	1 foot.
4. Hollpfeife	8 feet.	10. Cornett, IV ranks.	
5. Octave	4 feet.	11. Trompette	8 feet.
6. Flaut	4 feet.	12. Clarion	4 feet.

Choir, 12 Stops.

13. Prestant	8 feet.	20. Flautina	2 feet.
14. Viol di Gamba	8 feet.	21. Quint-flaut	1⅓ foot.
15. Hollpfeife	8 feet.	22. Carillon, II ranks	4 feet.
16. Flaut Traversière, Discant	8 feet.	23. Vox Humana	8 feet tone.
17. Octave	4 feet.	24. { Clarinett, Discant } { Hautbois, Bass } ...	8 feet.
18. Flaut	4 feet.		
19. Super-octave	2 feet.		

Echo, 6 Stops.

25. Hollpfeife	8 feet.	29. Hautbois, Discant	8 feet.
26. Gemshorn	4 feet.	30. { Vox Humana, Discant } { Vox Humana, Bass }	8 feet tone.
27. Flaut	4 feet tone.		
28. Super-octave	2 feet.		

Pedal, 10 Stops.

31. Bourdon	16 feet.	36. Octave	4 feet.
32. Viol di Gamba	8 feet.	37. Posaune	16 feet.
33. Prestant	8 feet.	38. Trompette	8 feet.
34. Gemshorn	8 feet.	39. Clarion	4 feet.
35. Quint	5⅓ feet.	40. Clarino	2 feet.

Accessory Stops, Movements, &c.

1. Great to Pedal. | 2. Tremulant Echo. | 3. Tremulant Positif.

Compass.

Manuals, CC to f³ in alt., 54 notes. | Pedal, CCC to Gamut A, 22 notes.

31. COLOGNE.

The organ in the Church of St. Columba, at Cologne, was made by König, in 1753, and presents the remarkable peculiarity, for a German organ of the size, of being entirely without Pedal Stops.   The following is a list of the contents of the above-named instrument :—

Great, 12 Stops.

1. Prestant	16 feet.	7. Super-octave	2 feet.
2. Principal	8 feet.	8. Sesqualtera, III ranks	2⅔ feet.
3. Viol di Gamba	8 feet.	9. Mixture, IV ranks	2 feet.
4. Gedact	8 feet tone.	10. Posaune	16 feet.
5. Octava	4 feet.	11. Trompette	8 feet.
6. Flaut Douce	4 feet.	12. Clarion	4 feet.

Choir, 9 Stops.

13. Gedact	8 feet tone.	18. Quint-flaut	1½ foot.
14. Prestant	4 feet.	19. Carillon, II ranks.	
15. Flaut Traversière	4 feet.	20. Clarinett, Discant	8 feet tone.
16. Flaut Douce	4 feet.	21. Vox Humana	8 feet tone.
17. Octava	2 feet.		

32. COLOGNE.

The organ in the Church of St. Ursula is a new instrument, and was built by Heinrich, of Cologne. It contains 25 stops, 2 Manuals, and a Pedal of 6 stops. The following is a list of its contents :—

Great, 11 Stops.

1. Bourdon	16 feet tone.	7. Quint	2¾ feet.
2. Principal	8 feet.	8. Octave	2 feet.
3. Bourdon	8 feet tone.	9. Mixture, IV ranks.	
4. Gamba	8 feet.	10. Cornett.	
5. Octave	4 feet.	11. Trompette	8 feet.
6. Flote	4 feet.		

Choir, 8 Stops.

12. Prestant	8 feet.	16. Flaut	4 feet.
13. Bourdon	8 feet tone.	17. Octave	2 feet.
14. Salicional	8 feet.	18. Oboe	8 feet.
15. Fernflote	4 feet.	19. Basset Horn	8 feet.

Pedal, 6 Stops.

20. Sub-bass	16 feet.	23. Posaune	16 feet.
21. Violoncello	8 feet.	24. Trompette	8 feet.
22. Octave Bass	8 feet.	25. Clarion	4 feet.

33. BONN.

There is a fine old organ in the Cathedral at Bonn, containing 29 sounding stops, among which is a particularly fine 16-foot Posaune on the Pedal, of wood. The instrument has 2 Manuals and Pedal, among which the stops are thus distributed :—

Great, 12 Stops.

1. Bourdon	16 feet tone.	7. Quint	3 feet.
2. Principal	8 feet.	8. Super-octave	2 feet.
3. Bourdon	8 feet tone.	9. Octavine	1 foot.
4. Gamba	8 feet.	10. Mixture.	
5. Salicional	8 feet.	11. Trompette	8 feet.
6. Octave	4 feet.	12. Clarion	4 feet.

Choir, 11 Stops.

13. Bourdon	8 feet tone.	19. Octave	2 feet.
14. Flote, Discant	8 feet.	20. Mixture.	
15. Principal	4 feet.	21. Trompette	8 feet.
16. Octave	4 feet.	22. Bassoon	8 feet.
17. Rohrflote	4 feet tone.	23. Vox Humana	8 feet.
18. Quint	3 feet.		

Pedal, 6 Stops.

24. Sub-bass	16 feet tone.	27. Posaune	16 feet.
25. Principal	8 feet.	28. Posaune	8 feet.
26. Violoncello	8 feet.	29. Posaune	4 feet.

34. BONN.

The organ in the Protestant Church at Bonn, by Weil, is an excellent instrument. It has 19 stops, of which the following is a list :—

Great, 9 Stops.

1. Bourdon	16 feet tone.	6. Flute	4 feet.
2. Principal	8 feet.	7. Salicional	4 feet.
3. Bourdon	8 feet tone.	8. Super-octave	2 feet.
4. Gamba	8 feet.	9. Trompette	8 feet.
5. Octave	4 feet.		

Choir, 7 Stops.

10. Flote	8 feet.	14. Rohrflote	4 feet.
11. Hohlflote	8 feet.	15. Super-octave	2 feet.
12. Harmonica	8 feet.	16. Krumhorn	8 feet.
13. Principal	4 feet.		

Pedal, 3 Stops.

17. Principal... 16 feet.	18. Sub-bass... 16 feet tone.	19. Octave... 8 feet.

35. COBLENTZ.

The organ in the Church of Castor, at Coblentz, has 39 stops, distributed among 3 Manuals and Pedal, as follow :—

Great, 16 Stops.

1. Gross Gedact	16 feet tone.	10. Quint	2⅔ feet.
2. Principal	8 feet.	11. Super-octave	2 feet.
3. Viol di Gamba	8 feet.	12. Vox Angelica	2 feet.
4. Hollpfeife	8 feet.	13. Terz	1⅗ foot.
5. Quintadena	8 feet tone.	14. Mixture	1 foot.
6. Coppel	8 feet.	15. Cornett.	
7. Octave	4 feet.	16. { Trompette, Treble	8 feet.
8. Salicional	4 feet.	{ Trompette, Bass	
9. Flaut	4 feet.		

Choir, 9 Stops.

17. Bourdon	8 feet tone.	22. Octave	2 feet.
18. Flaut Ravena	8 feet.	23. Mixture.	
19. Principal	4 feet.	24. Krumhorn	8 feet tone.
20. Flaut	4 feet.	25. Vox Humana	8 feet tone.
21. Quint	2⅔ feet.		

Echo, 7 Stops.

26. Bourdon	8 feet tone.	30. Octave	2 feet.
27. Flaut	4 feet.	31. Trompette	8 feet.
28. Salicional	4 feet.	32. Vox Humana	8 feet tone.
29. Quint	2⅔ feet.		

Pedal, 7 Stops.

33. Violon Bass	16 feet.	37. Posaune Bass	16 feet.
34. Sub-bass	16 feet tone.	38. Clarion Bass	4 feet.
35. Principal Bass	8 feet.	39. Cornet Bass	2 feet.
36. Octave Bass	4 feet.		

Accessory Stops, Movements, &c.

1. Choir to Great.	2. Great to Pedal.	3. Tremulant Echo.

Compass.

Manuals, CC to d³ in alt., 51 notes.	Pedal, CCC to Gamut G, 20 notes.

36. Strasbourg.

Strasbourg has long been famous for its bell-founders, clock-makers, organ-builders, and for its Freemasons. So early as the 13th century there were several organs in its cathedral very curious in their structure, and sonorous in their tone. The present instrument was built by Silbermann, of Strasbourg, and was completed in August, 1716. It has 42 sounding stops, of which number 7 are on the Pedal; 2,242 pipes; and 6 bellows, 12 feet by 6. The organ is placed on the north side of the nave, where it projects from the triforium about 50 feet above the pavement of the cathedral. The following are the particulars of the instrument :—

Great, 13 Stops.

1. Bourdon .... 16 feet tone.	9. Cymbale.	
2. Montre, tin .... 8 feet.	10. Cornet, V ranks.	
3. Bourdon .... 8 feet tone.	11. { Trompette, Discant } ... 8 feet.	
4. Prestant....................... 4 feet.	{ Trompette, Basse }	
5. Nazard .... 2⅔ feet.	12. Trompette .... 8 feet.	
6. Doublette .... 2 feet.	13. { Clarion, Discant } ...... 4 feet.	
7. Tierce .... 1⅗ foot.	{ Clarion, Basse }	
8. Fourniture.		

Choir, 11 Stops.

14. Montre, tin .... 8 feet.	20. Tierce .... 1⅗ foot.
15. Bourdon .... 8 feet tone.	21. Larigot...................... 1⅓ foot.
16. Prestant....................... 4 feet.	22. Fourniture.
17. Flute ......,................. 4 feet.	23. Cymbale.
18. Nazard .... 2⅔ feet.	24. { Cromorne, Discant } ... 8 feet.
19. Doublette .... 2 feet.	{ Cromorne, Basse }

Echo, 11 Stops.

25. Montre, tin .... 8 feet.	31. Flute Magique .... 4 feet.
26. Gamba .... 8 feet.	32. Doublette...................... 2 feet.
27. Bourdon .... 8 feet tone.	33. Hautbois .... 8 feet.
28. Salicional .... 8 feet.	34. Voix Humaine .... 8 feet.
29. Prestant....................... 4 feet.	35. { Trompette, Discant } ... 8 feet.
30. Flute .... 4 feet.	{ Basson, Basse }

Pedal, 7 Stops.

36. Montre, tin .... 16 feet.	40. Bombarde .... 16 feet.
37. Bourdon .... 16 feet tone.	41. Trompette .... 8 feet.
38. Montre .... 8 feet.	42. Clarion........................ 4 feet.
39. Prestant....................... 4 feet.	

Accessory Stops, Movements, &c.

Tremulant to Great.	Tremulant to Echo.

The Echo and Choir Manuals couple to the Great by being drawn out a little.

Compass.

Manuals, CC to c³ in alt., 49 notes.	Pedal, CCC to tenor c, 25 notes.

37. STRASBOURG.

The organ in St. Thomas's Church is also the work of Silbermann, and bears the date of 1740. It has undergone some alterations by Weltzer, a resident organ-builder in Strasbourg. It contains 36 sounding stops, of which number 7 are on the Pedal. The distribution of the stops is as follows :—

Great, 13 Stops.

1.	Bourdon, stopped metal to the tenor c key, then wood	16 feet tone.	8.	Doublette	2 feet.
2.	Montre	8 feet.	9.	Fourniture, IV ranks.	
3.	Bourdon, metal	8 feet tone.	10.	Cornet, V ranks.	
4.	Salicional	8 feet.	11.	Trompette, Discant } Trompette, Basse } ...	8 feet.
5.	Prestant	4 feet.	12.	Clarion, Discant } Clarion, Basse }	4 feet.
6.	Flute	4 feet.	13.	Voix Humaine	8 feet.
7.	Nazard	2⅔ feet.			

Choir, 8 Stops.

14.	Bourdon, metal	8 feet tone.	18.	Flute	4 feet.
15.	Quintadena	8 feet.	19.	Nazard	3 feet.
16.	Prestant	4 feet.	20.	Doublette	2 feet.
17.	Cordedain	4 feet.	21.	Cromorne	8 feet.

Echo, 8 Stops.

22.	Montre	8 feet.	27.	Cordedain, a kind of flaut traverse, of metal	4 feet.
23.	Viol di Gamba	8 feet.	28.	Trompette	8 feet.
24.	Bourdon, metal	8 feet tone.	29.	Basson	8 feet.
25.	Salicional	8 feet tone.			
26.	Flute	4 feet.			

Pedal, 7 Stops.

30.	Principal, wood	16 feet.	34.	Bombarde, wood	16 feet.
31.	Octave	8 feet.	35.	Trompette, metal	8 feet.
32.	Quint	6 feet.	36.	Clarion, metal	4 feet.
33.	Prestant	4 feet.			

Compass.

Manuals, CC to c³ in alt., 49 notes. | Pedal, CCC to tenor c, 25 notes.
The Echo and Choir Manuals move and couple to Great.

38. STRASBOURG.

The organ in the Protestant Church, called the "Temple neuf," the work of Silbermann, was destroyed, together with the building in which it stood, during the Prussian War, and, like the last, an excellent instrument, being especially remark-able for the beauty of its Diapasons and Metal Flutes. It had 46 stops, 3 Manuals, and Pedal, as follows :—

Great, 14 Stops.

1.	Bourdon	16 feet tone.	9.	Tierce	1⅗ foot.
2.	Montre	8 feet.	10.	Fourniture, III ranks	1 foot.
3.	Bourdon	8 feet tone.	11.	Cymbale, III ranks	2 feet.
4.	Quintaton	8 feet.	12.	Cornet, V ranks.	
5.	Prestant	4 feet.	13.	Trompette, Discant } Trompette, Basse } ...	8 feet.
6.	Flute	4 feet tone.			
7.	Quint	2⅔ feet.	14.	Clarion, Discant } Clarion, Basse }	4 feet.
8.	Doublette	2 feet.			

Choir, 10 Stops.

15. Bourdon	8 feet tone.		20. Doublette	2 feet.
16. Salicional	8 feet.		21. Larigot	1⅓ foot.
17. Prestant	4 feet.		22. Hautbois, Discant	8 feet.
18. Flute	4 feet tone.		23. Cromorne	8 feet.
19. Jeu Celeste	4 feet.		24. Cor de basset	8 feet.

Echo, 13 Stops.

25. Bourdon	16 feet tone.		32. Sifflute	1 foot.
26. Montre	8 feet.		33. Fourniture, III ranks.	
27. Bourdon	8 feet tone.		34. Cornett, IV ranks.	
28. Viol di Gamba	8 feet.		35. Trompette	8 feet.
29. Prestant	4 feet.		36. Basson	8 feet.
30. Flute	4 feet tone.		37. Vox Humana	8 feet.
31. Doublette	2 feet.			

Pedal, 9 Stops.

38. Principal, wood	16 feet.		43. Plein jeu, II ranks.	
39. Bourdon (open wood)	16 feet.		44. Bombarde, metal	16 feet.
40. Octave	8 feet.		45. Trompette, metal	8 feet.
41. Violoncello	8 feet.		46. Clarion, metal	4 feet.
42. Prestant	4 feet.			

39. FREIBURG IN BRESGAU.

The Cathedral of Freiburg in Bresgau, so long celebrated for its beautiful Gothic spire, contains two organs, both of which are small, but of remarkably sweet and full tone. The one in the nave is very old, having been put up in 1520; that in the Choir, which is about the same size, was built in 1811. The Nave organ has 24 stops, 2 Manuals, and Pedal, of which the following are the particulars :—

Great, 10 Stops.

1. Bourdon	16 feet tone.		6. Nazard	2⅔ feet.
2. Principal	8 feet.		7. Super-octave	2 feet.
3. Bourdon	8 feet tone.		8. Mixture, III ranks.	
4. Octave	4 feet.		9. Cymbale, III ranks.	
5. Flote	4 feet tone.		10. Trompette	8 feet.

Choir, 10 Stops.

11. Principal	8 feet.		16. Flote	4 feet.
12. Bourdon	8 feet tone.		17. Waldflote	2 feet.
13. Salicional	8 feet.		18. Sesquialtera, II ranks	2⅔ feet.
14. Gamba	8 feet.		19. Cromorne	8 feet tone.
15. Octave	4 feet.		20. Vox-Humana	8 feet tone.

Pedal, 4 Stops.

21. Montre	16 feet.		23. Octave	8 feet.
22. Bourdon	16 feet tone.		24. Posaune, to FFF	16 feet.

Compass.

Manual, CC, short octave, up to a² in alt. | Pedal, CCC to CC, one octave complete.

40. FREIBURG IN BRESGAU.

The organ in the Lutheran Church at Freiburg in Bresgau was built about 300 years ago, but has lately been repaired. It has 2 Manuals and Pedal, and 32 stops, of which the following is a list :—

Great, 14 Stops.

1. Bourdon	16 feet tone.	8. Quint	2⅔ feet.
2. Principal	8 feet.	9. Super-octave	2 feet.
3. Hohlflote	8 feet.	10. Waldflote	2 feet.
4. Bourdon	8 feet tone.	11. Cymbale, III ranks.	
5. Octave	4 feet.	12. Mixture, II ranks.	
6. Flote	4 feet.	13. Cornett, V ranks.	
7. Fugara	4 feet.	14. Trompette	8 feet.

Choir, 10 Stops.

15. Principal	8 feet.	20. Gemshorn	4 feet.
16. Bourdon	8 feet tone.	21. Flote	4 feet.
17. Gamba	8 feet.	22. Rohrflote	4 feet tone.
18. Salicional	8 feet.	23. Super-octave	2 feet.
19. Octave	4 feet.	24. Trompette	8 feet.

Pedal, 8 Stops.

25. Montre	16 feet.	29. Bourdon	8 feet tone.
26. Bourdon	16 feet tone.	30. Mixture, III ranks.	
27. Quintaton	16 feet tone.	31. Posaune	16 feet.
28. Principal	8 feet.	32. Trompette	8 feet.

Compass.

Manuals, CC to f³ in alt., 54 notes.
Pedal, CCC to Gamut G, 1½ octave.

Coupler.

Choir to Great.

41. FRANKFORT.

The very large and fine organ in St. Paul's Church, Frankfort, was built by Walker, of Ludwigsburg, and was opened in the month of June, 1833. It contains 74 stops, 3 Manuals, and 2 Pedals, and 12 Bellows 14 feet long by 5½ broad. The draw-stops are placed over as well as at the sides of the Manuals. The quality and varied tones of the numerous 16, 8, and 4 feet Manual Flue stops are deserving of all praise. The following is an enumeration of the stops in this organ :—

Great, 23 Stops.

1. Manual-Untersatz	32 feet tone.	13. Gemshorn-terz	3⅕ feet.
2. Principal, in front	16 feet.	14. Quint	2⅔ feet.
3. Gamba major	16 feet.	15. Super-octave, II ranks	2 feet.
4. Tibia major	16 feet tone.	16. Waldflote	2 feet.
5. Octave	8 feet.	17. Terz Discant	1⅗ feet.
6. Viol di Gamba	8 feet.	18. Klein Octave	1 foot.
7. Gemshorn	8 feet.	19. Mixture, IV ranks.	
8. Jubalflote, 2 mouths	8 feet.	20. Scharf, V ranks.	
9. Quint	5⅓ feet.	21. Cornett, V ranks.	
10. Octave	4 feet.	22. Tuba	16 feet.
11. Hollpfeife	4 feet.	23. Trompette	8 feet.
12. Fugara	4 feet.		

Choir, 15 Stops.

24. Bourdon	16 feet tone.	32. Flauto Traverso	4 feet.
25. Principal, in front	8 feet.	33. Rohrflote	4 feet tone.
26. Salicional	8 feet.	34. Gemshorn Quint	2⅔ feet.
27. Dolce	8 feet.	35. Octave	2 feet.
28. Gedact	8 feet tone.	36. Mixture, V ranks	2 feet.
29. Quintaton	8 feet tone.	37. Posaune	8 feet.
30. Quintflote	5⅓ feet tone.	38. Vox Humana	8 feet.
31. Octave	4 feet.		

Echo, 14 Stops.

39. Quintaton	16 feet tone.	46. Dolcissimo	4 feet.
40. Principal	8 feet.	47. Flute d'amour	4 feet.
41. Harmonica	8 feet.	48. Gedact	4 feet tone.
42. Bifaro	8 feet.	49. Nazard	2⅔ feet.
43. Hohlflote	8 feet.	50. Flautino	2 feet.
44. Gedact, two mouths	8 feet tone.	51. Hautbois	8 feet.
45. Spitzflote	4 feet.	52. Physharmonica	8 feet.

First Pedal, 15 Stops.

53. Contra Bass, open	32 feet.	61. Terza	6⅖ feet.
54. Sub-bass, open	32 feet.	62. Quint	5⅓ feet.
55. Principal Bass, in front	16 feet.	63. Octave	4 feet.
56. Octave Bass	16 feet.	64. Posaune	16 feet.
57. Violon	16 feet.	65. Trompette	8 feet.
58. Quint	10⅔ feet.	66. Clarino	4 feet.
59. Octave	8 feet.	67. Cornettino	2 feet.
60. Violoncello	8 feet.		

Second Pedal, 7 Stops.

68. Sub-bass	16 feet tone.	72. Flote	4 feet.
69. Violon d'amour	16 feet.	73. Waldflote	2 feet.
70. Principal	8 feet.	74. Fagotto	16 feet.
71. Flote	8 feet.		

Accessory Stops, Movements, &c.

1. Choir to Great.	4. Choir to second Pedal.
2. Echo to Choir.	5. Second to first Pedal.
3. Great to first Pedal.	6 to 10. Five Wind-trunk valves.

Compass.

Manuals, CC to f⁵ in alt., 54 keys. | Pedal, CCC to tenor d, 27 keys.

42. FULDA.

The organ in the Town Church at Fulda was constructed by G. F. Ratzmann, of Ohrdruff. It has 48 sounding stops, 3 Manuals, and Pedal of 9 stops; also bellows measuring 12 feet by 8. The following is its disposition :—

Great, 15 Stops.
Large Scale and full intonation.

1. Principal, tin, the 16 feet octave in front	16 feet.	11. Octave, II ranks, tin	2 feet & 1 ft.
2. Bourdon, wood	16 feet tone.	12. Mixture, IV ranks, c¹, e¹, g¹, c²	2 feet.
3. Principal, tin, in front	8 feet.	13. Cymbale, III ranks, g¹, c², g²	1¼ foot.
4. Bourdon, wood	8 feet tone.	14. Cornett, III ranks, the first and second ranks, wood stopped, c, g. c	8 feet tone.
5. Hohlflote, wood	8 feet.		
6. Quint, wood Bass, tin Treble	5⅓ feet.		
7. Gamba Quint	5⅓ feet.		
8. Octave, tin	4 feet.	15. Trompette, tin, with free reeds	8 feet.
9. Hohlflote, wood	4 feet.		
10. Quint, tin	2⅔ feet.		

Choir, 12 Stops.

Smaller Scale and clear intonation.

16.	Principal, the bass and tenor octaves of wood, the treble of tin	16 feet.	21.	Octave, tin	4 feet.
17.	Principal, tin in front	8 feet.	22.	Flote, wood..................	4 feet.
18.	Gemshorn, the bass and tenor octaves of wood, the treble of tin	8 feet.	23.	Klein Gedact, tin	4 feet tone.
			24.	Waldflote, tin	4 feet.
			25.	Quint, tin.....................	2⅔ feet.
19.	Still Gedact, wood	8 feet tone.	26.	Octave, II ranks, tin......	2 feet & 1 ft.
20.	Quintaton, tin	8 feet tone.	27.	Mixture, IV ranks, tin, c¹. e¹, g¹, c²	2 feet.

Echo, 12 Stops.

Smaller Scale and delicate intonation.

28.	Quintaton, the bass octave of wood, the remainder of tin......................	16 feet tone.	34.	Spitzflote, tin	4 feet.
			35.	Flote Traversière, wood...	4 feet.
29.	Geigen Principal, tin in front	8 feet.	36.	Flageolet, tin	2 feet.
30.	Salicional	8 feet.	37.	Sifflote, tin	1 foot.
31.	Gedact, wood	8 feet tone.	38.	Mixture, III ranks, tin, c¹, g¹, c³	2 feet.
32.	Flote Traversière, wood ...	8 feet.			
33.	Octave, tin	4 feet.	39.	Clavioline	8 feet.

Pedal, 8 Stops.

Largest Scale and fullest intonation.

40.	Untersatz, wood	32 feet tone.	45.	Octaven Bass, wood	8 feet.
41.	Principal Bass, wood	16 feet.	46.	Violoncello, wood	8 feet.
42.	Violon, wood	16 feet.	47.	Traversen Bass	8 feet.
43.	Sub-bass, wood	16 feet tone.	48.	Posaune, wooden tubes ...	16 feet.
44.	Traversen Bass, wood......	16 feet.			

Accessory Stops, Movements, &c.

1.	Coupler Choir to Great.	5.	Tremulant.
2.	Coupler Echo to Great.	6, 7, 8, 9.	Four double action composition Pedals.
3.	Coupler Great to Pedal.		
4.	Coupler Choir to Pedal.		

Compass.

Manuals, CC to f³ in alt., 54 notes. | Pedal, CCC to tenor d, 27 notes.

43. GOTHA.

The organ in St. Augustine's Church, at Gotha, was built in 1841, by Schulze, and contains 34 stops, of which the following is a list :—

Great, 15 Stops.

1.	Bourdon to the fiddle g key	32 feet tone.	6.	Hohlflote......................	8 feet.
2.	Principal; bass and tenor octaves of wood; from the middle c¹ key upwards, of tin	16 feet.	7.	Octave	4 feet.
			8.	Hohlflote......................	4 feet.
			9.	Gedact	4 feet tone.
3.	Bourdon	16 feet tone.	10.	Quint	2⅔ feet.
4.	Octave; bass octave of wood; from tenor c upwards, of tin..............	8 feet.	11.	Octave	2 and 1.
			12.	Mixture, V ranks	2 feet.
			13.	Cymbale, III ranks	2 feet.
			14.	Cornett, III ranks.	
5.	Gamba	8 feet.	15.	Trompette	8 feet.

Choir, 11 Stops.

16. Lieblich Gedact	16 feet tone.	21. Lieblich Gedact	8 feet tone.
17. Geigen Principal; bass octave wood	8 feet.	22. Octave	4 feet.
18. Salicional	8 feet.	23. Flaute Douce	4 feet.
19. Flauto Traverso	8 feet.	24. Quinte	2⅔ feet.
20. Harmonica	8 feet.	25. Octave	2 feet.
		26. Scharf, III ranks	2 feet.

Pedal, 8 Stops.

27. Principal Bass	16 feet.	31. Violoncello	8 feet.
28. Violon Bass	16 feet.	32. Gedact Bass	8 feet tone.
29. Sub-bass	16 feet tone.	33. Posaune	32 feet.
30. Octave Bass	8 feet.	34. Posaune	16 feet.

44. GOTHA.

The organ in the Church of St. Margaret, at Gotha, was also built by Schulze. It contains 26 stops, distributed as follows :—

Great or Lower Manual, 13 Stops.

1. Principal	16 feet.	8. Quint, stopped wood	5⅓ feet tone.
2. Bourdon	16 feet tone.	9. Octave	4 feet.
3. Principal	8 feet.	10. Flote	4 feet.
4. Gamba	8 feet.	11. { Quint	2⅔ feet.
5. Hohlflote	8 feet.	{ Octave	2 feet.
6. Gedact	8 feet tone.	12. Mixture, V ranks	2 feet.
7. Harmonica	8 feet.	13. Scharf, III ranks	2 feet.

Choir or Upper Manual, 7 Stops.

14. Lieblich Gedact	16 feet tone.	18. Flauto Traverso	8 feet.
15. Geigen Principal	8 feet.	19. Principal	4 feet.
16. Salicional	8 feet.	20. Flauto Traverso	4 feet.
17. Lieblich Gedact	8 feet tone.		

Pedal, 6 Stops.

21. Principal Bass	16 feet.	24. Octaven Bass	8 feet.
22. Violon	16 feet.	25. Violoncello	8 feet.
23. Sub-bass	16 feet tone.	26. Posaune	16 feet.

45. HAARHAUSEN.

The organ in the Church at Haarhausen, in the Dukedom of Gotha, has 2 Manuals and Pedal, and 22 stops. The following is its disposition :—

Great, 10 Stops.

1. Quintaton	16 feet tone.	6. Octave	4 feet.
2. Principal, English tin	8 feet.	7. Quint	2⅔ feet.
3. Gedact	8 feet tone.	8. Super-octave	2 feet.
4. Gamba	8 feet.	9. Mixture, IV ranks	2 feet.
5. Hohlflote, of wood	8 feet.	10. Cymbale, III ranks	1 foot.

Choir, 8 Stops.

11. Flote, to tenor c	8 feet.	15. Nachthorn	4 feet.
12. Still Gedact	8 feet tone.	16. Octave	2 feet.
13. Quintaton	8 feet tone.	17. Sesquialtera, II ranks	2⅔ feet.
14. Principal, English tin	4 feet.	18. Mixture, IV ranks	1 foot.

Pedal, 4 Stops.

19. Violon Bass	....	16 feet.	21. Octaven Bass	.... 8 feet.
20. Sub-bass	....	16 feet tone.	22. Posaunen Bass	.... 16 feet.

Accessory Stops, &c.

1. Choir to Great.	3, 4, 5. Three Wind-trunk valves.
2. Great to Pedal.	

46. ELTSLEBEN.

The organ in the Church at Eltsleben, in the Princedom of Schwartzburg, was built by Francis Volkland, of Erfurt. It has 2 Manuals and Pedal, and 28 stops, the names and distribution of which latter are as follow :—

Great, 12 Stops.

1. Quintaton	....	16 feet tone.	7. Quint	.... 2¾ feet.
2. Principal, English tin	......	8 feet.	8. Super-octave	.... 2 feet.
3. Bourdon	....	8 feet tone.	9. Sesquialtera, II ranks	..... 2⅔ feet.
4. Gamba	....	8 feet.	10. Mixture, VI ranks	.... 2 feet.
5. Flauto Traverso	....	8 feet.	11. Cymbale, IV ranks	.... 1 foot.
6. Octave	....	4 feet.	12. Trompette	.... 8 feet.

Choir, 10 Stops.

13. Gedact	....	8 feet tone.	18. Hohlflote	.... 4 feet.
14. Quintaton	....	8 feet tone.	19. Octave	.... 2 feet.
15. Principal, English tin	......	4 feet.	20. Sesquialtera, II ranks	... 2¾ feet.
16. Nachthorn	....	4 feet.	21. Mixture, IV ranks	.... 1⅓ foot.
17. Spitzflote	....	4 feet.	22. Vox Humana	.... 8 feet tone.

Pedal, 6 Stops.

23. Violon Bass	....	16 feet.	26. Violon Bass	.... 8 feet.
24. Sub-bass	....	16 feet tone.	27. Hohlfloten Bass	.... 4 feet.
25. Octaven Bass	....	8 feet.	28. Posaunen Bass	.... 16 feet.

Accessory Stops, Movements, &c.

1. Coupler Choir to Great.	4, 5, 6. Three Wind-trunk valves to Manuals
2. Coupler Great to Pedal.	and Pedal.
3. Tremulant to Choir.	7. Cymbelstern, g, h, d, g.
	8. Cymbelstern, c, e, g, c.

47. WALTERSHAUSEN.

The fine organ at Waltershausen, in the Dukedom of Gotha, was built by G. H. Trost, of Altenbourg, in the years 1726 to 1730. It contains 3 Manuals and Pedal, and 50 sounding stops; the names and distribution of which latter are as follow :—

Great, 17 Stops.

1. Bourdon	....	16 feet tone.	10. Rohrflote	.... 4 feet tone.
2. Quintaton	....	16 feet tone.	11. Salicional	.... 4 feet.
3. Prestant, Eng. tin, in front		8 feet.	12. Quint	.... 2¾ feet.
4. Bourdon	....	8 feet tone.	13. Super-octave	.... 2 feet.
5. Gamba	....	8 feet.	14. Sesquialtera, II ranks	... 2¾ feet.
6. Gemshorn	....	8 feet.	15. Mixture, VIII ranks	...... 2 feet.
7. Quintaton	....	8 feet tone.	16. Fagotto	.... 16 feet.
8. Unda Maris	....	8 feet tone.	17. Trompette	.... 8 feet.
9. Octave	....	4 feet.		

Choir, 12 *Stops.*

18. Spitzflote Major	8 feet.
19. Nachthorn	8 feet.
20. Principal, Eng. tin, in front	4 feet.
21. Quintaton	4 feet tone.
22. Gemshorn......................	4 feet.
23. Flauto Douce	4 feet.
24. Gemshorn Quint............	2⅔ feet.
25. Nasat	2⅔ feet.
26. Octave	2 feet.
27. Sesquialtera	1⅗ foot.
28. Mixture, IV ranks	2⅔ feet.
29. Hautbois	8 feet.

Echo, 7 *Stops.*

30. Geigen Principal, Eng. tin, in front	8 feet.
31. Doppel-Flute	8 feet.
32. Hohlflote	8 feet.
33. Flauto Traverso	8 feet.
34. Spitzflote	4 feet.
35. Still Gedact	4 feet tone.
36. Hohlflote....................	2 feet.

Pedal, 14 *Stops.*

37. Gross Untersatz	32 feet tone.
38. Gross Principal, Eng. tin, in front	16 feet.
39. Quintaton	16 feet tone.
40. Violon	16 feet.
41. Untersatz	16 feet tone.
42. Octaven Principal	8 feet.
43. Bourdon	8 feet tone.
44. Viol di Gamba	8 feet.
45. Quint	5⅓ feet.
46. Octave	4 feet.
47. Rohrflote	4 feet tone.
48. Mixture	2 feet.
49. Posaune	16 feet.
50. Trompette	8 feet.

Accessory Stops, Movements, &c.

1. Coupler Choir to Great.	4. Tremulant to Choir.
2. Coupler Echo to Great.	5. Cymbelstern.
3. Coupler Great to Pedal.	6, 7, 8, 9. Four Wind-valves.

48. ZERBST.

The new organ in the Church of St. Nicholas, Zerbst, was built by Zuberier and his partner, Geibelin, of Dresden, in 1840. It contains 37 Stops, 2 Manuals, and a Pedal of 9 stops. The details of the instrument are as follow :—

Great, 15 *Stops.*

1. Principal, in front	16 feet.
2. Quintaton	16 feet tone.
3. Octave	8 feet.
4. Gedact	8 feet tone.
5. Viol di Gamba..............	8 feet.
6. Hohlflote	8 feet.
7. Quint	5⅓ feet.
8. Super-octave	4 feet.
9. Gedact	4 feet tone.
10. Gemshorn	4 feet.
11. Quint	2⅔ feet.
12. Quint decima	2 feet.
13. Mixture, VI ranks.	
14. Cornett, IV ranks.	
15. Trompette	8 feet.

Choir, 13 *Stops.*

16. Bourdon	16 feet tone.
17. Principal	8 feet.
18. Gedact	8 feet tone.
19. Quintaton	8 feet tone.
20. Flauto Traverso	8 feet.
21. Octave	4 feet.
22. Salicet	4 feet.
23. Flaut Douce	4 feet.
24. Quint	2⅔ feet.
25. Super-octave	2 feet.
26. Waldflote....................	2 feet.
27. Tertia	1⅗ foot.
28. Mixture, IV ranks	2⅔ feet.

Pedal, 9 *Stops.*

29. Untersatz	32 feet tone.
30. Principal, in front	16 feet.
31. Sub-bass	16 feet tone.
32. Violon	16 feet.
33. Octave	8 feet.
34. Violoncello	8 feet.
35. Super-octave	4 feet.
36. Posaune	16 feet.
37. Trompette	8 feet.

Accessory Stops, Movements, &c.

1. Coupler Great to Pedal.	2, 3, 4. Three Wind-trunk valves.

Six Bellows, 10 feet by 5.

49. LANGENSULZA.

The new organ in the Church of St. Boniface, at Langensulza, contains 34 stops, distributed among 2 Manuals and Pedal in the following manner :—

Great, 14 Stops.

1. Bourdon, of wood	16 feet tone.	8. Spitzflote	4 feet.
2. Principal, of English tin...	8 feet.	9. Quint	2⅔ feet.
3. Bourdon	8 feet tone.	10. Super-octave	2 feet.
4. Gemshorn	8 feet.	11. Mixture, VI ranks	2 feet.
5. Viol di Gamba...	8 feet.	12. Cymbale, III ranks	1 foot.
6. Flauto Major	8 feet.	13. Cornett, III ranks.	
7. Octave	4 feet.	14. Trompette	8 feet.

Choir, 13 Stops.

15. Quintaton	16 feet tone.	21. Flach-flote, pear-tree wood	4 feet.
16. Principal, of English tin...	8 feet.	22. Octave, metal	2 feet.
17. Gedact, wood	8 feet tone.	23. Sesquialtera, II ranks ...	2⅔ feet.
18. Flauto Traverso, pear-tree wood	8 feet.	24. Mixture, IV ranks	2 feet.
		25. Scharf, IV ranks	1 foot.
19. Klein Gedact, metal	4 feet tone.	26. Cymbal, III ranks	½ foot.
20. Nachthorn	4 feet.	27. Vox Humana	8 feet tone.

Pedal, 7 Stops.

28. Gross Untersatz, wood	32 feet tone.	32. Traversen Bass, wood ...	16 feet.
29. Principal Bass, wood	16 feet.	33. Octaven Bass, wood	8 feet.
30. Violon Bass, wood	16 feet tone.	34. Posaunen Bass, wood ...	16 feet.
31. Sub-bass, wood	16 feet tone.		

Accessory Stops, Movements, &c.

1. Coupler Choir to Great.	4. Tremulant to Choir.
2. Coupler Great to Pedal.	5, 6, 7. Three Wind-trunk valves.
3. Coupler Choir to Pedal.	8. Cymbelstern.

50. MUHLHAUSEN.

The organ in the Church at Muhlhausen has 60 sounding stops, 3 Manuals and Pedal. The following is a list of the stops :—

Great, 15 Stops.

1. Bourdon	16 feet tone.	9. Super-octave	2 feet.
2. Surdun	16 feet tone.	10. Waldhorn	2 feet.
3. Principal	8 feet.	11. Sexte	2⅔ feet.
4. Spitzflote	8 feet.	12. Sifflote	1 foot.
5. Salicional	8 feet.	13. Mixture, VII & VIII ranks.	
6. Octave	4 feet.	14. Mixture, VI ranks.	
7. Offeneflote	4 feet.	15. Zink, reed	8 feet.
8. Quint	2⅔ feet.		

Choir, 14 Stops.

16. Principal	8 feet.	23. Super-octave	2 feet.
17. Gedact	8 feet tone.	24. Gemshorn	2 feet.
18. Quintaton	8 feet tone.	25. Tertian	2 feet.
19. Hohlflote	4 feet.	26. Sifflote	1 foot.
20. Quintaton	4 feet tone.	27. Mixture, VI ranks.	
21. Querflote	4 feet.	28. Dulcian	16 feet.
22. Quint	2⅔ feet.	29. Krummhorn	8 feet tone.

Echo, 13 Stops.

30. Salicional	16 feet.	37. Waldflote	2 feet.
31. Principal	8 feet.	38. Tertia	2 feet.
32. Viol di Gamba	8 feet.	39. Cymbale, IV ranks.	
33. Hohlflote	8 feet.	40. Harfen-regal	16 feet.
34. Spitzflote	4 feet.	41. Hautbois	8 feet.
35. Flote Douce	4 feet.	42. Trompette	4 feet.
36. Quint	2⅔ feet.		

Pedal, 18 *Stops*.

43.	Sub-bass	32 feet tone.	52.	Super-super-octave	1 foot.
44.	Principal	16 feet.	53.	Mixture, X ranks.	
45.	Sub-bass	16 feet tone.	54.	Posaune	32 feet.
46.	Octave	8 feet.	55.	Posaune	16 feet.
47.	Waldflote	8 feet.	56.	Dulcian	16 feet.
48.	Octave	4 feet.	57.	Trompete	8 feet.
49.	Quintaton	4 feet tone.	58.	Krummhorn	8 feet tone.
50.	Nachthorn	4 feet.	59.	Schalmey	4 feet tone.
51.	Super-octave	2 feet.	60.	Cornett	2 feet.

51. MERSEBURG.

The organ in the Cathedral Church, at Merseburg, in Saxony, originally erected in the year 1629, and enlarged in 1698, was considerably augmented and improved by Herr Ladegast, in the year 1853. It now contains 5686 pipes, and the following 81 sounding stops. The compass of the Manuals is from CC to g in alt.; and the Pedal, from CCC to tenor f.

Hauptwerk, 20 *Stops*.

1.	Sub-Bourdon, to tenor c key, CCC pipe	32 feet tone.	11.	Gedact, metal	4 feet.
2.	Principal, in front, Eng. tin	16 feet tone.	12.	Gemshorn, metal	4 feet.
3.	Bourdon, wood	16 feet tone.	13.	Quint, metal	2⅔ feet.
4.	Principal, in front tin	8 feet.	14.	Octave, metal	2 feet.
5.	Doppel Gedact, wood	8 feet tone.	15.	Doublette, II ranks	4 & 2 feet.
6.	Gamba, tin	8 feet.	16.	Mixture, IV ranks.	
7.	Hohlflote, wood	8 feet.	17.	Scharf, IV ranks.	
8.	Gemshorn, tin	8 feet.	18.	Cornet, III to V ranks.	
9.	Quint Gedact, tin	5⅓ feet tone.	19.	Fagotto	16 feet.
10.	Octave, tin	4 feet.	20.	Trompette	8 feet.

Oberwerk, 16 *Stops*.

21.	Quintaton, metal	16 feet tone.	29.	Spitzflote, wood	4 feet.
22.	Principal, tin	8 feet.	30.	Quint, metal	2⅔ feet.
23.	Rohrflote, tin	8 feet tone.	31.	Waldflote, metal	2 feet.
24.	Gamba, tin	8 feet.	32.	Tern, metal	1⅗ foot.
25.	Gedact, tin	8 feet tone.	33.	Sifflote, metal	1 foot.
26.	Flaute Amabile, wood	8 feet.	34.	Mixture, IV ranks.	
27.	Octave, metal	4 feet.	35.	Schalmey, metal	8 feet tone.
28.	Rohrflote, metal	4 feet tone.	36.	Stahlspiel.	

Rückpositiv, 11 *Stops*.

37.	Bourdon, wood	16 feet tone.	43.	Gedact, metal	4 feet tone.
38.	Principal, Eng. tin	8 feet.	44.	Octave, metal	2 feet.
39.	Flauto Traverso, wood	8 feet.	45.	Mixture, IV ranks.	
40.	Quintaton, metal	8 feet tone.	46.	Cornett, II to V ranks.	
41.	Fugara, tin	8 feet.	47.	Oboe	8 feet.
42.	Octave, metal	4 feet.			

Brustwerk, 14 *Stops*.

48.	Lieblich Gedact, wood	16 feet tone.	56.	Salicional, metal	4 feet.
49.	Geigen Principal, tin	8 feet.	57.	Nasat, metal	2⅔ feet.
50.	Lieblich Gedact, wood	8 feet tone.	58.	Octave, metal	2 feet.
51.	Salicional	8 feet.	59.	Cymbale, III ranks.	
52.	Flauto Dolce, wood	8 feet.	60.	Progressiv-Harmonica, II to	
53.	Unda Maris, II ranks, tin	8 feet.		IV ranks.	
54.	Octave, tin	4 feet.	61.	Æoline	16 feet.
55.	Zartflote, wood	4 feet.			

M M

Pedal, 20 Stops.

62.	Untersatz, wood	32 feet.	72. Rohr Quint, metal	5½ feet.
63.	Principal, Eng. tin, in front	16 feet.	73. Octave, metal	4 feet.
64.	Sub-bass.......................	16 feet tone.	74. Flote, wood	4 feet.
65.	Violin Bass	16 feet.	75. Scharf-flote, metal	4 feet.
66.	Salicet Bass	16 feet.	76. Mixture, IV ranks.	
67.	Grossnasat	10⅔ feet.	77. Cornett, IV ranks.	
68.	Principal	8 feet.	78. Posaune	32 feet.
69.	Bass-flote	8 feet.	79. Posaune	16 feet.
70.	Violoncello	8 feet.	80. Dulcian.......................	16 feet.
71.	Terz, metal	6⅘ feet.	81. Trompette	8 feet.

Accessory Stops, Movements, &c.

82-84. Three Manual Couplers.	96. Collectivzug to Pedal.
85-87. Three Pedal Couplers.	97. Calcantenruf.
88-91. Four Wind-valves to Manuals.	98. Cymbelstern.
92-94. Three Wind-valves to Pedals.	99. Echozug.
95. Tremulant.	100. Vacant.

52. HALLE.

The old organ in the Church of St. Maurice, at Halle, was made by Isaac Compenius, of Brunswick, in 1625. The present instrument was built by Schulze, and contains 40 stops, distributed between 3 Manuals and Pedal. The soundboards are made to slope upwards from front to back, so that the stops stand in terrace form.

Great, 14 Stops.

1. Bourdon to the fiddle g key	32 feet tone.	8. Quint	5⅓ feet.
2. Principal	16 feet.	9. Octave	4 feet.
3. Bourdon	16 feet tone.	10. Flote	4 feet.
4. Octave	8 feet.	11. Quint and Octave......	2⅔ & 2 feet.
5. Gedact	8 feet tone.	12. Mixture, V ranks	2 feet.
6. Gamba	8 feet.	13. Cornett, III ranks.	
7. Hohlflote	8 feet.	14. Trompette..................	8 feet.

Choir, 10 Stops.

15. Bourdon.....................	16 feet tone.	20. Octave	4 feet.
16. Principal	8 feet.	21. Hohlflote	4 feet.
17. Gedact	8 feet tone.	22. Quint	2⅔ feet.
18. Flote	8 feet.	23. Octave	2 feet.
19. Salicional	8 feet.	24. Scharf, V ranks	2 feet.

Echo, 8 Stops.

25. Lieblich Gedact	16 feet tone.	29. Harmonica	8 feet.
26. Geigen Principal	8 feet.	30. Schweizerflote	8 feet.
27. Lieblich Gedact	8 feet tone.	31. Geigen Principal	4 feet.
28. Flauto Traverso	8 feet.	32. Gedact	4 feet tone.

Pedal, 8 Stops.

33. Principal Bass	16 feet.	37. Gedact Bass	8 feet tone.
34. Sub-bass	16 feet tone.	38. Violoncello	8 feet.
35. Violone	16 feet.	39. Posaune	32 feet.
36. Octave Bass	8 feet.	40. Posaune	16 feet.

53. LOIZ.

The organ in the Marien-Kirche at Loiz, built by Johann Frederic Schulze, has 34 sounding stops, 2 Manuals, and Pedal. The following is a list of its contents :—

Great, 14 Stops.

1. Bourdon to the fiddle g key	32 feet tone.	8. Octave	4 feet.
2. Bourdon	16 feet.	9. Gedact-flöte	4 feet.
3. Principal	8 feet.	10. Quint	2⅔ feet.
4. Gedact	8 feet tone.	11. Octave	2 feet.
5. Gamba	8 feet.	12. Mixture, V ranks	2 feet.
6. Hohlflöte	8 feet.	13. Scharf, III ranks	2 feet.
7. Quint	5⅓ feet.	14. Trompette	8 feet.

Choir, 12 Stops.

15. Lieblich Gedact	16 feet tone.	21. Octave	4 feet.
16. Geigen Principal	8 feet.	22. Flauto Traverso	4 feet.
17. Lieblich Gedact	8 feet tone.	23. Quint	2⅔ feet.
18. Salicional	8 feet.	24. Octave	2 feet.
19. Flauto Traverso	8 feet.	25. Scharf, III ranks	2 feet.
20. Harmonica	8 feet.	26. Æoline	8 feet.

Pedal, 8 Stops.

27. Violone	16 feet.	31. Gedact	8 feet tone.
28. Sub-bass	16 feet tone.	32. Violoncello	8 feet.
29. Gross Quint	10⅔ feet.	33. Posaune	32 feet.
30. Octaven Bass	8 feet.	34. Posaune	16 feet.

Compass.

Manuals, CC to f³ in alt., 54 tones.	Pedal, CCC to tenor d, 28 tones.

54. KATSCHER.

The organ in the Catholic Church at Katscher was built by Müller, sen., in 1843. It has 21 sounding stops, distributed among 2 Manuals and Pedal in the following manner :—

Great, 11 Stops.

1. Bourdon, maple-wood in the treble, pine in bass	16 feet tone.	5. Portunalflaut	8 feet.
2. Principal, ¼ tin, in front	8 feet.	6. Principal	4 feet tone.
3. Salicet, maple-wood to tenor c, remaining octave, pine	8 feet.	7. Doppel-rohrflöte, of oak	4 feet tone.
		8. Gemshorn quint, metal	2⅔ feet.
4. Doppel-rohrflöte, oak to middle c¹, pine for the remaining two octaves	8 feet tone.	9. Super-octave, metal	2 feet.
		10. Mixture, probe tin, V ranks.	
		11. Trompette	8 feet.

Choir, 6 Stops.

12. Principal, in front	8 feet.	15. Salicet	4 feet.
13. Salicet, of probe tin in the treble, pine in the bass	8 feet.	16. Portunal, of maple and pear-tree woods to tenor c; the last octave of pine	4 feet.
14. Flaut major, oak in the treble, pine in the bass	8 feet tone.	17. Violini, 14 loth, probe tin	2 feet.

Pedal, 4 Stops.

18. Violon, of pine-wood	16 feet.	20. Violon, of pine wood	8 feet.
19. Sub-bass, of pine-wood	16 feet tone.	21. Posaune, peartree-wood	16 feet.

Accessory Stops, &c.

1. Wind to Great.
2. Wind to Choir.
3. Wind to Pedal.

Compass, &c.

Manuals, CC to d³ in alt.
Pedal, CCC to tenor d.
3 Bellows, 9 feet by 4½.

55. ERDMANNSDORF.

The organ in the Church at Erdmannsdorf was built by Buckow, in 1840 ; and has 19 sounding stops, of which the following is a list :—

Great, 9 Stops.

1. Bourdon, wood............... 16 feet tone.
2. Principal, of Eng. tin in front 8 feet.
3. Gemshorn, 14 loth. tin ... 8 feet.
4. Principal octave, Eng. tin in front .... 4 feet.
5. Gemshorn, 14 loth. tin ... 4 feet.

6. Nazard (conical) 12 loth. tin 3 feet.
7. Super-octave, 14 loth. tin 2 feet.
8. Cornetti, 12 loth. tin, of conical pipes, III ranks 2 feet.
9. Progressio, 14 loth. tin, III and IV ranks .... 2 feet.

Choir, 6 Stops.

10. Salicional, Eng. tin......... 8 feet.
11. Viola di Gamba .... 8 feet.
12. Flauto Douce, 10 loth. metal, lower octaves of wood... 8 feet.
13. Principal, Eng. tin .... 4 feet.

14. Flaut d'amour, 10 loth. metal 4 feet.
15. Flautino, 12 loth. probe tin, conical pipes .... 2 feet.
16. Slide for a reed stop of ... 8 feet.

Pedal, 4 Stops.

17. Violon, wood .... 16 feet.
18. Sub-bass, wood .... 16 feet tone.

19. Violoncello, the upper notes of probe tin .... 8 feet.
20. Posaune .... 16 feet.

Accessory Stops, &c.

1. Coupler, Choir to Great. | 2. Coupler, Great to Pedal. | 3, 4, 5. Three Wind-trunk valves.

Compass, &c.

Manuals, CC to f³ in alt. | Pedal, CCC to tenor d.

56. KRUMOLS.

The organ in the new Catholic Church at Krumols has 22 sounding stops, of which the following is a list :—

Great, 10 Stops.

1. Bourdon, metal treble, wood bass .... 16 feet tone.
2. Principal, Eng. tin, polished, and in front .... 8 feet.
3. Gemshorn, 14 loth. Eng. tin 8 feet.
4. Hohlflote, the upper 3½ octave in 10 loth. metal, the remainder in wood ...... 8 feet.

5. Octave, 12 loth. Eng. tin 4 feet.
6. Gemshorn, 12 loth. Eng. tin 4 feet.
7. Quint, 12 loth. Eng. tin 2⅔ feet.
8. Super-octave, 12 loth. Eng. tin .... 2 feet.
9. Progressio, 12 loth. Eng. tin, III, IV, and V ranks ... 2 feet.
10. Trompette..................... 8 feet.

Choir, 8 Stops.

11. Viola di Gamba, 15 loth. Eng. tin .... 8 feet.
12. Flaut Douce, 10 loth. metal to tenor c, last octave wood .... 8 feet.
13. Principal, 14 loth. Eng. tin, in front.................... 4 feet.

14. Flaut d'amour, 10 loth. metal 4 feet.
15. Quinta dulcis .... 2⅔ feet.
16. Flautino, 12 loth. Eng. tin 2 feet.
17. Flauto Piccolo, 12 loth. Eng. tin..................... 1 foot.
18. Cornetti, 12 loth. Eng. tin, III ranks.

Pedal, 4 Stops.

19. Principal, wood	16 feet.	21. Octave, 12 loth tin	8 feet.
20. Sub-bass, wood	16 feet tone.	22. Posaune	16 feet.

Accessory Stops, Movements, &c.

1. Coupler, Choir to Great.	3, 4, 5. Three Wind-trunk valves.
2. Coupler, Great to Pedal.	

Compass.

Manuals, CC to f³ in alt. | Pedal, CCC to tenor d. | Three Bellows, 10 feet long.

57. HALBERSTADT.

The organ in the great church at Halberstadt was almost completely re-built by J. F. Schulze, in the year 1838. It has 65 sounding-stops, and about 4,250 pipes. There are 4 Manuals and a Pedal organ of 18 Stops. The specification of the stops is as follows :—

First Manual, 15 Stops.

1. Principal	16 feet.	9. Octave	2 feet.
2. Octave	8 feet.	10. Mixture, VI ranks	2 feet.
3. Gemshorn	8 feet.	11. Scharf, IV ranks	2 feet.
4. Gedact	8 feet tone.	12. Cornett, IV ranks.	
5. Nasat	5⅓ feet.	13. Contra-bourdon	32 feet tone.
6. Octave	4 feet.	14. Trompette	16 feet.
7. Gedact	4 feet tone.	15. Trompette	8 feet.
8. Quint	2⅔ feet.		

Second Manual, 13 Stops.

16. Gedact	16 feet tone.	23. Flute Douce	4 feet.
17. Quintaton	8 feet.	24. Quint	2⅔ feet.
18. Principal	8 feet.	25. Octave	2 feet.
19. Viola di Gamba	8 feet.	26. Mixture, V ranks	2 feet.
20. Hohlflote	8 feet.	27. Cymbale, III ranks	1 foot.
21. Gedact	8 feet tone.	28. Hautbois	8 feet.
22. Octave	4 feet.		

Third Manual, 11 Stops.

29. Bourdon	16 feet tone.	35. Nasat	2⅔ feet.
30. Principal	8 feet.	36. Octave	2 feet.
31. Salicional	8 feet.	37. Mixture, IV ranks.	
32. Gedact	8 feet tone.	38. Cornett, III ranks.	
33. Octave	4 feet.	39. Vox humana	8 feet tone.
34. Spitzflote	4 feet.		

Fourth Manual, 8 Stops.

40. Lieblich Gedact	16 feet tone.	44. Lieblich Gedact	8 feet tone.
41. Terpodion	8 feet.	45. Principal	4 feet.
42. Harmonica	8 feet.	46. Flauto Traverso	4 feet.
43. Flauto Traverso	8 feet.	47. Phyzharmonica	8 feet.

Pedal, 18 Stops.

48. Untersatz	32 feet tone.	57. Tertia	6⅖ feet.
49. Principal	16 feet.	58. Nasat	5⅓ feet.
50. Violone	16 feet.	59. Octave	4 feet.
51. Sub-bass	16 feet tone.	60. Mixtur, IV ranks	4 feet.
52. Sub-bass	16 feet.	61. Cornett, V ranks.	
53. Grossnasat	10⅔ feet.	62. Posaune	32 feet.
54. Octave	8 feet.	63. Posaune	16 feet.
55. Violoncello	8 feet.	64. Trompette	8 feet.
56. Gedact	8 feet tone.	65. Trompette	4 feet

58. HIRSCHBERG.

The large organ in Christ Church, Hirschberg, has 62 sounding stops, 4 Manuals, Pedal of 16 stops, and 3,844 pipes. The stops are disposed in the following manner :—

First Manual, 16 *Stops.*

1.	Principal, $\frac{3}{4}$ tin	16 feet.	9.	Quint, tin	$2\frac{2}{3}$ feet.
2.	Quintaton, metal	16 feet tone.	10.	Vigesima secunda, tin	2 feet.
3.	Principal, Eng. tin	8 feet.	11.	Rauschquint, II ranks, tin	$1\frac{1}{3}$ foot.
4.	Gemshorn, metal	8 feet.	12.	Mixture, V ranks, tin	2 feet.
5.	Hohlflote, wood	8 feet.	13.	Scharf, IV ranks, tin	$1\frac{1}{3}$ foot.
6.	Nazard, tin	$5\frac{1}{3}$ feet.	14.	Cymbale, III ranks, tin	1 foot.
7.	Super-octave, tin	4 feet.	15.	Tromba, $\frac{3}{4}$ tin	16 feet.
8.	Flute Douce, wood	4 feet.	16.	Trompette, $\frac{3}{4}$ tin	8 feet.

Second Manual, 13 *Stops.*

17.	Bourdon, oak-wood	16 feet tone.	24.	Super-octave, tin	2 feet.
18.	Principal, in front, tin	8 feet.	25.	Terz, tin	$1\frac{3}{5}$ foot.
19.	Gedact, metal	8 feet tone.	26.	Flageolet, tin	1 foot.
20.	Quintaton, metal	8 feet tone.	27.	Mixture, VI ranks, tin	2 feet.
21.	Octave, tin	4 feet.	28.	Cymbale, III ranks, tin	$1\frac{1}{3}$ foot.
22.	Gemshorn, tin	4 feet.	29.	Vox humana, $\frac{3}{4}$ tin	8 feet tone.
23.	Quint, tin	$2\frac{2}{3}$ feet.			

Third Manual, 10 *Stops.*

30.	Principal, Eng. tin	8 feet.	35.	Quint	$2\frac{2}{3}$ feet.
31.	Fugara, pine and maple-wood	8 feet.	36.	Super-octave	2 feet.
32.	Gedact, oak-wood	8 feet tone.	37.	Mixture, IV ranks.	
33.	Octave	4 feet.	38.	Sesquialtera, II ranks.	
34.	Rohrflote, metal	4 feet tone.	39.	Schalomo, tin	8 feet tone.

Fourth Manual, 7 *Stops.*

40.	Prestant, tin	8 feet.	44.	Super-octave, tin	2 feet.
41.	Flaut Douce, wood	8 feet.	45.	Cornett, II ranks, tin	$1\frac{1}{3}$ foot.
42.	Octave, tin	4 feet.	46.	Oboe im descant, wood / Fagotto im bass, wood	8 feet.
43.	Flaut Traversière, wood	4 feet.			

Pedal, 16 *Stops.*

47.	Untersatz, wood	32 feet tone.	55.	Super-octave, tin	4 feet.
48.	Principal, Eng. tin	16 feet.	56.	Nachthorn, tin	2 feet.
49.	Violon	16 feet.	57.	Mixture, V ranks, tin	$2\frac{2}{3}$ feet.
50.	Quintaton	16 feet tone.	58.	Rauschquint, II ranks, tin	
51.	Sub-bass	16 feet.	59.	Contra-posaune, wood	32 feet.
52.	Octave, wood and metal	8 feet.	60.	Posaune, wood	16 feet.
53.	Violoncello	8 feet.	61.	Trompette, $\frac{3}{4}$ tin	8 feet.
54.	Quint, metal	$5\frac{1}{3}$ feet.	62.	Clarino, $\frac{3}{4}$ tin	4 feet.

Accessory Stops, &c.

1, 2, 3, 4. Couplers for all 4 Manuals.
5. Coupler, Great to Pedal.
6 to 12. Seven Wind-trunk valves.
13. Tremulant.

59. NAUMBERG.

The organ in the Church of St. Wenzel, in Naumberg, contains 52 sounding stops, 3 Manuals, and a Pedal of 12 stops; 3,000 pipes, and 7 large pairs of bellows. The oldest parts of the instrument date as far back as 1613, to which additions were made in 1734 (by Hildebrand, of Leipzig), in 1737 and in 1810. The present contents of the organ are as follow :—

Great, 15 Stops.

1.	Principal	16 feet.	9. Quint	3 feet.
2.	Quintaton	16 feet tone.	10. Octave	2 feet.
3.	Octave	8 feet.	11. Weitpfeife	2 feet.
4.	Spitzflote	8 feet.	12. Mixture, V ranks.	
5.	Gedact	8 feet tone.	13. Cornett, V ranks.	
6.	Prestant	4 feet.	14. Bombard	16 feet.
7.	Spitzflote	4 feet.	15. Trompette	8 feet.
8.	Gedact	4 feet tone.		

Echo, 14 Stops.

16.	Bourdon	16 feet tone.	23. Gemshorn	4 feet.
17.	Principal	8 feet.	24. Gedact	4 feet.
18.	Principal Undamar	8 feet.	25. Quint	3 feet.
19.	Hohlflote	8 feet.	26. Octave	2 feet.
20.	Flauto Traverso	8 feet.	27. Waldflote	2 feet.
21.	Clav. Æoline	8 feet.	28. Sifflote	1 foot.
22.	Prestant	4 feet.	29. Mixture, V ranks.	

Choir, 11 Stops.

30.	Tibia major	16 feet tone.	36. Quintaton	8 feet tone.
31.	Principal	8 feet.	37. Prestant	4 feet.
32.	Gemshorn	8 feet.	38. Rohrflote	4 feet tone.
33.	Viola di Gamba	8 feet.	39. Octave	2 feet.
34.	Fugara	8 feet.	40. Mixture, V ranks	3 feet.
35.	Rohrflote	8 feet tone.		

Pedal, 12 Stops.

41.	Principal	16 feet.	47. Octave	4 feet.
42.	Violon	16 feet.	48. Octave	2 feet.
43.	Sub-bass	16 feet tone.	49. Mixture, V ranks	3½ feet.
44.	Octave Bass	8 feet.	50. Posaune	32 feet.
45.	Violon	8 feet.	51. Posaune	16 feet.
46.	Quint	6 feet.	52. Trompette	8 feet.

60. TREBNITZ.

The organ in the Catholic Church at Trebnitz has 33 sounding stops, which are distributed as follows :—

Great, 13 Stops.

1. Bourdon, wood	16 feet.	7. Gemshorn Quint, metal ...	5⅓ feet.
2. Principal, Eng. tin, in front	8 feet.	8. Octave, English tin in front	4 feet.
3. Salicet, ⅛ tin to tenor f, wood bass	8 feet.	9. Doppel-rohrflote, maple-wood	4 feet.
4. Gemshorn, metal, except the bottom octave, which is of wood	8 feet.	10. Quint, metal	2⅔ feet.
5. Quintaton, half tin	8 feet tone.	11. Super-octave, metal	2 feet.
6. Rohrflote, metal, except the 8 feet octave, which is of wood	8 feet.	12. Mixture, V ranks.	
		13. Trompette, ⅛ tin	8 feet.

Choir, 9 Stops.

14. Principal, Eng. tin	8 feet.	18. Salicet, tin	4 feet.
15. Salicet, ⅛ the lowest octave of wood	8 feet.	19. Portunal	4 feet.
16. Portunalflote, wood	8 feet.	20. Gemshorn Quint, ⅛ tin ...	3 feet.
17. Flaut major, wood	8 feet tone.	21. Super-octave, metal	2 feet.
		22. Cymbale, III ranks.	

Pedal, 11 Stops.

23.	Principal, wood	16 feet.	29.	Salicet, wood	8 feet.
24.	Gamba, wood	16 feet.	30.	Doppelflaut, wood	8 feet tone.
25.	Salicet, wood	16 feet.	31.	Super-octave	4 feet.
26.	Sub-bass, wood	16 feet tone.	32.	Posaune, wood	16 feet.
27.	Quinten Bass, wood	10⅔ feet.	33.	Trompette, ⅛ tin	8 feet.
28.	Octaven Bass, wood	8 feet.			

Accessory Stops, &c.

1. Coupler, Choir to Great.
2. Coupler, Great to Pedal.

3, 4. Two Wind-trunk valves.
Four Bellows, 9 feet by 4½.

Compass.

Manuals, CC to f³ in alt. | Pedal, CCC to tenor d.

61. SALZWEDEL.

The organ in the Church of St. Catharine, in the new town of Salzwedel, has 42 sounding stops, and was built by Frederick Turley, Treuenbritzen, in 1838.

Great, 15 Stops.

1.	Principal, in front	16 feet.	9.	Quint	2⅔ feet.
2.	Octave	8 feet.	10.	Super-octave	2 feet.
3.	Spitzflote	8 feet.	11.	Cornett, IV ranks, 6, 4, 3⅓, and 2 feet.	
4.	Gedact	8 feet tone.	12.	Scharf, IV ranks, 2, 1⅓, 1⅓, and 1 foot.	
5.	Quint	5⅓ feet.	13.	Cymbale, III ranks, 1, ½, and ⅓ foot.	
6.	Super-octave	4 feet.	14.	Trompette	16 feet.
7.	Rohrflote	4 feet tone.	15.	Trompette	8 feet.
8.	Lieblich Gedact	4 feet tone.			

Choir, 13 Stops.

16.	Bourdon	16 feet tone.	23.	Gemshorn	4 feet.
17.	Principal, in front	8 feet.	24.	Nasat	3 feet.
18.	Viola di Gamba	8 feet.	25.	Super-octave	2 feet.
19.	Salicional	8 feet.	26.	Mixture, IV ranks, 2, 1⅓, 1, and ½ feet.	
20.	Quintaton	8 feet tone.	27.	Æoline	16 feet.
21.	Lieblich Gedact	8 feet tone.	28.	Hautbois, to c¹	8 feet.
22.	Octave	4 feet.			

Pedal, 14 Stops.

29.	Principal, in front	16 feet.	36.	Nasat	6 feet.
30.	Violon	16 feet.	37.	Super-octave	4 feet.
31.	Sub-bass	16 feet tone.	38.	Compensation Mixture, V ranks.	
32.	Grossnasat	12 feet.	39.	Posaune	16 feet.
33.	Octave	8 feet.	40.	Dulcian	16 feet.
34.	Gedact	8 feet tone.	41.	Trompette	8 feet.
35.	Tertia	6⅓ feet.	42.	Clarion	4 feet.

Accessory Stops, &c.

1. Coupler, Choir to Great.
2. Tremulant.

3, 4, 5. Three Wind-trunk valves.
Six Bellows.

62. WEISSENFELS.

The organ in the Lock Church at Weissenfels was built by Schulze. It has 19 stops, 2 Manuals, and Pedal. The following is a list of its contents:—

Great, 10 Stops.

1.	Bourdon	16 feet tone.	6.	Octave	4 feet.
2.	Principal	8 feet.	7.	Quint	2⅔ feet.
3.	Viola di Gamba	8 feet.	8.	Octave	2 feet.
4.	Hohlflote	8 feet.	9.	Mixture, V ranks	2 feet.
5.	Gedact	8 feet tone.	10.	Scharf, III ranks	2 feet.

Choir, 5 Stops.

11. Lieblich Gedact	16 feet tone.		14. Lieblich Gedact	8 feet tone.
12. Salicional	8 feet.		15. Principal	4 feet.
13. Flauto Traverso	8 feet.			

Pedal, 4 Stops.

16. Gedact	16 feet tone.		18. Gedact	8 feet tone.
17. Principal	8 feet.		19. Posaune	16 feet.

Accessory Stops.

1. Coupler, Choir to Great. | 2. Coupler, Great to Pedal.

Compass.

Manuals, CC to f^a in alt. | Pedal, CCC to tenor d.

63. CELLE.

The organ in the Ludwigs Church at Celle has 15 stops, 2 Manuals, and Pedal. The following are the names of the stops :—

Great, 7 Stops.

1. Bourdon, metal to middle c^1, remaining 2 octaves wood	16 feet tone.		4. Octave, 4 loth. metal	4 feet.
2. Principal, 12 loth. tin, in front	8 feet.		5. Gemshorn, 4 loth. metal	4 feet.
3. Rohrflote, metal treble, wood bass	8 feet tone.		6. Octave, 4 loth. metal	2 feet.
			7. Mixture, III ranks.	

Choir, 4 Stops.

8. Salicional	8 feet.		10. Rohrflote, 4 loth. metal	4 feet tone.
9. Gedact, metal treble, wood bass	8 feet tone.		11. Waldflote, 4 loth. metal	2 feet.

Pedal, 4 Stops.

12. Sub-bass, wood	16 feet tone.		14. Octave, 4 loth. metal	4 feet.
13. Principal, 12 loth. metal	8 feet.		15. Posaune	16 feet.

64. VERDEN.

The organ in the pretty little Cathedral at Verden is a particularly fine instrument, built by Schulze, containing 34 sounding stops, of which the following is a list :—

Great, 14 Stops.

1. Bourdon	32 feet tone.		8. Octave	4 feet.
2. Bourdon	16 feet tone.		9. Flote	4 feet.
3. Principal	8 feet.		10. Hohlflote	4 feet.
4. Gedact	8 feet tone.		11. Quint and Octave	2⅔ & 2 feet.
5. Gamba	8 feet.		12. Mixture, V ranks	2 feet.
6. Hohlflote	8 feet.		13. Cymbale, III ranks	2 feet.
7. Quint	5⅓ feet.		14. Cornett, III ranks	4 feet.

Choir, 11 Stops.

15. Lieblich Gedact	16 feet tone.		21. Geigen Principal	4 feet.
16. Lieblich Gedact	8 feet tone.		22. Flauto Traverso	4 feet.
17. Geigen Principal	8 feet.		23. Quint and Octave	2⅔ & 2 feet.
18. Salicional	8 feet.		24. Scharf, III ranks.	
19. Flauto Traverso	8 feet.		25. Æoline	8 feet.
20. Harmonica	8 feet.			

Pedal, 9 *Stops.*

26. Principal Bass	16 feet.	31. Gedact-bass	8 feet tone.
27. Sub-bass.......................	16 feet tone.	32. Violoncello	8 feet.
28. Violon	16 feet.	33. Posaune	32 feet.
29. Quinten Bass..................	10¾ feet tone.	34. Posaune	16 feet.
30. Octave Bass	8 feet.		

Compass.

Manuals, CC to f³ in alt, 54 notes. | Pedal, CCC to tenor d, 27 notes.

65. BREMEN.

The organ in the Cathedral Church at Bremen was built by Schulze, and contains 59 stops, 16 of which are devoted to the Pedal. It presents the peculiarities of having a stop of 32-feet tone on the Choir as well as on the Great Manual, and of having a Great stopped Quint of 21⅓ feet on the Pedal. The following is the specification of the above-named instrument :—

Great, 16 *Stops.*

1. Bourdon, to tenor c key ...	32 feet tone.	9. Octave	4 feet.
2. Principal	16 feet.	10. Flote	4 feet.
3. Bourdon.......................	16 feet.	11. Quint and Octave	2⅔ & 2 feet.
4. Principal	8 feet.	12. Mixture, V ranks............	2 feet.
5. Gedact	8 feet tone.	13. Cymbale, III ranks	2 feet.
6. Gamba	8 feet.	14. Cornett, III ranks	4 feet.
7. Hohlflote	8 feet.	15. Trompette.....................	16 feet.
8. Quint	5⅓ feet.	16. Trompette	8 feet.

Choir, 13 *Stops.*

17. Bourdon, to tenor c key ...	32 feet tone.	24. Flote	4 feet.
18. Bourdon.......................	16 feet tone.	25. Spitzflote	4 feet.
19. Salicional	8 feet.	26. Quint and Octave	2⅔ & 2 feet.
20. Gedact	8 feet tone.	27. Mixture, V ranks............	2 feet.
21. Flote	8 feet.	28. Scharf, III ranks	2 feet.
22. Principal	8 feet.	29. Phyzharmonica	8 feet.
23. Octave	4 feet.		

Swell, 14 *Stops.*

30. Lieblich Gedact	16 feet tone.	37. Geigen Principal	4 feet.
31. Geigen Principal	8 feet.	38. Flauto Traverso	4 feet.
32. Harmonica	8 feet.	39. Zart-flote	4 feet.
33. Lieblich Gedact	8 feet tone.	40. Quint...........................	2⅔ feet.
34. Terpodion	8 feet.	41. Octave	2 feet.
35. Gedact-flote	8 feet tone.	42. Mixture, III ranks	2 feet.
36. Flauto Traverso	8 feet.	43. Æoline	8 feet.

Pedal, 16 *Stops.*

44. Principal Bass	32 feet.	52. Gedact Bass............,......	8 feet tone.
45. Gross Quinten Bass	21½ feet tone.	53. Floten Bass	8 feet.
46. Principal Bass	16 feet.	54. Violoncello	8 feet.
47. Major Bass	16 feet.	55. Octave	4 feet.
48. Violon	16 feet.	56. Posaune	32 feet.
49. Sub-bass	16 feet tone.	57. Reim	16 feet.
50. Quinten Bass	10¾ feet tone.	58. Posaune	16 feet.
51. Octaven Bass	8 feet.	59. Trompette	8 feet.

HAMBURG.

The ancient city of Hamburg was long celebrated for the number (namely, 5) and excellence of its 32-feet organs, two of which, however, perished in the great conflagration of 1842. Of the 3 which remain that in the present church of St. Michael is the best known, and is also the most modern one.

66. CHURCH AND ORGAN OF ST. MICHAEL'S, HAMBURG.

The old church of St. Michael being struck by lightning and burnt down, the present edifice was commenced in 1750, from the designs of Mr. Ernest George Sonnin, and opened for service in 1762. The height of the church inside is 93 feet, its length 249 feet, and its breadth 178 feet. The organ stands at the west end, and contains the following stops :—

Great Organ, 18 Stops.

1.	Principal, tin	16 feet.	10.	Nasat, metal	2⅔ feet.
2.	Quintadena, wood and metal	16 feet tone.	11.	Octave, tin	2 feet.
			12.	Rauschpfeife, II ranks, tin	2⅔ feet.
3.	Octave, tin	8 feet.	13.	Mixture, VIII ranks, tin	2 feet.
4.	Gedact, wood and metal	8 feet tone.	14.	Scharf, V ranks, tin	1⅓ foot.
5.	Gamba, tin	8 feet.	15.	Cornet, V ranks, tin	8 feet.
6.	Gemshorn, metal	8 feet.	16.	Trompette, tin	16 feet.
7.	Quint, tin	5⅓ feet.	17.	Trompette, tin	8 feet.
8.	Octave, tin	4 feet.	18.	Oboe, from tenor f, tin	8 feet.
9.	Gemshorn, metal	4 feet.			

Choir Organ, 16 Stops.

19.	Rohrflote, wood and metal	16 feet tone.	27.	Nasat, tin	2⅔ feet.
20.	Principal, tin	8 feet.	28.	Octave, tin	2 feet.
21.	Principal, to fiddle g	8 feet.	29.	Flach-flote, metal	2 feet.
22.	Rohrflote, metal	8 feet tone.	30.	Quint, tin	1⅓ foot.
23.	Flauto Traverso, wood	8 feet.	31.	Rauschpfeife, II ranks, tin	2⅔ feet.
24.	Klein-Gedact, wood	8 feet tone.	32.	Cymbale, V ranks, tin	
25.	Octave, tin	4 feet.	33.	Chalumeau, tin	8 feet.
26.	Rohrflote, metal	4 feet tone.	34.	Trompette, tin	4 feet.

Upper-work and Swell on the same Manual, 20 stops :—

Upper-work, 16 Stops.

35.	Bourdon, wood and metal	8 feet tone.	43.	Octave, tin	2 feet.
36.	Principal, tin	8 feet.	44.	Rauschpfeife, II ranks, tin	2⅔ feet.
37.	Quintadena, wood and metal	8 feet tone.	45.	Cymbale, V ranks, tin	1⅓ foot.
			46.	Echo cornett, to fiddle g, V ranks	8 feet.
38.	Spitzflote, metal	8 feet.			
39.	Unda Maris, to fiddle g	8 feet.	47.	Trompette	8 feet.
40.	Octave, tin	4 feet.	48.	Vox humana, tin	8 feet.
41.	Spitzflote, metal	4 feet.	49.	Cremona to tenor f	8 feet.
42.	Quint, tin	2⅔ feet.	50.	Glockenspiel to tenor f	8 feet.

Swell, 4 Stops.

51.	Octave	8 feet.	53.	Cornett, V ranks in the treble, II in bass.	
52.	Octave	4 feet.	54.	Trompette	8 feet.

Pedal, 16 Stops.

55.	Principal, tin	32 feet.	63.	Gedact, tin	8 feet tone.
56.	Sub-bass, wood	32 feet tone.	64.	Octave, tin	4 feet.
57.	Principal, tin	16 feet.	65.	Mixture, tin, X ranks.	
58.	Sub-bass, open, wood	16 feet.	66.	Posaune, tin	32 feet.
59.	Sub-bass, stopped, wood	16 feet tone.	67.	Posaune, tin	16 feet.
60.	Violone, wood	16 feet.	68.	Fagotto	16 feet.
61.	Rohr-quint, metal	10⅔ feet tone.	69.	Trompette, tin	8 feet.
62.	Octave, tin	8 feet.	70.	Clarion, tin	4 feet.

Accessory Stops.

1. Tremulant to Great Manual.	4. Wind to Choir Organ.
2. Cymbalstar.	5. Wind to Upper-work.
3. Wind to Great Organ.	6. Wind to Pedal Organ.

The case presents a handsome front, 60 feet in height and 60 feet in width. The 32-feet pipe stands in the centre by itself, in an immense pilaster; the remainder of the 32-feet stop in two great concave compartments, one on each side, and every pipe is supported below by a base, and finished off above with a Corinthian capital, gilded, the pipes themselves forming the shafts, being of their natural bright silvery colour.

The organ is finely laid out inside, in four stories, to each of which free access is obtained by wide staircases with hand-rails. Passage-boards occur in abundance, and any pipe in this immense instrument can be got at without disturbing a second one.

There are no "conveyanced off" pipes, except those which appear in the front of the case, the site of the organ being so favourable as to allow of the soundboards being made of ample dimensions.

Those of the Great organ are made "in halves," each half measuring from 8¼ to 9 feet in length, and the pipes of every stop stand in a single row, even to the 16-feet double trumpet.

The CCCC pipe in the middle of the front is made of pure tin, is 35 feet 6 inches in length, weighs upwards of 960 pounds, is 20 inches in diameter, and the body was cast in one sheet.

The diameter of the 32-feet Posaune is 16 inches at the bell, and of the 16-feet Posaune, 10 inches. A light sieve of metal wire, with wide meshes, placed over the bell of each of the large reed pipes, keeps out the birds—a most necessary and excellent precaution. The tops of a great portion of the large metal pipes also have an addition that is by no means common. This consists of a sliding cylinder, introduced to aid the process of tuning, which is drawn up or pressed down according as the pitch of the pipe may require flattening or sharping. The top of the pipe is further covered with leather outside to prevent the cylinder slipping. None of the pipes are pressed out of shape, none present bent or ragged tops, as is too frequently the case in English organs, but all preserve their symmetry of outline.

Silbermann, the celebrated organ-builder, of Dresden, was invited to construct the new St. Michael's organ, which invitation he accepted; but, dying shortly afterwards, the execution of the work was entrusted to his principal workman, Hildebrand. This was about the year 1768. T. Matheson, the celebrated composer and theorist, left, by will, £4,000 towards paying for this organ, which sum, however, did not nearly equal the amount expended in its fabrication.

67. ST. CATHERINE'S CHURCH, HAMBURG.

An organ stood in this church as early as the year 1501. A portion of the present instrument was made in 1540, including a Principal, on the Pedal, of 26 feet. This latter was removed, on account of its damaged state and feeble tone, in 1670, after being in use at least 130 years, and the present stop of 32 feet, of the best English tin, polished, substituted. Sebastian Bach, when a youth, made frequent journeys to Hamburg to hear the then organist of St. Catherine's Church, John Adam Reinkin, who was at that time very famous; and he remembered to his latest years, with lively satisfaction, this organ, with its magnificent 32-feet Pedal, on which, in after life, he sometimes publicly performed. In 1867 an organ committee was formed, consisting of four gentlemen connected with the administration of the Church, and the present organist, Herr H. Dagenhardt, who entered into a contract with the organ-builder, Mr. Heinr. Wolfsteller, junr., for the cleansing, improvement, and enlarging of the instrument, according to a design prepared by the organist.   The organ now contains the following stops :—

Hauptwerk.

1. Principal	16 feet.		7. Octave	4 feet.
2. Quintaton	16 feet tone.		8. Octave	2 feet.
3. Principal	8 feet.		9. Rauschpfeife, II ranks.	
4. Octave	8 feet.		10. Mixture, VI to X ranks.	
5. Salicet	8 feet.		11. Trompette	16 feet.
6. Hohlflote	8 feet.		12. Trompette	8 feet.

Oberwerk.

13. Bourdon	16 feet tone.		19. Waldflote	2 feet.
14. Principal	8 feet.		20. Scharf, III to V ranks.	
15. Gedact	8 feet tone.		21. Trompette	8 feet.
16. Rohrflote	8 feet tone.		22. Trompette	4 feet.
17. Octave	4 feet.		23. Vox humana	8 feet.
18. Flote	4 feet.		24. Glockenspiel.	

Rückpositiv.

25. Bourdon	16 feet tone.		31. Nasat	3 feet.
26. Principal	8 feet.		32. Octave	2 feet.
27. Quintaton	8 feet tone.		33. Sesqualtera, II ranks.	
28. Gedact	8 feet tone.		34. Scharf, V ranks.	
29. Octave	4 feet.		35. Dulcian	16 feet.
30. Hohlflote	4 feet.		36. Hautbois d'Amour	8 feet.

Brustwerk (Swell).

37. Principal	8 feet.		41. Scharf, V ranks.	
38. Gedact	8 feet tone.		42. Trompette	8 feet.
39. Octave	4 feet.		43. Oboe	8 feet.
40. Quintaton	4 feet tone.		44. Cimbalstern.	

Pedal.

45. Principal	32 feet.		52. Octave	4 feet.
46. Principal	16 feet.		53. Rauschpfeife, II ranks.	
47. Sub-bass	16 feet tone.		54. Posaune	32 feet.
48. Violon	16 feet.		55. Posaune	16 feet.
49. Quint	10⅔ feet.		56. Dulcian	16 feet.
50. Octave	8 feet.		57. Trompette	8 feet.
51. Bourdon	8 feet tone.		58. Trompette	4 feet.

68. HAMBURG.

The fine organ in the Church of St. Jacobi, at Hamburg, was built by the Abbe Schnittker, and was completed towards the close of the seventeenth century. Sebastian Bach, when a young man, was very desirous to obtain the appointment of organist to this church, on account of the great excellence of the instrument it contained ; but, in spite of the excitement which his wonderful playing created, he did not succeed ; the reason being that a clerical amateur, of mediocre talent, offered a sum of money for the appointment, which temptation had more weight with the authorities than the transcendent skill of the great master.   The organ has 60 sounding stops, 4 Manuals, and Pedal of 14 stops.   The following is the disposition :—

Great, 12 Stops.

1. Principal	16 feet.		7. Rohrflote	4 feet tone.
2. Quintadena	16 feet tone.		8. Quint	2⅔ feet.
3. Octave	8 feet.		9. Super-octave	2 feet.
4. Viola di Gamba	8 feet.		10. Mixtur, VI and VIII ranks.	
5. Spitzflote	8 feet.		11. Rauschpfeife.	
6. Octave	4 feet.		12. Trompette	16 feet.

Choir, 13 *Stops.*

13. Principal	8 feet.		20. Octave	2 feet.
14. Bauerpfeife	8 feet.		21. Sifflote	1 foot.
15. Quintadena	8 feet tone.		22. Sesquialtera, II ranks	2⅔ feet.
16. Gedact	8 feet tone.		23. Scharf, VI and VIII ranks.	
17. Octave	4 feet.		24. Dulcian	8 feet.
18. Blockflote	4 feet.		25. Trompette	8 feet.
19. Nasat	2⅔ feet.			

Echo, 13 *Stops.*

26. Principal	8 feet.		33. Gemshorn	2 feet.
27. Hohlflote	8 feet.		34. Cymbale, III ranks.	
28. Rohrflote	8 feet tone.		35. Scharf, VI ranks.	
29. Octave	4 feet.		36. Trompette	8 feet.
30. Spitzflote	4 feet.		37. Oboe, to middle c^1	8 feet.
31. Nasat	2⅔ feet.		38. Vox humana	8 feet tone.
32. Octave	2 feet.			

Swell, 8 *Stops.*

39. Principal	8 feet.		43. Sesquialtera, II ranks	2⅔ feet.
40. Octave	4 feet.		44. Scharf, VI and VIII ranks.	
41. Hohlflote	4 feet.		45. Dulcian	8 feet.
42. Waldflote	2 feet.		46. Trichter-regal	8 feet.

Pedal, 14 *Stops.*

47. Principal, in front	32 feet.		54. Rauschpfeife, II ranks.	
48. Octave	16 feet.		55. Posaune	32 feet.
49. Sub-bass	16 feet tone.		56. Posaune	16 feet.
50. Octave	8 feet.		57. Dulcian	16 feet.
51. Octave	4 feet.		58. Trompette	8 feet.
52. Nachthorn	2 feet.		59. Trompette	4 feet.
53. Mixtur, VI and VIII ranks.			60. Cornet	2 feet.

The 4 Manuals can be coupled together.

Accessory Stops.

1 to 5. Five Wind-trunk valves.		7. Glockenspiel.
6. Cymbalstar.		8. Trommel.

The name of the builder of the above excellent organ is held in great veneration in Germany ; where his instruments are as highly prized for their stability, as they are justly celebrated for their dignified and impressive tone. The Abbe Schnittker resided at a place about thirty-six English miles from Hamburg, in the Hanoverian territories, in a house that has gone by the name of "the organ-builder's box" or villa ever since.

The three fine instruments, just noticed, form most interesting objects for examination to an English admirer of the organ ; not simply on account of the very distinct character in the tone of each, but because they so closely resemble, in quality, the organs of three of the most celebrated builders of this country of past times ; and they therefore picture to the hearer what the instruments of those builders would have been, had the art in England been in a more advanced state in their day.

The organ in the Church of St. Catherine, which is the oldest of the three, is strikingly like Harris's in tone ; clear, ringing, and dashing in the Mixtures. That in the church of St. Jacobi calls to mind the instruments of Father Smith ; resonant, solemn, and dignified ; with somewhat less fire than that at St. Catherine's, but rather more fulness. The organ at St. Michael's, the most recently constructed one of the three, also the largest in scale, is less powerful than the others, but very musical and pleasing ; and, in all these respects, forcibly calls to mind the excellent instruments of Green.

69. HAMBURG.

The organ that lately stood in the Church of St. Nicholas, at Hamburg, had 67 sounding stops, and, like the last, was built by Schnittker, who completed it in the year 1686. The following is a list of the stops that were contained in this instrument :—

Great, 14 Stops.

1. Principal	16 feet.	8. Spitzflote	4 feet.
2. Quintadena	16 feet tone.	9. Rauschpfeife, III ranks ...	2⅔ feet.
3. Octave	8 feet.	10. Super-octave	2 feet.
4. Spitzflote	8 feet.	11. Mixture, VI to IX ranks.	
5. Salicional, wood	8 feet.	12. Scharf, III ranks.	
6. Viola di Gamba	8 feet.	13. Trompette	16 feet.
7. Octave	4 feet.	14. Trompette	8 feet.

Echo, 14 Stops.

15. Quintadena	16 feet tone.	22. Flachflote	2 feet.
16. Octave	8 feet.	23. Scharf, IV to VI ranks.	
17. Quintadena	8 feet tone.	24. Cymbale, III ranks.	
18. Rohrflote	8 feet tone.	25. Trompette	8 feet.
19. Octave	4 feet.	26. Trompette	4 feet.
20. Rohrflote	4 feet.	27. Krumhorn	8 feet tone.
21. Nasat	2⅔ feet.	28. Vox humana	8 feet tone.

Choir, in front, 13 Stops.

29. Bourdon	16 feet tone.	36. Sifflote	2 feet.
30. Principal	8 feet.	37. Querflote	2 feet.
31. Quintadena	8 feet tone.	38. Scharf, VI to IX ranks.	
32. Gedact	8 feet tone.	39. Dulcian	16 feet.
33. Octave	4 feet.	40. Trompette	8 feet.
34. Rohrflote	4 feet tone.	41. Trompette to middle c¹ ...	8 feet.
35. Sesquialtera, II ranks	2⅔ feet.		

Brustwerk, 10 Stops.

42. Principal	8 feet.	47. Rauschpfeife, II ranks ...	2⅔ feet.
43. Bauerpfeife	8 feet.	48. Waldflote	2 feet.
44. Blockflote, wood	8 feet.	49. Nasat	1⅓ foot.
45. Principal	4 feet.	50. Scharf, III to VI ranks.	
46. Blockflote, wood	4 feet.	51. Dulcian	8 feet.

Pedal, 16 Stops.

52. Principal	32 feet.	60. Nachthorn	2 feet.
53. Octave	16 feet.	61. Mixture, VI to X ranks.	
54. Quint	10⅔ feet.	62. Posaune	32 feet.
55. Octave	8 feet.	63. Posaune	16 feet.
56. Violoncello	8 feet.	64. Dulcian	16 feet.
57. Rauschpfeife, III ranks ...	5⅓ feet.	65. Trompette	8 feet.
58. Octave	4 feet.	66. Krumhorn	8 feet tone.
59. Gedact	4 feet tone.	67. Trompette	4 feet.

Accessory Stops.

1. Cymbalstar.	3. Tremulant.	5 to 10. Six Wind-trunk valves.
2. Glockenspiel.	4. Riegal.	11. Coupler, Choir to Pedal.

70. HAMBURG.

The organ that stood in St. Peter's Church, previous to the fire, was the most ancient one in the city. It is not known when or by whom it was originally built ; but the last two Manuals, which were subsequent additions, were made upwards of

300 years ago, *i.e.*, in 1548, at Hartzogenbuch, in Brabant, and sent thither by sea. The stops in the above organ were as follows :—

Great, 11 Stops.

1. Principal	16 feet.	7. Octave	4 feet.
2. Gedact	16 feet tone.	8. Rauschpfeife, II ranks ...	2⅔ feet.
3. Octave	8 feet.	9. Mixture, IV ranks.	
4. Rohrflote	8 feet tone.	10. Scharf, III ranks.	
5. Viola di Gamba	8 feet.	11. Trompette	16 feet.
6. Quint	5⅓ feet.		

Echo, 14 Stops.

12. Quintadena	16 feet tone.	19. Sesquialtera, II ranks	2⅔ feet.
13. Principal	8 feet.	20. Mixture, IV ranks.	
14. Principal	8 feet.	21. Cornett, V ranks.	
15. Gedact	8 feet tone.	22. Trompette	8 feet.
16. Octave	4 feet.	23. Trompette	8 feet.
17. Spitzflote	4 feet.	24. Oboe Discant	8 feet.
18. Nasat	2⅔ feet.	25. Vox Humana	8 feet tone.

Choir, in front, 12 Stops.

26. Principal	8 feet.	32. Flote	2 feet.
27. Quintadena	8 feet tone.	33. Sifflote	1 foot.
28. Gedact	8 feet tone.	34. Scharfe, IV ranks.	
29. Octave	4 feet.	35. Dulcian	16 feet.
30. Blockflote	4 feet.	36. Trompette	8 feet.
31. Sesquialtera, II ranks. ...	2⅔ feet.	37. Trompette, tenor c	8 feet.

Pedal, 13 Stops.

38. Principal	32 feet.	45. Posaune	32 feet.
39. Untersatz	16 feet.	46. Posaune	16 feet.
40. Octave	8 feet.	47. Dulcian	16 feet.
41. Rohr-quint	5⅓ feet tone.	48. Trompette	8 feet.
42. Octave	4 feet.	49. Trompette	4 feet.
43. Mixture, VI ranks.		50. Cornett	2 feet.
44. Rauschpfeife, II ranks.			

71. LUBECK.

The Marien Kirche, in the ancient town of Lubeck, contains two organs ; the largest of which stands at the west end of the church, a stately Gothic edifice, measuring upwards of 120 English feet in height inside, and about 300 feet in length. It was built in the year 1518; the choir organ being added in the year 1561, which date is ingeniously recorded among the ornamental carving on the top. The case presents a most noble and magnificent, though not elaborate, façade ; and is from 70 to 80 feet in height, 40 in width, and 7 in depth. It has the 32-feet metal pipes in front, the largest of which is 19 inches in diameter. All the front pipes are of pure tin, burnished; and are slightly but exquisitely diapered about the mouth. The case is made of a handsome dark wood, probably walnut, and has a great quantity of carved and gilt work about it, which gives a gorgeous effect to the whole.

Diederich Buxtehude was organist of this church in the early part of the last century, and was so celebrated, that Sebastian Bach, then a youth, undertook a journey on foot to Lubeck to hear him. Among Buxtehude's compositions for the organ, there is one with a *double* pedal part, with which Bach seems to have been acquainted.

The Lubeck organ has just had a new inside put to it, by J. F. Schulze, of Paulinzelle, from a specification drawn up by H. Jimmerthal, the organist to the church. It is laid out in four stories, the swell occupying the upper one. The frame-work and sound-boards are almost entirely of oak ; the front-boards of the latter being of polished mahogany, handsomely inlaid with ebony. The front-boards are fastened on with *wooden* screws having large six-sided heads, which present the great advantage of being capable of being turned by the fingers unaided. The beams that support the organ are built into the wall behind, and the organ hangs, pendant fashion, therefrom, with the most elegant effect.

The organ has 82 sounding stops, distributed among 4 Manuals and 2 Pedals, and includes 3 stops of 32 feet, 17 of 16 feet, and 30 of 8 feet.

The following is a detailed account of its contents :—

Great, 21 Stops.

1. Bourdon to the tenor c key	32 feet tone.	11. Octave ... 4 feet.
2. Principal	16 feet.	12. Spitzflote ... 4 feet.
3. Viola Major	16 feet.	13. Gambette ... 4 feet.
4. Bourdon	16 feet tone.	14. Nasat ... 2⅔ feet.
5. Principal	8 feet.	15. Rausch-quint, II fach ... 2⅔ & 2 feet.
6. Gemshorn	8 feet.	16. Mixture, V fach ... 2 feet.
7. Hohlflote	8 feet.	17. Cymbale, III fach ... 2 feet.
8. Viol di Gamba	8 feet.	18. Cornett, IV fach.
9. Gedact	8 feet tone.	19. Trompette ... 16 feet.
10. Quint	5⅓ feet.	20. Trompette ... 8 feet.
		21. Trompette ... 4 feet.

Choir, 16 Stops.

22. Principal	16 feet.	30. Gemshorn ... 4 feet.
23. Bourdon	16 feet tone.	31. Rohrflote ... 4 feet tone.
24. Principal	8 feet.	32. Quint ... 2⅔ feet.
25. Salicional	8 feet.	33. Octave ... 2 feet.
26. Spitzflote	8 feet.	34. Mixture, V fach ... 2 feet.
27. Czakan Flote	8 feet.	35. Scharf, III fach ... 2 feet.
28. Gedact	8 feet tone.	36. Phyzharmonica ... 16 feet.
29. Octave	4 feet.	37. Trompette ... 8 feet.

Echo, 14 Stops.

38. Lieblich Gedact	16 feet tone.	45. Zartflote ... 4 feet.
39. Geigen Principal	8 feet.	46. Flauto Traverso ... 4 feet.
40. Terpodion	8 feet.	47. Quint ... 2⅔ feet.
41. Lieblich Gedact	8 feet tone.	48. Waldflote ... 2 feet.
42. Flauto Traverso	8 feet.	49. Mixture, V fach ... 2 feet.
43. Doppelflote	8 feet tone.	50. Æoline ... 8 feet.
44. Geigen Principal	4 feet.	51. Oboe ... 8 feet.

Swell, 10 Stops.

52. Quintaton	16 feet tone.	57. Principal ... 4 feet.
53. Principal	8 feet.	58. Viola d'amour ... 4 feet.
54. Fugara	8 feet.	59. Mixture, III fach ... 2 feet.
55. Gedact	8 feet tone.	60. Æoline ... 16 feet.
56. Harmonica	8 feet.	61. Clarinetto ... 8 feet tone.

Great Pedal, 16 Stops.

62. Gross Principal	32 feet.	70. Terz ... 6⅖ feet.
63. Principal Bass	16 feet.	71. Quint ... 5⅓ feet.
64. Basso Magiore	16 feet.	72. Octave ... 4 feet.
65. Violon	16 feet.	73. Cornett, V fach.
66. Quint	10⅔ feet.	74. Contra Posaune ... 32 feet.
67. Principal Bass	8 feet.	75. Posaune ... 16 feet.
68. Basso Minore	8 feet.	76. Trompette ... 8 feet.
69. Violoncello	8 feet.	77. Clarine ... 4 feet.

Choir Pedal, 5 Stops.

78. Sub-bass	16 feet tone.	81. Gedact ... 8 feet tone.
79. Doppelflotenbass	16 feet tone.	82. Fagotto ... 16 feet.
80. Violoncello	8 feet.	

Accessory Stops, &c.

1. Wind to Great.
2. Wind to Choir.
3. Wind to Echo.
4. Wind to Swell.
5. Wind to Great Pedal Basses.

6. Wind to Pedal Reed-work.
7. Wind to Choir Pedal.
8. Coupler, Choir to Great.
9. Coupler, Echo to Great.
10. Coupler, Great to Pedal.

72. LUBECK.

The second organ in this church—the "little organ," as it is called—contains 33 stops, 3 Manuals, and a Pedal ; has a 16 feet speaking front, and has the Choir organ in front. The specification is as follows :—

Great, 8 Stops.

1. Quintaton	16 feet tone.	
2. Principal	8 feet.	
3. Spitzflote	8 feet.	
4. Octave	4 feet.	
5. Flote	4 feet.	
6. Rausch-quint, II ranks	2⅔ & 2 feet.	
7. Mixture, IV and V ranks.		
8. Trompette	8 feet.	

Choir, 11 Stops.

9. Principal	8 feet.
10. Quintadena	8 feet tone.
11. Rohrflote	8 feet tone.
12. Octave	4 feet.
13. Rohrflote	4 feet tone.
14. Flote	2 feet.
15. Sesquialtera, II ranks	2⅔ & 1⅗ feet.
16. Mixture, IV ranks.	
17. Scharf, V ranks.	
18. Fagotto	16 feet tone.
19. Regal	8 feet.

Swell, 4 Stops.

20. Gedact	8 feet tone.
21. Gedact	4 feet tone.
22. Cornett, III ranks.	
23. Trompette	8 feet.

Pedal, 10 Stops.

24. Principal, in front	16 feet.
25. Gross Quint, stopped	10⅔ feet tone.
26. Octave	8 feet.
27. Gedact	8 feet tone.
28. Octave	8 feet.
29. Octave	4 feet.
30. Mixture, III ranks	2⅔ feet.
31. Posaune	16 feet.
32. Trompette	8 feet.
33. Schalmey	4 feet tone.

73. LUBECK.

The organ in the second church, not the cathedral, has 4 Manuals, and Pedal and 45 stops, of which the following is a list :—

Great, 9 Stops.

1. Principal	16 feet.
2. Quintaton	16 feet tonc.
3. Octave	8 feet.
4. Viol di Gamba	8 feet.
5. Octave	4 feet.
6. Flote	4 feet.
7. Rauschpfeife, II ranks	2⅔ feet.
8. Mixture, VIII ranks.	
9. Scharf, VI ranks.	

Choir, 10 Stops.

10. Principal	8 feet.
11. Gedact	8 feet tone.
12. Quintaton	8 feet tone.
13. Barpfeife	8 feet.
14. Octave	4 feet.
15. Flote	4 feet.
16. Sifflote	2 feet.
17. Mixture, IV ranks.	
18. Schalmey	8 feet tone.
19. Regal	8 feet.

Echo, 10 Stops.

20.	Principal	8 feet.	25.	Nasat	2⅔ feet.
21.	Hohlflote	8 feet.	26.	Waldflote	2 feet.
22.	Zink	8 feet.	27.	Cymbale, III ranks.	
23.	Principal	4 feet.	28.	Trompette	8 feet.
24.	Flote	4 feet.	29.	Vox humana	8 feet tone.

Swell, 7 Stops.

30.	Gedact	8 feet tone.	34.	Scharf, IV ranks.	
31.	Octave	4 feet.	35.	Dulcian	16 feet tone.
32.	Quintaton	8 feet tone.	36.	Regal	8 feet.
33.	Waldflote	2 feet.			

Pedal, 9 Stops.

37.	Principal	16 feet.	42.	Octave	4 feet.
38.	Sub-bass	16 feet tone.	43.	Mixture, IV ranks.	
39.	Octave	8 feet.	44.	Posaune	16 feet.
40.	Violoncello	8 feet.	45.	Trompette	8 feet.
41.	Gedact	8 feet tone.			

74. WISMAR.

The organ in St. Mary's Church, at Wismar, was built by J. F. Schulze, and was finished in 1840. It has 56 sounding stops, 8 bellows, and 3 Manuals and Pedal. The following is a list of the stops :—

Great, 15 Stops.

1.	Bourdon to g	32 feet tone.	9.	Octave	4 feet.
2.	Principal	16 feet.	10.	Gemshorn	4 feet.
3.	Quintaton	16 feet tone.	11.	Scharf, V ranks.	
4.	Octave	8 feet.	12.	Cymbale, III ranks.	
5.	Hohlflote	8 feet.	13.	Cornett, III ranks.	
6.	Terpodion	8 feet.	14.	Trompette	16 feet.
7.	Gedact	8 feet tone.	15.	Trompette	8 feet.
8.	Quint	5⅓ feet.			

Choir, 13 Stops.

16.	Bourdon	16 feet.	23.	Spitzflote	4 feet.
17.	Principal	8 feet.	24.	Flote	4 feet.
18.	Gemshorn	8 feet.	25.	Quint and Octave, II ranks	2⅔ & 2 feet.
19.	Gamba	8 feet.	26.	Mixture, IV ranks	1⅓ foot.
20.	Flauto Traverso	8 feet.	27.	Phyzharmonica	16 feet.
21.	Gedact	8 feet tone.	28.	Trompette	8 feet.
22.	Octave	4 feet.			

Swell, 11 Stops.

29.	Lieblich Gedact	16 feet.	35.	Octave	4 feet.
30.	Geigen Principal	8 feet.	36.	Fugara	4 feet.
31.	Salicional	8 feet.	37.	Waldflote	2 feet.
32.	Zartflote	8 feet.	38.	Mixture, III ranks.	
33.	Flauto Traverso	8 feet.	39.	Æoline	8 feet.
34.	Lieblich Gedact	8 feet tone.			

Pedal, 17 Stops.

40.	Principal Bass	32 feet.	49.	Gedact Bass	8 feet tone.
41.	Principal	16 feet.	50.	Octave	4 feet.
42.	Quintaton	16 feet.	51.	Mixture, V ranks.	
43.	Major Bass	16 feet.	52.	Posaune	32 feet.
44.	Sub-bass	16 feet tone.	53.	Posaune	16 feet.
45.	Quint	10⅔ feet.	54.	Bombarde	16 feet.
46.	Octaven Bass	8 feet.	55.	Trompette	8 feet.
47.	Violone	8 feet.	56.	Clarino	4 feet.
48.	Minor Bass	8 feet.			

75. PERLEBERG.

The organ in the Church at Perleberg was built by Tobias Turley and his son, John F. Turley, in 1831, and has 36 sounding stops :—

Great, 14 Stops.

1. Bourdon	16 feet tone.
2. Principal, Eng. tin, in front	8 feet.
3. Spitzflote, metal to tenor c, lowest octave wood......	8 feet.
4. Hohlflote, metal to tenor c, lowest octave wood......	8 feet.
5. Rohrflote, metal	8 feet tone.
6. Octave, Prussian tin	4 feet.
7. Gemshorn, metal............	4 feet.
8. Lieblich Gedact, metal ...	4 feet tone.
9. Quint, Prussian tin	3 feet.
10. Super-octave, Prussian tin	2 feet.
11. Scharf, V ranks, Prussian tin................2, 1⅗, 1⅓, 1, and ⅔ feet.	
12. Cymbale, III ranks, Prussian tin ....1, ½, and ¼ foot.	
13. Cornett, III ranks, Eng. tin ....2⅔, 2, and 1⅗ feet.	
14. Trompette	8 feet.

Choir, 12 Stops.

15. Bourdon, metal, except the lowest octave, which is of wood.....................	16 feet tone.
16. Principal, in front	8 feet.
17. Viol di Gamba, Eng. tin to tenor c, last octave wood	8 feet.
18. Flauto Traverso, pear-tree wood......................	8 feet.
19. Gedact, metal...............	8 feet tone.
20. Octave.........................	4 feet.
21. Rohrflote.....................	4 feet tone.
22. Nasat.........................	2⅔ feet.
23. Super-octave	2 feet.
24. Mixture, III ranks......1⅓, 1, and ⅔ foot.	
25. Æoline, wood..............	16 feet.
26. Hautbois, treble...........	8 feet.

Pedal, 10 Stops.

27. Untersatz, wood	32 feet tone.
28. Principal, in front	16 feet.
29. Sub-bass, wood	16 feet tone.
30. Gross Nasat, wood	10⅔ feet.
31. Octave, wood	8 feet.
32. Gedact-bass, wood	8 feet tone.
33. Terz, wood	6⅖ feet.
34. Super-octave, metal	4 feet.
35. Posaune	16 feet.
36. Trompette	8 feet.

76. BERLIN.

The organ in St. Mary's Church at Berlin was originally built, in 1722, by Joachim Wagner, but has received subsequent additions at the hands of Buchholz, of Berlin. It now has 40 sounding stops, 3 Manuals, a Pedal of 9 stops, and 6 pairs of bellows, 9 feet long by 4½ broad. The stops are distributed as follows :—

Great, 12 Stops.

1. Bourdon	16 feet tone.
2. Principal	8 feet.
3. Rohrflote	8 feet tone.
4. Viol di Gamba...............	8 feet.
5. Octave	4 feet.
6. Spitzflote	4 feet.
7. Quint	2⅔ feet.
8. Super-octave	2 feet.
9. Cornett, V ranks.	
10. Scharf, V ranks.	
11. Cymbale, III ranks.	
12. Trompette	8 feet.

Choir, 9 Stops.

13. Salicional	8 feet.
14. Gemshorn.....................	8 feet.
15. Gedact	8 feet tone.
16. Quintaton	8 feet tonc.
17. Octave	4 feet.
18. Fugara.........................	4 feet.
19. Lieblichflote	4 feet tone.
20. Nazard.........................	2⅔ feet.
21. Super-octave	2 feet.

Echo, 10 Stops.

22. Quintaton	16 feet tone.
23. Principal	8 feet.
24. Gedact	8 feet tonc.
25. Octave	4 feet.
26. Rohrflote	4 feet tonc.
27. Nazard	2⅔ feet.
28. Super-octave	2 feet.
29. Sifflote........................	1 foot.
30. { Mixture, major { Mixture, minor } IV ranks.	
31. { Hautbois, discant { Fagotto, bass } ... 8 feet.	

Pedal, 9 Stops.

32. Principal, in front	16 feet.	37. Bass-flote	8 feet tone.
33. Sub-bass	16 feet tone.	38. Octave	4 feet.
34. Violon	16 feet.	39. Contra-Posaune	32 feet.
35. Gross Nazard	10⅔ feet.	40. Posaune	16 feet.
36. Gemshorn	8 feet.		

Accessory Stops.

1. Coupler, Choir to Great.	3. Coupler, Great to Pedal.
2. Coupler, Echo to Great.	4, 5, 6, 7. Four Wind-trunk valves.

77. BERLIN.

The organ in the Garrison Church at Berlin was built, in 1725, by Joachim Wagner, and contains 49 stops, 3 Manuals, and Pedal of 12 stops. The names and distribution of the stops are as follow :—

Great, 13 Stops.

1. Bourdon	16 feet tone.	8. Quint	2⅔ feet.
2. Principal	8 feet.	9. Octave	2 feet.
3. Rohrflote	8 feet tone.	10. Mixture, IV ranks.	
4. Viol di Gamba	8 feet.	11. Cornett, V ranks.	
5. Flauto Traverso	8 feet.	12. Scharf, VI ranks.	
6. Octave	4 feet.	13. Fagotto	16 feet.
7. Spitzflote	4 feet.		

Echo, 11 Stops.

14. Gedact	8 feet tone.	20. Flageolet	2 feet.
15. Quintaton	8 feet tone.	21. Terz	1⅗ foot.
16. Principal	4 feet.	22. Quint	1⅓ foot.
17. Rohrflote	4 feet tone.	23. Cymbale, IV ranks.	
18. Nasat	2⅔ feet.	24. Vox humana	8 feet tone.
19. Octave	2 feet.		

Choir, 13 Stops.

25. Quintaton	16 feet tone.	32. Octave	2 feet.
26. Principal	8 feet.	33. Waldflote	2 feet.
27. Gedact	8 feet tone.	34. Sifflote	1 foot.
28. Salicional	8 feet.	35. Scharf, V ranks.	
29. Octave	4 feet.	36. Cymbale, III ranks.	
30. Fugara	4 feet.	37. Trompette Discant / Trompette Bass	8 feet.
31. Quint	2⅔ feet.		

Pedal, 12 Stops.

38. Principal, in front	16 feet.	44. Quint	2⅔ feet.
39. Violon	16 feet.	45. Mixture, VIII ranks.	
40. Octave	8 feet.	46. Posaune	32 feet.
41. Gemshorn	8 feet.	47. Posaune	16 feet.
42. Quint	5⅓ feet.	48. Trompette	8 feet.
43. Nachthorn	4 feet.	49. Clarion	4 feet.

78. KRONSTADT.

The fine organ in the Cathedral Church at Kronstadt was built from the plans of C. Buchholz, of Berlin, in 1839. It contains 63 sounding stops, 4 Manuals, and Pedal of 17 stops, and 9 large pairs of bellows. The stops are distributed as follows :—

Great, 15 Stops.

1. Principal	16 feet.	9. Spitzflote	4 feet.
2. Quintaton	16 feet tone.	10. Waldflote	4 feet.
3. Principal	8 feet.	11. Quint	2⅔ feet.
4. Rohrflote	8 feet tone.	12. Super-octave	2 feet.
5. Gemshorn	8 feet.	13. Cornett, V ranks.	
6. Viol di Gamba	8 feet.	14. Scharf, V ranks.	
7. Nasat	5⅓ feet.	15. Cymbale, V ranks.	
8. Octave	4 feet.		

Echo, 13 Stops.

16. Bourdon	16 feet tone.	23. Rohrflote	4 feet tone.
17. Principal	8 feet.	24. Fugara	4 feet.
18. Gedact	8 feet tone.	25. Nasat	2⅔ feet.
19. Salicional	8 feet.	26. Super-octave, II ranks ...	2 feet.
20. Hohlflote	8 feet.	27. Mixture, V ranks.	
21. Quintaton	8 feet tone.	28. Hautbois	8 feet.
22. Octave	4 feet.		

Choir, 11 Stops.

29. Salicional	16 feet.	35. Viol d'amour	4 feet.
30. Principal	8 feet.	36. Flauto Douce	4 feet.
31. Gedact	8 feet tone.	37. Gemshorn Quint	2⅔ feet.
32. Viol di Gamba	8 feet.	38. Decima Quint	2 feet.
33. Flauto Traverso	8 feet.	39. Progressio harmonica, III	
34. Octave	4 feet.	to V ranks.	

Reed-work Manual, 7 Stops.

40. Fagotto	16 feet.	44. Rohrflote	8 feet tone.
41. Trompette	8 feet.	45. Violon	8 feet.
42. Clarionett	8 feet.	46. Principal	4 feet.
43. Vox Angelica	8 feet.		

Nos. 44, 45, and 46 are Lip Stops.

Pedal, 17 Stops.

47. Principal	32 feet.	56. Gemshorn	8 feet.
48. Untersatz	32 feet tone.	57. Quint	5⅓ feet.
49. Principal	16 feet.	58. Octave	4 feet.
50. Sub-bass	16 feet tone.	59. Mixture, IV ranks.	
51. Violon	16 feet.	60. Contra-Posaune	32 feet.
52. Nasat	10⅔ feet.	61. Posaune	16 feet.
53. Principal	8 feet.	62. Trompette	8 feet.
54. Bass-flote	8 feet tone.	63. Cornett	4 feet.
55. Violon	8 feet.		

Accessory Stops, Movements, &c.

1, 2, 3. Three Manual Couplers.	5 to 9. Five Wind-trunk valves.
4. Pedal Coupler.	

Compass.

Manuals, CC to g³ in alt, 56 notes.	Pedal, CCC to fiddle g, 32 notes.

79. LEIPZIG.

The organ in the University Church at Leipzig is a very fine instrument, but the touch is so heavy that playing on it is a great labour. It has 3 Manuals and Pedal, and 58 stops, of which latter the following is an enumeration :—

Great, 18 Stops.

1. Principal	16 feet.	10. Quint	2⅔ feet.
2. Bourdon	16 feet tone.	11. Octave	2 feet.
3. Octave	8 feet.	12. Tertia	1⅗ feet.
4. Gemshorn	8 feet.	13. Mixture, VI ranks.	
5. Gamba	8 feet.	14. Cymbale, III ranks.	
6. Rohrflote	8 feet tone.	15. Cornett, V ranks.	
7. Quinta	5⅓ feet.	16. Fagotto	16 feet.
8. Octave	4 feet.	17. Trompette	8 feet.
9. Gemshorn	4 feet.	18. Clarion	4 feet.

Choir, 12 *Stops.*

19.	Salicional	8 feet.	25.	Nasat	2 feet.
20.	Flote	8 feet.	26.	Octave	2 feet.
21.	Rohrflote	8 feet tone.	27.	Quint	1½ foot.
22.	Principal	4 feet.	28.	Flageolet	1 foot.
23.	Flote	4 feet.	29.	Mixture, IV ranks.	
24.	Gedact	4 feet tone.	30.	Oboe	8 feet.

Echo, 14 *Stops.*

31.	Quintaton	16 feet tone.	38.	Rohrflote	4 feet tone.
32.	Principal	8 feet.	39.	Quint	2⅔ feet.
33.	Spitzflote	8 feet.	40.	Octave	4 feet.
34.	Fugara	8 feet.	41.	Mixture, VI ranks.	
35.	Quintaton	8 feet tone.	42.	Cornett, III ranks.	
36.	Gedact	8 feet tone.	43.	Phyzharmonica	8 feet tone.
37.	Octave	4 feet.	44.	Vox humana	8 feet tone.

Pedal, 14 *Stops.*

45.	Principal	32 feet.	52.	Quint	5⅓ feet.
46.	Octave	16 feet.	53.	Octave	4 feet.
47.	Violon	16 feet.	54.	Mixture, V ranks.	
48.	Sub-bass	16 feet tone.	55.	Posaune	32 feet.
49.	Quint	10⅔ feet.	56.	Posaune	16 feet.
50.	Octave	8 feet.	57.	Trompette	8 feet.
51.	Violoncello	8 feet.	58.	Clarion	4 feet.

Accessory Stops, Movements, &c.

1. Echo to Great.	4. Tremulant Echo.
2. Choir to Great.	5, 6, 7. Three Wind-trunk valves.
3. Great to Pedal.	

Compass.

Manuals, CC to e³ in alt.	Pedal, CCC to tenor e.

DRESDEN.

The five principal churches in the city of Dresden all contain very fine organs, four of which are by Silbermann, one of the most renowned German organ builders of the last century, and whose name (Silbermann) very well describes the sparkling and chaste tone of his instruments. In the *Ramble among the Musicians of Germany*, a most interesting volume, written by the late Mr. Edward Holmes, and published in 1828, the author, in describing these instruments, observes :—"In glancing over the list of contents, the musical reader may please his imagination by fancying with what effect a piece of florid and artful counterpoint comes out of a German organ, where the player sits with a flood of sound ready to the touch of his fingers and store of thunder lying harmless at his feet. The thickness, depth, and independence of the Pedals here vindicate supremely the poetical ascendancy of the fugue over every other class of musical composition ; and in slow subjects, when the bass rolls in its ponderousness—there is no disputing it—it is like the *fiat* of the Omnipotent. As a matter of science, it is worthy consideration how far the structure of our organs might be improved by uniting the sweet *cathedral* quality of tone for which those of the Temple, Westminster Abbey, &c., are noted with the magnificence of Silbermann. If there lived now in England a mechanic capable of associating the best points of the two, a perfect specimen of the kind would be the result." Since the above excellent observations on the effect of the Dresden organs were written, a considerable advance has been made in the art of organ-building in England.

The largest of Silbermann's four Dresden organs stands in the Royal Catholic Church.

80. DRESDEN.

The fine organ in the Royal Catholic Church is esteemed Silbermann's masterpiece. Gottfried Silbermann died during its progress, and it was finished by his nephew, John Daniel Silbermann, of Strasbourg, who had assisted him in the work; and was completed and erected in the year 1754. It has 48 stops, distributed in the following manner :—

Great, 16 Stops.

1.	Principal	16 feet.	9.	Octave	2 feet.
2.	Bourdon	16 feet tone.	10.	Terz	1⅗ foot.
3.	Principal	8 feet.	11.	Mixture, IV ranks.	
4.	Viol di Gamba	8 feet.	12.	Cymbale, III ranks.	
5.	Rohrflote	8 feet tone.	13.	Cornett, V ranks.	
6.	Octave	4 feet.	14.	Fagotto	16 feet.
7.	Spitzflote	4 feet.	15.	Trompette	8 feet.
8.	Quint	2⅔ feet.	16.	Clarion	4 feet.

Echo, 14 Stops.

17.	Quintaton	16 feet tone.	24.	Nasat	2⅔ feet.
18.	Principal	8 feet.	25.	Octave	2 feet.
19.	Gedact	8 feet tone.	26.	Terz	1⅗ foot.
20.	Quintaton	8 feet tone.	27.	Flageolet	1 foot.
21.	Unda Maris	8 feet tone.	28.	Mixture, IV ranks.	
22.	Octave	4 feet.	29.	Echo, V ranks.	
23.	Rohrflote	4 feet tone.	30.	Vox humana	8 feet tone.

Choir, 10 Stops.

31.	Gedact	8 feet.	36.	Quint	1⅓ foot.
32.	Principal	4 feet.	37.	Sifflote	1 foot.
33.	Rohrflote	4 feet tone.	38.	Mixture, III ranks.	
34.	Nasat	2⅔ feet.	39.	Sesquialtera, II ranks.	
35.	Octave	2 feet.	40.	Chalumeau	8 feet tone.

Pedal, 8 Stops.

41.	Untersatz	32 feet tone.	45.	Mixture, VI ranks.	
42.	Principal	16 feet.	46.	Posaune	16 feet.
43.	Octave-bass	8 feet.	47.	Trompette	8 feet.
44.	Octave	4 feet.	48.	Clarion	4 feet.

Accessory Stops, &c.

1. Echo to Great.	3. Tremulant Echo.
2. Great to Pedal.	4. Tremulant Great.

Compass.

Manuals, CC to d³ in alt.	Pedal, CCC to tenor c.

81. DRESDEN.

The organ in the Royal Church of the Evangelists, at Dresden, was completed and erected by Silbermann in the year 1720. It has 32 sounding stops, distributed among 2 Manuals and Pedal, in the following manner :—

Great, 14 Stops.

1.	Bourdon	16 feet tone.	8.	Octave	2 feet.
2.	Principal	8 feet.	9.	Terz	1⅗ foot.
3.	Spitzflote	8 feet.	10.	Mixture, IV ranks.	
4.	Rohrflote	8 feet tone.	11.	Cymbale, III ranks.	
5.	Octave	4 feet.	12.	Cornett, IV ranks.	
6.	Gemshorn	4 feet.	13.	Trompette	8 feet.
7.	Quint	2⅔ feet.	14.	Clarion	4 feet.

Choir, 13 *Stops.*

15. Quintaton	16 feet tone.	22. Nasat	2⅔ feet.
16. Principal	8 feet.	23. Octave	2 feet.
17. Gedact	8 feet tone.	24. Quint	1⅓ foot.
18. Quintaton	8 feet tone.	25. Sifflote	1 foot.
19. Unda Maris	8 feet tone.	26. Mixture, III ranks.	
20. Octave	4 feet.	27. Vox humana	8 feet.
21. Rohrflote	4 feet tone.		

Pedal, 5 *Stops.*

28. Principal Bass	16 feet.	31. Posaune	16 feet.
29. Sub-bass	16 feet tone.	32. Trompette	8 feet tone.
30. Violon	8 feet.		

82. DRESDEN.

The organ in St. Mary's Church was completed in the year 1736. It has 43 Stops, 3 Manuals, and a Pedal of 8 stops, including a covered stop of 32-feet tone. The distribution of the stops is as follows :—

Great, 14 *Stops.*

1. Principal	16 feet.	8. Octave	2 feet.
2. Octave	8 feet.	9. Terz	1⅗ foot.
3. Viol di Gamba	8 feet.	10. Mixture, IV ranks.	
4. Rohrflote	8 feet tone.	11. Cymbale, III ranks.	
5. Octave	4 feet.	12. Cornett, V ranks.	
6. Spitzflote	4 feet.	13. Fagotto	16 feet.
7. Quint	2⅔ feet.	14. Trompette	8 feet.

Echo, 11 *Stops.*

15. Quintadena	16 feet tone.	21. Nasat	2⅔ feet.
16. Principal	8 feet.	22. Octave	2 feet.
17. Gedact	8 feet tone.	23. Terz	1⅗ foot.
18. Quintaton	8 feet tone.	24. Mixture, IV ranks.	
19. Octave	4 feet.	25. Vox humana	8 feet tone.
20. Rohrflote	4 feet tone.		

Choir, 10 *Stops.*

26. Gedact	8 feet tone.	31. Gemshorn	2 feet.
27. Principal	4 feet.	32. Quint	1⅓ foot.
28. Rohrflote	4 feet tone.	33. Sifflote	1 foot.
29. Nasat	2⅔ feet.	34. Mixture, III ranks.	
30. Octave	2 feet.	35. Chalumeau	8 feet tone.

Pedal, 8 *Stops.*

36. Untersatz	32 feet tone.	40. Mixture, VI ranks.	
37. Principal Bass	16 feet.	41. Posaune	16 feet.
38. Octave Bass	8 feet.	42. Trompette	8 feet.
39. Octave	4 feet.	43. Clarion	4 feet.

Neben Register.

1. Tremulant. | 2. Schwebung. | 3. Bass Ventil. | 4. Coppel. | 5. Klingel.

83. DRESDEN.

The organ in the Church of St. Sophia, at Dresden, was built by Silbermann, about the year 1750, and is a very fine instrument. It contains 33 stops, which are distributed among 2 Manuals and Pedal in the following manner :—

Great, 15 *Stops.*

1. Bourdon	16 feet tone.	9. Octave	2 feet.
2. Quintaton	16 feet tone.	10. Terz	1⅗ foot.
3. Principal	8 feet.	11. Mixture, V ranks.	
4. Spitzflote	8 feet.	12. Cymbale, III ranks.	
5. Rohrflote	8 feet tone.	13. Cornett, V ranks.	
6. Octave	4 feet.	14. { Trompette Discant / Trompette Bass }	8 feet.
7. Gemshorn	4 feet.	15. Clarion	4 feet.
8. Quint	2⅔ feet.		

Choir, 12 Stops.

16.	Quintaton	16 feet.	22.	Rohrflote	4 feet tone.
17.	Principal	8 feet.	23.	Nasat	2⅔ feet.
18.	Gedact	8 feet tone.	24.	Octave	2 feet.
19.	Quintaton	8 feet tone.	25.	Super-octave	1 foot.
20.	Unda Maris	8 feet tone.	26.	Mixture, III ranks.	
21.	Octave	4 feet.	27.	Vox humana	8 feet tone.

Pedal, 6 Stops.

28.	Principal	16 feet.	31.	Cornett, VIII ranks.	
29.	Bourdon	16 feet tone.	32.	Posaune	16 feet.
30.	Sub-bass	16 feet.	33.	Trompette	8 feet.

Accessory Stops, &c.

1. Coupler, Choir to Great.
2. Coupler, Great to Pedal.
3. Tremulant to Choir.

Compass.

Manuals, CC to d³ in alt.
Pedal, CCC to tenor c.

84. DRESDEN.

The organ in the Church of the Holy Cross, built by Jagermann, of Dresden, is altogether a very fine instrument. It is the largest in the city, and contains 56 sounding stops, 3 Manuals, and Pedal of 32 feet. The following is a list of its contents :—

Great, 16 Stops.

1.	Principal	16 feet.	9.	Quint	2⅔ feet.
2.	Bourdon	16 feet tone.	10.	Octave	2 feet.
3.	Gross-octave	8 feet.	11.	Terz	1⅗ foot.
4.	Gamba	8 feet.	12.	Mixture, VI ranks.	
5.	Gemshorn	8 feet.	13.	Cymbale, V ranks.	
6.	Rohrflote	8 feet tone.	14.	Cornett, V ranks.	
7.	Octave	4 feet.	15.	Fagotto	16 feet.
8.	Gemshorn	4 feet.	16.	Trompette	8 feet.

Choir, 10 Stops.

17.	Lieblich Gedact	8 feet tone.	22.	Octave	2 feet.
18.	Rohrflote	8 feet tone.	23.	Quint	1⅓ foot.
19.	Principal	4 feet.	24.	Sifflote	1 foot.
20.	Rohrflote	4 feet tone.	25.	Mixture, IV ranks.	
21.	Nasat	2⅔ feet.	26.	Cromorne	8 feet tone.

Echo, 14 Stops.

27.	Quintaton	16 feet tone.	34.	Quint	2⅔ feet.
28.	Principal	8 feet.	35.	Octave	2 feet.
29.	Schwiegel	8 feet.	36.	Flageolet	1 foot.
30.	Gedact	8 feet tone.	37.	Mixture, V ranks.	
31.	Quintaton	8 feet.	38.	Cymbale, IV ranks.	
32.	Octave	4 feet.	39.	Cornett, V ranks.	
33.	Rohrflote	4 feet tone.	40.	Vox humana	8 feet tone.

Pedal, 16 Stops.

41.	Gross Principal Bass	32 feet.	49.	Koppel	8 feet.
42.	Principal Bass	16 feet.	50.	Quint Bass	5⅓ feet.
43.	Violon Bass	16 feet.	51.	Octave Bass	4 feet.
44.	Sub-bass	16 feet tone.	52.	Octave Bass	2 feet.
45.	Gedact Quint Bass	10⅔ feet tone.	53.	Mixture Bass, VI ranks.	
46.	Principal Bass	8 feet.	54.	Posaune Bass	16 feet.
47.	Quintaton Bass	8 feet tone.	55.	Trompette Bass	8 feet.
48.	Violon Bass	8 feet.	56.	Clarion Bass	4 feet.

Accessory Stops, &c.

1. Coupler, Great to Pedal.
2. Coupler, Echo to Great.
3. Tremulant Echo.
4, 5, 6. Three trunk valves.

Couplers.

Manuals, CC to d³ in alt. | Pedal, CCC to tenor d.

85. FREIBERG IN SAXONY.

The cathedral at Freiberg, in Saxony, contains one of Silbermann's largest and finest organs, comprising 45 stops, 3 Manuals, and a Pedal of 10 stops. The following is a list of the several stops contained therein :—

Great, 13 Stops.

1. Bourdon, wood in the bass 16 feet tone.
2. Principal, Eng. tin .... 8 feet.
3. Viol di Gamba, tin .... 8 feet.
4. Rohrflote, tin .... 8 feet tone.
5. Octave, tin .... 4 feet.
6. Quint, tin .... 2⅔ feet.
7. Super-octave, tin........... 2 feet.
8. Tierce .... 1⅗ foot.
9. Fourniture, IV ranks, Eng. tin.
10. Cymbale, III ranks, Eng. tin.
11. Cornett, V ranks, Eng. tin.
12. Trompette, Eng. tin ...... 8 feet.
13. Clarion, Eng. tin .... 4 feet.

Choir, 13 Stops.

14. Quintaton, Eng. tin ...... 16 feet tone.
15. Principal, Eng. tin .... 8 feet.
16. Bourdon, metal treble, wood bass............. 8 feet tone.
17. Octave, Eng. tin .... 4 feet.
18. Flute, Eng. tin.............. 4 feet.
19. Nazard, metal .... 2⅔ feet.
20. Super-octave, Eng. tin ... 2 feet.
21. Tierce, Eng. tin .... 1⅗ foot.
22. Fourniture, III ranks, Eng. tin.
23. Cymbale, III ranks, Eng. tin.
24. Echo Cornett, V ranks, metal.
25. Cromorne, Eng. tin ...... 8 feet tone.
26. Vox humana, Eng. tin ... 8 feet tone.

Echo, 9 Stops.

27. Bourdon, metal .... 8 feet tone.
28. Principal, Eng. tin .... 4 feet.
29. Rohrflote, Eng. tin ....:.. 4 feet tone.
30. Nazard, metal .... 2⅔ feet.
31. Octave, Eng. tin .... 2 feet.
32. Tierce, metal .... 1⅗ foot.
33. Quint, Eng. tin .... 1⅓ foot.
34. Sifflote, Eng. tin .... 1 foot.
35. Fourniture, III ranks, Eng. tin.

Pedal, 10 Stops.

36. Untersatz, wood .... 32 feet tone.
37. Principal Bass, Eng. tin... 16 feet.
38. Sub-bass, wood .... 16 feet tone.
39. Octave, wood .... 16 feet.
40. Octave Bass, tin .... 8 feet.
41. Super-octave, tin .... 4 feet.
42. Fourniture, VI ranks, tin.
43. Bombarde, tin.............. 16 feet.
44. Trompette, tin .... 8 feet.
45. Clarion, tin................. 4 feet.

Accessory Stops, &c.

Coupler, Great to Pedal.
Wind-trunk valves.
Two Tremulants.
Six bellows.

86. PRAGUE.

The organ in the Church of St. Dominico, at Prague, is a very large and most interesting instrument. It has 4 Manuals and Pedal and 71 stops, distributed in the following manner :—

Great, 14 Stops.

1. Principal .... 16 feet.
2. Gross Gedact .... 16 feet tone.
3. Octave .... 8 feet.
4. Gedact .... 8 feet tone.
5. Octave .... 4 feet.
6. Offenflote .. .. 4 feet.
7. Quint........................... 2⅔ feet.
8. Super-octave .... 2 feet.
9. Spitzflote...................... 2 feet.
10. Sexte .... 2⅔ feet.
11. Quint .... 1⅓ foot.
12. Kuzialflote .... 1 foot.
13. Mixture, X ranks.
14. Cymbale, IV ranks.

Echo, 12 Stops.

15. Quintaton	16 feet tone.	21. Nachthorn	4 feet.
16. Surdun	16 feet tone.	22. Super-octave	2 feet.
17. Principal	8 feet.	23. Rauschpfeife, III ranks...	2⅔ feet.
18. Gemshorn	8 feet.	24. Koppel Quint	1⅓ foot.
19. Hohlflote	8 feet.	25. Mixture, VI ranks.	
20. Octave	4 feet.	26. Cromorne	8 feet tone.

Inside Choir, 9 Stops.

27. Gedact	8 feet tone.	32. Sedecima	1 foot.
28. Gedact	4 feet tone.	33. Cymbale, III ranks.	
29. Quintaton	4 feet tone.	34. Jungfern regal	16 feet.
30. Octave	4 feet.	35. Regal	8 feet.
31. Quint	1⅓ foot.		

Front Choir, 18 Stops.

36. Principal	16 feet.	45. Super-octave	2 feet.
37. Salicional	16 feet.	46. Gemshorn	2 feet.
38. Principal	8 feet.	47. Waldflote	2 feet.
39. Rohrflote	8 feet tone.	48. Sexte	1⅗ foot.
40. Quintaton	8 feet tone.	49. Sifflote	1 foot.
41. Octave	4 feet.	50. Mixture, V ranks.	
42. Blockflote	4 feet.	51. Cornett, III ranks.	
43. Querflote	4 feet.	52. Dulcian, of wood	16 feet.
44. Quint	2⅔ feet.	53. Trompette	8 feet.

Pedal, 18 Stops.

54. Principal	32 feet.		Quint, III ranks.
55. Octave	16 feet.		Super-octave, II ranks.
56. Principal	16 feet.	65.	Tertian, II ranks.
57. Salicional	16 feet.		Koppel, III ranks.
58. Octave	8 feet.	66. Mixture, VIII ranks.	
59. Gross Quint	5⅓ feet.	67. Posaune	32 feet.
60. Super-octave	4 feet.	68. Posaune	16 feet.
61. Nachthorn	4 feet.	69. Dulcian	16 feet.
62. Spitzflote	2 feet.	70. Trompette	8 feet.
63. Koppel	2 feet.	71. Schalmey	4 feet.
64. Bauerflote	1 foot.		

87. GOERLITZ.

The organ in the Church of St. Peter and St. Paul, at Goerlitz, in Upper Lusatia, was built by Eugenius Casparini and his son, Adam Horatius, in six years; and was consecrated by a solemn service, August 19th, 1703. It has 82 stops, 55 of which are whole stops, and 3,270 pipes, 522 of which are of metal. The front of the organ case shows above 280 pipes of polished tin, the largest of which is the FFFF in the Pedal, 24 feet long. The organ has 3 Manuals and 12 pairs of bellows. The following is an enumeration of the whole stops :—

Great, 16 Stops.

1. Principal, in front	16 feet.	9. Quint	2⅔ feet.
2. Octave Principal	8 feet.	10. Sedecima	2 feet.
3. Viol di Gamba	8 feet.	11. Quint	1⅓ foot.
4. Quintadena	8 feet tone.	12. Mixture, V ranks.	
5. Gedact	8 feet tone.	13. Rauschpfeife, III ranks.	
6. Flote-quint	5⅓ feet.	14. Bombarde	16 feet.
7. Super-octave	4 feet.	15. Trompette	8 feet.
8. Salicional	4 feet.	16. Vox humana	8 feet tone.

Echo, 8 Stops.

17. Gedact	8 feet tone.	21. Nason	1⅓ foot.
18. Principal	4 feet.	22. Sedecima	1 foot.
19. Octave	2 feet.	23. Mixture, III ranks.	
20. Flageolet	2 feet.	24. Hautbois	8 feet.

Choir, 12 Stops.

25.	Quintadena, cypress-wood	16 feet tone.	31.	Sedecima	2 feet.
26.	Principal	8 feet.	32.	Flageolet	2 feet.
27.	Unda Maris, cypress-wood	8 feet tone.	33.	Super-sedecima	1 foot.
28.	Octave	4 feet.	34.	Cornett, V ranks.	
29.	Flote	4 feet tone.	35.	Mixture, II ranks.	
30.	Quint	2⅔ feet.	36.	Cymbale, II ranks.	

Pedal, 19 Stops.

37.	Gross Principal, tin	32 feet.	47.	Rustic	2 feet.
38.	Violon Bass	16 feet.	48.	Mixture, V ranks.	
39.	Bourdon	16 feet tone.	49.	Scharf, II ranks.	
40.	Tubalflote	8 feet.	50.	Cymbale, II ranks.	
41.	Quintadena	8 feet tone.	51.	Posaune	16 feet.
42.	Quint	5⅓ feet.	52.	Fagotto	16 feet.
43.	Super-octave	4 feet.	53.	Trompette	8 feet.
44.	Virgin royal	4 feet.	54.	Schalmey-bass	8 feet tone.
45.	Tubalflote	4 feet.	55.	Corno	8 feet.
46.	Tubalflote	2 feet.			

Compass of Pedals, 2 Octaves, from CCC to tenor c.

88. GOERLITZ.

The organ in St. Mary's Church, at Goerlitz, has 16 sounding stops, and was built by Buckow, in 1838.

Great, 8 Stops.

1.	Bourdon, wood	16 feet tone.	6.	Super-octave, 12 loth. Eng. tin	2 feet.
2.	Principal, 14 loth. Eng. tin, in front	8 feet.	7.	Mixture, 12 loth. Eng. tin, IV ranks	2 feet.
3.	Flaut grave, wood	8 feet.	8.	Cornett to fiddle g, III ranks	2 feet.
4.	Principal-octave, 14 loth. Eng. tin, in front	4 feet.	9.	Slide for a Trompette	8 feet.
5.	Gemshorn-quint, 12 loth. Eng. tin	2⅔ feet.			

Choir, 4 Stops.

10.	Viol di Gamba, 12 loth. Eng. tin	8 feet.	12.	Dulcian, wood	8 feet.
11.	Flaut Douce, wood	8 feet.	13.	Flaut d'amour, wood	4 feet tone.

Pedal, 3 Stops.

14.	Violon, pine-wood	16 feet tone.	16.	Posaune	16 feet.
15.	Violoncello, pine-wood	8 feet.			

Accessory Stops.

1. Coupler, Choir to Great.	2. Coupler, Great to Pedal.

89. LIEGNITZ.

The organ in the Church of St. Peter and St. Paul, at Liegnitz, was erected by Buckow, in the year 1839. It has 3 Manuals and Pedal, and 42 sounding stops, the names and distribution of which are as follow :—

Great, 13 Stops.

1.	Bourdon, wood	16 feet tone.	8.	Flaut Douce, metal	4 feet.
2.	Principal, tin	8 feet.	9.	Quint, metal	2⅔ feet.
3.	Gemshorn, tin	8 feet.	10.	Super-octave, metal	2 feet.
4.	Viol d'amour, tin	8 feet.	11.	Flautino, metal	2 feet.
5.	Flaut grave	8 feet.	12.	Progressio, III, IV, and V ranks	2 feet.
6.	Flaut Douce, wood	8 feet.	13.	Cornett, III ranks	5⅓, 4, 3⅓ ft.
7.	Octave, tin	4 feet.			

Choir, 8 Stops.

14. Quintaton, tin ; the great octave of wood .... 16 feet tone.
15. Salicional, ¼ Eng. tin...... 8 feet.
16. Pyramidflote, wood......... 8 feet.
17. Prestant, ¼ Eng. tin ...... 4 feet.

18. Piffaro, ¼ Eng. tin......... 4 feet.
19. Flautino, ¼ Eng. tin ...... 2 feet.
20. Cornett, III ranks, Eng. tin .... 2⅔, 2, 1⅓ ft.
21. Oboe .... 8 feet.

Echo, 9 Stops.

22. Prestant, ¼ tin .... 8 feet.
23. Viola di Gamba, ¼ tin...... 8 feet.
24. Flaut amabile, metal, the bass octave of wood ... 8 feet.
25. Principal, ¼ Eng. tin ...... 4 feet.

26. Flaut amoroso, metal ... 4 feet.
27. Spitzflote-quint, tin ...... 2⅔ feet.
28. Octave, tin .... 2 feet.
29. Flaut Piccolo, tin .... 1 foot.
30. Mixture, III ranks......... 1⅓ feet.

Pedal, 12 Stops.

31. Principal, polished tin, in front .... 16 feet.
32. Violon, oak .... 16 feet.
33. Prestant, oak .... 16 feet.
34. Sub-bass .... 16 feet tone.
35. Principal .... 8 feet.
36. Violoncello, wood .... 8 feet.

37. Bass-flote, wood........... 8 feet tone.
38. Quint, tin and wood ...... 5⅓ feet.
39. Super-octave .... 4 feet.
40. Octave........................ 2 feet.
41. Posaune .... 16 feet.
42. Trompette .... 8 feet.

Accessory Stops.

1. Coupler, Choir to Great.
2. Coupler, Echo to Great.

3. Coupler, Great to Pedal.
4, 5, 6, 7. Four Wink-trunk valves.

90. BRESLAU.

The Cathedral Church of St. John, at Breslau, contains no less than 3 distinct organs ; one in the nave, a second in the choir, and a third in one of the small chapels. The Great organ has 60 sounding stops, 3 Manuals, and a Pedal of 18 stops ; 4,700 pipes, and 12 bellows. The following are the details of the largest organ :—

Great, 16 Stops.

1. Principal, in front, tin ... 16 feet.
2. Quintaton, metal.......... 16 feet tone.
3. Octave, in front, tin ...... 8 feet.
4. Gemshorn, metal.......... 8 feet.
5. Salicet, metal .... 8 feet.
6. Quintaton, metal........... 8 feet tone.
7. Flaut major, wood .... 8 feet.
8. Quint, metal............ ...... 5⅓ feet.

9. Super-octave, metal ...... 4 feet.
10. Rohrflote, metal........... 4 feet tone.
11. Gemshorn, metal .... 4 feet.
12. Quint, metal .... 2⅔ feet.
13. Sedecima, metal........... 2 feet.
14. Scharf, metal, IV ranks.
15. Mixture, metal, VII ranks.
16. Trompette, tin .... 8 feet.

Echo, 14 Stops.

17. Bourdon, maple-wood...... 16 feet tone.
18. Principal, tin .... 8 feet.
19. Salicet, tin .... 8 feet.
20. Flaut allemande, metal ... 8 feet.
21. Doppel Rohrflote, maple 8 feet tone.
22. Octave, tin .... 4 feet.
23. Salicet, tin .... 4 feet.

24. Spitzflote, metal........... 4 feet.
25. Doppel Rohrflote, maple 4 feet tone.
26. Nasat, metal .... 2⅔ feet.
27. Super-octave, metal ...... 2 feet.
28. Cymbale, metal, III ranks.
29. Mixture, metal, VI ranks.
30. Clarinett, tin .... 8 feet tone.

Choir, 12 Stops.

31. Principal, in front, tin ... 8 feet.
32. Gamba, metal .... 8 feet.
33. Flaut Traverse.......... ... 8 feet.
34. Quintaton.................. 8 feet tone.
35. Flaut Douce................. 8 feet.
36. Flaut major .... 8 feet.

37. Octave, metal.............. 4 feet.
38. Flaut minor, wood........ 4 feet.
39. Quint, metal .... 2⅔ feet.
40. Super-octave, metal ...... 2 feet.
41. Mixture, metal, IV ranks.
42. Hautbois, metal .... 8 feet.

Pedal, 18 Stops.

43. Principal, of tin to FFFF sharp, and in front ; the lower pipes of wood ..... 32 feet.	51. Gemshorn, metal .... 8 feet.
44. Octave, metal .... 16 feet.	52. Violoncello, wood .... 8 feet.
45. Violon, wood................. 16 feet.	53. Doppelflöte, of oak........ 8 feet tone.
46. Gamba, wood .... 16 feet.	54. Quint, metal .... 5⅓ feet.
47. Sub-bass, of oak .... 16 feet tone.	55. Sedecima, metal .... 4 feet.
48. Quintaton, of oak........... 16 feet tone.	56. Nachthorn, of oak .... 4 feet.
49. Gemshorn-quint, metal ... 10⅘ feet.	57. Posaune, wood .... 32 feet.
50. Principal, tin................. 8 feet.	58. Posaune, wood .... 16 feet.
	59. Fagotto, wood .... 16 feet.
	60. Trompette, tin .... 8 feet.

Accessory Stops, &c.

1. Echo to Great.
2. Choir to Great.
3. Great to Pedal.
4. Wind-valve to Great.
5. Wind-valve to Choir.

6. Wind-valve to Echo.
7. Wind-valve to great Pedal Sound-board.
8. Wind-valve to Pedal Reed-work and 32 feet Principal.

Compass.

Manuals, CC to f³ in alt. | Pedal, CCC to tenor c.

91. BRESLAU.

The Choir organ :—

Manual, 9 Stops.

1. Principal .... 8 feet.	6. Doppel Rohrflöte .... 4 feet tone.
2. Gamba .... 8 feet.	7. Nasat-quint .... 2⅔ feet.
3. Flaut allemande .... 8 feet.	8. Super-octave .... 2 feet.
4. Flaut major .... 8 feet tone.	9. Mixture, IV ranks.
5. Octave .... 4 feet.	

Pedal, 3 Stops.

10. Sub-bass .... 16 feet tone.	12. Super-octave .... 4 feet.
11. Octave Bass .... 4 feet.	

Compass.

Manual, CC to f³ in alt. | Pedal, CCC to tenor c. | Coupler, Manual to Pedal.

91B. BRESLAU.

The little organ in one of the Chapels :—

1. Salicet .... 8 feet.	5. Flaut allemande .... 4 feet.
2. Quintaton .... 8 feet tone.	6. Quint........................ 2⅔ feet.
3. Principal .... 4 feet.	7. Super-octave .... 2 feet.
4. Flaut amabile .... 4 feet.	8. Mixture, III ranks.

92. BRESLAU.

The old part of the large organ in the Church of St. Mary Magdalen, at Breslau, is the work of Joh. Roder, of Berlin, who constructed it in 1725 ; to whose work additions were made by Engler in 1821. The organ has now 55 sounding stops, 3 Manuals, and Pedal of 16 stops ; 3,415 pipes, and 10 pairs of bellows. There is, besides the large organ, a small one in the choir, of 12 stops. Contents of the large organ :—

Great, 14 Stops.

1. Contra Principal, of tin, in front .... 16 feet.	8. Rohrflöte, metal .... 4 feet tone.
2. Quintaton, metal .... 16 feet tone.	9. Quint, metal .... 2⅔ feet.
3. Principal, metal .... 8 feet.	10. Super-octave, metal ..... 2 feet.
4. Salicet, tin.... .... 8 feet.	11. Scharf, IV ranks.......... 1 foot.
5. Flautallemande major, wood 8 feet tone.	12. Mixture, VIII ranks ...... 1⅓ foot.
5. Quinteten .... 8 feet tone.	13. Rausch-quint, II ranks ... 2⅔ feet.
Octave .. .. 4 feet.	14. Trompette, metal .... 8 feet.

Echo, 13 Stops.

15. Principal, of tin, in front...	8 feet.	22. Quint, metal	2⅔ feet.
16. Gemshorn, metal	8 feet.	23. Super-octave, metal	2 feet.
17. Salicet to tenor f, tin	8 feet.	24. Waldflote, metal	2 feet.
18. Flaut major, wood	8 feet tone.	25. Mixture, VI ranks, metal	1½ foot.
19. Octave, metal	4 feet.	26. Cymbale, III ranks, metal	1⅓ foot.
20. Doppel Spitzflote, wood ...	4 feet.	27. Vox humana, wood	8 feet tone.
21. Fugara, metal	4 feet.		

Choir, 12 Stops.

28. Principal, of tin, in front...	8 feet.	34. Doppelflote, wood	4 feet tone.
29. Salicet to fiddle g, wood...	8 feet.	35. Quint, metal	2⅔ feet.
30. Flaut allemande, metal ...	8 feet.	36. Super-octave, metal	2 feet.
31. Flaut amabile, wood	8 feet.	37. Cymbale, II ranks	1½ foot.
32. Octave, metal	4 feet.	38. Mixture, IV ranks	1 foot.
33. Spitzflote, metal	4 feet.	39. Oboe, metal	8 feet.

Pedal, 16 Stops.

40. Principal	32 feet.	48. Flauten Bass, wood	8 feet.
41. Octave, metal	16 feet.	49. Quint, metal	5⅓ feet.
42. Violon, wood	16 feet.	50. Super-octave, metal	4 feet.
43. Salicet, wood	16 feet.	51. Mixture, V ranks, metal...	4 feet.
44. Sub-bass, wood	16 feet tone.	52. Posaune, wood	32 feet.
45. Octave Bass	8 feet.	53. Posaune	16 feet.
46. Violoncello, wood	8 feet.	54. Fagotto, metal	16 feet.
47. Doppelflote Bass, wood ...	8 feet tone.	55. Trompette, tin	8 feet.

Accessory Stops, &c.

1. Choir to Great.	6. Wind-valve to Pedal Flue-work.
2. Echo to Great.	7. Wind-valve to Pedal Reed-work.
3. Wind-valve to Great.	8. Glockenspiel to Great.
4. Wind-valve to Choir.	9. Glockenspiel to Pedal.
5. Wind-valve to Echo.	

Compass.

Manuals, CC to c³ in alt, without CC sharp. | Pedal, CCC to tenor d, without CCC sharp.

93. BRESLAU.

The large organ in St. Elizabeth's Church, Breslau, was built by Michael Engler, in 1750, and has since been enlarged (1830) by Müller. It has 54 sounding stops, 3 Manuals, and Pedal of 14 stops; and 8 large pairs of bellows. In the Choir there is a smaller organ, containing 17 stops. The details of the chief organ are as follow :—

Great, 16 Stops.

1. Salicet, tin	16 feet.	9. Nachthorn	4 feet.
2. Quintaton, tin	16 feet tone.	10. Quint	2⅔ feet.
3. Bourdon, wood	16 feet tone.	11. Super-octave	2 feet.
4. Principal, tin	8 feet.	12. Cymbale, III ranks.	
5. Gemshorn, tin	8 feet.	13. Mixture, VI ranks.	
6. Salicet, tin	8 feet.	14. Muset Bass	16 feet.
7. Flaut major, wood	8 feet tone.	15. Trompette, metal	8 feet.
8. Octave, tin	4 feet.	16. Vox humana, tin (labial)	8 feet.

Echo, 14 Stops.

17. Bourdon, wood	16 feet tone.	24. Rohrflote, wood	4 feet tone.
18. Principal, tin	8 feet.	25. Quint, metal	2⅔ feet.
19. Salicet, tin	8 feet.	26. Super-octave	2 feet.
20. Fugara, tin	8 feet.	27. Terz	1⅗ foot.
21. Flaut amabile, wood	8 feet.	28. Rausch-quint	2⅔ feet.
22. Octave, tin	4 feet.	29. Mixture, IV ranks.	
23. Spitzflote, wood	4 feet.	30. Schalmey, metal	8 feet tone.

Choir, 10 *Stops.*

31. Principal	8 feet.	36. Portunal, wood	4 feet.
32. Flaut allemande, tin	8 feet.	37. Quint, metal	2⅔ feet.
33. Flaut amabile, wood	8 feet.	38. Super-octave	2 feet.
34. Quintaton, wood	8 feet tone.	39. Mixture, III ranks.	
35. Octave, tin	4 feet.	40. Oboe, metal	8 feet.

Pedal, 14 *Stops.*

41. Major Bass, wood	32 feet tone.	48. Bassflote, wood	8 feet tone.
42. Principal, of tin, in front	16 feet.	49. Gemshorn Quint, metal	5⅓ feet.
43. Salicet, of tin and wood	16 feet.	50. Super-octave, tin	4 feet.
44. Violon, wood	16 feet.	51. Mixture, metal, V ranks.	
45. Sub-bass, wood	16 feet tone.	52. Posaune	32 feet.
46. Quintaton, wood	16 feet tone.	53. Posaune, wood	16 feet.
47. Principal, tin, in front	8 feet.	54. Trompette, tin	8 feet.

Accessory Stops, &c.

1. Choir to Great.	5. Wind-valve to Choir.
2. Echo to Great.	6. Wind-valve to Pedal flue-work.
3. Wind-valve to Great.	7. Wind-valve to Pedal reed-work.
4. Wind-valve to Echo.	

Compass.

Manuals, CC to c³ in alt., without CC sharp. | Pedal, CCC to tenor e, without CCC sharp.

94. BRESLAU.

Contents of the small organ in Choir :—

Manual, 12 *Stops.*

1. Principal, in front	8 feet.	7. Flaut minor	4 feet.
2. Quintaton	8 feet tone.	8. Quint	2⅔ feet.
3. Salicet	8 feet.	9. Super-octave	2 feet.
4. Flaut major	8 feet.	10. Cymbale, II ranks.	
5. Principal	4 feet.	11. Mixture, IV ranks.	
6. Octave	4 feet.	12. Vox humana	8 feet tone.

Pedal, 5 *Stops.*

13. Violon	16 feet.	16. Doppelflote	8 feet.
14. Sub-bass	16 feet tone.	17. Super-octave	4 feet.
15. Octave Bass	8 feet.		

Compass.

Manual, CC to c³ in alt., 4 octaves. | Pedal, CCC to tenor c, 2 octaves.

95. BRESLAU.

The organ in the Church of St. Bernhardin was built by Casparini in 1705, and enlarged by Hartig in 1831. It has 35 sounding stops, 2 Manuals, and Pedal of 12 stops. Besides the large organ, there is a small one in the church which has 14 stops. The specifications are as follow :—

LARGE ORGAN.

Great, 13 *Stops.*

1. Bourdon	16 feet tone.	8. Doppelflote	4 feet.
2. Quintaton	16 feet tone.	9. Quint	2⅔ feet.
3. Principal, in front	8 feet.	10. Super-octave	2 feet.
4. Gamba	8 feet.	11. Mixture, V ranks.	
5. Flaut major	8 feet.	12. Cymbale, II ranks.	
6. Portunal	8 feet.	13. Trompette	8 feet.
7. Octave	4 feet.		

O O

Choir, 10 *Stops.*

14. Principal, in front	8 feet.	19. Quint	2⅔ feet.
15. Salicet	8 feet.	20. Super-octave	2 feet.
16. Flaut amabile	8 feet.	21. Mixture, IV ranks.	
17. Octave	4 feet.	22. Cymbale, II ranks.	
18. Flaut minor	4 feet.	23. Oboe	8 feet.

Pedal, 12 *Stops.*

24. Major	32 feet.	30. Doppelflote	8 feet.
25. Principal, in front	16 feet.	31. Quintaton	8 feet tone.
26. Violon	16 feet.	32. Super-octave	4 feet.
27. Sub-bass	16 feet tone.	33. Posaune	32 feet.
28. Major Quint	10⅔ feet.	34. Posaune	16 feet.
29. Violon	8 feet.	35. Trompette	8 feet.

Accessory Stops, &c.

1. Choir to Great.	4. Wind-valve to Choir.
2. Great to Pedal.	5. Wind-valve to Pedal flue stops.
3. Wind-valve to Great.	6. Wind-valve to Pedal reed stops.

96. SMALL ORGAN.

Manual, 10 *Stops.*

1. Principal	8 feet.	6. Flaut Traverso	4 feet.
2. Gamba	8 feet.	7. Quint	2⅔ feet.
3. Quintaton	8 feet tone.	8. Super-octave	2 feet.
4. Portunal	8 feet.	9. Mixture, IV ranks.	
5. Octave	4 feet.	10. Cymbale, II ranks.	

Pedal, 4 *Stops.*

11. Violon	16 feet.	13. Octave	8 feet.
12. Sub-bass	16 feet tone.	14. Super-octave	4 feet.

97. BRESLAU.

The organ in the Church of St. Vincent, at Breslau, has the very unusual proportion of half as many Pedal stops as there are Manual stops; that is to say, 15 of the former to 30 of the latter. The specification is as follows :—

Great, 15 *Stops.*

1. Quintaton	16 feet tone.	9. Gemshorn	4 feet.
2. Principal	8 feet.	10. Octave	2 feet.
3. Gemshorn	8 feet.	11. Rauschquint Bass.	
4. Salicional	8 feet.	12. Mixture, VI ranks.	
5. Portunal	8 feet.	13. Cymbale, III ranks.	
6. Flaut	8 feet tone.	14. Cornett, IV ranks.	
7. Unda Maris	8 feet.	15. Trompette	8 feet.
8. Octave	4 feet.		

Choir, 15 *Stops.*

16. Prestant	8 feet.	24. Flaut	4 feet.
17. Gamba	8 feet.	25. Flaut Traverso	4 feet.
18. Fugara	8 feet.	26. Octave Bass.	
19. Trinona	8 feet.	27. Quint, III ranks.	
20. Flaut	8 feet.	28. Mixture, IV ranks.	
21. Quintaton	8 feet tone.	29. Cymbale, III ranks.	
22. Principal	4 feet.	30. Clarinett	8 feet tone.
23. Trinona	4 feet.		

Pedal, 15 Stops.

31. Major	32 feet tone.	39. Violon	8 feet.
32. Principal	16 feet.	40. Violoncello	8 feet.
33. Gamba	16 feet.	41. Flaut	8 feet.
34. Violon	16 feet.	42. Gemshorn-quint	5¼ feet.
35. Sub-bass	16 feet tone.	43. Octave	4 feet.
36. Quintaton	16 feet tone.	44. Posaune	16 feet.
37. Octave	8 feet.	45. Trompette	8 feet.
38. Gamba	8 feet.		

Accessory Stops, Couplers, &c.

1. Choir to Great.	3, 4, 5. Three wind-trunk valves.
2. Great to Pedal.	Five Bellows.

98. BRESLAU.

The organ in the Church of St. Ethelbert, in Breslau, was built by the elder Müller, and completed in 1837. It has 24 sounding stops, 2 Manuals, and Pedal of 5 stops. The following is a list of the stops :—

Great, 12 Stops.

1. Bourdon	16 feet tone.	7. Octave	4 feet.
2. Principal, in front	8 feet.	8. Doppel-rohrflote	4 feet tone.
3. Salicet	8 feet.	9. Quint	2⅔ feet.
4. Gemshorn	8 feet.	10. Super-octave	2 feet.
5. Bourdon	8 feet tone.	11. Mixture, V ranks.	
6. Gemshorn Quint	5⅓ feet.	12. Clarinette	8 feet tone.

Choir, 7 Stops.

13. Salicet	8 feet.	17. Portual	4 feet.
14. Flaut major	8 feet.	18. Super-octave	2 feet.
15. Portual	8 feet.	19. Cymbale, II ranks.	
16. Principal	4 feet.		

Pedal, 5 Stops.

20. Principal	16 feet.	23. Octave	8 feet.
21. Gamba	16 feet.	24. Posaune	16 feet.
22. Sub-bass	16 feet tone.		

Accessory Stops, &c.

1. Choir to Great.	4. Wind-valve to Choir.
2. Great to Pedal.	5. Wind-valve to Pedal.
3. Wind-valve to Great.	

Compass.

Manuals, CC to d³ in alt.	Pedal, CCC to tenor c.

99. BRESLAU.

The organ in the Church of the Eleven Thousand Virgins, at Breslau, was built by Müller, sen., in 1826; and has 27 sounding stops, 2 Manuals, and Pedal. The following is a list of its contents :—

Great, 11 Stops.

1. Bourdon	16 feet tone.	7. Rohrflote	4 feet tone.
2. Principal	8 feet.	8. Quint	2⅔ feet.
3. Gamba	8 feet.	9. Super-octave	2 feet.
4. Portual	8 feet.	10. Mixture, V ranks.	
5. Doppelflote	8 feet.	11. Clarinett	8 feet tone.
6. Octave	4 feet.		

Choir, 9 Stops.

12.	Salicet	8 feet.	17. Nasat-quint	2⅔ feet.
13.	Quintaton	8 feet tone.	18. Super-octave	2 feet.
14.	Flaut major	8 feet.	19. Mixture, III ranks.	
15.	Principal	4 feet.	20. Vox humana (labial)	8 feet.
16.	Flauto Traverso	4 feet.		

Pedal, 7 Stops.

21.	Violon	16 feet.	25. Doppelflote	8 feet tone.
22.	Gamba	16 feet.	26. Octave	4 feet.
23.	Sub-bass	16 feet tone.	27. Posaune	16 feet.
24.	Octave	8 feet.		

Accessory Stops, &c.

1. Choir to Great.	4. Wind-valve to Choir.
2. Great to Pedal.	5. Wind-valve to Pedal.
3. Wind-valve to Great.	Compass of Manuals, CC to f³ in alt.

100. BRESLAU.

The organ in the Church of St. Salvator, in Breslau, has 19 stops, of which number 8 are on the Pedal. The following shows the disposition :—

Manual, 11 Stops.

1.	Principal, in front	8 feet.	7. Flaut minor	4 feet.
2.	Salicet	8 feet.	8. Quint	2⅔ feet.
3.	Quintaton	8 feet tone.	9. Super-octave	2 feet.
4.	Flaut major	8 feet.	10. Mixture, IV ranks.	
5.	Octave	4 feet.	11. Cymbale, II ranks.	
6.	Gemshorn	4 feet.		

Pedal, 8 Stops.

12.	Violon	16 feet.	16. Quint	5⅓ feet.
13.	Sub-bass	16 feet tone.	17. Super-octave	4 feet.
14.	Octave Bass	8 feet.	18. Mixture, III ranks.	
15.	Flote Bass	8 feet tone.	19. Posaune	16 feet.

101. BRESLAU.

The organ in the Cemetery Church at Breslau has 12 stops, as follows :—

Great, 6 Stops.

1.	Principal	8 feet.	4. Flaut major	8 feet.
2.	Salicet	8 feet.	5. Octave	4 feet.
3.	Quintaton	8 feet tone.	6. Spitzflote	4 feet.

Choir, 3 Stops.

7. Dulcian (labial) 8 feet. | 8. Flaut amabile 8 feet. | 9. Doppelflote ...... 4 feet.

Pedal, 3 Stops.

10. Sub-bass ... 16 feet tone. | 11. Quintaton 16 feet tone. | 12. Octave-bass ...... 8 feet.

Couplers, &c.

1. Great to Pedal.

Compass of Manuals, CC to c³ in alt. | Compass of Pedal, CCC to tenor e.

102. BRESLAU.

The organ in the Church of St. Mauritius, in Breslau, has 9 stops, of which the following is a list :—

Manual, 7 Stops.

1.	Principal	8 feet.	5. Gemshorn	4 feet.
2.	Hohlflote	8 feet.	6. Quint	2⅔ feet.
3.	Gedact	8 feet tone.	7. Super-octave	2 feet.
4.	Octave	4 feet.		

Pedal, 2 Stops.

8. Sub-bass .... 16 feet tone. | 9. Octave Bass .... 8 feet.

103. BRESLAU.

The organ in the Church of St. Barbara, at Breslau, has 21 sounding stops, of which the following is a list :—

Great, 8 Stops.

1. Quintaton	16 feet tone.	5. Octave	4 feet.
2. Principal	8 feet.	6. Quint	2⅔ feet.
3. Salicet	8 feet.	7. Super-octave	2 feet.
4. Flote	8 feet tone.	8. Mixture, V ranks.	

Upper Manual, Choir, 7 Stops.

9. Salicet	8 feet.	13. Quint	2⅔ feet.
10. Flote	8 feet tone.	14. Super-octave	2 feet.
11. Principal	4 feet.	15. Mixture, II ranks.	
12. Doppelflote	4 feet tone.		

Pedal, 6 Stops.

16. Sub-bass	16 feet tone.	19. Quint Bass	5⅓ feet.
17. Octave Bass	8 feet.	20. Gemshorn	4 feet.
18. Flote Bass	8 feet tone.	21. Fagotto	16 feet.

104. BRESLAU.

The organ in the Music-room of the University at Breslau has 14 stops, distributed in the following manner :—

First Manual, 6 Stops.

1. Principal	8 feet.	4. Doppel-rohrflote	4 feet tone.
2. Portunal	8 feet.	5. Quint	2⅔ feet.
3. Octave	4 feet.	6. Super-octave	2 feet.

Upper Manual, 4 Stops.

7. Salicional, metal	8 feet.	9. Rohrflote	4 feet tone.
8. Gedact, metal, treble	8 feet tone.	10. Waldflote, metal	2 feet.

Pedal, 4 Stops.

11. Violon	16 feet.	13. Violon	8 feet.
12. Sub-bass	16 feet tone.	14. Principal	4 feet.

Compass, &c.

Manuals, CC to f³ in alt.	3 Bellows, 8 feet by 4.	Pedals, CCC to tenor e.

105. CRACOW.

The organ in the Evangelist's Church at Cracow has 15 stops, of which the following is a list :—

Great, 9 Stops.

1. Bourdon, wood	16 feet.	6. Hohlflote, wood	4 feet.
2. Principal, tin	8 feet.	7. Quint, tin	2⅔ feet.
3. Gamba, tin	8 feet.	8. Super-octave, tin	2 feet.
4. Flote, wood	8 feet.	9. Mixture, II ranks	2 feet.
5. Octave, tin	4 feet.		

Choir, 3 Stops.

10. Salicet...8 feet.	11. Portunal...8 feet.	12. Portunal...4 feet.

Pedal, 3 Stops.

13. Violon...16 feet.	14. Sub-bass...16 feet tone.	15. Violon...8 feet.

106. WARSAW.

The organ in the Lutheran Church at Warsaw has 27 sounding stops. It was built in 1827-9 by Robert Müller, jun., of Breslau, and has 6 bellows, 10 feet long by 5 in breadth. The following is an enumeration of the stops :—

Great, 10 Stops.

1. Principal, tin, in front......	16 feet.	6. Octave, tin	4 feet.
2. Principal, tin	8 feet.	7. Doppel-rohrflote, wood...	4 feet tone.
3. Gemshorn, tin	8 feet.	8. Quint, tin	2⅔ feet.
4. Portunal wood	8 feet.	9. Octave, tin	2 feet.
5. Doppelflote, wood	8 feet tone.	10. Mixture, tin, IV ranks.	

Choir, 8 Stops.

11. Salicet, tin	8 feet.	15. Principal, tin	4 feet.
12. Flauto, wood	8 feet.	16. Salicet, tin	4 feet.
13. Flaut Traverso, wood......	8 feet.	17. Violini, tin	2 feet.
14. Quintaton, tin	8 feet tone.	18. Clarinett	8 feet tone.

Pedal, 9 Stops.

19. Major, wood.................	32 feet tone.	24. Quint, wood	5⅓ feet.
20. Violon, wood	16 feet.	25. Octave, tin	4 feet.
21. Gamba, wood	16 feet.	26. Posaune, wood	16 feet.
22. Sub-bass wood..............	16 feet tone.	27. Trompette, wood	8 feet.
23. Octave Bass, wood	8 feet.		

107. VIENNA.

The organ in the Cathedral Church of St. Stephen, at Vienna, is a very old one. It has 41 stops, distributed among 2 Manuals and Pedal in the following manner :—

Great, 18 Stops.

1. Major Flute	16 feet.	10. Fugara..........................	4 feet.
2. Quintaton	16 feet tone.	11. Nachthorn	4 feet.
3. Principal	8 feet.	12. Quint	2⅔ feet.
4. Bourdon	8 feet tone.	13. Super-octave	2 feet.
5. Gamba	8 feet.	14. Mixture, VIII ranks.	
6. Salicional	8 feet.	15. Sesquialtera, IV ranks.	
7. Octave	4 feet.	16. Cymbale, VIII ranks.	
8. Spitzflote	4 feet.	17. Scharf, IV ranks.	
9. Gamba	4 feet.	18. Trompette	8 feet.

Choir, 10 Stops.

19. Coppel	8 feet.	24. Flote	4 feet.
20. Rohrflote	8 feet tone.	25. Dulcian	4 feet.
21. Flote amabile	8 feet.	26. Nazard.........................	2⅔ feet.
22. Quintaton	8 feet tone.	27. Octave	2 feet.
23. Principal	4 feet.	28. Mixture, V ranks.	

Pedal, 13 Stops.

29. Principal, metal	16 feet.	36. Octave.......................	4 feet.
30. Sub-bass, wood	16 feet.	37. Mixture, VI ranks.	
31. Bourdon	16 feet tone.	38. Cornett, IV ranks.	
32. Principal, metal	8 feet.	39. Bombarde	16 feet.
33. Octave, wood	8 feet.	40. Posaune	16 feet.
34. Violoncello	8 feet.	41. Trompette	8 feet.
35. Quint............................	5⅓ feet.		

Accessory Stops, &c.

1. Choir to Great.	3. Tremulant.
2. Great to Pedal.	4, 5, 6, Three Wind-trunk valves.

Compass.

Manuals, CC to d⁸ in alt.	Pedal, CCC to tenor c.

108. VIENNA.

The organ in St. Michael's Church, at Vienna, is a very old instrument. It has 3 Manuals, Pedal, and 40 stops, the distribution and names of which are as follow :—

Great, 16 Stops.

1. Bourdon	16 feet tone.		9. Nachthorn	4 feet.
2. Principal	8 feet.		10. Feldflote	4 feet.
3. Piffaro	8 feet.		11. Quint	2⅔ feet.
4. Quintaton	8 feet tone.		12. Tierce	1⅗ foot.
5. Salicional	8 feet.		13. Mixture, II ranks.	
6. Octave	4 feet.		14. Sesquialtera, III ranks.	
7. Fugara	4 feet.		15. Cymbale, V ranks.	
8. Spitzflote	4 feet.		16. Super-octave	1 foot.

Choir, 10 Stops.

17. Coppel	8 feet.		22. Flote minor	4 feet.
18. Flote major	8 feet.		23. Quint	2⅔ feet.
19. Principal	4 feet.		24. Octave	2 feet.
20. Octave	4 feet.		25. Super-octave	1 foot.
21. Coppel	4 feet.		26. Mixture, II ranks.	

Echo, 4 Stops.

27. Coppel	8 feet.		29. Flote	4 feet.
28. Principal	4 feet.		30. Octave	2 feet.

Pedal, 10 Stops.

31. Principal, metal	16 feet.		36. Coppel	8 feet.
32. Sub-bass, wood	16 feet.		37. Octave	4 feet.
33. Bourdon, wood	16 feet tone.		38. Cornett, III ranks.	
34. Octave, metal	8 feet.		39. Posaune	16 feet.
35. Octave, wood	8 feet.		40. Trompette	8 feet.

Accessory Stops, &c.
1. Choir to Great.
2. Echo to Great.

Compass.
Manuals, CC to c³ in alt., short octaves.
Pedal, CCC short to A.

109. VIENNA.

The organ in the Lutheran Church, at Vienna, was built by Deutschmann, of that city, and has 2 Manuals and Pedal, and 23 stops, of which the following is a list :—

Great, 9 Stops.

1. Principal	8 feet.		6. Quint	2⅔ feet.
2. Gamba	8 feet.		7. Super-octave	2 feet.
3. Flote	8 feet.		8. Mixture, IV ranks.	
4. Octave	4 feet.		9. { Hautbois Discant } { Fagotto, Bass }	8 feet.
5. Fugara	4 feet.			

Choir, 6 Stops.

10. Coppel	8 feet.		13. Octave	2 feet.
11. Principal	4 feet.		14. Super-octave	1 foot.
12. Dulciana	4 feet.		15. Vox humana	8 feet tone.

Pedal, 8 Stops.

16. Bourdon, open	16 feet.		20. Octave	8 feet.
17. Sub-bass	16 feet tone.		21. Octave	4 feet.
18. Principal	8 feet.		22. Posaune	16 feet.
19. Violoncello	8 feet.		23. Trompette	8 feet.

Accessory Stops, &c.
1. Choir to Great.
2. Tremulant to Choir.

Compass.
Manuals, CC to d³ in alt.
Pedal CCC to A.

110. VIENNA.

The organ in the Church of the Minorites, at Vienna, which is a very old one, has lately been renovated by Deutschmann of that city. It has two Manuals and Pedal, and 24 stops, of which the following is a list :—

Great, 10 Stops.

1. Principal	8 feet.	6. Nachthorn	4 feet.
2. Quintaton	8 feet tone.	7. Quint	2⅔ feet.
3. Waldflöte	8 feet.	8. Super-octave	2 feet.
4. Octave	4 feet.	9. Mixture, V. ranks.	
5. Rohrflöte	4 feet tone.	10. Cymbale, II ranks.	

Choir, 8 Stops.

11. Principal	8 feet.	15. Flöte	4 feet.
12. Coppel	8 feet.	16. Octave	2 feet.
13. Salicional	8 feet.	17. Quint	1⅓ foot.
14. Principal	4 feet.	18. Super-octave	1 foot.

Pedal, 6 Stops.

19. Coppel	16 feet.	22. Octave	8 feet.
20. Violon	16 feet.	23. Quint	5⅓ feet.
21. Principal	8 feet.	24. Cornett, III ranks.	

Accessory Stops.

1. Choir to Great.   2. Great to Pedal.

Compass.

Manuals, CC short to f³ in alt.   Pedal, CCC short to A.

111. VIENNA.

The organ in St. Peter's Church is a very old instrument. It has 30 stops 3 Manuals, and Pedal of 6 stops. There are no reeds in the organ, and the Mixtures are harsh; but the 16, 8, and 4 feet stops are good. The following is a specification of the stops :—

Great, 12 Stops.

1. Principal	8 feet.	7. Gemshorn	4 feet.
2. Coppel	8 feet.	8. Nachthorn	4 feet.
3. Gamba	8 feet.	9. Fugara	4 feet.
4. Salicional	8 feet.	10. Quint	2⅔ feet.
5. Quintaton	8 feet tone.	11. Octave	2 feet.
6. Octave	4 feet.	12. Mixture, VI ranks.	

Echo, 8 Stops.

13. Coppel	8 feet.	17. Flageolet	2 feet.
14. Principal	4 feet.	18. Quint	1⅓ foot.
15. Flöte	4 feet.	19. Octave	1 foot.
16. Octave	2 feet.	20. Mixture, IV ranks.	

Choir, 4 Stops.

21. Coppel	8 feet.	23. Flöte	4 feet.
22. Principal	4 feet.	24. Octave	2 feet.

Pedal, 6 Stops.

25. Coppel	16 feet.	28. Octave	8 feet.
26. Sub-bass	16 feet tone.	29. Octave	4 feet.
27. Principal	8 feet.	30. Cornett, IV ranks.	

Compass.

Compass of Manuals, CC short to c³ in alt. | Compass of Pedal, CCC short to A.

112. FREIBURG, IN SWITZERLAND.

In the Cathedral Church of St. Nicholas, at Freiburg, in Switzerland, is a particularly fine organ, built by Aloise Moser in 1834. It has 4 Manuals, 2 Pedals, 61 stops, and 4,165 pipes. The draw-stops do not operate in the usual way, *i.e.*, forwards, but they slide to the right and left. The case is of dark walnut-tree wood, very elaborately ornamented with gilded carved work. The Vox humana in the Echo is described as being a singularly successful stop. The following is a list of the contents of this admirable instrument :—

Great, 16 Stops.

1.	Montre	16 feet.	9.	Doublette	2 feet.
2.	Bourdon	16 feet tone.	10.	Fourniture, VI and VII ranks.	
3.	Octave	8 feet.	11.	Cymbale, III ranks	2 feet.
4.	Principal	8 feet.	12.	Scharf, VIII ranks	2 feet.
5.	Bourdon	8 feet.	13.	Petit Cornett, III ranks.	
6.	Gamba	8 feet.	14.	Grand Cornett, a reed	16 feet.
7.	Prestant	4 feet.	15.	Trombone	8 feet.
8.	Dulcian	4 feet.	16.	Clarion	4 feet.

Choir, 14 Stops.

17.	Quintadena	16 feet tone.	24.	Flûte à cheminée	4 feet tone.
18.	Principal	8 feet.	25.	Nazard	2 feet.
19.	Principal	8 feet.	26.	Doublette	2 feet.
20.	Gamba	8 feet.	27.	Flageolet	1 foot.
21.	Flute Douce	8 feet.	28.	Fourniture, IV and V ranks	2 feet.
22.	Octave	4 feet.	29.	Cornett, V ranks	8 feet.
23.	Flute	4 feet.	30.	Trompette	8 feet.

Positif, 12 Stops.

31.	Montre	8 feet.	37.	Flûte bouchée	4 feet.
32.	Bourdon	8 feet tone.	38.	Dulcian	4 feet.
33.	Viola	8 feet.	39.	Quintflote	2⅔ feet.
34.	Salicional	8 feet.	40.	Flageolet	2 feet.
35.	Prestant	4 feet.	41.	Cornett, V ranks.	
36.	Calcan	4 feet.	42.	Cromorne	8 feet tone.

Echo, 8 Stops.

43.	Montre	8 feet.	47.	Quint Flute	4 feet.
44.	Bourdon	8 feet tone.	48.	Flageolet	2 feet.
45.	Flute	8 feet.	49.	Vox humana	8 feet.
46.	Salicional	8 feet.	50.	Cornett	8 feet.

Great Pedal, 6 Stops.

51.	Bass Bourdon	32 feet tone.	54.	Prestant	4 feet.
52.	Sub-bass	16 feet.	55.	Bombarde	16 feet.
53.	Octave	8 feet.	56.	Trombone	8 feet.

Choir Pedal, 5 Stops.

57.	Montre	16 feet.	60.	Prestant	4 feet.
58.	Principal	8 feet.	61.	Trompette	8 feet.
59.	Flute	8 feet tone.			

Accessory Stops, &c.

1. Choir to Great.		3. Tremulant Great.
2. Great to Pedal.		4. Tremulant Echo.

Compass.

Manuals, CC to f³ in alt.	Pedals, CCC to tenor c.

113. HANOVER.

The organ in the Market Church at Hanover is a very fine instrument, the work of Herr Meyer. It contains 47 sounding stops, three Manuals, and a separate Pedal. The following is a list of the stops of this organ :—

Great, 15 Stops.

1. Principal, in front	16 feet.	9. Octave	4 feet.
2. Bourdon	16 feet.	10. Rohrflote	4 feet.
3. Principal	8 feet.	11. Octave	2 feet.
4. Gemshorn	8 feet.	12. Mixture, V ranks.	
5. Gamba	8 feet.	13. Cornett, IV ranks.	
6. Doppelflote	8 feet.	14. Trompette	16 feet.
7. Rohrflote	8 feet.	15. Trompette	8 feet.
8. Quint	5⅓ feet.		

Choir, 12 Stops.

16. Bourdon	16 feet tone.	22. Querflote	4 feet.
17. Principal	8 feet.	23. Nasat	2⅔ feet.
18. Gedact	8 feet tone.	24. Octave	2 feet.
19. Quintaton	8 feet.	25. Mixture, III ranks.	
20. Octave	4 feet.	26. Dulcian	16 feet.
21. Quintaton	4 feet.	27. Oboe	8 feet.

Swell, 6 Stops.

28. Geigen Principal	8 feet.	31. Salamine	4 feet.
29. Salicional	8 feet.	32. Waldflote	2 feet.
30. Gedact	8 feet.	33. Æoline	8 feet.

Pedal, 14 Stops.

34. Principal	16 feet.	41. Octave	4 feet.
35. Violon	16 feet.	42. Flote	2 feet.
36. Sub-bass	16 feet tone.	43. Mixture, III ranks.	
37. Quint	10⅔ feet tone.	44. Posaune	32 feet.
38. Principal	8 feet.	45. Posaune	16 feet.
39. Violon	8 feet.	46. Trompette	8 feet.
40. Bourdon	8 feet.	47. Trompette	4 feet.

Accessories.

10 Bellows :—6 for Manuals ; 4 for Pedal Organ. 4 Wind-trunk valves.	Forte Pedal and Piano Pedal; the latter leaves stops Nos. 35, 36, 39, and 40 in operation.

114. HANOVER.

The organ in the Chapel Royal at Hanover was made by Meyer, and contains the following 40 stops :—

Great, 13 Stops.

1. Bourdon	16 feet tone.	8. Flote	4 feet.
2. Principal	8 feet.	9. Quint	2⅔ feet.
3. Gemshorn	8 feet.	10. Octave	2 feet.
4. Gamba	8 feet.	11. Mixture, V ranks.	
5. Rohrflote	8 feet tone.	12. Trompette	16 feet.
6. Quintaton	8 feet.	13. Trompette	8 feet.
7. Octave	4 feet.		

Choir, 10 Stops.

14. Quintaton	16 feet tone.	19. Doppelflote	4 feet.
15. Principal	8 feet.	20. Nasat	2⅔ feet.
16. Gamba	8 feet.	21. Octave	2 feet.
17. Rohrflote	8 feet.	22. Mixture, III ranks.	
18. Octave	4 feet.	23. Oboe	8 feet.

Swell, 7 Stops.

24. Geigen Principal	8 feet.	28. Spitzflote	4 feet.
25. Salicional	8 feet.	29. Waldflote	2 feet.
26. Gedact	8 feet tone.	30. Oboe	8 feet.
27. Octave	4 feet.		

Pedal, 10 *Stops.*

31. Principal	16 feet.	36. Octave	4 feet.
32. Sub-bass	16 feet tone.	37. Posaune	16 feet.
33. Quint	10⅔ feet tone.	38. Trompette	8 feet.
34. Octave	8 feet.	39. Trompette	4 feet.
35. Bourdon	8 feet tone.	40. Cornett	2 feet.

Accessories.

8 Bellows ; 5 for the Manuals, 3 for the Pedals. | 4 Wind valves ; Forte and Piano Pedals for the Pedal Organ.

115. HANOVER.

The new organ in St. John's, Hanover, contains 44 stops, and, like the two preceding, was built by Meyer, who is a resident of the town :—

Great, 15 *Stops.*

1. Principal	16 feet.	9. Octave	4 feet.
2. Bourdon	16 feet tone.	10. Gemshorn	4 feet.
3. Principal	8 feet.	11. Octave	2 feet.
4. Spitzflote	8 feet.	12. Mixture, V ranks.	
5. Rohrflote	8 feet tone.	13. Cornett, IV ranks.	
6. Hohlflote	8 feet.	14. Trompette	16 feet.
7. Quintaton	8 feet tone.	15. Trompette	8 feet.
8. Quint	5⅓ feet tone.		

Choir, 11 *Stops.*

16. Quintaton	16 feet tone.	22. Flote	4 feet.
17. Principal	8 feet.	23. Quint	2⅔ feet.
18. Gamba	8 feet.	24. Octave	2 feet.
19. Gedact	8 feet tone.	25. Mixture, IV ranks.	
20. Doppelflote	8 feet.	26. Dulcian	16 feet.
21. Octave	4 feet.		

Swell, 6 *Stops.*

27. Geigen Principal	8 feet.	30. Salamine	8 feet.
28. Salicional	8 feet.	31. Spitzflote	4 feet.
29. Gedact	8 feet tone.	32. Hohlflote	4 feet.

Pedal, 12 *Stops.*

33. Principal	16 feet.	39. Bourdon	8 feet tone.
34. Violon	16 feet.	40. Octave	4 feet.
35. Sub-bass	16 feet tone.	41. Posaune	32 feet.
36. Quint	10⅔ feet tone.	42. Posaune	16 feet.
37. Principal	8 feet.	43. Trompette	8 feet.
38. Violoncello	8 feet.	44. Trompette	4 feet.

116. ULM.

The Cathedral at Ulm has, for upwards of two centuries and a half, enjoyed the high reputation of possessing an organ ranking among the finest specimens of its kind and time, not only in regard to excellence, but also as to completeness. So far back as the year 1591 it was furnished with an instrument, then quite new, reputed to have been the united work of three distinct firms ; Andre Schneider, of Silicie, Conrad Schott, of Suabe, and Pierre Grunwalder, of Nuremberg, being mentioned as having taken part in its construction. This joint production, after being repaired, in 1630, by Jean Meyer, the builder of the organ recently burnt in the cathedral at Frankfort, yielded at length to the ravages of time, and was, in the year 1730, replaced by a new 32-feet organ, made by the Schmahls, father and son, which contained 45 stops, 2 Manuals and Pedal, and 16 bellows. The largest pipe in this instrument measured 13 inches in diameter, and the entire work was enclosed in an elaborate case, measuring 93 feet in height and 28 feet in width. In the course of time this organ, also, like its predecessor, became decayed and infirm, and the erection of a new one in its place was some years since accordingly agreed upon. The execution of this great work was entrusted to Walcker, of Ludwigsburg, who, with Schulze, of Paulinzelle, near Erfurt, shares the highest reputation among the present generation of German organ-builders, and also the most extensive and important practice. Walcker's first specification was prepared in the year 1838 ; a second one, for an organ of 80 stops, was drawn out in 1845, and a third one in 1846, for an instrument of 94 stops. It was not, however, until the 11th of January, 1849, that the agreement of Mr. Walcker was finally made out and signed, which was then for an instrument to contain 100 stops, 4 Manuals, and 2 Pedals, 6,564 pipes, 18 bellows, &c. The removal of the old organ occupied the period between the 22nd of January and the 17th of March, 1849 ; and the erection and completion of the new one in the church from May, 1854, to October 13th, 1856, on which latter day it was formally inaugurated with a concert of organ music.

This new Ulm organ contains, as already stated, 100 stops, which are appropriated in the following manner, viz. :—

		Stops.
To the First Manual (Great Organ)	....	30
,, Second Manual (Choir Organ)	....	23
,, Third Manual (Swell Organ)	....	16
,, First (or loud) Pedal	....	24
,, Second (or soft) Pedal	....	7
		100

The scheme of the stops stands thus :—

First Manual, 30 Stops.

1. Untersatz to tenor c key, the CCC pipe .... 32 feet.	17. Octave........................ 2 feet.
2. Principal .... 16 feet.	18. Waldflote .... 2 feet.
3. Tibia major .... 16 feet.	19. Octave........................ 1 foot.
4. Viol di Gamba............... 16 feet.	20. Sesquialtera, II ranks ... 2⅔ feet.
5. Octave .... 8 feet.	21. Cornett, V ranks, all
6. Gemshorn..................... 8 feet.	through..................... 10⅔ feet.
7. Gedact .... 8 feet.	22. Mixture, V ranks .... 4 feet.
8. Salicional .... 8 feet.	23. Mixture, V ranks .... 2⅔ feet.
9. Flote (open wood) .... 8 feet.	24. Scharf, V ranks........... 2 feet.
10. Viol di Gamba............... 8 feet.	*25. Contra fagotto .... 16 feet.
11. Quint .... 5⅓ feet.	*26. Fagotto, wood, small ... 16 feet.
12. Octave .... 4 feet.	*27. Posaune .... 8 feet.
13. Flote............................ 4 feet.	*28. Trompette .... 8 feet.
14. Rohrflote .... 4 feet.	*29. Clarine .... 4 feet.
15. Fugara .... 4 feet.	*30. Clarinett, flue pipes in
16. Terz .... 3⅕ feet.	the treble.................. 2 feet.

Second Manual, 23 Stops.

31. Salicional, lowest octave wood........................ 16 feet.	42. Viola .... 4 feet.
32. Gedact .... 16 feet.	43. Traverso flute............... 4 feet.
33. Principal .... 8 feet.	44. Klein Gedact .... 4 feet.
34. Flote .... 8 feet.	45. Octave........................ 2 feet.
35. Piffaro, small scale with beard and ears........... 8 feet.	46. Piccolo, metal .... 2 feet.
	47. Mixture, VIII ranks...... 2⅔ feet.
36. Dolce........................... 8 feet.	48. Cymbale, III ranks ...... 1 foot.
37. Gedact .... 8 feet.	*49. Posaune .... 8 feet.
38. Quintaton .... 8 feet.	*50. Trompette .... 8 feet.
39. Quintflote..................... 5⅓ feet.	*51. Fagotto .... 8 feet.
40. Octave .... 4 feet.	*52. Clarinett..................... 8 feet.
41. Spitzflote .... 4 feet.	*53. Corno .... 4 feet.

Third Manual, 16 Stops.

54. Bourdon	16 feet.	62. Dolce	4 feet.
55. Principal	8 feet.	63. Nazard	2⅔ feet.
56. Spitzflote	8 feet.	64. Octave	2 feet.
57. Piffaro	8 feet.	65. Flautino	2 feet.
58. Harmonica	8 feet.	66. Mixture, V ranks	2 feet.
59. Gedact	8 feet.	*67. Vox humana	8 feet.
60. Octave	4 feet.	68. Phyzharmonica	8 feet.
61. Gemshorn	4 feet.	*69. Oboe	4 feet.

Fourth Manual, 13 Reed Stops.

Belonging to the other Manuals, which borrowed stops are distinguished by an asterisk on their respective Manuals.

25. Contra fagotto	16 feet.	52. Clarinett	8 feet.
26. Fagotto	16 feet.	67. Vox humana	8 feet.
27. Posaune	8 feet.	29. Clarine	4 feet.
28. Trompette	8 feet.	53. Corno	4 feet.
49. Posaune	8 feet.	69. Oboe	4 feet.
50. Trompette	8 feet.	30. Clarinett	2 feet.
51. Fagotto	8 feet.		

First Pedal, 24 Stops.

70. Principal Bass, in front	32 feet.	82. Terz	6⅖ feet.
71. Grand Bourdon	32 feet.	83. Quint	5⅓ feet.
72. Octave Bass	16 feet.	84. Octave	4 feet.
73. Principal Bass	16 feet.	85. Cornett, V ranks	4 feet.
74. Violon Bass	16 feet.	86. Bombardon, free reed	32 feet.
75. Bourdon	16 feet.	87. Posaune	16 feet.
76. Sub-bass	16 feet.	88. Fagotto	16 feet.
77. Quint	10⅔ feet.	89. Posaune	8 feet.
78. Octave	8 feet.	90. Trompette	8 feet.
79. Flote Bass	8 feet.	91. Clarine	4 feet.
80. Violoncello	8 feet.	92. Corno-basso	4 feet.
81. Viola	8 feet.	93. Cornettino	2 feet.

Second Pedal, 7 Stops.

94. Violon Bass	16 feet.	98. Hohlflote	2 feet.
95. Gedact Bass	16 feet.	99. Serpent	16 feet.
96. Flauto	8 feet.	100. Basset horn	8 feet.
97. Flauto	4 feet.		

Couplers.

1. First and second Manual.	6. Fourth and first Manual.
2. Second and third Manual.	7. First Manual and first Pedal.
3. First and third Manual.	8. Second Manual and second Pedal.
4. Fourth and third Manual.	9. First and second Pedal.
5. Fourth and second Manual.	

Crescendo to the Phyzharmonica.
Crescendo and Decrescendo to the entire work.

Among the most striking features of this specification must be classed the great amount and variety of 16, 8, and 4 feet flue-work therein included. Although not comprehending everything—the French Harmonic Flute and the English Dulciana class of stops being absent—yet the double, unison, and octave flue stops on the Manuals present, on the whole, facilities for tone-colouring such as are to be found scarcely in any other organ in existence. Another point worthy of attention is the composition of the chorus stops. The size, which is given, of the longest rank of each of those in the Great organ, clearly indicates that the mixtures are not simply composed of small ranks of pipes, which would do little more than add to the general din of the instrument, but are so compounded that while each one is qualified to do its individual share in imparting brightness to the general effect, each can also do its individual share in toning down that brightness by strengthening and giving additional roundness to some of the sounds which lie below. The Great organ, too, contains, as do all the modern first-class instruments in Germany, a stop of 32-feet tone (Untersatz), while the great Cornett includes the Mutation aliquots of the pitch.

The internal, mechanical, and other arrangements present many peculiarities and excellencies which are worth noting. The bellows are formed after the fashion of gasometers ; that is to say, they each consist of an upper cylinder working inside a lower. By this plan side-ribs are done away with, and the strength of the wind produced is absolutely equal at all times. Every stop in the organ is placed on a little sound-board of its own, the object of which is to prevent the possibility of any stops robbing others of wind when they are all in use. Each little sound-board is furnished with as many pallets as there are keys on the controlling clavier, and the pallets, which may be familiarly described as being of mushroom shape, are arranged vertically, and operate by being lifted up instead of drawn down. To prevent the touch being disagreeably heavy from the concentration of so many pallets on each key, Barker's pneumatic lever is introduced, which removes all unpleasant resistance from the finger. The pipes of most of the stops are placed in their natural or semitonal order, that is to say, with the largest pipe to the extreme left, and the smallest to the extreme right, Walcker giving the preference to this arrangement over all others on acoustical grounds. As there are numerous small sound-boards, instead of one or more large ones, slides, which are only required for securing the use of the stops independently, are unnecessary, and the stops are each brought into play, or the reverse, by opening or closing a ventil at one end of the little sound-board. One great merit of this separate sound-board system consists in the facility which it offers for borrowing stops from one Manual for the use of another. In the present instance no less than *thirteen* reed stops, collected from the three Manuals, are concentrated on a fourth, thus forming what the French term a " Bombarde Organ ;" and all this is accomplished mainly by the introduction of an additional ventil placed at the second end of the sound-board of each of the borrowed stops.

One of the most effective and important novelties in this organ is the " Crescendo and Decrescendo " to the entire work. This movement draws every stop in the entire instrument in the best succession, so that a perfectly gradual crescendo can be produced from the most delicate *pianissimo* up to the most overwhelming *fortissimo*. The movement can, moreover, be checked at any stage, and there allowed to remain, or it can be reversed, so as to produce a partial piano, then advanced again, and so on. The apparatus itself seems to be the most complete and simple for the purpose that has yet been devised. It is worked by a wheel, of which there are two, one placed on each side of the pedal claviers, and can, therefore, be controlled by either foot.

The instrument stands at the west end of the church, the most favourable place for it in one respect, but so far back as to be in the tower (with its front just under the tower arch), which is somewhat damaging to its effect. The cost of the organ was 28,000 florins, or about £2,240 sterling.

117. FRANCE.

The organ in the Cathedral of Carcassaune was built by Cavaillé-Coll, and contains 40 sounding stops, of which the following is a list :—

Grand Orgue.

1. Montre	16 feet.	5. Flute harmonic	8 feet.
2. Bourdon	16 feet.	6. Viole de Gamba	8 feet.
3. Montre	8 feet.	7. Prestant	4 feet.
4. Bourdon	8 feet.	8. Viole d'amour	4 feet.

Jeux de Combinaison.

9. Octave	4 feet.	13. Cymbale, III ranks.	
10. Quint	3 feet.	14. Bombarde	16 feet.
11. Doublette	2 feet.	15. Trompette	8 feet.
12. Fourniture, IV ranks.		16. Clarion	4 feet.

Positif, 10 Stops.

17. Montre	8 feet.	22. Quint	3 feet.
18. Bourdon	8 feet.	23. Doublette	2 feet.
19. Salicional	8 feet.	24. Plein Jeu, III ranks.	
20. Prestant	4 feet.	25. Trompette	8 feet.
21. Flute Douce	4 feet.	26. Cromorne	8 feet.

Recit. Expressif, 4 Stops.

27. Flute Harmonic	8 feet.	29. Viole d'amour	8 feet.
28. Flute Douce	8 feet.	30. Flute Octaviante	4 feet.

Jeux de Combinaison.

31. Octavin	2 feet.	33. Bassoon et Hautbois	8 feet.
32. Trompette Harmonic	8 feet.	34. Voix humaine	8 feet.

Clavier Pedales.

35. Contre-bass	16 feet.	37. Octave	4 feet.
36. Basse	8 feet.		

Jeux de Combinaison.

38. Bombarde	16 feet.	40. Clarion	4 feet.
39. Trompette	8 feet.		

Eleven Pedals de Combinaison, &c.

118. PARIS, NOTRE-DAME-DE-LORETTE.

This organ was constructed, in 1836, by Cavaillé-Coll, father and son, and is the first instrument built by them after their establishment in Paris. It has 3 Manuals, a separate Pedal of 6 stops, and 47 sounding stops, of which the following is a list :—

Great Organ, 19 Stops; Compass, CC to f³, 54 Notes.

1. Montre, the bass of wood	16 feet.	12. Grand Cornet, commencing at f, VII ranks.	
2. Bourdon	16 feet tone.		
3. Montre	8 feet.	13. Gross Fourniture, IV ranks.	
4. Salicional	8 feet.	14. Petite Fourniture, IV ranks.	
5. Bourdon	8 feet tone.	15. Cymbale, IV ranks.	
6. Prestant	4 feet.	16. Bombarde, the Bass octave in unison with the Trompette	16 feet.
7. Flute	4 feet.		
8. Dessus de Flûte conique	4 feet.		
9. Nazard	2⅔ feet.	17. Trompette	8 feet.
10. Quatre de Nazard	2 feet.	18. Clarion	4 feet.
11. Doublette	2 feet.	19. Voix humaine	8 feet tone.

Choir Organ, 12 Stops; Compass, CC to f³, 54 Notes.

20. Bourdon	8 feet tone.	26. Tierce	1⅗ foot.
21. Flute	8 feet.	27. Plein Jeu, V ranks.	
22. Prestant	4 feet.	28. Cornet, V ranks.	
23. Flute	4 feet.	29. Trompette	8 feet.
24. Nazard	2⅔ feet.	30. Clarion	4 feet.
25. Doublette	2 feet.	31. Bassoon	8 feet.

Swell, 10 Stops; Compass, Tenor f to f³, 37 Notes.

32. Bourdon	8 feet tone.	37. Cornet, III ranks.	
33. Flute Traversière	8 feet.	38. Trompette	8 feet.
34. Flute	4 feet.	39. Hautbois	8 feet.
35. Flute Octaviante	4 feet.	40. Voix humaine	8 feet tone.
36. Flageolet	2 feet.	41. Cor Anglais	8 feet.

Pedal, 6 Stops; Compass, CCC to Tenor c, 25 Notes.

42.	Flute ouverte	16 feet.	45.	Trompette	16 feet.
43.	Flute	8 feet.	46.	Trompette	8 feet.
44.	Flute	4 feet.	47.	Clarion	4 feet.

119. PARIS, SAINT GENEVIEVE.

The organ in this Church was built by Cavaillé-Coll in 1852-3, and contains the 21 sounding stops mentioned below :—

Great, 9 Stops; Compass, CC to f³, 54 Notes.

1.	Bourdon	16 feet tone.	6.	Gamba	4 feet.
2.	Montre	8 feet.	7.	Doublette	2 feet.
3.	Salicional	8 feet.	8.	Trompette	8 feet.
4.	Bourdon	8 feet tone.	9.	Clarion	4 feet.
5.	Prestant	4 feet.			

Swell, 8 Stops; Compass, Tenor c to f³, 42 Notes.

10.	Flute harmonic	8 feet.	14.	Octavin	2 feet.
11.	Bourdon	8 feet.	15.	Trompette	8 feet.
12.	Viole di Gamba	8 feet.	16.	Cor Anglais et Hautboy	8 feet.
13.	Flute Octaviante	4 feet.	17.	Voix humaine	8 feet tone.

Pedal, 4 Stops; Compass, CCC to Gamut g, 20 Notes.

18.	Sub-bass	16 feet.	20.	Trompette	8 feet.
19.	Bass	8 feet.	21.	Clarion	4 feet.

120. ELBERFELD.

The new Church in Elberfeld contains a very fine new organ built by J. F. Schulze and Son, in 1858. It has three Manuals and Pedals, and the stops mentioned below :—

Great Organ, 11 Stops.

1.	Principal	16 feet.	7.	Gemshorn	4 feet.
2.	Bourdon	16 feet tone.	8.	{ Twelfth	2⅔ feet.
3.	Principal	8 feet.		{ Fifteenth	2 feet.
4.	Viole di Gamba	8 feet.	9.	Mixture, V ranks	2 feet.
5.	Hohlflote	8 feet.	10.	Cornett, III ranks	2⅔ feet.
6.	Octave	4 feet.	11.	Trompette	8 feet.

Choir Organ, 9 Stops.

12.	Lieblich Bourdon	16 feet tone.	17.	Rohrflote	4 feet tone.
13.	Geigen Principal	8 feet.	18.	Nazard	2⅔ feet.
14.	Gemshorn	8 feet.	19.	Flautino	2 feet.
15.	Rohrflote	8 feet tone.	20.	Oboe	8 feet.
16.	Octave	4 feet.			

Third Clavier.

21.	Lieblich Gedact	8 feet tone.	24.	Flauto Traverso	8 feet.
22.	Harmonica	8 feet.	25.	Viola d'amour	4 feet.
23.	Vox Angelica	8 feet.	26.	Flute Harmonic	4 feet.

Pedal.

27.	Violon	16 feet.	31.	Gedact-bass	8 feet tone.
28.	Sub-bass	16 feet tone.	32.	Octave	4 feet.
29.	Quint	10⅔ feet tone.	33.	Posaune	16 feet.
30.	Violoncello	8 feet.	34.	Trompette	8 feet.

121. BASLE.

The fine new organ in the Minster Church at Basle is the work of Frederick Haas, and contains 60 sounding stops, of which the following is a list :—

Great, 17 Stops.

1. Principal, Eng. tin, in front	16 feet.	8. Quint, wood	5½ feet tone.
2. Bordun, wood, double mouths, from tenor c pipe	16 feet tone.	9. Octave, Eng. tin	4 feet.
3. Octave, Eng. tin	8 feet.	10. Gemshorn, probe tin	4 feet.
4. Gemshorn, probe tin	8 feet.	11. Hohlflote, wood	4 feet.
5. Viol di Gamba, Eng. tin	8 feet.	12. Quint, probe tin	2⅔ feet.
6. Bordun, wood, double mouths, from tenor c pipe	8 feet tone.	13. Waldflote, probe tin	2 feet.
		14. Mixture, probe tin, V ranks	4 feet.
		15. Cornet, probe tin, III ranks	5⅓, 4, & 3⅕ ft.
7. Flauto, wood, double mouths, from fiddle g pipe	8 feet.	16. Fagotto	16 feet.
		17. Trompette, tin	8 feet.

Choir, 15 Stops.

18. Quintaton	16 feet tone.	26. Fugara	4 feet.
19. Principal	8 feet.	27. Klein Gedact	4 feet tone.
20. Bordun	8 feet tone.	28. Quinte	2⅔ feet.
21. Viola d'amour	8 feet.	29. Octave	2 feet.
22. Salicional	8 feet.	30. Mixtur, IV ranks	2 feet.
23. Dolce	8 feet.	31. Cornet, V ranks.	
24. Octave	4 feet.	32. Fagott and Clarinett	8 feet.
25. Flauto Traverso	4 feet.		

Swell, 14 Stops.

33. Lieblich Bordun	16 feet tone.	40. Flûte d'amour	4 feet.
34. Spitzflote	8 feet.	41. Quinte	2⅔ feet.
35. Harmonika	8 feet.	42. Flautino	2 feet.
36. Flauto Traverso	8 feet.	43. Phyzharmonika	16 feet.
37. Still Gedact	8 feet tone.	44. Phyzharmonika	8 feet.
38. Spitzflote	4 feet.	45. Vox humana	8 feet.
39. Dolcissimo	4 feet.	46. Vox humana	8 feet.

Pedal, 14 Stops.

47. Untersatz, open, wood	32 feet.	54. Violoncello, proof tin	8 feet.
48. Octave Bass, wood	16 feet.	55. Flote, wood	8 feet.
49. Violon Bass, Eng. tin	16 feet.	56. Quintflote, wood	5⅓ feet.
50. Violon Bass, wood	16 feet.	57. Octave	4 feet.
51. Sub-bass, wood	16 feet tone.	58. Posaune	16 feet.
52. Quinte, stopped wood	10⅔ feet.	59. Trompette	8 feet.
53. Octave Bass, proof tin	8 feet.	60. Clarine	4 feet.

Accessory Stops, &c.

Coupler, Choir to Great.	Registerzug for the Pedal.
Coupler, Great to Pedal.	Registerzug for the Great Manual.
Calcantenwecker.	Registerzug for the Choir Manual.

122. QUITTELSDORF.

The organ in the village Church of Quittelsdorf, near Paulinzelle, was built by Andreas Schulze, in the year 1791. It has 21 sounding stops, two Manuals, and separate Pedal.

Great Organ, 10 Stops.

1. Bordun	16 feet.	6. Octave	4 feet.
2. Principal	8 feet.	7. Vogelflote	4 feet.
3. Viol di Gamba	8 feet.	8. Sesquialtera, II ranks.	12, 17, 2⅔ & 1⅗ ft.
4. Gedact	8 feet.	9. Mixtur, VI ranks.	2 feet.
5. Hohlflote	8 feet.	10. Cimbel, IV ranks.	

Choir Organ, 7 Stops.

11. Lieblich Gedact	8 feet.	15. Rohrflote	4 feet.
12. Quintaton	8 feet.	16. Waldflote	2 feet.
13. Flauto Traverso	8 feet.	17. Scharf, III ranks	2 feet.
14. Principal	4 feet.		

Pedal, 4 Stops.

| 18. Violon | 16 feet. | 20. Octave Bass | 8 feet. |
| 19. Sub-bass | 16 feet. | 21. Posaun Bass | 16 feet. |

Compass.

| Pedal CCC to tenor c. | Manual CC (no C♯) to c (4 octaves). |

Accessory Stops, Couplers, &c.

| Manual to Pedal. | Accord-glocks. |
| Choir to Great. | Tremulant. |

123. MILBEITZ.

The organ in the village Church of Milbeitz, near Paulinzelle, was made by Andreas Schulze, the grandfather of the present organ-builders, and contains the 21 sounding stops mentioned below :—

Great Organ, 9 Stops.

1. Bordun	16 feet tone.	6. Octave	4 feet.
2. Principal	8 feet.	7. Flote	4 feet.
3. Gedact	8 feet.	8. Sesquialtera	12, 17, 2⅔ & 1⅗ feet.
4. Hohlflote	8 feet.	9. Mixtur, V ranks	2 feet.
5. Gamba	8 feet.		

Choir Organ, 7 Stops.

10. Lieblich Gedact	8 feet tone.	14. Rohrflote	4 feet.
11. Salicet	8 feet tone.	15. Quint	2⅔ feet.
12. Flauto Traverso	8 feet.	16. Octave	2 feet.
13. Principal	4 feet.		

Pedal Organ, 5 Stops.

17. Violin	16 feet.	20. Violin	8 feet.
18. Sub-bass	16 feet.	21. Posaune Bass	16 feet.
19. Octave Bass	8 feet.		

Couplers.

| Accord-glocks. | Tremulant. |

Compass.

| Pedal, CCC to tenor c. | Manuals, CC to C³ (no CC♯). |

124. ANGSTADT.

The organ in this Church was built by J. F. Schulze about the year 1838. It contains 21 sounding stops, 2 Manuals, and Pedal. The following is a list of its contents :—

Great Organ, 8 Stops.

1. Principal, to middle c key, Bordun below	16 feet.	5. Octave	4 feet.
2. Principal	8 feet.	6. Flote	4 feet.
3. Gambe	8 feet.	7. Mixtur, V ranks	2 feet.
4. Hohlflote	8 feet.	8. Cymbel, III ranks	2 feet.

Choir Organ, 8 Stops.

9. Bordun	16 feet tone.	13. Salicional	4 feet.
10. Principal	8 feet.	14. Dolzflote	4 feet.
11. Flauto Traverso	8 feet.	15. Octave	2 feet.
12. Gedact	8 feet.	16. Scharf, III ranks	2 feet.

Pedal Organ, 5 Stops.

17. Violin	16 feet.	20. Octave Bass	8 feet.
18. Sub-bass	16 feet.	21. Violon	8 feet.
19. Principal Bass	8 feet.		

2 Couplers.

125. LUCERNE.

The organ in the Cathedral at Lucerne, in Switzerland, was built by Geissler, of Salzburg, in the year 1651. It has 48 stops, 3 Manuals, and Pedal of 13 stops, among which is a particularly fine Sub-bass of 32 feet in metal. It is proposed to rebuild this organ very shortly.

Over the Manuals is the following quaint account of the organ :—

"ORGAN IN THE COLLEGIATE CHURCH AT LUCERNE."

"This organ is the masterpiece of John Geissler, native of Salzburg. It was commenced and finished in the space of 17 years. The first use made of it dates from 1651, when the son of this famous artist, elected chaplain of this college, was celebrating his first Mass. The whole work consists of 3 Manuals ; of a Pedal with two octaves ; and 2826 Pipes, composed, for the most part of them, of English pewter. The largest of these measures 2 feet in diameter [Qy.], 37 feet in length, and should contain very easily 1308 French pints of any liquor. The Mixtures of this admirable work may be varied 7 times ; and, besides this advantage, there are several registers whereby one may make use of the three Manuals together, or one or two of them separately. This masterpiece was first tried and approved of by four organists belonging to foreign princes, and cost about 12,000 Rhenish florins, a sum which is esteemed very valuable for that time."

The following is a list of the stops in the Lucerne organ :—

Great, 12 Stops.

1. Nachthorn	16 feet.	7. Nazard	2⅔ feet.
2. Prestant	8 feet.	8. Spitzflote	2 feet.
3. Hohlflote	8 feet.	9. Quintadena	2 feet tone.
4. Salicional	8 feet.	10. Sesquialtera, V ranks	2⅔ feet.
5. Gemshorn	4 feet.	11. Trompet	8 feet.
6. Quintflote	2⅔ feet tone.	12. Vox humana	8 feet.

Choir, 11 Stops.

13. Principal	8 feet.	19. Mixtur, III ranks.	
14. Hohlflote	8 feet.	20. Cymbel, III ranks.	
15. Quint	5⅓ feet.	21. Cornet, V ranks.	
16. Octave	4 feet.	22. Schalmey	8 feet tone.
17. Quintflote	2⅔ feet tone.	23. Hornlein, a small reed	8 feet.
18. Terzflote	1⅗ foot tone.		

Echo, 12 Stops.

24. Principal	16 feet.	30. Gross-terz	3⅕ feet.
25. Octave	8 feet.	31. Duodecima	2⅔ feet.
26. Solo Principal	8 feet.	32. Quintadena	2 feet tone.
27. Viola	8 feet.	33. Klein-terz	1⅗ foot.
28. Quint	5⅓ feet.	34. Sesquialtera, IV ranks	2⅔ feet.
29. Super-octave	4 feet.	35. Mixtur, III ranks.	

Pedal, 13 Stops.

36.	Sub-bass, metal	32 feet.	43.	Super-octave	4 feet.
37.	Bass, metal	16 feet.	44.	Mixtur, V ranks.	
38.	Principal, metal	16 feet.	45.	Bombarde	16 feet.
39.	Holz-bass, wood	16 feet.	46.	Posaune	8 feet.
40.	Bourdon, wood	16 feet tone.	47.	Portune	4 feet.
41.	Octave	8 feet.	48.	Horn	2 feet.
42.	Klein Octave ....,.	8 feet.			

Accessory Stops, &c.

1.	Echo to Great.	3. Great to Pedal.
2.	Choir to Great.	4. Echo to Choir.

Compass.

Manuals, CC to e³ in alt., short octaves. | Pedal. CCC to tenor c, short octaves.

126. WINTERTHUR.

The organ in the principal Church at Winterthur, near Zurich, was built partly by Hasse and partly by Moser, of Freiburg. It contains 44 sounding stops, 3 Manuals, and a Pedal of 9 stops. Among the latter is a very fine 32-feet Sub-bass, of wood. The following is a list of the stops :—

Great, 14 Stops.

1.	Principal	16 feet.	8.	Octav	4 feet.
2.	Bourdon	16 feet tone.	9.	Fugara........................	4 feet.
3.	Octav	8 feet.	10.	Quinte	2¾ feet.
4.	Bourdon	8 feet tone.	11.	Waldflote	2 feet.
5.	Viol di Gamba	8 feet.	12.	Mixture, V ranks.	
6.	Flote, dopp lab.	8 feet.	13.	Cornet, V ranks.	
7.	Quintflote...................	5⅓ feet tone.	14.	Trompette	8 feet.

Choir, 11 Stops.

15.	Bourdon	16 feet tone.	21.	Rohrflote......................	4 feet tone.
16.	Principal	8 feet.	22.	Flauto Traverso	4 feet.
17.	Viol di Gamba...............	8 feet.	23.	Octave	2 feet.
18.	Bourdon	8 feet tone.	24.	Mixture, IV ranks.	
19.	Dolce	8 feet.	25.	{ Clarinet Treble } { Bassoon Bass }	8 feet.
20.	Gemshorn	4 feet.			

Swell, 10 Stops.

26.	Principal	8 feet.	31.	Spitzflote	4 feet.
27.	Lieblich Gedact	8 feet tone.	32.	Flauto d'amore	4 feet.
28.	Harmonica	8 feet.	33.	Flautino	2 feet.
29.	Salicional.....................	8 feet.	34.	Phyzharmonica, free reeds	8 feet.
30.	Lieblich-flote	8 feet tone.	35.	Vox humana	8 feet tone.

Pedal, 9 Stops.

36.	Sub-bass, wood	32 feet.	41.	Violoncello	8 feet.
37.	Octav Bass, wood	16 feet.	42.	Octav	4 feet.
38.	Sub-bass, wood	16 feet tone.	43.	Posaune	16 feet.
39.	Octav Bass, metal	8 feet.	44.	Trompette	8 feet.
40.	Flote Bass, wood	8 feet tone.			

Accessory Stops, Movements, &c.

1.	Coupler, Choir to Great.	5, 6. 7. Three Wind-trunk Valves.
2.	Ditto Swell to Choir.	8. Tremulant to Swell.
3.	Ditto Great to Pedal.	9, 10. Two Composition Pedals.
4.	Ditto Choir to Pedal.	

Compass.

Manuals, CC to f³ in alt., 54 notes. | Pedal, CCC to tenor c, 25 notes.

127. CONSTANCE.

The organ in the Cathedral at Constance, in Switzerland, was originally built in the year 1518, which date appears on the case of the instrument. It stands at the west end of the nave, and has the front pipes richly decorated with diaper and scroll work. The organ has 2 Manuals and Pedal, and 27 sounding stops, of which the following is a list :—

Great, 11 Stops.

1. Bourdon	16 feet tone.	7. Quinte .... 2⅔ feet.
2. Principal	8 feet.	8. Super-octave .... 2 feet.
3. Viol di Gamba	8 feet.	9. Mixtur, VI ranks .... 2 feet.
4. Gedact	8 feet tone.	10. Cymbel, IV ranks .... 1 foot.
5. Octave	4 feet.	11. Dulcian...................... 8 feet.
6. Flote Gedact	4 feet tone.	

Choir, 8 Stops.

12. Principal	8 feet.	16. Octave .... 4 feet.
13. Gemshorn	8 feet.	17. Rohrflote .... 4 feet tone.
14. Bourdon	8 feet tone.	18. Quinte .... 2⅔ feet.
15. Salicional	8 feet.	19. Mixtur, III ranks .... 2 feet.

Pedal, 8 Stops.

20. Principal Bass	16 feet.	24. Rausch-quinte, II ranks... 2⅔ feet.
21. Nassat Major	12 feet tone.	25. Mixtur, IV ranks........... 2 feet.
22. Octave Bass	8 feet.	26. Posaune .... 16 feet.
23. Prestant Bass	4 feet.	27. Trompette .... 8 feet.

Accessory Stops.	*Compass.*
1. Choir to Great.	Manuals, CC to f⁸ in alt.
2. Great to Pedal.	Pedal, CCC to Gamut G.

128. STUTGARD.

An organ was erected in the Stiftskirche, at Stutgard, by Conrad Schott, about the year 1591. The instrument now standing there was built in the year 1737, for the Benedictine Abbey of Zwiefalten, by Martin, of Hayengen, partner of the celebrated organ-builder, Gabler. It has been repaired and enlarged by Walker, of Ludwigsburg, and is a particularly fine instrument. It has 4 Manuals and 2 Pedals, and contains 70 sounding stops, of which the following is a list :—

Great Organ, 16 Stops.

1. Bourdon	32 feet tone.	9. Octav .... 4 feet.
2. Principal, tin, in front	16 feet.	10. Dolce .... 4 feet.
3. Bourdon	16 feet tone.	11. Fugara .... 4 feet.
4. Octav	8 feet.	12. Super-octav .... 2 feet.
5. Gamba	8 feet.	13. Mixtur, IV ranks... 4, 2⅔, 1⅓, & 1 feet.
6. Gedact	8 feet tone.	14. Cornet, IV ranks .... 10⅔ feet tone.
7. Piffara, II ranks	8 & 4 feet.	15. Tuba .... 16 feet.
8. Quint	5⅓ feet.	16. Trompette.................. 8 feet.

Second Manual, 13 Stops.

17. Bourdon	16 feet tone.	24. Flote...................... 4 feet.
18. Principal	8 feet.	25. Rohrflote .... 4 feet tone.
19. Gedact	8 feet tone.	26. Nazard .... 2⅔ feet
20. Viola	8 feet.	27. Super-octave .... 2 feet.
21. Salicional	8 feet.	28. Mixtur, IV ranks........... 2 feet.
22. Piffara	8 feet.	29. Clarinet .... 8 feet tone.
23. Octave	4 feet.	

Choir, or 3rd Organ, 11 Stops.

30.	Salicional	16 feet.	36.	Octav	4 feet.
31.	Principal	8 feet.	37.	Travers-flote	4 feet.
32.	Gedact	8 feet tone.	38.	Flageolet	2 feet.
33.	Viola	8 feet.	39.	Mixtur, II ranks.	
34.	Harmonica	8 feet.	40.	Phyzharmonica	8 feet.
35.	Flote	8 feet.			

Echo Organ, 9 Stops.

41.	Principal	8 feet.	46.	Flote	4 feet.
42.	Gedact	8 feet tone.	47.	Salicet	2 feet.
43.	Dolce	8 feet.	48.	Super-octav	2 feet.
44.	Viola	4 feet.	49.	Sesquialtera, II ranks	2⅔ & 1⅗ feet.
45.	Octav	4 feet.			

First Pedal, 14 Stops.

50.	Sub-bass, wood	32 feet.	57.	Quint	5⅓ feet.
51.	Principal, metal	16 feet.	58.	Octav	4 feet.
52.	Octav, wood	16 feet.	59.	Posaune	32 feet.
53.	Violon, II ranks	16 & 8 feet.	60.	Posaune	16 feet.
54.	Quint	10⅔ feet.	61.	Trompette ·	8 feet.
55.	Octav	8 feet.	62.	Clarion	4 feet.
56.	Quintadon	8 feet tone.	63.	Clarion	2 feet.

Second Pedal, 7 Stops.

64.	Bourdon	16 feet tone.	68.	Flautino	2 feet.
65.	Violoncello	8 feet.	69.	Serpent	16 feet.
66.	Bourdon	8 feet tone.	70.	Basset Horn	8 feet.
67.	Flote	4 feet.			

Accessory Stops.

1. First Pedal to Second Pedal.	4. Second Manual to Second Pedal.
2. First and Second Manual.	5. Second and Third Manual.
3. First Manual to First Pedal.	6. Third and Fourth Manual.

Compass.

Four Manuals, CC to d⁵ in alt.	Two Pedals, CCC to tenor d.

129. STUTGARD.

The organ in the Jews' Synagogue was built by Weigle in the year 1860. It has 2 Manuals, Pedal, and 22 stops, of which the following is a list :—

Great Organ, 11 Stops.

1.	Bourdon	16 feet tone.	7.	Rohrflote	4 feet tone
2.	Principal	8 feet.	8.	Quint	2⅔ feet.
3.	Gedact	8 feet tone.	9.	Super-octave	2 feet.
4.	Viol di Gamba	8 feet.	10.	Mixtur, IV ranks.	
5.	Flaut dolce	8 feet.	11.	Trompette	8 feet.
6.	Octave	4 feet.			

Choir Organ, 7 Stops.

12.	Principal	8 feet.	16.	Gemshorn	4 feet.
13.	Lieblich Gedact	8 feet tone.	17.	Traverso	4 feet.
14.	Dolce	8 feet.	18.	Phyzharmonica	8 feet.
15.	Salicional	8 feet.			

Pedal, 4 Stops.

19.	Violon	16 feet.	21.	Octave	8 feet.
20.	Bourdon	16 feet tone.	22.	Posaune	16 feet.

Couplers, &c.

Choir to Great.	Great to Pedal.	Choir to Pedal.	Glock.

130. WEINGARTEN.

The central dome and the two west towers of the great Church of the Benedictine Monastery at Weingarten are seen to great advantage from the Ravensburg Railway. The monastery is approached by a flight of twenty steps, leading to a paved "place," with the west end of the Church in front ; a house, with gateway leading to monastic buildings, to the right ; a fine prospect of the country to the left, with the steps, the town, and a view of Ravensburg, and country between and beyond, in the remaining direction. The organ in the monastery was being cleaned and repaired, at the time of our visit, by Weigle, of Stutgard. We could not, therefore, form any opinion of its general effect ; but we tried several of the pipes separately, and obtained a general idea of the scale of some of the stops. The 32-feet pipe, of tin, in front, measures between 15 and 16 inches in diameter ; the largest stopped pipe, 32 feet tone, about 11 by 13 inches inside, of yellow deal ; the Violoncello, 8 feet, on the Pedal, is harmonic, 16 feet in length, of tin, 3½ inches in diameter ; the Violon and Octave Bass, 16 feet, are of wood, the latter about 10 inches across the mouth. The "Coppel" is of metal, stopped, with sliding cap ; large scale, the CC pipe (4 feet length) being over 4 inches in diameter, probe tin, very thick, with arched lip ; tone full and pure, like that of very good wood pipes. The Principal Tutti, large scale, CC, 5¼ to 6 inches, and very heavy pipes ; tone very strong. The Carillon on third Manual, composed of real bells, shaped like those attached to skeleton clocks, of bright metal ; very musical and pure in tone. Bombarde Bass, 32 feet, of wood, like pear tree in the upper part, painted white outside. Scale small, tenor d about 2 inches square inside. Largest pipes have metal boots and sockets, wooden reeds, leathered, and brass tongues.

The draw stops are arranged in six horizontal rows on each side, six in a row, with two additional on each side, making 76 draw stops in the total. Knobs of turned ivory ; the draws also of ivory, ⅜ of an inch square. The names of the stops, on plates of ivory, are let into the fittings.

Great, 16 Stops.

1.	Prestant	16 feet.	9. Querflote	4 feet.
2.	Principal	8 feet.	10. Hohlflote	2 feet.
3.	Rohrflote	8 feet tone.	11. Super-octave	2 feet.
4.	Piffara	8 feet.	12. Sesquialtera, VIII ranks	2⅔ feet.
5.	Quintaton	8 feet tone.	13. Mixture, XX ranks	2 feet.
6.	Octave	4 feet.	14. Cornet, VIII ranks	2 feet.
7.	Rohrflote	4 feet tone.	15. Trompetten (new)	8 feet.
8.	Flote Douce	4 feet.	16. Cymbelstern.	

Choir, 12 Stops.

17.	Bordun	16 feet tone.	23. Salicional	8 feet.
18.	Principal tutti (strong) ...	8 feet.	24. Octav Douce	4 feet.
19.	Violoncello	8 feet.	25. Viola	4 feet.
20.	Coppel	8 feet.	26. Nasat	2 feet.
21.	Hohlflote	8 feet.	27. Mixture, XXI ranks	4 feet.
22.	Unda Maris	8 feet.	28. Cymbal, II ranks	2 feet.

Echo, 13 Stops.

29.	Bordun	16 feet tone.	36. Piffaro	4 feet.
30.	Principal	8 feet.	37. Super-octave	2 feet.
31.	Quintaton	8 feet tone.	38. Mixture, XII ranks	2 feet.
32.	Viola Douce	8 feet.	39. Cornet, IV ranks	1 foot.
33.	Flauten	8 feet.	40. Clarinet (new)	8 feet.
34.	Octave	8 feet.	41. Carillon, from tenor f upwards.	
35.	Hohlflote	4 feet.		

Positif, 12 Stops.

42. Principal Douce, in front...	8 feet.	48. Rohrflote	4 feet tone.
43. Violoncello	8 feet.	49. Querflote	4 feet.
44. Quintaton	8 feet.	50. Flageolet	4 feet.
45. Flute Douce	8 feet.	51. Cornet, XII ranks	2 feet.
46. Piffaro	4 feet.	52. Hautbois	8 feet.
47. Flauto Traverso	4 feet.	53. Voix humaine	8 feet.

Pedal, 17 Stops.

54. Contra-bass, tin, in front..	32 feet.	63. Sesquialtera Bass, II and	
55. Sub-bass, wood	32 feet tone.	III.ranks	2¾ feet.
56. Octave Bass, wood	16 feet.	64. Mixturen Bass, V ranks...	8 feet.
57. Violon Bass, wood	16 feet.	65. Bombarde Bass	32 feet.
58. Quintaton Bass	16 feet.	66. Posaune Bass	16 feet.
59. Super-octave Bass, in front	8 feet.	67. Trompette Bass	8 feet.
60. Flote Douce Bass	8 feet.	68. Fagott Bass	8 feet.
61. Violoncello Bass	8 feet.	69. Cornet Bass	4 feet.
62. Hohlflote Bass	4 feet.	70. Carillon Pedal.	

Compass.

Manuals, CC to c³ in alt. | Pedals, CCC to tenor d.

Flat pitch.

Accessory Stops, Movements, &c.

1. Coupler, Echo to Great.	4. Rosignal.
2. Tremulant.	5. Cymbals.
3. Cuckoo.	6. La Force.

131. MUNICH.

The organ in the Odéon Concert-room, at Munich, is a little gem. It was built, in 1851, by Walker, of Ludwigsburg, and contains 20 stops, distributed among two Manuals and Pedal. The Phyzharmonica is on a separate wind, and is managed, by a new Pedal contrivance, so as to produce the most exquisite effects of delicate *crescendo* and *diminuendo*. The following is the specification of the above-named organ :—

Great, 10 Stops.

1. Bourdon, wood	16 feet.	6. Octave, metal	4 feet.
2. Principal, metal	8 feet.	7. Flote, wood	4 feet.
3. Gamba, wood	8 feet.	8. Octave, metal	2 feet.
4. Rohrflote, metal	8 feet tone.	9. Cornet, VII ranks	16 feet tone.
5. Gedact, wood	8 feet tone.	10. Trompette	8 feet.

Echo, 6 Stops.

11. Salicional, metal	8 feet.	14. Spitzflote, metal	4 feet.
12. Flote, wood	8 feet.	15. Dolce, metal	4 feet.
13. Gedact, wood	8 feet tone.	16. Phyzharmonica	8 feet.

Pedal, 4 Stops.

17. Sub-bass, wood, open	16 feet.	19. Violoncello, metal	8 feet.
18. Viol di Gamba, metal	16 feet.	20. Fagotto	16 feet.

Accessory Stops.

1. Echo to Great. | 2. Great to Pedal.

Compass.

Manuals, CC to f³ in alt. | Pedal, CCC to tenor d.

132. RATISBON.

The organ in the Church of St. Emmeran, at Ratisbon, was built about 250 years ago. It has 28 stops distributed among 2 Manuals and Pedal in the following manner :—

Great, 10 Stops.

1.	Principal	8 feet.	6.	Flote	4 feet.
2.	Bourdon	8 feet tone.	7.	Quint	2⅔ feet.
3.	Gamba	8 feet.	8.	Super-octave	2 feet.
4.	Coppel	8 feet.	9.	Mixtur, III ranks.	
5.	Octave	4 feet.	10.	Mixtur, minor, II ranks.	

Choir, 8 Stops.

11.	Coppel	8 feet.	15.	Octave	4 feet.
12.	Salicional	8 feet.	16.	Flote	4 feet.
13.	Allemande	8 feet.	17.	Spitzflote	4 feet.
14.	Principal	4 feet.	18.	Super-octave	2 feet.

Pedal, 8 Stops.

19.	Gross-bass	16 feet.	23.	Quint	5⅓ feet.
20.	Violone	16 feet.	24.	Octave	4 feet.
21.	Principal	8 feet.	25.	Super-octave	2 feet.
22.	Violoncello	8 feet.	26.	Mixtur, V ranks.	

Accessory Stops.

1. Choir to Great.   2. Great to Pedal.

Compass.

Manuals, CC to c³ in alt.   Pedal, CCC to A.

133. BOTZEN.

The organ in the Parish Church at Botzen, Tyrol, was built by Hess, and repaired by Carlo Mauracher. It has 2 Manuals and Pedal, and 30 stops, of which the following is a list :—

Great, 12 Stops.

1.	Coppel	16 feet.	7.	Flauto duodecimo	2⅔ feet.
2.	Gamba	8 feet.	8.	Super-octave	2 feet.
3.	Flaut amabile	8 feet.	9.	Mixtur.	
4.	Flauto stoppo	8 feet tone.	10.	Cornet.	
5.	Quintadena	8 feet tone.	11.	Trombe	8 feet.
6.	Octave	4 feet.	12.	Vox humana	8 feet tone.

Choir, 10 Stops.

13.	Coppel	8 feet.	18.	Sesquialtera, II ranks	2⅔ feet.
14.	Viola	8 feet.	19.	Flageolet	2 feet.
15.	Salicional	8 feet.	20.	Tibia Silvest	2 feet.
16.	Principal	4 feet.	21.	Cymbal	1⅓ foot.
17.	Flauto	4 feet.	22.	Dulcian	8 feet.

Pedal, 8 Stops.

23.	Principal Bass	16 feet.	27.	Octave Bass	8 feet.
24.	Violon Bass	16 feet.	28.	Mixtur Bass	4 feet.
25.	Sub-bass	16 feet tone.	29.	Posaune	8 feet.
26.	Principal	8 feet.	30.	Clarion	4 feet.

Compass.

Manuals, CC to f³ in alt.   Pedal, CCC to FF.

134. St. Peter's, at Rome.

So little is generally known in England concerning the organs of Italy that it is presumed the following accounts of some of the large cathedral and celebrated church organs of that country will be perused with much interest. It will be perceived, from the particulars relating to the subject appended to the specifications in question, that the compass most usually adopted by the Italian organ-builders for the Manuals of their instruments is that descending to the CCC or 16-feet key. Occasionally this range is met with "complete," as in the organ at St. Alessandro, at Milan, and therefore corresponding almost exactly with the downward compass of the Great organ Manuals at St. Paul's Cathedral, Westminster Abbey, &c. The stops of a Manual of such range are just double the size of the usually quoted lengths; that is to say, the Principal (Open Diapason) is 16 feet actual measurement, and not 8; the Ottava (Principal) is 8 feet, and not 4, and so on; and the Pedal organ of such instruments usually consists of but a very few stops, as the deeper tones of the Manual serve as a sort of substitute for it in general effects. Sometimes the Manuals are of the compass denominated "CCC short;" that is, they have the 16-feet key for the lowest note, but with certain tones omitted from the scale, and such an arrangement of the remaining keys as is shown in the following scheme :—

	EEE		FFF♯		GG♯		BB♭	
CCC		FFF	DDD	GG	EEE	AA	BB	CC

Sometimes the Italian Manuals descend to FFF, as in the two large organs at Milan Cathedral, corresponding with the compass adopted by Green for his organs at St. George's Chapel, Windsor, Salisbury Cathedral, Greenwich Hospital, &c. The length of the stops in all such FFF Manuals is half as large again as the corresponding stops of CC organs; thus the Manual and Pedal Diapasons are not simply 8 and 16 feet in length, but 12 and 24 feet respectively. In a few instances CC Manuals are met with, as in two of the Geneva organs, with, of course, a somewhat larger proportionate Pedal organ by way of "Bass."

Among other peculiarities in the Italian system of organ-building will be ·noticed that of placing one more Open Diapason (Principale) in the treble of the Manual than in the bass, evidently with the view of preserving an equal strength between the upper and lower tones of the gamut, as in the organs at St. Peter's at Rome, Milan Cathedral, &c. In some instances this plan for strengthening the acute sounds will be found extended to the Principal (Ottava), as in organs at Milan, Como, &c. Another feature in connection with the Italian schemes is the plan of making a greater number of the small ranks of pipes draw separately than is the custom in any other country. Thus we find not only the 19th and 22nd frequently appearing as separate stops, but also the 26th, 29th, and even the 33rd and 36th, disposed in a similar manner. Among the most striking features in the Italian organs, however, is the constant presence of the Octave and Sub-octave couplers, which so materially increase the number of distinct combinations, as well as augment the general power of instruments possessing them.

In the Church of St. Peter's, at Rome, there are *four* organs ; all of which, however, are small for so spacious an edifice. The largest one of the number was originally built about 150 years since, but has recently been reconstructed and enlarged by Priori, an organ-builder in Rome. It has 2 Manuals and Pedal, and 27 stops, of which the following are the names. As, however, many of the names are probably new to many English readers, a list of equivalent terms is placed in parallel columns therewith, which will serve to elucidate their meaning :—

Great, 17 Stops.

1. Principale doppio, Soprano e Basso	Double Diapason, Treble and Bass.
2. Principale 1mo Soprano	First Open Diapason, Treble.
Principale 1mo Basso	First Open Diapason, Bass.
3. Principale 2ndo Soprano	Second Open Diapason, Treble.
Principale 2ndo Basso.....................	Second Open Diapason, Bass.
4. Principale 3zo, Soprano	Third Open Diapason, Treble.
5. Flauto Traverso, Soprano e Basso........	German Flute, Treble and Bass.
6. Flauto Tedesca, Soprano	A kind of Clarabella.
7. Ottava Soprano	Octave or Principal Treble.
Ottava Basso	Octave or Principal Bass.
8. Duodecima	Twelfth.
9. Decima quinta	Fifteenth.
10. Ottavini, Basso e Soprano	Piccolo, Bass and Treble.
11. Decima nona	Nineteenth or Larigot.
12. Vigesima seconda..........................	Twenty-second or Octave Fifteenth.
13. Vigesimanona	Twenty-ninth or Super-octave Fifteenth.
14. Ripieno di quattro	Chorus or Mixture, IV ranks.
15. Cornetto Soprano, di cinque	Cornet, Treble, V ranks.
16. Tromba Soprano	Trumpet, Treble.
Trombone Basso	Trombone, Bass.
17. Corno Inglese, Soprano	English Horn, Treble.
Fagotto, Basso............................	Bassoon, Bass.

Swell, 6 Stops.

18. Principale, Soprano........................	Open Diapason, Treble.
Principale, Basso...........................	Open Diapason, Bass.
19. Ottava	Octave or Principal.
20. Decima quinta	Fifteenth.
21. Ripieur, di cinque	Mixture, V ranks.
22. Oboe, Soprano.............................	Hautboy, Treble.
23. Tromba, Soprano...........................	Trumpet, Treble.
Corno, Basso	Horn, Bass.

Pedal, 4 Stops.

24. Contra-Basso, di 16.......................	Open Diapason, wood .... 16 feet.
25. Principale, di 16	Diapason .... 16 feet.
26. Principale, di 8	Principal .... 8 feet.
27. Reinforza a lingue	Free Reed, without tubes ...... 16 feet tone.

Accessory Stops, Movements, &c.

1. Coupler, Swell to Great.	4, 5. Octave and Sub-octave on Great Manual.
2. Coupler, Great to Pedal.	6, 7, 8. Three Composition Pedals.
3. Coupler, Swell to Pedal.	9. Drum Pedal.

Compass.

Manuals, CCC short to f³ in alt.	Pedal, CCC short to tenor c.

135. ROME.

The organ that ranks as second in point of size in St. Peter's, at Rome, was built by Priori, of that city, and has 1 Manual and Pedal, and 21 stops, of which the following is a list :—

Mannal, 17 Stops.

1. Contra-Bassi, Soprano e Basso.
2. Principale, 1mo Soprano.
   Principale, Basso.
3. Principale, 2ndo Soprano.
4. Flauto Traverso, Soprano e Basso.
5. Flauto Tedesco, Soprano.
6. Ottava, Soprano.
   Ottava, Basso.
7. Duodecima.
8. Decima quinta
9. Ottavini ne Basso.

10. Decima nona.
11. Vigesima seconda.
12. Vigesima nona.
13. Ripieno di cinque.
14. Cornetto di quattro, Soprano.
15. Voce Umana (*not* a reed).
16. Tromba, Soprano.
    Trombone, Basso.
17. Corno Inglese, Soprano.
    Fagotto, Basso.

Pedal, 4 Stops.

18. Contra-Basso, di 16.
19. Principale,   di 8.

20. Ottava,   di 4.
21. Bombarde, di 16.

Accessory Stop.
Drum.

The Church of St. John, of Lateran, at Rome, has an organ of 36 stops. It was first built in 1549, and is the largest instrument in the city.

136. MILAN CATHEDRAL.

In Milan Cathedral there are two organs, one on each side of the choir ; both of which are exceedingly effective, and suit admirably the noble building in which they are placed. Neither of them contains any Reed stops ; stops of that nature being expressly forbidden by the Ambrosian rite. Both instruments were made by the brothers Serassi, of Bergamo. That which stands on the north-side of the choir was completed in 1842, has 1 Manual and Pedal, and the following stops :—

Manual, 28 Stops.

1. Doppio ne Soprani, di 24 Piedi. (Double Treble.)
   Contra-Basso, di 24 Piedi. (Double Bass.)
2. Principale, 1mo Soprano. (Open Treble.)
   Principale, 1mo Basso ......(Open Bass.)
3. Principale, 2ndo Soprano.(Open Treble.)
   Principale, 2ndo Basso ......(Open Bass.)
4. Principale, 3zo Soprano (Open Treble.)
5. Violone Soprano ....(Violin.)
   Violono Basso ....(Bass.)
6. Flautone, Soprano.........(Met. St. Dn.)
   Flautone, Basso............(Stopped Bass.)
7. Flauto Tedesca ....(Clarabella.)
8. Ottava, 1mo Soprano ....(Prin. Tre.)
   Ottava, 1mo Basso............(Prin. Bass.)
9. Ottava, 2ndo Soprano ......(Prin. Tre.)
   Ottava, 2ndo Basso ......(Prin. Bass.)
10. Ottava, 3zo Soprano ....(Prin. Tre.)
11. Viola Soprano............(Octave Gamba.)
    Violoncello Basso ....(Gamba Bass.)
12. Flauto Traverso ....(German Flute.)
13. Duodecimo ....(12th.)
14. Decima quinta, 1mo ....(15th.)

15. Decima quinta, 2ndo ....(15th.)
16. Flautino ....(Piccolo.)
17. Decima nona, e .... 1mo.
    Vigesima seconda ....(19 and 22.)
18. Decima nona, e .... 2ndo.
    Vigesima seconda ....(19 and 22.)
19. Vigesima sesta, e)
    Vigesima nona   } ....(26 and 29.)
20. Vigesima quarto, e)
    Decima settima   } ......(24 and 17.)
21. Trigesima terza, e)
    Trigesima sesta   } ......(33 and 36.)
22. Trigesima prima, e)
    Trigesima sesta   } ......(31 and 36.)
23. Ripieno di quatro (Mixture IV ranks.)
24. Ripieno di tre (Mixture III ranks.)
25. Cornetto Soprano, a cinque (Cornet V ranks.)
26. Cornettino Sop. : a quattro (small Cornet IV ranks.)
27. Corno dolce, Soprano ......(Soft Horn.)
28. Voce Humana, Sop. ....(not a reed.)

Pedal, 4 Stops.

29. Contra Basso .... 24 feet.	31. Ottava .... 12 feet.
30. Basso Profundo .... 24 feet.	32. Principale .... 12 feet.

Accessory Stops, Movements, &c.

1. Terza Mano (third-hand, octave Coupler).	3. Tremblant.
2. Pedali armonichi (Pedal Coupler).	4, 5. Two Composition Pedals.

Compass.

Manual, FFF to f³ in alt., complete.	Pedal, FFF to tenor c, complete.

137. MILAN CATHEDRAL.

The organ on the south side of the Choir has 2 Manuals and 29 stops, of which the following is a list :—

Great, 21 Stops.

1. Contra Bassi.	10. Decima nona.
2. Principale, 1mo Soprano.	11. Vigesima seconda.
Principale, 1mo Basso.	12. Vigesima sesta.
3. Principale, 2ndo Soprano.	13. Vigesima nona.
Principale, 2ndo Basso.	14. Vigesima sesta e nona.
4. Flauto Traverso.	15. Trigesima terza.
5. Ottava Soprano.	16. Trigesima sesta.
Ottava Bassi.	17. Trigesima terza e sesta.
6. Ottava Soprano.	18. Quadragesima, e
Ottava Bassi.	Quadragesima, terza.
7. Flauto in Ottava.	19. Cornetta primo.
8. Duodecima.	20. Cornetta secunda.
9. Quinta decima.	21. Voce Umana.

Positif, 8 Stops.

22. Principale Soprani.	25. Quinta decima.
Principale Bassi.	26. Decima nona.
23. Flauto Soprani.	27. Vigesima secunda.
24. Ottava Soprani.	28. Vigesima sesta.
Ottava Bassi.	29. Vigesima nona.

Accessory Stops, Movements, &c.

1. Bassi Armonici ne Pedali.	3. Sub-octave Coupler.
2. Terzo Mano.	4. Piano and Forte movement.

Compass.

Manuals, FFF to g³ in altissimo.	Pedal Clavier, FFF to tenor b.

138. MILAN.

The organ in the Church of St. Alessandro, at Milan, has 49 stops, 2 Manuals, and a Pedal of 10 stops. The following is its specification :—

Great, 24 Stops.

1. Principale Soprano 1mo ... 32 feet.	11. Violino Soprano............ 8 feet.
Principale Basso 1mo ...... 32 feet.	Basso Viola.................. 8 feet.
2. Principale Sop. e Basso 2ndo 32 feet.	12. Quinta decima 1mo ..... 4 feet.
3. Violone Basso al CC........ 32 feet.	13. Quinta decima 2ndo ...... 4 feet.
4. Principale Soprano 1mo ... 16 feet.	14. Decima nona .... 3 feet.
Principale Basso 1mo ...... 16 feet.	15. Ottavino .... 2 feet.
5. Principale Soprano 2ndo ... 16 feet.	16. Ripieno di due.
Principale Basso 2ndo ...... 16 feet.	17. Ripieno di quattro.
6. Viola Soprano .... 16 feet.	18. Ripieno di tre.
Viola Basso................... 16 feet.	19. Ripieno di quattro.
7. Corno Flauto .... 16 feet.	20. Corno Inglese.............. 32 feet.
8. Ottava Soprano 1mo........ 8 feet.	21. Tromba Soprano .... 16 feet.
Ottava Basso 1mo .... 8 feet.	Tromba Basso............... 16 feet.
9. Ottava Sop. e Basso .... 8 feet.	22. Clarinetto Soprano........ 16 feet.
10. Flauto Soprano .... 8 feet.	Fagotto Basso .... 16 feet.
Flauto Basso .... 8 feet.	23. Tromba Allemano Basso 16 feet.
	24. Tromba Armoniche ...... 8 feet.

Swell, 15 Stops.

25.	Principale Soprano	16 feet.	31.	Flauto Traverso Soprano	8 feet.
	Principale Basso	16 feet.	32.	Viola Basso	8 feet.
26.	Voce flebile Soprano 1mo	16 feet.	33.	Decima quinta	4 feet.
	Voce flebile Basso	16 feet.	34.	Decima nona	3 feet.
27.	Voce flebile Sop. 2ndo	16 feet.	35.	Vigesima seconda	2 feet.
28.	Violetta Soprano 1mo	16 feet.	36.	Vigesima sesta e nona.	
	Violoncello Basso	16 feet.	37.	Clarinetto Soprano	16 feet.
29.	Violetta Soprano 2ndo	16 feet.	38.	Fagottone Basso	32 feet.
30.	Ottava	8 feet.	39.	Claroone Basso	8 feet.

Pedal, 10 Stops.

40.	Violone profondo	32 feet.	45.	Ripieno a tre	8, 6, & 4 feet.
41.	Contrabassi e rinforzi	16 feet.	46.	Bombardi	16 feet.
42.	Violoncello a lingur in la	16 feet.	47.	Tromboni	8 feet.
43.	Bassi Armonichi e duodecima.		48.	Corni da caccia	4 feet.
44.	Principali e ottava	8 & 4 feet.	49.	Timpani.	

Accessory Stops, Movements, &c.

1. Coupler, Swell to Great.
2. Coupler, Great to Pedal.
3. Seraphine, or Fisarmonica, on a separate wind.
4. Thunder Pedal.
5. Drums.
6, 7, 8. Three Composition Pedals.

Compass.

Great, CCC to c⁴ in altissimo, six complete octaves.
Swell, CC to c⁴ in altissimo, five complete octaves.
Pedal, CCC to Tenor c, two complete octaves.

139. COMO.

There are two organs in the Cathedral at Como. The oldest was built in 1596, and was afterwards much improved, but is now unplayable. The other was erected in 1650 by Hermann, a Jesuit, and is of exquisite tone. It has 3 Manuals and Pedal, and 48 stops, of which the following is a list :—

Great Organ, 20 Stops.

1.	Principale Soprano	32 feet.	11.	Duodecima	6 feet.
2.	Principale Soprano e Basso	32 feet.	12.	Quinta decima Soprano	4 feet.
3.	Principale Soprano 1mo	16 feet.		Quinta decima Basso	4 feet.
	Principale Basso 1mo	16 feet.	13.	Ottavius Soprano	4 feet.
4.	Principale Soprano 2ndo	16 feet.	14.	Decima nona	3 feet.
	Principale Basso 2ndo	16 feet.	15.	Vigesima seconda	2 feet.
5.	Principale Soprano 3zo	16 feet.	16.	Ripieno di quattro.	
6.	Flauto Soprano	16 feet.	17.	Ripieno di quattro.	
7.	Viola Basso profonda	16 feet.	18.	Tromba Soprano	16 feet.
8.	Ottava Soprano 1mo	8 feet.		Tromba Basso	16 feet.
	Ottava Bass 1mo	8 feet.	19.	Trombe di caccia Soprano	16 feet.
9.	Ottava Soprano e Basso	8 feet.		Fagotto Basso	16 feet.
10.	Flauto in Ottava, Soprano e Basso	8 feet.	20.	Voce Umana Soprano	16 feet.

Choir Organ, 17 Stops.

21.	Principale Soprano	16 feet.	28.	Flagioletta Soprano	4 feet.
	Principale Basso	16 feet.	29.	Decima nona	3 feet.
22.	Principale Soprano	16 feet.	30.	Vigesima seconda	2 feet.
23.	Flauto Allemanno Soprano	16 feet.	31.	Vigesima sesta e nona.	
24.	Violino Soprano	16 feet.	32.	Trigesima terza e sesta.	
	Violono Basso	16 feet.	33.	Cornetto Soprano di cinque.	
25.	Ottava Soprano	8 feet.	34.	Corno Inglese Soprano	32 feet.
	Ottava Basso	8 feet.	35.	Oboe Soprano	16 feet.
26.	Flauto in Ottava Soprano	8 feet.		Violoncello Basso (a reed)	16 feet.
	Flauto Basso	8 feet.	36.	Voce Umana Soprano	16 feet.
27.	Quinta Decima	4 feet.	37.	Tromba Armoniche Basso	8 feet.

Swell Organ, 7 Stops.

38. Principale Soprano .... 16 feet.	41. Corno dolce, Soprano ...... 32 feet.
Principale Basso .... 16 feet.	42. Corno Bassetto, Soprano... 32 feet.
39. Flauto in ottava .... 8 feet.	43. Voce Umana, Soprano ... 16 feet.
40. Ripieno di cinque.	44. Fagottone, Basso .... 16 feet.

Pedal Organ, 4 Stops.

45. Contra Bassi con rinforzi... 32 & 16 feet.	47. Bombardone .... 16 feet.
46. Contra Bassi dolci (stopped) 16 feet.	48. Tromboni .... 8 feet.

Accessory Stops, Movements, &c.

1. Coupler, Choir to Great.	4, 5. Octave and Double Couplers.
2. Coupler, Swell to Great.	6, 7, 8. Three Composition Pedals.
3. Coupler, Great to Pedal.	9. Drums.

Compass.

Manuals, CCC short to f⁵ in alt.	Pedal, CCC short to tenor d.

140. COMO.

The organ in the Church of the Santissimo Crocifisso, at Como, was built by the Brothers Serassi, of Bergamo. It has 2 Manuals, a Pedal of 8 Stops, and 39 stops, of which latter the following is a list :—

Great, 24 Stops.

1. Principale Soprano .... 32 feet.	Flauto Ottava, Basso ...... 8 feet.
Principale Basso .... 32 feet.	13. Duodecima .... 6 feet.
2. Principale Soprano .... 32 feet.	14. Quinta decima, Soprano ... 4 feet.
3. Corno dolce .... 32 feet.	Quinta decima, Basso ...... 4 feet.
4. Principale Soprano, 1mo... 16 feet.	15. Decima nona.................. 3 feet.
Principale Basso, 1mo ...... 16 feet.	16. Vigesima seconda............ 2 feet.
5. Principale Soprano, 2ndo 16 feet.	17. Ripieno di quattro.
6. Principale Soprano, 3zo ... 16 feet.	18. Ripieno di quattro.
7. Flauto Traverso Soprano... 16 feet.	19. Cornetto di cinque.
8. Violone Basso .... 16 feet.	20. Corno Inglese, Soprano ... 32 feet.
9. Ottava Soprano e Basso ... 8 feet.	21. Tromba Soprano .... 16 feet.
10. Ottava Soprano .... 8 feet.	22. Fagotti Basso .... 16 feet.
11. Viola Basso .... 8 feet.	23. Voce Umana, Soprano ... 16 feet.
12. Flauto Ottava, Soprano ... 8 feet.	24. Clarone, Basso .... 8 feet.

Swell Organ, 8 Stops.

25. Principale Soprano .... 16 feet.	28. Flauto in Ottava .... 8 feet.
Principale Basso .... 16 feet.	29. Decima quinta e nona.
26. Corna Musa .... 16 feet.	30. Ripieno di tre.
27. Ottava Soprano .... 8 feet.	31. Cornettino di tre, Soprano.
Ottava Basso .... 8 feet.	32. Serpentino Bass, al CC ... 32 feet.

Pedal Organ, 8 Stops.

33. Contra-bassi, al sol (GGG) 32 feet.	37. Bombardi .... 16 feet.
34. Contra-bassi con rinforzi ... 16 feet.	38. Tromboni .... 8 feet.
35. Ottavo .... 8 feet.	39. Trombe .... 4 feet.
36. Ripieno di cinque.	

Accessory Stops, Movements, &c.

1. Coupler, Swell to Great.	6. Timpani.
2. Coupler, Great to Pedal.	7. Bells.
3. Coupler, Swell to Pedal.	8. Thunder.
4. Octave Coupler.	9, 10. Two Composition Pedals.
5. Sub-octave Coupler.	

Compass.

Manuals, CCC short to f³ in alt.	Pedal, CCC short to tenor c.

141. FLORENCE.

The organ in the Church of St. Gaetano, at Florence, has 3 Manuals, embracing 34 stops, and a very good Contra-basso on the Pedal. The following is a list of the stops :—

Great, 14 Stops.

1.	Principale, Soprano	8 feet.	8.	Vigesima seconda	1 foot.
	Principale, Basso	8 feet.	9.	Ripieno di tre.	
2.	Ottava	4 feet.	10.	Cornetta di tre.	
3.	Flauto	4 feet.	11.	Cornettino di tre.	
4.	Nasardo	3 feet.	12.	Tromba, Soprano	8 feet.
5.	Decima quinta	2 feet.		Tromba, Basso	8 feet.
6.	Flautino, Soprano e Basso	2 feet.	13.	Voce Umana	8 feet.
7.	Decima nona	1½ foot.	14.	Clarone	4 feet.

Choir, 11 Stops.

15.	Corno dolce, Soprano	16 feet.	20.	Flauto	4 feet.
16.	Principale, Soprano	8 feet.	21.	Flautino	2 feet.
	Principale, Basso	8 feet.	22.	Corno Inglese, Soprano	16 feet.
17.	Voce Angelica	8 feet.	23.	Tromba, Basso e Soprano	8 feet.
18.	Flautone, metal	8 feet.	24.	Oboe, Soprano	8 feet.
19.	Ottava	4 feet.	25.	Voce Umana	8 feet.

Echo, 8 Stops.

26.	Principale	8 feet.	30.	Decima Quinta	2 feet.
27.	Ottava	4 feet.	31.	Ripieno di quattro.	
28.	Flauto	4 feet.	32.	Cornettino di tre.	
29.	Nasardo	3 feet.	33.	Tromba	8 feet.

Pedal, 1 Stop.

34. Rinforza de Contra-bassi (wood, open) ...... 16 feet.

Accessory Stops, Movements, &c.

1.	Coupler, Choir to Great.	4.	Great Sub-octave Coupler.
2.	Coupler, Echo to Great.	5.	Great to Pedal.
3.	Great Octave Coupler.	6, 7, 8.	Three Composition Pedals.

Compass.

Manuals, CC short to c³ in alt. | Pedal, CCC short to tenor c.

There are very excellent organs in the churches of St. Spirito and Santa Croce at Florence, the particulars of which, however, are not at hand. That in the church of St. Spirito has been rebuilt by Ducie, of Florence, and contains some remarkably fine reeds and a very effective 16 feet Principale on the Pedal.

142. GENOA.

The organ in the Church of Santa Maria des Vignes, at Genoa, was built by the Brothers Serassi, of Bergamo. It has 28 stops, of which the following is a list :—

Manual, 27 Stops.

1.	Soprano Doppio.	13.	Decima nona.
	Contra-basso.	14.	Vigesima seconda.
2.	Principale, 1mo Soprano.	15.	Vigesima sesta.
	Principale, 1mo Basso.	16.	Vigesima nona.
3.	Principale, 2ndo Soprano.	17.	Flageoletti ne Bassi.
	Principale, 2ndo Basso.	18.	Trigesima sesta.
4.	Flauto Tedesco.	19.	Ripieno di quattro.
5.	Flauto Francese, Soprano.	20.	Ripieno di tre.
6.	Ottava, Soprano.	21.	Cornetto di cinque.
	Ottava, Basso.	22.	Cornetto di tre.
7.	Traverso Ottava.	23.	Tromba, Soprano.
8.	Viola Basso.		Trombone, Basso.
9.	Duodecima.	24.	Cor Anglais, Soprano.
10.	Decima Quinta 1mo.	25.	Fagotti, Basso.
11.	Decima Quinta 2ndo.	26.	Timpani.
12.	Ottavini.	27.	Bells.

Pedal, 1 *Stop.*

28. Rinforzo di Contra Bassi (open, wood) .... 16 feet.

Accessory Stops, Movements, &c.

1. Octave Coupler. | 2. Sub-octave Coupler. | 3 to 8. Six Composition Pedals.

Compass.

Manual, CC short to c⁴ in alt. | Pedal, CCC short to tenor c.

143. GENOA.

The organ in the Carigrana Church, at Genoa, was built by Hermann. It contains 3 Manuals and 42 stops, of which the following is a list :—

Great, 25 *Stops.*

1. Contra Basso, Soprano e Basso.	13. Ottavini, Soprano e Basso.
2. Contra Basso, Soprano.	14. Decima nona.
3. Principale Soprano 1mo.	15. Vigesima seconda.
Principale Basso 1mo.	16. Vigesima nona.
4. Principale Soprano 2ndo.	17. Trigesima sesta.
Principale Basso 2ndo.	18. Sesquialtera di quattro.
5. Principale Soprano 3zo.	19. Ripieno di cinque.
6. Flauto Traverso, Soprano e Basso.	20. Cornetto di quattro.
7. Flauto Tedesco, Soprano e Basso.	21. Cornetto di tre.
8. Ottava Soprano 1mo.	22. Tromba Soprano.
Ottava Basso.	Trombone Basso.
9. Ottava Soprano 2ndo.	23. Tromba Real, Soprano.
10. Flautino.	Fagotto Basso.
11. Duodecima.	24. Voce Umana (a Reed).
12. Decima quinta.	25. Corna Musa, Soprano.

Choir, 5 *Stops.*

26. Principale.	28. Ottava.	30. Vox Pueri, Soprano.
27. Flautino.	29. Ripieno di cinque.	Vox Tauri, Basso.

Echo, 6 *Stops.*

31. Principale.	33. Ottava.	35. Oboe, Soprano.
32. Corno Dolce, Soprano.	34. Ripieno di quattro.	36. Tromba, Soprano.

Pedal, 6 *Stops.*

37. ContraBasso, al La(toAAA) 32 feet.	40. Principale .... 8 feet.
38. Principale .... 8 feet.	41. Tromba .... 16 feet.
39. Contra Basso .... 16 feet.	42. Clarone .... 8 feet.

Accessory Stops, Movements, &c.

1. Coupler, uniting all the Manuals.	7, 8. Two Bird stops, on Echo Manual.
2. Coupler, Great to Pedal.	9. Thunder, by means of a Pedal.
3, 4, 5. Three Composition Pedals.	10. Drum, by means of a Pedal.
6. Bells, on Choir Manual.	

Compass.

Great, CCC short to c³ in alt.	Swell, CC to c³ in alt.
Choir, CCC short to c³ in alt.	Pedal, CCC short to tenor d.

144. GENEVA.

The organ in the Cathedral Church of St. Pierre, at Geneva, was built by Gerger about 150 years ago. It has 4 Manuals, a Pedal of 2 octaves, and 45 stops, of which the following is a list :—

Great, 17 *Stops.*

1. Montre .... 16 feet.	10. Doublette .... 2 feet.
2. Grand Bourdon .... 16 feet tone.	11. Tierce .... 1⅗ foot.
3. Huit Pieds Ouverte .... 8 feet.	12. Cymballe.
4. Principal .... 8 feet.	13. Fourniture.
5. Flute .... 8 feet.	14. Cornette, V ranks.
6. Bourdon .... 8 feet tone.	15. Trompette des dessus...... 8 feet.
7. Prestant....................... 4 feet.	Trompette des bassus...... 8 feet.
8. Nazard .... 3 feet.	16. Clairon....................... 4 feet.
9. Quarte de Nazard......... ... 2 feet.	17. Voix Humaine .... 8 feet tone

Q Q

Choir, 10 Stops.

18. Bourdon	8 feet.	23. Cymballe.			
19. Prestant	4 feet.	24. Fourniture.			
20. Flute	4 feet.	25. Cornette.			
21. Doublette	2 feet.	26. Trompette	8 feet.		
22. Tierce	1⅗ foot.	27. Crom Horn	8 feet tone.		

Echo, 6 Stops.

28. Bourdon	8 feet tone.	31. Cornette, III ranks.	
29. Prestant	4 feet.	32. Trompette	8 feet.
30. Flute	4 feet.	33. Crom Horn	8 feet tone.

Orgue de Recit., 6 Stops.

34. Bourdon	8 feet tone.	37. Doublette	2 feet.
35. Flute Allemande	8 feet.	38. Cornette, IV ranks.	
36. Prestant	4 feet.	39. Trompette	8 feet.

Pedal, 6 Stops.

40. 16 Pieds Ouverte, to GG	16 feet.	43. Bombarde	16 feet.
41. Bourdon	16 feet tone.	44. Trompette	8 feet.
42. Huit Pieds Ouverte	8 feet.	45. Clairon	4 feet.

Accessory Stops, Movements, &c.

1. Coupler, Positif to Great. | 2. Coupler, Great to Pedal.

Compass.

Great, CC to d³ in alt. | Echo, Middle c¹ to d³ in alt.
Positif, CC to d³ in alt. | Pedal, CCC to tenor c.
Orgue de Recit, Fiddle g to d³ in alt. |

145. SIENA.

The organ in the cathedral is very small, yet a very effective instrument. It has but 1 Manual and 14 stops, of which the following is a list :—

Manual, 11 Stops.

1. Principale, Soprano.	6. Vigesima seconda.
Principale, Basso.	7. Ripieno di quattro.
2. Flauto Traverso.	8. Cornetto di cinque.
3. Ottava.	9. Tromba, Soprano e Basso.
4. Decima quinta.	10. Corno Inglese.
5. Decima nona.	11. Voce Umana (not a Reed).

Pedal, 3 Stops.

12. Contra Bassi, al La (AAA) 32 feet.	14. Rinforza de Contra Bassi
13. Contra Bassi, al La (AA)... 16 feet.	(Trombone) .... 16 feet.

Compass.

Manual, CCC short to d³ in alt. | Pedal, CCC short to FF.

Accessory Stops, Movements, &c.

1, 2. Manual Couplers, octave above and | 3. Manual to Pedal.
below. |

146. SEVILLE.

The large organ in Seville Cathedral has frequently been extolled by tourists for its magnitude and great power. There are several organs in the cathedral, the two principal of which stand, sideways, one on each side of the choir, and opposite each other. Each of these has a complete and beautifully adorned front, both behind as well as before; and also a handsome "Choir organ in front," not only towards the choir, but also another towards the aisle. The Reed stops which are unexampled for their number are placed outside the organs, and project horizontally from the several fronts in 2, 3, and 4 tiers. The largest pipes are uppermost, and are supported by iron bars. The mouths of the tubes are Trumpet-shaped.

The older of the two chief organs is the largest. According to most accounts, this has 110 stops and 5,300 pipes. It is evident, however, that many of the stops are, like those in the Italian organs just described, only "half stops." By no other means could such an aggregation of stops be accounted to comprise a number of pipes inferior to that contained in the Rotterdam, Weingarten, and some other organs, which have at the same time 30 or 40 stops less than the Seville organ. Still less could it otherwise be explained how there can be *two* "first" Mixtures, *two* "second" Mixtures, and so forth. The following account and translation of the large Seville organ has been prepared from memorandums made from the draw-stop handles by J. W. Fraser, Esq., of Manchester, and forwarded to Mr. Hill, the eminent organ-builder, who kindly furnished them to the writer. The figures, 13, 26, and 52, attached to certain stops, seem to correspond with the signs 8, 16, and 32, in the German tablature, in marking the size of the large Foundation stops :—

Great, 42 Stops, 62 Draw Stops.

1. Flauto de 26	Double Diapason.	(Treb.)
Flauto de 26	Double Diapason.	(Bass.)
2. Flauto de 26	Double Diapason.	(Treb.)
3 Violon de 26	Gamba Major, or Double Gamba.	(Treb.)
Violon de 26	Gamba Major, or Double Gamba.	(Bass.)
4. Tolosana de 26	Double stop; probably either invented or first made at Toulouse, and hence named after that place.	
5. Baxoncillo	Open Diapason. (T.)	"Baxon" is a Bassoon and
Baxoncillo	Open Diapason. (B.)	"illo" implies diminution;
6. Baxoncillo	Open Diapason. (T.)	but the Baxoncillo stop is
Baxoncillo	Open Diapason. (B.)	known to be the equivalent to
7. Baxoncillo	Open Diapason. (Treb.)	the English Open Diapason.
8. Tapadillo	Stopped Diapason.	(Treb.)
Tapadillo	Stopped Diapason.	(Bass.)
9. Tapadillo	Stopped Diapason.	(Treb.)
10. Flauta de 13	Unison Flute.	(Treb.)
Flauta de 13	Unison Flute.	(Bass.)
11. Flauta de 13	Unison Flute.	(Treb.)
12. Flauta Traversa	German Flute.	(Treb.)
13. Violon de 13	Gamba.	(Treb.)
Violon de 13	Gamba.	(Bass.)
14. Violon de 13	Gamba.	(Treb.)
15. Tolosana	Unison stop. See No. 6 above.	
16. Docena de 26	Twelfth to the 26-feet stops. Fifth to the 13-feet stops. Quint.	
17. Octava	Octave or Principal. (Treb.)	
Octava	Principal. (Bass.)	
18. Octava	Principal.	
19. Docen y 26°	Twelfth and 26th (Octave Larigot).	
20. Quincena	Fifteenth.	
21. Lleno 1°	First Mixture.	(Treb.)
Lleno 1°	First Mixture.	(Bass.)
22. Lleno 2°	Second Mixture.	(Treb.)
Lleno 2°	Second Mixture.	(Bass.)
23. Lleno	Mixture.	
24. Corneta	Cornet.	
25. Corneta	Cornet.	
26. Trompa de 52	Double Double Trumpet.	
27. Trompa de 26	Double Trumpet.	(Treb.)
Tromba de 26	Double Trumpet.	(Bass.)

28. Trompa Real	Royal or Grand Trumpet. (Treb.)
Trompa Real	Royal or Grand Trumpet. (Bass.)
29. Trompa Real	Royal or Grand Trumpet. (Treb.)
Trompa Real	Royal or Grand Trumpet. (Bass.)
30. Trompa de Batalla	Battle Trumpet. (Treb.)
Trompa Magna	Great Trumpet. (Bass.)
31. Trompa 8...................................	Octave Trumpet, probably.
32. Oboe..........	Hautboy.
Fagot	Bassoon.
33. Cremona	Cremona.
34. Vox de 13	Vox Humana.
35. Viejos	"Viejos," the eyebrows. This stop takes its
Viejos	name from the shape of the cover or plug at the top of the pipe.
36. Clarin Real	Royal or Grand Clarion. (Treb.)
Clarin Real	Royal or Grand Clarion. (Bass.)
37. Clarin Real	Royal or Grand Clarion.
38. Clarin de Batalla	Battle Clarion. (Treb.)
Clarin de Batalla	Battle Clarion. (Bass.)
39. Clarin Claro	Clear Clarion.
40. Clarin en 15	Octave Clarion. (Treb.)
Clarin en 15	Octave Clarion. (Bass.)
41. Clarin en 15	Octave Clarion.
42. Orlo	Orlo, shawn; "Cink" of Dutch and "Zincke" of German organs. The original instrument exists only in the German saying : "In heaven the angels only play fiddles and shawms."

Forte de Echo, 10 Stops; 12 Draw Stops.

43. Baxoncillo	Open Diapason.
44. Tapadillo....................................	Stopped Diapason.
45. Flauta Traverso	German Flute.
46. Flauta	Flute.
47. Corneta	Cornet.
48. Trompa Real	Grand Trumpet.
Trompa Magna	Great Trumpet.
49. Trompa Bastarda	"Bastarda," a piece of ordnance. [Trumpet. Bombarde or Great Reed. Probably a Double
50. Vox Contralto.............................	Contralto Voice.
51. Oboe..........	Hautboy.
Fagot	Bassoon.
52. Clarin Sordina	Soft Clarion.

Echo, 12 Stops; 14 Draw Stops.

53. Baxoncillo	Open Diapason.
54. Tapadillo....................................	Stopped Diapason.
55. Violon de 13	Gamba.
56. Tolosana	Unison stop.
57. Flauto Traverso	German Flute.
58. Flauto de 13e 8va	Flute, of Octave as well as Unison pitch.
59. Docena.....................................	Twelfth.
60. Quincena	Fifteenth.
61. Lleno	Mixture.
62. Corneta	Cornet.
63. Trompa Real	Royal Trumpet.
Trompa Magna	Great Trumpet.
64. Vox de 13	Vox Humana.
Vox Contralto................................	Contralto Voice.

Contra Pedale, 7 Stops.

65. Trompa de 26	Trumpet of 26 feet.
66. Trompa de 26	Trumpet of 26 feet.
67. Trompa de 15	Trumpet of 13 feet.
68. Trompa de Octave.........................	Octave Trumpet (6¼ feet).
69. Trompa de 15	Twelfth Trumpet (4⅖ feet).
70. Trompa en 15.............................	Fifteenth Trumpet (3¼ feet).
71. Trompa en 17	Tierce Trumpet.

Compass.

Manuals, CC to g³ in altissimo. | Pedal, One Octave.

The above organ has several more stops, the names of which are not on the stop-handles.   These are probably Couplers, Wind-valves, and other Accessory stops.

Great............................	42 stops.	62 draw-stops.
Forte de Echo	10	12
Echo	12	14
Pedal...........................	7	7
Couplers, wind-valves, &c.		15
	———	———
	71	110

The mode of blowing the bellows of the above organ is peculiar.   Instead of working with his hands, a man walks backwards and forwards along an inclined plane of about 15 feet in length, which is balanced in the middle on its axis. These communicate with five other pair, united by a bar ; and the latter are so contrived that, when they are in danger of being overstrained, a valve is lifted up, and gives them relief.

Passing ten times along the inclined plane fills all these vessels, which are so ample that, when stretched, they supply the full organ fifteen minutes.

147. SEVILLE.

The second organ in Seville Cathedral has 71 draw-stops, 3 Manuals, and Pedal.   The contents of the several Manual organs were not placed separately in the memorandum from which the following account was prepared :—

Manual Stops.

1. Violata	Small Viol, or Gambette.	
2. Baxoncillo......................................	Open Diapason.	
3. Trompeta de Batalla	Battle Trumpet.	
4. Viejos...	See 35 in No. 146.	
5. Orlo	Cink. A small Reed.	
6. Clarin en 22ª	Super-octave Clarion.	
7. Clarin en 15ª	Octave Clarion.	
8. Clarin Claro	Clear Clarion.	
9. Clarin de Campana	Hunting Horn.	
10. Chirimia	Clarion.	
11. Violata Suave	Soft Viola.	
12. Baxoncillo......................................	Open Diapason.	
13. Trompeta en 15	Octave Clarion.	
14. Trompeta en 8	Clarion.	
15. Trompeta en 26	Double Trumpet.	
16. Mudo	Mute. Wind-valve ?	
17. Nasardo...	Twelfth.	
18. Corneta de 26	Double Reed.............................. 26 feet.	
19. Octava de Nasardo	Nineteenth, or Larigot.	
20. Quincena Tapada..............................	Stopped Fifteenth. Stopped Piccolo.	
21. Octava Tapada.................................	Stopped Octave. Stopped Flute.	
22. Violon de 13...................................	Gamba.	
23. Lleno de 8......................................	Mixture.	
24. Diezmonovena	Nineteenth, or Larigot.	
25. Quincena	Fifteenth.	
26. Docena	Twelfth.	
27. Octava	Octave, or Principal.	
28. Flauta de 13	Unison Flute.	
29. Flautada de 13.................................	Large Unison Flute.	
30. Flautada de 26.................................	Double Diapason.	
31. Violon.		

32.	Contra Baxo	Double Bass.
33.	Clarin en 15ᵃ	Octave Clarion.
34.	Baxoncillo	Open Diapason.
35.	Trompeta Real	Grand Trumpet.
36.	Trompeta Real	Grand Trumpet.
37.	Tolosana	Unison stop.
38.	Lleno	Mixture.
39.	Diezmonovena	Nineteenth, or Larigot.
40.	Quincena	Fifteenth.
41.	Docena	Twelfth.
42.	Octava	Octave.
43.	Flautada de 13	Large Unison Flute.
44.	Preparacion	Preparation. Probably a wind-valve, or a bell to give notice to the blower.
45.	Trompa	Trumpet.
46.	Serpenton	Great Serpent. Double Reed.
47.	Vox Humana	Vox Humana.
48.	Clarin en 15	Octave Clarion.
49.	Clarin de Sordino	Soft Clarion.
50.	Clarinete	Clarinet.
51.	Fagot	Bassoon.
52.	Nasardo en 19ᵃ	Twelfth and Larigot.
53.	Nasardo en 17ᵃ	Twelfth and Tierce. Sesquialtera.
54.	Nasardo en 15ᵃ	Twelfth and Fifteenth. Rausch-quint.
55.	Lleno	Mixture.
56.	Diezmonovena	Larigot.
57.	Quincena	Fifteenth.
58.	Octava	Principal.
59.	Violon de 13	Gamba.

Pedal, 9 Stops.

60.	Flautada de 26	Great Flute or Diapason of ... 26 feet.
61.	Contra de 26	Double, of ... 26 feet.
62.	Contra 8	Double Octave.
63.	Contra 15	Double 15.
64.	Contra 22	Double 22.
65.	Contra 29	Double 29.
66.	Bombarda de 26	Great Reed ... 26 feet.
67.	Bombarda de 13	Great Reed ... 13 feet.
68.	Contra de Clarin	Great Clarion ... 2¼ feet.
69, 70, 71.	Three stops without names.	

Compass.

Manuals, AA to c⁴ alt., in 5½ octaves.

148. COLOGNE CATHEDRAL.

An account of the Organ in Cologne Cathedral has already been given ; but a new one, of first-class dimensions, has been projected by A. W. Gottschalg, of which the following are the particulars :—

Choir Organ, CC to G.

1.	Principal	16 feet.
2.	Flute Conique	16 feet.
3.	Contra Fagotto	16 feet.
4.	Principal	8 feet.
5.	Double Gedackt	8 feet.
6.	Salicional	8 feet.
7.	Rohrflote	8 feet.
8.	Dolce	8 feet.
9.	Quintaton	8 feet.
10.	Bassoon and Clarionet	8 feet.
11.	Trompette Harmonique	8 feet.
12.	Quint Flute	5⅓ feet.
13.	Gambette	4 feet.
14.	Octave Flute	4 feet.
15.	Fugara	4 feet.
16.	Viola	4 feet.
17.	Clarion Conique	4 feet.
18.	Gemshorn Quinte	2⅔ feet.
19.	Wald Flute	2 feet.
20.	Doublette	2 feet.
21.	Cornet, V ranks.	
22.	Mixture, V ranks.	

Great Organ, CC to G.

23. Manual Untersatz (Sub-Bourdon)	32 feet.
24. Principal (Double Diapason)	16 feet.
25. Gamba	16 feet.
26. Flauto Major	16 feet.
27. Bombarde	16 feet.
28. Principal, No. 1. (in English tin)	8 feet.
29. Principal, No. 2. (small scale)	8 feet.
30. Viol di Gamba	8 feet.
31. Double Flute	8 feet.
32. Fugara	8 feet.
33. Hohlflote	8 feet.
34. Tromba	8 feet.
35. Trombone	8 feet.
36. Quint	5⅓ feet.
37. Octave	4 feet.
38. Rohrflote	4 feet.
39. Gemshorn	4 feet.
40. Clarion	4 feet.
41. Twelfth	2⅔ feet.
42. Fifteenth	2 feet.
43. Clarinet, with divided lips.	
44. Octave Fifteenth	1 foot.
45. Grand Cornet, V ranks (commencing with the Fifth above)	16 feet tone.
46. Mixture, XV ranks (commencing with)	4 feet tone.
47. Mixture, V ranks (commencing with Twelfth).	
48. Sharp Mixture, V ranks (commencing with Fifteenth).	

Swell, CC to G.

49. Bourdon	16 feet.
50. Euphone	16 feet.
51. Gemshorn	8 feet.
52. Flute Harmonique	8 feet.
53. Keraulophon	8 feet.
54. Bourdon	8 feet.
55. Cor Anglais	8 feet.
56. Bassoon Oboe	8 feet.
57. Vox Humana	8 feet.
58. Voix Celeste	8 feet.
59. Trompette Harmonique	8 feet.
60. Viole d'Amour	8 feet.
61. Rohr Quint	5⅓ feet.
62. Violin Principal	4 feet.
63. Traversflote	4 feet.
64. Dulciana	4 feet.
65. Clarion	4 feet.
66. Piccolo Harmonique	2 feet.
67. Echo Cornet, V ranks, from	4 feet tone.
68. Sesquialtera, II ranks, Twelfth and Seventeenth.	
69. Harmonia Ætheria, IV ranks, from Fifteenth.	

Solo Organ, CC to G.

70. Lieblich Gedackt	16 feet.
71. Fernflote (Distant Flute)	8 feet.
72. Echo Dulciana	8 feet.
73. Vox Angelica	8 feet.
74. Harmonica	8 feet.
75. Corno di Bassetto	8 feet.
76. Tuba Mirabilis (with Swell Effect).	
77. Klein Gedackt	4 feet.
78. Orchestral Flute	4 feet.
79. Violin	4 feet.
80. Flageolet	2 feet.

Pedal Organ, CCC to D.

81. Principal Bass (English tin, the ten largest pipes standing in the front)	32 feet.
82. Grand Bourdon	32 feet.
83. Contra Bombarde	32 feet.
84. Contra Bass	16 feet.
85. Principal Bass	16 feet.
86. Sub-Bass	16 feet.
87. Violin Bass	16 feet.
88. Bourdon	16 feet.
89. Contra Fagotto	16 feet.
90. Bass Trombone	16 feet.
91. Quint Bass	10⅔ feet.
92. Violoncello	8 feet.
93. Octave Bass	8 feet.
94. Flute Bass	8 feet.
95. Gedackt Bass	8 feet.
96. Bassoon	8 feet.
97. Trombone	8 feet.
98. Posaune	8 feet.
99. Great Third	6⅖ feet.
100. Octave Quint	5⅓ feet.
101. Fifteenth	4 feet.
102. Octave Flute	4 feet.
103. Juba Clarion	4 feet.
104. Cornet, V ranks (commencing from Fifteenth).	

Accessory Stops.

1. Copulas—Choir to Pedals.
2. „ Great to Pedals.
3. „ Swell to Pedals.
4. „ Solo to Pedals.
5. „ Solo to Great.
6. „ Solo to Swell.
7. „ Swell to Great.
8. „ Swell to Choir.
9. „ Great to Pneumatic Action.
10. Copulas—Choir to Great.
11. Octave Copula on Solo.
12. Octave Copula on Great.
13. Sub-Octave Swell to Choir.
14. Super-Octave Swell to Choir.
15. Bellows Signal.
16. Tremulant for Vox Humana of Swell.

Composition Pedals.

17. Closing Ventil for Pneumatic Stops of Pedals.
18. „ „ Choir.
19. „ „ Great.
20. „ „ Swell.
21. „ „ Solo.
22. Copula for Forte Pedal.
23. Combination for Piano on Pedal, Choir, Great, and Swell.
24. „ Mezzo Forte on the same Organs.
25. „ Forte on the same Organs.
26. „ Fortissimo on the same Organs.
27. „ Full Power on the Three Manuals and Pedal.
28. General Crescendo Pedal for the whole Organ.
29. Diminuendo „ „
30. Swell Effect for the Three Manuals.
31. Combination for Swelling Tuba Mirabilis of Solo, and separate Swell of Vox Humana and Bassoon of the Swell Organ.

149. ST. PETER'S, ROME.

An organ of the first magnitude has been designed for the Cathedral Church of St. Peter, at Rome, by M. Aristide Cavaillé-Coll, the great organ-builder of Paris, to contain 124 sounding stops, 5 Manuals, of five octaves each, in compass, from CC to c in altmo., and a Pedal of 30 notes from CCC to tenor F. The following is a list of its proposed contents :—

Pedal Organ.

1. Principal-Bass .... 32 feet.
2. Front Bass (Double Open Diapason), metal ...... 32 feet.
3. Great Bourdon .... 32 feet.
4. Acoustic Bass .... 32 feet.
5. Great Flute .... 16 feet.
6. Contra-Bass .... 16 feet.
7. Violone .... 16 feet.
8. Sub-bass .... 16 feet.
9. Great Quint .... 10⅔ feet.
10. Flute .... 8 feet.
11. Principal...................... 8 feet.
12. Violoncello .... 8 feet.
13. Stopped Flute .... 8 feet.
14. Tierce .... 6⅖ feet.
15. Quint .... 5⅓ feet.
16. Seventh .... 4⅔ feet.
17. Fifteenth .... 4 feet.
18. Contra-Bombarde ...... 32 feet.
19. Bombarde .... 16 feet.
20. Quint-Bombarde .... 10⅔ feet.
21. Trumpet .... 8 feet.
22. Clarion .... 4 feet.

First Manual: Great Organ (1st Division).

23.	Front Double Open Diapason	16 feet.
24.	Bourdon	16 feet.
25.	Front Open Diapason ...	8 feet.
26.	Harmonic Flute	8 feet.
27.	Diapason	8 feet.
28.	Viol di Gamba	8 feet.
29.	Bourdon	8 feet.
30.	Dulciana	8 feet.
31.	Quint	5⅓ feet.
32.	Principal	4 feet.
33.	Flute	4 feet.
34.	Octave	4 feet.
35.	Twelfth	2⅔ feet.
36.	Fifteenth	2 feet.
37.	Great Furniture, IV ranks.	
38.	Great Cymbal, V ranks.	
39.	Furniture, III ranks.	
40.	Cymbal, IV ranks.	
41.	Bassoon	16 feet.
42.	Harmonic Trumpet	8 feet.
43.	Bassoon	8 feet.
44.	Clarion	4 feet.

Great Choir (2nd Division).

45.	Acoustic Bass	16 feet.
46.	Great Harmonic Flute	16 feet.
47.	Violoncello	8 feet.
48.	Harmonic Flute	8 feet.
49.	Diapason	8 feet.
50.	Unda Maris, tenor c	8 feet.
51.	Principal	4 feet.
52.	Flute	4 feet.
53.	Piccolo	2 feet.
54.	Cornet, V ranks	8 feet.
55.	Sesquialtera, III ranks	8 feet.
56.	Tuba Magna	16 feet.
57.	Tuba Mirabilis	8 feet.
58.	Quint Trumpet	5⅓ feet.
59.	Clarion	4 feet.
60.	Octave Clarion	2 feet.

Second Manual: Bombard Organ.

61.	Principal Bass	16 feet.
62.	Quintaton	16 feet.
63.	Harmonic Flute	8 feet.
64.	Cone Flute	8 feet.
65.	Keraulophon	8 feet.
66.	Stopped Diapason	8 feet.
67.	Great Flute	4 feet.
68.	Principal	4 feet.
69.	Great Tierce	3⅕ feet.
70.	Quint	2⅔ feet.
71.	Seventh	2⅘ feet.
72.	Octave (Fifteenth)	2 feet.
73.	Great Cornet, V ranks	16 feet.
74.	Bombard	16 feet.
75.	Trumpet	8 feet.
76.	Clarion	4 feet.

Third Manual: Choir Organ.

77.	Violone	16 feet.
78.	Bourdon	16 feet.
79.	Traverse Flute	8 feet.
80.	Diapason	8 feet.
81.	Salicional	8 feet.
82.	Night-Horn	8 feet.
83.	Vox Angelica, tenor c	8 feet.
84.	Dulcet Flute	4 feet.
85.	Dulciana	4 feet.
86.	Twelfth	2⅔ feet.
87.	Fifteenth	2 feet.
88.	Full Mixture, V ranks	8 feet.
89.	Full Horn	16 feet.
90.	Harmonic Trumpet	8 feet.
91.	Cremona	8 feet.
92.	Bassoon and Oboe	8 feet.

Fourth Manual: Swell Organ.

93.	Bourdon	16 feet.
94.	Dulcet Horn	16 feet.
95.	Harmonic Flute	8 feet.
96.	Pavilion Flute	8 feet.
97.	Gamba	8 feet.
98.	Voix Celeste, tenor c	8 feet.
99.	Dulcette	4 feet.
100.	Flute	4 feet.
101.	Principal	4 feet.
102.	Flageolet	2 feet.
103.	Cornet, V ranks	8 feet.
104.	Bassoon	16 feet.
105.	Musette	8 feet.
106.	Vox Humana	8 feet.
107.	Harmonic Trumpet	8 feet.
108.	Harmonic Clarion	4 feet.

Fifth Manual: Solo Organ.

109.	Sub-bass	16 feet.	117.	Tierce	1⅗ foot.
110.	Conic-Flute	16 feet.	118.	Larigot	1⅓ foot.
111.	Traverse-Flute Harmonic	8 feet.	119.	Seventh	1⅐ foot.
112.	Diapason	8 feet.	120.	Super-Piccolo	1 foot.
113.	Quintaton	8 feet.*	121.	Cor Anglais	16 feet.
114.	Flute	4 feet.	122.	Clarinette	8 feet.
115.	Twelfth	2⅔ feet.	123.	Harmonic Trumpet	8 feet.
116.	Fifteenth	2 feet.	124.	Violin Harmonic	4 feet.

Combination Stops.

There are 7 of these, one to each Clavier, with the exception of the Great, which has 2, one to each of its divisions. Each knob is present in duplicate on each side of the Manual, thus making, of course, 14 in all.

8. Bell.

Composition Stops.

There are 15 of these in all, 3 to the Pedale, 4 to the Great, and 2 to each of the remaining Manuals; one stop governs the foundation, or, as we would say, unison work, the other the mutation, chorus, and reeds; for the Pedale there is a further division into 32 and 16 feet. These stops are placed over the Solo Manual.

Pedals of Effect.

1. Storm Pedal.

Coupling Pedals.

2. Great to Pedals.	10. Great to Pneumatic.
3. Great Choir to Pedals.	11. Great Choir to Pneumatic.
4. Bombarde to Pedals.	12. Bombarde to Great (Pneumatic).
5. Choir to Pedals.	13. Choir to Great.
6. Swell to Pedals.	14. Swell to Great.
7. Solo to Pedals.	15. Solo to Great.
8. Sub-Octave to Great.	16. Swell to Choir.
9. Sub-Octave to Bombarde.	17. Solo to Bombarde.

Tremulant Pedals.

18. Tremulant to Swell. | 19. Tremulant to Solo.

Composition Pedals Proper.

These do not act on arbitrary combinations, as with English work, but on previous arrangements prepared by hand at pleasure, and of course giving any composition that the stops admit of; there is thus necessity for but 7 of these, 2 to the Great, and 1 to each of the other Claviers.

Swell Pedals.

27. Swell Pedal. | 28. Solo Pedal.

These 28 Pedals are to be arranged, properly grouped, in two rows, one above the other in the usual position.

---

* We think this must be a misprint.

150. BOMBAY CATHEDRAL.

The following is a description of the large and fine organ built by Messrs. Bishop and Starr for the Cathedral, Bombay. The case and wood pipes are made of solid mahogany :—

Great, 10 *Stops ; Compass, CC to G in alt.*

1. Open Diapason	....	8 feet.	6. Flute	....	4 feet.
2. Bell Diapason	....	8 feet.	7. Twelfth	....	3 feet.
3. Stopped Diapason, Bass ...		8 feet tone.	8. Fifteenth	....	2 feet.
4. Clarabella	....	8 feet tone.	9. Sesquialtera, III ranks.		
5. Principal	....	4 feet.	10. Trumpet	....	8 feet.

Choir, 8 *Stops ; Compass, CC to G in alt.*

1. Dulciana	....	8 feet.	5. Metallic Flute	....	4 feet.
2. Stopped Diapason, Bass ...		8 feet tone.	6. Principal	....	4 feet.
3. German Flute	....	8 feet tone.	7. Piccolo	....	2 feet.
4. Keraulophon	....	8 feet.	8. Cremona	....	8 feet.

Swell, 7 *Stops ; Compass, CC to G in alt.*

1. Double Diapason	....	16 feet tone.	5. Fifteenth	....	2 feet.
2. Open Diapason	....	8 feet.	6. Cornopean	....	8 feet.
3. Stopped Diapason	....	8 feet tone.	7. Hautboy	....	8 feet.
4. Principal	....	4 feet.			

Pedal, 6 *Stops ; Compass, CCC to E.*

1. Open Diapason, Bass, wood		16 feet.	4. Principal, metal	....	8 feet.
2. Ditto,	ditto,	metal 16 feet.	5. Fifteenth, metal	....	4 feet.
3. Bourdon	....	16 feet tone.	6. Prepared for Reed.		

Accessory Stops, Movements, &c.

1. Great to Pedals.	6. Sub Swell to Choir.
2. Choir to ditto.	7. Super Swell to Great.
3. Swell to ditto.	8. Three Composition Pedals to Great.
4. Ditto to Great.	9. Two ditto ditto to Choir.
5. Ditto to Choir.	10. One ditto ditto to Swell.

151. BOMBAY.

The organ in the Town Hall, Bombay, was built by Messrs. Bishop and Starr. It has 4 Manuals, a separate Pedal, and 40 Sounding stops, of which the following is a list :—

Great Organ, Compass CC to A, 58 *notes.*

1. Sub Open Diapason	......	16 feet.	4. Principal	....	4 feet.
2. Open Diapason	....	8 feet.	5. Mixture (12th and 15th)		3 and 2 feet.
3. Clarabella (open throughout)	....	8 feet.	6. Sesquialtera, III and IV ranks	....	Various.

Solo Great Organ, Compass CC to A, 58 notes.

7.	Bell Diapason (grooved in No. 8)	8 feet.	10. Wald Flute.................	4 feet.
8.	Harmonic Flute	8 feet.	11. Harmonic Piccolo	2 feet.
9.	Geigen Principal...........	4 feet.	12. Trumpet	8 feet.
			13. Clarion	4 feet.

The Solo organ is on the same Manual as the Great organ, but is on a higher pressure of wind. The same pneumatic pallet acts on both, by means of a novel mechanical arrangement.

Swell Organ, CC to A, 58 notes.

14.	Lieblich Bourdon	16 feet.	20. Fifteenth.....................	2 feet.
15.	Open Diapason	8 feet.	21. Mixture, III ranks........	Various.
16.	Salicional (grooved into No. 15)	8 feet.	22. Contra-fagotto	16 feet.
17.	Clarinet Flute	8 feet.	23. Cornopean	8 feet.
18.	Principal	4 feet.	24. Hautboy	8 feet.
19.	Lieblich Flute	4 feet	25. Vox Humana	8 feet.

Choir Organ, CC to A, 58 notes.

26.	Dulciana	8 feet.	31. Flageolet	2 feet.
27.	Keraulophon	8 feet.	32. Orchestral Oboe, C	8 feet.
28.	Suabe Flute.................	8 feet.	33. Cremona } .... 8 feet.	
29.	Salicet	4 feet.	34. Bassoon Bass }	
30.	Hohl Flute	4 feet.		

Pedal Organ, CCC to F, 30 notes.

35.	Grand Open Diapason,, metal	16 feet.	37. Grand Bourdon	16 feet.
36.	Grand Open Diapason, wood......................	16 feet.	38. Grand Principal...........	8 feet.
			39. Grand Fifteenth...........	4 feet.
			40. Grand Bombarde	16 feet.

Couplers, &c.

1. Swell to Great.	5. Choir to Great.
2. Swell to Pedals.	6. Great to Pedal.
3. Swell to Choir.	7. Tremulant to Swell.
4. Choir to Pedals.	8. Sforzando.

49 to 57. Composition Pedals.

Four pairs of bellows with pressures of wind varying from 2½ to 5 inches.

C. K. K. Bishop's Patent Simplified Pneumatic Actions applied to the Great and Swell Manuals.

The interior metal pipes are of " Spotted Metal," except the Keraulophon, which contains a still higher percentage of tin.

The exterior metal pipes are of zinc, which metal will better sustain the shaking it will experience in its long voyage. The wood pipes are all of Mahogany.

The rest of the wood-work is of Mahogany, Oak, and Cedar, and is varnished throughout, to protect it from the effects of changes of climate.

The rollers are of tubular iron, the squares of gilded brass, and the wire-work of a metal made expressly for this organ instead of the usual tinned iron wire, which speedily rusts in India.

The bellows are provided with Messrs. Bishop and Starr's "Unalterable Pallet" for extreme climates, and all the leather-work is poisoned to protect it from· the attacks of white ants.

152. TREMONT TEMPLE, BOSTON.

The following is an account of the large organ built by Messrs. E. an G. Hook for the Tremont Temple, United States, which is reprinted from the description circulated by the builders at the time of the opening of the instrument in 1854. The Swell is throughout, and there is an independent Pedal organ. Wind is supplied by three bellows at different pressures. It contains 70 registers, comprising every variety of tone, and embracing all the novelties of the most celebrated European organs.

It occupies a space at the end of the hall, 50 feet high and 50 feet wide, and is concealed by an open-work screen. The following are the stops in this instrument :—

Great, 15 *Stops; Compass, CC to A in alt.,* 58 *Notes.*

1. Tenoroon, Open Diapason.	9. Grand Fifteenth.
2. Grand Open Diapason.	10. Fifteenth.
3. Open Diapason.	11. Sesquialtera, II ranks.
4. Melodia.	12. Mixture, III ranks.
5. Stopped Diapason.	13. Furniture, IV ranks.
6. Grand Principal.	14. Trumpet.
7. Principal.	15. Clarion.
8. Twelfth.	

Choir, 10 *Stops; Compass, CC to A in alt.,* 58 *Notes.*

16. Open Diapason.	21. Mixture, III ranks.
17. Dulciana.	22. Hohl Flute.
18. Stopped Diapason.	23. Viol d'Amour.
19. Principal.	24. Clarionet.
20. Fifteenth.	25. Bassoon.

Swell, 15 *Stops; Compass, CC to A in alt.,* 58 *Notes.*

26. Sub-bass.	34. Fifteenth.
27. Double Diapason.	35. Sesquialtera, III ranks.
28. Open Diapason.	36. Trumpet, Bass.
29. Viol di Gamba.	37. Trumpet, Treble.
30. Stopped Diapason.	38. Hautboy.
31. Principal.	39. Clarion.
32. Night Horn.	40. Double Trumpet.
33. Twelfth.	

Solo, 6 *Stops; Compass, CC to A in alt.,* 58 *Notes.*

41. Horn Diapason.	44. Wald Flute.
42. Gamba.	45. Piccolo.
43. Clarabella.	46. Trumpet.

Pedal, 10 *Stops; Compass, CCC to D,* 27 *Notes.*

47. Double Diapason .... 32 feet.	52. Violoncello .... 8 feet.
48. Bourdon .... 16 feet.	53. Quint .... 6 feet.
49. Open Diapason, wood ... 16 feet.	54. Principal .... 4 feet.
50. Open Diapason, metal...... 16 feet.	55. Trombone.................... 8 feet.
51. Open Diapason.............. 8 feet.	56. Posaune .... 16 feet.

Accessory Stops, Movements, &c.

1. Swell to Great, Unison.	8. Great to Pedals.
2. Swell to Great, Super-octave.	9. Choir to Pedals.
3. Choir to Great, Sub-octave.	10. Pedal Octaves.
4. Swell to Choir, Unison.	11. Pedal Bourdon, Separation.
5. Swell to Solo, Unison.	12. Pedal Open Diapason, Separation
6. Solo to Great, Unison.	13. Solo Organ Signal.
7. Swell to Pedals.	14. Bellows Signal.

153. MUSIC HALL, BOSTON.

The grand organ in the Music Hall, Boston, United States (described as the "Great Monster Organ of the New World"), was built by E. F. Walcker and Son, of Ludwigsburg, Wurtemberg. It was begun in 1857, and finished in 1863.

Some of the most important stops are the Bifra, in the Choir, with its double set of pipes and Tremolo ; the Physharmonica, in the Choir, a free Reed without pipes, with a Swell of its own ; the great Mixture of 5 ranks in the Pedal, which gives a ground tone of 32 feet in Harmonics, Sub-bass 16 feet, Quint 10⅔ feet, Octave 8 feet, Tenth 5⅓ feet, and Fifteenth 4 feet ; and a Vox Humana in the Solo, with double pipes, Swell, and Tremulant of its own.

There are six pairs of large bellows-feeders, which gather the wind into a huge reservoir containing about 400 cubic feet. There are several smaller ones, distributors, making in all fifteen pairs of bellows. These are worked by a machine, which is propelled by water derived from the reservoirs. The case, or *orgel-gehause*, is of black walnut, and is covered with carved statues, busts, masks, and figures in bold relief. It is about 47 feet in width ; the two projecting central towers are 60 feet high.

The following is a synopsis of the contents of this organ :—

Great, 25 Stops.

1. Principal, or Double Diapason .... 16 feet.
   Of pure English tin ; the 24 largest pipes displayed in front.
2. Tibia Major .... 16 feet.
   Of pine wood ; borrows the lower octave from Principal.
3. Viola Major .... 16 feet.
4. Basson (Bassoon) } .... 16 feet.
5. Ophicleid .... } .... 8 feet.
   Complements to each other. Free Reeds, tuned by a screw. Chiefly of wood, but bells of upper octaves tin.
6. Principal (Diapason) ...... 8 feet.
7. Flote (Flute).................. 8 feet.
   Wood, double width, with double mouths.
8. Gemshorn..................... 8 feet.
9. Viola di Gamba, pure tin 8 feet.
10. Gedackt (Stop Diapason) 8 feet.
11. Trombone..................... 8 feet.
12. Trumpet, of proof tin ...... 8 feet.
13. Octave (Engl. Principal), pure tin.
14. Fugara, pure tin .... 8 feet.
15. Hohlflote (hollow-toned flute), metal .... 4 feet.

16. Flute d'Amour, of pine and pear-wood, slender 4 feet.
17. Clairon (Clarion) .... 4 feet.
    Reed stop, of proof tin, trumpet-like ; in the highest octave 2 open flue pipes in unison replace the Reeds.
18. Waldflote (Flute of the Woods), proof tin ...... 2 feet.
19. Quint (Fifth), proof tin .... 5⅓ feet.
20. Terz (Tenth), proof tin ... 3⅕ feet.
21. Quintflote (Flute Twelfth), proof tin .... 2⅔ feet.
22. Terz Discant (Seventeenth), proof tin...... 1⅗ foot.
23. Cornet, V ranks............ 5⅓ feet.
    Harmonics of 16 feet tone ; take their ground tones from Quint. Compass from G to A 3, 38 notes.
24. Mixtur, VI ranks .... 2⅔ feet.
    Harmonics of 8 feet tone. Proof tin.
25. Scharff, IV ranks .... 1⅓ foot.
    Harmonics of 4 feet tone. Proof tin.

Choir, 15 Stops.

26. Gedackt ... . 16 feet.
27. Principal Flute.............. 8 feet.
    Pure English tin ; larger pipes displayed.
28. Spitzflote .... 8 feet.
    A pointed or conical flute of tin.
29. Bifra, II ranks .... 8 & 4 feet.
    Of tin ; each note has 2 pipes, one stopped, the other (its octave) open and slender. It has also a Tremolo.
30. Gedackt, wood.............. 8 feet.
31. Clarin Bass .... 4 feet.
32. Clarin Discant .... 4 feet.
    Reeds, trum et-like, of proof tin.

33. Viola, proof tin .... 8 feet.
    Of soft intonation, like the piano in Physharmonica.
34. Physharmonica .. .. 8 feet.
    Purely metal Reeds with a Swell.
35. Hohlpfeife .... 4 feet.
    Lowest octaves of maple, the rest of metal. Very bright and liquid flute tone.
36. Principal Flute, tin ...... 4 feet.
37. Dolce (Dulciana), tin...... 4 feet.
38. Flautino (Octave Flute)... 2 feet.
39. Sesquialtera, II ranks ... 2⅔ & 1⅗ feet.
40. Super-octave, tin .... 1 foot.

Swell, 18 *Stops.*

41. Bourdon (Double Stop Diapason)........................ 16 feet.
42. Principal, proof tin .... 8 feet.
43. Salicional .... 8 feet.
   Proof tin, slender. Tone like a Dulciana of reedy quality, but a little stronger.
44. Dolce (Dulciana) .... 8 feet.
   Of metal; one of the softest stops.
45. Quintaton .... 8 feet.
   A stop pipe of tin, sounding its Harmonic Fifth (or Twelfth) with the ground tone.
46. Gedackt (Stop Diapason) 8 feet.
   Wood, double width; double mouths in upper octaves. Very full round tone, with other stops.
47. Trombone Bass (Trombone) 8 feet.
48. Trombone Disct. (Trumpet), bells of brass ...... 8 feet.
49. Bassoon Bass (Bassoon) ... 8 feet.
50. Hautbois (Oboe)............ 8 feet.
51. Principal Octave, proof tin 4 feet.
52. Rohrflote .... 4 feet.
   What English builders call a "half-stopped pipe," of metal. French: *Flute-à-Cheminée.*
53. Traversflote (Traverse Flute) .... 4 feet.
   The lowest octaves of fir and pear-wood, square, slender. The rest of maple, turned, like the actual German flute; double length, pierced in the middle; and overblown, *i.e.*, sounding the octave.
54. Cornettino .... 4 feet.
   Soft, trumpet-like, of tin, 12 highest pipes doubled, and flue pipes.
55. Quintflote .... 5⅓ feet.
56. Nasard (Twelfth), tin .. 2⅔ feet.
57. Octave, tin .... 2 feet.
58. Mixtur, V ranks............ 2 feet.

Solo, 11 *Stops.*

59. Bourdon (Stopped Diapason)........................ 16 feet.
   Two lowest octaves of wood, the rest of metal.
60. Gamben Principal, pure tin 8 feet.
61. Æoline .... 8 feet.
   The softest and most string-like stop of all; lower octave of wood, continuation, of proof tin, very slender.
62. Concert Flute .... 8 feet.
   Of finest pine-wood, square. From C upward double length, pierced, and blowing the octave.
63. Corno Basetto .... 8 feet.
   Reed stop of clarionet-like tone; bells of tin.
64. Vox Humana .... 8 feet.
   Of metal, with two pipes to each note, one of them a Reed pipe, and partly with double reeds. Also has a special Swell and Tremulant.
65. Gemshorn, proof tin ...... 4 feet.
66. Piffaro, II ranks............ 4 & 2 feet.
67. Vox Angelica .... 4 feet.
   A delicate Reed stop.
68. Quint .... 2⅔ feet.
   A covered pipe of metal.
69. Piccolo (Octave Flute), metal....................... 2 feet.

Pedal, 20 *Stops.*

70. Principal Bass (Double Double Diapason)........ 32 feet.
   Six of the largest pipes of pure English tin, the rest of wood.
71. Grand Bourdon, V ranks... 32 feet.
   A compound stop, having for foundation Sub-bass 16 feet, which, with four ranks of Harmonic tones, gives the 32 feet sound.
72. Bombardon .... 32 feet.
   A monster Reed tone, with screw tuning apparatus.
73. Octave Bass .... 16 feet.
   Pure tin; 13 pipes in front.
74. Sub-bass .... 16 feet.
   Strong wood, open, of very wide scale.
75. Trombone...................... 16 feet.
   Powerful Reed tone; bells of zinc.
76. Contra Violon, wood ...... 16 feet.
77. Octave Bass, tin............ 8 feet.
78. Hohlfloten Bass (Hollow Flute Bass) .... 8 feet.
79. Violoncello, tin .... 8 feet.
80. Trumpet .... 8 feet.
81. Corno-Basso .... 4 feet.
82. Octave, tin .... 4 feet.
83. Cornettino, tin .... 2 feet.
   N.B.—The following stops are placed in the Swell-box.
84. Bourdon (Double Stopped Diapason)................... 16 feet.
85. Viola .... 8 feet.
   Of tin; soft Gamba tone.
86. Flute, wood.................. 8 feet.
87. Flute .... 4 feet.
88. Basson (Bassoon) .... 16 feet.
   A very powerful deep Reed tone, tuned with screw.
89. Waldflote, metal .... 2 feet.

There are 12 Pedal combination movements for producing various changes and connections.

1. Zungen Stimmen, draws all the Reeds of the Great organ.
2. Fortissimo Hauptwerk, draws all the Great organ except Scharff, Cornet, and Reeds.
3. Forte Hauptwerk, draws one 16 feet, five 8 feet, and four 4 feet stops of the Great organ.
4. Piano Hauptwerk, draws the 8 feet stops of the Great organ.
5. Solo Orgel, draws Corno and Bassetto of Solo organ.
6. Volleswerk, draws Full organ.
7 to 12. Pedal Couplers.

There is, situated over the Manuals of the Great organ, within the reach of the thumbs of the performer, a set of small knobs—couplers—which control the couplings of the several Manuals. One of the most important mechanical contrivances is the crescendo and diminuendo Pedal, by which the performer is enabled to bring out, one by one, *ad. lib.*, each stop of the organ to its fullest capacity, and *vice versâ*.

Over the Manuals, on a tablet of black marble, in letters of gold is this inscription :—

E. F. WALCKER & CO.

LUDWIGSBURG, KDM. WURTEMBERG

O. P. C. C.

BEGUN, FEB. 1857. FINSHED, OCT. 1863.

154. NEW YORK.

The new organ in Trinity Church, New York, was built by Mr. Henry Erben in 1846, from a specification prepared by Dr. Hodges, and has recently been enlarged by the same firm. It has now 39 sounding stops and 11 Couplers ; 3 Manual organs, of 16, 8, and 4 feet compass respectively ; a Swell Bass of 2 stops, and a 32-feet Pedal stop. The instrument, which stands at the west end of the church, is enclosed in a bold Gothic case, designed by Richard Upjohn, Esq., the architect of the church. The Choir organ is in front, and has an 8-feet speaking front ; while the Great organ has a 16-feet speaking front. All the Manuals descend to CCC, 16 feet ; and the Swell ascends an extra octave also. The following is a list of the stops in the above-named instrument :—

Great Organ.

1. Strong Open Diapason.
2. Clear Open Diapason.
3. Stopped Diapason.
4. Strong Principal.
5. Bright Principal.
6. Flute.
7. Double Octave.
8. Twelfth.
9. Sesquialtera.
10. Mixture.
11. Trumpet.
12. Clarion.

Choir Organ.

13. Stopped Diapason.
14. Dulciana.
15. Principal.
16. Flute.
17. Fifteenth.
18. Clarionet.
19. Bassoon.

Swell Organ.

20. Double Diapason.
21. Open Diapason.
22. Dulciana.
23. Stopped Diapason.
24. Principal.
25. Cornet.
26. Hautboy.
27. Trumpet.
28. Vox Humana.

Swell Bass.

29. Dulciana. | 30. Serpent.

Solo Organ.

31. Double Diapason.
32. Horn Diapason.
33. Gamba.
34. Melodia.

35. Harmonic Flute.
36. Tuba Mirabilis.
37. Cornopean.

Pedal Organ.

38. Grand Double Open Diapason. | 39. Grand Open Diapason.

Couplers.

1. Swell to Great.
2. Swell and Great at octaves.
3. Swell to Choir.
4. Choir to Great.
5. Choir and Swell at octaves.
6. Great to Pedal, 16 feet pitch.

7. Great to Pedal, 8 feet pitch.
8. Choir to Pedal.
9. Swell Bass to Pedal.
10. Pedal pipes in 32 feet pitch.
11. Pedal pipes in 16 feet pitch.

Compass.

Great, CCC to f³ in alt., 66 keys. 16 feet compass.
Choir, CC to f³ in alt., 54 keys, 8 feet compass.
Swell, tenor c to f¹ in alt., 54 keys, 4 feet compass.
Swell Bass, two octaves.
Pedal Stop, CCCC to tenor c, 37 pipes, 32 feet compass.
Pedal Clavier, CCC to tenor c, 25 keys.

155. NEW YORK.

The organ in the Church of the Annunciation, New York, United States, was built by George Jardine, of New York, in 1853. It contains 3 Manual organs, of 8 feet compass, and a separate Pedal, and also 30 sounding stops. The following is a list of its contents :—

Great, 9 Stops.

1. Double Diapason .... 16 feet.
2. Open Diapason .... 8 feet.
3. Stopped Diapason .... 8 feet tone.
4. Melodia .... 8 feet.
5. Principal .... 4 feet.

6. Twelfth .... 2⅔ feet.
7. Fifteenth .... 2 feet.
8. Sesquialtera, IV ranks.
9. Trumpet .... 8 feet.

Choir, 8 Stops.

10. Open Diapason .... 8 feet.
11. Viola di Gamba .... 8 feet.
12. Stopped Diapason .... 8 feet tone.
13. Principal .... 4 feet.

14. Flute .... 4 feet tone.
15. Fifteenth .... 2 feet.
16. Clarinet, Treble .... 8 feet tone.
17. Bassoon, Bass.............. 8 feet.

Swell, 10 Stops.

18. Bourdon .... 16 feet tone.
19. Open Diapason .... 8 feet.
20. Stopped Diapason .... 8 feet tone.
21. Dulciana .... 8 feet.
22. Principal .... 4 feet.

23. Fifteenth .... 2 feet.
24. Mixture, III ranks.
25. Trumpet .... 8 feet.
26. Oboe .... 8 feet.
27. Clarion .... 4 feet.

R R

Pedal, 3 Stops.

28. Open Diapason .... 16 feet.	30. Octave .... 8 feet.
29. Bourdon .... 16 feet tone.	

Couplers.

1. Swell to Great.	6. Great to Pedal.
2. Swell Octave to Great.	7. Choir to Pedal.
3. Swell to Choir.	8. Swell to Pedal.
4. Choir to Great.	9. Pedal Organ Octave.
5. Choir Sub-octave to Great.	

Compass.

Great, CC to f³ in alt.	Swell, CC to f³ in alt.
Choir, CC to f³ in alt.	Pedal, CCC to tenor c.

By means of Mr. G. Jardine's pallet the touch is relieved from all disagreeable stiffness, although there are 5 Manual Couplers, upwards and downwards, as well as in the unison.

156. NEW YORK.—BROOKLYN TABERNACLE.

This admirable organ was built by Messrs. Jardine and Son, and consists of (1) Great Organ, divided into three compartments, namely, Diapason Organ, Chorus Organ, and Solo Organ, controlled by eight piston combination knobs ; (2) a Swell Organ ; (3) an Orchestral Organ ; and (4) a separate Pedal Organ. The dimensions of the organ are 50 feet wide, 14 feet deep, and 50 feet high. The bellows are supplied by three hydraulic engines. There are altogether fifty-two registers, of which the following are the details :—

Great Organ.

1. Double Open Diapason, metal, deep tone .... 16 feet.	4. Doppel Diapason, wood, very full and pervading 8 feet.
2. Open Diapason Major, metal, full sonorous ...... 8 feet.	5. Melody Diapason, wood, clear and ringing ...... 8 feet.
3. Open Diapason minor, metal, clear and round 8 feet.	

Chorus Organ.

6. Quint, metal, harmonic intonation .... 6 feet.	10. R. Cymbal, metal, consisting of the 17th and 19th tones above the Diapasons............... ..
7. Principal, metal, round yet clear tone .... 4 feet.	11. R. Sesquialtera, metal, 15th, 22nd, and 29th tones, and breaking into 8th, 12th, and 15th tone 2 feet.
8. Nasard, metal, round and subdued tone .... 3 feet.	
9. Piccolo, metal, round and brilliant . ... 2 feet.	

Solo Organ.

12. Gamba, metal, crisp, light tone .... 8 feet.
13. Dulcissima, metal, sweet, singing tone .... 8 feet.

14. Harmonic, pure and imitative .... 4 feet.
15. Clarionet, very orchestral 4 feet.
16. Trumpet, round and mellow 8 feet.
17. Quint ....

Second Manual, or Swell.

18. Bourdon, wood and metal, deep, pervading tone ... 16 feet.
19. Open Diapason, metal, very full........................... 8 feet.
20. Clariona, metal, reedy, clear 8 feet.
21. Clarionet Flute, wood and metal, round and pure 8 feet.
22. Dulciana, metal, very delicate .... 8 feet.
23. Violono, metal, brilliant tone 4 feet.
24. Piccolo, metal, brilliant tone .... 2 feet.

25. R. Cornet, metal, very rich 3 or 4 feet.
26. Cornopean, metal, new scale, very round and mellow .... 8 feet.
27. Oboe with Bassoon, imported reeds, new scale 8 feet.
28. Vox Humana, metal, imported reeds, this new score from Cavaille of Paris .... 8 feet.
29. Echo Flute, distant, soft tone .... 4 feet.

Third Manual, Orchestral Organ.

30. Song Trumpet, metal ...... 8 feet.
31. Concert Flute, wood, a stop of immense power ...... 8 feet.

32. Horn, metal, clear and ringing .... 8 feet.
33. Flute à Pavillon, sparkling tone .... 4 feet.

Pedal Organ.

34. Open Diapason, powerful and deep .... 16 feet.
35. Violin, metal, rich, deep tone 16 feet.
36. Contra-Bourdon, pervading, full..................... 16 feet.
37. Gross-Quint, wood producing 32 feet effect ... 12 feet.

38. Violoncello, stringy and imitative .... 8 feet.
39. Flute, metal, round and orchestral .... 4 feet.
40. Trombone, metal, pure and broad tone .... 16 feet.

Pneumatic Piston Knobs.

1. Open Diapason major, mezzo power.
2. Gamba, piano power.
3. Dulcissima, pianissimo power.
4. Harmonic Flute, mezzo power.

5. Diapason Organ, forte power.
6. Solo Organ, fortissimo power.
7. Solo and Diapason Organ, FF.
8. Diapason, Solo, and Chorus Organ.

Bells.

1. 8 feet. 2½ octaves of real Bells, operated by the Swell or Great Organ keyboards; they are struck with a piano action, are imported by the maker, 32 Bells.
2. 8 feet. Sharp effect on Bells.

Couplers.

1. Swell Manual to Great Organ.
2. Orchestral to Great Manual.

3. Bellows.

These Couplers, made on an improved system, are free from friction.

Pedals of Combinations.

1. Great Manual to Pedal. | 2. Orchestral to Pedal.
                                  3. Swell Manual to Pedal.

1. The Sforzando Pedal is a new effect introduced, by which, in a moment, from the softest effect the full power of the organ can be thrown on.
2. Balance Swell Pedal with vertical shades, introduced from Europe.

Summary.

Great Organ Manual—

Sub-divisions.	Diapason Organ	5 registers.
	Chorus Organ	6 registers.
	Solo Organ	5 registers.
	Piston Combination..	8 registers.
Swell Organ (Manual)		12 registers.
Orchestral Organ (Manual)		4 registers.
Bells, 32		2 registers.
Couplers		3 registers.
Pedals of Combination, 5..		

Total : 32 Bells ; 5 Pedals ; 52 Registers.

157. Trinity Chapel, New York.

The organ in Trinity Chapel was built by Messrs. J. H. & C. S. Odell from a specification prepared by Mr. W. B. Gilbert. It contains the 33 sounding stops, &c., mentioned below :—

Great Organ.

1. Contra Gamba, ... 16 feet.	6. Twelfth .... 3 feet.
2. Stopped Diapason .... 8 feet.	7. Fifteenth..................... 2 feet.
3. Open Diapason .... 8 feet.	8. Sesquialtera, IV ranks, pure tin,
4. Gamba .... 4 feet.	9. Trumpet, pure tin .... 8 feet.
5. Principal .... 4 feet.	10. Clarion ,, ... 4 feet.

Swell Organ.

11. Bourdon .... 16 feet tone.	17. Principal..................... 4 feet.
12. Stopped Diapason .... 8 feet.	18. Mixture, IV ranks.
13. Dulciana .... 8 feet.	19. Oboe .... 8 feet.
14. Salicional .... 8 feet.	20. Cornopean .... 8 feet.
15. Open Diapason .... 8 feet.	21. Contra Trumpet............ 16 feet.
16. Dulcet Flute.................. 4 feet.	

Choir Organ.

22. Melodia........................ 8 feet.	25. Concert Flute............... 4 feet.
23. Dolce............................ 8 feet.	26. Principal .... 4 feet.
24. Keraulophon .... 8 feet.	27. Clarionette .... 8 feet.

Pedal Organ.

28. Sub-Bourdon .... 32 feet tone.	31. Open Diapason .... 16 feet.
29. Bourdon .... 16 feet.	32. Violoncello .... 8 feet.
30. Bell Gamba .... 16 feet.	33. Trombone .... 16 feet.

Couplers, &c.

1. Swell to Great.	4. Great to Pedal.
2. Swell to Choir.	5. Swell to Pedal.
3. Choir to Pedal.	6. Signal to blowers.

Composition Pedals.

Three double action on Great Organ. | Two double action on Swell Organ.

Compass.

Manuals, CC to a³, 58 notes.   Pedal, CCC to e, 29 notes.

158. CALIFORNIA.

The organ in the Presbyterian Church, Oakland, San Francisco, built by Messrs. Bevington and Son, has two Manuals, separate Pedal, and 24 sounding stops of which latter the following is a list :—

Great Organ.

1.	Open Diapason	8 feet.	6.	Fifteenth	2 feet.
2.	Dulciana	8 feet.	7.	Full Mixture, III ranks...	3 feet.
3.	Claribel	8 feet.	8.	Clarionet	8 feet.
4.	Flute Harmonique	4 feet.	9.	Bassoon	
5.	Principal	4 feet.	10.	Trumpet	8 feet.

Swell Organ.

11.	Bourdon	16 feet.	17.	Principal	4 feet.
12.	Double Diapason	16 feet.	18.	Twelfth	3 feet.
13.	Open Diapason	8 feet.	19.	Fifteenth	2 feet.
14.	Lieblich Gedact	8 feet.	20.	Cornopean	8 feet.
15.	Bell Gamba	8 feet.	21.	Oboe	8 feet.
16.	Wald Flute	4 feet.			

Pedal Organ.

22.	Great Open Diapason, wood	16 feet.	24.	Bourdon	16 feet.
23.	Great Open Diapason, metal	16 feet.			

Couplers, &c.

Swell to Great.	Great to Pedal.
Swell to Pedal.	Tremulant to Swell by Pedal.
Swell Sub-Octave to Great.	Three Composition Pedals to Great.
Swell Octave to Great.	Three Composition Pedals to Swell.

Compass.

Manuals, CC to g³, 56 notes. | Pedal, CCC to F, 30 notes.

159. ST. JOHN'S CATHEDRAL, NEWFOUNDLAND.

The organ in St. John's Cathedral, Newfoundland, was built by Robson in 1853.   It contains 46 sounding stops, as follows :—

Great Organ, 16 Stops ; Compass, CC to G in alt., 56 Notes.

1.	Double Diapason, Bass Double Diapason	16 feet tone.	8.	Twelfth	3 feet.
			9.	Fifteenth	2 feet.
2.	Large Open Diapason	8 feet.	10.	Sesquialtera, III ranks.	
3.	Open Diapason	8 feet.	11.	Mixture, III ranks.	
4.	Stopped Diapason	8 feet tone.	12.	Furniture, III ranks.	
5.	Quint	6 feet.	13.	Contra Fagotto	16 feet.
6.	Principal	4 feet.	14.	Posaune	8 feet.
7.	Tenth	3⅕ feet.	15.	Clarion	4 feet.

Choir Organ, 11 *Stops; Compass, CC to G in alt., 56 Notes.*

16. Dulciana	8 feet.	
17. Viol di Gamba..............	8 feet.	
18. Stopped Diapason	8 feet tone.	
19. Clarabella Flute	8 feet.	
20. Celestina Viol	4 feet.	
21. Principal	4 feet.	
22. Flute	4 feet.	
23. Piccolo.......................	2 feet.	
24. Mixture, Dulciana Scale, III ranks.		
25. Bassoon } Clarionet }	.... 8 feet tone.	

Swell Organ, 13 *Stops; Compass, CC to G in alt., 56 Notes.*

26. Double Diapason, Bass } Double Diapason :........ }	16 feet tone.
27. Open Diapason	8 feet.
28. Stopped Diapason	8 feet tone.
29. Principal	4 feet.
30. Twelfth	3 feet.
31. Fifteenth	2 feet.
32. Sesquialtera } Mixture ... } V ranks.	
33. Horn...........................	8 feet.
34. Oboe	8 feet.
35. Clarion	4 feet.
36. Octave Clarion..............	2 feet.

Pedal Organ, 6 *Stops; Compass, CCC to F, 30 Notes.*

37. Open Diapason...............	16 feet.
38. Stopped Diapason	16 feet tone.
39. Principal	8 feet.
40. Basso-flauto	8 feet tone.
41. Trombone.....................	16 feet.
42. Trumpet	8 feet.

Couplers.

1. Swell to Great.	3. Great to Pedals.
2. Ditto to Pedals.	4. Choir to ditto.

160. ST. PAUL, WELLINGTON, NEW ZEALAND.

This organ, comprising two complete Manuals and separate Pedal, was built by Mr. T. C. Lewis, and contains the following 17 sounding stops :—

Great Organ, CC to G, 56 *notes.*

1. Lieblich Gedact	16 feet.
2. Open Diapason	8 feet.
3. Lieblich Gedact	8 feet.
4. Salicional (tenor c, grooved for bass)	8 feet.
5. Octave	4 feet.
6. Flute	4 feet.
7. Mixture, III ranks.........	2 feet.

Swell Organ, CC to G, 56 *notes.*

8. Rohrflote	8 feet.
9. Geigen Principal	8 feet.
10. Viol di Gamba	8 feet.
11. Voix Céleste...................	8 feet.
12. Geigen Principal............	4 feet.
13. Flautina	2 feet.
14. Horn	8 feet.
15. Oboe and Bassoon	8 feet.

Pedal Organ, CCC to F, 30 *notes.*

16. Open Bass....................	16 feet.
17. Sub-Bass	16 feet.

Couplers.

Great to Pedals.	Swell to Pedals.	Swell to Great.

Three Pedals of Combination.

161. MELBOURNE, AUSTRALIA.

Description of the new organ for the Town Hall, Melbourne, Australia, by Messrs. William Hill and Son. Compass of each Manual, CC to C, 61 notes :—

Great Organ.

1. Double Open Diapason ...	16 feet.	
2. Bourdon	16 feet.	
3. Open Diapason	8 feet.	
4. Open Diapason	8 feet.	
5. Gamba	8 feet.	
6. Stopped Diapason	8 feet.	
7. Principal	4 feet.	
8. Principal	4 feet.	
9. Harmonic Flute	4 feet.	
10. Twelfth	3 feet.	
11. Fifteenth	2 feet.	
12. Mixture, IV ranks.		
13. Mixture, III ranks.		
14. Double Trumpet	16 feet.	
15. Posaune	8 feet.	
16. Trumpet	8 feet.	
17. Clarion	4 feet.	

Choir Organ.

18. Bourdon	16 feet.	
19. Salicional	8 feet.	
20. Dulcian	8 feet.	
21. Gedact (metal treble)	8 feet.	
22. Gamba	4 feet.	
23. Principal	4 feet.	
24. Gemshorn Twelfth	3 feet.	
25. Gemshorn Harmonic	2 feet.	
26. Dulcian Mixture, II ranks.		
27. Clarionet	8 feet.	

Swell Organ.

28. Bourdon	16 feet.	
29. Open Diapason	8 feet.	
30. Cone Gamba	8 feet.	
31. Pierced Gamba	8 feet.	
32. Stopped Diapason (metal treble)	8 feet.	
33. Principal	4 feet.	
34. Suabe Flute	4 feet.	
35. Twelfth	3 feet.	
36. Fifteenth	2 feet.	
37. Mixture, IV ranks.		
38. Double Trumpet	16 feet.	
39. Cornopean	8 feet.	
40. Oboe	8 feet.	
41. Clarion	4 feet.	

Solo Organ.

42. Lieblich Bourdon, tenor c	16 feet.	
43. Harmonic Flute, wood bass	8 feet.	
44. Vox Angelica, Tenor c, II ranks	8 feet.	
45. Flute Octaviante	4 feet.	
46. Piccolo	2 feet.	
47. Glockenspiel, tenor c, II ranks.		
48. Bassoon, tenor C	16 feet.	
49. Clarionet	8 feet.	
50. Orchestral Oboe, tenor c	8 feet.	
51. Vox Humana	8 feet.	
52. Oboe Clarion	4 feet.	
53. Tuba Mirabilis	8 feet.	
54. Tuba Mirabilis	4 feet.	

Pedal Organ, Compass CCC to F, 30 notes.

55. Double Open Diapason, metal	32 feet.	
56. Open Diapason, metal	16 feet.	
57. Open Diapason, wood	16 feet.	
58. Bourdon	16 feet.	
59. Quint	12 feet.	
60. Principal	8 feet.	
61. Violon	8 feet.	
62. Twelfth	6 feet.	
63. Fifteenth	4 feet.	
64. Mixture, III ranks.		
65. Trombone	16 feet.	
66. Clarion	8 feet.	

Couplers, &c.

Swell to Great.	Choir to Great (Sub-Octave).	Choir to Pedal.
Swell to Great (Sub-Octave).	Solo to Great.	Great to Pedal.
Swell to Choir.	Solo to Pedal.	Swell to Pedal.

4 Composition Pedals to Great, 3 do. to Swell, 2 do. to Choir, and 4 Combination stops (by hand) to Solo Organ. Solo Tremulant. Total, 79 stops, and 4373 pipes.

162. ADELAIDE.

Description of the organ for the Town Hall, Adelaide, Australia, built by Hill and Son in 1876. Three Manuals, compass of each, CC to A, 58 notes, and Pedal Clavier, CCC to F, 30 notes.

Great Organ.

1. Double Diapason, wood ...	16 feet.	7. Twelfth, metal .... 3 feet.
2. Open Diapason, metal ...	8 feet.	8. Fifteenth, metal .... 2 feet.
3. Open Diapason, No. 2, metal	8 feet.	9. Full Mixture, metal, III ranks.
4. Stopped Diapason, wood..	8 feet.	10. Sharp Mixture, metal, II ranks.
5. Principal, metal ...	4 feet.	11. Posaune, metal .... 8 feet.
6. Harmonic Flute, ,, ...	4 feet.	12. Clarion, ,, ... 8 feet.

Choir Organ.

13. Cone Gamba, metal...	8 feet.	17. Gemshorn, metal... 4 feet.
14. Dulciana (C grooved) ,, ...	8 feet.	18. Lieblich Flute, ,, ... 4 feet.
15. Voix Celeste (tenor c) ,, ...	8 feet.	19. Flageolet, ,, ... 2 feet.
16. Lieblich Gedact, wood ...	8 feet.	20. Clarionet, tenor c, ,, ... 8 feet.

Swell Organ.

21. Lieblich Bourdon, wood...	16 feet.	27. Fifteenth, metal............ 2 feet.
22. Open Diapason, metal......	8 feet.	28. Mixture, metal, III ranks.
23. Pierced Gamba (C grooved) metal........................	8 feet.	29. Double Trumpet, metal ... 16 feet.
24. Hohl Flute, wood	8 feet.	30. Cornopean, ,, ... 8 feet.
25. Principal, metal	4 feet.	31. Oboe, ,, ... 8 feet.
26. Rohr Flute, ,, ...	4 feet.	32. Clarion, ,, ... 8 feet.

Pedal Organ.

33. Double Open Diapason, wood	32 feet.	36. Violoncello, wood .... 8 feet.
34. Open Diapason, wood	16 feet.	37. Trombone, wood .... 16 feet.
35. Bourdon, wood	16 feet.	

Couplers.

1. Swell to Great.	5. Choir to Pedal.
2. Swell to Sub-Octave.	6. Great to Pedal.
3. Swell to Octave.	7. Swell to Pedal.
4. Swell to Choir.	

Four Composition Pedals to Great Organ. | Three Composition Pedals to Swell Organ.
Pneumatic action to Great and Couplers.

BRITISH ORGANS.

LONDON AND ITS ENVIRONS.

163. St. Paul's Cathedral.

The organ built by Father Smith for this Cathedral in 1697 consisted of a "Great and Choir organ," with probably a small Echo. The Great extended down to CCC (16 feet), without the CCC♯; while the Choir ranged to FFF, BB♭ being the first semitone. Towards the latter part of the last century a Swell of 7 stops was added by Crang; and at the commencement of the present century the pitch of the whole organ, which had previously been very high, was lowered a semitone, an entirely new series of pipes being introduced for the lowest key. Subsequently "new trebles" were put to the Chorus stops, and after that entire new stops were substituted for some of the old ones, until at length very little of the original organ remained. In 1874 an almost entirely new organ was supplied by Mr. Henry Willis, who divided the fine old case into two parts, repairing and preserving the two original 16-feet metal Diapasons as the front pipes. The organ now consists of 4 complete Manuals from CC to A, 58 notes, and two octaves and a half of concave and radiating Pedals from CCC to F, 30 notes.

Solo.

1. Flute harmonique	....	8 feet.
2. Concert Flute	....	4 feet.
3. Corno-di-Bassetto	....	8 feet.
4. Oboe	....	8 feet.
5. Tuba Major	....	8 feet.
6. Clarion	....	4 feet.

Swell.

7. Contra Gamba	....	16 feet.
8. Open Diapason	....	8 feet.
9. Lieblich Gedact	....	8 feet.
10. Salicional	....	8 feet.
11. Vox Angelica	....	8 feet.
12. Principal	....	4 feet.
13. Fifteenth	....	2 feet.
14. Echo Cornet.		
15. Contra Posaune	....	16 feet.
16. Cornopean	....	8 feet.
17. Hautboy	....	8 feet.
18. Clarion	.....	4 feet.

Great.

19. Double Diapason	....	16 feet.
20. Open Diapason	....	8 feet.
21. Open Diapason	....	8 feet.
22. Claribel Flute	....	8 feet.
23. Quint	....	6 feet.
24. Flute harmonique	....	4 feet.
25. Principal	....	4 feet.
26. Octave Quint	....	3 feet.
27. Super Octave	....	2 feet.
28. Fourniture.		
29. Mixture.		
30. Trombone	....	16 feet.
31. Tromba	....	8 feet.
32. Clarion	....	4 feet.

Choir.

33. Bourdon	....	16 feet.
34. Open Diapason	....	8 feet.
35. Dulciana	....	8 feet.
36. Violoncello	....	8 feet.
37. Claribel Flute	....	8 feet.
38. Lieblich Gedact	....	8 feet.
39. Flute harmonique	....	4 feet.
40. Principal	....	4 feet.
41. Flageolet	....	2 feet.
42. Corno-di-Bassetto	....	8 feet.
43. Cor Anglais	....	8 feet.

Pedale.

44. Double Open Diapason, wood	....	32 feet.
45. Open Diapason, wood	...	16 feet.
46. Violone, metal	....	16 feet.
47. Violoncello, metal	....	8 feet.
48. Octave, metal	....	8 feet.
49. Mixture, metal.		
50. Contra Posaune	....	32 feet.
51. Grand Bombard	....	16 feet.
52. Clarion	....	8 feet.

Couplers.

53. Solo to Great.
54. Choir to Great.
55. Swell to Great, Sub-Octave.
56. Swell to Great, Unison.
57. Swell to Great, Super-Octave.

58. Swell to Pedals.
59. Great to Pedals.
60. Choir to Pedals.
61. Solo to Pedals.
62. Ventil Pedale.

Four patent Pneumatic Combination Pistons for acting upon the different stops are applied to each Manual organ. Four Pneumatic Combination Pedals for Pedal organ acting also on the pistons of the Great organ. A double acting Pedal for Great to Pedal Coupler. A Pedal for Swell to Great Unison Coupler. The Pneumatic lever is applied to the Great organ.

The Swell and Choir organs, which are on the opposite side of the Choir, are acted upon by the patent pneumatic tubular apparatus connected with a Pneumatic lever of a peculiar construction which has the advantage of working noiselessly, and never failing. The draw-stop movement is treated in a similar manner.

The Pedal organ which is on the floor of the cathedral, behind the Choir stalls and standing away from the other portion of the instrument, is acted upon by the same means.

The organ derives its wind from three very powerful bellows placed in the crypt, having each 4 feeders ; these bellows are worked with 3 hydraulic engines, and supply the wind to the different reservoirs placed above in the organ automatically, *i.e.*, when the bellows' reservoirs are full the water supply is cut off, and, as the wind is consumed, the engine or engines are again brought into action.

164. WESTMINSTER ABBEY.

The present organ in Westminster Abbey was originally built in 1730 by Schreider & Jordan. It then consisted of Great and Choir, ranging from GG ($10\frac{2}{3}$ feet compass), up to d³ in alt., and a Swell with 4 Unison stops to Fiddle g ($2\frac{2}{3}$ feet compass). A Pedal-board from GG to Gamut A, with an octave of Unison open pipes, was added by Avery during the time Dr. Cooke was organist. In 1828 an octave of GGG Pedal pipes, and a new (soft) Trumpet and Clarion, in place of the old Reeds, were introduced by Elliott. Subsequently a new Swell to tenor c, with 8 stops, was added by Hill ; and a Dulciana and Open Diapason put into the Choir organ in place of the Fifteenth and Cremona. In 1848 the organ was entirely re-constructed by Mr. Hill, and divided ; the Great organ with new and larger sound-boards, movements, &c., being placed on the south side of the screen, and the Swell on the north ; leaving the centre unoccupied, so that an uninterrupted view of the upper part of the minster may be obtained from one end to the other. The Choir organ remains in its old place over the doorway leading from the nave into the choir, and the 32 feet Pedal Diapasons are laid horizontally along the screen. The Claviers are placed crossways behind the Choir organ.

The alterations in 1848 comprised an extension of the Great organ down to CCC (16 feet compass), with the addition of a new Open Diapason ; the conversion of one of the old Diapasons into a Double ; the insertion of a Quint ; a Posaune, and three additional ranks of Mixture. The compass was also extended up to f³ in alt. An entirely new Swell to CC (8 feet compass) was introduced ; a Hohl Flute and Cromorne added to the Choir, and two Open Diapasons, 16 and 32 feet, appropriated to the Pedal ;—such of the old Pedal pipes as were available being used in the latter.

A Solo organ has subsequently been added, and the Instrument now contains 38 sounding stops, of which the following is a list :—

Great, CCC (16 feet compass), 14 Stops.

1. Double Diapason to CC key.
2. Open Diapason (throughout).
3. Open Diapason to CC.
4. Stopped Diapason.
5. Principal.
6. Principal (throughout).
7. Stopped Flute to CC key.
8. Twelfth.
9. Fifteenth.
10. Sesqualtera, V ranks.
11. Mixture, III ranks.
12. Double Trumpet to tenor c key.
13. Posaune (throughout).
14. Clarion.

Swell, CC (8 feet compass), 10 Stops.

15. DoubleDiapason.
16. Open Diapason.
17. Stopped Diapason.
18. Principal.
19. Fifteenth.
20. Sesqualtera, III ranks.
21. Contra Fagotto, to tenor c key.
22. Cornopean.
23. Hautboy.
24. Clarion.

Choir, GG (10⅔ feet compass), 6 Stops.

25. Open Diapason to Gamut G.
26. Hohl Flute.
27. Stopped Diapason.
28. Principal.
29. Flute.
30. Cromorne.

Solo Organ, CC (8 feet compass).

		Pipes.			Pipes.
31. Bourdon, wood	8 feet ...	56	34. Tuba Mirabilis, metal	8 feet ...	56
32. Open Diapason, metal	8 feet ...	56	35. Vox humana, metal	8 feet ...	56
33. Harmonic Flute, metal	8 feet ...	56	36. Orchestral Oboe, metal	8 feet ...	56

Pedal, CCC (16 feet compass), 2 Stops.

37. Great Open Diapason, 32 feet.
38. Open Diapason, 16 feet.

Accessory Stops, Movements, &c.

1. Coupler Swell to Great.
2. Great to Pedal, 16-feet pitch.
3. Great to Pedal, 8-feet pitch.
4. Choir to Pedal, 16-feet pitch.
5. Swell to Pedal, 8-feet pitch.
6, 7, 8. Three Composition Pedals.

165. TEMPLE CHURCH.

The fine organ in the Temple Church was built by Father Smith, in the year 1688. From the time of its first construction it had fourteen notes in each octave, instead of the usual twelve only, the extra notes or "quarter tones" being D sharp and A flat, which were quite distinct from the usual notes, G sharp and E flat. The keys for these added notes were provided, externally, by those for G sharp and E flat being divided crossways, the back halves serving for the special keys being made to rise as much above the front portions as did the latter above the long keys. Internally the keys were necessarily of *half* width only, so that on each side of the pin-hole very little substance could remain. This defect caused the keys at times to "spring," and so render the touch uncertain. The original compass of the organ was from c³ in alt. down to FFF, and, while there were the quarter notes in the upper octaves, there was but one semitonic key between the five lower tones from CC down to FFF, namely BB flat.

The following is a copy of Father Smith's original disposition of stops :—

THE SCHEDULE.

Great Organ.

1. Prestant, of mettle	61 pipes	12 foote tone.
2. Hohlflute, of wood and mettle	61 pipes	12 foote tone.
3. Principall, of mettle	61 pipes	06 foote tone.
4. Quinta, of mettle	61 pipes	04 foote tone.
5. Super-Octave	61 pipes	03 foote tone.
6. Cornett, of mettle	112 pipes	02 foote tone.
7. Sesquialtera, of mettle	183 pipes	03 foote tone.
8. Gedackt, of waines-cott	61 pipes	06 foote tone.
9. Mixture, of mettle	226 pipes	03 foote tone.
10. Trumpett, of mettle	61 pipes	12 foote tone.

Choir Organ.

11. Gedackt, of waines-cott	61 pipes	12 foote.
12. Hohlflute, of metal	61 pipes	06 foote.
13. A Sadt, of mettle	61 pipes	06 foote.
14. Spitzflute, of mettle	61 pipes	03 foote.
15. A Violl and Violin, of mettle	61 pipes	12 foote.
16. Voice Humaine, of mettle	61 pipes	12 foote.

366 pipes.

Ecchos.

17. Gedackt, of wood	61 pipes	06 foote tone.
18. Sup. Octave, of mettle	61 pipes	06 foote tone.
19. Gedackt, of wood	29 pipes.	
20. Flute, of mettle	29 pipes.	
21. Cornett, of mettle	87 pipes.	
22. Sesquialtera	105 pipes.	
23. Trumpett	29 pipes.	

401
366
948

With three full sets of keys and quarter notes.

21st June, 1688.   (Signed)   BER. SMITH.

When the organ was first built the pipes were crowded together in a most inconvenient and irregular manner, but which arrangement was unavoidable, on account of the contracted dimensions of the site destined for its reception, under the centre arch separating the round church from the choir.

Some years after the re-erection of the organ in the organ-chamber (*i.e.*, in 1856), new and more extensive sound-boards, admitting of a more orderly and systematic arrangement of the pipes were constructed, larger and more capacious bellows were provided, and new mechanism was introduced ; though the case remaining where it was originally set up, some 5 or 6 feet within the recess, necessarily deprived the instrument of much room that would have been of the greatest value at the time that it was being laid out afresh. The Swell was at the same time carried down from tenor c to CC, by the late Mr. T. J. F. Robson. Several new stops were also introduced which were at the time new to this country, in the construction and voicing of which Mr. Hopkins had the good fortune to secure the assistance of Mr. Edward Schulze, the eminent organ-builder of Paulinzelle, near Erfurt. The organ, which is blown by two of Joy's patent hydraulic engines, now contains the following stops :—

Great Organ, 16 Stops.

1. Double Diapason............ 16 feet tone.	8. Octave, clear and strong 4 feet tone.
2. Open Diapason, smooth and mellow .... 8 feet tone.	9. Nason Flute, Stopped ... 4 feet.
	10. Twelfth .... 2⅔ feet tone.
3. Open Diapason, clear and strong .... 8 feet tone.	11. Fifteenth .... 2 feet tone.
	12. Full Mixture, III ranks... 2 feet tone.
4. Stopped Diapason, metal, to tenor c sharp .... 8 feet tone.	13. Sharp Mixture, V ranks 2 feet tone.
5. Hohlflote, Bass octave Gedact .... 8 feet tone.	14. Small Trumpet, old, re-voiced .... 8 feet.
	15. Large Trumpet, new...... 8 feet.
6. Viol di Gamba .... 8 feet tone.	16. Clarion .... 4 feet tone.
7. Principal, smooth and mellow .... 4 feet tone.	

Swell Organ, 12 Stops.

17. Bourdon .... 16 feet tone.	23. Mixture, IV ranks......... 1½ foot tone.
18. Open Diapason .... 8 feet tone.	24. Double Bassoon............ 16 feet tone.
19. Rohr Gedact................ 8 feet tone.	25. French Horn .... 8 feet tone.
20. Principal .... 4 feet tone.	26. Hautboy .... 8 feet tone.
21. Rohrflote .... 4 feet tone.	27. Clarion...................... 4 feet tone.
22. { Twelfth .... 2⅔ feet. { Fifteenth .... 2 feet tone.	28. Oboe .... 8 feet tone.

Choir Organ, 11 Stops.

29. Lieblich Bordun .... 16 feet tone.	35. Gemshorn .... 4 feet.
30. Spitzflote .... 8 feet.	36. Violino....................... 4 feet.
31. Violin Diapason .... 8 feet.	37. Lieblich-Flote .... 4 feet tone.
32. Dulciana .... 8 feet.	38. Flautino .... 2 feet.
33. Lieblich-Gedact .... 8 feet.	39. Corno di Bassetto .... 8 feet.
34. Flauto Traverso .... 8 feet.	

Pedal Organ, 8 Stops.

40. Sub-Bass to FFFF .... 32 feet.	45. Violoncello .... 8 feet.
41. Open-Bass .... 16 feet.	46. { Twelfth Bass .... 5⅓ feet. { Fifteenth Bass............ 4 feet.
42. Stopped Bass .... 16 feet tone.	
43. Violin .... 16 feet.	47. Trombone .... 16 feet.
44. Quint .... 10⅔ feet tone.	

Compass of all the Manuals CC to g³ in alt. | Compass of Pedals CCC to tenor f.

Accessory Stops, Movements, &c.

1. Swell to Great.	7, 8, 9, 10, 11. Five Composition Pedals, acting on the Great and Pedal organs in combinations
2. Choir Sub Octave to Great	
3. Swell to Choir.	
4. Great to Pedal.	12, 13, 14. Three Composition Pedals, acting on the Swell organ.
5. Swell to Pedal.	15. Soft Pedal organ.
6. Choir to Pedal.	16. Pedal acting on "Great to Pedal."
	17. Tremulant.

166. Exeter Hall.

The large organ in Exeter Hall was built expressly for the Sacred Harmonic Society, in the year 1839, by Mr. Joseph William Walker, of Francis Street, Tottenham Court Road. The exterior, which corresponds with the architecture of the Hall, was designed by Mr. Robert R. Banks. The width of the instrument is 30 feet, and the height 40 ; the depth in the lower part is 4 feet 6 inches only, the Directors of the Hall having limited the builder to these dimensions, to prevent a loss of space on the platform when public meetings are held. Within this lower part, the bellows, 4 in number, are placed ; while above, at the height of 12 feet from the floor, comes the main body of the organ, carried out on projecting cantilions or consoles. Over each console rises a circular turret of gilt pipes, surmounted by an ornament imitative of that beautiful ancient specimen, the choragic monument of Lysicrates. The two centre towers are considerably higher than the outer ones, and project 5 feet each beyond the body of the instrument ; the longest pipes in these towers measure 20 feet from the base, and 16 from the body (C and C sharp) ; the circumference is 45 inches, the diameter 15 inches, and the weight of each 4 cwt. The whole front of the organ, including the circular ends (which are novel features in the design), is divided into eleven compartments of gilt pipes. The keys are so arranged that the organist, when playing, faces the conductor and the audience, instead of sitting with his back towards them. In 1849 the Pneumatic action for lightening the touch was added to the organ, this being the first instance of its employment by any of the London builders. Larger and more powerful Reed Stops were at the same time introduced into the Great organ and Swell. Still more recently the instrument was enlarged and partly remodelled, under the direction of the late Mr. Brownsmith, the then organist to the Society for which it was built. Two Reeds on a heavy pressure of wind were added to the Swell, and the Double Diapason turned into a Second Unison Open ; the compass of the Swell was extended from FF down to CC ; a third Open Diapason and a Second Principal were introduced into the Great organ, and the system of equal temperament adapted for the tuning ; the latter improvement was at the suggestion of Sir M. Costa.

The organ now contains 42 sounding stops, of which the following is a list :—

Great, 13 Stops.

1. Open Diapason.	8. Fifteenth.
2. Open Diapason, large.	9. Sesquialtera, III ranks.
3. Open Diapason, small.	10. Mixture, II ranks.
4. Stopped Diapason.	11. Furniture, II ranks.
5. Principal, large.	12. Trumpet.
6. Principal.	13. Clarion.
7. Twelfth.	

Choir, 7 Stops.

14. Open Diapason.	18. Metal Flute.
15. Stopped Diapason.	19. Fifteenth.
16. Dulciana to FF.	20. Cremona to fiddle g.
17. Principal.	

Swell, 13 Stops.

21. Open Diapason.	28. Sesquialtera, III ranks.
22. Open Diapason, large.	29. Horn.
23. Stopped Diapason.	30. Oboe.
24. Dulciana.	31. Clarion.
25. Principal.	32. Ophicleide, 8 feet } on a
26. Metal Flute.	33. Ophicleide, 4 feet } heavy wind.
27. Fifteenth.	

Pedal, 9 Stops.

34. Double Open, to FFFF ... 32 feet.	39. Fifteenth .... 4 feet.
35. Open Diapason, wood ... 16 feet.	40. Sesquialtera, III ranks.
36. Open Diapason, metal ... 16 feet.	41. Trombone .... 16 feet.
37. Bourdon .... 16 feet.	42. Trumpet .... 8 feet.
38. Principal .... 8 feet.	

Accessory Stops, Movements, &c.

1. Swell to Great.	5 to 11. Seven Composition Pedals; viz., 3
2. Choir to Great.	to Great, 2 to Swell, and 2 to
3. Great to Pedal.	Pedal.
4. Choir to Pedal.	12. Pneumatic attachment.

Compass.

Great and Choir, FFF to g³ in alt. | Swell, CC to g³ in alt.

Pedal, CCC to tenor e.

167. ROYAL ALBERT HALL.

The instrument in the Royal Albert Hall, constructed by Mr. Henry Willis, of Camden Town, London, consists of 5 Claviers. The compass of the 4 Manual Claviers extends from CC to C in alt. (5 complete octaves, or 61 notes), and that of the Pedal from CCC to G (2⅗ octaves, or 32 notes). The following is the disposition of the stops :—

Choir, 20 Stops.

1. Violone .... 16 feet.	11. Flageolet..................... 2 feet.
2. Viol di Gamba.............. 8 feet.	12. Piccolo (harmonic)......... 2 feet.
3. Dulciana .... 8 feet.	13. Super-octave .... 2 feet.
4. Lieblich Gedact .... 8 feet.	14. Mixture, III ranks.
5. Open Diapason .... 8 feet.	15. Corni di Bassetto .... 16 feet.
6. Vox Angelica .... 8 feet.	16. Clarionet .... 8 feet.
7. Principal (harmonic) ...... 4 feet.	17. Cor Anglais.................. 8 feet.
8. Gemshorn..................... 4 feet.	18. Oboe .... 8 feet.
9. Lieblich Flöte .... 4 feet.	19. Trompette harmonique ... 16 & 8 feet.
10. Celestiana..................... 4 feet.	20. Clarion .... 4 feet.

The pipes in this organ are of metal. The effect of wood is imparted by the harmonic construction, and the disadvantage of using wood for small pipes is therefore avoided. The stops numbered 1, 3, 6, 8, 9, 11, 14, and 17 are intended to represent what is called the "Echo Organ" in some large organs, and in them placed on a fifth Clavier.

Great, 25 Stops.

21. Flute conique, partly harmonic .... 16 feet.	33. Viola .... 4 feet.
22. Contra Gamba.............. 16 feet.	34. Octave .... 4 feet.
23. Violone..................... 16 feet.	35. Quinte Octaviante .... 3 feet.
24. Bourdon .... 16 feet.	36. Piccolo Harmonique ...... 2 feet.
25. Open Diapason .... 8 feet.	37. Super-octave .... 2 feet.
26. Open Diapason .... 8 feet.	38. Furniture, V ranks.
27. Viol di Gamba......... ..... 8 feet.	39. Mixture, V ranks.
28. Claribel.......................... 8 feet.	40. Contra Posaune .... 16 feet.
29. Flute Harmonique .... 8 feet.	41. Posaune .... 8 feet.
30. Flute à Pavillon .... 8 feet.	42. Trompette Harmonique... 16 & 8 feet.
31. Quint............................ 6 feet.	43. Tromba .... 8 feet.
32. Flute Octaviante Harmonique .... 4 feet.	44. Clarion Harmonique ...... 8 & 4 feet.
	45. Clarion .... 4 feet.

Of the above stops only the basses of the Bourdon and Claribel are of wood.

Swell, 25 Stops.

46. Double Diapason............	16 feet.	
47. Bourdon	16 feet.	
48. Salicional	8 feet.	
49. Open Diapason	8 feet.	
50. Viol di Gamba..............	8 feet.	
51. Flutes à Cheminées........	8 feet.	
52. Claribel Flute	8 feet.	
53. Quint...........................	6 feet.	
54. Flute Harmonique	4 feet.	
55. Viola...........................	4 feet.	
56. Principal	4 feet.	
57. Quinte Octaviante	3 feet.	
58. Super-octave	2 feet.	

59. Piccolo Harmonique	2 feet.	
60. Sesquialtera, V ranks.		
61. Mixture, V ranks.		
62. Contra Posaune	16 feet.	
63. Contra Oboe	16 feet.	
64. Baryton	16 feet.	
65. Voix Humaine	8 feet.	
66. Oboe	8 feet.	
67. Cornopean	8 feet.	
68. Tuba Major	8 feet.	
69. Tuba	4 feet.	
70. Clarion	4 feet.	

Of these stops only the basses of the Bourdon and Claribel Flute are of wood.

Solo, 20 Stops.

71. Contra Basso	16 feet.	
72. Flute à Pavillon	8 feet.	
73. Viol d'Amore	8 feet.	
74. Flute Harmonique	8 feet.	
75. Claribel Flute	8 feet.	
76. Voix Celeste................	8 feet.	
77. Flute Traversière	4 feet.	
78. Concert Flute	4 feet.	
79. Piccolo Harmonique	2 feet.	
80. Cymbale		

81. Corno di Bassetto	16 feet.	
82. Clarionet.....................	8 feet.	
83. Bassoon	8 feet.	
84. French Horn	8 feet.	
85. Ophicleide	8 feet.	
86. Trombone	8 feet.	
87. Oboe	8 feet.	
88. Bombardon	16 feet.	
89. Tuba Mirabilis	8 feet.	
90. Tuba Clarion	4 feet.	

Nos. 81, 82, 83, 84, and 87 are inclosed in a swell box.

Pedal, 21 Stops.

91. Double Open Diapason, wood	32 feet.	
92. Double Open Diapason, metal	32 feet.	
93. Contra Violone, metal ...	32 feet.	
94. Open Diapason, wood ...	16 feet.	
95. Open Diapason, metal ...	16 feet.	
96. Bourdon, wood	16 feet.	
97. Violone, metal	16 feet.	
98. Great Quint, metal	12 feet.	
99. Violoncello, metal........	8 feet.	
100. Octave, wood..............	8 feet.	

101. Quint, metal	6 feet.	
102. Super-octave, metal......	4 feet.	
103. Furniture, V ranks.		
104. Mixture, III ranks.		
105. Contra Posaune, wood...	32 feet.	
106. Contra Fagotto, wood...	16 feet.	
107. Bombarde, metal	16 feet.	
108. Ophicleide, wood	16 feet.	
109. Trombone, metal	16 feet.	
110. Fagotto, wood	8 feet.	
111. Clarion, metal	8 feet.	

The inside pipes belonging to those stops that contribute to the front are similarly shaped in mouth, body, and foot.

Couplers.

1. Solo Sub-Octave (on itself).	8. Swell to Choir.
2. Solo Super-Octave (on itself).	9. Solo to Choir.
3. Swell Sub-Octave (on itself).	10. Solo to Pedals.
4. Swell Super-Octave (on itself).	11. Swell to Pedals.
5. Unison Solo to Great.	12. Great to Pedals.
6. Unison Swell to Great.	13. Choir to Pedals.
7. Unison Choir to Great.	14. Sforzando.

A double-acting vertical movement, struck by the heel of either foot, instantly detaches and connects the movement of the Pedal organ from all but the Bourdon, Violone, Open Diapason (metal), and Octave, and also draws and withdraws the Pedal Coupler to Great organ.

Eight patent Pneumatic Combination Pistons govern the whole of the stops of each Manual organ. These thirty-two pistons appear immediately below and in front of each Clavier, concentrated so as to be at all times within reach of the hands of the performer.

Six Pedals govern the stops of the Pedal organ by means of ventils. Two Pedals apply and detach a movement that causes the aforesaid six Pedals governing the Pedal organ to act also upon the combination movement of the Great organ. Six Pedals govern and combine in various ways all the other accessories, and thus, by one instantaneous operation of the performer, vary the effect of the whole instrument at once. Two Tremulants, governed by Pedals (one to the Swell, the other to the Solo organ), are applied. These Tremulants act only upon suitable stops. The Sforzando is brought in action by means of a Pedal. Two Pedals govern the Great to Pedal Coupler. The patent atmospheric contrivance of 1862 for actuating the Swell independently of the Swell Pedals is also applied.

The general construction of the instrument is of the most elaborate and beautiful kind, of the best materials and workmanship. The internal metal pipes consist of 5-9ths lamb-stamp commercial tin and 4-9ths soft lead, and the scales of these, as well as those of the front, are suitable to the proportions of the building. All the front pipes are made of tin 90 and lead 10 in 100 parts, and are burnished and polished in the same manner as those in the best Continental organs. The key-fittings are elegant in design, the combination pistons being plated with gold and engine-turned. The claviers are made of very thick ivory.

The main reservoirs in which the compressed air is forced are placed in a chamber prepared in a clean and dry locality. The feeders supplying the air by steam power are of the most ample size, and constructed to receive their wind from the room above, and not from the locality in which they are placed. To carry out this arrangement (of the highest importance), passages are provided for the wind-shafts to and from the organ to the chamber in which the main reservoirs are placed. The main reservoirs deliver their wind to numerous reservoirs in immediate connection with the pipes.

168. WESTMINSTER AQUARIUM.

The large organ in the Royal Aquarium and Summer and Winter Gardens, Westminster, was built by Mr. Henry Jones, under the direction of Dr. Sullivan. It has three complete Manuals, extending from CC to C, 61 notes. The Pedal organ is of the full compass, CCC to F, 30 notes ; and every stop is of the full range.

Great Organ, CC to C, 61 Notes.

1. Double Diapason, metal...	16 feet.	
2. Open Diapason, metal ...	8 feet.	
3. Harmonic Diapason, metal	8 feet.	
4. Gamba, metal	8 feet.	
5. Gedact, wood and metal	8 feet.	
6. Octave, metal	4 feet.	
7. Harmonic Flute, metal ...	4 feet.	
8. Twelfth, metal...............	2⅔ feet.	
9. Fifteenth, metal	2 feet.	
10. Octavine Harmonic, metal	2 feet.	
11. Mixture, III ranks, metal	various.	
12. Mixture, II ranks, metal	various.	
13. Contra Posaune, metal ...	16 feet.	
14. Posaune, metal	8 feet.	
15. Trumpet, metal	8 feet.	
16. Clarion, metal...............	4 feet.	
17. Spare Slide.		

Swell Organ, CC to C, 61 Notes.

18. Double Diapason, wood and metal	16 feet.
19. Open Diapason, metal ...	8 feet.
20. Gamba, metal	8 feet.
21. Salicional, metal	8 feet.
22. Voix Celeste, metal	8 feet.
23. Gedact, wood and metal	8 feet.
24. Harmonic Flute, metal ...	4 feet.
25. Principal, metal	4 feet.
26. Octave, metal	2 feet.
27. Mixture, III ranks, metal	various.
28. Contra Fagotto, metal ...	16 feet.
29. Horn, metal	8 feet.
30. Harmonic Trumpet, metal	8 feet.
31. Orchestral Oboe, metal...	8 feet.
32. Clarion, metal	4 feet.
33. Voix Humaine, metal ...	8 feet.
34. Spare Slide.	

Choir Organ, CC to C, 61 Notes.

35. Open Diapason, metal ...	8 feet.
36. Dulciana, metal	8 feet.
37. Stopped Diapason, wood	8 feet.
38. Octave Keraulophon, metal	4 feet.
39. Harmonic Flute, metal...	4 feet.
40. Piccolo, wood and metal	2 feet.
41. Hautbois, metal	8 feet.
42. Clarionet, metal	8 feet.

Pedal Organ, CCC to F, 30 Notes.

43. Double Open Diapason, wood	32 feet.
44. Great Unison, wood	16 feet.
45. Bass Gamba, metal	16 feet.
46. Bourdon, wood	16 feet.
47. Bass Flute, wood	8 feet.
48. Violoncello, wood	8 feet.
49. Trombone, wood	16 feet.
50. Bassoon, metal	8 feet.
51. Spare slide.	

Couplers.

52. Swell to Great.	57. Choir to Pedals.
53. Choir to Great.	58. Octave Great.
54. Swell to Choir.	59. Space prepared.
55. Swell to Pedals.	60. Space prepared.
56. Great to Pedals.	

Accessory Movements.

1, 2, 3, 4. Composition Pedals acting on Great and Pedal organs.
5, 6, 7, 8. Composition Pedals acting on Swell organ.
9, 10. Tremulant acting on Swell, by Pedal.
11. Crescendo Pedal.

2½ Octaves of German Pedals.

General Summary.

	Stops.	Pipes.
Great Organ	17	1,159
Swell Organ	17	1,098
Choir Organ	8	488
Pedal Organ	9	240
Couplers	9	
Total	60	2,985

Preparation has been made for the addition of a fourth or Solo organ, in addition to the extra slides on Great, Swell, and Pedals, as mentioned above. Four large bellows (placed beneath) supply the instrument with wind at different pressures. These bellows are driven by steam power, but are so arranged that manual labour can be employed should any mishap occur among the steam machinery. An improved Pneumatic Lever is attached to the Great and Swell organ keys, by which means a light touch is obtained, and the Couplers (when in use) cause no extra weight on the Manuals. It is also fitted with Radiating and

Concave Pedals, Diagonal Draw-stops, Overhanging keys, and every modern improvement to bring the whole instrument comfortably within the control of the performer. The Reed stops are voiced on a heavy pressure wind, while the scaling of the pipes throughout has been carefully selected from the best authorities, both English and Foreign. To ensure the variety that is necessary for orchestral purposes, the lighter Solo stops have been manufactured and voiced by two of the most eminent Firms in Paris.

169. CRYSTAL PALACE.

The following is a description of the large organ built by Messrs. Gray and Davison, expressly for the Great Handel Festival at the Crystal Palace in 1857.

The space it occupies in the centre transept is 40 feet in width by 24 in depth, exclusive of the platform for the bellows. Of these reservoirs there are altogether 16, by which a great variety of pressure is obtained, which gives increased brilliancy to the treble portion of the registers, and brings out the tone of some of the more commanding stops. The weight of the instrument is about 20 tons.

Great Organ, CC to A in alt., 19 Stops.

1. Double Open Diapason ...	16 feet.	11. Flageolet Harmonique ...	2 feet.
2. Double Dulciana............	16 feet.	12. Mixture, IV ranks.	
3. Open Diapason	8 feet.	13. Furniture, III ranks.	
4. Flautà Pavillon	8 feet.	14. Cymbal, V ranks.	
5. Claribel Flute	8 feet.	15. Contra Trombone	16 feet.
6. Flute Harmonique	8 feet.	16. Posaune	8 feet.
7. Quint...........................	6 feet.	17. Trumpet Harmonique ...	8 feet.
8. Flute Octaviante	4 feet.	18. Clarion......................	4 feet.
9. Twelfth	3 feet.	19. Octave Clarion	2 feet.
10. Super-octave.................	2 feet.		

Choir Organ, CC to A in alt., 12 Stops.

20. Bourdon	16 feet.	26. Claribel Flute..............	4 feet.
21. Gamba	8 feet	27. Spitz Flute	2 feet.
22. Salicional	8 feet.	28. Piccolo	2 feet.
23. Voix céleste	8 feet.	29. Mixture, III ranks.	
24. Clarinet Flute	8 feet.	30. Cor Anglais and Bassoon	8 feet.
25. Gemshorn	4 feet.	31. Trumpet	8 feet.

Swell Organ, CC to A in alt., 17 Stops.

32. Bourdon	16 feet.	41. Mixture, IV ranks.	
33. Open Diapason	8 feet.	42. Furniture, III ranks.	
34. Vox Humana	8 feet.	43. Piccolo Harmonique	2 feet.
35. Keraulophon.................	8 feet.	44. Contra Fagotto	16 feet.
36. Concert Flute	8 feet.	45. Cornopean	8 feet.
37. Octave	4 feet.	46. Oboe	8 feet.
38. Flute Octaviante	4 feet.	47. Clarion......................	4 feet.
39. Twelfth	3 feet.	48. Echo Tromba	8 feet.
40. Super-octave.................	2 feet.		

Solo Organ, 5 Stops.

49. Flute Harmonique	8 feet.	52. Corni di Bassetto	8 feet.
50. Flute Octaviante	4 feet.	53. Grand Tromba	8 feet.
51. Open Diapason	8 feet.		

Pedal Organ, CCC to F, 12 *Stops.*

54. Contra Bass	32 feet.	60. Octave	8 feet.
55. Contra Bombarde	32 feet.	61. Twelfth	5⅓ feet.
56. Open Diapason, wood	16 feet.	62. Super-octave	4 feet.
57. Open Diapason, metal	16 feet.	63. Mixture, IV ranks.	
58. Violone	16 feet.	64. Trumpet	8 feet.
59. Bombarde	16 feet.	65. Clarion	4 feet.

Couplers.

1. Swell to Great.	3. Swell to Choir.	6. Solo to Great.
2. Swell Octave, and Sub-octave.	4. Choir to Great.	Each Manual to Pedals.
	5. Choir to Octave.	Tremulant.

Total number of stops .... 65 | Total number of pipes 4568

170. ALEXANDRA PALACE.

The organ in the Alexandra Palace, Muswell Hill, was built by Mr. Henry Willis, of London. The distribution of the stops is as follows :—

Solo, 14 *Stops.*

1. Violoncello (imitative)	8 feet.	8. Bombardon	16 feet.
2. Viola (imitative)	4 feet.	9. Trumpet (Harmonic)	8 feet.
3. Flute Harmonique	8 feet.	10. Ophicleide	8 feet.
4. Flute Octaviante	4 feet.	11. Bassoon	8 feet.
5. Concert Flute (imitative)	4 feet.	12. Oboe (Orchestral)	8 feet.
6. Piccolo (imitative)	2 feet.	13. Clarionette (Orchestral)	8 feet.
7. Claribel	8 feet.	14. Clarion	4 feet.

Swell, 21 *Stops.*

15. Double Diapason	16 feet.	26. Fifteenth	2 feet.
16. Bourdon	16 feet.	27. Sesquialtera, V ranks.	
17. Open Diapason	8 feet.	28. Mixture, III ranks.	
18. Open Diapason	8 feet.	29. Contra Posaune	16 feet.
19. Salicional	8 feet.	30. Contra Fagotto	16 feet.
20. Lieblich Gedact	8 feet.	31. Cornopean	8 feet.
21. Flute Harmonique	8 feet.	32. Trumpet	8 feet.
22. Flute Octaviante	4 feet.	33. Hautboy	8 feet.
23. Flauto Traverso	4 feet.	34. Vox Humana	8 feet.
24. Principal	4 feet.	35. Clarion	4 feet.
25. Twelfth	3 feet.		

Great, 20 *Stops.*

36. Double Diapason	16 feet.	46. Quinte Octaviante	3 feet.
37. Bourdon	16 feet.	47. Super-octave	2 feet.
38. Open Diapason	8 feet.	48. Piccolo	2 feet.
39. Open Diapason	8 feet.	49. Sesquialtera, V ranks.	
40. Open Diapason	8 feet.	50. Mixture, III ranks.	
41. Viol di Gamba	8 feet.	51. Trombone	16 feet.
42. Claribel	8 feet.	52. Bombard	8 feet.
43. Quinte	6 feet.	53. Trumpet	8 feet.
44. Principal	4 feet.	54. Posaune	8 feet.
45. Flute Traversière	4 feet.	55. Clarion	4 feet.

Choir, 17 Stops.

56. Contra Gamba	16 feet.	
57. Viol di Gamba	8 feet.	
58. Salicional	8 feet.	
59. Claribel	8 feet.	
60. Flute Harmonique	8 feet.	
61. Lieblich Gedact	8 feet.	
62. Vox Angelica	8 feet.	
63. Flute Octaviante	4 feet.	
64. Gemshorn	4 feet.	

65. Viola	4 feet.
66. Lieblich Flote	4 feet.
67. Flageolet	2 feet.
68. Mixture.	
69. Trompette Harmonique	8 feet.
70. Clarion	4 feet.
71. Corno di Bassetto	8 feet.
72. Corno Inglese	8 feet.

Pedale.

73. Double Diapason, open wood	32 feet.
74. Double Diapason, open metal	32 feet.
75. Sub-Bourdon	32 feet.
76. Open Diapason, wood	16 feet.
77. Violone, metal	16 feet.
78. Bourdon	16 feet.
79. Contra Basso, open wood	16 feet.

80. Octave	8 feet.
81. Principal	8 feet.
82. Super-octave	4 feet.
83. Sesquialtera, III ranks.	
84. Mixture, III ranks.	
85. Bombard	32 feet.
86. Trombone	16 feet.
87. Ophicleide	16 feet.
88. Clarion	8 feet.

Accessories.

89. Solo to Great.	
90. Solo Sub-octave on itself.	
91. Solo Super-octave on itself.	
92. Solo to Choir.	
93. Swell to Great, Unison.	
94. Swell to Great, Sub-octave.	
95. Swell to Great, Super-octave.	
96. Swell to Choir.	

97. Choir to Great.	
98. Pedale in Octaves on Nos. 86, 87, 88.	
99. Pedale in Octaves on Nos. 82, 83, 84.	
100. Solo to Pedals.	
101. Swell to Pedals.	
102. Great to Pedals.	
103. Choir to Pedals.	

Compass.

Four Manuals, CC to C, 61 notes. | Pedal Organ, CCC to G, 32 notes.

To enable the performer to command these stops and accessories, there are eight pneumatic combining pistons to each clavier, which arrange in fixed selections the stops of each organ by the mere pressure of the finger.

Six Pedals govern the stops of the Pedal organ by a similar pneumatic arrangement. The Sforzando is brought into action by means of a Pedal. Two Pedals, or a double-acting Pedal, actuate the Great to Pedal Coupler. Two Tremulants, governed by Pedals, are applied to suitable stops—one to the Swell, the other to the Solo organ.

The metal pipes throughout the organ to 4 feet are made of the finest spotted metal.

The wind is derived from bellows placed in the basement. Two of these are blown by a steam engine of 12-horse power, and supply ordinary pressures of air. Another bellows (heavy pressure, and of prodigious strength) is blown in connection with a vacuum apparatus by a second engine of 8-horse power. From the bellows in the basement the wind passes into numerous reservoirs placed in the localities of the various sections of each organ.

Each Manual is furnished with a pneumatic lever of the most approved construction as an intermediary power between the keys and the valves of the organ. The Pedal organ is played throughout by means of the novel and beautiful pneumatic tubular apparatus patented by the builder.

The whole draw-stop movement is upon an entirely new principle, each stop being drawn and withdrawn by a pneumatic lever of a peculiar construction in connection with a reciprocating apparatus commanded by the ordinary draw-stop rod, the motor being highly compressed air for the one and highly attenuated air for the other. By this means the ordinary draw-stop movements, such as levers, shafts of iron, rods, centres, &c., are entirely got rid of. For this invention, and for other contrivances in connection with the wind, the builder has obtained a patent.

171. Bow and Bromley Institute.

This instrument, built by Messrs. Brindley and Foster, of Sheffield, in 1874, comprises two key-boards, each from CC to A, four octaves and three-quarters, a Pedal-board from CCC to G, two octaves and a half, and 27 sounding stops, of which the following is a list :—

Great Organ, 11 Stops.

1. Bourdon, wood and metal	16 feet.	7. Flute Harmonique, wood and metal	4 feet.
2. Open Diapason, metal ...	8 feet.	8. Grave Mixture, II ranks...	2⅔ feet.
3. Lieblich Gedact, wood and metal	8 feet.	9. Full Mixture, III ranks...	2 feet.
4. Hohlflote, wood	8 feet.	10. Trumpet, metal	8 feet.
5. Vox Angelica, metal	8 feet.	11. Clarinet and Bassoon	8 feet.
6. Principal, metal	4 feet.		

Swell Organ, 10 Stops.

12. Lieblich Bourdon, wood and metal	16 feet.	16. Voix Célestes, metal	8 feet.
13. Open Diapason, metal ...	8 feet.	17. Principal, metal	4 feet.
14. Lieblich Gedact, wood and metal	8 feet.	18. Piccolo, metal	2 feet.
15. Viol di Gamba, metal	8 feet.	19. Full Mixture, III ranks...	2 feet.
		20. Cornopean, metal	8 feet.
		21. Hautbois, metal	8 feet.

Pedal Organ, 6 Stops.

22. Contra-bass, metal	16 feet.	25. Flute Bass, wood	8 feet.
23. Sub-bass, wood	16 feet.	26. Trombone, metal	16 feet.
24. Principal Bass, metal	8 feet.	27. Trumpet, metal	8 feet.

The Pneumatic action is applied to the Great and Swell organs.

Five Couplers acted upon by Small Pedals.

1. Swell to Pedals.	4. Swell Sub-octave, on its own key-board.
2. Great to Pedals.	5. Swell Super-octave, ditto.
3. Swell to Great.	

Seven Ventil Combination Pedals; four acting on the Great and Pedal organs simultaneously, the remaining three on the Swell.

172. "The Hall," Regent's Park.

The organ at the residence of Mr. Nathl. J. Holmes, the Hall, Primrose Hill Road, Regent's Park, was constructed from the designs of Mr. W. T. Best by Messrs. Bryceson Brothers and Morten, London; commenced in 1872, finished 1875. It

has 4 key-boards, each from C to C, 5 octaves in extent ; the Pedal-board from C
to F, two octaves and a half ; and contains the following registers :—

Great Organ.
(Lowest Key-board.)

1.	Double Diapason	16 feet.	8. Principal	4 feet.
2.	Open Diapason	8 feet.	9. Flute Harmonique	4 feet.
3.	Viola	8 feet.	10. Twelfth	3 feet.
4.	Hohlflote	8 feet.	11. Fifteenth	2 feet.
5.	Flauto Traverso	8 feet.	12. Full Mixture, III ranks.	
6.	Salicional	8 feet.	13. Trombone	8 feet.
7.	Dulciana	8 feet.	14. Clarion	4 feet.

Choir Organ.
(Second Key-board.)

15.	Lieblich Bourdon	16 feet.	21. Octave Viola	4 feet.
16.	Spitzflote	8 feet.	22. Flute Harmonique	4 feet.
17.	Viol di Gamba	8 feet.	23. Lieblich Flote	4 feet.
18.	Echo Dulciana	8 feet.	24. Piccolo	2 feet.
19.	Lieblich Gedact	8 feet.	25. Cor Anglais	8 feet.
20.	Vienna Flute	8 feet.	26. Clarionet and Bassoon	8 feet.

Swell Organ.
(Third Key-board.)

27.	Double Diapason	16 feet.	35. Octave Flageolet	1 foot.
28.	Open Diapason	8 feet.	36. Echo Cornet, III ranks.	
29.	Keraulophon	8 feet.	37. Contra Fagotto	16 feet.
30.	Hohl Flote	8 feet.	38. Cornopean	8 feet.
31.	Lieblich Gedact	8 feet.	39. Hautbois	8 feet.
32.	Voix Célestes	8 feet.	40. Vox Humana	8 feet.
33.	Principal	4 feet.	41. Corno di Bassetto	8 feet.
34.	Lieblich Flote	4 feet.	42. Clarion	4 feet.

Solo Organ.
(Fourth Key-board.)

43.	Clarionet (in a separate Swell)	8 feet.	46. Tromba	8 feet.
44.	Orchestral Flute	8 feet.	47. Contra Trombone	16 feet.
45.	Piccolo	2 feet.	48. Carillon (a gamut of 61 bells)	4 feet.

Echo Organ.
(Fourth Key-board.)

49.	Bourdon Doux	16 feet.	52. Voix Célestes	8 feet.
50.	Corno Dolce	8 feet.	53. Flute Douce	4 feet.
51.	Viole d'Amour	8 feet.	54. Harmonica, III ranks.	

Pedal Organ.

55.	Double Open Diapason	32 feet.	61. Super Octave	4 feet.
56.	Contra Bass	16 feet.	62. Contra Bombarde	32 feet.
57.	Sub-Bass	16 feet.	63. Trombone	16 feet.
58.	Violon	16 feet.	64. Bassoon	8 feet.
59.	Violoncello	8 feet.	65. Trumpet	8 feet.
60.	Bass Flute	8 feet.		

Couplers, &c.
(On the Left Side.)

1. Solo to Pedals.	4. Great to Pedals.
2. Swell to Pedals.	5. Ventil to Pedal Organ.
3. Choir to Pedals.	6. Ventil to Echo Organ.

(On the Right Side.)

7. Solo to Great.
8. Swell Super-octave, on its own keyboard.
9. Swell Sub-octave, on its own keyboard.

10. Swell to Great.
11. Swell to Choir.
12. Ventil to Choir.

The necessary changes of tone are effected by means of eight Combination Pedals, and a series of eight small pistons placed between the key-boards, both of a new construction.

The sound-boards receive the wind at various pressures from 15 separate reservoirs, which derive their supply from the main bellows, placed in the basement, and blown by a steam engine of 11-horse power. The regulation of the wind supply is automatic.

The key-boards are detached from the organ itself, and reversed in position, so that the player faces the audience, and is enabled to hear the various effects of tone produced without difficulty.

Every stop extends throughout the entire Manual compass, and the key-boards are constructed so that a passage of organ music can be readily played on two adjoining rows of keys by the same hand.

The various stop-handles are within convenient reach of either hand, and do not descend below the level of the fourth key-board.

The pneumatic touch is applied to the Great, Swell, and Pedal claviers.

The two Swell Pedals, usually to the right of the player, are here placed in the centre.

The Couplers, and other accessory appliances, are acted upon by a system of small Pedals ; and a Tremulant (also brought into operation by means of a Pedal), can be applied to any of the nine reed-stops in the Swell and Solo organs.

There are 65 sounding stops in the organ, 9 Couplers, 21 adjusting Pedals, &c., and 4,209 pipes.

The Echo organ is placed at the opposite end of the concert-room on a raised corbel, 30 feet from the floor, and at a distance of 100 feet away from the key-boards, and it is provided with the new electric action. It is controlled from the fourth Manual of the Great organ. Vacuum pneumatic instantaneous draw-stop action (Messrs. Bryceson Brothers & Mortem, patentees), is applied both to the Great and Echo organs.

The Great organ stands 50 feet high, 30 feet wide, and 30 feet deep. The largest pipe in the organ is to be found in the centre tower ; it belongs to the Pedal Double Diapason, and is in metal, 38 feet high, 20 inches in diameter, vibrating 33 times in a second, and sounding the lowest C of the musical gamut. The weight of the organ is 87 tons.

173. ROYAL NORMAL COLLEGE AND ACADEMY OF MUSIC FOR THE BLIND,

UPPER NORWOOD, S.E.

The organ in the Hall of the above College was built by Messrs. Forster and Andrews. It contains the 26 sounding stops mentioned below :—

Great Organ, CC to A.

	Feet Tone.	Pipes.		Feet Tone.	Pipes.
1. Open Diapason, metal	8	58	5. Harmonic Flute, metal	4	58
2. Gamba, metal	8	58	6. Fifteenth, metal	2	58
3. Hohlflöte, wood	8	58	7. Mixture, III ranks, metal		174
4. Principal, metal	4	58	8. Trumpet, metal	8	58

Swell Organ, CC to A.

9. Lieblich Bourdon, wood ...16 58	13. Voix Célestes, metal......... 8 46
10. Open Diapason, wood and metal 8 58	14. Principal, metal 4 58
	15. Harmonic Piccolo, metal... 2 58
11. Rohrflote, metal 8 58	16. Horn, metal 8 58
12. Salicional, metal 8 58	17. Oboe, metal 8 58

Choir Organ, CC to A.

18. Dulciana, metal 8 58	21. Flautino, metal............... 2 58
19. Lieblich Gedact, wood 8 58	22. Corno di Bassetto, metal... 8 58
20. Flauto Traverso, metal...... 4 58	

Pedal Organ, CCC to F.

23. Open Diapason, wood 16 30	25. Quint, wood ....10¾ ... 30
24. Bourdon, wood......... ......16 30	26. Flute, wood 8 30

Couplers.

1. Swell to Great.	4. Great to Pedals.
2. Swell to Pedals.	5. Choir to Pedals.
3. Swell to Octave.	6. Swell to Choir.

Six Composition Pedals.

Case of pitch pine, having angular projecting towers and decorated front pipes.

The above, with two other organs for the same Institution, are supplied with blowing power from a gas engine in the base of the building.

174. CHAPEL ROYAL, WHITEHALL.

This organ was originally built by Father Schmidt. The case and some of the original wood pipes remain to this day. It is in oak, of noble design, with four towers, and most elaborately carved, about 24 feet high by 16 feet in breadth, surmounted with the royal arms. It was rebuilt in 1814 by Elliot; it then had 20 stops. In 1844 Messrs. Hill and Son added an entire new Swell, of large dimensions, and other improvements, at the suggestion of the organist, Mr. Massey. The organ now contains 4 Manuals and 33 sounding stops. Compass, from GG to F in alt. Pedal pipes from FFF up, twenty-one notes to D, with Choir organ in front of the gallery.

Great, 8 Stops.

1. Open Diapason.	5. Fifteenth.
2. Stopped Diapason.	6. Sesqualtera, III ranks.
3. Principal.	7. Mixture, II ranks.
4. Twelfth.	8. Trumpet.

Choir, 6 Stops.

9. Open Diapason.	12. Viol di Gamba.
10. Stopped Diapason, Treble.	13. Principal.
11. Stopped Diapason, Bass.	14. Bassoon.

Swell, 14 Stops.—Down to FF.

15. Bourdon.	22. Fifteenth.
16. Tenoroon.	23. Sesqualtera.
17. Open Diapason.	24. Mixture.
18. Clarabella.	25. Corno, Basso.
19. Stopped Diapason, Bass.	26. Cornopean.
20. Flageolet.	27. Clarion.
21. Principal.	28. Hautboy.

Solo, 4 Stops.

29. Open Diapason. | 30. Stopped Diapason. | 31. Flute. | 32. Cromorne.

Pedal, 1 Stop.

33. Open Pipes to FFF, 12 feet.

Couplers.

1. Pedal to Great.
2. Pedal to Choir.

3. Swell to Great.
4. Swell to Choir (Octave below).

175. ST. MARGARET'S, WESTMINSTER.

The fine organ in St. Margaret's Church, Westminster, was built by Avery, in 1804, and cost eight hundred guineas and the old organ by Father Smith, for which Avery allowed two hundred pounds. The organ was rebuilt in 1859 by Mr. G. M. Holditch, and the following is a description of the organ as it now stands :—

Great Organ, CC to F in alt.

1. Open Diapason, front ...... 8 feet.
2. *Open Diapason .... 8 feet.
3. Stopped Diapason and Clarabella .... 8 feet.
4. Principal .... 4 feet.
5. Twelfth .... 3 feet.

6. Fifteenth .... 2 feet.
7. Tierce .... 1¾ foot.
8. Sesquialtera.
9. Mixture.
10. Trumpet .... 8 feet.

Choir Organ, CC to F in alt.

11. Dulciana .... 8 feet.
12. Stopped Diapason .... 8 feet.
13. Stopped Diapason, Bass... 8 feet.
14. Principal .... 4 feet.

15. Flute .... 4 feet.
16. *Slide for Unison Stop.
17. *Cremona.

Swell Organ, CC to F in alt.

18. *Bourdon .... 16 feet.
19. *Double Diapason............ 16 feet.
20. *Open Diapason, Bass ...... 8 feet.
21. Open Diapason, Treble ... 8 feet.
22. Stopped Diapason .... 8 feet.
23. Principal .... 4 feet.

24. Twelfth .... 3 feet.
25. Fifteenth .... 2 feet.
26. *Sesquialtera.
27. *Double Trumpet .... 16 feet.
28. *Cornopean .... 8 feet.
29. Hautboy .... 8 feet.

Pedal Organ, extending to CCC, 16 feet.

30. Open Diapason .... 16 feet.
31. Stopped Diapason .... 16 feet.
32. Principal .... 8 feet.
33. Fifteenth .... 4 feet.

34. Sesquialtera.
35. Mixture.
36. Trumpet .... 16 feet.

There are only 4 notes at present in the Pedal organ extending to GG, but not including GG sharp.

Accessory Stops, Movements, &c.

1. Pedals to Great.
2. Pedals to Choir.
3. Pedals to Swell.
4. 16 feet Pedals to Great.
5. Swell to Great.

6. Choir to Swell.

Three Composition Pedals to Great.
Three Composition Pedals to Swell.
Two Octaves and a third of German Pedals.

The stops marked thus (*) are not at present in the organ, but the mechanism for them is provided. None of the stops extend through in the Swell organ. The old Swell organ had only 35 notes in compass ; the present one has 54 notes compass. The bellows are of peculiar construction, very large, and will afford an ample supply of wind when the organ has all the stops of pipes completed.

176. St. James's, Piccadilly.

The organ, by Harris, that was placed in this church immediately after its erection, was given by Queen Mary, in 1691, having been before "in ye Greate Chappell at Whitehall, which heretofore ye Papist possessed." In 1852 an entirely new inside was put to the instrument, with the exception of a fine Metal Stopped Diapason and the front Open Diapason, which are retained. The handsome old case is also preserved; the new Choir organ being enclosed in a new and separate case, placed in front of the gallery. The present instrument, built by J. C. Bishop and Son, contains 36 sounding stops, distributed among 3 Manuals and Pedal in the following manner :—

Great, 12 Stops.

1.	Open Diapason	8 feet.	7.	Twelfth	2⅔ feet.
2.	Open Diapason	8 feet.	8.	Fifteenth	2 feet.
3.	Stopped Diapason, metal, Treble	8 feet tone.	9.	Sesquialtera, III ranks	1⅗ foot.
4.	German Flute	8 feet.	10.	Mixture, III ranks	⅘ foot.
5.	Principal	4 feet.	11.	Posaune	8 feet.
6.	Flageolet	4 feet.	12.	Clarion	4 feet.

Swell, 11 Stops.

13.	Bourdon	16 feet tone.	19.	Mixture, III ranks	⅘ foot.
14.	Open Diapason	8 feet.	20.	Contra Fagotto	16 feet.
15.	Stopped Diapason	8 feet tone.	21.	Cornopean	8 feet.
16.	Principal	4 feet.	22.	Hautboy	8 feet.
17.	Fifteenth	2 feet.	23.	Clarion	4 feet.
18.	Sesquialtera, III ranks	1⅗ foot.			

Choir, 9 Stops.

24.	Open Diapason	8 feet.	29.	Harmonic Flute	4 feet.
25.	{ Lieblich Gedact / Stopped Bass }	8 feet.	30.	Fifteenth	2 feet.
26.	Dulciana	8 feet.	31.	Piccolo	2 feet.
27.	Viol de Gamba	8 feet.	32.	{ Cremona Treble / Bassoon Bass }	8 feet.
28.	Principal	4 feet.			

Pedal, 4 Stops.

33.	Open Diapason	16 feet.	35.	Principal	8 feet.
34.	Bourdon	16 feet tone.	36.	Trombone	16 feet.

Accessory Stops, Movements, &c.

1. Coupler, Swell to Great.	5. Coupler, Swell to Pedal.
2. Coupler, Choir to Great.	6. Coupler, Choir to Pedal.
3. Coupler, Swell to Choir.	7 to 15. Nine Composition Pedals.
4. Coupler, Great to Pedal.	

Compass.

All the Manuals, CC to f³ in alt. | Pedal, CCC to tenor e.

177. CHAPEL ROYAL, ST. JAMES'S.

The organ in the Chapel Royal, St. James's, built by Messrs. Wm. Hill and Son, contains 27 Sounding stops, 3 Manuals, compass of each CC to G, 56 notes, and a Pedal Clavier CCC to F, 30 notes.

Great Organ.

		Pipes.			Pipes.
1. Open Diapason, metal	8 feet	56	5. Twelfth, metal .... 3 feet	56
2. Cone Gamba, metal ...	8 feet	56	6. Fifteenth, metal ...... 2 feet	56
3. Stopped Diapason and			7. Mixture, metal, 11	
Clarabella, wood	8 feet	56	ranks......................................	112
4. Principal, metal	4 feet	56	8. Trumpet, metal ...... 8 feet	56

Choir Organ.

9. Open Diapason, metal	8 feet	56	12. Gemshorn, metal ...... 4 feet	56
10. Dulciana (gamut g, groove No. 3), metal..................	8 feet	44	13. Suabe Flute, wood ... 4 feet	56
			14. Clarionet, tenor c, metal.................. 8 feet	44
11. Lieblich Gedact, wood	8 feet	56		

Swell Organ.

15. Lieblich Bourdon, wood	16 feet	56	19. Principal, metal ...... 4 feet	56
16. Open Diapason, metal	8 feet	56	20. Celestina, metal ...... 4 feet	56
17. Keraulophon, metal...	8 feet	56	21. Fifteenth, metal ...... 2 feet	56
18. Stopped Diapason, wood	8 feet	56	22. Mixture, metal, III ranks	168
			23. Horn, metal .... 8 feet	56
			24. Oboe, metal............ 8 feet	56

Pedal Organ.

25. Open Diapason, wood 16 feet	30	27. Violon, wood .... 8 feet	30
26. Bourdon, wood ...... 16 feet	30		

Couplers.

1. Swell to Great.	4. Great to Pedal.
2. Swell to Super-Octave.	5. Choir to Pedal.
3. Swell to Choir.	6. Swell to Pedal.

Three Composition Pedals to Great organ.
Two Composition Pedals to Swell organ.

178. ST. KATHERINE'S, REGENT'S PARK.

The organ in St. Katherine's Church, Regent's Park, removed from the demolished Collegiate Church of the same name near the Tower, is one of Green's finest instruments. It was built in 1778, under the direction of Joah Bates; and comprises Great and Choir organs from GG (10$\frac{2}{3}$ feet compass) up to e³ in alt. ; and a Swell down to Gamut G (5⅓ feet compass), a most extensive and excellent range for the period. Below G, the Swell keys act on the Choir organ. The following is a list of the stops in the above-mentioned instrument :—

Great, 10 Stops.

1. Open Diapason.
2. Open Diapason.
3. Stopped Diapason.
4. Principal.
5. Twelfth.
6. Fifteenth.
7. Sesquialtera, III ranks.
8. Mixture, II ranks.
9. Trumpet.
10. Cornet, IV ranks.

Choir, 5 Stops.

11. Stopped Diapason.
12. Principal.
13. Flute.
14. Fifteenth.
15. Bassoon.

Swell, 6 Stops.

16. Open Diapason.
17. Stopped Diapason.
18. Principal.
19. Cornet, III ranks.
20. Trumpet.
21. Hautboy.

Pedal, 1 Stop.

22. An Octave of Open Pipes to CCC, 16 feet length.
Pedal Clavier to GG.

179. ST. MARTIN-IN-THE-FIELDS.

This organ, originally built, in 1854, by Messrs. Bevington, for the Parish Church of St. Martin-in-the-Fields, was subsequently re-modelled by Messrs. Hill and Son. It contains 3 Manuals, from CC to G in alt. (56 keys) and Pedal organ, 2½ octaves (30 keys) ; 2 pairs of double-action bellows, with inverted rib, 10 feet long by 7 feet wide, and 43 Register stops.

The whole is enclosed in two richly carved cases of solid wainscoat oak, from the designs of Thomas Allom, Architect, M.I.B.A. The large case, 29 feet in height by 19 in width, contains the Great, the Swell, and the Pedal organs, all the gilt front pipes forming the lower notes of the Diapasons, the centre pipe, CCC, being 18 feet in length. The smaller case in front of the lower gallery, 10 feet wide by 12 feet in height, contains the Choir organ, the front gilt pipes also forming a portion of the interior stops.

Great Organ, Compass CC to G, 56 Notes.

1. Double Open Diapason ... 16 feet.
2. Open Diapason, No. 1 ... 8 feet.
3. Open Diapason, No. 2 ... 8 feet.
4. Stopped Diapason .... 8 feet.
5. Principal .... 4 feet.
6. Harmonic Flute .... 4 feet.
7. Twelfth .... 3 feet.
8. Fifteenth .... 2 feet.
9. Mixture, IV ranks.
10. Posaune .... 8 feet.
11. Clarion .... 4 feet.

Swell Organ, Compass CC to G, 56 Notes.

12. Double Open Diapason ... 16 feet.
13. Open Diapason .... 8 feet.
14. Dulciana to tenor c .... 8 feet.
15. Stopped Diapason, wood 8 feet.
16. Principal, metal .... 4 feet.
17. Flute, wood .... 4 feet.
18. Twelfth, metal .... 3 feet.
19. Fifteenth, metal .... 2 feet.
20. Mixture, II ranks.
21. Oboe .... 8 feet.
22. Horn .... 8 feet.
23. Double Trumpet............ 16 feet.
24. Clarion....................... 4 feet.

Choir Organ, Compass CC to G, 56 Notes.

25.	Double Open Diapason, wood	16 feet.	31.	Stopped Diapason, Bass, wood	8 feet.

25. Double Open Diapason, wood .... 16 feet.
26. Bourdon, wood .... 16 feet.
27. Open Diapason, metal ... 8 feet.
28. Dulciana, to tenor c, metal 8 feet.
29. Keraulophon, metal ...... 8 feet.
30. Claribel, wood .... 8 feet.

31. Stopped Diapason, Bass, wood .... 8 feet.
32. Principal, metal .... 4 feet.
33. Flute, wood.................. 4 feet.
34. Flautina, metal .... 2 feet.
35. Clarionet, to tenor c ...... 8 feet.
36. Bassoon .... 16 feet.

Pedal Organ, Compass CCC to F, 29 Notes.

37. Great Open Diapason, wood 16 feet.
38. Bourdon, wood .... 16 feet.
39. Bass Flute, wood............ 8 feet.
40. Principal, metal .... 8 feet.

41. Fifteenth, metal .... 4 feet.
42. Great Trombone, metal... 16 feet.
43. Clarion, metal................ 8 feet.

Couplers.

1. Swell to Great.
2. Swell to Choir.
3. Great to Pedals.

4. Choir to Pedals.
5. Swell to Pedals.

Six Composition Draw stop Pedals acting ; three on the Great and three on the Swell organ.

180. CHRIST CHURCH, NEWGATE STREET.

The fine organ in Christ Church, Newgate Street, was originally built by Harris in 1690. After receiving various additions, it was entirely remodelled by Mr. Hill about the year 1835, when all the Manual organs were re-constructed to the CC compass ; but at that time the Pedal organ had but one octave of pipes to each stop, and the Pedal reeds only four notes to each stop ; the Open Diapason in Choir ceased at Gamut G ; and the organ had no Composition Pedals. The touch was extremely heavy ; the number of speaking stops then being 39.

In the years 1867-68 extensive improvements were suggested by the present organist, Joseph Thomas Cooper, F.R.A.S., and by the liberality of the united parishes of Christ Church, Newgate Street, and St. Leonard's, Foster Lane, the work was executed by Messrs. Hill & Son. The instrument now contains the following stops :—

Great Organ, 13 Stops.

1. Double Open Diapason ... 16 feet.
2. Open Diapason .... 8 feet.
3. Open Diapason .... 8 feet.
4. Stopped Diapason .... 8 feet tone.
5. Principal .... 4 feet.
6. Twelfth........................ 2⅔ feet.
7. Fifteenth .... 2 feet.

8. Sesqualtera, V ranks.
9. Mixture, V ranks.
10. Doublette, II ranks ...... 2 feet.
11. Double Trumpet............ 16 feet.
12. Posaune .... 8 feet.
13. Clarion .... 4 feet.

Swell Organ, 11 Stops.

14. Double Diapason............ 16 feet tone.
15. Open Diapason .... 8 feet.
16. Stopped Diapason .... 8 feet tone.
17. Principal .... 4 feet.
18. Flageolet .... 4 feet.
19. Fifteenth .... 2 feet.

20. Mixture, V ranks.
21. Corno .... 8 feet.
22. Trumpet .... 8 feet.
23. Hautbois...................... 8 feet.
24. Clarion........................ 4 feet.

Choir Organ, 8 Stops.

25. *Open Diapason (now extended to CC) .... 8 feet.
26. Stopped Diapason .... 8 feet tone.
27. *Dulciana .... 8 feet.
28. *Clarionet (to CC)........... 8 feet.
29. Principal .... 4 feet.

30. *Lieblich Flute.............. 4 feet.
31. Fifteenth..................... 2 feet.
32. *Flute Piccolo (converted from the previous Stopped Flute)...................... 2 feet.

Pedal Organ, 10 Stops.

33. *Sub-Bass (converted from the previous Double Open Diapason, and now carried throughout) ...... 32 feet.
34. Open Wood.................. 16 feet.
35. Montre, open metal......... 16 feet.
36. *Bourdon .... 16 feet tone.

37. Principal .... 8 feet.
38. Twelfth .... 5⅓ feet.
39. Fifteenth..................... 4 feet.
40. Larigot Mixture, V ranks.
41. Trombone .... 16 feet.
42. Octave Trombone .... 8 feet.

Accessory Stops, Movements, &c.

1. Coupler, Great to Pedal.
2. Coupler, Swell to Pedal.
3. Coupler, Choir to Pedal.

4. Coupler, Swell to Great.
5. Coupler, Choir to Great.
6. Coupler, Choir to Swell.

Composition Pedals.

Three to Great organ. | Two to Choir organ.

Compass.

Great CC to f³ in alt.
Swell CC to f³ in alt.
Choir CC to f³ in alt.

Pedal Organ, CCCC, to tenor f.
Pedal Clavier, CC, to f¹ ; two octaves and a half.

The improvements made in 1867-68, were :—New Manuals, new radiating Pedal-board ; the Pneumatic action applied to the Great organ and all the Couplers ; a new Dulciana, Clarionet, and Lieblich Flute added to Choir ; the Open Diapason Choir extended from Gamut G to CC ; the Old Stopped Flute in Choir converted into a Piccolo ; a new Bourdon stop added to Pedal organ ; one of the open wood, 16-feet Pedals converted into a Sub-bass, 32-feet (these new stops and conversions are marked *). All the Pedal stops extended to the complete compass, two octaves and a half ; and the five Composition Pedals.

181. ST. LAWRENCE JEWRY, GUILDHALL.

This organ was built by Gray and Davison, 1875, the handsome old case by Harris being retained. It has 33 stops, 5 couplers, 3 Manuals, CC to A, and Pedal CCC to F.

Great Organ.

1. Double Diapason............ 16 feet.
2. Open Diapason .... 8 feet.
3. Open Diapason .... 8 feet.
4. Clarabella..................... 8 feet.
5. Octave .... 4 feet.

6. Flute Octaviante............ 4 feet.
7. Quint .... 2⅔ feet.
8. Super Octave .... 2 feet.
9. Mixture, V ranks.
10. Trumpet .... 8 feet.

Swell Organ.

11. Lieblich Bourdon	16 feet.		16. Geigen Principal	4 feet.
12. Open Diapason	8 feet.		17. Mixture, III ranks.	
13. Keraulophon	8 feet.		18. Cornopean	8 feet.
14. Rohr Flute	8 feet.		19. Oboe	8 feet.
15. Voix Céleste	8 feet.		20. Clarion	4 feet.

Choir Organ.

21. Lieblich Bourdon	16 feet.		25. Suabe Flute	4 feet.
22. Salicional	8 feet.		26. Flageolet Harmonic	2 feet.
23. Lieblich Gedact	8 feet.		27. Corno di Bassetto	8 feet.
24. Viol d'Amour	4 feet.			

Pedal Organ.

28. Open Diapason	16 feet.		31. Violoncello	8 feet.
29. Violon	16 feet.		32. Super Octave	4 feet.
30. Quint	10¾ feet.		33. Trombone	16 feet.

Couplers.

1. Swell to Great.
2. Swell to Pedals.
3. Swell to Choir.

4. Great to Pedals.
5. Choir to Pedals.

7 Composition Pedals. 4 to the Great and Pedal Organs, and 3 to the Swell.

The Pedal Couplers are acted on by Pedals as well as by hand.

The case has three fronts, and is of oak, very richly carved, with the case of the Choir organ, which is now inside the larger case in front.

182.—ROYAL SARDINIAN CHAPEL, LINCOLN'S INN FIELDS.

The organ in the Sardinian Chapel, Lincoln's Inn Fields, was built by Messrs. Bishop, Starr, & Richardson. It has 3 Manuals, a separate Pedal, and 40 Stops, of which the following is a list :—

Great Organ, Compass CCC to A, 70 Notes.

1. Double Diapason	16 feet.		8. Principal	4 feet.
2. Open Diapason, Bass, metal	16 feet.		9. Wald Flute	4 feet.
3. Open Diapason, Treble, metal	8 feet.		10. Twelfth	3 feet.
			11. Fifteenth	2 feet.
4. Open Diapason, Bright	8 feet.		12. Block Flute	2 feet.
5. Stop Diapason and Clarabella	8 feet.		13. Sesquialtera, IV ranks.	
6. Harmonic Flute	8 feet.		14. Mixture, III ranks.	
7. Principal	8 feet.		15. Posaune	8 feet.
			16. Trumpet	16 feet.
			17. Clarion	8 feet.

Choir Organ, Compass CC to A, 58 Notes.

18. Dulciana, Bass	8 feet.		23. Principal	4 feet.
19. Dulciana, tenor c	8 feet.		24. Flute	4 feet.
20. Viol di Gamba	8 feet.		25. Fifteenth	2 feet.
21. Stopped Diapason, Bass	8 feet.		26. Bassoon	8 feet.
22. Stopped Diapason, tenor c, metal	8 feet.		27. Cremona	8 feet.

Swell Organ, CC to A, 58 Notes.

28. Double Diapason	16 feet.	33. Mixture, III ranks.	
29. Open Diapason	8 feet.	34. Contra Fagotto	16 feet.
30. Stop Diapason	8 feet.	35. Horn	8 feet.
31. Principal	4 feet.	36. Hautboy	8 feet.
32. Fifteenth	2 feet.	37. Clarion	4 feet.

Pedal Organ, CC to E, 29 Notes.

38. Contra Bourdon	32 feet.	40. Bourdon	16 feet.
39. Open Bass	16 feet.		

Couplers.

41. Great to Pedals	16 feet.	45. Choir to Great	
42. Great to Pedals	8 feet.	46. Swell to Great	
43. Choir to Pedals		47. Swell to Choir	
44. Swell to Pedals			

Accessory Movements.

Two Octaves and one-third of Pedals.	Three Composition Pedals to Swell.
Four Composition Pedals to Great.	Movement to take on and off 16ft. Pedal Stop.

This organ has five large pairs of bellows, with different pressures of wind.

183. CHURCH OF ST. PETER, EATON SQUARE.

Organ built by Mr. T. C. Lewis. The following is a synopsis of its contents :—

Great Organ, CC to A, 58 Notes.

Front Sound-board (3½-inch wind).

1. Open Diapason	16 feet.	10. Clarion	4 feet.
2. Open Diapason, No. 1	8 feet.	This Sound-board is governed by a Ventil, with a stop-handle.	
3. Hohlflote	8 feet.	Back Sound-board (3½-inch wind).	
4. Viol di Gamba	8 feet.	11. Bourdon	16 feet.
5. Octave	4 feet.	12. Open Diapason, No. 2	8 feet.
6. Hohlflote	4 feet.	13. Viola	8 feet.
7. Great Mixture, V ranks	2 feet.	14. Stopped Diapason	8 feet.
This Sound-board is governed by a Ventil, with a stop-handle.		15. Quint	2½ feet.
Middle Sound-board (5½-inch wind.)		16. Gemshorn	4 feet.
8. Trumpet	16 feet.	17. Full Mixture, II ranks	1½ feet.
9. Trumpet	8 feet.	18. Mixture, IV ranks	1½ feet.

Swell Organ, CC to A, 58 Notes.

19. Bourdon	16 feet.	26. Flute Harmonique	4 feet.
20. Rohrflote	8 feet.	27. Mixture, V ranks	2 feet.
21. Geigen Principal	8 feet.	28. Trumpet	16 feet.
22. Flute Harmonique	8 feet.	29. Trumpet	8 feet.
23. Gamba	8 feet.	30. Oboe and Bassoon	8 feet.
24. Voix Célestes, tenor c	8 feet.	31. Clarion	4 feet.
25. Geigen Principal	4 feet.	32. Voix Humaine	8 feet.

Choir Organ, CC to A, 58 Notes.

33. Lieblich Gedact	16 feet.	39. Lieblich Gedact	4 feet.
34. Lieblich Gedact	8 feet.	40. Flauto Traverso	4 feet.
35. Salicional	8 feet.	41. Lieblich Gedact	2 feet.
36. Vox Angelica	8 feet.	42. Mixture, III ranks	2 feet.
37. Flauto Traverso	8 feet.	43. Orchestral Oboe	8 feet.
38. Salicet	4 feet.	44. Clarionet	8 feet.

T T

Pedal Organ, CCC to G, 32 Notes.

Back Sound-board (4 inch wind).
45. Great Bass, wood.............. 16 feet.
Middle Sound-board (4-inch wind).
46. Quint Bass .... 10¾ feet.
47. Octave Bass .... 8 feet.
These Sound-boards are governed by a Ventil,
with a Stop-handle.
Front Sound-board (5¼-inch wind).
48. Posaune........................... 16 feet.
49. Trumpet .... 8 feet.
This Sound-board is governed by a Ventil,
with a Stop-handle.

North Sound-board (4-inch wind).
50. Violon .... 16 feet.
51. Violoncello .... 8 feet.
This Sound-board is governed by a Ventil,
with a Stop-handle.
South Sound-board (4-inch wind).
52. Sub-bass .... 16 feet.
53. Flute Bass........................ 8 feet.

Couplers and other Movements.

1. Great to Pedals.
2. Swell to Pedals.
3. Choir to Pedals.
4. Swell to Great.
5. Choir to Great.
6. Great organ Reed Ventil.

7. Front Great organ Ventil.
8. Great Bass, Quint Bass, Octave Bass
Ventil.
9. Pedal Reed Ventil.
10. Violon and Violoncello Ventil.

Sixteen Combination and other Pedals.

Choir to Pedals, on and off.
Swell to Pedals, on and off.
Three Combinations to Swell.
Four Combinations to Great.
Great and Pedal Reeds, on and off.
Pedal to bring out all Ventil Stops, and
Great to Pedal Coupler.

Pedal to take in all Ventil Stops, and
Great to Pedal Coupler.
Choir Swell Pedal.
Voix Humaine Swell Pedal.
Swell Pedal.
Tremulant.

184. FOUNDLING HOSPITAL.

The new organ at the Foundling Hospital was built by Bevington, from a specification prepared by Mr. Willing, the organist to the chapel. It consists of 49 sounding stops, 3 Manuals, and Pedal. The following is a list of the stops which it contains :—

Great, 18 Stops.

	Pipes.	Feet.
1. Double Open Diapason to the tenor c key ...	49 ...	16
2. Bourdon, CCC to BB...	12 ...	16 tone.
3. Open Diapason, No. 1..	61 ...	8
4. Open Diapason, No. 2..	61 ...	8
5. Open Diapason, No. 3, large scale ...	61 ...	8
6. Stopped Diapason through	61 ...	8 tone.
7. Clarabella to fiddle g ...	42 ...	8
8. Principal, No. 1	61 ...	4

	Pipes.	Feet.
9. Principal, No. 2	61 ...	4
10. Wald Flute to tenor c	49 ...	4
11. Twelfth	61 ...	2⅔
12. Fifteenth	61 ...	2
13. Sesquialtera	244 ...	IV ranks.
14. Mixture	183 ...	III ranks.
15. Furniture	183 ...	III ranks.
16. Trumpet	61 ...	8
17. Tromba, solo stop ...	49 ...	8
18. Clarion	61 ...	4

Choir, 11 Stops.

	Pipes.	Feet.
19. Dulcian, Treble	49 ...	8
20. Dulcian, Bass	12 ...	8
21. Viol di Gamba, tenor c	49 ...	8
22. Stopped Diapason	61 ...	8 tone.
23. Principal	61 ...	4
24. Wald Flute, tenor c ...	49 ...	4

	Pipes.	Feet.
25. Suabe Flute, tenor c ...	49 ...	4
26. Fifteenth	61 ...	2
27. Piccolo, tenor c	49 ...	2
28. Double Bassoon, tenor c	49 ...	16
29. Clarionette, tenor c...	49 ...	8 tone.

Swell, 15 Stops.

	Pipes.	Feet.		Pipes.	Feet.
30. Double Open Diapason to fiddle g key	42	16	37. Principal	61	4
31. Bourdon Bass, CCC to FF♯	19	16 tone.	38. Open Flute, tenor c	49	4
32. Open Diapason	61	8	39. Triplet	183	III ranks.
33. Stopped Diapason, Treble	49	8 tone.	40. Doublette	122	II ranks.
34. Stopped Diapason, Bass	12	8 tone.	41. Trombone	61	16
35. Dulciana, tenor c	49	8	42. Cornopean	61	8
36. Viol di Gamba, tenor c	49	8	43. Oboe	61	8
			44. Clarion	61	4

Pedal, 5 Stops.

	Pipes.	Feet.		Pipes.	Feet.
45. Open Diapason, wood	30	16	48. Principal, metal	30	8
46. Open Diapason, metal	30	16	49. Trombone, metal	30	16
47. Bourdon, wood	30	16 tone.			

Also by means of an octave coupler and an additional octave of pipes above tenor f :—

	Pipes.	Feet.		Pipes.	Feet.
a. Octave, wood	12	8	d. Fifteenth, metal	12	4
b. Principal, metal	12	8	e. Trumpet, metal	12	8
c. Bass Flute, wood	12	8 tone.			

Accessory Stops, Movements, &c.

1. Swell to Great.	5. Pedal to Choir.
2. Swell to Choir.	6. Octave up to Great.
3. Pedal to Great.	7 to 15. Nine Composition Pedals.
4. Pedal to Swell.	

Compass.

Great, CC to c⁴ in altissimo, 5 complete octaves.	Swell, CC to c⁴ in altissimo, ditto.
Choir, CC to c⁴ in altissimo, ditto.	Pedal Organ, CCC to Middle f¹, 3½ octaves.
	Pedal Clavier, CCC to Tenor F, 2½ octaves.

185. Christ Church, Westminster Road.

This organ, by Mr. T. C. Lewis, has 36 sounding stops, 3 Manuals, and a separate Pedal organ. The following is its disposition :—

Great Organ, CC to G, 56 Notes.

1. Bourdon	16 feet.	7. Hohlflote	4 feet.
2. Open Diapason, No. 1	8 feet.	8. Octave Quint	2⅔ feet.
3. Open Diapason, No. 2	8 feet.	9. Super-octave	2 feet.
4. Stopped Diapason	8 feet.	10. Mixture, IV ranks	1½ foot.
5. Hohlflote	8 feet.	11. Trumpet	16 feet.
6. Octave	4 feet.	12. Trumpet	8 feet.

Swell Organ, CC to G, 56 Notes.

13. Lieblich Gedact	16 feet.	19. Mixture, III ranks	2 feet.
14. Geigen Principal	8 feet.	20. Trumpet	16 feet.
15. Gamba	8 feet.	21. Trumpet	8 feet.
16. Voix Célestes, tenor c	8 feet.	22. Oboe	8 feet.
17. Rohrflote	8 feet.	23. Clarion	4 feet.
18. Geigen Principal	4 feet.		

Choir Organ, CC to G, 56 Notes.

24. Lieblich Gedact	8 feet.	
25. Salicional	8 feet.	
26. Vox Angelica	8 feet.	
27. Salicet	4 feet.	
28. Flauto Traverso	4 feet.	
29. Flautina	2 feet.	
30. Clarionet	8 feet.	

Pedal Organ, CCC to F, 30 Notes.

31. Open Bass	16 feet.	
32. Sub-bass	16 feet.	
33. Quint Bass	10⅔ feet.	
34. Octave Bass	8 feet.	
35. Flute Bass	8 feet.	
36. Posaune	16 feet.	

Couplers.

1. Choir to Pedals.
2. Great to Pedals.
3. Swell to Pedals.
4. Swell to Great.

Pedals of Combination.

4 to the Great organ.   3 to the Swell organ.

186. SAINT JOHN THE EVANGELIST, WILTON ROAD, PIMLICO.

This organ, by Mr. T. C. Lewis, has 3 complete Manuals, a separate Pedal organ, and the 32 sounding stops mentioned below:—

Great Organ, CC to A, 58 Notes.

1. Bourdon	16 feet.	
2. Open Diapason, No. 1	8 feet.	
3. Open Diapason, No. 2	8 feet.	
4. Stopped Diapason	8 feet.	
5. Hohlflote	8 feet.	
6. Octave	4 feet.	
7. Hohlflote	4 feet.	
8. Octave Quint	2⅓ feet.	
9. Super-octave	2 feet.	
10. Mixture, IV ranks	1½ foot.	
11. Trumpet	8 feet.	

Swell Organ, CC to A, 58 Notes.

12. Lieblich Gedact	16 feet.	
13. Geigen Principal	8 feet.	
14. Rohrflote	8 feet.	
15. Gamba	8 feet.	
16. Voix Célestes, tenor c	8 feet.	
17. Æolian	8 feet.	
18. Geigen Principal	4 feet.	
19. Mixture, III ranks	2 feet.	
20. Trumpet	16 feet.	
21. Trumpet	8 feet.	
22. Oboe	8 feet.	
23. Voix Humaine	8 feet.	
24. Clarion	4 feet.	

Choir Organ, CC to A, 58 Notes.

25. Lieblich-Gedact	8 feet.	
26. Salicional	8 feet.	
27. Vox Angelica	8 feet.	
28. Concert Flute	4 feet.	
29. Salicet	4 feet.	

Pedal Organ, CCC to F, 30 Notes.

Independent Pedal action, 16-feet pitch.

30. Open Bass	16 feet.	
31. Sub-bass	16 feet.	
32. Posaune	16 feet.	

Independent Pedal action, 8 feet pitch.

1. Octave	8 feet.	
2. Flute Bass	8 feet.	
3. Trumpet	8 feet.	

Couplers.

1. Choir to Pedals.	4. Swell to Great.
2. Great to Pedals.	5. Swell to Choir.
3. Swell to Pedals.	

Pedals of Combination.

4 to the Great organ.	4 to the Swell organ.

187. ST. GABRIEL'S CHURCH, PIMLICO.

This organ was built by Bevington, from a specification prepared by the late Mr. Brownsmith, organist to the church. It contains 32 draw stops, commanding the sounding stops, and 6 Couplers. The following is a list of its contents :—

Great, 11 *Stops.*

	Pipes.		Pipes.
1. Open Diapason	59	8. Sesquialtera	177
2. Open Diapason	59	9. Mixture	118
3. Stopped Diapason	59	10. Trumpet	59
4. Principal	59	11. Clarion	59
5. Flute	59		—
6. Twelfth	59		826
7. Fifteenth	59		

Swell, 11 *Stops.*

		Pipes.		Pipes.
12. Double Diapason, Bass	} 47		19. Mixture	94
13. Double Diapason, Treble			20. Horn	47
14. Open Diapason		47	21. Oboe	47
15. Dulciana		47	22. Clarion	47
16. Stopped Diapason		47		—
17. Principal		47		517
18. Flute		47		

Choir, 8 *Stops.*

	Pipes.		Pipes.
23. Dulciana	47	28. Fifteenth	59
24. Stopped Diapason	59	29. Bassoon	59
25. Principal	59	30. Cremona	} 59
26. Flute, Bass	} 59		
27. Flute, Treble			342

Pedal, 2 *Stops.*

31. Open Diapason to CCC, 16 feet length	20	32. Trombone to CCC, 16 feet length	20
			40

Accessory Stops, Movements, &c.

1. Swell to Great.	5. Pedals to Great.
2. Octave down, Choir to Great.	6. Pedals to Choir.
3. Octave up, Great.	7 to 11. Five Composition Pedals.
4. Octave down, Choir.	

Compass.

Great, GG, with GG♯ up to f³ in alt.	Pedal organ, Gamut G down to CCC, 16
Choir, GG, with GG♯ up to f³ in alt.	feet length, then repeating.
Swell organ, Gamut G, up to f³ in alt.	Pedal Clavier, GG to Fiddle g, two octaves.
Swell Clavier, down to GG, acting on	
Choir organ below Gamut G.	

The organ is enclosed in a Gothic screen case of solid oak, with gilt speaking pipes, designed by Thomas Cundy, Esq., the architect of the church.

188. St. Paul's, Wilton Place, Knightsbridge.

This organ, built by Gray and Davison in 1843, was enlarged by the builders in 1871, and re-erected in an organ chamber on the north side of the church. It consists of four rows of keys, 42 sounding stops, and has an independent Pedal organ, an octave lower than the Manuals, of two octaves and three notes in compass, CCC, 16 feet, to E, with *nine* ranks of pipes throughout. The following is a list of the stops :—

Great, 13 Stops.

1. Double Diapason, Bass ...	16 feet.	8. Fifteenth	2 feet.
2. Double Diapason, Treble	16 feet.	9. Sesquialtera, IV ranks	
3. Open Diapason	8 feet.	10. Mixture, II ranks.	
4. Open Diapason	8 feet.	11. Harmonic Flute	4 feet.
5. Stopped Diapason	8 feet.	12. Trumpet	8 feet.
6. Principal	4 feet.	13. Clarion	4 feet.
7. Twelfth	3 feet.		

Choir, 11 Stops.

14. Dulciana	8 feet.	20. Principal	4 feet.
15. Keraulophon	8 feet.	21. Piccolo	2 feet.
16. Stopped Diapason, Bass...	8 feet.	22. Fifteenth	2 feet.
17. Stopped Diapason, Treble	8 feet.	23. Suabe Flute	4 feet.
18. Voix Celeste..................	8 feet.	24. Clarionet	8 feet.
19. Flute	4 feet.		

Swell, 13 Stops.

25. Double Diapason, Bass ...	16 feet.	32. Sesquialtera, III ranks.	
26. Double Diapason, Treble	16 feet.	33. Mixture, II ranks.	
27. Open Diapason	8 feet.	34. Hautboy	8 feet.
28. Stopped Diapason	8 feet.	35. Cornopean	8 feet.
29. Principal	4 feet.	36. Trumpet	8 feet.
30. Flute	4 feet.	37. Clarion	2 feet.
31. Fifteenth	2 feet.		

Pedal, 6 Stops.

38. Open Diapason	16 feet.	41. Fifteenth.....................	4 feet.
39. Stopped Diapason	16 feet.	42. Trombone	16 feet.
40. Principal	8 feet.		

Couplers.

1. Swell to Great Manual.	4. Great Manual to Pedals.
2. Swell to Choir Manual.	5. Choir Manual to Pedals.
3. Swell Manual to Pedals.	6. Tremulant to Swell.

The Swell organ is of the same compass as the Great and Choir organs —CC, 8 feet—and is of an improved construction. The four reed stops, Hautboy, Cornopean, Trumpet, and Clarion, as well as the Double Diapason of 16 feet, are throughout the whole compass of this part of the instrument. The Keraulophon was introduced *for the first time* in this instrument. There are eight Composition Pedals, to change the stops in the various organs.

189. The Oratory, Brompton.

This instrument was built by Messrs. Bishop and Starr, and contains 59 sounding stops, distributed among 4 Manuals and Pedal in the following manner :—

Great Organ, CC to A, 58 Notes.

	Pipes.	Feet.		Pipes.	Feet.
1. Sub Open Diapason, metal	58	16	9. Twelfth	58	3
2. Open Diapason	58	8	10. Fifteenth	58	2
3. Bell Diapason	58	8	11. Block Flute	58	2
4. Clarabella	58	8	12. Sesquialtera, IV ranks	232	
5. Stop Diapason	58	8	13. Mixture, III ranks	174	
6. Principal	58	4	14. Posaune	58	8
7. Wald Flute	58	4	15. Clarion	58	4
8. Harmonic Flute	39	8			

Swell Organ, CC to A, 58 Notes.

	Pipes.	Feet.		Pipes.	Feet.
16. Double Diapason	58	16	23. Sesquialtera, III ranks	174	
17. Open Diapason	58	8	24. Mixture, III ranks	174	
18. Salicional	46	8	25. Contra Fagotto	58	16
19. Stopped Clarionette Flute	58	8	26. Cornopean	58	8
20. Principal	58	8	27. Hautboy	58	8
21. Keraulophon	58	4	28. Clarion	58	4
22. Fifteenth	58	2			

Choir Organ, CC to F, 58 Notes.

	Pipes.	Feet.		Pipes.	Feet.
29. Bourdon, Bass	12	19	37. German Flute	46	4
30. Sub-Dulciana	42	16	38. Hohl Flute	58	4
31. Open Diapason, C grooved			39. Fifteenth	58	2
Bass	46	8	40. Piccolo	58	2
32. Dulciana	58	8	41. Dulciana Mixture, III ranks	174	
33. Stopped Diapason, Bass	12	8	42. Bassoon, Bass	12	8
34. Metallic Flute	46	8	43. Bassoon	46	8
35. Viol di Gamba	46	8	44. Cremona	46	8
36. Principal	58	4			

Solo Organ, CC to A, 58 Notes.

	Pipes.	Feet.			Feet.
45. Tuba	58	8	47. Octave Tuba (prepared)		4
46. Flute Harmonique	58	8			

Pedal Organ, CCC to E, 29 Notes.

	Pipes.	Feet.		Pipes.	Feet.
48. Space for		32	54. Stopped Flute	41	8
49. Open Diapason, metal	41	16	55. Fifteenth	41	4
50. Open Diapason, wood	29	16	56. Sesquialtera	82	
51. Violon	29	16	57. Mixture	82	
52. Bourdon	41	16	58. Bombardone	29	16
53. Principal	41	8	59. Clarion	41	8

Couplers.

1. Solo to Great.
2. Solo to Swell.
3. Swell to Great.
4. Choir to Great.
5. Swell to Choir.
6. Solo to Pedals.

7. Swell to Pedals.
8. Great to Pedals.
9. Choir to Pedals.
10. Pedal Super-octave.
11. Tremulant.
12. Steam.

Accessory Stops.

Four Composition Pedals to Choir
Three Composition Pedals to Great.

Three Composition Pedals to Swell.
Three Composition Pedals to Pedals.

The organ has four large pairs of bellows, with different pressures of wind, operated upon by steam power. It is 24 feet wide, 18 feet deep, and 31 feet high, and is surrounded by large metal pipes, which for the present are left in their metallic lustre.

190. Parish Church, Kensington.

Description of the organ in the Parish Church, Kensington, built by Hill and Son in 1872. Three Manuals, compass of each, CC to G, 56 notes, and Pedal Clavier, CCC to F, 30 notes.

Great Organ.

		Pipes.				Pipes.
1.	Double Diapason, wood and metal	16 feet ... 56	6.	Principal, metal	4 feet ...	56
2.	Open Diapason, wood and metal	8 feet ... 56	7.	Harmonic Flute, metal...	4 feet ...	56
			8.	Twelfth, metal	3 feet ...	56
3.	Open Diapason, No. 2, wood and metal	8 feet ... 56	9.	Fifteenth, metal	2 feet ...	56
			10.	Mixture, metal, IV ranks.	...	224
4.	Gamba, wood and metal...	8 feet ... 56	11.	Posaune, metal	8 feet ...	56
5.	Stopped Diapason, wood	8 feet ... 56	12.	Clarion, metal	8 feet ...	56

Choir Organ.

13.	Open Diapason, metal ...	8 feet ... 56	17.	Wald Flute, wood	4 feet ...	56
14.	Dulciana, metal	8 feet ... 56	18.	Flautina, metal	2 feet ...	56
15.	Gedact, wood	8 feet ... 56	19.	Clarionet, metal	8 feet ...	56
16.	Gemshorn, metal	4 feet ... 56				

Swell Organ.

20.	Bourdon, wood	16 feet ... 56	26.	Twelfth, metal	3 feet ...	56
21.	Open Diapason, metal ...	8 feet ... 56	27.	Fifteenth, metal	2 feet ...	56
22.	Salicional, metal	8 feet ... 56	28.	Mixture, metal, IV ranks.	...	224
23.	Stopped Diapason, wood	8 feet ... 56	29.	Horn, metal	8 feet ...	58
24.	Principal, metal	4 feet ... 56	30.	Oboe, metal	8 feet ...	58
25.	Suabe Flute, wood	4 feet ... 56	31.	Clarion, metal	8 feet ...	58

Pedal Organ.

32.	Sub-Bourdon, wood	32 feet ... 30	36.	Principal, metal	8 feet ...	30
33.	Open Diapason, wood ...	16 feet ... 30	37.	Fifteenth, metal	4 feet ...	30
34.	Violone, wood	16 feet ... 30	38.	Trombone, wood	16 feet ...	30
35.	Bourdon, wood	16 feet ... 30				

Couplers.

1. Swell to Great.
2. Swell to Choir.
3. Great to Pedal.

4. Choir to Pedal.
5. Swell to Pedal.

Four Composition Pedals to Great and Pedal. | Three Composition Pedals to Swell Organ.

191. Church of St. Mary Aldermary, Queen Victoria Street.

The organ in this church, built in 1781 by England and Russell, was rebuilt and enlarged by G. M. Holdich in 1877, and now contains 30 sounding stops.

Great Organ, CC to G.

1. Double Diapason	16 feet.	6. Principal	4 feet.
2. Open Diapason	8 feet.	7. Twelfth	3 feet.
3. Gamba	8 feet.	8. Fifteenth	2 feet.
4. Stopped Diapason	8 feet.	9. Sesquialtera, III ranks.	
5. Wald Flute	4 feet.	10. Trumpet	8 feet.

Choir Organ, CC to G.

11. Dulciana	8 feet.	15. Piccolo Flute	2 feet.
12. Stopped Diapason	8 feet.	16. Oboe	8 feet.
13. Flute	4 feet.	17. Cremona to tenor c	8 feet.
14. Principal	4 feet.		

Swell Organ, CC to G.

18. Open Diapason	8 feet.	23. Mixture, III ranks.	
19. Stopped Diapason	8 feet.	24. Horn	8 feet.
20. Salicional	8 feet.	25. Hautboy	8 feet.
21. Principal	4 feet.	26. Clarion	4 feet.
22. Fifteenth	2 feet.		

Pedal Organ, CCC to F.

27. Double Open Diapason	16 feet.	29. Octave	8 feet.
28. Bourdon	16 feet.	30. Trombone	16 feet.

Compass.

1. Great to Pedals.	4. Swell to Great.
2. Choir to Pedals.	5. Swell to Choir.
3. Swell to Pedals.	6. Sub-octave Swell.

Three Composition Pedals to Great.   Two Composition Pedals to Swell.

192. St. Sepulchre's.

The organ in St. Sepulchre's Church, Snow Hill, was originally built by Renatus Harris, in 1670, and is supposed to be the oldest instrument of his make now existing in London. It consisted at first of a Great and Choir organ only, the compass being from GG, short octaves, to d³ in alt. On the instrument undergoing an extensive repair by the elder Byfield, about the year 1730, a small Tenor f Swell was added, and a new Trumpet, Clarion, and Open Diapason Bass put to the Great organ. In 1817 the compass was carried up to e³ in alt., and made "long octaves" in the Bass by Mr. Hancock; another Open Diapason was added throughout the Great organ, a Dulciana put in the Choir organ, in place of the Vox Humana ; and an Octave of GG Pedals and Unison Pedal Pipes applied. In 1827 the Swell was extended in compass down to Gamut G by Mr. Gray, and two octaves of CCC Pedals laid down ; also two Couplers, Great and Choir to Pedal, introduced. In 1835 Mr. Gray made a further extension of the Swell, and added the Great Pedal Diapason, which is the identical one that was used in the organ erected for the Festival in Westminster Abbey, in 1834. A new sound-board was also made to the Great organ for facilitating the tuning, and for improving and preserving the instrument. The organ has since been considerably enlarged and improved by Gray and Davison, through the liberality of the parish and the munificence of a private gentleman. The new work consisted of an independent Pedal organ of 10 stops, the Keraulophon and Clarionet stops in the Choir organ, an extension of the Swell Double Diapason, new Manuals, &c. ; and " it now requires only a Double Diapason and a new Open Diapason in the Great organ, the Double Diapason in the Swell to be completed, and a Contra Fagotto or Double Reed throughout the same Manual, with new Draw-Stop Action, Composition Pedals, &c., to make this truly magnificent instrument complete."* It contains 42 sounding stops, of which the following is a list :—

Great Organ, 15 Stops.

1. Open Diapason, No. 1 ...	8 feet.	9. Tierce	1⅗ foot.
2. Open Diapason, No. 2 ...	8 feet.	10. Larigot	1⅓ foot.
3. Stopped Diapason	8 feet.	11. Sesquialtera, III ranks ...	1½ foot.
4. Clarabella Treble	8 feet.	12. Mixture, II ranks	⅔ foot.
5. Principal, No. 1	4 feet.	13. Furniture, III ranks	1⅗ foot.
6. Principal, No. 2	4 feet.	14. Trumpet	8 feet.
7. Twelfth.......................	3 feet.	15. Clarion......................	4 feet.
8. Fifteenth	2 feet.		

Swell Organ, 10 Stops.

16. Double Diapason, Bass ...	16 feet.	21. Sesquialtera, III ranks ...	1¼ feet.
17. Open Diapason	8 feet.	22. Horn	8 feet.
18. Stopped Diapason	8 feet.	23. Trumpet	8 feet.
19. Principal	4 feet.	24. Hautbois	8 feet.
20. Fifteenth	2 feet.	25. Clarion	4 feet.

Choir Organ, 7 Stops.

26. Stopped Diapason	8 feet.	30. Flute	4 feet.
27. Dulcian.......................	8 feet.	31. Fifteenth	2 feet.
28. Keraulophon	8 feet.	32. Clarionet	8 feet.
29. Principal	4 feet.		

Pedal Organ, 10 Stops.

33. Grand Open Diapason, wood........	16 feet.	38. Grand Fifteenth	4 feet.
		39. Grand Mixture, V ranks.	
34. Grand Violon, metal	16 feet.	40. Grand Posaune	16 feet.
35. Grand Bourdon	16 feet.	41. Grand Trumpet	8 feet.
36. Grand Principal	8 feet.	42. Grand Clarion..............	4 feet.
37. Grand Twelfth..............	6 feet.		

Accessory Stops, Movements, &c.

1. Coupler, Great to Pedal, 16 feet pitch.	7. Choir, Sub-octave to Great.
2. Coupler, Great to Pedal, 8 feet pitch.	8. Sforzando Coupler, Great to Swell.
3. Coupler, Choir to Pedal, 8 feet pitch.	9 to 15. Seven Composition Pedals.
4. Coupler, Swell to Pedal, 16 feet pitch.	16. Pneumatic Lever attachment.
5. Coupler, Swell to Great.	17. Tremulant Swell.
6. Coupler, Swell to Choir.	Two Horizontal Bellows.

Compass.

Great, GG to e³ in alt.	Swell, GG to e³ in alt.
Choir, GG to e³ in alt.	Pedal, CCC to tenor f.

---

* Advertisement to the late Mr. Cooper's *Organist's Manual.*

193. ST. ANDREW'S, HOLBORN.

Description of the organ in St. Andrew's Church, Holborn, built by Hill and Sons in 1872. Three Manuals, compass of each CC to G, 56 notes, and Pedal Clavier, CCC to F, 30 notes.

Great Organ.

1. Double Diapason, wood...	16 feet.	7. Twelfth, metal............	3 feet.
2. Open Diapason, metal ...	8 feet.	8 Fifteenth ,, ...	2 feet.
3. Open Diapason, No. 2, metal	8 feet.	9. Sesquialtera ,, ...	3 ranks.
4. Stopped Diapason, wood	8 feet.	10. Mixture ,, ...	4 ranks.
5. Principal, metal	4 feet.	11. Posaune ,, ...	8 feet.
6. Harmonic Flute, metal ...	4 feet.	12. Clarion ,, ...	8 feet.

Choir Organ.

13. Lieblich Gedact, wood ...	16 feet.	18. Principal, metal...........	4 feet.
14. Open Diapason, metal ...	8 feet.	19. Suabe Flute, wood.........	4 feet.
15. Gamba, metal	8 feet.	20. Fifteenth, metal...........	2 feet.
16. Dulciana, metal	8 feet.	21. Clarionet, tenor c, metal	8 feet.
17. Claribel, wood..............	8 feet.		

Swell Organ.

22. Bourdon, wood	16 feet.	29. Mixture, metal	5 ranks.
23. Open Diapason, metal ...	8 feet.	30. Double Trumpet, metal...	16 feet.
24. Viol d'amour, metal	8 feet.	31. Cornopean, metal	8 feet.
25. Stopped Diapason, wood	8 feet.	32. Trumpet, metal	8 feet.
26. Principal, metal	4 feet.	33. Oboe, metal	8 feet.
27. Wald Flute, wood	4 feet.	34. Clarion, metal	8 feet.
28. Fifteenth, metal	2 feet.		

Pedal Organ.

35. Open Diapason, wood ...	16 feet.	39. Twelfth, metal	6 feet.
36. Open Diapason, metal ...	16 feet.	40. Fifteenth, metal...........	4 feet.
37. Bourdon, wood	16 feet.	41. Trombone, wood	16 feet.
38. Principal, metal	8 feet.	42. Trumpet, metal	8 feet.

Couplers.

1. Swell to Great.	4. Great to Pedal.
2. Swell to Great (Sub-Octave).	5. Choir to Pedal.
3. Choir to Swell.	6. Swell to Pedal.

Three Composition Pedals to Great Organ and Pedal. | Three Composition Pedals to Swell Organ.

Pneumatic Action to Great Organ and Couplers.

194. ST. PETER'S, CORNHILL.

The organ in St. Peter's Church, Cornhill, was originally built by Father Smith, in 1681, at a cost of £210, inclusive of painting and gilding. It then contained the following 13 Stops; compass, GG, short octaves, to d in alt., viz. :—

Great, 9 Stops.

1. Open Diapason.	4. Twelfth.	7. Mixture, II ranks.
2. Stopped Diapason.	5. Fifteenth.	8. Trumpet.
3. Principal.	6. Sesquialtera, III ranks.	9. Cornet to Middle c♯, V ranks.

Choir, 4 Stops.

10. Stopped Diapason.	11. Principal.	12. Fifteenth.	13. Cremona.

To which Crang added a tenor f Swell of 6 stops. The "Chorus" of Smith's organ was originally a very fine one, but had been in very bad hands. A new inside was put to the organ, and the case widened, by the insertion of a centre tower, by Mr. Hill, about the year 1840. On removing the old instrument, it was found to contain many wooden pipes of Smith's construction, which the mellowing hand of time had rendered of more than ordinary value, and which were accordingly incorporated with the new work. The present organ, which is considered one of the finest in London, contains the following stops :—

Great, 20 *Draw Stops*.

1. Tenoroon Diapason to tenor c key	16 feet.	11. Stopped Flute	4 feet tone.
2. Bourdon to meet No. 1	16 feet tone.	12. Twelfth	2⅔ feet.
3. Principal Diapason	8 feet.	13. Fifteenth	2 feet.
4. Stopped Diapason, Treble	8 feet tone.	14. Tierce	1⅗ foot.
5. Stopped Diapason, Bass	8 feet tone.	15. Sesquialtera, II ranks	1½ foot.
6. Dulciana to tenor c	8 feet.	16. Mixture, II ranks	⅔ foot.
7. Claribel Flute to tenor c	8 feet.	17. Doublette, II ranks	2 feet.
8. Principal Octave	4 feet.	18. Corno Trombone	8 feet.
9. Wald Flute	4 feet.	19. Corno Clarion	4 feet.
10. Oboe Flute	4 feet.	20. Cremorne to tenor c	8 feet tone.

Swell, 18 *Draw Stops*.

21. Tenoroon Dulcian to tenor c key	16 feet.	30. Fifteenth	2 feet.
22. Bourdon to meet No. 21	16 feet tone.	31. Piccolo to tenor c	2 feet.
23. Principal Diapason	8 feet.	32. Sesquialtera, III ranks	1⅗ foot.
24. Stopped Diapason, Treble	8 feet tone.	33. Mixture, II ranks	⅔ foot.
25. Stopped Diapason, Bass	8 feet tone.	34. Echo Dulcian Cornet, V ranks.	
26. Principal Octave	4 feet.	35. Cornopean	8 feet.
27. Suabe Flute to tenor c	4 feet.	36. Tromba	8 feet.
28. Flageolet to tenor c	4 feet.	37. Hautboy	8 feet.
29. Twelfth	2⅔ feet.	38. Clarion	4 feet.

Pedal, 2 *Draw Stops*.

39. Great Diapason	16 feet.	40. Contra Posaune	16 feet.

Accessory Stops, Movements, &c.

1. Coupler, Swell to Great.	4. Octave Pedal.
2. Coupler, Great to Pedal.	5, 6, 7, 8. Four Composition Pedals.
3. Coupler, Swell to Pedal.	

Compass.

Great Organ, CC to f³ in alt., 54 notes.	Pedal Organ, CCC to BB, 12 notes.
Swell Organ, CC to f³ in alt., 54 notes.	Pedal Clavier, CCC to tenor a, 27 keys.

195. St. Michael's Cornhill.

The organ in St. Michael's Church, Cornhill, was originally built by Renatus Harris, A.D., 1684. In the year 1789 a Swell was added, and other improvements made, by Green ; and in 1849 the organ was entirely re-constructed by Messrs. Robson, under the direction of the late Mr. Limpus. The electric action has lately been applied to the instrument.

Great Organ, 12 Stops.

	Feet.	Pipes.			Feet.	Pipes.
1. Double Open Diapason, metal	16	56	7. Twelfth		3	56
2. Large Open Diapason	8	56	8. Fifteenth		2	256
3. Open Diapason	8	56	9. Sesquialtera, IV ranks		2	224
4. Stopped Diapason	8	56	10. Mixture, IV ranks		1	24
5. Principal	4	56	11. Trumpet		8	56
6. Wald Flute	4	56	12. Clarion		4	56

Choir Organ, 8 Stops.

	Feet.	Pipes.			Feet.	Pipes.
13. Dulcian	8	64	17. Flute, metal		4 tone.	56
14. Viol di Gamba	8	54	18. Fifteenth		2	56
15. Stopped Diapason	8 tone.	56	19. Bassoon		8	56
16. Principal	4	56	20. Clarionet		8 tone.	44

Swell Organ, 12 Stops.

	Feet.	Pipes.			Feet.	Pipes.
21. Double Open Diapason	16 tone.	56	27. Piccolo		2	56
22. Open Diapason	8	56	28. Sesquialtera, III ranks		$1\frac{1}{3}$	168
23. Dulcian	8	56	29. Mixture, II ranks		$\frac{3}{4}$	112
24. Stopped Diapason	8 tone.	56	30. Oboe		8	56
25. Principal	4	56	31. Horn		8	56
26. Fifteenth	2	56	32. Clarion		4	85

Pedal, 3 Stops.

	Feet.	Pipes.			Feet.	Pipes.
33. Open Diapason	16	30	35. Trombone		16	30
34. Stopped Diapason	16 tone.	30				

Accessory Stops, Movements, &c.

1. Swell to Great.
2. Swell to Choir.
3. Great to Pedal.
4. Choir to Pedal.

5. Swell to Pedal.
6. Octave Pedal.
7, 8, 9, 10. Four Composition Pedals.

Compass.

All the Manuals, CC to g³ in alt. | Pedal, CCC to tenor f.

Summary of Stops.

	Stops.	Pipes.		Stops.	Pipes.
Great Organ	12	1008		32	2260
Swell Organ	12	828	Pedal Organ	3	90
Choir Organ	8	424	Copulas	6	
	32	2260		41	2350

196. St. Stephen's Church, Walbrook.

This organ, originally built by George England about the year 1760, has been considerably enlarged and improved by Messrs. Hill and Son. It now contains the 34 sounding stops mentioned below :—

Great Organ.

1. Open Diapason	8 feet.		6. Twelfth	3 feet.
2. Open Diapason	8 feet.		7. Fifteenth	2 feet.
3. Stopped Diapason, metal, Treble	8 feet.		8. Mixture, IV ranks.	
			9. Furniture, III ranks.	
4. Principal	4 feet.		10. Trumpet	8 feet.
5. Nason, open, wood	4 feet.		11. Clarion	4 feet.

Swell Organ.

12. Bourdon	16 feet.	16. Principal	4 feet.
13. Open Diapason	8 feet.	17. Twelfth and Fifteenth ...	3 and 2 feet.
14. German flute, metal, grooved to open in Bass octave	8 feet.	18. Mixture, IV ranks.	
		19. Double Trumpet	16 feet.
		20. Oboe	8 feet.
15. Stopped Diapason, metal Treble	8 feet.	21. Trumpet	8 feet.
		22. Clarion	4 feet.

Choir Organ.

23. Keraulophon	8 feet.	27. Stopped Flute, open, metal, Treble	4 feet
24. Dulcian, grooved to Keraulophon in Bass octave	8 feet.	28. Fifteenth	2 feet.
		29. Clarionet	8 feet.
25. Stopped Diapason, metal, Treble	8 feet.	30. French Horn	8 feet.
26. Principal	4 feet.	31. Vox Humana	8 feet.

Pedal Organ.

32. Open Diapason	16 feet.	34 Trombone	16 feet.
33. Bourdon	16 feet.		

Couplers.

1. Swell to Great.	4. Great to Pedal.
2. Swell to Choir.	5. Choir to Pedal.
3. Swell to Pedals.	

Three Composition Pedals to Great, and two to Swell.

Compass.

Manuals, CC to g in altissimo, 56 feet. | Pedal, CC to f, 30 notes.

197. ST. MARY-AT-HILL.

The organ at St. Mary-at-Hill is a very fine instrument, and was built in 1849 by Messrs. Hill and Co. It contains 30 sounding stops, distributed among two Manuals and Pedal in the following manner : —

Great, 15 Stops.—Every Stop throughout.

1. Bourdon and Open Diapason	16 feet.	9. Walde Flute	4 feet.
2. Open Diapason	8 feet.	10. Flageolet	2 feet.
3. Gamba	8 feet.	11. Sesquialtera, III ranks.	
4. Stopped Diapason	8 feet.	12. Mixture, ... III ranks.	
5. Quint	6 feet.	13. Posaune	8 feet.
6. Octave	4 feet.	14. Clarion	4 feet.
7. Octave Quint	3 feet.	15. Krum Horn	8 feet.
8. Super-octave	2 feet.		

Swell, 12 Stops.

16. Bourdon and Open Diapason	16 feet.	22. Octave Quint	3 feet.
17. Open Diapason	8 feet.	23. Super-octave	2 feet.
18. { Stopped Diapason, Bass / Stopped Diapason, Treble }	8 feet.	24. Sesquialtera, III ranks.	
		25. Cornopean	8 feet.
19. Hohl Flute	8 feet.	26. Hautboy	8 feet.
20. Octave	4 feet.	27. Clarion	4 feet.
21. Suabe Flute	4 feet.		

Pedal, 3 Stops.

28. Open Diapason, 16 feet. | 29. Octave, 8 feet. | 30. Trombone.

Accessory Stops, Movements, &c.

1. Coupler, Swell to Great.
2. Coupler, Great to Pedal.
3. Coupler, Swell to Pedal.
4, 5, 6. Three Composition Pedals.

Compass.

Great, CC to f³ in alt. | Swell, CC to f³ in alt. | Pedal, CCC to tenor e.

198. ST. MICHAEL'S, CHESTER SQUARE.

This instrument, built by T. J. Robson, in 1847, consists of three Manual organs, viz., Swell, Great, and Choir, together with an independent Pedal organ. The Manuals are of the orthodox range, from CC, ascending from thence to g³ in altissimo, 56 notes. The Pedal-board, with the Pedal organ running *throughout*, extends from CCC to tenor f, 30 notes, being the *first* Pedal organ erected in London of this complete compass.

Great, 12 Stops.

1. Double Stopped Diapason	16 feet tone.	7. Fifteenth	2 feet.
2. Open Diapason	8 feet.	8. Piccolo, open, wood	2 feet.
3. Stopped Diapason	8 feet tone.	9. Sesquialtera, III ranks	1½ foot.
4. Principal	4 feet.	10. Mixture, II ranks	½ foot.
5. Flute, open, wood	4 feet.	11. Trumpet	8 feet.
6. Twelfth	2⅔ feet.	12. Clarion	4 feet.

Choir, 10 Stops.

13. Dulciana	8 feet.	19. Fifteenth	2 feet.
14. Viol di Gamba	8 feet.	20. Furniture, II ranks	1½ foot.
15. Stopped Diapason, Treble	8 feet tone.	21. Bassoon throughout	8 feet.
16. Stopped Diapason, Bass	8 feet tone.	22. Clarionet and Corno di	
17. Principal	4 feet.	Bassetto	8 feet tone.
18. Flute	4 feet.		

Swell, 12 Stops.

23. Double Dulciana	16 feet.	29. Fifteenth	2 feet.
24. Open Diapason	8 feet.	30. Mixture, III ranks	1½ foot.
25. Stopped Diapason	8 feet tone.	31. Double Bassoon	16 feet.
26. Principal	4 feet.	32. Horn	8 feet.
27. Celestina	4 feet.	33. Hautboy	8 feet.
28. Twelfth	2⅔ feet.	34. Clarion	4 feet.

Pedal, 3 Stops.

35. Open Diapason	16 feet.	37. Trombone, metal	16 feet.
36. Stopped Diapason	16 feet tone.		

Accessory Stops, Movements, &c.

1. Swell to Great.
2. Swell to Choir.
3. Great to Pedals.
4. Choir to Pedal.
5. Pedal Octave.
6, 7, 8. Three Composition Pedals.

199. St. Saviour's, Southwark.

The organ in St. Saviour's Church, Southwark, possesses a fine bold tone, and originally was enclosed in a splendid case, with the 16 feet metal Double Diapason in front. The instrument was built in the year 1703, and has been attributed to Schrider and to Schwarbrook, but the work appears more like that of Harris. The Great and Choir organs were originally "short octave, GG," and ascended to e³ in alt.; the Swell to fiddle g was a subsequent addition, having been made by Byfield. In 1818 the organ was considerably enlarged by Davis, who made the Great and Choir organs "long octaves," and added the f³ in alt. above. The Swell was extended to tenor c; an octave and a half of G Pedals were laid down; a similar compass of GGG Pedal pipes applied; and a Swell and two Pedal Couplers were also introduced.

Subsequently, Mr. Bishop put in a Cremona in place of the Vox Humana in the Choir organ; a Clarabella in the room of the 5-rank Cornet in the Great organ; a new Twelfth and Fifteenth; and a Pedal Octave Coupler. In 1841 the organ was removed from its previous position between the Transepts to the west-end of the new Nave, just then rebuilt on the site of the old one. The Swell was then extended down to Gamut G by Bishop, and two horizontal bellows provided. At the same time the magnificent old case was superseded by the present one, designed and provided by the architect of the building, and the largest pipes of the original front were placed inside. The organ now contains 28 sounding stops, of which the following is a list :—

Great, 13 Stops.

1. Double Open Diapason.	8. Twelfth.
2. Open Diapason.	9. Fifteenth.
3. Open Diapason.	10. Sesquialtera, IV ranks,
4. Stopped Diapason.	11. Furniture, III ranks.
5. Clarabella.	12. Trumpet.
6. Principal.	13. Clarion.
7. Stopped Flute.	

Choir, 7 Stops.

14. Open Diapason.	18. Fifteenth.
15. Stopped Diapason.	19. Mixture, III ranks.
16. Principal.	20. Cremona.
17. Stopped Flute.	

Swell, 7 Stops.

21. Open Diapason.	25. Trumpet.
22. Stopped Diapason.	26. Oboe.
23. Principal.	27. Clarion.
24. Sesquialtera, III ranks.	

Pedal, 1 Stop.

28. Open wood Pipes, CC to Gamut GGG ...... 21½ feet length.

Compass.

Great, GG to f³ in alt.	Swell Gamut, G to f³ in alt.
Choir, GG to f³ in alt.	Pedal, GG to tenor c.

Accessory Stops, Movements, &c.

1. Swell to Great. | 2. Choir to Great. | 3. Great to Pedal. | 4. Choir to Pedal.

200. ST. OLAVE'S, SOUTHWARK.

" This organ, of a 32 feet Manual Gamut, was designed by Mr. H. J. Gauntlett, commenced by Mr. Lincoln, 1844, and perfected by Mr. William Hill, 1846." The foregoing inscription appears on a brass plate between the Manuals. The organ is about to be rebuilt. At present it contains 40 sounding stops, of which the following is a list :—

Great, 27 Stops.

1.	Sub-bourdon to tenor c key	32 feet.	
2.	Tenoroon to tenor c key	16 feet.	
3.	Bourdon	16 feet tone.	
4.	Unison, open	8 feet.	
5.	Unison, treble, closed	8 feet tone.	
6.	Unison, bass, closed	8 feet tone.	
7.	Viol di Gamba to tenor c	8 feet.	
8.	Salicional to tenor c	8 feet.	
9.	Clarabella to tenor c	8 feet.	
10.	Quint	6 feet.	
11.	Octave	4 feet.	
12.	Wald Flute to tenor c	4 feet.	
13.	Decima	3½ feet.	
14.	Duo decimo	3 feet.	
15.	Super-octave	2 feet.	
16.	Piccolo to tenor c	2 feet.	
17.	Octave decima	1¾ foot.	
18.	Sesquialtera, III ranks.		
19.	Mixture, II ranks.		
20.	Furniture, III ranks.		
21.	Doublette, II ranks.		
22.	Glockenspiel, II ranks.		
23.	Posaune	8 feet.	
24.	Clarion	4 feet.	
25.	Octave Clarion	2 feet.	
26.	Cromhorn to tenor c	8 feet tone.	
27.	Corno Flute to tenor c	8 feet.	

Swell, 10 Stops.

28.	Tenoroon	16 feet.	
29.	Unison, open	8 feet.	
30.	Unison, closed	8 feet tone.	
31.	Octave	8 feet.	
32.	Suabe Flute	4 feet.	
33.	Super-octave	2 feet.	
34.	Flageolet	2 feet.	
35.	Octave Fifteenth	1 foot.	
36.	Cornopean	8 feet.	
37.	Hautbois	8 feet.	

Pedal, 3 Stops.

38.	Contra Bourdon	32 feet tone.	
39.	Principal Contra Bass	16 feet.	
40.	Bass Trombone	16 feet.	

Couplers, &c.

1.	Grand organ combined.	3.	Grand to Pedal.
2.	Swell to Grand.	4.	Swell to Pedal.

Compass.

Great CC to f³ in alt. | Swell, tenor c to f³ in alt. | Pedal, CCC to tenor d.

The Great organ has two separate sound-boards, which accounts for the Coupler denominated " Grand organ combined."

201. ST. JAMES'S, BERMONDSEY.

This organ was built by Bishop in 1829, and contains the following 29 stops :-

Great, 10 Stops.   59 Notes, from GG to F.

1.	Open Diapason.	6.	Fifteenth.
2.	Open Diapason.	7.	Sesquialtera, III ranks.
3.	Stopped Diapason.	8.	Mixture, II ranks.
4.	Principal.	9.	Trumpet.
5.	Twelfth.	10.	Clarion.

U U

Choir, 8 Stops.　59 Notes, from GG to F.

11. Open Diapason.	15. Flute.
12. Stopped Diapason.	16. Fifteenth.
13. Dulciana, from Gamut G.	17. Cremona, Treble.
14. Principal.	18. Bassoon, Bass.

Swell, 8 Stops.　47 Notes, from Gamut G to F.

With keys continued to GG, acting on the Choir organ.

19. Open Diapason.	23. Cornet (originally 12th, 15th, and Sesquialtera ; now, unfortunately, only 12th and 15th).
20. Open Diapason.	
21. Stopped Diapason.	24. French Horn.
22. Principal.	25. Trumpet.
	26. Hautboy.

Pedal, 3 Stops.

27. Double Diapason, 25 Notes, from GGG...21½ feet length.
28. Unison.............. Ditto .... GG...10¾ ,, ,,
29. Trombone .... Ditto .... GG...10⅜ ,, ,,

Couplers.

1. Swell to Great.	4. Pedals to Great.
2. Swell to Choir.	5. Pedals to Choir.
3. Great to Choir.	

Composition Pedals, &c.

1. Full.	4. Shifting movement for shutting off all Swell but the Diapasons.
2. Full, without Reeds.	
3. Diapasons.	5. Pedal for coupling Swell to Great.

There is a key-board at the side, by means of which a second performer can play the Pedals.

202. QUEBEC CHAPEL.

This organ was built, in 1868, by Gray and Davison. It has 3 complete Manuals from CC to A, and Pedal from CCC to F.

Swell Organ.

1. Bourdon .... 16 feet.	6. Fifteenth .... 2 feet.
2. Open Diapason .... 8 feet.	7. Mixture, III ranks.
3. Stopped Diapason .... 8 feet.	8. Cornopean .... 8 feet.
4. Keraulophon .... 8 feet.	9. Oboe .... 8 feet.
5. Principal .... 4 feet.	10. Clarion......................... 4 feet.

Great Organ.

11. Double Diapason............ 16 feet.	16. Principal .... 4 feet.
12. Open Diapason .... 8 feet.	17. Twelfth .... 3 feet.
13. Flute Harmonique .... 8 feet.	18. Fifteenth .... 2 feet.
14. Stopped Diapason .... 8 feet.	19. Mixture, IV ranks.
15. Flute Octaviante .... 4 feet.	20. Posaune .... 8 feet.

Choir Organ.

21. Dulciana .... 8 feet.	24. Gemshorn .... 4 feet.
22. Lieblich Gedact .... 8 feet.	25. Piccolo......................... 2 feet.
23. Wald Flute .... 4 feet.	26. Corno di Bassetto .... 8 feet.

Pedal Organ.

27. Grand Open Diapason ... 16 feet.	29. Grand Principal .... 8 feet.
28. Grand Bourdon .... 16 feet.	30. Grand Trombone .... 16 feet.

Couplers.

1. Swell to Great Manual.	5. Choir Manual to Pedals.
2. Swell to Choir Manual.	7 Composition Pedals. 4 to Great organ
3. Swell Manual to Pedals.	and 3 to Swell.
4. Great Manual to Pedals.	

The organ is placed in the gallery, at the north side of the chancel, and the key-boards, &c., brought down to the floor so that the organist sits near the singers.

203. St. Pancras Church.

This organ, originally built by Gray and Davison (1856) for the Music Hall, Birmingham, was rebuilt and erected by the same firm in St. Pancras Church. It has three Manuals, CC to A, and Pedals, from CCC to F, and contains 37 stops and 7 couplers.

Great Organ.

1. Double Diapason .... 16 feet.	8. Twelfth .... 3 feet.
2. Open Diapason .... 8 feet.	9. Fifteenth .... 2 feet.
3. Gamba .... 8 feet.	10. Sesquialtera, III ranks.
4. Stopped Diapason .... 8 feet.	11. Mixture, III ranks.
5. Flute Harmonic .... 8 feet.	12. Posaune .... 8 feet.
6. Octave .... 4 feet.	13. Clarion....................... 4 feet.
7. Flute Octaviante .... 4 feet.	

Swell Organ.

14. Bourdon .... 16 feet.	19. Sesquialtera, III ranks.
15. Open Diapason .... 8 feet.	20. Cornopean .... 8 feet.
16. Stopped Diapason .... 8 feet.	21. Oboe .... 8 feet.
17. Octave .... 4 feet.	22. Clarion .... 4 feet.
18. Fifteenth .... 2 feet.	Tremulant.

Choir Organ.

23. Salicional .... 8 feet.	27. Gemshorn .... 4 feet.
24. Vox Celeste .... 8 feet.	28. Flute d'Amour .... 4 feet.
25. Stopped Diapason Bass ... 8 feet.	29. Piccolo .... 2 feet.
26. Concert Flute .... 8 feet.	30. Clarionet..................... 8 feet.

Pedal Organ.

31. Contra Bourdon .... 32 feet.	35. Fifteenth .... 4 feet.
32. Open Diapason .... 16 feet.	36. Trombone .... 16 feet.
33. Bourdon .... 16 feet.	37. Trumpet .... 8 feet.
34. Octave .... 8 feet.	

Couplers.

1. Swell to Great Manual.	5. Swell to Choir.
2. Swell to Great, Sub-octave.	6. Great Manual to Pedals.
3. Swell to Great, Super-octave.	7. Choir Manual to Pedals.
4. Swell to Pedals.	

Composition Pedals.

4 to the Great ; 3 to the Swell ; and 1 to the Pedal organ.

204. KENSINGTON PARK, ALL SAINTS.

This organ was built by Gray and Davison in 1860. It has 3 Manuals, CC to F, and Pedals, CCC to E.

Great Organ.

1.	Double Diapason	16 feet.	7.	Twelfth	3 feet
2.	Open Diapason	8 feet.	8.	Fifteenth	2 feet.
3.	Gamba	8 feet.	9.	Mixture, III ranks.	
4.	Stopped Diapason	8 feet.	10.	Furniture, III ranks.	
5.	Principal	4 feet.	11.	Trumpet	8 feet.
6.	Flute Harmonic	4 feet.			

Choir Organ.

12.	Dulciana	8 feet.	15.	Gemshorn	4 feet.
13.	Stopped Diapason	8 feet.	16.	Piccolo	2 feet.
14.	Flute	4 feet.	17.	Corno di Bassetto	8 feet.

Swell Organ.

18.	Bourdon	16 feet.	24.	Fifteenth	2 feet.
19.	Open Diapason	8 feet.	25.	Mixture, III ranks.	
20.	Keraulophon	8 feet.	26.	Cornopean	8 feet.
21.	Stopped Diapason, Bass...	8 feet.	27.	Oboe	8 feet.
22.	Clarionet Flute	8 feet.	28.	Clarion	4 feet.
23.	Principal	4 feet.		Tremulant.	

Pedal Organ.

29.	Grand Open Diapason	16 feet.	31.	Principal	8 feet.
30.	Violon	16 feet.	32.	Trombone	16 feet.

Couplers.

1.	Swell to Great.	5. Swell to Choir.
2.	Swell to Pedals.	6. Swell to Great Octave.
3.	Great to Pedals.	7. Swell to Great Sub-octave.
4.	Choir to Pedals.	

Composition Pedals.

4 to the Great and Pedal organs; 2 to the Swell organ.

205. CITY TEMPLE.

This organ, erected by Forster and Andrews, Hull, has 3 Manuals, a separate Pedal organ, and 32 sounding stops. The Pedal-board is concave and radiating. The case is of classic design, with circular towers, and carried out in selected pitch pine; and the front pipes are handsomely decorated. The following is a list of its stops :—

Great Organ, CC to G.

		Pipes.	Feet.			Pipes.	Feet.
1.	Double Open Diapason, metal	56	16	6. Harmonic Flute, metal ...	56	4
2.	Open Diapason Major, metal	56	8	7. Twelfth, metal	56	$2\frac{2}{3}$
3.	Open Diapason Minor, metal	56	8	8. Fifteenth, metal	56	2
4.	Hohlflote, wood	56	8	9. Mixture, V ranks, metal..	280	—
5.	Principal, metal	56	4	10. Posaune, metal	56	8
				11. Clarion, metal	56	4

Choir Organ, CC to G.

	Pipes.	Feet.			Pipes.	Feet.
12. Violin Diapason, metal.....	56	8	15. Flauto Traverso, metal ...		56	4
13. Lieblich Gedact, wood ...	56	8	16. Flautino, metal		56	2
14. Dulciana (grooved into No. 13), metal	44	8	17. Clarionet, metal.............		44	8

Swell Organ, CC to G.

	Pipes.	Feet.			Pipes.	Feet.
18. Lieblich Bourdon, wood ...	56	16	22. Principal, metal		56	4
19. Open Diapason, wood and metal......................	56	8	23. Harmonic Piccolo, metal		56	2
20. Gamba, wood and metal...	56	8	24. Mixture, III ranks, metal		168	—
21. Viol d'Amour (grooved into No. 20), metal	44	8	25. Horn, metal..................		56	8
			26. Oboe, metal.................		56	8
			27. Clarion, metal.............		56	4

Pedal Organ, CCC to F.

	Pipes.	Feet.			Pipes.	Feet.
28. Large Open Diapason, wood	30	16	31. Violoncello, wood		30	8
29. Bourdon, wood..............	30	16	32. Trombone, wood and metal		30	16
30. Quint, wood	30	10⅔				

Couplers.

1. Swell to Great.	4. Swell to Choir.
2. Swell to Pedals.	5. Great to Pedals.
3. Swell Octave.	6. Choir to Pedals.

6 Composition Pedals to Great and Swell organ.

Recapitulation.

Great organ	11	Registers	840	Pipes.
Choir organ	6	,,	312	,,
Swell organ	10	,,	660	,,
Pedal organ	4	,,	120	,,
Couplers	6	,,	—	,,
Grand Total	37	Registers	1932	Pipes.

206. St. Giles, Camberwell.

The organ at this church was built by Mr. J. C. Bishop, in 1844, from a specification prepared by the late Dr. S. S. Wesley. It contains 41 sounding stops.

Great, 14 Stops.

1. Open Diapason	8 feet.	8. Fifteenth	2 feet.
2. Open Diapason	8 feet.	9. Sesquialtera, III ranks.	
3. Open Diapason, wood, large	8 feet.	10. Mixture, III ranks.	
4. Clarabella.....................	8 feet.	11. Furniture, II ranks.	
5. Principal	4 feet.	12. Doublette, II ranks.	
6. Principal	4 feet.	13. Trumpet	8 feet.
7. Twelfth.......................	2⅔ feet.	14. Clarion......................	4 feet.

Choir, 10 Stops.

15. Open Diapason, metal throughout	8 feet.	20. Flute	4 feet.
16. Dulciana, metal throughout	8 feet.	21. Fifteenth	2 feet.
17. Stopped Diapason	8 feet tone.	22. Mixture, II ranks	1⅓ foot.
18. Clarabella.....................	8 feet.	23. Cremona	8 feet tone.
19. Principal	4 feet.	24. Bassoon	8 feet.

Swell, 14 Stops.

25. Bourdon	16 feet tone.	32. Sesquialtera, III ranks ...	1⅓ foot.
26. Double Diapason	16 feet.	33. Mixture, II ranks	⅔ foot.
27. Open Diapason	8 feet.	34. Doublette, II ranks	2 feet.
28. Open Diapason	8 feet.	35. Horn	8 feet.
29. Stopped Diapason	8 feet tone.	36. Trumpet	8 feet.
30. Principal	4 feet.	37. Hautboy	8 feet.
31. Fifteenth	2 feet.	38. Clarion	4 feet.

Pedal, 3 Stops.

39. Double Diapason	16 feet.	41. Double Trumpet	16 feet.
40. Open Diapason, large scale, metal	8 feet.		

Accessory Stops, Movements, &c.

1. Swell to Pedals.	4. Swell to Great.
2. Great to Pedals.	5. Wood, open, to Pedals separately.
3. Choir to Pedals.	6 to 13. Eight Composition Pedals.

207. HOLY TRINITY, PADDINGTON.

The new organ for the above church was built by Mr. T. C. Lewis. It has 3 Manuals, a separate Pedal organ, and the 29 stops mentioned below :—

Great Organ, CC to G, 56 Notes.

1. Bourdon	16 feet.	5. Octave Quint	2⅔ feet.
2. Open Diapason	8 feet.	6. Super-octave	2 feet.
3. Rohrflote	8 feet.	7. Mixture, IV ranks	1⅓ foot.
4. Octave	4 feet.	8. Trumpet	8 feet.

Swell Organ, CC to G, 56 Notes.

9. Lieblich-gedact	16 feet.	14. Geigen Principal	4 feet.
10. Geigen Principal	8 feet.	15. Mixture, III ranks	2 feet.
11. Lieblich Gedact	8 feet.	16. Trumpet	8 feet.
12. Gamba	8 feet.	17. Oboe	8 feet.
13. Voix Celeste, tenor c	8 feet.	18. Vox Humana	8 feet.

Choir Organ, CC to G, 56 Notes.

19. Lieblich Gedact	16 feet.	23. Flute Harmonique	4 feet.
20. Salicional	8 feet.	24. Clarionet	8 feet.
21. Vox Angelica	8 feet.	25. Flautina	2 feet.
22. Salicet	4 feet.		

Pedal Organ, CCC to F, 30 Notes.

6. Open Bass	16 feet.	28. Sub-bass	16 feet.
7. Sub-bass	32 feet.	29. Posaune	16 feet.

Couplers.

1. Choir to Pedals.	4. Swell to Great.
2. Swell to Pedals.	5. Swell to Choir.
3. Great to Pedals.	Five Pedals of Combination.

The Pedal organ is carried up an octave beyond the compass of the Pedal-board, 42 notes to each stop, and furnished with an octave coupler.

208. West London Synagogue.

This organ was built by Gray and Davison in the year 1869. It has three complete Manuals, from CC, 8 feet, to A, and Pedal organ from CCC to E.

Great Organ.

1. Double Diapason .... 16 feet.	6. Principal .... 4 feet.
2. Open Diapason .... 8 feet	7. Piccolo Harmonic .... 2 feet.
3. Flute Harmonique .... 8 feet.	8. Ottavina .... 2 feet.
4. Stopped Diapason .... 8 feet.	9. Mixture, IV ranks.
5. Flute Octaviante .... 4 feet.	10. Posaune .... 8 feet.

Swell Organ.

11. Bourdon .... 16 feet.	17. Mixture, III ranks.
12. Open Diapason .... 8 feet.	18. Cornopean .... 8 feet.
13. Stopped Diapason .... 8 feet.	19. Oboe .... 8 feet.
14. Keraulophon .... 8 feet.	20. Clarion .... 4 feet.
15. Principal .... 4 feet.	Tremulant.
16. Fifteenth .... 2 feet.	

Choir Organ.

21. Dulciana .... 8 feet.	24. Suabe Flute .... 4 feet.
22. Lieblich Gedact .... 8 feet.	25. Flageolet..................... 2 feet.
23. Flute d'Amour .... 4 feet.	26. Corno di Bassetto .... 8 feet.

Pedal Organ.

27. Open Diapason .... 16 feet.	30. Principal .... 8 feet.
28. Violone......................... 16 feet.	31. Trombone .... 16 feet.
29. Bourdon .... 16 feet.	

Couplers, &c.

1. Swell to Great Manual.	4. Swell Manual to Pedals.
2. Swell to Choir Manual.	5. Great Manual to Pedals.
3. Swell to Great Manual octave.	6. Choir Manual to Pedals.

4 Composition Pedals to the Great and Pedal organ, and 4 to the Swell.

209. South Hackney Church.

This organ was built by Gray and Davison in 1873, and consists of 3 Manuals, CC to G, and Pedals, CCC to E.

Great Organ.

1. Double Diapason............ 16 feet.	6. Quint .... 2⅔ feet.
2. Open Diapason .... 8 feet.	7. Super-octave .... 2 feet.
3. Hohl Flute .... 8 feet.	8. Mixture, IV ranks.
4. Stopped Diapason, Bass... 8 feet.	9. Trumpet .... 8 feet.
5. Octave .... 4 feet.	

Swell Organ.

10. Bourdon .... 16 feet.	15. Super-octave .... 2 feet.
11. Open Diapason .... 8 feet.	16. Mixture, III ranks.
12. Keraulophon, tenor c ...... 8 feet.	17. Cornopean .... 8 feet.
13. Stopped Diapason .... 8 feet.	18. Oboe .... 8 feet.
14. Octave .... 4 feet.	19. Clarion........................ 4 feet.

Choir Organ.

20.	Dulciana	8 feet.	24. Flute	4 feet.
21.	Viol di Gamba	8 feet.	25. Piccolo	2 feet.
22.	Stopped Diapason	8 feet.	26. Clarionet	8 feet.
23.	Gemshorn	4 feet.		

Pedal Organ.

27.	Open Diapason	16 feet.	29. Violoncello	8 feet.
28.	Bourdon	16 feet.	30. Trombone	16 feet.

Couplers.

1. Swell to Great.
2. Swell to Choir.
3. Swell to Pedals.

4. Great to Pedals.
5. Choir to Pedals.

Some of the pipes of the former organ have been re-voiced and retained in this organ.

210. St. Mary's, Stoke Newington.

This organ was erected by Gray and Davison in 1858, and completed in 1875. It has 3 Manuals, CC to F, and Pedals from CCC to F. It is placed in a gallery in the south transept, and the key-boards are brought down and turned round. The disposition of the stops is as follows :—

Great Organ.

1.	Bourdon	16 feet.	7. Octave	4 feet.
2.	Open Diapason	8 feet.	8. Twelfth	3 feet.
3.	Open Diapason	8 feet.	9. Super-octave	2 feet.
4.	Flute Harmonic	8 feet.	10. Mixture, IV ranks.	
5.	Stopped Diapason	8 feet.	11. Posaune	8 feet.
6.	Flute Octaviante	4 feet.	12. Clarion	4 feet.

Swell Organ.

13.	Double Diapason	16 feet.	19. Super-octave	2 feet.
14.	Open Diapason	8 feet.	20. Mixture, III ranks.	
15.	Keraulophon	8 feet.	21. Cornopean	8 feet.
16.	Stopped Diapason, Bass	8 feet.	22. Oboe	8 feet.
17.	Concert Flute	8 feet.	23. Clarion	4 feet.
18.	Octave	4 feet.	Tremulant.	

Choir Organ.

24.	Salicional	8 feet.	29. Flute d'Amour	4 feet.
25.	Viol di Gamba	8 feet.	30. Super-octave	2 feet.
26.	Stopped Diapason, Bass	8 feet.	31. Piccolo	2 feet.
27.	Clarionet Flute	8 feet.	32. Corno di Bassetto	8 feet.
28.	Gemshorn	4 feet.		

Pedal Organ.

33.	Open Diapason	16 feet.	36. Super-octave	4 feet.
34.	Violon	16 feet.	37. Trombone	16 feet.
35.	Octave	8 feet.		

Couplers, &c.

1. Swell to Great.
2. Swell to Pedals.
3. Swell to Choir.

4. Choir to Pedals.
5. Great to Pedals.

4 Composition Pedals to Great.   3 Composition Pedals to Swell.
2 Composition Pedals to Pedals.

211. ST. MATTHEW'S, UPPER CLAPTON.

This organ was built by Gray and Davison in 1867, and consists of three Manuals, from CC to G, 56 notes, and two octaves and a fourth of Pedals, from CCC to F, 30 notes.

Great Organ.

1. Double Diapason .... 16 feet.	6. Harmonic Flute .... 4 feet.
2. Open Diapason .... 8 feet.	7. Twelfth .... 3 feet.
3. Gamba .... 8 feet.	8. Fifteenth..................... 2 feet.
4. Clarinet Flute .... 8 feet.	9. Mixture, IV ranks.
5. Principal .... 4 feet.	10. Trumpet .... 8 feet.

Swell Organ.

11. Bourdon .... 16 feet.	16. Fifteenth .... 2 feet.
12. Open Diapason .... 8 feet.	17. Mixture, II ranks.
13. Keraulophon .... 8 feet.	18. Cornopean .... 8 feet.
14. Concert Flute .... 8 feet.	19. Oboe .... 8 feet.
15. Principal .... 4 feet.	20. Clarion....................... 4 feet.

Choir Organ.

21. Open Diapason .... 8 feet.	25. Suabe Flute .... 4 feet.
22. Viol di Gamba............ .... 8 feet.	26. Piccolo....................... 2 feet.
23. Lieblich Gedact .... 8 feet.	27. Corno di Bassetto .... 8 feet.
24. Gemshorn .... 4 feet.	

Pedal Organ.

28. Grand Open Diapason ... 16 feet.	30. Grand Principal .... 8 feet.
29. Grand Bourdon .... 16 feet.	

Couplers.

1. Swell to Great Manual.	4. Swell to Choir Manual.
2. Swell Octave to Great Manual.	5. Great Manual to Pedals.
3 Swell Manual to Pedals.	6. Choir Manual to Pedals.

Composition Pedals.

4 to Great Organ. | 3 to Swell.

This organ is placed in an organ chamber at the south side of the chancel, and the key-board, &c., brought down.

212. ST. ANN'S, LIMEHOUSE.

The new organ in St. Ann's, Limehouse, was made by Gray and Davison, and is the same which those builders erected in the Great Exhibition building in 1851. It contains 34 stops, of which the following is a list :—

Great, 13 Stops.

1. Double Open Diapason ... 16 feet.	8. Fifteenth .... 2 feet.
2. Open Diapason .... 8 feet.	9. Flageolet, open .... 2 feet.
3. Open Diapason .... 8 feet.	10. Sesquialtera, III ranks ... 1¾ foot.
4. Stopped Diapason .... 8 feet tone.	11. Mixture, II ranks .... ⅔ foot.
5. Octave .... 4 feet.	12. Posaune .... 8 feet.
6. Stopped Flute .... 4 feet tone.	13. Clarion .... 4 feet.
7. Twelfth .... 2⅔ feet.	

Choir, 8 Stops.

14. Dulciana	8 feet.	18. Octave	4 feet.
15. Keraulophon	8 feet.	19. Flute, open	4 feet.
16. Clarinet Flute	8 feet tone.	20. Fifteenth	2 feet.
17. Stopped Diapason Bass ...	8 feet tone.	21. Clarinet	8 feet tone.

Swell, 9 Stops.

22. Bourdon	16 feet tone.	27. Sesquialtera, III ranks.	
23. Open Diapason	8 feet.	28. Cornopean	8 feet.
24. Stopped Diapason	8 feet tone.	29. Oboe	8 feet.
25. Octave	4 feet.	30. Clarion	4 feet.
26. Fifteenth	2 feet.		

Pedal, 4 Stops.

31. Grand Open Diapason ...	16 feet.	33. Grand Octave	8 feet.
32. Grand Bourdon	16 feet tone.	34. Grand Bombarde	16 feet.

Accessory Stops, Movements, &c.

1. Swell to Great.	3. Great to Pedal.	5. Swell to Pedal.
2. Swell to Choir.	4. Choir to Pedal.	6. Sforzando Pedal.
	7 to 12. Six Composition Pedals.	

Compass.

Great, CC to f³ in alt.
Choir, CC to f³ in alt.
Swell organ, tenor c (4 feet compass) to f³ in alt.

Swell Clavier down to CC, acting on Choir organ below tenor c.
Pedal, CCC to tenor e.

213. CHRIST CHURCH, SPITALFIELDS.

The organ in this fine Church is one of the largest and best in the metropolis. It was originally built by Bridge, in 1730, for the sum of £600, scarcely half its real value. In 1822 it was repaired by Mr. Bishop, who introduced the Dulcian into the Choir organ, in place of the III-rank Mixture. The instrument afterwards suffered materially from water, during the fire that occurred in the steeple, and was subsequently repaired and enlarged by Lincoln, in 1837, who added the Pedal pipes to GGG, and extended the Swell to tenor c, besides adding several new stops. In 1852 the organ underwent further enlargement, owing to the spirit and musical taste of the Rev. Mr. Stone, the Rector, which amplification was effected by Messrs. Gray and Davison, under the direction of Mr. J. S. Noble, the then organist of the Church. The Spitalfields organ now contains 45 sounding stops, distributed among 3 Manuals and Pedal, in the following manner :—

Great Organ, 16 Stops.

1. Open Diapason.	9. Fifteenth.
2. Open Diapason.	10. Tierce.
3. Stopped Diapason.	11. Sesquialtera, V ranks.
4. Clarabella.	12. Mixture, II ranks.
5. Principal.	13. Furniture, III ranks.
6. Principal.	14. Posaune.
7. Twelfth.	15. Trumpet.
8. Fifteenth.	16. Clarion.

Swell Organ, 14 Stops.

17. Double Diapason.
18. Bourdon.
19. Open Diapason.
20. Open Diapason to tenor c.
21. Stopped Diapason to tenor c.
22. Stopped Diapason Bass.
23. Principal.

24. Fifteenth.
25. Sesqualtera, III ranks.
26. Mixture, II ranks.
27. Contra Fagotto.
28. Cornopean.
29. Oboe.
30. Clarion.

Choir Organ, 11 Stops.

31. Open Diapason.
32. Stopped Diapason.
33. Dulciana.
34. Principal.

35. Flute.
36. Fifteenth.
37. Flageolet.
38. French Horn to tenor c.

39. Trumpet to tenor c.
40. Cremona.
41. Bassoon.

Pedal Organ, 4 Stops.

42. Open Diapason. | 43. Bourdon. | 44. Principal. | 45. Trombone.

Accessory Stops, Movements, &c.

1. Coupler, Swell to Great.
2. Coupler, Choir to Great.
3. Coupler, Swell to Choir.
4. Coupler, Great to Swell (Sforzando).
5. Coupler, Choir Sub-octave to Great.
6. Coupler, Great to Pedal.

7. Great Sub-octave to Pedal.
8. Choir to Pedal.
9. Swell to Pedal.
10. Octave Pedal Coupler.
11 to 17. Seven Composition Pedals.

Compass.

Great, GG to f³ in alt............ 59 notes.
Choir, GG to f³ in alt .... 59 notes.

Swell, CC to f³ in alt .... 54 notes.
Pedal, partly GG to middle e... 34 notes.

Summary of Stops and Pipes.

Great .... 16 stops .... 1328 pipes.
Choir .... 11 stops .... 551 pipes.
Swell .... 14 stops .... 798 pipes.
Pedal .... 4 stops .... 92 pipes.

45 stops.   2769 pipes.

Couplers............... 9

214. ST. LUKE'S CHURCH, OLD STREET ROAD.

The organ in St. Luke's Church, Old Street Road, was originally built by Bridge, but has been re-modelled and entirely re-constructed by Gray and Davison. It now consists of 3 Manual organs of complete compass, an independent Pedal, and 32 stops, of which the following is a list :—

Great, 14 Stops.

1. Sub-octave, stopped ...... 16 feet tone.
2. Principal, open .... 8 feet.
3. Principal, open .... 8 feet.
4. Stopped Principal .... 8 feet tone.
5. Octave .... 4 feet.
6. Piccolo Flute .... 4 feet.
7. Twelfth...................... 3 feet.

8. Fifteenth .... 2 feet.
9. Ottavina .... 2 feet.
10. Seventeenth.................. 1⅗ foot.
11. Sesqualtera, II ranks ... 1⅓ foot.
12. Mixture, II ranks .... ⅔ foot.
13. Trumpet .... 8 feet.
14. Clarion...................... 4 feet.

Choir, 7 Stops.

15. Stopped Flute, Treble ...	8 feet tone.	19. Flageolet	4 feet.
16. Stopped Bass	8 feet tone.	20. Fifteenth	2 feet.
17. Dulciana	8 feet.	21. Clarinet	8 feet tone.
18. Octave	4 feet.		

Swell, 9 Stops.

22. Sub-octave, Stopped	16 feet tone.	27. Sesquialtera, III ranks ...	1¾ foot.
23. Principal	8 feet.	28. Hautboy	8 feet.
24. Concert Flute	8 feet.	29. Cornopean	8 feet.
25. Octave	4 feet.	30. Clarion	4 feet.
26. Fifteenth	2 feet.		

Pedal, 2 Stops.

31. Grand Principal	16 feet.	32. Grand Octave..............	8 feet.

Accessory Stops, Movements, &c.

1. Coupler, Swell to Great.
2. Coupler, Swell to Great, Sub-octave.
3. Coupler, Swell to Great, Super-octave.
4. Coupler, Great to Pedal.
5. Coupler, Choir to Pedal.
6. Coupler, Swell to Pedal.
7, 8, 9, 10. Four Composition Pedals.
11. Tremulant Swell.

Compass.

Great, CC to f³ in alt.
Choir, CC to f³ in alt.

Swell, CC to f³ in alt.
Pedal, CCC to Tenor c.

215. St. Mary's Catholic Chapel, Moorfields.

The organ in St. Mary's Catholic Chapel, Moorfields, was built by Bevington and Son. It contains 31 sounding stops, of which the following is a list :—

Great, 13 Stops.

1. Open Diapason, metal, No. 1.
2. Open Diapason, ditto, No. 2.
3. Open Diapason, small, No. 3.
4. Stopped Diapason, No. 1.
5. Stopped Diapason, No. 2.
6. Principal, large, No. 1.
7. Principal, No. 2.
8. Twelfth.
9. Fifteenth.
10. Sesquialtera, IV ranks.
11. Mixture, III ranks.
12. Trumpet.
13. Clarion.

Choir, 8 Stops.

14. Open Diapason.
15. Stopped Diapason.
16. Dulciana.
17. Principal.
18. Flute.
19. Fifteenth.
20. Mixture, III ranks.
21. Cremona.

Swell, 9 Stops.

22. Double Diapason.
23. Open Diapason.
24. Stopped Diapason
25. Claribel.
26. Principal.
27. Cornet, III ranks.
28. Trumpet.
29. Clarion.
30. Oboe.

Pedal, 1 Stop.

31 Open Pipes from CC down to FFFF..............24 feet length.

Accessory Stops, Movements, &c.

1, 2, 3. Three Couplers.   4 to 12. Nine Composition Pedals.

Compass.

Great, FFF to f³ in alt.   Swell, FF to f³ in alt.
Choir, FFF to f³ in alt.   Pedal, FFF to Tenor c.

216. GREENWICH.

The organ in the chapel of the Royal Hospital, at Greenwich, is a most admirable specimen of Green's work. It cost £1,000, exclusive of the case, and contains the following 26 stops :—

Great, 12 Stops.

1. Open Diapason.
2. Open Diapason.
3. Stopped Diapason.
4. Clarabella, in lieu of IV rank Cornet.
5. Principal.
6. Metal Flute.
7. Twelfth.
8. Fifteenth.
9. Sesquialtera, III ranks.
10. Mixture, III ranks.
11. {Trumpet, Treble. {Trumpet, Bass.
12. Clarion.

Choir, 5 Stops.

13. Stopped Diapason.
14. Principal.
15. Flute.
16. Fifteenth.
17. Cremona.

Swell, 8 Stops.

18. Open Diapason.
19. Dulciana.
20. Stopped Diapason.
21. Principal.
22. Dulciana Principal.
23. Cornet, III ranks, 12, 15, 17.
24. Hautboy.
25. Trumpet.

Pedal, 1 Stop.

26. Open Diapason, CC down to CCC ; then return BB to FFF.

Accessory Stops, Movements, &c.

1. Coupler, Swell to Great.
2. Coupler, Choir to Great.
3. Coupler, Great to Pedal.
4. Coupler, Choir to Pedal.

Compass.

Great, FFF to e³ in alt. ; no FFF♯   Swell, FF to e³ in alt. ; keys below FF acting.
Choir, FFF to e³ in alt. ; no FFF♯   Pedal Clavier, FFF to tenor c.

217. LEE CHURCH, KENT.

This fine organ was built by Bishop in 1850. It has 29 sounding stops, of which the following is a list :—

Great, 9 Stops.

1. Open Diapason	8 feet.	6. Fifteenth	2 feet.
2. Stopped Diapason	8 feet tone.	7. Sesquialtera, III ranks.	
3. German Flute	8 feet.	8. Mixture, II ranks.	
4. Principal	4 feet.	9. Trumpet	8 feet.
5. Twelfth	2⅔ feet.		

Choir, 8 Stops.

10.	Open Diapason	8 feet.	14.	Principal	4 feet.
11.	Dulciana	8 feet.	15.	Flute	4 feet.
12.	Stopped Diapason	8 feet tone.	16.	Fifteenth	2 feet.
13.	Viol di Gamba	8 feet.	17.	Cremona	8 feet tone.

Swell, 10 Stops.

18.	Bourdon, Bass	16 feet tone.	23.	Twelfth	2⅔ feet.
19.	Tenoroon	16 feet.	24.	Fifteenth	2 feet.
20.	Open Diapason	8 feet.	25.	Sesquialtera, III ranks.	
21.	Stopped Diapason	8 feet tone.	26.	Horn	8 feet.
22.	Principal	4 feet.	27.	Hautboy	8 feet.

Pedal, 2 Stops.

28.	Open Diapason	16 feet.	29.	Stopped Diapason	16 feet tone.

Couplers, &c.

1.	Pedals to Choir organ.	5.	Swell to Great.
2.	Ditto to Great organ.	6.	Choir to Great.
3.	Ditto to Swell.	7 to 13.	Seven Composition Pedals, viz.,
4.	Swell to Choir.		3 to Great organ, 4 to Swell.

Compass.

All the Manuals, CC to f³ in alt. | Pedal, CCC to tenor c.

218. St. Mary's, Clapham.

This organ was built by Mr. J. C. Bishop in 1845. It has three complete rows of keys, from CC to F, and 28 sounding stops :—

Great, 8 Stops.

1.	Open Diapason	8 feet.	5.	Twelfth	2⅔ feet.
2.	Stopped Diapason	8 feet tone.	6.	Fifteenth	2 feet.
3.	German Flute	8 feet.	7.	Sesquialtera, III ranks.	
4.	Principal	4 feet.	8.	Trumpet	8 feet.

Choir, 8 Stops.

9.	Open Diapason	8 feet.	14.	Flute	4 feet.
10.	Dulciana	8 feet.	15.	Fifteenth	2 feet.
11.	Stopped Diapason	8 feet tone.	16.	Clarionet	8 feet tone.
12.	Clarabella	8 feet.	17.	Double Diapason, Bass...	16 feet tone.
13.	Principal	4 feet.			

Swell, 10 Stops.

18.	Open Diapason	8 feet.	23.	Sesquialtera, III ranks.	
19.	Stopped Diapason	8 feet tone.	24.	Mixture, II ranks.	
20.	Principal	4 feet.	25.	Horn	8 feet.
21.	Twelfth	2⅔ feet.	26.	Hautboy	8 feet.
22.	Fifteenth	2 feet.	27.	Clarion	4 feet.

Pedal, 1 Stop.

28. Open Diapason... .... 16 feet.

Accessory Stops, Movements, &c.

1. Swell to Pedal.
2. Great to Pedal.
3. Choir to Pedal.
4. Swell to Great.
5. Choir to Great.
6. Swell to Choir.

7. Swell to Great, octave higher.
8, 9, 10. Three Composition Pedals to Great.
11, 12, 13. Three Composition Pedals to Choir.

Compass.

Great, CC to f ³ in alt.
Choir, CC to f ³ in alt.

Swell, CC to f ³ in alt.
Pedal, CCC to tenor c.

219. HAMPTON COURT PALACE.

The organ in the Chapel Royal, Hampton Court Palace, is a most excellent and interesting little instrument, built by Father Smith. It has been enlarged and much improved by Hill, who added the Pedal pipes, and also a Cremona to the Choir organ. The organ now contains 20 sounding stops, of which the following is a list :—

Great, 9 Stops.

1. Open Diapason.
2. Stopped Diapason.
3. Principal.
4. Flute (*Quintaton*).
5. Twelfth.

6. Fifteenth.
7. Sesqualtera, III ranks.
8. Cornet, III ranks.
9. Trumpet.

Choir, 5 Stops.

10. Stopped Diapason.
11. Principal.
12. Flute.

13. Fifteenth.
14. Cremona.

Swell, 5 Stops.

15. Open Diapason.
16. Stopped Diapason.
17. Principal.

18. Hautboy.
19. Trumpet.

Pedal, 1 Stop.

20. Open Pipes, Gamut G down to CCC, 16 feet length ; repeating on lowest ½ octave of Pedal.

Couplers.

1. Swell to Great. | 2. Great to Pedal. | 3. Choir to Pedal.

Compass.

Great, GG to e³ in alt.
Choir, GG to e³ in alt.
Swell, Tenor f to f³ in alt

Pedal Stop, CCC to gamut G.
Pedal Clavier, GG to fiddle g.

COUNTRY ORGANS.

220. WINDSOR.

THE organ that was built by Father Smith, in the reign of Charles the Second, for St. George's Chapel, Windsor, was, on the completion of the present instrument by Green, presented to Windsor Church by King George the Third. Green's organ was opened on Sunday, October 17, 1790. It was originally enclosed in a " general Swell ; " but this was removed many years ago. Considerable additions have been made to the instrument by Gray and Davison ; among the most important of which may be mentioned the extension of the Swell to FF, together with the introduction of six new stops ; the application of open Pedal pipes to FFFF ; the substitution of a Mixture and a Clarabella in place of the Furniture and a IV rank Cornet in the Great organ, and of a Keraulophon in lieu of the Fifteenth in the Choir. The organ now contains 33 sounding stops, of which the following is a list :—

Great, 12 Stops.

1. Open Diapason, Nave Front.
2. Open Diapason, Choir Front.
3. Stopped Diapason.
4. Clarabella Flute.
5. Principal.
6. Twelfth.
7. Fifteenth.
8. Sesquialtera, III ranks.
9. Mixture, II ranks.
10. Trumpet, Treble.
11. Trumpet, Bass.
12. Clarion.

Choir, 7 Stops.

13. Dulciana to FF.
14. Stopped Diapason.
15. Principal.
16. Octave Flute.
17. Keraulophon.
18. Bassoon.
19. Clarionet.

Swell, 12 Stops.

20. Double Diapason.
21. Open Diapason.
22. Stopped Diapason.
23. Dulciana.
24. Dulciana Principal.
25. Principal.
26. Fifteenth.
27. Sesquialtera, III ranks.
28. Cornopean.
29. Hautboy.
30. Trumpet.
31. Clarion.

Pedal, 2 Stops.

32. Double Open Diapason to FFFF............... 24 feet length.
33. Open Diapason to FFF.......................... 12 feet length.

Couplers.

Swell to Great.
Choir to Pedal.

Great to Pedals.
Swell to Pedals.

221. WINDSOR.

The organ in St. George's Hall, Windsor Castle, was built by Messrs. Hill and Co. It contains 29 sounding stops, 2 complete Manuals, and an independent Pedal of 3 stops. It is also furnished with two sets of movements, draw-stops, claviers, &c., so that it can be used in the Chapel as well as in the Hall. The following is a list of the stops :—

Great, 12 Stops.

1. Double Open and Bourdon 16 feet.	7. Flute .... 4 feet.
2. Open Diapason .... 8 feet.	8. Twelfth .... 3¾ feet.
3. Cone Gamba .... 8 feet.	9. Fifteenth...................... 2 feet.
4. Stopped Diapason .... 8 feet tone.	10. Sesquialtera, III ranks.
5. Quint .... 5⅓ feet.	11. Posaune .... 8 feet.
6. Principal .... 4 feet.	12. Clarion .... 4 feet.

Choir, 6 Stops.

13. Open Diapason, throughout 8 feet.	16. Gemshorn .... 4 feet.
14. Clarabella and Stopped Bass 8 feet.	17. Flute .... 4 feet.
15. Salicional to tenor c ...... 8 feet.	18. Cromorne .... 8 feet tone.

Swell, 8 Stops.

19. Double Diapason............ 16 feet.	23. Fifteenth...................... 2 feet.
20. Open Diapason .... 8 feet.	24. Sesquialtera, II ranks.
21. Stopped Diapason .... 8 feet tone.	25. Cornopean .... 8 feet.
22. Principal .... 4 feet.	26. Oboe .... 8 feet.

Pedal, 3 Stops.

27. Open Diapason .... 16 feet.	29. Trombone .... 16 feet.
28. Principal .... 8 feet.	

Accessory Stops, Movements, &c.

1. Swell to Great.	2. Great to Pedal.	3. Swell to Pedal.

Compass.

Great, CC to f³ in alt.	Swell, CC to f³ in alt.	Pedal, CCC to tenor d.

222. TORQUAY.

Description of the organ in St. John's Church, Torquay, built by Hill and Son in 1873. 4 Manuals, compass of each CC to G, 56 notes, and Pedal Clavier CCC to F, 30 notes :—

Great Organ.

	Labelled.
1. Bourdon	Tibia Pileata Gravis, XVI.
2. Open Diapason	Regula Primaria, VIII.
3. Hohl Flute	Tibia Fistulata, VIII.
4. Octave	Octava, IV.
5. Harmonic Flute	Tibia Transversa, IV.
6. Twelfth	Duodecima, III.
7. Fifteenth	Quintadecima, II.
8. Mixture, IV ranks	Miscella Quadruplex.
9. Posaune	Tuba Magna, VIII.

X X

Choir Organ.

10.	Pierced Salicional	Tibia Salicionalis. VIII.
11.	Wald Flute	Tibia Silvestris, VIII.
12.	Rohr Flute	Tibia Arundinacea. IV.
13.	Viol d'Amour Pierced	Fides Amoris, IV.
14.	Spitz Flote	Tibia Acuta. II.
15.	Bassoon	Fascis, VIII.
16.	Sub-octave Coupler	Sub-octave Copula.
17.	Tremulant	Flatus Tremulus.

Swell Organ.

18.	Bourdon	Tibia Pileata Gravis, XVI.
19.	Open Diapason	Regula Primaria, VIII.
20.	Lieblich Gedact	Tibia Pileata Amabilis, VIII.
21.	Octave	Octava, IV.
22.	Suabe Flute	Tibia Suavis, IV.
23.	Mixture, III ranks	Miscella Triplex.
24.	Horn	Cornu, VIII.
25.	Oboe	Calamus.
26.	Sub-octave Coupler	Sub-octava Copula.
27.	Tremulant	Flatus Tremulus.

Solo Organ. (*In Double Swell.*)

28.	Viol di Gamba	Fides Cruralis, VIII.
29.	Unda Maris, tenor c	Unda Maris, VIII.
30.	Dulciana	Tibia Dulcis, VIII.
31.	Vox Humana	Vox Humana, VIII.
32.	Cremona	Cantus Cremonensis, VIII.
33.	Tremulant	Flatus Tremulus.
34.	Duplicate handle	Manual 2 ad Pedals.

Pedal Organ.

35.	Sub-bass	Tibia Pileata Gravissima, XXXII.
36.	Open Diapason, metal	Regula Primaria, XVI.
37.	Open Diapason, wood	Tibia Aperta Magna, XVI.
38.	Bourdon	Tibia Pileata, XVI.
39.	Principal	Octava, VIII.
40.	Fifteenth	Quintadecima, IV.
41.	Trombone	Tuba Ductilis, XVI.

Couplers.

1.	Swell to Great	Manual III and Manual II.
2.	Choir to Great	,, I and ,, II.
3.	Swell to Choir	,, III and ,, I.
4.	Sub-octave in Swell	(Second Swell.)
5.	Sub-octave in Choir	(Second Choir.)
6.	Swell to Pedal	Manual III and Pedal.
7.	Great to Pedal	,, II and ,,
8.	Choir to Pedal	,, I and ,,

Tremulant on Solo, Swell, and Choir. Three Composition Pedals to Great. Two Composition Pedals to Pedal. Three Swell Pedals, one to Swell, two to Solo,

223. GLOUCESTER CATHEDRAL.

This organ was originally built by the elder Harris, in conjunction with his son, Renatus, in the year 1670. In 1847 the instrument was considerably enlarged by Henry Willis, of London, who added a Swell of 12 stops, all of which are entirely new (with its movement), excepting some old pipes which are derived from the old Twelfth in the Great organ and the old Swell. The continuation of the Great organ from GG to CCC, and the entire re-arrangement of the Pedals and mechanism, including new Couplers, &c., and the addition of a Mixture and Clarion to the Great organ, are also by Willis. The instrument now contains 29 sounding stops, of which the following is a list :—

Great, 11 *Stops.*

1. Open Diapason.
2. Open Diapason.
3. Stopped Diapason.
4. Clarabella.
5. Principal.
6. Twelfth.
7. Fifteenth.
8. Sesquialtera, IV ranks.
9. Mixture, II ranks.
10. Trumpet.
11. Clarion.

Choir, 5 *Stops.*

12. Dulciana.
13. Stopped Diapason.
14. Principal.
15. Flute, metal.
16. Fifteenth.

Swell, 12 *Stops.*

17. Open Diapason.
18. Open Diapason.
19. Stopped Diapason.
20. Dulciana.
21. Principal.
22. Flute.
23. Fifteenth.
24. Sesquialtera.
25. Trumpet.
26. Hautboy.
27. Cremona.
28. Clarion.

Pedal, 1 *Stop.*

29. Open Diapason.

Accessory Stops, Movements, &c.

1. Coupler, Swell to Great.
2. Coupler, Choir to Great.
3. Coupler, Swell to Choir.
4. Coupler, Pedals to Great.
5. Coupler, Pedals to Choir.
6. Coupler, Pedal to Great.

Compass.

Great, CCC to f³ in alt.
Choir, GG to f³ in alt.

Swell, CC to f³ in alt.
Pedal, CCC to tenor e₁

224. TEWKESBURY.

Part of the organ now standing in the Abbey Church of Tewkesbury formed a portion of that which originally stood in Magdalen College, Oxford ; whence it was removed to its present locality in 1740, on the completion of Schwarbrook's organ for the College just mentioned. The Tewkesbury organ, however, has been entirely re-modelled and greatly enlarged by Willis. But little of the original work remains, except a few Diapasons and the Principal, together with the East or Choir front, which, although thin, are valuable, as they are made of tin, alloyed with about eight pounds of lead in the cwt. The organ contains 22 stops.

Great, 13 Stops, from CC to F.

1. Open Diapason	8 feet.	8. Fifteenth	4 feet.
2. Open Diapason	8 feet.	9. Sesquialtera.	
3. Stopped Diapason	8 feet tone.	10. Mixture.	
4. Clarabella	8 feet.	11. Trumpet	8 feet.
5. Dulciana	8 feet.	12. Clarion	4 feet.
6. Principal	4 feet.	13. Cremona	8 feet tone.
7. Twelfth	2⅔ feet.		

Swell, 7 Stops, from CC to F.

14. Open Diapason	8 feet.	18. Sesquialtera, III ranks ...	1¾ foot.
15. Stopped Diapason	8 feet tone.	19. Trumpet (only prepared for).	
16. Principal	4 feet.	20. Hautboy	8 feet.
17. Fifteenth	2 feet.		

Pedal, 2 Stops, 2 Octaves and a Major Third, from CCC to E.

21. Double Open Diapason ...	16 feet.	22. Double Trumpet	16 feet.

Couplers.

1. Swell to Great.	2. Swell to Pedals.	3. Great to Pedal.

225. HEREFORD CATHEDRAL.

This organ, originally built by Renatus Harris in 1686, was a present from King Charles the Second. Byfield afterwards added the Choir organ ; and the instrument has since been successfully repaired by Snetzler, Green, Avery, Lincoln, Elliott, who, in 1806, put Pedals and Pedal pipes ; and, by Bishop, who introduced the present Swell and Pedal pipes.

Since the close of 1862 it has undergone a number of alterations and additions, amounting to an entire re-modelling, at the hands of Messrs. Gray and Davison. In fact, it may be described as a new instrument, rather than a restored organ, although such of the old pipes as were in good condition, having been re-voiced, are again used.

The site selected is underneath the westernmost arch of the south aisle of the Choir, the Swell being in the triforium, and the bellows, erected in a framework of wood, in the passage leading to the robing room.

The pneumatic action, for lightening the touch, &c., is applied to the Great organ and its Couplers, also to the whole of the Draw stop and Composition Action throughout. It is intended to blow the instrument by hydraulic power, but at present three handles are used for the purpose. The pipes of the Pedal Violone (some of the largest in England) are placed in front, and from their great height, as well as from their elaborate decorations, designed by Sir Gilbert Scott, present a most imposing appearance. There are 2230 pipes in the organ.

Great Organ, 16 Stops.

1. Bourdon .... 16 feet.	9. Gamba.
2. Open Diapason .... 8 feet.	10. Open Diapason .... 8 feet.
3. Stopped Diapason .... 8 feet.	11. Clarabella .... 8 feet.
4. Principal .... 4 feet.	12. Principal, metal .... 4 feet.
5. Twelfth.	13. Fifteenth.
6. Tierce.	14. Larigot.
7. Furniture, IV ranks.	15. Mixture, II ranks.
8. Trumpet .... 8 feet.	16. Clarion....................... 4 feet.

Choir Organ, 7 Stops.

17. Stopped Diapason.	21. Dulciana.
18. Principal.	22. Spitzflote.
19. Flute.	23. Flageolet.
20. Cremona.	

Swell Organ, 10 Stops.

24. Bourdon .... 16 feet.	29. Open Diapason .... 8 feet.
25. Keraulophon .... 8 feet.	30. Soft Diapason.............. 8 feet.
26. Principal .... 4 feet.	31. Fifteenth.
27. Mixture.	32. Cornopean .... 8 feet.
28. Oboe .... 8 feet.	33. Clarion .... 4 feet.

Pedal Organ, CCC to F, 7 Stops.

34. Bourdon .... 16 feet.	38. Violone, metal .... 16 feet.
35. Grand Open Diapason ... 16 feet.	39. Principal .... 8 feet.
36. Fifteenth .... 4 feet.	40. Trombone .... 16 feet.
37. Trumpet .... 8 feet.	

Compass.

1. Pedals to Swell.	4. Pedals to Great.
2. Pedals to Choir.	5. Swell to Great.
3. Swell to Choir.	

Total—45 stops. There are 6 Composition Pedals.

226. WORCESTER CATHEDRAL.

The Choir organ was built by Messrs. Hill and Co. in the year 1842. It contains 39 sounding stops, of which the following is a list :—

Great, 14 Stops.

1. Tenoroon .... 16 feet.	8. Wald Flote .... 4 feet.
2. Bourdon, to meet No. 1... 16 feet tone.	9. Twelfth .... 2⅔ feet.
3. Open Diapason, back...... 8 feet.	10. Fifteenth .... 2 feet.
4. Open Diapason, front ..... 8 feet.	11. Sesquialtera, III ranks ... 1⅗ foot.
5. Stopped Diapason .... 8 feet tone.	12. Mixture, II ranks .... ⅔ foot.
6. Quint .... 5⅓ feet.	13. Doublette, II ranks ...... 2 feet.
7. Principal .... 4 feet.	14. Posaune .... 8 feet.

Choir, 8 Stops.

15. Dulciana	8 feet.	19. Stopped Flute	4 feet tone
16. Clarabella	8 feet.	20. Oboe Flute	4 feet.
17. Stopped Diapason	8 feet tone.	21. Fifteenth	2 feet.
18. Principal	4 feet.	22. Cremona	8 feet tone.

Swell, 11 Stops.

23. Double Dulciana	16 feet.	29. Flageolet	2 feet.
24. Open Diapason	8 feet.	30. Doublette, II ranks	2 feet.
25. Stopped Diapason	8 feet tone.	31. Echo Cornet.	
26. Dulciana	8 feet.	32. Oboe	8 feet.
27. Principal	4 feet.	33. Cornopean	8 feet.
28. Suabe Flute	4 feet.		

Pedal, 6 Stops.

34. Open Diapason	16 feet.	37. Fifteenth	4 feet.
35. Stopped Diapason	16 feet tone.	38. Sesquialtera, V ranks.	
36. Principal	8 feet.	39. Trombone	16 feet.

Accessory Stops, Movements, &c.

1. Coupler, Swell to Great.	4. Coupler, Pedals to Choir.
2. Coupler, Swell to Choir.	5 to 9. Five Composition Pedals.
3. Coupler, Pedals to Great.	

Compass.

Great, CC to f³ in alt.	Swell, tenor c to f³ in alt.
Choir, CC to f³ in alt.	Pedal, CCC to tenor e.

227. WORCESTER.

Description of the organ built by Hill and Son for Worcester Cathedral transept in 1875. Four Manuals, compass of each, CC to A, 58 notes, and Pedal Clavier, CCC to F, 30 notes.

Great Organ.

1. Double Open Diapason, metal	16 feet.	7. Principal, metal	4 feet.
		8. Harmonic Flute, metal	4 feet.
2. Bourdon, wood	16 feet.	9. Twelfth, metal	3 feet.
3. Open Diapason, metal	8 feet.	10. Fifteenth, metal	2 feet.
4. Open Diapason, No. 2, metal	8 feet.	11. Full Mixture, metal, III ranks.	
		12. Sharp Mixture, metal, IV ranks.	
5. Gamba, metal	8 feet.	13. Posaune, metal	8 feet.
6. Stopped Diapason, wood	8 feet.	14. Clarion, metal	4 feet.

Choir Organ.

15. Open Diapason, metal	8 feet.	19. Principal, metal	4 feet.
16. Dulciana, metal	8 feet.	20. Waldflote, wood	4 feet.
17. Salicional, grooved, No. 2, metal	8 feet.	21. Flautina, metal	2 feet.
		22. Dulciana Mixture, metal, II ranks.	
18. Hohlflote, wood	8 feet.	23. Clarionet, metal	8 feet.

Solo Organ.

24. Tuba Mirabilis, metal	8 feet.	26. Vox Humana, metal	8 feet.
25. Vox Angelica, metal, II ranks.		27. Harmonic Flute, metal	4 feet.

Swell Organ.

28. Bourdon, wood	16 feet.	
29. Open Diapason, metal	8 feet.	
30. Salicional, metal	8 feet.	
31. Stopped Diapason, wood	8 feet.	
32. Principal, metal	4 feet.	
33. Lieblich Flute, metal	4 feet.	
34. Twelfth, metal	3 feet.	
35. Fifteenth, metal	2 feet.	
36. Mixture, metal, III ranks.		
37. Double Trumpet, metal	16 feet.	
38. Cornopean, metal	8 feet.	
39. Oboe, metal	8 feet.	
40. Clarion, metal	8 feet.	

Pedal Organ.

41. Double Open Diapason, metal	32 feet.
42. Double Open Diapason, wood	32 feet.
43. Open Diapason, metal	16 feet.
44. Open Diapason, wood	16 feet.
45. Violone, wood	16 feet.
46. Bourdon, wood	16 feet.
47. Principal, metal	8 feet.
48. Violoncello, wood	8 feet.
49. Twelfth, metal	6 feet.
50. Fifteenth, metal	8 feet.
51. Mixture, metal, III ranks.	
52. Trombone, wood	16 feet.
53. Clarion, metal	8 feet.

Couplers.

1. Swell to Great.	6. Great to Pedal.
2. Swell to Octave.	7. Choir to Pedal.
3. Swell to Sub-octave.	8. Swell to Pedal.
4. Solo to Great.	9. Pedal "Forte" ventil.
5. Swell to Choir.	

4 Composition Pedals to Great and Pedal.
3 Composition Pedals to Swell organ.

3 Composition Pedals to Pedal organ.
Pneumatic action to Great, Swell and Couplers.

228. STRATFORD-ON-AVON.

The organ in the Parish Church at Stratford-on-Avon was built by Hill, in 1841, from a specification prepared by Mr. F. Marshall, of Leamington. It contains 36 sounding stops, of which the following is a list :—

Great, 18 Stops.

1. Tenoroon Diapason	16 feet.	
2. Bourdon	16 feet tone.	
3. Principal Diapason	8 feet.	
4. Stopped Diapason, Treble	8 feet tone.	
5. Stopped Diapason, Bass	8 feet tone.	
6. Dulciana	8 feet.	
7. Quint	5⅓ feet.	
8. Principal Octave	4 feet.	
9. Waldflöte	4 feet.	
10. Oboe Flute	4 feet.	
11. Twelfth	2⅔ feet.	
12. Fifteenth	2 feet.	
13. Octave Fifteenth	1 foot.	
14. Sesquialtera	1⅓ foot.	
15. Mixture	⅔ foot.	
16. Corno Trombone	8 feet.	
17. Corno Clarion	4 feet.	
18. Cromorne	8 feet tone.	

Swell, 12 Stops.

19. Tenoroon Diapason	16 feet.	
20. Bourdon, to meet No. 1	16 feet tone.	
21. Principal Diapason	8 feet.	
22. Stopped Diapason, Treble	8 feet tone.	
23. Stopped Diapason, Bass	8 feet tone.	
24. Principal Octave	4 feet.	
25. Suabe Flute	4 feet.	
26. Flageolet	2 feet.	
27. Doublette, II ranks	2 feet.	
28. Echo Dulciana Cornet, V ranks	1⅗ foot.	
29. Oboe	8 feet.	
30. Cornopean	8 feet.	

Pedal, 6 Stops.

31. Open Diapason	16 feet.	34. Fifteenth	4 feet.
32. Bourdon	16 feet tone.	35. Mixture, V ranks	4 feet.
33. Principal	8 feet.	36. Posaune	16 feet.

Accessory Stops, Movements, &c.

1. Coupler, Swell to Great.	4. Octave Pedal.
2. Great to Pedal.	5 to 7. Three Composition Pedals.
3. Swell to Pedal.	

Compass.

Great and Swell, CC to f⁸ in alt. | Pedal CCC to tenor d.

229. BIRMINGHAM.

The splendid organ in the Town Hall, Birmingham, was built by Mr. William Hill, of London, and cost about £3,000. The height of the case is 40 feet; it is 35 feet wide, and 15 feet deep. The bellows contains 300 square feet of surface, and upwards of three tons' weight upon the bellows is required to give the necessary pressure. The trackers, if laid out in a straight line, would reach above five miles. The principal metal pipe, standing in front of the organ, is 35 feet 3 inches long, and 5 feet 8 inches in circumference. The largest wood pipe, CCCC, 32 feet, is 12 feet in circumference, and its interior measurement is 224 cubic feet. Originally the Great and Choir organs were of 16 feet compass; but, on the occasion of the instrument being re-modelled, they were altered to the CC or 8-feet range; the Great being at the same time converted into a " 16-feet Manual," in the German acceptation of the term. The Pedal stops were also increased in number from four to *fifteen*. The organ has a *fourth* Manual, in connection with a Combination or Solo organ, upon which, by an ingenious contrivance, can be played any stop or stops out of the Swell or Choir organs, without interfering with their previous arrangement on their separate Manuals. There are two Octaves and five notes of Pedals. The timber alone used in this instrument weighs between twenty and thirty tons; and the metal and other materials employed in its formation raise it to a total weight of at least forty tons.

The Birmingham organ has 53 sounding stops, of which the following is a list :—

Great, 19 Stops.

1. Double Open Diapason ...	16 feet.	11. Doublette, II ranks	2 feet.
2. Open Diapason	8 feet.	12. Sesquialtera, V ranks.	
3. Open Diapason	8 feet.	13. Mixture, V ranks.	
4. Open Diapason	8 feet.	14. Furniture, V ranks.	
5. Stopped Diapason	8 feet tone.	15. Contra or Double Trumpet	16 feet.
6. Quint	5½ feet tone.	16. Posaune	8 feet.
7. Principal	4 feet.	17. Clarion	4 feet.
8. Principal	4 feet.	18. Octave Clarion	2 feet.
9. Twelfth	2⅔ feet.	19. Great Ophicleide, on a	
10. Fifteenth	2 feet.	heavy pressure of wind	8 feet.

Swell, 10 Stops.

20. Double Diapason	16 feet.	25. Sesquialtera, V ranks ...	1¾ foot.
21. Open Diapason	8 feet.	26. Horn	8 feet.
22. Stopped Diapason	8 feet tone.	27. Trumpet	8 feet.
23. Principal	4 feet.	28. Hautboy	8 feet.
24. Fifteenth	2 feet.	29. Clarion	4 feet.

Choir, 9 Stops.

30. Open Diapason	....	8 feet.
31. Dulciana	....	8 feet.
32. Stopped Diapason	....	8 feet tone.
33. Principal	....	4 feet.
34. Flute	....	4 feet.
35. Oboe Flute	....	4 feet.
36. Waldflote	....	4 feet.
37. Fifteenth	....	2 feet.
38. Cornopean	....	8 feet.

Pedal, 15 Stops.

39. Contra Open Diapason, metal	....	32 feet.
40. Contra Open Diapason, wood	....	32 feet.
41. Open Diapason, metal	...	16 feet.
42. Open Diapason, metal	...	16 feet.
43. Open Diapason, wood	...	16 feet.
44. Stopped Diapason	....	16 feet tone.
45. Principal	....	8 feet.
46. Twelfth	....	6 feet.
47. Fifteenth	....	4 feet.
48. Sesquialtera, V ranks.		
49. Mixture, V ranks.		
50. Contra Posaune	....	32 feet.
51. Posaune	....	16 feet.
52. Trumpet	....	8 feet.
53. Clarion	....	4 feet.

COMBINATION OR SOLO ORGAN.

Choir, 8 Stops.

1. Open Diapason.	5. Harmonica.
2. Cornopean.	6. Flute.
3. Dulciana.	7. Cremona.
4. Stopped Diapason.	8. Bells.

Swell, 9 Stops.

9. Hautboy.	14. Clarabella.
10. Clarion.	15. Principal.
11. Trumpet.	16. Stopped Diapason.
12. Horn.	17. Open Diapason.
13. Fifteenth.	

Accessory Stops, Movements, &c.

1. Swell to Great.	5. Pedals only.
2. Choir to Great.	6. Combination Choir.
3. Pedals to Great.	7. Combination Swell.
4. Pedals to Choir.	8 to 14. Seven Composition Pedals.

Compass.

All four Manuals, CC to f³ in alt.	Pedal, CCC to tenor f.

230. LICHFIELD CATHEDRAL.

The old organ, now removed, was erected by Samuel Green in 1789. In 1860 the present organ was erected by Mr. G. M. Holditch. It was a present from J. Spode, Esq., of Hawkesyard Park, in the county of Stafford.

The organ consists of 3 whole rows of keys, and a large independent Pedal organ. The compass of the Manuals is from CC to F in alt.

Great Organ, 19 Stops.

	Feet.		Pipes.			Feet.		Pipes.
1. Sub-bass	16	...	12	12. Super-quint	3	...	54
2. Tenoroon	16	...	42	13. Super-octave	2	...	54
3. Open Diapason	8	...	54	14. Tierce	1⅗	...	54
4. Open Diapason	8	...	42	15. Sesquialtera	1⅓	...	108
5. Open Diapason, Bass	8	...	12	16. Doublette	2	...	108
6. Bell Gamba	8	...	42	17. Mixture		...	108
7. Clarabella	8	...	54	18. Posaune	8	...	54
8. Stopped Diapason	8	...	54	19. Clarion	8	...	54
9. Octave	4	...	54				
10. Gamba Octave	4	...	54				1056
11. Waldflote	4	...	42				

Choir Organ, 7 Stops.

	Feet.		Pipes.			Feet.		Pipes.
20. Dulciana	8	...	54	25. Fifteenth	2	...	54
21. Stopped Diapason, Bass	8	...	12	26. Cremona	8	...	42
22. Stopped Diapason, Treble	8	...	42				
23. Principal	4	...	54				312
24. Flute	4	...	54				

Swell Organ, 17 Stops.

	Feet.		Pipes.			Feet.		Pipes.
27. Bourdon	16	...	12	37. Mixture		...	108
28. Double Diapason	16	...	12	38. Cornopean, Bass	8	...	12
29. Open Diapason	8	...	42	39. Cornopean, Treble	8	...	42
30. Open Diapason, Bass	8	...	12	40. Trumpet	8	...	54
31. Keraulophon	8	..	42	41. Hautboy	8	...	42
32. Stopped Diapason	8	...	54	42. Tromba	16	...	42
33. Principal	4	...	54	43. Clarion	4	...	54
34. Fifteenth	2	...	54				
35. Tierce	1⅗	...	54				828
36. Sesquialtera	1⅓	...	108				

Pedal Organ, 10 Stops ; Compass from CCC to E, 2 Octaves and a Third.

	Feet.		Pipes.			Feet.		Pipes.
44. Double Double Open Diapason	32	...	12	50. Sesquialtera		...	58
45. Double Open Diapason	16	...	29	51. Mixture		...	58
46. Montre	16	...	29	52. Grand Trombone	16	...	29
47. Grand Bourdon	16	...	29	53. Grand Trumpet	8	...	29
48. Octave	8	...	29				
49. Super-octave	4	...	29				811

Couplers.

1. Pedals to Great.
2. Pedals to Swell.
3. Pedals to Choir.
4. Swell to Great.

5. Great to Choir.
6. Swell to Choir.
7. Octave Coupler Pedals.

Number of Pipes.

Great organ	1056
Choir organ	312
Swell organ	828
Pedal organ	311
Total number of pipes	2507

Number of Stops.

Great organ	19
Choir organ	7
Swell organ	17
Pedal organ	10
Couplers	7
Total number of stops	60

There are 8 Composition Pedals to change the various stops.

The Great and Pedal organs have the pneumatic action applied. The whole organ is supplied by three pairs of bellows, with double feeders. The organ is constructed in a peculiar way, and the large 32-feet CCCC pipes are laid down, as the instrument stands in the side aisle of the transept of the cathedral, and the keys brought through the wall into the side aisle of the choir.

231. SHREWSBURY.

The organ in St. Mary's, Shrewsbury, is a fine instrument, and was built by Harris and Byfield in 1729. In 1847 it was enlarged and improved by Gray and Davison, and now contains 23 sounding stops.

Great, 8 Stops, from CC to E, 53 Notes.

	Pipes.		Pipes.
1. Open Diapason	53	6. Sesquialtera, III ranks	147
2. Stopped Diapason	53	7. Mixture, II ranks	65
3. Principal	53	8. Trumpet	53
4. Twelfth	53		—
5. Fifteenth	53		530

Choir, 5 Stops.

9. Stopped Diapason	53	12. Flute	53
10. Dulciana to tenor c	41	13. Fifteenth	53
11. Principal	53		—
			253

Swell, 9 Stops, from tenor c.

14. Double Diapason	41	19. Sesquialtera	123
15. Open Diapason	41	20. Hautboy	41
16. Stopped Diapason	41	21. Cornopean	41
17. Principal	41	22. Clarion	41
18. Fifteenth	41		—
			451

Pedal, 1 Stop.

23. Open Diapason, from CCC to D 27

Total number of pipes..................... 1261

Couplers.

1. Swell to Great.	2. Pedals to Great.	3. Pedals to Choir.

232. SHREWSBURY.

The organ in St. Chad's, Shrewsbury, was built by Gray in 1794, and enlarged and improved by Gray and Davison in 1848.

Great, 9 Stops, from CC to F, 54 Notes.

	Pipes.		Pipes.
1. Stopped Diapason	54	6. Twelfth	54
2. Open Diapason	54	7. Fifteenth	54
3. Open Diapason to tenor c, in place of II rank Mixture	42	8. Sesquialtera, III ranks	150
4. Clarabella to Middle c¹, in place of IV rank Cornet	30	9. Trumpet	54
5. Principal	54		546

Choir, 8 *Stops.*

	Pipes.		Pipes.
10. Stopped Diapason, Treble		15. Flute	42
11. Stopped Diapason, Bass	54	16. Cremona	42
12. Keraulophon	42	17. Bourdon, CCC to BB	12
13. Dulciana	42		
14. Principal	54		288

Swell, 9 *Stops, from tenor c.*

	Pipes.		Pipes.
18. Double Diapason	42	24. Hautboy.................................	42
19. Stopped Diapason	42	25. Cornopean.............................	42
20. Open Diapason	42	26. Clarion	42
21. Principal	42		
22. Fifteenth	42		462
23. Sesquialtera............................	126		

Pedal, 1 *Stop.*

27. Open Diapason, from CCC to E 29

Total number of pipes.................... 1325

Couplers, *&c.*

1. Swell to Great.	4 to 8. Five Composition Pedals ; *viz.*
2. Pedals to Great.	3 to the Great organ,
3. Pedals to Choir.	2 to the Swell.

233. CHESTER CATHEDRAL.

This organ was built by Messrs. Gray and Davison in 1844, and contained 36 sounding stops, of which the following is a list. It has recently been re-erected, and perhaps somewhat altered.

Great, 14 *Stops, CC to F.*

1. Double Diapason.	8. Twelfth.	
2. Open Diapason.	9. Fifteenth.	
3. Open Diapason.	10. Sesquialtera, III ranks.	
4. Stopped Diapason.	11. Furniture, II ranks.	
5. Fifth, stopped.	12. Mixture, II ranks.	
6. Principal.	13. Trumpet.	
7. Flute.	14. Clarion.	

Choir, 7 *Stops, GG to F.*

15. Open Diapason.	18. Principal.	20. Fifteenth.
16. Dulciana.	19. Flute.	21. Clarion.
17. Stopped Diapason.		

Swell, 9 *Stops, FF to F.*

22. Double Diapason.	25. Principal.	28. Hautboy.
23. Open Diapason.	26. Fifteenth.	29. Cornopean.
24. Stopped Diapason.	27. Sesquialtera, III ranks.	30. Clarion.

Pedal, 6 *Stops, CCC to D.*

31. Open Diapason .... 16 feet.	34. Fifteenth .... 4 feet.
32. Stopped Diapason .... 16 feet.	35. Tierce .... 3¼ feet.
33. Principal .... 8 feet.	36. Sesquialtera, II ranks.

Couplers.

1. Swell to Great.	3. Choir to Great.	5. Choir to Pedals.
2. Swell to Choir.	4. Great to Pedals.	

234. LIVERPOOL.

The organ in Great George Street Chapel was built by Hill in 1841, and contains 52 sounding stops, of which the following is a list :—

Great, 16 Stops.

1.	Tenoroon to tenor c key...	16 feet.	9.	Tenth	3⅕ feet.
2.	Bourdon, to meet No. 1	16 feet tone.	10.	Twelfth	2⅔ feet.
3.	Open Diapason	8 feet.	11.	Fifteenth	2 feet.
4.	Open Diapason	8 feet.	12.	Sesquialtera, III ranks...	1⅗ foot.
5.	Stopped Diapason	8 feet tone.	13.	Mixture, III ranks	½ foot.
6.	Quint	5⅓ feet.	14.	Doublette, II ranks	2 feet.
7.	Principal	4 feet.	15.	Posaune	8 feet.
8.	Flute	4 feet.	16.	Clarion	4 feet.

Swell, 20 Stops.

17.	Tenoroon to tenor c key ...	16 feet.	27.	Flageolet	2 feet.
18.	Bourdon to meet No. 17	16 feet tone.	28.	Sesquialtera, III ranks ...	1⅗ foot.
19.	Open Diapason	8 feet.	29.	Mixture, II ranks	½ foot.
20.	Dulciana	8 feet.	30.	Echo Cornet, V ranks.	
21.	Stopped Diapason	8 feet tone.	31.	Contra Fagotto	16 feet.
22.	Quint	5⅓ feet.	32.	Cornopean	8 feet.
23.	Principal	4 feet.	33.	Trumpet	8 feet.
24.	Suabe Flute	4 feet.	34.	Oboe	8 feet.
25.	Twelfth	2⅔ feet.	35.	Corno Flute	8 feet.
26.	Fifteenth	2 feet.	36.	Clarion	4 feet.

Choir, 8 Stops.

37.	Open Diapason	8 feet.	42.	Stopped Flute	4 feet tone.
38.	Dulciana	8 feet tone.	43.	Waldflote	4 feet.
39.	Stopped Diapason	8 feet.	44.	Oboe Flute	4 feet.
40.	Clarabella	8 feet.	45.	Cremona	8 feet tone.
41.	Principal	4 feet.			

Solo Organ, 1 Stop.

46. Tuba Mirabilis .... 8 feet.

Pedal, 6 Stops.

47.	Open Diapason	16 feet.	50.	Fifteenth	4 feet.
48.	Bourdon	16 feet tone.	51.	Sesquialtera, V ranks ...	3⅕ feet.
49.	Principal	8 feet.	52.	Trombone	16 feet.

Accessory Stops, Movements, &c.

1.	Swell to Great.	4.	Swell to Pedal.
2.	Choir to Great.	5.	Choir to Pedal.
3.	Great to Pedal.	6 to 10.	Five Composition Pedals.

Compass.

Great, CC to f³ in alt.	Swell, CC to f³ in alt.
Choir, CC to f³ in alt.	Pedal, CCC to tenor d.

235. ST. GEORGE'S HALL, LIVERPOOL.

The organ in this magnificent building was erected in 1855 by Henry Willis, of London, in accordance with the plans of the late Dr. S. S. Wesley.

In 1867 the Corporation ordered the entire re-construction of the instrument, which important undertaking was carried out by Mr. Willis, under the superintendence of Mr. W. T. Best, who has acted here as organist since 1855. The organ now contains exactly one hundred "sounding" stops, disposed between four Claviers and Pedal. The compass of each key-board is five octaves and two notes ; (GG to A in alt.)—the Pedal range is two octaves and a half—(CCC to F). Every stop extends throughout the entire Manual compass. The Choir organ contains 18 stops ; the Great, 25 ; the Swell, 25 ; the Solo organ, 15 ; and the Pedal, 17. The accessory appliances consist of 10 Couplers and 42 pneumatic pistons, which places the varied tone-character of the immense instrument at the immediate disposal of the player. No zinc is employed in the construction of the pipes. The wind is derived from two large bellows, placed in the basement of St. George's Hall, blown by a steam engine of eight horse power. These bellows supply fourteen reservoirs, placed in various departments of the instrument ; the wind pressure ranges from three-and-a-half inches to twenty. Each key-board possesses the pneumatic lever, as an intermediary agent between the keys and the valves of the organ. The pedal board has two pneumatic levers for the same purpose. The entire cost of the organ, including every detail, amounted to £10,000.

First Manual (Choir), 18 Stops.

1.	Bourdon	16 feet.	10. Octave Viola	4 feet.
2.	Open Diapason	8 feet.	11. Twelfth	3 feet.
3.	Clarabella	8 feet.	12. Fifteenth	2 feet.
4.	Lieblich Gedact	8 feet.	13. Flageolet	2 feet.
5.	Dulciana	8 feet.	14. Sesquialtera, IV ranks.	
6.	Viol di Gamba	8 feet.	15. Tromba	8 feet.
7.	Voix Céleste	8 feet.	16. Clarionet	8 feet.
8.	Principal	4 feet.	17. Orchestral Oboe	8 feet.
9.	Harmonic Flute	4 feet.	18. Clarion	4 feet.

Second Manual (Great), 25 Stops.

19.	Double Open Diapason, metal	16 feet.	31. Decima	3½ feet.
20.	Open Diapason	8 feet.	32. Twelfth	3 feet.
21.	Open Diapason	8 feet.	33. Fifteenth	2 feet.
22.	Clarabella	8 feet.	34. Fifteenth	2 feet.
23.	Flute à Pavillon	8 feet.	35. Doublette, II ranks	2 and 1 feet.
24.	Lieblich Gedact	8 feet.	36. Sesquialtera, V ranks.	
25.	Violoncello	8 feet.	37. Mixture, IV ranks.	
26.	Quint	6 feet.	38. Contra Trombone	16 feet.
27.	Octave Viola	4 feet.	39. Trombone	8 feet.
28.	Principal	4 feet.	40. Ophicleide	8 feet.
29.	Principal	4 feet.	41. Trumpet	8 feet.
30.	Flauto Traverso	4 feet.	42. Clarion	4 feet.
			43. Clarion	4 feet.

Third Manual (Swell), 25 Stops.

44.	Double Diapason	16 feet.	57. Doublette, II ranks	2 & 1 feet.
45.	Open Diapason	8 feet.	58. Sesquialtera, V ranks.	
46.	Open Diapason	8 feet.	59. Contra Trombone	16 feet.
47.	Echo Dulciana	8 feet.	60. Contra Fagotto	16 feet.
48.	Lieblich Gedact	8 feet.	61. Ophicleide	8 feet.
49.	Voix Céleste	8 feet.	62. Trumpet	8 feet.
50.	Principal	4 feet.	63. Corno Dolce	8 feet.
51.	Gemshorn	4 feet.	64. Oboe	8 feet.
52.	Waldflote	4 feet.	65. Corno di Bassetto	8 feet.
53.	Twelfth	3 feet.	66. Vox Humana	8 feet.
54.	Fifteenth	2 feet.	67. Clarion	4 feet.
55.	Fifteenth	2 feet.	68. Clarion	4 feet.
56.	Piccolo	2 feet.	Tremulant to Swell,	

Fourth Manual (Solo Organ), 15 Stops.

69. Bourdon	16 feet.	78. Orchestral Oboe	8 feet.
70. Flauto Dolce	8 feet.	79. Clarion	4 feet.
71. Lieblich Gedact	8 feet.	80. Tromba	8 feet.
72. Flute Harmonique	4 feet.	81. Ophicleide	8 feet.
73. Piccolo Harmonique	2 feet.	82. Cornopean	8 feet.
74. Contra Fagotto	16 feet.	83. Trompette Harmonique	4 feet.
75. Trombone	8 feet.		
76. Bassoon	8 feet.		
77. Clarionet	8 feet.		

These last four registers are on a heavy wind-pressure, ranging from 15 to 20 inches.

Pedal Organ, 17 Stops.

84. Double Open Diapason, wood	32 feet.	92. Flute	8 feet.
85. Double Open Diapason, metal	32 feet.	93. Quint	6 feet.
86. Contra Trombone	32 feet.	94. Fifteenth	4 feet.
87. Open Diapason, wood	16 feet.	95. Fourniture, V ranks.	
88. Open Diapason, metal	16 feet.	96. Mixture, IV ranks.	
89. Violone, metal	16 feet.	97. Trombone	16 feet.
90. Bourdon	16 feet.	98. Ophicleide	16 feet.
91. Principal	8 feet.	99. Trompette	8 feet.
		100. Clarion	4 feet.

Couplers.

1. Swell to Great, Unison.	6. Solo to Choir.
2. Swell to Great, Sub-octave.	7. Great to Pedals.
3. Swell to Great, Super-octave.	8. Swell to Pedals.
4. Choir to Great.	9. Choir to Pedals.
5. Solo to Great.	10. Solo to Pedals.

236. LIVERPOOL.

The organ in the Collegiate Institution, Liverpool, was built by Mr. Jackson, of Liverpool, in 1850. It contains the 40 sounding stops mentioned below :—

Great, 20 Stops, 16 Ranks.

1. Tenoroon	16 feet.	8. Fifteenth	2 feet.
2. Bourdon, to meet No. 1	16 feet tone.	9. Sesqualtera, III ranks.	
3. Great Open Diapason	8 feet.	10. Mixture, III ranks.	
4. Small Open Diapason	8 feet.	11. Sharp twentieth.	
5. Stopped Diapason	8 feet tone.	12. Trumpet	8 feet.
6. Principal	4 feet.	13. Clarion	4 feet.
7. Twelfth	2⅔ feet.		

Choir, 11 Stops.

14. Open Diapason	8 feet.	20. Flute	4 feet.
15. Stopped Diapason	8 feet.	21. Piccolo	2 feet.
16. Clarabella	8 feet.	22. Fifteenth	2 feet.
17. Keraulophon	8 feet.	23. Bassoon	8 feet.
18. Dulciana	8 feet.	24. Clarionet	8 feet.
19. Principal	4 feet.		

Swell, 9 Stops.

25. Double Diapason	16 feet.	30. Echo Dulciana Cornet, III ranks.	
26. Open Diapason	8 feet.	31. Cornopean	8 feet.
27. Stopped Diapason	8 feet.	32. Oboe	8 feet.
28. Principal	5 feet.	33. Clarion	4 feet.
29. Fifteenth	2 feet.		

Pedal, 7 Stops.

34. Great Open Diapason ...... 16 feet.	38. Fifteenth .... 4 feet.
35. Bourdon .... 16 feet.	39. Mixture, VI ranks.
36. Principal .... 8 feet.	40. Posaune .... 16 feet.
37. Twelfth........................ 5⅓ feet.	

Accessory Stops, Movements, &c.

1. Swell to Great.	5. Choir to Pedals.
2. Choir to Swell.	6. Great to Pedals.
3. Sub-octave Choir to Great.	7. Super-octave to Pedals.
4. Swell to Pedals.	8 to 13. Six Composition Pedals.

Compass.

All the Manuals, CC to g³ in altissimo.	Pedal, CCC to Fiddle g.

237. LIVERPOOL.

Description of the organ in St. Margaret's Church, Liverpool, built by Hill and Son in 1873. 3 Manuals, compass of each, CC to G, 56 notes, and Pedal Clavier, CCC to F, 30 notes :—

Great Organ.

	Feet.	Pipes.		Feet.	Pipes.
1. Double Open Diapason, wood	16	12	8. Principal, metal	4	56
2. Tenoroon Diapason, wood	16	44	9. Harmonic Flute, metal ...	4	56
3. Open Diapason, metal......	8	56	10. Twelfth, metal	3	56
4. Flute à Pavillon, wood ...	8	56	11. Fifteenth, metal	2	56
5. Gamba, metal	8	56	12. Mixture, metal, IV ranks.		224
6. Hohlflote, wood	8	56	13. Trumpet, metal	8	56
7. Stopped Diapason, wood	8	56	14. Clarion, metal...............	4	56

Choir Organ.

	Feet.	Pipes.		Feet.	Pipes.
15. Dulciana, metal	8	56	19. Harmonic Piccolo, metal	2	56
16. Gamba, metal	8	56	20. Clarionet, metal	8	56
17. Clarabella, wood............	8	56	21. Orchestral Oboe, metal...	8	56
18. Lieblich Flute, wood	4	56			

Swell Organ.

	Feet.	Pipes.		Feet.	Pipes.
22. Bourdon, wood	16	56	29. Contra Trumpet, metal ...	8	56
23. Open Diapason, metal ...	8	56	30. Cornopean, metal	8	56
24. Lieblich, wood...............	8	56	31. Oboe, metal	8	56
25. Keraulophon, tenor c, metal	8	44	32. Clarion, metal	8	56
			33. Vox Humana, metal	8	56
26. Principal, metal	4	56	34. Vox Angelica, II ranks, to tenor c, Gedact, bass	8	100
27. Fifteenth, metal	2	56			
28. Mixture, metal, III ranks		68	35. Tremulant		

Pedal Organ. (Radiating and Concave.)

	Feet.	Pipes.		Feet.	Pipes.
36. Double Open Diapason, wood......................	32	30	39. Bourdon, wood	16	30
37. Open Diapason, wood......	16	30	40. Violoncello, wood	8	30
38. Violone, wood ,.............	16	30	41. Mixture, metal, III ranks.		90
			42. Trombone, wood	16	30

Couplers.

1. Swell to Great.
2. Swell to Octave.
3. Swell to Sub-octave.
4. Choir to Great.

5. Swell to Choir.
6. Swell to Great.
7. Great to Pedal.
8. Swell to Pedal.

4 Composition Pedals to Great organ.
1 Composition Pedal to Choir organ.
3 Composition Pedals to Swell organ.
Pneumatic action to Great and Couplers.

238. LIVERPOOL.

The following is the description of the organ at the Wesley Chapel, Stanhope Street, built by Gray and Davison in 1874 :—

Choir Organ.

1.	Geigen Principal	8 feet.	5.	Piccolo Harmonique	2 feet.
2.	Salicional	8 feet.	6.	Clarionet	8 feet.
3.	Clarabella	8 feet.	7.	Orchestral Oboe	8 feet.
4.	Waldflote	4 feet.			

(Nos. 6 and 7 are placed in a separate Swell box, and Tremulant applied to them.)

Great Organ.

8.	Contra Gamba	16 feet.	14.	Mixture, V ranks	various.
9.	Open Diapason	8 feet.	15.	Hohlflote	8 feet.
10.	Viola	8 feet.	16.	Flute Octaviante	4 feet.
11.	Principal	4 feet.	17.	Posaune	8 feet.
12.	Twelfth	3 feet.	18.	Clarion	4 feet.
13.	Fifteenth	2 feet.			

Swell Organ.

19.	Lieblich Gedact	16 feet.	26.	Mixture, IV ranks	various.
20.	Spitz Flote	8 feet.	27.	Sifflote	2 feet.
21.	Viol d'Amour	8 feet.	28.	Contra Trumpet	16 feet.
22.	Voix Céleste	8 feet.	29.	Cornopean	8 feet.
23.	Gedact	8 feet.	30.	Oboe	8 feet.
24.	Gemshorn	4 feet.	31.	Clarion	4 feet.
25.	Flute d'Amour	4 feet.		Tremulant.	

Pedal Organ.

32.	Open Diapason	16 feet.	36.	Bass Flute	8 feet.
33.	Violone	16 feet.	37.	Violoncello	8 feet.
34.	Bourdon	16 feet.	38.	Trombone	16 feet.
35.	Grosse Quint	12 feet.			

Couplers and Accessory Stops.

1. Choir Manual to Pedals.
2. Great Manual to Pedals.
3. Swell Manual to Pedals.
4. Choir Manual to Great Manual.
5. Swell Manual to Choir Manual.
6. Swell Sub-octave to Great Manual.
7. Swell Manual to Great Manual.

8. Swell Octave to Great Manual.
9. Choir Sforzando.
10. Swell Sforzando.
11. Solo to Choir.
12. Solo to Great.
13. Solo to Swell.
14. Clochette.

Accessory Pedals.

1. Choir Tremulant.
2. Choir Sforzando.
3. Solo to Swell.
4. Solo to Choir.
5 to 8. Swell Combinations.
9. Solo to Great.

10 to 13. Great Combinations.
14. Swell Sforzando.
15. Great Manual to Pedals.
16. Swell Crescendo.
17. Choir Crescendo.

General Remarks.

The stops numbered 15, 16, 17, 18, are on a heavy pressure of wind, and so arranged that they can be used on any Manual.

Pneumatic levers attached to the Great organ and Couplers.

By a peculiar mechanical arrangement the Great organ Diapasons can be detached and used with Choir organ for loud accompaniments.

Three complete Manuals, CC to A.................. 56 notes.
Pedal organ, CCC to F .... 30 notes.

239. HUDDERSFIELD.

The organ in Buxton Road Chapel, Huddersfield, was built by T. J. Robson, of London, and consists of 3 Manuals—Great, Choir, and Swell—with an independent Pedal organ of 9 stops. It contains 40 sounding stops, of which the following is a list :—

Great, 15 Stops, CC to C in alt., 61 Notes.

1. Double Open Diapason, metal throughout ...... 16 feet.
2. Large Open Diapason ... 8 feet.
3. Open Diapason .... 8 feet.
4. Stopped Diapason .... 8 feet tone.
5. Quint........................... 6 feet.
6. Principal .... 4 feet.
7. Wald Flute .... 4 feet.

8. Twelfth .... 3 feet.
9. Fifteenth .... 2 feet.
10. Piccolo .... 2 feet.
11. Sesqualtera, III ranks ... 1½ foot.
12. Mixture, II ranks .... ½ foot.
13. Furniture, III ranks.
14. Trumpet .... 8 feet.
15. Clarion .... 4 feet.

Choir, 4 Stops, CC to C in alt., 61 Notes.

16. Stopped Diapason and Clarabella .... 8 feet tone.
17. Dulciana .... 8 feet.

18. Viol di Gamba .... 8 feet.
19. Principal...................... 4 feet.

Swell, 12 Stops, CC to C in alt., 61 Notes.

20. Double Diapason............ 16 feet tone.
21. Open Diapason .... 8 feet.
22. Stopped Diapason .... 8 feet tone.
23. Viol di Gamba.............. 8 feet.
24. Principal .... 4 feet.
25. Fifteenth .... 2 feet.
26. Sesqualtera, III ranks ... 1½ foot.

27. Contra Fagotto, metal ... 16 feet.
28. Clarionet and Corni di Bassetto .... 8 feet.
29. Hautboy .... 8 feet.
30. Horn ...!..................... 8 feet.
31. Clarion .... 4 feet.

Pedal, 9 Stops.

The compass of the pipes, CCC to F (42 notes), three and a half octaves, the upper octave being added for the purpose of completing the Octave Copula.

32. Open Diapason	16 feet.	37. Sesquialtera, V ranks	3⅕ feet.
33. Violone	16 feet tone.	38. Posaune, metal	16 feet.
34. Principal	8 feet.	39. Trumpet	8 feet.
35. Quint	6 feet.	40. Clarion	4 feet.
36. Fifteenth	4 feet.		

Couplers, &c.

1. Swell to Great. | 2. Great to Pedals. | 3. Choir to Pedals. | 4. Octave Pedals.
5 to 10. Six Composition Pedals.

Summary of Stops and Pipes.

	Stops.		Pipes.
Great organ	15	......	1232
Swell organ	12	......	854
Choir organ	4	......	220
Pedal organ	9	......	546
Couplers	4	......	
	44		2852

240. ASHTON-UNDER-LYNE.

The organ in the Parish Church of Ashton-under-Lyne was the noble gift of Edward Brown, Esq., of the Firs, and was built by Hill in the year 1845. It contains 55 sounding stops, besides 8 Couplers, 3 Manuals, and a Pedal of 6 stops. The following is its disposition :—

Great, 21 Stops.

	Pipes.	Feet.		Pipes.	Feet
1. Tenoroon Diapason	42	16	12. Fifteenth	54	2
2. Bourdon, CCC to BB	12	16 tone.	13. Tierce	54	1⅗
3. Open Diapason	54	8	14. Sesquialtera, III ranks	162	1⅗
4. Open Diapason	54	8	15. Mixture, III ranks	162	⅔
5. Stopped Diapason to tenor c	42	8 tone.	16. Doublette, II ranks	108	2
6. Stopped Diapason, Bass	12	8 tone.	17. Tenoroon Trumpet	42	16
7. Quint	54	5⅓	18. Double Trumpet, CCC to BB	12	16
8. Principal	54	4	19. Posaune	54	8
9. Wald Flute to tenor c	42	4	20. Clarion	54	4
10. Tenth	54		21. Octave Clarion	54	2
11. Twelfth	54	2⅔			

Swell, 18 Stops.

22. Tenoroon Dulciana	42	16	31. Fifteenth	54	2
23. Bourdon, CCC to BB	12	16 tone.	32. Flageolet, tenor c	42	2
24. Open Diapason	54	8	33. Sesquialtera, III ranks	162	1⅗
25. Echo Dulciana to tenor c	42	8	34. Mixture, II ranks	108	⅔
26. Stopped Diapason, Treble	42	8 tone.	35. Echo Dulciana Cornet to tenor c, V ranks	210	
27. Stopped Diapason, Bass	12	8 tone.	36. Tenoroon Trumpet to tenor c	42	16
28. Principal	54	4	37. Cornopean	54	8
29. Suabe Flute to tenor c	42	4	38. Oboe	54	8
30. Twelfth	54	2⅔	39. Clarion	54	8

Choir, 10 Stops.

	Pipes.	Feet.			Pipes.	Feet.
40. Open Diapason	54	8		45. Oboe Flute to tenor c	42	4
41. Claribel to tenor c	42	8		46. Stopped Flute to tenor		
42. Viol di Gamba to tenor				c	42	4 one.
c	42	8		47. Fifteenth	54	2
43. Stopped Diapason, Bass	12	8 tone.		48. Piccolo to tenor c ...	42	2
44. Principal	54	4		49. Cremona to tenor c...	42	8 tone.

Pedal, 6 Stops.

	Pipes.	Feet.			Pipes.	Feet.
50. Open Diapason	27	16		53. Fifteenth	27	4
51. Bourdon	27	16 tone.		54. Mixture, V ranks	135	3¼
52. Principal	24	8		55. Trombone	27	16

Accessory Stops, Movements, &c.

1 to 8. Eight Couplers. | 9 to 14. Six Composition Pedals. | 15. Sforzando Pedal.

Compass.

Great Organ, CC to f³ in alt. ...... 54 notes. | Choir Organ, CC to f³ in alt. ...... 54 notes.
Swell Organ, CC to f³ in alt. ...... 54 notes. | Pedal Organ, CCC to tenor d ...... 27 notes.

Summary of Pipes and Stops.

Great organ	1230	 21
Swell organ	1134	 18
Choir organ	426	 10
Pedal organ	270	 6
Total...............	3060	 55

241. STOCKPORT.

The organ in the large room of the Stockport Sunday School was built in 1853 by Kirtland and Jardine, of Manchester, according to a scheme drawn up by the late George Cooper, Esq., of London. The instrument contains 23 sounding stops, distributed among 2 complete Manuals and Pedal in the following manner :—

Great, 12 Stops.

	Feet.	Pipes.			Feet.	Pipes.
1. Open Diapason, major ...	8	54		8. Fifteenth	2	54
2. Open Diapason, minor ...	8	59		9. Sesqualtera, IV ranks ...	1¼	216
3. Stopped Diapason	8 tone.	54		10. Trumpet	8	54
4. Dulciana	8	54		11. Clarion	4	54
5. Wald Flute	4	54		12. Cremona to fiddle g	8	35
6. Principal	4	54				
7. Twelfth	2⅔	54		Number of pipes...............		636

Swell, 10 Stops.

	Feet.	Pipes.			Feet.	Pipes.
13. Double Stopped Diapason	16	54		19. Fifteenth	2	54
14. Open Diapason...............	8	54		20. Sesqualtera, III ranks ...	1¼	162
15. Stopped Diapason	8	54		21. Cornopean	8	54
16. Keraulophon to tenor c ...	8	42		22. Hautboy	8	54
17. Principal	4	54				
18. Hohlflute	4	54		Pipes in Swell............		636

Pedal, 1 Stop.

23. Open Diapason ....16 feet.

Accessory Stops, Movements, &c.

1. Swell to Great, Unison.
2. Swell to Great, Sub-octave.
3. Swell to Great, Octave.
4. Great to Pedal.
5. Swell to Pedal.
6 to 9. Four Composition Pedals to Great organ.

10 and 11. Two Composition Pedals to Swell organ.
12. Pedal, Sub-octave Swell.
13. Pedal, Unison Octave Swell.
14. Pedal, Octave Swell.
15. Sforzando Pedal, acting simultaneously upon the three Swell Couplers.

Compass.

Great, CC to f³ in alt. | Swell, CC to f³ in alt. | Pedal, CCC to tenor f.

242. OLDHAM.

The organ in the Parish Church at Oldham was built in the year 1830 by Elliott and Hill, of London. It contains 31 sounding stops, of which the following is a list :—

Great, 14 Stops.

1. Double Diapason, Treble.
2. Double Diapason, Bass.
3. Open Diapason, No. 1.
4. Open Diapason, No. 2.
5. Stopped Diapason.
6. Principal, No. 1.
7. Principal, No. 2.

8. Twelfth.
9. Fifteenth.
10. Sesquialtera, IV ranks.
11. Mixture, III ranks.
12. Trumpet, Treble.
13. Trumpet, Bass.
14. Clarion.

Choir, 8 Stops.

15. Open Diapason.
16. Stopped Diapason.
17. Principal.
18. Flute.

19. Fifteenth.
20. Flageolet.
21. Cremona.
22. Bassoon.

Swell, 8 Stops.

23. Double Diapason.
24. Open Diapason.
25. Stopped Diapason.
26. Dulciana.

27. Principal.
28. Mixture, III ranks.
29. Trumpet.
30. Hautboy.

Pedal, 1 Stop.

31. Pedal pipes.

Accessory Stops, Movements, &c.

1. Coupler, Swell to Great.
2. Coupler, Great to Pedal.

3. Coupler, Choir to Pedal.
4, 5, 6. Three Composition Pedals.

Compass.

Great, GG to f³ in alt.
Choir, GG to f³ in alt.
Swell organ, tenor c to f³ in alt.

Swell Clavier, down to GG, and acting on Choir organ below tenor c.
Pedal Clavier, GG to tenor d.

243. SALISBURY CATHEDRAL.

The new organ in Salisbury Cathedral, built by Mr. Henry Willis, has 4 Manuals, separate Pedal, and the 55 sounding stops mentioned below :—

Great Organ.

1.	Double Open Diapason, metal	16 feet.		
2.	Open Diapason, large, metal	8 feet.		
3.	Open Diapason, small, metal	8 feet.		
4.	Stopped Diapason, metal	8 feet.		
5.	Claribel Flute, closed, Bass, wood	8 feet.		
6.	Principal, metal	4 feet.		
7.	Flute Harmonique, metal	4 feet.		

8. Twelfth, metal	3 feet.
9. Fifteenth, metal	2 feet.
10. Piccolo, metal	2 feet.
11. Mixture, full, IV ranks, metal	2 feet.
12. Double Trumpet, metal	16 feet.
13. Cornopean, metal	8 feet.
14. Clarion, metal	4 feet.

Solo Organ.

15. Flute Harmonique, metal	8 feet.
16. Flute Harmonique, metal	4 feet.
17. Orchestral Oboe, metal	8 feet.

18. Tuba, metal	8 feet.
19. Corno di Bassetto, metal	8 feet.
20. Clarion, metal	4 feet.

Swell Organ.

21. Contra Gamba, metal	16 feet.
22. Viol di Gamba, metal	8 feet.
23. Open Diapason, metal	8 feet.
24. Lieblich Gedact, metal	8 feet.
25. Vox Angelica (undulating to tenor c), metal	8 feet.
26. Octave, metal	4 feet.
27. Flute Harmonique, metal	4 feet.

28. Super-octave, metal	2 feet.
29. Mixture, metal, IV ranks.	
30. Contra Fagotto, metal	16 feet.
31. Trumpet, metal	8 feet.
32. Hautboy, metal	8 feet.
33. Clarion, metal	4 feet.
34. Vox Humana, metal	8 feet.

Choir Organ.

35. Lieblich Gedact, metal	16 feet.
36. Lieblich Gedact, metal	8 feet.
37. Lieblich Gedact, metal	4 feet.
38. Flute Harmonique, metal	8 feet.
39. Flute Harmonique, metal	4 feet.

40. Salicional, metal	8 feet.
41. Gemshorn, metal	4 feet.
42. Flageolet, metal	2 feet.
43. Corno di Bassetto, metal	8 feet.
44. Cor Anglais, metal	8 feet.

Pedal Organ.

45. Double Open Diapason, metal	32 feet.
46. Open Diapason, metal	16 feet.
47. Violone, metal	16 feet.
48. Octave, metal	8 feet.
49. Open Diapason, wood	16 feet.

50. Flute, open, wood	8 feet.
51. Mixture, metal, IV ranks.	
52. Contra Posaune, wood	32 feet.
53. Ophicleide, metal	16 feet.
54. Clarion, metal	8 feet.
55. Bourdon, wood	16 feet.

Couplers.

Swell to Great, Unison.	Solo to Pedals.
Swell to Great, Super-octave.	Swell to Pedals.
Swell to Great, Sub-octave.	Great to Pedals.
Solo to Great.	Choir to Pedals.
Choir to Great.	Tremulant to Swell, Vox Humana.

Four Patent Pneumatic Combination Pistons to each Clavier ; Four Combination Pedals to Pedal Organ ; a double-acting Pedal to Great, to Pedal Coupler ; four complete Manuals from CC to A, 58 notes, and 2 octaves and a half of Concave and Radiating Pedals from CCC to F, 30 notes.

244. HALIFAX.

The fine organ in the Parish Church at Halifax was built by Snetzler in 1766. It has received several additions since then, and now contains 26 sounding stops, of which the following is a list :—

Great, 11 Stops.

1. Open Diapason, throughout	8 feet.	7. Sesquialtera, IV ranks ...	2 feet.
2. Open Diapason, throughout	8 feet.	8. Mixture, III ranks.........	1 foot.
3. Stopped Diapason	8 feet tone.	9. Mounted Cornet, to Middle	
4. Principal	4 feet.	c¹, V ranks	8 feet tone.
5. Twelfth........................	2⅔ feet.	10. Trumpet	8 feet.
6. Fifteenth	2 feet.	11. Clarion........................	4 feet.

Swell, 7 Stops.

12. Double Diapason............	16 feet tone.	16. Sesquialtera, III ranks ...	2⅔ feet.
13. Open Diapason	8 feet.	17. Cornopean	8 feet.
14. Stopped Diapason	8 feet tone.	18. Oboe	8 feet.
15. Principal	4 feet.		

Choir, 7 Stops.

19. Open Diapason, throughout	8 feet.	23. Flute	4 feet tone.
20. Stopped Diapason	8 feet tone.	24. Fifteenth	2 feet.
21. Dulciana to Gamut G......	8 feet.	25. { Bassoon Treble }	8 feet.
22. Principal	4 feet.	{ Bassoon Bass }	

Pedal, 1 Stop.

25. Great Open Diapason, wood, DD down to GGG, 21⅓ feet length.

245. ALL SOULS' CHURCH, HALIFAX.

This organ, built by Messrs. Forster and Andrews, has 4 complete Manuals, from CC to A, Pedals from CCC to F, and 53 sounding stops, as follows :—

Great Organ.

	Feet Tone.	Pipes.		Feet Tone.	Pipes.
1. Double Diapason, closed, wood	16 ...	58	8. Twelfth, metal	2⅔ ...	58
2. Open Diapason, metal......	8 ...	58	9. Fifteenth, metal............	2 ...	58
3. Violon Diapason, metal ...	8 ...	58	10. Full Mixture, II & III ranks, metal...............		150
4. Hohlflote, wood	8 ...	58	11. Bright Mixture, III ranks, metal.........................		174
5. Stopped Diapason, wood..	8 ...	58	12. Trumpet, metal	8 ...	58
6. Principal, metal	4 ...	58	13. Clarion, metal...............	4 ...	58
7. Harmonic Flute, metal ...	4 ...	58			

Swell Organ.

	Feet Tone.	Pipes.		Feet Tone.	Pipes.
14. Bourdon, wood..............	16 ...	58	21. Fifteenth, metal	2 ...	58
15. Open Diapason, metal......	8 ...	58	22. Mixture, III ranks, metal		175
16. Salicional, metal	8 ...	46	23. Contra Fagotto, metal ...	16 ...	46
17. Rohrflote, wood and metal	8 ...	58	24. Horn, metal.................	8 ...	58
18. Principal, metal	4 ...	58	25. Oboe, metal	8 ...	58
19. Viola d'Amour, metal	4 ...	58	26. Voix Humaine, metal ...	8 ...	58
20. Twelfth, metal	2⅔ ...	58	27. Clarion, metal	4 ...	58

Choir Organ.

	Feet tone.	Pipes.			Feet tone.	Pipes.
28. Lieblich Bourdon, wood...	16	... 46		32. Salicional, metal............	4	... 58
29. Dulciana, metal	8	... 58		33. Lieblich Flote, wood......	4	... 58
30. Lieblich Gedact, wood and				34. Flautino(Harmonic), metal	2	... 58
metal........................	8	... 58		35. Krummhorn, metal	8	... } 58
31. Bell Gamba, metal	8	... 46		36. Bassoon, metal	8	... }

Echo Organ.

	Feet tone.	Pipes.			Feet tone.	Pipes.
37. Tibia Major, wood	16	... 46		41. Flauto Traverso, wood ...	8	... 58
38. Vox Angelica, metal	8	... }		42. Flauto Dolcissimo, wood	4	... 58
39. Salamine, metal	8	... } 92		43. Celestina, metal............	4	... 58
40. Flauto Amabile, wood and				44. Harmonica Ætheria, metal $\{\begin{smallmatrix}2\frac{2}{3}\\2\end{smallmatrix}\}$ ..		116
metal........................	8	... 58				

Pedal Organ.

	Feet tone.	Pipes.			Feet tone.	Pipes.
45. Open Diapason, wood......	16	... 30		50. Flute, wood	8	... 30
46. Violon, metal	16	... 30		51. Fifteenth, metal............	4	... 30
47. Bourdon, wood..............	16	... 30		52. Trombone, metal	16	... 30
48. Gross Quint, wood	10⅔	... 30		53. Trumpet, metal	8	... 30
49. Violoncello, metal	8	... 30				

Couplers, &c.

1. Great to Pedals.	6. Swell to Choir.
2. Choir to Pedals.	7. Swell Octave to Great.
3. Swell to Pedals.	8. Choir Sub-octave to Great.
4. Pedal Pipes, wind.	9. Swell to Echo, by Pedal.
5. Swell to Great.	

Accessory Stops.

1, 2, 3. Composition Pedals to Great Organ. | 4, 5, 6. Composition Pedals to Swell Organ.
7. Tremulant to Swell by Pedal.

The organ is placed in the North Chapel. The case is of selected Memel wainscoat oak (designed by Sir G. G. Scott, A.R.A., the architect of the Church). On the impost stand the large 16 and 8 feet pipes, enclosed by a wrought-iron band, and decorated on the spotted metal of which they are made. The various bellows, by means of which the organ is supplied with five different pressures of wind, are blown by a patent hydraulic engine, with provision for the usual hand-blowing action. Nearly the whole of the metal pipes, including the 16-foot Pedal Violon, are made of the finest spotted metal.

246. BRADFORD.

The organ in Eastbrook Chapel, Bradford, was built by Hill in 1844-45. It has 3 Manual organs of complete compass, a Pedal of 7 stops, and 44 stops, of which the following is a list :—

Great, 15 Stops.

1. Tenoroon	16 feet.	9. Tenth	3⅕ feet.
2. Bourdon, metal	16 feet.	10. Twelfth	2⅔ feet.
3. Open Diapason	8 feet.	11. Fifteenth.....................	2 feet.
4. Open Diapason	8 feet.	12. Sesqualtera, V ranks ...	1⅗ foot.
5. Stopped Diapason	8 feet tone.	13. Mixture, III ranks.........	⅗ foot.
6. Quint...........................	5⅓ feet.	14. Posaune	8 feet.
7. Principal	4 feet.	15. Clarion......................	4 feet.
8. Wald Flute	4 feet.		

Swell, 14 Stops.

16.	Tenoroon	16 feet.	23. Twelfth	2⅔ feet.
17.	Bourdon	16 feet.	24. Fifteenth	2 feet.
18.	Open Diapason	8 feet.	25. Flageolet	2 feet.
19.	Stopped Diapason	8 feet tone.	26. Sesquialtera, III ranks...	1⅓ foot.
20.	Dulciana to tenor c	8 feet.	27. Cornopean	8 feet.
21.	Principal	4 feet.	28. Hautboy	8 feet.
22.	Flute	4 feet.	29. Clarion	4 feet.

Choir, 8 Stops.

30.	Open Diapason	8 feet.	34. Wald Flute	4 feet.
31.	Stopped Diapason	8 feet tone.	35. Fifteenth	2 feet.
32.	Viol di Gamba	8 feet.	36. Cremona	8 feet tone.
33.	Principal	4 feet.	37. Bassoon	8 feet.

Pedal, 7 Stops.

38.	Open, wood, to GGG	32 feet.	42. Fifteenth	2 feet.
39.	Open, metal	16 feet.	43. Sesquialtera, V ranks ...	3⅓ feet.
40.	Principal	8 feet.	44. Trombone	16 feet.
41.	Twelfth	6 feet.		

Accessory Stops, Movements, &c.

1. Coupler, Swell to Great.
2. Coupler, Great to Pedal.
3. Coupler, Swell to Pedal.

4. Coupler, Choir to Pedal.
5, 6, 7. Three Composition Pedals.

Compass.

Great, CC to f³ in alt., 54 notes.
Swell, CC to f³ in alt., 54 notes.

Choir, CC to f³ in alt., 54 notes.
Pedal, CCC to tenor d, 27 notes.

247. LEEDS TOWN HALL.

The grand organ which stands in the Leeds Town Hall was built by Messrs. Gray and Davison, from plans prepared by Mr. Henry Smart, of London, and Dr. William Spark, of Leeds. It was commenced in 1857, completed in 1859, and inaugurated by two public performances on the 7th of April.

The case was designed by Mr. Broderick, architect of the Town Hall. The lower part, which is of oak, was made in Leeds by Messrs. Thorp and Atkinson. The ornaments are all of carved wood, and are exceedingly well executed by Mr. Matthews, also of Leeds.

The total cost, including the case and hydraulic engines, was about £6000.

The organ has 4 Manual claviers, the compass of each, from CC to C in altissimo, 61 notes, and a Pedal Clavier, from CCC to F, 30 notes.

The *Orchestral Solo organ* (uppermost Clavier) contains the following stops :—

By Pipes on Sound Boards.

	Feet.	Pipes.		Feet.	Pipes.
1. Bourdon	8	61	6. Oboe	8	49
2. Concert Flute, Harmonic..	8	42	7. Cor Anglais and Bassoon,		
3. Piccolo, Harmonic	4	49	free reed	8	61
4. Ottavina, Harmonic	2	61	8. Tromba	8	61
5. Clarinet	8	61	9. Ophicleide	8	81

By Mechanical Combination.

10. Clarinet and Flute, in Octaves.
11. Oboe and Flute, in Octaves.
12. Clarinet and Bassoon, in Octaves.
13. Clarinet and Oboe, in Octaves.
14. Oboe and Bassoon, in Octaves.

15. Flute, Clarinet, and Bassoon, in Double Octaves.
16. Flute, Oboe, and Bassoon, in Double Octaves.

The *Swell organ* (second Clavier) contains the following stops :—

		Feet.		Pipes.			Feet.		Pipes.
1.	Bourdon	16	...	61	11. Fifteenth	2	...	61
2.	Open Diapason	8	...	61	12. Piccolo	2	...	61
3.	Stopped Diapason, Treble.	8	...	49	13. Sesquialtera, IV ranks ...		...	244
4.	Stopped Diapason, Bass ...	8	...	12	14. Mixture, III ranks	1	...	183
5.	Keraulophon	8	...	49	15. Contra Fagotto	16	...	61
6.	Harmonic Flute	8	...	49	16. Trumpet	8	...	61
7.	Octave	4	...	61	17. Cornopean	8	...	61
8.	Gemshorn	4	...	61	18. Oboe	8	...	61
9.	Wood Flute	4	...	·61	19. Vox Humana	8	...	61
10.	Twelfth	3	...	61	20. Clarion	4	...	61

The *Great organ* (third Clavier) contains, in reality, two complete and distinct organs, of different powers and qualities. One, called the "*Front Great organ,*" contains the following stops :—

		Feet.		Pipes.			Feet.		Pipes.
1.	Double Diapason, open, metal	16	...	61	7. Twelfth	3	...	61
2.	Open Diapason	8	...	61	8. Fifteenth	2	...	61
3.	Spitz Gamba	8	...	61	9. Quint Mixture, IV ranks		...	244
4.	Stopped Diapason	8	...	61	10. Tierce Mixture, V ranks		...	305
5.	Octave	4	...	61	11. Trumpet	8	...	61
6.	Wald Flute	4	...	61	12. Clarion	4	...	61

The contents of the *Back Great organ* are as follows :—

		Feet.		Pipes.			Feet.		Pipes.
13.	Bourdon	16	...	61	20. Piccolo Harmonic	2	...	61
14.	Flute à Pavillon	8	...	61	21. Cymbal, III ranks		...	183
15.	Viola	8	...	61	22. Furniture, IV ranks		...	244
16.	Flute Harmonic	8	...	61	23. Contra Trombone	16	...	61
17.	Quint	6	...	61	24. Trombone	8	...	61
18.	Octave	4	...	61	25. Trumpet Harmonic	8	...	61
19.	Flute Octaviante	4	...	54	26. Tenor Trombone	4	...	61

The *Choir Organ* (lowermost Clavier) contains the following stops :—

		Feet.		Pipes.			Feet.		Pipes.
1.	Sub-dulciana	16	...	61	9. Flute Harmonic	4	...	49
2.	Open Diapason	8	...	61	10. Twelfth	3	...	61
3.	Rohrflote, metal	8	...	49	11. Fifteenth	2	...	61
4.	Stopped Diapason, Bass, wood	8	...	12	12. Ottavina, wood	2	...	61
5.	Salicional	8	...	61	13. Dulciana Mixture, V ranks		...	305
6.	Viol di Gamba	8	...	49	14. Euphone, free reed	16	...	61
7.	Octave	4	...	61	15. Trumpet	8	...	61
8.	Suabe Flute	4	...	49	16. Clarion	4	...	61

The *Echo Organ,** which can be played on either the Solo or Choir Clavier, contains the following stops :—

		Feet.		Pipes.			Feet.		Pipes.
1.	Bourdon, wood	16	...	49	5. Flute d'Amour, metal	4	...	61
2.	Dulciana, metal	8	...	49	6. Dulciana Mixture, metal, IV ranks		...	244
3.	Lieblich Gedact, wood	8	...	61	7. Carillons.			
4.	Flute Traverso, wood	4	...	61				

---

* The Echo organ was added in 1865 ; it formed part of the original plan, and was only omitted at first on the score of expense.

The *Pedal Organ* contains the following stops :—

	Feet.	Pipes.			Feet.	Pipes
1. Sub-bass, open metal	32	30	10. Twelfth		6	30
2. Contra Bourdon, wood	32	30	11. Fifteenth		4	30
3. Open Diapason, metal	16	30	12. Mixture, V ranks			150
4. Open Diapason, wood	16	30	13. Contra Bombard, free			
5. Violon, wood	16	30	reed		32	30
6. Bourdon, wood	16	30	14. Bombard		16	30
7. Quint, open, wood	12	30	15. Fagotto		16	30
8. Octave	8	30	16. Clarion		8	30
9. Violoncello	8	30				

The *Coupling Stops* are as follows :—

1. Solo organ to Great Clavier.
2. Great organ to Solo Clavier.
3. Solo organ, Super-octave (on its own Clavier).
4. Solo organ, Sub-octave (on its own Clavier).
5. Swell organ to Great Super-octave.
6. Swell organ to Great Unison.
7. Swell organ to Great Sub-octave.
8. Swell organ to Choir Clavier.
9. Choir organ to Great Unison.
10. Swell organ to Pedal Clavier.
11. Choir organ to ditto.
12. Great organ to ditto.
13. Full Pedal organ.
14. Solo organ to Pedal Clavier.
15. Echo organ to Solo Clavier.
16. Echo organ to Choir Clavier.
17. Tremulant to Echo organ.

The *Pedals*, &c., for various purposes of mechanical adjustment, are as follows :—

1. Swell Pedal.
2. Swell Pedal for Solo organ.
3. Swell Tremulant Pedal.
4. Pedal admitting wind to the back Great organ.
5. Pedal coupling the back Great organ to Swell Clavier.
6, 7, 8, 9. Composition Pedals.
10. Crescendo Pedal.
11. Diminuendo Pedal.
12 to 15. Indexes to Composition Pedals.
16 and 17. Wind Couplers to Composition Pedals.

Summary of Draw Stops, &c.

Solo organ	9	Echo organ		8
Combination Pedal	7	Pedal organ		16
Swell organ	20	Coupling Stops		17
Great organ—Front 12, back 14	26			
Choir organ	16	Making a total of		117

Summary of Pipes.

Solo organ	500	Echo organ		520
Swell organ	1440	Pedal organ		600
Great organ	2311			
Choir organ	1123	Total		6500

248. YORK MINSTER.

This instrument was built after the fire at the Minster in 1829 by Messrs. Elliott and Hill, under the superintendence of the late organist, Dr. Camidge. It was considered the *largest* in the world, containing 80 stops, and 8000 pipes; it cost about £5000, including the original gift of the late Earl of Scarborough (who was the senior prebendary of the Cathedral at the time the first fire occurred), of £3000. Unhappily, his lordship died before the completion of the instrument, so that the remaining £2000 had to be furnished by the Chapter, assisted by subscriptions from the neighbouring nobility, gentry, and clergy. It was, however, his lordship's desire and intention to have supplied the sum wanting, beyond that contracted for ; but, as his death occurred so suddenly, they were deprived of this advantage. The Great Manual contained 4818 pipes ; the Swell organ, 1586 ; the Choir organ, 1399 ; and the Pedal organ, 200 pipes.

In connection with the York Minster organ various improvements were suggested at different times, and carried out by the late Dr. Camidge, to assist in making up for the defects in its original construction. Still, however, these defects were appreciably visible to all persons conversant with the anatomy of a cathedral organ ; and, in the spring of the year 1863, the Dean and Chapter instituted an examination of the instrument, when it was found that it had become considerably impaired in power. It was, therefore, determined that it should undergo a thorough renovation and re-construction ; and an appeal was made to the public for subscriptions to carry out the object, which was liberally responded to. The construction of the organ was carried out by Messrs. Hill, under the superintendence of Dr. Monk, the present organist.

The following is a description of the large screen organ as it now stands :—

Great, 24 Stops, CC to G in alt.

1. Double Open Diapason, metal	16 feet.	13. Twelfth, metal	3 feet.
2. Gedact, wood	16 feet.	14. Fifteenth, metal	2 feet.
3. Open Diapason, East, metal...	8 feet.	15. Octave Flute, wood	2 feet.
4. Open Diapason, West, metal...	8 feet.	16. Full Mixture, IV ranks.	
5. Open Diapason, No. 3, metal...	8 feet.	17. Sharp Mixture, III ranks.	
6. Gamba, metal	8 feet.	18. Tierce Mixture, III ranks.	
7. Stopped Diapason, wood	8 feet.	19. Cornet, IV ranks.	
8. Quint	6 feet.	20. Glockenspiel, II ranks.	
9. Octave	4 feet.	21. Double Trumpet, metal	16 feet.
10. Octave	4 feet.	22. Posaune, metal	8 feet.
11. Open Diapason	8 feet.	23. Trumpet, metal	8 feet.
12. Harmonic Flute	4 feet.	24. Clarion, metal	4 feet.

Choir, 9 Stops, CC to G in alt.

25. Gedact, wood	16 feet.	30. Wald Flute, wood	4 feet.
26. Open Diapason, metal	8 feet.	31. Fifteenth, metal	2 feet.
27. Dulciana, metal	8 feet.	32. Mixture, II ranks.	
28. Stopped Diapason, metal	8 feet.	33. Clarionet	8 feet.
29. Gemshorn	4 feet.		

Swell, 14 Stops, CC to G in alt.

34. Bourdon, wood	16 feet.	41. Dulciana Mixture, III ranks.	
35. Open Diapason, metal	8 feet.	42. Double Bassoon	16 feet.
36. Dulciana, metal	8 feet.	43. Horn	8 feet.
37. Stopped Diapason	8 feet.	44. Trumpet	8 feet.
38. Octave, metal	8 feet.	45. Oboe	8 feet.
39. Fifteenth, metal	2 feet.	46. Vox Humana	8 feet.
40. Full Mixture, III ranks.		47. Clarion	4 feet.

Solo, 3 Stops, CC to G in alt.

48. Tuba, metal	16 feet.	50. Harmonic Flute	4 feet.
49. Tuba, metal	8 feet.		

Pedal, 19 Stops, CCC to F, 30 notes.

51. Double Open Diapason, wood	32 feet.	61. Flute Bass, wood .... 8 feet.
52. Double Open Diapason, metal	32 feet.	62. Twelfth, wood .... 6 feet.
53. Open Diapason, wood	16 feet.	63. Fifteenth, wood .... 4 feet.
54. Sub-Bass, wood	16 feet.	64. Mixture, V ranks .... 3½ feet.
55. Open Diapason, metal	16 feet.	65. Sackbut, wood .... 32 feet.
56. Violone, wood...................	16 feet.	66. Trombone .... 16 feet.
57. Bourdon	16 feet.	67. Bassoon, metal .... 16 feet.
58. Quint (Stopped)	12 feet.	68. Clarion, metal .... 8 feet.
59. Octave, metal	8 feet.	69. Octave Clarion .... 4 feet.
60. Octave Bass, wood	8 feet.	

Couplers.

1. Great to Pedals.	4. Swell to Choir.	6. Solo to Swell.
2. Swell to Pedals.	5. Swell to Great.	7. Swell to Great.
3. Choir to Pedals.		

Composition Pedals.

2 to Pedal.	2 to Swell.	4 to Great.	2 Tremulants.

Summary of Stops.

Great 24	Solo.............................. 3
Choir 9	Pedal 19
Swell 14	

249. THE NAVE ORGAN, YORK MINSTER.

This instrument, which was erected in September, 1863, under the third arch of the north aisle, by Messrs. Hill and Son, from a specification of the present organist, Dr. Monk, is intended for the "Special Services" in the nave, to accompany and support large bodies of singers; for this purpose it has been designed, scaled, and voiced.

It consists of 3 complete Manual organs, and a Pedal organ, viz. :—

Great, 11 Stops, CC to A, 58 Notes.

1. Bourdon, wood..............	16 feet tone.	7. Twelfth, metal .... 2⅔ feet.
2. Open Diapason, No. 1 ...	8 feet.	8. Fifteenth, metal .... 2 feet.
3. Open Diapason, No. 2 ...	8 feet.	9. Mixture, IV ranks, metal 1½ foot.
4. Stopped Diapason, wood	8 feet tone.	10. Posaune, metal .... 8 feet.
5. Octave, metal	4 feet.	11. Clarion, metal .... 4 feet.
6. Harmonic Flute, metal ...	4 feet.	

Choir, 7 Stops, CC to A, 58 Notes.

12. Cone Gamba, throughout, metal........................	6 feet.	15. Gemshorn, metal .... 4 feet.
13. Dulciana to tenor c, metal	8 feet.	16. Lieblich Flote, wood...... 4 feet tone.
14. Lieblich Gedact, wood ...	8 feet tone.	17. Piccolo, wood............... 2 feet.
		18. Clarinet to tenor c......... 8 feet tone.

Swell, 9 Stops, CC to A, 58 Notes.

19. Bourdon, wood	16 feet tone.	24. Mixture, IV ranks .... 1½ foot.
20. Open Diapason, metal ...	8 feet.	25. Corno .... 8 feet.
21. Stopped Diapason	8 feet tone.	26. Oboe .... 8 feet.
22. Octave	4 feet.	27. Clarion....................... 4 feet.
23. Fifteenth	2 feet.	

Pedal, 6 Stops, CCC to tenor f, 30 Notes.

28.	Open Diapason, wood ...	16 feet.	31. Octave, metal ....,......	8 feet.
29.	Sub-bass, wood	16 feet tone.	32. Fifteenth, metal	4 feet.
30.	Violone, wood	16 feet.	33. Trombone, wood	16 feet.

Couplers, Accessory Stops, &c.

1. Swell to Great.	6. Swell to Pedals.
2. Swell Sub-octave to Great.	7 to 10. Four Composition Pedals.
3. Choir to Great.	Radiating and Concave Pedal Board, and
4. Great to Pedals.	Draw-stop Jambs, placed at an angle, so
5. Choir to Pedals.	that the stops draw towards the performer.

250. YORK.

The new organ at New Street Wesleyan Chapel, York, was built by Messrs. Forster and Andrews, of Hull. The following is a synopsis of the stops of the instrument :—

Great Organ, CC to G.

	Feet.	Pipes.		Feet.	Pipes.
1. Open Diapason, metal......	8	56	6. Principal, metal	4	56
2. Hohlflote, wood	8	56	7. Twelfth, metal..............	2⅔	56
3. Dulciana, metal	8	56	8. Fifteenth	2	56
4. Lieblich Gedact, wood......	8	56	9. Clarionet	8	44
5. Flauto Traverso, metal ...	4	56			

Swell Organ CC to G.

	Feet.	Pipes.		Feet.	Pipes.
10. Lieblich Bourdon, wood...	16	56	14. Principal, metal	4	56
11. Open Diapason, wood and			15. Flageolet, wood	2	59
metal.......................	8	56	16. Mixture, II ranks, metal		112
12. Salicional (12 stopt), metal	8	56	17. Horn, metal..................	8	56
13. Voix Célestes, metal	8	44	18. Oboe, metal..................	8	56

Pedal Organ, CCC to F.

	Feet.	Pipes.		Feet.	Pipes.
19. Open Diapason, wood......	16	30	20. Bourdon, wood	16	30

Couplers.

1. Great to Pedals.	3. Swell to Great.
2. Swell to Pedals.	4. Swell Octave.

Pipes.

Great organ	492
Swell organ	548
Pedal organ	60
	1100

3 Composition Pedals to Great and 3 to Swell. Radiating Pedal-board. Front pipes handsomely decorated.

251. TANKERSLEY, YORKSHIRE.

This organ, built by Messrs. Brindley and Foster in 1874, has 3 Manuals, separate Pedal of good proportion, and 34 sounding stops. The following is its specification :—

Great Organ, 9 Stops.

1. Double Stopped Diapason	16 feet.	6. Rohrflote	4 feet.
2. Open Diapason	8 feet.	7. Grave Mixture, II ranks.	
3. Gamba	8 feet.	8. Great Mixture, V ranks.	
4. Hohlflote	8 feet.	9. Trumpet	8 feet.
5. Principal	4 feet.		

Swell Organ, 10 Stops.

10. Lieblich Bourdon	16 feet.	16. Horn	8 feet.
11. Violin Diapason	8 feet.	17. Oboe	8 feet.
12. Vox Angelica	8 feet.	18. Clarion	4 feet.
13. Voix Célestes, undulating	8 feet.	19. Vox Humana, in second	
14. Principal	4 feet.	swell box	8 feet.
15. Mixture, III ranks.			

Choir Organ, 8 Stops.

20. Salicional	8 feet.	24. Flauto Traverso	4 feet.
21. Dulciana	8 feet.	25. Dulcet Twelfth	3 feet.
22. Lieblich Gedact	8 feet.	26. Piccolo	2 feet.
23. Salicet	4 feet.	27. Clarionet	8 feet.

Pedal Organ, 7 Stops.

28. Open Bass	16 feet.	32. Flute Bass	8 feet.
29. Sub-bass	16 feet.	33. Trombone Bass	16 feet.
30. Quint Bass	10¾ feet.	34. Trumpet Bass	8 feet.
31. Principal Bass	8 feet.		

Couplers.

1. Swell to Great.	5. Swell to Pedal.
2. Swell to Choir.	6. Great to Pedal.
3. Choir to Pedal.	7. Choir to Great.
4. Swell Sub-octave.	8. Tremulant.

5 Composition Pedals.

Compass.

Manuals, CC to g³, 56 notes. | Pedals, CCC to e, 29 notes.

252. CHRIST CHURCH, MACCLESFIELD.

This organ was built by Messrs. Gray and Davison in 1876. It consists of 3 Manuals, from CC to G, and Pedals, from CCC to F, two octaves and a fourth.

Great Organ.

1. Double Diapason	16 feet.	6. Flute Octaviante	4 feet.
2. Open Diapason	8 feet.	7. Quinte	2¾ feet.
3. Gamba	8 feet.	8. Super-octave	2 feet.
4. Clarionet Flute	8 feet.	9. Mixture, IV ranks.	
5. Octave	4 feet.	10. Trumpet	8 feet.

Swell Organ.

11. Lieblich Bourdon	16 feet.		18. Mixture, III ranks.	
12. Open Diapason	8 feet.		19. Cornopean	8 feet.
13. Keraulophon	8 feet.		20. Orchestral Oboe	8 feet.
14. Voix Céleste	8 feet.		21. VoxHumana (in a separate	
15. Concert Flute	8 feet.		box)	8 feet.
16. Octave	4 feet.		22. Clarion	4 feet.
17. Super-octave	2 feet.		Tremulant.	

Choir Organ.

23. Dulciana, tenor c	8 feet.		27. Suabe Flute	4 feet.
24. Viol di Gamba	8 feet.		28. Flageolet Harmonique	2 feet.
25. Lieblich Gedact	8 feet.		29. Clarionet	8 feet.
26. Gemshorn	4 feet.		30. Corno di Bassetto	8 feet.

Pedal Organ.

31. Grand Open Diapason	16 feet.		33. Violoncello	8 feet.
32. Grand Bourdon	16 feet.		34. Trombone	16 feet.

Couplers.

1. Swell to Great Manual.		4. Great Manual to Pedals.
2. Swell to Choir Manual.		5. Choir Manual to Pedals.
3. Swell Manual to Pedals.		

7 Composition Pedals ; 4 to Great and 3 to the Swell organ.

253. St. Mary's Church, Beverley.

The organ in St. Mary's Church, Beverley, was built by Messrs. Forster and Andrews in 1869. The case, designed by Sir G. G. Scott, is of oak, richly carved. The front and pipes at west side are handsomely decorated. The pneumatic movement is applied to the Great organ and its couplers, and the whole is blown by three different pressures of wind. The following is the specification :—

Great Organ, CC to G, 11 Stops.

1. Double Open Diapason	16 feet.		7. Twelfth	2⅔ feet.
2. Open Diapason	8 feet.		8. Fifteenth	2 feet.
3. Gamba	8 feet.		9. Mixture, V ranks.	
4. Stopped Diapason	8 feet.		10. Posaune	8 feet.
5. Principal	4 feet.		11. Clarion	4 feet.
6. Harmonic Flute	4 feet.			

Swell Organ, CC to G, 10 Stops.

12. Bourdon	16 feet.		17. Flageolet	2 feet.
13. Open Diapason	8 feet.		18. Mixture, IV ranks.	
14. Flute d'Amour	8 feet.		19. Horn	8 feet.
15. Stopped Diapason	8 feet.		20. Oboe	8 feet.
16. Principal	4 feet.		21. Clarion	4 feet.

Choir Organ, CC to G, 7 Stops.

22. Dulciana	8 feet.		26. Lieblich Flote	4 feet.
23. Bell Gamba	8 feet.		27. Flautino Harmonic	2 feet.
24. Lieblich Gedact	8 feet.		28. Corno di Bassetto	8 feet.
25. Flauto Traverso	4 feet.			

Pedal Organ, CCC to F, 5 Stops.

29. Open Diapason	16 feet.		32. Flute	8 feet.
30. Violon	16 feet.		33. Trombone	16 feet
31. Bourdon	16 feet.			

Couplers.

1. Great to Pedals.
2. Swell to Pedals.
3. Choir to Pedals.
4. Swell to Choir.

5. Swell Octave to Great.
6. Swell to Great.
7. Swell Sub-octave to Great.

3 Composition Pedals to Great organ.

3 Composition Pedals to Swell organ.

254. HOLY TRINITY CHURCH, HULL.

The organ in Holy Trinity Church was built by Messrs. Forster and Andrews, and, although not the largest in Yorkshire, it is one possessing very exceptional features in quality of tone and in mechanical appliances for variety of effect. The pneumatic movement is applied to Great, Swell, and Pedal keys, and all couplers in connection therewith. The Pedal-board is of the latest improved construction; and the wind is supplied at various pressures suitable for the different qualities of tone. The dimensions of the organ are 36 feet high, 16 feet 16 inches wide, and 22 feet deep. The following description indicates what is complete and what is prepared for :—

Great Organ, CC to A.

	Feet.	Pipes.		Feet.	Pipes.
1. Double Open Diapason, metal	16	58	7. Waldflute, metal	4	58
2. Large Open Diapason, metal	8	58	8. Twelfth, metal	$2\frac{2}{3}$	58
3. Gamba, metal	8	58	9. Fifteenth, metal	2	58
4. Flute Harmonic, wood	8	58	10. Mixture, IV ranks, metal		230
5. Stopped Diapason, wood	8	58	11. Posaune, metal	8	58
6. Principal, metal	4	58	12. Clarion, metal	4	58

Swell Organ, CC to A.

	Feet.	Pipes.		Feet.	Pipes.
13. Bourdon, wood	16	58	20. Mixture, V ranks, metal		290
14. Open Diapason, metal	8	58	21. Double Trumpet (space only), metal	16	58
15. Rohrflote, wood	8	58	22. Horn, metal	8	58
16. Salicional, metal	8	58	23. Oboe, metal	8	58
17. Principal, metal	4	58	24. Clarion, metal	4	58
18. Flute (space only) metal	4	58			
19. Fifteenth, metal	2	58			

Choir Organ, CC to A.

	Feet.	Pipes.		Feet.	Pipes.
25. Lieblich Bourdon (space only), wood	16	58	29. Lieblich Gedact, wood	8	58
26. Dulciana, metal	8	58	30. Flauto Traverso, metal	4	58
27. Voix Céleste, metal	8	58	31. Lieblich Flote, wood	4	58
28. Bell Gamba, metal	8	58	32. Piccolo, metal	2	58
Lower Octave do. (space only), metal		12	33. Corno di Bassetto, metal	8	58

Pedal Organ, CCC to F.

	Feet.	Pipes.		Feet.	Pipes.
34. Contra Diapason, Open (space only), wood	32	30	38. Grosse Quint, wood	$10\frac{2}{3}$	30
35. Open Diapason, wood	16	30	39. Principal, metal	8	30
36. Violon, metal	16	30	40. Flute, wood	8	30
37. Bourdon, wood	16	30	41. Trombone, wood and metal	16	30
			42. Trumpet, metal	8	30

Couplers.

1. Swell to Great.
2. Swell to Octave.
3. Swell to Sub-octave.
4. Swell to Pedals.

5. Choir to Pedals.
6. Choir to Pedals.
7. Swell to Choir.

Accessory Movements.

8 Pneumatic Combination Pedals, acting upon Great, Swell, and Pedal stops, Tremulant to Swell by Pedal, Sforzando Pedal.

Summary.

Great Organ	868 Pipes		12 Registers.
Swell Organ	928 ,,		12 ,,
Choir Organ	510 ,,		9 ,,
Pedal Organ	270 ,,		9 ,,
Couplers			7 ,,
	2576 ,,		49 ,,

255. WYCLIFFE CONGREGATIONAL CHURCH, HULL.

The organ in Wycliffe Congregational Church was built by Messrs. Forster and Andrews, of Hull, and contains the stops mentioned below —

Great Organ, CC to G.

	Feet.	Pipes.		Feet.	Pipes.
1. Double Open Diapason, metal	16 ...	56	6. Waldflote, wood	4 ...	56
2. Open Diapason, metal	8 ...	56	7. Twelfth, metal	2⅔ ...	56
3. Violin Diapason, metal	8 ...	56	8. Fifteenth, metal	2 ...	56
4. Hohlflote, wood	8 ...	56	9. Mixture, metal, IV ranks.		224
5. Principal, metal	4 ...	56	10. Trumpet, metal	8 ...	56

Swell Organ, CC to G.

	Feet.	Pipes.		Feet.	Pipes.
11. Lieblich Bourdon, wood	16 ...	56	16. Fifteenth, metal	2 ...	56
12. Open Diapason, metal	8 ...	56	17. Mixture, metal, V ranks		280
13. Salicional, metal	8 ...	56	18. Horn, metal	8 ...	56
14. Stopped Diapason, wood	8 ...	56	19. Oboe, metal	8 ...	56
15. Principal, metal	4 ...	56	20. Clarion, metal	4 ...	56

Choir Organ, CC to G.

	Feet.	Pipes.		Feet.	Pipes.
21. Dulciana, metal	8 ...	56	25. Lieblich Flote, wood	4 ...	56
22. Bell Gamba, metal	8 ...	56	26. Flautino, metal	2 ...	56
23. Lieblich Gedact, wood	8 ...	56	27. Corno di Bassetto, metal.	8 ...	44
24. Flauto Traverso, metal	4 ...	56			

Pedal Organ, CCC to F.

	Feet.	Pipes.		Feet.	Pipes.
28. Open Diapason, wood	16 ...	30	30. Violoncello, wood	8 ...	30
29. Bourdon, wood	16 ...	30	31. Flute, wood	8 ...	30

Couplers.

1. Swell to Great.
2. Swell to Pedals.
3. Swell Octave to Great,

4. Swell Sub-octave to Great.
5. Great to Pedals.
6. Choir to Pedals.

There are three Composition Pedals to the Great organ and three to the Swell organ. The pneumatic movement is applied to the Great organ and its Couplers. The whole is blown by three pressures of wind. The Swell is enclosed in a double-framed box. The new French pitch, or "Normal Diapason," has been adopted as more useful for Congregational accompaniment. The case is stained deal. On either side are angular towers, containing the Open Diapason pipes. Behind the centre pipes are the 16-feet Double Open Diapasons, presenting a fine appearance.

256. DONCASTER.

The present organ in the Parish Church of St. George, at Doncaster, was built by Herr Edmund Schulze, the celebrated organ builder of Paulinzelle, near Erfurt. It was commenced in 1857, and completed in 1862. The following is a list of its stops :—

Great, 21 Stops; CC to A in alt., 58 Notes.

1.	Sub Bourdon to tenor c ...	32 feet.	12. Twelfth	$2\frac{2}{3}$ feet.
2.	Double Open Diapason ...	16 feet.	13. Fifteenth	2 feet.
3.	Bourdon	16 feet.	14. Mixture, V ranks.	
4.	Open Diapason	8 feet.	15. Cymbal, III to V ranks.	
5.	Octave	8 feet.	16. Cornet to tenor c, IV ranks.	
6.	Hohlflote	8 feet.	17. Double Trumpet	16 feet.
7.	Stopped Diapason	8 feet.	18. Trumpet	8 feet.
8.	Great Quint	$5\frac{1}{3}$ feet.	19. Posaune	8 feet.
9.	Principal	4 feet.	20. Horn	8 feet.
10.	Gemshorn	4 feet.	21. Clarion	4 feet.
11.	Stopped Flute	4 feet.		

Choir, 13 Stops; CC to A in alt., 58 Notes.

22.	Lieblich Gedact	16 feet.	29. Lieblich Flute	4 feet.
23.	Geigen Principal	8 feet.	30. Flauto Traverso	4 feet.
24.	Viol di Gamba	8 feet.	31. Quintaton	4 feet.
25.	Flauto Traverso	8 feet.	32. Flautino	2 feet.
26.	Salicional	8 feet.	33. Mixture, III ranks.	
27.	Lieblich Gedact	8 feet.	34. Clarionet	8 feet.
28.	Geigen Principal	4 feet.		

Swell, 18 Stops; CC to A in alt., 58 Notes.

35.	Bourdon	16 feet.	44. Viol d'Amour	4 feet.
36.	Open Diapason	8 feet.	45. Mixture, V ranks.	
37.	Gemshorn	8 feet.	46. Scharf, III ranks.	
38.	Terpodion	8 feet.	47. Cornet to tenor c, IV ranks.	
39.	Harmonic Flute	8 feet.	48. Double Bassoon	16 feet.
40.	Rohrflute	8 feet.	49. Hautboy	8 feet.
41.	Principal	4 feet.	50. Trumpet	8 feet.
42.	Harmonic Flute	4 feet.	51. Horn	8 feet.
43.	Stopped Flute	4 feet.	52. Clarion	4 feet.

Solo (most of which is taken from the Swell), 9 Stops; CC to A in alt., 58 Notes.

53.	Gemshorn	8 feet.	58. Double Bassoon	16 feet.
54.	Harmonic Flute	8 feet.	59. Hautboy	8 feet.
55.	Rohrflote	8 feet.	60. Horn	8 feet.
56.	Harmonic Flute	4 feet.	61. Vox Humana	8 feet.
57.	Stopped Flute	4 feet.		

Echo, 8 Stops; CC to A in alt., 58 Notes.

62. Tibia Major	16 feet.	66. Flauto Amabile .... 8 feet.
63. Vox Angelica	8 feet.	67. Celestina .... 4 feet.
64. Harmonica	8 feet.	68. Flauto Dolcissimo .... 4 feet.
65. Flauto Traverso	8 feet.	69. Harmonica Ætheria, II ranks.

Pedal, 25 Stops; CCCC to E, 29 Notes.

70. Sub-principal	32 feet.	83. Fifteenth, Bass	4 feet.
71. Major, Bass	16 feet.	84. Tierce	3⅕ feet.
72. Principal, Bass	16 feet.	85. Mixture, II ranks.	
73. Sub-bass	16 feet.	86. Cymbal, II ranks.	
74. Open Diapason, Bass	16 feet.	87. Contra Posaune	32 feet.
75. Violone	16 feet.	88. Posaune	16 feet.
76. Minor, Bass	8 feet.	89. Bombarde	16 feet.
77. Octave, Bass	8 feet.	90. Contra Fagotto	16 feet.
78. Violoncello	8 feet.	91. Trumpet	8 feet.
79. Flute, Bass	8 feet.	92. Horn	8 feet.
80. Great Quint	10⅔ feet.	93. Fagotto	8 feet.
81. Quint, Bass	5⅓ feet.	94. Clarion	4 feet.
82. Great Tierce	6⅘ feet.		

Accessory Stops, &c.

1. Great to Pedal		6 and 7. Composition stops for Great.
2. Swell to Great		8. Combination for the Pedals.
3. Choir to Great	By Pedals.	9 and 10. Combination stops for Swell.
4. Tremulant for Swell		11. Combination for Choir organ.
5. Thunder Stop.		

257. SHEFFIELD.

The organ by Messrs. T. C. Lewis and Co., for St. Marie's Catholic Church, at Sheffield, is to have 3 Manuals, with separate pedal, and the 23 sounding stops enumerated below :—

Great Organ, CC to A, 58 Notes.

1. Bourdon	16 feet.	5. Octave Quint .... 2⅔ feet.
2. Open Diapason	8 feet.	6. Super-octave .... 2 feet.
3. Stopped Diapason	8 feet.	7. Mixture, IV ranks .... 1½ foot.
4. Octave	4 feet.	8. Trumpet .... 8 feet.

Swell Organ, CC to A, 58 Notes.

9. Geigen Principal	8 feet.	13. Flautino .... 2 feet.
10. Rohrflote	8 feet.	14. Horn .... 8 feet.
11. Æolian	8 feet.	15. Oboe .... 8 feet.
12. Geigen Principal	4 feet.		

Choir Organ, CC to A, 58 Notes.

16. Salicional	8 feet.	19. Salicet .... 4 feet.
17. Vox Angelica	8 feet.	20. Flute Harmonique .... 4 feet.
18. Lieblich Gedact	8 feet.	21. Clarionet .... 8 feet.

Pedal Organ, CCC to F, 30 Notes.

22. Open Bass	16 feet.	23. Sub-bass .... 16 feet.

Couplers.

1. Choir to Pedals.	4. Swell to Great.
2. Great to Pedals.	5. Swell to Choir.
3. Swell to Pedals.	

Three Pedals of Combination.

258. CARLISLE CATHEDRAL.

This organ was built by Mr. Willis, in 1856, from a specification prepared by Mr. Ford, the organist, and Mr. W. T. Best, of Liverpool. The compass is 4½ octaves, from CC to g in alt. It has a Pedal-board containing 30 notes, or 2½ octaves, from CCC to F, and all the registers extend throughout the compass of the key-boards, without exception.

Great, 11 Stops.

1. Double Open Diapason, metal	16 feet.	6. Fifteenth, metal	2 feet.
2. Open Diapason, metal ...	8 feet.	7. Sesquialtera, V ranks, metal.	
3. Stopped Diapason, wood..	8 feet.	8. Furniture, III ranks, metal.	
4. Principal, metal	4 feet.	9. Trombone, metal	8 feet.
5. Twelfth, metal..............	3 feet.	10. Trumpet, metal	8 feet.
		11. Clarion, metal	4 feet.

Choir, 6 Stops.

12. Open Diapason, metal ...	8 feet.	15. Gamba, metal..............	8 feet.
13. Clarabella, wood............	8 feet.	16. Harmonic Flute, metal...	4 feet.
14. Dulciana, metal	8 feet.	17. Clarionette, metal	8 feet.

Swell, 11 Stops.

18. Double Diapason, metal...	16 feet.	24. Contra Fagotto, wood ...	16 feet.
19. Open Diapason, metal ...	8 feet.	25. Horn, metal	8 feet.
20. Stopped Diapason, wood..	8 feet.	26. Oboe, metal	8 feet.
21. Principal, metal	4 feet.	27. Clarion, metal	4 feet.
22. Flageolet, wood	2 feet.	28. Vox Humana, metal	8 feet.
23. Echo Cornet, V ranks, the lowest rank of wood, the remaining IV of metal.		Tremulant.	

Pedal, 7 Stops.

29. Open Diapason, wood......	16 feet.	33. Fifteenth, metal	4 feet.
30. Violone, metal	16 feet.	34. Trombone, metal	16 feet.
31. Bourdon, wood	16 feet.	35. Trumpet, metal	8 feet.
32. Principal, metal	8 feet.		

Couplers.

1. Swell to Great.	4. Pedal to Swell.
2. Choir to Great.	5. Pedal to Choir.
3. Pedal to Great.	

Number of Pipes.

Great organ	952
Swell organ	840
Choir organ	336
Pedal organ	210
Total	2338

259. St. Peter's Roman Catholic Church, Scarborough.

This organ was built by Messrs. Forster and Andrews in 1874. The following is a list of the stops :—

Great Organ, 10 Stops; Compass, CC to G, 56 Pipes.

1. Double Stopped Diapason......	16 feet.	6. Waldflote	4 feet.
2. Open Diapason	8 feet.	7. Twelfth..............	2⅔ feet.
3. Violin Diapason	8 feet.	8. Fifteenth	2 feet.
4. Stopped Diapason	8 feet.	9. Mixture, IV ranks.	
5. Principal	4 feet.	10. Trumpet	8 feet.

Swell Organ, 7 Stops; Compass, CC to G, 56 Pipes.

11. Lieblich Bourdon.................	16 feet.	15. Spitzflote	4 feet.
12. Gedact	8 feet.	16. Cornopean	8 feet.
13. Open Diapason	8 feet.	17. Oboe.........................	8 feet.
14. Flute d'Amour	8 feet.		

Choir Organ, 4 Stops; Compass, CC to G, 56 Pipes.

18. Gedact	8 feet.	20. Harmonic Flute	4 feet.
19. Dulciana	8 feet.	21. Krummhorn	8 feet.

Pedal Organ, 3 Stops; Compass, CCC to D, 27 Notes.

22. Open Bass	16 feet.	24. Violoncello...........................	8 feet.
23. Bourdon Bass.......................	16 feet.		

Couplers.

1. Swell to Great.	4. Swell to Pedals.
2. Swell Octave.	5. Choir to Pedals.
3. Great to Pedals.	

4 Composition Pedals.

260. Scarborough Bar Congregational Church.

This organ was built by Messrs. Forster and Andrews in 1870. The case is of pitch pine, with angular towers supporting the 16 feet pipes, which, with the remainder of the front, are richly gilded. The stops are as follows :—

Great Organ, 10 Stops, CC to G.

1. Double Open Diapason ...	16 feet.	6. Harmonic Flute............	4 feet.
2. Open Diapason	8 feet.	7. Twelfth	2⅔ feet.
3. Gamba	8 feet.	8. Fifteenth	2 feet.
4. Hohlflote	8 feet.	9. Mixture, IV ranks.	
5. Principal	4 feet.	10. Trumpet	8 feet.

Swell Organ, 10 Stops, CC to G.

11. Lieblich Bourdon	16 feet.	16. Fifteenth	2 feet.
12. Open Diapason	8 feet.	17. Mixture, V ranks.	
13. Salicional	8 feet.	18. Horn	8 feet.
14. Rohrflote	8 feet.	19. Oboe	8 feet.
15. Principal	4 feet.	20. Clarion.......................	4 feet.

Choir Organ, 5 Stops, CC to G.

21. Dulciana	8 feet.	24. Flautino	2 feet.
22. Lieblich Gedact	8 feet.	25. Corno di Basset'o	8 feet.
23. Flauto Traverso	4 feet.		

Pedal Organ, 3 Stops, CCC to F.

26. Open Diapason	16 feet.	28. Flute	8 feet.
27. Bourdon	16 feet.		

Couplers.

1. Swell to Great.	4. Swell to Choir.
2. Swell to Pedals.	5. Swell Octave to Great.
3. Great to Pedals.	6. Choir to Pedals.

5 Composition Pedals.

261. CHORLEY PARISH CHURCH.

This organ was built by Messrs. Forster and Andrews in 1872. The case has angular towers and decorated front pipes. The stops are as follows :—

Great Organ, 10 Stops, CC to G.

1.	Double Open Diapason ...	16 feet.	6.	Harmonic Flute	4 feet.
2.	Open Diapason	8 feet.	7.	Twelfth	2⅔ feet.
3.	Dulciana	8 feet.	8.	Fifteenth	2 feet.
4.	Stopped Diapason	8 feet.	9.	Mixture, IV ranks.	
5.	Principal	4 feet.	10.	Trumpet	8 feet.

Swell Organ, 7 Stops, CC to G.

11.	Bourdon	16 feet.	15.	Flageolet	2 feet.
12.	Open Diapason	8 feet.	16.	Cornopean	8 feet.
13.	Flute d'Amour	8 feet.	17.	Oboe	8 feet.
14.	Principal	4 feet.			

Choir Organ, 5 Stops, CC to G.

18.	Viol d'Amour	8 feet.	21.	Flautino	2 feet.
19.	Lieblich Gedact	8 feet.	22.	Corno di Bassetto	8 feet.
20.	Flauto Traverso	4 feet.			

Pedal Organ, 2 Stops, CCC to F.

23.	Open Diapason	16 feet.	24.	Bourdon	16 feet.

Couplers.

1. Swell to Great.		4. Choir to Pedals.
2. Great to Pedals.		5. Swell Octave.
3. Swell to Pedals.		

5 Composition Pedals.

262. PETERSFIELD.

The organ in Petersfield Parish Church was built by Messrs. Forster and Andrews in 1874. It has 19 stops, of which the following is a list :—

Great Organ, 10 Stops; Compass, CC to G, 56 Notes.

1.	Open Diapason	8 feet.	6.	Harmonic Flute	4 feet.
2.	Hohlflote	8 feet.	7.	Twelfth	2⅔ feet.
3.	Dulciana	8 feet.	8.	Fifteenth	2 feet.
4.	Gamba	8 feet.	9.	Mixture, III ranks.	
5.	Principal	4 feet.	10.	Trumpet	8 feet.

Swell Organ, 7 Stops; Compass, 2 Stops, CC to G, 56 Notes.

11.	Lieblich Bourdon	16 feet.	15.	Mixture, II ranks.	
12.	Open Diapason	8 feet.	16.	Horn	8 feet.
13.	Viol d'Amour	8 feet.	17.	Oboe	8 feet.
14.	Principal	4 feet.			

Pedal Organ, 2 Stops, CCC to F, 30 Notes.

18.	Open Diapason	16 feet.	19.	Bourdon	16 feet.

Couplers.

1. Swell to Great.		3. Swell to Pedals.
2. Swell Octave.		4. Great to Pedals.

6 Composition Pedals.

263. DURHAM CATHEDRAL.

The fine new organ in this Cathedral was built by Mr. Henry Willis. It is supplied with wind by six large bellows, blown by three hydraulic engines. The 55 sounding stops are as follows :—

Great Organ, CC to A, 58 Notes.

1. Open Diapason, metal ... 16 feet.
2. Open Diapason (large), metal .... 8 feet.
3. Open Diapason (small), metal .... 8 feet.
4. Gamba (throughout), metal 8 feet.
5. Stopped Diapason, wood 8 feet.
6. Claribel Flute, wood ...... 8 feet.
7. Octave, metal .... 4 feet.
8. Harmonic Flute, metal... 4 feet.
9. Twelfth, metal .... 2⅔ feet.
10. Fifteenth, metal .... 2 feet.
11. Piccolo, wood.............. 2 feet.
12. Mixture, IV ranks, metal.
13. Double Trumpet, metal... 16 feet.
14. Cornopean, metal .... 8 feet.
15. Clarion, metal.............. 4 feet.

Swell Organ, CC to A, 58 Notes.

16. Double Diapason, metal and wood................. 16 feet.
17. Open Diapason, metal ... 8 feet.
18. Open Diapason (small), metal .... 8 feet.
19. Viol d'Amour, metal ..... 8 feet.
20. Lieblich Gedact, wood ... 8 feet.
21. Octave, metal .... 4 feet.
22. Harmonic Flute, metal ... 4 feet.
23. Fifteenth, metal .... 2 feet.
24. Piccolo, wood.............. 2 feet.
25. Mixture, V ranks, metal.
26. Contra Fagotto, metal ... 16 feet.
27. Trumpet, metal .... 8 feet.
28. Oboe, metal .... 8 feet.
29. Vox Humana, metal ...... 8 feet.
30. Clarion, metal .... 4 feet.

Choir Organ, CC to A, 58 Notes.

31. Lieblich Gedact, metal and wood................. 16 feet.
32. Lieblich Gedact, metal and wood................. 8 feet.
33. Salicional, metal........... 8 feet.
34. Vox Angelica, metal ...... 8 feet.
35. Flauto Traverso, wood ... 8 feet.
36. Lieblich Gedact, metal ... 4 feet.
37. Gemshorn, metal .... 4 feet.
38. Flauto Traverso, wood ... 4 feet.
39. Corno di Bassetto .... 8 feet.

Solo Organ, CC to A, 58 Notes.

40. Harmonic Flute, metal ... 8 feet.
41. Orchestral Oboe, metal ... 8 feet.
42. Corno di Bassetto, metal 8 feet.
43. Tuba, metal .... 8 feet.
44. Concert Harmonic Flute, metal .... 4 feet.
45. Clarion, metal .... 4 feet.

Pedal Organ, CCC to F, 30 Notes.

46. Open Diapason, wood ... 32 feet.
47. Open Diapason, wood ... 16 feet.
48. Open Diapason, metal ... 16 feet.
49. Violon, metal .... 16 feet.
50. Bourdon, wood .... 16 feet.
51. Octave, metal.............. 8 feet.
52. Flute, wood .... 8 feet.
53. Mixture, IV ranks, metal.
54. Posaune, metal .... 16 feet.
55. Cornopean, metal .... 8 feet.

Couplers, &c., &c.

1. Swell to Great, Unison.
2. Swell to Great, Octave.
3. Swell to Great, Sub-octave.
4. Choir to Great.
5. Solo to Great.
6. Solo to Pedals.
7. Swell to Pedals.
8. Great to Pedals.
9. Choir to Pedals.
10. Tremulant to Swell.

4 Composition Pedals to Great organ.
3 Composition Pedals to Swell organ.

3 Composition Pedals to Pedal organ.
1 Double action Pedal, Great to Pedals.

264. LINCOLN CATHEDRAL.

This organ was built, in 1826, by W. Allen, and extended by his son Charles Allen in 1851.

Great, 11 Stops; Compass of Great and Choir, from GG to F in alt.

1. Large Open Diapason.
2. Small Open Diapason.
3. Stopped Diapason.
4. Clarabella.
5. Principal.
6. Twelfth.

7. Fifteenth.
8. Cornet, Treble, IV ranks.
9. Sesquialtera, Bass, III ranks.
10. Trumpet, Treble.
11. Trumpet, Bass.

Choir, 6 Stops.

12. Stopped Diapason.
13. Dulciana.

14. Viol di Gamba.
15. Principal.

16. Flute.
17. Fifteenth.

Swell, 9 Stops; Gamut to F in alt.

18. Double Diapason.
19. Open Diapason.
20. Stopped Diapason.

21. Principal.
22. Flute.
23. Twelfth.

24. Fifteenth.
25. Hautboy.
26. Horn.

Pedal, 7 Stops.

27. Sub-bourdon .... 32 feet.
28. Open Diapason .... 16 feet.
29. Principal .... 8 feet.
30. Twelfth........................ 6 feet.

31. Fifteenth .... 4 feet.
32. Sesquialtera.
33. Trombone .... 16 feet.

Accessory Stops, Movements, &c.

1. Swell to Great.
2. Swell to Choir.
3. Pedal to Great.

4. Swell to Choir.
5 to 9. Five Composition Pedals.

Compass.

Great, GG to f³ in alt.
Choir, GG to f³ in alt.
Swell Gamut, G to f³ in alt.
Pedal Clavier, CCC to fiddle g.

Pedal stops, Nos. 27 and 28, CCC to fiddle g ; Nos. 29 to 33, CCC to FFF ♯, seven semitones, to meet Great organ at GG.

265. BOSTON.

The large organ in the Centenary Chapel, Boston, Lincolnshire, was built by Gray and Davison in the year 1850. It has Great and Choir Manuals, from CC, 8 feet, to F in alt. ; Pedal organ, two octaves and a fourth : CCC, to tenor f, and Swell to tenor c.

There are two bellows—one for the Manuals, the other for the Pedal organ ; and four Composition Pedals ; also a Sforzando Pedal.

The sides, as well as the front of the case, contain speaking pipes ; and the dimensions of the instrument are 26 feet high, 23 feet wide, and 18 feet deep.

There are 42 stops, and 2490 Pipes.

Great, 14 Stops.

1. Double Open Diapason ...	16 feet.	
2. Open Diapason	8 feet.	
3. Open Diapason	8 feet.	
4. Stopped Diapason	8 feet.	
5. Quint............................	6 feet.	
6. Octave	4 feet.	
7. Flute............................	4 feet.	
8. Octave Quint	8 feet.	
9. Super-octave	2 feet.	
10. Flageolet......................	2 feet.	
11. Sesquialtera, III ranks.		
12. Furniture, III ranks.		
13. Posaune	8 feet.	
14. Clarion........................	4 feet.	

Choir, 12 Stops.

15. Open Diapason	8 feet.	
16. Gamba	8 feet.	
17. Keraulophon	8 feet.	
18. Stopped Diapason, Bass...	8 feet.	
19. Clarionet Flute	8 feet.	
20. Octave	4 feet.	
21. Flute	4 feet.	
22. Gemshorn	4 feet.	
23. Super-octave	2 feet.	
24. Flageolet.........	2 feet.	
25. Sesquialtera, III ranks.		
26. Corno di Bassetto	8 feet.	

Swell, 10 Stops.

27. Bourdon	16 feet.	
28. Open Diapason	8 feet.	
29. Stopped Diapason	8 feet.	
30. Octave	4 feet.	
31. Super-octave	2 feet.	
32. Sesquialtera, III ranks.		
33. Contra Fagotto	16 feet.	
34. Cornopean	8 feet.	
35. Oboe	8 feet.	
36. Clarion	4 feet.	

Pedal, 6 Stops.

37. Grand Open Diapason ...	16 feet.	
38. Grand Violon	16 feet.	
39. Grand Bourdon	16 feet.	
40. Grand Octave...............	8 feet.	
41. Grand Super-octave	4 feet.	
42. Grand Trombone	16 feet.	

Couplers.

1. Swell to Great Manual.	
2. Choir to Great Manual.	
3. Swell to Choir Manual.	
4. Swell Manual to Pedals.	
5. Great Manual to Pedals.	
6. Choir Manual to Pedals.	
7. Sforzando Pedal.	

266. PARISH CHURCH, BOSTON, LINCOLNSHIRE.

The old organ in the Parish Church, Boston, Lincolnshire, was built by Christian Smith, at the end of the 17th century. The following is a list of its stops and pipes :—

Great, 12 Stops; CC to F in alt., 54 Notes.

	Pipes.	Feet.		Pipes.	Feet.
1. Open Diapason, Front ...	54	8	7. Twelfth	54	3
2. Open Diapason, Back	54	8	8. Fifteenth	54	2
3. Stopped Diapason	54	8	9. Sesquialtera, III ranks ...	162	
4. Principal	54	4	10. Mixture, II ranks	108	
5. Flute à Bec	46	4	11. Cornet.........................	30	
6. Clarabella	30	8	12. Trumpet	54	8

Choir, 5 Stops; CC to F in alt., 54 Notes.

	Pipes.	Feet.			Pipes.	Feet.
13. Dulciana, ...	47	... 8	15. Principal		54	... 4
14. Lieblich Gedact, or Stopped			16. Flute		54	... 4
Diapason, wood and metal	54	... 8	17. Cremona		42	... 8

Swell, 9 Stops; Tenor C to F in alt., 42 Notes.

	Pipes.	Feet.			Pipes.	Feet.
18. Double Diapason	42	... 16	23. Cornet, II ranks		84	... 2
19. Open Diapason	42	... 8	24. Cornopean		42	... 8
20. Stopped Diapason	42	... 8	25. Hautboy		42	... 8
21. Principal	42	... 4	26. Clarion		42	... 4
22. Fifteenth	42	... 2				

Pedal, 3 Stops; CCC to E, 29 Notes.

27. Diapason	29	... 16	29. Trumpet		29	... 16
28. Bourdon	29	... 16				

Accessory Stops, &c.

1. Swell to Great.	Three Composition Pedals to Great.
2. Great to Pedals.	Tremulant to Swell.
3. Choir to Pedals.	

267. SOUTHWELL.

The organ in Southwell Collegiate Church was originally built by Father Schmidt, but, having been damaged by fire, it was repaired by Snetzler, whose bill, dated January, 1766, is still in the possession of the Chapter. Compass of Great and Choir organs, from GG to d⁹ in alt.; of the Swell, from fiddle g to d⁸ in alt.; and of the Pedal Clavier, GG to tenor c. The general effect of the instrument is excellent, considering the smallness of the number of its stops; and the Diapasons are very fine.

Great, 8 Stops.

1. Open Diapason.	5. Fifteenth.
2. Stopped Diapason.	6. Sesquialtera, III ranks.
3. Principal.	7. Trumpet.
4. Twelfth.	8. Cornet to Middle c¹, V ranks.

Choir, 5 Stops.

9. Stopped Diapason.	12. Flute.
10. Dulciana to Gamut G.	13. Fifteenth.
11. Principal.	

Swell, 4 Stops.

14. Open Diapason.	16. Principal.
15. Stopped Diapason.	17. Fifteenth.

268. NOTTINGHAM.

The former organ of St. Mary's Church, Nottingham, was sold to St. Andrew's Church, Nottingham, where it still contains Snetzler's original Diapasons, Flute, and Mixture. In 1871 the old organ was replaced at St. Mary's by a fine instrument, built by Messrs. Bishop and Starr; this is placed on the north side of the chancel in a very handsome Gothic bracket case of carved oak, designed by Sir Gilbert Scott. The pipes shown in front of this case are of spotted metal, and all the interior metal pipes are composed of 25 parts tin to 75 parts lead. The pneumatic lever is applied to the Great and Swell Manuals, and Bishop's simplified pneumatic action to the Choir organ. The following is the specification :—

Great Organ, CC to G, 12 Stops.

	Feet.	Pipes.		Feet.	Pipes.
1. Sub-open Diapason, metal	16 ...	56	7. Twelfth, metal	2⅔ ...	56
2. Open Diapason, metal......	8 ...	56	8. Fifteenth, metal	2 ...	56
3. Bell Diapason, metal	8 ...	56	9. Sesqualtera, IV ranks, metal		... 224
4. Clarabella and Stopped Diapason, wood	8 tone	56	10. Mixture, III ranks, metal		... 168
5. Principal, metal	4 ...	56	11. Posaune, metal	8 ...	56
6. Harmonic Flute, metal ...	4 ...	56	12. Clarion	4 ...	56

Swell Organ, CC to G, 12 Stops.

	Feet.	Pipes.		Feet.	Pipes.
13. Double Diapason, Stopped, wood	16 tone	56	19. Grave Mixture, II ranks, metal ....2⅔ and 2		... 112
14. Open Diapason, metal......	8 ...	56	20. Acute Mixture, III ranks, metal........................		... 168
15. Salicional, tenor c, metal...	8 ...	44	21. Contra Fagotto, metal ...	16 ...	56
16. Stopped Diapason and Metallic Flute, wood and metal........................	8 tone	56	22. Cornopean, metal	8 ...	56
			23. Hautboy, metal	8 ...	56
17. Principal, metal	4 ...	56	24. Clarion, metal...............	8 ...	56
18. Lieblich Gedact, wood ...	4 tone	56			

Choir Organ, CC to G, 9 Stops.

	Feet.	Pipes.		Feet.	Pipes.
25. Dulciana, metal	8 ...	56	30. Fifteenth, metal	2 ...	56
26. Viol di Gamba, tenor c, metal........................	8 ...	44	31. Piccolo, wood and metal	2 ...	56
27. German Flute, wood	8 ...	56	32. Dulciana Mixture, III ranks, metal		... 168
28. Geigen Principal, metal ...	4 ...	56	33. Cremona and Bassoon ...	8 ...	56
29. Hohlflote, wood	4 ...	56			

Pedal Organ, CCC to F, 4 Stops.

	Feet.	Pipes.		Feet.	Pipes.
34. Open Diapason, wood......	16 ...	30	36. Principal, metal	8 ...	30
35. Bourdon, wood...............	16 tone	30	37. Bombardone, wood	16 ...	30

Couplers.

1. Swell to Great.	4. Great to Pedals.
2. Swell to Pedals.	5. Choir to Pedals.
3. Swell to Choir.	6. Choir to Great.

10 Composition Pedals.

Total number of pipes.................. 2422.

The Stopped Diapason and Metallic Flute of the Swell and the Dulciana of the Choir organ are arranged in half stops to draw treble and bass separately. There are three pairs of bellows, worked by one of Joy's hydraulic engines.

269. MECHANICS' HALL, NOTTINGHAM.

The organ originally built for this hall by Bevington, and afterwards enlarged and improved by Groves, of London, was destroyed by fire in 1867. The present instrument was erected in 1869, at a cost of £800, by Messrs. Hill and Son. It contains the following stops :—

Great Organ, CC to G, 10 Stops.

	Feet.	Pipes.			Feet.	Pipes.
1. Bourdon, wood	16 tone	56	6. Waldflote, wood		4	56
2. Open Diapason, metal	8	56	7. Twelfth, metal		2⅔	56
3. Gamba, metal	8	56	8. Fifteenth, metal		2	56
4. Stopped Diapason, wood	8 tone	56	9. Mixture, III ranks, metal			168
5. Principal, metal	4	56	10. Trumpet, metal		8	56

Swell Organ, CC to G, 10 Stops.

	Feet.	Pipes.			Feet.	Pipes.
11. Lieblich Bourdon, wood	16 tone	56	16. Fifteenth, metal		2	56
12. Open Diapason, metal	8	56	17. Mixture, II ranks, metal			112
13. Keraulophon to tenor c, metal	8	44	18. Cornopean, metal		8	56
			19. Oboe, metal		8	56
14. Stopped Diapason, wood	8 tone	56	20. Clarion, metal		4	56
15. Principal, metal	4	56				

Choir Organ, CC to G, 7 Stops.

	Feet.	Pipes.			Feet.	Pipes.
21. Dulciana, metal	8	56	25. Lieblich Flute, metal		4	56
22. Voix Céleste, tenor c, metal	8	44	26. Piccolo, metal		2	56
23. Gedact, wood	8 tone	56	27. Clarionet, tenor c, metal		8	44
24. Gemshorn, metal	4	56				

Pedal Organ, CCC to F, 6 Stops.

	Feet.	Pipes.			Feet.	Pipes.
28. Open Diapason, wood	16	30	31. Violon, wood		8	30
29. Bourdon, wood	16 tone	30	32. Bass Flute, wood		8	30
30. Great Quint, wood	10⅔	30	33. Trombone, wood		16	30

Couplers.

1. Swell to Great.	4. Choir to Pedals.
2. Swell to Choir.	5. Swell to Pedals.
3. Great to Pedals.	
3 Composition Pedals to Great organ.	2 Composition Pedals to Swell organ.

270. DERBY ROAD CHAPEL, NOTTINGHAM.

This organ was built in 1873 by Messrs. Conacher and Co., of Huddersfield, to the specification of Mr. W. Shelmerdine. It is placed in a chamber on the north side of the chancel, and occupies a space of about 10 feet by 14 feet, and 25 feet high. The bellows, blown by a Duncan's double action hydraulic engine, are placed under the floor of the chapel. The motive power is under perfect control from the organist's seat, and an automatic governor increases or reduces the speed of the engine, as the quantity of wind in use may require. A copper air-vessel on the supply pipe protects the engine from the slightest shock from variations of water pressure, and concussion valves in the air trunks further steady the wind; the result is an ample supply on the most sudden demand and perfect evenness of pressure under intermittent use. The stops draw at an angle of 45°, and every stop, without exception, runs through the entire compass. The Manuals are beaked and overhang ; the pedals radiating and concave.

Great Organ, CC to G, 8 Stops.

	Feet.	Pipes.		Feet.	Pipes
1. Open Diapason, metal	8	56	6. Fifteenth, metal	2	56
2. Horn Diapason, spotted			7. Sesqualtera, III ranks,		
metal	8	56	metal		168
3. Stopped Diapason, oak	8 tone	56	8. Trumpet, metal	8	56
4. Principal, spotted metal	4	56			
5. Harmonic Flute, spotted					
metal	4 tone	56			

Choir Organ, CC to G, 8 Stops.

	Feet.	Pipes.		Feet.	Pipes
9. Dulciana, metal	8	56	13. Nason, oak	4 tone	56
10. Keraulophon, metal, with			14. Gemshorn, metal	4	56
mouth of tin	8	56	15. Piccolo, spotted metal,		
11. Flauto Traverso, pine, tri-			stopped	2 tone	56
angular pipes	8	56	16. Clarionet, spotted metal	8	56
12. Suabe Flote, wood	4	56			

Swell Organ, CC to G, 11 Stops.

	Feet.	Pipes.		Feet.	Pipes
17. Lieblich Gedact, wood	16 tone	56	23. Fifteenth, metal	2	56
18. Open Diapason, metal	8	56	24. Mixture, III ranks, metal		168
19. Salicional, spotted metal	8	56	25. Cornopean, spotted metal	8	56
20. Rohrflote, metal and wood	8 tone	56	26. Oboe, spotted metal	8	56
21. Principal, metal	4	56	27. Clarion, metal	4	56
22. Waldflote, wood	4	56			

Pedal Organ, CCC to F, 3 Stops.

	Feet.	Pipes.		Feet.	Pipes
28. Open Diapason, wood	16	30	30. Violoncello, metal	8	30
29. Bourdon, wood	16 tone	30			

Couplers.

1. Swell to Great.	4. Choir to Great.
2. Swell to Choir.	5. Choir to Pedals.
3. Swell to Pedals.	6. Great to Pedals.

8 Composition Pedals.　Tremulant to Great organ and Swell.

271. UNITARIAN CHAPEL, NOTTINGHAM.

The following is the description of the organ at the Unitarian Chapel, High Pavement, Nottingham, erected by Bishop and Son in 1876 :—

at Organ, CC to G, 56 Notes.

	Feet.	Pipes.		Feet.	Pipes.
1. Sub-open Diapason	16	56	6. Harmonic Flute	4	56
2. Open Diapason	8	56	7. Grave Mixture (12th and		
3. Viola	8	56	15th), II and III ranks		112
4. Clarabella	8	56	8. Sesqualtera	3	168
5. Principal	4	56	9. Trumpet	8	56

Swell Organ, CC to G.

	Feet.	Pipes.			Feet.	Pipes.
10. Lieblich Bourdon	16	56	15. Fifteenth		2	56
11. Violin Diapason	8	56	16. Mixture, III ranks		various	168
12. Rohrflote	8	56	17. Cornopean		8	56
13. Voix Célestes, C	8	44	18. Bassoon and Oboe		8	56
14. Principal	4	56	19. Clarion		4	56

Choir Organ, CC to G.

	Feet.	Pipes.			Feet.	Pipes.
20. Viol di Gamba	8	56	24. Flauto Traverso		4	56
21. Dulciana, C, grooved bass	8	44	25. Harmonic Piccolo		2	56
22. Lieblich Gedact	8	56	26. Euphone (free reed)		8	56
23. Salicet	4	56				

Pedal Organ, CCC to F, 30 Notes.

	Feet.	Pipes.			Feet.	Pipes.
27. Grand Open Diapason	16	30	30. Violoncello		8	30
28. Bourdon	16 tone	30	31. Prepared for Trombone		16	
29. Violone	16	30				

Couplers.

1. Swell to Great.
2. Choir to Great.
3. Swell to Choir.

4. Swell to Pedal.
5. Choir to Pedal.
6. Great to Pedal.

4 Composition Pedals to Great.   3 Composition Pedals to Swell.

The Great organ is furnished with C. K. K. Bishop's diminutive pneumatic action, which also controls the Manual couplers.

272. NORTHAMPTON.

The organ in All Saints' Church, Northampton, was built by Mr. Hill about twenty-two years ago ; a great portion of the previous organ being used up in the new work. It contains 44 sounding stops, 3 Manuals, and an independent Pedal of 7 stops. The following is a specification of the instrument as left by Mr. Hill :—

Great, 16 Stops, CC to F.

1. Double Open	16 feet.	9. Fifteenth	2 feet.
2. Double Stopped throughout	16 feet.	10. Sesquialtera, III ranks ...	1¾ foot.
3. Open Diapason	8 feet.	11. Doublette, II ranks	2 feet.
4. Open Diapason	8 feet.	12. Furniture, IV ranks	¾ foot.
5. Stopped Diapason	8 feet.	13. Double Trumpet	16 feet.
6. Quint	6 feet.	14. Posaune	8 feet.
7. Principal	4 feet.	15. Trumpet	8 feet.
8. Twelfth	3 feet.	16. Clarion	4 feet.

Choir, 6 Stops, CC to F.

17. Dulciana	8 feet.	20. Flute	4 feet.
18. Stopped Dulciana	8 feet.	21. Fifteenth	2 feet.
19. Principal	4 feet.	22. Cremona	8 feet.

Swell, 15 Stops, CC to F.

23. Double Diapason	16 feet.	31. Mixture, II ranks.	
24. Open Diapason	8 feet.	32. Contra Fagotto	16 feet.
25. Stopped Diapason	8 feet.	33. Cornopean	8 feet.
26. Dulciana	8 feet.	34. Trumpet	8 feet.
27. Principal	4 feet.	35. Oboe	8 feet.
28. Twelfth	3 feet.	36. Clarion	4 feet.
29. Fifteenth	2 feet.	37. Flute	4 feet.
30. Sesquialtera, III ranks.			

Pedal, 7 Stops, CCC to tenor d.

38. Open, wood	16 feet.	42. Sesquialtera, V ranks.	
39. Sub-bass	16 feet.	43. Trombone	16 feet.
40. Principal	8 feet.	44. Trumpet	8 feet.
41. Fifteenth	4 feet.		

Couplers.

3 Pedal Couplers.	1 Manual Coupler.

273. NORTHAMPTON.

The organ in the Exchange Room, at Northampton, is the German instrument that was placed in the Great Exhibition building of 1851 by Schulze, of Paulinzelle, near Erfurt. It is an admirable organ, and presents varieties of tone, both in regard to character and strength, quite unusual in an instrument with so few stops. It contains 16 sounding stops, of which the following is a list :—

Great, 8 Stops.

1. Bourdon	16 feet tone.	6. Octave	4 feet.
2. Open Diapason	8 feet.	7. {Quint and } drawing	2⅔ feet.
3. Gamba	8 feet.	{Super-octave} together	2 feet.
4. Hohlflote	8 feet.	8. Mixture, V ranks	2 feet.
5. Gedact	8 feet tone.		

Choir, 6 Stops.

9. Lieblich Gedact to Gamut G key (GG pipe)	16 feet tone.	12. Flauto Traverso	8 feet.
10. Geigen Principal	8 feet.	13. Geigen Principal	4 feet.
11. Lieblich Gedact	8 feet tone.	14. Flauto Traverso and Lieblich Gedact, on 1 slider	4 feet.

Pedal, 2 independent Stops, and 2 by communication.

A. Sub-bass, borrowed from Manual Bourdon	16 feet tone.	B. Flute Bass, borrowed from Manual Gedact	8 feet tone.
15. Octave Bass, wood	8 feet.	16. Posaune, free reeds	16 feet tone.

Couplers.

1. Great to Pedals.	2. Choir, Sub-octave to Great.

Compass.

Great, CC to f³ in alt.	Choir, CC to f³ in alt.	Pedal, CCC to tenor d.

The Pedal Clavier is concave in section, consequently the extreme keys are much more within convenient reach than usual.

274. ST. MARY'S CATHEDRAL, NEWCASTLE-ON-TYNE.

This fine organ was built by Messrs. Thos. C. Lewis and Co., of Shepherd's Lane, Brixton, London, and is a noble example of high-class work. It is in the Gothic style, after the designs of John F. Bentley, Esq., and harmonises well with the structure of the Cathedral, an edifice by the elder Pugin. The instrument occupies a gallery which extends across the entire width of the nave, its dimensions are 25 feet 6 inches wide, 15 feet deep, and 21 feet high. The front—the plan of which recedes in two breaks on either side of the organ to the depth of 9 feet— is divided into seven compartments, five of which are occupied above the impost by the two Diapasons of the Great organ, the remainder having small panels filled with gilt ornaments; the massive case is deeply moulded and battlemented, the lower part being filled with rich panelling, and the upper part with cusped headings, the posts buttressed and surmounted by finial terminations. The front rank of Diapason pipes alone weighs upwards of 4½ cwt., and the richness in pure tin of the metal pipes in this work may be inferred from the fact that this organ contains 40 cwt., or 2 tons, of the finest spotted metal. The organ has 3 Manuals, CC to A, 58 notes; has 35 sounding stops, and a total of 2035 pipes.

Choir, 7 Stops.

1.	Lieblich Gedact, wood and metal .... 16 feet.	4.	Vox Angelica .... 8 feet.
2.	Lieblich Gedact, wood and metal .... 8 feet.	5.	Salicet .... 4 feet.
3.	Salicional .... 8 feet.	6.	Flute Harmonique .... 4 feet.
		7.	Clarionet and Bassoon ... 8 feet.

Great, 10 Stops.

8.	Bourdon, wood and metal 16 feet.	13.	Gemshorn .... 4 feet.
9.	Open Diapason .... 8 feet.	14.	Octave Quint .... 2⅔ feet.
10.	Open Diapason, small ... 8 feet.	15.	Super-octave .... 2 feet.
11.	Hohlflote, wood and metal 8 feet.	16.	Mixture, III ranks......... 8 feet.
12.	Octave .... 4 feet.	17.	Trumpet .... 8 feet.

Swell, 12 Stops.

18.	Bourdon, wood and metal 16 feet.	24.	Mixture, II ranks .... 2⅔ feet.
19.	Geigen Principal .... 8 feet.	25.	Bassoon .... 16 feet.
20.	Lieblich Gedact, wood and metal .... 8 feet.	26.	Oboe and Bassoon .... 8 feet.
21.	Viol di Gamba .... 8 feet.	27.	Trumpet .... 8 feet.
22.	Voix Célestes, tenor c ... 8 feet.	28.	Voix Humaine .... 8 feet.
23.	Geigen Principal .... 4 feet.	29.	Clarion........................ 4 feet.

Pedal, 6 Stops (42 pipes to each stop).

30.	Great Bass, wood .... 16 feet.	33.	Great Quint, wood and metal .... 10⅔ feet.
31.	Open Diapason, metal and zinc........................... 16 feet.	34.	Posaune .... 16 feet.
32.	Sub-bass, wood .... 16 feet.	35.	Octave.

Accessory Movements, &c.

1.	Couplers, Choir to Pedals.	3.	Couplers, Swell to Pedals.
2.	Couplers, Great to Pedals.	4.	Couplers, Swell to Great.

Three Pedals of combination to Great organ and three to Swell organ. Pedal to take off Great to Pedals. Pedal to Voix Humaine. Two Swell Pedals, Nos. 1 and 2, and Tremulant.

The bellows to this organ are on a new plan, and are arranged in a peculiar manner. Two storage bellows are placed on either side of the organ, and these are filled by two double-action vertical feeders; the supply from one of these two bellows flows according to demand into a large air reservoir, occupying the whole central space of the floor of the organ, and is then regulated by an automatic movement, which at all times renders the wind perfectly steady, because all communication with the Pedal sound-board is avoided. The Pedal sound-board takes its supply solely from the other storage bellows, which is of ample dimensions for every demand upon it. The bellows and reservoir measure together 150 superficial feet, and contains 160 cubic feet of air.

The Swell box, again, is treated on a novel system, being fitted with Venetian shutters, both back and front, for the purpose of equalising the temperature between the Manuals by leaving both sets of shutters freely open when the organ is not in use. The plan has proved most excellent to the organist for removing that trying perplexity of the Swell being out of tune by reason of differences of temperature between that and the other organs. The Voix Humaine is enclosed in a box inside the Swell, has its mechanism of shutters, and is acted upon by a special Pedal. The Swell within the Swell produces most delicate contrasts of tone, and the two sets of shutters, through the action of separate pedals, allow more finely graduated crescendo, and a more prompt and powerful sforzando than is ordinarily commanded.

275. TOWN HALL, NEWCASTLE-ON-TYNE.

This organ was built by Gray and Davison in 1858. It contains 3 Manuals, CC to A, and Pedals, CCC to F.

Great Organ.

1. Double Diapason	16 feet.	8. Twelfth	2⅔ feet.
2. Open Diapason	8 feet.	9. Super-octave	2 feet.
3. Flute à Pavillon	8 feet.	10. Mixture, III ranks.	
4. Flute Harmonic	8 feet.	11. Furniture, III ranks.	
5. Stopped Diapason	8 feet.	12. Contra Fagotto	16 feet.
6. Octave	4 feet.	13. Posaune	8 feet.
7. Flute Octaviante	4 feet.	14. Clarion	4 feet.

Swell Organ.

15. Bourdon	16 feet.	22. Super-octave	2 feet.
16. Open Diapason	8 feet.	23. Mixture, III ranks.	
17. Keraulophon	8 feet.	24. Cornopean	8 feet.
18. Stopped Diapason, Bass	8 feet.	25. Oboe	8 feet.
19. Clarionet Flute	8 feet.	26. Clarion	4 feet.
20. Octave	4 feet.	Tremulant.	
21. Twelfth	3 feet.		

Choir Organ.

27. Salicional	8 feet.	32. Gemshorn	4 feet.
28. Voix Céleste	8 feet.	33. Suabe Flute	4 feet.
29. Gamba	8 feet.	34. Piccolo	2 feet.
30. Stopped Diapason, Bass	8 feet.	35. Fifteenth	2 feet.
31. Concert Flute	8 feet.	36. Corno di Bassetto	8 feet.

Pedal Organ.

37. Contra Bourdon	32 feet.	41. Octave	8 feet.
38. Open Diapason	16 feet.	42. Super-octave	4 feet.
39. Violon	16 feet.	43. Trombone	16 feet.
40. Bourdon	16 feet.		

Couplers.

1. Swell to Great, Unison.
2. Swell to Sub-octave.
3. Swell to Super-octave.
4. Swell to Choir.
5. Swell to Pedals.
6. Choir to Pedals.
7. Great to Pedals.
8. Sforzando Coupler.
9. Great to Swell by Pedal.

4 Composition Pedals to Great ; 3 to Swell ; 2 to Pedals,

276. LUDLOW CHURCH.

This organ was built by Gray and Davison in 1860. It contains 4 Manuals, CC to G ; and Pedals, CCC to E.

Great Organ.

1. Double Diapason	16 feet.	7. Fifteenth	2 feet.
2. Open Diapason	8 feet.	8. Mixture, III ranks.	
3. Stopped Diapason	8 feet.	9. Furniture, III ranks.	
4. Spitz Flute	8 feet.	10. Trumpet	8 feet.
5. Principal	4 feet.	11. Clarion	4 feet.
6. Twelfth	3 feet.		

Choir Organ.

12. Open Diapason	8 feet.	16. Flute	4 feet.
13. Stopped Diapason	8 feet.	17. Piccolo	2 feet.
14. Dulciana	8 feet.	18. Clarionet	8 feet.
15. Principal	4 feet.		

Solo Organ.

19. Grand Tuba	8 feet.	21. Cornet, V ranks.
20. Harmonic Flute	8 feet.	

Swell Organ.

22. Bourdon	16 feet.	27. Fifteenth	2 feet.
23. Open Diapason	8 feet.	28. Mixture, II ranks.	
24. Stopped Diapason	8 feet.	29. Cornopean	8 feet.
25. Principal	4 feet.	30. Oboe	8 feet.
26. Keraulophon	8 feet.	Tremulant.	

Pedal Organ.

31. Open Diapason	16 feet.	34. Principal	8 feet.
32. Bourdon	16 feet.	35. Fifteenth	4 feet.
33. Violon	16 feet.	36. Trombone	16 feet.

Couplers.

1. Swell to Great.	5. Choir to Pedals.
2. Swell to Pedals.	6. Choir to Great.
3. Great to Pedals.	7. Solo to Great.
4. Swell to Choir.	

3 Composition Pedals to Great and 2 to Swell. Some of the pipes and case of former organ, by Snetzler, have been retained.

277. SHERBORNE ABBEY.

This organ was built by Gray and Davison in 1856, and enlarged and improved by them in 1876. It contains 3 Manuals, CC to F. Swell throughout, and Pedals, from CCC to F.

Great Organ.

1. Double Diapason	16 feet.	7. Fifteenth	2 feet.
2. Open Diapason	8 feet.	8. Sesquialtera, III ranks.	
3. Open Diapason	8 feet.	9. Harmonic Flute	4 feet.
4. Stopped Diapason	8 feet.	10. Posaune	8 feet.
5. Octave	4 feet.	11. Clarion	4 feet.
6. Twelfth	3 feet.		

Choir Organ.

12.	Gamba.			
13.	Dulciana	8 feet.	17. Flute	4 feet.
14.	Stopped Diapason, Bass...	8 feet.	18. Fifteenth	2 feet.
15.	Clarionet Flute	8 feet.	19. Piccolo	2 feet.
16.	Gemshorn	4 feet.	20. Clarionet	8 feet.

Swell Organ.

21. Bourdon	16 feet.	27. Super-octave	2 feet.
22. Open Diapason	8 feet.	28. Sesquialtera.	
23. Keraulophon	8 feet.	29. Cornopean	8 feet.
24. Stopped Diapason	8 feet.	30. Oboe	8 feet.
25. Octave	4 feet.	31. Clarion	4 feet.
26. Harmonic Flute	4 feet.	Tremulant.	

Pedal Organ.

32. Open Diapason	16 feet.	35. Super-octave	4 feet.
33. Bourdon	16 feet.	36. Trombone	16 feet.
34. Octave	8 feet.		

Couplers.

1. Great Manual to Pedals.
2. Choir Manual to Pedals.
3. Swell Manual to Pedals.
4. Swell to Great Manual.
5. Swell to Choir Manual.
6. Swell to Great and Octave.
7. Sforzando Great to Swell by Pedal.

3 Composition Pedals to Great, and 2 to Swell.

278. LYNN REGIS.

The old organ at St. Margaret's, Lynn Regis, Norfolk—partly the work of Dallans, and partly the production of some more ancient workman—was given to the church by " John Tinner," in 1679. The present fine instrument was built by the celebrated Snetzler, under the direction of Dr. Burney, in the year 1754. It is the largest instrument Snetzler ever made in England ; slightly exceeding in this respect his other celebrated piece of handiwork at Halifax. The Lynn organ originally contained a III-rank Furniture in the Great organ, *in addition* to the IV-rank Sesquialtera (as at Halifax) ; also a separate Tierce, and a Bourdon, *in metal*, to CC, excepting the two lowest pipes, which were of wood. These three stops were at some time cancelled, and a second Open Diapason, Principal, and Fifteenth placed in their stead ; a Clarabella has also been inserted in the Choir organ, in place of the Vox Humana. In the Swell there were originally three unison Reeds (Hautboy, Trumpet, and French Horn) ; but there are now but two. The organ was repaired in 1796 by Lincoln, and underwent a second renovation in 1816. About eighteen years since it received the important addition of a Pedal Diapason to GGG, which was added by Holdich, of London. The organ now contains 27 sounding stops, of which the following is a list :—

Great, 12 Stops.

1. Open Diapason.
2. Open Diapason.
3. Stopped Diapason.
4. Principal.
5. Principal.
6. Twelfth.
7. Fifteenth.
8. Fifteenth.
9. Sesquialtera, IV ranks.
10. Cornet to c¹, V ranks.
11. Trumpet.
12. Clarion.

Choir, 7 Stops.

13. Dulciana.
14. Stopped Diapason.
15. Clarabella.
16. Principal.

17. Flute.
18. Fifteenth.
19. Bassoon up to middle g¹.

Swell, 7 Stops.

20. Open Diapason.
21. Stopped Diapason.
22. Principal.
23. German Flute.

24. Cornet, IV ranks.
25. Trumpet.
26. Hautboy.

Pedal, 1 Stop.

27. Open Diapason, to GGG, 21½ feet length.

Couplers.

1. Swell to Great. | 2. Pedals to Great. | 3. Pedals to Choir.

Compass.

Great, GG to e³ in alt.
Choir, GG to e³ in alt.

Swell, tenor f to e³ in alt.
Pedals, down to GG.

The Swell Clavier descends to GG, and acts on the Bass of the Choir Stopped Diapason, Dulciana, and Flute, below tenor f, which are made to draw separately and independently for that purpose, whereby the apparent number of sounding stops is increased from 27 to 30.

This is the first English organ that had a Dulciana; a stop that, in this example, runs through to GG in metal.

279. NORWICH CATHEDRAL.

This organ has an elaborately carved Gothic oak case; it stands over the screen, and consequently has a double front, containing, in the western, the open Diapason (said to be of Harris's make), and, in the Choir front, an open Diapason of Byfield's. The organ underwent a considerable change some time since, it being removed to its present situation, when the Choir organ was taken from its usual position and placed on the south side of the instrument, and the Swell organ on the opposite side, both being on a level with the base of the Great organ, and unseen from the Choir. At this time Double Diapason Pedal pipes, down to GGG, were added by Bishop, and located on the north side of the building, under the triforium, having separate bellows and a long movement. The instrument contains :—

Great, 10 Stops.

1. Open Diapason.
2. Open Diapason.
3. Stopped Diapason.
4. Clarabella, in place of V-rank Cornet.
5. Principal.

6. Twelfth.
7. Fifteenth.
8. Tierce.
9. Sesquialtera.
10. Trumpet.

Choir, 6 *Stops.*

11. Dulciana to tenor c.
12. Stopped Diapason.
13. Principal.

14. Stopped Flute.
15. Fifteenth.
16. Cremona to tenor f.

Swell, 5 *Stops.*

17. Open Diapason.
18. Stopped Diapason.
19. Principal.

20. Hautboy.
21. Trumpet.

Pedal, 1 *Stop.*

22. Open Diapason to GGG............21½ feet length.

Accessory *Stops, Movements, &c.*

1. Coupler, Swell to Great.
2. Coupler Great to Pedal.

3. Coupler, Choir to Pedal.
4, 5, 6. Three Composition Pedals.

Compass.

Great, GG to f³ in alt.
Choir, GG to f³ in alt.
Swell, tenor c to f³ in alt.

Swell Clavier to GG, acting on Choir
organ below tenor c.

280. NORWICH.

The organ in the Church of St. Peter Mancroft, Norwich, is a fine instrument,
originally built by Harris, and afterwards repaired by England, who added the
Dulciana to the Choir organ, and put in a new Swell. The following is a list of
its stops, as drawn by the late Mr. Russell :—

Great, 12 *Stops.*

1. Open Diapason.
2. Stopped Diapason.
3. Principal.
4. Twelfth.
5. Fifteenth.
6. Tierce.
7. Larigot.

8. Sesquialtera, III ranks.
9. Mixture, II ranks.
10. Furniture, III ranks.
11. Cornet, mounted, to middle c¹,
     V ranks.
12. Trumpet.

Choir, 8 *Stops.*

13. Dulciana to Gamut G.
14. Open Diapason to tenor d.
15. Stopped Diapason to tenor d.
16. Principal to tenor d.

17. Flute.
18. Fifteenth.
19. Vox Humana throughout.
20. Bassoon, throughout.

Swell, 6 *Stops.*

21. Open Diapason.
22. Stopped Diapason.
23. Principal.

24. Cornet, III ranks.
25. Hautboy.
26. Trumpet.

The Open Diapason, Stopped Diapason, and Principal in the Choir organ,
are borrowed from the corresponding stops of the Great organ, from tenor d

281. St. Nicholas Church, Great Yarmouth.

Description of the organ at St. Nicholas Church, Great Yarmouth, as originally built by Jordan, Bridge, and Byfield in 1733, and recently re-constructed by Messrs. Bishop and Son.

Great Organ, CC to G.

	Feet.	Pipes.			Feet.	Pipes.
1. Double Open Diapason, metal	16	56	9. Harmonic Flute, metal		4	56
2. Open Diapason, large, metal	8	56	10. Twelfth, metal		3	56
3. Open Diapason, small, metal	8	56	11. Fifteenth		2	56
4. Viola, metal and wood	8	56	12. Mixture, III ranks, metal, various			168
5. Stopped Diapason, metal Treble	8	56	13. Sesquialtera, V ranks, metal, various			280
6. Clarabella C, wood	8	44	14. Double Trumpet, metal		16	56
7. Principal, metal	4	56	15. Posaune, metal		8	56
8. Octave, metal	4	56	16. Trumpet, metal		8	56
			17. Clarion, metal		4	56

Choir Organ.

	Feet.	Pipes.			Feet.	Pipes.
18. Open Diapason	8	56	24. Fifteenth		2	56
19. Hohlflote, closed, Bass	8	56	25. Cremona		8	56
20. Dulciana	8	56	26. Mixture, II ranks, and one			
21. Keraulophon, C grooved, Bass	8	44	prepared		various	112
22. Flute, metal	4	56	27. Orchestral Oboe, prepared		8	
23. Principal	4	56				

Swell Organ.

	Feet.	Pipes.			Feet.	Pipes.
28. Lieblich Bourdon, wood	16 tone	56	37. Mixture, IV ranks		various	224
29. Open Diapason	8	56	38. Contra Fagotto		16	56
30. Stopped Diapason, wood and metal	8 tone	56	39. Horn		8	56
31. Gamba, C grooved, Bass	8	44	40. Trumpet		8	56
32. Voix Célestes C	8	44	41. Hautboy		8	56
33. Principal	4	56	42. Clarion		4	56
34. Suabe Flute	4	56	43. Vox Humana, in a distinct			
35. Piccolo, wood	2	56	box at back, and inside of			
36. Fifteenth	2	56	Great Swell box		8	56

Pedal Organ, CCC to F, 30 Notes.

	Feet.	Pipes.			Feet.	Pipes.
44. Double Open Diapason	32	30	48. Principal		8	30
45. Open Diapason	16	30	49. Trombone		16	33
46. Violon	16	30	50. Prepared slide for Mixture.			
47. Bourdon	16 tone	30				

Solo Organ.

At present the keys alone of this organ are inserted.

Couplers, &c.

1. Swell to Pedals.	7. Choir to Great.
2. Choir to Pedals.	8. Swell Sub-octave.
3. Swell to Great.	9. Tremolo to Swell organ.
4. Swell Octave.	10. Compositions to Pedal organ.
5. Great to Pedals.	11. Compositions to Swell organ.
6. Swell to Choir.	12. Compositions to Great organ.

The instrument is " divided," the two halves being placed in the aisles, and the key-boards in the chancel amongst the choir seats. The whole of the mechanism, even to the Swell and Tremolo actions, is planned on the tubular pneumatic system, but dispensing with exhaust bellows. In the north aisle are placed the Great organ and a portion of the Pedal organ, contained in the original fine case. In the south aisle are the Swell and Choir organs with the remainder of the Pedal organ, contained in the fine case from St. Peter à Mancroft at Norwich, which was purchased purposely.

282. ELY CATHEDRAL.

This organ, erected by Hill in 1851, is placed in the triforium, and projects out from the arches about six feet. The keys are placed in a stone gallery, behind the top of the stalls, and communicate with the organ by means of a long movement. The instrument is enclosed in a handsome case of oak, made according to a design prepared by Sir Gilbert Scott. The organ contains :—

Great, 13 Stops.

1. Double Diapason	16 feet.	8. Super-octave	2 feet.
2. Open Diapason	8 feet.	9. Sesquialtera, III ranks.	
3. Open Diapason	8 feet.	10. Mixture, III ranks.	
4. Stopped Diapason	8 feet.	11. Posaune	8 feet.
5. Quint	6 feet.	12. Trumpet	8 feet.
6. Octave	4 feet.	13. Clarion	4 feet.
7. Octave Quint	3 feet.		

Choir, 7 Stops.

14. Open Diapason	8 feet.	18. Flute	4 feet.
15. Clarabella, throughout	8 feet.	19. Super-octave	2 feet.
16. Stopped Diapason	8 feet.	20. Cremona	8 feet.
17. Octave	4 feet.		

Swell, 6 Stops.

21. Double Diapason	16 feet.	24. Octave	4 feet.
22. Open Diapason	8 feet.	25. Trumpet	8 feet.
23. Stopped Diapason	8 feet.	26. Hautboy	8 feet.

Pedal, 6 Stops.

27. Open, wood	16 feet.	30. Super-octave	4 feet.
28. Open, metal	16 feet.	31. Sesquialtera, III ranks.	
29. Octave	8 feet.	32. Trombone	16 feet.

Accessory Stops, Movements, &c.

1. Swell to Great.	3. Pedals to Great.
2. Choir to Great.	4. Pedals to Choir.

Compass.

Great, CC to f³ in alt.	Swell, tenor c, to f³ in alt.
Choir, CC to f³ in alt.	Pedal, CCC to tenor d.

283. TRINITY COLLEGE, CAMBRIDGE.

Description of the organ in Trinity College, Cambridge, built by Hill and Son in 1871. Four Manuals, compass of each CC to G, 56 notes, and Pedal Clavier, CCC to F, 30 notes :—

Great Organ.

	Feet.	Pipes.		Feet.	Pipes.
1. Double Open Diapason, metal	16	56	8. Principal, metal	4	56
2. Open Diapason, metal	8	56	9. Wald Flute, wood	4	56
3. Open Diapason, No. 2, metal	8	56	10. Nason, wood	4	56
			11. Twelfth, metal	3	56
4. Salicional, metal	8	56	12. Fifteenth, metal	2	56
5. Pierced Gamba, metal	8	56	13. Full Mixture, metal, III ranks		168
6. Stopped Diapason, wood	8	56	14. Sharp Mixture, metal II ranks		112
7. Quint, metal	6	56	15. Trumpet, metal	8	56
			16. Clarion, metal	4	56

Choir Organ.

	Feet.	Pipes.			Feet.	Pipes.
17. Double Dulciana, metal ...	16	56	22. Stopped Diapason, wood	8	56
18. Dulciana, metal	8	56	23. Stopped Flute, wood......	4	56
19. Open Diapason, metal ...	8	56	24. Principal, metal	4	56
20. Claribel, c grooved, wood	8	44	25. Flautina, metal	2	56
21. Viol di Gamba, metal	8	56	26. Cremona, metal	8	56

Solo Organ.

	Feet.	Pipes.			Feet.	Pipes.
27. Harmonic Flute, metal ...	8	56	31. Lieblich Flute, metal ...	4	56
28. Harmonic Flute, metal ...	4	56	32. Tuba Mirabilis, metal ...	8	56
29. Vox Angelica, metal, II ranks		112	33. Vox Humana, metal	8	56
30. Piccolo, metal	2	56	34. Orchestral Oboe, metal...	8	56

(All in box but Tuba and Flute Harmonic.)

Swell Organ.

	Feet.	Pipes.			Feet.	Pipes.
35. Double Diapason, wood...	16	56	42. Fifteenth, metal	2	56
36. Open Diapason, metal ...	8	56	43. Mixture, metal, III ranks		168
37. Salicional, metal	8	56	44. Double Trumpet, metal...	16	56
38. Cone Gamba, metal	8	56	45. Trumpet, metal	8	56
39. Stopped Diapason, wood..	8	56	46. Cornopean, metal	8	56
40. Suabe Flute, wood	4	56	47. Oboe, metal	8	56
41. Principal, metal	4	56	48. Clarion, metal...............	8	56

Pedal Organ.

	Feet.	Pipes.			Feet.	Pipes.
49. Sub-bourdon, wood........	32	30	55. Bass Flute, wood.........	8	30
50. Open Diapason, wood ...	16	30	56. Fifteenth, metal	4	30
51. Open Diapason, metal ...	16	30	57. Mixture, metal, III ranks		90
52. Violon, wood	16	30	58. Trombone, wood	16	30
53. Bourdon, wood	16	30	59. Clarion, metal...............	8	30
54. Principal, metal	8	30			

Couplers.

1. Swell to Great.	6. Great to Pedal.
2. Choir to Great.	7. Choir to Pedal.
3. Solo to Great.	8. Solo to Pedal.
4. Solo to Swell.	9. Swell to Pedal.
5. Swell to Choir.	

4 Composition Pedals to Great and Pedal combined. 3 Composition Pedals to Swell organ. Tremulant to Swell organ and Solo organ. Pneumatic Action to Great and Couplers.

284. ST. JOHN'S COLLEGE, CAMBRIDGE.

The organ in the chapel of St. John's College, Cambridge, was built by Hill in 1839. It is not complete, preparation being made for five more stops.

Great, 10 Stops; Compass, FFF to f³ in alt.

1. Open Diapason.	6. Clarabella.
2. Stopped Diapason.	7. Twelfth and Fifteenth on one side.
3. Double Dulciana.	8. Fifteenth, No. 2.
4. Principal.	9. Sesquialtera.
5. Flute.	10. Trumpet.

Choir, 6 Stops; FFF to f in alt.

11. Open Diapason throughout.	14. Flute.
12. Stopped Diapason.	15. Principal.
13. Dulciana.	16. Cremona.

Swell, 9 Stops; FF to f in alt.

17. Open Diapason.
18. Stopped Diapason.
19. Dulciana.
20. Principal.
21. Harmonica.

22. Sesqualtera, IV ranks.
23. Hautboy.
24. French Horn.
25. Clarion.

Pedal, 1 Stop.

26. Open Diapason, to FFF.

Couplers.

1. Swell to Great. | 2. Octave Swell to Great. | 3. Choir to Great.

285. BEDFORD.

The organ in St. Paul's Wesleyan Chapel was built by Wadsworth, Manchester, in 1869. The following are its stops :—

Great, 12 Stops; CC to G.

	Feet.	Pipes.		Feet.	Pipes.
1. Bourdon, wood and metal	16	56	7. Flute Harmonique, metal	2	56
2. Open Diapason, metal	8	56	8. Fifteenth, metal	2	56
3. Violin Diapason, metal	8	44	9. Mixture, II ranks, metal		112
4. Hohlflote	8	56	10. Furniture, II ranks, metal		112
5. Rohr Gedact, wood and metal	8	56	11. Trumpet, metal	8	56
6. Principal, metal	4	56	12. Clarionet, metal	4	56

Swell, 12 Stops; CC to G.

	Feet.	Pipes.		Feet.	Pipes.
13. Lieblich Bourdon, wood and metal	16	56	19. Fifteenth, metal	2	56
14. Open Diapason, metal	8	56	20. Mixture, III ranks, metal		112
15. Flute d'Amour, metal	8	56	21. Cornopean, metal	8	56
16. Keraulophon, metal	8	44	22. Hautboy, metal	8	56
17. Spitzflote, metal	4	56	23. Clarion, metal	4	56
18. Flute Céleste, wood	4	56	24. Vox Humana	8	56
			Tremulant to Swell.		

Choir, 6 Stops; CC to G.

	Feet.	Pipes.		Feet.	Pipes.
25. Lieblich Gedact, wood and metal	8	56	28. Lieblich Gedact, metal	4	56
26. Dulciana, metal	8	56	29. Flageolet, metal	2	56
27. Viola, metal	8	44	30. Clarionet, metal	8	56

Pedal, 5 Stops; CCC to G.

	Feet.	Pipes.		Feet.	Pipes.
31. Open Diapason, wood	16	29	34. Octave, wood	8	29
32. Sub-bass	16	29	35. Trombone, wood	8	29
33. Principal, wood	8	29			

Accessory Stops, Movements, &c.

Coupler, Swell to Great.
Coupler, Swell to Great Sub-octave.
Coupler, Swell to Pedals.
Coupler, Great to Pedals.

Coupler, Choir to Pedals.
Coupler, Choir to Great Sub-octave.
5 Composition Pedals.

The metal pipes are of the best tin metal of the most approved substance, and all the trebles, except the reeds, are of spotted metal; it is tuned to the "Normal Diapason pitch." The reeds and flue work on the Great and Swell are of different pressures. The Pedals are radiating and concave. The bellows are horizontal, double-leathered, with double feeders and compensating folds, and the case is of polished pitch pine.

286. ROCHESTER CATHEDRAL.

This organ, originally built by Samuel Green, was enlarged by Hill in 1835. A few years ago it was divided, the work being commenced by Walker, and completed by Messrs. Forster and Andrews, of Hull, who introduced the two Front 16 feet Metal Diapasons.

Great, 10 Stops; GG to F in alt., 59 Notes.

1. Double Open Diapason ... 16 feet.
2. Open Diapason.............. 8 feet.
3. Open Diapason.............. 8 feet.
4. Stopped Diapason .... 8 feet tone.
5. Principal .... 4 feet.
6. Flute, tenor c .... 4 feet.
7. Twelfth .... 2⅔ feet.
8. Fifteenth .... 2 feet.
9. Sesquialtera, III ranks.
10. Mixture, II ranks.
11. Trumpet............ .... 8 feet.

Choir, 7 Stops; GG to F in alt., 59 Notes.

12. Dulciana .... 8 feet.
13. Stopped Diapason .... 8 feet tone.
14. Gamba .... 8 feet.
15. Principal .... 4 feet.
16. Wald Flute (CC) .... 4 feet.
17. Fifteenth .... 2 feet.
18. Clarionet (CC) .... 8 feet tone.

Swell, 11 Stops; CC to F in alt., 54 Notes.

19. Bourdon........................ 16 feet.
20. Open Diapason.............. 8 feet.
21. Stopped Diapason, metal... 8 feet tone.
22. Dulciana, Gamut G .... 8 feet.
23. Principal .... 4 feet.
24. Dulciana Principal .... 4 feet.
25. Cornet, III ranks.
26. Dulciana Mixture, IV ranks.
27. Horn .... 8 feet.
28. Hautboy........................ 8 feet.
29. Clarion .... 4 feet.

Pedal, 5 Stops; CCC to F, 30 Notes.

30. Sub-bass (GGG) .... 32 feet tone.
31. Open Diapason, wood...... 16 feet.
32. Violone .... 16 feet.
33. Open Diapason, metal ... 16 feet.
34. Principal, or Violoncello... 8 feet.
35. Posaune........................ 16 feet.

Accessory Stops, Movements, &c.

1. Swell to Great.
2. Choir Sub-octave to Great.
3. Swell to Pedal.
4. Great to Pedal.
5. Choir to Pedal.
6. Four Composition Pedals to Great.
7. Two Composition Pedals to Swell.

287. TONBRIDGE WELLS.

The organ in Trinity Church, Tonbridge Wells, was built by Gray in 1840 The following is the specification :—

Great, 8 Stops; Compass, GG to F in alt.

1. Stopped Diapason.
2. Open Diapason.
3. Open Diapason.
4. Principal.
5. Twelfth.
6. Fifteenth.
7. Sesquialtera, III ranks.
8. Trumpet.

Choir, 6 Stops; GG to F in alt.

9. Stopped Diapason.
10. Open Diapason.
11. Principal.

12. Fifteenth.
13. Flute.
14. Cremona to fiddle g.

Swell, 5 Stops; Compass, from Tenor C to F in alt.

15. Open Diapason.
16. Stopped Diapason.
17. Principal.

18. Trumpet.
19. Hautboy.

Pedal, 1 Stop.

20. Open Diapason, CC to CCC, one octave...... 16 feet length.

Accessory Stops, Movements, &c.

Coupler to Great Organ.
Four Composition Pedals.

Two Octaves and a note of German Pedals, from CCC.

288. CANTERBURY CATHEDRAL.

It is not known who was the original builder of the organ in Canterbury Cathedral; but it was re-built by Samuel Green, in 1784, who put in new Diapasons and enlarged the scale of the pipes. It was removed, in 1827, from above the screen, by Longhurst, sen., who put in new keys and a long movement of upwards of 90 feet; he also re-built the Swell organ, and extended the compass to tenor c. The organist now sits in the Choir behind the Decani Lay Clerks. The organ, which is very inefficient, is placed over the south aisle; has 3 sets of keys; Compass, from GG to E; two octaves of Pedals, and one octave of Pedal Pipes from CCC to CC.

Great, 12 Stops.

1. Open Diapason.
2. Open Diapason.
3. Stopped Diapason.
4. Clarabella, Treble, in place of V-rank Cornet.
5. Principal.
6. Fifteenth.

7. Twelfth.
8. Sesquialtera, III ranks.
9. Mixture, II ranks.
10. Trumpet, Treble.
11. Great Trumpet (throughout).
12. Clarion (throughout).

Choir, 6 Stops.

13. Stopped Diapason.
14. Dulciana.
15. Stopped Flute.

16. Open Flute.
17. Principal.
18. Cremona.

Swell, 10 Stops.

19. Stopped Diapason.
20. Double Open Diapason.
21. Unison Open Diapason.
22. Principal.
23. Fifteenth.

24. Twelfth.
25. Sesquialtera, III ranks.
26. Cornopean.
27. Trumpet.
28. Hautboy.

Pedal, 2 Stops.

29. Stopped Diapason, wood.

30. Open Diapason, wood.

Couplers.

1. Swell to Great.
2. Pedal to Great.
3. Pedal to Choir.

289. CRANBROOK.

The organ in the Parish Church at Cranbrook, Kent, was built by Mr. Willis in 1854, and consists of two complete rows of keys, of the Compass from CC to F in alt., fifty-four notes, and two octaves and a half of Pedals, of the Compass CCC to F, thirty notes. It contains the following stops :—

Great, 11 *Stops.*

1.	Double Diapason, closed, wood	16 feet.	
2.	Large Open Diapason, metal	8 feet.	
3.	Small Open Diapason, metal	8 feet.	
4.	Stopped Diapason and Clarabella, wood	8 feet.	
5.	Dulciana, metal	8 feet.	
6.	Flute (Harmonic), metal	4 feet.	
7.	Principal, metal	4 feet.	
8.	Twelfth, metal	3 feet.	
9.	Fifteenth, metal	2 feet.	
10.	Sesqualtera, V ranks, metal	1⅗ foot.	
11.	Trumpet, metal	8 feet.	

Swell, 10 *Stops.*

12.	Double Diapason, closed, wood	16 feet.
13.	Open Diapason, metal ...	8 feet.
14.	Stopped Diapason, wood	8 feet.
15.	Gamba to tenor c, metal	8 feet.
16.	Principal, metal	4 feet.
17.	Fifteenth, metal	2 feet.
18.	Mixture, III ranks, metal.	
19.	Contra Hautboy, metal	16 feet.
20.	Hautboy, metal	8 feet.
21.	Trumpet, metal	8 feet.

Pedal, 1 *Stop.*

22. Grand Open Diapason, wood............................ 16 feet.

Couplers.

1. Swell to Great. | 2. Swell to Pedals. | 3. Great to Pedals.

290. CHICHESTER CATHEDRAL.

This organ was built by Renatus Harris in 1678, and originally had but one Manual ; no Pedals ; only one Open Diapason, which stood in the west front of the case, diapered and gilded ; and no Reed stop. In the year 1725 Byfield added the Choir organ, and put a Trumpet stop into the Great organ. In 1778 the east front Open Diapason was added by Knight, who at the same time built the Swell. In 1806 England considerably improved the organ, by introducing new and larger sound-boards ; at the same time making the Great and Choir Manuals long Octaves ; putting a II-rank Mixture into the Great organ ; placing a Hautboy in the room of the Swell Trumpet, and a Dulciana to Gamut G, in lieu of the Choir Cremona. The old pipes were at the same time rounded out and repaired. For these repairs and improvements England received 200 guineas. A Pedal Clavier, of the same compass, GG to tenor c, was also laid down by England, acting on the Bass keys of the Great Manual. In 1829 Pilcher added a set of Unison Pedal pipes from FFF to tenor c, and placed a Clarabella in the Swell in the room of the IV-rank Cornet. He also put in a new horizontal bellows, using the old diagonals as the two feeders, and also re-gilt the Choir front pipes. The cost was about £100. In 1844 a set of Double Open Pedal pipes, FFFF to CC, and a separate bellows, were added by Gray and Davison, the largest pipes being laid horizontally at the back of the organ, in the organ loft. The Swell Clavier was at the same time extended to GG, communicating with and pulling down the corresponding keys of the Choir organ ; a Clarabella stop was inserted in place of the V-rank Cornet in the Great organ ; a Cremona was put into the Choir ; a Coupler, Swell to Great, was applied ; also two Composition Pedals ; and the whole of the pipes were repaired, and many much improved. The cost was £218. In 1851 a Swell of 8 stops was added by Hill, the organ then containing the following stops :—

Great, 10 Stops.

1. Open Diapason.	6. Twelfth.
2. Open Diapason.	7. Fifteenth.
3. Stopped Diapason.	8. Sesquialtera, III ranks.
4. Clarabella, in place of V-rank Cornet.	9. Mixture, II ranks.
5. Principal.	10. Trumpet, draws in halves.

Choir, 6 Stops.

11. Dulciana to Gamut G.	14. Flute.
12. Stopped Diapason.	15. Fifteenth.
13. Principal.	16. Cremona to fiddle g.

Swell, 8 Stops.

17. Double Diapason.	21. Fifteenth.
18. Open Diapason.	22. Sesquialtera, III ranks.
19. Stopped Diapason.	23. Hautboy.
20. Principal.	24. Cornopean.

Pedal, 2 Stops.

25. Great Open Bass, to FFFF, 24 feet. | 26. Open Diapason, to FFF, 12 feet.

Accessory Stops, &c.

1. Swell to Great.	3. Choir to Pedal.
2. Great to Pedal.	4, 5. Two Composition Pedals.

Compass.

Great, GG to d³ in alt.	Swell Clavier, GG to d³ in alt.
Choir, GG to d³ in alt.	Pedal, FFF to tenor c, 20 notes.
Swell, tenor c to d³ in alt.	

291. WINCHESTER.

The fine organ in Winchester Cathedral was built by Willis, under the direction of Dr. S. S. Wesley. It comprises 4 Manuals, an independent 32-feet Pedal of 8 stops, and, altogether, 48 sounding stops, nearly all of which are whole stops. The following is the scheme. :—

Great, 13 Stops.

1. Double Diapason	16 feet.	8. Fifteenth		2 feet.
2. Open Diapason	8 feet.	9. Sesquialtera.		
3. Open Diapason	8 feet.	10. Mixture.		
4. Stopped Diapason	8 feet tone.	11. Trombone		8 feet.
5. Principal	4 feet.	12. Trumpet		8 feet.
6. Principal	4 feet.	13. Clarion		4 feet.
7. Twelfth	2⅔ feet.			

Swell, 13 Stops.

14. Double Diapason	16 feet.	21. Sesquialtera.		
15. Open Diapason	8 feet.	22. Mixture.		
16. Stopped Diapason	8 feet tone.	23. Trumpet		16 feet.
17. Principal	4 feet.	24. Trumpet		8 feet.
18. Flute	4 feet.	25. Hautboy		8 feet.
19. Twelfth	2⅔ feet.	26. Clarion		4 feet.
20. Fifteenth	2 feet.			

Choir, 8 Stops.

27. Open Diapason .... 8 feet.
28. Stopped Diapason .... 8 feet tone.
29. Dulciana .... 8 feet.
30. Principal .... 4 feet.

31. Flute .... 4 feet.
32. Fifteenth .... 2 feet.
33. Sesqualtera.
34. Cremona .... 8 feet tone.

Solo, 6 Stops.

35. Harmonic Flute .... 8 feet.
36. Harmonic Flute .... 4 feet.
37. Piccolo .... 2 feet.

38. Horn .... 8 feet.
39. Orchestral Hautboy ...... 8 feet.
40. Corno di Bassetto .... 8 feet tone.

Pedal, 8 Stops.

41. Double Double Diapason 32 feet.
42. Double Open Diapason ... 16 feet.
43. Double Dulciana .... 16 feet.
44. Open Diapason .... 8 feet.

45. Principal .... 4 feet.
46. Mixture.
47. Trombone .... 16 feet.
48. Tromba .... 8 feet.

Compass of all the Manuals, CC. Pedal, CCC.

Couplers.

1. Swell to Great.
2. Choir to Great.

3. Great to Pedal.
4. Choir to Pedal.

5. Swell to Pedal.

292. RIPON CATHEDRAL.

The new organ for the Cathedral at Ripon is being built by Mr Lewis, and is to consist of 3 complete Manuals, a 32-feet Pedal, and to contain the following specified stops :—

Great Organ, CC to A, 58 Notes.

1. Bourdon .... 16 feet.
2. Open Diapason, large .... 8 feet.
3. Open Diapason, small ... 8 feet.
4. Viola........................... 8 feet.
5. Hohlflote .... 8 feet.
6. Stopped Diapason .... 8 feet.
7. Octave .... 4 feet.

8. Hohlflote.................... 4 feet.
9. Octave Quint .... 2⅔ feet.
10. Super-octave .... 2 feet.
11. Full Mixture, IV ranks... 1⅓ foot.
12. Contra Trumpet........... 16 feet.
13. Trumpet .... 8 feet.

Swell Organ, CC to A, 58 Notes.

14. Bourdon .... 16 feet.
15. Geigen Principal .... 8 feet.
16. Rohrflote (old organ) ...... 8 feet.
17. Pierced Gamba .... 8 feet.
18. Dulciana (old organ) ...... 8 feet.
19. Geigen Principal........... 4 feet.
20. Rohrflote (old organ) ...... 4 feet.

21. Dulcet .... 4 feet.
22. Flautina .... 2 feet.
23. Mixture, III ranks........ 2 feet.
24. Contra Trumpet........... 16 feet.
25. Horn .... 8 feet.
26. Oboe .... 8 feet.
27. Clarion .... 4 feet.

Choir Organ, CC to A, 58 Notes.

28. Lieblich Gedact .... 16 feet.
29. Salicional (old organ)...... 8 feet.
30. Lieblich Gedact .... 8 feet.
31. Stopped Diapason (old organ) .... 8 feet.
32. Dolce .... 8 feet.

33. Vox Angelica .... 8 feet.
34. Lieblich Gedact .... 4 feet.
35. Flauto Dolce .... 4 feet.
36. Lieblich Gedact .... 2 feet.
37. Clarionet..................... 8 feet.

Pedal Organ, CCC to F, 30 Notes.

38. Sub-bass	32 feet.	42. Flute Bass.....................	8 feet.
39. Open Diapason	16 feet.	43. Octave	8 feet.
40. Bourdon	16 feet.	44. Trombone.....................	16 feet.
41. Quint Bass	10⅔ feet.		

Couplers.

Choir to Pedals	Swell to Great.
Great to Pedals.	Swell to Choir.
Swell to Pedals.	

7 Pedals of Combination.

293. WELLS CATHEDRAL.

The old organ in this Cathedral was built by Father Smith in 1664; and re-built by Green in 1786. An octave and a half of Pedals and Double Pedal pipes were added by Smith, of Bristol, about the year 1830. It contained 23 sounding stops. The present organ was erected by Mr. Henry Willis in 1857.

Great, 13 Stops; CC to G in alt., 56 Notes.

1. Double Diapason, metal	16 feet.	8. Fifteenth, metal	2 feet.
2. Open Diapason, metal	8 feet.	9. Sesquialtera, III ranks, metal.	
3. Open Diapason, metal	8 feet.	10. Mixture, III ranks, metal.	
4. Stopped Diapason, wood	8 feet.	11. Posaune, metal	16 feet.
5. Principal, metal	4 feet.	12. Trombone, metal.................	8 feet.
6. Principal, metal	4 feet.	13. Clarion, metal	4 feet.
7. Twelfth, metal....................	3 feet.		

Choir, 9 Stops; CC to G in alt., 56 Notes.

14. Douple Diapason, wood	16 feet.	19. Flute Harmonique, metal	4 feet.
15. Open Diapason, metal	8 feet.	20. Piccolo Harmonique	2 feet.
16. Dulciana, metal	8 feet.	21. Clarinet and Corno di Bassetto	8 feet.
17. Stopped Diapason, wood	8 feet.	22. Oboe (Orchestral), from fiddle	
18. Principal, metal	4 feet.	G...............................	8 feet.

Swell, 10 Stops; CC to G in alt., 56 Notes.

23. Double Diapason and Dulciana	16 feet.	28. Echo Cornet, III ranks.	
		29. Contra Fagotto, wood	16 feet.
24. Open Diapason, metal	8 feet.	30. Trumpet, metal	8 feet.
25. Stopped Diapason, wood	8 feet.	31. Hautboy, metal	8 feet.
26. Principal, metal	4 feet.	32. Clarion, metal	4 feet.
27. Fifteenth, metal	2 feet.		

Pedal, 7 Stops; CCC to F, 30 Notes.

33. Double Diapason, wood........	16 feet.	37. Mixture, III ranks, metal.	
34. Violone, Open, metal............	16 feet.	38. Trombone, wood.................	8 feet.
35. Principal, metal	8 feet.	39. Posaune, metal	16 feet.
36. Fifteenth, metal	4 feet.		

Couplers.

1. Swell to Great.	3. Swell to Pedals.	5. Choir to Pedals,
2. Choir to Great.	4. Great to Pedals.	

294. VICTORIA ROOMS, BRISTOL.

This organ, originally built for the Panopticon, Leicester Square, by Messrs. Hill and Co., in 1853, has been re-erected in the above rooms by Messrs. Bryceson Brothers, who have partly re-constructed it. It has 4 Manual organs, all of the CC or 8-feet compass; a separate Pedal of 10 stops and 6 bellows at different pressures.

All the musical scales have alike been rendered available to the performer on this instrument, by the adoption of the admirable system of equal temperament.

The following is a list of the stops in this organ :—

Great Organ, 16 Stops.

1. Double Open Diapason, metal and wood .... 16 feet.	8. Octave Quint, metal ...... 3 feet.
2. Open Diapason, metal ... 8 feet.	9. Super-octave, metal ...... 2 feet.
3. Open Diapason, No. 2, metal .... 8 feet.	10. Sesquialtera, III ranks, metal.
4. Stopped Diapason, wood.. 8 feet tone.	11. Mixture, III ranks, metal.
5. Salicional .... 8 feet.	12. Furniture, III ranks, metal.
6. Octave, metal .... 4 feet.	13. Trumpet, metal .... 16 feet.
7. Wald Flute, wood .... 4 feet.	14. Posaune, metal .... 8 feet.
	15. Trumpet, metal .... 8 feet.
	16. Clarion, metal .... 4 feet.

Choir Organ, 12 Stops.

17. Bourdon, wood.............. 16 feet tone.	23. Super-octave, metal ...... 2 feet.
18. Gamba, metal .... 8 feet.	24. Sesquialtera, II ranks, metal.
19. Open Diapason .... 8 feet.	25. Stopped Flute, metal...... 4 feet tone.
20. Stopped Diapason, metal and wood.................. 8 feet tone.	26. Flageolet..................... 2 feet.
21. Octave .... 4 feet.	27. { Bassoon Bass, wood..... } 8 feet. { Clarionet Treble, wood }
22. Octave Quint, metal ...... 3 feet.	28. Trumpet, metal .... 8 feet.

Solo Organ, 9 Stops.

29. Tuba Organ. { 1. Grand Tuba Mirabilis, metal ... 8 feet.	34. Doublette, II ranks, metal 2 feet.
30. { 2. Do. Clarion, metal 4 feet.	35. Vox Angelica, II ranks, metal .... 8 feet.
31. Claribel, wood .... 8 feet.	36. Krum Horn, metal ...... 8 feet tone.
32. Harmonic Flute, metal ... 4 feet.	37. Vox Humana, metal ...... 8 feet tone.
33. Piccolo .... 2 feet.	

Swell Organ, 13 Stops.

38. Bourdon .... 16 feet.	45. Sesquialtera, V ranks, metal.
39. Open Diapason, metal ... 8 feet.	46. Suabe Flute, wood........ 4 feet.
40. Salicional, metal .... 8 feet.	47. Cornopean, metal .... 8 feet.
41. Stopped Diapason, wood.. 8 feet.	48. Trumpet, metal .... 8 feet.
42. Octave, metal .... 4 feet.	49. Hautboy, metal .... 8 feet.
43. Octave Quint, metal ...... 3 feet.	50. Clarion, metal.............. 4 feet.
44. Super-octave, metal ...... 2 feet.	

Pedal Organ, 10 Stops.

51. Double Open Diapason, wood........................ 32 feet.	57. Super-octave, metal ...... 4 feet.
52. Open Diapason, wood ... 16 feet.	58. Sesquialtera, V ranks, metal .... 3 feet.
53. Open Diapason, metal ... 16 feet.	59. Trombone, metal .... 16 feet.
54. Bourdon, wood .... 16 feet tone.	60. Octave Trombone, metal 8 feet.
55. Octave, metal .... 8 feet.	61. Drums CC—C.
56. Octave Quint .... 6 feet.	

Accessory Stops, Movements, &c.

1. Coupler, Swell to Great.
2. Choir to Great.
3. Solo to Great.
4. Pedal to Great.
5. Pedal to Choir.
6. Pedal to Swell.

7. Pedal to Solo.
8 to 16. Nine Composition Pedals.
17, 18. Two Tremulants.
19. Pneumatic Lever attachment.
20. Crescendo and Diminuendo Pedal.

No. of Sounding Stops.

Great Organ	16
Choir	12
Swell	13
Solo	9
Pedal	10
	60

No. of Pipes.

Great Organ	1276
Choir	754
Swell	932
Solo	626
Pedal	416
	4004

295. BRISTOL.

The organ in St. James's Church has been re-built by Mr. W. G. Vowles, Bristol. It has 44 sounding stops, 6 Couplers, 6 Composition Pedals, 4 Manuals, and Pedal organ. Pneumatic action is attached to Great Manual and Couplers, with 3 large reservoirs and 6 feeders to supply them with wind. The contents are as follows :—

Great Organ, CC to G in alt., 56 Notes.

	Feet.	Pipes.		Feet.	Pipes.
1. Double Diapason, wood and metal	16 tone	56	6. Suabe Flute, wood	4	56
2. Open Diapason, large, metal	8	56	7. Twelfth, metal	3	56
3. Open Diapason, small, metal	8	56	8. Fifteenth, metal	2	56
4. Stopped Diapason, wood	8	56	9. Mixture, 4 ranks, metal	various	224
5. Principal, metal	4	56	10. Trumpet, metal	8	56
			11. Clarion, metal	4	56

Grand Swell, CC to G in alt., 56 Notes.

	Feet.	Pipes.		Feet.	Pipes.
12. Lieblich Gedact, wood	16	56	19. Twelfth, metal	3	56
13. Open Diapason, metal	8	56	20. Piccolo, metal	2	56
14. Stopped Diapason, wood	8	56	21. Mixture, III ranks, metal, various		168
15. Dulciana, metal	8	56	22. Cornopean, metal	8	56
16. Vox Angelica, metal	8	56	23. Hautboy, metal	8	56
17. Principal, metal	4	56	24. Clarion, metal	4	56
18. Stopped Flute, metal	4	56			

Echo Swell, tenor c to G, 44 Notes.

	Feet.	Pipes.		Feet.	Pipes.
25. Open Diapason, metal	8	44	30. Tierce, metal.		
26. Stopped Diapason, wood	8	44	31. Trumpet, metal	8	44
27. Principal, metal	4	44	32. Oboe, metal	8	44
28. Twelfth, metal	3	44	33. Clarionette, metal, (octave)	4	44
29. Fifteenth, metal	2	44			

Choir Organ, CC to G in alt., 56 Notes.

	Feet.	Pipes.		Feet.	Pipes.
34. Dulciana, metal	8	56	38. Stopped Flute, metal	4	56
35. Gamba, metal	8	56	39. Piccolo, wood	2	56
36. Stopped Diapason, wood	8	56	40. Clarionette and Bassoon, metal	8	56
37. Flute Harmonique, metal	4	56			

Pedal Organ, CCC to G.

	Feet.	Pipes.		Feet.	Pipes.
41. Grand Open Diapason, wood	16	30	43. Bourdon, wood	16	30
42. Violone, wood	16	30	44. Principal, metal	8	30

The old Echo Swell has been preserved intact, although a few of the stops might have been advantageously cancelled for new ones.

296. COLSTON HALL, BRISTOL.

The instrument consists of 4 sets of Manuals, from CC to C in alt., 61 notes, and concave and radiating Pedals, from CCC to G, 32 notes.

Great Organ.

1. Grand Double Diapason........ 16 feet.	7. Quint............................... 3 feet.
2. Open Diapason .... 8 feet.	8. Super-octave .... 2 feet.
3. Open Diapason .... 8 feet.	9. Fourniture, IV ranks.
4. Violoncello .... 8 feet.	10. Trombone........................... 16 feet.
5. Flute Harmonique .... 8 feet.	11. Tromba Harmonic .... 8 feet.
6. Octave .... 4 feet.	12. Clarion .... 4 feet.

Swell.

13. Contra Gamba .... 16 feet.	20. Echo Cornet, III ranks.
14. Salicional .... 8 feet.	21. Contra Posaune .... 16 feet.
15. Open Diapason .... 8 feet.	22. Cornopean .... 8 feet.
16. Lieblich Gedact .... 8 feet.	23. Hautboy .... 8 feet.
17. Vox Angelica .... 8 feet.	24. Clarionet .... 8 feet.
18. Principal .... 4 feet.	25. Vox Humana .... 8 feet.
19. Fifteenth .... 2 feet.	26. Clarion .... 4 feet.

Choir.

27. Dulciana .... 8 feet.	32. Flageolet .... 2 feet.
28. Lieblich Gedact .... 8 feet.	33. Corno di Bassetto .... 8 feet.
29. Claribel Flute .... 8 feet.	34. Bassoon............................ 8 feet.
30. Violoncello .... 8 feet.	35. Posaune............................ 8 feet.
31. Flute Octaviante Harmonique 4 feet.	

Solo.

36. Flute Harmonique .... 8 feet.	40. Corno di Bassetto .... 8 feet.
37. Concert Flute .... 4 feet.	41. Oboe (Orchestral) .... 8 feet.
38. Viol di Gamba.................... 8 feet.	42. Tuba Major Harmonic .... 8 feet.
39. Violin .... 4 feet.	43. Clarion .... 4 feet.

Pedal.

44. Double Diapason, wood........ 32 feet.	49. Octave, wood .... 8 feet.
45. Open Diapason, wood .... 16 feet.	50. Mixture, III ranks.
46. Violone, metal.................... 16 feet.	51. Grand Bombard .... 16 feet.
47. Bourdon, wood .... 16 feet.	52. Contra Posaune } Prepared { 32 feet.
48. Violoncello, metal .... 8 feet.	53. Clarion .... } for only { 8 feet.

Accessories, &c.

1. Solo to Great.	6. Solo to Pedals.
2. Swell to Great, Sub-octave on itself.	7. Swell to Pedals.
3. Swell to Great, Unison.	8. Great to Pedals.
4. Swell to Great, Super-octave on itself.	9. Choir to Pedals.
5. Choir to Great.	

Tremulant to Vox Humana Swell.

The patent atmospheric combinations movement is applied in 4 changes to each of the Manuals. Four Pedals acting on those of the Great organ also affect the Pedal organ, and adapt it to the power then obtained in the Great organ. Four Pedals act on the Couplers, as Composition Pedals act on ordinary stops. A double acting Pedal produces a *pp* effect, even when the *tutti* Pedal is arranged.

The Swell and Great organs are played through the agency of the pneumatic lever. The wind is supplied from bellows placed in a chamber beneath the organ and blown by means of two hydraulic engines. These bellows draw their air down from an altitud esomewhat above the pipes in the organ ; the wind thus obtained then passes into numerous reservoirs peculiarly constructed to obtain absolute steadiness, and from them passes to the various sections of the wind chests at suitable pressures for the different variety of stops ; the wind chests being furnished with the patent prize medal valves of 1862.

297. BRISTOL CATHEDRAL.

The old organ was built by Renatus Harris in 1685. Upon its removal (on the re-building of the present organ) it was found to be completely worn out and worm-eaten. Upon the restoration of the Cathedral, the present organ was erected in the north aisle. The inside wood-work was entirely renewed. The wood pipes were retained, as also the front pipes, which are of pure tin, and formed the two Open Diapasons of the Great organ from GG to middle C, and the lowest octave of the two Principals. With the exception of the above, and the Trumpet and Clarion of the Great organ, the whole of the other part was renewed, but the old metal was used as far as possible. The whole of the metal pipes are spotted metal. The present organ was re-built by Mr. W. G. Vowles, of Bristol, in 1861.

Great, 12 Stops, GG to G.

1. Open Diapason (large scale).	7. Twelfth.
2. Open Diapason (small scale).	8. Fifteenth.
3. Clarabella to Gamut G.	9. Sesquialtera, IV ranks.
4. Stopped Diapason.	10. Mixture, II ranks.
5. Principal.	11. Trumpet.
6. Principal.	12. Clarion.

Choir, 7 Stops, GG to G.

13. Stopped Diapason.	17. Principal.
14. Dulciana to Gamut G.	18. Piccolo, wood.
15. Viol di Gamba to Gamut G.	19. Cremona to tenor c.
16. Flute.	

Swell, 11 Stops, Gamut G to G.

20. Double Dulciana.	26. Fifteenth.
21. Open Diapason.	27. Mixture, II ranks.
22. Stopped Diapason.	28. Cornopean.
23. Harmonic Flute.	29. Trumpet.
24. Principal.	30. Hautboy.
25. Twelfth.	

Pedal, 3 Stops, CCC to F.

31. Open Diapason, wood. | 32, Bourdon, wood. | 33. Principal, metal.

Couplers.

1. Swell to Choir.	5. Pedals to Great, Unison.
2. Swell to Great, Unison.	6. Pedals to Great, Octaves.
3. Swell to Great, Octaves.	7. Pedal organ in Octaves.
4. Pedals to Choir.	

Composition Pedals.

3 to the Great organ.	2 acting on the Couplers and Pedal
5 to the Swell organ.	organ Draw-Stops.

The old case, which is very richly carved (said to be the work of Grinling Gibbons), has been carefully preserved and adapted to the enlarged instrument. The Choir organ case, at the back of the organist, is entirely new, and, being of Gothic design, contrasts strangely with the old organ case.

298. LLANDAFF CATHEDRAL.

This organ was built by Gray and Davison in 1857. It consists of 3 Manuals CC to F, and Pedals, CCC to E.

Great Organ.

1. Bourdon	16 feet.	6. Harmonic Flute	4 feet.
2. Open Diapason	8 feet.	7. Twelfth	3 feet.
3. Gamba	8 feet.	8. Fifteenth	2 feet.
4. Stopped Diapason	8 feet.	9. Mixture, IV ranks.	
5. Principal	4 feet.	10. Trumpet	8 feet.

Swell Organ.

11. Double Diapason	16 feet.	16. Fifteenth	2 feet.
12. Open Diapason	8 feet.	17. Mixture, II ranks.	
13. Keraulophon	8 feet.	18. Cornopean	8 feet.
14. Stopped Diapason	8 feet.	19. Oboe	8 feet.
15. Principal	4 feet.	20. Clarion	4 feet.

Choir Organ.

21. Double Diapason	16 feet.	26. Gemshorn	4 feet.
22. Spitz Flute	8 feet.	27. Flute	4 feet.
23. Dulciana	8 feet.	28. Piccolo	2 feet.
24. Stopped Diapason, Bass	8 feet.	29. Clarinet, tenor c	8 feet.
25. Clarinet Flute	8 feet.		

Pedal Organ.

30. Open Diapason	16 feet.	32. Principal	8 feet.
31. Bourdon	16 feet.	33. Trombone	16 feet.

Couplers.

1. Swell to Great Manual.	4. Great to Pedals.
2. Swell to Choir Manual.	5. Choir to Pedals.
3. Swell to Pedals.	

4 Composition Pedals to Great ; 2 Composition Pedals to Swell.

299. EXETER CATHEDRAL.

The organ made by John Loosemore, in 1665, has recently undergone considerable alteration at the hands of Mr. Speechly, who has put in new Choir and Swell organs. The original Great organ sound-board, the large double metal pipes, and the handsome old case, are still retained. The organ now contains 31 sounding stops, of which the following is a list :—

Great Organ, Compass GG to F, 58 Notes (no G♯).

	Feet.		Pipes.		Feet.		Pipes
1. Double Diapason, wood and metal	16	...	58	7. Flute Harmonique, metal	4	...	58
				8. Twelfth, metal	2⅔	...	58
2. Open Diapason, metal	8	...	58	9. Fifteenth, metal	2	...	58
3. Open Diapason, metal	8	...	58	10. *Mixture, 11 ranks, metal	various		110
4. Stopped Diapason, wood and metal	8	...	58	11. *Mixture, III ranks, metal	various		174
5. Clarabella, wood	8	...		* Formerly one stop.			
6. Principal, metal	4	...	58	12. Trumpet, metal	8	...	58
				13. Clarion, metal	4	...	58

Swell Organ, Compass CC to F, 54 Notes (prepared, CC to G, 56 Notes).

		Feet.	Pipes.			Feet.	Pipes.
14.	Double Diapason, wood...	16	... 54	18.	Octave, metal	4	... 54
15.	Open Diapason, metal......	8	... 54	19.	Mixture, III ranks, metal, various		162
16.	Stopped Diapason, wood			20.	Cornopean, metal	8	... 54
	and metal	8	... 54	21.	Oboe, metal................	8	... 54
17.	Salicional, metal	8	... 42	22.	Clarion, metal...............	4	... 54

Choir Organ, Compass CC to F, 54 Notes (prepared, CC to G, 56 Notes).

		Feet.	Pipes.			Feet.	Pipes.
23.	Gamba, metal	8	... 54	26.	Wald Flute, wood	4	... 54
24.	Lieblich Gedact, wood and			27.	Gemshorn, metal............	4	... 54
	metal	8	... 54	28.	Corno di Bassetto, metal	8	... 54
25.	Dulciana, metal	8	... 54				

Pedal Organ, Compass of Pipes GGG to F (35), G♯ added.

Compass of Pedals CCC to F, 30 Notes.

29.	Open Diapason, metal......	32	... 35	31.	Bourdon, wood	16	... 30
30.	Open Diapason, from No.						
	1, metal....................	16	... 30				

Couplers, &c.

1. Swell to Pedal.	4. Choir to Pedal.
2. Great to Pedal, GG.	5. Swell to Great.
3. Great to Pedal, CC.	6. Swell to Choir.

4 Composition Pedals to the Great organ.
4 Composition Pedals to the Swell organ.
A double action Pedal for governing the Great to Pedal Coupler.

300. St. Jude's, Southsea.

This organ was built by Gray and Davison in 1872. It consists of 3 Manuals, from CC to G, and Pedals, from CCC to F.

Great Organ.

1.	Double Diapason............	16 feet.	7.	Twelfth	3 feet.
2.	Open Diapason	8 feet.	8.	Fifteenth	2 feet.
3.	Gamba	8 feet.	9.	Mixture, III ranks.	
4.	Stopped Diapason	8 feet.	10.	Trumpet	8 feet.
5.	Harmonic Flute	4 feet.	11.	Clarion	4 feet.
6.	Principal	4 feet.			

Swell Organ.

12.	Double Diapason............	16 feet.	18.	Sesquialtera, III ranks.	
13.	Open Diapason	8 feet.	19.	Cornopean	8 feet.
14.	Keraulophon	8 feet.	20.	Oboe	8 feet.
15.	Stopped Diapason	8 feet.	21.	Clarion	4 feet.
16.	Principal	4 feet.		Tremulant.	
17.	Fifteenth	2 feet.			

Choir Organ.

22.	Dulciana	8 feet.	26.	Suabe Flute	4 feet.
23.	Viol di Gamba..............	8 feet.	27.	Flageolet....................	2 feet.
24.	Lieblich Gedact	8 feet.	28.	Corno di Bassetto	8 feet.
25.	Gemshorn	4 feet.			

Pedal Organ.

29. Open Diapason .... 16 feet.	31. Principal .... 8 feet.
30. Bourdon .... 16 feet.	32. Trombone .... 16 feet.

Couplers.

1. Swell to Great Manual.	4. Great Manual to Pedals.
2. Swell to Choir Manual.	5. Choir Manual to Pedals.
3. Swell Manual to Pedals.	

4 Composition Pedals to Great ; 4 Composition Pedals to Swell.

Some of the pipes, re-voiced, have been retained.

301. ST. JOHN'S CHURCH, MARGATE.

This organ was built by Gray and Davison in 1876. It has three Manuals, CC to G, Pedals, from CCC to F, and contains the following stops :—

Great Organ.

1. Double Diapason .... 16 feet.	8. Twelfth .... 3 feet.
2. Open Diapason .... 8 feet.	9. Fifteenth.......................... 2 feet.
3. Gamba .... 8 feet.	10. Sesquialtera, III ranks.
4. Stopped Diapason.................. 8 feet.	11. Mixture, II ranks.
5. Clarinet Flute .... 8 feet.	12. Trumpet .... 8 feet.
6. Principal........................... 4 feet.	13. Clarion .... 4 feet.
7. Flute Harmonic..................... 4 feet.	

Swell Organ.

14. Lieblich Bourdon .... 16 feet.	19. Fifteenth............................ 2 feet.
15. Open Diapason .... 8 feet.	20. Mixture, III ranks.
16. Keraulophon .... 8 feet.	21. Oboe .... 8 feet.
17. Stopped Diapason.................. 8 feet.	22. Cornopean .... 8 feet.
18. Principal........................... 4 feet.	23. Clarion .... 4 feet.

Choir Organ.

24. Open Diapason .... 8 feet.	28. Flute .... 4 feet.
25. Dulciana .... 8 feet.	29. Flageolet .... 2 feet.
26. Lieblich Gedact .... 8 feet.	30. Corno di Bassetto .... 8 feet.
27. Gemshorn .... 4 feet.	

Pedal Organ.

31. Grand Open Diapason .... 16 feet.	33. Violoncello .... 8 feet.
32. Grand Bourdon .... 16 feet.	34. Trombone .... 16 feet.

Couplers.

1. Swell to Great Manual.	5. Great Manual to Pedals.
2. Swell Manual to Pedals.	6. Choir Manual to Pedals.
3. Swell Octave.	7. Pedal Octave.
4. Swell to Choir Manual.	

4 Composition Pedals to the Great and Pedal Organ, and 3 to the Swell.

302. BRIGHTON.

The instrument in the Great Concert Hall, built by Bryceson and Co., has four complete Manuals, compass CC to A, 58 notes, viz., Solo, Swell, Great, and Choir organs, also an independent Pedal organ, CCC to F, 30 notes, the largest pipe being CCCC, 32 feet. The Great organ and Manual Couplers are played by means of the pneumatic apparatus. The Combination Pedals also act by pneumatic power. The bellows supply three pressures of wind. The case is of Italian design, introducing ornamental wrought ironwork, and 16 feet metal pipes, arranged in two towers; a double tier of 8 feet pipes, and projecting trumpets, forming the centre front. The front pipes are richly decorated with gold and colours. Dimensions, 37 feet high, 25 feet wide, and 16 feet deep. The necessary atmospheric temperature for tuning and maintaining *band pitch* is secured by the introduction of a self-regulating high-pressure hot-water apparatus (Perkins's patent) placed beneath the organ especially for this purpose.

Solo, 6 Stops.

		Pipes.	Feet.			Pipes.	Feet.
1.	Corno Dolce, metal	58	8	4. Orchestral Oboe and Bassoon, metal		58	8
2.	Orchestral Flute, metal	58	4	5. Tromba (Harmonic), metal		58	8
3.	Corno di Bassetto, metal	58	8	6. Clarion, metal		58	4

Swell, 14 Stops.

		Pipes.	Feet.			Pipes.	Feet.
7.	Bourdon and Double Diapason, wood	58	16	14. Twelfth and Fifteenth, metal		116	3 & 2
8.	Open Diapason, metal	58	8	15. Mixture (19, 22), metal		116	
9.	Viola, wood and metal	58	8	16. Double Trumpet, metal		58	16
10.	Rohrflote, wood and metal	58	8	17. Voix Humane, metal		58	8
11.	Principal, metal	58	4	18. Cornopean, metal		58	8
12.	Echo Flute, metal	58	4	19. Oboe, metal		58	8
13.	Flageolet, metal	58	2	20. Clarion, metal		58	4

(Tremulant acting on Swell.)

Great, 12 Stops.

		Pipes.	Feet.			Pipes.	Feet.
21.	Double Open Diapason wood and metal	58	16	27. Waldflote, wood and metal		58	4
22.	Great Open Diapason, metal	58	8	28. Twelfth, metal		58	3
23.	Violin Open Diapason, metal	58	8	29. Fifteenth, metal		58	2
24.	Hohlflote, wood and metal	58	8	30. Mixture (19, 22), metal		116	
25.	Salicional, wood and metal	58	8	31. Trumpet, metal		58	8
26.	Principal, metal	58	4	32. Clarion, metal		58	4

Choir, 8 Stops.

		Pipes.	Feet.			Pipes.	Feet.
33.	Dulciana, metal	58	8	37. Harmonic Flute, metal		58	4
34.	Flauto Traverso, metal	58	8	38. Stopped Flute, metal		58	4
35.	Voix Céleste, metal	58	8	39. Harmonic Piccolo, metal		58	2
36.	Lieblich Gedact, wood and metal	58	8	40. Clarionet and Bassoon, metal		58	8

Pedal, 9 Stops.

		Pipes.	Feet.			Pipes.	Feet.
41.	Sub-bass, wood	30	32	46. Flute, wood		30	8
42.	Open Diapason, wood	30	16	47. Bombarde, metal		30	32
43.	Violon, metal	30	16	48. Trombone, metal		30	16
44.	Bourdon, wood	30	16	49. Trumpet, metal		30	8
45.	Violoncello, metal	30	8				

Couplers.

1. Super-solo to Choir.		9. Choir to Great.
2. Sub-solo to Choir.		10. Solo to Pedals.
3. Solo to Choir.		11. Swell to Pedals.
4. Solo to Great.		12. Great to Pedals.
5. Super-swell to Great.		13. Choir to Pedals.
6. Sub-swell to Great.		14.
7. Swell to Great.		15.
8. Swell to Choir.		

Summary.

	Stops.		Pipes.
Solo Organ	6		348
Swell Organ	14		928
Great Organ	12		754
Choir Organ	8		464
Pedal Organ	9		270
Couplers	15		
Total	64		2764

4 Combination Pedals to Swell Organ.
4 Combination Pedals to Great Organ.

4 Combination Pedals to Pedal Organ.
4 Combination Pedals to Couplers.

303. BRIGHTON.

The organ in the Concert Room of the Dome Pavilion, Brighton, was built by Mr. Henry Willis. It has 4 complete Manuals, from CC to A, 58 notes, and two octaves and a half of Pedals, from CCC to F, 30 notes.

Solo Organ, 6 Stops.

1. Tuba Major Harmonic	8 feet.		4. Oboe	8 feet.
2. Clarion	4 feet.		5. Concert Flute	8 feet.
3. Clarionet	8 feet.		6. Flute Octaviante	4 feet.

Swell Organ, 12 Stops.

7. Salicional	16 feet.		13. Mixture.	
8. Salicional	8 feet.		14. Contra Posaune	16 feet.
9. Open Diapason	8 feet.		15. Cornopean	8 feet.
10. Lieblich Gedact	8 feet.		16. Hautboy	8 feet.
11. Principal	4 feet.		17. Vox Humana	8 feet.
12. Flageolet	2 feet.		18. Clarion	4 feet.

Great Organ, 11 Stops.

19. Double Open Diapason	16 feet.		25. Quint Octaviante	3 feet.
20. Open Diapason	8 feet.		26. Super-octave	2 feet.
21. Open Diapason	8 feet.		27. Furniture.	
22. Viola	8 feet.		28. Bombard Harmonic	8 feet.
23. Claribel Flute	8 feet.		29. Clarion Harmonic	4 feet.
24. Principal	4 feet.			

Choir Organ, 9 Stops.

30. Viol di Gamba	8 feet.		35. Flute Dolce	4 feet.
31. Dulciana	8 feet.		36. Flageolet	2 feet.
32. Vox Angelica	8 feet.		37. Viola	4 feet.
33. Flute Harmonique	8 feet.		38. Corno di Bassetto	8 feet.
34. Gemshorn	4 feet.			

Pedal Organ, 6 Stops.

39. Double Diapason	32 feet.	42. Octave		8 feet.
40. Open Diapason	16 feet.	43. Furniture.		
41. Bourdon	16 feet.	44. Ophicleide		16 feet.

Couplers.

1. Swell to Great, Super-octave.
2. Swell to Great, Unison.
3. Swell to Great, Sub-octave.
4. Swell to Pedals.
5. Solo to Pedals.

6. Great to Pedals.
7. Choir to Pedals.
8. Choir to Great.
9. Solo to Great.
10. Tremulant.

The wind is supplied by two hydraulic engines.

304. ST. MARGARET'S CHURCH, BRIGHTON.

This organ was built by Gray and Davison in the year 1874. It contains 31 stops, which are distributed among 3 Manuals and Pedal in the following manner. The blowing is by hydraulic power.

Great Organ.

1. Double Diapason	16 feet.	7. Quint		$2\frac{2}{3}$ feet.
2. Open Diapason	8 feet.	8. Super Octave		2 feet.
3. Gamba	8 feet.	9. Mixture, IV ranks		
4. Clarionet Flute	8 feet.	10. Trumpet		8 feet.
5. Octave	4 feet.	11. Clarion		4 feet.
6. Harmonic Flute	4 feet.			

Swell Organ.

12. Lieblich Bourdon	16 feet.	18. Mixture, II ranks.		
13. Open Diapason	8 feet.	19. Cornopean		8 feet.
14. Keraulophon	8 feet.	20. Oboe		8 feet.
15. Concert Flute	4 feet.	21. Clarion		4 feet.
16. Octave	4 feet.		Tremulant.	
17. Octavina	2 feet.			

Choir Organ.

22. Dulciana	8 feet.	25. Suabe Flute		4 feet.
23. Viol di Gamba	8 feet.	26. Flageolet		2 feet.
24. Lieblich Gedact	8 feet.	27. Clarinet		8 feet.

Pedal Organ.

28. Grand Open Diapason	16 feet.	30. Quint		12 feet.
29. Grand Bourdon	16 feet.	31. Violon		8 feet.

Couplers.

1. Swell to Great Manual.
2. Swell to Choir Manual.
3. Swell Manual to Pedals.
4. Great Manual to Pedals.

5. Choir Manual to Pedals.
6. Swell Octave on its own Manual.
7. Choir Sub-octave on its own Manual.
8. Pedal Octave.

Composition Pedals.

3 to Great. | 3 to Swell.

305. MAGDALEN COLLEGE.

The new organ in Magdalen College Chapel, Oxford, was built by Gray and Davison, and completed in the early part of 1855. It contains 35 sounding stops, distributed among 4 Manuals and Pedals in the following manner :—

Great, 10 Stops.

1. Open Diapason	8 feet.	6. Twelfth .... 3 feet.
2. Open Diapason	8 feet.	7. Super-octave .... 2 feet.
3. Stopped Diapason	8 feet.	8. Sesquialtera, III ranks.
4. Octave	4 feet.	9. Mixture, II ranks.
5. Flute	4 feet.	10. Posaune .... 8 feet.

Choir, 8 Stops.

11. Salicional	8 feet.	15. Octave...................... 4 feet.
12. Gamba	8 feet.	16. Flute d'Amour .... 4 feet.
13. Stopped Diapason, Bass...	8 feet.	17. Piccolo .... 2 feet.
14. Concert Flute	8 feet.	18. Corno di Bassetto .... 8 feet.

Swell, 11 Stops.

19. Bourdon	16 feet.	25. Super-octave .... 2 feet.
20. Open Diapason	8 feet.	26. Sesquialtera, III ranks.
21. Stopped Diapason, Bass...	8 feet.	27. Cornopean .... 8 feet.
22. Clarionet Flute	8 feet.	28. Oboe .... 8 feet.
23. Keraulophon	8 feet.	29. Clarion .... 4 feet.
24. Octave...	4 feet.	

Solo, 2 Stops.

30. Flute Harmonique	8 feet.	31. Tromba .... 8 feet.

Pedal, 4 Stops.

32. Grand Open Diapason ...	16 feet.	34. Grand Octave............... 8 feet.
33. Grand Bourdon	16 feet.	35. Trand Trombone .... 16 feet.

Accessory Stops, Movements, &c.

1. Swell to Great Manual.	8. Swell to Great Super-octave.
2. Swell to Choir Manual.	9. Solo to Swell Manual.
3. Swell Manual to Pedals.	10. Tremulant Swell.
4. Great Manual to Pedals.	11 to 16. Six Composition Pedals.
5. Choir Manual to Pedals.	17 and 18. Two Pedals for taking on and
6. Choir Sub-octave to Great Manual.	off the Coupling Stops.
7. Swell to Great Sub-octave.	19. Pneumatic Lever attachment.

There are several reservoirs, producing different weights of wind; and the increasing pressure system has been applied to the Great organ. The Solo organ is also voiced to a heavy weight of wind. To prevent the numerous Couplers disagreeably affecting the touch, the pneumatic apparatus is applied to the Great organ Manual and all that it affects.

306. KEBLE COLLEGE, OXFORD.

The organ in the Chapel of this College was erected by Messrs. Hill and Son in 1876. It contains three Manuals, a separate Pedal, and 30 stops, of which latter the following is a list :—

Great Organ, 10 Stops.

1. Double Diapason...,.........	16 feet.	6. Wald Flute .... 4 feet.
2. Open Diapason	8 feet.	7. Twelfth .... 3 feet.
3. Open Diapason	8 feet.	8. Fifteenth .... 2 feet.
4. Stopped Diapason	8 feet.	9. Mixture, III ranks.
5. Principal	4 feet.	10. Trumpet .... 8 feet.

Choir Organ, 7 Stops.

11. Gamba	8 feet.	15. Suabe Flute .... 4 feet.
12. Dulciana	8 feet.	16. Flautina .... 2 feet.
13. Gedact	8 feet.	17. Clarionet .... 8 feet.
14. Gemshorn.....................	4 feet.	

Swell Organ, 10 Stops.

18. Bourdon	16 feet.	23. Lieblich Flute .... 4 feet.
19. Open Diapason	8 feet.	24. Fifteenth .... 2 feet.
20. Salicional	8 feet.	25. Mixture .... 2 feet.
21. Hohlflote	8 feet.	26. Cornopean .... 8 feet.
22. Principal	4 feet.	27. Oboe .... 8 feet.

Pedal Organ, 3 Stops.

28. Open Diapason	16 feet.	30. Violoncello .... 8 feet.
29. Bourdon	16 feet.	

Couplers, &c.

5 Composition Pedals.

Compass.

Manual, CC to G³, 56 notes. | Pedals, CCC to tenor f, 30 notes.

307. CHRIST CHURCH CATHEDRAL, OXFORD.

This organ was built by Gray and Davison in 1870. It consists of 3 Manuals, CC to G, and Pedals, from CCC to F.

Great Organ.

1. Open Diapason	8 feet.	6. Fifteenth .... 2 feet.
2. Open Diapason	8 feet.	7. Sesquialtera, III ranks.
3. Stopped Diapason	8 feet.	8. Mixture, II ranks.
4. Principal	4 feet.	9. Trumpet .... 8 feet.
5. Twelfth........................	3 feet.	

Choir Organ.

10. Dulciana	8 feet.	13. Flute .... 4 feet.
11. Stopped Diapason	8 feet.	14. Cremona .... 8 feet.
12. Principal	4 feet.	

Swell Organ.

15. Double Diapason .... 16 feet.	20. Fifteenth .... 2 feet.
16. Open Diapason .... 8 feet.	21. Mixture, II ranks.
17. Keraulophon .... 8 feet.	22. Cornopean .... 8 feet.
18. Stopped Diapason .... 8 feet.	23. Oboe .... 8 feet.
19. Principal .... 4 feet.	24. Clarion .... 4 feet.

Pedal Organ.

25. Grand Open Diapason ... 16 feet.	27. Grand Principal .... 8 feet.
26. Grand Bourdon .... 16 feet.	28. Grand Trombone .... 16 feet.

Couplers.

1. Swell to Great Manual.	4. Choir Manual to Pedals.
2. Swell to Choir Manual.	5. Great Manual to Pedals.
3. Swell Manual to Pedals.	

4 Composition Pedals to Great; 2 to Swell.

Some of the pipes of the former organ, by Father Schmidt and Case, have been retained.

308. RADLEY.

The organ in St. Peter's College, Radley, near Oxford, was built by Messrs. Telford, of Dublin. It consists of 3 complete Manuals, an independent Pedal of 10 stops, and 47 sounding stops, of which the following is a list :—

Great, 16 Stops.

1. Double Open Diapason, metal .... 16 feet.	8. Tenth, metal .... 3½ feet.
2. Open Diapason, Great, metal .... 8 feet.	9. Twelfth, metal .... 2⅔ feet.
3. Open Diapason, small, metal .... 8 feet.	10. Fifteenth, metal........... 2 feet.
4. Stopped Diapason, wood 8 feet tone.	11. Octave Flute, wood ...... 2 feet.
5. Quint, metal................... 5½ feet.	12. Sesquialtera, metal, IV ranks.
6. Principal, Great, metal ... 4 feet.	13. Mixture, metal, III ranks.
7. Principal, small, metal ... 4 feet.	14. Double Trumpet, metal 16 feet.
	15. Trumpet, metal .... 8 feet.
	16. Clarion, metal .... 4 feet.

Choir, 8 Stops.

17. Stopped Diapason, wood 8 feet tone.	21. Wald Flute, wood .... 4 feet.
18. Dulciana, metal .... 8 feet.	22. Fifteenth, metal .... 2 feet.
19. Viol di Gamba, metal...... 8 feet.	23. Mixture, metal .... 1½ foot.
20. Principal, metal .... 4 feet.	24. Cremona, metal........... 8 feet.

Swell, 13 Stops.

25. Double Diapason, metal and wood................. 16 feet.	31. Twelfth, metal .... 2⅔ feet.
26. Open Diapason, metal ... 8 feet.	32. Fifteenth, metal........... 2 feet.
27. Dulciana, metal .... 8 feet.	33. Twenty-second, metal ... 1 foot.
28. Stopped Diapason, wood 8 feet tone	34. Sesquialtera, metal, III ranks.
29. Principal, metal .... 4 feet.	35. Cornet (Dulciana), metal, III ranks.
30. Principal, small, metal ... 4 feet.	36. Trumpet, metal .... 8 feet.
	37. Oboe, metal .... 8 feet.

Pedal, 10 Stops.

38. Double Double Open Diapason, wood .... 32 feet.	42. Principal, metal........... 4 feet.
39. Double Open Diapason, wood...................... 16 feet.	43. Twelfth, metal .... 2⅔ feet.
40. Double Open Diapason, metal...:.................... 16 feet.	44. Fifteenth, metal........... 2 feet.
41. Open Diapason, metal ... 8 feet.	45. Sesquialtera, metal, IV ranks.
	46. Double Trumpet, metal 16 feet.
	47. Trumpet, metal .... 8 feet.

Accessory Stops, Movements, &c.

1. Coupler, Swell to Great.
2. Coupler, Swell to Choir.
3. Coupler, Swell to Pedal.

4. Coupler, Great to Pedal.
5 to 10. Six Composition Pedals.

Compass.

Great, CC to g³ in altissimo.
Choir, CC to g³ in altissimo.

Swell, CC to g³ in altissimo.
Pedal, CCC to fiddle g.

309. HENLEY-ON-THAMES.

The organ in the Church at Henley-on-Thames was built by Mr. Holdich in 1854. It contains 36 sounding stops, of which the following is a list :—

Great, 12 *Stops.*

1. Large Open Diapason...... 8 feet.	7. Fifteenth .... 2 feet.
2. Open Diapason .... 8 feet.	8. Tierce .... 1⅗ foot.
3. Clarabella Treble, and	9. Sesqualtera.................. 1⅓ foot.
Stopped Diapason, Bass 8 feet.	10. Mixture .... ½ foot.
4. Principal .... 4 feet.	11. Trumpet .... 8 feet.
5. Flute........................... 4 feet.	12. Clarion .... 4 feet.
6. Twelfth .... 2⅔ feet.	

Choir, 8 *Stops.*

13. Dulciana .... 8 feet.	17. Flute .... 4 feet.
14. Clarabella.................... 8 feet.	18. Fifteenth .... 2 feet.
15. Stopped Diapason, Bass... 8 feet.	19. Piccolo....................... 2 feet.
16. Principal .... 4 feet.	20. Cremona..................... 8 feet tone.

Swell, 12 *Stops.*

21. Double Diapason........... 16 feet.	28. Tierce .... 1⅗ foot.
22. Bourdon .... 16 feet.	29. Sesqualtera .... 1⅓ foot.
23. Open Diapason .... 8 feet.	30. Double Trumpet .... 16 feet.
24. Stopped Diapason .... 8 feet.	31. Cornopean .... 8 feet.
25. Viol di Gamba.............. 8 feet.	32. Hautboy .... 8 feet.
26. Principal .... 4 feet.	Diaocton.
27. Fifteenth .... 2 feet.	

Pedal, 4 *Stops.*

33. Grand Double Diapason... 16 feet.	35. Grand Principal .... 8 feet.
34. Grand Bourdon .... 16 feet.	36. Grand Trombone .... 16 feet.

Compass.

Manuals, CC to f³ in alt. | Pedal, down to CCC.

310. BEDDINGTON CHURCH, SURREY.

This organ is a very handsome and costly structure, built by Messrs. Thomas C. Lewis & Co., of Shepherd's Lane, Brixton, London. It is most skilfully planned in every detail ; the case is well designed by Mr. Joseph Clark, and is decorated and illuminated in a highly artistic and elaborate manner by Morris Marshall & Co., of Queen Square, Bloomsbury.

Choir, 5 *Stops, CC to G,* 56 *Notes.*

1. Lieblich Gedact, wood and metal .... 8 feet.	3. Salicet .... 4 feet.
2. Salicional .... 8 feet.	4. Flute Harmonique........ 4 feet.
	5. Clarionet and Bassoon ... 8 feet.

Great, 8 Stops.

6. Bourdon, wood and metal	16 feet.	10. Octave Quint	2⅓ feet.
7. Open Diapason	8 feet.	11. Super-octave	2 feet.
8. Rohrflote, wood and metal	8 feet.	12. Mixture, III ranks.........	2 feet.
9. Octave	4 feet.	13. Trumpet	8 feet.

Swell Organ, 9 Stops.

14. Lieblich Gedact, wood and metal	16 feet.	18. Voix Célestes, tenor c ...	8 feet.
15. Geigen Principal............	8 feet.	19. Geigen Principal	4 feet.
16. Lieblich Gedact, wood and metal	8 feet.	20. Mixture, II ranks	2⅓ feet.
		21. Trumpet	8 feet.
17. Gamba	8 feet.	22. Oboe and Bassoon.........	8 feet.

Pedal, 5 Stops, CCC to F, 30 Notes (42 Notes to each Stop).

23. Open Diapason, metal and zinc	16 feet.	25. Quint, wood	10⅔ feet.
24. Sub-bass, wood	16 feet.	26. Posaune, metal	16 feet.
		27. Octave Coupler.	

Couplers, &c.

1. Choir to Pedals. | 2. Great to Pedals. | 3. Swell to Pedals. | 4. Swell to Great.

5 Pedals of Combination and Tremulant.

The bellows is placed in a chamber beneath the organ, the feeders are worked by two three-throw crank axles, with which fly-wheels are connected; there is also a distinct air reservoir, communicating directly with the Manual sound-boards, obviating the necessity for the ordinary concussion bellows. The metal pipes are all of fine spotted metal.

311. St. Asaph's Cathedral.

This organ was built by Hill in 1834. In 1859 additions and improvements to the organ, under the superintendence of the organist, Mr. Robert Augustus Atkins, were carried out by Hill and Son, much to the satisfaction of the Dean and Chapter.

Great, 11 Stops, GG to F in alt.

1. Open Diapason	8 feet.	7. Wald Flute.................	4 feet.
2. Open Diapason	8 feet.	8. Twelfth	3 feet.
3. Gamba	8 feet.	9. Fifteenth	2 feet.
4. Stopped Diapason	8 feet.	10. Sesquialtera, III ranks.	
5. Principal	4 feet.	11. Trumpet	8 feet.
6. Nason Flute..................	4 feet.		

Choir, 6 Stops, GG to F in alt.

12. Open Diapason	8 feet.	15. Principal	4 feet.
13. Stopped Diapason	8 feet.	16. Suabe Flute ,...............	4 feet.
14. Viol di Gamba...............	8 feet.	17. Cromorne	8 feet.

Swell, 10 *Stops, tenor c to F in alt.*

18. Double Diapason............ 16 feet.		23. Fifteenth .... 2 feet.	
19. Open Diapason .... 8 feet.		24. Mixture, III ranks.	
20. Vox Angelica, II ranks ... 8 feet.		25. Cornopean .... 8 feet.	
21. Stopped Diapason .... 8 feet.		26. Oboe .... 8 feet.	
22. Principal .... 4 feet.		27. Tremulant.	

Pedal, 2 Stops.

28. Open Diapason .... 16 feet. | 29. Bourdon .... 16 feet tone.

Couplers.

1. Swell to Great. | 2. Great to Pedals. | 3. Choir to Pedals.

312. ST. DAVID'S CATHEDRAL.

The organ in St. David's Cathedral was originally built by Father Schmidt, of whose workmanship (excepting the old oak case) only the Open Metal Diapason pipes remain ; the rest is the production of Mr. Lincoln, and was supplied about twenty-five years ago. The Compass of the Great organ is from CC to F in alt., Mr. Lincoln having added five notes to the original range, which was CC to C in alt.

Of the reeds in the Great organ, the Posaune only is complete ; but the instrument is pierced and ready for the Clarion, although there are as yet no pipes for it. There is no Choir organ, which is a sad defect, as it is so much required in the cathedral service.

Great, 12 Stops.

1. Double Diapason (*i.e.*, Bourdon and Tenoroon).	7. Twelfth.
2. Open Metal Diapason (Schmidt's).	8. Fifteenth.
3. Open Wood Diapason.	9. Sesquialtera, III ranks.
4. Quint.	10. Mixture.
5. Principal.	11. Posaune (very fine).
6. Wald Flute.	12. Clarion (no pipes as yet).

Swell, 9 Stops, from tenor c.

13. Double Diapason.	18. Doublette.
14. Diapason, metal.	19. Cornopean.
15. Diapason, wood.	20. Hautboy.
16. Principal.	21. Clarion.
17. Piccolo.	

Pedal, 1 Stop.

22. Open Diapason from CCC .... 16 feet.

Couplers.

1. Swell to Great. | 2. Pedals to Manuals. | 3. Two octaves of Pedals.

There is a Tremulant to the Swell ; six composition Pedals to the Great organ stops, two for the Swell, and the pneumatic lever for lightening the touch. The last four stops of the Great (the Harmonic flutes and reeds) are placed on a distinct sound-board, and supplied with air at a higher pressure than that allotted to the rest of the Great organ. By a peculiar mechanical arrangement these four stops can be thrown out of connection with the Great organ keys, and placed under the command of the Swell Manual.

313. LANCASTER.

The organ in St. Thomas's Church, Lancaster, was the noble gift of the Rev. Colin Campbell to his church and its congregation. It was built by Banfield, of Birmingham, and is an extensive instrument, consisting of 35 sounding stops, comprising 3 complete Manuals, and an independent Pedal of 4 stops. The organ is enclosed in a very beautiful case of oak, made by Hatch, of Lancaster, from a design by Messrs. Sharpe & Paley, the architects.

The Pedal clavier is made on the radiating principle ; and the doors which close up the organ are furnished with plate-glass panels. The specification of the above-named organ is as follows :—

Great, 11 Stops.

		Pipes.		Feet.
1.	Open Diapason	54	...	8
2.	Open Diapason	54	...	8
3.	Clarabella	54	...	8
4.	Stopped Diapason	54	...	8 tone.
5.	Principal	54	...	4
6.	Twelfth	54	...	2⅔
7.	Fifteenth	54	...	2
8.	Sesquialtera, III ranks	162	...	1⅗
9.	Mixture, II ranks	108	...	⅔
10.	Trumpet	54	...	8
11.	Clarion	54	...	4
		756		

Choir, 9 Stops.

		Pipes.		Feet.
12.	Dulciana, throughout	54	...	8
13.	Keraulophon	42	...	8
14.	Stopped Diapason, Treble	42	...	8 tone.
15.	Stopped Diapason, Bass	12	...	8 tone.
16.	Principal	54	...	4
17.	Celestiana	54	...	4
18.	Flute	54	...	4
19.	Ottevena	54	...	2
20.	Cremona	35	...	8 tone.
		401		

Swell, 11 Stops.

		Pipes.		Feet.
21.	Double Diapason, CCC	54	...	16
22.	Open Diapason	54	...	8
23.	Stopped Diapason	54	...	8 tone.
24.	Principal	54	...	4
25.	Twelfth	54	...	2⅔
26.	Fifteenth	54	...	2
27.	Mixture, III ranks	162	...	1⅗
28.	Horn	54	...	8
29.	Trumpet	54	...	8
30.	Hautboy	54	...	8
31.	Clarion	54	...	10
		702		

Pedal, 4 Stops.

		Pipes.		Feet.
32.	Grand Open Diapason	29	...	16
33.	Grand Bourdon	29	...	16 tone.
34.	Grand Principal	29	...	8
35.	Grand Mixture, III ranks	...		87
				174

Making a total of 2033 pipes.

Couplers.

1. Great organ to Pedals.
2. Choir organ to Pedals.
3. Swell organ to Pedals.
4. Pedal organ in Octaves.
5. Swell to Great,
6. Swell to Choir.
7. Swell and Choir to Great.
8. Great to Swell Sub-octave.
9. Great to Choir Sub-octave.

314. PRESTON.

The organ in Preston Parish Church was originally built by Davis, of London, in 1802, and had a Great organ from GG to F in alt., and a Swell to fiddle g. No Pedals or Pedal pipes—Diagonal Bellows. It has subsequently received several additions, made by Gray and Davison, Jackson, of Liverpool, &c., at the expense of S. Horrocks, Esq., Guild Mayor; W. A. Cross, Esq., of Red Scar. Mr. Greaves, the organist, added the ♯ Twentieth. The organ has now 36 sounding stops, of which the following is a list :—

Great, 16 Stops.

1. Double Diapason, Bass ⎱ in metal.	9. Fifteenth, metal.
2. Double Diapason, Treble. ⎰	10. Fifteenth, wood.
3. Stopped Diapason.	11. Sesquialtera, III ranks.
4. Open Diapason, large scale.	12. Mixture, II ranks.
5. Open Diapason.	13. ♯ Twentieth.
6. Principal, metal.	14. Trumpet, Bass.
7. Principal, wood.	15. Trumpet, Treble.
8. Twelfth.	16. Clarion.

Choir, 7 Stops.

17. Stopped Diapason.	20. Principal.	22. Fifteenth.
18. Clarabella.	21. Flute.	23. Cromorne.
19. Dulciana.		

Swell, 9 Stops.

24. Double Diapason.	27. Keraulophon.	30. Mixture.
25. Stopped Diapason.	28. Principal.	31. Hautboy.
26. Open Diapason.	29. Fifteenth.	32. Cornopean.

Pedal, 4 Stops.

33. Open Diapason .... 16 feet.	35. Fifteenth .... 4 feet.
34. Principal .... 8 feet.	36. Sesquialtera, III ranks.

Accessory Stops, Movements, &c.

1. Coupler, Pedals to Great.	5. Coupler, Octave Coupler Swell.
2. Coupler, Pedals to Choir.	6, 7. Three Composition Pedals for
3. Coupler, Swell to Great.	Great organ stops.
4. Coupler, Choir to Swell.	

Compass.

Great and Choir organs, from CC to f³ in alt. | Swell, from tenor c to f³ in alt.
Pedal, CCC to tenor e.

315. WARRINGTON.

The organ in the Parish Church, Warrington, was built by Gray and Davison in 1876. It consists of 3 Manuals, CC to G, and Pedals, CCC to F, two octaves and a fourth.

Great Organ.

1. Double Open Diapason ... 16 feet.	7. Twelfth .... 3 feet.
2. Open Diapason .... 8 feet.	8. Fifteenth .... 2 feet.
3. Viola .... 8 feet.	9. Furniture, III ranks.
4. Hohlflote .... 8 feet.	10. Mixture, IV ranks.
5. Principal .... 4 feet.	11. Trombone .... 8 feet.
6. Flute Harmonique .... 4 feet.	12. Clarion...................... 4 feet.

Swell Organ.

13.	Lieblich Bourdon	16 feet.	20. Sifflote	2 feet.
14.	Open Diapason	8 feet.	21. Mixture, IV ranks.	
15.	Keraulophon	8 feet.	22. Double Trumpet	16 feet.
16.	Voix Angelique	8 feet.	23. Cornopean	8 feet.
17.	Gedact	8 feet.	24. Oboe	8 feet.
18.	Gemshorn	4 feet.	25. Clarion	4 feet.
19.	Flute d'Amour	4 feet.	Tremulant.	

Choir Organ.

26.	Lieblich Gedact	16 feet.	30. Waldflute	4 feet.
27.	Geigen Principal	8 feet.	31. Celestina	4 feet.
28.	Clarabella	8 feet.	32. Piccolo Harmonique	2 feet.
29.	Dulciana	8 feet.	33. Clarionet	8 feet.

Pedal Organ.

34.	Sub-bass	32 feet.	38. Flute Bass	8 feet.
35.	Open Diapason	16 feet.	39. Violoncello	8 feet.
36.	Violone	16 feet.	40. Bombarde	16 feet.
37.	Bourdon	16 feet.		

Couplers.

1. Swell Manual to Choir.
2. Swell Manual to Great.
3. Swell Manual to Great Sub-octave.
4. Swell Manual to Great Octave.

5. Swell Manual to Pedals.
6. Great Manual to Pedals.
7. Choir Manual to Pedals.
8. Choir Manual to Great.

8 Composition Pedals : 4 to the Great ; 4 to the Swell.

316. DUNHAM MASSEY.

The organ in St. Margaret's Church, as rebuilt by M. August Gern, and erected in 1876, has 3 Manuals, an independent Pedal, and 29 stops, of which latter the following is a list :—

Great Organ, 10 Stops.

1.	Open Diapason	8 feet.	7. Octave Quint	2⅔ feet.
2.	Flute Harmonique	8 feet.	8. Super-octave	2 feet.
3.	Clarabella	8 feet.	9. Sesqualtera, III ranks.	
4.	Viol di Gamba	8 feet.	10. Trumpet	8 feet.
5.	Octave	4 feet.	Pneumatic Action.	
6.	Flute Octaviante	4 feet.		

Swell Organ, 9 Stops.

11.	Double Diapason	16 feet.	16. Octavin	2 feet.
12.	Open Diapason	8 feet.	17. Cornopean	8 feet.
13.	Salicional	8 feet.	18. Hautbois	8 feet.
14.	Voix Céleste	8 feet.	19. Voix Humaine	8 feet.
15.	Octave	4 feet.	Pneumatic Action.	

Choir Organ, 7 Stops.

20.	Flute Traversière	8 feet.	24. Wald Flute	4 feet.
21.	Dulciana	8 feet.	25. Piccolo	2 feet.
22.	Lieblich Gedact	8 feet.	26. Clarionet	8 feet.
23.	Gemshorn	4 feet.		

Pedal Organ, 3 Stops.

27.	Open Diapason	16 feet.	29. Fagotto	16 feet.
28.	Sub-bass	16 feet.		

Compass.

Manuals, CC to g³, 56 notes.　|　Pedals, CCC to e, 29 notes.

Couplers, &c.

1. Swell to Great.	6. Great to Pedal.
2. Choir to Great.	7. Swell to Pedal.
3. Choir Sub-octave to Great.	8. Choir to Pedal.
4. Swell Octave.	9. Pedal Octave.
5. Swell Sub-octave.	10. Tremulant to Swell.

4 Combination Pedals to Great, with Pneumatic Action ; 3 Combination Pedals to Swell.

The organ is placed in the north transept, on each side and over the large window, the Swell being placed above, directly under the roof of the church. The console is at a distance of 25 feet from the wall, the length of trackers from the Swell organ being 60 feet. The organ has one large bellows and four reservoirs, one being placed directly under each sound-board. The feeders are worked by a gas steam engine, supplied by Mr. W. T. Mabley, of Manchester.

317. WEDNESBURY.

The Town Hall organ, the munificent gift of Alexander Brogden, Esq., and costing about £3000, was built by Forster and Andrews. It has three Manuals of the complete range of 58 keys, CC to A in altissimo, and a Pedal of 30, from CCC to F. It consists of Great, Swell, and Choir organs, all of the full compass of the Manuals, and a Pedal organ of the same compass as the Pedal keys, and contains the following stops arranged in the various organs as below :—

Great Organ.

	Feet.	Pipes.		Feet.	Pipes.
1. Double Open Diapason, metal	16	58	7. Twelfth, metal	2½	58
2. Open Diapason, metal	8	58	8. Fifteenth, metal	2	58
3. Violin Diapason, metal	8	58	9. Mixture, metal, IV ranks		232
4. Hohlflote, wood	8	58	10. Trumpet, metal	4	58
5. Principal, metal	4	58	11. Clarion, metal	8	58
6. Harmonic Flute, metal	4	58			

Swell Organ.

	Feet.	Pipes.		Feet.	Pipes.
12. Bourdon, wood	16	58	17. Fifteenth, metal	2	58
13. Open Diapason, metal	8	58	18. Mixture, metal, III ranks		174
14. Salicional, metal	8	46	19. Horn, metal	8	58
15. Rohrflote, metal	8	58	20. Oboe, metal	4	58
16. Principal, metal	4	58			

Choir Organ.

	Feet.	Pipes.		Feet.	Pipes.
21. Dulciana, metal	8	58	24. Flauto Traverso, metal	4	58
22. Lieblich Gedact, wood	8	58	25. Harmonic Piccolo, metal	2	58
23. Lieblich Gedact, wood	4	58	26. Krummhorn, metal	8	58

Pedal Organ.

	Feet.	Pipes.		Feet.	Pipes.
27. Grand Open Diapason, wood	16	30	29. Violoncello, wood	8	30
28. Bourdon, wood	16	30	30. Trombone, metal	16	30

Summary of Pipes.

Great	812
Swell	626
Choir	348
Pedal	120

The Pedal keys and Manuals are connected or isolated by the following couplers :—

1. Pedal to Great.
2. Pedal to Swell.
3. Pedal to Choir.
4. Great to Swell.

5. Great to Choir.
6. Swell Sub-octave.
7. Swell Super-octave.

There are also three combination Pedals, producing various mixtures to the Great organ, and two to the Swell. The entire number of draw-stops, including the Trombone, is 38.

The wind is supplied by two pairs of bellows, fixed underneath the organ platform, and both being under the immediate control of the performer. To one pair are fixed diagonal feeders, which are moved by hand, and to the other are fixed French feeders, worked by Duncan's patent hydraulic engines, supplied by Messrs. G. Forester and Co., of Liverpool.

The front bears the following inscription :—" Presented by A. Brogden, Esq., M.P., the first member returned for the borough of Wednesbury, June 26, 1872."

The case is from designs by Messrs. Loxton Brothers, architects, of Wednesbury. The pipes presented to view are decorated and enriched in colour and gold, and extend round the sides of the case as well as across the front.

318. BOLTON.

The Great organ erected in the Town Hall, Bolton, is by Messrs. Gray and Davison. It has 4 key-boards, each from C to C, five octaves in extent ; a Pedal-board, from C to G, two octaves and a half, and 48 sounding stops, as follows :—

Choir Organ.

(Lowest Key-board.)

1. Bourdon .... 16 feet.
2. Violin Diapason .... 8 feet.
3. Vox Angelica .... 8 feet.
4. Lieblich Gedact .... 8 feet.

5. Flauto Traverso .... 4 feet.
6. Piccolo........................ 2 feet.
7. Echo Dulciana Cornet, V ranks.
8. Trumpet .... 8 feet.

Great Organ.

(Second Key-board.)

9. Double Open Diapason ... 26 feet.
10. Open Diapason .... 8 feet.
11. Viola.......................... 8 feet.
12. Claribel Flute .... 8 feet.
13. Principal .... 4 feet.
14. Flute Octaviante .... 4 feet.

15. Quint Mixture, II ranks.
16. Great Mixture, V ranks.
17. Double Trombone .... 6 feet.
18. Harmonic Trumpet ...... 8 feet.
19. Clarion .... 4 feet.

Solo Organ.

(Third Key-board.)

20. Concert Open Diapason... 8 feet.
21. Flute Harmonique .... 8 feet.
22. Flute Octaviante Harmonique .... 4 feet.

23. Cor Anglais .... 8 feet.
24. Clarionet and Bassoon ... 8 feet.
25. Tuba Mirabilis .... 8 feet.
26. Carillon (Bells) .... 4 feet.

Swell Organ.
(Highest Key-board.)

27.	Lieblich Bourdon	16 feet.	34.	Flautino	2 feet.
28.	Open Diapason	8 feet.	35.	Mixture, III ranks.	
29.	Viol di Gamba	8 feet.	36.	Vox Humana	8 feet.
30.	Voix Célestes	8 feet.	37.	Corno di Bassetto	8 feet.
31.	Lieblich Gedact	8 feet.	38.	Hautbois	8 feet.
32.	Salicet	4 feet,	39.	Trumpet	8 feet.
33.	Nazard	2⅔ feet.	40.	Clarion	4 feet.

Pedal Organ.

41.	Double Open Diapason	32 feet.	45.	Clarabella Bass	8 feet.
42.	Contra Bass	16 feet.	46.	Violoncello	8 feet.
43.	Bourdon	16 feet.	47.	Trombone	16 feet.
44.	Violon	16 feet.	48.	Trumpet	8 feet.

Couplers.

1. Swell to Great.
2. Solo to Great.
3. Swell to Choir.
4. Solo to Choir.
5. Swell Sub-octave, on its own key-board.
6. Swell Super-octave, on its own key-board.
7. Solo Sub-octave, on its own key-board.
8. Solo Super-octave, on its own key-board.
9. Choir to Pedals.
10. Great to Pedals.
11. Solo to Pedals.
12. Swell to Pedals.

The key-boards are so constructed, that a passage of organ music can be readily played on two adjoining rows of keys by the fingers of the same hand.

All the stop-handles are within convenient reach of either hand, and do not ascend beyond the level of the fourth key-board.

The pneumatic touch is applied to the Great, Solo, and Swell key-boards.

There are two Tremulants ; one to the Swell Reed stops, and the other to the Cor Anglais and Clarionet, in the Solo organ.

The stops in the Solo organ (Nos. 25 and 26), are enclosed in a separate Swell.

There are two Swell Pedals, which can be arrested in their action at any point desired.

Instead of effecting the necessary changes of tone by means of " Composition Pedals," or other appliances, the varied tone-character of this instrument is governed by a system of " Ventils," which admit the wind to various sections of the organ, without affecting the stop-handles in any way.

The Ventils are brought into operation by fixing down a series of small Pedals. Of these the Great and Pedal organs are provided with 4, and the Swell organ with 3.

The Couplers, Nos. 1, 2, 10, and 11 (Swell to Great, Solo to Great, Great to Pedals, Solo to Pedals) are actuated by small Pedals on the right and left of the player. The remaining 8 Couplers (having stop-handles) are placed in front, immediately above the Swell key-board. The cost of the organ and case, with the accessories, was about £4000.

319. St. Matthew's, Bolton.

This organ was built by Gray and Davison in 1876. It consists of 3 Manuals, CC to G, and Pedals, from CCC to F. The stops are as follows :—

Great Organ.

1.	Double Diapason	16 feet.	6.	Flute Octaviante	4 feet.
2.	Open Diapason	8 feet.	7.	Quint	2⅔ feet.
3.	Gamba	8 feet.	8.	Super-octave	2 feet.
4.	Clarionet Flute	8 feet.	9.	Mixture, IV ranks.	
5.	Octave	4 feet.	10.	Trumpet	8 feet.

Swell Organ.

11. Lieblich Bourdon	16 feet.	17. Mixture, III ranks.	
12. Open Diapason	8 feet.	18. Cornopean	8 feet.
13. Keraulophon	8 feet.	19. Oboe	8 feet.
14. Concert Flute	8 feet.	20. Vox Humana	8 feet.
15. Octave	4 feet.	21. Clarion	4 feet.
16. Super-octave	2 feet.	Tremulant.	

Choir Organ.

22. Dulciana, tenor c	8 feet.	26. Suabe Flute	4 feet.
23. Viol di Gamba	8 feet.	27. Flageolet Harmonique	2 feet.
24. Lieblich Gedact	8 feet.	28. Corno di Bassetto	8 feet.
25. Gemshorn	4 feet.		

Pedal Organ.

29. Grand Open Diapason	16 feet.	31. Violon	8 feet.
30. Grand Bourdon	16 feet.	32. Trombone	16 feet.

Couplers.

1. Swell to Great Manual.	4. Great Manual to Pedals.
2. Swell to Choir Manual.	5. Choir Manual to Pedals.
3. Swell Manual to Pedals.	

7 Composition Pedals ; 4 to Great ; 3 to Swell.

320. ALL SAINTS', BOLTON.

The organ in All Saints', Bolton, was built by Gray and Davison in 1876. It contains three complete Manuals, from CC to G, and Pedals, from CCC to E, and the following stops :—

Great Organ.

1. Double Diapason	16 feet.	5. Quint	2⅔ feet.
2. Open Diapason	8 feet.	6. Super-octave	2 feet.
3. Clarionet Flute	8 feet.	7. Mixture, IV ranks.	
4. Octave	4 feet.	8. Trumpet	8 feet.

Swell Organ.

9. Lieblich Bourdon	16 feet.	14. Mixture, II ranks.	
10. Open Diapason	8 feet.	15. Oboe	8 feet.
11. Keraulophon	8 feet.	16. Cornopean	8 feet.
12. Concert Flute	8 feet.	Tremulant.	
13. Octave	4 feet.		

Choir Organ.

17. Dulciana	8 feet.	20. Flageolet Harmonic	2 feet.
18. Lieblich Gedact	8 feet.	21. Clarionet	8 feet.
19. Flute	4 feet.		

Pedal Organ.

22. Grand Open Diapason	16 feet.	24. Violon	8 feet.
23. Grand Bourdon	16 feet.		

Couplers.

1. Swell to Great Manual.	4. Great to Pedals.
2. Swell to Choir Manual.	5. Choir to Pedals.
3. Swell to Pedals.	

Accessory Movements.

3 Composition Pedals to Great.	3 Composition Pedals to Swell.

321. ST. LUKE'S, MANCHESTER.

The organ in St. Luke's, Manchester, was built by Hill in 1840. The following is the specification :—

Great, 10 *Stops; CC to F in alt.*

1. Double Open Diapason ... 16 feet.	6. Twelfth .... 3 feet.
2. Open Diapason .... 8 feet.	7. Sesquialtera, III ranks.
3. Stopped Diapason .... 8 feet.	8. Mixture, II ranks.
4. Principal .... 4 feet.	9. Octave Fifteenth .... 1 foot.
5. Fifteenth .... 2 feet.	10. Posaune.

Choir, 10 *Stops; CC to F in alt.*

11. Open Diapason .... 8 feet.	16. Fifteenth .... 2 feet.
12. Stopped Diapason .... 8 feet.	17. Oboe Flute .... 4 feet.
13. Clarabella .... 8 feet.	18. Wald Flute .... 4 feet.
14. Principal .... 4 feet.	19. Piccolo...................... 2 feet.
15. Dulciana .... 8 feet.	20. Cremona .... 8 feet.

Swell, 7 *Stops; tenor c to F in alt.*

21. Double Open Diapason ... 16 feet.	25. Doublette, II ranks ...... 2 feet.
22. Open Diapason .... 8 feet.	26. Cornopean .... 8 feet.
23. Stopped Diapason .... 8 feet.	27. Oboe .... 8 feet.
24. Principal .... 4 feet.	

Pedal, 3 *Stops; One Octave, CCC to CC.*

28. Open Diapason .... 16 feet.	30. Trombone .... 16 feet.
29. Bourdon .... 16 feet.	

Couplers.

1. Choir to Great.	5. Swell to Pedals.
2. Swell to Great.	6, 7. Two Composition Pedals to Swell.
3. Great to Pedals.	8, 9, 10. Three Composition Pedals to
4. Choir to Pedals.	Great.

322. HOLY TRINITY, MANCHESTER.

The organ in Holy Trinity Church, Manchester, was built in 1852 by Kirtland and Jardine, of Manchester. It has 4 Manuals, Great organ, Choir, Swell, and Solo, besides an independent Pedal, and contains 49 stops, of which the following is a list :—

Great, 14 *Stops; CC to F, 54 Notes.*

1. Bourdon .... 16 feet.	8. Clear Flute .... 4 feet.
2. Open Diapason .... 16 feet.	9. Twelfth .... 2⅔ feet.
3. Salicional .... 8 feet.	10. Fifteenth .... 2 feet.
4. Stopped Diapason, Bass... } 8 feet.	11. Sesquialtera, III ranks ... 1⅗ foot.
5. Clarabella..................... }	12. Mixture, III ranks......... 1 foot.
6. Quint........................ .... 5⅓ feet.	13. Trumpet .... 8 feet.
7. Principal .... 4 feet.	14. Clarion...................... 4 feet.

Choir, 11 *Stops; CC to F, 54 Notes.*

15. *Bourdon .... 16 feet.	21. Rohrflute, tenor c .... 4 feet.
16. Dulciana .... 8 feet.	22. Twelfth .... 2⅔ feet.
17. Stopped Diapason, Bass... } 8 feet.	23. Fifteenth .... 2 feet.
18. Stopped Diapason, Treble }	24. Flageolet, tenor c .... 2 feet.
19. Viol di Gamba, tenor c ... 8 feet.	25. Bassoon and Clarinet...... 8 feet.
20. Principal .... 4 feet.	

Swell, 10 Stops; CC to F, 54 Notes.

26.	Bourdon	16 feet.	31.	Fifteenth	2 feet.
27.	Open Diapason	8 feet.	32.	Mixture, III ranks	1⅓ foot.
28.	Stopped Diapason	8 feet.	33.	Cornopean	8 feet.
29.	Principal	4 feet.	34.	Hautboy	8 feet.
30.	Twelfth	2⅔ feet.	35.	Clarion	4 feet.

Solo, 5 Stops; tenor c to F, 42 Notes.

36.	*Gamba	8 feet.	39.	*Flute Harmonique	4 feet.
37.	*Vox Angelica	8 feet.	40.	*Æoline	8 feet.
38.	*Flauto Traverso	4 feet.			

Pedal, 9 Stops; CCC to F, 30 Notes.

41.	Open Diapason	16 feet.	46.	Fifteenth	4 feet.
42.	Stopped Diapason	16 feet.	47.	Mixture (19, 22, 26, 29).	
43.	Quint	10⅔ feet.	48.	*Posaune	16 feet.
44.	Principal	8 feet.	49.	*Clarion	8 feet.
45.	Twelfth	5⅓ feet.			

Couplers.............. 6 | Ventils.............. 4 | Composition Pedals... 6

The keys are 25 feet from the organ, yet the " touch " is *remarkably* crisp, and pleasant to the performer. The keys of the Solo, Swell, and Great organs each project an inch over the keys next below them ; by this means the top set (Solo) is brought 3 inches nearer to the performer than in keys made in the usual manner. The stops marked (*) have no pipes in, but are " prepared " to receive them.

323. FREE TRADE HALL, MANCHESTER.

The fine organ in the Free Trade Hall, Manchester, was built by Messrs. Kirtland and Jardine in 1857. It has 60 draw stops, of which 52 are sounding stops, several of which are modelled from the inventions of the most celebrated organ builders of France and Germany. The Hohlflote, Gamba, Harmonica, and Posaune (16 feet) are from the German ; the Voix Céleste, Voix Humaine, Flute Harmonica, Euphone, &c., from the French. The Posaune, Euphone, and Harmonica, are " free reeds," which are seldom used in English organs. The organ is constructed on the "Simplification System" invented by the Abbé Vogler, of Mannheim, and introduced into this country by Messrs. Kirtland and Jardine. By this system every pipe stands directly over the air chamber supplying it with wind. There are 4 wind reservoirs. These are supplied with air by 6 feeders, put in motion by means of 2 hydraulic engines. The various organs have different pressures of wind, and thus the desired intonation and true character of the stops are more perfectly obtained. The pipes are scaled in accordance with the theory of Professor Topfer, of Weimar, and the instrument is tuned on the equal temperament system.

Great Organ, 15 Stops; CC to G in alt., 56 Notes.

1.	Double Open Diapason	16 feet.	9.	Clear Flute	4 feet.
2.	Open Diapason	8 feet.	10.	Twelfth	2⅔ feet.
3.	Violin Diapason	8 feet.	11.	Fifteenth	2 feet.
4.	Hohlflote	8 feet.	12.	Mixture, V ranks.	
5.	Open Diapason	8 feet.	13.	Double Trumpet	16 feet.
6.	Quint	5⅓ feet.	14.	Posaune	8 feet.
7.	Principal	4 feet.	15.	Clarion	4 feet.
8.	Gamba	4 feet.			

Swell Organ, 20 Stops ; CC to G in alt., 56 Notes.

16.	Bourdon	16 feet.	26.	Twelfth	2⅔ feet.
17.	Open Diapason	8 feet.	27.	Fifteenth	2 feet.
18.	Salicional	8 feet.	28.	Mixture, V ranks.	
19.	Stopped Diapason	8 feet.	29.	Euphone	16 feet.
20.	Dulciana	8 feet.	30.	Cornopean	8 feet.
21.	Voix Céleste	8 feet.	31.	Oboe	8 feet.
22.	Quint	5⅓ feet.	32.	Voix Humaine	8 feet.
23.	Principal	4 feet.	33.	Clarion	4 feet.
24.	Hohlflote	4 feet.	34.	Octave Clarion	2 feet.
25.	Rohrflote	4 feet.		Tremulant.	

Solo Organ, 8 Stops ; CC to G in alt., 56 Notes.

35.	Hohlflote	8 feet.	39.	Bassoon and Clarionet	8 feet.
36.	Gamba	8 feet.	40.	Tuba	8 feet.
37.	Corno Dolce	8 feet.	41.	Harmonica	4 feet.
38.	Flute Harmonique	4 feet.	42.	Tuba	4 feet.

Pedal Organ, 10 Stops ; CCC to E, 29 Notes.

43.	Sub-bass	32 feet.	48.	Violoncello	8 feet.
44.	Open Diapason	16 feet.	49.	Twelfth	5⅓ feet.
45.	Bourdon	16 feet.	50.	Fifteenth	4 feet.
46.	Quint	10⅔ feet.	51.	Posaune	16 feet.
47.	Principal	8 feet.	52.	Trumpet	8 feet.

Accessory Stops, Movements, &c.

1.	Swell to Great, Unison.	6. Solo to Pedals.
2.	Swell to Great, Octave.	7. Clochette.
3.	Solo to Great.	Four Combination Pedals to Great.
4.	Swell to Pedals.	Two Combination Pedals to Swell.
5.	Great to Pedals.	Two Combination Pedals to Pedals.

324. St. Peter's, Manchester.

The organ in St. Peter's Church, Manchester, was built in 1856 by Kirtland and Jardine. It contains the following stops :—

Great Organ, 17 Stops ; CC to G in alt., 56 Notes.

1.	Double Open Diapason	16 feet.	10.	Clear Flute	4 feet.
2.	Grand Open Diapason	8 feet.	11.	Twelfth	2⅔ feet.
3.	Open Diapason	8 feet.	12.	Fifteenth	2 feet.
4.	Gamba	8 feet.	13.	Full Mixture, V ranks.	
5.	Flute à Pavillon	8 feet.	14.	Sharp Mixture, IV ranks.	
6.	Stopped Diapason	8 feet.	15.	Double Trumpet	16 feet.
7.	Quint	5⅓ feet.	16.	Trompette Harmonique	8 feet.
8.	Grand Principal	4 feet.	17.	Clarion	4 feet.
9.	Principal	4 feet.			

Choir Organ, 14 Stops ; CC to G in alt., 56 Notes.

18.	Bourdon	16 feet.	25.	Flauto Traverso, Harmonic	4 feet.
19.	Spitzflote	8 feet.	26.	Rohrflote	4 feet.
20.	Dulciana	8 feet.	27.	Fifteenth	2 feet.
21.	Viol di Gamba	8 feet.	28.	Mixture, IV ranks.	
22.	Gedact	8 feet.	29.	Euphone and Bassoon	16 feet.
23.	Voix Célestes	8 feet.	30.	Trumpet	8 feet.
24.	Gemshorn	4 feet.	31.	Voix Humaine	8 feet.

Swell Organ, 14 Stops; CC to G in alt., 56 Notes.

32. Bourdon	16 feet.	
33. Open Diapason	8 feet.	
34. Hohlflöte	8 feet.	
35. Stopped Diapason	8 feet.	
36. Principal	4 feet.	
37. Gedact Flute	4 feet.	
38. Twelfth	2⅔ feet.	
39. Fifteenth	2 feet.	
40. Clear Mixture, V ranks.		
41. Contra Fagotto	16 feet.	
42. Cornopean	8 feet.	
43. Hautboy	8 feet.	
44. Cor Anglais	8 feet.	
45. Clarion	4 feet.	

Solo Organ, 5 Stops.

46. Open Diapason, Harmonic	8 feet.
47. Concert Flute, Harmonic	8 feet.
48. Flageolet, Harmonic	2 feet.
49. Tromba	8 feet.
50. Corno di Bassetto and Clarionet	8 feet.

Pedal Organ, 11 Stops; CCC to tenor f, 30 Notes.

51. Sub-bass	32 feet.
52. Open Diapason	16 feet.
53. Violon	16 feet.
54. Stopped Diapason	16 feet.
55. Grosse Quint	10⅔ feet.
56. Principal	8 feet.
57. Violoncello	8 feet.
58. Twelfth	5⅓ feet.
59. Fifteenth	4 feet.
60. Posaune	16 feet.
61. Trumpet	8 feet.

Accessory Stops, Movements, &c.

1. Solo to Great.	10. Pedal Organ Attachment.
2. Swell to Great, Unison.	11. Clochette.
3. Swell to Great, Octave.	Tremulant Swell.
4. Swell to Great, Sub-octave.	Tremulant to Choir.
5. Choir to Great.	Sforzando Pedal.
6. Solo to Great.	4 Combination Pedals to Great.
7. Swell to Pedals.	2 Combination Pedals to Pedals.
8. Great to Pedals.	2 Combination Pedals to Swell.
9. Choir to Pedals.	

325. MANCHESTER CATHEDRAL.

The new organ in Manchester Cathedral was built by Messrs. Hill and Son in 1871. It has 4 Manuals, independent Pedal, and 51 sounding stops, of which the following is a list :—

Great Organ, CC to G.

	Feet.	Pipes.		Feet.	Pipes.
1. Double Open Diapason (and Bourdon, Bass), wood and metal	16	56	8. Twelfth, metal	3	56
			9. Fifteenth, metal	2	56
2. Open Diapason, metal	8	56	10. Full Mixture, III ranks, metal		168
3. Harmonic Flute, metal	8	56			
4. Gamba, metal	8	56	11. Sharp Mixture, IV ranks, metal		224
5. Stopped Diapason, wood	8	56			
6. Principal, metal	4	56	12. Posaune, metal	8	56
7. Harmonic Flute, metal	4	56	13. Clarion, metal	4	56

Choir Organ, CC to G.

	Feet.	Pipes.		Feet.	Pipes.
14. Open Diapason, metal	8	56	18. Wald Flute, wood	4	56
15. Dulciana, metal	8	56	19. Principal, metal	4	56
16. Salicional (grooved), metal	8	44	20. Flautina, metal	2	56
17. Stopped Diapason and Claribel, wood	8	56	21. Clarionet	8	56

Swell Organ, CC to G.

		Feet.		Pipes.				Feet.		Pipes.
22.	Lieblich Bourdon, wood...	16	...	56	31.	Dulciana Mixture, II ranks, metal		...		112
23.	Open Diapason, metal......	8	...	56						
24.	Keraulophon, metal.........	8	...	56	32.	Sharp Mixture, III ranks, metal		...		168
25.	Dulciana, metal	8	...	56						
26.	Stopped Diapason, wood	8	...	56	33.	Double Trumpet, metal...	16	...	56
27.	Principal, metal	4	...	56	34.	Cornopean, metal	8	...	56
28.	Dulcet, metal	4	...	56	35.	Oboe, metal..................	8	...	56
29.	Suabe Flute, wood	4	...	56	36.	Clarion, metal..............	4	...	56
30.	Flageolet, wood	2	...	56	37.	Vox Humana, metal	8	...	56

Solo Organ (enclosed in a Swell).

		Feet.		Pipes.				Feet.		Pipes.
38.	Tuba Mirabilis, metal......	8	...	56	40.	Voix Céleste, II ranks, metal		...		100
39.	Harmonic Flute, metal ...	4	...	56						
					41.	Orchestral Oboe, metal...	8	...	56

Pedal Organ, CCC to F.

		Feet.		Pipes.				Feet.		Pipes.
42.	Double Open Diapason, wood	32	...	30	47.	Principal, metal	8	...	30
43.	Open Diapason, metal......	16	...	30	48.	Bourdon, wood	16	...	30
44.	Open Diapason, wood ...	16	...	30	49.	Fifteenth, metal	4	...	30
45.	Violon, wood	8	...	30	50.	Trombone, wood............	16	...	30
46.	Violon, metal	8	...	30	51.	Clarion, metal................	8	...	30

Couplers.

1.	Swell to Great.	6. Swell to Pedal.
2.	Swell to Octave.	7. Choir to Pedal.
3.	Swell to Sub-octave.	8. Swell to Pedal.
4.	Swell to Choir.	9. Solo to Pedal.
5.	Solo to Great.	

Pneumatic apparatus to Great, Swell, and Pedal organ.
Great Pneumatic acts on Manual Coupler connected with it.
A Pedal to take on and off Great to Pedal.
Tremulant to the Swell organ.
The Swell box has shutters at the back and front.

ORGANS IN SCOTLAND AND IRELAND.

326. City Hall, Glasgow.

This instrument was built by Gray and Davison in 1853. It was considerably enlarged in 1855, and great improvements have recently (Christmas, 1876) been made to it by the same builders. It has 4 Manuals, 57 Stops, 12 Couplers, &c., and each Manual has a range of five complete octaves, or sixty-one notes, extending from CC to C in altissimo. The Pedal organ has a compass of two octaves and a third. The general contents of the instrument are as follows:—

Choir Organ.

1.	Lieblich Gedact	16 feet.	8. Flute	4 feet.
2.	Open Diapason	8 feet.	9. Fifteenth	2 feet.
3.	Salicional	8 feet.	10. Celestina	4 feet.
4.	Voix Céleste..................	8 feet.	11. Sesquialtera, III ranks.	
5.	Stopped Diapason, Bass...	8 feet.	12. Trumpet	8 feet.
6.	Clarionet Flute...............	8 feet.	13. Corno di Bassetto	8 feet.
7.	Octave	4 feet.		

Great Organ.

14. Double Diapason	16 feet.	
15. Open Diapason	8 feet.	
16. Viola	8 feet.	
17. Stopped Diapason	8 feet.	
18. Octave	4 feet.	
19. Twelfth	3 feet.	
20. Fifteenth	2 feet.	
21. Flute d'Amour	4 feet.	
22. Sifflote	2 feet.	
23. Mixture, IV ranks.		
24. Furniture, III ranks.		
25. Posaune	8 feet.	
26. Clarion	4 feet.	
27. Flute Harmonique	8 feet.	
28. Flute Octaviante	4 feet.	

Swell Organ.

29. Bourdon	16 feet.	
30. Open Diapason	8 feet.	
31. Keraulophon	8 feet.	
32. Stopped Diapason, Bass	8 feet.	
33. Clarionet Flute	8 feet.	
34. Octave	4 feet.	
35. Flute	4 feet.	
36. Fifteenth	2 feet.	
37. Flageolet	2 feet.	
38. Sesquialtera, III ranks.		
39. Mixture, II ranks.		
40. Contra Fagotto	16 feet.	
41. Cornopean	8 feet.	
42. Oboe	8 feet.	
43. Voix Humaine	8 feet.	
44. Clarion	4 feet.	

Solo Organ.

45. Flute Harmonique	8 feet.	
46. Flute Octaviante	4 feet.	
47. Piccolo	2 feet.	
48. Clarionet	8 feet.	
49. Orchestral Oboe	8 feet.	
50. Tromba	8 feet.	
51. Carillons.		

Pedal Organ.

52. Contra Bourdon	32 feet.	
53. Open Diapason	16 feet.	
54. Bourdon	16 feet.	
55. Principal	8 feet.	
56. Violoncello	8 feet.	
57. Bombarde	16 feet.	

Couplers.

1. Choir to Pedals.	7. Swell to Great.
2. Great to Pedals.	8. Swell to Great Sub-octave.
3. Swell to Pedals.	9. Swell to Great Octave.
4. Solo to Pedals.	10. Choir to Great Sub-octave.
5. Solo to Great.	11. Storm Pedal.
6. Solo to Swell.	12. Tremulant to Swell.

There are eight Combination and Composition Pedals acting on the stops of the Great and Swell organs. A new and larger wind-chest for the Great organ has been introduced on the ventil system, and so constructed that every pipe has its own valve and stands over its own wind, with the exception of the front pipes

327. GLASGOW.

The organ for the Public Hall, Glasgow, is being built by Mr. Lewis, and will have 4 Manuals and Pedal Organ, and 64 sounding stops. The following will be its specification :—

Front Great Organ, CC to C, 61 Notes.

1. Double Open Diapason	16 feet.	
2. Open Diapason, large	8 feet.	
3. Open Diapason, small	8 feet.	
4. Rohrflote	8 feet.	
5. Octave	4 feet.	
6. Twelfth	$2\frac{2}{3}$ feet.	
7. Fifteenth	2 feet.	
8. Sesquialtera, IV ranks	$1\frac{1}{3}$ foot.	
9. Trumpet	8 feet.	

Back Great Organ.

10. Bourdon	16 feet.	15. Mixture, V ranks	2 feet.
11. Viola	8 feet.	16. Double Trumpet	16 feet.
12. Hohlflote	8 feet.	17. Trombone	8 feet.
13. Harmonic Flute	4 feet.	18. Clarion	4 feet.
14. Octave Viola	4 feet.		

Swell Organ, CC to C, 61 Notes.

19. Bourdon	16 feet.	28. Fifteenth	2 feet.
20. Open Diapason	8 feet.	29. Full Mixture, IV ranks...	1½ foot.
21. Spitzflote	8 feet.	30. Echo Dulciana Cornet,	
22. Viol di Gamba	8 feet.	VI ranks	8 feet.
23. Voix Céleste	8 feet.	31. Contra Fagotto	16 feet.
24. Flauto Dolce	8 feet.	32. Trumpet	8 feet.
25. Octave	4 feet.	33. Cornopean	8 feet.
26. Suahe Flote	4 feet.	34. Oboe	8 feet.
27. Nazard	2⅔ feet.	35. Clarion	4 feet.

Solo Organ, CC to C, 61 Notes (enclosed in Swell).

36. Tuba	8 feet.	40. Cor Anglais	8 feet.
37. Tromba	8 feet.	41. Oboe	8 feet.
38. Harmonic Flute	8 feet.	42. Clarionet	8 feet.
39. Octave Flute	4 feet.		

Choir Organ, CC to C, 61 Notes.

43. Lieblich Bourdon	16 feet.	48. Lieblich Flote	4 feet.
44. Violin Diapason	8 feet.	49. Gemshorn	4 feet.
45. Dulciana	8 feet.	50. Piccolo	2 feet.
46. Flauto Traverso	8 feet.	51. Vox Humana ⎰ Enclosed ⎰ 8 feet.
47. Lieblich Gedact	8 feet.	52. Clarionet ... ⎱ in a Swell ⎱ 8 feet.

Pedal Organ.

53. Double Open Diapason ...	32 feet.	59. Violoncello	8 feet.
54. Open Diapason, wood ...	16 feet.	60. Grave Mixture, II ranks	5⅓ feet.
55. Open Diapason, metal ...	16 feet.	61. Trombone	16 feet.
56. Violon Dulciana	16 feet.	62. Contra Fagotto	16 feet.
57. Quint	10⅔ feet.	63. Trumpet	8 feet.
58. Octave	8 feet.	64. Clarion	4 feet.

Total number of Sounding Stops.

Solo organ, 7; Swell organ, 17; Choir organ, 10; Great organ, 18; Pedal organ, 12. Total, 64.

Couplers, &c.

1. Full Pedal organ.	8. Swell to Great Super-octave.
2. Great to Pedal.	9. Choir to Great.
3. Choir to Pedal.	10. Swell to Choir.
4. Swell to Pedal.	11. Solo to Great.
5. Solo to Pedal.	12. Great to Solo.
6. Swell to Great Sub-octave.	13. Solo Sub-octave, on its own Clavier.
7. Swell to Great Unison.	14. Solo Super-octave, on its own Clavier.

Thirteen Combination and other Pedals. Three Combination Pedals for the Swell organ. Four Combination Pedals for the Great and Pedal organs. Ventil Pedal, admitting wind to the stops of the "Back Great organ." Swell "Crescendo" Pedal. Solo "Crescendo" Pedal. Choir "Crescendo" Pedal. Tremulant to Choir. Tremulant to Swell.

Coupling Pedals.

Solo to Pedals. Great to Pedals, on the left. Solo to Great, Swell to Great, on the right.

328. EDINBURGH UNIVERSITY.

This organ, built for Professor Donaldson in 1861 by Hill & Son, has, since Professor Oakeley's succession to the Chair of Music, received many additions and improvements. It has also (through the munificence of Sir David Baxter, Bart., a great benefactor to the University) been enclosed in a handsome oak case, and the larger pipes in the side wings or towers have been gilded. In the centre are placed the arms of General Reid, the founder of the Chair of Music. Some additions to the Pedal organ were from the first contemplated, which have now probably been supplied.

Great, 12 Stops, CC to G.

1. Double Open Diapason, to C, metal .... 16 feet.
2. Open Diapason, metal ... 8 feet.
3. Stopped Diapason, wood 8 feet.
4. Gamba, metal .... 8 feet.
5. Principal, metal .... 4 feet.
6. Harmonic Flute, to C, metal...................... 4 feet.
7. Twelfth, metal .... 2⅔ feet.
8. Fifteenth, metal........... 2 feet.
9. Mixture, IV ranks, metal
10. Trumpet, metal .... 8 feet.
11. Clarion, metal .... 4 feet.
12. Harmonic Mixture, XIV ranks, tenor c.

Swell, 13 stops, same Compass.

13. Bourdon, wood .... 16 feet.
14. Open Diapason, metal .... 8 feet.
15. Stopped Diapason, wood 8 feet.
16. Dulciana, metal .... 8 feet.
17. Principal, metal .... 4 feet.
18. Flute, metal .... 4 feet.
19. Fifteenth, metal .... 2 feet.
20. Mixture, II ranks.
21. Oboe, metal................. 8 feet.
22. Horn, metal .... 8 feet.
23. Clarion, metal............. 4 feet.
24. Vox Humana, metal ...... 8 feet.
25. Contra Fagotto, metal ... 16 feet.

Choir, 10 stops, same Compass.

26. Double Diapason, wood... 16 feet.
27. Open Diapason, wood ... 8 feet.
28. Stopped Diapason, wood 8 feet.
29. Dulciana, metal .... 8 feet.
30. Salicional, metal........... 8 feet.
31. Gamba, metal .... 8 feet.
32. Gemshorn, to tenor c, metal...................... 8 feet.
33. Suabe flute, wood .... 4 feet.
34. Gemshorn, metal .... 4 feet.
35. Piccolo, wood and metal 2 feet.

Solo, 9 Stops, same Compass.

36. Hohl Flute, wood .... 8 feet.
37. Flute d'Amour, metal, lower octave, wood...... 8 feet.
38. Salicional, to C, metal ... 8 feet.
39. Flauto Traverso, metal ... 4 feet.
40. Dolcean, metal .... 4 feet.
41. Clarionet, metal........... 8 feet.
42. Orchestral Oboe, to G, metal...................... 8 feet.
43. Voix Humaine .... 8 feet.
44. Cor Anglais, metal........ 16 feet.

Pedal, 10 Stops, CCC to F.

45. Double Open Diapason, wood .... 32 feet.
46. Open Diapason, wood ... 16 feet.
47. Keraulophon, metal ...... 16 feet.
48. Violon, wood .... 8 feet.
49. Fifteenth, metal .... 4 feet.
50. Trombone, wood .... 16 feet.
51. Trumpet, metal .... 8 feet.
52. Mixture, III ranks.
53. Violon .... 16 feet.
54. Double Open Diapason, metal...................... 32 feet.

Couplers.

1. Pedal to Great.
2. Pedal to Swell.
3. Pedal to Choir.
4. Choir to Great.
5. Solo to Great.
6. Solo to Swell.
7. Swell Unison to Great.
8. Swell Sub-octave to Great.
9. Swell Super-octave to Great.
10. Swell to Choir.

Composition Pedals : 3 to Great ; 2 to Swell ; Tremulant to Swell.

329. EDINBURGH.

The organ in the Music Hall, at Edinburgh, was built in the year 1843 by Mr. Hill, of London, and contains 38 sounding stops, of which the following is a list :—

Great, 14 *Stops.*

1. Tenoroon .... 16 feet.	8. Wald Flute.................. 4 feet.
2. Bourdon, to meet No. 1... 16 feet tone.	9. Duodecima .... 2⅔ feet.
3. Unison, open .... 8 feet.	10. Super-octave .... 2 feet.
4. Unison, closed, Treble ... 8 feet tone.	11. Sesquialtera, III ranks... 1⅗ foot.
5. Unison, closed, Bass ...... 8 feet tone.	12. Mixture, II ranks .... ⅔ foot.
6. Quint.......................... 5⅓ feet.	13. Doublette, II ranks ...... 2 feet.
7. Octave .... 4 feet.	14. Posaune .... 8 feet.

Choir, 11 *Stops.*

15. Clarabella..................... 8 feet.	21. Oboe Flute.................. 4 feet.
16. Unison, closed, Bass ...... 8 feet tone.	22. Piccolo .... 2 feet.
17. Salicional .... 8 feet.	23. Cremona .... 8 feet tone.
18. Viol di Gamba............... 8 feet.	24. Corno Flute .... 8 feet.
19. Closed Flute................. 4 feet tone.	25. Cornopean, Bass........... 8 feet.
20. Celestina .... 4 feet.	

Swell, 10 *Stops.*

26. Tenoroon Dulciana......... 16 feet.	31. Flageolet..................... 2 feet.
27. Unison, open .... 8 feet.	32. Doublette, II ranks ...... 2 feet.
28. Unison, closed.............. 8 feet tone.	33. Echo Cornet, IV ranks.
29. Octave .... 4 feet.	34. Oboe .... 8 feet.
30. Suabe Flute .... 4 feet.	35. Cornopean .... 8 feet.

Pedal, 3 *Stops.*

36. Contra Bass, open .... 16 feet.	38. Trombone, wood .... 16 feet.
37. Bourdon, stopped .... 16 feet tone.	

Accessory Stops, Movements, &c.

1. Coupler, Swell to Great.	4. Coupler, Choir to Pedal.
2. Coupler, Choir to Great.	5, 6, and 7. Three Composition Pedals.
3. Coupler, Great to Pedal.	

Compass.

Great, CC to f³ in alt.	Swell, tenor c to f³ in alt.
Choir, CC to f³ in alt.	Pedal, CCC to tenor d.

The Case is 35 feet in height, and 17½ feet in width.

330. DUNDEE, KINNAIRD HALL.

This organ, built by Messrs. Forster and Andrews, has 4 complete Manuals, from CC to A, and a Pedal organ, from CCC to F.

Great Organ.

	Ft. Tone.	Pipes.		Ft. Tone.	Pipes.
1. Double Diapason, closed, wood and metal	16	58	9. Fifteenth, metal	2	58
2. Open Diapason, metal......	8	58	10. Full Mixture, V ranks, metal		290
3. Violin Diapason, metal ...	8	58	11. Sharp Mixture, III ranks, metal		174
4. Hohlflote, wood	8	58			
5. Stopped Diapason, wood...	8	58	12. Double Trumpet, metal ...	16	58
6. Principal, metal	4	58	13. Posaune, metal..............	8	58
7. Harmonic Flute, metal ...	4	58	14. Trumpet, metal	8	58
8. Twelfth, metal	2⅔	58	15. Clarion, metal	4	58

Choir Organ.

		Feet.	Pipes.
16.	Bourdon, wood and metal	16	... 58
17.	Dulciana, metal	8	... 58
18.	Lieblich Gedact, wood and metal	8	... 58
19.	Viol d'Amour, metal	4	... 58
20.	Gedact Flote, metal	4	... 58
21.	Flautino, metal	2	... 58
22.	Krummhorn, metal	8	... 46

Swell Organ.

		Feet.	Pipes.
23.	Double Stopped Diapason, wood	16	... 58
24.	Open Diapason, metal	8	... 58
25.	Viol di Gamba, metal	8	... 58
26.	Stopped Diapason, wood and metal	8	... 58
27.	Principal, metal	4	... 58
28.	Flauto Traverso Harmonic, metal	4	... 58
29.	Mixture, IV ranks, metal		... 232
30.	Contra Fagotto, metal	16	... 58
31.	Horn, metal	8	... 58
32.	Hautboy, metal	8	... 58
33.	Clarion, metal	8	... 58
34.	Tremulant, metal		...

Solo Organ.

		Feet.	Pipes.
35.	Harmonic Flute, metal	8	... 58
36.	Orchestral Clarionet, metal	8	... 46
37.	Orchestral Oboe, metal	8	... 46
38.	Tuba, metal	8	... 58
39.	Flute Octaviante, metal	4	... 58

All the Solo Organ, except the Tuba, is enclosed in a Swell box.

Pedal Organ.

		Feet.	Pipes.
40.	Double Open Diapason, (preparation only), wood	32	...
41.	Large Open Diapason, wood	16	... 30
42.	Open Diapason, metal	16	... 30
43.	Violon, wood	16	... 30
44.	Bourdon, wood	16	... 30
45.	Quint, wood	$10\frac{2}{3}$	... 30
46.	Principal, metal	8	... 12
47.	Flute, wood	8	... 12
48.	Violoncello, wood	8	... 12
49.	Trombone, metal	16	... 30
50.	Trumpet, metal	8	... 30

Couplers.

1. Solo to Great organ.
2. Swell to Great organ.
3. Choir to Great organ, Sub-octave.
4. Great organ to Pedals.
5. Swell organ to Pedals.
6. Choir organ to Pedals.
7. Great organ Reeds.

Four Combination Movements to draw in and out the stops of the Great and Pedal organs simultaneously.

Three Combination Movements to draw in and out the stops of the Swell organ.

Summary.

Great organ	1218 pipes	15	registers.
Swell organ	812 ,,	12	,,
Choir organ	394 ,,	7	,,
Solo organ	266 ,,	5	,,
Pedal organ	846 ,,	11	,,
Couplers		7	,,
	2936 ,,	57	,,

This organ is one of the largest in Scotland. It occupies a space of nearly 40 feet in width, by about 17 feet in depth ; and is upwards of 30 feet in height. The instrument is supplied with wind, at various pressures, both by hand and hydraulic power, the former being available should the latter fail through any cause. The bellows are placed in an apartment below the orchestra, on which the organ is built.

331. PAISLEY ABBEY.

This organ, by M. Cavaillé-Coll, was erected in 1874. It contains 24 sounding stops, 2 complete Manuals, and a separate Pedal, of which the following are the particulars :—

Great Organ, 12 Stops.

1. Bourdon, wood and tin ...	16 feet.	7. Octave, tin		4 feet.
2. Principal, tin throughout	8 feet.	8. Doublette, tin		2 feet.
3. Flute Harmonique, wood		9. Plein Jeu, VI ranks.		
and tin	8 feet.	10. Bassoon		16 feet.
4. Bourdon, wood and tin ...	8 feet.	11. Trompette		8 feet.
5. Salicional, wood and tin...	8 feet.	12. Clarion		4 feet.
6. Prestant, tin	4 feet.			

Swell Organ, 8 Stops.

13. Viol di Gamba, tin	8 feet.	17. Flute Octaviante, tin		4 feet.
14. Flute Traversière Harmo-		18. Trompette		8 feet.
nique	8 feet.	19. Hautbois and Bassoon ...		8 feet.
15. Bourdon, wood and tin ...	8 feet.	20. Voix Humaine		8 feet.
16. Voix Céleste, to tenor c	8 feet.			

Pedal Organ, 4 Stops.

21. Contre Basse Ouverte, wood	16 feet.	23. Violoncello, metal		8 feet.
22. Bourdon, wood and tin ...	16 feet.	24. Bombard, tin		16 feet.

Compass.

Manuals, CC to g³, 56 notes. | Pedal, CCC to tenor f, 30 notes.
11 Coupler and Combination Pedals.

The instrument is built in two divisions at the west end of the church, the Great organ being placed on the south, and the Swell on the north side of the large stained window.

332. KILMARNOCK.

The organ in the Corn Exchange Hall was built by Forster and Andrews in 1871. The following is the specification :—

Great Organ, 11 Stops; CC to C in alt., 61 Notes.

1. Double Open Diapason ...	16 feet.	7. Fifteenth		2 feet.
2. Open Diapason	8 feet.	8. Piccolo		2 feet.
3. Violin Diapason	8 feet.	9. Mixture, IV ranks.		
4. Hohlflote	8 feet.	10. Trumpet		8 feet.
5. Principal	4 feet.	11. Clarion		4 feet.
6. Harmonic Flute	4 feet.			

Swell Organ, 9 Stops; CC to C in alt., 61 Notes.

12. Lieblich Bourdon	16 feet.	17. Flageolet		2 feet.
13. Open Diapason	8 feet.	18. Mixture, III ranks.		
14. Salicional	8 feet.	19. Horn		8 feet.
15. Stopped Diapason	8 feet.	20. Oboe		8 feet.
16. Principal	4 feet.			

Echo Organ, 3 Stops; CC to C in alt., 61 Notes.

21. Echo Dulciana	8 feet.	23. Echo Flautino		2 feet.
22. Echo Celestina	4 feet.			

Solo Organ, 4 Stops; CC to C in alt., 61 Notes.

24.	Orchestral Flute	8 feet.	26.	Orchestral Oboe	8 feet.
25.	Orchestral Clarionet and Bassoon	8 feet.	27.	Tromba	8 feet.

Pedal Organ, 3 Stops; CCC to F, 30 Notes.

28.	Open Diapason	16 feet.	30.	Violoncello	8 feet.
29.	Bourdon	16 feet.			

Couplers, &c.

1.	Great to Pedals.	5.	Solo Octave.
2.	Swell to Pedals.	6.	Swell to Great.
3.	Pedal Octave.	7.	Solo to Pedals.
4.	Swell Octave.	8.	Solo to Great.

7 Composition Pedals.

The design of case is suited to the building, with richly decorated pipes in front, symmetrically arranged and supported by perforated bands.

333. ST. ANDREW'S CATHEDRAL, INVERNESS.

This instrument, the gift of Miss Macpherson-Grant, of Aberlour, was built by Messrs. Hill and Son, of London, from the specification, and under the superintendence of Professor Oakeley, and contains the following stops:—

Great, CC to G, 10 Stops.

1.	Bourdon	16 feet.	6.	Wald Flute	4 feet.
2.	Open Diapason	8 feet.	7.	Twelfth	3 feet.
3.	Cone Gamba	8 feet.	8.	Fifteenth	2 feet.
4.	Stopped Diapason	8 feet.	9.	Mixture, III ranks	1½ foot.
5.	Principal	4 feet.	10.	Trumpet	8 feet.

Swell, CC to G, 8 Stops.

11.	Bourdon and Double Open	16 feet.	15.	Mixture, III ranks.	
12.	Open Diapason	8 feet.	16.	Cornopean	8 feet.
13.	Stopped Diapason	8 feet.	17.	Oboe	8 feet.
14.	Principal	4 feet.	18.	Vox Humana	8 feet.

Choir, CC to G, 5 Stops.

19.	Dulciana	8 feet.	22.	Suabe Flute	4 feet.
20.	Gedact	8 feet.	23.	Clarionet	8 feet.
21.	Gemshorn	4 feet.			

Pedal, CCC to E, 3 Stops.

24.	Open Diapason	16 feet.	25. Bourdon	16 feet.	26. Violone	8 feet.

Couplers.

1.	Swell to Great.	3.	Great to Pedal.
2.	Swell to Pedal.	4.	Choir to Pedal.

Composition Pedals.

3 to Great Organ | 2 to Swell. | Tremulant to Swell.
The total number of pipes is 1590.

The organ is provided with 3 Manuals, and is blown by one of Joy's patent water engines.

It was the original intention of the Committee to have placed the organ in the small chamber to the left, but the presentation of so handsome a gift rendered this fortunately impossible, and the end of the south transept was selected—a position which has met with the approval of all musical authorities.

Room is provided for additional stops, with 32-feet Open Diapason on the Pedal.

334. ST. PATRICK'S CATHEDRAL, DUBLIN.

The original organ in St. Patrick's Cathedral, Dublin, was built by Renatus Harris in 1697 ; in confirmation of which, the following is extracted from the Chapter book :—" 12th August, 1695. The Dean and Chapter agree with Renatus Harris, of London, organ builder, to make and set up a double organ for the sum of £505. In the Great organ, Open Diapason of metal, Stopped Diapason of wood, Principal of metal, Nason of wood, a Great Twelfth of metal, Fifteenth of metal, Sesquialtera of metal, a Mixture of metal, a Cornet of metal. In the Little organ—a Principal of metal, Stopped Diapason of wood, Fifteenth of metal, Nason of wood, being in all 13 stops, consisting of 800 pipes, sound-board, &c., &c. The pipes of the old organ to be removed, and to allow £65 for the same."

" 11th March, 1697. Organ erected and examined by the several vicars." " 10th May, 1697. Further contract for additional stops for £350, to be paid at Strongbow's Tomb, in Christ Church, on stated times named—viz., Trumpet stop, Echo stop, *Time stop* (?), entire Open Diapason, Flute of metal, Great Furniture of III ranks."

The organ as it now stands contains the following stops :—

Great, 11 *Stops, GG to F in alt.*

1. Open Diapason.	7. Tierce.
2. Large Open Diapason.	8. Sesquialtera, III ranks.
3. Stopped Diapason.	9. Furniture, III ranks.
4. Principal.	10. Cornet, from tenor c, V ranks.
5. Twelfth.	11. Great Trumpet.
6. Fifteenth.	

Choir, 4 *Stops, GG to E in alt.*

12. Stopped Diapason.	15. Large Principal, stopped and
13. Dulciana.	open, borrowed from the Great
14. Flute.	organ by means of tubes.

Swell, 8 *Stops, from Gamut G.*

16. Double Diapason.	20. Twelfth.
17. Open Diapason.	21. Fifteenth.
18. Stopped Diapason.	22. Hautboy.
19. Principal.	23. Trumpet.

Pedal, 2 *Stops ; from CCC to E, two Octaves and two Notes.*

24. Double Diapason, 16 feet.	25. Stopped Diapason, 8 feet, Unison.

Couplers.

1. Great to Swell.	2. Pedals to Great.

335. CHRIST CHURCH CATHEDRAL, DUBLIN.

The organ in Christ Church Cathedral, Dublin, was originally built by Byfield, of London, in A.D. 1751, but has been altered by various builders, and numerous additions made at different times. It originally consisted of 2½ rows of keys, Great and Choir organs, GG long octaves to d³ in alt., Swell from fiddle g to d³ in alt. An excellent Swell was added in 1845, from CC to F in alt. The older organ formed a portion of the one built by Renatus Harris for the Temple Church, London. Upon the erection of the present instrument by Byfield, he took the old organ in exchange as part of payment, which instrument was sold, after his death, for £500, and placed in Wolverhampton Church. This organ originally contained a Double Bassoon to the DD key (DDD Pipe), which appears to have been the first double Reed introduced into any British organ.

Great, 10 Stops, GG to F in alt.

1. Double Open Diapason.
2. Open Diapason, No. 1.
3. Open Diapason, No. 2.
4. Stopped Diapason.
5. Principal.
6. Twelfth.
7. Fifteenth.
8. Doublette, 8ve, 15th, and 22nd.
9. Sesquialtera, III ranks (useless).
10. Trumpet (entirely useless).

Choir, 5 Stops, GG to F in alt.

11. Open Diapason, from middle D upwards.
12. Dulciana.
13. Stopped Diapason.
14. Principal.
15. Flute.

Swell, 11 Stops, CC to F in alt.

16. Double Stopped Diapason.
17. Open Diapason.
18. Dulciana.
19. Stopped Diapason.
20. Principal.
21. Twelfth.
22. Fifteenth.
23. Doublette, 8ve, 15th, and 22nd.
24. Sesquialtera.
25. Oboe.
26. Trumpet.

Pedal, 2 Stops; CC to D, two Octaves and two Notes.

27. Open Diapason, 16 feet.
28. Principal, 8 feet.

Coupling Actions.

Swell to Great. | Swell to Pedals. | Great to Pedals.

336. TRINITY COLLEGE CHAPEL, DUBLIN.

The greater portion of the organ in Trinity College Chapel, Dublin, was built by Telford, of Dublin, in 1838. It occupies the case of an organ built by Green, of London. The Choir of Green's instrument was not removed, on account of its excellence ; the Swell, Great, and Pedal organs are alone new.

Great, 8 Stops, GG to F in alt.

1. Open Diapason.
2. Open Diapason.
3. Stopped Diapason.
4. Principal.
5. Twelfth.
6. Fifteenth.
7. Sesquialtera.
8. Trumpet.

Choir, 4 Stops, GG to E in alt.

9. Stopped Diapason.
10. Dulciana.

11. Principal.
12. Fifteenth.

Swell, 9 Stops, C, 4 feet, to F in alt.

13. Double Stopped Diapason.
14. Open Diapason.
15. Dulciana.
16. Stopped Diapason.
17. Principal.

18. Principal.
19. Fifteenth.
20. Oboe.
21. Trumpet.

Pedal, 5 Stops, GG to F, Octave and a half.

22. Unison.
23. Principal.
24. Twelfth.

25. Fifteenth.
26. Trumpet.

Coupling Actions.

Swell to Great.

Great to Pedals.

337. DUBLIN.

The organ in the Roman Catholic Church of St. Nicholas, Dublin, was built by Telford, of Dublin.

Great, 12 Stops, FFF to F.

1. Great Open Diapason, metal 8 feet.
2. Open Diapason, metal ... 8 feet.
3. Dulciana, open, metal...... 8 feet.
4. Stopped Diapason, wood 8 feet.
5. Principal, metal .... 4 feet.
6. Second Principal, metal... 8 feet.

7. Twelfth, metal .... 2⅔ feet.
8. Fifteenth, metal........... 2 feet.
9. Sesquialtera, III ranks.
10. Mixture, II ranks.
11. Trumpet .... 8 feet.
12. Clarion......................... 4 feet.

Choir, 7 Stops, FFF to F.

13. Open Diapason, metal ... 8 feet.
14. Dulciana, metal .... 8 feet.
15. Stopped Diapason, wood 8 feet.
16. Principal, metal .... 4 feet.

17. Flute, wood.................. 4 feet.
18. Fifteenth, metal........... 2 feet.
19. Cremona, metal .... 8 feet.

Swell, 10 Stops, Gamut G to F.

20. Double Stopped Diapason,
       metal....................... 16 feet.
21. Open Diapason, metal ... 8 feet.
22. Dulciana, metal .... 8 feet.
23. Stopped Diapason, wood 8 feet.
24. Principal, metal .... 4 feet.

25. Twelfth, metal .... 2⅔ feet.
26. Fifteenth, metal........... 2 feet.
27. Sesquialtera, III ranks.
28. Trumpet .... 8 feet.
29. Hautboy .... 8 feet.

Pedal, 5 Stops, FFF to F.

30. Double, open, wood ...... 16 feet
31. Unison, open, metal ...... 8 feet
32. Octave .... 4 feet.

33. Twelfth .... 2⅔ feet.
34. Fifteenth .... 2 feet.

338. Dublin.

The organ in the Roman Catholic Church of St. Francis Xavier, Gardener Street, Dublin, was built by Flight and Robson, and finished and erected by Gray and Son.

Great, 13 Stops, FFF to G in alt.

	Feet.	Pipes.			Feet.	Pipes.
1. Double Diapason, metal and wood	16	51	7. Twelfth, metal		2⅔	63
2. Great Open Diapason, metal	8	63	8. Fifteenth, metal		2	63
3. Small Open Diapason, metal	8	51	9. Twenty-second, metal		1	63
4. Stopped Diapason, wood	8	63	10. Sesqualtera, III ranks, metal		1	189
5. Quint, metal	5⅓	51	11. Mixture, II ranks		1	126
6. Principal, metal	4	63	12. Trumpet, metal		8	63
			13. Clarion, metal		4	63

Choir, 8 Stops, FFF to G.

	Feet.	Pipes.			Feet.	Pipes.
14. Open Diapason, metal	8	63	18. Principal, metal		4	63
15. Dulciana, wood and metal	8	51	19. Flute, wood		4	51
16. Stopped Diapason, wood	8	63	20. Fifteenth, metal		2	64
17. Keraulophon, metal	8	44	21. Cremona, metal		8	39

Swell, 12 Stops, FF to G in alt.

	Feet.	Pipes.			Feet.	Pipes.
22. Double Stopped Diapason, Bass, wood	16		27. Flute, wood		4	51
23. Double Open Diapason, Treble, metal	16		28. Fifteenth, metal		2	51
24. Open Diapason, metal	8	51	29. Sesqualtera, III ranks			153
25. Stopped Diapason, wood	8	51	30. Cornopean, metal		8	51
26. Principal, metal	4	51	31. Trumpet, metal		8	51
			32. Hautboy, metal		8	51
			33. Clarion, metal		4	51

Pedal, 2 Stops, FFF to F.

	Feet.	Pipes.			Feet.	Pipes.
34. Double Open Diapason, wood	16	25	35. Unison Open Diapason		8	25

Accessory Stops, Movements, &c.

1 to 8. Eight Composition Pedals. | 9 to 12. Four Coupling Actions.

339. Belfast.

The organ in the New Church of St. Malachy, Belfast, was built by Telford, of Dublin, in 1849. It has 3 complete Manuals, from CC to F in alt., and a Pedal, from CCC to E—two octaves and four notes; also 33 sounding stops, of which the following is a list :—

Great, 13 Stops, CC to F in alt.

1. Bourdon, wood	16 feet.	8. Fifteenth, metal	2 feet.
2. Tenoroon, metal	16 feet.	9. Doublette, metal	1 foot.
3. Great Open Diapason, metal	8 feet.	10. Sesqualtera, metal, III ranks.	
4. Small Open Diapason, metal	8 feet.	11. Mixture, metal, II ranks.	
5. Stopped Diapason, wood	8 feet.	12. Posaune, metal	8 feet.
6. Principal, metal	4 feet.	13. Clarion, metal	4 feet.
7. Twelfth, metal	2⅔ feet.		

Choir, 7 Stops, CC to F in alt.

14. Dulciana, metal	8 feet.	18. Principal, metal	4 feet.
15. Stopped Diapason, wood	8 feet.	19. Wald Flute, wood	4 feet.
16. Clarabella, wood	8 feet.	20. Fifteenth, metal	2 feet.
17. Viol di Gamba, wood	8 feet.		

Swell, 10 Stops, CC to F in alt.

21. Double Stopped Diapason, wood	16 feet.	26. Fifteenth, metal	2 feet.
22. Open Diapason, metal	8 feet.	27. Doublette, metal	1 foot.
23. Dulciana, metal	8 feet.	28. Sesquialtera, metal, III ranks.	
24. Principal, metal	4 feet.	29. Cornopean, metal	8 feet.
25. Twelfth, metal	2¾ feet.	30. Hautbois, metal	8 feet.

Pedal, 3 Stops, CCC to E, 29 Notes.

31. Grand Double Open Diapason	16 feet.	32. Double Trombone	16 feet.
		33. Unison Trombone	8 feet.

Couplers, &c.

1. Swell organ to Great Manual.	4. Great organ to Pedals.
2. Swell organ to Choir Manual.	5 to 8. Four Composition Pedals.
3. Swell organ to Pedals.	

The largest pipe is 16 feet long ; the smallest, ⅜ of an inch.

340. CASHEL.

The organ in Cashel Roman Catholic Cathedral, Ireland, was erected, in 1846, by Bevington and Sons. It is one of the largest organs in the South of Ireland.

Great, 11 Stops, FFF to F.

	Pipes.		Pipes
1. Tenoroon, metal	} 60	7. Fifteenth	60
2. Bourdon Bass, FFFF		8. Sesquialtera, IV ranks	240
3. Open Diapason, FFF, metal	60	9. Mixture, III ranks	180
4. Stopped Diapason	60	10. Trumpet	60
5. Principal	60	11. Clarion	60
6. Twelfth	60		

Choir, 9 Stops.

12. Open Diapason, FFF, metal	60	17. Flute, FFF	60
13. Dulciana, FF	49	18. Fifteenth	60
14. Stopped Diapason, Treble	} 60	19. Clarionet	42
15. Stopped Diapason, Bass, FFF		20. Bassoon, Bass, FFF	18
16. Principal, FFF	60		

Swell, 8 Stops, tenor c to f.

21. Double Diapason	42	25. Flute, open, wood	42
22. Open Diapason	42	26. Cornet, III ranks	126
23. Stopped Diapason	42	27. Cornopean	42
24. Principal	42	28. Oboe	42

Pedal, 1 Stop.

29. Open, wood, CC to FFFF .... 24 feet.

Accessory Stops, Movements, &c.

1 to 6. Six Composition Pedals.	7 to 10. Four Coupling Movements.

	Pipes.		Pipes.
Great organ	900	Pedal	20
Choir	409		
Swell	420	Total	1749

341. KILKENNY.

The organ in the Cathedral Church of St. Canice, Kilkenny, was first erected in the Great Exhibition Building at Dublin, and was afterwards sold to the Dean and Chapter of the above Cathedral. The case is Gothic, handsomely carved. The organ contains 3 rows of keys—Great, Swell, and Choir ; and Pedal of 2 octaves and 2 notes.

Great, 11 *Stops ; CC to F in alt.,* 54 *Notes.*

		Pipes.			Pipes.
1.	Open Diapason, No. 1	54	7.	Fifteenth	54
2.	Open Diapason, No. 2	54	8.	Sesquialtera, III ranks	162
3.	Stopped Diapason }	54	9.	Mixture, II ranks	108
4.	Claribel }		10.	Trumpet	54
5.	Principal	54	11.	Clarion	54
6.	Twelfth	54			

Swell, 8 *Stops ; tenor c to F in alt.,* 42 *Notes.*

12.	Double Diapason	42	16.	Doublette, 15th and 22d	84
13.	Open Diapason	42	17.	Double Trumpet	42
14.	Stopped Diapason	42	18.	Cornopean	42
15.	Principal	42	19.	Clarion	42

Choir, 8 *Stops; CC to F in alt.,* 54 *Notes.*

20.	Double Diapason, Bass, closed wood	54	23.	Dulciana, tenor c	54
21.	Double Diapason, Treble, closed wood	54	24.	Viol di Gamba, tenor c	42
22.	Stopped Diapason	54	25.	Principal, CC	54
			26.	Flute, tenor c	42
			27.	Cremona, G	35

Pedal, 1 *Stop ; CCC to C,* 27 *Notes.*

28. Great Open Diapason .... 16 feet ...... 27 pipes.

Coupling Actions.

1. Swell to Great.		4. Pedals to Choir.
2. Swell to Choir.		5. Pedals to Swell.
3. Pedals to Great.		

342. CORK.

The organ in SS. Peter and Paul's Catholic Church, Cork, was built by Bryceson Brothers and Morten in 1876. It is enclosed in a handsome carved Gothic case, of Memel wood, 36 feet high, 30 feet wide, 12 feet deep, with four towers of 16 feet metal pipes, the whole frontage of pipes and woodwork richly illuminated in gold and colours.

The pneumatic lever apparatus is applied to both Swell and Great organs separately, as well as to Manual couplers. Tubular pneumatic power is introduced in addition, so that a pallet is now placed beneath each large front pipe, instead of a conveyance being used for its supply of wind.

The Great organ reeds are on an increased pressure of wind, and enclosed in the same box with the Swell organ. Each Manual sound-board is divided and supplied by two distinct reservoirs of its own for Treble and Bass. Pedal sound-boards have two large reservoirs. There are three main bellows, with double feeders to each for filling reservoirs. Every draw-stop knob represents a sounding stop throughout, excepting Voix Céleste. Couplers act by hitching pedals only. Pitch, French Diapason normal. Concave and radiating Pedal-board. Draw-stop knobs placed at an angle to performer.

Great Organ, CC to A.

	Pipes.	Feet.		Pipes.	Feet.
1. Double Open Diapason. metal	58	... 16	7. Harmonic Flute, metal ...	58	... 4
2. Open Diapason, metal ...	58	... 8	8. Flautina, metal	58	... 2
3. Open Flute, wood and metal	58	... 8	9. Full Mixture, IV ranks, metal	232	
4. Viola, metal	58	... 8	10. Double Trumpet, metal...	58	... 16
5. Stopped Diapason, wood and metal	58	... 8	11. Trumpet, metal	58	... 8
6. Principal, metal	58	... 4	12. Clarion, metal...............	58	... 4

Swell Organ, CC to A.

	Pipes.	Feet.		Pipes.	Feet.
13. Double Diapason, wood and metal	58	... 16	18. Principal, metal	58	... 4
14. Open Diapason, wood and metal	58	... 8	19. Echo Flute, metal	58	... 4
15. Viol di Gamba, metal	58	... 8	20. Harmonic Piccolo, metal	58	... 2
16. Voix Célestes, metal	46	... 8	21. Mixture, III ranks, metal	174	
17. Lieblich Gedact, wood and metal	58	... 8	22. Cornopean, metal	58	... 8
			23. Oboe, metal.................	58	... 8
			24. Vox Humana, metal	58	... 8
			Tremulant acting on Swell.		

Choir Organ, CC to A.

	Pipes.	Feet.		Pipes.	Feet.
25. Dulciana, metal	58	... 8	29. Lieblich Flote, metal......	58	... 4
26. Viol d'Amour, metal	58	... 8	30. Flageolet, metal	58	... 2
27. Rohrflote, wood and metal	58	... 8	31. Clarionet and Bassoon, metal	58	... 8
28. Gemshorn, metal	58	... 4			

Pedal Organ, CCC to F.

	Pipes.	Feet.		Pipes.	Feet.
32. Contra Bass, wood	30	... 32	36. Violoncello, metal	30	... 8
33. Open Diapason, wood......	30	... 16	37. Bass Flute, wood	30	... 8
34. Violone, metal	30	... 16	38. Trombone, wood	30	... 16
35. Bourdon, wood..............	30	... 16			

Couplers by Pedals.

1. Swell to Great.	6. Great to Pedals.
2. Swell to Choir.	7. Choir to Pedals.
3. Sub-choir to Great.	8. Trombone on and off.
4. Great Reeds to Swell.	9. Swell Tremulant.
5. Swell to Pedals.	

Summary.

Swell organ	12 stops	800 pipes.
Great organ	12 ,, ...	870 ,,
Choir organ	7 ,, ...	398 ,,
Pedal organ	7 ,, ...	210 ,,
Total sounding stops......	38 ,,	2278 ,,

4 Combination Pedals to Great and Pedal Organs.   3 Combination Pedals to Swell Organ

NOTES.

After paragraph No. 200, p. 49.—The following account and date of the first use of a "reversed key-board" will be read with interest. It has been kindly furnished to Mr. Hopkins by Mr. W. H. Cummings, who discovered it :—

"An organ made by Mr. Jordan, being the first of its kind, the contrivance of which is such that the master, when he plays, sits with his face to the audience (and the keys being but 3 feet high), sees the whole company, and would be very useful in churches. This organ has but one set of keys, but is so contrived that the Trumpet Bass and Trumpet Treble, the Sesquialtera and Cornet stops are put off and on by the feet, singly, or altogether, at the master's discretion, and as quick as thought, without taking the hand off the keys. The said Mr Jordan invites all masters, gentlemen and ladies, to come and hear this performance at his workhouse, against St. George's Church, Southwark, and will give his attendance from 2 till 4 o'clock, all next week, Ash Wednesday only excepted. N.B.—This organ was played on and approved by several masters in public, the latter end of November, and is fit for any small church or chappel."—Advertisement in the *London Journal*, Saturday, Feb. 7, 1729—30.

After paragraph No. 266, p. 68.—Among other motors for blowing organs, gas engines have been introduced. These start at full power at a moment's notice ; and common gas is said to feed the engine at one penny an hour per horse power.

After paragraph No. 307, p. 87.—The "pneumatic tubular transmission system" remains here to be noticed. This recent improvement promises to supersede the ordinary tracker "long-movement" for the distant departments of all large organs. The germ of this application is found in the late Mr. Booth's contrivance already referred to on p. 59, consisting of a tube receiving compressed wind at one end and having a "motor" at the other ; but it was not until the year 1867 that the principle was turned to the present admirable account, when it was applied to an organ publicly shown at the Paris Exhibition in that year. The tube-pneumatic was first introduced to the English public by Mr. Henry Willis, in his recent re-build of the organ in St. Paul's Cathedral. It is also extensively used by the same builder in his Great organ in the Alexandra Palace ; by Messrs. Bryceson, in the organ removed by them from St. Paul's to the Victoria Rooms, Bristol ; by the Messrs. Bishop, in the Yarmouth organ as recently re-built by them ; and by Mr. Lewis, for the Pedal organ of his new instrument in Ripon Cathedral.

After paragraph No. 559, p. 133.—Among the future improvements of the organ the introduction of string stops promises to be one of considerable importance. For some years experiments have been carried on to perfect an arrangement by which the vibrations of a reed are communicated direct to a string, and the sound produced is that of the string. This has been the subject of a series of patents. The plan is in so forward a state that a small separate instrument, called the "wind-viol," has been successfully tried, producing sounds of organ-like power, but with the true string tone. A series of apparatus to illustrate the invention was exhibited in the Loan Collection of Scientific Apparatus at South Kensington, the description of which occupies two pages of the official catalogue (pages 170 and 171, 2nd edition). The last patent shows the invention as applied to a separate instrument, by superseding the bow by the use of wind governed by the keys of an ordinary Manual, so that with a string for each note a complete stop is formed, and it is perfectly understood that the production of new and original stops for the organ is the ultimate object of Mr. J. B. Hamilton and the other patentees, and that the great value of the patent lies in that direction. The patentees at present appear only desirous to complete their invention and secure their rights.

After paragraph No. 1165, p. 282.—The most convenient height for the surface of the organ-stool above the pedals is twenty inches.

A LIST OF FOREIGN AND ENGLISH EQUIVALENT TERMS.

As many of the names which appear in the foregoing accounts of Continental organs may not be familiar to some readers, the following table of the chief Foreign Stops, with their English equivalents, when they exist, and a brief notice of them when they do not, has been prepared, which, it is hoped, may assist those who may not be able to decipher the foreign nomenclature.

Manual Stops.

Grosse Principal, 32 feet.—Double Double Open Diapason, 32 feet.

Montre, 32 feet.—The same, "mounted," or in "front."

Sub-Bourdon, 32 feet tone.—Double Double Stopped Diapason, 32 feet tone.

Manual-Untersatz, 32 feet tone.—The same.

Bourdon, or Bordun, 32 feet tone.—The same.

Principal, 16 feet.—Double Open Diapason, 16 feet.

Montre, 16 feet.—The same, "mounted," or in "front."

Prestant, 16 feet.—The same.

Gamba Major, 16 feet.—Great, or Double Gamba, 16 feet.

Salicional, 16 feet.—Reedy Double Dulciana, 16 feet.

Bourdon, or Bordun, 16 feet tone.—Double Stopped Diapason, 16 feet tone.

Tibia Major, 16 feet tone.—The same.

Gross Gedact, 16 feet tone.—The same.

Lieblich Gedact, 16 feet tone.—Double Stopped Diapason, of slender scale and sweet intonation.

Rohrflote, 16 feet tone.—Double Stopped Diapason, of metal pipes with chimneys.

Quintaton, 16 feet tone.—Double Stopped Diapason, of rather small scale, producing the Twelfth of the fundamental sound, as well as the ground tone itself—*i.e.*, sounding the 16 and 5⅓ feet tones—16 feet tone.

Octave, 8 feet.—Octave to the "Principal" or *Double* Open Diapason of 16 feet, and therefore identical with the *Unison* Open Diapason, 8 feet.

Principal, 8 feet.—Open Diapason, 8 feet.

Montre, 8 feet.—The same.

Flute, 8 feet.—The same.

Geigen Principal, 8 feet.—Violin or crisp-toned Diapason, 8 feet.

Gamba, or Viol di Gamba, 8 feet.—Bass Viol Unison stop, of smaller scale and thinner, but more pungent tone than the Violin Diapason, 8 feet.

Fugara, 8 feet.—A species of small-scale Gamba, of bright and cutting tone, and slow speech, 8 feet.

Salicional, 8 feet.—Dulciana of reedy quality, 8 feet.

Flauto Traverso, 8 feet.—German Flute, formed of cylindrical pipes of pear-tree wood, and sounding their octave in the Treble, 8 feet.

Hohlflote, 8 feet.—Hollow Flute, a kind of Clarabella, 8 feet.

Harmonica, 8 feet.—A unison open wood stop, sometimes smaller in the treble and larger in the bass than the Hohlflote, 8 feet.

Spitzflote, 8 feet.—Spire or Taper Flute, a unison open metal stop, formed of pipes with conical bodies, 8 feet.

Gemshorn, 8 feet.—Goat Horn, a unison open metal stop, more conical than the Spitzflote, 8 feet.

Connel, 8 feet.—Coupling-flute, a kind of stopped Diapason or Clarabella, intended to be used chiefly in combination with some other stop—as the Stopped Diapason is used with the Clarinet in England—hence its name, 8 feet.

Portunal-flaut, 8 feet.—An open wood stop, of the Clarabella species, the pipes of which are larger at top than at bottom, and producing a tone of Clarionet quality, 8 feet.

Bifara, 8 feet.—A unison open stop, formed of pipes having two mouths, the speech of which is accompanied by a pleasing undulation, 8 feet.

Unda Maris, 8 feet.—Wave of the Sea. A unison open stop, tuned rather sharper than the other stops, and producing an undulating or waving effect when drawn in conjunction with another stop, 8 feet.

Voix Céleste, 8 feet.—A stop of II ranks, resembling Dulcianas, one of which is tuned sharper than the other, producing an undulating effect like that of the Unda Maris, 8 feet.

Blockflote, 8 feet.—Common or ordinary Flute, formed of pipes larger than Diapason scale, 8 feet.

Portunal, 8 feet.—An open wood stop, of the Clarabella species, but with the pipes larger at top than at bottom, and producing a tone like that of the Clarionet, 8 feet.

Flauto Dolce, 8 feet.—A unison Flute stop, of tranquil and agreeable tone, well adapted for cantabile music, for which an Open Diapason would be both too strong and too full, 8 feet.

Gedact, 8 feet tone.—Covered stop. Stopped Diapason, 8 feet tone.

Lieblich Gedact, 8 feet tone.—Stopped Diapason, of slender scale and sweet intonation, 8 feet tone.

Still Gedact, 8 feet tone.—Stopped Diapason, of quiet tone, 8 feet tone.

Rohrflote, 8 feet tone.—Reed Flute. Metal Stopped Diapason, with reeds, tubes, or chimneys, 8 feet tone.

Quintaton, 8 feet tone.—Stopped Diapason, producing the Twelfth as well as the ground-tone—i.e., sounding the 8 and 2⅔ feet tones—8 feet tone.

Nacht Horn, 8 feet tone.—Night Horn. Nearly identical with the foregoing, but of larger scale, and more horn-like in tone, 8 feet tone.

Quint, 5⅓ feet.—Fifth-sounding stop. In this case producing the Fifth above the Diapason, 5⅓ feet.

Grosse-Nazard, Nasard, Nassat, Nasat, 5⅓ feet.—Fifth to the Unison Diapason, 5⅓ feet.

Gemshorn-quint, 5⅓ feet.—Fifth composed of Gemshorn pipes, 5⅓ feet.

Quint Gedact, 5⅓ feet tone.—Stopped Fifth, 5⅓ feet tone.

Roer-quint, 5⅓ feet tone.—Stopped Fifth, formed of metal pipes with chimneys, 5⅓ feet tone.

Super-octave, 4 feet.—The second octave or Fifteenth above the "Principal," or Double Open Diapason of 16 feet, identical with the English Principal, 4 feet.

Octave, 4 feet.—The Octave to the Open Diapason of 8 feet. The English Principal, 4 feet.

Principal, 4 feet.—Principal, 4 feet.

Prestant, 4 feet.—The same, 4 feet.

Spitzflote, 4 feet.—Octave stop, formed of conical pipes, 4 feet.

Geigen Principal, 4 feet.—Violin Principal, 4 feet.

Gambette, 4 feet.—Small Gamba, or Octave Gamba, 4 feet.

Salicional Octave, 4 feet.—Octave Salicional, 4 feet.

Flauto Traverso, 4 feet.—German Flute, the Treble pipes sounding their Harmonic, or Octave, 4 feet.

Hohlflote, 4 feet.—A kind of Octave Clarabella, 4 feet.

Flaut-à-becq, 4 feet.—Flute with beak or mouth-piece at one end. The old English Flute, 4 feet.

Klein Gedact, 4 feet tone.—Small Covered stop. Stopped Flute, 4 feet tone.

Rohrflote, 4 feet tone.—Stopped metal Flute, with reeds, tubes, or chimneys, 4 feet tone.

Grosse Tierce, 3⅕ feet.—Great Third-sounding Stop. In this case producing the Third above the Principal. Tenth or Decima, 3⅕ feet.

Quinte, 2⅔ feet.—Fifth-sounding stop when of this size, producing the Fifth above the Principal Twelfth, or Duodecimo, 2⅔ feet.

Gemshorn-quint, 2⅔ feet.—Twelfth, formed of Gemshorn pipes, 2⅔ feet.

Nasard, 2⅔ feet.—Twelfth, 2⅔ feet.

Sedecima, 2 feet.—The third octave, Octave Fifteenth, or Twenty-second, above the "Principal" or Double Open Diapason of 16 feet. Identical with the English "Fifteenth," 2 feet.

Super-octave, 2 feet.—The second Octave above the Unison "Principal." The Fifteenth, 2 feet.

Octave, 2 feet.—Octave to the Principal of 4 feet, 2 feet.

Doublette, 2 feet.—The same, 2 feet.

Quarte de Nazard, 2 feet.—The same.

Quinta-decima, 2 feet.—The Fifth above the Tenth—*i.e.*, the Fifteenth, 2 feet.
Gemshorn, 2 feet.—Gemshorn Fifteenth, 2 feet.
Waldflote, 2 feet.—Forest-flute, 2 feet.
Hohlflote, 2 feet.—Hollow Flute, of Fifteenth pitch, 2 feet.
Rausch-pfeif, $2\frac{2}{3}$ feet.—Twelfth and Fifteenth on one slider, $2\frac{2}{3}$ feet.
Rausch-quint, $2\frac{2}{3}$ feet.—The same.
Flageolet, 2 feet.—Flageolet, 2 feet.
Terz, $1\frac{3}{5}$ foot.—Tierce, when of this size, sounding the Third above the Fifteenth, $1\frac{3}{5}$ feet.
Sexte, $2\frac{2}{3}$ feet.—Sixth. A II-rank Mutation stop, sounding the interval of a major sixth. A Twelfth and Tierce on one slider, $2\frac{2}{3}$ feet.
Sesquialtera, $2\frac{2}{3}$ feet.—Sesquialtera, II ranks; the same, $2\frac{2}{3}$ feet.
Quinta, $1\frac{1}{3}$ foot.—Fifth-sounding stop, producing the Fifth above the Fifteenth. The Nineteenth or Larigot, $1\frac{1}{3}$ foot.
Tertian, $1\frac{3}{5}$ foot.—A II-rank Mutation stop, sounding the interval of a minor third. A Tierce and Larigot on one slider, $1\frac{3}{5}$ foot.
Sedecima, 1 foot.—Twenty-second or Octave Fifteenth, 1 foot.
Mixture, 2 feet.— A mixed Stop—*i.e.*, consisting of Foundation and Mutation ranks of pipes, compounded together, the largest rank being usually a Fifteenth, 2 feet.
Scharf, $1\frac{1}{3}$ foot.—Sharp, also a mixed stop, composed of smaller pipes than the Mixture, or on a smaller scale, and sometimes containing a Tierce, particularly if the Mixture has not one, $1\frac{1}{3}$ foot.
Cymbel, 1 foot.—The most acute of the bright stops, being very small in scale, and high in pitch—it is sometimes formed exclusively of octave ranks—1 foot.
Cornet.—Cornet, frequently a Compound stop, formed of pipes several scales larger than Diapason measure, and producing a "horny" tone; hence its name. Sometimes the Cornet is a large Manual Reed, as at Freiburg and Seville; in other examples it is a small Pedal Reed, as at Muhlhausen, Merseburg, &c.
Contra Fagott, 32 feet.—Double Double Bassoon, 32 feet.
Tromba, 16 feet.—Double Trumpet, 16 feet.
Tuba, 16 feet.—The same.
Trompet, 16 feet.—The same.
Dulcian, 16 feet.—Dulcian means, literally, a small Bassoon. In this case, a Double Bassoon, 16 feet.
Fagotto, 16 feet.—Double Bassoon, 16.
Bombarde, 16 feet.—Double Reed, 16 feet.
Euphone, 16 feet.—Double Reed, 16 feet.
Phisarmonica, 16 feet.—Double Reed, with Free Reeds, and Tubes of half length, 16 feet tone.
Grand Cornet, 16 feet.—Double Reed, 16 feet.
Corneta—Double Reed.
Trompette, 8 feet.—Trumpet, 8 feet.
Trompette Harmonique, 8 feet.—Harmonic Trumpet, 8 feet.
Hautbois, 8 feet.—Hautboy, 8 feet.
Cor Anglais, 8 feet.—English Horn, 8 feet.
Dulcian, 8 feet.—Bassoon, 8 feet.
Fagotto, 8 feet.—The same.
Krumhorn, 8 feet tone.—Clarionet, 8 feet tone.
Cromhorn, 8 feet tone.—The same.
Schalmay, 8 feet tone.—The same.
Vox Humana, 8 feet tone.—Human Voice, 8 feet tone.
Clarin, 4 feet.—Clarion, 8 feet tone.

Pedal Stops.

Sub-principal, 32 feet.—"Under Principal," *i.e.*, below the Pedal Diapason pitch. Double Open Bass, 32 feet.
Gross Principal, 32 feet.—Great or Double Diapason Bass, 32 feet.
Prestant, 32 feet.—The same.

Flute Ouverte, **32 feet.**—The same.

Untersatz, **32 feet tone.**—"Below position," *i.e.*, under the Pedal Unison pitch. Double Stopped Bass, 32 feet tone.

Sub-bass **32 feet tone.**—"Under Bass," or Double Stopped Bass, 32 feet tone.

Quintaton, **32 feet tone.**—Double Stopped Bass, sounding the Twelfth as well as the ground tone, in this case producing the 32 and 10⅔ feet tones.

Grand Bourdon, **32 feet tone.**—Great or Double Bourdon, 32 feet tone.

Gross Quinten Bass, **21⅓ feet tone.**—Fifth to the Great Bass of 32 feet, 21⅓ feet tone.

Principal Bass, **16 feet.**—Open Diapason Bass, 16 feet.

Octave, **16 feet.**—The same.

Prestant, **16 feet.**—The same. Where there is a Metal "Principal" of 16 feet on the same Pedal, the name Prestant is applied to a *wood* Open Bass of the same size.

Flute Ouverte, **16 feet.**—The same.

Violone, **16 feet.**—Double Bass. A unison open wood stop, of much smaller scale than the Diapason, and formed of pipes that are a little wider at the top than at the bottom, and furnished with ears and beard at the mouth. The tone of the Violone is crisp and resonant, like that of the orchestral Double Bass; and its speech being a little slow, it has the Stopped Bass always drawn with it; 16 feet.

Gamba, **16 feet.**—Gamba Bass, 16 feet.

Salicet, **16 feet.**—Dulciana Bass, 16 feet.

Sub-bass, **16 feet tone.**—Stopped Bass, usually, but sometimes Open wood, 16 feet, 16 feet tone.

Bourdon, **16 feet tone.**—This name is very rarely applied to a Pedal stop. When it is so, it is generally to a Stopped Bass, though occasionally to a wood open Bass, 16 feet, 16 feet tone.

Quintaton, **16 feet tone.**—A small scale unison covered stop, sounding the Twelfth as well as the ground tone—*i.e.*, producing the 16-feet and 5⅓ feet tones—16 feet tone.

Gross Quint, Stopped, **10⅔ feet tone.**—Great Fifth, Stopped, 10⅔ feet tone.

Roer-quint, **10⅔ feet tone.**—Stopped Fifth, formed of pipes with reeds, tubes, or chimneys, 10⅔ feet tone.

Octave, **8 feet.**—Octave, or Principal to the Diapason of 16 feet, 8 feet.

Violoncello, **8 feet.**—Crisp-toned open stop, of small scale. The "Octave" to the Violone of 16 feet, 8 feet.

Bass Flute, **8 feet tone.**—Flute Bass. The Stopped Octave to the Stopped Bass of 16 feet tone, 8 feet tone.

Tertia, **6⅖ feet.**—Tenth, or Great Tierce, 6⅖ feet.

Quint, **5⅓ feet.**—Twelfth, 5⅓ feet.

Rohr-quint, **5⅓ feet tone.**—Stopped Twelfth, 5⅓ feet tone.

Super-octave, **4 feet.**—Fifteenth, 4 feet.

Mixtur, **V ranks.**—Mixtur, V ranks, 4 feet.

Cornet, **VIII ranks.**—Pedal Cornet.

Contra Posaune, **32 feet.**—Double Trombone, 32 feet.

Posaune, **16 feet.**—Trombone, 16 feet.

Bombarde.—Large Unison Pedal Reed, 16 feet.

Fagotto, **16 feet.**—Bassoon, 16 feet.

Dulcian, **16 feet.**—Small Bassoon, 16 feet.

Trompet, **8 feet.**—Trumpet, 8 feet.

Trombone, **8 feet.**—Large Octave Reed, 8 feet.

Basson, **8 feet.**—Octave Bassoon, 8 feet.

Krummhorn, **8 feet.**—Cremona, 8 feet tone.

Clairon, **4 feet.**

Cornet, **4 feet.**

Cinq, **2 feet.**

Cornet, **2 feet.**

Clarion, **4 feet.**

Cornet.—A small Reed Clairon, 4 feet.

Octave Clarion, **2 feet.**

Octave Clairon, **2 feet.**

INDEX TO HISTORY OF THE ORGAN.

INDEX TO CONSTRUCTION OF THE ORGAN.

———————>◦<◦———————

INDEX TO BRITISH AND FOREIGN ORGANS.

Music and Books published by Travis & Emery Music Bookshop:

on.: Hymnarium Sarisburiense, cum Rubricis et Notis Musicis.

on.: Säcularfeier des Geburtstages von Ludwig van Beethoven

ricola, Johann Friedrich from Tosi: Anleitung zur Singkunst.

ch, C.P.E.: edited W. Emery: Nekrolog or Obituary Notice of J.S. Bach.

teson, Naomi Judith: Alcock of Salisbury

the, William: A Briefe Introduction to the Skill of Song

x, Arnold: Symphony #5, Arranged for Piano Four Hands by Walter Emery

rney, Charles: The Present State of Music in France and Italy

rney, Charles: The Present State of Music in Germany, The Netherlands …

rney, Charles: An Account of the Musical Performances ... Handel

rney, Karl: Nachricht von Georg Friedrich Handel's Lebensumstanden.

rns, Robert: The Caledonian Musical Museum ..The Best Scotch Songs. (1810)

bbett, W.W.: Cobbett's Cyclopedic Survey of Chamber Music. (2 vols.)

rrette, Michel: Le Maitre de Clavecin

imp, Bryan: Dear Mr. Rosenthal … Dear Mr. Gaisberg …

imp, Bryan: Solo: The Biography of Solomon

otch, William: Substance of Several Courses of Lectures on Music

Indy, Vincent: Beethoven: Biographie Critique

Indy, Vincent: Beethoven: A Critical Biography

Indy, Vincent: César Franck (in French)

schhof, Joseph: Versuch einer Geschichte des Clavierbaues. (Faksimile 1853).

rescobaldi, Girolamo: D'Arie Musicali per Cantarsi. Primo & Secondo Libro.

eminiani, Francesco: The Art of Playing the Violin.

andel; Purcell; Boyce; Geene et al: Calliope or English Harmony: Volume First.

äuser: Musikalisches Lexikon. 2 vols in one.

awkins, John: A General History of the Science and Practice of Music (5 vols.)

erbert-Caesari, Edgar: The Science and Sensations of Vocal Tone

erbert-Caesari, Edgar: Vocal Truth

opkins and Rimboult: The Organ. Its History and Construction.

unt, John: - see separate list of discographies at the end of these titles

saacs, Lewis: Hänsel and Gretel. A Guide to Humperdinck's Opera.

saacs, Lewis: Königskinder (Royal Children) A Guide to Humperdinck's Opera.

astner: Manuel Général de Musique Militaire

acassagne, M. l'Abbé Joseph : Traité Général des élémens du Chant.

ascelles (née Catley), Anne: The Life of Miss Anne Catley.

Mainwaring, John: Memoirs of the Life of the Late George Frederic Handel

Malcolm, Alexander: A Treaty of Music: Speculative, Practical and Historical

Marx, Adolph Bernhard: Die Kunst des Gesanges, Theoretisch-Practisch

May, Florence: The Life of Brahms

May, Florence: The Girlhood Of Clara Schumann: Clara Wieck And Her Time.

Mellers, Wilfrid: Angels of the Night: Popular Female Singers of Our Time

Mellers, Wilfrid: Bach and the Dance of God

Mellers, Wilfrid: Beethoven and the Voice of God

Mellers, Wilfrid: Caliban Reborn - Renewal in Twentieth Century Music

Mellers, Wilfrid: Darker Shade of Pale, A Backdrop to Bob Dylan

Mellers, Wilfrid: François Couperin and the French Classical Tradition

Mellers, Wilfrid: Harmonious Meeting
Mellers, Wilfrid: Le Jardin Retrouvé, The Music of Frederic Mompou
Mellers, Wilfrid: Music and Society, England and the European Tradition
Mellers, Wilfrid: Music in a New Found Land: ... ... American Music
Mellers, Wilfrid: Romanticism and the Twentieth Century (from 1800)
Mellers, Wilfrid: The Masks of Orpheus: ...... the Story of European Music.
Mellers, Wilfrid: The Sonata Principle (from c. 1750)
Mellers, Wilfrid: Vaughan Williams and the Vision of Albion
Panchianio, Cattuffio: Rutzvanscad Il Giovine
Pearce, Charles: Sims Reeves, Fifty Years of Music in England.
Pettitt, John: Philharmonia Orchestra: A Record of Achievement, 1948-1985
Playford, John: An Introduction to the Skill of Musick.
Purcell, Henry et al: Harmonia Sacra ... The First Book, (1726)
Purcell, Henry et al: Harmonia Sacra ... Book II (1726)
Quantz, Johann: Versuch einer Anweisung die Flöte trave   rsiere zu spielen.
Rameau, Jean-Philippe: Code de Musique Pratique, ou Methodes.
Rameau, Jean-Philippe: Erreurs sur La Musique dans l'Encyclopédie
Rastall, Richard: The Notation of Western Music.
Rimbault, Edward: The Pianoforte, Its Origins, Progress, and Construction.
Rousseau, Jean Jacques: Dictionnaire de Musique
Rubinstein, Anton : Guide to the proper use of the Pianoforte Pedals.
Sainsbury, John S.: Dictionary of Musicians. (1825). 2 vols.
Serré de Rieux, Jean de : Les dons des Enfans de Latone
Simpson, Christopher: A Compendium of Practical Musick in Five Parts
Spohr, Louis: Autobiography
Spohr, Louis: Grand Violin School
Tans'ur, William: A New Musical Grammar; or The Harmonical Spectator
Terry, Charles Sanford: Bach's Chorals – Parts 1, 2 and 3.
Terry, Charles Sanford: John Christian Bach
Terry, Charles Sanford: J.S. Bach's Original Hymn-Tunes for Congregational Use.
Terry, Charles Sanford: Four-Part Chorals of J.S. Bach. (German & English)
Terry, Charles Sanford: Joh. Seb. Bach, Cantata Texts, Sacred and Secular.
Terry, Charles Sanford: The Origins of the Family of Bach Musicians.
Tosi, Pierfrancesco: Opinioni de' Cantori Antichi, e Moderni
Tosi, Pierfrancesco: Observations on the Florid Song.
Van der Straeten, Edmund: History of the Violoncello, The Viol da Gamba ...
Van der Straeten, Edmund: History of the Violin, Its Ancestors... (2 vols.)
Walther, J. G. [Waltern]: Musicalisches Lexikon [Musikalisches Lexicon]
Wagner, Richard: Beethoven (Leipzig 1870)
Wagner, Richard: Lebens-Bericht (Leipzig 1884)
Wagner, Richard: The Musaic of the Future (Translated by E. Dannreuther).
Zwirn, Gerald: Stranded Stories From The Operas

Travis & Emery Music Bookshop
17 Cecil Court, London, WC2N 4EZ, United Kingdom.
Tel. (+44) (0) 20 7240 2129
© Travis & Emery 2011

Discographies by Travis & Emery:
Discographies by John Hunt.

More 20th Century Conductors: 7 Discographies: Eugen Jochum, Ferenc Fricsay, Carl Sch uricht, Felix Weingartner, Josef Krips, Otto Klemperer, Erich Kleiber.

More Giants of the Keyboard: 5 Discographies: Claudio Arrau, Gyorgy Cziffra, Vladim Horowitz, Dinu Lipatti, Artur Rubinstein.

More Musical Knights: 4 Discographies: Hamilton Harty, Charles Mackerras, Simon Rattl John Pritchard.

Musical Knights: 6 Discographies: Henry Wood, Thomas Beecham, Adrian Boult, John Ba birolli, Reginald Goodall, Malcolm Sargent.

Philharmonic Autocrat 1: Discography of: Herbert Von Karajan [Third Edition]

Philharmonic Autocrat 2: Concert Register of Herbert Von Karajan Second Edition.

Philips Minigroove: Second Extended Version of the European Discography.

Pianists For The Connoisseur: 6 Discographies: Arturo Benedetti Michelangeli, Alfred Cor tot, Alexis Weissenberg, Clifford Curzon, Solomon, Elly Ney.

Sächsische Staatskapelle Dresden: Complete Discography.

Singers of the Third Reich: 5 Discographies: Helge Roswaenge, Tiana Lemnitz, Franz Voelk er, Maria Mueller, Max Lorenz.

Singers on the Yellow Label: 7 Discographies: Maria Stader, Elfriede Troetschel, Annelie Kupper, Wolfgang Windgassen, Ernst Haefliger, Josef Greindl, Kim Borg

Six Wagnerian Sopranos: 6 Discographies: Frieda Leider, Kirsten Flagstad, Astrid Varnay Martha Moedl, Birgit Nilsson, Gwyneth Jones.

Sviatoslav Richter: Pianist of the Century: Discography.

Teachers and Pupils: 7 Discographies: Elisabeth Schwarzkopf, Maria Ivoguen, Maria Ce botari, Meta Seinemeyer, Ljuba Welitsch, Rita Streich, Erna Berger

Tenors in a Lyric Tradition: 3 Discographies: Peter Anders, Walther Ludwig, Fritz Wun derlich.

The Art of the Diva: 3 Discographies: Claudia Muzio, Maria Callas, Magda Olivero.

The Furtwaengler Sound Sixth Edition: Discography and Concert Listing.

The Great Dictators: 3 Discographies: Evgeny Mravinsky, Artur Rodzinski, Sergiu Celi bidache.

The Lyric Baritone: 5 Discographies: Hans Reinmar, Gerhard Huesch, Josef Metternich, Her mann Uhde, Eberhard Waechter.

The Post-War German Tradition: 5 Discographies: Rudolf Kempe, Joseph Keilberth, Wolf gang Sawallisch, Rafael Kubelik, Andre Cluytens.

Wagner Im Festspielhaus: Discography of the Bayreuth Festival.

Wiener Philharmoniker 1 - Vienna Philharmonic and Vienna State Opera Orchestras: Discog raphy Part 1 1905-1954.

Wiener Philharmoniker 2 - Vienna Philharmonic and Vienna State Opera Orchestras: Discog raphy Part 2 1954-1989.

Discography by Stephen J. Pettitt, edited by John Hunt:
Philharmonia Orchestra: Complete Discography 1945-1987

Travis & EmeryMusic Bookshop.
17 Cecil Court, London, UK.
(+44) (0) 20 7 240 2129.   sales@travis-and-emery.com .
© Travis & Emery 2011